# CHILD DEVELOPMENT

# CHILD DEVELOPMENT

THOMAS J. BERNDT

*Purdue University*

second edition

Brown & Benchmark
PUBLISHERS

Madison, WI   Dubuque   Guilford, CT   Chicago   Toronto   London
Mexico City   Caracas   Buenos Aires   Madrid   Bogotá   Sydney

**Book Team**

Executive Publisher  *Edgar J. Laube*
Acquisitions Editor  *Steven Yetter*
Project Editor  *Ted Underhill*
Production Editor  *Gloria G. Schiesl*
Proofreading Coordinator  *Carrie Barker*
Art Editor  *Rita Hingtgen*
Photo Editor  *Rose Deluhery*
Permissions Coordinator  *Patricia Barth*
Production Manager  *Beth Kundert*
Production/Costing Manager  *Sherry Padden*
Design and New Media Development Manager  *Linda Meehan Avenarius*
Marketing Manager  *Carla Aspelmeier*
Proofreader  *Mary Svetlik Anderson*

Basal Text  *10/12 Cochin*
Display Type  *Cochin*
Typesetting System  *Macintosh® QuarkXPress*
Paper Stock  *45# Mirror Matte*

Executive Vice President and General Manager  *Bob McLaughlin*
Vice President, Business Manager  *Russ Domeyer*
Vice President of Production and New Media Development  *Victoria Putman*
National Sales Manager  *Phil Rudder*
National Telesales Director  *John Finn*

 **A Times Mirror Company**

The credits section for this book begins on page 711 and is considered  an
extension of the copyright page.

Cover design by Elise Lansdon

Interior design by Christopher E. Reese

Cover image: "Baby Reaching for an Apple," 1893, Mary Cassatt/Virginia Museum of Fine Arts, Richmond, VA. Gift of Ivor and Anne Massey.
Photo: Grace Wen Hwa Ts'ao, © 1994 Virginia Museum of Fine Arts.

Copyedited by Laurie McGee; proofread by Francine Buda Banwarth

Library of Congress Catalog Card Number: 96–86612

ISBN 0–697–27549–3 (paperbound)
ISBN 0–697–35967–0 (casebound)

Printed in the United States of America by Times Mirror Higher Education Group, Inc.,
2460 Kerper Boulevard, Dubuque, IA 52001

10  9  8  7  6  5  4  3  2  1

TO MY
PARENTS

# BRIEF CONTENTS

# CONTENTS

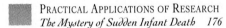
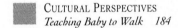

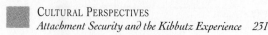

*C h a p t e r   N i n e*

# COGNITIVE DEVELOPMENT: INFORMATION-PROCESSING COMPONENTS   330
(WITH LUCIA A. FRENCH, UNIVERSITY OF ROCHESTER)

*C h a p t e r   T e n*

# INTELLIGENCE AND ACADEMIC ACHIEVEMENT   376

*C h a p t e r   E l e v e n*

# PARENTING AND FAMILY RELATIONSHIPS    424

*Chapter Fourteen*

# SEX-ROLE DEVELOPMENT  562

*Chapter Fifteen*

# MORAL DEVELOPMENT  604

# PREFACE

A s I prepared the second edition of this textbook, I kept in mind the goals that I had for the first edition. One goal was to encourage students to think critically about the development of children and the field of child development. Another goal was to write a text that could be used successfully in an introductory course, a student's first course in child development. I view these two goals as complementary. On one hand, students must understand the basic concepts and issues in a field of study before they can think critically about the field. On the other hand, giving students an understanding of basic concepts and issues should be the purpose of an introductory course. For this edition, I have retained the elements of the first edition that have helped students gain an understanding of child development.

In other respects, this edition differs greatly from the first one. During the past five years, researchers have made significant discoveries about all facets of children's development. These discoveries are described in every chapter of the book. In addition, many instructors and students who used the first edition have made insightful comments about how the book could be improved. While preparing the second edition, I carefully considered all of their comments.

The blend of the old and the new in this edition can be seen in every major feature of the book. This preface provides an overview of the book's major features. In choosing each feature, my aim was to increase the book's effectiveness in helping students understand children's development.

## Research Focus

Understanding depends on knowledge. In child development, knowledge comes from systematic research. Therefore, a focus on research is a central feature of this book.

Thousands of researchers around the world are continually adding to knowledge about children's development. In each chapter of this book, I have reviewed the most recent and important research findings. I have also scanned computer databases (e.g., PsycLit, Medline) and the tremendous variety of materials on the Internet. Consequently, this edition includes more varied and up-to-date information than would have been possible five years ago.

If not presented carefully, however, new information can reduce rather than enhance students' understanding. Students may be offered an unending series of "newsbites," without the context necessary to think critically about them. To avoid this problem, I have used the same strategy for presenting research findings as in the first edition.

First, the methods and results of the most significant studies are described in detail. Second, tables and figures are used liberally, so students can see what researchers did and what they found. Many tables and figures were created specifically for this edition from data in research reports. Finally, I have prepared students for the strong research emphasis by including a chapter on methodology as the second chapter in this book.

## Focus on Theories

Findings about children's development are more meaningful when they are related to the questions that researchers are trying to answer. Those questions often derive from developmental theories. A second feature of this book is a focus on theories intended to describe and

explain children's development. To prepare students for this focus, chapter 1 includes an overview of issues relevant to all developmental theories. Then the most important theories are introduced.

## Focus on Practical Applications

People immediately see the value of theories and research that can be applied to enhance children's development or solve problems that children have. Students often take courses in child development because they are interested in such applications. Another important feature of this text is a focus on practical applications. In the second edition, each chapter includes a boxed section titled, "Practical Applications of Research." Each section provides a closer look at research that has implications for promoting a specific aspect of development.

## Focus on Social Relationships

A new feature of the second edition is a consistent focus on the role of social relationships in children's development. Children's ability to form positive relationships with other people is a good indicator of their healthy development. These relationships also have a powerful influence on children's lives.

Despite the obvious significance of social relationships, many textbooks confine their comments about them to a couple chapters at the end of the book. By contrast, every chapter in this book ends with a section that explores the link between social relationships and the topics of the chapter. To signal this section, a graphic symbol appears in the margin beside the section's heading. These sections remind students about the social context of development and unify the book.

## Cultural Perspectives on Child Development

As in the first edition, I invite students to think about the cultural context of development as they begin each chapter. Sometimes students read a brief story adapted from observations in another culture. Sometimes students read about research in which children's development in different cultures was compared. These introductions make students aware that they should try to understand the development of children in all cultures.

For the second edition, the coverage of cultural influences has been significantly broadened. Besides including examples of the cross-cultural research, this edition includes examples of the cultural diversity (or multiculturalism) within a single nation. In addition, each chapter includes a boxed section titled, "Cultural Perspectives." This section provides an in-depth look at research either among geographically separated groups or among different cultural groups within one country. Often, this section is linked to the story or brief research summary that begins the chapter, which adds coherence to the chapter.

## A Writing Style That Is Easy to Comprehend

In writing the first edition, I chose a conversational style. I wrote as if I were talking to my readers rather than lecturing to them or reciting a list of facts. As I received reviews of the first edition, I was gratified to learn that instructors approved of this writing style. Some reviewers applauded the clear description of difficult ideas; some commented on the clarity of the tables and figures; some labeled the first edition as the most readable textbook of its kind. Because of these positive reactions, I have kept the same writing style for this edition.

I have also retained, and tried to improve, the pedagogical aids in the book. An *outline* that shows the major topics and their sequence precedes the content of each chapter. The explorations of cultural diversity that begin each chapter serve as a *preview*, introducing themes that students can carry through the chapter. Each chapter ends with a *summary* that has headings matching those in the chapter outline.

When technical terms are used for the first time, they are printed in **boldface.** All boldfaced terms are defined in a *glossary* at the end of the book. In this second edition, each term is also defined in the margin of the page on which the term is first used. This marginal glossary makes it easy for students to identify and review the new vocabulary in a chapter.

Finally, many instructors ask students to go beyond their textbook and explore some aspect of development in more detail. To help students with papers, reports, or other assignments, the first edition included annotated *suggested readings* after each chapter. This edition includes an updated list of readings.

## Organization and Content: What's New?

Reviewers of the first edition generally approved of both its topical organization and the emphasis that specific topics received. However, reviewers often suggested topics to add or to cover in more depth. By contrast, some reviewers suggested that the final chapter on developmental psychopathology was not as central to an introductory child-development course as the other chapters. To expand the coverage of other topics without making the book's length excessive, that chapter has been dropped, but some of its content (e.g., on principles of family therapy) has been moved to other chapters.

In addition, every chapter has been thoroughly revised and updated. To indicate the types of changes made, I will briefly describe the topics of each chapter and the new material in this edition.

As mentioned earlier, chapter 1 examines central issues and major theories in child development. What's new includes:

- a table outlining the positions of major theories on central issues in child development.
- data on the ethnicity of children in the United States, which is linked to the theoretical issue of cultural specificity.

Chapter 2, on research methods, includes major sections on measurement and on research design. What's new includes:

- procedures for validating measures used with children from different ethnic groups.
- comments about how social relationships between researchers and research participants can affect the quality of a study.

Chapter 3 provides an introduction to genetic influences on development. Models of gene-environment interaction receive special attention. What's new includes:

- information about chromosomal abnormalities such as fragile X syndrome and Huntington's disease.
- a discussion of how much parents' genes, rather than their childrearing practices, affect their children's development.

Chapter 4 is on prenatal development, birth, and the effects of birth complications. What's new includes:

- evidence that drug treatment can reduce the transmission of the AIDS virus from a pregnant woman to her fetus.
- more evidence on the father's role during pregnancy and birth.

Chapter 5 covers aspects of development that are closely linked to biological changes: physical growth, brain development, motor development, and early perceptual development. What's new includes:

- information about programs for reducing childhood malnutrition around the world.
- greater coverage of the dynamic-systems approach to motor development.

Chapter 6 describes the earliest phases of social development, including early emotional development and infant-parent attachments. What's new includes:

- ideas about the intergenerational transmission of attachment.
- added information about infants' relationships with caregivers other than their parents.

Chapter 7 deals primarily with children's acquisition of their first spoken language, but sign language and second-language learning are also considered. What's new includes:

- current age norms for vocabulary growth.
- new data on the language comprehension of nonhuman primates.

Chapters 8 and 9 were completely rewritten for this edition. The new versions were prepared in collaboration with Professor Lucia A. French of the University of Rochester. Chapter 8 now focuses on Piaget's and Vygotsky's theories of cognitive development. What's new includes:

- an evaluation of Piagetian curricula for elementary and secondary schools.
- thorough coverage of Vygotsky's theory and its extensions by Brown, Rogoff, Wertsch, and others.

Chapter 9 is focused on specific components of information processing such as perception and remembering. I describe this chapter's focus as information-processing components rather than information-processing theories because the chapter includes research linked to other theories (e.g., Gibson's theory of perceptual learning). What's new includes:

- a section on mental representation that explores concept formation, event schemas, and understanding of scale models.
- a discussion of educational interventions that combine aspects of information-processing and Vygotsky's theory.

Chapter 10 links the topics of intelligence and academic achievement. I first describe research on children's IQ scores and then examine achievement motivation and actual achievement. What's new includes:

- recent data about the effects of schooling on IQ.
- a description of multiple models of achievement motivation.

Chapter 11 deals with family relationships. One section describes how variations in family structure can influence children. What's new includes:

- data from the U.S. Census Bureau about the changes in families during the past 25 years.
- an expanded discussion of interventions for children with divorced parents.

Chapter 12, on peer relationships, includes information on topics ranging from the peer interactions of infants to the cliques of adolescents. What's new includes:

- evidence that "Just Say No" programs for reducing adolescents' drug use are sometimes counterproductive.
- recent data on the effects of child-care centers on peer relationships.

Chapter 13 is concerned with the development of social cognition. Major topics include self-esteem and understanding of other people. What's new includes:

- evidence that programs for gifted children may lower their self-esteem.
- new data on the young child's theory of mind.

Chapter 14, on sex-role development, examines the elements of, and explanations for, sex typing. What's new includes:

- recent data documenting hormonal influences on sex typing.
- a discussion of recent debates about parents' and teachers' contributions to children's sex typing.

Chapter 15 reviews developments in reasoning about morality, the moral emotions (e.g., guilt), and moral behavior. What's new includes:

- cross-cultural research that suggests a need for a broader definition of morality itself.
- information about moral exemplars, adults whose lives illustrate unusual moral commitment.

## Supplements

The publisher and ancillary team have worked together to produce an outstanding integrated teaching package to accompany *Child Development*. The authors of the ancillaries are all experienced teachers in the child development course. The ancillaries have been designed to make it as easy as possible to customize the entire package to meet the unique needs of professors and students.

The **Instructor's Manual,** the key to this teaching package, was created by T. Bridgett Perry of Framingham State College. The manual provides many useful tools to enhance teaching, assist preparation, and increase your enjoyment. For each chapter of the text, the manual provides student objectives and goals (summarized to reflect those in the study guide and test bank), detailed chapter summaries, lecture strategies and highlights, classroom and student activities, lists of key people and terms, essay/study questions, transparency suggestions, and film catalogue with distributors.

The **Test Item File** was constructed by Francine Blumberg of Fordham University. Francine has worked extensively with the Educational Testing Service (ETS) as a writer of test items for the Advanced Placement Test for Psychology. This comprehensive test bank includes over 1,200 multiple-choice test questions that are keyed to the text and learning objectives. Each item is designated as factual, conceptual, or applied as defined by the first three levels of Benjamin Bloom's *Taxonomy of Educational Objectives* (1956).

The questions in the Test Item File are available on *MicroTest III*, a powerful but easy-to-use test-generating program by Chariot Software Group. MicroTest is available for DOS, Windows, and Macintosh. With MicroTest, you can easily select questions from the Test Item File and print a test and an answer key. You can customize questions, headings, and instructions, you can add or import questions of your own, and you can print your test in a choice of fonts if your printer supports them. You can obtain a copy of MicroTest III by contacting your local Brown & Benchmark Sales Representative or by phoning Educational Resources at 1–800–338–5371.

The **Study Guide** was also created by T. Bridgett Perry of Framingham State College. For each chapter of the text, the student is provided with an outline, a guided review, key persons matching exercise, and study questions (key persons and study questions sections included for self-testing). The study guide includes a section designed to help students study more effectively and efficiently.

The **Brown & Benchmark Human Development Transparency/Slide Set,** Second Edition, consists of 141 acetate transparencies or slides. These full-color transparencies include graphics from various outside sources and were expressly designed to provide comprehensive coverage of all major topic areas generally covered in human development courses. A comprehensive annotated guide provides a brief description for each transparency and helpful suggestions for use in the classroom.

A **Customized Transparency Program** is available to adopters of *Child Development*, Second Edition, based on the number of textbooks ordered. Consult your Brown & Benchmark Sales Representative for ordering policies.

**The Human Development Electronic Image Bank CD-ROM** contains more than 100 useful images and a computer projection system divided into two separate programs: The Interactive Slide Show and the Slide Show Editor. The Interactive Slide Show allows you to play a preset slide show containing selected images from Times Mirror Higher Education Group textbooks. The Slide Show Editor allows you to customize and create your own

slide show. You can add slides anywhere you like in the presentation and incorporate any audio or visual files you'd like, as well as create title screens. You also may use the CD-ROM images with your own presentation software (PowerPoint, etc.). Images are available in both PICT and BMP formats (Macintosh and Windows compatible).

Several **Videotapes** are also available to instructors. Among them is the highly acclaimed series *Seasons of Life,* which captures the psychology of child development including sections covering infancy, early childhood, and childhood and adolescence. Availability is based upon the number of textbooks ordered from Brown & Benchmark Publishers by your bookstore.

The **Human Development Interactive Videodisc Set** produced by Roger Ray of Rollins College brings life-span development to life with instant access to over 30 brief video segments from the highly acclaimed *Seasons of Life* series. The two-disc set can be used alone for selecting and sequencing excerpts, or in tandem with a Macintosh computer to add interactive commentary capability, as well as extra video and search options. Consult your Brown & Benchmark Sales Representative for details.

**The Critical Thinker,** written by Richard Mayer and Fiona Goodchild of the University of California, Santa Barbara, uses excerpts from introductory psychology textbooks to show students how to think critically about psychology. This publication is available at no charge to first-year adopters of our textbook, or can be purchased separately.

# B&B CourseKits™

B&B CourseKits™ are course-specific collections of for sale educational materials custom packaged for maximum convenience and value. CourseKits offer you the flexibility of customizing and combining Brown & Benchmark course materials (B&B CourseKits™, Annual Editions®, Taking Sides®, etc.) with your own or other material. Each CourseKit contains two or more instructor-selected items conveniently packaged and priced for your students. For more information on B&B CourseKits™, please contact your local Brown & Benchmark Sales Representative.

## Annual Editions®

Magazines, newspapers, and journals of the public press play an important role in providing current, first-rate, relevant educational information. If you are interested in exposing students in your child development course to a wide range of current, well-balanced, carefully selected articles from some of the most important magazines, newspapers, and journals published today, you may want to consider *Annual Editions: Child Growth and Development,* published by the Dushkin Publishing Group, a unit of Brown & Benchmark Publishers. *Annual Editions: Child Growth and Development* is a collection of over 40 articles on topics related to the latest research and thinking in child development. *Annual Editions,* which is updated each year, has a number of features designed to make it particularly useful, including a topic guide, an annotated table of contents, and unit overviews. Consult your Brown & Benchmark Sales Representative for more details.

## Taking Sides®

Are you interested in generating classroom discussion? In finding a tool to more fully involve your students in their experience of your course? Would you like to encourage your students to become more active learners? To develop their critical thinking skills? Lastly, are you intrigued by current controversies related to issues in childhood and development? If so, you should be aware of a publication from the Dushkin Publishing Group, a unit of Brown & Benchmark Publishers: *Taking Sides: Clashing Views on Controversial Issues in Childhood and Society,* edited by Professors Robert L. DelCampo and Diane S. DelCampo of New Mexico State University. *Taking Sides,* a reader that takes a pro/con approach to issues, is designed to introduce students to controversies in childhood and development. The readings, which represent the arguments of leading child behaviorists and social commentators, reflect a variety of viewpoints and have been selected for their liveliness, currency, and substance. Consult your Brown & Benchmark Sales Representative for more details.

## CourseMedia™

As educational needs and methods change, Brown & Benchmark adds innovative, contemporary student materials for the computer, audio, and video devices of the 1990s and beyond. These include:

- Stand-alone materials
- Study guides
- Software simulations
- Tutorials
- Exercises

CourseMedia™ also includes instructional aids you can use to enhance lectures and discussions, such as:

- Videos
- Level I and III videodiscs
- CD-ROMs

## CourseWorks

CourseWorks (formerly Kinko's CourseWorks in the United States) is the Brown & Benchmark custom publishing service. With its own printing and distribution facility, CourseWorks gives you the flexibility to add current material to your course at any time. CourseWorks provides you with a unique set of options:

- Customizing Brown & Benchmark CourseBooks
- Publishing your own material
- Including any previously published material for which we can secure permissions
- Adding photos
- Performing copyediting
- Creating custom covers

## Acknowledgments

Publishing a textbook requires the combined efforts of many people. I would like to thank Michael Lange, who was psychology editor at Brown & Benchmark when the initial plan for the second edition was outlined. I also want to thank Steven Yetter, who took over as Brown & Benchmark's psychology editor and who has guided the progress of this revision. Steven and I were greatly aided by Ted Underhill, senior developmental editor for psychology. I have been impressed in my many contacts with Ted by his good sense, graciousness, and patience.

I also want to thank the experts who provided me with invaluable feedback on the drafts of chapters for the first edition, the final form of the first edition, and the drafts of revised chapters. Their thoughtful comments about the content, organization, and style that are appropriate for an introductory text gave me very clear directions for improving the book. To acknowledge the time and effort of these individuals, I would like to mention each of them:

**Margarita Azmitia**    University of California, Santa Cruz
**Leonard Abbeduto**    University of Wisconsin — Madison
**Linda Baker**    University of Maryland, Baltimore County
**Dana Birnbaum**    University of Maine
**Nathan Brody**    Wesleyan University
**Celia Brownell**    University of Pittsburgh
**Toni Campbell**    San Jose State University
**James Doyle**    Roane State Community College
**Laura Freberg**    California Polytechnic State University
**Hill Goldsmith**    University of Wisconsin — Madison
**Peter Gordon**    University of Pittsburgh
**Dana Gross**    St. Olaf College

**Walter Hapkewicz**   Michigan State University
**Karen Hayes**   University of New Mexico
**Paul Jose**   Loyola University
**Andrew Kinney**   Mohawk Valley Community College
**Claire Kopp**   Claremont Graduate School
**Rosemary Krawczyk**   Mankato State University
**Daniel Lapsley**   Brandon University
**Andrew Newcomb**   University of Richmond
**Thomas Parish**   Kansas State University
**Kathleen Preston**   Humboldt State University
**Elizabeth Rider**   Elizabethtown College
**Nan Ratner**   University of Maryland
**Paul Roodin**   State University of New York at Oswego
**Helen Ross**   San Diego State University
**Ellin Scholnick**   University of Maryland
**Susan Siaw**   California State Polytechnic University at Pomona
**Robert Siegler**   Carnegie-Mellon University
**Robert Sternberg**   Yale University
**Michael Stevenson**   Ball State University
**Robert Stewart**   Oakland University
**Granville Sydnor**   San Jacinto College
**Donna Fisher Thompson**   Niagara University
**Nadia Webb**   Rutgers University

My secretary at Purdue, Jeannie Wade, also helped in countless ways, from copying source material to typing references and printing the final manuscript of the book. Once the manuscript of the book was ready, several people helped to make it into the book you are reading, including Gloria Schiesl, production editor; Christopher E. Reese, designer; Leslie Dague and Rose Deluhery, photo editors; Rita Hingtgen, art editor; and Patricia Barth, permissions coordinator. Many other people contributed to the book in special ways, and I am grateful to all of them.

Finally, I want to thank my wife and children for their patience during my absence and occasional distraction as I tried not to fall hopelessly behind the schedule for this project. They serve as a constant reminder of the importance of child-development research for improving the lives of children and their families.

# CHILD DEVELOPMENT

*Chapter One*

# CURRENT ISSUES AND THEORIES

*T*he development of children involves a fascinating combination of processes and events. At birth, children become part of a complex social world. Their parents are usually the central figures in this new world, but even young infants are greatly affected by the larger culture that they enter at birth.

One team of researchers studied infants and parents in two cultures, that of middle-class parents in the United States and that of Mayan parents in Guatemala (Morelli et al., 1992). The results of the study are the basis for the two stories that follow. Fictitious names are used in the stories, but each story accurately describes the cultural differences in one facet of childrearing, infants' sleeping arrangements.

John and Mary Smith brought their newborn daughter Katherine home from the hospital when she was two days old. For the next few weeks Katherine slept in a bassinet in her parents' bedroom. Mary said, "We were nervous at first, so we wanted to be able to look and see that she was still there and still breathing."

After three months, Katherine was moved to her own bedroom, where she slept in a crib. Her parents felt Katherine was old enough to be by herself and that she "should have her own space." They also thought both their sleep and her sleep would be less disrupted if they were in different rooms.

The Smiths' arrangements for their infant daughter probably seem commonplace to you, because you were probably treated similarly during infancy. But notice how their arrangements contrast with those of rural Mayan infants:

With the help of a midwife, Maria Lopez gave birth to her daughter, Herlinda, at home on a hot summer afternoon. Her husband, Juan, was working in the fields outside their town when Herlinda was born. He saw his daughter for the first time when he returned in the evening. That night, Herlinda slept in her parents' bed by her mother's side. Maria did not wake up to feed Herlinda at night. She simply placed Herlinda close to her breast so that the infant could nurse whenever she wanted to.

Herlinda slept in her parents' bed until she was 2 years old. Then Maria became pregnant again. Juan told Maria that it was time to move Herlinda out of their bed. When the new baby arrived, Herlinda would need to move to another bed, and Juan said it was better to get her adjusted to sleeping somewhere else before then. So Herlinda started sleeping in a second bed in her parents' bedroom. Her father slept beside her in the same bed.

The contrasts between the U.S. and Mayan patterns are striking, and you will read more about them later. For now, the stories serve to illustrate that children's development differs across cultures. And though these two stories involve geographically separated cultures, cultural differences also exist within any large and diverse society. In the United States, for example, Black infants are more likely than White infants to sleep with their parents during the night (Lozoff, Wolf, & Davis, 1984). To understand children's development fully, you need to appreciate differences between countries and differences among ethnic groups within one country. You will learn in this book about both kinds of differences.

The U.S. and Mayan stories illustrate another fact about child development that is equally important. In both cultures—and every other culture around the world—infants normally receive their primary care from their parents. That is, parental care during infancy is universal to the human species. As children grow, parental care remains important, but children also form relationships with other adults and with peers. These relationships then influence their development.

A central theme of this book is that social relationships are central to child development. Sometimes you will read about the development of relationships themselves. For example, you will discover which experiences would help Katherine Smith and Herlinda Lopez to develop good relationships with their parents. You will also read about the effects of social relationships on children. For example, you will find out how Katherine's parents and Herlinda's parents can influence their achievement in school and their self-esteem. To highlight the role of relationships in child development, each chapter of the book concludes with

a section on the importance of social relationships to the topics examined in the chapter. Those concluding sections are indicated by a graphic symbol for social relationships in the margin.

The stories of the Smith and Lopez families illustrate a third point. Both Katherine's parents and Herlinda's parents had firm ideas about how infants change with age. That is, they had definite assumptions about child development. In addition, the girls' parents had ideas about which kinds of sleeping arrangements are good for infants. As you will see later, these ideas were part of a general theory about how children develop and how to enhance their development.

During the past century, many scholars and researchers have presented formal theories of child development. This chapter provides a survey of the most important theories. The chapter begins with an explicit definition of child development as a subject and a scientific discipline. Next, four issues critical for understanding theories of child development are presented. The following section, which makes up the bulk of the chapter, describes the essential elements of a theory and the major principles of developmental theories.

# WHAT IS CHILD DEVELOPMENT?

In informal use, *child development* refers to changes in children's height, weight, behavior, or other characteristics as they grow older. However, not all changes with age are developmental. Suppose that a boy receives a bicycle for his sixth birthday and begins riding the bicycle for hours each day. Would this change in his daily activities be an example of development? No, it would not, because it is due to a change in the boy's access to a bicycle, not a systematic change in the boy's own characteristics.

Stated formally, **child development** refers to age changes in children's characteristics that are systematic rather than haphazard, and successive rather than independent of earlier conditions (Lerner, 1986). An infant's shift from sucking milk from the mother's breast to eating solid foods is an example of a developmental change. This change is part of a systematic shift toward a mature eating pattern. It depends on earlier conditions, such as the infant's physical growth and the gradual maturation of the digestive system.

Some theorists have proposed an even stricter definition of development. Heinz Werner (1957) argued that changes are developmental only when they are from a global form of organization to a more differentiated and complex form. Thus, if children simply grew taller as they grew older, Werner would not consider that a developmental change. He would also look for—and, in this case, find—changes in children's underlying biological organization.

Theorists like Werner do not consider purely quantitative changes, such as changes in height, as developmental. They reserve the term for qualitative changes, changes in organization or structure (Green, 1989; Miller, 1993). For example, the shift at the end of infancy from simply making sounds to speaking in words reflects a qualitative change in communication.

Other theorists adopt a broader definition of development because they assume that many important age changes in children's characteristics are quantitative rather than qualitative. For example, these theorists would argue that gradual improvements in communication occur throughout infancy and childhood. Before infants use their first words, they develop the ability to communicate through facial expressions and gestures. After infants say their first words, they still need to develop many abilities before they can communicate successfully in various settings. Thus, as you will see shortly, whether development involves mostly qualitative or mostly quantitative changes is an issue on which developmental theories are divided.

Another definition of child development is the scientific discipline that focuses on the changes that occur as human beings grow to maturity. To understand these changes, you need to start at the beginning, the moment of conception. For full understanding, you need to consider even earlier events. In particular, you need to know about the production of the egg and sperm cells that join at conception. Both those early events, and the developmental changes between conception and birth, will be examined in this book. Then you will follow the development of human beings through infancy, childhood, and adolescence.

**child development**
*Age changes in children's characteristics that are systematic rather than haphazard, and successive rather than independent of earlier conditions; also, the scientific discipline that focuses on these age changes.*

Child development is multifaceted, so individuals with many kinds of expertise belong to the discipline. One facet involves physical development. The size and complexity of the human body change dramatically between conception and maturity. Pediatricians, nurses, and other health-care professionals devote their lives to studying normal physical development and working with children whose physical development is abnormal.

Another facet of children's development involves the increase with age in cognitive or intellectual abilities. What children know, learn, and can remember improves greatly as they grow. Psychologists, educators, and neuroscientists work to identify the processes responsible for these improvements and to help children whose cognitive abilities lag behind those of their peers.

Yet another facet of children's development involves emotional expressions and social behavior. Newborns have only limited ability to participate in social interactions. Before those infants reach adulthood, they learn how to recognize others' emotions, how to express their own emotions appropriately, and how to behave competently in various social situations. In short, they become mature members of their society and their culture. Psychologists, sociologists, and anthropologists share an interest in understanding these facets of development and devising interventions to help children who deviate from the normal developmental path.

All the facets of children's development are connected to one another. For example, poor nutrition can not only stunt children's physical growth but also retard their cognitive development and cause them to be apathetic in social situations. These connections explain why studies of the role of nutrition in development often bring together scientists with different areas of specialization. Nutrition is not a special case, however. In this book you will find many examples in which experts from several disciplines worked together to increase understanding of child development.

# CURRENT ISSUES IN CHILD DEVELOPMENT

Most questions about children's development fall into two broad categories. The first category includes questions about what happens during development. For example, when do children usually start walking independently? When do they become able to reason logically? How do their relationships with parents change as they move through adolescence? These questions call for a *description* of specific aspects of development.

The second category focuses not on *what* develops but on *why* it does so. For example, why do 5-year-olds typically spend more time in cooperative play with peers than 3-year-olds do? Why do some 5-year-olds spend less time cooperating with peers than playing alone? These questions call for an *explanation* of specific aspects of development. The first question is about the explanation of developmental changes. The second question refers instead to the explanation of differences between children who are the same age.

Some theories of child development emphasize the accurate and comprehensive description of developmental changes. Other theories emphasize the explanation of individual differences between children. Few theories give equal emphasis to the description and to the explanation of development. These contrasts among theories are highlighted in the following section.

However, four issues cut across theories of development. These issues are not novel. Philosophers discussed them long before the emergence of child development as a scientific discipline. The four issues have also provoked intense controversies during recent decades. Therefore, understanding them will give you a basis for analyzing and comparing developmental theories.

## Qualitative Versus Quantitative Change

Earlier you read that Werner (1957) considered only qualitative changes as truly developmental. He did not view purely quantitative changes, like changes in size, as developmental changes. Many theorists question Werner's definition of development, but all agree that he raised an important issue (Lerner, 1986). Is the average child a "little adult," who is only

smaller, less intelligent, and less socially skilled than an adult? Or are children qualitatively different from adults, with biological systems, thoughts, and behaviors that are different in kind from those of adults?

Some historians have argued that children were viewed as "little adults" in Western societies throughout most of recorded history (e.g., Aries, 1962). Other historians dispute this conclusion (Borstelmann, 1983; Pollock, 1987). Those historians cite comments by ancient and medieval writers about children's special characteristics and their need for careful training. For example, ancient Roman writers divided the years from birth to adulthood into distinct periods. Most often, they compared infancy with childhood or childhood with adolescence (French, 1977).

On the other hand, periods of development received relatively little attention until the 1700s. One provocative and influential writer of that century was Jean Jacques Rousseau. In the book *Emile*, Rousseau argued that children move through stages of development that reflect qualitative changes in all aspects of their psychological makeup.

The stage of infancy extends from birth to about age 2. Rousseau considered the development of walking and speaking as the hallmarks of this stage. The second stage, early and middle childhood, extends from 2 to 12 years of age. Rousseau believed that children in this stage can think logically, but only about objects that they can see, hear, or touch.

The third stage, late childhood, starts around age 12 and ends with puberty, the biological changes that accompany the development of sexual maturity. Rousseau did not try to state a definite age for the end of this stage because he believed that the onset of puberty varies in different climates and cultures. (As you will discover in chapter 5, his belief was correct.) Rousseau argued that children's intellectual ability increases rapidly during this third stage. However, children are not yet able to understand truly abstract ideas.

The final stage of development is adolescence, which begins at puberty and ends with the attainment of adulthood. To emphasize the importance of this stage, Rousseau called it a "second birth." During adolescence the capacity for truly abstract thinking is coupled with great emotional turbulence. Rousseau's statements in *Emile* about the onset of adolescence dramatically illustrate his view that development involves qualitative change:

> As the roaring of the waves precedes the tempest, so the murmur of rising passions announces this tumultuous change; a suppressed excitement warns us of the approaching danger. A change of temper, frequent outbursts of anger, a perpetual stirring of the mind, make the child almost ungovernable. He becomes deaf to the voice he used to obey; he is a lion in a fever; he distrusts his keeper and refuses to be controlled. (1762/1979, p. 172)

Keep Rousseau's outline of developmental stages in mind as you continue reading. His description is similar in several respects to the cognitive-developmental theory of Jean Piaget. You will see that Piaget's theory has been criticized partly because of his view that development should be described in terms of stages, or qualitative changes.

## Continuity Versus Discontinuity

A second issue concerning the description of development deals not with the typical or normal path of development but with individual differences in development. Many proverbs suggest that individual differences show great **continuity,** or stability over time. In other words, once children start on a path of development, they are likely to stay on the same path. This idea is expressed in sayings such as, "The child is father of the man"; "As the twig is bent, so grows the tree"; and, "Train a child in the way he should go, and when he is old he will not turn from it" (Prov. 22:6).

The meaning of continuity in development can be stated more precisely with a figure. Figure 1.1 shows how the reading level of three hypothetical children changed during the six grades of a traditional elementary school. Child A was already reading at the third-grade level in first grade. Child B was an average student, reading at the first-grade level in first grade. Child C was a below-average student in first grade. When tested, this child could not read at all.

**continuity**
*Stability over time, or the degree to which a child follows the same path of development from birth to maturity. More precisely, the degree to which differences between children present at one point in development are preserved as the children grow to maturity.*

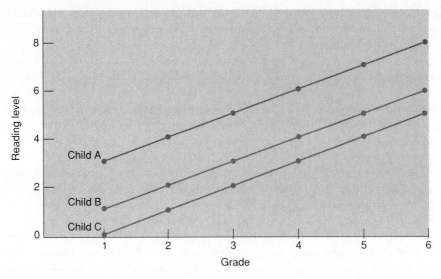

## FIGURE 1.1

The reading levels of these children show perfect continuity. Each child's reading level improves as each moves to higher grades, but the differences among the children remain constant.

**discontinuity**

*Instability over time, or substantial changes in children's developmental paths between birth and maturity. More precisely, the degree to which differences between children present at one point in development are altered as the children grow to maturity (see **continuity**).*

All the children improved greatly in reading during their elementary school years. In that sense, all experienced a developmental change. Even so, the differences in their reading ability showed great stability. The reading level of Child A remained two years above grade level. The reading level of Child B remained at grade level. Child C's reading level remained a year below grade level. This pattern reflects perfect continuity in development, or perfect stability of individual differences.

Figure 1.2 illustrates **discontinuity,** or great instability of individual differences in development over time. This figure shows the scores of three children whose relative performance in reading changed dramatically during the elementary grades. Child D was advanced in reading in first grade but lagged behind the other two children by sixth grade. Child F was delayed in reading in first grade but was far above grade level by sixth grade. In short, the ranking of the three children shifted sharply over six years, or showed little stability.

Researchers look for evidence of continuity not in sets of three children but in large and representative samples. With such samples, researchers can estimate the degree of continuity in specific characteristics for all children. Continuity also varies for different characteristics. For example, individual differences in academic achievement show greater continuity between the preschool years and adolescence than do individual differences in passivity (Kagan & Moss, 1962).

Discovering the degree of continuity in specific facets of development is important for both theoretical and practical reasons. Many theorists have argued that experiences early in life have especially powerful and lasting effects because they place children on a path of development that is difficult to alter. These theorists take evidence of high continuity in development as support for their argument (see Clarke & Clarke, 1976).

The idea that early experiences have stronger effects than those later in life has a long history. John Locke (1632–1704), an English philosopher, argued for the importance of early experience using a metaphor of the flow of water in rivers. He said:

> The little or almost insensible impressions on our tender infancies have very important and lasting consequences; and there 'tis, as in the fountains of some rivers, where a gentle application of the hand turns the flexible waters in channels, that make

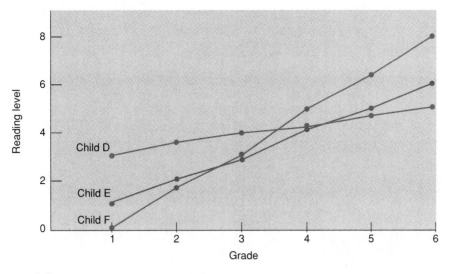

## FIGURE 1.2

The reading levels of these children show considerable discontinuity. The relative positions of children D, E, and F change greatly between the first and sixth grades.

them take quite contrary courses: and by this direction given them at first in the source, they receive different tendencies, and arrive at last at very remote and distant places. (1693/1947, p. 210)

The practical importance of information about continuity derives from its link to prediction and intervention. When an aspect of development shows high continuity, children's future performance can be predicted from their performance at a young age. In particular, children who are likely to have problems later in life can be identified early, and adults can intervene to head off those problems. For example, children who are not reading in first grade can be given extra help right away. With such help, children who are having reading difficulties may improve to an average level or better, and stay at that level throughout their school years. By contrast, if an aspect of development shows little continuity, deciding which children should be given extra help is difficult.

## Nature Versus Nurture

Probably no issue in the field of child development has aroused more heated controversy than that of nature versus nurture. Unlike the first two issues, questions about nature versus nurture deal with the explanation of development rather than its description. **Nature** refers to the influence of genetic inheritance, or heredity, on children's development. **Nurture** refers to the influence of the environment on children's development. In this context, *environment* is defined broadly, including children's learning, training, education, and other experiences. Questions about the relative importance of nature and nurture have been the subject of vigorous debates not only among scientists but also among laypeople (see figure 1.3).

## A Philosopher's View

An early discussion of the nature-nurture issue is in the writings of Plato, the greatest philosopher of ancient Greece. Plato (427?–347 B.C.) presented a model for an ideal government in his *Republic*. He laid out a detailed plan for the rearing and education of the children from whom a nation's leaders would be selected. Those children would be separated from their parents at birth. They would be reared together by nurses who would carefully control their experience. Even the stories that the children heard at bedtime would be censored. In short, Plato advocated total control over the children's nurture based on a master plan that would specify all their experiences.

**nature**
*A general term that refers to the effects of heredity or genetic influence on children's development.*

**nurture**
*A general term that refers to the effects of learning, training, education, and other environmental influences on children's development.*

## FIGURE 1.3

Some people make bets about the importance of heredity (or nature) and environment (or nurture) in human development. The question has also been a source of theoretical controversy. You will discover as you read that the question is still open but that the final answer will not be as simple as Gladys or her husband think.

*The Born Loser* reprinted by permission of Newspaper Enterprise Association, Inc.

Plato did not dismiss the importance of nature or heredity. He wrote metaphorically that some men—the best men—are made of gold, others of silver, and still others of brass and iron. He asserted that these characteristics "will generally be preserved in [their] children" (1942, p. 303). Thus, Plato strongly believed in inherited differences among people.

How did Plato integrate his ideas about nurture and nature? His proposals were radical for his time—and for the present. He argued that the survival and prosperity of the state depended on the government's control over all mating and childrearing. In his words, "the best of either sex should be united with the best as often, and the inferior with the inferior, as seldom as possible; and [the rulers] should rear the offspring of the one sort of union; but not of the other, if the flock is to be maintained in first-rate condition" (p. 346). That is, Plato wanted government leaders to control both the nurture and the nature of their successors.

Plato's radical proposals show the importance of the nature-nurture issue. The political implications of assuming that heredity greatly affects children's development can be revolutionary, and sometimes alarming (Baumrind, 1993; Herrnstein & Murray, 1994; Horgan, 1993; Jackson, 1993). So can the implications of assuming that children's development is greatly affected by their environments.

Still, Plato's position on the nature-nurture issue was more moderate than that of many scholars who followed him. Plato explicitly acknowledged the joint influences of nature and nurture on children's development. Many later writers phrased the issue as an "either-or," suggesting that either nature or nurture largely determines children's development.

## Gesell and the Principle of Maturation

One extreme advocate of the influence of nature was a pediatrician named Arnold Gesell (1880–1961). Gesell argued that heredity influences children's status at birth (e.g., the color

FIGURE 1.4
Gesell took many films of the identical twin girls who participated in his research on training, maturation, and motor development. You cannot tell from this photograph which girl received special training. Even if you saw the entire film, you would find it hard to judge which girl was trained because her twin showed the same skill in climbing stairs once she reached the normal age for the development of climbing.

of their eyes) and their pattern of growth between infancy and adulthood. He defined **maturation** as the process by which genes control the course of development.

To show the importance of maturation, Gesell did several experiments with identical twins. For example, he gave one toddler girl special training in motor skills like climbing stairs (see figure 1.4). Her twin sister received no special training. Although the trained girl learned to climb stairs earlier than her untrained sister did, Gesell did not conclude that nurture has a strong influence on development. Instead, he extended the experiment to see whether the girl who had received special training continued to show more advanced motor skills than her sister.

The answer was no. Almost as soon as the untrained sister reached the age when most children learn to climb stairs, she did so as well as the trained twin. Gesell found similar results for other motor skills. Special training was effective, but the untrained girl quickly caught up with her trained sister once she reached the normal age for the development of each skill. Gesell took these findings as evidence that maturation controls children's rate of development.

Unfortunately, Gesell could not specify how maturation operated. The concept remained somewhat of a mystery. Gesell did years of research in which he carefully recorded the average age at which children can perform various behaviors such as grasping objects or playing a piano. Yet he could not convincingly explain why some children performed these behaviors earlier or later than the average child did. His research failed to show how maturation led either to the normal course of development or to differences in development.

**maturation**
*The process by which children's genes control the course of their development.*

## Watson and Classical Conditioning

During the early years of Gesell's career, John B. Watson (1878–1958) presented an equally extreme argument for the influence of nurture or experience on development. In one book he boasted, "Give me a dozen healthy infants, well-formed, and my own specified world to bring them up in, and I'll guarantee to take any one at random and train him to become any type of specialist I might select—doctor, lawyer, artist, merchant-chief, and yes, even beggar-man and thief, regardless of his talents, penchants, tendencies, abilities, vocations, and race of his ancestors" (1930, p. 104).

**FIGURE 1.5**

Pavlov and his assistants prepare for an experiment in classical conditioning with their usual subject, a dog.

**classical conditioning**
*A type of learning that results from the repeated pairing of two stimuli. The response that naturally follows one stimulus (e.g., the presentation of food) begins to occur following the other stimulus (e.g., a bell), after the two stimuli are repeatedly paired.*

**unconditioned stimulus**
*In classical conditioning, the term for the signal or event that elicits the unconditioned response.*

**unconditioned response**
*In classical conditioning, the natural, spontaneous, or unlearned response to an unconditioned stimulus.*

**conditioned stimulus**
*The term in classical conditioning for the stimulus that begins to elicit a response after it is repeatedly paired with another stimulus that spontaneously elicits the same response (see classical conditioning).*

**conditioned response**
*The term in classical conditioning for an organism's reaction to a conditioned stimulus.*

Of course, Watson was not forced (or allowed) to make good his boast. He never took charge of a dozen newborns and tried to control their development from that point to adulthood. He did complete several experiments showing the influence of experiences in infancy on emotional development. These experiments were based on the principle of classical conditioning.

**Classical conditioning** is a type of learning that occurs when two stimuli are repeatedly paired. The response that normally follows one stimulus (e.g., salivation after seeing food) begins to occur following the second stimulus (e.g., hearing a bell) after the two have been paired several times. Classical conditioning was first described by Ivan Pavlov (1849–1936), a Russian psychologist.

Pavlov noted that dogs produce saliva when they see a piece of meat or another type of food (see figure 1.5). Pavlov described the sight of food as an **unconditioned stimulus** that elicited the **unconditioned response** of salivation. The stimulus and response are *unconditioned* because they are not the result of special experiences: They occur naturally or spontaneously.

Pavlov discovered that if he regularly rang a bell just before presenting the food, dogs would start to salivate at the sound of the bell. In Pavlov's terms, the pairing of the bell with the food was a form of conditioning that made the bell a **conditioned stimulus** for salivation. The dogs' salivation after hearing the bell was a **conditioned response.** The change in the dogs' behavior after they had experienced the repeated pairing of the bell with the food was an illustration of classical conditioning.

During the 1920s Watson (1928) studied the classical conditioning of fear in infants. His most famous experiment was with a 9-month-old boy whom he called Little Albert. First Watson showed the boy a white rabbit. The boy initially enjoyed looking at and touching the rabbit.

Then Watson changed the situation. When Albert touched the rabbit, Watson hammered on a steel bar that was a foot behind Little Albert's head. The loud clang of the hammer on the bar frightened the boy and he started to cry. Eventually, he calmed down and reached for the rabbit again. But when he touched it, Watson again hammered on the steel bar behind his head. After the boy's reaching for the rabbit was paired a few times with the clanging of the bar, his behavior changed greatly. He not only did not try to touch the rabbit, he also showed fear whenever he saw the rabbit. In other words, Little Albert learned to fear rabbits through classical conditioning.

Watson concluded that classical conditioning is the source of most fears in childhood. He advised parents to use classical conditioning to produce desirable fears, like fear of fire, and eliminate undesirable fears, like fear of the dark. More generally, Watson asserted that parents could mold their children to become whatever they wanted by controlling what the children learned. In short, Watson argued that nurture determines children's development.

## Combined and Interactive Effects of Nature and Nurture

Gesell and Watson presented their arguments about the significance of nature and nurture more than half a century ago. Nevertheless, the issue that they debated remains unresolved. Controversies about the relative importance of nature and nurture have persisted to the present. You will read more about these controversies in chapter 3, which focuses on the contributions of heredity to children's development.

One theme of chapter 3 is that these controversies persist because some scholars continue to phrase the issue as one of nature *versus* nurture. For most aspects of development, the issue is better phrased in terms of the joint influences of nature *and* nurture. Most often, children differ from each other because of differences in both their genes and their environments, as Plato proposed long ago.

In addition, some aspects of development depend on more complex interactions between nature and nurture. For children with a certain genetic makeup, one kind of experience may be especially beneficial or especially harmful. For children with a different genetic makeup, the same experience may have little or no effect.

Consider the effects of sunbathing, or getting a suntan by spending hours in direct sunlight. Sunbathing is especially hazardous for children with fair skin because they sunburn easily. Children with darker skin are less affected by their time in the sun than are those with fair skin. Thus the experience of sunbathing has different effects on children who differ in their genetic makeup. In chapter 3, you will read more about such interactions between the effects of nature and nurture.

# Cultural Specificity Versus Developmental Universals

The last issue that cuts across major theories of development concerns the significance of culture. Unlike the other three issues, this issue involves both the description and the explanation of development. Some researchers have argued that cultural variations have powerful effects on children's development. These variations affect when (or if) children develop certain skills and which influences on their development are most powerful. Theories that emphasize these variations include implicit or explicit assumptions about **cultural specificity.** Advocates for cultural specificity assume that the most accurate descriptions and explanations of children's development will vary across cultures.

Other theories place little emphasis on cultural variations. These theories include implicit or explicit assumptions that the most significant aspects of children's development are similar in every culture. Theorists who accept such assumptions believe that human beings—and human children—are more alike than different from one another. This belief leads directly to hypotheses about **developmental universals.** Advocates for developmental universals assume that children in different cultures develop important skills at roughly the same ages through a single, universal set of processes.

To understand this issue fully, you need to know how culture is defined. Although definitions differ, the central meaning of a **culture** is a pattern of behaviors, beliefs, arts, language use, values, ideas, and social institutions that is characteristic of a human group and that is transmitted from one generation to the next. The elements of a culture can be abstract (ideas) or concrete (arts). Whether abstract or concrete, the elements of a culture must be shared by, or common to, a group of people. In addition, they must be socially transmitted, through experience, rather than passed on through genetic inheritance.

Certain characteristics of a culture are especially relevant to child development. Super and Harkness (1986) described these characteristics as defining the **developmental niche** of

**cultural specificity**
*An assumption that descriptions and explanations of children's development are specific to a culture and vary across cultures.*

**developmental universals**
*Descriptions or explanations of children's development that are assumed to hold in every culture.*

**culture**
*A pattern of behaviors, beliefs, arts, language use, values, ideas, and social institutions that is characteristic of a human group and that is transmitted from one generation to the next.*

**developmental niche**
*The cultural context in which children are reared and to which they are adapted.*

a culture. In biology, a niche is the place within an environment where an organism makes its home and to which it is adapted. The developmental niche for children refers to the cultural context in which they are reared and to which they are adapted.

Super and Harkness (1986) proposed that a developmental niche has three major components. The first is the physical and social settings in which children live. Earlier you read about infants' sleeping arrangements in the United States and in rural Guatemala. Infants' sleeping arrangements fall into this first component of a developmental niche.

The second component includes the customs of child care and childrearing in a culture. How parents arrange infants' sleeping and their daily routines are part of this component. *Cultural Perspectives*: "A Cross-Cultural Study of Infants' Sleeping Arrangements" gives some details about the contrasting patterns in U.S. and Guatemalan families.

The third component of a developmental niche is the psychology of the adults who care for children. This component includes parents' beliefs about what children need to be taught. For example, in some cultures parents believe infants must be taught to walk and to talk (Super & Harkness, 1986). Also included in this component are parents' beliefs about the goals of childrearing. *Cultural Perspectives*: "A Cross-Cultural Study of Infants' Sleeping Arrangements" describes how infants' sleeping arrangements in the United States and rural Guatemala are linked to parents' beliefs about children's independence and about strong family ties.

To examine cultural influences on development, researchers have used two general approaches. **Cross-cultural research** involves the study of children in two or more human groups that are geographically separated and part of distinct societies or nations. *Cultural Perspectives:* "A Cross-Cultural Study of Infants' Sleeping Arrangements" is an example, and you will encounter many other examples in later chapters. Child development researchers have studied children on every inhabited continent in both modern and preindustrial societies (Harkness, 1992; Munroe, Munroe, & Whiting, 1981; Whiting & Edwards, 1988).

The second approach can be described as the study of **multiculturalism,** the examination of cultural diversity within a single nation. Most large countries include people from various cultural backgrounds. Researchers are now exploring not only how the development of children in these groups differs but also how the relations among groups affect children's development (Greenfield, 1993; Harrison et al., 1990; McLoyd, 1990a; Spencer, 1990).

Most children in the United States are White, but many belong to other cultural groups. Writers disagree about the best terms to use for these groups. Whites are sometimes called European Americans. Blacks are sometimes called African Americans. People whose ancestors were among the original inhabitants of North America are sometimes called Native Americans but more often called American Indians. Another group, Hispanics, includes people defined by their origin rather than their race.

Moreover, every large cultural group can be subdivided. American Indians often prefer to identify themselves by their tribe (e.g., Sioux, Cherokee, or Navaho) rather than by the general label. Hispanics who came from Puerto Rico are often distinguished from those who came from other Caribbean islands or from Central and South America.

In this book, cultural and ethnic groups are described with the most specific label possible. For example, research on Mexican American children is described using that label rather than the more general label of Hispanic children. When a general label is appropriate, those used by the U.S. Bureau of the Census are used in this book. In the 1990 census, people identified themselves as White, Black, American Indian (including Eskimos and Aleuts), or Asian (including Pacific Islanders), and as being or not being of Hispanic origin.

Figure 1.6 shows the Census Bureau's labels, slightly abbreviated. The figure also shows the distribution of the U.S. population of children in 1992. For comparison, the projected distribution of the U.S. population of children in 2010 is shown. Most U.S. children in 1992 were White, and that ethnic group is still projected to be the majority in 2010. However, the percentage of children in other ethnic groups is expected to increase between 1992 and 2010. The greatest increases are expected in the Hispanic and Asian groups.

**cross-cultural research**
*The study of children in two or more human groups that are geographically separated and part of distinct societies or nations.*

**multiculturalism**
*Concerned with the cultural diversity, or the differences among cultural groups, within a single nation.*

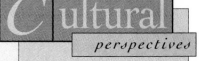

A CROSS-CULTURAL
STUDY OF INFANTS'
SLEEPING
ARRANGEMENTS

Deciding where an infant should sleep may seem like a simple matter. However, parents in different cultures make decisions about infants' sleeping arrangements that reveal a great deal about the cultural context of childhood.

Gilda Morelli and her colleagues (1992) interviewed 18 White middle-class mothers in the United States who had a child between 2 and 28 months old. They also interviewed 14 Mayan mothers in rural Guatemala who had a child between 12 and 22 months old. The interviews focused on the mothers' decisions about where that child slept, and the mothers' reasons for their decisions.

Most U.S. mothers had placed their newborns in a bassinet near their own bed. None slept with their infants in their own bed. In explaining this decision, mothers said that night feedings were easier when the infant was in the same room. They also liked being able to check at night to make sure the infant was okay.

Most mothers moved their infants out of their room before the infants were 3 months old. These mothers felt 3-month-olds were old enough to be by themselves. In addition, mothers said they didn't want to wake the infant when they went to bed later or awoke earlier than the infant did. These comments suggest one aspect of the developmental niche for U.S. children, different schedules of waking and sleeping for infants and for parents.

More than a third of the U.S. mothers said they moved their infants out of their room to encourage the infants' independence and give the infants their own territory. They also wanted to make the infants more able to accept separations from parents. In broader terms, mothers' decisions about where their infants slept reflected their ideas about child development and their goals in parenting.

In contrast to U.S. infants, no Mayan infants slept in a bed by themselves. All slept in their mother's bed from birth until 2 or 3 years of age. This arrangement was convenient because mothers could feed their infants simply by making the breast accessible, without even waking up. But Mayan mothers also felt infants would be very upset if they slept alone. They wanted their infants to form a positive relationship to them, and they felt sleeping together would promote that goal. As in the United States, Mayan infants' sleeping arrangements reflected their mothers' beliefs about children and their parenting goals.

Can you say which sleeping arrangements are better? Probably not, if you adopt the viewpoint of cultural specificity. According to Morelli et al. (1992), each pattern fits the values of the parents in that culture. Mayan parents choose sleeping arrangements that express the value they place on close family relationships and interdependence. U.S. parents choose sleeping arrangements that express the value they place on self-reliance and independence. In this way, the care of infants reveals and reinforces the values of a culture.

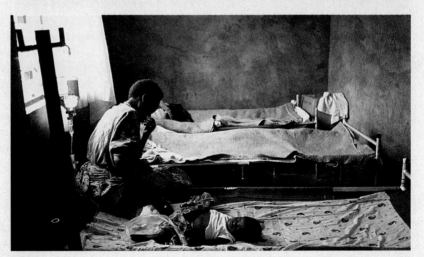

Most U.S. parents prefer to have their infants sleep in a separate room that is clearly designed for the infants. Parents in many other cultures, including this African mother, prefer to sleep in the same room and in the same bed as their infants. In these ways, infants' sleeping arrangements reflect the emphasis that adults in different cultures place on independence versus interpendence.

FIGURE 1.6

In 1992 more than two-thirds of U.S. children under 18 years of age were White. The Census Bureau estimates that by 2010, the percentage of White children in the United States will decrease as the percentages of other racial and ethnic groups increase.

Source: U.S. Census Bureau.

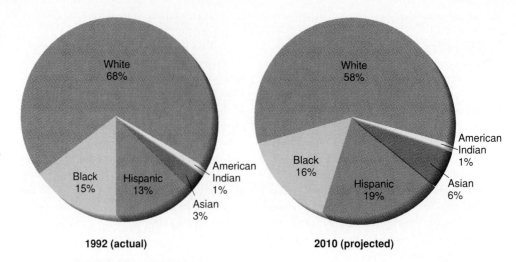

1992 (actual)          2010 (projected)

The United States is not unusual in becoming more culturally diverse over time. People around the world are leaving their native countries to escape from war and oppression or to search for a better life. These global changes give special emphasis to the issue of whether children's development shows great cultural specificity or impressive universality.

# THEORIES OF CHILD DEVELOPMENT

Many scholars have tried to describe and explain children's development. The most detailed, coherent, and influential of these accounts are regarded as theories of development. This section begins with a formal definition of a developmental theory and some guidelines for comparing theories. Then the distinctive features of several major theories are discussed.

## Defining and Comparing Developmental Theories

When used by laypeople, the word *theoretical* can have a negative connotation. As secondary definitions of the term, one dictionary lists "lacking verification or practical application" and "unproved or uncertain" (Morris, 1981). This view of theory underlies statements like "The plan is purely theoretical," or, to excuse some wild idea, "It's just a theory."

Scientists view theories much more positively. You can understand why if you read the primary definition of a theory in the same dictionary. A **theory** is "systematically organized knowledge applicable in a relatively wide variety of circumstances; especially, a system of assumptions, accepted principles, and rules of procedure devised to analyze, predict, or otherwise explain the nature or behavior of a specified set of phenomena."

The basic elements of a theory are its assumptions and accepted principles. Some assumptions or principles are stated as definitions of abstract concepts. For example, Sigmund Freud assumed that people have a psychological structure called the *id* that seeks pleasure through the gratification of instinctive drives. In psychological theories, entities like the id that cannot be observed directly are often called **constructs.** Intelligence and hyperactivity are other psychological constructs.

Other assumptions or principles are stated as general laws about phenomena. John B. Watson, for example, treated classical conditioning as a law of learning. He assumed that classical conditioning occurs whenever two stimuli are repeatedly paired.

Equally central to theories are **hypotheses,** statements that have not yet been proved, which are derived from the assumptions and principles of a theory. A theory is tested when experiments are done to examine its hypotheses. If a prediction implied by a hypothesis is confirmed, the theory is strengthened or becomes more convincing. If the prediction is not confirmed, the theory is weakened or becomes more doubtful.

**theory**
*A system of assumptions, accepted principles, and rules of procedure devised to analyze, predict, or otherwise explain a set of phenomena.*

**constructs**
*Entities that are part of some psychological theory but that cannot be observed directly (e.g., intelligence and hyperactivity).*

**hypotheses**
*Statements that have not yet been proved, which are derived from the assumptions and principles of a theory.*

Today, many children not only watch network television programs but also view movies on videotape. What would you predict (or, what is your theory) about the effects of viewing on children's behavior? If these boys watch a movie with many violent episodes, will they become more aggressive, or will viewing such a movie reduce the boys aggressive impulses? If you think viewing violent episodes could have both effects, you must explain more clearly when and why. Without such an explanation, your theory of the effects of viewing violent behavior on television would not be falsifiable—or useful.

## Attributes of an Ideal Theory

Experiments done to test hypotheses provide one way of evaluating and comparing theories. However, theories can be evaluated in other ways. Three attributes of a good theory are suggested by its definition. Researchers often add two more, giving a total of five attributes of an ideal theory:

1. *Accurate Predictions and Useful Explanations.* The goal of any theory is the explanation of phenomena. Often, the most convincing test of an explanation is an accurate prediction of some event. For example, some theories include hypotheses about how children are affected by viewing aggressive behavior (e.g., Bandura, 1977b). These theories suggest that children who watch aggressive television programs will behave more aggressively than those who watch nonaggressive programs. If an experiment confirms this prediction, you can conclude that the theory is useful in explaining children's aggression.

A theory of this kind would also be useful in suggesting a way to reduce children's aggression. That is, children should not be exposed to aggressive television programs. More generally, a theory is useful when it suggests techniques for enhancing desirable behaviors and healthy development.

2. *Hypotheses That Are Capable of Being Disconfirmed.* A good theory contains a sort of self-destruct mechanism. That is, the theory includes hypotheses whose disconfirmation would lead to the collapse of the entire theory. Researchers refer to this criterion by saying that the theory is **falsifiable.** A falsifiable theory always passes this critical test: Experiments can be designed that can conclusively show whether the theory is right or wrong. If designing such studies was impossible, then researchers would have no way to find out whether the theory was right *or* wrong.

Suppose, for example, that a theory includes two assumptions. First, children learn to be aggressive by watching aggressive television programs. Second, children's aggressive impulses can be defused by watching aggressive television programs. The two assumptions lead to contradictory predictions. Because the theory can account for either an increase or a decrease in children's aggression after watching aggressive TV programs, it fails the falsifiability criterion.

**falsifiable**
*A property of a good theory, indicating that experiments can be designed to show conclusively whether the theory is right or wrong. A falsifiable theory contains one or more hypotheses whose disconfirmation would lead to a rejection of the entire theory.*

3. *Systematically Organized, Logically Consistent Propositions.* The assumptions, principles, and hypotheses of a theory cannot be thrown together haphazardly. They must have some structure and be consistent with one another. This criterion may seem easy to meet, but as a theory increases in scope and complexity, or changes over time, contradictions can easily creep in. Additions to a theory may, therefore, weaken rather than strengthen it.

4. *Broadly Applicable Knowledge.* Suppose one theorist said that he could explain why young children are afraid of the dark. Suppose another theorist said that she could explain all fears that children express during infancy, childhood, and adolescence. You would probably be more impressed with the theory that seemed more broadly applicable, and most researchers would, too. That is, researchers view theories as better when those theories are more broadly applicable.

Nevertheless, theorists may (to use an old saying) "bite off more than they can chew." A theorist who proposes to explain too much may not provide a good explanation of anything. For this reason, an uneasy balance exists between so-called "grand theories" and theories that focus on a few behaviors in specific conditions. In this book, you will read about grand theories that were rejected after more specific theories were proposed. You will also read about small-scale theories that were gradually expanded to account for more findings about development.

5. *Heuristic Value.* The final attribute of a good theory is more subjective than the previous ones. The word *heuristic* means guiding discovery or learning. A theory is of great **heuristic value** when it leads to a large amount of productive research designed to evaluate, to extend, or even to discredit the theory. No scientific field can advance without new ideas, so theories with heuristic value are prized even when some of their assumptions are inaccurate or misleading.

**heuristic value**
*One criterion for the evaluation of a theory. A theory is of great heuristic value when it provokes a great deal of research designed to evaluate, expand, or even to disconfirm the theory.*

## Comparing Theories of Development: When and Why?

Is there a single, ideal theory of child development? There isn't now, and there probably never will be. One reason is that no theory tries to answer all questions about children's development. Some theories focus on questions about personality development, whereas others focus on questions about cognitive or social development. Even when two theories deal with the same aspect of development, they may be complementary rather than contradictory. One theory may offer only a description of developmental changes. The other may instead offer an explanation of differences between children the same age.

Of course, theories sometimes offer competing explanations for the same phenomena. That raises the question, "Who's right?" When the conflict is central to the field, researchers often take sides. They conduct experiments and publish papers in which they defend their position and criticize their proponents. Often, popular writers become interested in the controversy because it makes science more personal and dramatic. These writers prepare articles with titles like, "The Revolution in Psychologists' Ideas about Children."

Sometimes all the hoopla is justified. Some controversies are critical to our understanding of children. Some shed light on basic questions about the origins and future of the human species. Some have important implications for childrearing and public policy.

You should recognize, however, that such controversies do not go on indefinitely. Eventually, they are resolved. The weight of the evidence accumulated by many researchers supports one side, the other side, or some blend of the two.

In the rest of this chapter, you will read about some theories that currently are well accepted and others that currently are controversial. All the theories are worth your attention because they raise important questions about children's development. Table 1.1 lists the theories that will be reviewed. The table also summarizes the position of each theory on the four developmental issues. Not all issues are central to every theory, so some cells in the table are blank. Examining the table now will give you a framework for understanding the detailed information that follows.

**TABLE 1.1** *Positions of Major Theories on Four Developmental Issues*

| THEORY | QUALITATIVE VS. QUANTITATIVE CHANGES | CONTINUITY VS. DISCONTINUITY | NATURE VS. NURTURE | CULTURAL SPECIFICITY VS. DEVELOPMENTAL UNIVERSALS |
|---|---|---|---|---|
| Psychoanalytic theory (Freud and Erikson) | Qualitative changes (stages of personality development) are emphasized. | Substantial continuity from childhood to adulthood is expected. | Erikson emphasized nurture more than nature, but both theorists assumed nature and nurture jointly influence development. | Erikson attached more importance to culture than Freud did, but both theorists assumed stages of personality development are similar across cultures. |
| Learning theories | No qualitative changes (or stages) are assumed. | Children's behavior shows continuity if their environments do. | Nurture or environment is emphasized more than nature. | The major principles of learning are assumed to hold universally. |
| Piaget's genetic epistemology | Qualitative changes (stages) are described. | | Nature and nurture interact as children construct their knowledge of the world. | Cognitive stages and the factors influencing their development are assumed to be universal. |
| Information-processing approaches | Qualitative and quantitative changes, but no general stages, are assumed. | | | |
| Ethological theories | | Moderate continuity across childhood is expected. | Both nature and nurture are considered important. | Characteristics universal to the human species are emphasized. |
| Vygotsky's theory | Qualitative and quantitative changes, but no general stages, are described. | | Both nature and nurture are important, but effects of nurture are emphasized. | Cultures have a great influence on what develops and how it develops. |
| Bronfenbrenner's ecological systems theory | | | Nurture is important, but children's nature affects their response to environments. | Effects of specific influences are assumed to depend heavily on the cultural context. |

*Note.* Blanks indicate issues not important in a particular theory.

## Psychoanalytic Theories

The first major theory of child development was designed to explain why some adults become mentally ill. Sigmund Freud (1856–1939) used the method of psychoanalysis to explore both normal and abnormal personality development. Later, Erik Erikson (1902–1994) modified Freud's ideas while presenting an outline of development through life.

### Freud's Theory of Personality Development

Freud was trained as a physician and then specialized in neurology, the study of the nervous system and its disorders. Freud saw many patients whose physical ailments had no apparent biological causes. He invited these patients to talk at length, without interruption, about their past lives and their current thoughts, wishes, and emotions (see figure 1.7). Freud called this method of treatment **psychoanalysis.** As he tried to explain what happened during his sessions with patients, he devised the first psychoanalytic theory.

Most of Freud's patients were adults. After listening to them talk about themselves, Freud became convinced that their psychological problems originated in childhood. Moreover, he argued that his ideas about the causes of adults' problems were critical to understanding normal personality development. He formulated several sets of ideas about personality development during his career, and he revised his ideas over time (Emde, 1992; Miller, 1993). Best known, however, are his hypotheses about (a) stages in personality development and (b) the development of the basic components of personality.

**psychoanalysis**
*A treatment for mental illness devised by Sigmund Freud in which patients talk at great length and with virtually no interruptions about their past experiences and their current thoughts, wishes, and emotions.*

## FIGURE 1.7

Freud's exploration of the human mind began in surroundings like these. As Freud's patients reclined on the couch, he practiced the form of therapy called psychoanalysis. During therapy sessions, Freud gained the insights that led to his psychoanalytic theory. This couch and room are not Freud's original ones from Vienna, however. They are in London, where Freud moved after Hitler's takeover of Germany during the 1930s.

**libido**
*Freud's term for a fund of sexual energy that is focused on different bodily organs during different periods in development.*

**psychosexual stages**
*Developmental phases proposed by Freud that reflect changes in the focus of sexual energy on different bodily organs. The stages describe the psychological consequences of transformations in sexuality.*

**Oedipal crisis**
*According to Freud, a stage between 3 and 6 years of age when boys are sexually attracted to their mothers, and are hostile to their fathers, but are not fully conscious of their feelings.*

**Electra complex**
*According to Freud, a stage between 3 and 6 years of age when girls are sexually attracted to their fathers and hostile to their mothers.*

**identification**
*According to Freud, the process that motivates children to try to become like their same-sex parent in all important respects.*

***Stages of Psychosexual Development***    Freud assumed that all human beings are endowed from birth with **libido,** which is sexually charged psychological energy. This energy is focused on different bodily organs at different ages. When the focus of libido changes, changes in behavior occur. These changes define a series of **psychosexual stages.** Freud called the stages *psychosexual* because they reflect the psychological consequences of the various modes of early sexuality. The stages occur in the following sequence.

1. *Oral stage.* Immediately after birth, infants' sexual energy is focused on the mouth. Some behaviors that show the infants' oral focus are sucking, spitting, and biting.

2. *Anal stage.* During the second year of life, toddlers' sexual energy is focused on the anus. They show great interest in the expulsion or retention of feces. Of course, this period is also when most parents begin to toilet train their children.

3. *Phallic (or early genital) stage.* Freud believed that boys around 3 years of age begin to seek sexual pleasure by handling their penis (for which the Latin word is *phallus*). Young girls recognize that they lack a penis and begin to envy boys.

According to Freud, boys also go through the **Oedipal crisis** between 3 and 6 years of age (Emde, 1992). Freud took the name for this crisis from the Greek myth of Oedipus, who murdered his father and married his mother without knowing that he was related to either. Freud assumed that preschool boys are sexually attracted to their mothers and hostile to their fathers, although they are not fully conscious of their feelings. He also assumed that preschool girls become sexually attracted to their fathers and hostile to their mothers. He described this combination of feelings and motives as the **Electra complex,** taking this name from another Greek myth.

Children in the phallic stage are largely unaware of their sexual and aggressive impulses toward parents, but they are still distressed by them. In response, children repress their impulses and identify with the parent of the same sex. **Identification,** to Freud, meant a desire to become like the parent in all important respects.

4. *Latency stage.* After children repress their unacceptable impulses toward parents by identifying with the parents, they move into the next psychosexual stage. This stage lasts

from roughly 6 years of age to puberty. It is called the latency stage because sexual impulses are under control and out of sight.

5. *Genital stage.* At puberty, sexual impulses arise again. According to Freud, puberty does not bring another form of infantile or childish sexuality. Instead, adolescents reach the end point of psychosexual development. Freud argued that humans enter the genital stage during adolescence and remain in that stage throughout adulthood.

***Components of Personality and Their Development*** According to Freud, the structure of personality also changes during early and middle childhood. Freud proposed that infants' behavior is controlled by the **id,** the component of personality that seeks the immediate gratification of instinctive desires. No other component exists in early infancy, so the young infant is continually trying to increase feelings of pleasure and reduce tension.

As infants grow older, they face demands from parents to restrain their impulses. To resolve the conflicts between instinctive desires and external demands, a second component of personality develops. This component, the **ego,** tries to satisfy the impulses of the id, but not always immediately or directly. The ego may delay the expression of impulses, or divert them into more acceptable channels, so that they create fewer problems. In this way the ego helps children cope with reality.

A third component of personality, the **superego,** emerges in early childhood. The superego represents the norms and standards of the culture as children have internalized them. One part of the superego, the **conscience,** represents the punitive side of norms. It instructs children about what they should not do and makes them feel guilty if they go against it. Another part of the superego, the **ego ideal,** represents the positive side of cultural norms. It encourages children to become models of desirable behavior and achievement.

Freud's idea that conscience is not present at birth but, instead, emerges during the first few years of life was not novel. More novel were Freud's hypotheses about disciplinary techniques by parents that lead children to develop either a strong or weak superego. For several decades child development researchers tried to test these hypotheses (see Maccoby, 1980). The findings of this research were often inconclusive or contrary to Freud's predictions. As a result, many of Freud's ideas are not accepted by current researchers.

Nevertheless, large numbers of therapists continue to use psychoanalysis to treat mental disorders. In addition, some researchers continue to explore Freud's writings for significant insights about children's development (Emde, 1992). As the model of psychosexual stages implies, Freud emphasized the long-term significance of experiences in infancy and early childhood. As the comments about the conflicts between the id, ego, and superego imply, Freud emphasized the influence of nonconscious processes on children's behavior. You will see that these ideas have echoes in modern theories of social and personality development.

## Erikson's Outline of Psychosocial Stages

Freud's many disciples often proposed significant revisions in his theory. For the field of child development, the most important variant of Freud's psychoanalytic theory is that of Erik Erikson.

Erikson was born in Germany but moved to the United States during the 1930s. In the United States he studied patterns of childrearing in several cultural groups, including the Sioux of South Dakota and the Yurok of California. Perhaps because of these experiences, Erikson emphasized the impact of culture on personality development. He also believed that children's social relationships greatly influence their personality. By contrast, Erikson viewed sexual instincts as less important than Freud did.

Erikson proposed eight **psychosocial stages** that express, in capsule form, the key experiences and events of the human life cycle. As figure 1.8 shows, Erikson's stages for infancy and childhood roughly correspond to those of Freud. Yet even during those years, Erikson viewed social experiences as more critical for development than sexually charged energy. For example, he suggested that oral pleasure in infancy is less important for later development than is an infant's sense of trust in parents and the world. Trust reflects confidence in

**id**
*In Freud's theory, the component of personality that always seeks the immediate gratification of instinctive desires.*

**ego**
*In Freud's theory, the component of personality that tries to resolve the conflicts that arise between instinctive desires and reality.*

**superego**
*In Freud's theory, the component of personality that represents cultural norms and standards as internalized by the child.*

**conscience**
*Defined by Freud as the part of the superego that represents the punitive side of norms, telling children what they should not do and making them feel guilty if they do so.*

**ego ideal**
*Defined by Freud as the part of the superego that represents the positive side of norms, which encourages children to model desirable behavior and achievement.*

**psychosocial stages**
*Erikson's description of the distinct phases of development that are consequences of the social experiences and major events of the human life cycle.*

FIGURE 1.8

A comparison of Freud's *psychosexual* stages and Erikson's *psychosocial* stages. Notice the correspondence between the two sequences of stages in infancy and childhood. Yet Erikson, unlike Freud, identified distinct stages of personality development in adulthood. He also emphasized themes in development rather than the connection of sexual energy to specific bodily organs.

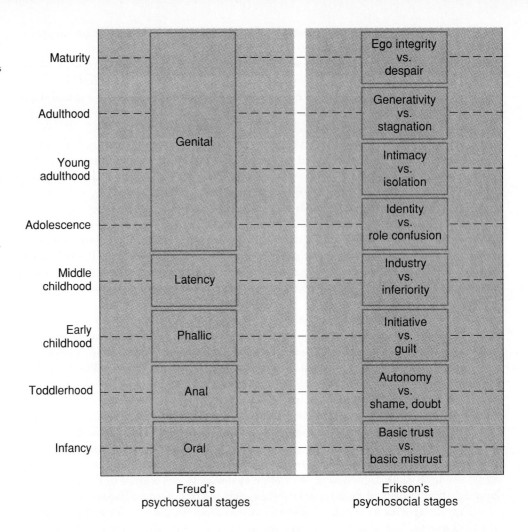

**generativity**
*Erikson's term for the trait of producing and giving to others, which ideally develops in adulthood.*

caregivers' consistency and in one's own ability to control urges. According to Erikson, whether infants develop basic trust or mistrust depends on how responsive their parents are to their needs. That is why he viewed his stages as psycho*social* rather than psycho*sexual*.

In Erikson's second stage, toddlers begin to experiment in the world. Some of this experimentation involves testing the limits imposed by adults. If adults allow experimentation but are firm when necessary, toddlers gain a sense of autonomy. If adults' control is ineffective, toddlers experience shame and doubt.

Erikson's later stages also contrast positive and negative outcomes for personality development. Early childhood brings increased activity that may contribute either to healthy initiative or to guilt over one's acts. Entering middle childhood means entering school and beginning the work of becoming an educated person. The school years can give children a sense of accomplishment (industry) or, if they are unsuccessful, feelings of inferiority.

Erikson diverged further from Freud by not treating adolescence as the final stage of personality development. Erikson argued that the primary task of adolescence is not to develop a mature sexuality but to form a sense of identity. Adolescents especially need to choose a career that answers the question, "What shall I do with my life?" If they cannot answer this question successfully, they fall into role confusion.

Erikson assumed that mature sexuality comes in young adulthood, when youth form intimate relationships. A failure to form such relationships leaves adolescents isolated from other people. Conversely, forming such relationships normally leads, in Erikson's sketch of human life, to childbearing and childrearing. The facet of personality most important for childrearing is **generativity,** the trait of producing and giving to others. Adults without

children who do not give to other people in comparable ways are likely to suffer from personal stagnation and self-indulgence.

Finally, Erikson believed that older people look back on their experiences and accomplishments. If they do so with a sense of pride or, at least, acceptance, they end life with a sense of **ego integrity.** If they do so with a sense of anger or disappointment, they end life in despair.

Erikson's psychosocial stages are not a complete theory of development. Rather, they are a description of facets of personality whose development may be linked to specific life tasks. In later chapters you will learn more about these facets and the social experiences to which they are linked.

## Developmental Issues and Psychoanalytic Theory

In their many writings, Freud and Erikson discussed all four issues that cut across developmental theories (see table 1.1 on page 19). Their hypotheses about psychosexual or psychosocial stages reflect a belief that qualitative changes are central to personality development. Freud's hypotheses about the gradual emergence of the ego and superego also reflect a belief in qualitative change. In other words, neither Freud nor Erikson thought of children as "little adults." These theorists viewed children as taking several distinct steps between birth and maturity.

On the issue of continuity versus discontinuity, Freud's views were especially definite. Once children reached the latency stage, Freud thought that their personality was almost set. In his words, "the little human being is frequently a finished product in his fourth or fifth year, and only gradually reveals in later years what lies buried in him" (1920/1965, p. 364). With the resolution of the crises of the phallic stage, a child's personality takes its basic form. According to Freud, an adult's personality and relationships are determined by experiences during the early years of life.

Erikson did not assume that an individual's personality was set by 5 years of age. He assumed that personality could change throughout life as individuals faced new life tasks. Yet like Freud, he assumed that early experiences have lasting effects on children's ideas about the world and sense of self. This assumption implies that individual differences in personality should show substantial continuity.

On the issue of nature versus nurture, the positions of Freud and Erikson were more moderate. Freud believed that relationships with parents during early childhood strongly affect people's personalities. He also believed in the importance of instinctive drives and in a hereditary component to personality. In short, he acknowledged that both nurture and nature affect children's development (Emde, 1992).

Erikson emphasized the influence of the larger culture on children's development more than Freud did. Still, Erikson did not deny that heredity influenced personality development. Neither Freud nor Erikson offered specific hypotheses about the relative importance of nature versus nurture.

Finally, both Freud and Erikson emphasized developmental universals rather than cultural specificity. Freud assumed that his model of personality development was true for all humans, not merely adults in Europe in the early twentieth century. Erikson assumed that children's personalities are influenced by the dominant values and practices in their culture. However, he did not suggest any cultural specificity to his stages of psychosocial development. On the contrary, he assumed that the stages reflected the interaction of an unfolding personality with a series of universal life tasks. In sum, both theorists tried to present a universal portrait of personality development.

## Learning Theories

What do Plato, John Locke, and John B. Watson have in common? One answer is that they all emphasized the importance of learning for children's development. **Learning** is a change in behavior in a specific situation due to experience in that situation (Stevenson, 1983). Children's behavior in a specific situation can also change if they become tired or distracted. Changes involve learning only if they are the result of children's experience rather than these other causes.

**ego integrity**
*Erikson's term for the ideal end point of personality development, when people look back on their experiences and accomplishments with a sense of pride or, at least, acceptance.*

**learning**
*A change in behavior in a specific situation due to experience rather than to fatigue or other causes.*

One aim of learning theorists is to identify the processes by which learning occurs. That is, they seek to define basic principles of learning. Earlier you read about classical conditioning, which is one important principle of learning. Other principles have been emphasized in more recent theories.

## Skinner and Operant Conditioning

Children learn to repeat behaviors that are rewarded and not to repeat behaviors that are punished. The principle of learning that explains these effects was stated most precisely by B. F. Skinner (1904–1990), the best-known psychologist of this century.

**operants**
*Skinner's term for behaviors that are emitted spontaneously by an organism.*

Skinner defined behaviors that are emitted spontaneously by an organism as **operants.** He chose this term because these behaviors show how the organism "operates" on the environment. He proposed that operants are controlled by their consequences. Operants that are rewarded or followed by reinforcement are strengthened and become more likely in the future. Operants that are followed by punishment are weakened and become less likely. Skinner defined the control of behaviors by their consequences as **operant conditioning.**

**operant conditioning**
*Defined by Skinner as the type of learning that reflects the control of behavior by rewards and punishments.*

Skinner spent his entire life elaborating the theory of operant conditioning. He compared the effectiveness of reinforcement versus punishment as techniques for changing behavior. He also discussed two processes for learning new behaviors. To explain the acquisition of language, he emphasized the importance of imitation (Skinner, 1957). To explain the learning of other behaviors, he emphasized the process of **shaping.** In this process, spontaneous behaviors are reinforced when they more and more closely match a desired new behavior. Today many professionals use techniques of operant conditioning to change children's behavior and reduce behavioral problems.

**shaping**
*In Skinner's term, the process of reinforcing spontaneous behaviors that more and more closely match a desired new behavior.*

## Bandura's Social Learning Theory

Albert Bandura (1977b) extended previous learning theories in several ways. First, he argued that people can learn behaviors rapidly and efficiently by observing other people who model the behaviors. Children, for example, often learn how to cook or use tools by watching their parents. Bandura defined the principle of learning from models as **observational learning.** He called his theory **social learning theory** because it emphasized learning from other people.

**observational learning**
*The principle in social learning theory that refers to learning from observing other people's behavior.*

**social learning theory**
*A theory of learning that emphasizes not only the control of behavior by rewards and punishments but also learning by observation of other people.*

Second, Bandura pointed out that people do not imitate all the behaviors that they observe. People only imitate a model's behavior if they think they will be rewarded or, at least, not punished for doing so. For example, although preschool boys sometimes watch girls playing with dolls, they rarely imitate the girls' play. Boys don't imitate the girls' behavior because they think they would be teased if they did—and they are probably right.

This example shows one link between social learning theory and the theory of operant conditioning. Bandura agreed that learning depends on reinforcement and punishment. Yet he proposed that children learn not only from reinforcements and punishments that they receive but also from those given to their models for behavior.

Third, Bandura (1986, 1992) gradually refined his theory by adding assumptions and hypotheses about thinking and reasoning. The usual term in psychology for the processes of thinking and reasoning is **cognition.** Thus theories allied with that of Bandura became known as *cognitive social learning theories* (see Mischel, 1973).

**cognition**
*The processes of thinking and reasoning.*

Bandura described several cognitive processes that intervene between children's observation of a model and their imitation of the model. To learn from a model, children must first attend to the model's behavior. Then they must retain or remember that behavior. Later, they must produce a replica of the behavior they have observed by retrieving and processing the information they have retained. In short, attention, memory, and information processing must be integrated to ensure observational learning and later imitation. To emphasize the importance of these processes, Bandura (1986) redefined his theory as *social cognitive theory.*

Fourth, Bandura added assumptions about how children regulate their behavior. Besides considering how other people might respond to a behavior, children develop internal standards for evaluating their own behavior (Bandura, 1977a; Grusec, 1992). A major element in this self-regulation is children's self-efficacy. **Self-efficacy** refers to children's beliefs about their ability to behave in a way that produces desired outcomes. For example, children

**self-efficacy**
*Beliefs about one's ability to behave in a way that produces desired outcomes.*

are high in self-efficacy with respect to academic tasks if they think they can get high grades by working hard. Children are low in academic self-efficacy if they think they can't get high grades even if they work hard.

Finally, Bandura (1978) added the idea of **reciprocal determinism,** the mutual influences of children's thoughts, behaviors, and environments on each other. He said that children are not completely controlled by their environments because they partly create these environments. For example, children's interests affect their choices of television programs. In making these choices, children create their viewing environment. That environment, in turn, affects their future behavior. Stated more formally, the idea of reciprocal determinism describes "the opportunity for people to shape their destinies as well as the limits of self-direction" (Bandura, 1978, p. 357).

**reciprocal determinism**
*The mutual influence of people's thoughts, behaviors, and environments on each other, which implies both that people can shape their destiny and that self-direction has limits.*

## Developmental Issues and Learning Theories

Learning theorists have neither proposed general stages of development nor accepted other theorists' hypotheses about stages. Thus they have rejected the idea that development involves a regular sequence of qualitative changes (see table 1.1, p. 19). Moreover, learning theorists have assumed that the same principles of learning are valid for infants, children, and adults. For these reasons, many writers describe learning theories as nondevelopmental (Stevenson, 1983).

To questions about continuity in development, learning theorists give a qualified answer. They argue that children's behavior should show continuity over time if the features of their environments undergo little change. For example, if children are consistently rewarded for certain behaviors and punished for other behaviors, their behavior should not change much as they grow. If patterns of reinforcement and punishment change, children's behavior should also change.

These predictions may seem like common sense, but their implications are profound. Recall that Freud and Erikson assumed experiences early in life have lasting effects on children. To a learning theorist, early experiences are neither more nor less important than later ones. At all ages, children respond to the current features of their learning environments. At all ages, children shift to new paths of development if their environments change.

On the issue of nature versus nurture, learning theorists uniformly emphasize the effects of experience more than heredity. John B. Watson took an extreme position on this issue, and Skinner largely agreed with him. Contemporary learning theorists like Bandura have taken a more moderate position. They admit that heredity plays a role in children's development, but they are less interested in defining this role than in exploring the effects of children's environments.

Finally, learning theorists recognize that children's development differs greatly across cultures. However, they argue that these variations can be explained by differences in children's environments. These theorists assume that the same principles of learning apply in all cultures. At the most important level, then, they argue not for cultural specificity but for developmental universals.

# Theories of Cognitive Development

Although Bandura (1977a, 1992) discussed the role of cognition in observational learning, he did not study age changes in cognition directly. Most studies of cognitive development have derived from two theoretical perspectives. The first is the comprehensive and intriguing theory of the Swiss psychologist Jean Piaget. The second is not a single theory but a variety of perspectives on cognition labeled collectively as information-processing approaches.

## Piaget's Genetic Epistemology

Jean Piaget (1896–1980) was the most prolific and provocative developmental psychologist of this century. During a career that spanned more than 60 years, Piaget formulated a detailed theory of cognitive development. Piaget tried to describe and explain the developmental changes in all forms of thinking, reasoning, and intellectual activity from birth to adulthood.

Piaget did not call himself a cognitive-developmental theorist or even a developmental psychologist. He preferred to call his field of study **genetic epistemology.** Epistemology is the branch of philosophy that involves the study of knowledge, asking questions such as

**genetic epistemology**
*Piaget's term for the study of the development of children's knowledge of their own thoughts and the external world.*

Jean Piaget watching young children at play. When Piaget was a young man, he spent many hours observing children's play, games, and conversations. As he grew older, he more often studied children's performance on structured tasks. Piaget's discoveries are considered in several chapters, but especially in chapter 8.

**assimilation**
*A cognitive function defined by Piaget as the integration of external elements into existing cognitive structures.*

**accommodation**
*A cognitive function that, in Piaget's theory, describes the modification of existing cognitive structures by new elements.*

"What is knowledge?" and "Where does knowledge come from?" The adjective *genetic*, as Piaget used it, referred not to genes or heredity but to development itself. In short, Piaget claimed as his domain the developmental changes in children's knowledge about their own thoughts and the external world. His theory has two basic principles, organization and adaptation.

***Cognitive Organization***    Stages of Reasoning. Piaget argued that thinking is organized at all ages because organization is necessary for reasoning. For example, suppose you hear that a boy named Alonzo is 46 inches tall and that another boy named Zachary is 10 inches taller. You can deduce, logically, that Zachary is 56 inches tall. You can make that deduction because you understand the basic logic of measurement, a logic that allows you to organize the facts you have and recognize their implications.

The claim that adults' thinking is organized and logical is neither surprising nor novel. Piaget went further by claiming that young children's thinking is also organized and logical. Yet, according to Piaget, the organization of children's thinking is qualitatively different from that of adults. That is, children differ from adults in the logic they use to make deductions and solve problems.

Piaget described distinct forms of logic, or cognitive organization, for different periods of development. He viewed these forms of organization as defining a sequence of cognitive stages. His descriptions of these stages have been examined in thousands of studies. In later chapters you will learn about the specific features of each stage.

Besides outlining the logic of each stage, Piaget stated three assumptions that applied to the entire stage sequence. First, he assumed that cognitive stages are not tied to specific types of cognitive problems but are completely general. He argued that all of a child's thinking and reasoning reflects one mode of cognitive organization, or one cognitive stage. Therefore, a child's thinking and reasoning should be highly consistent across cognitive tasks.

Second, Piaget assumed that children move through the stages of cognitive development in an invariant sequence. Children cannot move from a low stage to a high stage without going through the intermediate stages. Also, children cannot regress to lower stages. Just as children crawl before they walk and do not return to crawling after they start walking, children move through cognitive stages without any skipping or regression.

Third, Piaget assumed that his stages of cognitive development are universal. That is, all human beings pass through the same general stages of thinking as they grow. Piaget argued that his cognitive stages represent basic ways of viewing oneself and the world. Therefore, they are not affected by variations in education or other cultural influences.

If the features of cognitive stages do not vary across cultures, what does affect them? In particular, why do children move to higher stages as they get older? These questions relate to the second principle in Piaget's theory, adaptation.

***Processes of Cognitive Adaptation to the World***    Piaget (1970) defined two cognitive functions that help children adapt to their world. These functions also lead gradually to the qualitative changes in adaptation that reflect movement to higher stages. The first function, **assimilation,** allows the integration of external elements into existing structures of an organism. Piaget defined assimilation in general terms rather than in terms of cognition alone to emphasize the parallels between biological and cognitive assimilation.

When you eat an ice-cream cone, you assimilate the ice cream and the cone into your body through the process of digestion. In a similar way, cognitive assimilation means incorporating objects or events into existing cognitive structures. For example, a preschool boy may push a wooden block across the floor and make sounds like a car as he does so. The boy thus assimilates the block into an existing cognitive structure for playing with toy cars. Piaget felt that assimilation was important not only for play but also for other aspects of thinking, from recognition of objects to problem solving.

Children could not get far in life if they were capable only of assimilation. Each day they confront new situations or events that call for changes in their behavior. A second cognitive function, **accommodation,** allows the modification of structures in response to

external elements. In the biological realm, accommodation occurs when the body adjusts to hot or cold foods, or sweet and sour foods. In the cognitive realm, imitation is an example of pure accommodation. When children imitate another person's actions, they change the cognitive structures governing their actions to make them more like the other person's.

Children also accommodate to new situations on their own, without modeling their behavior on other people's. When an adolescent confronts a new algebra problem, for example, he or she probably will try to solve it by modifying strategies previously used to solve other problems. These modifications in strategies are the result of accommodation.

Several years after Piaget introduced the concepts of assimilation and accommodation, he added a new principle of adaptation that he called **equilibration.** He defined equilibration as a process of self-regulation by which children change their cognitive structures in response to events. He argued that children try to change these structures when they feel a sense of disequilibrium, or cognitive conflict. For example, children may notice that a deduction they have made using their immature logic doesn't match reality. As they try to resolve this conflict, they may develop a more adequate form of reasoning. This process, repeated many times, leads gradually to the development of the new logic that defines a higher cognitive stage.

This child is acting on the world and constructing part of his own world. Piaget proposed that children also construct their logic, or their cognitive structures, through their actions on the world.

**equilibration**
*According to Piaget, the process of self-regulation by which children change their cognitive structures in response to events.*

*Piaget's Position on Developmental Issues*   Piaget's hypotheses about general cognitive stages place him with theorists who emphasize qualitative rather than quantitative changes in development. Piaget granted that there are quantitative changes in development. For example, certain types of logical thinking are consolidated or strengthened through repetition. Still, the centerpiece of Piaget's theory is his hypothesis that qualitative changes in thinking occur during infancy, childhood, and adolescence.

Piaget said much less about the issue of continuity versus discontinuity. Throughout his career Piaget focused on the normal course of development rather than the differences among children the same age. He recognized that some children are more advanced in their thinking and reasoning than other children, but he did not discuss the origins of such differences. Similarly, he did not discuss whether those differences should show any continuity over time.

On the issue of nature versus nurture, Piaget expressed a unique position. He agreed that cognitive development depends partly on maturation, but he viewed the role of maturation as limited. The maturation of the brain does create new possibilities for thinking and reasoning. Yet whether these possibilities are realized depends on children's own activity: their assimilation, accommodation, and equilibration.

Similarly, Piaget agreed that children can learn from their experiences, but experiences can have no effect if children are not prepared for them. In particular, children must be ready to assimilate new information, accommodate to it, or respond to the disequilibrium that it causes. Thus, according to Piaget, what children learn depends less on their experiences than on their cognitive activity.

Piaget therefore argued for a complex interaction of maturation and learning, or nature and nurture. To describe the form of this interaction, Piaget often called himself a **constructivist.** He believed that children actively construct their knowledge of the world—and build their cognitive structures—through their activity.

Finally, Piaget believed in developmental universals rather than cultural specificity. In one article Piaget (1972) suggested that children's performance on specific cognitive tasks may vary across cultures because schooling and other experiences vary. But Piaget considered these variations as superficial. He strongly asserted that the same sequence of cognitive stages is found in all cultures. He also assumed that the same principles of cognitive adaptation hold in all cultures, because those principles are rooted in human biology.

**constructivist**
*A theorist who believes, as Piaget did, that children actively construct their knowledge of the world, and build their cognitive structures, through their activity.*

## Information-Processing Approaches

Piaget drew analogies between biological and cognitive processes because he assumed cognitive development is a special case of biological development. Other psychologists view cognition differently. They see analogies between human thinking and the operation of a computer. The analogy between human thinking and computer operations is central to information-processing approaches to cognitive development.

*Exploring the Analogy Between Humans and Computers*   Viewed abstractly, the components of a computer system are similar to those of the human information-processing system. First, both systems need devices for receiving input. Computers can receive input through a keyboard, a mouse, a modem, or more sophisticated devices like a musical instrument. Input to the human information processor comes through the five senses and is received through the processes of perception and attention.

Second, both systems need components that retain information. Computers have various types of memory and pieces of hardware (e.g., hard disks or CD-ROM drives) for storing information. Human beings also have different types of memories for information that must be retained for a short or a long period.

Third, both systems need components to interpret and integrate new information and stored information. For example, a computer interprets keystrokes by comparing them with information in memory. Human beings interpret speech sounds by comparing those sounds with memories of a specific language. In a computer, the central processing unit handles this interpretation and integration. In models of human information processing, no consensus exists about the best label for this component. Theorists have focused less on defining the component than on exploring how it operates.

Finally, both systems produce output when processing is completed. A computer may direct its output to a monitor screen, a printer, or another device. The output of the human information processor is some type of behavior—verbal, physical, or both.

The abstract similarities between human and computer information processing are acknowledged by many researchers. However, these researchers do not always agree on how developmental changes in children's thinking should be described. Because of these disagreements among researchers, this section refers not to a single information-processing approach but to multiple approaches (Klahr, 1989, 1992).

*Three Information-Processing Approaches*   One approach is to focus on a single component of the information-processing system. For example, many researchers have studied memory development. A major question that these researchers have tried to answer is how and why memory improves with age. One reason is that older children and adults use various strategies for remembering. If you needed to remember the number 4947692 for a minute or two, you would probably repeat the number, aloud or mentally, after hearing it. Young children are less likely to use such a rehearsal strategy. The increased use of memory strategies partly explains why remembering improves with age (Kail, 1990). But why does the use of memory strategies increase with age? You learn the answer to this question, and much more about the components of human information processing, in chapter 9.

Another approach taken by many researchers is to study the operation of the entire information-processing system when children are engaged in problem solving. Consider, for example, the balance scale shown in figure 1.9. If you ask 5-year-olds to explain how the balance works, they will usually say that the side with more weight on it will go down. If the weight on both sides is equal, they say the scale will balance (Siegler, 1976).

This simple rule sometimes works but often does not. Think about what would happen if the weight on both sides was equal, but one weight was farther from the center than the other. As children get older, they are better able to predict what would happen in that situation. Their predictions improve because they devise more complex rules that better reflect the physics of a balance scale.

In a third approach, researchers take the analogy between humans and computers even more literally. These researchers assume that full understanding of children's problem

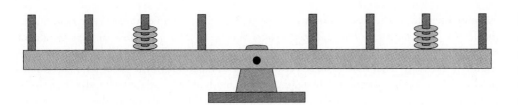

solving is shown by the ability to write a computer program that behaves the same way (Klahr, 1992). Therefore, the central goal of these researchers is to construct computer simulations of children's performance on cognitive tasks. Moreover, these researchers seek to write programs that do more than mimic children's reasoning at specific ages; they want programs that modify themselves, or "learn," as children do.

Critics of this approach have argued that children are not like computers (Brown, 1982). Computers do not spontaneously change their hardware and software. Unlike children, they do not grow or develop. A distinction should be made, however, between a computer as a physical device and a computer program. To illustrate the point, David Klahr (1992, p. 300) said that "Meteorologists who run computer simulations of hurricanes do not believe that the atmosphere works like a computer." Similarly, researchers who construct computer simulations of children's reasoning do not believe that children are exactly like computers. Rather, they believe that theories of cognitive development can be made more precise and tested more rigorously if they are expressed in computer programs.

***Information-Processing Approaches and Developmental Issues*** Piaget's idea that children progress through a series of general cognitive stages is rejected by all information-processing theorists. These theorists argue that children's performance on cognitive tasks improves with age because of improvements in specific components of information processing. The components responsible for these improvements vary across tasks. Therefore, age changes in children's reasoning should not show the consistency that hypotheses about general stages imply.

Although information-processing theorists reject the idea of general stages, they assume that children's performance on some tasks changes qualitatively with age. For example, older children use different rules to make predictions about the balance scale than younger children do. However, cognitive development also involves quantitative changes. In particular, children become faster and more efficient at processing information as they grow. For an information-processing theorist, then, an accurate description of cognitive development must include both qualitative and quantitative changes (Miller, 1993).

The issue of continuity versus discontinuity in development has so far been tangential to research on information processing. Information-processing theorists have focused on the normal changes in cognitive processes as children get older. Questions about individual differences and their continuity over time have received little attention.

Table 1.1 (p. 19) lists no position for information-processing approaches on the nature-nurture issue, because theorists have taken different positions (see Flavell, 1984; Flavell, Miller, & Miller, 1993). Some have suggested that children differ from adults only because they have had less experience. These theorists imply that with proper training children at any age could succeed on almost any cognitive task. Other theorists believe that nature, or maturation, limits the complexity of children's thinking and the kinds of cognitive tasks that they can do.

Finally, information-processing theorists have not taken a definite position on the issue of cultural specificity versus developmental universals. Only a few researchers have explored how children's cultural context might affect their information processing (Miller, 1993). These explorations suggest that information-processing theorists will consider the issue of cultural specificity more carefully in the future.

# Ethological Theory

Charles Darwin (1809–1882) published his master work, *The Origin of Species*, in 1859. According to Darwin, the millions of plant and animal species on earth evolved from a few

common ancestors. Their evolution was governed by the principle stated in the book's subtitle, *Natural Selection, or the Preservation of Favored Races in the Struggle for Life.* In the struggle for existence, only a few members of any species survive and bear offspring. Only these few contribute to the next generation. The selection of which members of the species do and do not produce offspring is not random. Instead, those individuals who adapt best to their environment most often survive and procreate. This means that the population of the "child" generation is different from that of the "parent" generation. The differences between any two generations are small, but over long periods of time—and natural selection—great differences arise that amount to the emergence of new species.

Darwin's theory of evolution through natural selection is fundamental to modern biology. One branch of biology that is strongly based on evolutionary theory is **ethology,** which can be defined as the study of animal behavior in natural settings. Ethologists are most interested in behaviors that are (a) universal, or shown by all members of a species, and (b) instinctive, or genetically programmed.

Once ethologists identify a behavioral pattern that is species-universal and instinctive, they try to discover its evolutionary significance. That is, they try to find out how the pattern contributes to the survival of the species. Initially, ethologists concentrated on birds, fish, or other nonhuman species. In the 1960s, however, they began to extend their theories to human beings. For example, Konrad Lorenz (1963) drew parallels between human beings and other animals in his best-selling book, *On Aggression.* Other ethologists began to study the nature and functions of aggressive behavior and other social behaviors in children, especially during the preschool years (see Blurton Jones, 1972).

## The Ethological Theory of Infant-Parent Attachment

In child development, the most important ethological theory was proposed by John Bowlby (1907–1990). Bowlby was a British psychiatrist who focused throughout his career on the relationships between infants and mothers. During the 1940s and 1950s, Bowlby (1951) used Freudian theory as the foundation for his writings on the mother-infant relationship. However, after reading the work of Lorenz and other ethologists, Bowlby concluded that ethological principles better explain the special attachment of infants to their mothers.

Bowlby (1969, 1988) was attracted to ethological theory because it accounted for the combined influence of nature and nurture on mother-infant relationships. During human evolutionary history, infants have become genetically prepared to form an attachment to their mother, because the mother provides them with food and protection in a dangerous world. Conversely, mothers have become genetically prepared to feed and care for their infants. Infants who do not form a close attachment to their mothers, or whose mothers do not care for them, are unlikely to survive childhood and contribute to the next generation.

On the other hand, the characteristics of mother-infant relationships are not entirely programmed genetically. Each infant must learn who his or her mother is. Each mother must learn to adapt to the unique features of her infant's personality. Moreover, infants and mothers must transform their relationship as the infant grows older and needs less intensive care and supervision. This kind of learning gives human behavior its variety and adaptability.

The blend of nature and nurture in the formation of infant-mother attachments is complex and controversial. Ethological attachment theory includes hypotheses about the infant-care arrangements to which infants can adapt. It also includes hypotheses about arrangements in which infants will not thrive. Because of the practical significance of these hypotheses, chapter 6 includes a detailed look at the theory.

## Ethological Theory and Developmental Issues

Bowlby (1969) did not argue for stages of social development. He assumed that both qualitative and quantitative changes occur as infant-parent attachments develop, but he was not especially concerned about the balance between the two. By contrast, the issue of continuity versus discontinuity is central to attachment theory. Bowlby assumed that the quality of infants' attachments to their parents had an enduring influence on their social and personality development. In

**ethology**
*The study of an organism's behavior in its natural habitat, with special attention to behavioral patterns that contribute to the survival of a species.*

particular, infants whose parents fail to give them consistent, responsive care are not likely, as children, to be well adjusted psychologically. In other words, Bowlby accepted Freud's and Erikson's assumptions about the lasting importance of experiences early in life.

You've already read about Bowlby's position on the nature-nurture issue. To repeat briefly, Bowlby assumed that certain behaviors are instinctively programmed because they enhance the survival of the human species. Bowlby and other ethologists also assume that nurture or experience affects development. In particular, the quality of infant-parent attachments depends on the nurture provided by parents. Thus, nature and nurture jointly influence development.

Finally, ethological theorists emphasize species-universal behaviors and minimize the importance of cultural variations. Bowlby assumed that infants in all cultures need their parents to feed and protect them. Therefore, cultural variations in attachment should be small. As you will see in chapter 6, this hypothesis has been challenged by researchers who argue for important cultural influences on the earliest relationships between infants and parents.

## Theories of the Context for Development

Table 1.1 (p. 19) shows that every theory discussed so far takes a position in favor of developmental universals rather than cultural specificity. That's not surprising when you think about the attributes of an ideal theory. Such a theory contains "broadly applicable knowledge," and theorists can claim greater applicability by arguing that their theory applies to all children around the world. In recent decades, however, two theories that emphasize cultural specificity have received increasing attention.

### Vygotsky's Sociocultural Theory

During the 1980s, many researchers argued that children's development is powerfully shaped by their social and cultural context. For these researchers, **context** refers to the social relationships in which children are involved, the features of their culture that influence how they are reared, and the social institutions that affect the beliefs and behaviors of parents and other caregivers. Theorists who emphasize the importance of the social and cultural context are called **contextualists.** One early theorist in this group was Lev Vygotsky.

Lev Vygotsky was born in Russia in 1896. He first studied law and literature but then became a teacher of psychology in a small town. His career in child development really began in 1924 when he gave a brilliant speech to a distinguished group of psychologists. A senior psychologist then offered him a position in the Institute of Psychology in Moscow. For the next ten years he published more than 100 books and articles on his theory and research.

Unfortunately, Vygotsky died of tuberculosis in 1934, when he was only 37 years old. Shortly afterward, his publications were banned by the Communist government because he had often referred in his writings to Piaget and other Western psychologists. In addition, Communist officials disliked his use of intelligence testing and his assertions about the cognitive differences between people from different cultural backgrounds in Russia (Miller, 1993). As a result, Vygotsky's ideas were almost forgotten for more than 40 years.

During the late 1970s, interest in Vygotsky's theory revived, spurred partly by the publication of his major writings in *Mind in Society* (Vygotsky, 1978). The title of the book suggests Vygotsky's primary interest, which was mental or cognitive development. The title also suggests his central idea, which is that the cognitive functioning of individuals has its origins in their social interactions.

***The Social and Cultural Context of Cognitive Development*** One of Vygotsky's principal hypotheses was that cognitive development partly results from the transformation of social speech into inner speech or thought. Children learn a great deal about the world through conversations with adults. In these conversations children ask questions and adults answer them. As a result, the children not only learn the answers to specific questions; they also learn the form of an intellectual dialogue. Gradually, they internalize this form. Children say to themselves, for example, "How can I solve this problem?" To highlight the importance of such internalization, Vygotsky defined thinking as *inner speech* (Wertsch & Tulviste, 1992).

**context**
*The social relationships in which children are involved, the features of their culture that influence how they are reared, and the social institutions that affect the beliefs and behaviors of parents and other caregivers.*

**contextualists**
*Theorists who emphasize the importance of children's social and cultural context.*

# RECIPROCAL TEACHING: WORKING IN THE "ZONE"

For more than 10 years, Ann Brown and her colleagues have studied the benefits of interactive learning environments in schools and homes (Brown et al., 1991). These researchers have given special attention to cooperative learning groups including a teacher and several students. In these groups children learn through **reciprocal teaching,** where students and an adult teacher take turns leading a discussion of part of a text that they have just read.

To begin the discussion, the leader asks a question about the main idea in the text. As the group discusses the question, the leader clarifies points others have misunderstood. When the group members reach a consensus about the answer to the question, the leader summarizes the answer. Then the leader asks the group to predict the content of the next part of the text.

One goal of the discussion is to help the students understand and remember the material they have read. An equally important goal is to teach students strategies that they can use when reading independently. In Vygotsky's terms, the group works in the students' zone of proximal development. The leader models several strategies for reading comprehension, including questioning, seeking

**V**ygotsky's theory emphasizes the value of expanding students' zone of proximal development by asking questions, clarifying ideas, and summarizing the discussion. Such techniques can be part of reciprocal teaching in groups like this one.

**reciprocal teaching**
*A method of classroom learning in which students and an adult teacher take turns leading a group discussion of some topic or material.*

**zone of proximal development**
*The distance between children's apparent level of cognitive development when working independently and their level when solving problems under adult guidance or working with more capable peers.*

Vygotsky also discussed the educational implications of his ideas about the social origins of thinking. He defined the **zone of proximal development** as the distance between children's apparent level of cognitive development when working independently and their level when solving problems under adult guidance or working with more capable peers (Vygotsky, 1978). He suggested that children's performance when working with adults or more capable peers is a better index of their cognitive level than is their performance working alone.

Vygotsky proposed that educators should try to work within their students' zone of proximal development. When students are working on cognitive problems, a more experienced person should direct their attention to important details about the problems, remind them of significant facts, and otherwise support their efforts at problem solving. In this way, the other person expands the students' zone of proximal development and brings them a step closer to solving such problems independently. A real-life application of these ideas is described in *Practical Applications:* "Reciprocal Teaching."

Another of Vygotsky's principal hypotheses was that the social context of children's development gives them access to tools for thought (Vygotsky, 1981). The most powerful tool is language. Language is, in part, a cognitive tool that children acquire through participation in a culture. Children's language gives them a set of symbols that can be used to represent things in the world. These symbols allow children not only to talk with others but also to think more precisely about objects, emotions, actions, and ideas.

Besides exposing children to a language, every human culture provides children with other tools for thought. These tools may be abstract, like language. For example, children may learn systems for remembering the names of all their ancestors, or many pairs of states and their capitals. Children may learn systems for counting the sheep in a herd or the money in a set of coins.

clarification, summarizing, and making predictions about what comes next. In the group, the other students learn to use these strategies. They can later apply them when reading on their own. Brown and her colleagues describe this procedure as teaching "in anticipation of competence." In other words, educators help students read better than they could on their own by placing them in an interactive learning environment.

Does this kind of teaching work? One experiment included seventh graders who were randomly assigned to different conditions. Students in the reciprocal-teaching condition spent one month working on reading in small groups. Students in another condition received explicit instruction in reading strategies and then completed paper and pencil exercises in which they applied the strategies to reading passages. However, students in this condition never worked in groups.

Figure 1.10 shows the students' scores on tests of reading comprehension given at the beginning and end of the experiment. Notice that the comprehension of students in the reciprocal-teaching group was far superior to that of students in the other group. The students involved in reciprocal teaching also improved more than the other students in their scores on standardized reading tests. These findings illustrate the benefits of social interactions that take place within a student's zone of proximal development.

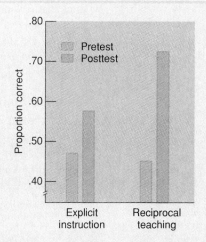

## FIGURE 1.10

Seventh graders' reading comprehension improved greatly from pretest to posttest if they worked in small groups that used techniques of reciprocal teaching. Students' comprehension improved little if they simply received instruction in reading strategies (Source: Palincsar and Brown, 1984.)

Other tools for thought include educational skills and physical objects. For example, most children learn to write. Among its many purposes writing serves to structure and direct thinking. Writing can be integrated with other tools like a word processor to change the ways people think, communicate, and work together. Objects like maps, calculators, and computers also affect children's thinking.

In summary, Vygotsky presented a sociocultural theory of cognitive development. He argued that all thinking is social in origin, because it is the internalization of speech. In addition, thinking is shaped by the social context because children use the tools for thought that exist in their culture. Children in different cultures learn to use different cognitive tools, so the nature of cognitive development depends on children's cultural context.

***Vygotsky's Position on Developmental Issues***   Vygotsky assumed that the normal pattern of cognitive development includes both qualitative and quantitative changes (Miller, 1993). For example, the shift from purely social speech to inner speech is an example of a qualitative change. The gradual improvement in children's performance as adults work with them in their zone of proximal development is an example of a quantitative change. By contrast, Vygotsky said little about whether individual differences in development show continuity or discontinuity.

On the issue of nature versus nurture, Vygotsky took a more definite position. By emphasizing the effects of the social and cultural context on development, Vygotsky obviously put more weight on nurture than on nature. Even so, Vygotsky was not an extreme environmentalist (Wertsch & Tulviste, 1992). He admitted that cognitive development is influenced by maturation, but he did not try to explain this influence precisely. Instead, he and his followers focused on the role of social interactions and the broader culture in development.

Vygotsky's position on the issue of cultural specificity versus developmental universals varied over time (Wertsch & Tulviste, 1992). In his last writings, however, he argued that children's

thinking is so strongly affected by the cultural context that a universal description of cognitive development cannot be presented. Children learn to use different tools of thought in different cultures, and the value of the tools used in a specific culture cannot be judged on an absolute scale. Contemporary researchers who have adopted Vygotsky's theory have also assumed that development can only be understood and evaluated within a specific cultural context.

## Bronfenbrenner's Ecological Systems Theory

A second contextualist theory is most concerned not with children's development itself but with the environments in which children develop. Urie Bronfenbrenner (1979, 1986, 1992) has encouraged researchers to study the changing relations between children and the environments in which they live. As a framework for such studies, Bronfenbrenner proposed an ecological systems theory. **Ecology** is the science of the relationships between organisms and their environments. Bronfenbrenner's theory deals with the ecology of child development, or the environmental systems that affect how children develop.

*Five Types of Environmental Systems* Bronfenbrenner distinguished five levels of children's environments (see figure 1.11). The lowest level, the **microsystem,** refers partly to the setting for a child's behavior and partly to the activities, participants, and roles in that setting. For example, one microsystem might include a backyard in which a 7-year-old girl is throwing a Frisbee with her 9-year-old brother. This microsystem has a specific setting (the backyard) with specific participants (two siblings) in specific roles (playing Frisbee).

If the children's father came into the backyard and started playing with them, another microsystem would be created. A new microsystem would be created even if the father was not playing with them but was sitting in a lounge chair. The siblings' interactions with each other would be likely to change when the father entered, even if he did not interact with them. To understand their behavior fully, all elements of their microsystem must be considered.

The next level of the environment is the **mesosystem.** The arrows in figure 1.11 are intended to show that the mesosystem is defined by the connections among microsystems. In other words, the mesosystem reflects the relations among the various settings in which children spend their time. For many children, the mesosystem includes links between home, school or child-care center, neighborhood, church, and athletic teams or other extracurricular activities. Especially in complex societies like that of the United States, children spend time in many different environments that affect one another.

The third level of the environment, the **exosystem,** includes settings that children do not enter but that affect them indirectly. For example, few children in the United States visit the places where their parents work. Even so, what happens in those settings affects them because it affects their parents' emotions, attitudes, and behavior. Exosystem influences also include those of television, radio, and the other mass media. Few children contribute directly to the content of mass-media programs, but all children are affected by the programs that they watch or hear.

The most global level of the environment is the **macrosystem.** This level refers to the consistencies in the systems at lower levels across an entire society or culture. For example, schools are similar in their structure and operation throughout the United States, but U.S. schools are different from those in other countries (Goodlad, 1984; Stevenson, 1992). The similarities in social institutions like schools partly define the macrosystem.

In addition, the macrosystem includes the values and beliefs that accompany and maintain the similarities in social institutions. In the United States, values and beliefs differ among people who differ in social class and ethnicity. They also differ among people who live in cities and rural areas. People in each of these groups can be viewed as living in somewhat different macrosystems (Bronfenbrenner, 1992).

The final level of Bronfenbrenner's model deals with variations not in space or extent but in time. The **chronosystem** refers to the patterns of stability and change in children's environments over time. As children grow older, they typically move from preschool to elementary school and so on. Many children also experience changes in the home environment

### ecology
*The science of the relationships between organisms and their environments.*

### microsystem
*In Bronfenbrenner's model, the lowest level of the environment, which includes the setting for a child's behavior and the activities, participants, and roles in that setting.*

### mesosystem
*In Bronfenbrenner's ecological model, the level of the environment that reflects the connections among microsystems (e.g., between a child's home and school).*

### exosystem
*In Bronfenbrenner's model, the level of the environment that includes settings that children do not enter but that affect them indirectly (e.g., their parents' workplace).*

### macrosystem
*In Bronfenbrenner's model, the most global level of the environment, which describes the consistencies in lower-level systems across a society or culture.*

### chronosystem
*In Bronfenbrenner's model, the patterns of stability and change in children's environments over time.*

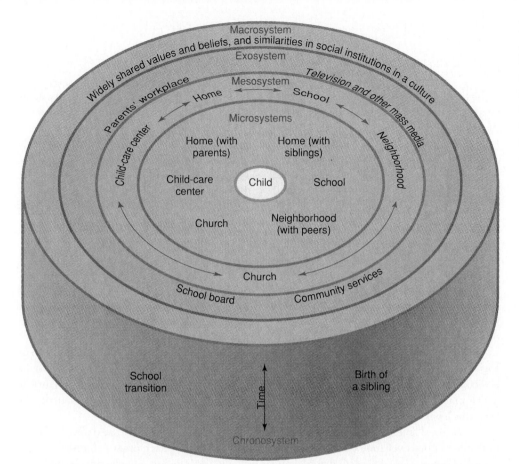

FIGURE 1.11
A schematic diagram of the five levels in Bronfenbrenner's ecological model. The arrows in the mesosystem level indicate the connections between microsystems such as home and school.

when their mother has a new baby or an older sibling leaves home. Such life transitions must be considered in an ecological model because children can be affected not only by their current environment but also by a change in environments.

***Ecological Systems Theory and Developmental Issues*** Because Bronfenbrenner wanted primarily to emphasize the characteristics and effects of children's environments, he did not take a strong position on whether developmental changes are mostly qualitative or quantitative. In addition, he did not argue explicitly for continuity or discontinuity of individual differences in development.

Given the focus of Bronfenbrenner's theory, you might have expected him to take the *nurture* side on the nature-nurture issue. Bronfenbrenner does assume that children are greatly influenced by their environments, but he also assumes that children play an active role in their own development. Any two children will differ in how they respond to the same environment. In addition, children partly choose the environments in which they will spend their time. In short, Bronfenbrenner asserts that both nature and nurture have significant effects on development.

Finally, more than any other theorist Bronfenbrenner argues for cultural specificity in development. His theory considers the differences between geographically separated cultures like those of the United States and Guatemala. It also considers the differences among ethnic groups in one country. Furthermore, Bronfenbrenner expects the aspects of a culture that define a macrosystem to influence the characteristics of other ecological systems. Therefore, he believes researchers should take as their highest goal the understanding of children's development in specific social and cultural contexts.

# ISSUES, THEORIES, AND LEVELS OF SOCIAL COMPLEXITY

At birth, children become part of a complex social world. The first time you read this statement, at the beginning of the chapter, it may have seemed like a truism. Why mention something so obvious? The answer is that this truism has been largely ignored by many theorists. In addition, the truism gains more meaning when the complexity of children's social worlds is analyzed more carefully. Robert Hinde (1987) has identified several levels of social complexity that shed light on the developmental issues and theories discussed in this chapter.

The first level deals with an individual. At this level children's social worlds are not considered, so the truism stated earlier is either rejected or considered unimportant. This level is the primary focus of theorists who emphasize the influence of *nature* on development. These theorists assume that the genetic makeup of individual children has more influence on their development than their social environment does. The level of the individual child is also the primary focus of theorists who argue for developmental universals. These theorists assume that the cultural variations in social worlds have little effect on children's development. A focus on this level is perhaps greatest in Piaget's theory and the information-processing approaches, because these theories portray development as occurring primarily as solitary individuals try to solve cognitive problems.

The second level of social complexity deals with social interactions. The importance of social interactions with other people who reward, punish, and serve as models for behavior is recognized in modern learning theories. All theorists who emphasize the role of nurture in development recognize the effects of social interactions on children. All acknowledge at least this level of complexity in children's social environments.

The third level of social complexity deals with **relationships,** which are defined by multiple interactions over time between two individuals who know each other (Hinde, 1987). A complete description of a relationship includes not only the individuals' behavior toward each other but also their related attitudes, hopes, expectations, and emotions. In addition, because relationships involve interactions over time, they have psychological significance even when the two individuals are not interacting with each other.

Plato's guidelines for rearing children show that he attached little importance to relationships of this kind. Similarly, relationships were not emphasized by John B. Watson or other learning theorists. By contrast, relationships are central to the developmental theories of Freud, Erikson, and Bowlby. In these theories, relationships are viewed not only as important for children's development; the formation of relationships is viewed as one aspect of development.

Hinde's (1987) next level of social complexity involves the networks of relationships that make up social groups. In most developmental theories this level receives little attention. However, Bronfenbrenner's ideas about the microsystem, and changes in microsystems when new individuals enter a setting, involve this level of analysis of social environments.

Finally, the highest level of social complexity deals with the cultural context for each lower level. As an ethologist, Hinde (1987) is unusual in emphasizing the influence of cultures. You should recall that ethological theorists have typically argued for developmental universals rather than cultural specificity. However, Hinde assumes that culture is "a uniquely human attribute" (1987, p. 3) not found in other species. Not surprisingly, Hinde endorses the central ideas of Vygotsky and Bronfenbrenner, the two theorists who have most strongly advocated contextualist theories of child development.

Should you conclude, then, that contextualist theories are better than all others? Not necessarily. Remember that each theory has its domain of applicability. Remember, too, that a theory can become so "grand" that it does not yield accurate predictions and useful explanations. Therefore, instead of trying to judge developmental theories in terms of abstract criteria, see how well the theories account for the particular aspects of development examined in later chapters.

**relationships**
*Ties between individuals who know each other that are defined by their multiple interactions over time.*

# SUMMARY

## What Is Child Development?

Child development refers to age-related changes in children's characteristics that are systematic rather than haphazard, and successive rather than independent of earlier conditions. Theorists and researchers in the field of child development focus on the changes that occur as human beings grow to maturity. These theorists and researchers try to describe and explain the age changes in physical features, cognitive processes, and social relationships.

## Current Issues in Child Development

Four issues cut across major theories of child development. Each can be stated as a question. First, is the normal course of development better described in terms of qualitative changes or quantitative changes? Second, do individual differences in development show mostly continuity or mostly discontinuity over time? Third, can children's development be better explained by their nature (heredity) or their nurture (environment)? Finally, is there significant cultural specificity in children's development, or are the major patterns of development culturally universal?

## Defining and Comparing Developmental Theories

Theories of child development consist of systematically organized knowledge that is intended to explain and predict phenomena. Theories are evaluated using several criteria, such as the accuracy of their predictions and their heuristic value.

## Psychoanalytic Theories

Freud proposed a sequence of psychosexual stages between infancy and adolescence.

Later, his stage sequence was revised by Erikson, who proposed eight psychosocial stages between infancy and the end of life. These psychoanalytic theories are no longer in the mainstream of child development, but several of their assumptions have become part of current theories.

## Learning Theories

John B. Watson presented the first learning theory in child development. He emphasized the principle of classical conditioning. Later, Skinner proposed the principle of operant conditioning. Most recently, Bandura developed social learning theory and its current refinement, social cognitive theory. Bandura emphasized the principle of observational learning.

## Theories of Cognitive Development

Jean Piaget described cognitive organization as changing qualitatively with age. Each qualitative change moves children to a new, general stage of cognitive development. To explain the changes, Piaget defined processes of assimilation, accommodation, and equilibration.

Information-processing theorists draw an analogy between human reasoning and the operation of computers. They reject Piaget's hypothesis of general stages of development. Instead, they focus on single components of the information-processing system, on analyses of specific cognitive tasks, or on the construction of computer simulations of children's reasoning.

## Ethological Theory

Ethologists are most interested in behavioral patterns that are species-universal, instinctive, and critical for the survival of a

species. Bowlby's theory of infant-parent attachment offers an explanation of the special relationship that infants develop with their parents. The formation of this relationship reflects a complex interaction between genetic programming and social experience.

## Theories of the Context for Development

Vygotsky proposed that cognitive development depends heavily on children's social and cultural context. One important step in cognitive development, according to Vygotsky, is the internalization of social speech to form inner speech or thought. Also important is the acquisition of language and other tools for thought.

Bronfenbrenner argued that researchers need a more differentiated picture of the environments in which children develop. He proposed an ecological systems theory that focuses on children's microsystems, mesosystems, exosystems, macrosystem, and chronosystem.

## Issues, Theories, and Levels of Social Complexity

Not all theorists pay attention to the complex social world in which children are reared. Some focus primarily on the lowest level of social complexity, that of individual children. Others focus on the higher level of social interactions or the patterns of interactions that define relationships. Only a few focus on social groups or the connections among groups in a culture. However, each theory should be judged by how well it describes or explains a particular aspect of development.

# SUGGESTED READINGS

Bornstein, M. H., & Lamb, M. E. (Eds.). (1992). *Developmental psychology: An advanced textbook.* Hillsdale, NJ: Erlbaum.   Unlike most texts, this book is a collection of chapters written by various experts in child development. Several chapters offer a more detailed look at the developmental theories about which you have read. You can also consult the book for further information about specific topics in development.

Kessen, W. (1965). *The child.* New York: Wiley.   For this book, Kessen selected excerpts from the writings of the major early theorists on child development.

Kessen added illuminating and often witty comments about the salient features of each theorist's work and the connections between theorists and their predecessors, contemporaries, and followers.

Miller, P. H. (1993). *Theories of developmental psychology* (3rd ed.). New York: W. H. Freeman.   Each of the major theories of development is discussed in one chapter of this book. Both the strengths and weaknesses of the theories are reviewed. Some chapters also provide an overview of research based on a theory. The book ends with general reflections on developmental theories.

Pollock, L. (1987). *A lasting relationship: Parents and children over three centuries.* Hanover, NH: University Press of New England.   How were children treated in previous centuries? This book lets you answer that question after reading accounts of childhood from 1600 to 1900. The book is a compilation of diaries, memoirs, autobiographies, and letters. The authors range from the nobility of England (e.g., Queen Victoria) to famous Americans (e.g., Thomas Jefferson) to people who had neither position nor fame.

### Chapter Two

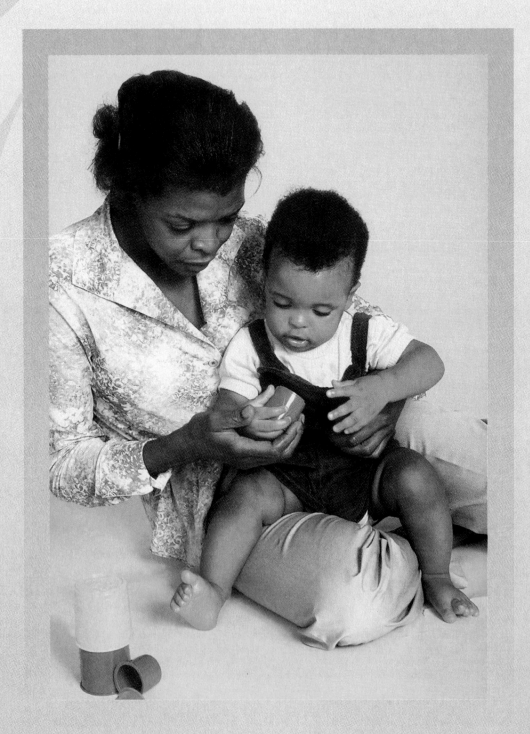

# STUDYING CHILDREN'S DEVELOPMENT: A PRIMER ON METHODS

A group of people called the Ache lives in the dense forests of eastern Paraguay in South America. Before their first peaceful contacts with outsiders during the 1970s, the Ache lived entirely as hunter-gatherers (see figure 2.1). Even into the 1980s, they spent much of their time hunting for monkeys, armadillos, snakes, insects, and other animals. They also collected oranges, honey, and other plant products (Kaplan & Dove, 1987).

The Ache way of life is very different from that in the United States. Ache infants do not move about as freely as do infants in the United States. In a dense forest, straying from parents can be dangerous. Infants not under their parents' watchful eyes can be bitten by snakes or harmed by other animals, so their mothers keep them close by (see figure 2.2).

If you watched Ache infants and young children carefully, you would discover that they don't start walking independently until they are nearly 2 years old. You might ask, then, whether their overall motor development is slower than that of children in the United States. You might also ask whether their parents' control over their movement delays their motor development.

To find the answers to these questions, you would need to study the development of Ache children systematically, and you would need a variety of methods to do so. This chapter describes methods you could use to examine not only Ache motor development but any question about children's development. To make the presentation simpler, the discussion focuses on one aspect of research methods at a time. As its subtitle states, the chapter is only a primer on methods.

While reading about the various research methods you should keep two general points in mind. First, every method has advantages and disadvantages. After learning the disadvantages of each method, you might conclude that all research in child development has important limitations and, therefore, that none of the findings can be trusted. You are right in saying that all research has limitations, but you are wrong in concluding that none of the findings can be trusted. How is that possible?

The answer relates to the second general point. Research in child development, as in all science, is cumulative. Each new study builds on previous research. If the results of one study are confirmed by those in a later study with different methods, you can feel more confident that the results are trustworthy.

## FIGURE 2.1

The Ache people of eastern Paraguay get much of their food from hunting monkeys, snakes, and other animals. Here they prepare their weapons for a hunting trip.

FIGURE 2.2
Ache mothers keep their infants close to protect them from the dangers of the forest. Ache mothers keep busy while watching their infants by preparing food, weaving, or doing other tasks.

In more technical terms, the science of child development rests on the replication of research. **Replication** refers to the test of a hypothesis, or the investigation of a research question, using multiple samples and, often, using different but parallel methods. If the results of one study with certain methods replicate those in another study with different methods, then researchers are more willing to accept those results as valid. Similarly, a study with a single sample can be strengthened by including multiple measures of important constructs. As with replication across studies, the use of multiple measures with complementary advantages and disadvantages increases confidence in the findings of research.

**replication**
*The test of a hypothesis or the investigation of a research question with multiple samples of subjects and, often, with different but parallel methods.*

As you read, then, consider the specific methods that are discussed as the building blocks of the science of child development. Just as a single block does not make a solid wall, research with a single method does not yield completely solid conclusions. But when several methods have been used in several studies, researchers have obtained trustworthy information about children's development.

# MEASUREMENT

Critical to any research method is the measurement of important phenomena. One definition of **measurement** is a set of rules for assigning numbers to objects in such a way as to represent quantities of attributes (Nunnally, 1978). For example, simple rules specify how to use a yardstick to measure the size of a room or the height of a young child. However, the rules become more complex when children's behavior or aspects of their development are measured.

**measurement**
*A set of rules for assigning numbers to objects in such a way as to represent quantities of attributes.*

Imagine that you were a researcher who wanted to measure the motor development of Ache children. To begin, you would need to find out when the children are first able to perform specific behaviors such as walking independently. Judging when a child can walk independently is not always easy to do. For example, would you say that a 1-year-old girl can walk independently if she must hold onto someone's finger? What if she can take only one step on her own? What if she can take only three steps? These questions show why researchers must establish rules about when to credit a child with independent walking.

Your second task would be to create a measure of overall motor development. To complete this task, you would need to define other indicators of motor development besides walking, and then establish rules for measuring them. For example, you might measure when Ache infants can sit without being supported by adults. You might measure when older Ache children can balance on one foot for at least 5 seconds (Kaplan & Dove, 1987).

Next, you would need to decide how to combine the information on all the indicators of motor development that you have measured. One simple way is to give children one point for every indicator of motor development on which they succeed. For example, they get a point if they can walk independently. They get no points for indicators of motor development on which they fail. The total number of points that children receive would serve as a measure of their motor development.

Similar measurement procedures apply to other constructs besides motor development. Researchers always begin by selecting several indicators of a construct and deciding how each should be measured. Then they decide how to combine the information from those indicators into a single measure.

Researchers do not have a manual or guidebook that tells exactly how to make these decisions. On many topics in child development, previous research can be used as a guide. In addition, advanced textbooks spell out general principles of measurement (e.g., Nunnally, 1978).

Almost always, however, researchers must use their own judgment in making some decisions about measurement. When a decision is a matter of judgment, different researchers will often make different decisions. This does not mean that one researcher will have good measures and the other researchers will have bad ones. Sometimes different measures are appropriate for testing hypotheses derived from different theories. Sometimes different measures can show that a hypothesis should be revised, because it is confirmed with certain measures of a construct but not with other measures.

How, then, can you evaluate whether a researcher's decisions about measurement were good ones? You will find answers to this question in the following sections. The next section introduces different measurement techniques and reviews criteria for judging the adequacy of specific measures obtained with each technique.

## Techniques of Measurement

So far you have read about only one technique of measurement, the observation of children's spontaneous behavior. A second technique is to derive measures from verbal reports. Researchers may interview children, ask them to complete a questionnaire, or give interviews or questionnaires to other people who know the children. A third technique is to assess children's performance on structured tasks.

Table 2.1 lists the three general techniques, a few of their subtypes, and the major purpose of each. The table also lists some questions that should be considered when choosing a measurement technique or evaluating a measure that was obtained by using a specific technique. Reading the entries in the table will give you a framework for understanding the following discussion of specific techniques.

### Behavioral Observation

For many decades, the observation of children's spontaneous behavior has been a primary method of child development research. Piaget (1926/1971; 1937/1954), Vygotsky (1934/1962), and other pioneers in the field carefully observed their own children and other children. Today behavioral observation continues to be a powerful technique for measuring important aspects of child development. The study of Ache children (Kaplan & Dove, 1987) is an example of observation done in natural settings, the places where children normally spend their days. Observation is also done in laboratory settings. These two types of observation have different purposes and raise different issues.

***Naturalistic Observation***   To understand children's daily lives and their normal behavior, many researchers have observed children in their homes, their classrooms, or their playgrounds. Because these settings define the natural environment for children, this measurement technique is called **naturalistic observation.** Its major purpose is to measure children's typical behavior directly. In addition, this technique is sometimes used to measure the environmental influences on children's behavior.

**naturalistic observation**
*A technique for measuring children's typical behavior by observing them in their homes, classrooms, playgrounds, or other natural settings.*

## TABLE 2.1  Types of Measurement Techniques in Child Development Research

| Measurement Technique | Major Purpose | Issues |
|---|---|---|
| **Behavioral Observation** | | |
| Naturalistic observation | To measure children's typical behavior and, sometimes, to measure the environmental influences on their behavior. | How adequate is the sample of children's behavior? How representative is the behavioral sample? How reactive are children to the observers? |
| Laboratory observation | To measure children's behavior under conditions controlled by a researcher. This control simplifies the collection of meaningful data and the testing of causal hypotheses. | How reactive are children to the laboratory setting? Does children's behavior in the laboratory correspond to that in natural settings? |
| **Verbal Reports** | | |
| Children's self-reports | To understand children's thoughts and feelings. | Are answers affected by a social-desirability bias? Are children's memories accurate? |
| Reports by parents or teachers | To obtain information about children's behavior and adjustment. | Are reports biased toward socially desirable answers? Do parents and teachers have accurate information about children's behavior? |
| Peers' reports | To obtain information about children's behavior toward peers, determine children's reputation with peers, and assess their popularity. | Do peers know how a child thinks and feels? How much information do peers have about other children's behavior? Are reports biased by a peer's liking for a particular child? |
| **Assessments of Task Performance** | To see how children's cognitive performance improves with age, and to find out which cognitive processes contribute to improved performance. | What is the theoretical significance of a task? What is its practical importance? How good is the evidence on cognitive processes? |
| **Cross-Cultural Research** | To examine the cultural specificity or universality of children's development and of the influences on their development. | Are measures culturally appropriate? Are scores on measures equivalent across cultures? Are there good measures of the cultural context? |

Procedures for naturalistic observation differ, depending on the specific setting and the behaviors under observation. The goal of one study (Wachs et al., 1993) was to see how the development of children between 17 and 30 months of age was related to the caregiving that they received. The study included more than 150 young children and their caregivers from a village near Cairo, Egypt. Children and their caregivers were first observed for 30 minutes when they were 17 months old. The observations were repeated twice a month until the children were 30 months old.

Observing and recording every behavior that children display in a natural setting would be impossible, so all observational research focuses on a selected set of behaviors. The goals of a study determine which behaviors are recorded systematically. In the Egyptian study, the observers recorded the behaviors listed in table 2.2. Notice that the codes refer to broad categories of behavior. For example, the observers recorded the number of vocalizations that toddlers made, not the words they spoke. The observers recorded whether a caregiver responded to a toddler's vocalization, not exactly how the caregiver responded. Using broad categories makes a coding system simpler, which makes it easier for observers to record the types of behavior accurately.

Table 2.2 also shows that observers did not use the same procedure for all behaviors. The procedure for observing some behaviors was **continuous real-time measurement** (Sackett, 1978); that is, the observer recorded every occurrence of a behavior during the 30-minute period of observation. For example, each time the toddler vocalized, the observer added to the count for the number of toddler vocalizations. As noted in the table, vocalizations were

**continuous real-time measurement**
*Recording every occurrence of a behavior during a set period of observation.*

**TABLE 2.2** *Behaviors Recorded During Naturalistic Observation of Egyptian Children and Their Caregivers*

| CHILDREN'S BEHAVIORS | DESCRIPTION |
|---|---|
| ***Continuous Real-Time Measurement*** | |
| Vocalizations | Counted each time the child produced a languagelike sound. Vocalizations were counted separately when they were separated by at least 3 seconds. |
| Distress episodes | Counted each time a child cried for more than 3 seconds. Episodes were counted separately when they were separated by at least 60 seconds. |
| ***Time Sampling*** | |
| Person involvement | Child was involved in interaction with an adult, sibling, or peer. |
| Object involvement | Child was playing with an object. |
| Simultaneous involvement | Child was involved with persons and objects at the same time. |
| Alert state | Child's state was coded as irritable, wide awake and alert, drowsy, or falling asleep. |
| Near home | Child was at home or no more than 5 yards from home. |
| CAREGIVERS' BEHAVIORS | |
| ***Continuous Real-Time Measurement*** | |
| Vocalizations | The caregiver vocalized to the child, without the child having vocalized in the past 3 seconds. |
| Response to child vocalization | The caregiver responded within 3 seconds to a child's vocalization verbally or nonverbally. |
| Physical contact (duration) | The amount of time the child was picked up or held or carried. |
| Physical contact (frequency) | The number of times the child was picked up, held, or carried. |
| No response to child distress | The number of times the caregiver did not respond to the child's distress and the child stopped showing distress. |
| ***Time Sampling*** | |
| Number of persons | The number of persons in the same room as the child, or the number within 5 feet of the child if the child was outside. |
| Responsible caregiver | Whether an adult, a sibling, or no caregiver was close to the child and responsible for the child's safety. |
| Caregiver in reach | Whether the caregiver could touch the child without moving from where he or she was. |

© *The Society for Research in Child Development, Inc.*

counted as separate only when they were separated from other vocalizations by at least 3 seconds. As you see, the rules for measuring this behavior had to be defined explicitly and precisely.

Continuous real-time measurement provides the kind of data necessary for **sequential analysis,** analysis of the antecedents and consequences of behavior (Gottman & Roy, 1990). For example, this analysis could show whether toddlers' distress consistently led to vocalizations or to physical contact by the caregiver. It could also show whether either the caregiver's vocalizations or her physical contact consistently reduced the child's distress.

Recording and analyzing sequences of behavior can be very illuminating (see, e.g., Gottman, 1983). This procedure is not for everyone, however. The analysis of behavior sequences is complex and time-consuming, and there are simpler alternatives. The researchers who studied Egyptian toddlers (Wachs et al., 1993) decided to code directly for a few behavioral sequences (e.g., caregivers' reactions to toddlers' vocalizations) rather than to use sequential analyses to identify them.

Another coding procedure used in the Egyptian study was a form of **time sampling,** in which observers record the occurrence of specific behaviors only for certain time periods. At the end of every 5-minute period, observers recorded whether the toddler's caregiver was within reach of the toddler.

Time sampling is most often used when researchers are studying not one child but most or all the children in an interacting group. Suppose that a researcher wanted to assess the aggressive behavior of young children in preschool classrooms. The researcher would

**sequential analysis**
*A procedure for judging the antecedents and consequences of behavior that is based on the analysis of sequences of behaviors by one or more people.*

**time sampling**
*A procedure in which an observer watches a specific child for a set time that is divided into smaller intervals. The observer records whether the child displays a specific behavior (or behaviors) during each interval.*

probably decide to observe individual children for short periods, instead of trying to observe all children in the group simultaneously. For example, the researcher might watch one child for 5 minutes and then begin observing another child for the next 5 minutes. Often, the 5-minute period is divided into shorter intervals of, say, 10 seconds each. At the end of each interval, the researcher would record whether the focal child displayed any aggressive behavior during those 10 seconds. That is, the observer would record the presence or absence of behaviors, not their frequency (Sackett, 1978). Some information is lost when present-absent coding is used, but children normally display only a few behaviors during intervals as short as 10 seconds.

Three issues are important to consider when evaluating measures derived from naturalistic observation. Each can be stated as a question.

1. *Do the observations provide an adequate sample of children's behavior?* The term *time sampling* indicates that naturalistic observation gives researchers only a sample of children's normal behavior. Small samples of behavior may not accurately show how children typically behave. For example, if you tried to measure children's aggressive behavior by observing them for 5 minutes on one day, you would not obtain good measures. You might by chance observe a generally nonaggressive boy during 5 minutes when he got entangled in a quarrel with a group of other boys. You might by chance observe a generally aggressive girl during 5 minutes when she was intensely concentrating on an art project and so not interacting with anyone.

How large a sample of observations is adequate? In the Egyptian study (Wachs et al., 1993), children and their caregivers were observed for 30 minutes twice a month for more than a year. To derive final measures, the researchers combined scores for the 6 hours of observation during each six-month period. Most researchers would agree that this sample is adequate for judging the relations between young children's behavioral competence and their interactions with caregivers. By contrast, if the researchers had observed children and their caregivers for only 5 minutes each month, most researchers would have viewed their samples of behavior as inadequate.

Researchers always prefer larger samples of behavior (or longer periods of observation). However, no general rule for the size of behavioral samples exists. This is, again, a matter of judgment. A researcher's judgments about this issue, and other issues mentioned later in this section, are tested when measures are evaluated using the general criteria presented later.

2. *Do the observations provide a **representative sample** of children's behavior?* A sample of behavior is *representative* when it reflects all of children's experiences, not a biased selection of them. Suppose that you wanted to observe children in a day-care center, but you only did observations inside the center between 9:00 A.M. and noon. If you observed for the entire morning, you would probably have an adequate sample of children's behaviors. However, your sample of behaviors would not be representative because you would not know how children behaved on the playground outside or during the afternoons. Naturalistic observations yield more accurate measures when they are done in multiple settings throughout the day.

3. *Do children show high reactivity to the observers?* **Reactivity** refers to children's responses to the observers or to the conditions of observation. When children's reactivity is high, their behavior while under observation is very different from their normal behavior.

Many writers question whether either adults or children behave normally when they know they are being observed (e.g., Miller, 1987). To avoid this problem, researchers sometimes arrange special circumstances for observation. Figure 2.3 shows an observer who is watching a group of toddlers and their caregiver from behind a one-way mirror. The toddlers cannot tell whether an observer is behind the mirror, so reactivity should not be a problem.

Another option, used in the Egyptian study (Wachs et al., 1993), is to have one or more observation sessions before collecting actual data. The initial sessions acclimate children to the observations and make their behavior more natural when data collection begins. Researchers typically find that adults and children soon ignore an observer who does not interact with them. The observer also shows no visible response to their behavior, so they soon go about their daily business. In short, reactivity to observers can be a problem in naturalistic observation, but careful attention to the procedures for observation can greatly lessen its impact.

**representative sample**
*A sample of children's behavior that reflects all of the children's experiences, not a biased selection of them.*

**reactivity**
*Children's responses to observers or to conditions of observation.*

The adult in the foreground is observing the behavior of several young children from behind a one-way mirror. Child development researchers have spent years observing the behavior of young children in natural settings like this preschool classroom. Such observations are the primary source of data on children's social behavior. They are also valuable for describing children's motor skills, problem-solving ability, play patterns, and other characteristics.

*Laboratory Observation*   Researchers who do naturalistic observation have little control over the conditions of observation. For example, they cannot control whether a young child's caregiver is the mother, the father, a sibling, or someone else. When a child is a member of a large group, as in a preschool classroom, the researcher cannot control the behavior of classmates toward a particular child. A researcher can have control over these conditions when observations are done in laboratory settings.

Control over the conditions of observation is often necessary for collecting meaningful data. Suppose that you wanted to judge infants' visual perception, or how well they can see. You might guess what infants could and could not see by watching them at home, but verifying your guesses would be difficult.

Much more accurate measures of infants' visual perception have been obtained in the laboratory. For example, to assess how well infants can see patterns, researchers have shown them checkerboards of black and white squares (Banks & Salapatek, 1983). When each square on the checkerboard is large, infants can easily see the pattern. As the size of the squares decreases, infants find it harder to distinguish them. When the squares are too small for infants to see, the checkerboard looks to them like a uniform shade of gray.

How do the researchers judge whether infants see the black and white squares? They have used several methods. One of the most sophisticated is the measurement of evoked potentials, the electrical activity of the brain, by placing electrodes on infants' heads (see figure 2.4). Then the infants are shown squares that change phase (black to white and back) several times each second. Measures of evoked potentials show whether the infants' eyes and brain respond to the shifts in phase.

Accurate recording of evoked potentials can only be done in an environment where lighting, infants' positions, and the presentation of stimuli are carefully controlled. Such control would be impossible to achieve in infants' homes—unless you changed part of the home into a laboratory! For studies of this kind, observations in laboratory settings are both necessary and appropriate.

For testing hypotheses about the causes of children's behavior, control over the conditions of observation may also be necessary. Suppose that you wanted to compare children's

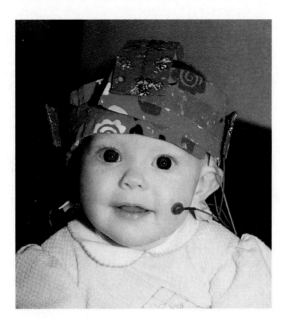

FIGURE 2.4
This baby is really "wired"! The wires connect to electrodes on her head that record her brain's electrical activity when she sees a stimulus. That is, they measure her visual-evoked (electrical) potential.

behavior toward friends with their behavior toward other classmates. This comparison would be difficult to make in natural settings because children interact much more often with friends than with other classmates. Moreover, friends are likely to engage in different activities when they are together than mere classmates do. To ensure meaningful comparisons of friends' and classmates' behavior, you would need to arrange standard conditions for observations of both. Those conditions are easier to arrange in a laboratory setting.

One team of researchers examined friends' and classmates' behavior during situations that elicited conflicts (Hartup et al., 1993). These researchers used a large van that had been converted into a mobile research laboratory. The van, which included two research rooms, was parked on the grounds of an elementary school.

To begin the study, the third and fourth graders in the school were asked to name their best friends. Then the researchers paired each child either with a mutual friend or with another classmate. The pairs of children were brought to the mobile laboratory, one at a time. Each child was then taken into a separate room where each was taught the rules of a board game called "Snake Pit." Next, the children played the game together in one room while their interaction was recorded on videotape.

Although the children did not know it, they were taught different rules for the game. For example, one child was taught that a player who landed on the same space as the other player received an extra turn. The other child was taught that this player had to return to the starting point on the board. Children were taught different rules to make conflicts more likely during the game. In other words, the researchers arranged the game so that they could be sure of seeing the type of behavior that was the focus of the study. By controlling the children's experiences, the researchers increased the odds that their study would be successful.

Two issues are especially important to consider when evaluating measures derived from laboratory observation. Again, these issues can be stated as questions:

1. *Are children highly reactive to the laboratory setting?* This question matches one asked about naturalistic observation. Stated differently, the question is whether children act unnaturally in a laboratory setting because they realize they are under observation. This question is difficult to answer conclusively, so researchers try to minimize reactivity in all ways possible.

In the study of friends' conflicts (Hartup et al., 1993), children's behavior while playing the game was recorded on videotape, but the video camera was in a separate room behind a one-way mirror. Children were unlikely to react to the camera that they could not see. They

probably reacted mostly to the behavior of their opponent in the Snake Pit game. Moreover, both friends and other classmates were in the same conditions, so differences in their behavior cannot easily be explained in terms of reactivity.

2. *Does children's behavior in the laboratory correspond to that in natural settings?* To increase the match between laboratory observation and "real life," researchers often introduce realistic elements into laboratory tasks. For example, the board game used to elicit friends' conflicts was new, but it was created by using parts of commercially available games (Hartup et al., 1993). The children played the game in an unfamiliar van, but the van was parked near their regular school building.

Still, the meaningfulness of measures obtained through laboratory observation remains controversial (Berkowitz & Donnerstein, 1982; Miller, 1987). When evaluating research using this measurement technique, you should pay attention to any information provided about the conditions of observation and children's reactions to them. Researchers might, for example, report that children said little about the experimenters or the laboratory furnishings when under observation by a hidden camera.

In addition, you should pay attention to researchers' comments about the natural settings in which similar behaviors could be expected. For example, the study of friends' conflicts might show how friends behave when playing games in a natural setting. That study might not show how friends behave when having a conversation or working together on schoolwork. If you analyze the laboratory conditions carefully, you will be more able to draw conclusions about the applicability of observations in those conditions to natural settings.

## Verbal Reports

Often, behavioral observations are impractical or cannot provide the kind of information that a researcher needs. One alternative is to use interviews, questionnaires, or other forms of verbal reports. Children can report their thoughts, feelings, or behaviors. Parents or other adults can report on the children they know, or children's peers can report their impressions of them. Data from each of these sources have special value for certain purposes.

***Children's Self-Reports*** When researchers want to understand children's thoughts and feelings, the best measurement technique is to ask the children themselves. Suppose you want to know how positively children feel about themselves. In other words, you want to measure their *self-esteem*. Structured questions can provide information about various facets of self-esteem, including children's beliefs about their school performance, social relationships, and general self-worth.

Table 2.3 shows some sample items and the response options for one measure of children's self-esteem (Harter, 1985). Notice that each item includes a sentence about two kinds of children. Some children are said to feel good about themselves. For example, they "are pretty pleased about themselves." Other children are said to feel bad about themselves. For example, they "are often unhappy with themselves."

Children decide to which other children they are most similar and whether the statement about those other children is "really true" or "sort of true" for themselves. Children get higher scores when they choose the high self-esteem alternatives as more true for themselves. Total scores are derived by averaging the scores children receive on all items of one type.

Of course, children can complete questionnaires only if they can read. A researcher might try to make a questionnaire suitable for children who cannot read by converting it into an interview and reading the questions to children. But more than a change in mode of presentation is often necessary. For instance, the wording of the questions may also need to be simplified.

Some questions may not be meaningful for young children no matter how they are worded. If you asked other adults about their attitudes toward capital punishment, most of them would readily understand what you meant. Asking a 4-year-old the same question would probably yield a blank stare. Indeed, you might find no way to state a question about capital punishment so that it makes sense to a 4-year-old. All measures based on verbal reports must, therefore, be appropriate for a child's developmental level.

TABLE 2.3 *Sample Items and Response Options on Harter's Self-Perception Profile for Children*

| | Really true for me | Sort of true for me | | | | | Sort of true for me | Really true for me |
|---|---|---|---|---|---|---|---|---|
| **Global Self-Worth** | ☐ | ☐ | | Some kids are often *unhappy* with themselves | *but* | Other kids are pretty *pleased* with themselves. | ☐ | ☐ |
| **Scholastic Competence** | ☐ | ☐ | | Some kids feel that they are very *good* at their school work | *but* | Other kids *worry* about whether they can do the school work assigned to them. | ☐ | ☐ |
| **Social Acceptance** | ☐ | ☐ | | Some kids find it *hard* to make friends | *but* | Other kids find it's pretty *easy* to make friends. | ☐ | ☐ |
| **Athletic Competence** | ☐ | ☐ | | Some kids do very *well* at all kinds of sports | *but* | Other kids *don't* feel that they are very good when it comes to sports. | ☐ | ☐ |
| **Physical Appearance** | ☐ | ☐ | | Some kids are *happy* with the way they look | *but* | Other kids are *not* happy with the way they look. | ☐ | ☐ |
| **Behavioral Conduct** | ☐ | ☐ | | Some kids often do *not* like the way they *behave* | *but* | Other kids usually *like* the way they behave. | ☐ | ☐ |

From Professor Susan Harter, *Self-Perception Profile for Children*. Reprinted by permission.

The most important issues in evaluating children's self-reports concern whether children are willing and able to provide accurate reports. Stated as questions, these issues are as follows:

1. *Are children's answers affected by a **social-desirability bias,** a bias to give responses that are perceived as socially desirable?* During an interview, children may not respond truthfully because they want to please the interviewer. When completing a questionnaire, children may give false answers because they want whoever reads their answers to form a positive impression of them. In short, measures that are distorted by strong social-desirability biases are inaccurate. Responses on these measures merely show which answers children think will make them look good.

Some researchers try to minimize social-desirability biases by making questionnaires anonymous. Alternatively, researchers judge the strength of this bias by relating scores on self-report measures to scores on other types of measures. For example, Harter (1982) reported that students higher in self-reported athletic competence received higher ratings from their physical education teachers for their athletic ability. These relations suggest that the students reported honestly about their perceptions of their athletic competence.

2. *Are children's memories accurate?* The ability to provide accurate reports sometimes depends on children's memory. This influence of memory is most significant when children report on their behavior. Suppose, for example, that you asked children about their classroom involvement. In particular, you asked them how often they participated in class discussions during the past week. Even if children are willing to report this information, they may not remember how often they volunteered an answer to a teacher's question or made other comments in class. Partly for this reason, self-report measures of behavior are less common than

**social-desirability bias**
*A bias to give responses that are perceived as socially acceptable.*

are self-report measures of thoughts and feelings. More accurate information on children's behavior can often be obtained from their parents and teachers.

***Parents' and Teachers' Reports*** For one study (Ladd & Golter, 1988), parents recorded the out-of-school contacts that their preschool children had with peers. On six days (including weekdays and weekends), they recorded with whom their children played, where, and how long the play lasted. An outside observer would have had great difficulty getting this information. The study included 58 children, so the observer would have needed at least 348 days (58 children × 6 days each) to collect the same data. Of course, an observer also would have been more intrusive and so may have obtained less accurate data than parents did.

Parents can also report on problem behaviors that their children show. The Child Behavior Checklist is used to assess a comprehensive set of behavioral problems (Achenbach, 1991). Parents read items such as "argues a lot," "likes to be alone," and "nightmares," and then indicate how true each item is of their child. Thousands of parents of both children without behavioral problems and children referred for psychological treatment have completed the checklist. A comparable checklist is used by teachers to report the behavior of children in their classes. With the data now available, clinicians can compare the behavioral profile of any child with the normal profile for the child's age and sex.

The major questions about parents' and teachers' reports are similar to those mentioned for children's self-reports.

1. *Are reports biased toward socially desirable answers?* Adults' reports about children may be biased. For example, parents may not report accurately on their child's misbehavior. They may, instead, exaggerate their child's virtues. Teachers may do the same, if they feel that their students' behavior reflects on their own competence.

By contrast, parents and teachers who have poor relationships with particular children may exaggerate the children's vices rather than their virtues. These biases may reflect either unwillingness to say honestly how the children behave or unconscious distortions due to a specific parent's or teacher's attitudes toward a specific child.

2. *Do parents and teachers have accurate information about children's behavior?* Even parents do not know everything about their children's behavior. Unless children talk freely with their parents, the parents may not know how well their children get along with their classmates at school. Unless teachers spend time in the school cafeteria and on the playground, they may not know how often children are involved in fights with their classmates. Moreover, parents and teachers know about children's thoughts and feelings only indirectly, if at all.

Nevertheless, these limitations of adults' reports should not be exaggerated. Parents spend many hours with their children, and they are usually willing to report frankly on their children's characteristics. Teachers not only interact with the same groups of children for many months; they also see the variations among children and so have a basis for comparing them. Because of these strengths, measures based on adults' reports are valuable in developmental research, yielding findings that have stood the tests of time and replication.

***Peers' Reports*** Peers or classmates can provide detailed information about a child's behavior. Classmates see countless examples of other children's behavior in settings ranging from the classroom to the playground. Classmates also hear conversations about behaviors by other children that they did not observe directly. For instance, they may learn who had a fight with whom, or what grade a child got on a test.

One way to tap this source of information is to describe specific behaviors to children and ask them to say which of their classmates shows the behavior most frequently. To make this procedure more interesting, researchers often tell them to "pretend that you are the director of a play starring the students in this classroom. The director of the play has to do many things but the most important job is to select the right people to act in the play. So, your job is to choose the students who could play each part or role best" (Masten, Morison, & Pellegrini, 1985, p. 525).

| TABLE 2.4 | *Sample Items for the Revised Class Play and the Dimensions to Which They Refer* | | |
|---|---|---|---|

| SOCIABILITY–LEADERSHIP | AGGRESSIVE–DISRUPTIVE | SENSITIVE–ISOLATED |
|---|---|---|
| 1. Good leader | 1. Picks on other kids | 1. Often left out |
| 2. Everyone likes to be with | 2. Too bossy | 2. Feelings get hurt easily |
| 3. Has many friends | 3. Teases other children too much | 3. Usually sad |
| 4. Good sense of humor | 4. Gets into a lot of fights | 4. Rather play alone than with others |
| 5. Everyone listens to | | |
| 6. Good ideas for things to do | | |
| 7. Makes new friends easily | | |

Adapted from A. S. Masten, et al., "A revised class play method of peer assessment," in *Developmental Psychology*, 21:523–533. Copyright © 1985 by The American Psychological Association. Adapted with permission.

Children name classmates for positive roles like "has a good sense of humor," and for negative roles like "gets into a lot of fights" (see table 2.4). Children are allowed to name the same classmate more than once if that classmate fits several roles well. By counting the number of times a given child is named for the positive and negative roles, a researcher can assess the child's general reputation with classmates. By subdividing the categories for positive and negative roles, a researcher can assess more specific behaviors such as a child's reputation for aggression, helpfulness, and so on.

The questions most important when evaluating peers' reports are similar to those mentioned for other types of verbal reports, so they can be listed briefly.

1. *Do peers know how a child thinks or feels?* Because peers may know little about other children's thoughts and feelings, peer reports usually focus not on such characteristics but on observable behaviors.

2. *Do peers have information about the behavior on which they are asked to report?* Peers are likely to have little or no information about certain behaviors, such as how hard a child works on homework. Therefore, whether peers have had sufficient opportunity to observe specific types of behaviors should be considered when evaluating the items on a peer-report measure.

3. *Are peers' reports biased by how much they like or dislike a classmate?* Children may say that their best friends have a good sense of humor, even if most of their classmates think their friends' jokes are stupid. Conversely, children who dislike a particular classmate may say that the classmate is bossy, even if that opinion is not shared by other children in the class.

For some researchers, how much other classmates like a particular child is not a source of bias but of revealing data. With those data, researchers can estimate how popular the child is or, conversely, the degree to which the child is rejected by peers (Asher & Coie, 1990). Chapter 12 includes more information about this measurement technique and its value in judging children's social competence.

## Assessments of Task Performance

Some researchers take as their primary goal the assessment of children's performance on specific tasks. For example, they want to find out how often children at various ages give the right answer to certain types of logical problems. If children give the wrong answer, these researchers may also want to find out which cognitive processes led them astray.

The best-known assessments of task performance are part of intelligence and achievement tests. Chapter 10 focuses on these tests, but one example is useful now. For part of one intelligence test (Wechsler, 1989), preschool children must make designs with blocks. For example, the children must arrange four small blocks to make a larger design that matches a model (see figure 2.5). The examiner scores whether children successfully complete the design and, if so, how quickly they complete it. The speed with which children complete the design is taken as a measure of their perceptual motor ability.

**FIGURE 2.5**

Can you see how to put together the four blocks to make the design on the right? If you can, you passed one intelligence test item—for preschoolers.

Separate blocks

Completed design

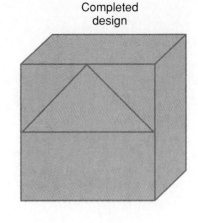

**FIGURE 2.6**

Piaget's procedure for testing children's understanding of the conservation of liquid quantity.

First step

Is there the same amount of water in glasses A and B?

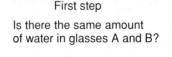

Second step

Now does glass C have the same amount of water as glass A?

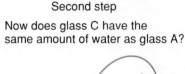

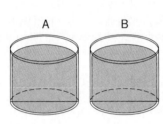

A          B

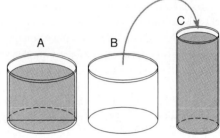

A          B          C

**conservation of liquid quantity**
*Piaget's term for one property of liquids, which is that their amount does not change if you pour them from one container into another. Also refers to Piaget's task for testing children's understanding of this property.*

An intelligence test can serve as one measure of a child's intellectual ability, but a test score by itself does not explain why a child does well or poorly. Jean Piaget recognized this limitation of intelligence testing early in his career. He then tried to devise methods of discovering more about children's reasoning. Over the years, Piaget created hundreds of tasks to study many facets of children's cognitive development. Figure 2.6 illustrates the procedure for his most famous task. A child is shown the two glasses of water in the first panel of the figure and asked whether they have the same amount of water. The child sees that the water in both glasses reaches the same height and usually says yes.

Then the water from one glass is poured into a taller, thinner glass—as the child watches. (See the second panel of the figure.) The child is asked whether the two glasses with water now have the same amount. Usually the child says, "No, the tall one has more." If asked why, the child says something like, "The water comes up higher here [in the tall glass], so it has more."

This answer implies that the child does not realize that an amount of water does not change when it is poured from one glass to another. Piaget discovered that most 5-year-olds do not appreciate this principle, which he called **conservation of liquid quantity.** By 7 years of age, most children recognize that pouring a liquid from one container to another does not change its quantity. In Piaget's terms, 7-year-olds are conservers. Piaget viewed the shift from nonconservation to conservation as a sign that a child has moved to a higher cognitive stage.

Researchers who adopt the information-processing approach to cognitive development often use tasks different from Piaget's. Figure 2.7 illustrates an experimental apparatus for studying the speed with which children react to letters or numbers in unusual orientations (Kail, 1986). The child is looking at a computer screen that shows a letter *F* tilted on its side

**FIGURE 2.7**
Is this child looking at a standard *F* or a backward *F* that has been tilted from the vertical? How quickly children can answer this question and press the correct key tells us about their speed of mental rotation. That is, it tells us how fast they can mentally rotate the letter to the vertical so that they can "see" whether it is a standard *F* or a backward *F*.

(30 degrees from the vertical). Mentally rotating the letter backward to the vertical position confirms that the letter is truly an *F*. On other trials children see mirror images of letters, for example, a letter *F* written backward. These letters are also tilted to varying degrees. The children's task is to decide, as fast as they can, whether the letter they see on a trial is a true letter or a mirror image.

Children react more slowly when letters are farther from the vertical because they mentally rotate each letter to the vertical before deciding whether it is a letter or a mirror image. Therefore, differences in children's reaction times for letters tilted to differing degrees measure their speed of mental rotation. In other words, the task lets researchers measure how fast children think.

When evaluating measures of task performance, the adequacy of specific tasks is a central concern. This general concern is linked to three issues, which are expressed in the following questions.

1. *What is the theoretical significance of a task?* Consider the conservation task in figure 2.6. Does the shift to correct answers on this task actually signal a new stage of cognitive development? This question is best answered by comparing children's performance on a conservation task with their performance on other tasks that are, in theory, related.

2. *What is the practical importance of a task?* You might wonder why anyone cares whether young children give correct answers on the conservation task or the mental-rotation task. One answer is that performance on these tasks is expected to relate to performance on more strictly academic tasks such as reading, doing arithmetic, and understanding scientific principles. If these relations exist, research on the tasks can increase understanding of children's performance on strictly academic tasks.

3. *Do measures of task performance provide good evidence about underlying cognitive processes?* Piaget asserted that children's responses on the conservation task provide evidence for his theory of cognitive stages. You will see in chapter 8 that information-processing researchers disagree with Piaget about the cognitive processes involved in conservation. Assessments of task performance are more valuable when they do not allow this ambiguity about cognitive processes.

## Cross-Cultural Research

One issue featured in chapter 1 was whether specific aspects of development vary across cultures or are universal to the human species. Cross-cultural research provides evidence on this issue. Another purpose of cross-cultural research is to see if the processes influencing development are or are not similar in different cultures.

All the measurement techniques discussed earlier can be adapted to achieve these purposes. The Egyptian study (Wachs et al., 1993) mentioned earlier was implicitly cross-cultural, despite including children from only one country, because the methods matched those in previous studies with U.S. children. In the study of infants' sleeping arrangements discussed in chapter 1 (Morelli et al., 1992), the primary measures were obtained from parents' verbal reports. In addition, Piagetian tasks and other assessments of task performance have been used in many cross-cultural studies (Dasen, 1977).

The requirements for measurement are more stringent for cross-cultural research than for research within one culture. The following questions address three issues important in evaluating cross-cultural research.

1. *Are the measures appropriate for participants from every culture involved?* Intense debates have occurred over the cultural appropriateness of measures derived from laboratory observations. For example, Levine and Miller (1990) questioned whether laboratory procedures used in the United States to assess infants' attachments to their parents yield meaningful data when used in other cultures. This debate is reviewed in chapter 6.

Some measures devised for use in one culture can be modified so they are appropriate in other cultures. The researchers who assessed Ache children's motor development had to drop several items on a measure devised for U.S. children because those items did not fit the Ache context (Kaplan & Dove, 1987). An item on children's ability to pedal a tricycle could not be used because Ache children don't ride tricycles in the forest. Items about drawing on paper were dropped because Ache children have little access to paper. Even after these exclusions, the researchers had enough items to compare Ache and U.S. children's motor development, as you will see in chapter 5.

2. *Are scores on important measures equivalent across cultures?* The equivalence of measures can be evaluated on several levels (Knight et al., 1992). The individual items on a measure are equivalent across cultures if scores on each item show the same relations to scores on other items in all cultures. Entire measures are equivalent if they relate similarly to measures of other constructs in all cultures. When measures are fully equivalent, a particular score on a measure represents the same degree or intensity of a construct in all cultures.

For example, a mother's warmth or acceptance of her children might be measured on a scale from 1 (low) to 5 (high). This measure provides equivalent scores for Anglo-American and Hispanic mothers if an Anglo-American mother with a score of 4 is just as warm toward her children as a Hispanic mother with the same score. Several measures used in child development have passed even this stringent test of equivalence, as *Cultural Perspectives:* "Parenting and Children's Mental Health in Hispanic and Anglo-American Families" explains.

3. *How well are important aspects of the culture measured?* In cross-cultural studies, researchers want to find out not only how children's development differs across cultures but also how the differences should be explained. To make their explanations convincing, researchers need information about the cultural context, the major features of children's developmental niche (Super & Harkness, 1986). Unfortunately, few cross-cultural studies have included systematic information about cultural contexts (Harkness, 1992).

**ethnographic research**
*A collection of methods designed to provide a comprehensive and objective account of all aspects of a culture.*

Careful description of the cultural context is the hallmark of **ethnographic research.** The goal of ethnographic research is to provide a comprehensive and objective account of all aspects of a culture (Barry, 1981). Ethnographers base their accounts on intensive involvement in a culture. They typically live in a single community for several months. Each day they take detailed notes on people's conversations, behaviors, and daily routines. In addition, they interview community leaders and elders who can explain cultural patterns and describe historical changes in these patterns.

PARENTING AND CHILDREN'S MENTAL HEALTH IN HISPANIC AND ANGLO-AMERICAN FAMILIES

Do Hispanic and Anglo-American parents treat their children differently? If so, do these differences affect the children's mental health? These questions deal with important issues about cultural diversity within the United States. Answering the questions is not easy, because researchers must show that their measures of parenting and of children's mental health are equivalent for Hispanics and Anglo-Americans. Recently, George Knight, Lynn Virdin, and Mark Roosa (1994) examined the equivalence of several widely used measures.

The researchers interviewed 70 Hispanic children who ranged from 9 to 13 years of age. They also interviewed 161 Anglo-American children similar in age. During the interviews the children reported on their mother's child-rearing practices and their own depression and conduct problems. In addition, the children completed the self-esteem measure (Harter, 1985) that was described earlier in the chapter.

The interviews were conducted in the children's homes with their mothers' knowledge and consent. A second interviewer talked to the children's mothers while the first interviewer talked to the children. Mothers reported on their childrearing practices and on their children's depression and conduct problems. The use of parallel measures derived from mothers' and children's reports strengthens this study.

Anglo-American mothers described themselves as less rejecting and controlling than did Hispanic mothers. Anglo-American children also described their mothers as less rejecting and controlling than did the Hispanic children. The researchers noted that these differences may result from greater environmental risk in Hispanic families or from the emphasis of Hispanics on traditional values and obedience to adults.

On most measures of mental health, the Hispanic and Anglo-American children did not differ significantly, whether their mental health was judged from their self-reports or their mothers' reports. Hispanic children reported greater depression, but the self-report measure of depression used in the study seemed not to be equivalent across the two ethnic groups. Even when the two groups of children reported similar parenting, Hispanic children had higher scores on the depression measure than did Anglo-American children. This pattern suggests that scores on the measure need to be interpreted differently for Hispanic and Anglo-American children.

On the other measures of children's mental health, and on all the parenting measures, scores seemed equivalent for the two ethnic groups. Therefore, the data can be used to answer the two initial questions. Hispanic and Anglo-American mothers treat their children differently, but these differences do not noticeably affect their children's mental health.

The researchers cautioned that their Hispanic families were Mexican Americans who were fluent in English. Different results may be found for other segments of the Hispanic population. Nevertheless, it is reassuring to know that the equivalence of measures intended for use in different ethnic groups can be rigorously evaluated and demonstrated.

Hispanic parents treat their children somewhat differently than do Anglo-American parents, but most parenting measures show the same relations to children's mental health in both ethnic groups, which suggests the measures are fully equivalent for the two groups of parents.

Kaplan and Dove (1987) were ethnographers who lived with the Ache people. They supplemented their daily observations and interviews with standard assessments of motor development. Ethnographers usually obtain additional information from official sources, for example, on land ownership or crime statistics (Fry, 1992).

Ethnographic accounts can be extremely valuable in understanding the development of children in a specific culture. Understanding is enhanced because the ethnographer's goal is to take the perspective of the people in a culture, not that of an outside observer (Kramer, 1991). Consequently, ethnographic methods are a valuable complement to other measurement techniques in cross-cultural research.

## Reliability and Validity of Measures

Suppose that you have created a new measure of motor development, self-esteem, or speed of information processing. How can you tell whether your new measure is a good one? Or, to shift perspective from creator to critic, how can you judge the quality of other researchers' measures? To make these judgments, you need to examine two general criteria for the adequacy of measures: reliability and validity.

### Reliability

**Reliability** refers to the precision of a measure, defined as the consistency with which a characteristic is measured. Suppose that you gave an observer a set of rules for measuring Ache children's ability to walk independently. Then you did a quick check of the reliability of the measure. You asked the observer to watch each of three children on three occasions, two weeks apart. On each occasion, the observer was to give each child a "pass" or a "fail" based on his or her apparent walking ability at each time.

After completing the observations, the observer gave you the following scores:

| Child | Time | | |
|-------|------|------|------|
| | 1 | 2 | 3 |
| A | pass | pass | pass |
| B | fail | pass | pass |
| C | pass | fail | pass |

Child *A* received a pass every time, so for this child your measure gave consistent results. Child *B* failed the first time but passed the later times. Although these results are inconsistent, you might assume that this child learned to walk between Time 1 and Time 2.

The results for Child *C* are more difficult to explain. Why would this child be able to walk at Time 1 and unable to do so at Time 2? This inconsistent pattern seems to reflect **random error,** errors of measurement that reduce the consistency of scores. More reliable measures have less random error and so yield more consistent results.

The example also shows one method for judging the reliability of a measure. You repeat a series of measurements several times and examine the consistency of the scores across times. Each time is one *test*; the later times are *retests*. The relation between the scores for the first test and a later retest estimates the **test-retest reliability.** When measures are reliable, children's scores on a test are strongly related to their scores on a retest.

The pattern of scores for Child *B* suggests another requirement for test-retest reliability. The interval between tests must be short enough to minimize the possibility of true changes in children's characteristics. Most psychological constructs (e.g., self-esteem and IQ) are fairly stable over months or years, so retest intervals of a few weeks are usually acceptable.

You could—and should—use a second method for assessing the reliability of your measure of walking ability. You need to see whether two independent observers can agree on the score that a particular child should receive. In technical terms, you need an estimate of **interobserver agreement.** When observers more often agree on the scores assigned to specific children, the resulting measures are more reliable.

Researchers routinely assess interobserver agreement when they study children's social behavior in natural settings. Similar estimates of reliability are necessary for other types of measures if scoring children's responses involves some degree of subjectivity. When giving

**reliability**
*The precision of a measure, or the consistency with which a particular characteristic is measured.*

**random error**
*Errors of measurement that reduce the consistency of scores and therefore lower the reliability of measures.*

**test-retest reliability**
*The correlation between the scores for some sample of children on a first test and a later test (or retest).*

**interobserver agreement**
*An index of reliability based on the correspondence between the scores that two observers assign to specific children when they observe the children simultaneously.*

| **TABLE 2.5** | *A Valid Item for Testing the Mathematical Ability of Adolescent Boys and Girls?* |
|---|---|

A high school basketball team has won 40 percent of its first 15 games. Beginning with the sixteenth game, how many games in a row does the team now have to win in order to have a 55 percent winning record?

(A) 3
(B) 5
(C) 6
(D) 11
(E) 15

From Linn & Hyde, 1989.

Piaget's conservation tasks, for example, researchers often ask children to explain the reasons for their answers. Then they code these reasons into categories. Such coding involves human judgment. Therefore, researchers need to assess the reliability of coding, or the agreement between two people who independently code the reasons given by a sample of children.

A third method of assessing reliability applies to measures of broad constructs like motor development or self-esteem. Recall that researchers typically combine scores for many indicators or items to obtain measures of these constructs. You might ask, then, whether the scores on the various indicators or items are consistent.

Table 2.3 showed some items on one measure of self-esteem (Harter, 1985). That measure has six items for each facet of self-esteem. For example, six items are designed to assess children's global self-worth. You would expect children who report high self-esteem on one of these items to report high self-esteem on most of the other items. You would expect a similar consistency from children who report moderate or low self-esteem on one item. By comparing the scores for different items, you can estimate the **internal consistency** of the measure, the extent to which all items yield similar scores. Internal consistency is higher for more reliable measures.

**internal consistency**
*An index of the reliability of multiitem measures based on the correlations between items, or the degree to which all items yield similar scores for particular children.*

No measure is perfectly reliable. Remember that reliability refers to precision of measurement, and precision is always relative. However, some measures yield highly reliable scores, scores highly consistent across times, observers, and items. Researchers place most confidence in studies using such measures.

## Validity

The **validity** of a measure refers to its accuracy, or the extent to which scores on the measure reflect children's actual characteristics rather than extraneous factors. If children's scores are not measured precisely (with high consistency), they cannot be measured accurately. Therefore, a measure that is unreliable cannot be valid. However, highly reliable measures may still be low in validity.

**validity**
*The accuracy of a measure, or the extent to which differences in scores on the measure match differences in children's actual characteristics.*

Problems of validity can be subtle. Suppose that you want to measure adolescents' mathematical ability. You construct a test that includes various math problems, including the one in table 2.5, which was used on one version of the Scholastic Aptitude Test.

Would you consider this item a valid measure of mathematical ability? It certainly deals with math, and you must do some calculations to get the right answer (which is B). Still, many people would regard the item as biased in favor of boys. The item deals with basketball, a sport in which more boys than girls have a strong interest. So if boys do better than girls on the item, as they do (Linn & Hyde, 1989), the sex difference might reflect a difference not in mathematical ability but in experience with basketball statistics.

Judging the validity of this item, or an entire test with such items, is not easy. In contrast to reliability assessment, no standard methods exist for assessing the validity of measures. Researchers rely on one general rule: If a measure is valid, scores on the measure will relate to scores on other measures in sensible, theoretically meaningful ways.

Suppose you compared boys' and girls' scores on the basketball item with their scores on a test of mathematical ability that included no items about sports. You also compared boys' and girls' scores on the basketball item with their scores on a test of basketball knowledge. That test included items about the rules of basketball, the best-known players, and so on.

For simplicity's sake, consider only two possible results. One possibility is that both boys and girls who did well on the basketball item also did well on the other test of math ability. This result would suggest that the item accurately measures differences in boys' and girls' math ability.

The other possibility is that boys did better than girls on the basketball item and the test of basketball knowledge but not on the other math test. This result would suggest that the basketball item is not a valid measure of math ability.

These two results can be described more formally. Suppose that you created a math test with many items like the basketball item. If students who receive high scores on your test also receive high scores on other measures of math ability, you have shown the **convergent validity** of your new measure. The convergent validity of a measure is high when scores on the measure are strongly related to scores on other measures of the same construct.

Also important for assessing validity are the relations of a new measure to measures of other constructs. If students who receive high scores on your new test do *not* consistently receive high scores on tests of basketball knowledge, you have shown the **discriminant validity** of your measure. The discriminant validity of a measure is high when scores on the measure are unrelated to scores on measures of different constructs.

Evidence on a measure's convergent and discriminant validity is crucial for judging its **construct validity.** Construct validity refers to the degree to which a measure captures the psychological construct it is supposed to measure. For example, a measure of math ability is high in construct validity when it accurately measures differences in people's ability to solve mathematical problems. When a measure has high convergent and discriminant validity, it is by definition high in construct validity.

Bronfenbrenner (1977, 1979), the prime architect of the ecological model discussed in chapter 1, emphasized the importance of the **ecological validity** of measures. He defined ecological validity as high when participants in research perceive the research setting as having the properties that the researcher assumes it has. Bronfenbrenner was particularly concerned about research done in a laboratory setting. He argued that children often react primarily to the unfamiliarity of the setting rather than to the specific conditions arranged by the researcher.

Bronfenbrenner stated this argument dramatically when he described most developmental research as *"the science of the strange behavior of children in strange situations with strange adults for the briefest possible periods of time"* (1979, p. 19, italics original). He called for more research on spontaneously occurring behavior, in natural settings, with parents or familiar peers rather than unfamiliar adult experimenters.

Nevertheless, Bronfenbrenner was not arguing that all research in laboratory settings is low in ecological validity. As his definition states, laboratory research can be high in validity if the setting is understood similarly by the researcher and by the children being studied. In the study of friends' conflicts (Hartup et al., 1993), the children who played the Snake Pit game seemed to interpret the game as the researchers intended. Likewise, infants whose visual perception is under investigation apparently interpret visual stimuli in the way that researchers intend.

Yet just as reliability is never perfect, neither is validity. All measures are limited because researchers cannot measure any aspect of children's development with 100 percent accuracy. Nevertheless, researchers have devised many measures that are high in validity. In later chapters, you will learn about the discoveries that researchers have made by using these measures.

# RESEARCH DESIGN

The measures used in a research project define its content, or the phenomena under investigation. These measures must be integrated into a **research design,** which refers to the structure of a research project. Stated informally, a research design specifies *what* is done to *whom* and *when* (Kerlinger, 1986).

**convergent validity**
*A type of validity that is high when a measure is strongly correlated with other measures that are presumed to assess the same construct.*

**discriminant validity**
*A type of validity that is high when a measure of one construct is not correlated with measures of different constructs.*

**construct validity**
*The degree to which a measure provides an accurate assessment of the psychological construct it is supposed to measure.*

**ecological validity**
*A type of validity that is high when participants in research perceive the research setting as having the properties that the researcher assumes it has.*

**research design**
*The structure of a research project, including the characteristics of the participants, the participants' experiences, and the schedule of measurements and treatments.*

The first component of a research design concerns the whom, the participants in the research. Do they include boys, girls, or children of both sexes? Are they infants, young children, adolescents, or individuals from several age groups? The purposes of a study largely determine how these questions are answered.

The number of participants is also important. Suppose that you wanted to examine the relation between elementary-school children's self-esteem and their academic achievement. Assessing every elementary-school child in the United States would be impossible, so you would need to select a sample from that population. If your sample included only 30 children from one classroom, you could not feel very confident about your results. If you included 3,000 students from 100 classrooms, you could better estimate the relation between self-esteem and achievement in the entire population.

Besides differing in size and in individuals' characteristics, samples can differ in how representative they are of a population. Many schools assign students either to regular classes or to advanced or remedial classes. Suppose, then, that a researcher did a study of fourth graders, but only recruited them from regular classes. Because the sample for the study did not include students from advanced or remedial classes, the findings would not necessarily apply to the entire population of fourth graders. Researchers try to recruit participants so that they obtain **representative samples,** ones that include the full range of children in the population under study.

**representative samples**
*Samples that include children from all segments or subgroups of the population under study.*

The second component of a research design concerns the what, the experiences of the participants. Are they given some special manipulation, exposed to a carefully selected set of stimulus situations, or treated in another unusual way? Or does the researcher simply measure certain of the participants' characteristics without altering or manipulating their experiences? In other words, does the research design include special *treatments* or consist solely of *measurements?*

Recall the question about Ache children's motor development. To answer that question, a research design that included only measurements would be most appropriate. The primary goal of the research would be to measure the children's motor development in their current ecological and cultural context. You will see later, though, that you could better understand their motor development if you supplemented this design with certain treatments.

The third component of a research design is the when, the schedule of measurements and treatments. Are children's characteristics measured only once, or several times? If they receive some treatment, are their characteristics measured beforehand, as the treatment is given, afterward, or at all these times?

The schedule of measurements and treatments in a research design has important developmental implications. Researchers who measure the same children's characteristics at different times are also measuring their characteristics at different ages. In other words, they are examining their course of development. Several research designs are used to describe the course of development, as table 2.6 shows.

Designs that include both a treatment and later observations of children's behavior can examine the effects of the treatment on children's development. Knowing the effects of a specific treatment can, in turn, provide clues about the causes of children's development. That is, it can partly answer questions about the explanation of development. As table 2.6 shows, two general types of designs are used to explore possible explanations of children's development.

Finally, table 2.6 lists some complex designs that combine features of the basic designs. You'll read about those designs after learning more about the basic designs.

## Basic Designs for Describing Development

Research designs for describing children's development differ in their complexity, their efficiency, and the kinds of questions they can answer. As you'll see, the simplest and most efficient designs are widely used but leave some questions unanswered.

### The Cross-Sectional Design

Child-development researchers rely most often on the **cross-sectional design** for answering questions about how children change with age. Two or more groups of children who differ

**cross-sectional design**
*A research design in which two or more groups of children who differ in age are assessed at roughly the same time.*

TABLE 2.6 *Research Designs Used to Describe and Explain Children's Development*

| RESEARCH DESIGN | DISTINCTIVE FEATURES | MAJOR PURPOSE | ISSUES |
|---|---|---|---|
| **Designs for Describing Development** | | | |
| Cross-sectional | Children in different age groups are assessed at about the same time. | To estimate the age changes in children's behavior. | Most efficient design of this type, but the developmental paths of individuals cannot be charted. |
| Longitudinal | The same children are assessed multiple times as they grow older. | To examine age changes for groups and individuals. | Provides information about continuity in development but may be affected by attrition and retesting. |
| **Designs for Explaining Development** | | | |
| Correlational | Two or more measures of children's characteristics are assessed at one time and correlated. | To see how variations in different characteristics are related and, sometimes, to obtain tentative evidence about the causes of differences among children. | An easy design to implement, but tests of causal hypotheses are weak because reverse causation and third variables cannot be ruled out. |
| Experimental | An independent variable or treatment is under the experimenter's control. | To test hypotheses about how children's experiences affect their characteristics. | Valuable for showing which experiences *can* affect children but may not show which experiences have the strongest effects in real life. |
| **More Complex Designs** | | | |
| Cohort-sequential | Children from two or more birth cohorts are studied longitudinally, as they grow. | To accelerate the progress of a longitudinal study or to chart historical trends in children's behavior. | Ideal for examining some questions, but, for many questions, basic designs are adequate and less expensive. |
| Experimental intervention | Children are either given or not given a special treatment designed to enhance their development, and then followed as they grow. | To find out the long-term effects of changing children's experiences. | Superior to other designs for judging the effects of programs that affect children's daily lives but can be compromised if attrition is high. |
| Meta-analysis | The statistical analysis of data from many studies on the same issue. | To obtain more accurate estimates of differences between groups. | All available data must be included, and the quality of the original studies may need to be considered. |

in age are assessed at about the same time. Figure 2.8 outlines a cross-sectional design for studying children's development between 5 and 11 years of age.

Notice that the time of measurement is 1998. What the researcher measures is not stated because measurement is not part of a research design. Notice, also, that children from four age groups are included in the sample. Different names are listed on the figure at 5, 7, 9, and 11 years to show that different children are in each group. With the data from all four groups, a researcher could estimate the changes in children's characteristics between 5 and 11 years of age.

The greatest advantage of the cross-sectional design is its efficiency. A researcher can study children's development across several years in no more time than it takes to collect data on several groups of children. Therefore, many researchers choose cross-sectional designs to test hypotheses about age changes in behavior. Piaget, for example, used cross-sectional designs in nearly all the research that he conducted over 60 years.

Cross-sectional designs are also useful for finding **age norms,** the average ages at which children reach developmental milestones. Suppose you wanted to find out the average age at which Ache children begin to walk. You could observe young children who differed in age and pinpoint the earliest age at which most children were walking. Then you could

**age norms**
*The average ages at which children master specific developmental tasks, such as learning to walk.*

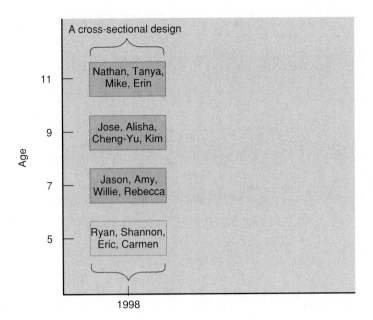

**FIGURE 2.8**
A cross-sectional design. In 1998, a researcher measures some characteristic of two or more groups of children who differ in age.

compare the age norm for Ache children with previously determined norms for U.S. children. You would find that the average Ache child starts walking several months later than do U.S. children (Kaplan & Dove, 1987). One disadvantage of cross-sectional designs is that they do not show how children change as they get older. Instead, they show how children of different ages differ in their behavior. Consequently, a cross-sectional design only allows researchers to *estimate* the changes in children's behavior.

When would estimates of age changes from a cross-sectional study be inaccurate? One answer is when important changes are occurring in the larger social environment. For example, suppose you wanted to use the design in figure 2.8 to study some aspect of cognitive development. However, in 1997, the year before your study began, the government changed its educational policy and required all 4-year-olds to enter kindergarten. Previously, children had started school at age 6.

As a result, your assessments in 1998 include 5-year-olds who started school at age 4 and 7-year-olds who started school at age 6. In technical terms, the 5-year-olds belong to the 1993 birth **cohort,** the group of all children born in 1993. The 7-year-olds belong to the 1991 birth cohort. Children in both cohorts will have had one year of schooling when you test them. The differences between these two cohorts might not match those found in a later cross-sectional study that included children from cohorts in which everyone started school at age 4. In those later cohorts, the 5- and 7-year-olds would differ not only in age but also in years of schooling.

Most historical changes, though, are less dramatic or have little impact on children's development. For example, historical changes seem not to have affected patterns of motor development. Cross-sectional designs can, therefore, yield accurate information about these patterns.

A more serious disadvantage of cross-sectional designs is that they cannot tell us about the developmental paths of individual children. Remember from chapter 1 that information about individual developmental paths is critical for deciding whether children show continuity or discontinuity over time. To assess continuity in development, assessments of the same child at different ages are necessary.

## The Longitudinal Design

A **longitudinal design** is ideal for examining the continuity in children's development. In a longitudinal design, the characteristics of one group of children are assessed several times as they grow. Figure 2.9 illustrates the contrast between a cross-sectional and longitudinal design.

**cohort**
*In research design, the term used to refer to all children born during the same year.*

**longitudinal design**
*A research design in which children are assessed on multiple occasions over periods of months or years.*

FIGURE 2.9

A comparison of a cross-sectional and a longitudinal design. For the longitudinal design, a researcher measures some characteristic of a group of 5-year-olds in 1998. The researcher returns to measure the same characteristic of the same children in 2000, 2002, and 2004.

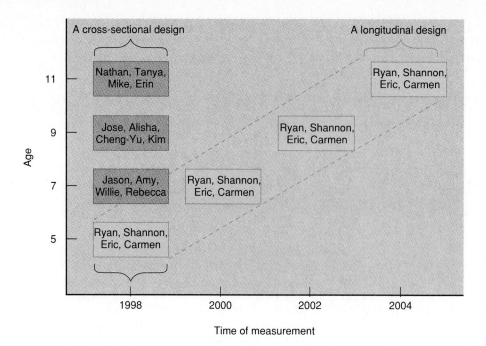

For the longitudinal design, the same children's names are listed at each of four ages. These children will be assessed four times during a six-year period. Therefore, the time course of the study will match the progress in the children's development.

With a longitudinal design, researchers can directly measure the age changes in children's characteristics, not just the differences among children in different age groups. Researchers also can chart the pattern of change for each child and then analyze the continuity of the individual differences among children.

In addition, researchers use longitudinal designs to test hypotheses about long-term effects of early experiences. Recall that Ache children start walking several months later than U.S. children, perhaps because Ache mothers greatly restrict their infants' movements. You might wonder whether this early restriction has lasting effects, causing delays in motor development that persist throughout childhood.

Kaplan and Dove (1987) suggested that the delays in Ache motor development do not persist. Once children reach about 5 years of age, Ache mothers no longer try to keep them close by. By 10 years of age, Ache children have developed exceptional motor skills. For example, the children climb trees more than 80 feet tall and practice chopping branches with machetes while high in the trees! Still, to confirm that their early experiences did not have lasting effects, researchers would need to observe the same children during infancy, early childhood, and later childhood. That is, they would need a longitudinal design.

Longitudinal studies do not always take years to complete. A short-term longitudinal study may continue for only a few months. Studies of this kind can be useful in judging the influence of children's social relationships on their behavior (e.g., Berndt & Keefe, 1995). However, the best-known longitudinal studies have continued for decades.

Several large longitudinal studies were done by teams of researchers at Stanford University and the University of California at Berkeley. These studies began in the late 1920s and early 1930s with newborn infants or with early adolescents. Nancy Bayley coordinated the first study of infants, which focused initially on the development of mental abilities and motor skills. Based on her observations, Bayley devised scales for measuring individual differences in mental and motor development. You will learn more about the Bayley scales in chapter 10.

With older children and adolescents, the emphasis on mental abilities and physical development was supplemented by an emphasis on intelligence, personality, and social behavior. Lewis Terman of Stanford began a longitudinal study in which gifted children were

followed into adulthood. As these adults married and had children, the researchers added their children and, eventually, their grandchildren to the samples. Chapter 10 includes more information about this study.

Although all longitudinal studies are valuable, they have several disadvantages. They are more expensive than comparable cross-sectional studies, partly because they last longer. Keeping the sample intact is a major task, especially in a mobile society such as the United States. Attrition from the sample because children move out of town, decide not to continue, or are lost for other reasons can threaten the entire study.

Attrition is a problem because statistical analyses are less adequate with smaller samples. In extreme cases, the sample may become so small that no firm conclusions can be drawn from the study. More often, the problem is not the amount of attrition but the degree to which attrition is selective or nonrandom. If the children who do not continue in the study are more talented than those who do, data from the study will not be representative of the original population.

Another concern is the repeated testing of children. If children recall their previous answers, they may respond differently than if they were taking a test for the first time. Such effects of retesting make it difficult to interpret changes in scores across times.

Finally, the data from a longitudinal study apply to children growing up in one historical period. The problem of cohort differences was mentioned in connection with the cross-sectional design. A different but analogous problem exists with the longitudinal design. All children in a longitudinal study belong to the same cohort, and results for that cohort may not hold for children in other cohorts. For example, figure 2.9 illustrates a longitudinal study of children from the 1993 cohort, because children who are 5-year-olds in 1998 were born in 1993. These children's experiences may be very different from those of children in the major longitudinal studies that began during the 1920s and 1930s.

In summary, historical changes may complicate the interpretation of data from both cross-sectional and longitudinal studies. To avoid these problems, researchers have sometimes turned to more complex designs. Those designs are discussed after the basic designs for explaining development.

## Basic Designs for Explaining Development

Child development researchers do not seek merely to describe children's development but also to explain it. For example, you now know that Ache children's motor development is delayed compared with that of U.S. children. This knowledge immediately raises the question: Why? To answer questions about the explanation of development, researchers most often choose between correlational and experimental designs.

### Correlational Designs

Researchers using a **correlational design** obtain a sample of children and then examine the relations between the children's scores on various measures. The strength of the relations between measures is often expressed by a statistic called the **correlation coefficient,** or *correlation* for short.

A correlation shows the degree to which two measures are related. If the measures are unrelated, the correlation between them is zero (.00). If higher scores on one measure go with higher scores on the other, then the correlation between them is positive, somewhere between .00 and 1.0. If higher scores on one measure go with lower scores on the other, the correlation between them is negative, between −1.0 and .00. A correlation is **statistically significant** when the relation between two measures is stronger than would be expected by chance.

The link between correlational designs and correlation coefficients illustrates the close connection between research design and statistics. The two are not completely parallel, however. Researchers often use correlational designs without presenting their results in the form of correlation coefficients. For example, Patterson and Stouthamer-Loeber (1984) examined the relation between delinquent behavior by adolescents and the failure of the adolescents' parents to monitor their activities adequately. For one analysis, the researchers divided the sample of parents into those who did and those who did not monitor their adolescents

**correlational design**
*A design in which a researcher examines the relation between the scores of children (or adults) on two or more measures.*

**correlation coefficient**
*A statistic that indicates the strength of the relation between two measures.*

**statistically significant**
*A relation between two measures that is stronger than would be expected by chance.*

FIGURE 2.10
Various hypotheses could account for a positive correlation between two measures such as low parental monitoring and delinquent behavior in adolescents. Besides the hypothesis that the first causes the second, the data could be explained by the hypotheses of reverse causation or a third variable.

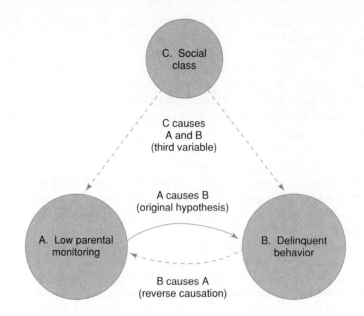

adequately. Then they divided the sample of adolescents into those who were and those who were not delinquent. The researchers found that 76 percent of the delinquent adolescents were poorly monitored by their parents. Only 10 percent of the adolescents who were not delinquent were poorly monitored.

Although the researchers reported percentages instead of correlation coefficients, the design of their study was correlational. The researchers examined the relation between the naturally occurring variations in adolescents' delinquency and in their parents' monitoring. The study did not involve any manipulation or treatment. When researchers simply measure the observed variations in children's scores or in children's and parents' scores, they are using a correlational design.

Correlational designs are ideal for testing hypotheses about the relations among measures. For example, have you ever wondered if children with higher grades are less well liked by their classmates (or if "brains" are unpopular)? To find out, you could recruit a sample of children and measure both their grades and their popularity. Past research suggests that your hypothesis about the relation between the two would be disconfirmed (Newcomb, Bukowski, & Pattee, 1993). The correlation between grades in school and popularity is not always strong, but it is positive rather than negative—more academically successful children are more popular.

A more difficult question is whether a correlational design is useful in explaining the differences in children's behavior. Can it help researchers determine the influences on children's behavior? Can it help them find out what causes one child to behave differently from another?

Strictly speaking, the answer is no. Correlational designs cannot be used to test hypotheses about cause and effect. This point is often expressed in a brief phrase: Correlation does not imply causation.

Think about the study of delinquency and parental monitoring (Patterson & Stouthamer-Loeber, 1984). The hypothesis driving that study was that inadequate monitoring by parents leads to delinquent behavior by adolescents. Conversely, adequate monitoring by parents reduces adolescents' opportunities for delinquent behavior. This cause-effect relationship is shown in figure 2.10 by the solid arrow from parental monitoring to delinquency.

Yet even when researchers find a positive correlation between low parental monitoring and delinquency, they cannot conclude that low monitoring causes delinquency. A positive correlation would also exist if adolescents' delinquent behavior reduced their parents' monitoring. The parents of delinquents might say to themselves, "If Johnny is going to get into trouble, I'd rather not know about it."

Stated more formally, the presumed cause (inadequate monitoring) might be the effect, and vice versa. This is the hypothesis of **reverse causation,** which suggests that the true cause-effect relation is the opposite of that assumed by the researchers. Figure 2.10 shows this alternative hypothesis by the dashed arrow from delinquency to parental monitoring.

The figure shows still another possibility. A correlation between two variables (a **variable** is anything that varies or can be varied) might be due to a **third variable** that caused both of them. For example, delinquent behavior and inadequate parental monitoring might be symptoms of a lifestyle that is more common in lower-class families than in middle-class families. In other words, no cause-effect relation exists between adolescent delinquency and inadequate parental monitoring. They are correlated because both reflect more general features of a lower-class lifestyle. Figure 2.10 shows this hypothesis by the dotted arrows from social class to the other two variables.

**reverse causation**
*A hypothesis that the true cause-effect relation between two variables is in the direction opposite to that assumed by a researcher.*

**variable**
*Anything that varies or can be varied.*

**third variable**
*In correlational designs, an unmeasured variable that accounts for the relation between two variables that are measured.*

Sometimes a researcher can use evidence from other research to cast doubt on hypotheses about reverse causation and third variables. Suppose that other research showed that social class is not related to delinquent behavior and parental monitoring. Then a researcher could reject the hypothesis that social class accounts for the correlation between them.

In addition, a correlational design can provide evidence against a causal hypothesis. Suppose measures of parental monitoring were not correlated with measures of adolescent delinquency. Then you would need to be skeptical about the hypothesis that one causes the other.

Few researchers would eagerly choose a design that could provide strong evidence *against* their hypothesis but only weak evidence *for* it. Yet that is often the only choice that child development researchers have. Child development researchers have used correlational designs in many studies because good alternatives are seldom available.

Consider the case of the Ache again. Suppose you wanted a definitive test of the hypothesis that Ache children's motor development is delayed by their mothers' restrictions on their movements. To test this hypothesis, you might consider telling one group of Ache mothers to let their children move about more freely. Then you could measure the differences between their children's motor development and that of other Ache children. Such an experiment would be unethical because the unrestricted children might be exposed to serious danger in the forest. If their mothers are right about the hazards of forest life, you could not justify doing an experiment that would increase their children's risks.

You might, instead, consider telling one group of Ache mothers to restrict their children's movements even more than they normally would. Then you would see what effect the added restrictions have on the children's motor development. Such an experiment would also be unethical, because your hypothesis is that the added restrictions would further delay their motor development.

This example illustrates why child development researchers have relied so often on correlational designs. These designs do not allow conclusive tests of hypotheses about cause and effect, but they can provide data that are consistent or inconsistent with those hypotheses. Therefore, they are useful tools for researchers whose goal is explaining children's development.

## Experimental Designs

For more conclusive tests of hypotheses about causality, researchers rely on **experimental designs.** Figure 2.11 outlines a simple experimental design.

Central to the experimental design is an **independent variable.** This term refers to a stimulus, experience, manipulation, or treatment that can be varied by an experimenter because it is under the experimenter's control. In particular, the experimenter can choose to expose some subjects to the independent variable while not exposing other subjects to it. The independent variable can also be defined from a theoretical perspective as the presumed cause of some behavior or outcome.

In one classic experiment (Bandura, Ross, & Ross, 1963), the independent variable was exposure to a film in which an adult model behaved aggressively toward a plastic Bobo doll. In other words, the film was a treatment that some children in the experiment received. The researchers decided how the adult model would behave and which children would be

**experimental designs**
*Designs that allow conclusive tests of hypotheses about cause and effect because the presumed cause is under the researcher's control.*

**independent variable**
*In experimental designs, a manipulation or treatment by the experimenter that is the presumed cause of some behavior or event.*

FIGURE 2.11

An outline of an experimental design with two groups of children assigned randomly to an experimental condition or a control condition.

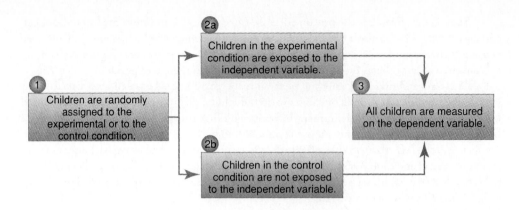

experimental condition
*In experimental designs, the condition in which children are exposed to the independent variable.*

control condition
*In experimental designs, the condition in which children are not exposed to the independent variable.*

random assignment
*A procedure in which chance determines in which condition children in an experimental study are placed.*

dependent variable
*In experimental designs, a measure that a researcher expects to be affected by the independent variable or treatment.*

baseline
*In experiments testing the effects of reinforcement, the initial phase before any change in reinforcement patterns is made.*

treatment
*The phase in some experiments in which reinforcement patterns are changed. More generally, the independent variable to which participants in an experiment are exposed.*

reversal
*In experiments testing the effects of reinforcement, the phase in which the pattern of reinforcements is returned to that of the baseline phase.*

exposed to the model. In short, they controlled both the form of the independent variable and who received it.

Researchers typically describe children who are exposed to the independent variable as in the **experimental condition.** Children not exposed to the independent variable are in the **control condition.** The two groups of children are assumed to be equivalent before the experiment begins. Usually, researchers try to ensure their equivalence by a procedure of **random assignment** to conditions. For example, a researcher may flip a coin to decide whether a specific child should be in the experimental condition or the control condition.

After children are assigned to conditions, exposure to the independent variable occurs. In the Bobo-doll experiment, children in the experimental condition saw the film of the adult model. Children in the control condition did not see the film.

In the final phase of an experiment, all children's scores on a **dependent variable** are assessed. A dependent variable is a measure that, in theory, should be affected by the independent variable. One experiment may have several dependent variables. The dependent variables in the Bobo-doll experiment were various measures of children's aggressive behavior. The researchers expected children who saw the aggressive film to be more aggressive afterward, and they were. These results support the hypothesis that seeing models of aggressive behavior causes children to become more aggressive.

Not all experiments are done in laboratory settings, and not all have the design outlined in figure 2.11. One experiment done in a natural setting examined teachers' influence on cooperative cross-sex play in preschool classrooms (Serbin, Tonick, & Sternglanz, 1977). Typically, preschool children spend most of their time playing with children of the same sex. However, the researchers assumed that cross-sex play would increase if teachers gave positive reinforcement to boys who played with girls and vice versa.

The experiment was unusual because children were not assigned randomly to experimental and control conditions. However, it was a true experiment because the researchers had control over an independent variable and could conclusively show its effects on a dependent variable.

During the first, **baseline** phase of the study, the researchers simply measured the rate of cooperative cross-sex play. After two weeks, the **treatment** phase began. When teachers saw boys and girls who were playing together cooperatively, they said something like, "I like the tower John and Kathy are building with the blocks." Teachers made these comments loud enough for the rest of the class to hear. After two weeks of treatment, the experiment moved into the **reversal** phase. Teachers stopped giving positive reinforcement for cross-sex play. That is, the pattern of reinforcements was reversed, returned to that of the baseline phase.

Figure 2.12 shows the rate of cooperative cross-sex play during each phase of the experiment. Notice that the rate increased when teachers began to reinforce such play but decreased when teachers no longer reinforced it. Because the changes in children's behavior exactly matched the changes in teachers' behavior, the researchers could conclude that teachers' reinforcement increases cooperative cross-sex play. More generally, the findings support the hypothesis that reinforcement affects preschoolers' rate of cross-sex play.

One limitation of the baseline-treatment-reversal design is that some behaviors do not "turn on" and "turn off" as quickly as the design requires. Consider, again, the question of Ache children's motor development. Suppose that you devised an exercise program that you assumed would accelerate children's motor development. To evaluate the program's effects you might observe children's motor development for a three-month baseline period, then arrange a three-month treatment phase in which children did the exercises, and finally have a three-month reversal phase with no exercise program.

During the reversal phase, you would not expect children's motor skills to return to their pretreatment level. Development doesn't work that way. Many behaviors that emerge during development persist on their own, so the baseline-treatment-reversal design is not adequate for testing hypotheses about their causes.

More generally, experimental studies show only how children are affected by specific experiences. They do not show whether or how often children have those experiences in natural settings. Therefore, experiments only provide a partial explanation of development. They clarify which experiences *can* lead to differences among children but not necessarily which ones *do* cause the differences that are normally observed (McCall, 1977).

## More Complex Research Designs

Some questions about children's development cannot be answered with the basic designs discussed thus far. Other questions receive only partial answers when examined using the basic designs. For these cases, a variety of more complex designs are available.

### The Cohort-Sequential Design

For describing developmental changes, a **cohort-sequential design** is more powerful than either the cross-sectional or the longitudinal design. As figure 2.13 shows, this design includes samples of children from more than one birth cohort whose characteristics are measured more than once. Other combinations of the basic designs for describing development have been discussed (Baltes, Reese, & Nesselroade, 1977), but that shown in the figure is perhaps the most common.

Notice that two age groups are tested at each time of measurement, as in a cross-sectional study. In addition, the children in each cohort are tested several times, as in a longitudinal study. By putting the two together, or examining longitudinal sequences, a researcher gains valuable data. The longitudinal facet of the design means a researcher can assess age changes directly, rather than merely estimating them. The design can also answer questions raised by a longitudinal design. For example, effects of repeated testing can be evaluated by comparing children from different cohorts who are the same age but who are taking a test for the first or for the second time.

Moreover, cohort-sequential designs make longitudinal research more efficient. The design in figure 2.13 would provide data about age changes between 5 and 13 years of age—an eight-year span—but the study would take only six years to complete. This **accelerated longitudinal design** has recently been used to study the age changes in children's behavioral problems (Stanger, Achenbach, & Verhulst, 1994).

Finally, cohort-sequential designs are often used to examine historical changes in children's behavior. For example, a public-health goal in the United States is to reduce cigarette smoking. To judge the changes over time in children's and adolescents' smoking, one team of researchers surveyed 6th- to 12th-grade students in 1980 (Chassin et al., 1987). Students in the same grades were surveyed again in 1981, 1982, and 1983.

Antismoking messages seemed to have affected the 6th to 9th graders, because the students in the later cohorts smoked less. For example, in 1980 only 37 percent of 9th graders said they had never smoked a cigarette. By 1983 about 52 percent of 9th graders said they had never smoked. Unfortunately, these historical changes were not found for 10th to 12th graders. About the same percentage of 10th to 12th graders were smokers in 1983 as in 1980.

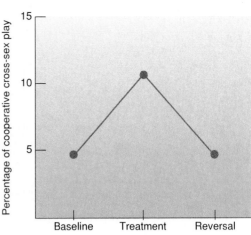

**FIGURE 2.12**

The results of a study with the baseline-treatment-reversal design. Note that cooperative cross-sex play was rare in the baseline phase, increased in the treatment phase, and returned to baseline in the reversal phase. (Adapted from Serbin et al., 1977.)

**cohort-sequential design**
*A research design in which the characteristics of multiple cohorts of children are measured on more than one occasion.*

**accelerated longitudinal design**
*Use of a cohort-sequential design to examine changes over a greater age span than that for which any specific child is assessed.*

## FIGURE 2.13

A comparison of a cohort-sequential design with the cross-sectional and longitudinal designs. The sequential design has certain features of both the simpler designs. It involves a comparison of children of different ages at one time, like the cross-sectional design. It also involves a comparison of the same children at different ages (and different times), like the longitudinal design.

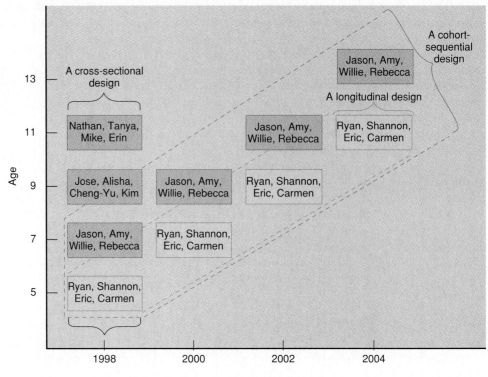

Apparently, new messages or methods are needed to reduce smoking by high-school students. More generally, these findings illustrate the value of cohort-sequential designs in understanding and possibly altering the historical trends in adolescents' behavior.

## Experimental Interventions

Combining a basic design for describing development with one for explaining development can be very rewarding. Suppose that you wanted to examine the effects of exercise on motor development. You could recruit parents of newborns and assign their infants randomly to either an experimental condition that included an exercise program or a no-exercise, control condition. For infants assigned to the experimental condition, the exercise program would begin at 3 months of age and continue for one year. After the program ended, you would observe infants in both conditions for three years.

Which design are you using? You are not only conducting an experiment but also including elements of a longitudinal design. In other words, you are studying the effects of an experimental manipulation longitudinally, to see whether it has a lasting influence on children's development. When an experimental manipulation is intended to enhance development, it is often called an **intervention.** *Practical Applications of Research:* "Improving Children's Intelligence" describes the results of a unique intervention designed to enhance the intellectual development of disadvantaged children.

**intervention**
*An experimental manipulation that is intended to enhance children's development.*

## Meta-Analysis

A single study rarely provides a definitive answer to questions about child development. Even large-scale studies may leave some questions open. Researchers often do additional studies to replicate or extend the findings of earlier research. On some issues, dozens or even hundreds of studies may provide relevant data. Is it possible to integrate the results of these studies systematically?

Yes, it is. **Meta-analysis** is the statistical analysis of a large collection of analysis results from separate studies (Glass, 1976). In other words, it is an analysis of analyses, or a statistical comparison of the data from multiple studies.

**meta-analysis**
*The statistical analysis of a large collection of analysis results from separate studies.*

# IMPROVING CHILDREN'S INTELLIGENCE: THE CAROLINA ABECEDARIAN PROJECT

In 1972 some new parents in North Carolina were invited to participate in a unique experiment called the Abecedarian Project (Campbell & Ramey, 1994). An abecedarian is a person who is learning the alphabet. (Think of an "a–b–c–d"–erian.) The goal of the experiment was to see whether a special preschool program could improve children's learning not only of the alphabet but of many other intellectual skills.

More specifically, the experiment was designed to show whether a preschool program could increase the IQ scores of young children from poor families. The parents invited to participate in the experiment had extremely low incomes: The median earned income reported by the families was none! Only about one-quarter of the families included both biological parents. About half the mothers in these families were under 20 years of age, and most mothers had not finished high school.

Parents were told that if they agreed to participate in the experiment, their infants would be randomly assigned either to the experimental condition or to the control condition. If assigned to the experimental condition, infants would be enrolled in a special day-care center when they were about 4 months of age. They would attend the center for 40 hours a week, 50 weeks a year. The center's daily program would include activities designed to enhance children's cognitive, language, perceptual, motor, and social development. If assigned to the control condition, infants would not receive day care but would get free formula and disposable diapers until they were toilet trained.

Random assignment was crucial to this project, but it can be difficult to achieve with projects that so profoundly affect children's lives. Fortunately, almost all parents who were contacted agreed to participate in the experiment. Almost all stayed with the experiment after learning whether their infants were assigned to the experimental condition or to the control condition. Moreover, attrition was low throughout the study, which lasted until the children were 12 years old.

When the children reached kindergarten age, they were randomly assigned to receive either a school-age intervention or no intervention. Children receiving the intervention were paired with an adult who gave them extra educational activities and helped build relationships between teachers and parents. This intervention continued for three years.

The children were given IQ tests throughout their infancy and childhood. Figure 2.14 shows their test scores between 3 months (before the preschool program began) and 12 years of age. Soon after the program began, infants in the program began to show higher IQ scores than those in the control condition. These gains were maintained through age 12. The school-age intervention had much weaker effects.

The practical significance of this experimental intervention is obvious. As the researchers stated, "Better early environments can improve the chances that poor children will acquire the preparation they need for academic success" (Campbell & Ramey, 1994, p. 696).

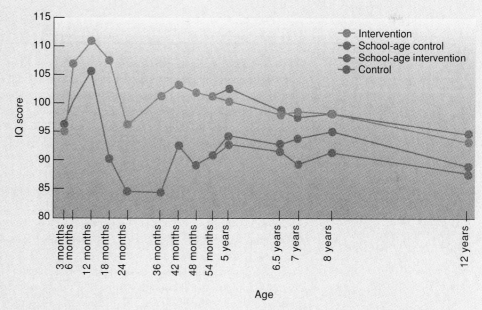

## FIGURE 2.14

Participation in the Abecedarian Project, an intensive intervention for infants and preschool children, significantly raised children's IQ scores. An intervention that began when the children reached kindergarten age had much weaker effects. (Adapted from Campbell & Ramey, 1994.)

For example, many researchers have reported that boys have faster reaction times than girls on the mental-rotation tasks discussed earlier in the chapter. Boys also receive higher scores than girls on other tasks that seem to assess spatial abilities. However, the size of the sex difference varies across studies.

To estimate the sex differences in spatial abilities more accurately, a meta-analyst first computes an **effect size** for the sex difference in every available study on the topic. The effect size, symbolized by $\partial$, corresponds to the difference between the mean scores for boys and girls expressed in units of standard deviations. A **standard deviation** is an index of the variability of the scores in a group. Therefore, a $\partial$ of .50 indicates that the mean scores for boys and girls are half a standard deviation apart. A $\partial$ of .10 indicates that boys' and girls' scores differ by only one-tenth of a standard deviation. Once effect sizes are computed for each study, the mean effect size across studies can be computed.

A recent meta-analysis of 286 studies of sex differences in spatial abilities confirmed that males receive higher scores than females on tests of spatial abilities (Voyer, Voyer, & Bryden, 1995). The mean effect size for the sex difference was a $\partial$ of .37, or slightly more than one-third of a standard deviation. However, more refined analyses showed that sex differences were nonsignificant on many tests before 13 years of age. That is, the results suggested that males first begin to show better spatial abilities than females during adolescence.

Meta-analyses can produce misleading results if they are not part of a systematic approach to research synthesis (Cooper & Hedges, 1994). A researcher needs to be sure that all relevant studies are included in the meta-analysis. The quality of the studies may also need to be evaluated systematically, to ensure that conclusions do not depend on studies with poor measures or weak designs. When used with care, meta-analytic techniques can lead to more conclusive answers to many questions about human development.

# ETHICAL ISSUES IN DEVELOPMENTAL RESEARCH

You read earlier about the ethical problems that make it difficult to study Ache children's motor development experimentally. Ethical issues are not relevant only to experimental manipulations. Some issues are important in all phases of all types of research. The ethical standards that should be observed in child development research have been stated by several organizations (e.g., American Psychological Association, 1992; Society for Research in Child Development, 1993). The following points summarize those standards.

1. *Obtain informed consent.* Most research begins with the recruitment of the children who will participate. These children normally need to give their **informed consent** before they can be included in the research. That is, the children need to be fully informed about the procedures for the research, and their consent must be obtained, before they become part of the sample. Children should also be informed that they can end their participation in the study at any time without penalty.

This general guideline does not always apply. Suppose that you want to observe the behavior of children on a school playground. Would you need to inform them of your plans and get their consent to be observed? The answer is no, if the children are in a public place, they are anonymous, and they would not suffer any negative consequences from the research.

Suppose, instead, that you were studying the visual perception of 3-month-old infants. Do you need to get their informed consent? Again the answer is no, because 3-month-olds would be unable to understand your explanation of the research and, therefore, could not give informed consent. You would, instead, need to get the informed consent of their parents before including them in the study. In addition, you would still have an obligation to safeguard the infants' welfare and watch for signs that your procedures are unpleasant or harmful to them (Thompson, 1990).

Parents' informed consent should normally be obtained even when their children are old enough to understand a verbal description of a study's procedures. Parents should be

---

**effect size**
*The difference between the means for two groups expressed in standard deviation units.*

**standard deviation**
*An index of the variability of the scores in a group.*

**informed consent**
*Children's agreement to participate in a research project after they have been fully informed about its procedures.*

Before this infant can be included in a research project, the researcher must have the informed consent of his parents. The researcher must explain the procedures for the study in terms that the parents can understand and inform them of their right to withdraw their child from the study at any time.

informed about all aspects of a research project that may affect their willingness to participate. Then their written consent for their child's participation should be obtained.

The requirement to obtain informed consent can pose problems in research. Sometimes children need *not* to know about certain procedures; sometimes actual deception is needed for an experiment. Is not "telling all" to children, or telling them something that is not true, always unethical in child development research?

Researchers have debated this question extensively, and their general answer is no. Withholding information or providing false information may be acceptable if doing so has no negative consequences for children. Think back to the study of friends' behavior when playing the Snake Pit game (Hartup et al., 1993). The children were not informed that they would be taught different rules for playing the game. Unless children asked, they were not even told about the different rules after the game. The researchers noted that all children enjoyed the game and, therefore, "telling them that they had been taught different rules would create more problems than it would resolve" (p. 448).

2. *Obtain approval from a review board.* Researchers do not make decisions about withholding information or using deception either lightly or without consultation. Before beginning a study, researchers usually present a complete description of their plans and procedures to a review board at their university or research institution. The members of the board evaluate whether the plans and procedures are acceptable in terms of the protection for subjects and the likely benefits and costs of the research.

3. *Avoid physical or psychological harm to children.* A review board tries to ensure that no procedures are used that would harm children either physically or psychologically. This guideline does not bar all procedures that might be uncomfortable or distressing to children. Some procedures may be unpleasant (e.g., inoculation with an experimental drug) but have some therapeutic value. The issue is whether the benefits of the research for the children outweigh its costs.

Other research may make some children mildly uncomfortable, but not to a level greater than that common in daily life. For example, you will read in chapter 6 about research in which infants' arm movements were restricted so that their emotional reactions (including anger) could be observed. Although some infants become distressed in this research, they obviously do

not have totally free movement in daily life. The mild and brief restraint in the research is, therefore, acceptable.

4. *Respect participants' confidentiality.* All information obtained from children involved in a study must be kept confidential. In all reports on the research, the children's names should not be used. Even in casual conversations with students or colleagues, their names should not be mentioned.

Under extreme conditions, this guideline can and must be ignored. Sometimes children who are being interviewed for a study provide information that suggests they are being abused. Both ethical standards and many state laws require that this information be given to responsible officials who can investigate the case thoroughly. More generally, researchers must inform parents, guardians, teachers, or other adults in authority if they obtain any information regarding threats to a child's well-being. For example, a researcher who discovers that a child is seriously depressed should contact people who can arrange for psychological help.

5. *Be careful when reporting research results.* Researchers have two types of ethical obligations when reporting their results. First, they should report their general findings to the children who participated, and to their parents, in terms that they can understand. Also, researchers must be cautious about making evaluative statements or giving advice, because children and parents may exaggerate the significance of their comments.

Second, researchers must consider how their findings might be interpreted when published in scientific journals or other places. Could the findings be misinterpreted? How could their publication affect social attitudes or public policies? Researchers should try to answer these questions to lessen the likelihood that their findings will be misused.

Judging the ethics of research is not always easy. Think again about the classic Bobo-doll experiment (Bandura et al., 1963). You might say that this experiment was designed to increase the aggressive behavior of preschool children by showing them an aggressive film. Is such an experiment ethical?

Increasing children's aggression can hardly be considered as desirable, so you might view this experiment as violating the guideline not to use any procedures that may harm children psychologically. On the other hand, prime-time television programs often expose children to acts of aggression much more serious than the adult model's attacks on a Bobo doll. To understand how this diet of television viewing affects children, experimental studies are necessary. Whether the risks of an experiment can be accepted because of its benefits to children or to society is a decision that researchers and review boards must make before the research begins.

# RELATIONSHIPS BETWEEN RESEARCHERS AND PARTICIPANTS

You read in this chapter about several kinds of research on children's relationships. Some examples are the studies of caregiver-child interaction in Egypt (Wachs et al., 1993) and of parenting in Hispanic and Anglo-American families (Knight et al., 1994).

Social relationships are more than a topic of study, however. The success of any research project depends partly on the relationships between researchers and the participants (children or adults) in the research. This may seem surprising. Some comments in the chapter might suggest that relationships between researchers and children are obstacles to accurate measurement of children's characteristics.

Recall the earlier discussion of reactivity in naturalistic and laboratory observation. The main point of this discussion was that researchers do not want children to react to the observers. Therefore, observers should never interact with the children, and certainly never form relationships with them. To achieve this goal, observers are kept as invisible as possible, for example, behind a one-way mirror.

Similarly, recall the discussion of social-desirability biases in verbal reports. Researchers worry that children, parents, or other people providing verbal reports will give answers that they think will please the interviewer, rather than reporting frankly and fully. Therefore, researchers instruct interviewers to be as noncommittal (or unsociable?) as possible. These instructions are intended to prevent interviewers from giving the people being interviewed any cues about which responses would be socially desirable.

By contrast, many researchers would argue that all human activities, including research, are inherently social. Even when no interaction occurs between researchers and the children they are studying, the researchers must accurately interpret the children's social world. Suppose, for example, that you were observing preschool children's aggressive behavior. You see a child knock down another child's tower of blocks. How do you interpret this behavior? Was it an aggressive act, done as an attack on the other child's playthings? Was it part of a game that the two children were playing—and enjoying? Was it simply an accident? To code the behavior correctly, you need to understand the perspective of the children involved. Your understanding might be greater if you knew the children well, or even formed relationships with them.

Ethnographers, especially, emphasize the social relationships between researchers and participants. Rather than remaining aloof and "objective," ethnographers embed themselves in the social world of the people they study. They are less concerned about reactivity than about misunderstanding other people's behavior because of their ignorance about the social context.

So, should developmental researchers keep their distance from the children they study, or should they try to build relationships? Debates over this question continue because each position has merit. Moreover, issues regarding the social relationships between researchers and participants are not relevant only to measurement. They are also relevant to research design.

Think, in particular, about the longitudinal design. The success of a longitudinal study depends heavily on retaining a representative sample. In other words, attrition must be kept to a minimum. How do you do that? One proven technique is remaining in close contact with the participants. Researchers send the participants birthday cards, letters with interesting news about the study, and other useful information. Researchers may also have parties in which participants and researchers have fun together. If researchers do not foster positive relationships with participants, some participants will lose interest in the study and refuse to continue with it.

In summary, developmental researchers always have some sort of social relationship with the children whom they study. This relationship may last years and become closer over time. It may, instead, be brief and limited. But some relationship is necessary for full understanding between researchers and participants. That kind of understanding is essential for meaningful and interpretable research.

# SUMMARY

**Measurement**
Measurement is a set of rules for assigning numbers to objects in such a way as to represent quantities of attributes. When creating a measure, researchers usually identify several indicators of a broad construct, establish rules for scoring children's status on those indicators, and then combine the information on all indicators.

**Techniques of Measurement**
Child development researchers use various techniques to measure children's characteristics. Those techniques include naturalistic observations (with continuous real-time measurement or time sampling)

and laboratory observation. They also include verbal reports from children themselves, or from their parents, teachers, and peers. Other techniques are assessments of task performance and the construction of measures that yield equivalent scores in different cultures.

**Reliability and Validity of Measures**
Reliability refers to the precision of a measure, or the consistency with which children's attributes can be measured. Consistency can be judged by test-retest reliability, interobserver agreement, and the internal consistency of a set of items.

Validity refers to the accuracy of a measure, or the extent to which scores

reflect children's actual characteristics rather than extraneous factors. To judge the validity of a construct, researchers evaluate its convergent and discriminant validity. Bronfenbrenner emphasized the importance of a measure's ecological validity.

**Research Design**
Research design refers to the structure of an investigation, what is done to whom and when. The structure includes the participants in the research, whether the investigation includes any treatments or solely measurements, and when the measurements and treatments are scheduled.

### Basic Designs for Describing Development

The most efficient design for describing the changes as children grow is the cross-sectional design. However, cross-sectional designs only provide estimates of the age changes in children's behavior. A longitudinal design allows researchers to measure age changes directly, but repeated testing of children can pose problems.

### Basic Designs for Explaining Development

The relations among multiple characteristics of the same group of children can be examined with a correlational design. Correlational designs are also used for preliminary tests of causal hypotheses, but correlational designs allow only weak tests of such hypotheses. Experimental studies allow definitive tests of hypotheses about how an independent variable affects one or more dependent variables.

### More Complex Research Designs

Cohort-sequential designs, which combine elements of the cross-sectional and the longitudinal designs, are used to study age changes and historical trends in children's behavior. Experimental interventions are used to find the effects of children's experiences on their development. Interventions have often been used to examine the effects of educational programs on children's academic achievement. Methods of meta-analysis allow the systematic integration of data from multiple studies.

### Ethical Issues in Developmental Research

Many professional organizations have adopted ethical standards for child development research. These standards require that researchers obtain informed consent from participants, that they submit their plans to a review board, that they avoid causing physical or psychological harm to participants, that they respect participants' confidentiality, and that they consider the likely responses of their audience when reporting their results.

### Relationships Between Researchers and Participants

The success of a research project depends partly on the relationships between the researchers and the children or adults who are participants. These relationships may enhance reactivity during behavioral observation or increase social-desirability biases in verbal reports. However, ethnographers argue that forming relationships with participants is necessary to understand their behavior. Forming relationships may also be essential for avoiding attrition in longitudinal studies.

# SUGGESTED READINGS

Appelbaum, M. I., & McCall, R. B. (1983). Design and analysis in developmental psychology. In P. H. Mussen (Series Ed.), W. Kessen (Vol. Ed.), *Handbook of child psychology. Vol. 1. History, theory, and methods* (pp. 414–476). New York: Wiley. This chapter is from a multivolume handbook for specialists in child development. The authors link discussions of research design with discussions of the statistical analysis of data obtained. It is a valuable reference but not easy reading.

Irwin, D. M., & Bushnell, M. M. (1980). *Observational strategies for child study.* New York: Holt, Rinehart and Winston. This book has long been used as an introduction to methods of naturalistic observation. The book describes the various types of observation methods and includes laboratory assignments that allow students to practice each method.

Miller, S. A. (1987). *Developmental research methods.* Englewood Cliffs, NJ: Prentice-Hall. Miller begins by reviewing general principles of measurement and research design. Then he reviews recent research in infancy, cognitive development, social development, and aging. Finally, he considers some issues of data analysis, ethics, and reporting research results.

Pellegrini, A. D. (1991). *Applied child study: A developmental approach* (2nd ed.). Hillsdale, NJ: Erlbaum. Several types of research methods are discussed in this book. In addition, several developmental theories are outlined. Pellegrini argues that theories are needed to make observations of children meaningful. He also argues for "action research," research done to solve practical problems, especially those in educational environments.

*Chapter Three*

# UNDERSTANDING GENETIC INFLUENCES ON DEVELOPMENT

*T*he simplest studies sometimes have the most provocative results. One cross-cultural study was done with Chinese infants from Beijing, Irish infants from Dublin, and Caucasian infants from the Boston area (Kagan, Arcus, & Snidman, 1993). All the infants were 4 months old. They were shown various toys and mobiles for a few seconds each. They also heard a woman's voice repeating syllables like *ga* a few times. As they watched or listened, observers recorded whether the infants waved their arms, kicked their feet, or showed other motor activity. In addition, the observers recorded whether the infants vocalized, fretted, or cried.

All measures showed the same pattern of results. The Chinese infants had the lowest scores for motor activity, vocalizing, fretting, and crying. The U.S. infants had the highest scores for these behaviors, and the Irish infants' scores were intermediate.

What accounts for these differences? You already know the answer, in general terms. They probably reflect some combination of differences in nature or heredity and differences in nurture or environment. The infants in the three groups came from different populations and so may have differed in their heredity. The infants were being brought up by parents living in different cultures, so their environments also differed.

This chapter focuses on the first part of that combination, the influences of heredity. Scientists now know a great deal about the processes of genetic inheritance. Those processes explain why every child is different from every other child and why children resemble, but are different from, their parents. The chapter begins with a review of the basic principles of human genetics. This review will give you a foundation for understanding how children's genetic makeup influences their development.

The processes by which genetic information is transferred from parents to children are not foolproof. Some human infants are born with genetic defects that cause abnormal development. Fortunately, these defects are rare, but they deserve your attention for two reasons. First, they clarify the process of genetic transmission. Research on children with genetic defects has greatly increased knowledge about human genetics. Second, the studies of these children have proved that children's heredity does not totally determine their destiny. Children with genetic defects can often develop normally if brought up in an appropriate environment. That is, genetic and environmental influences interact throughout development.

Studies of abnormal development do not tell the whole story of genetic influence. Also important is research on normal human variation. The study of infants in China, Ireland, and the United States (Kagan et al., 1993) is one example, and you will read more about that study later. You will also learn about current models for describing how children's genetic makeup and their environments jointly influence their development. Finally, you will discover how researchers estimate the degree to which heredity accounts for the normal variation in human characteristics.

# THE BIOLOGY OF HEREDITY

To explain how children's heredity influences their development, knowledge of the principles of genetics is necessary. A review of those principles will make it easier to understand the following information about genetic influences on development.

## How the Genetic Code Is Stored and Duplicated

A human being is a highly complex organism composed of trillions of cells with specialized functions and structures (see figure 3.1). Almost all these cells contain a nucleus, or command center, that controls the processes that occur in the cell. Each cell's nucleus contains the complete genetic code for the development of an individual. Inside the nucleus are molecular structures that store a genetic blueprint for the individual. These structures contain all the information needed to organize the individual's behavior and development.

Figure 3.1 shows that the genetic code for an individual is carried by structures within the cell nucleus called **chromosomes.** *Chromosome* comes from the Greek words for color (*chromo*) and body (*soma*), so chromosomes are literally "colored bodies." Biologists gave them this name because they were sensitive to dyes or stains. The chromosomes can be seen under a microscope if an appropriate dye is placed in a cell just before it begins to divide.

**chromosomes**
*Threadlike structures within the nucleus of every cell that contain the DNA or genetic material of an organism.*

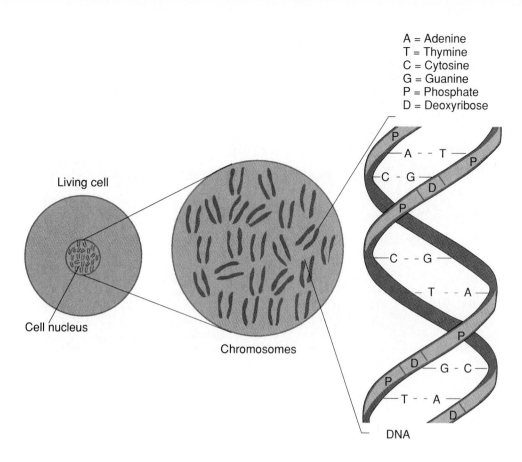

A = Adenine
T = Thymine
C = Cytosine
G = Guanine
P = Phosphate
D = Deoxyribose

Living cell

Cell nucleus

Chromosomes

DNA

FIGURE 3.1

A schematic description of the biological structures that carry genetic information. In the nucleus of every living cell are chromosomes that contain DNA, which holds the genetic information for the organism's development.

Normally, the cells of a human being contain 46 chromosomes. Each chromosome holds, in biochemical form, part of the genetic information that makes each person both a unique individual and a member of the human species. This information is encoded in a chemical called **deoxyribonucleic acid,** or **DNA.** The amount of DNA in any cell is extremely small, less than a billionth of a gram, but the amount of genetic information coded in the DNA is enormous.

In the early 1950s, Watson and Crick (1953) discovered that DNA has the form of a double helix. That is, a DNA molecule has a backbone consisting of two strands of sugar (deoxyribose) and phosphate molecules that twist around each other (see figure 3.1). Between the two strands, linking them to each other, are nucleotide bases. Each base links at one end to the backbone and at the other end—or across the middle of the double helix—to the other base.

The links between nucleotide bases are highly constrained. DNA includes only four nucleotide bases: adenine, thymine, guanine, and cytosine. Each base can link across the DNA strands to only one other base. As figure 3.1 shows, adenine (A) always pairs with thymine (T) and guanine (G) always pairs with cytosine (C).

The form of the DNA molecule is critical for the copying of its genetic code into new cells. The duplication of DNA is a complex process involving many biochemical substances and several steps. Figure 3.2 illustrates only the beginning and ending points of this process.

As the process begins, the two strands of the original DNA molecule disconnect in the middle and twist apart. Then new nucleotide bases that are floating, unattached, in the cell nucleus join to each strand. As the new bases are attached, a new sugar-phosphate backbone forms. Because each base pairs with only one other base, the sequence of bases on the two new DNA strands matches that on the original DNA strands. Thus, as the figure shows, the original double helix is transformed into two new helixes that are identical to the original: Each new helix contains one strand from the original and one that was copied.

**deoxyribonucleic acid (DNA)**
*The substance on the chromosomes that carries the genetic information for the production and regulation of proteins that, in turn, affect the observable characteristics of an organism.*

With an electron microscope, you can actually see the long DNA molecule that contains the genetic information for human development and functioning.

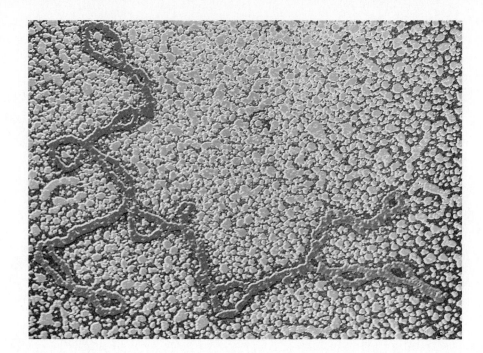

## FIGURE 3.2
A simplified model of DNA replication. The two strands of DNA disconnect and twist apart. Then new nucleotide bases join to each strand, and a new backbone links the new bases together.

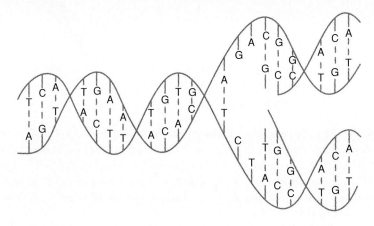

**mitosis**
*A process of cell division in which two new cells with exactly the same DNA are formed from a single cell.*

**sister chromatids**
*Two copies of a single chromosome that are formed during the first step in mitosis.*

The duplication of DNA normally occurs during a process of cell division called **mitosis.** During the growth of human beings (and all other organisms), new cells form almost constantly. The first step in mitosis is the duplication of the DNA and, thus, the formation of duplicate copies of each chromosome called **sister chromatids.** During the next step, the chromatids separate and move to opposite sides of the cell. Gradually, the two sides of the cell pull apart, and a membrane or wall forms along the boundary between them. There are, then, two cells joined to each other. Finally, the cells separate, yielding two cells that (as with the DNA helixes) each contain original and new material. The process of DNA replication during mitosis explains why every cell in an organism contains the same genetic information.

## Genes and Protein Synthesis
The structure of the DNA molecule makes it a simple yet powerful genetic code for life. In an abstract sense, a DNA molecule gives instructions for the production of specific proteins. Proteins make up the structure of the body (e.g., hair, skin) and control the biochemical processes within cells. Some sequences of nucleotide bases on the DNA molecule provide the genetic code for the sequences of amino acids in specific proteins. Other sequences of bases on the DNA provide instructions for when a protein should be produced and how much should be produced.

A **gene** is, in biochemical terms, a specific segment of the DNA that is responsible for the production of a particular protein (Scarr & Kidd, 1983). Some observable characteristics depend on the presence or absence of single proteins and, therefore, on a single gene. You will read about some of these characteristics shortly. Because of this link between specific genes and specific characteristics, a gene can also be defined as the unit of genetic inheritance.

A single chromosome containing a long DNA molecule may include thousands of genes. These genes follow one another on a chromosome like the words in a very long sentence. Biologists estimate that the human **genome,** the total genetic material on all human chromosomes, includes more than 200,000 genes (McKusick, 1994). These genes vary greatly in size. Some have only a few hundred pairs of nucleotide bases while others have millions.

During the late 1980s, biological researchers in the United States launched the Human Genome Project, an effort to identify the exact sequence of the 3 billion nucleotide base pairs on the 46 human chromosomes (Jaroff, 1989). Advocates of the project have described it as the Holy Grail of biology, as "cracking the genetic code of life" (Lee, 1991). Mapping the human genome would greatly simplify the identification of genes causing inherited disorders. It would also increase the possibility of **genetic engineering,** placing normal genes into the cells of people with genetic disorders in order to cure those disorders.

However, completing a map of the human genome is an enormous task. Even if high-tech laboratory equipment and high-speed computers allowed researchers to identify 100,000 base pairs each day, they would have to work for 30,000 days or more than 80 years to map the estimated 3 billion base pairs. Fortunately, teams of researchers from several countries are working on different parts of the task, and all are trying to devise techniques to increase the speed of identification.

One negative side effect of the Human Genome Project may be an increase in mistaken ideas about genetic influence. Popular writers sometimes suggest that the DNA in a particular person's cells is a precise program for the development and functioning of the person. If taken literally, this suggestion is false, because DNA does not control development and functioning directly. Instead, DNA controls biological processes and, especially, protein synthesis.

Even protein synthesis is not controlled entirely by the DNA. Also important is the biological environment of a cell. For example, the proteins synthesized from the DNA in bone cells are different from those synthesized in muscle cells. The difference in proteins is what makes one cell "bone" and the other cell "muscle." Even at a biological level, then, heredity (or DNA) and environment jointly influence development.

## Mechanisms of Genetic Inheritance

So far you've read about the structure of the genetic code and the processes of gene action. The next part of the story of life concerns the transmission of genetic information across generations. How does the genetic makeup of parents affect that of their children? What mechanisms account for this genetic inheritance?

To answer these questions, a more detailed look at human chromosomes is necessary. Recall that chromosomes absorb dyes that make them visible under a microscope. Figure 3.3 is a photograph, taken through a microscope, of the chromosomes from a normal human male. Notice that the chromosomes differ in size. Because of their reactions to the dyes, they also have some regions that are lighter than others. The specific positions of the lighter and darker regions define a chromosome's **banding pattern.**

The differences in chromosome size and in banding patterns are largely consistent across individuals. After examining many sets of chromosomes photographed this way, researchers devised a standard procedure for arranging and labeling them. Photographs of chromosomes arranged according to this standard procedure are called **karyotypes.**

Figure 3.4 shows karyotypes of a normal human male and a normal human female. Notice that most of the chromosomes are grouped into pairs. More specifically, 44 of the chromosomes of each person are grouped into 22 pairs. The chromosomes in each pair are similar in their size, banding patterns, and genetic makeup. That is, the composition and sequence of the genes on them are similar. Consequently, the two chromosomes in a pair are called **homologous.** The 22 pairs of homologous chromosomes are called **autosomes.** In a

**gene**
*A segment of the DNA that carries instructions for the production of a particular protein. Also, the units of heredity that determine specific characteristics such as hair color.*

**genome**
*The total genetic material on all the chromosomes of an organism.*

**genetic engineering**
*The placement of normal genes into the cells of people with genetic disorders in order to cure those disorders.*

**banding pattern**
*The pattern of lighter and darker regions on a chromosome after the chromosome has absorbed specific dyes.*

**karyotypes**
*Photographs of individuals' chromosomes in which the chromosomes are arranged in order of their size and labeled according to a standard procedure.*

**homologous**
*A term for pairs of chromosomes that are similar in size, banding patterns, and genetic makeup.*

**autosomes**
*The 44 human chromosomes that can be grouped into pairs of chromosomes similar in size and gene sequence.*

## FIGURE 3.3

The chromosomes of a normal male. This photograph was taken after cells grown in a laboratory culture were treated so that they could be stained at a point partway through the process of mitosis.

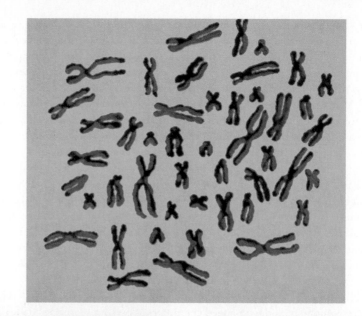

## FIGURE 3.4

Karyotypes of a normal human male and female. The pairs of chromosomes are arranged in order and numbered from largest to smallest. The sex chromosomes are shown after the 22 pairs of autosomes. The karyotype with two X chromosomes is female; the one with X and Y chromosomes is male.

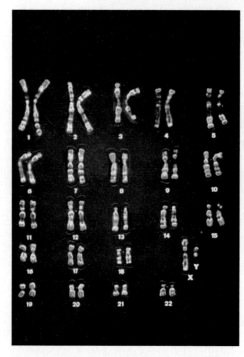

Male

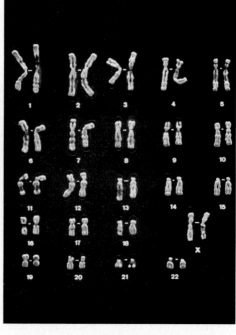

Female

karyotype the autosomes are arranged in order from largest to smallest with the largest labeled as number 1 and the smallest as number 22.

The two karyotypes in the figure differ most obviously in the 23rd pair of chromosomes. On the karyotype of the normal female, the last two chromosomes are both labeled X. On the karyotype of the normal male, the last pair includes one X and one Y. Genetically, a normal female is XX and a normal male is XY. Because this difference in chromosomes is the basis for sex differentiation in humans, the X and Y chromosomes are called **sex chromosomes.**

The differences in the sex chromosomes suggest a more specific question about the mechanisms of genetic inheritance. Each human being has a father, who has XY sex chromosomes, and a mother, who has XX sex chromosomes. How can a father and mother

**sex chromosomes**
*The pair of chromosomes in human beings that is responsible for sex differentiation.*

During the first step of meiosis, the sister chromatids of homologous chromosomes remain close to each other. (This illustration shows the chromatids of a single pair of homologous chromosomes.)

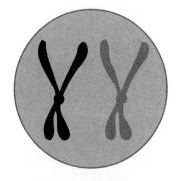

Then the chromosomes exchange corresponding segments of DNA as part of each chromosome breaks off and attaches to its partner.

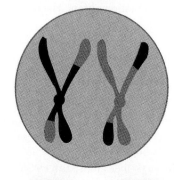

During the second step, the homologous chromosomes separate and the cell divides, creating two new cells.

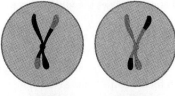

In the third step of meiosis, the chromosomes are segregated into separate gametes during cell division.

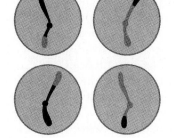

FIGURE 3.5
The crossing over of chromosome segments during meiosis.

produce some children (their daughters) who have XX chromosomes, and other children (their sons) who have XY chromosomes?

The answer to this question, and to the earlier questions about genetic inheritance, lies in the process of sexual reproduction. Sexual reproduction depends on a process of cell division called **meiosis.** Meiosis takes place only in the bodily organs designed for reproduction: the male testes and the female ovaries.

Biologists divide the process of meiosis into many phases (Mange & Mange, 1990). Its general characteristics can be understood, however, by distinguishing three steps. First, each chromosome duplicates itself, forming sister chromatids that remain attached to each other. Moreover, homologous autosomes also remain close to each other (see figure 3.5). The proximity between the corresponding members of each pair of chromosomes allows an exchange of genetic material known as **crossing over.** As the figure shows, segments of matching chromosomes break off and trade places with each other during this step of meiosis.

**meiosis**
*A process of cell division that prepares the way for sexual reproduction by producing new cells that have only half the number of chromosomes in normal body cells.*

**crossing over**
*An exchange of genetic material during meiosis that occurs when segments of homologous chromosomes break off and reattach to the other chromosome in the pair.*

How much crossing over takes place and where the chromosomes break and reattach is largely due to chance. The result of this process is the formation of new chromosomes that differ from those a person inherited from his or her parents. Thus, crossing over increases the uniqueness of offspring and the genetic diversity of the human species.

During the second step in meiosis, the homologous chromosomes (each with its sister chromatids) move to opposite sides of the cell and the cell divides. This division produces two new cells.

During the third step, the sister chromatids in the two new cells separate and move to opposite sides of their new cells. Then those cells divide. This time, each new cell has only 23 chromosomes. These new cells are called **gametes.** The gametes created in the male testes are called *sperm*; those created in the female ovaries are called *ova*, or egg cells. However, meiosis results in the formation of four viable gametes (as shown in figure 3.5) only in males. In females, the successive divisions of one cell lead to the production of one egg cell, or *ovum*, and three very small cells that do not mature into ova.

The shuffling of chromosomes during the creation of gametes is random, with one very important constraint. As mentioned earlier, the autosomes and the sex chromosomes are paired. Each gamete receives one chromosome from each autosome pair and one sex chromosome. Which one of the two goes into which gamete is a matter of chance.

For example, look again at the male karyotype in figure 3.4. At the end of meiosis, one of this male's sperm could contain the chromosome on the left in autosome pair 1, that on the right in pair 2, that on the left in pair 3, and so on. When another one of his cells divides, the shuffling of chromosomes into sperm cells could be entirely different. The chances of having two identical sperm cells at the end of this process are less than 8 million to 1, even without considering crossing over. The chances of identical crossing over *and* identical assignment of chromosomes to sperm cells are extremely small. In short, the scrambling of chromosomal material during meiosis ensures the uniqueness of each human being.

The transfer of genetic material from parents to children is completed at conception, when a sperm fertilizes an ovum. Then a new cell called a **zygote** is formed that contains the genetic material from the father and the mother. This new cell includes the 23 chromosomes from the father's sperm and the 23 chromosomes from the mother's egg. That is, the zygote has the 46 chromosomes normal for a human being.

Because of the random processes involved in the production of sperm and egg cells, almost no chance exists for two zygotes from the same parents to be genetically identical. How, then, can there be identical twins?

Identical twins have the same genetic material because they develop from one zygote. This zygote divides shortly after fertilization into two cells that develop into separate fetuses. Because the two fetuses develop from a single zygote, they are called **monozygotic** (meaning one-zygote), or MZ, **twins.**

By contrast, fraternal twins develop when the mother releases two egg cells that are fertilized at about the same time by two sperm cells. That is, fraternal twins develop from different zygotes and are called **dizygotic** (two-zygote), or DZ, **twins.** Dizygotic twins are no more similar, genetically, than any other pair of siblings. Because they are the same age and develop in the same prenatal environment, they are often compared with identical twins in behavior-genetics research.

About 4 of every 1,000 pregnancies involves MZ twins (Mange & Mange, 1990). The rate varies little among ethnic groups and seems unrelated to the mother's age or the number of previous children she has had. DZ twins are more common, but their rate varies with ethnicity and other factors. Women in West Africa, and American women of West African descent, have more DZ twins than European and European American women. Some groups of Asian women have fewer DZ twins than do women in other ethnic groups. In all ethnic groups, DZ twins are most common among mothers who are about 35 years of age, and lower among either younger or older mothers.

Among Whites in the United States, the rate of DZ twin births increased between 1970 and 1990 (Luke, 1994). So did the rate of triplets and even larger numbers of multiple births (Kiely, Kleinman, & Kiely, 1992). Most triplets come from two eggs, so they include

**gametes**
*Cells with only 23 chromosomes that are created during the process of meiosis. The gametes created in the male testes are called sperm; those created in the female ovaries are called ova or egg cells.*

**zygote**
*The new cell formed when a sperm cell with 23 chromosomes fertilizes an egg cell with 23 chromosomes. The new cell has the 46 chromosomes that are normal for a human being.*

**monozygotic twins**
*Twins that develop from a single zygote that separates into two zygotes shortly after fertilization; also known as identical twins.*

**dizygotic twins**
*Twins that result from the fertilization of two egg cells by two sperm cells at roughly the same time; also called fraternal twins.*

one set of MZ twins and one singleton (Guttmacher & Kaiser, 1986). Twins, triplets, and other kinds of multiple births have probably increased because more women who have had difficulty in starting a pregnancy are using fertility drugs. These drugs stimulate ovulation and so increase the chance that two or more eggs will be released simultaneously.

Finally, while mothers determine how many births will result from one pregnancy, fathers determine the sex of those children. Because females have two X chromosomes, they produce gametes (ova) that only have X chromosomes. Because males have X and Y chromosomes, their gametes (sperm) can have either sex chromosome. Therefore, whether a particular child is a boy or a girl depends on his or her father. The child will be a boy if one of the father's sperm cells that contains a Y chromosome fertilizes the ovum. The child will be a girl if one of the father's sperm cells that contains an X chromosome fertilizes the ovum.

# GENOTYPES, PHENOTYPES, AND ABNORMAL DEVELOPMENT

The ability of living organisms to reproduce themselves while preserving both genetic diversity and the uniformity of their species is truly amazing. The structure of human genetic material is complex, and the transfer of this material to later generations involves multiple processes, each including several steps. Do these processes always function properly? Is the genetic code always transmitted without error?

Unfortunately, the answer to these questions is no. The processes of genetic transmission sometimes go awry. Scientists have learned about errors in genetic transmission by examining variations in people's appearance or behavior that are outside the normal range. Often, scientists have worked backward, using evidence on people's characteristics to make inferences about their genetic makeup.

A child's genetic makeup is defined more formally as the child's **genotype.** All the observable characteristics of a child define the child's **phenotype.** The derivation of *genotype* from genes is obvious. *Phenotype* comes from the Greek word *phanein*, meaning "to show or to display." In other words, the phenotype refers to the characteristics of a person that you can see.

Using children's phenotypes to infer their genotypes can be difficult for two reasons. First, the phenotype does not express all the genetic information in a particular child's DNA. Some genes cancel or prevent the expression of other genes. Second, the phenotype is determined jointly by children's genes and by their experiences. In a broad sense, phenotypes describe children's developmental status, which is the product of both heredity and environment.

Nevertheless, some phenotypes are so distinctive and so clearly linked to genetic inheritance that inferences about genotypes can be made. In addition, chromosomal abnormalities that are observed in karyotypes can be related to abnormalities in children's development. Other abnormalities can be traced to single genes that have been identified or that are likely to be identified when the Human Genome Project is completed.

Geneticists have cataloged thousands of physical and behavioral characteristics that seem to be related, strongly or weakly, to differences in genotypes (McKusick, 1994). The genetic variations that lead to important disorders can be classified into two main types. Some disorders are due to abnormal autosomes or sex chromosomes; others are due to abnormalities in single genes.

Table 3.1 lists a few disorders that are caused by chromosomal abnormalities. The disorders listed are relatively common and have been thoroughly studied. Therefore, they provide good illustrations of the effects of children's genotypes on their behavior and development.

**genotype**
*The genetic makeup of an individual.*

**phenotype**
*The observable characteristics of an individual.*

## Chromosomal Abnormalities

Occasionally, sperm or ova (gametes) are produced that have more or fewer than the normal 23 chromosomes. During the process of crossing over, chromosomal fragments may not accurately separate and reattach. During the next steps in meiosis, a pair of autosomes or sex chromosomes may end up in the same gamete. Another gamete then is missing a chromosome from that pair.

**TABLE 3.1** *Examples of Chromosomal Abnormalities*

| DISORDER | DESCRIPTION | INCIDENCE | PHYSICAL SIGNS | DEVELOPMENT |
|---|---|---|---|---|
| *Disorders of the Autosomes* | | | | |
| Down syndrome | Most have an extra 21st chromosome, so the disorder is also called trisomy-21 | 12 in 10,000 births, but more likely with older mothers | Flattened face, small nose, almond-shaped eyes because of large eyelid folds, respiratory and heart problems that lower life expectancy | Initially normal development but retarded intellectual development before one year; moderate to severe mental retardation in childhood and adulthood |
| Trisomy 13 | Three chromosomes of type 13 | 1–2 in 10,000 births | Small head, malformed ears, eye disorders, abnormal brain structures, heart defects | Severe mental retardation; nearly all die in less than a year |
| *Disorders of the Sex Chromosomes* | | | | |
| Turner syndrome | 45-X or X0 (only one sex chromosome, an X) | 1–4 in 10,000 female births | Female in appearance but sterile; short stature and minor physical abnormalities | Normal verbal intelligence but poor visual-spatial ability |
| Klinefelter syndrome | 47-XXY (two X chromosomes and one Y; some cases have more than two X chromosomes and more than one Y chromosome | 5–20 in 10,000 male births | Male in appearance and above average in height; secondary sex characteristics do not develop normally and most are sterile | Usually normal intelligence; sometimes retarded language development |
| XYY | 47-XYY (two Y chromosomes and one X; some cases have more than two Y chromosomes and a single X) | 10 in 10,000 male births | Unusually tall | May show lower intelligence but findings are inconsistent |
| Fragile X syndrome | An X chromosome has a pinched-in region that is associated with a gene in which a sequence of three nucleotide bases is repeated many times. | 8 in 10,000 male births; 5 in 10,000 female births | In males, large testicles and a long, narrow face with enlarged ears; in females, few or no physical abnormalities | In males, mental retardation and behavior problems (e.g., hyperactivity and poor eye contact); in females, either no problems or mild mental retardation |

Mistakes during meiosis are significant only if a flawed gamete becomes part of a zygote. In other words, the mistakes cause problems if a sperm with the wrong number of chromosomes fertilizes a normal ovum or vice versa. Even then, the mistakes may not be obvious because the zygote will often be spontaneously aborted. This type of abortion occurs, in part, because the faulty zygote does not contain the correct genetic instructions for normal prenatal development. Often, the zygote aborts so early in pregnancy that the mother is never aware that she was pregnant.

Some chromosomal abnormalities are not lethal but result in abnormal development. The developmental consequences of these genetic mistakes typically are more severe when they involve the autosomes rather than the sex chromosomes. Table 3.1 lists two autosomal abnormalities that do not always result in spontaneous abortion but that are associated with greatly abnormal development and with a shortened life expectancy.

## Down Syndrome

The most common autosomal defect is **Down syndrome.** Its name derives from the person—Dr. Langdon Down—who gave an early, careful description of the disorder (Kessler, 1988; Moore, 1988). Another name used for the syndrome is **trisomy-21.** This name refers to the

**Down syndrome**
*A chromosomal abnormality that leads to unusual physical features (e.g., relatively flat faces and almond-shaped eyes), an increased likelihood of medical problems, and severe mental retardation.*

**trisomy-21**
*The chromosomal abnormality that most often causes Down syndrome, which is the presence of three rather than the normal two chromosomes of type 21.*

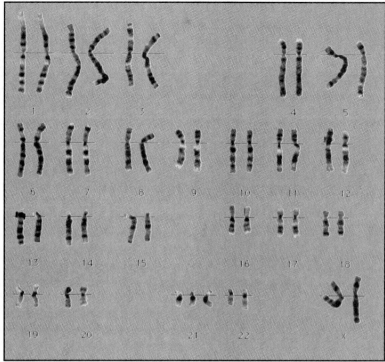

(b)

(a)                                                                                              (c)

## FIGURE 3.6

The young skier has Down syndrome. So does the boy in the classroom with his hand raised. Notice their rounded heads, relatively flat faces, and (especially on the skier) eyelid folds that give their eyes an almond shape. Photo (b) is a karyotype of a Down syndrome child. Notice the three chromosomes of type 21, where normally there are only two. Notice, also, that this chromosomal abnormality did not prevent the boys in the other photographs from achieving some success in life and being part of children's groups.

genotypic variation that is the most common cause of the syndrome. Most children with Down syndrome have three chromosomes (thus *tri*-somy) of type 21 (see the karyotype in figure 3.6) rather than the normal two. In about 75 percent of cases, the extra 21st chromosome comes from the mother (Mange & Mange, 1990). That is, the mother's ovum contained both chromosomes in her 21st pair rather than one.

Down syndrome children have distinctive physical features (see figure 3.6). They have somewhat flat faces with eyelid folds that give their eyes an almond shape. Their noses are small, and their heads are more rounded than is typical. They are below average in height, have a stocky build, and have generally poor muscle tone. They are also likely to have respiratory problems, heart malformations, and leukemia. For these reasons, Down syndrome

children have a higher mortality rate and a shorter life expectancy than normal children. They often die before age 20, although improved medical care has allowed a larger proportion to survive into adulthood (Carr, 1994; Vandenberg, Singer, & Pauls, 1986).

The psychological profile of Down syndrome children is unusual. During early infancy they seem to develop normally, but their rate of development slows after 6 months of age. By 10 months of age, Down syndrome infants receive lower scores than normal infants on measures of intellectual development (Kopp, 1983). During early childhood, their rate of intellectual development remains slower than that of normal children, so they fall further behind the norms for their age. During the school years, Down syndrome children show moderate to severe mental retardation, with IQ scores about 50 points below the norm of 100 (Kessler, 1988).

The developmental level reached by Down syndrome children is not entirely fixed by their genes. Their rearing environment also makes a difference (Shapiro, 1994). Down syndrome children who live at home reach a higher level of intellectual and social maturity than do children who are raised in institutions. Enrichment programs for Down syndrome infants can also enhance their development.

Early-intervention programs yield the most consistent gains in adaptive social behaviors and in fine motor skills like grasping and cutting. These programs show less impressive gains in gross motor ability, linguistic skills, and cognitive or academic performance (Gibson & Harris, 1988). The intellectual performance of people with Down syndrome may improve even in adulthood, but the improvements are modest. The mean IQ of adults with Down syndrome is about 45, although some adults reach an IQ of 70 (Carr, 1994). More intensive interventions that begin in childhood and continue into adulthood might have stronger effects.

Other researchers have focused on the origins of Down syndrome. Older mothers more often have Down syndrome infants. With mothers under 30 years of age, Down syndrome occurs in less than 1 of every 1,000 births. With mothers over 45 years of age, Down syndrome occurs in more than 8 of every 100 births (Mange & Mange, 1990). The rate of Down syndrome may also be higher when the father is older, but the evidence on this point is inconsistent (Mange & Mange, 1990; Vandenberg et al., 1986).

Why should older mothers have more Down syndrome infants? The best answer to this question is not clear, but most hypotheses focus on a curious feature of human reproduction. Males begin to produce sperm cells in adolescence, when they reach puberty. Females, by contrast, prepare all the ova that they will ever have before they are born. In other words, before birth a human female completes the first phases of meiosis for all the several hundred thousand egg cells that she will ever produce. These cells remain in her ovaries until puberty. Then they begin to mature. They complete meiosis at a steady rate during the woman's childbearing years.

Many researchers have suggested that Down syndrome reflects problems with the aging egg cells in a woman's ovaries. Because of biochemical changes in the woman's body, the reproductive system and meiosis in particular may not operate as flawlessly in older women. Alternatively, the problems may arise in the outside environment. Some researchers have suggested that women's exposure to the low levels of radiation present in normal environments may have harmful effects, over time, on their ova. However, current evidence regarding the effects of such low-level radiation is inconsistent (Mange & Mange, 1990).

In sum, the exact cause of the higher rate of Down syndrome in infants with older mothers is not yet known. Research continues, and someday doctors may be able to identify parents who have the greatest risk of conceiving a Down syndrome child. Future research may also suggest ways that these parents can reduce their risk.

## Disorders Linked to the Sex Chromosomes

Abnormal sex chromosomes are more common but have less serious consequences than abnormal autosomes. In particular, children with an abnormal number of sex chromosomes do not consistently suffer from mental retardation. However, they often differ from normal children in their physical features, biological functioning, social behavior, and patterns of intellectual abilities. Table 3.1 lists three of the most common disorders that are due to abnormalities of the sex chromosomes.

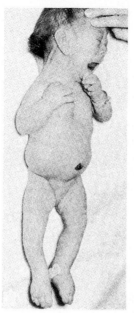

**FIGURE 3.7**

The Turner syndrome karyotype is abnormal because there is only one sex chromosome, an X. The infant in the top photograph has Turner syndrome. Notice that the infant has the external sex organs of a female. She also has the somewhat webbed neck of Turner syndrome females.

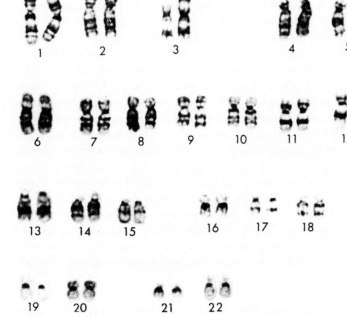

*Turner Syndrome*   Children with **Turner syndrome** have only one sex chromosome, an X. They have neither the second X chromosome of a normal female nor the Y chromosome of a normal male (see figure 3.7). Therefore, the syndrome is also called X0 (that is, X-zero) or 45-X, meaning that the child has only 45 chromosomes and only one X chromosome. The most common cause is an error in the production of sperm, so that the child receives an X chromosome from the mother but no sex chromosome from the father (Mange & Mange, 1990).

Children with Turner syndrome have the sex organs of a normal female, so they are brought up as girls. They are usually sterile, though, and they rarely develop breasts and other secondary sex characteristics during adolescence. They are relatively short, have a webbed or shortened neck, and have short, stubby fingers. Except for their short stature, the physical abnormalities are slight and may not be obvious to an untrained observer.

**Turner syndrome**
*A chromosomal abnormality that results from the presence of only one sex chromosome, an X. Children with this syndrome are phenotypically female but sterile.*

Most Turner syndrome girls score in the normal range on verbal intelligence, but their verbal and spatial abilities are relatively poor (McCauley et al., 1987; Pennington et al., 1982). Consequently, they often have below-normal scores on IQ tests that include both verbal and visual or spatial subtests. In addition, girls with Turner syndrome have poorer handwriting than normal girls and, occasionally, show deficits in memory and attention.

Turner syndrome girls generally are lower in social maturity than normal girls. They have fewer friends and fewer positive interactions with their friends. They have lower self-concepts, especially about their physical appearance. These differences exist even when girls with Turner syndrome are compared with other girls who are unusually short or physically immature but chromosomally normal (McCauley et al., 1987).

Some physical abnormalities associated with Turner syndrome can be eliminated by administering replacement hormones during childhood; for example, hormone therapy can increase the height of Turner syndrome girls. In adolescence, giving female hormones can lead to the development of normal secondary sex characteristics. These benefits of hormone therapy show again that children's development is affected jointly by their genes and their environments. Giving hormones to Turner syndrome girls is a biological intervention, but it is also an external intervention, which reflects the influence of nurture rather than nature.

**Klinefelter syndrome**
*A chromosomal abnormality that usually results from the presence of two X chromosomes and one Y chromosome. Children with the syndrome are phenotypically male but never produce sperm.*

*Klinefelter Syndrome*    The problem in Turner syndrome is a deficit in genetic material, one fewer sex chromosome than is normal. Other genetic disorders are caused by an excess of genetic material. Table 3.1 lists two sex-chromosome disorders of this kind. Of those two, **Klinefelter syndrome** is more distinctive. Children with this syndrome usually have two X chromosomes and one Y chromosome, so their genotype is 47-XXY. The extra chromosome can come from either the mother or the father. Errors in the production of the mother's ova are more common, especially among older mothers (Mandoki et al., 1991).

Children with Klinefelter syndrome are phenotypically male. Their physical appearance is largely normal, although they are above average in height. Often, the syndrome is not often recognized until puberty, when some boys begin to show some breast development. Although the boys do not produce sperm, their sexual behavior is usually normal.

Some boys with Klinefelter syndrome are mildly retarded, so the syndrome is more common among patients in mental institutions. Their retardation is greatest in verbal intelligence, and they show delayed language development. During the school years, their reading and spelling ability may be poor (Mandoki et al., 1991; Money, 1993). However, most boys with Klinefelter syndrome are normal in intelligence.

Testosterone treatment during adolescence can enhance the development of secondary sex characteristics in these boys (Mange & Mange, 1990). Hormone treatment cannot correct their infertility, because their reproductive organs are structurally abnormal. However, infertility is often the only serious problem encountered by males with this relatively common chromosomal disorder.

**fragile X syndrome**
*A chromosomal abnormality in which one region on the X chromosome is pinched in. Children with the syndrome are often mentally retarded.*

*Fragile X Syndrome*    Some genetic disorders do not involve changes in the number of chromosomes children have, but rather abnormal chromosome structure. The **fragile X syndrome** gets its name from a pinched-in region near the tip of the long arm on an X chromosome. The abnormal structure of this region makes the tip of the chromosome more fragile or vulnerable to breaking off.

The change in chromosome structure is associated with a specific gene that has an abnormal sequence of nucleotide bases (Caskey et al., 1992). In normal individuals, one portion of the gene includes about 30 repeats of the sequence cytosine-guanine-guanine. In individuals with fragile X syndrome, this sequence is repeated more than 200 times.

Fragile X syndrome is often associated with mental retardation. Some researchers estimate that this chromosomal defect is the most common cause of inherited mental retardation (deVries et al., 1994). However, the effects of the defect differ greatly for the two sexes.

Most boys with fragile X syndrome are distinctive in their physical appearance (Lachiewicz et al., 1994). They have a long, narrow head with large ears. Especially after puberty, they have large testicles. They may also have other physical signs such as calluses on

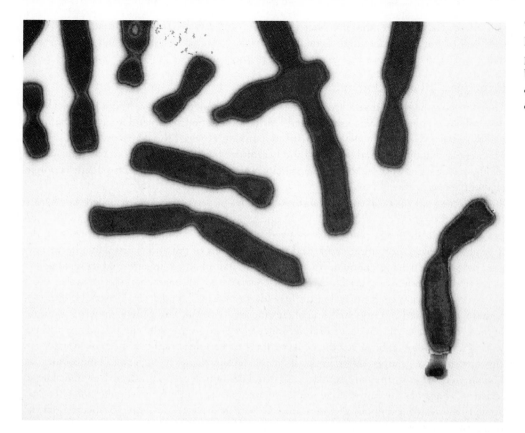

The X chromosome on the lower right in this photo has a pinched-in region near the bottom. The abnormal chromosome structure is the cause of fragile X syndrome.

their hands and an unusually high palate. Girls with the syndrome show few distinctive physical features, probably because the fragile X chromosome is not active in all their cells, and they have another, normal X chromosome.

Boys with fragile X syndrome are usually retarded, often so severely that they are placed in institutions. However, about one-fifth of boys with the syndrome are normal in intelligence. Girls with the syndrome tend only to have mild or borderline mental retardation (Ashley et al., 1993). These boys and girls may, however, transfer the defective X chromosome to their children or grandchildren, who may then display the full syndrome.

Many boys with fragile X syndrome show severe behavioral problems. Some common problems are hyperactivity, an unwillingness to make eye contact with other people, an avoidance of being touched by others, and a tendency to bite or flap hands. These problems are also characteristic of children with **autism,** a severe developmental disorder characterized by impaired social interactions and repetitive, self-stimulating behavior. In addition, both fragile X syndrome and autism are more common among boys than girls.

Because of these parallels, some researchers have suggested that the fragile X chromosomal defect is a cause of autism. However, not all boys with fragile X are diagnosed as autistic (Lachiewicz et al., 1994). Not all autistic boys show the mental retardation of boys with fragile X (Howlin & Yule, 1990; Schreibman & Charlop, 1989). Fragile X and autism therefore appear to be distinct disorders.

Still, both disorders have a genetic basis (Bolton et al., 1994; deVries et al., 1994), and research on the relations between them could lead to greater understanding of both. Greater understanding might, in turn, result in more specific ideas for their prevention and treatment.

**autism**
*A pervasive developmental disorder whose symptoms include an absence or impairment of social relationships and ritual or self-stimulating behavior.*

## Gene Expression and Single-Gene Defects

Many genetic disorders are linked not to the number or the structure of children's chromosomes but to the composition of specific genes. Although some genetic disorders involve

multiple genes, disorders that involve a single gene are easier to trace and to describe. However, before you can understand single-gene defects, you must first understand the principles that govern the expression of a genotype in a phenotype.

## Principles of Gene Dominance

The genes on the 46 human chromosomes do not act independently. Many biological and psychological characteristics are affected by the joint action of several genes. In the nineteenth century, Gregor Mendel, an Austrian monk, discovered the major principles of gene interaction. Although Mendel studied the hereditary transmission of characteristics in pea plants, scientists now know that these principles explain important aspects of gene action in all complex organisms.

For several years, Mendel cross-bred varieties of pea plants and recorded the characteristics of the new plants that resulted. In one experiment, Mendel found that breeding tall pea plants with short pea plants did not produce new plants of medium height. Instead, the new plants were either tall or short, and the proportions of tall and short plants in the new generation were usually unequal. Most often, more tall plants than short plants resulted.

In the twentieth century, geneticists discovered many human characteristics that show patterns of inheritance comparable to those described by Mendel (McKusick, 1994). Geneticists also gained an understanding of chromosomes, DNA, and genetic material. Because of these discoveries, the patterns of inheritance observed by Mendel can be fully explained.

First, though, a brief review of some facts of heredity might be helpful. Recall that chromosomes are grouped into pairs, and the two chromosomes in each pair of autosomes are homologous. That is, they are similar in size and contain genes that affect the same characteristics. The genes are in the same sequence, so genes that affect a particular characteristic are in the same place on both chromosomes. Geneticists call the position of a specific gene its **locus,** the Latin word for *place.*

Geneticists use the term **allele** to refer to each of the two genes at the same locus on homologous chromosomes. More specifically, an allele refers to the genetic information, or the form of a gene, encoded at a particular locus on a chromosome (Scarr & Kidd, 1983). Mendel's patterns of inheritance depend on the joint effect of two alleles on two homologous chromosomes.

Consider the example of hair color. To simplify the example, assume that only one gene with two alleles controls hair color. One allele leads normally to dark hair. The other allele leads normally to blond hair. People can have two alleles of the same type or one allele of each type. A person who has two alleles of the same type is **homozygous** for hair color. A person who has two different alleles is **heterozygous** for hair color.

People have dark hair if they have two alleles for dark hair. They have blond hair if they have two alleles for blond. But what if they have one allele of each type? Rather than having hair that is intermediate between blond and dark, their hair will be dark. The allele for dark hair is **dominant,** which means that this characteristic is expressed even if a person has a second allele for blond hair. The allele for blond hair, by contrast, is **recessive,** meaning that this characteristic is expressed only when a person has two alleles of this type.

Suppose, now, that a man with dark hair marries a woman who also has dark hair. Suppose that they have four children. What color will their children's hair be? To answer this question, you need to know more than their parents' hair color. You also need to know which alleles the parents carry, that is, the parents' genotype. The parents' phenotype (i.e., their actual hair color) does not tell us fully about their genotype. The mother and father might each be homozygous and have two alleles for dark hair. Or each parent might be heterozygous and have one dominant allele for dark hair and one recessive allele for blond hair.

If both parents are homozygous for dark hair, their children will all have dark hair, because the parents can only give them the alleles for dark hair. If both parents are heterozygous, their children will, on the average, show the pattern in figure 3.8. That is, three children will have dark hair, although two of them will be heterozygous for hair color. One of their children will have blond hair, because he or she will receive the blond alleles from both parents.

Now a puzzle for you. A man and his wife both have dark hair, but their four sons all have blond hair. How is that possible?

**locus**
*The term in genetics for the position of a specific gene on a chromosome.*

**allele**
*The genetic information, or the form of a gene, encoded at a particular locus on a chromosome.*

**homozygous**
*In genetics, the condition of having two alleles of the same type on homologous chromosomes.*

**heterozygous**
*In genetics, having two different alleles at the corresponding locations on homologous chromosomes.*

**dominant**
*The allele for a characteristic (e.g., hair color) that is expressed even if a person has a different allele for the same characteristic on the homologous chromosome.*

**recessive**
*The allele for a characteristic (e.g., hair color) that is expressed only if a person does not have a different allele for the same characteristic on the homologous chromosome.*

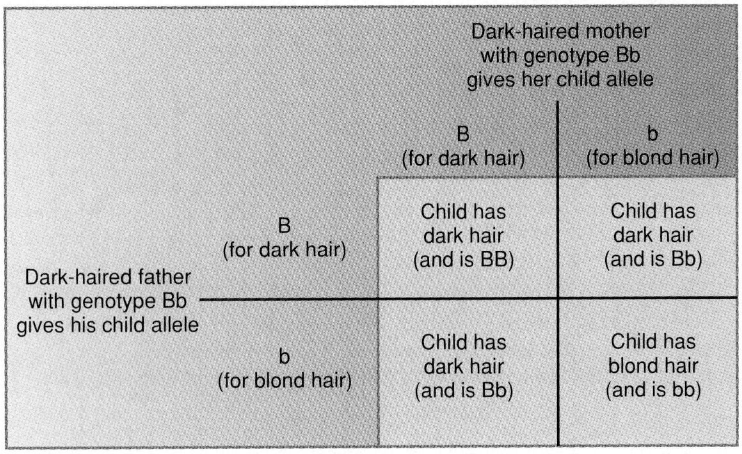

FIGURE 3.8
When two parents with dark hair have four children, what color will the children's hair be? This figure shows what outcome can be expected, on the average, when both parents are heterozygous for hair color. That is, each parent has a dominant allele for dark hair, symbolized by B, and a recessive allele for blond hair, symbolized by b.

It's possible because the pattern in figure 3.8 only holds "on the average." To understand what is really happening, think back to the discussion of meiosis. Remember that the shuffling of chromosomes into gametes—sperm cells and ova—is a random process. Therefore, the shuffling of alleles into gametes is also random. The processes that lead to the fertilization of a specific ovum by a specific sperm introduce more randomness into the transfer of genes from parents to children.

The processes of gene transfer lead on the average to the pattern in figure 3.8, but the pattern may not hold for a particular set of four children. You can get four "heads" in a row when flipping a coin, although the probability of a "head" is 50 percent on each throw. You can also get four blond-haired boys from two dark-haired parents, provided the parents are heterozygous. Although the probability of having blond hair is 25 percent for each child, some heterozygous parents will have no blond-haired children, and others will have all blond-haired children.

The principle of dominance has many important implications. One is that a person's phenotype is an incomplete expression of his or her genotype. Because people have dominant alleles that mask the expression of recessive alleles, their observable characteristics do not give us full information about their genetic makeup. In other words, the principle of dominance is one reason that people with different genotypes may have the same phenotype.

## Autosomal Genetic Disorders

Many genetic disorders that afflict human beings are caused by recessive alleles. A smaller number reflect the expression of dominant alleles. Still other disorders do not fit into the previous two groups because they involve the sex chromosomes rather than the autosomes. Table 3.2 lists some examples of all three types. A closer look at three disorders will show you more precisely how single-gene defects are expressed.

*Phenylketonuria: An Autosomal Recessive Disorder*   During the 1930s, a Scandinavian physician noticed that some severely retarded children had an unusual odor about them. Laboratory tests showed that these children had large amounts of phenylpyruvic acid in their urine. Later researchers discovered that the children accumulated phenylpyruvic acid because they lacked the enzyme that converts phenylalanine, an amino acid present in many foods, into other chemicals. Phenylpyruvic acid belongs to a class of organic compounds called *ketones,* so the syndrome was called **phenylketonuria,** or **PKU.**

Researchers soon discovered that PKU is an autosomal recessive characteristic. The locus of the alleles responsible for PKU is on one of the autosomes, and children have the disorder only if they inherit the recessive allele from both parents. During the 1980s, researchers discovered that these alleles are on the tip of the long arm of chromosome 12 (Mange & Mange, 1990). The parents of children with PKU rarely have the disorder because they have one normal allele that is dominant over the allele responsible for PKU.

**phenylketonuria (PKU)**
*An autosomal recessive disorder that makes children unable to break down the amino acid phenylalanine. Unless placed on a restricted diet early in life, children with the disorder suffer severe mental retardation.*

## TABLE 3.2    Examples of Single-Gene Defects

| DISORDER | DESCRIPTION | INCIDENCE | PHYSICAL SIGNS | DEVELOPMENT |
|---|---|---|---|---|
| **Autosomal Recessive Disorders** | | | | |
| Phenylketonuria (PKU) | Absence of the enzyme that breaks down phenylalanine | 1 in 10,000 births | Fair skin, light hair color, prone to spasms | Severe mental retardation if untreated; fairly normal if kept on low-phenylalanine diet |
| Sickle-cell anemia | Leads to sickle-shaped (crescent-shaped) blood cells with abnormally low capacity to carry oxygen | 20 in 10,000 African American births, but also common in other groups who live in or emigrated from areas where malaria is common | Weakness, pain in joints and abdomen because of ruptured blood cells, bacterial infections, degeneration of organs | Increases infant and childhood mortality |
| Tay-Sachs disease | Enzyme disorder that affects brain metabolism | 2–3 in 10,000 births to Jews from Eastern Europe | No obvious deformities | Apparently normal for the first few months of life; then regression in motor development, lack of social responsiveness, blindness, and brain deterioration causing death, usually before age 3. |
| **Autosomal Dominant Disorders** | | | | |
| Huntington's disease | A central nervous system disorder caused by an abnormal DNA segment linked to a genetic marker on chromosome 4 | 3–7 in 100,000 births | Usually none in childhood or adolescence | Onset of muscle spasms and personality disorders usually after age 30, with mental deterioration and death within 20 years |
| Marfan syndrome | Affects connective tissues in the skeleton, eyes, and heart | 4–6 in 100,000 births | Unusually tall with long limbs and fingers, a deformed spinal column, nearsightedness and eye deformities, and heart defects | Heart defects can lead to early death, but surgery or drug treatment is sometimes helpful |
| **Disorders Caused by Recessive Genes on the X Chromosome** | | | | |
| Hemophilia | Lack of substances that allow normal blood clotting | 1 in 10,000 male births; very rare in females | Children bruise easily and bleed excessively when injured | Normal in intelligence but below average in school achievement |
| Duchenne's muscular dystrophy | Causes progressive muscular degeneration | 2–3 in 10,000 males | Gradual weakening of muscles with some heart and skeletal defects | Loss of strength after three years that usually confines children to a wheelchair by 12 or 13 years of age; respiratory failure and death before age 20 |

Sources: Lee, 1991; Mange & Mange, 1990; McKusick, 1994; Schneider et al., 1990; Vandenberg, Singer, & Pauls, 1986.

Because children with PKU cannot break down phenylalanine, the amounts that are in their food accumulate in their blood. The high levels of phenylalanine then cause abnormal brain development. Within a few months after birth, infants with untreated PKU begin to show delays in motor and mental development. Most never learn to talk and some never learn to walk.

Fortunately, these negative outcomes can be prevented by eliminating the buildup of phenylalanine in the blood. Almost all infants in the United States are now screened for PKU shortly after birth. If they show the elevated levels of phenylalanine that indicate the

disorder, they are placed on a low-phenylalanine diet. They receive a special infant formula that provides protein but that, unlike mother's milk or cow's milk, is lacking in phenylalanine. When kept on the special diet, children with PKU develop normal or nearly normal IQs (Barclay & Walton, 1988).

Maintaining a diet low in phenylalanine is not easy for parents and children. Most common foods, especially high-protein foods, contain phenylalanine. The low-phenylalanine, artificial substitutes are not always tasty and can be a monotonous diet. Moreover, children must be carefully monitored to ensure that their level of phenylalanine does not become either too high or too low (Mange & Mange, 1990).

In previous decades, parents of children with PKU often kept them on the low-phenylalanine diet only until they were 5 or 10 years old. These parents and their doctors assumed that maintaining the special diet was not necessary for more than a few years because brain development was largely completed during early childhood.

Newer data suggest that long-term continuation of a low-phenylalanine diet can improve children's cognitive performance. A diet low in phenylalanine may also contribute to higher social competence (Reber, Kazak, & Himmelberg, 1987). In short, children with PKU may develop to their full potential only if they make a permanent change in one aspect of their environment—what they eat. Therefore, clinicians now recommend that people with PKU stay on a low-phenylalanine diet indefinitely.

A second reason for long-term continuation of a low-phenylalanine diet involves not the PKU children themselves but *their* children. If a woman with PKU becomes pregnant when she is not on the special diet, the outcomes for her developing fetus are disastrous. Although the fetus will not have PKU if the father provides a normal allele for breakdown of phenylalanine, the fetus will be affected by the mother's disorder.

A pregnant woman with PKU who is not on a restricted diet is likely to have high levels of phenylalanine in her blood. Her phenylalanine passes into the circulation system of the fetus and causes abnormal brain development. The fetus is then born with the brain damage that leads to mental retardation. In this way, the mother's genetic disorder creates a harmful environment for the development of her genetically normal child. But if a pregnant woman with PKU eats foods low in phenylalanine, she can ensure that her fetus develops normally.

PKU is another illustration of the interaction between genotypes and environments. In the normal environment before 1930, all children with PKU were destined to moderate or severe retardation (Katz, 1978). In the altered environment of a low-phenylalanine diet, children with PKU experience fairly normal brain development. They still have a genetic disorder and they can still transmit it to their children, but in a carefully managed environment, they and their children can have phenotypes within the normal range.

### Huntington's Disease: An Autosomal Dominant Disorder

Disorders like PKU that are caused by recessive alleles are more common than those caused by dominant alleles. If an allele causing a serious disorder is dominant, every person with even one allele will show the disorder. Disorders that seriously affect development are also likely to affect a person's ability to reproduce. Therefore, the chances that the dominant alleles will be passed to a new generation are usually small.

**Huntington's disease** is an exception to this rule because of its unusual time course. This rare disorder results from a dominant allele linked to a genetic marker on chromosome 4 (see table 3.2). People with the allele usually show normal development during childhood and adolescence. Between 35 and 50 years of age, however, they begin to experience muscle spasms and irritability, depression, or other personality disorders. They also experience memory impairments and other signs of brain deterioration (Vandenberg et al., 1986). Death normally follows within 15 years after diagnosis of the disorder.

Despite the severity of the disorder, the dominant allele remains in the gene pool because many people with Huntington's bear children before any symptoms of the disease are apparent. One famous example is the folk singer Woody Guthrie. Even more famous among geneticists is a European man who moved to Venezuela seven generations ago. His

**Huntington's disease**
*A rare, autosomal dominant disorder that does not affect early development but does lead to physical and mental problems and early death in adulthood.*

gene for Huntington's disease has now been traced through a family tree that includes more than 10,000 people (Lee, 1991).

Most often, a person with Huntington's disease carries only one allele for the disorder. The chances that the person will give that allele to his or her children are 50 percent, because the person could instead give them the normal allele. Genetic screening can be done to find out whether a specific child is affected. However, no way of preventing the disease or slowing its progress currently exists. Researchers hope that more research on the disorder will lead to effective treatments.

## Hemophilia: An X-linked Genetic Disorder

Single-gene defects on the sex chromosomes cause several genetic disorders. Nearly all these disorders involve genes on the X chromosome. The karyotype in figure 3.4 showed that the Y chromosome is small, and it apparently contains few genes. Disorders caused by genes on the X chromosome are described as **X-linked.**

One serious X-linked disorder is **hemophilia.** Children with hemophilia lack a substance that leads to normal clotting of blood. As a result, they bleed uncontrollably when cut or bruised. Some children are more severely affected than others, because several gene defects can cause hemophilia and some disrupt blood clotting more than others (Mange & Mange, 1990; McKusick, 1994).

Most people with hemophilia are male because the primary disorder results from a recessive allele on the X chromosome. Females would develop hemophilia if they received the recessive allele from both their mothers and their fathers, but the probability of this event is about 1 in 100 million (Mange & Mange, 1990). Females who receive the recessive allele for hemophilia from their mothers usually receive a normal allele from their fathers. Sons, however, lack this protection. The Y chromosome that sons receive from their fathers does not have the allele for blood clotting, so they always develop hemophilia if they receive the allele for hemophilia from their mothers.

Hemophilia is another example of the incomplete expression of the genotype in the phenotype. Women can carry the gene for hemophilia without being affected themselves. Men with hemophilia do not pass this gene to their sons, because they pass their Y chromosome, not their X chromosome, to sons. The X chromosome with the gene for hemophilia is passed to daughters, who are protected by their normal X chromosome. These daughters, however, can pass the hemophilia gene to their sons. Because X-linked recessive genes are transferred in this way, they seem to skip a generation. That is, the actual disease appears not in fathers and their sons, but in fathers and their grandsons.

Hemophilia is yet another illustration of the interactions between genotypes and environments. Boys with hemophilia are normal in intelligence but have below-average scores for academic achievement (Colgrove & Huntzinger, 1994; Loveland et al., 1994). The most likely explanation is that these boys are often absent from school because of illness. Consequently, their school performance suffers.

Hemophilia is also a tragic example of historical trends in human illnesses. During the 1980s, the AIDS virus spread in the United States and contaminated the nation's blood supply. Many hemophiliacs receive frequent blood transfusions as part of their treatment, and many became infected with AIDS. More than half the hemophiliac children and adolescents in most samples now have the AIDS virus (Loveland et al., 1994). Fortunately, this problem should not recur in the 1990s, because methods of detecting the AIDS virus have been developed and all contaminated blood is quickly destroyed.

Hemophilia and many other genetic disorders can now be detected during the prenatal period. Several procedures are used to obtain information about the genotype of a developing fetus. *Practical Applications of Research:* "Genetic Counseling and Prenatal Diagnosis" describes these procedures and the programs of genetic counseling that are associated with them.

## Beyond the Principle of Dominance

For many human characteristics, the principle of dominance does not hold. Gene interaction is often more complicated than the principle implies. Many other patterns of gene expression occur, but three are especially significant.

**X-linked**
*A term for genetic disorders that can be traced to genes on the X chromosome.*

**hemophilia**
*A serious X-linked disorder in which people lack a substance that leads to normal clotting of blood.*

First, the alleles that affect certain characteristics are not clearly dominant or recessive. Human blood types are a good example. Children who inherit the alleles for type A blood from one parent and type B blood from the other parent are neither type A nor type B but AB. That is, their blood shows a combination of types A and B. Both their alleles are expressed in their phenotypes. This pattern of gene expression is called **codominance.**

Second, alleles at a single locus may not act on their own. Their operation may be affected by other genes called **modifier genes.** For example, not all children with PKU show the same buildup of phenylalanine when on an unrestricted diet. Several genes that govern the production of several enzymes affect the breakdown of phenylalanine in the body. All these genes affect the amount of phenylalanine in the blood and, therefore, affect the phenotype of children with PKU (Mange & Mange, 1990).

Third, many human characteristics are affected by multiple genes on multiple chromosomes. Some researchers estimate that many genes have important and potentially measurable effects on human cognitive abilities, personality, and psychological disorders (Plomin, Owen, & McGuffin, 1994). When the effects of these genes combine in a simple, additive fashion, the pattern is called **polygenic inheritance** (Mange & Mange, 1990).

Scarr and Kidd (1983) argued that genetic models based on the principle of dominance "are largely irrelevant to human behavioral genetics, because most behavioral traits show patterns that are called **multifactorial inheritance**" (p. 365). Their definition of multifactorial inheritance includes the ideas of codominance, modifier genes, and polygenic inheritance. Their definition also allows for interactions or correlations between children's genotypes and the environments in which they grow up.

In summary, researchers have learned a great deal by using the assumptions about gene expression that Mendel described more than a century ago. The discoveries of the causes of PKU and hemophilia are two examples. However, many human characteristics show patterns of genetic influence that go beyond the principle of dominance. Later in the chapter, you will see how researchers explore the more complex patterns of multifactorial inheritance.

## Genetic Defects or Genetic Diversity?

One question not yet considered is the origin of genetic defects. What was the source of the gene that causes PKU, for example? Once the gene appeared, why did it survive? Genetic disorders usually decrease an individual's fitness in an evolutionary sense. Why, then, doesn't natural selection eliminate them?

Let's take the question about origins first. The appearance of a genetic defect requires a change in the DNA. A defect that involves a single gene results from a change in an allele at a particular locus on a chromosome. Other types of changes may involve multiple genes. All such changes in genetic material are **mutations.**

Mutations often occur without any obvious external cause. In the duplication of DNA during meiosis, nucleotide bases may be displaced or omitted, thus changing the genetic code. The rate of mutations increases when reproductive cells containing DNA are exposed to high heat or radiation. In addition, exposure to toxic chemicals and even viruses can increase the rate of mutations.

From one perspective, mutations always represent genetic mistakes. That is, they result from a failure of the DNA to reproduce itself accurately. From another perspective, mutations are genetic experiments that, on occasion, may improve the species. In that sense, they are the "raw material for natural selection" (Scarr & Kidd, 1983, p. 347) because they increase genetic diversity. Therefore, they increase the ability of a species to respond to diverse or varying environments.

Most mutations must be judged as failed experiments because they are harmful or even fatal to a developing organism. However, some mutations are beneficial under certain conditions. For example, the recessive allele that leads to PKU may increase resistance to rickets, a disease that leads to defective bone growth. Children with both the recessive allele for PKU and one normal allele may be less susceptible to rickets than those with two normal alleles (Vandenberg et al., 1986).

**codominance**
*A pattern of gene expression in which both alleles on homologous chromosomes contribute to the phenotype.*

**modifier genes**
*Genes that affect the expression or functioning of genes at other loci on the chromosomes.*

**polygenic inheritance**
*A pattern of gene expression in which multiple genes that affect the phenotype combine in a simple, additive fashion.*

**multifactorial inheritance**
*Patterns of genetic inheritance involving the action of multiple genes that do not follow the principle of dominance; also allows for interactions or correlations between children's genotypes and the environments in which they grow up.*

**mutations**
*Permanent changes in the DNA that lead to changes in the observable characteristics of an organism.*

# GENETIC COUNSELING AND PRENATAL DIAGNOSIS

Because hemophilia and many other genetic disorders have distinct patterns of inheritance, it is often possible to judge whether parents are likely to bear a child with a disorder. Genetic counselors have special training for making these judgments and additional training in counseling prospective parents. The process of genetic counseling can be broken into two steps.

The first step occurs before the conception of a child. Parents concerned about the risks of birth defects can consult with a genetic counselor to see whether their concern is justified. Consultation is especially important for prospective parents who have relatives with genetic disorders such as hemophilia or PKU. Parents who come from high-risk populations are also good candidates for genetic counseling. Jews in the United States are a high-risk group for the disorder known as Tay-Sachs (see table 3.2), and many of them have participated in genetic counseling programs (Merz, 1987).

Some prospective parents may be aware that they have a higher than normal risk for other reasons. For example, older mothers have a higher risk of conceiving a child with Down syndrome. Therefore, genetic counseling is often advised for mothers over 35 years of age.

Genetic counselors can offer two types of information to parents before conception. First, they can estimate the prospective parents' risk more precisely by preparing a detailed family history for both the man and the woman. With this history, a counselor can judge the likelihood that either parent is a carrier of the alleles for many genetic disorders.

Second, a genetic counselor can get more definite information about the parents' genotypes from a karyotype, a blood test, or other laboratory tests. These tests can show whether the parents carry recessive alleles for certain genetic disorders. A counselor who has done both a family history and genetic testing may be able to tell parents that they are unlikely to pass genes for any known disorders to their children. When the parents have recessive alleles for a specific disorder, a counselor can tell them their chances of bearing a child with those disorders.

Suppose that two parents receive a clean bill of health after this first step in counseling. Both their family histories and the laboratory tests imply that they are not carriers of any known disorders. Can they feel confident that their children will be genetically normal?

Unfortunately, the answer is no. Remember that some genetic disorders, particularly those involving chromosomal abnormalities, are not caused by defects in the parents' DNA but by the faulty separation of chromosomes into gametes during meiosis. Testing all the gametes is impossible, so problems in meiosis can be detected only after conception.

Prenatal diagnosis of genetic abnormalities is the second step in genetic counseling. Since the 1960s physicians have obtained information about the genetic makeup of a fetus through **amniocentesis.** For this procedure, a physician puts a hollow needle through the abdominal wall of a pregnant woman into the woman's uterus (see figure 3.9). Then the physician draws some of the amniotic fluid that surrounds the fetus into the needle.

Amniotic fluid contains cells shed by the fetus that can be used to create a karyotype. Examination of the karyotype can show whether the fetus has any chromosomal abnormalities. Other analyses of the fetal cells can show whether the fetus has some specific single-gene defects such as hemophilia.

Amniocentesis has some risks. Placement of the needle in the uterus is guided by ultrasound, a technique in which the uterus is scanned with ultrasonic waves that provide a "motion picture" of the fetus and the needle. However, incorrect placement of the needle can damage the fetus or placenta, or trigger a spontaneous miscarriage. Because of this risk, most doctors recommend amniocentesis only when there is an above-normal chance of birth defects.

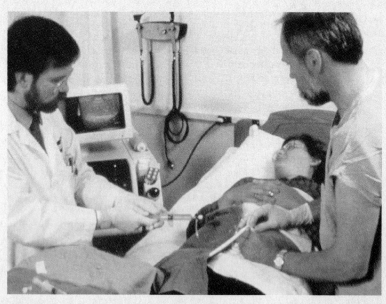

**FIGURE 3.9**

This woman is undergoing the procedure of amniocentesis. The doctor in the white coat has inserted a needle through the woman's abdomen into her uterus. He will then withdraw some amniotic fluid.

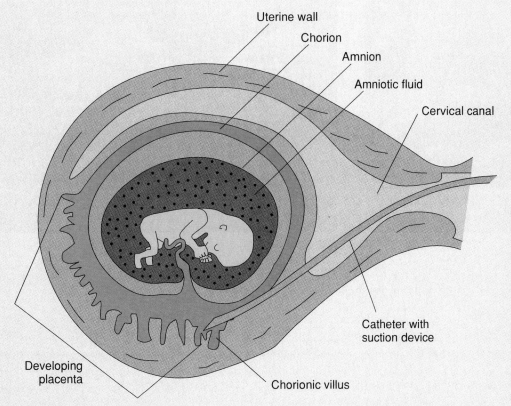

Uterine wall
Chorion
Amnion
Amniotic fluid
Cervical canal
Catheter with
suction device
Chorionic villus
Developing
placenta

**FIGURE 3.10**

Chorionic villus sampling (CVS) can be done by inserting a slender, flexible tube (catheter) through a woman's cervical canal into her uterus. The end of the tube is moved next to the chorionic villi. Then suction is applied to draw villi cells into the tube. The genetic makeup of these cells matches that of the fetus.

The greatest disadvantage of amniocentesis is that the results are not available until pregnancy is nearly half over. Little amniotic fluid is available to withdraw for analysis until about the 16th week of pregnancy. Completion of the tests on the fetal cells takes at least another two weeks. Amniocentesis can be done only 10 to 13 weeks after conception, but doing so seems to decrease the rate of successful pregnancies (Nicolaides et al., 1994).

A newer procedure that provides information earlier in pregnancy is **chorionic villus sampling,** or **CVS.** For this procedure, a physician inserts a slender, flexible tube through the woman's cervical canal (see figure 3.10). The tube is then moved near the **chorion,** the membrane that surrounds the fetus during early pregnancy. This membrane has hairlike projections called *villi* (singular, *villus*). A sample of the villi cells is drawn into the tube and then analyzed. These cells can be used to diagnose the condition of the fetus because the cells of the villi and the fetus are genetically identical.

CVS can be done as early as the eighth or ninth week of pregnancy. The results are available in about a week. Moreover,

the procedure seems to pose no greater risk to the mother and fetus than amniocentesis (Ammala et al., 1993).

Physicians can also diagnose the condition of a fetus by literally looking inside the uterus. In a procedure called **fetoscopy,** physicians place in the uterus a tube containing a small light that allows them to see the fetus. In addition, physicians can obtain a sample of fetal blood from the placenta or umbilical cord. This procedure can be done during the same period as CVS or amniocentesis to obtain more information about the fetus (Plouffe & Donahue, 1994).

If the various techniques of prenatal diagnosis reveal no abnormalities, the job of the genetic counselor is easy. If these techniques reveal that the fetus is genetically abnormal, the counselor may discuss the couple's options either to end the pregnancy or to plan for raising a child with a genetic disorder. Fortunately, the options for remedying the problems associated with genetic defects improve each year. Parents who know that their developing child has PKU, for example, can today avoid most consequences of the disorder by dietary restrictions. With continuing medical advances, this option should become attractive for more disorders.

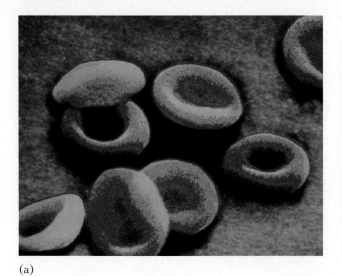

(a)

(b)

## FIGURE 3.11

(a) Photo showing normal blood cells. (b) Photo showing the flattened and curved (or sickle-shaped) blood cells of a person with sickle-cell anemia.

**sickle-cell anemia**
*A genetic disorder of which one symptom is that blood cells are curved like a sickle rather than having the rounded shape of normal red blood cells. Other symptoms can include increased bacterial infections, episodes of blocked circulation, and problems of organ degeneration.*

The benefits, under certain conditions, of apparently harmful mutations are clearest for the blood disorder **sickle-cell anemia.** The name for the disorder comes from the shape of the red blood cells in people who have it. These cells are curved like a sickle rather than round like normal red blood cells (see figure 3.11).

Sickle-cell anemia results from a recessive allele that affects the amino acids in human hemoglobin. Children with two recessive alleles show all the symptoms of the disorder. They have increased bacterial infections, episodes of blocked circulation, and problems of organ degeneration. Without careful medical treatment, they often die before the age of 5. Children with only one recessive allele show no symptoms or much milder anemia (Diamond, 1989).

Although the gene mutation that causes sickle-cell anemia has occurred repeatedly in human evolutionary history, its distribution and frequency are not random. The disorder is most common in areas where malaria is also common. Malaria is an infectious disease, transmitted through mosquito bites, that affects more than 100 million people each year and is a major cause of death in childhood (Diamond, 1989).

The match between the geographic distributions of sickle-cell anemia and malaria is a clue to the persistence of this genetic disorder. Stated most simply, the sickle-cell allele provides protection against malaria. Children who have one allele for sickle-cell anemia (but not two) are less likely to die of malaria than are children with two normal alleles. In malarial regions, this benefit of having one sickle-cell allele outweighs the cost of the anemia for children with two sickle-cell alleles.

In the United States, sickle-cell anemia is most common in Blacks. Of course, the ancestors of most Blacks in the United States came to this country from Africa, where malaria is a serious problem. Because malaria is not a problem in the United States and sickle-cell anemia is, the frequency of the sickle-cell allele should be lower in the United States than in Africa. Moreover, the disorder should decrease across generations, although at a slow rate (Mange & Mange, 1990).

That all genetic defects have hidden benefits seems doubtful. Some defects may persist simply because the corresponding gene mutations recur in each new generation. That is, the genetic code may be scrambled or misinterpreted in the same way across many generations.

However, the examples of PKU and sickle-cell anemia suggest that judgments about the harmfulness of genetic defects should not be made without thorough study. Additional research may reveal other examples of defects that have some advantages for people with only

one mutant allele. For this reason, researchers hesitate to conclude that any mutation which increases genetic diversity is entirely harmful to the human species.

# GENE-ENVIRONMENT INTERACTION AND NORMAL HUMAN VARIATION

The previous section focused on genetic causes of abnormal development because they illustrate the principles of genetic influence most simply and dramatically. However, children's genotypes do not merely affect whether their development is normal or abnormal. They also affect the position of children within the normal range. To understand how genotypes affect normal human variation, you need to understand current models of the interactions between genotypes and environments.

## Models of Gene-Environment Interaction

Two children with the same genotypes (i.e., identical twins) can, as adults, have different phenotypes. Two children with different genotypes can develop similar phenotypes. The outcomes in both cases depend on the environments in which the children are brought up. One question for child development theorists is how to describe the joint action of genetic and environmental influences.

### Reaction Range

Gottesman (1963) proposed that every genotype has its own **reaction range.** This range reflects the degree to which variations in environments affect the development of individuals with a particular genotype. In other words, it defines how much environments can influence the transformation of the genotype into a phenotype.

Figure 3.12 shows hypothetical reaction ranges for three genotypes. The ranges are given for one measure of the phenotype, IQ scores. You could substitute another measure, such as social skill or athletic ability, and interpret the figure in much the same way. The reaction ranges are hypothetical, rather than based on actual data, because directly measuring children's genotypes is impossible. That is, researchers cannot directly measure children's genetic potential for IQ (or any other characteristic).

**reaction range**
*The degree to which variations in environments can affect the development of individuals with a particular genotype and, thus, affect their mature phenotypes.*

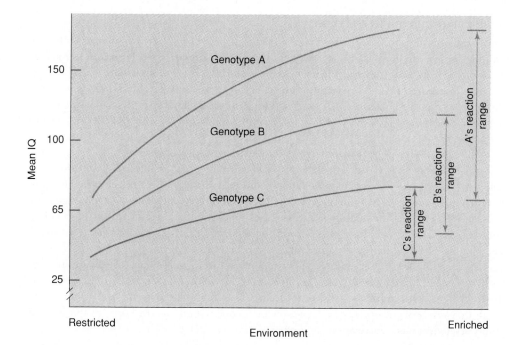

**FIGURE 3.12**
Hypothetical reaction ranges for the IQ scores of children with different genotypes. Notice that children with all genotypes develop higher IQs in enriched environments. In the same environment, children with different genotypes develop different IQs. However, a change in environments affects the A genotype more than the B and C genotypes: The genotypes have different reaction ranges.
Source: Gottesman, 1963.

Even so, the figure is based on two plausible assumptions. The first assumption is that enriched environments promote the development of a high IQ more than restricted environments do. Also, this effect holds for all genotypes. That's why all the lines in the figure slope upward. Children with all genotypes develop higher IQ scores in enriched environments than in restricted environments.

The second assumption is that differences in children's genotypes affect their measured intelligence. You already know that children's genotypes affect whether they have normal intelligence or are severely retarded. For example, children with the chromosomal abnormality that leads to Down syndrome are always retarded. Children with the normal complement of 46 chromosomes are less often retarded. However, children with Down syndrome do vary in their measured IQs. So do children with normal chromosomes. The figure implies that these differences are due partly to differences in genotypes, as shown by the separation of the lines for Genotypes A, B, and C.

Implicit in figure 3.12 is a more speculative hypothesis about reaction ranges for IQ. The figure shows larger reaction ranges for children with "better" genotypes, or greater genetic potential for a high IQ. For Genotype A, the reaction range is from an IQ of around 65 to an IQ of greater than 150, or about 100 points. The reaction range for Genotype C is much smaller. The figure thus implies that variations in environments have dramatic effects on children with high intellectual potential but little effect on those with low intellectual potential.

Is this hypothesis correct? The question is very difficult to answer because, again, children's genotypes cannot be measured directly. Their genetic potential can be estimated with data on their biological relatives. In addition, the degree to which their environment is enriched or restricted can be measured. When both kinds of data are available, inferences can be drawn about how different environments affect children with different genotypes.

Data from research with such designs suggest that children with greater genetic potential are more influenced by certain variations in environments, as figure 3.12 implies (Bergeman & Plomin, 1989). Other variations in environments seem to have more effect on children with less genetic potential. Yet these two patterns are less common than a third pattern in which environmental variations have similar effects on children with all genotypes.

In summary, current evidence suggests that for general characteristics like IQ, reaction ranges are approximately equal for all genotypes (Rutter, Silberg, & Simonoff, 1993). This means that improvements in environments are likely to benefit children with "poor" genotypes as much as those with "better" genotypes. Conversely, rearing children in impoverished environments is likely to have equally negative effects on all children.

## Gene-Environment Correlations

Scarr and McCartney (1983) presented a model of genetic and environmental influence that emphasizes the importance of the **genotype-environment correlation.** A genotype-environment correlation exists when children with different genotypes are regularly exposed to, or reared in, environments that are systematically related to their genotypes. Plomin, DeFries, and Loehlin (1977) defined three kinds of genotype-environment correlations that Scarr and McCartney (1983) took as the foundation for a more general developmental model.

First, a **passive genotype-environment correlation** describes a relation between the genes that parents give to their children and the environments that parents provide for their children. For example, parents with high math ability are likely to transfer genes to their children that give them a high aptitude for math. These parents are also likely to encourage their children's growing understanding of mathematics. In particular, they might buy their young children computer games that provide training in math. When their children enter school, they may pay special attention to their math achievement.

In such families, a relation exists between the children's genotypes (a high aptitude for math) and their environments (a strong emphasis on learning and using math). However, the children themselves influence neither the genes that they have nor the environments in which they are brought up. They are passive recipients of both, as the label for this kind of genotype-environment correlation suggests.

**genotype-environment correlation**
*A systematic relation between variations in children's genotypes and variations in their rearing environments.*

**passive genotype-environment correlation**
*A relation between the genes that parents give to their children and the environments that they provide for their children.*

Why did these boys join this athletic team? According to Scarr and McCartney (1983), one reason might be that the children's genotypes gave them the ability and motivation for success in athletics. The children realized that athletics was a niche in which they could succeed, so they joined a team. This explanation refers to an active genotype-environment correlation.

Second, an **evocative genotype-environment correlation** describes a relation between the genes children have and the reactions of other people to their appearance or behavior. Various expressions of children's genotypes are likely to evoke distinctive reactions from other people. For example, children whose genotypes predispose them to be cooperative with adults are likely to elicit positive responses from adults. Therefore, these children are likely to have a pleasant and stimulating social environment. By contrast, children whose genotypes predispose them to be uncooperative are not as likely to have positive interactions with adults.

The two types of children have different social environments because their social behavior, which is influenced by their genotypes, leads adults to behave differently toward them. Stated more informally, the second kind of genotype-environment correlation emphasizes children's ability to change their environments merely by behaving naturally.

Third, an **active genotype-environment correlation** refers to children's attempts to find environments compatible with their genotypes. For example, children whose genotypes give them the ability and the motivation for success in athletics may join athletic teams and spend considerable time improving their athletic skills. Scarr and McCartney used the term **niche picking** to describe children's attempts to find an environment—a niche—that matches their talents and interests.

Scarr and McCartney proposed that the importance of the three kinds of genotype-environment correlations changes as children grow. In particular, active genotype-environment correlations become more significant as children get older. Young children are mostly under their parents' control. Adolescents and adults have more freedom to choose or to create the environment that they prefer. Scarr and McCartney (1983) summarize their argument by saying that "genes direct the course of human experience, but experiential opportunities are also necessary for development to occur" (p. 433).

Other researchers disagree with the assertion that genes direct the course of human experience (e.g., Baumrind, 1993; Jackson, 1993; Wachs, 1993). These researchers argue that growing up in particular environments has powerful effects on children's development. In their view, genes and environments, nature and nurture, are codirectors of children's development. Moreover, these researchers argue that variations in environments have stronger effects on some aspects of development than do variations in genotypes.

To evaluate these contrasting positions, researchers have done several types of studies. Some of their results are presented in the next section. In later chapters, you will find more detailed information about genetic influences on specific aspects of development.

**evocative genotype-environment correlation**
*A relation between children's genes and the reactions they evoke from other people. Those reactions partly define the environments in which the children grow up.*

**active genotype-environment correlation**
*A relation between children's genotypes and their environments that results from children's efforts to seek environments compatible with their genotypes.*

**niche picking**
*A term used by Scarr and McCartney to describe children's attempts to find an environment—a niche—that matches their talents and interests.*

## Estimating Genetic Influence

**behavior genetics**
*A subfield of science whose goal is the exploration of the genetic contribution to variations among individuals.*

Accurately estimating how well variations in genotypes account for variations in psychological characteristics is central to the field of **behavior genetics** (Plomin, DeFries, & McClearn, 1990). Behavior-genetics researchers use several methods to study the genetic influence on specific characteristics. These methods, and the estimates of genetic influence they yield, can be illustrated with examples from three domains: intelligence, personality, and mental illness.

### Genes and Intelligence: How Strong Is the Connection?

As mentioned earlier, children's genotypes can have dramatic effects on their measured intelligence. An abnormal genotype, such as that linked to Down syndrome, is often accompanied by abnormally low IQ scores. The question now, though, is how much genotypes affect the variations in IQ within the normal range. Most of the evidence on this question has come from studies of twins.

Behavior-genetics researchers often study twins because they know exactly how similar twins are genetically. Identical, or monozygotic (MZ), twins have the same genotypes. Fraternal, or dizygotic (DZ), twins share half their genes, on the average, because they have the same parents but develop from different zygotes. Stated quantitatively, the genetic similarity of MZ twins is 1.0 (or 100 percent); the genetic similarity of DZ twins averages .50 (or 50 percent).

If genetic similarity affects phenotypic similarity, MZ twins will be more similar to each other than will DZ twins. Researchers can estimate the genetic influence on a characteristic from the difference between MZ and DZ twins' similarity. These estimates are often phrased in terms of **heritability.** A broad definition of heritability is the proportion of the variation in an observable characteristic that is due to variations in genotypes (Rowe, 1994).

So, what do the results of twin studies tell us about the heritability of IQ? Figure 3.13 summarizes the data from many published studies of twins (McGue et al., 1993). The figure shows the average correlation found in those studies between the IQ scores of MZ twins. It also shows the average correlation between the IQ scores of DZ twins. The correlations for 4- to 6-year-olds are based on data from more than 100 pairs of twins. Those for older children are based on data from more than 1,000 pairs of twins.

All the correlations in the figure are above .50 and some are above .80. Such strong correlations are uncommon in psychological research. They show that both MZ and DZ twins are quite similar in their measured intelligence.

For estimating genetic influence, however, the most important data concern the differences between the correlations for MZ and DZ twins. In every age period, MZ twins are more similar in their IQ scores than DZ twins. In other words, the twins who are more similar genetically are also more similar in measured intelligence.

The differences between the MZ and DZ correlations can be used to estimate the heritability of IQ. One simple formula for heritability is twice the difference between the simi-

**heritability**
*An estimate of the amount of genetic influence on a characteristic, or the proportion of the variation in an observable characteristic that is due to variations in genotypes.*

## FIGURE 3.13

These correlations show how similar monozygotic (MZ) and dizygotic (DZ) twins are in their IQ scores. Each data point indicates the average of the correlations found in several studies. Notice that similarity in IQ is always higher for MZ twins than for DZ twins.

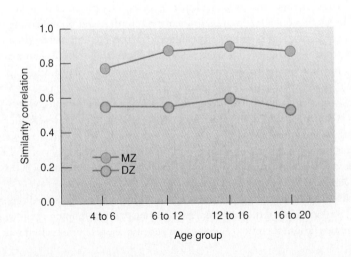

larity correlations for MZ and for DZ twins (Rowe, 1989). The differences in figure 3.13 range from about .20 to about .25, which suggests that the heritability of IQ is between .40 and .50. In other words, up to half the variability in twins' IQ scores can be attributed to the variability in their genotypes.

Studies of twins do not provide unambiguous estimates of genetic influence. These estimates depend on the assumption that genetic similarity is the only reason that MZ twins are more similar than DZ twins. You can probably think of other reasons that MZ twins might be similar. For example, MZ twins look alike, so parents and others might treat them more similarly than they do DZ twins. If so, MZ twins would have, in effect, more similar environments than DZ twins. Their greater similarity in IQ scores would, then, result from a combination of genetic and environmental similarity.

Researchers have found a way to test this hypothesis. Some MZ twins look different enough that their parents believe they are DZ twins, and some DZ twins look so similar that their parents believe they are MZ twins. Whether the twins are actually MZ or DZ can be determined with blood tests. Then researchers can see whether the twins' similarity in IQ is more strongly related to their parents' beliefs about them or to their actual genetic similarity.

A study of this kind was done by Scarr and Carter-Saltzman (1979). They found that parents' beliefs about their twins were not related to the twins' similarity in intellectual abilities. But as expected, the twins' similarity in intellectual abilities was higher if they actually were MZ rather than DZ twins.

Even when the assumptions for a twin study are met, the resulting estimates of heritability must be interpreted cautiously. These estimates always depend on the range of environments found in a given sample. If the range of environments increased, the proportion of the variation in specific characteristics that was apparently due to environmental variation would probably increase. Conversely, the proportion of variation that seemed to be due to genetic variation would probably decrease (Bronfenbrenner & Crouter, 1983).

Most estimates of the heritability of IQ, for example, come from samples of children who are all attending school. Suppose you increased the range of environments by including children who never attended school. Your estimate of environmental influence on IQ would probably go up, and your estimate of genetic influence of IQ would probably go down.

Behavior-genetics researchers counter this criticism by pointing out that few researchers have shown directly that differences in the range of environments greatly affect heritability estimates (Rowe & Waldman, 1993). Moreover, the goal of behavior-genetics research is not to explore all possible environments but to discover how much genotypes affect observed variations within the normal range of environments. In short, heritability estimates provide information about what *is*, not what *could be*.

## Genes and Personality: The Power of Environments

Children's genotypes may also influence their personality development. To estimate this influence, some researchers have compared children raised by their biological parents with adopted children. Children raised by their own parents receive both their genes and their family environment from those parents. Children adopted early in life receive their genes from their biological parents but their rearing environment from their adoptive parents.

Think about two siblings in the same family. If they have the same biological parents, they will be genetically related and raised in a common environment. If they were adopted and have different biological parents, they will not be genetically related but they will have a common environment. If genotypes influence personality, then biological siblings should be more similar in personality than adopted siblings. If a common environment also influences personality development, then adopted siblings should be more similar in personality than would be expected by chance.

What do the data show? One study included pairs of biological siblings and pairs of siblings with different parents who were adopted into the same family (Scarr et al., 1981). The adopted children were placed in their adoptive homes before they were 1 year old. The biological siblings and the adopted siblings completed personality questionnaires when they were between 16 and 22 years old.

FIGURE 3.14

How similar are siblings in their personality traits? The answer sometimes depends on whether they are biological or adopted siblings. On traits such as social potency, impulsivity, and neuroticism, biological siblings are much more similar than adopted siblings, probably because biological siblings have more similar genotypes. (Data from Scarr et al., 1981.)

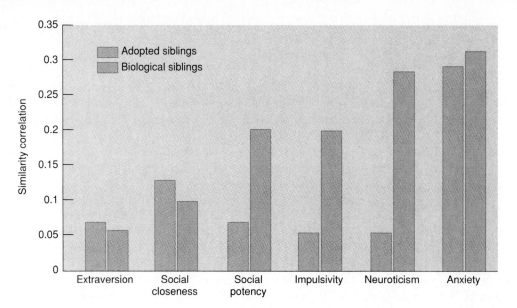

**nonshared environmental influences**
*Effects of features of the environment that are unique to a specific child, not shared by the child and his or her siblings.*

Figure 3.14 shows the correlations for the siblings' similarity on various measures of personality. None of the correlations is particularly strong. All are weaker than any correlation in figure 3.13 for twins' similarity in IQ scores. These data suggest that growing up in the same family does not make siblings very similar in personality.

Other studies have confirmed that a common family environment does not lead to substantial similarity between siblings in their social behavior or personality development (Dunn & Plomin, 1990). The development of siblings seems more affected by **nonshared environmental influences,** that is, influences of the unique environment in which each sibling lives (Plomin, 1989; Rowe, 1994). Each child in a family has a unique environment because parents treat each of them differently. For example, parents treat sons differently from daughters.

Siblings may also differ because they have different experiences outside the family. For example, siblings usually have different friends and different teachers at school. Less systematic factors that might contribute to differences between siblings are accidents, illnesses, or other events. These sources of influence, those not shared by all children in the same family, appear to have more impact on their personality development than does a shared family environment.

Of course, the correlations in figure 3.14 also provide evidence about genetic influence on personality development. On most measures, similarity is greater for biological siblings than for adopted siblings. Across all measures in the study (Scarr et al., 1981), the median correlation for biological siblings was .20; that for adopted siblings was only .07. The difference between these correlations (.13) suggests that the heritability of these personality traits is about .26 (2 × .13).

A closer look shows that the correlations for biological and adopted siblings differ most for the measure of neuroticism (i.e., shyness, low self-esteem, depression). The correlations differ hardly at all for the measure of extraversion (i.e., sociability, assertiveness, dominance). Does this mean that neuroticism is heritable and extraversion is not?

Although the correlations in the figure suggest that conclusion, several other studies suggest that most broad personality traits, including extraversion, have heritabilities of .40 to .50 (Plomin et al., 1994; Rowe, 1994). The other data come primarily from twin studies, which sometimes yield results different from those in studies of adopted children. Behavior-genetics researchers have offered possible explanations for the difference (e.g., Lykken et al., 1992), but the issue has not been fully resolved.

Nevertheless, two conclusions can be drawn. First, personality traits show a moderate degree of heritability, with most studies showing little variation in heritability estimates across traits. Second, the findings from one study may not precisely match those in other studies. As noted in chapter 2, findings replicated in several studies should be treated as most trustworthy.

Do people from different ethnic groups differ in temperament? More specifically, do they differ in the intensity of their emotional responses? Jerome Kagan, Doreen Arcus, and Nancy Snidman (1993) suggest that the answer to these questions is yes. They also suggest that the temperamental differences reflect differences in genotypes.

Kagan and his colleagues observed 4-month-old infants' responses to a structured set of experiences. To begin, infants were observed for 1 minute as their mother looked at them while smiling but not saying anything. Then the infants were shown toys and mobiles for short periods. Next, they heard a tape of a woman's voice repeating syllables like *ga* and *ma* either loudly or softly. Finally, the infants saw more toys and were observed for another minute as their mother looked at them without talking.

The sample for the study included 80 infants from Beijing, 106 infants from Dublin, and more than 600 Caucasian American infants from the Boston area. Figure 3.15 shows the mean scores for each group on the primary measures of emotional arousal. They included the number of seconds that infants cried, the percentage of trials on which they showed fretting or vocalizing, and the frequency of motor activities such as leg kicking.

On all behaviors, American children had the highest scores, Chinese children had the lowest scores, and Irish children were intermediate. In short, the infants differed in their level of emotional arousal. Kagan and his colleagues proposed that the differences reflected genetic differences among the groups. In addition, they speculated that the ethnic differences in temperament may be related to differences between Western and Eastern philosophies. In their view, Western philosophers have emphasized the need to control negative emotions of anxiety, fear, and guilt. Eastern philosophers have emphasized calmness, serenity, and the elimination of desire. Kagan et al. suggested that "perhaps nature and nurture come together even at the level of the deepest philosophical assumptions of a society" (p. 207).

These researchers' ideas are certainly provocative, but the evidence so far is inconclusive. The three groups of infants not only came from different ethnic groups but also lived in different environments. The children lived in countries that differed greatly. Patterns of parent-infant interaction may also have differed across groups, and these differences could have affected even 4-month-olds' emotional responses.

Therefore, judging whether the temperamental differences between groups are the result of nature or nurture is difficult. Additional studies with stronger research designs would be needed to make that judgment. Nevertheless, you should consider the findings in figure 3.15 as a valuable reminder of the diversity in human development.

## THE TEMPERAMENT OF AMERICAN, IRISH, AND CHINESE INFANTS

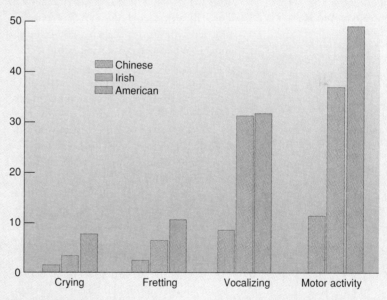

**FIGURE 3.15**

When 4-month-old infants are brought to a psychological laboratory and exposed to unfamiliar sights, sounds, and experiences, Chinese infants show less emotional arousal than Irish or American infants. Chinese infants cry and fret less, make fewer vocalizations, and show less motor activity. (Data from Kagan et al., 1993.)

Finally, genetic influences on personality have been explored with samples other than twins or adopted children. Another strategy is to compare children from different populations. The cross-cultural study of infants' behavior that introduced this chapter is one example (Kagan et al., 1993). *Cultural Perspectives:* "The Temperament of American, Irish, and Chinese Infants" includes more information about that study and its implications.

FIGURE 3.16

If one monozygotic (MZ) twin is schizophrenic, seriously depressed, or autistic, his or her cotwin often has the same mental illness. The concordance for these types of mental illness is much lower for dizygotic (DZ) twins. (Data from Gottesman, 1993; Plomin et al., 1994; Rutter et al., 1993.)

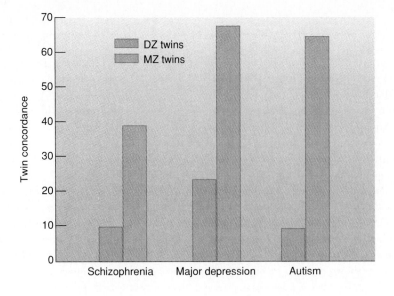

**concordance**
*In genetics, the percentage of genetically related persons who show similar characteristics (e.g., the percentage of twins who are either both schizophrenic or both nonschizophrenic).*

**schizophrenia**
*A broad category of psychological disorders that include such symptoms as delusions, hallucination, bizarre behavior, disturbances of thought, and a relative absence of emotional expression.*

**major depression**
*A serious impairment in psychological functioning with some combination of depressed mood, suicidal ideas, sleep disturbances, and social withdrawal.*

## Genes and Mental Illness: Concordance and Discordance

Many types of mental illness can be linked to people's genetic makeup. To estimate the genetic influence on specific categories of mental illness, researchers often assess the **concordance** in illness for genetically related individuals. For example, suppose that one MZ twin has been diagnosed with autism. If his or her cotwin is also autistic, the two twins are *concordant* for autism. When the concordance for a category of mental illness is higher for people whose genotypes are more closely related, some genetic influence on the illness can be assumed.

Figure 3.16 shows the percentage concordance between MZ twins and DZ twins for autism, schizophrenia, and major depression (Gottesman, 1993; Plomin et al., 1994; Rutter et al., 1993). The symptoms of autism were described earlier. **Schizophrenia** refers to a broad category of psychological disorders with symptoms that include delusions, hallucination, bizarre behavior, disturbances of thought, and a relative absence of emotional expression. **Major depression** refers to a serious impairment in psychological functioning with some combination of depressed mood, suicidal ideas, sleep disturbances, and social withdrawal.

For all three disorders, the concordance is higher for MZ than DZ twins. For instance, if one MZ twin is autistic, the chances that his or her cotwin will also be autistic are about 60 percent. By contrast, if a DZ twin is autistic, the chances that his or her cotwin will also be autistic are less than 10 percent. This difference implies that children can inherit a tendency toward autism.

Concordance can be assessed between relatives who are not twins. For example, many studies of parents and children suggest some genetic influence on the development of schizophrenia. The base rate for schizophrenia in human populations is between 1 and 3 percent. Among children with one schizophrenic parent, the rate is about 10 percent. Among children with two schizophrenic parents, the rate is between 35 and 45 percent (Gottesman, 1993; Rowe, 1994).

Viewed from another perspective, the concordance rates in figure 3.16 show the influence of the *environment* on mental illness. Although MZ twins have the same genotype, they are discordant for each illness (i.e., one twin has the illness and the other does not) between 30 and 60 percent of the time. Furthermore, no disorder has a concordance of 100 percent for MZ twins, so all disorders are influenced partly by the specific (nonshared) environment in which twins are reared.

Stated more generally, children's genotypes do not entirely determine their destiny. Children who have a biological relative with a serious mental illness are not fated to succumb to mental illness themselves. In a favorable environment, these children often become normal, well-functioning adults (Hanson, Gottesman, & Heston, 1990).

For example, children who have a schizophrenic parent are less likely to become schizophrenic themselves if their mother has an uncomplicated pregnancy and a normal delivery (Walker & Emory, 1983). They are less likely to become schizophrenic if they are brought up in families that are psychologically healthy and low in conflicts (Tienari et al., 1991). These kinds of positive environments reduce the chances that a genetic propensity will become an actual mental illness.

# BEHAVIOR GENETICS AND THE EFFECTS OF PARENTING

Studies of genetic influences on children's development are extremely controversial (Baumrind, 1993; Jackson, 1993; Rowe, 1994; Scarr, 1992, 1993; Wachs, 1993). Arguments rage over many issues of theory, methods, and interpretation of research findings. Some of these issues, such as the assumptions underlying twin studies, were mentioned earlier. Other issues relate to specific topics that are discussed in later chapters.

Perhaps the most controversial issue concerns the role of social relationships in children's development. This issue is central to the age-old debate over the effects of nature and nurture on development. In recent writings, the issue has been phrased specifically in terms of the effects of parent-child relationships.

Some behavior-genetics researchers have argued that normal variations in parenting (i.e., excluding extremes of abuse and neglect) have little or no influence on the variations in children's development. In a major address to child development researchers, Sandra Scarr (1992) asserted that "parental *differences* in rearing styles, social class, and income have small effects on the measurable *differences* in intelligence, interests, and personality among their children" (p. 10, italics in original). Similarly, David Rowe (1994) suggested that "the environmental variables most often named in socialization [research] (e.g., social class, parental warmth, and one- vs. two-parent households) may exert little influence on personality development over the life course" (p. 1).

How can Scarr and Rowe draw these conclusions? You read earlier that the heritability of IQ and of personality traits probably does not exceed .50. Doesn't that mean that at least 50 percent of the variance in IQ and personality must be caused by variations in children's environments and, specifically, variations in parenting?

Scarr (1992, 1993) and Rowe (1994) say no. They point to the evidence that shared environmental influences, those common to all children in a family, seem to have little influence on children's development. More important are nonshared environmental influences, those unique to each child in a family. And as noted earlier, nonshared influences need not involve family relationships. They may, instead, reflect the effects of children's relationships with friends, teachers, or other people.

By contrast, other researchers argue strongly that parent-child relationships are a major part of the nonshared environment (Hoffman, 1991). For example, suppose that a father read to his first son for 30 minutes each night when the son was a preschooler. Then the father got a new job with a long commute. Because he got home from work late, he could not read regularly to his second son when that son was a preschooler. Therefore, the two sons did not share the experience of having their father read regularly to them. Any effects of this difference in their experience could be defined both as parental influences and as nonshared environmental influences.

Behavior-genetics researchers have largely ignored this type of nonshared influence because they have rarely included measures of parenting in their studies. Fortunately, this situation is changing. Several large projects that involve both behavior-genetics researchers and researchers with expertise in parent-child relationships are now under way (Plomin, 1993). The data from these projects should provide a better understanding of the joint effects of children's genotypes and their family relationships.

Another proposition of Scarr (1992, 1993) and Rowe (1994) relates to the earlier discussion of active genotype-environment correlations and niche picking. These researchers

have argued that parents mainly provide an environment in which their children can develop their unique genetic potential. In other words, parents give opportunities to children to find their own niche—a niche consistent with their genotypes. According to Scarr (1992, p. 2), "children actually construct their own environments." That is, children create an environment that allows them to develop in the direction set by their genes.

According to some researchers (e.g., Baumrind, 1993), this view of development exaggerates children's independence or individualism. No children can create a separate little world in which they control whatever happens to them. No children have unlimited opportunity to develop their genetic potential. Opportunities are most limited for poor children and children from disadvantaged minority groups. In the language of Scarr and McCartney (1983), these children have few niches from which to pick when constructing their environments.

Even within a family, children's opportunities to create their own environments are limited. Children do not live alone; they live with parents and siblings who have different interests, goals, and patterns of behavior. Consider a family with two parents and two daughters who are planning their summer vacation. One daughter is interested in U.S. history and wants to visit Washington, D.C. The other daughter enjoys amusement parks and wants to go to Disney World. Which girl gets to create her own summer vacation environment and which does not?

The answer, in this hypothetical example, is neither. Instead of going to Disney World or to Washington, D.C., the girls' parents decide on a more relaxing vacation in a cottage on a lake. Their daughters, then, go swimming and boating rather than touring the White House or riding a roller coaster. In real life, too, parents exert considerable control over their children's environments; that is, parents decide which opportunities will and will not be available to their children (Baumrind, 1993).

Nevertheless, parents' influence is also limited. Children are born with genotypes that affect their development. Consequently, parents cannot mold their children into precisely the kind of adults they would most prefer. Although children are social beings who are influenced by their relationships, they are also unique individuals. Future research should lead to more detailed models of the processes by which children's genetic makeup and their social relationships jointly influence their development.

# SUMMARY

**The Biology of Heredity**
The principles of genetics explain why every child is unique, not exactly like his or her parents or anyone else. They also explain why every child resembles his or her parents.

**How the Genetic Code Is Stored and Duplicated**
The genetic code for the development of a child is carried in the child's DNA. The duplication of DNA normally occurs during a process of cell division called mitosis that results in the creation of new cells.

**Genes and Protein Synthesis**
DNA carries instructions for the production of proteins that form biological structures (e.g., bones, muscles) and regulate biological processes. Specific segments of DNA that control the production of particular proteins are called genes. A gene can also be defined as the unit of genetic inheritance.

**Mechanisms of Genetic Inheritance**
A normal human being has 46 chromosomes, including 22 pairs of autosomes and one pair of sex chromosomes. Chromosomes are scrambled and prepared for transmission from parents to children during meiosis. Conception occurs when a sperm from the father combines with an ovum from the mother to form a zygote.

**Genotypes, Phenotypes, and Abnormal Development**
Children's genetic makeup defines their genotype. Their observable characteristics define their phenotype. Errors during meiosis can lead to abnormalities in children's genotypes and, therefore, to abnormal development.

**Chromosomal Abnormalities**
Down syndrome is a serious disorder that results from the presence of three chromosomes of type 21. Disorders involving the sex chromosomes include Turner, Klinefelter, and fragile X syndromes.

**Gene Expression and Single-Gene Defects**
Genetic disorders can involve a single gene. The inheritance of these disorders often follows the principle of dominance. PKU is caused by an autosomal recessive gene. Huntington's disease is caused by an autosomal dominant gene. Other disorders such as hemophilia are caused by gene defects on the X chromosome, so they are called X-linked.

**Gene-Environment Interaction and Normal Human Variation**
Children's genotypes affect not only whether their characteristics are normal or abnormal. They also affect children's positions within the normal range.

**Models of Gene-Environment Interaction**
The reaction range is one way to describe the interplay between genes and environments during development. This interplay can also be described in terms of passive, evocative, and active genotype-environment correlations.

**Estimating Genetic Influence**
To estimate the heritability of specific characteristics, behavior-genetics researchers have compared the similarity of MZ and DZ twins. Other approaches include the comparison of biological and adopted siblings, and the comparison of children from different ethnic groups or populations.

**Behavior Genetics and the Effects of Parenting**
Some researchers have suggested that the shared family environment does not have powerful effects on children's development. Other researchers have gone further and argued that children largely create their own environments and that parents do little more than provide opportunities for children to express their genetic potential. This position has been challenged by researchers who argue that children's control over their environments is limited by their parents' control and by their position in society.

# SUGGESTED READINGS

Plomin, R., & McClearn, G. E. (Eds.). (1993). *Nature, nurture, and psychology.* Washington, DC: American Psychological Association. This volume includes chapters by many important behavior-genetics researchers. It also includes chapters by researchers who emphasize environmental influences on children's development. The authors consider genetic and environmental influences on cognitive abilities, personality, and psychopathology.

Rowe, D. C. (1994). *The limits of family influence: Genes, experience, and behavior.* New York: Guilford. Rowe covers some of the same ground as the authors in Plomin and McClearn, but he gives more attention to weaknesses in common arguments for environmental influence. As his title suggests, he focuses on the ambiguous evidence for parents' influence.

Shapiro, R. (1991). *The human blueprint: The race to unlock the secrets of our genetic script.* New York: St. Martin's Press. The Human Genome Project may be the largest international program of research in biology. The book is an accurate and clearly written account of the project. It also describes how the project became a high priority for research funding in the United States and elsewhere.

Watson, J. D. (1968). *The double helix.* New York: Atheneum. When first published, this book was a best-seller. It describes the discovery of the structure of the DNA molecule by James Watson and Francis Crick. This book is most interesting, though, because Watson does not focus only on the scientific work that led to that discovery. He also tells you about the scientists, including himself.

### Chapter Four

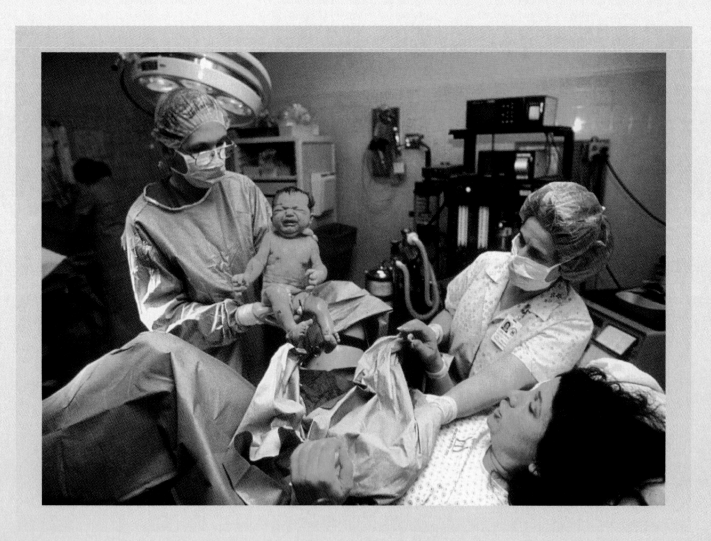

# PRENATAL DEVELOPMENT, BIRTH, AND THE NEWBORN

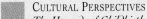

*T*he birth of a new child is an amazing, life-changing event for all concerned. In every culture, special preparations are made for a child's birth (Jordan, 1978; Mead & Newton, 1967). Every culture also has distinctive rules and customs for parents' behavior during the nine months of pregnancy that precede birth. Other rules and customs specify how a new baby should be treated. The following story illustrates how pregnancy and birth were arranged in one traditional culture. The story is based on ethnographic research done in northern India during the 1950s (Minturn & Hitchcock, 1963).

Mrs. Singh was pleased as she counted the days since her last menstrual period. It had been almost two months, so she assumed she must be pregnant. She already had one child, a daughter, so she knew what to expect. Actually, this would be her third pregnancy. Her second had ended in miscarriage. She hoped that this one would end normally, this time with a healthy boy, because her husband wanted a son to continue the family line.

The Singh family was part of the Rajput clan. They lived in Khalapur, a village with about 5,000 people. The Rajputs believed that their ancestors were warriors who had ruled India in ancient times. Now they were landowners and farmers whose fields lay outside the village on a fertile plain between the Ganges and Jumna Rivers. To the south, 90 miles away, was the city of Delhi. To the north were the Himalayas, their snow-covered peaks easily visible on clear days.

Mrs. Singh lived in the women's house of her extended family with her mother-in-law and the wives of her husband's two brothers. She told them about her pregnancy and accepted their congratulations. She told her husband, too, because they were expected to refrain from sexual intercourse during the pregnancy. He did not tell the other men in his family, because male relatives were not supposed to know when a woman was pregnant.

Throughout the pregnancy Mrs. Singh did her usual tasks. She made unleavened bread and other food for meals, wove and mended cotton clothing, and kept the courtyard clean. She changed her diet, refraining from pickles and other spicy foods, cold rice, and milk. She also developed a craving for mud and occasionally would eat some.

Mrs. Singh had first realized she was pregnant one day in July, during the heat and rain of the summer monsoon. Now it was March. The men were busy harvesting the winter crops and planting the spring crops. One morning after the men had left for the fields, she began to feel regular contractions of her uterus. She was in labor. She asked her sister-in-law to send for their midwife and then went to her room. Her mother-in-law placed a knife, a sickle, and a plowshare next to her bed.

By the time the midwife arrived, Mrs. Singh could feel the baby coming. She squatted on the floor, let the midwife take the baby as it came, and smiled when she saw it was a healthy and vigorous boy. She expelled the afterbirth, or placenta, a few minutes later. Then the midwife cut the umbilical cord with the knife. Next, the midwife rubbed the baby's body with flour and used her fingers to clean his eyes and nose. Finally, she buried the afterbirth in a rubbish heap and washed the baby.

To announce the boy's birth, Mrs. Singh's mother-in-law hired a man to beat a drum in front of their house. Soon afterward, women who were friends of Mrs. Singh came to sing special songs for the boy.

Some Rajput customs related to pregnancy and birth are distinctive to that culture. For example, not all cultures require women to refrain from sexual intercourse during pregnancy. In some cultures intercourse is encouraged, especially in early pregnancy (Mead & Newton, 1967).

In three important respects, however, pregnancy and birth are the same in northern India, the United States, and every other country in the world. First, the course of pregnancy is set by the biology of the human species, so it is the same universally. Chapter 3 examined the process of sexual reproduction up to the moment of conception, when a sperm and an ovum join to form a zygote. Roughly nine months of development separate the zygote from

The period from conception to birth is one of momentous changes. To an outsider, only the growth in the size of the baby is obvious. The mother notices much more about the development of her child. Even she, though, cannot really tell what her child will be like until the pregnancy is over and her baby is born.

the newborn infant. This period of *prenatal* (i.e., before birth) development is one of rapid and dramatic changes. Those changes are described in the first section of the chapter. The changes that parents experience during this period are also considered.

Second, people in all cultures recognize that pregnancies do not always progress normally. As Mrs. Singh knew, pregnancies sometimes end in miscarriage, or spontaneous abortion. Miscarriages can be caused by problems in the developing organism itself, problems with the uterus that shelters that organism, or problems in the environment outside the mother's body. These sources of potential problems are discussed in the second section of the chapter.

Third, pregnant women in most cultures try to reduce the hazards of pregnancy by changing their diet, their activities, or both (Mead & Newton, 1967). Mrs. Singh, for example, stopped eating pickles and other spicy foods. She also stopped drinking milk. During the 1950s, when the study of Rajput families was done, some Rajputs believed, mistakenly, that milk during pregnancy would make the baby grow too big (Minturn & Hitchcock, 1963).

Medical research has provided a vast amount of evidence about the real hazards of the prenatal period. Many of these hazards are under the parents' control. That is, parents can adjust their lives to reduce the risks of the prenatal period. This chapter describes many actions that parents can take to ensure that prenatal development proceeds normally.

The final section of the chapter deals with the birth process itself and the capabilities of the newborn. The long-term effects of birth complications such as prematurity and low birth weight are also examined. You will see that these complications do not always have lasting effects on children's development. With proper care, many children who have problems before or around the time of birth move back onto the normal track of development.

**TABLE 4.1** *The Three Periods of Prenatal Development*

| | LENGTH (MILLIMETERS) | WEIGHT (GRAMS) | DEVELOPMENTS |
|---|---|---|---|
| **The Germinal Period** | | | |
| Weeks 1–2 | 0.1 | < 1 | The zygote divides into a round mass of cells. About six days after conception, the mass of cells begins to implant in the uterus and connect with the mother's circulatory system. |
| **The Period of the Embryo** | | | |
| Weeks 3–4 | 5 | 1 | The germ disc at the center of the cell mass differentiates into the ectoderm, mesoderm, and endoderm. Then the spinal cord, jaws, brain, and limbs begin to form. Soon the heart starts beating. |
| Weeks 5–6 | 13 | 1 | The nose and other facial features become visible. The hands and feet become distinct, and the ovaries and testes start to develop. |
| Weeks 7–8 | 30–40 | 8 | The embryo becomes recognizably human. The brain divides into hemispheres and internal organs differentiate. The embryo starts to move independently. |
| **The Period of the Fetus** | | | |
| 3rd month | 100 | 45 | Body proportions become more like an infant's. The sex of the fetus is obvious. Muscles continue to develop and swallowing occurs. |
| 4th month | 200 | 200 | The fetus is so large and fetal movements are so strong that they can be felt by the mother. The fetus responds to lights, shows facial expressions, and develops fingerprints. |
| 5th–6th months | 300–350 | 800–1,000 | The fetus accumulates body fat and a skin covering called *vernix caseosa*. Fetal behavior becomes more regular, and the fetus reacts to loud sounds. |
| 7th–9th months | 400–500 | 1,600–3,400 | Fetal weight doubles during these months, as length increases and body fat accumulates. The skin becomes less wrinkled, and hair grows on the fetus's head. Brain development continues, and fetal hearing and memory are functional. |

*Sources:* Guttmacher & Kaiser, 1986; Moore & Persaud, 1993.

# FROM CONCEPTION TO BIRTH: INFANT AND PARENT PERSPECTIVES

Prenatal development is divided into three major periods. The *germinal period* begins at the moment of conception and extends for roughly two weeks afterward. The *period of the embryo* follows the germinal period and extends until two months after conception. The *period of the fetus* includes the remaining seven months of prenatal life. The distinctions between periods correspond to important changes in the structure of the developing organism. Those changes are outlined in table 4.1.

**germinal period**
*The earliest phase in prenatal development, the period from fertilization to two weeks after conception.*

## The Germinal Period

The term **germinal period** comes from the same root as the word *germinate*, which derives from the Latin word for *sprout* or *offshoot*. The term refers to the earliest phase in prenatal development,

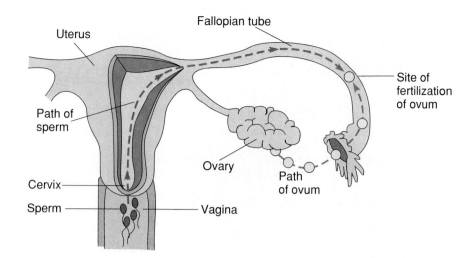

FIGURE 4.1

As an egg cell moves out of an ovary into the Fallopian tube, sperm cells move through the cervix and uterus on their way to meet it.

starting with conception. Because the fertilized cell formed by the union of a sperm and an ovum is called a zygote, another name for the germinal period is the *period of the zygote.*

Fertilization is a complex, precisely timed process. About halfway through a woman's menstrual cycle, a mature ovum bursts out of one of her ovaries and is drawn into a Fallopian tube (see figure 4.1). As it travels down the tube, it may be met by sperm released during sexual intercourse. During male orgasm, several hundred million sperm are released into the female vagina. Each sperm has a small, pointed head, which contains its genetic material, and a long tail that helps it swim in the vagina. Some sperm swim through the cervix and into the cervical canal and uterus. Only a small fraction of the original millions of sperm reach the Fallopian tube in which the ovum lies, and only a few hundred reach the ovum itself (Moore & Persaud, 1993).

The ovum is covered by a protective membrane that must be broken down before a sperm can enter. Many sperm cells surround the ovum, and each releases an enzyme that helps to dissolve the membrane. Only one sperm can enter and fuse its cell nucleus with that of the ovum. When fusion occurs, fertilization is complete—and a new life begins.

An ovum begins to deteriorate within 24 hours after it bursts from the ovary. Sperm have a longer life: They can survive for several days after intercourse. Therefore, fertilization is possible during only a few days each month. The highest probability of fertilization exists when sexual intercourse occurs either on the day when an ovum is released or on the day or two before ovulation (Wilcox, Weinberg, & Baird, 1995). Intercourse three to five days before ovulation can also result in fertilization of an ovum, but the probability is lower.

Several hours after the fusion of the nuclei from the sperm and ovum, the zygote begins to divide. In the process of mitosis, one cell becomes two. Then two cells become four, four become eight, and so on.

As noted in chapter 3, identical, or monozygotic (MZ), twins begin to develop if the zygote separates in two during these early cell divisions. If the zygote separates into three cells, identical triplets may develop. However, multiple births more commonly result from the release of multiple ova that are fertilized at about the same time. If two ova are fertilized by two sperm, fraternal, or dizygotic (DZ), twins start to develop. If three ova are released, fraternal triplets may be the result.

The next phases of development are similar regardless of whether the Fallopian tubes contain one or multiple zygotes. Repeated cell divisions change each zygote into a small round mass of cells. This mass continues to travel down the Fallopian tube and into the uterus.

About six days after conception, the mass of cells, now about .25 millimeters (1/100 of an inch) in diameter, settles on the lining of the uterus that will be its home for nearly nine months. The cell mass releases an enzyme that digests the cells of the uterus's lining. Then the entire cell mass lodges itself securely in a small hole within the lining. This process of **implantation** takes several days.

**implantation**
*During prenatal development, the process by which the small ball of cells that will become the embryo lodges itself in a hole in the lining of the uterus.*

FIGURE 4.2
A schematic diagram of the developing zygote near the end of the germinal period, around 12 days after conception. Notice the germ disc, the part that will gradually develop into the embryo and the fetus.

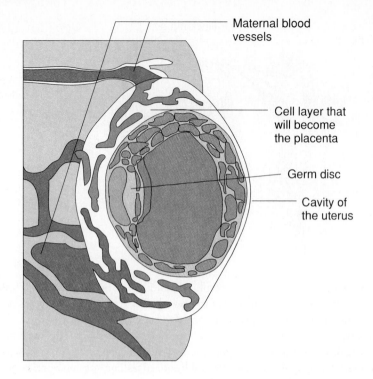

Maternal blood vessels

Cell layer that will become the placenta

Germ disc

Cavity of the uterus

**placenta**
*An organ that links the life-support systems of a pregnant woman and her embryo or fetus. It is attached both to the lining of the woman's uterus and to the umbilical cord that transfers oxygen and other substances to and from the embryo or fetus.*

**chorion**
*The outer of two membranes that surround the embryo or fetus.*

**amnion**
*The inner of two membranes that surround the embryo or fetus.*

**germ disc**
*The part of the cell mass during the germinal period of prenatal development that eventually becomes the fetus.*

After implantation, the mass of cells starts to link with the mother's blood vessels to obtain nourishment from the mother. In addition, the cell mass differentiates into several structures (see figure 4.2). The cells deepest in the uterine lining form blood vessels that ultimately will become the **placenta,** a critical element in a system connecting the developing organism to the mother. The placenta will allow the organism to receive nourishment from, and transfer waste products to, the mother's circulatory system. Other cells of the developing organism will differentiate to form an outer membrane called the **chorion** and an inner membrane called the **amnion.** As you recall from chapter 3, later in pregnancy physicians can use cells from the chorion or the fluid inside the amnion to judge the genetic makeup of the developing organism.

One of the smallest structures in the entire cell mass is the **germ disc,** shown in the center of figure 4.2. This disc will grow into the fetus. Notice how it is dwarfed, at this stage in development, by the surrounding protective structures. These structures provide the connection to the mother that will make development possible during the next eight months. If development proceeds normally, the germ disc will multiply thousands of times in size, becoming a fetus that fills almost the entire uterus.

Development does not always proceed normally. Between 20 and 45 percent of all fertilized eggs do not complete the germinal period and implant successfully (Moore & Persaud, 1993; Simpson, 1991). Abnormal development is most often caused by chromosomal abnormalities or lethal gene mutations in the zygote. In other words, genetic defects in the fertilized egg are a common reason for early miscarriage (Guttmacher & Kaiser, 1986).

Miscarriages also occur for other reasons. Sometimes the ball of cells begins to implant close to a large maternal blood vessel. As the cell mass digs into the lining of the uterus, the blood vessel may open and bleed, flushing out the cells. Then the blood vessel closes, just as in a typical menstrual period.

Most women are completely unaware of the problems during this period of pregnancy. Unless a woman has a pregnancy test shortly after conception occurs, she is not likely to guess that she is pregnant until more than two weeks have passed. Then she may realize that she has missed a menstrual period. If conception occurs but the zygote does not develop normally, her menstrual period will occur either on time or a few days late. If conception and implantation go smoothly, the missed menstrual period is likely to be—as it was for Mrs. Singh—the first signal that a baby is on the way.

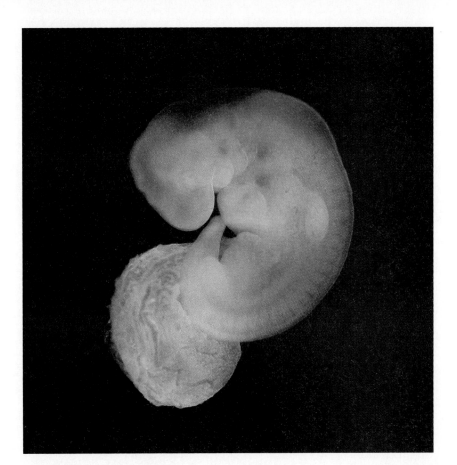

## The Period of the Embryo

The period of the embryo begins about 14 days after conception, when implantation is completed and the cells of the primitive germ disc begin to differentiate into layers. The word **embryo** comes from a Greek word meaning "something that grows in the body." The key feature of this definition, for our purposes, is that the "something" is at first not a recognizable human being. For the first few weeks of the embryonic period, the developing organism looks much like other mammals—even like other vertebrates such as fish and birds. Only near the end of the embryonic period does the embryo of human parents look distinctly human.

During the third week of life, the primitive germ disc differentiates into three layers. The outer layer, or *ectoderm* (which is, literally, "outside skin" in Greek), will gradually develop into the skin, hair, nails, and nervous system of the infant. The inner layer, or *endoderm* (which is, literally, "inside skin," in Greek), will gradually develop into the lungs, liver, glands, stomach, and other parts of the digestive system. A middle layer, or *mesoderm* (literally, "middle skin"), will become the muscles, the skeleton, and the blood, urinary, and reproductive systems.

Within days after the differentiation into layers, the ectoderm folds over to form a neural tube that will develop into the spinal cord. The "head" end of the tube expands, and the head begins to take shape. A primitive heart develops and starts beating by the beginning of the fourth week after fertilization.

A week later, the embryo is about 5 millimeters (⅕ inch) long (Miller & Persaud, 1993). Figure 4.3 shows that an embryo at this stage has a large, distinct head and a red, almost Valentine-shaped heart. The sockets for the eyes and ears are visible; also visible are two gill arches, below the largest part of the head, that all vertebrates have at this stage of prenatal development. The first arch will develop into the lower and upper jaws. The other arch will later disappear. At the opposite end of the body is a primitive tail, which covers the end of the spinal cord. It will disappear later, when the legs develop.

**embryo**
*The name given to the developing human from two to eight weeks after conception.*

FIGURE 4.4

A human fetus at 8 weeks of age. At this point, the beginning of the fetal period, the developing organism has begun to take on human form.

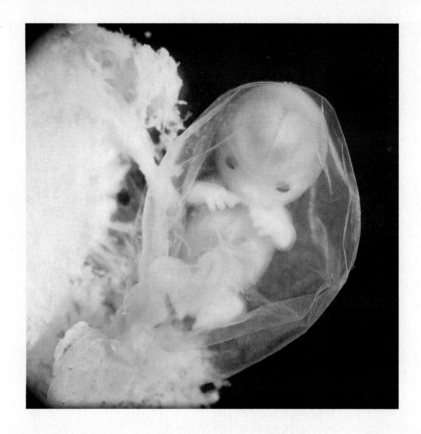

**cephalocaudal principle**
*The principle that development generally proceeds from the head to the foot. Body parts closer to the head develop earlier than those closer to the feet.*

**proximodistal principle**
*The principle that development usually proceeds from the center of the body outward. In particular, the arms develop earlier than the hands and fingers.*

During this stage the head is more developed than the rest of the body. Development generally proceeds from head to foot (or tail, as the case may be). This is known as the **cephalocaudal principle** of development, from the Greek word for head (*kephalos*) and the Latin word for tail (*cauda*).

In addition, the embryo at this stage has buds that will become arms and legs but no sign of hands or feet. This contrast illustrates another principle: Development usually progresses from the center of the body outward. This is known as the **proximodistal principle,** from the Latin words for near and distant. The cephalocaudal and proximodistal principles apply not only to the development of body structures before birth but also (as you will see in chapter 5) to the development of motor control after birth.

In the fifth and sixth weeks after fertilization, the embryo grows to a length of 13 millimeters (about ½ inch). Gradually, the jaws, nose, and other facial features become visible. The hands and feet become distinct from the arms and legs, and fingers and toes begin to appear. As the cephalocaudal principle implies, the hands develop more rapidly than the feet. Also, the cells that will become the ovaries of a female or the testes of a male begin to develop during these weeks. Biochemical signals from the DNA later in the embryonic period will determine whether the embryo becomes male or female.

In the seventh and eighth weeks, the embryo reaches 30 to 40 millimeters (1 to 1½ inches) in length but weighs less than 8 grams (less than a third of an ounce). All remaining body structures and organs begin to take shape.

By the end of the eighth week the face is completely formed, and the brain is divided into two hemispheres (see figure 4.4). Arms, hands, legs, and feet have all started to take human form. The liver, lungs, and other internal organs have begun to differentiate. These are only the first phases in the development of these structures and organs, though. They will not be completely developed until weeks or months later.

The signals for sex differentiation are also transmitted during the seventh and eighth weeks, so a trained examiner can soon tell whether this new human will be a boy or a girl. In addition, the embryo becomes able to move independently and exercise the developing muscles.

At this stage the mother does not notice the movements of the embryo because they are slight and are muffled by the amniotic fluid. Still, most mothers are well aware that they are pregnant. Mothers often feel unusually tired during these first two months, and often suffer from abdominal discomfort. People commonly refer to this discomfort as "morning sickness," although not all women feel the greatest discomfort in the morning. At least 30 percent of women have little discomfort at all (Cruikshank & Hays, 1991; Holt, 1988).

By contrast, a few women feel uncomfortable all day long and even have bouts of vomiting. Morning sickness usually overlaps with the embryonic period, beginning about two weeks after conception and ending six to eight weeks later. Fortunately, morning sickness does not often lead to more serious problems of weight loss or nutritional deficiencies.

For the mother, the embryonic period may be a time of heightened concern because miscarriages are relatively common during this phase of pregnancy. About 15 percent of pregnancies that reach the stage of successful implantation end in miscarriage, and these miscarriages usually occur during the embryonic period (Simpson, 1991). Defects in the embryo cause most miscarriages; maternal disease or problems with the uterus cause the remainder (Guttmacher & Kaiser, 1986). However, mothers who have one miscarriage do not have a high probability of a second one. The probability increases only after two or more miscarriages.

There is still another reason for special concern during the embryonic period, although some mothers are unaware of it. The developing organism is especially sensitive to harmful environmental influences during this period, because so many body structures and organs are forming. As you will see shortly, hazards in the environment can disrupt development, leading to misshapen or absent limbs, defects in the heart or other organs, and abnormalities in brain development.

## The Period of the Fetus

After eight weeks, the developing human gets a new name, the **fetus.** *Fetus* comes from the Latin word for "offspring," but it has a more specific meaning in this context. It refers to the developing organism once it has taken human form. Eight weeks after conception, the fetus looks like a human being. The changes that occur in the next seven months are more subtle than those in the previous two months, but they are not trivial. For optimal development, humans need these seven months in the supportive environment of the mother's uterus.

Early in the fetal period, the tissues of the chorion that surround the fetus are transformed into a fully functioning placenta. A membrane in the placenta separates the circulatory system of the fetus from that of the mother. However, many substances can pass through this membrane and so move from the mother's blood to the fetal blood supply.

The placenta is connected to the fetus itself by the **umbilical cord,** which is 1 to 2 centimeters in diameter and about 60 centimeters (2 feet) long. Two arteries inside the cord carry blood low in oxygen from the fetus to the placenta. One vein carries blood rich in oxygen back to the fetus.

The placenta and umbilical cord are a multifaceted life-support system for the fetus. These organs have three major functions (Moore & Persaud, 1993). First, as mentioned earlier, they allow for the transfer of substances necessary for fetal health. These substances include oxygen and other gases, vitamins, and antibodies that give the fetus immunity to some diseases such as measles. Second, the placenta itself produces fats and carbohydrates that provide nutrients and energy for the fetus. Third, tissues in the placenta synthesize hormones that ensure normal prenatal growth and the maintenance of a pregnancy.

Prenatal growth in length and weight is dramatic during the fetal period. During the third month, the length of the fetus triples and its weight increases more than five times. But even at the end of that month, an average fetus is only about 100 millimeters (4 inches) long; its weight is only about 45 grams (less than 2 ounces).

During the third month the body proportions of the fetus also begin to approach those of an infant (Miller & Persaud, 1993). The head, which earlier in the prenatal period was more than half the total body length, takes up a smaller proportion of body length as the arms and legs extend (see figure 4.5). In addition, the development of the external sex organs continues. Whether this new being will be a boy or a girl becomes increasingly obvious.

**fetus**
*The name of the developing human from eight weeks after conception, when it has begun to take human form, until birth.*

**umbilical cord**
*A long cord containing two arteries and one vein that carries oxygen, nutrients, and other substances between the placenta and the fetus.*

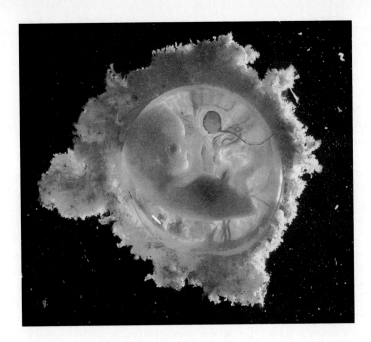

**FIGURE 4.5**
A human fetus at the beginning
of the fourth month, floating in
the amniotic fluid and
surrounded by the amnion and
chorion.

**vernix caseosa**
*A cheesy coating of dead cells and oils
that protects the skin of a fetus from
chapping in the amniotic fluid.*

Muscles continue their exercise during the third month: Legs kick, arms bend, and fingers grasp. All this movement is pure reflex, because the brain has not developed sufficiently to control it. The infant may also swallow amniotic fluid and release it as urine.

With the start of the fourth month, the mother enters her second trimester, that is, the second third of pregnancy. She is likely to feel better during this trimester than during the first one, because morning sickness is less common. In addition, during the fourth month or shortly afterward, mothers usually start to feel the movements of the fetus. The fetus now fills enough of the uterus so that its pushes and kicks are noticeable. The fetus also begins to respond to stimulation. In particular, it will move away if a bright light is directed at the mother's abdomen (Snow, 1989).

During the fifth and sixth months, the fetus accumulates body fat that will provide nutritional reserves and aid in temperature regulation after birth. The embryo who weighed less than 1 gram a month after conception becomes a fetus who weighs as much as 1,000 grams (2.2 pounds) five months later. The skin acquires a covering called **vernix caseosa,** which means "cheesy varnish" in Latin. This coating is composed of dead cells and oils that protects the fetus's skin from chapping in the amniotic fluid.

During these months the behavior of the fetus becomes more regular and coordinated. Often, the fetus will have predictable cycles of waking or activity and sleeping or rest. Body movements may even show recognizable patterns. With special photographic techniques, researchers once took a snapshot of a fetus sucking its thumb (figure 4.6).

For the mother, the second trimester is often the most enjoyable period in pregnancy. Morning sickness usually ends, although she still needs to adjust to her changing body. More important, the mother- and father-to-be learn from their doctor that they have passed the peak period for miscarriages. If they have gone through genetic counseling and taken advantage of techniques for prenatal diagnosis (as discussed in chapter 3), they may have information that the fetus is free from many genetic defects. Also, their ability to feel the fetal movement and hear the baby's heartbeat through a stethoscope is proof that "there really is a baby in there!"

During the third trimester, the seventh to ninth months of pregnancy, the fetus continues to grow in length and in weight. By the end of the ninth month, the typical fetus weighs about 3,400 grams (7.5 pounds) and is about 500 millimeters (or 20 inches) long. Additional body fat beneath the skin makes it less wrinkled than before and changes its skin color from red to white or bluish-pink.

Brain development continues steadily throughout the third trimester. As a result, more behavioral systems begin to operate normally. The lungs begin to function, and the fetus may make rhythmic chest movements that mimic breathing. In addition, fetal hearing is so well developed that the fetus can learn about common sounds and about human speech.

In one fascinating study (DeCasper & Spence, 1986), mothers were asked to read children's stories like Dr. Seuss's *The Cat in the Hat* aloud each day during the last six weeks of their pregnancy. Two days after birth, their newborns were taken to a hospital nursery where they were fitted with earphones and given a pacifier to suck.

Most newborns suck in bursts—several sucks followed by a pause, then another burst of sucks. Newborns can change the interval between bursts of sucks in response to stimulation. For this experiment, some infants who *decreased* their interval between sucks were reinforced by hearing the story their mothers had read before they were born. Other infants were reinforced by hearing that story if they *increased* the interval between sucks. If infants did not alter their sucking pattern, they heard a novel story that their mothers had never read aloud.

As the researchers expected, the newborn infants changed their sucking pattern so that they more often heard the story that their mother had read aloud while pregnant. The change in the newborns' behavior shows not only that they had heard the story but also that they remembered it. In other words, both their hearing and their memory were functional during their last months of prenatal development.

For parents-to-be, the third trimester is usually a time of learning. Many parents attend childbirth classes that describe the birth experience from the viewpoints of the baby, the mother, and the father. These classes often include information about the care of a new baby and the preparations that new parents should make for a baby. Such classes can diminish anxiety and give groups of expectant parents a chance to compare notes with one another (Holt, 1988). In this way, the classes can help first-time parents adjust to the new social roles, as father and mother, that they will have once their child is born.

Mothers often enjoy the third trimester less than the second. As the fetus gains weight and takes up more space, the mother usually becomes tired more easily and quickly. The fetus sometimes chooses to be most active when the mother is at rest, and so disturbs her sleep. In

addition, as the mother's uterus grows, it squeezes her other internal organs and may give her heartburn or other abdominal discomfort.

A mother's discomfort often decreases in the ninth month, because the uterus and fetus move down into the pelvis, away from the stomach. This movement typically occurs a few weeks before the baby's birth. It is a welcome signal to the mother that her pregnancy will soon be over.

# ENVIRONMENTAL INFLUENCES ON PRENATAL DEVELOPMENT

How does the environment outside the mother's uterus influence prenatal development? You might think that the uterus is a perfectly safe place for a growing organism. While floating in the amniotic fluid, the embryo or fetus seems protected from extremes in temperature, rough jolts, or other disturbances in the outside environment. For a long time, people also believed that the growing organism was protected from harmful substances that the mother ate or drank.

Many unhappy accidents of nature have proved that these optimistic assumptions about prenatal development are wrong. Scientists now know that the outside environment has an enormous effect on prenatal development. Almost anything that the mother eats or drinks can affect the embryo or fetus because most substances can pass through the placenta in one way or another. Prenatal development can also be affected by the mother's illnesses and the environmental hazards to which she is exposed.

**teratogens**
*Known causes of birth defects.*

**teratology**
*The field of study concerned with the causes and distribution of birth defects.*

Environmental influences are most obvious and most significant when they lead to birth defects. Known causes of birth defects are called **teratogens.** The field of study that focuses on the causes and distribution of birth defects is called **teratology.**

Teratogens are especially alarming because they are not always predictable. Substances that are harmless or even beneficial to an adult can have disastrous effects on a developing organism. Because of publicity about teratogens, the idea that the uterus is a perfectly safe environment has been replaced, in the minds of many prospective parents, by the idea that it is an especially vulnerable environment. These parents worry that the foods or medicines thought safe today will be shown tomorrow to cause birth defects.

This concern is partly justified. In recent decades, researchers have identified many common substances that can act as teratogens. As a result, doctors are cautious in prescribing any medicine to pregnant women. They also restrict the diet of pregnant women more than in the past.

Researchers have also learned more about how teratogens affect a developing organism. The major findings of the research can be stated as principles of environmental influence on prenatal development.

## Principles of Environmental Influence

Seven principles of environmental influence are consistent with the evidence from decades of research (Kopp, 1994; Sadler & Hunter, 1994; Vorhees & Mollnow, 1987).

1. *The placenta is not an effective barrier against harmful substances.* Most substances that enter the mother's bloodstream can pass into the bloodstream of the developing embryo or fetus through the placenta. Doctors originally thought that the placenta was a barrier against harmful substances because the blood of the mother and her developing child are separated and usually do not mix. However, small molecules in the mother's blood vessels can move through the placenta into the blood vessels of the embryo or fetus. Large molecules can be broken down on the mother's side of the placenta, pass into the fetal blood vessels, and recombine on that side. Therefore, the placenta can transfer not only oxygen, carbohydrates, and healthful antibodies from the mother to the fetus. It also can transfer viruses, alcohol, and harmful drugs or drug by-products.

2. *Teratogens have their greatest effects on developing structures.* The parts of a developing organism that are undergoing structural change are most susceptible to environmental influence and potential damage. Remember that the development of basic structures and organs occurs mostly during the period of the embryo, from roughly 2 to 8 weeks of age. As figure 4.7 shows, teratogens often have their greatest effect during this period. Therefore, the period of the embryo is a **critical period** for the development of many bodily structures and organs. The critical period for any specific part of a developing organism is the time when that part is affected by environmental influences that have little or no effect at other times. For example, the membrane between the ventricles of the heart is strongly affected by teratogens between the 3rd and 6th weeks after conception but not earlier or later (Lau & Kavlock, 1994). Therefore, those weeks define the critical period for the development of that membrane.

Some parts of the developing organism are always susceptible to teratogens but are more strongly affected at some times than at others. These times define **sensitive periods** in development (Bornstein, 1987). Figure 4.7 shows, for example, that the development of the brain (or central nervous system) can be affected by teratogens throughout the prenatal period. In the next chapter, you will learn that brain development can be negatively affected by environmental hazards even after birth. However, environmental influences are especially strong during the 3rd to 16th weeks of prenatal life. These weeks define a sensitive period for brain development.

The critical or sensitive periods for most bodily structures and organs fall into what, from the mother's perspective, is the first trimester of pregnancy. But as mentioned earlier, most mothers are not aware that they are pregnant until several weeks into the first trimester. Thus a mother may eat or drink something that harms the developing organism in her uterus without knowing that she was taking any risk. To prevent such harm, doctors now advise women to avoid all substances that could cause birth defects when any chance exists that they are pregnant or could become pregnant.

3. *The genotype of the mother and of her developing organism affect susceptibility to specific teratogens.* Not all infants who are exposed prenatally to teratogens have birth defects. The variations in outcomes partly explain why determining the causes of birth defects is so difficult. About 25 percent of birth defects can be attributed to genetic abnormalities like those examined in chapter 3. Perhaps another 10 percent can be attributed to specific teratogens, leaving about 65 percent due to unknown causes (Mortensen, Sever, & Oakley, 1991).

Many birth defects whose causes are unknown are likely to reflect the combination of a particular genotype with a particular environmental influence (Kolata, 1995). In other words, they illustrate the genotype-environment interactions discussed in the previous chapter. With growing knowledge about the human gene and its functioning, these combinations should become easier to identify.

One combination involves the mother's genotype and her diet (Mills et al., 1995). Some women whose diets are deficient in folic acid, a B vitamin found especially in fresh fruits and vegetables, bear infants with serious defects of the brain and spinal cord. However, other women with equally poor diets have normal infants.

The brain and spinal-cord defects are especially likely among mothers who have a gene that makes normal metabolism of common foods impossible without high levels of folic acid. If a mother has that specific gene, she must eat foods high in folic acid to avoid transferring toxic amounts of a specific amino acid to her fetus. In short, normal fetal development depends on an interaction between the mother's genotype and her nutrition.

Another illustration of this principle involves not the mother's genotype but that of her fetus. One category of birth defects involves a cleft palate, very small fingers and nails, a small head circumference, and mild mental retardation (Niebyl, 1991; Rutledge, 1994). This syndrome is found in fewer than 10 percent of infants whose mothers take the anticonvulsant phenytoin (also called Dilantin) during pregnancy. Infants show the syndrome if they lack an enzyme that breaks down one of the derivatives of phenytoin. Infants who have the genes necessary for production of that enzyme do not show the syndrome even if their mothers take phenytoin while pregnant.

**critical period**
*A time when a specific part of a developing organism is affected by environmental influences that have little or no effect at other times.*

**sensitive periods**
*A time interval, usually early in development, during which organisms are strongly affected by experiences that have weaker effects at other periods.*

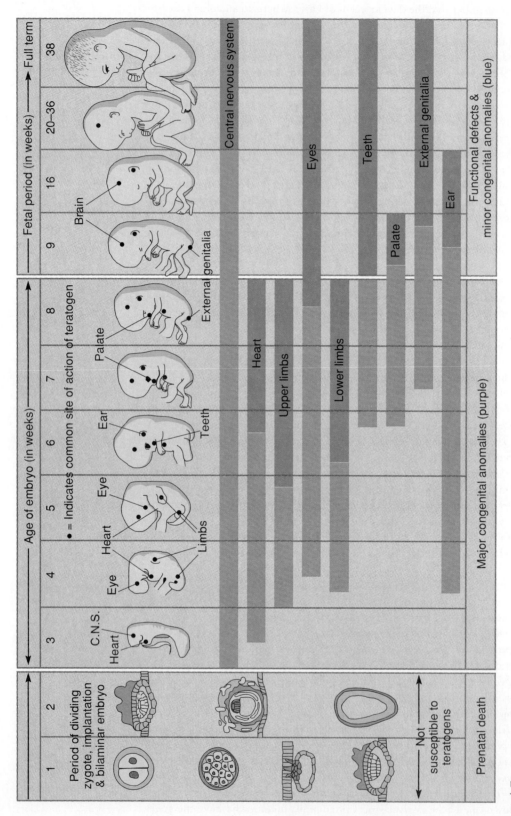

## FIGURE 4.7

A schematic illustration of the critical periods in human development. During the first two weeks, the developing organism has little susceptibility to teratogens. During those weeks, a substance either damages all or most cells, causing prenatal death, or damages only a few cells, allowing the embryo to recover without developing defects. The blue bars for later weeks indicate the most sensitive periods in the development of specific bodily parts and organs. Purple bars indicate less sensitive periods. (From Moore & Persaud, 1993.)

4. *The most sensitive measures of teratogen effects usually are behavioral rather than structural.* The effects of teratogens are most obvious when they produce structural deformities, so doctors and researchers immediately look for evidence of teratogens when newborn infants have deformed limbs, heads, or internal organs. But not all birth defects are so obvious. Some newborns who were prenatally exposed to teratogens are physically normal but display abnormal behavior. This pattern occurs, as you will see, in newborns whose mothers smoke cigarettes.

Many teratogens that have measurable effects on the behavior of a newborn can affect the development of bodily structures as well. With these teratogens, behavioral measures of prenatal damage usually are more sensitive. In other words, a fetus exposed to a small amount of the teratogen may have no noticeable structural deformities but still show behavioral impairments. For this reason, scientists who are evaluating the effects of specific substances on prenatal development pay attention both to bodily structures and to behavioral functioning.

5. *Greater doses of teratogens have greater effects.* Larger amounts of harmful substances have more negative effects on infants. This principle may seem self-evident, but its implications are important. For any specific teratogen, there should be a dose that has no noticeable effect on the developing organism. Determining this dose is often useful because some substances that are harmful in large doses may be beneficial to the mother in small doses. Examples include medicinal drugs like aspirin.

The principle also implies that a single exposure to a low dose of a drug will have less effect than repeated exposures. For example, you will read later that alcohol use by pregnant women can have extremely damaging effects on the developing fetus. Does this mean that a baby will be deformed if his or her mother has just one glass of wine during pregnancy? Most doctors would say no (Guttmacher & Kaiser, 1986). Alcohol is most harmful when a pregnant woman drinks frequently and heavily.

On the other hand, determining the "no-effect" level of a teratogen is difficult. Therefore, doctors usually recommend that pregnant women avoid all use of substances such as alcohol that are harmful in large doses, unless there are definite medical reasons for their use.

6. *The effects of teratogens may not be obvious at birth.* Some environmental influences on prenatal development are subtle. The damage resulting from small doses of certain teratogens may not be detected until an infant is a few weeks or months old—sometimes not even until a child enters school (Kopp, 1994). A few teratogens have effects that are not obvious until the children have reached adulthood and are ready to raise their own children.

This principle has the frightening implication that parents must wait years to find out whether their children are biologically normal. Fortunately, the principle focuses on the exceptional cases. The effects of most teratogens can be seen at birth or shortly after. Although some aspects of development are difficult to measure sensitively at birth, researchers are continuing to devise more sensitive measures of infants' characteristics. With these measures, early detection and treatment of developmental problems is more often possible.

7. *The long-term effects of many teratogens depend on postnatal care.* This principle is more optimistic than the previous one. Parents and other adults can often take steps to correct birth defects or reduce their negative consequences. Many physical deformities caused by teratogens can be surgically corrected. Many behavioral problems can be reduced or eliminated by responsive parenting or more specific interventions.

Sameroff and Chandler (1975) stated this principle, in its most general form, as a key assumption of their **transactional approach.** They proposed that children's development depends on the transactions between children and their environments. The contributions of children to these transactions depend on their biological and psychological makeup. For example, the transactions will be affected by any structural or behavioral defects and any developmental strengths that the children have at birth.

The contributions of forces in the environment to these transactions are many. They include the social interactions of the children with parents, siblings, peers, and other people. They also include the features of the physical environment in which the children are raised.

**transactional approach**
*A theoretical perspective that assumes children's development depends on the transactions (or interchanges) between the children and their environments. These transactions depend jointly on the children's characteristics and the characteristics of their environments.*

This child has deformed arms because his mother took the drug thalidomide during her pregnancy. By contrast, his legs and feet are normal. Children showed this pattern when their mothers took thalidomide during the fourth week after conception, when their arms were forming. The fourth week is, then, within the critical period for the development of the upper limbs.

**thalidomide**
*A drug that is a mild sedative for adults, but that causes severe birth defects if taken by pregnant women during the first trimester of pregnancy.*

Being reared in a supportive environment can have powerful effects on children who were exposed to teratogens prenatally. In such an environment, parents and other adults encourage the children's drives to master developmental tasks like learning to walk and learning to talk. This support and encouragement cannot reverse all negative effects of all teratogens. However, the environment after birth can help children with birth defects move in the direction of normal development.

Of course, this principle of environmental influence has a dark side. Not all children with prenatal teratogen exposure are raised in a supportive environment. When their parents are unconcerned, unresponsive, or unable to give them the encouragement they need, these children are likely to show continued problems that may even increase over time.

## Types of Teratogens and Their Effects

Many things in the environment outside a mother's womb can negatively affect the development of her embryo or fetus. As you read about all the types of teratogens, you could get the impression that most newborns have been exposed to some teratogens and so have some birth defects.

Fortunately, that's not true. Nearly all mothers who have regular prenatal care and uneventful pregnancies bear infants who are completely normal. To help you maintain a balanced perspective, this section includes information about the status of all teratogens. Also included is information about several substances that are harmless or even beneficial to pregnant women and their children.

Table 4.2 outlines four major types of teratogens: (1) medicines given to the mother, (2) illnesses that the mother has during pregnancy, (3) "social" drugs such as cocaine and alcohol, and (4) external influences such as radiation. Keep this framework in mind as you read about specific teratogens.

### Medical Drugs

Thousands of medical drugs are available to treat the range of illnesses, infections, and injuries experienced by humans. Many writers imply that the vast majority of these drugs are unsafe for pregnant women. Often, however, no careful testing has been done to show whether the drugs are safe or not, and some women may be avoiding drugs that could greatly improve their health (Holmes, 1994; Rubin, 1995). Still, being cautious is wise, because some drugs taken during pregnancy have disastrous effects on a developing embryo or fetus.

*Thalidomide* Pregnancy can be an uncomfortable period for women, involving nausea, fatigue, and difficulty in sleeping. Unfortunately, the medicines used to relieve these symptoms, even if safe for a woman, can be dangerous to an embryo or fetus.

In the early 1960s, some pregnant women in Europe began to take a new drug called **thalidomide.** The drug was a mild sedative that helped pregnant women get a peaceful night's sleep. But within a few months, doctors discovered that thalidomide also was a powerful teratogen. Women who took the drug during the first trimester of pregnancy often gave birth to infants with serious defects. The infants had deformed arms, legs, hands, feet, or facial features. Their specific deformities depended on exactly when their mothers had used thalidomide.

Consider a mother who had taken the drug in the seventh week after her last menstrual period. This would have been about three weeks into the period of the embryo, because conception is most probable about two weeks after a menstrual period. Her infant was likely to have had either no legs or deformed legs (Mortensen et al., 1991). If she had waited to take thalidomide until after the second month of pregnancy, her infant would probably not have had any structural abnormalities. By that time, most of her infant's basic bodily structures would have already formed. The close match between when mothers took thalidomide and which birth defects their infants showed is strong evidence for the principle that teratogens affect developing structures most.

## TABLE 4.2    *Examples of Various Types of Teratogens*

| TYPES | POSSIBLE BIRTH DEFECTS, AND STATUS |
|---|---|
| **Medical Drugs** | |
| Thalidomide | Causes deformities of arms, legs, hands, feet, fingers, and toes. Facial features may also be deformed. Heart and kidney defects are possible, and low IQs are typical. This drug is no longer prescribed for pregnant women. |
| Diethylstilbesterol (DES) | In women can cause abnormalities of the cervix, increased risk of one type of vaginal and cervical cancer, and difficulties in pregnancy. In men can cause minor abnormalities of the genital tract. Drug is no longer used. |
| Aspirin | Not a cause of birth defects but can increase bleeding by the fetus and the mother if normal doses are taken close to birth. Low doses can be useful in treatment of preeclampsia. Other pain relievers are safer. |
| Tetracycline | Not a cause of major deformities but can slow bone growth during the first trimester and put a yellow stain on teeth if taken during the second and third trimesters. Not recommended during pregnancy. |
| **Maternal Illnesses** | |
| Syphilis | Can cause deafness, abnormal teeth, bones, and facial features; liver damage, and brain damage leading to mental retardation. Fetal death is also likely. Incidence is increasing in the United States. |
| Herpes simplex | Can cause blindness, hearing loss, small head circumference, and mental retardation. Early infection can lead to fetal death; late infection can lead to premature birth. About 1 in 7,500 infants may be infected during labor and delivery. |
| Rubella (German measles) | Can cause deafness, eye cataracts, heart defects, small head circumference, and mental retardation. Prenatal risk can be avoided by vaccination. |
| HIV (Human Immunodeficiency Virus) | The virus that causes AIDS; can cause deformities of the head and face, frequent infections, and a high death rate. Several thousand cases in the United States and millions in the rest of the world. |
| **"Social" Drugs** | |
| Heroin | Causes addiction at birth, with withdrawal symptoms such as tremors and irritability. Few effects on growth or on mental and motor development by the preschool years. |
| Cocaine | May cause premature separation of the placenta, heart defects, and retarded motor and mental development, but not all studies show these effects. |
| Marijuana | Not a cause of structural deformities but may be linked to retarded prenatal growth and poor behavioral control at birth. Most commonly used illegal drug. |
| Alcohol | Can cause fetal alcohol syndrome, which includes facial abnormalities including a thin upper lip, small nose, and flattened face. Other symptoms are retarded prenatal growth, irritability, hyperactivity, and mental retardation. |
| Tobacco | Can cause miscarriage and low birth weight. Also linked to increased excitability in infants and asthma in children. Effects decrease as children get older. |
| Caffeine | No consistent evidence of negative effects, but high use may lower infants' birth weights, so avoiding it during pregnancy is prudent. |
| **Other Environmental Hazards** | |
| Radiation | In large doses, can cause abnormal brain development, skeletal deformities, and mental retardation. Medicinal use (e.g., in X rays) is not a source of concern. |
| Mercury | Can cause severe congenital deformities and mental retardation with cerebral palsy. Low doses resulting from maternal diets high in contaminated fish can delay motor and mental development. |
| PCBs | Can reduce birth weight and affect memory and verbal ability in childhood. These chemicals are concentrated in fish found in some lakes. |
| Lead | Can lead to lower birth rates and premature birth. Also associated with delayed intellectual development in childhood. |

*Sources:* Bellinger & Needleman, 1994; Day, Richardson, & McGauhey, 1994; Freij & Sever, 1988; Isada & Grossman, 1991; Moore & Persaud, 1993; Wendel, 1988.

Other research showed that thalidomide affected behavior as well as bodily structures (Vorhees & Mollnow, 1987). When tested in childhood, many thalidomide babies had subnormal IQ scores, which illustrates the principle that teratogens can affect both physical and psychological development.

In retrospect, the effects of thalidomide on intellectual development are not surprising. After all, the drug was a sedative intended to influence brain functioning. Unfortunately for many women and their infants, medical researchers discovered too late that the drug has catastrophic effects on a developing brain.

Infants in the United States were not affected by thalidomide because the drug was never approved for use in the United States. It was taken off the market in 1961, after doctors discovered its harmful effects, so this teratogen is not a source of birth defects today. Moreover, no other known teratogen produces the terrible arm and leg deformities found in infants prenatally exposed to thalidomide (Moore & Persaud, 1993).

*DES (diethylstilbesterol)*   From the 1940s through the 1960s, many doctors prescribed **diethylstilbesterol,** or **DES,** for pregnant women who had diabetes or who had suffered several previous miscarriages. The doctors thought this drug, an artificial form of the natural hormone estrogen, would increase the women's chances of having a successful pregnancy (Guttmacher & Kaiser, 1986). Not until many years later did they learn that the drug has teratogenic effects.

The delay occurred because no serious effects were apparent until the children of the women who took the drug reached adolescence. Then doctors noticed that the daughters of these women had an above-average risk of developing a special kind of vaginal and cervical cancer. By tracing medical records, the doctors linked this cancer to their mothers' use of DES during pregnancy.

Further research showed other negative effects of DES on daughters who did not develop cancer. When the daughters reached adulthood, they were more likely than other women to have difficulties in pregnancy themselves. In particular, they experienced more miscarriages and premature births than normal. The sons of mothers who took DES were not as severely affected as the daughters, but they showed minor physical abnormalities of the genital tract.

DES is the best example of the principle that the effects of teratogens are not always obvious at birth. This example can be viewed more optimistically, though. DES is the only important teratogen now known to have such delayed effects, and only a small fraction of the daughters of women who took DES experienced those effects. Only about 1 in 1,000 of these daughters developed the special type of vaginal and cervical cancer (Briggs, Freeman, & Yaffe, 1994).

In addition, although DES daughters have more difficulty bearing children, they finally succeed about as often as do women whose mothers did not use DES (Kolata, 1989). These data suggest that DES is not a powerful teratogen. And because it has not been prescribed for decades, it is not a current cause of birth defects.

*Aspirin*   What about the over-the-counter, nonprescription drugs? Are they safe during pregnancy? The most controversial nonprescription drug is aspirin. Repeated studies have not shown that normal doses of aspirin cause birth defects (Barr et al., 1990; Miller & Persaud, 1993; Mortensen et al., 1991), but continuous or excessive use may be harmful (Briggs et al., 1994).

Moreover, large doses of aspirin late in pregnancy can contribute to excessive bleeding in premature infants. Mothers also bleed more during childbirth if they have taken aspirin recently (Guttmacher & Kaiser, 1986; Mortensen et al., 1991). These problems do not arise with other pain relievers such as acetaminophen (Tylenol), so they are preferable to aspirin under most conditions (Mortensen et al., 1991).

Some women, however, benefit from taking small doses of aspirin during pregnancy. About 5 percent of women experience **preeclampsia** during their first pregnancy. This syndrome involves elevated blood pressure, swelling of the hands and feet, and the abnormal excretion of protein in the urine. Preeclampsia is less likely if women take a very low dose of

**diethylstilbesterol (DES)**
*A drug once given to pregnant women to decrease the risk of spontaneous abortions that, unfortunately, increased the risk their adolescent daughters would develop a specific type of vaginal and cervical cancer.*

**preeclampsia**
*A syndrome of pregnancy that involves elevated blood pressure, swelling of the hands and feet, and the abnormal excretion of protein into the urine.*

aspirin—60 mg or about ⅙ of a regular aspirin tablet—daily after their first trimester (Hauth et al., 1993; Sibai et al., 1993). Moreover, such a low dose neither increases the rate of birth defects nor causes serious complications during pregnancy and delivery.

*Antibiotics and Other "Good" Drugs*    Many medical drugs either have no negative effects on the developing embryo and fetus or have minor effects. Certain antibiotics, including penicillin, have not been shown to have any negative effects when used during pregnancy.

The example of antibiotics raises an important issue about medical drugs. Some writers imply that pregnant women can only ensure the safety of their fetus by avoiding all drugs. This view is shortsighted and may be dangerous. Occasionally, women develop serious illnesses in pregnancy, and they (along with their doctor) must weigh the risk to their life against known risks to prenatal development (Rubin, 1995).

Fortunately, many medical drugs benefit mother and fetus equally. In particular, penicillin can be used safely and successfully to treat maternal syphilis during pregnancy (Briggs et al., 1994; Isada & Grossman, 1991). This treatment also benefits the fetus because, as you will see shortly, a pregnant woman who is not treated can infect her fetus. The list of drugs that may not be safe in pregnancy is long. Still, there are many drugs whose use during pregnancy—under the direction of a doctor—is desirable or even vital.

## Maternal Illnesses

The physical health of a pregnant woman has a direct, obvious impact on the health of the developing organism in her uterus. If the mother has either a bacterial or a viral infection, her embryo or fetus may also get the infection. Moreover, these infections can have severe effects, causing birth defects or a spontaneous abortion.

*Syphilis*    At the beginning of the twentieth century, a common bacterial infection that had serious negative consequences for prenatal development was syphilis. Newborns whose mothers were infected with syphilis often had bone, liver, and brain damage—if they survived at all. Many of these newborns were premature and died soon after birth.

As just mentioned, syphilis can be treated early in pregnancy with antibiotics such as penicillin. Of course, the treatment can only be given to women who see a doctor for prenatal care early in pregnancy, and some women do not. For this reason, birth defects due to syphilis still occur, although less often than in earlier decades. During the early 1980s, only a few hundred children in the United States were born with congenital syphilis each year (Wendel, 1988).

Unfortunately, the historical trend reversed itself during the late 1980s. Because of increases in drug use and female prostitution, the rate of syphilis-infected newborns rose dramatically during the late 1980s (Isada & Grossman, 1991). In the early 1990s, several thousand U.S. infants were born with syphilis each year (Dehner & Gersell, 1994).

*Herpes Simplex*    More common than syphilis are infections caused by the herpes simplex virus. In a mother, this virus causes the pain, itching, and other symptoms of genital herpes. During pregnancy, the virus can travel from the mother through the placenta to the fetus. More often, the fetus is infected during the birth process when it comes in contact with infected tissues of the mother. Newborn infants do not have a fully developed immune system, so they are particularly sensitive to the virus. The viral infection can cause blindness, hearing loss, mental retardation, or death (Freij & Sever, 1988).

The harmful effects of the herpes virus are difficult to prevent for two reasons. First, many pregnant women who carry the virus have no symptoms and so are unaware of any risk to their fetus. If they are not checked carefully during pregnancy, they may infect the fetus without knowing it. Second, unlike bacterial infections, viral infections cannot be treated with antibiotics. Medical researchers are trying to create vaccines against these viruses, but progress has been slow.

Problems due to herpes can be greatly reduced if the fetus does not come in contact with infected tissues during the birth process. One way to arrange this is to deliver the baby by cesarean section rather than by a normal, vaginal delivery. The cesarean delivery

is considered later in more detail. For now, you need know only that it involves the removal of the fetus through an incision in the mother's abdomen and uterus. This procedure has some risks for the mother, but the risks are smaller than those that a herpes infection poses for her infant.

*Rubella*   Many other viruses besides herpes can have negative effects on the developing embryo and fetus. Rubella, or German measles, is a virus that, in adults, causes a light, itchy rash and low fever. These symptoms rarely last more than a couple of days. But if a woman becomes infected with the rubella virus early in pregnancy, the effects on the developing embryo can be extremely serious.

Prenatal rubella infections can cause deafness, eye cataracts, and heart defects. They can also contribute to growth retardation and disorders in brain development. These disorders affect more than half the infants of women who contract the virus during the embryonic period. The severity of these defects, and the high proportion of infected women whose infants suffer from them, show that rubella is a powerful teratogen.

In previous decades, epidemics of rubella led to large numbers of infants with birth defects. In the 1980s only a handful of infants were born each year with symptoms of prenatal rubella infection (Freij, South, & Sever, 1988). These infections have been largely eliminated because there is now an effective vaccine against the virus. This vaccine is given routinely to almost all schoolchildren.

Unfortunately, some women in the United States have never been vaccinated against rubella. Some schoolchildren in the United States have not been vaccinated against any of the common childhood diseases, including rubella. Therefore, as with syphilis, a resurgence of birth defects due to rubella occurred in the United States during the early 1990s (Ewart, Frederick, & Mascola, 1992). Until universal vaccination is achieved, rubella will continue to cause birth defects.

*AIDS (Acquired Immune Deficiency Syndrome)*   In the 1980s a terrifying new virus infected millions of people in the United States and other countries. Human immunodeficiency virus (HIV) causes Acquired Immune Deficiency Syndrome (AIDS). People with AIDS have difficulty resisting other infections. They increasingly suffer from diseases and medical conditions that are assumed to lead in all cases to death. The AIDS virus is thus the most powerful and lethal virus known.

In the 1980s AIDS spread fastest among homosexual men and intravenous drug users. Many other people contracted the virus through blood transfusions before effective HIV screening of donated blood was possible. Women sometimes contracted the virus through sexual relations with an infected man. Some of these women then became pregnant and transferred the virus to their embryo or fetus.

Estimates of the likelihood that a pregnant woman with HIV will infect her offspring range from 15 to 50 percent (Feinkind & Minkoff, 1988; Isada & Grossman, 1991; Scialli, 1994). Mothers are more likely to transfer the virus to a fetus when they have already begun to show the symptoms of AIDS. Unlike with other infections such as syphilis, the risk to the fetus is not reduced by cesarean delivery. However, transmission of the virus to a fetus is less likely if mothers with HIV take the drug zidovudine (AZT) during pregnancy (Connor et al., 1994). Regular use of the drug may be literally life-saving, reducing the risk of transmitting the virus to less than 10 percent.

By the early 1990s several thousand infants in the United States had been infected with HIV. Millions of infants and children had been infected in African countries, where HIV is more prevalent. The prospects for these infants are bleak. They have frequent infections, deformities of the head and face, neurological problems, and a high death rate (Zeichner & Plotkin, 1988). Most infants diagnosed with AIDS die between 3 and 4 years of age (Isada & Grossman, 1991).

In 1995 researchers reported a case study that offered some hope in dealing with this problem (Bryson et al., 1995). The researchers detected the AIDS virus in an infant boy whose mother also had the virus. The boy was tested again at 12 months of age, but that test

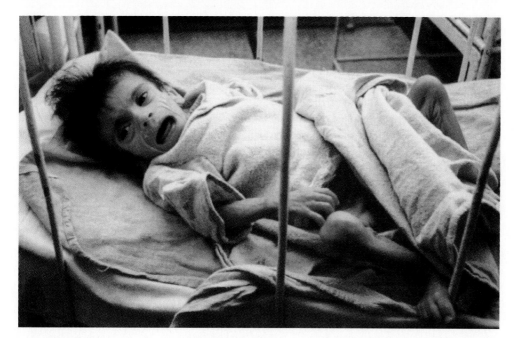

An infant with AIDS. These infants are often infected with the AIDS virus by their mothers during their prenatal development. They often spend their lives in hospitals and nearly all die in early childhood.

suggested he no longer had the virus. Numerous tests after the 12-month test have also revealed no evidence of the virus.

How this boy managed to clear the AIDS virus from his body is not yet clear. A few other children whose initial infection was less well documented also seem to have cleared the virus from their bodies. Further research on these children could not only show how best to treat infants whose mothers have HIV but also could suggest treatments for older children and adults who are infected with HIV.

## "Social" Drugs

Some pregnant women take drugs not for medical conditions or treatment of illness but for pleasure. Unfortunately, many drugs that cause pleasant changes in a pregnant woman's mood or state cause damage to her embryo or fetus.

*Illegal Drugs*   Many social drugs are illegal because they have negative effects on adults. Not surprisingly, they also have negative effects on development before birth. Narcotics such as heroin lead to addiction in adults. These drugs move through the mother's bloodstream into the placenta and then into the bloodstream of the developing child. At birth, infants of addicted women are addicts themselves. They must go through gradual withdrawal, just as older addicts do.

Heroin use is not consistently associated with structural deformities, and it apparently has few long-term consequences. Four-month-olds whose mothers were narcotics addicted during pregnancy show poorer motor coordination than normal but few social or cognitive deficits (Vorhees & Mollnow, 1987). By the preschool years, these children's motor skills and mental development are comparable to those of children whose mothers were not addicted to narcotics (Day, Richardson, & McGauhey, 1994).

Cocaine use during pregnancy has more serious effects than heroin use. Cocaine-using mothers have more miscarriages and more often experience premature separation of the placenta from the uterus, which greatly increases the risk of fetal death. However, these differences have not been found in all samples.

Some infants with cocaine-using mothers have heart defects, and some receive low scores on measures of motor development and intelligence (Moore & Persaud, 1993). Whether these results are due to their mothers' use of cocaine is difficult to say. Mothers who use cocaine often use other drugs and often fail to obtain any prenatal care. Their infants'

birth defects and developmental deficits may be caused by these environmental influences rather than cocaine use itself (Day et al., 1994; Lutiger et al., 1994).

Marijuana is the illegal drug most often used in the United States. Mothers who use this drug during pregnancy do not have infants with more structural deformities than other mothers. However, in some studies infants born to mothers who used marijuana heavily during pregnancy were smaller at birth (Day et al., 1994). Shortly after birth, these infants were more easily startled and displayed more trembling or shaking. By contrast, in another study, 2-year-olds whose mothers used marijuana during pregnancy did not differ in their behavior and abilities from 2-year-olds whose mothers did not use marijuana (Fried, 1986). These results imply that, as with narcotics, the effects of prenatal exposure weaken as children grow older. Even so, mothers who want to begin their transactions with their new infants most successfully should refrain from all illegal drugs during pregnancy.

**fetal alcohol syndrome**
*A pattern of birth defects caused by regular and heavy drinking of alcoholic beverages during pregnancy. It includes physical abnormalities of the face and internal organs, and problems in intellectual functioning and social behavior.*

***Alcohol*** Although alcohol is legal, it can cause severe birth defects. Mothers who drink alcohol regularly and heavily during pregnancy often bear infants with **fetal alcohol syndrome (FAS)**. Infants with the full syndrome have a thin upper lip, a small nose, widely spaced eyes, and a flattened face (see figure 4.8). They also have malformations of the heart, joints, and palate. Their physical growth is retarded prenatally and after birth. During childhood, they are hyperactive and distractible (Niebyl, 1991; Vorhees & Mollnow, 1987). Their brain is underdeveloped and they are often mentally retarded. Some researchers believe that prenatal exposure to alcohol is the most common cause of mental retardation in children (Moore & Persaud, 1993).

In the United States, about 0.2 percent of infants have FAS. Among mothers who have five or more alcoholic drinks per day, incidence of the syndrome may reach 30 percent (Vorhees & Mollnow, 1987). But even this figure underestimates the risks of alcohol use during pregnancy. Mothers who drink alcohol frequently also have more miscarriages or premature births.

Infants whose mothers drink only moderately during pregnancy rarely show the full fetal alcohol syndrome. However, their growth is often delayed, their IQ scores are below the norm, and their motor skills are worse than most other children's (Barr et al., 1990; Streissguth et al., 1989). Alcohol may, therefore, be the most important teratogen affecting human infants today.

The negative effects of alcohol use during pregnancy do not disappear as children grow (Streissguth et al., 1994). At 7 years of age, children whose mothers drank more alcohol during pregnancy have lower IQ scores, less positive ratings from their teachers, and poorer scores on laboratory tests of perception, attention, and memory. These results suggest that prenatal alcohol exposure has lasting effects on the development and functioning of the brain.

So far, researchers have not established a level of alcohol use during pregnancy that definitely has no effects on prenatal development (Barr et al., 1990; Niebyl, 1991). For this reason, most doctors advise pregnant women to avoid alcohol entirely. They also advise women to avoid regular use of medicines that contain alcohol.

Fortunately, this message seems to be getting across. In the 1960s few scientists believed that alcohol use during pregnancy posed any risks, and most women in the United States drank alcohol during pregnancy (Streissguth et al., 1994). In 1989 only a minority of U.S. women reported drinking during pregnancy, and the proportion dropped further by 1992 (Ventura et al., 1994). One result of this change should be a greater proportion of healthy, normal children.

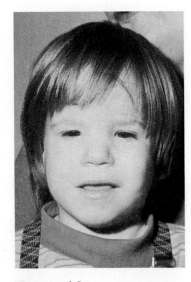

**Figure 4.8**
Because this boy's mother drank alcohol regularly and heavily during pregnancy, he was born with fetal alcohol syndrome. He has the thin upper lip, widely spaced eyes, small nose, and flattened face characteristic of this syndrome.

***Tobacco*** Another legal substance that has harmful effects on prenatal development is tobacco in the form of cigarettes. Smoking cigarettes increases the smoker's heart rate, blood pressure, and the level of carbon monoxide in the bloodstream. It also has negative effects on an embryo or fetus that receives the by-products of tobacco smoke through the placenta.

Women who are heavy smokers have a greater risk of miscarriage or premature birth. Their infants have lower birth weights than the infants of nonsmokers (Guttmacher & Kaiser, 1986; Streissguth et al., 1994). During the newborn period, infants born to heavy smokers show increased excitability and decreased attention to auditory stimuli (Fried et al.,

1987; Vorhees & Mollnow, 1987). In addition, they are more likely to develop asthma during infancy and childhood (Ventura et al., 1994).

These negative effects of cigarette smoking seem to depend partly on the nicotine in tobacco. Some writers estimate that when a woman smokes one cigarette, she receives one-tenth of a lethal dose of nicotine (Maurer & Maurer, 1988). The nicotine in the mother's body reduces blood flow to the placenta and so reduces the nutrients and oxygen available to the uterus.

Cigarette smoking also increases the level of carbon monoxide in a woman's bloodstream. Daphne and Charles Maurer (1988) described this increase as the equivalent of puffing on an auto's exhaust pipe. The carbon monoxide in the woman's blood passes into the bloodstream of the embryo or fetus, reducing the oxygen available to

**WHY START A LIFE UNDER A CLOUD?**

Smoking is harmful to your baby's health. Quit for both of you. For help call your American Cancer Society.

Why take the risk? That's the message of many public service advertisements that warn against the dangers of smoking to a pregnant woman and her embryo or fetus.

the developing brain and other organs. The evidence on carbon monoxide contamination is especially important because it suggests that smoking low-nicotine cigarettes may be nearly as harmful to a developing fetus as regular cigarettes.

Some researchers have found lower achievement test scores during the school years for children whose mothers were heavy smokers during pregnancy (Vorhees & Mollnow, 1987). The differences between children with smoking and nonsmoking mothers are usually small, though. In one well-controlled study (Lefkowitz, 1981), 10-year-olds whose mothers smoked during their pregnancies seemed as academically and socially competent as children with nonsmoking mothers.

Other researchers examined the effects of mothers' smoking during pregnancy on children's IQ scores at 4 and 7 years of age (Streissguth et al., 1994). These researchers also took account of the fact that women who smoke are also likely to drink more alcohol. When the researchers used statistical analyses to distinguish between the effects of the two substances, they found that children's IQ scores were negatively affected by their mothers' prenatal alcohol use but not by their mothers' smoking.

Even so, pregnant women should ask, "Why take the risk?" Some risks of smoking cannot be measured in long-term studies of infants and children, because these studies can include only data on successful pregnancies. Remember that cigarette smoking lowers the chances of a successful pregnancy and raises the chances of miscarriage. Also, cigarette smoking increases the risk of many illnesses for the mother herself. The safest course for women is not to smoke or to stop before they become pregnant.

*Caffeine*   Most adults regularly ingest caffeine by drinking coffee, tea (except herbal teas), cocoa, and caffeinated soft drinks. In addition, caffeine is often added to medicines because its stimulant properties offset the drowsiness-inducing properties of many medicinal drugs.

Whether caffeine intake during pregnancy has any effects on an embryo or fetus is difficult to judge. In theory, high doses of caffeine could reduce blood flow through the placenta and so decrease the flow of nutrients to the fetus. However, testing this hypothesis is difficult because women who drink caffeinated beverages also tend to drink alcoholic beverages and to smoke cigarettes (Niebyl, 1991). Attempts to examine the effects of caffeine alone have

suggested that it has little effect on prenatal development or infants' behavior after birth (Barr et al., 1990; Hronsky & Emory, 1987).

Given this limited evidence, physicians take different positions on caffeine use during pregnancy. Some suggest that moderate amounts of caffeine are not a problem (Guttmacher & Kaiser, 1986; Scialli, 1994). Others emphasize the possible effects of *high* caffeine intake through several cups of coffee, tea, or soft drinks daily (Miller & Persaud, 1993; Niebyl, 1991). One group of experts suggested that mothers who have several caffeinated drinks daily may have infants with lower birth weights (Institute of Medicine, 1990), so cutting down or eliminating caffeine during pregnancy is prudent.

## Other Environmental Hazards

The uterus is the most intimate environment for prenatal development. It lies inside another environment, the mother's body. The mother lives in a still larger environment, and the hazards that she encounters in her environment can affect her developing child as well.

Radiation in large doses can cause cancer and other illnesses in adults. Prenatal exposure to high levels of radiation leads to abnormal brain development, deformities in skeletal structures, and mental retardation. Radiation has its most negative effects on brain development when exposure occurs at the beginning of the fetal period (Moore & Persaud, 1993; Mortensen et al., 1991), when brain development is especially rapid. This is another example of the principle that teratogens have their greatest effects on developing structures.

The strongest evidence for harmful effects of radiation on prenatal development has come from studies of pregnant women in Japan who lived through the atomic-bomb blasts of World War II. Barring a nuclear war, exposure to radiation is not likely to be a serious problem for most pregnant women. Women may receive low doses of radiation from medical X rays, but physicians now use ultrasound techniques (described in chapter 3) with pregnant women more than X rays. If X rays are used, the doses are normally low and not a source of concern.

Environmental pollution that has little effect on adults can seriously affect an embryo or fetus. The most tragic case of environmental damage to unborn children occurred in Japan during the 1950s. A factory discharged waste products containing mercury into Minamata Bay. The mercury was absorbed by plants and then by fish that ate the plants. Then people who ate the fish were contaminated. Pregnant women with a heavy diet of fish bore children with congenital deformities, behavior problems like those of cerebral palsy, and severe mental retardation. These symptoms were the consequences of prenatal mercury poisoning (Moore & Persaud, 1993).

Not all mercury in the environment is the result of manufacturing or other kinds of environmental pollution. Some comes from natural processes that release mercury compounds, especially in oceans and lakes. These compounds move through the aquatic food chain, eventually becoming concentrated in large fish such as tuna, swordfish, and shark (Weiss, 1994). Pregnant women who regularly eat such fish can bear infants with mild mercury poisoning.

Low doses of mercury rarely cause congenital abnormalities, but they delay mental and motor development. This is another example of the principle that the most sensitive measures of teratogenic effects are usually behavioral rather than structural. How much fish pregnant women can safely include in their diets is currently unknown, but some scientists recommend that fish with a high mercury content (e.g., tuna fish) should not be part of the regular diets of pregnant women (Stern, 1993; Weiss, 1994).

Fish in the United States may be the source of other harmful chemicals besides mercury. A family of synthetic hydrocarbons called *polychlorinated biphenyls* (*PCBs*) was used for many years in electric transformers, paints, and other products. Although these chemicals are no longer made, they are part of industrial waste and have infiltrated the natural environment. They have, in particular, become concentrated in fish in the Great Lakes.

Pregnant women who eat large amounts of fish from these lakes have infants with lower birth weights and smaller heads than women with less fish in their diets. These infants have decreased responsiveness and poorer motor functioning a few days after birth. They also show poorer memory for visual stimuli at 7 months of age (Jacobson et al., 1985). At 4 years of age, these children received poorer scores on measures of verbal ability and memory than children

During their second and third trimesters, most pregnant women should take an iron supplement to ensure adequate nutrition for the fetus. Vitamin supplements may not be necessary, unless a woman's usual diet is deficient in important nutrients.

not exposed to PCBs prenatally (Jacobson & Jacobson, 1994). Fortunately, no children received high doses of PCBs prenatally, so neither their mental development nor their social behavior was seriously abnormal. Still, the effects are large enough to support recommendations that pregnant women avoid eating fish from lakes known to have these pollutants.

Other environmental pollutants can have negative effects on prenatal development (see table 4.2). However, prospective parents would be foolish to spend the nine months of pregnancy worrying about possible teratogens. Although many substances can act as teratogens, more than 95 percent of U.S. infants are born without serious problems, and teratogens account for only about 10 percent of the problems that occur (Miller & Persaud, 1993).

You should also remember that the most common causes of birth defects (e.g., alcohol use) are completely controllable. When pregnant women avoid obvious teratogens, their chances of bearing a child who has moved successfully through the stages of prenatal development are excellent.

## Maternal Characteristics Affecting Prenatal Risk

Prenatal development may be affected both by specific teratogens and by more general characteristics of a mother's life. Some important characteristics are the mother's nutrition during pregnancy, her age, and her emotional state.

### Nutrition

Women with a well-balanced diet before pregnancy can easily provide the developing fetus with adequate nourishment. Women who do not have well-balanced diets may need to increase their consumption of high-protein foods or to eat more fruits and vegetables that supply essential vitamins. All women need to eat more when they are pregnant than they usually do. They need the additional food to supply both their own nutritional requirements and the requirements of the fetus.

Most pregnant women in the United States take vitamin and mineral supplements during pregnancy. Whether these supplements are necessary, and whether they have any negative side effects, has long been debated. In 1990 a committee from the Institute of Medicine of the National Academy of Sciences recommended that pregnant women take iron supplements during their second and third trimesters (Institute of Medicine, 1990). Lack of iron may contribute to a craving for nonfood substances, such as laundry starch or clay (Rosso, 1990). In particular, Rajput women like Mrs. Singh may have had a craving for mud because of an iron deficiency, a calcium deficiency, or some other inadequacy in their diets.

The Institute of Medicine committee did not recommend routine vitamin and mineral supplements other than iron, especially during early pregnancy, because some vitamins can cause birth defects when taken in large doses (Rosso, 1990). Supplements of specific vitamins may be advisable for certain women. For example, complete vegetarians may benefit from supplements of vitamins D and $B_{12}$. Women who rarely drink milk may benefit from a calcium supplement, although they might also obtain calcium from other daily products such as cheese or yogurt (Guttmacher & Kaiser, 1986).

Probably the most common question about nutrition in pregnancy is, "How much weight should I gain?" A few decades ago, most doctors advised women not to gain more than 20 pounds during pregnancy. These doctors feared that excessive weight gain would lead to complications of pregnancy and more difficult births (Institute of Medicine, 1990).

Doctors now know that mothers who gain a few extra pounds have larger babies who adjust more rapidly to life outside the uterus. The Institute of Medicine committee suggested that women who are average in height and weight before pregnancy should gain between 25 and 35 pounds. Women whose prepregnancy weight is below average should gain between 28 and 40 pounds. Women whose prepregnancy weight is above average should gain at least 15 pounds.

For women with low incomes, or women in countries where food is scarce, malnutrition during pregnancy is a serious problem (Lozoff, 1989; Morgane et al., 1993). The consequences of prenatal malnutrition include greater prematurity and infant mortality, a lower birth weight, and poorer brain development. Also, the effects of chronic malnutrition may persist across generations. Children who are born to malnourished mothers tend to have less successful pregnancies themselves (Kopp & Kaler, 1989).

Other studies show that the destiny of children who were malnourished during the prenatal period is not completely fixed at birth. One team of researchers followed a group of Korean orphans who received inadequate nutrition not only during their mother's pregnancy but also during their infancy (Winick, Meyer, & Harris, 1975). These children were adopted into American middle-class families before they were 3 years of age. The researchers assessed the children's intellectual ability sometime during their first eight grades of school.

As figure 4.9 shows, three groups of infants took part in the study. The first group was extremely malnourished. Their height and weight when they first came to the adoption agency in Korea were below the 3rd percentile for Korean children of the same age. (That is, they were among the smallest and lightest 3 percent of Korean children.) The second group had more adequate nutrition, apparently, but their height and weight were still far below average: between the 3rd and 25th percentile for infants the same age. The third, well-nourished group was at or above the 25th percentile for height and weight.

After living in American middle-class families for six years or more, all three groups of children had mean IQ scores above the norm of 100. These results are encouraging, because they suggest that the effects of severe malnutrition during pregnancy and infancy are at least partly reversible. From another perspective, the results are discouraging, because they suggest that the effects of early malnutrition cannot be completely overcome. The mean score for the orphans who were severely malnourished was significantly lower than that for the well-nourished group. Even after being adopted into middle-class families, they did not catch up fully in intellectual development.

Of course, the results of this study do not answer the question about prenatal nutrition precisely. The orphans were malnourished, presumably, both before and after birth, during all the months before they came to the adoption agency. Therefore, distinguishing between the effects of prenatal malnutrition and the effects of malnutrition in infancy is impossible. However, some researchers have examined the effects of nutritional supplements with experimental designs in which pregnant women were randomly assigned to experimental (supplement) and control (no supplement) conditions. The results confirm that supplementing the diets of pregnant women improves their infants' development, particularly their motor development (Joos et al., 1983).

Experiments have also been done with rats and other animals (Morgane et al., 1993). Those experiments establish that improving nutrition after birth does not eliminate the

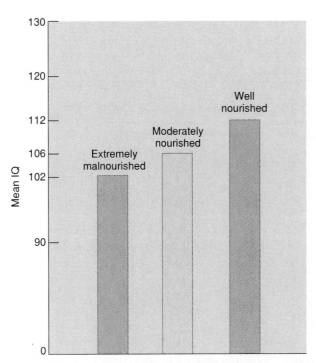

The mean IQs of the three nutrition groups

FIGURE 4.9

The mean IQ scores of Korean orphans who experienced different degrees of malnutrition before their adoption into middle-class U.S. families. All groups had IQ scores above the norm of 100, but differences between the three groups were still evident during their elementary school years.

From M. Winick et al., "Malnutrition and environmental enrichment by early adoption" in *Science*, 190:1173–1175. Copyright © 1975 American Association for the Advancement of Science. Reprinted with permission.

negative effects of malnutrition during the prenatal period. Because the prenatal period is critical for brain development, inadequate nutrition during that period leads to the abnormal development of brain structures. These structural defects cannot be completely repaired after birth. Therefore, good nutrition during pregnancy is essential for optimal development.

## Adolescent Pregnancy

The odds of a successful pregnancy are poorer for adolescents than for women in their twenties. Adolescents who become pregnant have more complications such as anemia and preeclampsia. They also have higher rates of labor and delivery complications. Their infants are more likely to be premature, to have neurological difficulties, and to die before age 1 (Osofsky, Osofsky, & Diamond, 1988; Ventura et al., 1994).

The increased risks are partly due to the failure of many pregnant adolescents to get adequate prenatal care. Some researchers have suggested that adolescents who receive adequate medical care do not have any greater risk of problem pregnancies than do older mothers (Lee & Corpuz, 1988). Indeed, some physicians have concluded that the late teen years — 18 to 20 — are, biologically, the ideal years for bearing children (Guttmacher & Kaiser, 1986).

This conclusion has been challenged. One team of researchers assessed the outcome of all pregnancies in Utah between 1970 and 1990 (Fraser, Brockert, & Ward, 1995). Women under 20 years of age more often had infants who were premature or low in birth weight. The difference between adolescent mothers and mothers in their twenties was still evident when the researchers focused exclusively on mothers who were married, had received prenatal care, and were similar in education. Because the effect of maternal age was apparent even when these demographic factors were taken into account, the researchers concluded that being a teenager itself increases the risk of poor birth outcomes.

Yet as always, data from a single study cannot be taken as definitive. Other research done mostly with urban Black women has suggested that early adolescent childbearing is not associated with poorer birth outcomes when differences in prenatal care and social class are taken into account (Goldenberg & Klerman, 1995). Moreover, arguments that adolescents are biologically less ready to bear children than are women in their twenties are difficult to defend, at least for mothers above 15 years of age (Cunningham et al., 1993).

The Children's Defense Fund is one of many organizations that try to inform adolescents about the problems that may accompany childbearing during adolescence. One problem is that adolescents may often defer or end their education before they finish high school. Not finishing high school lessens these adolescents' earning power and thus lessens their ability to provide for their young child.

# The one on the left will finish high school before the one on the right.

Adolescent pregnancy isn't just a problem in America, it's a crisis. To learn more about a social issue that concerns all of us, write: *Children's Defense Fund, 122 C Street, N.W., Washington, D.C. 20001.*

## The Children's Defense Fund.

For practical purposes, however, the biological risks associated with adolescent parenting are less important than are its social and economic consequences in a specific society. In the United States and many other modern societies, becoming a mother in the adolescent years often means dropping out of school or lowering educational aspirations. Adolescent mothers often have difficulty paying for good medical care and, therefore, less often receive good care. Once their infant is born, they are less able to pay for the infant's medical care, nutrition, and other expenses. Because of these problems, many public-education campaigns have been launched to reduce the rate of adolescent childbearing (Lawson & Rhode, 1993).

## Pregnancy After Age 35—or 40?

During the 1980s and 1990s, increasing numbers of women waited until they were 35 or even 40 years of age before having their first child. You remember from chapter 3 that as women grow older, their chances of conceiving a child with Down syndrome increase. In addition, older mothers suffer more from infertility. When they are successful in becoming pregnant, they have a higher rate of miscarriages and more complications of labor and delivery (Edge & Laros, 1993; Quenby & Farquharson, 1993). Their rate of low-birth-weight infants is higher than that of younger mothers; they also have a higher rate of infants whose birth weight is excessive—more than 8.8 pounds (Cunningham et al., 1993; Ventura et al., 1994).

Still, these problems are uncommon when women are in good health before becoming pregnant (Cunningham et al., 1993; Guttmacher & Kaiser, 1986). Moreover, older mothers are better educated than average and more often seek prenatal care (Ventura et al., 1994). For healthy, well-educated women over age 35, the chances of giving birth to a healthy, normal child may be as high as for women in their twenties.

## Emotional State

Do a pregnant woman's feelings about pregnancy or about other aspects of her life affect the developing organism in her uterus? Is a fetus harmed if the mother is unhappy, angry, or anxious? Does the fetus benefit if the mother is calm and happy?

Pregnant women who are more anxious do have more problems in pregnancy, more premature infants, and more irritable and restless infants (Norbeck & Tilden, 1983; Sameroff & Chandler, 1975). These findings are difficult to interpret, though. The data come from correlational designs and can be explained in several ways.

Some women might be anxious during pregnancy because they have had problems with previous pregnancies, or because their doctors have told them they are in a high-risk

group. If these mothers then have premature or irritable infants, the infants' problems could be caused not by the mothers' anxiety but by the risk factors that made them anxious.

To judge between these alternative explanations, a few researchers have measured both women's anxiety during pregnancy and their degree of medical risk (e.g., Lobel, Dunkel-Schetter, & Scrimshaw, 1992). Both measures were associated with premature births. That is, women who were more anxious during pregnancy had more premature infants; so did women who were judged to have a high medical risk.

Various mechanisms might account for the effects of mothers' emotional states on the outcome of their pregnancies. One possibility is that mothers' anxiety contributes to the release of hormones that, indirectly, reduce blood flow and oxygen to the fetus. Some hormones, such as epinephrine, might also increase the chances of premature labor. Another possibility is that mothers who are anxious and under stress less often maintain a good diet and less often get proper exercise and rest (Lobel et al., 1992). More research is needed to find which of these hypotheses is most accurate.

On the other hand, the effects of negative emotional states during pregnancy should not be exaggerated. Most women feel anxious sometime during pregnancy. No research suggests that occasional negative moods have any negative effects on an embryo or fetus. Negative effects are likely only if those moods are chronic or unusually intense.

# CHILDBIRTH AND THE NEONATAL PERIOD

The end point of prenatal development is the most momentous of all life transitions: birth. Many expectant parents begin preparing for this event months before it occurs. They attend classes for parents-to-be that describe the birth process and their roles in it. Earlier in the chapter, you learned that these classes may help parents cope with the long waiting period of pregnancy, but their primary goal is to help parents cope with the events surrounding the birth itself.

## Childbirth Education

A comedian could easily point out the humorous side of childbirth classes. Imagine a 70-year-old grandmother saying to her 25-year-old granddaughter and her husband, "So, you're going to have a baby. You need to take a class? In my day, it was a lot simpler."

The grandmother's comments contain a double-edged irony. In her day childbirth was simpler, at least from the pregnant woman's perspective. She arrived at the hospital in labor and was given a general anesthetic that made her unconscious. A few hours later, her doctor awakened her with the news that she had a new baby boy or girl. She may not have taken classes to prepare for this process, but her doctor certainly did!

The move away from general anesthesia during labor and delivery was spurred partly by mothers' beliefs that childbirth is a natural process. Throughout most of human history, mothers like Mrs. Singh bore children without the benefit of general anesthesia or doctors. The grandmother's joke is double-edged, though, because the modern perspective includes a touch of irony, too. If childbirth is such a natural process, why should prospective parents need to take classes on childbirth? Couldn't someone simply tell them to act naturally?

The advice to act naturally presumes too much. Yes, childbirth is a natural process, but natural processes do not always have what most people would consider successful outcomes. Women like Mrs. Singh, who go through labor and delivery without general anesthesia or doctors, sometimes have difficult labors that end with the death of the fetus. Sometimes labor and delivery are so difficult that they cause the death of the mother, too. And even when an infant is born alive, other aspects of the delivery may contribute to the infant's death within a few days. *Cultural Perspectives:* "The Hazards of Childbirth Under 'Natural' Conditions" describes these hazards of childbirth outside medical settings, with a special focus on the India of Mrs. Singh.

The advice to act naturally may also suggest to some women that, if they do, labor and delivery will be quick and painless. A relatively painless labor is possible but unusual. Most

THE HAZARDS
OF CHILDBIRTH
UNDER "NATURAL"
CONDITIONS

India, with over 900 million people, is second only to China in population. The United States, with over 260 million people, ranks third in population among all countries. India is a poorer country than the United States, and this difference is reflected in the life chances of its people from birth.

Figure 4.10 shows 1991–1993 statistics for four indicators of health in India and the United States. On each indicator, India has a poorer score than the United States, and the differences are often dramatic.

Infant mortality is defined by the number of infants who die before 1 year of age. In India, nearly 80 of every 1,000 infants—or 1 in 12—die in their first year. In the United States, the rate is less than 1 percent. Part of this difference is due, as the figure suggests, to the high percentage of Indian infants with a low birth weight.

Childbirth itself is much more hazardous for the mother in India than in the United States. Complications of delivery cause the death of almost 40 Indian mothers in every 10,000 births. The risk of maternal death in the United States is extremely small, less than 1 in 10,000 births. The difference between countries is partly due to the smaller percentage of mothers in India who have trained medical personnel to assist them during labor and delivery.

India is a vast country, however, and conditions differ greatly in its various regions.

Moreover, the health-care system in India has changed greatly in recent decades (Malhotra, 1990). Historical data make it possible to estimate the conditions that prevailed in Khalapur during the 1950s when anthropologists observed families like that of Mrs. Singh.

Khalapur is in one of the poorer states of India. Even in 1972, more than 1 in 5 infants born in rural areas of that state died before age 1. The rate was probably even higher in the 1950s. Most of these deaths resulted from neonatal tetanus, often caused by "using unclean instruments for cutting the umbilical cord" (Malhotra, 1990, p. 326). In other words, the dirty knives used by midwives who assisted women like Mrs. Singh often unwittingly caused the deaths of the infants whom they helped to deliver. The midwives' lack of standard hygienic practices must also have contributed to the high rates of maternal mortality at that time.

The Indian government is now working earnestly to improve the health of the population through education, better sanitation, greater access to prenatal care, and greater availability of trained medical personnel for women in labor. With increased resources and an improved system for primary health care, more infants and mothers can avoid the hazards of "natural" childbirth.

**FIGURE 4.10**
In poor countries like India, childbirth is much more hazardous for the infant and for the mother than in the United States. One reason for these differences is that trained medical personnel assist at childbirth more consistently in the United States than in India.

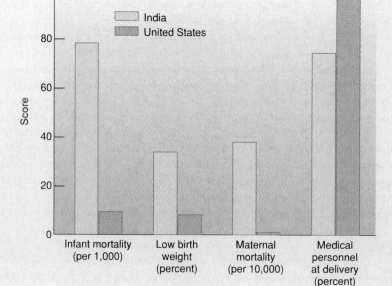

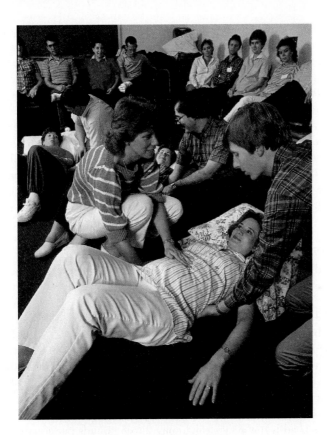

Women in a childbirth class practice techniques they will use during labor and delivery. Their partners act as their coaches during class, as they will do when the women are actually in labor.

women experience labor as painful, sometimes intensely so, and few women "naturally" know how to act to reduce this pain. Moreover, their lack of knowledge can increase their anxiety and make them experience the pain of labor and delivery more intensely.

More than 60 years ago, Grantly Dick-Read (1933) devised a program to prepare pregnant women for childbirth. One part of the program involved giving women information about what happens during labor and delivery. Dick-Read assumed that better-informed women would be less fearful when they began labor, and so would be less tense and feel less pain. Another part of his program involved exercises in relaxation and breathing that were designed to reduce the tension that enhances pain during childbirth.

A few decades later, a French physician named Ferdinand Lamaze (1970) devised a somewhat different program for childbirth education. Like Dick-Read, he included classes that described the normal course of labor and delivery. And like Dick-Read, he trained women in breathing and relaxation exercises. However, Lamaze explicitly based his breathing and relaxation techniques on Pavlov's principles of classical conditioning. Lamaze also assumed that women would benefit if they were coached, during labor, to use the breathing and relaxation techniques that they had learned. Usually, the woman's husband acted as her coach, attended classes with her, and gave her support throughout labor and delivery.

Today, most childbirth classes include some combination of the three key elements in the Dick-Read and Lamaze programs: (a) information about labor and delivery, (b) breathing and relaxation exercises, and (c) training of the father as the mother's coach and supporter (Broome & Koehler, 1986). Some classes also include pregnancy exercises, information about a specific hospital's procedures, and planning for the next life task: parenting (Stanway & Taubman, 1994).

Are these classes valuable? The evidence on this question is not conclusive because few experimental studies of childbirth education have been done. Still, you might be convinced by the following combination of anecdotal and systematic data.

Several years ago, one of my wife's sisters worked for a summer at a medical clinic in rural Korea. A young girl came to the clinic, obviously in labor. The girl was very frightened because no one had told her how the baby would get out of her body. Fortunately, the delivery went well anyway. This story may contain the best answer to the grandmother's question: You don't need a class to have a baby, but you'll probably feel better about it if you've taken one.

Parents who have attended childbirth classes do, indeed, feel better about the childbirth process than do parents who have not (Broome & Koehler, 1986; Leventhal et al., 1989; Wideman & Singer, 1984). In several studies, mothers who had attended classes reported that they experienced less pain during labor than mothers who had never attended. The mothers who had attended classes also received less pain medication during labor than those who did not. Fathers who had attended childbirth classes responded more positively to their newborns than those who had not. All these findings suggest that childbirth education makes labor and delivery a more positive experience for both parents.

## Normal Labor and Delivery

One topic in childbirth classes is the process of labor and delivery. This process is commonly divided into three stages, each of which ends with a significant event.

### The Stages of Labor

At the start of labor, the head of the fetus usually is just above the cervix (see figure 4.11). The first stage of labor begins with strong, rhythmic contractions of the uterus. These contractions push the amniotic fluid in the uterus against the cervix. Under this pressure, the cervix begins to enlarge, or dilate. The pressure also leads to the rupture of the membranes and the release of amniotic fluid, if the membranes were not ruptured already.

Then the uterine contractions press the head of the fetus against the cervix. The pressure on the baby's head is not very strong, only 2 to 5 pounds per square inch, but it is effective (Maurer & Maurer, 1988). As figure 4.11 shows, the cervix gradually stretches open and the baby's head begins to move through.

As labor proceeds, contractions become stronger, longer, and more frequent. Early contractions may occur every 10 or 15 minutes and last only about 30 seconds. Near the end of the first stage of labor, they may instead occur only 3 minutes apart and last more than a minute. This phase of transition between the first and second stages is sometimes more painful for the mother than any other part of labor. The intense contractions are especially likely when one part of the cervix does not dilate as quickly as the rest (Stanway & Taubman, 1994).

The first stage of labor is completed when the cervix is completely dilated, opening the vaginal canal for the passage of the fetus. Completion of this stage normally takes 6 to 12 hours when a woman is having her first child. It takes only 3 to 8 hours for the second and later children (Guttmacher & Kaiser, 1986; Moore & Persaud, 1993; O'Brien & Cefalo, 1991). For some women, though, this stage may be much longer or much shorter.

The second stage of labor begins at the point of full dilation of the cervix and ends with the delivery of the baby. During this stage the contractions of the uterus push the fetus through the vaginal canal. Contractions of the abdominal muscles add to the pressure on the fetus. This stage of labor lasts between 30 and 60 minutes in a woman's first delivery but only 10 to 30 minutes in later deliveries.

Once the baby is born, mothers sometimes think that the birth process is over, but a third stage of labor follows. During the third stage, the mother's body sheds the placenta (or *afterbirth*, so named because it comes after the child is born). As the uterus continues to contract, the placenta separates from the uterine wall. Once the placenta is expelled through the birth canal, more uterine contractions put pressure on the arteries that formerly supplied blood to the placenta. Under this pressure, the arteries close, to prevent excessive bleeding. This stage of labor usually lasts less than 10 minutes (Miller & Persaud, 1993).

After the placenta is expelled, or sometimes before, a healthy newborn may be placed on the mother's abdomen and given a chance to suck at her breast. Newborns usually do not receive milk from the mother's breast—the milk normally "comes in" a day or two later—but they will receive *colostrum*, a whitish liquid that is the precursor to milk.

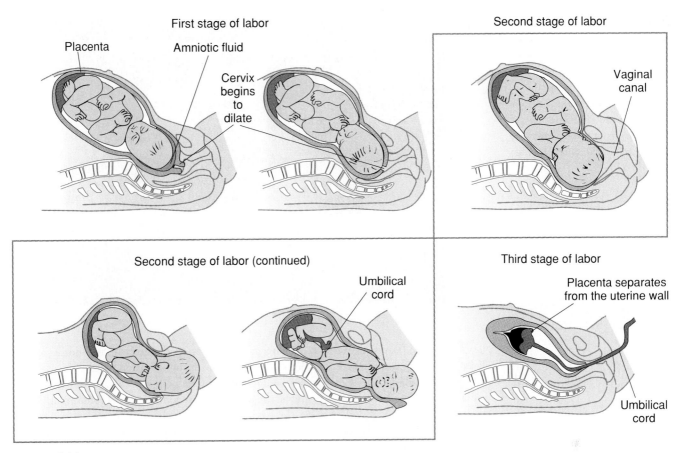

First stage of labor

Placenta    Amniotic fluid

Cervix begins to dilate

Second stage of labor

Vaginal canal

Second stage of labor (continued)

Umbilical cord

Third stage of labor

Placenta separates from the uterine wall

Umbilical cord

## FIGURE 4.11

The three stages of labor. During the first stage, the cervix dilates. During the second stage, the baby is delivered. During the third stage, the placenta is expelled, and the uterus contracts to stop the flow of blood to the arteries that supplied the placenta.

Physicians once believed that early contact between a mother and her newborn had great importance for later development. They believed this contact aided a process of **bonding** between a mother and infant (see Kennell & Klaus, 1988; Klaus & Klaus, 1985). This belief contributed to the establishment in many hospitals of a practice called *rooming in.* Newborns in these hospitals can spend most or all their time with their mother in her room rather than in a central nursery.

When there are birth complications, a mother may not be able to have contact with her newborn immediately after delivery. She may have only limited contact with the newborn during his or her first few days of life. The bonding hypothesis implied that such a mother might miss a critical period for bonding and so reduce her chances of forming a good relationship with her infant.

Fortunately for such mothers, studies suggest that the bonding hypothesis exaggerates the significance of early mother-infant contact (Klaus & Klaus, 1985). Extended contact in the first few hours or days of life may enhance mother-infant interaction slightly, but the effect is small and wanes over time (Campos et al., 1983). Mothers who lack this early contact can readily form a relationship with their infant once their medical problems or their infant's problems are resolved.

### A Profile of the Normal Newborn

**Neonate,** which comes from the Latin word for *newborn,* is a term applied to infants from birth to 4 weeks of age. Immediately after delivery, a normal neonate is not an especially pretty sight (see figure 4.12). A neonate's body may be covered with blood and other fluids. A neonate's

**bonding**
*The development of a relationship between a mother and her newborn infant after sustained contact early in the neonatal period.*

**neonate**
*The name for human infants during the first four weeks of life.*

FIGURE 4.12
This infant has just been born. Notice that the umbilical cord is still attached. The infant shows some signs of strain after the short (in distance) trip through the birth canal. The infant's mother, by contrast, seems very pleased to see the child she has carried so long.

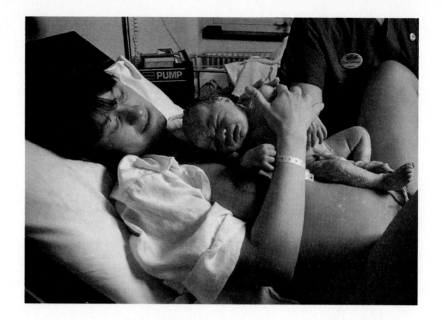

head may have been squeezed out of shape as it pushed past the bones in the mother's pelvis. Even so, neonates are amazingly complex creatures with sophisticated capabilities.

Almost all neonates are assessed immediately after birth with a scale devised by Virginia Apgar (1953). As table 4.3 shows, the scale takes account of heart rate, breathing, reflexes, muscle tone, and skin color. On each part of the scale, neonates receive a score of 0 (poor), 1 (fair), or 2 (good). Then the scores on all five parts are summed, so the total scale ranges from 0 to 10.

Usually, doctors give neonates Apgar scores at 1 minute after birth and at 5 minutes after birth. If the 5-minute Apgar score is low, the newborn is scored again at 10 minutes. Few infants receive perfect scores because few receive a score of 2 on skin color immediately after birth. Normal infants usually receive 5-minute scores between 7 and 9. An infant who receives a score of 3 or less at 1 minute needs intensive medical attention. If the score improves to the normal level by 5 minutes, the infant is likely to be perfectly normal later. If the score remains low, the survival and health of the infant are questionable.

T. Berry Brazelton devised a more extensive assessment of the newborn called the Neonatal Behavioral Assessment Scale, or NBAS (Brazelton, Nugent, & Lester, 1987). This assessment is not done routinely in hospitals, but it is an important tool for research on infants. Neonates are usually assessed on their second or third day of life. They may be assessed again when they are 7 to 10 days old, or at 2 weeks or 1 month of age. Repeated assessments provide a more accurate profile of the neonate than does a single assessment.

The goal of these assessments is to observe a neonate's best performance under ideal conditions. An examiner begins the assessment, ideally, when a neonate is asleep, roughly halfway between feedings. The examiner observes the infants' responses to lights, rattles or bells, and a prick of a pin on the foot. As the neonate slowly wakes up, the examiner observes his or her attention to visual stimuli and sounds. The examiner also checks the neonate's motor control, for example, when pulled to a sitting position. If the neonate becomes excited, the examiner records how quickly, and the highest level of excitement and irritability. Then the examiner seeks to calm the neonate and watches for his or her consolability and cuddliness. Finally, the examiner looks for involuntary movements such as tremors or startles, and attempts to elicit several reflexes found in normal newborns. (Some of these reflexes are discussed in the next chapter.)

Many researchers have used the NBAS to assess the developmental status of neonates who are in a high-risk group for some reason. Often, neonates are considered at high risk because they were prenatally exposed to harmful substances. For example, the NBAS showed

| TABLE 4.3 | *The Apgar Scale* | | |
|---|---|---|---|
| SIGN | | SCORE | |
| | 0 | 1 | 2 |
| Heart rate (beats/minute) | Not detectable | Less than 100 | 100 or more |
| Respiratory effort | Not breathing | Irregular or shallow breathing | Strong cry and breathing |
| Reflex irritability (when mucus is sucked from nose and throat) | No response | Weak response | Vigorous response |
| Muscle tone | Completely limp | Weak movement of limbs | Strongly flexes arms and legs |
| Skin color | Blue or pale | Partially pink | Pink body and limbs |

that newborns whose mothers were addicted to narcotics were less attentive to stimuli, had poorer motor control, and were less easily consoled than infants whose mothers did not abuse drugs (Chasnoff, Hatcher, & Burns, 1982).

## Birth Complications and Their Consequences

Complications sometimes arise during labor or delivery that call for special medical or surgical procedures. In addition, some infants are premature, born before they have completed the full nine months of normal prenatal development. Research on these conditions and on their long-term consequences has revealed a great deal about the vulnerability and the resilience of neonates.

### Oxygen Deprivation

The birth process is physically stressful for a fetus. One potentially serious problem is a decrease in the supply of oxygen to the fetus. During uterine contractions, the flow of maternal blood through the placenta and the flow of oxygen to the fetus decrease. When a fetus is in some positions, it can put pressure on the umbilical cord and reduce the flow of blood and oxygen through it.

A constant supply of oxygen is vital to the health of the fetus, especially for brain functioning, so oxygen deprivation during labor and delivery can cause serious problems (Petrie, 1991; Rosenberg, 1991). If prolonged, oxygen deprivation can cause the death of the fetus. Even if the fetus survives, many body organs may be damaged. The brain may be permanently affected, and cerebral palsy, epilepsy, or other neurological problems may appear as these children grow.

A great medical advance in recent decades was the invention of techniques for preventing these negative effects by monitoring blood flow to the fetus during labor (Petrie, 1991). A decrease in the flow of blood and oxygen to the fetus is often signaled by an abnormally high or low fetal heart rate. The fetal heart rate can be monitored through the mother's abdomen using an ultrasound device. Alternatively, a thin electrode can be passed through the vaginal canal and attached to the head of the fetus. In 1992 most women in the United States had one of these forms of electronic fetal monitoring during labor (Ventura et al., 1994).

If changes in fetal heart rate suggest that the fetus is in distress, the mother may be asked to shift her position to see whether that relieves pressure on the umbilical cord. She also may be asked to breathe air that is enriched in oxygen. If these strategies are ineffective or unsuitable, her doctor may recommend a cesarean delivery, which is discussed in detail next.

Unfortunately, electronic monitoring does not provide a completely accurate assessment of problems in labor. The monitors often suggest that a fetus is in distress when additional information suggests the opposite. An alternative to electronic fetal monitoring is the regular assessment of fetal heart rate with a stethoscope placed on the mother's abdomen. The

primary association of obstetricians, the American College of Obstetricians and Gynecologists, has concluded that this alternative is as adequate in assessing fetal problems as is electronic monitoring (Ventura et al., 1994).

However, some obstetricians disagree (Petrie, 1991). They argue that electronic monitoring is more practical in most hospitals and provides more precise data than does the alternative. In addition, electronic monitoring can be combined with other assessments that increase its accuracy in determining fetal distress. This combination decreases the probability of both fetal oxygen deprivation and unnecessary surgical procedures.

## Cesarean Section

A Roman historian, Pliny the Elder, wrote that Julius Caesar was not born in the natural way. Instead, someone cut through his mother's abdomen into her uterus. Then little Julius was lifted out alive and, perhaps, kicking and screaming. The story is probably false, but it is one attempt to explain why this method of delivery is called cesarean ("after Caesar") section (*cutting*).

**cesarean section**
*A method of delivery that involves cutting through the mother's abdominal wall and lifting the baby out of the uterus.*

A **cesarean section** is major surgery. The mother may be given general anesthesia to make her unconscious for some time. Alternatively, she may receive anesthesia that eliminates all sensation from the region of the operation but leaves her conscious (Chestnut & Gibbs, 1991).

Cesarean sections are more risky for mothers than are vaginal deliveries. The rate of maternal death is higher after cesarean delivery than vaginal delivery, although still less than 1 in 10,000 births (Depp, 1991). In about 10 percent of births, the incision into the abdomen and uterus becomes infected. The infection can be treated with antibiotics, but it increases the mother's discomfort after delivery and slows her recovery. The mother also loses blood during the operation, so she must be treated for anemia. Moreover, mothers must remain in the hospital longer after cesarean delivery than after vaginal delivery, increasing medical costs.

Despite its risks and costs, the rate of cesarean delivery increased dramatically in the United States during the twentieth century (Depp, 1991; Guttmacher & Kaiser, 1986). The increase was due partly to the belief that a woman who had one cesarean delivery must deliver later babies the same way. This belief is partly mistaken. The medical conditions that make a cesarean delivery necessary seldom recur. Moreover, the incision in the mother's uterus that allows a cesarean delivery may not increase the risks of a later, vaginal delivery, depending on how the incision is made.

A more important reason for the increasing rate of cesarean deliveries is that they are, under certain conditions, safer for the fetus. A long, hard labor can lead to fetal distress. Rather than prolong the labor, a doctor may recommend a cesarean. Also, a safe delivery may be possible only with a cesarean if the body of the fetus is sideways in the uterus or the feet of the fetus (rather than the head) are on top of the mother's cervix. These are poor positions for a vaginal delivery.

Still, most doctors believe that the rate of cesarean delivery in the United States is too high. In 1990 the U.S. Public Health Service set a goal of reducing the overall cesarean rate to 15 percent or less by the year 2000. In 1992 the rate was 22 percent (Ventura et al., 1994). More accurate fetal monitoring would help to reduce the cesarean rate. Also helpful would be an increase in the proportion of vaginal deliveries after an earlier cesarean delivery. Finally, doctors recommend more conservative judgments about when an infant's size or position in the uterus requires delivery by cesarean section.

## Drugs for Pain Relief During Labor

The strong uterine contractions during the first stage of labor are often painful. Even a woman who has practiced her breathing exercises and relaxation techniques may have a difficult labor with intense pain. If the labor is prolonged, some form of anesthesia may be needed for the health and safety of the mother (Chestnut & Gibbs, 1991). Remember, however, that most drugs given to the mother cross the placenta and affect the fetus. Is the fetus harmed by drugs that the mother receives for pain relief during pregnancy?

This question is controversial. On one hand, in several studies, infants whose mothers received pain medication during labor were less alert, more irritable, more fitful sleepers, and less consolable during the first few days of life (Brazelton et al., 1987; Maurer & Maurer, 1988). These effects were greater when mothers had longer labors, and when their infants were unusually small. Moreover, in one study small differences existed in the Brazelton Neonatal Behavior Assessment scores of 1-month-old infants whose mothers did and did not receive anesthesia during labor (Sepkoski et al., 1992).

On the other hand, few studies of pain medication have had experimental designs, and matching mothers in the groups that do and do not receive medication is difficult (Amiel Tison, Reynolds, & Cabral, 1994; Chestnut & Gibbs, 1991). Older studies often included mothers who received higher doses of pain medication than are commonly given today. Most important, when infants have been followed over time, no long-term effects of pain medication have been found (Maurer & Maurer, 1988). Still, doctors always try to use the minimum medication necessary, to ensure that even short-term effects on the fetus are small (Chestnut & Gibbs, 1991).

## Prematurity and Low Birth Weight

The neonatal period is most difficult for infants who are premature or low in birth weight. As you recall, a full-term infant spends about 38 weeks in the uterus from conception to birth. Infants are considered premature, or **preterm,** if they are born before they have completed the 37th week (Main & Main, 1991).

The average birth weight in the United States is about 3,400 grams (7.5 pounds). Infants weighing less than 2,500 grams (or 5.5 pounds) are considered as *low birth weight.* Infants weighing less than 1,500 grams (or 3.25 pounds) are *very low birth weight.* Infants weighing less than 1,000 grams (or 2.2 pounds) are *extremely low birth weight.*

Prematurity and birth weight are related but not synonymous. Most infants born with very low birth weights are premature; all infants with extremely low birth weights are premature (Hack & Fanaroff, 1988). However, only about half of all infants with low birth weights are preterm; only about half of preterm infants have low birth weights (Main & Main, 1991).

Infants' chances for survival after birth depend on their weight and on their maturity. Advances in medical care have lowered the minimum weight for an infant's survival. Some infants with birth weights under 400 grams (under 1 pound) have survived infancy and gone on to develop normally (Guttmacher & Kaiser, 1986). Similarly, the minimum age for survival has decreased. Some infants now survive after only 23 or 24 weeks of development inside the uterus. The threshold for survival is not likely to go any lower, even with improved medical care. The lungs and blood vessels are simply too immature to carry on the exchange of oxygen necessary for independent breathing until 23 weeks after conception.

Many infants who have a low birth weight do not survive the neonatal period. During the 1980s, about half of newborns with birth weights under 1,000 grams died during their first month of life (Hack & Fanaroff, 1988). More than one-third of newborns with birth weights less than 1,500 grams died before their first birthday (Ventura et al., 1994). Low-birth-weight infants who survive the first year often have serious handicaps such as blindness, other sensory impairments, or IQ scores below 70.

The picture is not completely grim, though. Many preterm and low-birth-weight infants do not show significant defects or delays in development. Moreover, the problems of these infants often decrease over time. In one study, infants with low (but not extremely low) birth weights who were healthy after birth showed poorer cognitive functioning at 12 months of age. By 2 years of age, they had caught up with their full-term peers (Greenberg & Crnic, 1988). The outcomes for preterm infants in another study depended on the quality of the family environment they entered after birth (Slater et al., 1987). Many other studies confirm that the environment after birth has powerful effects on the development of children who are preterm or low in birth weight (Bradley et al., 1994). *Practical Applications of Research:* "What Helps a Child Cope with Prenatal and Birth Complications?" describes one especially fascinating study.

**preterm**
*Infants born before they have completed the 37th week of prenatal development.*

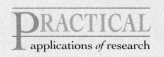

# WHAT HELPS A CHILD COPE WITH PRENATAL AND BIRTH COMPLICATIONS?

For more than 30 years, the Hawaiian island of Kauai was the location for a unique study of child development. Emmy Werner (1989) and her colleagues identified the entire population of 698 children born on Kauai during the year 1955. Werner's team assessed the development of most of these children at five different ages: 1 year, 2 years, 10 years, 18 years, and 31 or 32 years of age. In addition, they obtained records of their mothers' pregnancies and any complications of labor and delivery.

A few of the children experienced severe stress during the perinatal period (i.e., around the time of birth). For example, they experienced premature separation of the placenta, were born with congenital syphilis, or had a very low birth weight. Several of these children died before they were 2 years of age.

Another group of children experienced more moderate perinatal stress, for example, low (but not very low) birth weight or early pneumonia. Still another group experienced mild perinatal stress, including such problems as anemia, a brief delay in breathing after birth, or jaundice. Fortunately, most of the children suffered no appreciable stress prenatally and were born without complications.

The children then entered family environments that varied dramatically. Werner's team rated these environments for their stability. Families received low ratings if the parents divorced, the father was absent from the home, family discord was high, or parental alcoholism or mental illness led to repeated parent-child separations. Families received high ratings if the children had two supportive and mentally healthy parents throughout childhood. Between these two extremes were families that had an intermediate level of stability.

Werner found that the long-term outcomes for the Kauai children depended on both their perinatal stress and the stability of their families. Figure 4.13 shows the children's scores on a measure of developmental status at 20 months. Notice that scores are lower for children who had more severe perinatal stress. Scores are also lower for children from less stable families.

Measures of the children's development after 2 years of age were less affected by perinatal stress and more affected by current environmental influences. In other words, the influence of difficulties during the prenatal period and around birth decreased over time.

The features of children's environments that affected their development were extremely varied. Some children were positively influenced by grandparents or other relatives who provided care, support, and a positive role model. Other children benefited from close relationships with a teacher or another adult. Even children high in perinatal stress often developed normally if they had a supportive environment within the family or in their larger social world.

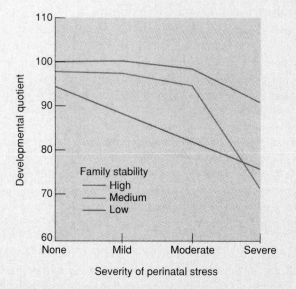

## FIGURE 4.13

Children on Kauai who experienced less perinatal stress scored better on developmental tests, or had higher developmental quotients, at 20 months of age. Children with more stable families also had higher developmental quotients. Thus both prenatal and birth complications, and experiences during the infant and toddler years, affect children's development.

Adapted from *Children of the Garden Island,* by Emmy E. Werner, and illustrated by Bob Conrad. Copyright © 1989 by Scientific American, Inc. All rights reserved.

Researchers continue to explore techniques for improving the life chances of preterm and underweight infants. For example, they have developed drugs that help to protect the immature lungs of preterm infants (Main & Main, 1991). Researchers have also shown that these infants can benefit from stimulation that is adapted to their individual needs (Thoman, 1993).

For example, preterm infants show more quiet sleep after leaving the hospital for their home if they are allowed in the newborn nursery to lie next to a stuffed bear that "breathes" (expanding and contracting as air is pumped in and out of tubes inside them) at the rate of a normal infant. The Breathing Bear is not intended to mimic the environment of the uterus,

because a preterm infant is fundamentally different from a fetus. However, the toy bear allows infants to have regular, soothing stimulation that is under their control because they can choose how close to stay to the bear.

Other researchers have intervened with the parents of preterm infants. These parents often need help in handling infants who are less responsive and more disoriented by normal sights and sounds than full-term infants. One intervention program was conducted by neonatal intensive care nurses (Rauh et al., 1988). The nurses used the procedures for the Neonatal Behavior Assessment Scale to show mothers (and fathers, if available) the abilities of their infants. The nurses also taught mothers how to recognize signs of distress in their infants and how to interact sensitively and responsively with them. After the mothers and infants left the hospital, the nurses visited them at home and helped mothers learn to interact positively and playfully with their infants.

Preterm and low-birth-weight infants often require special medical care and constant monitoring. With responsive care after birth, they often develop normally.

Four years later, the children of mothers in the intervention program were given a test of cognitive development and adaptive behavior. The test was also given to children who had been in the control condition. Children in the intervention had significantly higher scores. Other researchers have also shown the benefits of interventions with the parents of preterm infants (Bradley et al., 1994).

Unfortunately, the gains of early intervention are not always maintained after the intervention ends (Korner, 1987). When children with serious birth complications enter school, they often have significant educational or behavioral problems (Hoy, Bill, & Sykes, 1988; Main & Main, 1991). These problems are likely to be due partly to their prematurity or low birth weight, but other causes may also be involved.

Rates of prematurity and low birth weight are higher for women who receive no prenatal care, who are smokers, and who report alcohol use during pregnancy (Ventura et al., 1994). They are most likely to be teenagers with low levels of education and low incomes (Main & Main, 1991). Because of the overlap of these problems with birth complications, judging the impact of prematurity and low birth weight by themselves is difficult.

However, there is no doubt that infants get the best start in life when they are born a full nine months after conception with a normal birth weight. Therefore, the best solution to birth complications is to prevent them. The medical care of small, preterm infants is extremely expensive, highly risky, and sometimes more damaging than helpful (Kopp, 1983; Thoman, 1993). With adequate prenatal care, these costs can be avoided, and most humans can successfully complete the first phase of development in the shelter of their mother's womb.

# PREGNANCY AND BIRTH: A FATHER'S ROLE

In the story of Mrs. Singh that began this chapter, Mr. Singh played an extremely marginal role. Indeed, his relationship with his wife became more distant during pregnancy, because they stopped having sexual intercourse. In addition, he was not present during her labor, and he did not witness his son's birth.

Not all traditional cultures assign fathers the marginal role they had in Rajput society. In the Yucatan, fathers are expected to watch their wives' labor and delivery (Jordan, 1978). Other cultures have a practice of *couvade*, in which fathers lie in bed in a male simulation of labor while their wives are in labor (Mead & Newton, 1967). Whether couvade has any benefits for the mother—or the father—is difficult to say.

During most of the twentieth century, fathers in Western countries were not expected to participate in their wives' labor and delivery. As mentioned earlier, pregnant women were given a general anesthetic when they arrived at the hospital in labor. Meanwhile, their husbands were directed to the hospital's waiting room. After the doctor delivered the baby, he or she "delivered" the news about the baby to the waiting father.

Times have changed, and for the better. Today, most fathers in Western societies learn about labor and delivery in childbirth classes months before the event. Fathers are routinely invited to stay with their wives during labor. Fathers are also invited to watch the baby's delivery, even in most cases of cesarean delivery (Stanway & Taubman, 1994).

Greater involvement of the father benefits both mother and infant (Collins et al., 1993; Parke, 1981). Women adjust more successfully to pregnancy when they receive encouragement and other types of emotional support from their husbands. They bear infants with higher Apgar scores when their husbands give them more help, provide more financial assistance, and listen more sympathetically to their worries during pregnancy. Women require less pain medication during labor, and describe the birth process more positively, when their husbands are present to respond to their requests and coach them through the stages of labor.

Other social relationships also contribute to an enjoyable pregnancy and successful birth (Collins et al., 1993). Women bear infants with higher Apgar scores when they have received more emotional support, more information, and better overall care from doctors and nurses during pregnancy. In addition, infants' Apgar scores are higher when women receive more help with errands, child care, or household tasks from relatives and friends during pregnancy.

More generally, the research shows that social relationships can affect prenatal development as much as they affect later phases of life. Too often, however, these effects are overlooked. Many textbooks on pregnancy and prenatal development say little or nothing about fathers, leaving the impression that pregnancy and birth involve only a mother, her fetus, and a doctor (Cunningham et al., 1993; Gabbe, Niebyl, & Simpson, 1991; Moore & Persaud, 1993). Yet neither Mrs. Singh nor any other woman is socially isolated during this phase of life. Women's relationships with the father of their developing child strongly influence both their own experiences and the process of prenatal development.

# SUMMARY

### From Conception to Birth: Infant and Parent Perspectives
Prenatal development is divided into three major periods that correspond to important changes in the structure of the developing organism. From the parents' perspective, pregnancy is divided into three trimesters, each three months long.

### The Germinal Period
The germinal period begins at conception and ends with the implantation of a round mass of cells in the lining of the uterus. The period lasts about two weeks, but many zygotes do not implant successfully because of genetic defects or other causes.

### The Period of the Embryo
This period begins when implantation is completed and ends about six weeks later, when the developing organism has taken a distinctively human form. Development during these weeks is governed by the cephalocaudal and proximodistal principles. Morning sickness and miscarriages are relatively common during this period.

### The Period of the Fetus
The developing organism is called a fetus from eight weeks after conception until birth. Rapid growth in length and weight occurs, muscles are exercised, and the fetus starts to respond to lights and sounds.

### Environmental Influences on Prenatal Development
Environmental causes of birth defects are called teratogens. Even substances that are harmless to an adult can cross the placenta and cause birth defects.

### Principles of Environmental Influence
Decades of research on teratogens can be summarized in seven principles of environmental influence. One important principle is that teratogens have their greatest effects on developing structures. The period of the embryo is a critical or sensitive period for many body structures. Another important principle is that the genotypes of the mother and her developing organism affect susceptibility to teratogens.

### Types of Teratogens and Their Effects
Some teratogens are medical drugs such as thalidomide and DES. Other teratogens are the bacteria and viruses that cause maternal illnesses such as syphilis and AIDS. Still others are social drugs such as alcohol. Radiation and chemical pollutants can also cause birth defects.

### Maternal Characteristics Affecting Prenatal Risk
Prenatal malnutrition can cause poorer brain development and greater infant mortality. Good nutrition after birth can offset some but not all effects of malnutrition during the prenatal period. Prenatal risks are greater for women under 20 and over 35 years of age than for women in their twenties.

### Childbirth and the Neonatal Period
Childbirth is a momentous, and sometimes hazardous, life transition. Preparation for this event, and careful monitoring by trained medical personnel, increase the chances of a successful transition.

**Childbirth Education**

Classes for expectant parents provide information about labor and delivery, practice in breathing and relaxation exercises, and training of the father as a coach and supporter during labor. Attending the classes can lessen pain during labor and make the birth process a more positive experience for both parents.

**Normal Labor and Delivery**

During the first stage of labor, contractions of the uterus push the baby's head against the cervix and cause it to dilate. During the second stage, the baby moves through the vagina and is born. During the third stage, the placenta is expelled. The neonate is assessed immediately after birth with the Apgar scale.

**Birth Complications and Their Consequences**

In a difficult labor, the fetus may suffer from oxygen deprivation. Doctors may try to safeguard the fetus by doing a cesarean delivery. Doctors may also give the mother anesthetics that temporarily decrease infant alertness and increase infant irritability. Preterm and low-birth-weight infants often have more serious and enduring problems. The long-term outcomes for those who survive the neonatal period depend heavily on the quality of their postnatal environment.

**Pregnancy and Birth: A Father's Role**

Involvement of the father in pregnancy and childbirth benefits women and infants. Fathers' emotional support helps women adjust to pregnancy and is linked to greater health in neonates. Other friends and relatives can provide support for mothers that eases the stress of pregnancy and enhances prenatal development.

# SUGGESTED READINGS

Guttmacher, A. F., & Kaiser, I. H. (1986). *Pregnancy, birth, and family planning.* **New York: New American Library.** The first edition of this book appeared in 1937. It has remained popular with expectant parents for more than 50 years. The authors are obstetricians with many years of experience who offer wise advice on many issues.

Klaus, M. H., & Klaus, P. H. (1985). *The amazing newborn.* **Reading, MA: Addison-Wesley.** Marshall Klaus, one of the authors of this book, was one of the first physicians to emphasize the value of close mother-infant contact immediately after birth. This book includes many photographs that illustrate the remarkable abilities of the human newborn.

Maurer, D., & Maurer, C. (1988). *The world of the newborn.* **New York: Basic Books.** Daphne Maurer has done some of the most important research on infant visual perception; Charles Maurer is a science writer and photographer. In this book, they combined their talents to give us a fascinating glimpse of the earliest phase of human life.

Nilsson, L. (1990). *A child is born.* **London: Doubleday.** Lennart Nilsson pioneered the development of photographic techniques for recording human development inside the womb. This book is lavishly illustrated with his photographs. They capture the amazing detail and precision of development before birth.

### Chapter Five

# PHYSICAL, MOTOR, AND EARLY PERCEPTUAL DEVELOPMENT

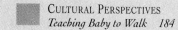

*P*arents in all cultures recognize that infancy is a hazardous period of life. Infants need special care to ensure their survival; they need appropriate experiences to ensure normal growth and development. Even so, the cultural differences in infants' treatment are great. For decades, researchers have tried to understand the long-term effects of these differences. The following story is based on a major study of this issue (Kagan et al., 1979).

Pablo didn't see much of the world during his first six months of life. Most of the day, his mother kept him tightly wrapped. When he was not crying or feeding, he spent his time in a cradle. Usually, the cradle was covered with a cloth so he couldn't see anything and no one could see him.

Pablo would not have seen much if his face hadn't been covered. He lived in a dark, one-room hut. His mother did not take him outside because she feared both illness and possible exposure to wicked people with magical powers (or the "evil eye"). She could not be expected to have more modern ideas about children's development. She had not gone to school and knew little about life beyond her small village in Guatemala.

Pablo's mother gave him more freedom after he was 6 months old. For example, she let his older brothers and sisters hold and play with him. After he was a year old, his mother began to encourage him to walk, and then his world widened further. He began to visit the other neighborhoods of his village, San Marcos La Laguna. Sometimes he went with his mother to a market in another town. He also began to do chores for the family, such as making rope and gathering water and wood. By the time he was 10, he spent most of his time working in the fields with his father or, occasionally, going to school.

Do you think that Pablo's limited experience during infancy would affect his development? If you guess that his development would be delayed, you are right. Jerome Kagan and Robert Klein (1973) observed infants between 5 and 12 months of age in San Marcos. They observed another sample of infants the same age from the United States, near Boston. The Guatemalan infants were less attentive to stimuli than the U.S. infants. Their motor skills and other psychological competencies also were retarded.

How, then, do you think Pablo and other children from his village would compare with U.S. children at 11 years of age? You might predict that they would still score below U.S. children on various measures of development. In other words, you might assume that there is continuity in development, that the differences between the two groups that existed in infancy would still be apparent at 11 years of age. Your prediction would also imply that the limits on Guatemalan infants' experience have lasting effects. In particular, their early experience in a dark hut without much social interaction affects their development for at least a decade.

Kagan and Klein (1973) challenged these assumptions. Besides testing infants in the two countries, they also tested 11-year-old children. On measures of perceptual analysis, perceptual inference, and memory, the scores of the two groups of 11-year-olds were similar. The researchers concluded that retardation in infancy does not guarantee continued retardation in adolescence. Children can recover from a lack of environmental stimulation in infancy if they shift to a richer and more varied environment as they get older. Children are, according to Kagan and Klein (1973), resilient and can overcome the negative effects of early experience.

Kagan and Klein's (1973) arguments for resilience, discontinuity in development, and a lack of permanent effects of early experience were controversial when they presented them. Those arguments are still controversial. Throughout this chapter, you will read about research in which the long-term effects of infants' experiences were examined.

However, the chapter is focused not on infancy itself but on aspects of development that are part of, or closely linked to, biological changes after birth. The first two sections deal with physical growth and brain development. You will learn about the changes in height, weight, and body proportions during infancy, childhood, and adolescence. You will also learn how both individual brain cells and overall brain functioning change with age.

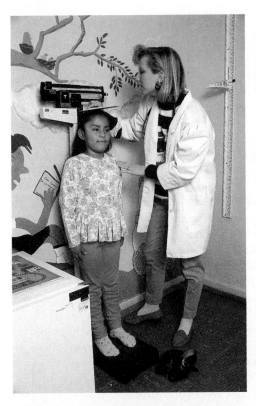

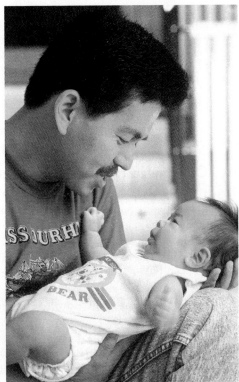

Most preschoolers are happy to have someone measure their height and show them how fast they are growing. Younger children express happiness when they master the developmental milestone of learning to walk. Their first steps also bring joy to those who watch them. Still younger children express interest in the sights of their world, especially the faces of other people. These photographs suggest some of the emotions linked to the topics of this chapter: physical growth, motor development, and early perceptual development.

The third section deals with motor development. One topic in that section will be the general change in infants' activity as they cycle through the states of sleep, vigorous activity, and crying. Another topic will be the gradual improvement with age in children's control over their body's movements.

The last section of the chapter deals with infants' changing experience of the world, or their early perceptual development. You will discover how well the five senses function in a newborn. Then you will find out how perception improves during the first year of life.

Perceptual development beyond infancy is not discussed in this chapter. As children grow older, their perception of the world becomes more closely tied to their thinking and reasoning. Perception is never a mindless process, but it is increasingly directed by children's thoughts and plans. These developments are discussed in chapter 9.

# PHYSICAL GROWTH

Recall from chapter 4 that the average newborn in the United States weighs about 3,400 g (7½ lb.) and is about 50 cm (20 in.) long at birth. Most infants lose about 10 percent of their body weight in the first few days after birth, in part because they dispose of excess water they had stored while in the uterus (Guttmacher & Kaiser, 1986). Infants do not regain this weight immediately because their mothers do not start to produce milk right away. Also, infants take a few days to learn to suck well and to digest milk efficiently. After those few days, infants begin to grow rapidly in both height and weight.

## Age Changes in Height and Weight

Figure 5.1 shows the mean height in samples of English boys and girls between birth and 19 years of age. Figure 5.2 shows the mean weight of the children in the same samples (Marshall & Tanner, 1986; Tanner, 1978). The comparable values for U.S. children are similar to those for English boys and girls (Eveleth & Tanner, 1990), but those for children in other countries sometimes differ greatly. For example, 4-year-old girls in the United States and England are about 101 cm (40 in.) tall; those in the Netherlands are about 105 cm (41 in.) tall and those in India are about 91 cm (36 in.) tall. Moreover, the differences between groups can vary across ages, because rates of growth also differ across countries.

Still, some aspects of human growth are universal. The figures show that growth is especially rapid during the first year of life. Between birth and 1 year of age, most infants increase in height by 25 cm (10 in.). Most infants double their birth weight before 6 months of age; they triple their birth weight to about 10 kg (22 lb.) by 1 year of age.

Growth in height and weight slows after the first year, fortunately. If you had gained 25 cm and 6.5 kg every year from birth on, by 18 years of age you would have been 5 m (over 16 ft.) tall and weighed over 120 kg (over 260 lb.). Although a few adults weigh that much, none has ever been that tall.

**FIGURE 5.1**
Age changes in the height of average boys and girls. (From Marshall & Tanner, 1986.)

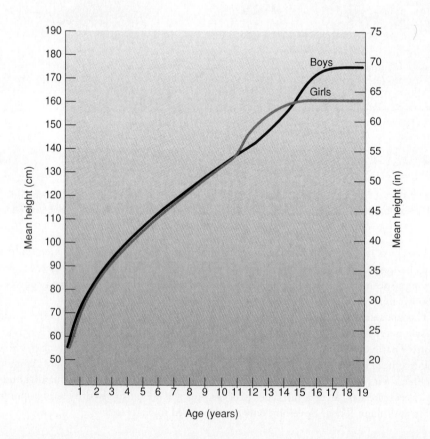

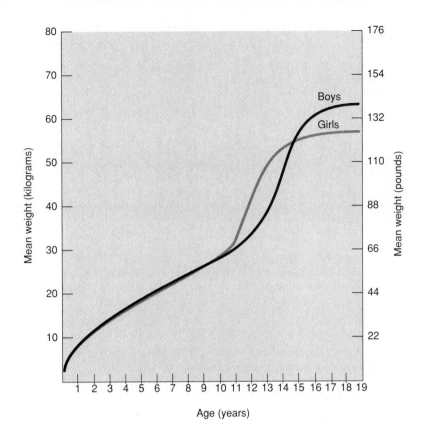

**FIGURE 5.2**

Age changes in the weight of average boys and girls. (Source: Tanner, 1978.)

Growth in height and weight speeds up again during the **adolescent growth spurt.** As the figures show, the average boy is slightly taller than the average girl from birth until 11 years of age. The average boy is slightly heavier than the average girl from birth until about 10 years of age. But for about three years after that, the average girl is taller and heavier than the average boy.

The reversal occurs because girls typically go through the adolescent growth spurt earlier than boys do. This growth spurt is one of the biological changes associated with puberty. Strictly speaking, **puberty** refers to the development of the capability for sexual reproduction. More generally, puberty refers to the physical and physiological changes that accompany the transition from childhood to adulthood.

The growth spurt of most European and European American girls peaks slightly before 12 years of age; that of Asiatic and African American girls occurs up to a year earlier (Eveleth & Tanner, 1990). The growth spurt of most European and European American boys peaks slightly before 14 years of age; most data suggest that Asiatic and African American boys experience this spurt up to a year earlier. In all groups, however, girls' growth spurt occurs about two years ahead of boys'. In other respects, too, girls' physical maturation is earlier than that of boys (Malina, 1990).

Another feature of physical growth is not obvious from the curves because they summarize the data across individuals. During all periods except the adolescent growth spurt, the physical growth of individual children shows a high degree of continuity and, therefore, predictability.

An old formula says that you can predict children's height in adulthood by doubling their height at age 2. To increase its accuracy, this formula should be stated differently for boys and for girls (Tanner, 1978). Boys reach approximately half their adult height shortly after their second birthday, so doubling their height at 24 months gives the best estimate of their adult height. Girls reach approximately half their adult height shortly after 18 months of age, so doubling their 18-month height gives the best estimate of their adult height. In particular, an average 18-month-old girl in the United States who is 81 cm (about 32 in.) tall

**adolescent growth spurt**
*A sharp increase in the rate of growth in height and weight early in the second decade of life.*

**puberty**
*The onset of the capability for sexual reproduction or childbearing. More generally, the physical and physiological changes that accompany adolescence and the development of reproductive ability.*

FIGURE 5.3

An illustration of the typical changes in body proportions from birth to 25 years of age. Notice how large the head is, proportionately, at birth.

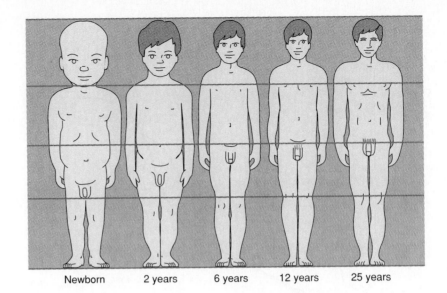

Newborn     2 years     6 years     12 years     25 years

becomes an average 18-year-old woman who is slightly over 163 cm (about 64 in.) tall (Barness, 1994). The sex-specific doubling formulas provide estimates of adult height that usually are within 3 inches of adults' actual heights (Tanner, 1978).

## Age Changes in Body Proportions

Not all body parts grow at the same rate during childhood and adolescence. Figure 5.3 is an idealized sketch of the changes in body proportions from birth to adulthood. Remember from chapter 4 that physical development usually proceeds from the head to the feet, as the *cephalocaudal* principle states. Before birth, the head develops rapidly, reaching more than two-thirds of its adult size. After birth, the head continues to grow but the rest of the body begins to catch up. In particular, the arms and legs grow more rapidly than does the head. You also read earlier about the *proximodistal* principle, which states that development usually proceeds from the center of the body outward. For example, the arms and legs grow faster than the hands and feet.

The two principles of development, like most general rules, have exceptions. Body proportions change in unusual ways during puberty. The extremities—hands and feet—grow to adult proportions sooner than does the center of the body, the trunk. This is why adolescents rapidly grow out of their shoes during the first part of their growth spurt, and rapidly grow out of their shirts near its end (Tanner, 1978).

In addition, sex differences in body proportions increase during puberty. Adolescent girls show an increase in the width of their hips, while boys increase in the width of their shoulders. The wider hips of the female leave more room for the birth canal and so make childbirth easier. The broader shoulders of the male, if matched by muscular development, make him more able to engage in heavy physical work or strenuous combat (Tanner, 1978).

Of course, the changes in body proportions at puberty have added psychological significance because they signal the achievement of maturity. Most adolescents respond positively to the signals of their increasing maturity (Simmons & Blyth, 1987). Adolescents' reactions depend to some degree, however, on whether they mature earlier, later, and at roughly the same time as most of their peers.

## Puberty and Its Psychological Correlates

The first evidence on the psychological significance of puberty came from the California longitudinal studies mentioned in chapter 2. Those studies generally suggested that early maturation is advantageous for boys (Clausen, 1975). Boys who went through puberty and the adolescent growth spurt before their peers were more self-confident than late-maturing boys. The early maturers also were more popular with peers and held more leadership posi-

tions in high school. The differences between the two groups decreased as they moved into adulthood. At age 38, the early maturers seemed more conventional in their personality and behavior than late maturers, but the two groups were similar in other respects.

By contrast, the California studies suggested that early maturation is disadvantageous for girls. In one longitudinal sample, early-maturing girls were lower in sociability and had more explosive tempers than late-maturing girls. In another sample, working-class girls who matured earlier than their peers were less self-confident and more submissive than girls who matured later. Among middle-class girls, however, early maturation was associated with greater self-confidence. As was true for boys, these differences between early- and late-maturing girls did not persist into adulthood (see Petersen & Taylor, 1980).

The California longitudinal studies began in the 1920s and 1930s, so their data on the correlates of early and late maturation are decades old. More recent studies have not always yielded comparable results. Some suggest advantages of early maturation for boys, but others show no significant differences between early and late maturers (Kimmel & Weiner, 1995; Richards, Abell, & Petersen, 1993). Some suggest disadvantages of early maturation for girls, but in others the differences between early and late maturers are found in some communities and not others (Richards et al., 1993). That is, the effects seem to depend on the larger social context in which boys and girls go through puberty.

Roberta Simmons and Dale Blyth (1987) studied hundreds of adolescents who were in the Milwaukee schools during the 1970s (Simmons & Blyth, 1987). Boys in their sample who went through puberty earlier than their peers felt more positively about their height, muscular development, and athletic ability than late-maturing boys. They also dated more than late-maturing boys. Yet surprisingly, the early maturers were less likely to rate themselves as "good-looking" than were late-maturing boys.

Girls in their sample who went through puberty earlier than their peers felt less positive about their height and weight than late-maturing girls. The early maturers also had poorer grades and engaged in more problem behaviors in school. However, the early maturers were more popular with boys and dated more than late maturers.

Simmons and Blyth (1987) suggested that boys often benefit from going through puberty earlier than their peers because other people perceive early maturers as more adultlike. In addition, our society values a tall, muscular physique in males. By contrast, early maturation may have more costs than benefits for girls. In particular, early maturation encourages girls to engage in behaviors, especially sexual behaviors, before they are fully prepared for them.

Simmons and Blyth (1987) cautioned, however, that the timing of puberty was significantly correlated with only a few measures of adolescent development. Early and late maturers did not differ in their scores on many other measures, including important indicators of psychological adjustment such as self-esteem. Also, the differences between early and late maturers decreased with age, especially for girls.

Finally, you should realize that differences between early and late maturers may not represent *effects* of pubertal timing (Graber, Brooks-Gunn, & Warren, 1995; Moffitt et al., 1992). Girls who go through puberty earlier tend to have mothers who also were early maturers. Their mothers tend to have married earlier in life and then to have been divorced. Therefore, these girls tend to grow up in families high in conflict or without a father in the home. These aspects of the family context may explain why early maturers differ from late maturers, when they do, better than does the timing of puberty itself.

## Influences on Physical Growth

Physical growth is influenced by children's heredity (or nature) and by their environment. Many kinds of research have revealed how the two types of influences interact in Western culture, in other cultures, and at different periods in history.

## Heredity

Taller parents generally have taller children. The correlation between parents' heights and their children's heights is partly due to the genes that parents pass to their children (Johnston, 1986). The influence of children's genotypes on their physical growth is also shown by

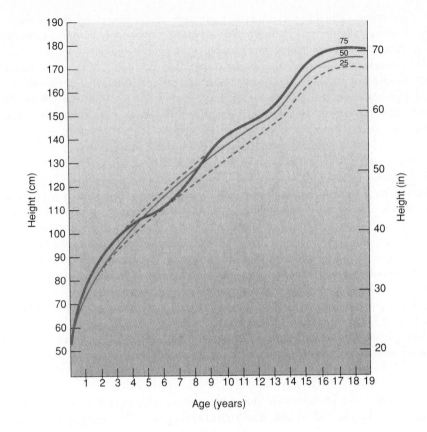

Age (years)

**catch-up growth**
*A period of rapid growth that follows a
period of abnormally reduced growth.*

twin studies (Wilson, 1976). If heredity affects physical growth, monozygotic (MZ) twins should be more similar in height than dizygotic (DZ) twins—and they are. At 4 years of age, the heights of DZ twins differ by an average of 3.2 cm (about 1¼ in.). At the same age, the heights of MZ twins differ by only 1.1 cm (less than ½ in.).

By contrast, at birth MZ twins differ in height (or length) as much as do DZ twins. These results suggest that heredity has a weaker effect on physical growth during the prenatal period than after birth. Growth in the uterus is influenced less by children's genes than by aspects of the prenatal environment. For example, one twin may receive more nourishment through the placenta than the other.

The influence of heredity on development after birth is shown most dramatically by the phenomenon of **catch-up growth,** a time of rapid growth following a time of growth restriction (Tanner, 1978).

Consider a boy who is above average in height from birth to age 4, most likely because his parents gave him genes that contribute to above-average height. However, the boy's growth rate slows after age 4, because of malnutrition, until age 6. Then the boy's nutrition improves.

One likely result of these events is shown in figure 5.4. Notice that the boy's height is at the 75th percentile from birth to age 4, but falls to the 25th percentile by age 6. After that age, the boy's growth rate accelerates, and his height again reaches the 75th percentile by age 9. That is, he completely catches up to his previous path of development in three years.

Consider another boy, and another form of catch-up growth. This boy is also above average in height from birth to age 4, and also has retarded growth from age 4 to age 6. However, once the cause of his growth retardation is removed, this boy does not show accelerated catch-up growth. Instead, he returns to his previous *rate* of development and reaches his genetically programmed height by growing for a longer time.

As figure 5.5 shows, this boy's adolescent growth spurt is delayed and he attains his adult height at age 19 rather than age 17. Despite the delay, his catch-up is complete: He reaches the 75th percentile in height, which was where he stood from birth to age 4.

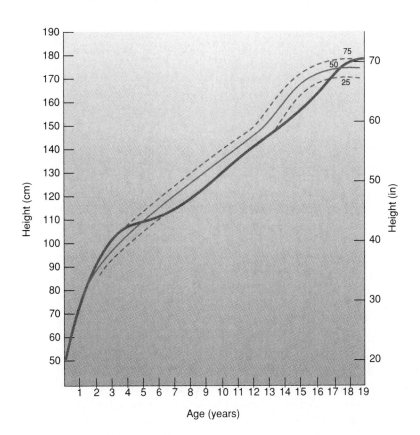

**FIGURE 5.5**
Another form of catch-up growth. The dark line is for the height of a boy who was at the 75th percentile for height from birth to age 4. The boy's growth rate slowed between age 4 and age 6, so his height dropped to the 25th percentile. Then his growth rate returned to normal, so he stayed at the 25th percentile until adolescence. His adolescent growth spurt did not begin until age 16, but then he grew to the 75th percentile in height.

Catch-up growth illustrates a principle of development called **canalization** (Waddington, 1957), which states that an organism tends to stay on the path of development (or the "canal") set by its heredity. If a temporary disturbance pushes it off that path, it tends to return to the path, or canal, set by its genotype.

When defining canalization, researchers need not specify the cause of children's delay in growth. They simply assume that once the cause is removed, children establish a growth trajectory that sooner or later returns them to their genetically programmed path of development. In particular, they eventually reach the height that their genotypes allow.

The principle of canalization implies that early experience does not have permanent effects on development. Unfavorable experiences may slow children's development temporarily, but children will catch up completely if given a chance later. Canalization is, then, an optimistic principle, one that fits Kagan and Klein's (1973) arguments about children's resilience.

However, the principle is wrong, at least under some conditions. Catch-up growth is not always complete. Some environmental causes of growth retardation have effects that last even after those causes no longer operate. For example, when one twin is larger at birth because of a more favorable position in the uterus, that twin usually continues to be slightly larger throughout childhood (Tanner, 1978). You will see other examples of the limits on catch-up growth, or the long-term effects of early experience, as you read about specific environmental influences on physical growth.

## Malnutrition

One horrifying but familiar image of childhood malnutrition is of a young child who is extremely thin, has wrinkled skin, and is obviously exhausted and close to death from starvation. Such a child is suffering from **marasmus,** a disease caused by a severe deficiency in caloric intake. These children have stopped growing and their tissues have begun to waste away.

Also familiar are images of children with their faces, legs, and bellies swollen with water. These children are not as close to death as those with marasmus. They have **kwashiorkor,** a disease of children whose diet provides sufficient calories but very little protein.

**canalization**
*A theoretical principle that states that an organism tends to return to its hereditarily determined path of development (or its own "canal") after being pushed off that path by a temporary disturbance.*

**marasmus**
*A disease caused by severe protein-energy undernutrition. Growth stops, the skin wrinkles, and the tissues begin to waste away.*

**kwashiorkor**
*A disease resulting from diets very low in protein but with adequate calories. The abdomen, face, and legs swell with water, the hair falls out, and sores develop on the skin.*

FIGURE 5.6
Guatemalan children who come from higher-SES families are taller during the elementary grades. The variations in height are probably related to variations in nutrition and health. (Source: Bogin & MacVean, 1983.)

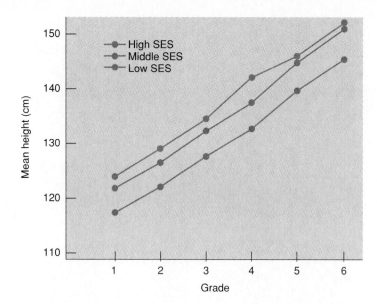

**protein-energy malnutrition (PEM)**
*A lack of protein, a lack of other foods that provide the body with energy, or both.*

**socioeconomic status (SES)**
*A composite measure of the wealth of a family and the prestige of the parents' occupations or roles in society.*

Besides body swelling, the symptoms of kwashiorkor include skin sores and hair that is brittle and starting to fall out (Snow, 1989).

Marasmus and kwashiorkor are the result of severe **protein-energy malnutrition (PEM),** caused by a lack of protein, a lack of other foods that provide the body with energy, or both. PEM weakens children so they are highly susceptible to fatal illnesses, if they do not die of starvation itself. PEM is rare, however, more rare than television and magazine stories might suggest. Even in the poorer countries of the Third World, fewer than 1 percent of children suffer from severe PEM (UNICEF, 1995). Higher percentages are found mainly in countries that are at war or experiencing severe famine.

Much more common is mild or moderate PEM, which afflicts more than one-third of all children under 5 years of age in Third World countries (Lozoff, 1989; UNICEF, 1995). Because of their lack of nutritious food, children with PEM are abnormally low in weight. For example, a 1-year-old child may weigh only 6 kg (13 lb.) rather than the normal 10 kg (22 lb.). Their low weight is associated with reduced height, or *stunting.*

Stunting due to malnutrition has been documented in many countries (Waterlow, 1988). Often, malnutrition is linked with child poverty or low socioeconomic status. **Socioeconomic status, or SES,** is a general measure of the wealth of a family and the prestige of the parents' occupations or roles in society. The relation of children's physical growth to their family's SES was examined in a study of children from the capital city of Guatemala (Bogin & MacVean, 1983).

Some children in the study were from low-SES families. Their parents had low-paying occupations and little education. Other children were from middle-SES families. Their parents had better-paying occupations, had received more education, and lived in more desirable areas than did those in the low-SES group. Still others were from high-SES families. Their parents had prestigious occupations, had received high levels of education, and lived in the best neighborhoods of the city.

The heights of the children in all three groups were measured in each of their first six grades of school. As figure 5.6 shows, children in the high-SES group were consistently taller than children in the middle-SES group. Those children, in turn, were taller than the children in the low-SES group. Barring changes in family circumstances, these differences in height were likely to persist into adulthood (Martorell, Mendoza, & Castillo, 1988).

The differences among the three SES groups were probably not due entirely to differences in the food they ate. Poor nutrition is often combined with other conditions that retard children's growth, such as a lack of adequate medical care. Frequent or severe illnesses that are not properly treated can greatly retard children's growth (Nabarro et al., 1988). Of course, medical care is most often inadequate in poor families.

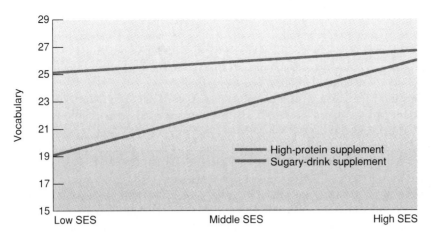

## FIGURE 5.7

In a long-term experiment in Guatemala, some children regularly received drinks high in protein while others received drinks high in sugar but low in protein. Among children receiving the sugary drink, those higher in SES had higher vocabulary scores in adolescence and early adulthood. Among children receiving the high-protein drink, the vocabulary advantage of children with a higher SES was minimal.

Even improvements in family circumstances may not reverse the negative effects of early poverty and malnutrition. You read in chapter 4 about Korean children who were adopted into middle-class American homes after suffering from malnutrition during infancy (Winick et al., 1975). Besides assessing the children's IQs, the researchers measured the children's height and weight.

During their elementary-school years, the children who were severely malnourished as infants were similar in weight to the children who had more adequate nutrition in infancy. The severely malnourished children were not as tall, though, as the other children. Thus, after early malnutrition these children experienced complete catch-up growth in weight but not in height.

Besides affecting physical growth, malnutrition affects children's behavior and psychological development. One team of researchers observed children in Kenya who experienced a severe but, fortunately, temporary food shortage (McDonald et al., 1994). During the shortage, children who were in school became less attentive in class and less active on the playground.

The long-term effects of malnutrition have been documented most conclusively in experiments (Grantham-McGregor et al., 1994; Scrimshaw, 1993; Super, Herrera, & Mora, 1990). Researchers in several countries have arranged for food supplements to be provided to some groups of pregnant women and young children. Other groups have received either no food supplements or supplements that are less nutritious (e.g., lower in protein).

For one study (Pollitt et al., 1993), people in entire villages were offered either a high-protein, high-calorie drink or a drink that was mostly sugar. The drinks were distributed twice daily in a central area in each village for eight years. More than a decade later, the researchers returned to test the intellectual ability of adolescents and young adults who had or had not received the nutritional supplements either prenatally or during the first seven years of life.

Adolescents and adults who had received the high-protein, high-calorie drink obtained higher scores on tests of knowledge, vocabulary, and reading and math ability than those who had received the sugary drink. Moreover, the effects were greatest for individuals who had received the nutritional supplements during the prenatal period and their first two years of life, when brain development is especially rapid.

On several tests, the nutritional supplements eliminated the typical advantage of children from high-SES families. Figure 5.7 shows the pattern of scores for the vocabulary test. Among children who received only the sugary drink, those from high-SES families had higher vocabulary scores. Among children who received the high-protein drink, variations in SES had little effect on vocabulary scores. In other words, adequate nutrition roughly equalized the vocabulary growth of children who came from richer and poorer families.

High protein is not all that is necessary for good nutrition. Children also need adequate supplies of vitamins and minerals. Iron deficiencies, in particular, cause fatigue, poor health, and poor cognitive development in childhood (Pollitt, 1994; Scrimshaw, 1991). Vitamin A deficiencies cause blindness and sometimes death (UNICEF, 1995). A lack of iodine in the diet can cause severe mental retardation (Jonsson, 1994).

Fortunately, reducing child malnutrition is possible even in poor countries (Jonsson, 1994). For example, iodine is added to salt in most industrialized countries (including the United States), and adding it to salt supplies in poor countries is not expensive. In addition, people can get vitamin A from green, leafy vegetables or from inexpensive tablets. Iron deficiencies can also be prevented by regular tablet supplements. With such simple methods, malnutrition can be cut greatly at low cost.

In the United States, several government programs help to prevent malnutrition in childhood (Children's Defense Fund, 1994; Pollitt, 1994). Many poor families receive food stamps, coupons that can be exchanged for food. Many low-income mothers participate in the Supplemental Food Program for Women, Infants, and Children (WIC), which provides vouchers for selected foods such as eggs and milk. In addition, schoolchildren from poor families often receive free or discounted breakfasts and lunches at school.

However, because of limits on funding, these programs are not available to all poor children. Therefore, malnutrition remains a problem in the United States. In the early 1990s, more than 20 percent of U.S. children lived in households with incomes below the poverty line. About 20 percent of U.S. children suffered from iron deficiencies (Pollitt, 1994). Unless these children receive adequate nutrition, they are unlikely to reach their full potential for physical growth and development.

## Overnutrition and Obesity

Some children suffer not from a lack of food but from too much food. Excessive eating leads to *obesity*, defined as weight greater than 120 percent of the average weight for one's height, age, and sex (Neumann & Jenks, 1992). This definition applies to about 15 to 25 percent of children in the United States (Giorgi, Suskind, & Catassi, 1992). Often, but not always, these children have low self-esteem and are unpopular with peers (Graves, Meyers, & Clark, 1988; von Almen, Figueroa-Colon, & Suskind, 1992). Like obese adults, they face increased risks of developing high blood pressure, breathing problems, and other problems that limit their physical activity (Epstein & Wing, 1987).

Children's weight is influenced by their genetic makeup. Children with heavier parents usually weigh more than children whose parents are lighter. The relation between parents' and children's obesity holds even when children are adopted and so are not raised by their biological parents (Stunkard et al., 1986). Twin studies also suggest a genetic influence on body weight. MZ twins are more similar in weight than DZ twins (Epstein & Cluss, 1986), even when the MZ twins are brought up in different families (Figueroa-Colon, von Almen, & Suskind, 1992).

Exactly how children's genotypes affect their odds of becoming obese is less clear. Some data suggest that genotypes influence whether children are thin or normal in weight but have little influence on whether children go beyond normal weight to obesity (Costanzo & Schiffman, 1989). Moreover, children's weight depends not only on how much they eat but also on their activity level. Some children eat a lot but do not get fat because they use great amounts of energy in vigorous activities like sports. In addition, children's metabolism, the speed with which their body naturally "burns off" calories, affects their weight. Some scientists have argued that children's genotypes may affect activity level and metabolism more than the amount and kind of food that they eat (Epstein & Cluss, 1986).

Whether children have a genetic propensity to become obese is not obvious at birth. Children's birth weights are not strongly related to their weight in later childhood and adulthood. Also, weight gains during the first year of life have little relation to obesity in childhood and adolescence. Some researchers have proposed that weight gains in infancy lead to the development of fat cells that increase the chances of obesity later, but careful studies have not supported this hypothesis. According to Alex Roche (1981), "There is no convincing evidence the obese infant

has more than a slight tendency to become an obese adult" (p. 38). More recent reviewers have drawn the same conclusion (Epstein & Wing, 1987; Salvioli & Faldella, 1992).

By contrast, the obese *child* does have an above-average risk of becoming an obese adult. In addition, the prediction of adult obesity improves as children grow older (Woolston, 1987). About two-thirds of obese 10- to 13-year-olds, for example, are likely to remain obese into adulthood (Epstein & Wing, 1987).

Health professionals have devised many programs for treating obese children (Epstein & Wing, 1987; Georgi et al., 1992; Neumann & Jenks, 1992). The most effective ones try to accomplish four goals: (1) reduce children's food intake enough to slow weight gain, or, in adolescence, to cause weight loss; (2) increase children's activity, through exercise, to use up food energy; (3) educate parents and siblings about how to reinforce and support obese children's efforts at controlling what they eat and getting adequate exercise; and (4) encouraging children and adolescents to take responsibility for regulating their eating and exercise.

Programs involving operant conditioning of eating and exercise seem especially effective (Neumann & Jenks, 1992). For example, children may be required to eat in only one place in their home, not anywhere they like. They may be rewarded for eating less or losing weight. They may be punished or lose rewards if they violate the rules of the program. Because parents have the most control over children's behavior, weight-loss programs are most effective when parents help to define and solve the problems leading to their children's obesity (Graves et al., 1988).

Any weight-loss program must be monitored carefully, because harmful side effects are possible. Without careful monitoring, children may not get all essential nutrients when their eating is restricted, and their growth in height may be reduced. In other words, a weight-loss program may replace the problem of overnutrition with that of undernutrition. When closely supervised, however, weight-loss programs have not had harmful consequences (Epstein & Wing, 1987).

Still, the best strategy is not to treat the problem of obesity after it arises but to prevent it. In school, children can receive instruction about healthful foods; they can also be involved in regular exercise programs. Parents can be encouraged to reduce the television watching and snacking that are associated with obesity (Neumann & Jenks, 1992; Rossi, 1992). Pediatricians can assess children's weight gain more carefully during regular exams. Pediatricians can advise parents about how to reduce food intake and increase the activity of children who are gaining too much (Salvioli & Faldella, 1992). With this multifaceted approach, fewer children will face the negative social and physical consequences of obesity.

## Secular Trends

Anyone who has watched professional basketball for a few years has probably noticed an increase in the height of the players. During the 1960s, a player 7 feet tall was exceptional. Now professional teams have many players over 7 feet tall. Even some high-school teams have 7-foot-tall players. What's happening here? Have human beings really gotten taller in the past few decades?

The answer is yes, but not in all populations in all countries. Figure 5.8 shows the mean height of White boys in North America from samples measured in different decades. The heights of the boys in some samples were measured around 1880; those of the boys in other samples were measured around 1960. The boys in the more recent samples were taller, and the differences at some ages were large. For example, 12-year-olds measured in 1960 were 4 inches taller than those measured in 1880.

The increase in American boys' height over an 80-year period is an example of a secular trend. *Secular* comes from a Latin word for "generation" or "age." Biologists define **secular trends** as changes in a population over generations or long time periods (Roche, 1979).

Most secular trends in human growth are increases in height, weight, and rates of physical maturation across decades. Increases in height between the nineteenth and twentieth centuries occurred in many countries besides the United States, including several European countries and Japan (Martorell et al., 1988). The same countries showed increases in children's mean weight and decreases in their mean age at puberty. One important pubertal event

**secular trends**
*Changes in human populations over generations or long time periods.*

FIGURE 5.8
Children in North America are taller now than a century ago. This figure, based on data from many sources, shows the mean height of White boys in North America in 1880 and 1960. (From Roche, 1979.)

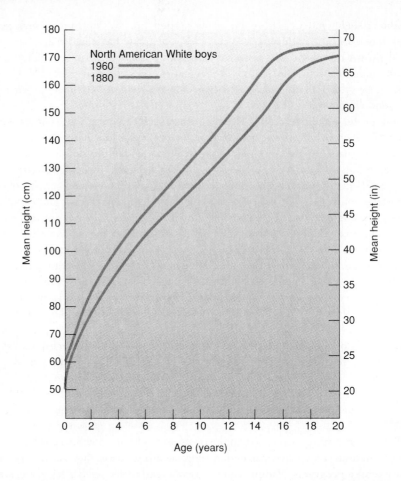

menarche
*The first occurrence of menstruation and the onset of regular menstrual cycles.*

in girls is **menarche,** the first occurrence of menstruation and the onset of regular menstrual cycles. Several studies suggest that the median age at menarche dropped approximately 3 years in the last century, from about 16 years around 1860 to about 13 years in the 1970s and 1980s (Malina, 1990; Roche, 1979).

Secular trends have not occurred in all countries. Where nutrition and medical care have changed little over the years, as in Guatemala and other Third World countries, no secular trend has been observed (Martorell et al., 1988). The greatest secular increases have occurred in countries where, broadly speaking, the conditions of life for children have improved. In these countries, infants and children receive more varied and nutritious food than they did a century ago. Perhaps more important, infants and children receive better medical care than they did earlier. Fewer children die in infancy and those who survive less often have severe, growth-retarding illnesses (Eveleth & Tanner, 1990; Malina, 1979).

Will secular increases in height and weight continue indefinitely? If we wait a few decades, will we begin to see basketball players who are over 8 feet tall? The answer seems to be no. Children's height continued to increase between 1965 and 1980 in the Netherlands (Eveleth & Tanner, 1990), but this result is unusual. Children growing up in high-SES families in the United States were no taller in the 1970s than their parents were as children. Also, national surveys in the United States showed little change in children's mean height between the 1960s and the 1970s (Roche, 1979). In short, secular trends are slowing or have stopped for children in most countries with high standards of nutrition and health care. Secular trends may still occur among less-advantaged children in other countries, if their conditions of life improve (Waterlow, 1988).

# GROWTH AND DEVELOPMENT OF THE BRAIN

Most pediatricians use another measure of growth during childhood besides height and weight. They measure the distance around the child's head, or head circumference. Increases

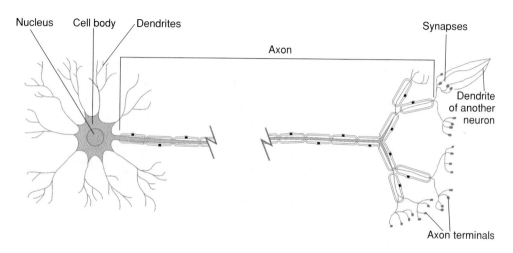

**FIGURE 5.9**

A schematic diagram of a neuron with its dendrites, axon, and synapses with other neurons.

in the size of the head tell a pediatrician something about the child's brain development. As the brain grows, the head grows to accommodate it.

Brain development is especially rapid between birth and age 2. The brain of an average newborn weighs about 350 grams, or about 25 percent of its adult weight (Nowakowski, 1987). During the first six months of life, the weight of the brain doubles. By 2 years of age, the brain reaches 75 percent of its adult weight (Tanner, 1978). This rapid increase in weight provides a hint of the dramatic changes in brain structure and functioning that occur during the first two years of life.

To understand more precisely how the brain develops, you need to think about a level of analysis more precise than brain weight or head circumference. You first need to know how individual nerve cells and cell networks change with age. Then you need to understand the changes in the functioning of larger regions of the brain.

## The Elaboration and Interconnection of Neurons

A human brain has many billions of nerve cells, or **neurons.** Each neuron has three major parts (see figure 5.9). In the nucleus of the *cell body* are the cell's DNA and other basic molecules necessary for cell life. The *dendrites* branch from the cell body and connect at their tips to other neurons. A long *axon* extends from the cell body in the opposite direction from the dendrites and connects to muscles, body organs, or other nerve cells.

The parts of a neuron cooperate in transferring biochemically coded information. The dendrites serve as inputs to the cell body; they receive information from muscles, organs, or the axon terminals of other nerve cells at *synapses* (see figure 5.9). The axon then serves as the output from the cell body, transferring the information to the next cell in the chain.

The billions of neurons in an adult brain all form before birth, but dramatic changes occur after birth in the connections of these neurons into neural networks. Figure 5.10 illustrates the changes in the portion of the brain that processes visual information. Each dark blot in the figure is the cell body of a neuron. The lines branching from the cell body are its axon and its dendrites. Notice that the number of dendrites and the length of the dendrites and axons increase between birth and 6 months of age. They increase still further between 6 months and 2 years of age. As a result, the number of synapses between neurons increases enormously. In the entire brain, thousands of new synapses may form each second during the first few months of life (Greenough, Black, & Wallace, 1987).

Not all synapses that form early in life survive. The infant's own experiences affect which synapses are maintained. At birth, several neurons may connect to a single muscle fiber or a single neuron may connect by multiple axon terminals to several muscle fibers. Over time, the duplicate connections drop out so that each neuron connects to one muscle fiber and vice versa. Synapses that are more often activated are more likely to be preserved (Greenough et al., 1987).

**neurons**
*Nerve cells.*

## FIGURE 5.10

Neurons in the visual context undergo dramatic development during the first two years of life. Note the increase in the number of dendrites on each neuron and the length of the dendrites and axons.

Reprinted by permission of the publisher from *The Postnatal Development of the Cerebral Cortex* by J. L. Conel, Cambridge, Mass.: Harvard University Press. Copyright © 1939, 1975 by the President and Fellows of Harvard College.

  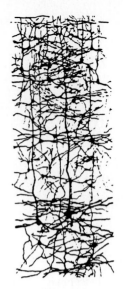

Neonate          Six months          Two years

The same process of overproduction of synapses followed by selective retention occurs with neurons that control perception. The effects of this process are most obvious in animals whose visual experience is altered experimentally. In one experiment (Hirsch & Tieman, 1987), newborn kittens were fitted with goggles that showed either horizontal lines or vertical lines. After the kittens had worn the goggles for a few weeks, researchers examined the dendrites on the neurons in the visual area of their brains. The dendrites in the two groups of kittens were oriented at right angles to each other, just as were the stripes on the kittens' goggles. The kittens' visual experience therefore affected which dendrite-synapse connections persisted and which did not.

Why does the body produce so many synapses and then retain only some? Although this strategy may seem inefficient or wasteful, it may be the most practical way to fine-tune the nervous system. There must be some method for deciding which muscles and sense organs should be connected to which neurons in the brain. The method used by human beings and other mammals (like kittens) is to let early motor and sensory experiences determine which connections between muscles, sense organs, and neurons to retain (Shatz, 1992).

The alternative would be to devise a genetic program that would define the "right" connections among the billions of neurons in the body and the brain. Such a program would contain a staggering amount of information that would strain the capacity of the DNA. Early experience in a normal environment can more easily accomplish the fine-tuning of the connections between body (muscles and sense organs) and brain (Gall, Ivy, & Lynch, 1986). Moreover, forming these connections on the basis of early experience guarantees that the nervous system is adapted to its environment.

The fine-tuning of the nervous system after birth depends on a process of **experience-expectant information storage** (Greenough et al., 1987). This term refers to early learning about aspects of the environment that exist everywhere and remain constant across times. Kittens not in experiments, for example, can expect to see both horizontal and vertical lines as soon as they open their eyes. Thus, in a normal environment kittens' visual experience helps them develop neurons that respond to all the visual stimulation in nature. In the same way, human infants develop neural networks that respond to the full range of stimulation in their early experience.

The process of experience-expectant information storage is most important during brief periods in early development. These periods fit the definition of *critical periods*, times when brain structures are strongly affected by experiences that have no effect at other times. Mature cats, for example, are not permanently affected by wearing goggles with horizontal or vertical stripes on them, because their visual system is already formed and is not fundamentally altered by changes in visual stimulation.

**experience-expectant information storage**
*A process especially important early in development that facilitates learning about aspects of the environment that exist everywhere and remain constant across times.*

Compare these two classrooms for preschool children. In both classrooms, children have something to do, but the classroom with more children is a richer environment in terms of social stimulation and play materials than is the other classroom. You should expect the classroom that provides a richer environment to have more positive effects on the children's brain development.

Human visual development has critical periods as well (Maurer & Maurer, 1988). For example, the two eyes normally receive slightly different impressions of a scene. By integrating the information from the two eyes, people can judge the distance of objects and the three-dimensionality of objects. Most of the neurons that respond to this information develop during the first year of life. If infants' visual experience is abnormal, which may happen if one eye is nearsighted or farsighted, their neurons are unlikely to become attuned to the differences in information from the two eyes.

In addition, when the two eyes do not work together, infants often stop using one eye. This problem can be avoided by providing infants with eyeglasses or contact lenses and covering the better eye with a patch so that the other eye must be used. If this treatment begins in the first year of life, children's vision almost always develops normally. If the treatment is delayed for 2 or 3 years, children's vision can never be fully restored to normal (Maurer & Maurer, 1988). The first year of life is, therefore, a critical period for the development of this aspect of the visual system.

Experience-expectant information storage is not the only process involved in brain development. Children need to do more than learn about universal features of sensory stimulation. They also must learn about the unique features of the environments in which they spend their days. This type of learning reflects a process of **experience-dependent information storage** (Greenough et al., 1987). Children learn, for example, who their own parents are, what aspects of their environments are dangerous, and how to play with specific toys or games. Exactly what children learn depends on what experiences they have.

Experience-dependent information storage results partly from the formation of new synapses in response to specific experiences. The potential for such refinements in neural networks exists throughout life. Throughout their lives, humans learn new information about the world. The process of experience-dependent information storage makes this learning possible.

Experience-dependent learning can be enhanced by environmental stimulation. Several decades ago, Donald Hebb (1949) compared the maze-learning ability of rats reared in a traditional laboratory environment with that of rats he reared at home as pets. He found that the rats reared in the enriched environment of a human home did better on maze learning than rats raised in individual cages in a psychology laboratory. Since then many researchers have studied rats reared in enriched environments—usually not in the researchers' homes but in large areas with other rats and a great variety of toys to explore. Rats reared in enriched environments learn faster than cage-reared rats and show greater brain development (Greenough et al., 1987; Rosenzweig, 1984). After living in an enriched environment, rats develop heavier brains with more dendrites per neuron and more synaptic connections per dendrite. These effects occur for mature rats as well as young rats.

**experience-dependent information storage**
*A process that facilitates learning about specific (nonuniversal) aspects of an environment (e.g., how to play with specific toys).*

FIGURE 5.11

A sketch of the major parts of the brain and some regions of the cerebral cortex.

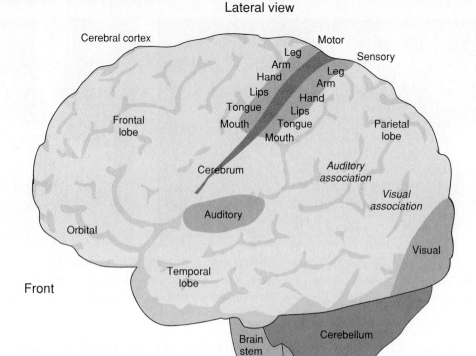

Lateral view

Cerebral cortex

Motor

Sensory

Leg
Arm
Hand
Lips
Tongue
Mouth

Leg
Arm
Hand
Lips
Tongue
Mouth

Frontal lobe

Parietal lobe

Cerebrum

*Auditory association*

*Visual association*

Auditory

Orbital

Visual

Front

Temporal lobe

Brain stem

Cerebellum

Back

Medulla

Spinal cord

The evidence on experience-dependent learning should be encouraging to people who are no longer in the phase of early development. They show, contrary to the old saying, that you can teach an old dog—or an old rat, or an old human being—new tricks. Stated more formally, they suggest that brain development can and does occur throughout life. Remember, though, that these conclusions hold only for organisms that have rich and varied experiences. Neither children nor adults will show continued brain development if they live in the human equivalent of a rat's cage!

## The Structure and Functioning of Specific Brain Regions

The different regions of the brain develop at different rates. The patterns of development for the brain regions are easiest to describe by focusing on the three physical dimensions of the brain: (a) from top to bottom, (b) from front to back, and (c) from left to right. Development on the first dimension proceeds generally from the bottom of the brain upward. The lowest portion of the brain, just above the spinal cord, is the **brain stem** (see figure 5.11). It regulates bodily functions, such as breathing, that are necessary for life. It also controls basic reflexes, discussed later in the chapter. The highest level of the brain is the **cerebral cortex.** The cortex consists of several thin layers of neurons that cover the **cerebrum,** the mass of nerve cells that is the largest part of the human brain. Neurons in the cerebrum and its cortex control voluntary motor movements, perception, and other psychological processes such as reasoning, remembering, and speaking.

Bodily functioning at birth is controlled mainly by the lower regions of the brain (Maurer & Maurer, 1988). By contrast, the cerebral cortex seems to have little influence on newborns' behavior. Newborns respond to all types of stimulation much like animals who have no cortex. For example, newborns stare for long periods at any small part of an object that catches their eye. When placed in the same situation, older children and adults typically engage in visual exploration of the entire object.

**brain stem**
*The lowest portion of the brain, just above the spinal cord, which regulates bodily functions such as breathing.*

**cerebral cortex**
*The highest level of the brain, consisting of several thin layers of neurons that cover the cerebrum.*

**cerebrum**
*The top and largest part of the human brain. Neurons in the cerebrum control voluntary motor movements, perception, and more complex psychological processes.*

During the first months of life, control by the cortex of perception and action emerges gradually. With greater cortical control, infants' behavior becomes more complex and more voluntary (Kinsbourne & Hiscock, 1983). Many examples of this age change are discussed in the next section of the chapter.

Descriptions of development on the second brain dimension, from front to back, have focused on the regions of the cerebral cortex. Cortical development does not proceed simply from front to back or vice versa. The earliest area to reach relative maturity is the motor cortex, which lies in front of the central fissure (or valley) that divides the cortex into two roughly equal parts (see figure 5.11). The neurons in this area control the movements of the arms, legs, hands, feet, lips, and other body parts that can be moved voluntarily.

The next area to reach a state of relative maturity is the somatosensory (or "body-sense") area behind the central fissure. This area contains neurons linked to the sense of touch. Next in order of development are the visual cortex at the back of the brain and the auditory cortex below the motor and somatosensory areas. Last to reach maturity are the association areas. These areas are necessary for memory, reasoning, and language (Tanner, 1978).

Although the speed of development in different cortical areas varies with age, all areas develop continuously. They begin to develop early in the prenatal period and continue to develop through the second decade of life. The first areas to develop show a slower rate of development after 2 years of age, but they do not stop developing entirely. Dramatic changes in many areas of the cortex take place between the ages of 6 and 8 years and again during adolescence (Rabinowicz, 1986).

When scientists talk about the third dimension of the brain, that going from left to right, they usually focus on the two halves of the cerebrum. The cerebrum is divided in two by a deep gap or fissure. Because the cerebrum itself is rounded like a sphere, the two halves are known as the left and right hemispheres.

Long ago, scientists learned that the nerve cells from the right side of the body cross in the brain stem and connect with neurons in the left hemisphere. Conversely, nerve cells from the left side of the body connect with neurons in the right hemisphere. Because of the crossing of neural pathways, people with strokes that damage the motor area of one hemisphere show weakness or paralysis on the opposite side of the body.

The two hemispheres are specialized in other ways. In adults, the left hemisphere plays a major role in language processing. The right hemisphere plays a major role in the processing of visual or spatial information and musical tones. Some popular writers have suggested that the **lateralization** of brain function, or the specialization of the left and right hemispheres, goes much further. They have suggested that the "left brain" is more logical and the "right brain" is more creative or intuitive. However, scientific research does not support these suggestions (Kinsbourne & Hiscock, 1983).

In normal adults, both sides of the brain cooperate in all kinds of reasoning and problem solving. This cooperation is possible because nerve impulses pass between the two hemispheres across the **corpus callosum,** a bundle of nerve fibers that links the hemispheres. Because of this link, and because few brain functions are completely lateralized, both cerebral hemispheres influence most aspects of cognitive functioning. For example, although language processing depends more on the left hemisphere, the right hemisphere is important for such language functions as verbal comprehension.

**lateralization**
*The process by which brain functions become specialized either in the left or in the right hemisphere.*

**corpus callosum**
*A bundle of nerve fibers that links the left and right hemispheres of the brain.*

## Brain Damage and Brain Plasticity

If the two cerebral hemispheres have specialized functions in adulthood, do they also have specialized functions in childhood? This question is important because it relates both to theories of brain development and to the practical issue of children's and adults' recovery from brain damage.

Eric Lenneberg (1967) proposed that the cerebral hemispheres do not have specialized functions at birth but become specialized during childhood. He based this conclusion on studies of people with left-hemisphere brain damage that impaired language functioning. In these studies, children less than 5 years old seemed to recover normal language after brain damage more quickly and completely than did adults. Lenneberg assumed that young

children respond to damage to the left hemisphere by shifting their language processing to the right hemisphere. Adults cannot do the same, according to Lenneberg, because their brains are already lateralized and the two hemispheres cannot modify themselves.

Lenneberg's (1967) hypothesis sparked a great deal of research because it posed two central questions about brain development. The first question concerns the development of brain lateralization. Evidence suggests, contrary to Lenneberg's hypothesis, that lateralization of brain functions is present at birth (Kinsbourne & Hiscock, 1983; Previc, 1991; Raz et al., 1994). Infants only a few weeks old respond more strongly to speech sounds they hear through their right ear than through their left ear. Because of the nerve-cell crossing in the brain stem mentioned earlier, sounds from the right ear are processed in the left hemisphere. Therefore, the stronger response by infants to right-ear speech demonstrates some specialization of language processing in the left hemisphere. Similar experiments show that infants process musical tones and other nonspeech sounds in the right hemisphere. Moreover, if children suffer brain damage due to bleeding around the time of birth, they show different patterns of cognitive performance depending on whether their left or right hemisphere was damaged.

Other evidence suggests that hemispheric lateralization does not change markedly after birth (Hiscock & Kinsbourne, 1995). In other words, the specialization of information processing by the two hemispheres does not increase with age. This conclusion is based partly on cross-sectional studies of children's listening to speech sounds through their right or left ears. Studies of visual perception and the exploration of objects by touch suggest the same conclusion.

The second question posed by Lenneberg's (1967) hypothesis is even more significant. His argument about age changes in recovery from brain damage points toward a broader issue of brain plasticity. As the term *plastic* implies, **brain plasticity** refers to the brain's flexibility, modifiability, or openness to change. Lenneberg (1967) assumed that adults were less able to recover from brain damage than were young children because brain plasticity is low after early childhood. Again, Lenneberg assumed that the undamaged regions of an adult's brain could not take over the functions of damaged regions.

No simple answer to questions about developmental changes in brain plasticity can be given. As Lenneberg (1967) assumed, young children often do show normal or nearly normal language development after left-hemisphere brain damage (Hiscock & Kinsbourne, 1995). Yet contrary to Lenneberg's assumptions, adults may recover as completely as children do when they suffer equally severe brain damage in the same brain regions (Snow, 1987). Thus, brain injuries do not always have more serious long-term consequences in adulthood than in childhood.

Recent studies also show that children do not recover completely from early brain injury. As the idea of cerebral lateralization would suggest, children who suffer left-hemisphere damage before and around the time of birth often show lasting impairments in verbal ability. Conversely, children who suffer right-hemisphere damage show lasting impairments in nonverbal or visual and spatial ability (Carlsson et al., 1994; Raz et al., 1994). In other words, brain plasticity is limited even early in life.

In some respects, brain plasticity may be *lower* in childhood than in adulthood. For example, children recover from brief periods of malnutrition less fully than do adults. That is, malnutrition has more lasting effects during childhood, when brain development is especially rapid, than during adulthood (Almli & Finger, 1987). Apparently, malnutrition reduces the rate of synapse formation. Some catch-up growth can occur if malnourished children receive adequate nutrition. But just as with physical development, the catch-up in brain development is not complete when early malnutrition is severe.

Taken together, current evidence indicates that brain plasticity depends not only on a person's age but also on the source of disruptions in development. Therefore, the belief that adults cannot recover from brain damage is overly pessimistic. Conversely, the belief that children can always recover from experiences that limit their brain development is overly optimistic.

**brain plasticity**
*The degree to which the brain is modifiable or open to change.*

# BEHAVIORAL ORGANIZATION AND MOTOR DEVELOPMENT

Physical growth and brain development are the basis for developmental changes in behavior. Changes in behavior can be described at several levels, starting with the most general level of behavioral states. A second, more specific level deals with patterns of movements. Especially important in infancy are the involuntary patterns of responses to stimuli called *reflexes*. A third level whose importance increases with age deals with voluntary motor behaviors such as walking.

## Sleep, Activity, and Crying: Age Changes in Behavioral States

Parents often wait eagerly for newborn babies to wake up and gaze at the world around them. Parents also wait eagerly for the first night that their young infant does *not* wake up around 3:00 A.M. to nurse and then gaze around the room. Obviously, infants have cycles of activity and rest that do not always match the preferred cycles of the adults who care for them. The infants' cycles illustrate the variations in their behavioral states.

### Five Behavioral States

A **behavioral state** refers to an infant's level of consciousness. More precisely, it refers to a person's position on the dimension from intense activity to quiet sleep. Researchers divide this single dimension into several distinct states, although they disagree about the number of states and their exact definition (Berg & Berg, 1987; Klaus & Klaus, 1985; Wolff, 1987; Zuckerman & Frank, 1992). Most researchers recognize at least the following five states:

**behavioral state**
*A general description of an infant's (or adult's) position on the dimension from intense activity to quiet sleep.*

1. *Quiet sleep.* Newborns who are sleeping quietly breathe slowly and regularly with their eyes closed. Their faces and their muscles are relaxed. They rarely move and are not easily awakened, even by noise or a touch.

2. *Active sleep.* In this state infants' eyes are usually closed but may be half-open. Often, the infants' eyes move rapidly, rolling around or jerking from one place to another. In addition, infants in active sleep have an irregular heartbeat, shallow and irregular breathing, and occasional periods a few seconds long when they do not breathe at all.

When adults are in the nearest equivalent to active sleep, showing rapid movement of the eyes, they normally report that they are dreaming. So far, researchers have not found a way to judge whether newborns are dreaming—and, if they are not, when children first begin to dream.

Premature infants and infants with medical problems show a different and potentially dangerous pattern of sleep states. They sometimes stop breathing during sleep for up to 20 seconds at a time. With these infants, such episodes occur more often during quiet sleep than active sleep. Some researchers believe that long periods without breathing are less likely in active sleep because the neural stimulation that leads to rapid eye movements also stimulates breathing (Berg & Berg, 1987). Researchers also suspect that nonbreathing episodes are related to the syndrome of Sudden Infant Death (see *Practical Applications of Research:* "The Mystery of Sudden Infant Death").

3. *Alert inactivity.* In the peaceful, alert state for which parents wait, a newborn's eyes are fully open and seem to move under conscious control. Newborns are relaxed, rarely move their limbs, and seem fully attentive to the world but calm.

4. *Waking activity.* As the intensity of newborns' activity increases, their alertness decreases. Newborns seem unable to control their attention and their muscles simultaneously. Their eyes remain open, but they seldom focus on objects. Their breathing is irregular, and they may moan or whimper as their legs and arms move about.

5. *Crying.* The extreme of newborns' activity is crying or fussing. While crying, newborns continue to move arms and legs in a disorganized fashion. Their faces are twisted and red; their eyes may be open or closed.

# THE MYSTERY OF SUDDEN INFANT DEATH

It is the grimmest of all mysteries: A 3-month-old baby boy is found dead in his crib. An autopsy reveals no apparent cause of death. Why did this baby die?

**Sudden Infant Death Syndrome,** or **SIDS,** is defined as the sudden death of an infant or young child that is unexpected by history and for which no adequate cause is revealed by a thorough postmortem examination (Carroll & Loughlin, 1994). Notice that SIDS is not, strictly speaking, a cause of death. Rather, it is a diagnosis applied to deaths for which there is no obvious cause.

In the United States and most other countries, between one and three of every 1,000 infants succumbs to SIDS. These deaths most often occur between 2 and 4 months of age. They are less common during the first month of life and during the second half-year of life (Hunt & Brouliette, 1987). They occasionally occur, although less often, after 1 year of age (Szybist, 1988).

SIDS more often claims the lives of infants who were preterm, had low birth weights, or had low Apgar scores. Also, SIDS infants are more likely to be male than female. These infants are small for their age, but neither this variable nor any other allows accurate identification of infants who will succumb to SIDS (Carroll & Loughlin, 1994).

SIDS is much more likely when the mother, father, or other people in the infants' homes smoke cigarettes (Klonoff-Cohen et al., 1995). Moreover, the risk of SIDS increases with the number of cigarettes smoked near the infant. In other words, so-called passive smoking can be deadly for an infant. Conversely, the rate of SIDS could be greatly reduced if all parents stopped smoking.

Other factors that increase the risk of SIDS include having a mother who is poorly educated, unmarried, or under 20 years old; having parents who use drugs; and living under crowded conditions (Carroll & Loughlin, 1994; Szybist, 1988). Still, many children with several of these risk factors survive infancy, and some with no risk factors die of SIDS (Hunt & Brouliette, 1987).

Some deaths attributed to SIDS might have simple explanations. One team of researchers visited the homes of 26 infants who were reported to have died of SIDS (Bass, Kravath, & Glass, 1986). They concluded that many of these deaths were accidental. Some infants seemed to have smothered in their cribs, for example, with their faces in a foam-rubber pillow. Other infants apparently suffocated when their mothers were breast-feeding them in bed and accidentally rolled over on them. Still other infants died in overheated rooms, and some seemed to be victims of child abuse. Findings like these have led many experts to call for a careful investigation of the scene of death before an infant is judged to have died of SIDS (Iyasu et al., 1994).

In addition, these and other findings have led to recommendations for lowering the risk of SIDS. Pediatricians in many countries have advised parents *not* to put infants to sleep lying on their stomachs, unless specific medical reasons for doing so exist. Instead, infants should be put down to sleep on their backs or on their sides, to reduce the risk of suffocation in a foam pillow or a soft mattress (Kattwinkel et al., 1994). SIDS rates in several countries have been cut in half as parents have stopped placing infants on their stomachs to sleep (Willinger, Hoffman, & Hartford, 1994).

Pediatricians have also tried to reduce the rate of SIDS by giving parents devices to monitor infant breathing and heart rate. If an infant stops breathing or has a greatly slowed heart rate, the monitor sounds an alarm so that parents can awaken the infant. The monitors have been tried because some infants who died of SIDS had long periods when they stopped breathing before they died. However, recent studies have shown that episodes of stopped breathing are not significantly related to the occurrence of an unexpected death (Carroll & Loughlin, 1994). Even so, the monitors are recommended for infants who are in a high-risk group for SIDS.

Other recommendations for parents involve proper infant care. In particular, parents should not allow their infants to become overheated. Infants should be clothed so that they become neither too cold nor too hot while sleeping. Parents should avoid the use of medications, such as the sedatives found in some cold remedies, that can affect infants' respiration and arousal. If all these recommendations are followed, fewer parents will suffer through the grim mystery of SIDS.

**Sudden Infant Death Syndrome (SIDS)**
*The sudden death of an infant or young child that is unexpected by history and for which no adequate cause is revealed by a thorough postmortem examination.*

On the average, newborns spend 16 to 18 hours a day in either quiet or active sleep. Some newborns sleep much less; others sleep even more. Newborns sleep about as much during the day as during the night, showing regular cycles of sleeping and waking that last about 4 hours. During most of each cycle, they are asleep. They are in the state of alert inactivity for a total of roughly 1 hour each day.

As the days and weeks pass, infants gradually develop sleep-wake cycles more like those of older children and adults. By the second month of life, they are sleeping substantially more during the night than during the day. They may not sleep through an entire night, though. They often awake for a feeding or two during the night.

By the end of the third month of life, infants are awake for roughly two-thirds of the day (Wolff, 1987). As they get older and gain greater muscle control, they develop a new state of *alert activity*, in which they not only attend to the world but also act on it. Achievement of this state sets the stage for infants' exploration of the world and even more rapid learning from experience.

## Changing Infant States: Social and Environmental Influences

From a parent's perspective, changes in an infant's state from minute to minute may be more important than changes from month to month. Can parents do anything, for example, to shift infants to a state of alert inactivity, to put them to sleep, or to stop them from crying? Answers to these questions would not only be useful to parents but also show how responsive infants are to different kinds of stimulation.

Researchers have identified one technique that can often change an infant's state to that of alert inactivity. Infants usually become more alert and less active if adults pick them up and hold them close to the shoulder (Korner & Thoman, 1972). Being held close limits infants' behavior; being in an upright position enhances infants' alertness.

Researchers have also identified one technique, the use of rhythmic stimulation, that can put an infant to sleep. For centuries, parents have used the rhythm of a rocking cradle, or the low, repetitive sounds of a lullaby. One high-technology alternative is the monotonous rumble of tires and wind in a car moving at highway speed. Some babies will even go to sleep to the sound of a vacuum cleaner.

Continuous and rhythmic stimulation can put babies to sleep because they change their state in response to environmental stimulation (Maurer & Maurer, 1988). If the level of environmental stimulation is high (but not painfully high), young infants reduce the stimulus input by going to sleep. Thus, paradoxically, faster rocking and louder sounds put babies to sleep more quickly and effectively than slower rocking and softer sounds. That conclusion holds only within limits, though. Young infants may experience high levels of stimulation as painful and start crying.

And what about crying? Are there effective techniques for quieting a crying baby? The answer to this question comes in four parts. First, some attempts to stop infants' crying are more effective than others. The mothers in one study (Bell & Ainsworth, 1972) used various techniques to soothe their crying infants. As you see from figure 5.12, the most effective technique was to pick up and hold the crying infant. This technique stopped the infant's crying more than 80 percent of the time. Feeding the infant was almost as effective. Giving infants a pacifier or toys stopped their crying about 60 percent of the time.

When mothers simply touched their infants without picking them up, or merely talked to their infants, they were less effective in soothing the infants. Approaching and touching the infant were more effective near the end of the first year of life than near the beginning, though. Older infants apparently depend less on close physical contact with the mother than do younger infants. In the next chapter, you will see how ethological theorists explain the importance of physical contact for soothing a crying infant.

Second, parents can more successfully soothe their infant if they know why the infant is crying. Parents can often guess the cause of their infant's crying simply by knowing the infant's schedule or circumstances. For example, infants who have not eaten for hours are likely to cry from hunger. Infants who have just been startled by a loud noise or a sudden jolt are likely to cry from fear.

Parents' wisdom—and infants' communication—seem to go even further. The pitch and rhythm of infants' cries differ when they are hungry versus in pain. Hunger cries, for example, become more intense over time. Pain cries are intense initially but then decrease in intensity (Zeskind et al., 1985). Even adults who are not parents appreciate this difference in types of cries. Adults also view hunger cries as becoming more urgent over time, while the reverse is true for pain cries (Green, Jones, & Gustafson, 1987).

Parents are not perfect, however, at judging why infants are crying. Parents sometimes assume that hungry infants are crying because they have a wet diaper or another source of moderate discomfort. Parents sometimes assume that infants who are in pain are crying

FIGURE 5.12

How can you soothe a crying infant? Here are some techniques that mothers in one study used, with the percentage of occasions on which each technique was effective. (Adapted from Bell & Ainsworth, 1972.)

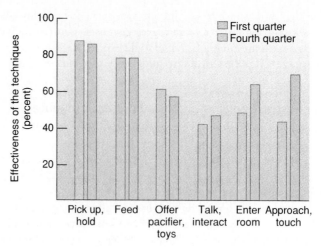

Techniques of soothing a crying infant

because they were startled or angry. These errors suggest that parents are better at judging a crying infant's level of discomfort—moderate or high—than at judging the specific reason the infant is crying (Gustafson & Harris, 1990).

Third, you may be reassured to learn that parents don't spend great amounts of time soothing crying infants because most infants spend little time crying (Bell & Ainsworth, 1972). Peter Wolff (1987) observed infants in their homes for several months after birth. He recorded full-blown cries during only 2 percent of the observation time. Mild fussiness occurred only 10 percent of the time. Moreover, crying and fussiness decreased over time. After the third month of life, many infants did almost no crying.

Parents of premature infants or infants with prenatal or birth complications have special problems. The cries of these infants are often higher in pitch than those of normal, full-term infants. Parents perceive these high-pitched cries as aversive and as signs that the infant is sick (Frodi et al., 1978; Zeskind & Lester, 1978). How parents respond to these distinctive cries is not entirely clear. Some parents may respond with special sensitivity to an infant whose cry suggests sickness. Other parents may withdraw from their infants or react angrily to them.

Finally, the importance of crying as a form of communication between infants and their parents deserves special emphasis. From birth on, parents have a special relationship with their children. Soon after birth, most mothers and many fathers can identify their infant from hearing the infant's cries (Gustafson, Green, & Cleland, 1994). Even adults who are not parents can accurately identify a specific infant's cry from as much as 30 m (100 ft.) away. Infants can, therefore, use crying as a signal of their need for food, protection, or comfort.

How parents interpret and respond to their infants' cries affects the formation of the parent-infant relationship. That relationship, in turn, affects the development of infants' patterns of communication (Bell & Ainsworth, 1972). After the first few weeks of life, infants' cries are less a sign of their behavioral state than a message to their parents. In the next chapter, you will see how this message is shaped by the relationship between infants and parents.

## Newborn Reflexes and the Transition to Voluntary Activity

Newborns are most active in the behavioral states of *waking activity* and *crying*. When in these states, the newborn's movements may seem uncontrolled and random. Yet when examined more closely, newborns show organized, amazingly complex patterns of behavior. The most distinctive and regular patterns of involuntary activity in response to specific stimuli are called **reflexes** (Cochran, 1994).

Several reflexes that can be elicited in newborns are essential for life. Breathing, for example, is a reflexive behavior. Sucking, which a newborn must do to get food from the mother's

**reflexes**
*Distinct and regular patterns of involuntary activity that are elicited by specific stimuli.*

breast, is another reflex. Also important in feeding is the **rooting reflex.** The light pressure of a finger on the cheek of newborns will cause them to turn their heads toward the finger, open their mouths, and close them on the finger. Newborns' tendency to "root around" for objects that touch them on the cheek can help them find the mother's nipple at feeding time.

Other reflexes protect newborns from danger. Newborns will close their eyes immediately if they suddenly see a bright light or feel a puff of air near their eyes. This **eyeblink reflex** can protect the eyes against potential damage. Newborns will flex a knee and move their foot away if they feel a pinprick on the sole of their foot, thus showing the **withdrawal reflex.** Newborns will grab and hold on if a stick is pressed against the palms of their hands. This **palmar grasp reflex** is quite strong. A newborn grasping onto a stick with both hands can be lifted off the ground like a gymnast holding onto a trapeze. (Don't try this with an infant, though, unless you have someone else ready to catch the infant if he or she lets go sooner than you expect.)

The **Moro reflex** is the most dramatic of the apparently protective reflexes. The reflex can be elicited by holding an infant in a horizontal position and then letting his or her head drop suddenly. In response to such a loss of support, infants arch their back and extend their legs. They throw both arms outward and then pull them back toward each other. If newborns who were holding onto a person started losing their grip, the Moro reflex combined with the palmar grasp could help them reattach to the person.

Still other newborn reflexes seem to be precursors of voluntary motor behaviors that emerge later in infancy. The **stepping reflex** is one example. To elicit this reflex, newborns are held upright with their feet just touching a smooth surface. Then their body is tilted alternately to the left and the right. In response, newborns will lift and move the right leg forward, then move the left, as if walking. Although newborns can't walk on their own, the coordination among muscles and joints that toddlers need to walk is partly present at birth.

The function of other reflexes is less clear, but these reflexes often provide information about a newborn's nervous system. The **Babinski reflex** can be elicited by stroking the sole of a newborn's foot with a finger, moving from the heel toward the toes. In response, the newborn will extend and spread the toes of the foot. This reflex is absent in infants with spinal-cord defects. Therefore, testing for this reflex can establish whether the connections between sensory and motor neurons are functioning normally. Partly for this reason, many reflexes are tested in the physical exam given to newborns (Cochran, 1994).

Many reflexes disappear a few months after birth. The palmar grasp, for example, cannot be elicited after about 4 months of age. The disappearance of reflexes after the newborn period is due partly to an increase in voluntary, cortical control (Bremner, 1994). Recall that brain development proceeds from the lowest level of the brain, the brain stem, to the highest level of the cortex. Reflexes are controlled by the brain stem or, occasionally, by the spinal cord. This lower-level control can be supplanted by the cortical control that allows true voluntary movement, so the transition from reflexes to voluntary activity reflects a change in brain functioning. Reflexes that persist beyond the point of normal disappearance can signal problems in brain development.

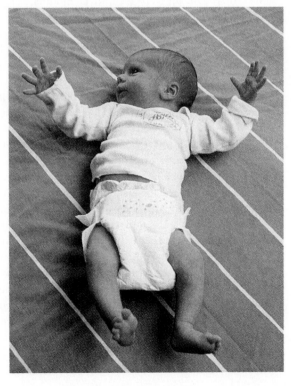

**rooting reflex**
*A newborn's response to a touch on the cheek — turning the head toward the object, opening the mouth, and closing it on the object.*

**eyeblink reflex**
*People's tendency to blink when they see a bright light or feel a puff of air near the eye.*

**withdrawal reflex**
*Newborns' tendency to flex their knee and move their foot away if they feel a pinprick on the sole of their foot.*

**palmar grasp reflex**
*Newborns' tendency to grab and hold onto a stick pressed against their palms.*

**Moro reflex**
*A reflex elicited by placing infants on their backs and abruptly reducing their support. In response, infants arch their back, extend their legs, and throw their arms outward and then pull them back toward each other.*

**stepping reflex**
*Newborns' tendency to make alternating movements of their two legs and feet if they are held, standing, and tilted slowly left and right.*

**Babinski reflex**
*A reflex elicited by stroking the sole of a newborn's foot, moving from the heel toward the toe. In response, normal newborns extend and spread their toes.*

This infant was startled by a loud noise or a sudden loss of support. In response, the infant is showing the Moro reflex, with arms outstretched, fingers extended, and legs spread. The infant will next bring the arms back toward each other in a grabbing gesture.

That reflexes disappear when infants begin to show voluntary behavior is only partly true. Some reflexes, such as the eyeblink in response to bright light, can be elicited in infants, children, and adults. Many reflexes that have a protective function last throughout life. Also, reflexes that seem to be precursors of voluntary behavior patterns do not simply disappear. The stepping reflex, for example, may play a critical role in the development of walking. As you will see in the next section, new discoveries have clarified how infants make the transition from the stepping reflex to voluntary walking.

## Early Developments in Controlled Motor Behavior

Voluntary walking is one of several milestones of motor development. Decades of research have established both the average age at which children pass these motor milestones and the variability among children in their attainment. This information is useful to pediatricians and other practitioners in identifying children with developmental delays.

Research on motor development can provide the answers to other questions, too. For example, what principles govern the development of voluntary motor behavior? Is the age at which children achieve the various motor milestones dependent solely on maturation (nature) or on maturation plus experience (nurture)? Finally, what is the long-term significance, if any, of early progress or retardation in motor development? As you read further, watch for the answers to these questions.

### Norms and Principles of Motor Development

Several scales for measuring children's motor development exist (e.g., Bayley, 1993; Capute & Shapiro, 1985; Frankenburg & Dodds, 1967; Frankenburg et al., 1981; Shirley, 1933; Sparrow, Balla, & Cicchetti, 1984). Most scales include two subscales. One is for **gross motor behavior,** movements of the entire body or major parts of the body. The other is for **fine motor behavior,** which refers mainly to eye-hand coordination and control of the arm, hand, and fingers.

Figure 5.13 shows the age norms for several indicators of gross motor development. The norms are based on large samples of infants and children throughout the United States. Although the norms reflect the average age at which children pass each item (or the 50th percentile), normal children may vary greatly from the average. For example, although most children first walk up steps around 17 months of age, about one-quarter do so before 14 months of age and another quarter do not do so until after 21 months of age.

Several items on the scale refer to widely recognized milestones. For example, the average age at which infants roll over is about 3 months. The average age at which they sit without support is between 5 and 6 months. The average age at which they walk well by themselves is just over 12 months.

The scale is more meaningful if you relate the items to each other. Then you can see more examples of the cephalocaudal principle. The first milestones of gross motor development involve lifting the head. The next milestones involve increasing control over the upper body, for example, lifting the chest and sitting without support. Next comes control of the lower body, indicated by standing and walking. In short, the development of motor control, like physical development, proceeds from the head to the foot.

Figure 5.14 shows the age norms for several indicators of fine motor development. The first few items refer to visual coordination, the infant's ability to track objects visually as they move. The next items deal with movements of the hands, alone or together. Again, these items are meaningful by themselves, but if viewed in sequence they also illustrate the proximodistal principle of development. An average infant can reach for objects with the entire arm around 4 months of age but cannot hold a small object in a pincer grasp—between the thumb and forefinger—until nearly 1 year of age. Infants have good control over their arms before their fingers because the arms are nearer the center of the body.

Motor-development scales are valuable because they show how motor control changes after infancy, up to age 6. Figure 5.13 indicates, for example, that most children cannot consistently catch a ball bounced to them until they are almost 4 years of age. Of course, motor

**gross motor behavior**
*Behavior that involves the movement of the entire body or major parts of the body (e.g., head, arms, legs).*

**fine motor behavior**
*Behavior that depends primarily on control of the hands and fingers, or eye-hand coordination.*

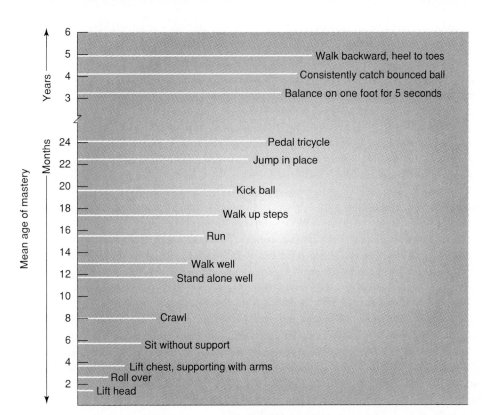

**FIGURE 5.13**

Age norms for various gross motor skills, involving movements of the whole body or major parts of the body. The norms, which are for U.S. children, are drawn from various measures of motor development. (Sources: Bayley, 1993; Frankenburg et al., 1981; Palmer & Caputo, 1994; Shonkoff, 1992.)

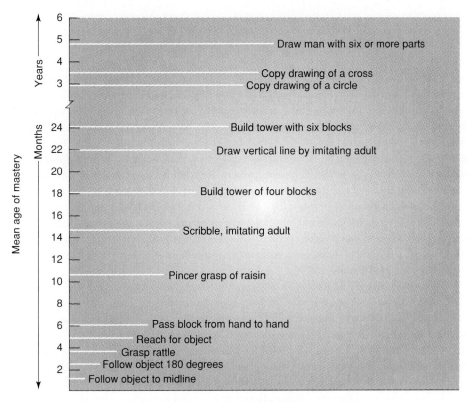

**FIGURE 5.14**

Age norms for various fine motor skills, involving coordinated movements of the eyes or the eyes and the hands. The norms, which are for U.S. children, are drawn from various measures of motor development. (Sources: Bayley, 1993; Frankenburg et al., 1981; Palmer & Caputo, 1994; Shonkoff, 1992.)

control continues to improve beyond age 6. To see this improvement most vividly, spend some time watching children of various ages playing sports like soccer or baseball.

One drawback of general scales for motor development is their lack of detail about any single achievement. Researchers have found that even apparently simple movements like reaching for an object show a long and complex developmental sequence.

When looking at an object, newborns will sometimes move an arm toward the object as if reaching for it. Yet they seldom get close enough to touch the object (Hofsten, 1984; Klaus & Klaus, 1985). This kind of "prereaching" decreases a few weeks after birth (Bremner, 1994). After two months, arm movements toward objects increase again, but the infant's hand now begins to open during the reach; that is, the hand prepares for grabbing the object.

The first successful reaching movements, around 3 to 5 months of age, are often visually guided; that is, infants watch their hand and the object simultaneously to guide the hand toward the object (Hofsten, 1984, 1989). However, infants can reach successfully without this visual guidance. If placed in the dark and shown a wooden egg that glows in the dark, 4- or 5-month-olds can successfully grasp the egg (Clifton et al., 1993). Even if a toy only rattles in the dark, infants of that age can grasp it successfully. They apparently do so because they have a mental representation of space that integrates external information (sights and sounds) with internal information about the positions of their own arms and hands.

Mature reaching is still more sophisticated (Bushnell, 1985; Clifton et al., 1993; Thelen et al., 1993). Infants learn to reach rapidly and accurately, moving straight toward the target and opening their hand the appropriate amount for the target's size and shape. The adjustments of the arm, hand, and other parts of the body that are involved in a skillful reach-and-grasp are so automatic and so coordinated that they seem simple. Think for a moment, though, about the movements of a professional dancer or athlete. What looks simple is often extremely difficult to do. The mature reaches of infants also result from months of practice and should be viewed as true milestones of motor development.

## Contributions of Maturation and Experience to Motor Development

Why do some infants walk earlier than others? More generally, why is motor development more rapid in some children than in others? For decades, arguments have raged over the answers to these questions.

***Nature Versus Nurture***   Remember from chapter 1 that Gesell (1954) believed motor development was controlled by maturation. He argued that all children learn to walk, reach, and grasp because these skills are part of a developmental program in the children's genes. And because children's genotypes differ, some mature faster than others. As evidence for these hypotheses, Gesell used the results of his training studies with identical twins (e.g., Gesell & Thompson, 1929). He viewed these studies as showing that motor training did not have any permanent effects on motor development. Instead, he argued, motor development depends on brain development, the maturation of the central nervous system (Gesell & Thompson, 1929).

This conclusion was accepted for a long time. Most child development researchers assumed that voluntary motor behaviors like walking emerge when the neural networks in the cortex reach maturity and take control over the motor neurons. Stated differently, researchers assumed that maturation involves the replacement of reflex control over movement by cortical control (Bremner, 1994).

Remember from chapter 2, however, that Ache children who were observed in Paraguay began to walk several months later than do children in the United States (Kaplan & Dove, 1987). Moreover, the Ache children's performance on a standard measure of gross motor development was much below the age norms for U.S. children. Recall that the researchers who studied Ache children argued that their motor development was delayed because their mothers did not allow them much freedom to move around. This hypothesis suggests that motor development is strongly influenced by infants' and children's experiences.

Other research supports the conclusion that early experience affects motor development. A few decades ago, Wayne Dennis (1960) examined the motor development of infants raised in institutions in Iran. In one institution, infants spent their days lying on their backs

This mother carries her infant close to her in cloths that restrict the infant's motor movements. Will this method of carrying the infant also delay his or her motor development? It might, but as you will read later, the delay is not likely to be permanent.

in cribs. They were only removed from their cribs for baths, which they only had every other day. No infants in this institution could walk alone before 2 years of age and few were walking even by age 3.

Additional evidence for the importance of early experience comes from other cross-cultural studies. The story about Pablo at the beginning of this chapter is one example. The infants in Pablo's village received better care than did the infants studied by Dennis (1960), but the movements of these village infants were still very restricted. And, when tested by Kagan and Klein (1973), their motor skills were retarded. By contrast, *Cultural Perspectives:* "Teaching Baby to Walk" describes cross-cultural studies that suggest early experiences can accelerate the development of motor skills.

***The Dynamic-Systems Approach to Motor Development***   Another perspective on motor development goes beyond the traditional categories of nature versus nurture. The central principle in this new perspective is that infants' movements are the product of a dynamic, self-organizing system (Fogel & Thelen, 1987; Smith & Thelen, 1993; Thelen, 1995; Thelen & Ulrich, 1991). In this **dynamic-systems approach,** patterns of behavior are viewed as the result of the cooperative functioning of many component processes. The processes change over time as a result of brain maturation, experience, or a combination of the two. These changes, in turn, lead to the emergence of new behavioral patterns.

The dynamic-systems approach has been applied to domains other than motor development (Smith & Thelen, 1993), but its value has been shown most clearly in research on motor skills. For example, Esther Thelen and her colleagues have argued that voluntary walking is the result of a long sequence of development that builds on the stepping reflex (Thelen, Kelso, & Fogel, 1987; Thelen & Ulrich, 1991). The emergence of walking also depends on other components, including some as elementary (and, in hindsight, as obvious) as an infant's muscle strength.

The stepping reflex shown by newborns is similar in form to the spontaneous kicks found in older infants (Thelen & Fisher, 1982). The form of the stepping reflex is also similar but not identical to that of mature walking (Thelen & Cooke, 1987). Why, then, does

**dynamic-systems approach**
*A theoretical perspective in which patterns of behavior are assumed to be the product of self-organizing systems involving many component processes. Changes in these processes over time lead to the emergence of new behavioral patterns.*

# TEACHING BABY TO WALK

If restricting infants' movement can delay their motor development, can encouraging infants' movement accelerate their motor development? Research findings summarized in table 5.1 suggest that the answer is yes.

Several decades ago, researchers discovered that infants in several African societies show precocious motor development (Super, 1981). One example is the !Kung, a group of people who live in the Kalahari desert in Southern Africa (Konner, 1976). As table 5.1 shows, the average !Kung infant begins walking independently around 10 months of age, two months earlier than the average age for U.S. children.

The !Kung infants' precocious development seems to be due partly to their great freedom of movement during infancy. When !Kung infants are carried by adults, they are placed in a sling that leaves their arms and legs free. !Kung parents also train infants to sit, stand, and walk. They view these achievements as too important to trust to maturation.

Early walking has also been documented among Jamaican infants who have immigrated to Great Britain (Hopkins & Westra, 1990). One sample of these infants began walking at an average age of 10 months, three months earlier than a sample of English infants in the same city. The Jamaican infants who were early walkers had mothers who gave them regular stretching exercises during the first months of life. These mothers also encouraged their development of walking, for example, by holding their infants' hands and practicing walking with them.

Other findings suggest that the differences between infants in Western and non-Western countries are due to experience (nurture) rather than to genetic potential (nature). First, the differences are not found when mothers do not give their infants special experiences to foster motor development. Table 5.1 shows that Jamaican infants whose mothers did not provide them with special motor training began walking around 12 months of age, about the same age as U.S. and English infants.

Second, differences between Western and non-Western infants are absent on motor skills not specifically trained by mothers. Mothers in non-Western cultures rarely attach any value to the achievement of crawling, so they rarely do exercises to promote the development of crawling. Not surprisingly, their infants show no precocity in crawling. In the study of Jamaican infants, the age norm for crawling was between 10 and 11 months for all groups (Hopkins & Westra, 1990). Moreover, several Jamaican mothers said their infants never went through a stage of crawling before learning to walk.

Taken together, the research shows that parents can help their infants acquire specific motor skills faster. More generally, it shows the importance of experience for motor development. However, parents do not change the course of their children's motor development greatly. Children gain an advantage only on skills closely related to those that their parents have encouraged and practiced with them.

---

**TABLE 5.1**  Motor Training and Age Norms in Different Cultures

| Group | Motor Training? | Mean Age of Walking (months) |
| --- | --- | --- |
| U.S. infants | No | 12 |
| !Kung infants | Yes, carrying in a sling and training in walking | 10 |
| Jamaican infants in England | Yes, stretching exercises and walking with hands held | 10 |
| English infants | No | 13 |
| Jamaican infants in England | No | 12 |

reflex stepping apparently disappear when an infant is a couple of months old? Why don't infants walk as soon as they can step, that is, at birth?

Maturation of the nervous system is part of the answer, but so are basic principles of physics. To perform the stepping reflex, infants must have the muscle strength to lift their legs. In the first few months of life, infants gain in weight and, especially, in body fat more than they gain in muscle strength. Therefore, stepping movements that a newborn can manage are difficult for a heavier 2-month-old to achieve.

To test this explanation, Thelen did several ingenious experiments (Thelen, Fisher, & Ridley-Johnson, 1984; Thelen & Ulrich, 1991). For example, she showed that the stepping reflex disappears first in infants who gain weight most rapidly after birth, as would be expected if their weight gain lessens their ability to display the reflex. By contrast, stepping movements increase if infants are held with their lower bodies in water. When infants' legs are submerged in water, the pull of gravity is reduced and their relatively weak muscles can more easily lift their relatively heavy legs.

Walking also depends on precise coordination between the stretching and contraction of leg muscles. As one leg is stretched back, the muscles of the other leg must contract and support the full weight of the body. This coordination is easier for infants who are allowed to walk on a motorized treadmill, so infants supported on a motorized treadmill display alternating stepping movements months before they can walk independently.

These examples illustrate only a few of the component abilities necessary for independent walking. The development of these abilities depends partly on neural maturation and partly on the universal forms of "body building." As infants crawl, they increase the muscle strength in their legs. As they stand or are held in a standing position, they improve their balance and the coordination of their muscle movements. When these and the other components for walking have emerged, infants start walking independently.

The dynamic-systems approach has its critics (Aslin, 1993; Hopkins, Beek, & Kalverboer, 1993). One question not answered by advocates of this approach is how children's genes and their environments work together to bring about motor development. Another question concerns exactly what role the brain plays as a director of movements and an influence on motor development.

Yet, as you read in chapter 1, no theory answers all questions about development. One virtue of the dynamic-systems approach is that it suggests testable hypotheses about the types of experiences that will promote or delay development. In addition, this approach adds rich meaning to the statement that children have both a body and a brain. The principles of physics that apply to the movements of stars, planets, and other heavenly bodies also apply to the movements of arms, legs, and other parts of children's bodies.

## Questions About Continuity in Motor Development

The evidence that early motor development is influenced by infants' experience raises important questions. Some of these questions are highly practical. For example, should parents worry if their infant's motor development is delayed? Should parents expect great athletic achievements from an infant whose motor development is advanced?

Other questions are more theoretical. For example, is there substantial continuity in motor development? Does an infant whose motor development is delayed show below-normal motor skills throughout childhood? Alternatively, do infants show the resilience emphasized by Kagan and Klein (1973) and usually overcome early disadvantages?

Because most data relevant to these questions are correlational, researchers cannot give conclusive answers. However, the available data consistently suggest that early delays in motor development have little long-term significance. Dennis (1960) reported that the retardation in motor skills that he found in institutionalized Iranian infants disappeared by adolescence. Kaplan and Dove (1987) suggested that Ache children in Paraguay reach or surpass the U.S. norms for gross motor development by 10 years of age. These studies imply that children given adequate motor experience after infancy can show complete catch-up growth in motor skills. We might, then, expect Pablo and other children from his village not to show any lasting deficits in motor development either.

However, this optimistic conclusion applies *only* to motor development. Early experiences may or may not have lasting effects, depending on the kind of experience and the aspect of development affected. You will see in later chapters that early experiences can and often do have lasting effects on children's cognitive development.

# EARLY PERCEPTUAL DEVELOPMENT

Some people believe that human infants, like kittens, don't see anything for the first few weeks after birth. These people are only half right. *Kittens* don't see for the first few weeks of life. They are born with their eyes closed (which makes them good subjects for certain experiments, as you read earlier). Human infants *can* see at birth, although not exactly as adults do.

People's confusion about what newborns can see is understandable, because newborns do not give clear signals about their perception of the world. Their repertoire of responses to environmental stimuli is small, so judging what they do perceive is difficult. But with each passing decade, researchers devise more ingenious techniques to find out how young infants experience their world: what they see, hear, taste, smell, and touch. Using these techniques, researchers have learned how rapidly and by which routes perception develops the accuracy and patterning found in adulthood. In the following sections you'll discover both what techniques researchers have devised and what they have learned about early perceptual development.

## Visual Perception

Because humans' visual experience of the world is so rich, questions about visual development are both fascinating and multifaceted. Even an apparently simple question about the accuracy of infants' visual perception requires a complex answer. One part of the answer deals with how well infants can see any visual stimulus. Another part deals with the meaning of specific visual stimuli to them. For example, researchers have asked if young infants recognize patterns like the arrangement of features on a human face. Yet another part of the answer deals with infants' visual perception of the third dimension, that is, distance (or depth) and the shape of solid objects.

### Visual Sensitivity

Remember the eye exams you had in elementary school? You saw a chart with letters of different sizes some distance away. The examiner asked you to read the letters on the chart. As the letters got smaller, they were more difficult to read. Eventually, you couldn't read them at all. If your vision was normal, you could read from 20 feet away the row of letters that most people without eye problems can read from that distance. Thus, your vision was 20/20.

**visual acuity**
*An index of the sharpness of a person's vision, or how well they can see objects.*

Researchers cannot use exactly the same technique with infants, so they have devised other ways to measure infants' **visual acuity,** how good their vision is. Infants usually prefer to look at stimuli that are complex. If you show an infant a plain gray square and a pattern of alternating black and white stripes, the infant will look longer at the stripes than the square because the stripes are more complex. But the thinner the stripes get, the less visible they are. If the stripes are very thin, they are hard to distinguish from the solid gray square. Moreover, infants who can't distinguish the thin stripes from the solid gray square can't show a preference for one over the other.

How thin can stripes be before infants stop showing a preference for looking at them? Most infants a week old cannot see stripes thinner than 0.1 of an inch wide from 1 foot away (Banks & Salapatek, 1983; Maurer & Maurer, 1988). This level of acuity corresponds to 20/600 vision measured on a standard eye chart. Other techniques for measuring infants' visual acuity, such as the analysis of evoked potentials mentioned in chapter 2, yield similar estimates of infants' visual acuity. If your vision were (still) that poor, you could not read this book. You might be legally blind.

Visual acuity improves greatly during the first year of life. By 8 months of age, infants can distinguish between a gray square and stripes only about 0.01 of an inch wide 1 foot away. This level of acuity is still lower than that in adulthood. At a distance of 1 foot, adults

with normal vision can see stripes only 0.003 of an inch wide. Children do not achieve this level of visual acuity until 5 or 6 years of age (Maurer & Maurer, 1988).

The deficits in newborn vision go beyond a low level of acuity. Young infants are relatively insensitive to contrasts or shading of stimuli. When researchers measure visual acuity, they use stimuli with maximum contrast. If they show infants stripes, the stripes are dark black or bright white. In the real world, though, many contrasts are less sharp.

Light on a human face, for example, creates a pattern of shading that helps us distinguish the cheeks from the chin, the nose, and the forehead. A newborn infant would be unable to see these differences in shading but would be sensitive to greater contrasts like that between a man's mustache and the skin of his face. Shortly after birth, infants are only about one-tenth as sensitive to differences in contrast or shading as adults are (Aslin, 1987; Maurer & Maurer, 1988). Their sensitivity to contrast improves nearly to adult levels around 6 months of age (Banks & Dannemiller, 1987).

A third limitation of young infants' vision is in **visual accommodation.** When you glance at an object a long distance away, eye muscles change the shape of your lens so that the object comes into focus. If you shift your glance to a nearby object, eye muscles automatically change the lens's shape to bring that object into focus. These adjustments of lens shape reflect the process of visual accommodation.

Early experiments suggested that newborn infants could not adjust their lens shape to focus on objects at different distances. That is, infants seemed incapable of visual accommodation. Then researchers carefully examined the stimuli used in the early experiments. These stimuli were so small or so lacking in contrast that young infants probably could not see them clearly. To exaggerate a bit, researchers were asking infants to focus on objects that they could barely see.

When the experiments were repeated with better stimuli, they showed that young infants do accommodate to objects at different distances. By shining a beam of light into an infant's eye and observing the beam as it is reflected from the retina, researchers found that even 1-month-olds adjust their focus when objects are at different distances (Aslin, 1987).

**visual accommodation**
*The process by which eye muscles change the shape of the lens to bring objects at different distances into focus.*

Even so, the eye movements responsible for visual accommodation were slower and less accurate in young infants than in adults. Infants also focused best on objects about 10 inches away. They focused less well on nearer and farther objects (Maurer & Maurer, 1988). During the first two to four months of life, visual accommodation becomes similar to that of adults (Bremner, 1994; Hainline & Abramov, 1992).

Another important feature of human vision is sensitivity to color. Infants' color vision might be examined by using the **preferential looking technique.** In this technique, an infant's ability to distinguish between two stimuli is tested by showing the stimuli simultaneously and observing whether the infant looks longer at one stimulus than the other. You read earlier about the use of this technique to study infants' visual acuity. A researcher might use the technique to study color vision by showing an infant two squares, one gray and one red. If the infant consistently looks more at one than the other, the researcher can conclude (if some other conditions are met) that the infant saw the difference between them.

But what if the infant doesn't look more at one than the other? One possible reason is that the infant can't see the difference between them. Yet another possible reason is that the infant sees the difference but doesn't prefer one color over the other. In general, the preferential looking technique provides more information about what infants *can* see than about what they *can't.*

Researchers sometimes use another technique for studying color vision that is based on the principle of **habituation.** Like children and adults, infants become bored and stop looking at stimuli that they have seen repeatedly. The decline in looking found after repeated presentations of the same stimulus is known as habituation. If an infant who has habituated to one stimulus is shown a new stimulus, the infant is likely to *dishabituate,* or show increased looking. The increase proves that the infant recognized the difference between the original stimulus and the new stimulus. More generally, researchers can use the habituation technique to find out when infants see two stimuli as the same (or similar) and when they see them as different.

The example of color vision can help in spelling out some details of the habituation technique. Suppose you show an infant a gray circle. The infant looks at the circle for a few seconds and then looks away. You remove the circle and, after a brief pause, present it again. The infant again looks at it but for less time than before. You repeat this sequence until the infant hardly looks at the circle when you present it.

Then, without any change in the timing, you substitute a red circle for the gray one. Even newborns will dishabituate, or show more looking, at that circle than at the previous one. The increase in looking shows that they can see the difference between gray and red. Using similar techniques, researchers have learned that newborns can also distinguish between gray and yellow and between gray and green. Newborns do not distinguish between gray and blue, nor between yellow and green (Maurer & Adams, 1987). Sensitivity to the differences between these colors emerges between birth and 3 months of age. Color vision in 3-month-olds is similar to that in adults (Teller & Bornstein, 1987).

The developments in visual acuity, sensitivity to contrast, accommodation, and color vision are caused by changes in multiple components of the visual system. Both newborns and adults have special neurons in the center of the retina, called *cones,* that allow the most sensitive vision, especially of color. In the newborn, however, these neurons are immature (Bremner, 1994; Maurer & Maurer, 1988). The neurons in the visual cortex are also immature at birth. As you learned earlier, they develop and are fine-tuned during the first months and years of life. In other words, the age changes in vision during the infant and toddler years are due to developments in both the eye and the brain (Banks & Dannemiller, 1987).

## Pattern Perception: Bull's-Eyes, Faces, and Many Points of Light

Within a few minutes after birth, most infants take their first look at the face of their mother and father. You know already that newborns can't see a face very well. But do they recognize the human face as a distinctive pattern? Is the human face a pattern that newborns identify and prefer?

Early research by Robert Fantz (1966) suggested that infants are more interested in human faces than in other visual patterns. Fantz showed infants pairs of visual stimuli

**preferential looking technique**
*Testing an infant's ability to distinguish between two visual stimuli by showing the stimuli simultaneously and observing whether the infant looks longer at one stimulus than the other.*

**habituation**
*A decrease in responding to stimuli presented repeatedly.*

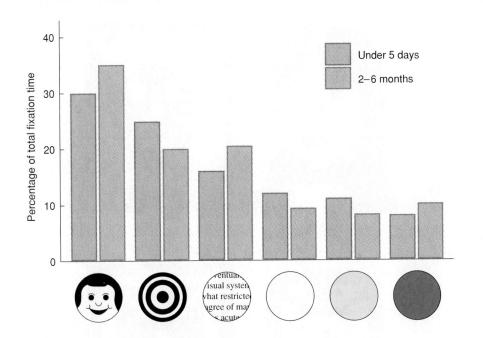

FIGURE 5.15

What do infants like to see? Both the newborns and the older infants in Fantz's (1966) study looked longer at a schematic face than at the other stimuli shown here. But as you will read in the text, later research suggests that the two groups of infants probably preferred the schematic face for different reasons.

(see figure 5.15), and recorded how long infants looked at each one. He was, in fact, the researcher who created the preferential looking technique.

The infants in Fantz's (1966) original study looked longer at the schematic diagram of a human face than at the other visual patterns such as a bull's-eye or a plain, colored disk. In later studies, Fantz scrambled the features of a human face. For example, he showed stimuli in which an eye was where the mouth should be, the nose was in the middle of the left cheek, and so on. He found that infants under 2 months of age did not consistently prefer the regular face over the face with scrambled features (see also Maurer & Barrera, 1981). These findings cast doubt on the hypothesis that young infants perceive the human face as a regular, distinctive pattern.

Other researchers then tried to figure out what features of visual stimuli are most attractive to young infants. They discovered many variations in visual patterns that influence infants' looking. For example, infants under 3 months of age prefer to look at patterns high in contour density, which means patterns with many shifts between light and dark areas. Infants also prefer concentric and symmetrical stimuli (like Fantz's bull's-eye) over stimuli that are less regular (Olson & Sherman, 1983).

As researchers gathered more data on infants' preferences, they tried to devise explanations for these preferences. Martin Banks and Arthur Ginsburg (1985) suggested that infants look longest at the stimuli that they see best. Because young infants are poor at detecting visual contrasts, they like to look at patterns high in contour density that have sharp contrasts. Also, young infants prefer patterns that are not highly complex (i.e., that do not have large numbers of distinct elements), because their poor acuity means they have trouble seeing the small elements in a complex pattern.

Why, then, don't infants prefer the simplest possible patterns, or even a plain disk? Marshall Haith (1980) suggested that young infants are genetically programmed to look at things that stimulate the visual system. When awake and alert, infants look at patterns that keep the neurons in the visual system active. As mentioned earlier, this neural activity is important during the first months of life in fine-tuning the links of visual input to neural networks.

What about faces, then? Faces have many characteristics that are attractive to infants. They are moderately complex stimuli that are partly symmetric (e.g., in the placement of the two eyes). They are high in contour density, especially at the boundaries between the skin, hair, eyes, and mouth. For these reasons alone, faces should be attractive to young

FIGURE 5.16
These computer-generated stimuli are similar in their complexity, contour density, and other characteristics, but only stimulus A looks like a schematic face. At 12 weeks of age, but not at 6 weeks, infants prefer stimulus A over the other patterns. (From Dannemiller & Stephens, 1988.)

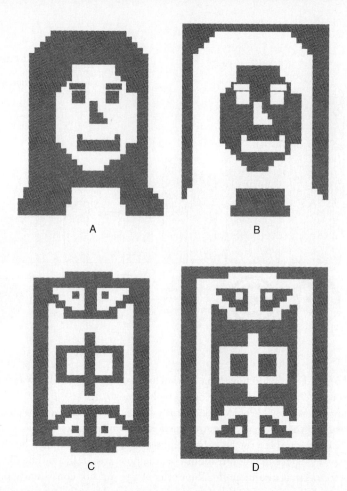

infants. They may be no more attractive, though, than other visual patterns that are similar in complexity, symmetry, contour density, and other features.

James Dannemiller and Benjamin Stephens (1988) tested these predictions with the stimuli shown in figure 5.16. As you can see, the stimulus that looks most like a human face is A. The two lower stimuli, C and D, are abstract geometric patterns. Pattern B looks a bit like a Halloween mask, but it lacks the contrast pattern of a human face. For example, the mouth is lighter rather than darker than the skin.

As previous research suggested, 6-week-old infants did not prefer the most facelike pattern (A) over the other patterns. When the complexity, contour density, and other features of a face were matched by these other patterns, infants showed no special fascination with a schematic human face. By 12 weeks of age, though, infants did prefer the schematic face over the other patterns. When given a choice between two stimuli, they looked at pattern A roughly 70 percent of the time.

Why don't 6-week-old infants prefer human faces more than other patterns? During the first month or so of life, infants rarely look at the features of a face. When shown a face, young infants focus most of their visual attention on the exterior boundary of the face, the outline of the head (Maurer & Salapatek, 1976). The outline is high in contour density, and that attracts young infants' attention. Thus they apparently see faces primarily as ovals with no internal features.

Around 2 months of age, infants begin to scan the internal features of faces. They focus especially on the eyes and mouth. Within the next month, or by 12 weeks of age, they start to see the human face as a distinctive visual pattern (Dannemiller & Stephens, 1988).

A limitation of most research on pattern perception is that the stimuli are highly artificial. One characteristic absent from the stimuli discussed so far—but typical of objects in

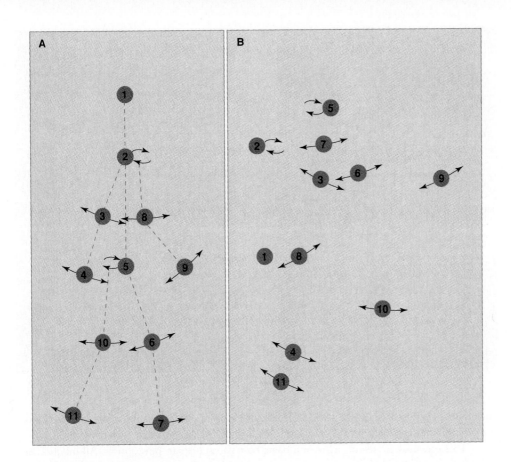

**FIGURE 5.17**

The 11 points of light in pattern A move in the directions indicated by the arrows. Even without the lines between the lights, you would perceive them as if they were attached to the head and the joints of a person walking. The lights in pattern B move in the same directions as the lights with the same numbers in pattern A, but their arrangement is haphazard. By 5 months of age, infants recognize the difference between these patterns and seem to interpret pattern A as that of a person walking in the dark.

the real world—is movement. Infants often see objects and people in motion. For example, they watch people approach them, move away from them, or do things around them.

An intriguing series of experiments suggests that infants' understanding of human motion changes dramatically during the first year of life. Infants in these experiments saw moving patterns of lights displayed on a computer monitor. Figure 5.17 shows two contrasting patterns.

Pattern A includes 11 points of light that move in the directions indicated by the arrows. The dotted lines between the lights are not part of the display shown to infants, but they illustrate that the pattern of lights matches the head, body, arms, and legs of a person. Adults who see pattern A in motion quickly judge that it shows a person walking in the dark with points of light attached to the head and the major joints of the body. Pattern B includes the same number of lights, and each light moves in the same directions as the light with the same number in pattern A. However, pattern B does not match that of a person in motion.

By 3 months of age but not before, infants look longer at pattern B than at pattern A, suggesting that they find the scrambled pattern more surprising (Bertenthal et al., 1987). This difference in looking does not, by itself, prove that the infants perceive what adults perceive in pattern A—a representation of a person walking. In other experiments, 3-month-olds responded similarly to pattern A and to a pattern in which the lights were inverted, as if the person was upside down (Proffitt & Bertenthal, 1990). By 5 months of age, however, infants respond differently to the "walking" pattern and to the inverted pattern, just as adults do. Apparently, perception of the normal pattern of human walking emerges around 5 months of age.

## Depth Perception

Now you know that newborns can see, although not as well as adults. You also know that infants gradually develop an appreciation of the significance of visual patterns such as human faces and

FIGURE 5.18

The checkerboard pattern is just under the plexiglass on the "shallow" side of the visual cliff apparatus, so the infant feels safe there. The pattern looks different on the deep side because it is a few feet below the plexiglass. The infant's hesitation to crawl on the deep side may be an indication of the perception of depth.

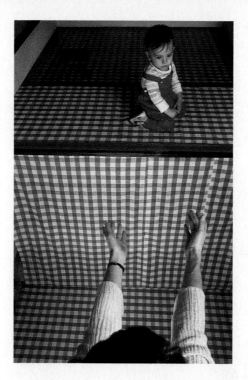 

movements. So far, though, you have read entirely about infants' perceptions of two-dimensional stimuli. Do infants, like adults, perceive the world as three-dimensional, as having depth?

This question arises because of a basic fact about human perception. All images sent from the eye to the brain are two-dimensional. Light is focused on the retina, a flat surface on the back of the eyeball. Neurons on this surface can easily represent visual information about the length and breadth of objects. Depth, however, must be judged by integrating the information from multiple neurons. Researchers have asked, then, whether newborns can perform this integration and, if not, when infants develop the ability to perceive depth.

One important experiment on infants' perception of depth was done more than 30 years ago. Eleanor Gibson and Richard Walk (1960) devised an apparatus called the visual cliff, which consists of a large platform covered with a sheet of plexiglass (see figure 5.18). On one half of the platform, a checkerboard pattern lies just under the sheet of plexiglass. On the other half, the checkerboard pattern is a few feet below the plexiglass, as if at the bottom of a cliff. Because plexiglass covers the entire platform, an infant can move on any part of it safely, and younger infants do. Most infants over 6 months of age, however, stay on one side of the platform: They will not crawl "over the cliff."

A later experiment showed that even 2-month-olds respond to the difference between the shallow and deep sides of the platform (Campos, Langer, & Krowitz, 1970). These infants' heart rates decreased when they were placed on the deep side and changed little on the shallow side, which suggests that they perceived the depth of the checkerboard pattern below them. On the other hand, the 2-month-olds may have simply responded to the difference in the appearance of the patterns on the two sides (Banks & Salapatek, 1983).

Around 7 to 9 months of age, infants show faster heart rates when they are lowered onto the deep side of the visual cliff (Bertenthal & Campos, 1987; Proffitt & Bertenthal, 1990). As in adults, infants' hearts beat faster when they are aroused and afraid. Therefore, their heart rate acceleration suggests the onset of a true fear of heights. This fear seems to arise around 7 to 9 months because infants typically begin to crawl around that age. Crawling or other kinds of self-produced movement provide the experience that causes infants to stay away from the deep side of the visual cliff.

Other research shows that infants can perceive depth before 7 months of age. New approaches to the study of depth perception came from examining the cues that adults use to judge depth. Some of these cues derive from the motion of objects.

Consider a simple experiment. You put on sound-deadening earphones and then stand in the middle of a street. Next, you look down the street and see a car apparently coming toward you at high speed. What do you do? Of course, you run out of the street.

But how did you know that you should run? You were wearing earphones, so you could not hear the sound of the car. How did you perceive that the car was coming toward you? One visual cue to the distance between you and the car is the change in the size of the car's retinal image. As the car gets closer, its image on the retina gets larger. You assumed that the car was approaching rapidly and that it might run you down, so you took defensive action.

Researchers have created a comparable illusion of impending collision by putting young infants in front of a screen with a dark shadow on it. As the infants watch, the shadow rapidly increases in size—as if an object is moving toward them. Do young infants take defensive action when faced with this cue to dangerously decreasing distance?

By 3 months of age, infants do react with a simple defensive action: They blink. By contrast, 1-month-olds do not blink more often in response to apparently approaching objects than to other visual patterns (Yonas & Owsley, 1987). Apparently, infants do not interpret the cues about objects' motion as cues about depth until sometime between 1 and 3 months of age (Gibson, 1987).

Adults use other cues to depth when looking at objects that are not in motion. Some cues derive from binocular information, information from the two eyes working together. Remember that the same scene creates slightly different images on the retinas of the two eyes, and that neurons develop in the visual cortex that are sensitive to this **retinal disparity.** Retinal disparity is one binocular cue to the distance of objects from the viewer.

Years ago, photographers used the phenomenon of retinal disparity to create souvenirs for tourists. They took two photographs of a scene, such as Niagara Falls, from slightly different angles. Then they mounted the two photographs in a special viewing instrument called a *stereoscope.* When people looked through the stereoscope, they saw one photograph with their left eye and another photograph with their right eye. The two photographic images were fused in the brain into an image of the scene with depth.

The human visual system provides a much more vivid experience of scenes with depth than any stereoscope. Yet it does so, apparently, only for infants above 3 months of age. Researchers have shown infants photographs like those prepared for an old-fashioned stereoscope. The photographs showed random-dot patterns, though, rather than an actual scene. If viewed through a stereoscope, part of the dot pattern looked like a shape raised above the background of random dots.

In several experiments, infants saw a series of stimuli in which the raised part of the pattern—for infants who picked up the binocular cues to depth—moved to different positions on different trials. When infants over 3 months of age saw these stimuli, they looked in the direction in which the raised part had moved. Infants under 3 months of age showed no consistent pattern of looking. The results suggest that 3-month-olds but not younger infants perceived the retinal disparity and interpreted it as a cue to depth in space (Yonas & Owsley, 1987).

Some cues to depth can be interpreted with visual input from just one eye. These cues are present even in a two-dimensional image, or picture, so they are called **pictorial cues.** For a sample of these cues, close one eye and look at figure 5.19. You probably perceive a half sphere jutting out on the left side and a hole on the right side. (If they look that way to you now, try turning the book over and see how that changes their appearance.) The differences in light and shading are pictorial cues to depth.

Infants become sensitive to most pictorial cues to depth between 5 and 7 months of age. Their sensitivity is evident from their responses to stimuli constructed to provide these cues. For example, the infants in one study were fitted with an eye patch so they could not take advantage of binocular cues to depth. Then they were shown the display in figure 5.19. At 7 months of age, infants reached mostly for the left side, which apparently shows a hemisphere

**retinal disparity**
*The difference in the images of the same scene in the two eyes. This difference is a binocular cue to the distance of objects from the viewer.*

**pictorial cues**
*Cues to depth that can be interpreted with visual input from just one eye.*

**FIGURE 5.19**

Which is the sphere, and which is the hole? (Now turn the book over and answer the same question.) This picture illustrates that we use cues like light and shading to judge depth, the third dimension of an object. So do 7-month-old infants. By contrast, 5-month-olds respond similarly to the "sphere" and the "hole."

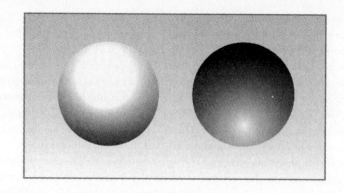

jutting toward them. At 5 months of age, infants reached for the two sides of the display equally (Granrud, Yonas, & Opland, 1985).

When infants first become able to perceive depth is uncertain. Infants may learn about depth and the third dimension during the first few months of life, as they apparently learn about the pattern of the human face. Another possibility is that some aspects of depth perception are present at birth. In other words, there may be an innate basis for depth perception (Kellman, Spelke, & Short, 1986). To test these contrasting hypotheses, researchers will need to devise new ways to determine how young infants interpret what they see.

## Perception of Sound and Sounds

In contrast to vision, the sense of hearing is well developed before birth. Remember from chapter 4 that infants respond to sounds during the last trimester of pregnancy. They also remember certain sequences of sounds that they have heard often, like the sounds of their mothers reading Dr. Seuss's *The Cat in the Hat* (DeCasper & Spence, 1986).

Still, newborns do not hear as well as adults. Researchers estimate what newborns can hear by recording the electrical activity of a newborn's brain in response to sounds. Studies using this procedure suggest that adults can hear sounds roughly 10 to 17 decibels softer than the softest sound newborns can hear (Aslin, 1987; Hecox, 1975). Auditory sensitivity improves steadily during infancy but does not reach adult levels until school age (Maurer & Maurer, 1988).

Newborns also turn their heads in the direction of sounds, which shows that they can locate sounds in space. For example, they turn their heads to the left if the loudspeaker presenting the sound is on their left side. Newborns respond very slowly in this situation, however, taking about 7 seconds to process a sound and turn in its direction (Morrongiello & Clifton, 1984; Muir & Field, 1979).

Newborns' head-turning toward sounds is reflexive rather than voluntary. Remember, voluntary responses are under cortical control and the cortex is immature at birth. As the cortex matures, reflexive turning in response to sounds decreases. By 5 months of age, infants' turning toward sounds seems to be part of a motivated search for the source of the sound, rather than a reflexive behavior (Muir & Clifton, 1985). The accuracy of sound localization also improves dramatically between birth and 6 months of age, with slower improvement after that age (Morrongiello, Fenwick, & Chance, 1990).

Researchers using an extension of the sound localization technique discovered an intriguing difference between the hearing of infants and adults (Clifton et al., 1981). They placed an infant between two loudspeakers and played a tape of a rattle through one speaker. They played the same tape through the other speaker, but with a delay of 0.007 of a second.

When adults are placed in this situation, they report that they heard only one sound, that coming from the loudspeaker that presented the sound first. Because the first sound takes precedence over the second one, this phenomenon is called the **precedence effect.** In the adult auditory system, the second sound is interpreted as an echo of the first and is

**precedence effect**
*The tendency to hear only the first sound if two identical sounds come from different directions a few milliseconds apart.*

therefore disregarded, or not truly heard. Sounds echo around us all the time. If we treated every echo as a distinct sound, our world would be very noisy and very confusing. (Of course, if the echo follows the first sound by a long period, like half a second, adults hear both the original sound and a distinct echo.)

The suppression of echoes that closely follow an original sound does not occur in the auditory nerve itself but at the higher level of the auditory cortex. Can you guess, then, how newborns with an immature cortex would behave in this experiment? Newborns should hear the original sound and its apparent echo as two distinct sounds. If they do, they should, literally, not know where to turn. That is exactly what the researchers found.

Newborns rarely turned their head in any direction when both loudspeakers played rattle sounds. When they did turn their heads, they turned as often toward the tape-delayed sound as toward the original sound. Five-month-olds, on the other hand, showed an adult-like precedence effect (Clifton, Morrongiello, & Dowd, 1984). The change between birth and 5 months illustrates the development of hearing and of the brain.

Hearing involves more than the detection of single sounds. Human beings must also interpret patterns of sounds, such as those in speech. Accurate perception of speech is essential for normal language development. Chapter 7, which is on language development, includes information about newborns' speech perceptions and the changes in speech perception during infancy.

## The Other Senses: Taste, Smell, and Touch

Human beings acquire information about the world through three other senses besides sight and hearing: taste, smell, and touch. These senses are surprisingly mature at birth.

### Taste

If you give newborns a drop of water sweetened with sugar, they display a slight smile that suggests they like the taste. If you place a drop of quinine water on newborns' tongues, they grimace or gag. If you give them a drop of citric acid, they pucker up their mouths. These reactions cannot be due to learning, because newborns react this way before they have tasted their mothers' milk or other liquids (Crook, 1987; Steiner, 1979).

The evidence on newborns' reactions to salty tastes is less consistent. Newborns do not respond with distinctive facial expressions when given salt water, even though highly salted water can be poisonous to them (Maurer & Maurer, 1988). Newborns suck in shorter bursts when given salted water rather than pure water, which shows that they are sensitive to the taste of salt (Crook, 1987). Yet newborns readily drink salty water if it is given to them. They will even drink large quantities of bitter solutions. Apparently their sense of taste does not regulate their intake of these fluids.

The newborns' behavior is less surprising when you recall that they drink for some time before they are born. Inside the uterus they swallow and digest amniotic fluid. This fluid is both salty and bitter, but the embryo benefits from the protein that it contains (Crook, 1987). Also, sucking and swallowing are part of a strong reflexive pattern in infancy, so infants will drink almost any fluid they are given, including poisons. This means, of course, that parents and other caregivers cannot count on infants to reject food that is dangerous to them.

Taste begins to regulate the intake of salty water by 1 year of age. One-year-olds will reject highly salted water that could be harmful for them. Even so, the prevalence of accidental poisoning is greater among 1-year-olds than among older children (Crook, 1987). Although taste influences what 1-year-olds eat, some substances that are poisonous in large doses taste good (e.g., sweetened medicines); other poisonous substances do not have a distinctly sour or bitter taste. For this reason, adults should not count on the sense of taste alone to protect young children from harm.

In contrast to salt, sweet tastes affect infants' behavior even at birth (Blass & Ciaramitaro, 1994). Newborns show the same ordering of preferences for sweets as adults do, for example, preferring sucrose (common sugar) to fructose (the sugar in honey). After receiving only one drop of sucrose, crying newborns often stop crying and show a decrease in heart rate. Moreover, newborns remain calm and alert for several minutes after receiving the sucrose.

These reactions prepare an infant for prolonged nursing. By lowering a distressed infant's activity level, they also help conserve energy so infant growth can proceed more rapidly.

## Smell

You have probably heard about bloodhounds that can follow the track of a person after sniffing a piece of clothing that the person has worn. Do you think you could accomplish the same feat? Is your sense of smell that keen?

You may assume that human beings don't have an especially good sense of smell, but experiments with newborns suggest the opposite. Newborns can perform like real bloodhounds when on the scent of their own mothers. Aidan MacFarlane (1975) asked breast-feeding mothers for the gauze pads that had absorbed milk that leaked out of their breasts. Then MacFarlane placed each mother's 6-day-old infant on a flat surface with one of her gauze pads on one side and a pad from another mother on the other side. Infants turned more toward their own mother's breast pad than toward the other pad, apparently because they recognized the smell of their own mothers.

Two-week-old infants who have been bottle-fed from birth still recognize the breast odors from their mothers, but they do not always show a preference for those odors (Porter et al., 1991). When given a choice between the smell of their mother's breast and the smell of the formula they have been fed for two weeks, these infants either choose the formula or show no clear preference.

However, when given a choice between the formula and the breast odors from another mother who is nursing, bottle-fed infants prefer the breast odors. Apparently, the breast odors of nursing mothers are attractive both to breast-fed and to bottle-fed infants (Porter et al., 1992). This attraction makes sense because those odors come from the natural food source for an infant. Infants might, therefore, be prepared by evolution to orient toward those odors.

Whether breast- or bottle-fed, infants also learn to recognize the distinctive smell of their own mothers. This learning is more rapid for breast-fed infants (Cernoch & Porter, 1985), perhaps because they have more intimate and prolonged contact with their mothers. Even so, all infants show that they prefer the smell of their own mothers within a few days after birth.

Shortly after birth, infants also discriminate between pleasant smells and sour or rotten smells. Infants respond negatively to the smell of rotten eggs; they respond positively to the smell of honey (Maurer & Maurer, 1988; Steiner, 1979). Infants also will turn away from the sharp, pungent odor of ammonia (Rieser, Yonas, & Wilkner, 1976).

By contrast, preschool children do not respond negatively to many odors that adults find unpleasant (Crook, 1987). Apparently, preschool children have not fully learned what adults believe "smells good" and "smells bad." This learning continues for years after the sense of smell is functional. Even adults can learn to recognize slight differences in the smells of different flowers, wines, or foods. Such recognition builds, however, on a foundation of sensitive smell at birth. Remember, newborns are partly like bloodhounds: They can smell where their next meal is coming from!

## Touch

You already know that newborns have a well-functioning sense of touch, because many reflexes depend on a response to a touch. In the rooting reflex, newborns respond to the touch of an object on their cheek. In the withdrawal reflex, newborns respond to a pinprick on their foot. These reflexes show two kinds of stimulation to which newborns are sensitive, light pressure and pain.

The sense of touch is even more complex, however. The nerve endings under the skin also are sensitive to the temperature, shape, and movement of objects in contact with the skin. If a cold glass tube is placed on the cheek of a day-old infant, the infant is likely to turn away from it. If the tube is warm, the infant is likely to open his or her mouth and turn toward it (Reisman, 1987).

By 6 months of age, infants even remember the temperature of objects they have played with (Bushnell, Shaw, & Strauss, 1985). Six-month-olds allowed to play with glass

tubes filled with hot water (110°F) eventually habituated or tired of playing with them. Infants' interest did not recover, or dishabituate, when they received a new tube filled with hot water, but interest did recover if the new tube was filled with cold water (40°F). These infants apparently remembered the temperature of the tube they had touched and considered temperature an important feature of that object.

By 1 month of age, infants can use their sense of touch to identify the shape of objects. Eleanor Gibson and Arlene Walker (1984) allowed 1-month-olds to suck either on a hard plastic rod or on a sponge cut in the same shape as the rod. Then they gave the infants a chance to look at two new rods as an experimenter moved them around. One rod did not change its shape as the experimenter waved it back and forth. An adult would view it as rigid, like the original plastic rod. The other rod was made of foam rubber, and the experimenter repeatedly squeezed it and released it to show that it was flexible, like the original sponge. As the experimenter displayed the objects, infants *looked* more at the type of object they had not *felt* before. If they had had the hard plastic rod in their mouth, they looked more at the flexible foam-rubber rod. If they had had the flexible sponge in their mouth, they looked more at the rigid rod.

The differences in looking suggest that infants remembered the feel of the objects they had previously had in their mouths. That is, they remembered whether the objects were rigid or flexible. Later, they wanted to see something new, something different from what they had felt. This shows that 1-month-olds not only have a refined sense of touch, at least for touch by mouth; they also link information about the feel of objects to their visual experience of objects.

## Links Between the Senses: Intermodal Perception

Gibson and Walker (1984) actually were less interested in the early sense of touch than in the links between touch and vision. In more technical terms, these investigators wanted to understand infants' **intermodal perception.** Each of the classic five senses provides information through a specific *modality:* vision through the eyes, hearing through the ears, and so on. Yet human beings are able to integrate information across modalities. For example, you can identify a golf ball either by its appearance or by the way it feels in your hand. You can identify your mother by her face or her voice and—in infancy at least—by her distinctive smell.

Most studies of intermodal perception have focused on the links between vision and hearing. One focus of research has been on 4-month-olds' ability to perceive correspondences between the movements of puppets and patterns of sounds (Spelke, Born, & Chu, 1983). Suppose that you saw two stuffed animals, a kangaroo and a donkey, jumping up and down at slightly different rates. On some occasions, you heard a metallic clang when the kangaroo hit the ground at the bottom of a jump. On other occasions, you heard a dull thud when the donkey hit the ground. However, you never heard both sounds at the same time.

When 4-month-old infants heard a clang as the kangaroo hit the ground, they looked mostly at the kangaroo. When they heard a thud as the donkey hit the ground, they looked mostly at the donkey. In other words, 4-month-olds looked most at the animal whose impact with the ground was synchronized with a sound.

In another study, 4-month-old infants heard sounds not when the animals touched the ground, but when they paused at the high points of their jumps. For example, infants heard a clang or a thud when the kangaroo or the donkey stopped at the top of a jump. Then the infants looked most at the animal that had a sound synchronized with the pauses in jumps. By 4 months of age, therefore, infants expected to hear sounds when animals made abrupt changes in movement.

From these and other experiments, Elizabeth Spelke (1987) concluded that young infants are primed to perceive certain basic properties of events and objects, regardless of their modality. She proposed that such direct perception of events and objects is an innate characteristic of the perceptual system.

Direct perception of events does not rule out learning. Eleanor Gibson (1969) presented a theory of perceptual learning that suggests humans perceive some properties of objects and events very early. Other properties are not perceived until infants acquire more experience in the world (Rose & Ruff, 1987; Thelen, 1995). If you hear a siren, for example,

**intermodal perception**
*The integration of information from two or more sensory modalities (e.g., vision and touch).*

you might look for a fire truck or a police car. Infants are less likely to expect the same correspondence between sounds and sights because they have never experienced them before.

Infants' lack of experience may partly explain why they do not demonstrate intermodal perception in all situations. In several studies (Lewkowicz, 1994), infants saw two balls bouncing at different speeds. They also heard a tone when one of the balls touched the ground. Neither 2-month-olds nor 5- and 8-month-olds looked longest at the ball whose rate of bouncing matched the rate of the sounds.

Many other experiments suggest that intermodal perception should not be described either as present at birth or as developing at a specific age. Instead, infants' ability to perceive correspondences across sensory modalities depends on the specific stimuli to which they are exposed and the specific types of correspondences involved (Bushnell, 1994; Smith, 1994; Walker-Andrews, 1994).

Sometimes infants can only match across modalities if they recognize specific stimuli. As mentioned earlier, infants need experience before they will look for a fire engine or police car when they hear a siren. Intermodal perception thus differs somewhat from the previous topics in this chapter because the important "facts" are not about what infants can do at a certain age. More important is an understanding of the processes by which infants integrate input from the various senses. Research on these processes should add greatly to understanding of perceptual learning. Perceptual learning continues throughout life, and you will read more about it in chapter 9.

# SOCIAL INFLUENCES ON PHYSICAL DEVELOPMENT

Aspects of individual development were emphasized most in this chapter. You learned about the physical growth of individual children, their brain development, and the improvements in their motor skills and perception. These developments can be greatly influenced, however, by children's social relationships. Three kinds of connections between social relationships and the various aspects of individual development can be specified.

First, social interactions influence the rate and sequence of individual development. Recall the story of Pablo that began the chapter. Pablo's mother slowed his rate of motor development by restricting his freedom of movement during infancy. By contrast, the !Kung mothers discussed in *Cultural Perspectives: "Teaching Baby to Walk"* accelerate their infants' motor development by giving them great freedom of movement and training them to walk. Jamaican mothers also accelerate their infants' walking by systematic exercises. Moreover, because Jamaican mothers do not view crawling as an important step toward walking, their infants sometimes learn to walk without going through a stage of crawling.

Second, developments in individual characteristics affect social relationships. Many individual achievements discussed in the chapter can be seen as preparing infants for full partnership in social relationships. For example, newborns learn to recognize their mothers' distinctive bodily odors, facilitating the formation of a special relationship with her. Newborns also show a preference for their mother's voice over that of an unfamiliar woman (De-Casper & Fifer, 1980), which promotes the development of the mother-infant relationship. As motor skills improve, infants like young Pablo form new relationships centered around play with siblings. With further progress in motor development, children like Pablo become productive members of their families, doing chores that ease their parents' workload.

Third, certain medical conditions dramatically illustrate the impact of social relationships on physical development. **Failure to thrive** is a medical condition defined by severely retarded growth. Infants and young children usually are diagnosed as showing failure to thrive if their weight is below the fifth percentile for their age on more than one occasion, or their weight is less than 80 percent of the typical weight for their age (Casey, 1992; Kirkland, 1994). Of all infants and young children admitted to hospitals for medical treatment, from 1 to 5 percent are diagnosed as having failure to thrive. Up to 20 percent of children seen in outpatient clinics in poor neighborhoods have this problem (Drotar, 1988).

**failure to thrive**
*A medical condition defined by severely retarded growth.*

Sometimes early growth retardation has a biological cause. In such cases children are defined as having *organic* failure to thrive. More often, no biological cause for the retarded growth is obvious. These children are defined as showing *nonorganic* failure to thrive. However, many researchers prefer to replace this implicit *nature* (organic) versus *nurture* (inorganic) classification with a transactional model like that mentioned in chapter 3 (Casey, 1992).

A transactional model can take account of both social and individual causes of failure to thrive. The problem often begins with a breakdown in parent-child interaction. Parents of failure-to-thrive children are less accepting of them and less responsive to them than the average parent (Bradley, Casey, & Wortham, 1984). These parents may not react sensitively to their children because of personality problems, marital problems, or a history of poor relationships with their own parents (Weston et al., 1993).

Children with failure to thrive may also contribute to a breakdown in parent-child interaction. These children are less active, less emotionally expressive, and less talkative than is typical (Powell, Low, and Speers, 1987). Also, they are more sickly, more fussy, and more difficult to interact with than other children (Bithoney & Newberger, 1987). Dealing with such children may be especially hard for parents when they are under stress for other reasons. Nonorganic failure to thrive is more common among poor families who often face financial and other stressors. When children with problems have parents with other problems, disruptions in the parent-child relationship are likely, and disturbances in the children's physical growth can be the result.

Severe cases of failure to thrive are often treated in hospitals. Most infants and young children with the syndrome show rapid weight gain and catch-up growth under hospital care. This treatment, however, may take months and is extremely expensive. The problems in families that led to the initial growth retardation may also be difficult to solve. If those problems cannot be solved, children may need to be placed in foster or adoptive homes after leaving the hospital (Casey, 1992; Singer, 1987).

Of course, the successful return of the child to his or her natural parents is the preferred option, so many programs for enhancing parent-child relationships have been devised. Unfortunately, little experimental research has been done on the effectiveness of these programs. Less systematic evaluations suggest that these programs can help parents build the kinds of relationships with their children that are necessary for normal physical growth (Drotar, 1988).

# SUMMARY

### Physical Growth
Physical growth involves changes in height, weight, body proportions, and the functioning of bodily organs. These changes are especially rapid during infancy and during early adolescence.

### Age Changes in Height and Weight
Between birth and age 1, infants usually increase in height by 25 cm and triple their birth weight to 10 kg. The adolescent growth spurt occurs about two years earlier in girls than in boys. Height and weight show high continuity and, therefore, predictability.

### Age Changes in Body Proportions
The cephalocaudal and proximodistal principles summarize the changes in body proportions from birth to puberty. During puberty, the hands and feet grow to adult size sooner than the center of the body.

### Puberty and Its Psychological Correlates
Going through puberty earlier than most peers may have advantages for boys and disadvantages for girls. These effects are temporary, vary with the social context, and may reflect differences in adolescents' families rather than the timing of puberty itself.

### Influences on Physical Growth
The influence of heredity on physical development is shown by the phenomenon of catch-up growth. Physical growth is also influenced by nutrition, the SES of a child's family, and physical illnesses. Secular trends in growth seem to depend on these influences.

### Growth and Development of the Brain
Brain development is especially rapid between birth and age 2. The changes during this period have been identified by examining the structure of neural networks and the functioning of larger brain regions.

### The Elaboration and Interconnection of Neurons
Brain development during infancy involves first the overproduction of synapses and then the retention of synapses more often activated. These changes reflect processes of experience-expectant information storage. Learning throughout life depends on processes of experience-dependent information storage.

### The Structure and Functioning of Specific Brain Regions
During infancy, control of bodily functioning shifts generally from the brain stem to the cortex. The earliest area of the brain to reach relative maturity is the motor cortex; last to reach maturity are the association areas.

### Brain Damage and Brain Plasticity

Recovery from brain damage does not vary consistently with age. Even infants may not recover completely from damage to specific hemispheres, and malnutrition damages infants' brains more than those of adults.

### Behavioral Organization and Motor Development

Age changes in behavior can be described at multiple levels, from the general levels of behavior states to that of voluntary motor behaviors such as walking.

### Sleep, Activity, and Crying: Age Changes in Behavioral States

Infants cycle through the states of quiet sleep, active sleep, alert inactivity, waking activity, and crying. Adults can change infants' states by changing their position, responding to their needs (e.g., for food), or exposing them to rhythmic stimulation.

### Newborn Reflexes and the Transition to Voluntary Activity

Reflexes are essential for life, protect infants from danger, or serve as precursors of voluntary motor behaviors. Some reflexes disappear with increasing age, as cortical control of movements is established.

### Early Developments in Controlled Motor Behavior

Gross motor and fine motor skills develop in an order consistent with the cephalocaudal and proximodistal principles. Both maturation and experience affect motor development. The dynamic-systems approach offers a novel perspective on the components necessary for skilled motor behavior.

### Early Perceptual Development

From birth, infants can perceive stimuli through all five senses. Their vision is relatively less mature than their other senses, but all senses develop significantly during infancy.

### Visual Perception

Developments in visual perception involve changes in visual acuity, contrast sensitivity, visual accommodation, and other processes. Infants also learn to recognize patterns such as the features on a human face and learn to use various cues for perceiving depth.

### Perception of Sound and Sounds

Although the sense of hearing is functional before birth, newborns do not hear as well as adults. Newborns will reflexively turn their heads toward a sound, but cortical control of hearing and orienting responses emerges several months later.

### The Other Senses: Taste, Smell, and Touch

Newborns react distinctively to sweet- and sour-tasting liquids. They also learn to recognize the distinctive odors of their own mothers within a few days after birth. By 1 month of age, infants can use their sense of touch to identify the shape of objects.

### Links between the Senses: Intermodal Perception

Under certain conditions, infants can perceive correspondences between visual stimuli and sounds, or between visual stimuli and objects they have felt. Such intermodal perception may reflect an innate ability to perceive objects and events directly. It may also reflect the exploration and analysis of stimuli, or infants' recognition of stimuli with which they have experience.

### Social Influences on Physical Development

Social relationships can affect the rate and sequence of physical, motor, and perceptual development. Nonorganic failure to thrive is an example of a physical disorder caused partly by problems in social relationships. Physical, motor, and perceptual development can also prepare infants for participation in social relationships. These facets of development may also be affected by the social and cultural context in which children are raised.

# SUGGESTED READINGS

**Bremner, J. G. (1994).** *Infancy* (2nd ed.). Oxford, England: Blackwell. This book includes additional information on all the topics discussed in this chapter. It also includes information on social and cognitive development during infancy.

**Johnson, R. V. (1994).** *Mayo Clinic complete book of pregnancy and baby's first year.* New York: Morrow. For questions you might ask a pediatrician, this book is likely to have the answer. Information is provided not only on the medical care of infants but also on issues of parenting. The book is heavily illustrated and simply written.

**Maurer, D., & Maurer, C. (1988).** *The world of the newborn.* New York: Basic. You may recall that this book was on the list of suggested readings for chapter 4. It is worth mentioning again because the authors are exceptionally good at describing and explaining what researchers have discovered about infants' development.

**Tanner, J. M. (1978).** *Fetus into man.* Cambridge, MA: Harvard University Press. For a long time, Tanner has been the world's foremost authority on human growth. In this book, Tanner describes human growth from birth to maturity and discusses the major influences on growth. He includes growth charts so you can compare yourself, your friends, and your children to the averages for a specific sex and age.

6

*Chapter  Six*

# FIRST STEPS IN SOCIAL DEVELOPMENT: EMOTIONS AND RELATIONSHIPS

Most Japanese mothers spend much of their time with their young infants. Japanese infants receive care from people other than their mothers less often than do infants in many other cultures. But infants in all cultures develop a close relationship, an attachment, to their mothers. And in all cultures, including Japan, infants also form relationships with people besides their mothers.

Tamaki did not know it, but she was about to have the strangest experience of her short life. It was just one week after her first birthday, and her mother was taking her on an outing. They traveled to a part of her city, Sapporo, Japan, that she had never seen before. They entered a large building where they met a woman who took them into a small room with a few toys. Tamaki began to play happily with the toys.

In a few minutes, another woman entered, chatted briefly with Tamaki's mother, and then started to talk to Tamaki. Shortly afterward, her mother left the room, without warning. Tamaki was somewhat frightened but did not stop playing entirely. After a few minutes, her mother returned and the other women left the room.

Then the situation became even worse from Tamaki's perspective. Tamaki's mother comforted her when she returned, but once Tamaki began playing with the toys again, her mother again left the room. This time, Tamaki was completely alone.

She cried immediately and loudly. She kept crying until her mother returned. (Her mother was gone for only a minute or so.) Tamaki immediately went to her mother, who picked her up and tried to comfort her. Tamaki was upset, but she felt safe in her mother's arms. As she listened to her mother's soothing words, she gradually stopped crying and began to feel better. In a few minutes, she was ready to start playing with the toys again.

Tamaki was particularly upset when her mother left because she had hardly ever been separated from her mother; she had certainly never been left alone. Her mother had never used a babysitter. If anyone else cared for Tamaki, which happened no more than twice a month, it was her father or her grandmother. At home, Tamaki's mother often carried her around on her back. Tamaki even took her bath with her mother. They slept in the same room and often in the same bed. So to have her mother leave her all alone, in a strange place, was an unfamiliar and distressing experience (Takahashi, 1990).

*Y*ou've probably guessed that this story about Tamaki and her mother were part of a study of infant social development. The procedure that Tamaki experienced was designed to assess certain aspects of her relationship with her mother. You will read in this chapter about the details of the procedure, the theory from which it derives, and the evidence on infant-mother relationships that it has yielded.

The procedure used with Tamaki and her mother was first used with infants and mothers from the United States. Infants and mothers from other cultures, such as Japan, sometimes behave differently from those in the United States. The story about Tamaki gives some hints about the possible origins of these differences. Later you will read about both the similarities and the differences in infant-mother relationships across cultures.

Before learning about relationships, however, you need to learn about the role of emotions in social interaction. The story referred to Tamaki's emotions several times: She played with the toys *happily.* Later she was *frightened* and *upset.* These emotions not only expressed her feelings and explained her behavior; they also were signals to the people around her. To understand the first social interactions among infants, their mothers, and other people, you must understand something about emotional development.

The first section of this chapter focuses on the earliest phases of emotional development. The later sections focus on the earliest social relationships, those that infants form with parents and other adults. As the chapter title suggests, this exploration of emotions and relationships deals with the first steps in children's social development. The next steps in social development are examined in later chapters on the family (chapter 11) and social cognition (chapter 13).

This chapter is also related to the ones that precede and follow it. As you read, you will see that social development in infancy is closely related to the developments in perception and motor skills discussed in chapter 5. When you read the next chapter, you will see that social interactions during infancy and early childhood have important effects on language development.

# EARLY EMOTIONAL DEVELOPMENT

Infants make their feelings known the moment they are born. Often, but not always, newborns cry in apparent distress as they emerge from the birth canal and enter a world of bright lights and loud sounds. As infants grow older, they express increasingly specific and complex emotions. In this section, you'll read about the types and functions of these emotional expressions.

## Expressing and Interpreting Emotions

Newborns often cry immediately after birth because they are overwhelmed by the new stimulation that they are receiving through all their senses (Maurer & Maurer, 1988). Their emotional response signals their distress or pain. Newborns display another negative emotion, too. Recall from chapter 5 that they express disgust if a drop of quinine water is placed on their tongues. By contrast, newborns often express interest when they are neither uncomfortable nor sleepy. That is, they look interested when they are in the state of alert inactivity.

### Differential Emotions versus Differentiation Theory

Researchers can identify pain, disgust, and interest in newborns because the newborns' facial expressions resemble those shown by adults experiencing these emotions. One hypothesis of Carroll Izard's differential emotions theory (Izard, 1991, 1994; Izard & Malatesta, 1987) is that infants are born with the ability to express a set of basic emotions—including pain, disgust, and interest—with the same facial features as adults.

Look, for example, at figure 6.1. What emotion would you guess that the infant in each photograph was experiencing? Izard would code the infant in (a) as showing interest, the one in (b) as showing pain, and the one in (c) as showing disgust. Would you agree with those judgments?

Adults label infants' emotional expressions as predicted by Izard's coding system more often than would be expected by chance (Izard, 1994; Izard & Malatesta, 1987). Other researchers, however, have used different procedures for obtaining adults' judgments and have reported findings inconsistent with differential emotions theory (Camras, Sullivan, & Michel, 1993; Matias & Cohn, 1993; Oster, Hegley, & Nagel, 1992). Adults sometimes judge an infant as expressing anger or sadness when Izard's coding system suggests that the infant is in pain. Adults sometimes judge infants as expressing a blend of different emotions when the coding system suggests they are expressing only one emotion.

The adults' judgments can be explained by a theory of differentiation in emotional development (Camras, 1994; Sroufe, 1979). This theory assumes that infants do not express discrete emotions at birth. Instead, they start life simply with the ability to express a general positive emotion ("I feel good") and a general negative emotion ("I feel terrible"). With increasing age, more specific emotions develop from these general emotions. For example, infants develop distinctive facial expressions for pain, sadness, and anger.

One problem for differentiation theory is that even young infants display distinctive facial expressions for several positive emotions. For example, adults can reliably judge when 2-month-olds are happy or expressing joy (Matias & Cohn, 1993). They can also distinguish between joy and other positive emotions such as surprise and interest. Remember, too, that adults can make distinctions among negative emotions, but only when certain procedures are used to obtain their judgments (Izard, 1994). Yet, even when those procedures are used, adults show less consensus in identifying infants' emotions than in identifying adults' emotions.

Taken together, the findings suggest that both differential emotions theory and differentiation theory are partly correct. Young infants regularly express discrete positive emotions such as joy and interest, which is consistent with differential emotions theory. Young infants less often express discrete negative emotions, as the theory of emotional differentiation implies, but young infants do not display only a single facial expression for negative emotion. Also consistent with differentiation theory, the distinctiveness of infants' facial expressions of negative emotions increases with age.

(a)

(b)

(c)

## FIGURE 6.1

(a) This infant is interested in what she sees. Her mouth is open and relaxed, and her brows are drawn together. (b) This infant is in pain, or physically distressed. Her brows are drawn down and inward, her eyes are tightly closed, and her mouth is opened in the shape of a square. (c) This infant is expressing disgust. His brows are lowered, his nose is wrinkled, his upper lip is raised, and his tongue is pushed out slightly.

A second controversial assumption of differential emotions theory is that infants feel what adults feel when their facial expressions are the same (Izard & Malatesta, 1987). For example, when infants' facial expressions match adults' expressions of sadness, the infants feel sad just as adults do. Izard (1994) assumes that this correspondence between facial expressions and inner feelings allows emotional communication between infants and adults and so contributes to infants' survival.

Other researchers argue that the many differences between infants and adults make it unwise to assume the same connections between facial expressions and feelings (Barrett & Campos, 1987; Camras, 1994; Oster et al., 1992). Infants' facial expressions sometimes suggest they are angry in situations when situational cues suggest they are simply in pain. Infants' expressions sometimes suggest they are not feeling any emotion when situational cues suggest they should be sad or angry. These mismatches between facial expressions and likely feelings imply that the correspondence between facial expressions and felt emotions may change during infancy rather than be adultlike at birth.

This controversy is more difficult to settle than the first one, because judging how infants feel is not as easy as photographing and analyzing their facial expressions. More research on when infants display specific expressions, and how their expressions change in response to others' behavior, may lead to more agreement about their emotional experience.

## Universal Emotional Expressions

Other conclusions about infants' emotional expressions are less often questioned. More than a century ago, Darwin (1872) proposed that all humans express distinct emotions in identical ways. Cross-cultural research with adults has largely confirmed Darwin's hypothesis about the universality of emotional expressions. In all cultures studied, adults have accurately identified several basic emotions from photographs of actors posing them, even when the actors were from another culture (e.g., Ekman, Friesen, & Ellsworth, 1982). Some researchers have disputed precisely how accurate this identification is (Russell, 1994), but the central findings have been confirmed with many samples of adults from many countries (Ekman, 1994; Izard, 1994).

By contrast, only a few researchers have explored the universality of infants' emotional expressions. For one study, 5- and 12-month-old infants from the United States and from Japan were videotaped as an adult held their arms folded across their stomach (Camras et al., 1992). Infants typically react negatively to this kind of restraint, struggling to get their arms free. The facial expressions of United States and Japanese infants placed in this situation were highly similar, lending support to the hypothesis that emotional expressions are universal even in infancy. Of course, studies in other cultures with procedures designed to evoke other emotions are needed to confirm the hypothesis.

## Changes in Emotional Expressions During Infancy

Infants do not display all the emotional expressions that adults do, at least not immediately after birth. Table 6.1 summarizes important age changes in emotional expression. The table also includes information about age changes in emotion recognition and interpretation that are discussed in the next section.

Newborns do not show the most common expression of happiness, a smile. In the first weeks of life, some infants show slight smiles in which the corners of the mouth lift briefly. However, these smiles often seem to be due to random nervous discharges, like those causing muscle spasms. Occasionally, newborns smile when mildly stimulated by gentle stroking or rocking, but these smiles are reflexive: They are patterns of muscle movement that are controlled by the brain stem, not the cortex.

By 2 months of age, infants smile at social stimuli, such as a human face. Their smiles elicit social behavior from other people and thus help to initiate social interactions. In this way, social smiles serve an adaptive function, helping infants form relationships with other people (Ellsworth, Muir, & Hains, 1993; Sroufe & Waters, 1976).

After 2 months of age, infants also smile at nonsocial stimuli. Once infants have seen a toy several times, they may smile at seeing it again (Kagan, Kearsley, & Zelazo, 1978). They

**TABLE 6.1** *Changes in Emotional Expression and Interpretation During Infancy*

| AGE | MARKER OF EMOTIONAL DEVELOPMENT |
| --- | --- |
| Birth | Expression of several emotions, including distress/pain, disgust, and interest |
| 2 months | First social smiles |
| 3 months | Discrimination between others' happy and sad expressions |
| 4–6 months | Laughter at sudden increases in stimulation |
| 7 months | Expressions of anger when inoculated or frustrated |
| | Discrimination between others' happy and surprised expressions |
| 8 months | Expressions of fear when placed on the visual cliff |
| 8–12 months | Social referencing: using others' emotional expressions to interpret ambiguous situations |
| 12 months | Laughter at mother's sucking on a baby bottle |
| After 12 months | Expressions of complex emotions such as shame and pride |

smile because they made a mental effort to interpret what they see, and they were successful in linking what they see to their memories of seeing it before. It is as if they said about the toy, "Aha, I remember you."

Why do infants (and adults) smile after a successful effort to assimilate some information? Do these nonsocial smiles have any adaptive significance? The answer is yes, because emotions are not just signals to other people. They also serve an organizing and motivating function for the person who experiences them (Izard & Malatesta, 1987; Sroufe & Waters, 1977).

When adults smile after solving a problem, they feel good and want to prolong that positive emotion. Consequently, they are encouraged to try other problems in the future. When infants smile after recognizing something, they feel good and are encouraged to engage in further exploration of their environments. In a sense, smiles reward infants for their cognitive activity, their efforts to understand the world.

By 4 months of age, infants not only smile but also laugh (Sroufe & Wunsch, 1972). At first, infants laugh mainly when their level of stimulation increases suddenly. Four-month-olds laugh loudly if their parents give them a vigorous kiss on the stomach. Six-month-olds laugh at sudden changes in sound patterns, like the sound of a frog's nighttime call (r-rr-rrr-rrrr-R-RR-RRR-RIBIPP!). By the end of the first year, infants react to the meaning of an event. They laugh, for example, at the incongruity of their mother sucking on a baby bottle.

Like smiling, laughter is valuable for infants. When infants laugh as their mother sucks on a baby bottle, they show their pleasure in the mother's game and encourage her to continue her interaction with them. Their laughter also suggests the pleasure that comes from a successful attempt to understand a novel and surprising event. Infants unable to understand such an event may turn away or even show fear (Maurer & Maurer, 1988; Sroufe & Waters, 1976).

Expressions of negative emotions, such as distress, can also be adaptive. When newborns show distress, they signal to other people that they want to escape from painful levels of stimulation. Similarly, when they show disgust, they signal their dislike for something they tasted or smelled. The expression of disgust may also serve a protective function, when infants spit out something with a bitter taste.

Other negative emotions, such as anger, become obvious only after 6 months of age. If you take a teething biscuit away from a 7-month-old who has just started chewing on it, the infant will often look angry (Stenberg, Campos, & Emde, 1983). When 7-month-olds receive a medical inoculation (or a "shot"), they may express either anger or pain (Izard, Hembree, & Huebner, 1987). After 1 year of age, expressions of anger after an inoculation become more common and pain expressions become less common. One interpretation of this age change is

that infants increasingly view an inoculation as an aggressive act. Therefore, they respond with anger that motivates defensive or aggressive reactions.

Another negative emotion that becomes obvious after 6 months of age is fear. You may recall from chapter 5 that researchers use the visual cliff to study infants' perception of depth. Researchers also have used the visual cliff to study the development of fear. Once infants are about 8 months of age and crawling independently, they look afraid when placed near the edge of the visual cliff (Bertenthal & Campos, 1987). Around the same age, many infants begin to show a fear of strangers. Remember that Tamaki was a little frightened when the strange woman tried to talk to her. We will examine fear of strangers more fully later because it is linked to theories of infant social relationships.

Emotional development continues after the first year of life. Between 1 and 2 years of age, more complex emotions emerge. Toddlers, for example, may express shame, guilt, and pride. These emotions are complex because they are linked to sophisticated social goals. For instance, shame reflects a failure to achieve the goal of maintaining other people's respect (Campos et al., 1983). Notice that this goal implies an understanding of self. To be ashamed, toddlers must understand the "I" in statements such as "Someone thinks that *I* did something bad." Children take a major step toward self-understanding during the toddler years. Chapter 13 examines the development of self-understanding from the toddler years through adolescence.

Some age changes in emotional expression are the result of explicit socialization. **Socialization** is a process by which children acquire the beliefs, attitudes, and behaviors expected of members of their society. Emotional expressions are behaviors, and they are a target of socialization. For example, children in the United States are expected to pretend that they are happy when they receive a present they don't like. As children grow, they learn more about the rules in their society for feigning or concealing emotions (Saarni, 1979).

The socialization of emotional expression begins in infancy and varies across cultures. Mothers in the United States are pleased when their young infants smile at them. Usually, mothers smile in return and attempt to prolong this positive interaction. By contrast, mothers who belong to the Gusii people of Kenya often look away when their infants smile at them. Their infants then shift to more neutral expressions themselves. This pattern of mother-infant interaction is culturally appropriate because, as adults, Gusii people try to maintain neutral facial expressions and avoid eye-to-eye contact (Tronick, 1989).

This example also illustrates that the socialization of emotions depends on infants' ability to respond appropriately to other people's emotional expressions. For example, U.S. infants must recognize their mother's smiles as an invitation to positive interaction. The ability to recognize and respond appropriately to others' emotional expressions also develops during infancy.

## Age Changes in Emotion Recognition

Think what your life would be like if you could not recognize other people's emotions. You would not know when people approved of your actions because you could not interpret their smiles or the positive tone in their voices. You would not know when other people were angry at you because you could not connect their distinctive facial features and voice tone to that negative emotion.

Not being able to recognize other people's emotions could even be dangerous. Imagine that you were taking a picture of your friends in a beautiful wilderness setting. You started to walk a few steps backward to get all your friends in the picture. As you continued to walk backward, you saw through the viewfinder that your friends' expressions changed. Unfortunately, you didn't recognize their new expressions as fear—and you suddenly stepped off the edge of a cliff!

This exercise in imagination should help you appreciate the experience of a newborn child. Newborns are unlikely to recognize differences in facial expressions because they cannot see these expressions clearly. Remember from chapter 5 that the visual system of newborns is immature and their visual acuity is poor. Newborns, then, have difficulty seeing the variations in facial features—smiles, frowns, raised eyebrows, and so on—that define distinct emotional expressions (Nelson, 1987).

**socialization**
*The process by which children acquire the beliefs, attitudes, and behaviors expected of members of their own society.*

By 3 months of age, infants' vision has improved enough so that they can discriminate between happy, smiling faces and sad, frowning faces (Barrera & Maurer, 1981). By 7 months of age, infants also recognize the similarities among different expressions of the same emotion. For example, if they see photographs of several women posing happy expressions, they gradually lose interest in the photographs, or habituate to them. If they then see a photograph of another woman posing a happy expression, they do not show increased looking, or dishabituation. They seem to say to themselves, "Ho, hum, it's just another happy face." By contrast, they look with renewed attention at a photograph of a woman with a surprised expression (Ludemann & Nelson, 1988). Thus, they discriminate between expressions of happiness and of surprise.

In addition, 7-month-olds recognize the correspondence between facial and vocal expressions of emotions (Soken & Pick, 1992). When people are happy, their voices often have a rapid, fluid rhythm. When people are angry, their voices are often intense, with an abrupt or staccato rhythm. If 7-month-olds hear an angry speech while viewing videotapes of actresses showing both happy and angry expressions, they look more at the picture of the angry actress. If they instead hear a happy speech, they look more at the picture of the happy actress. These patterns of looking demonstrate that 7-month-olds recognize and can match the visual and vocal cues to others' emotions.

## Infants' Emotional Reactions to Expressions of Emotion

Infants' understanding of others' emotional expressions is confirmed by their emotional reactions to them (Barrera & Maurer, 1981; Haviland & Lelwica, 1987; Termine & Izard, 1988). When the mothers of 9-month-olds express joy by smiling or talking in a positive tone to their infants, the infants express more joy themselves. Mothers' expressions of joy even elicit joyful expressions from 10-week-old infants. By contrast, when their mothers have a sad expression, young infants tend to express sadness, to suck their lips as if to soothe themselves, or to express anger. When their mothers express anger, young infants do the same or become so upset that the experimental procedure cannot be completed.

One-year-olds respond not only to emotions expressed toward them but also to emotions expressed by adults toward each other. Mothers report that 1-year-olds usually show affection when they see family members behave affectionately toward each other. Sometimes, though, 1-year-olds act as if they are jealous of the person receiving the affection (Cummings, Zahn-Waxler, & Radke-Yarrow, 1981). By contrast, conflicts between family members usually evoke expressions of distress from 1-year-olds. Expressions of anger in response to adults' anger are also common.

Among 2-year-olds, reactions to angry conflicts are distinctive and intense. For one experimental study (Cummings, Iannotti, & Zahn-Waxler, 1985), 2-year-olds visited a psychology laboratory with their mothers and one of their playmates. The laboratory was furnished like a typical apartment. While the 2-year-olds were in the kitchen of the apartment two unfamiliar women came in to clean the apartment. As they cleaned, they had a loud argument in which each woman accused the other of not doing her share of the work.

Figure 6.2 shows that the 2-year-olds were rarely distressed at being in the laboratory with the unfamiliar women, if the women were showing positive emotions toward each other. But when the women began their argument, the 2-year-olds' distress responses increased greatly. Counted among their distress responses were signs of anxiety, gestures of covering their faces, attempts to seek comfort from their mothers, and "freezing" without movement. After the argument, when the angry women were not in the room, the 2-year-olds showed a high level of aggression—hitting, shoving, or taking things from their playmate.

Some children came for a second visit to the laboratory in which they witnessed another argument. Figure 6.2 shows that the children again were distressed during the argument. They also were more aggressive afterward. The children reacted even more strongly to the second argument than to the first.

Fortunately, infants' distress responses decreased during both visits when the women began to respond positively to each other again. This pattern is consistent with that observed in natural settings. When adults resolve conflicts successfully, infants' and children's negative

FIGURE 6.2

Two-year-olds became distressed when they witnessed an angry argument between adults. Their distress decreased when the argument ended, but witnessing another argument on a second visit increased their distress even more than the first one did. (Data from Cummings, Iannotti, & Zahn-Waxler, 1985.)

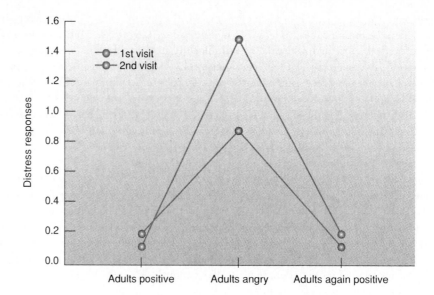

responses to witnessing their negative emotional expressions are greatly reduced (Davies & Cummings, 1994).

What if conflicts are not successfully resolved? What if the pervasive emotional climate of an infant's home is negative? Infants are negatively affected when they interact daily with parents whose own emotions are negative. For example, depressed mothers express less positive emotions toward their infants, display more anger, and look at their infants less often than do mothers who are not depressed. Infants of depressed mothers, in turn, express more sadness and anger themselves, look less at their mothers, and show more self-directed behaviors such as rocking or grasping themselves (Pickens & Field, 1993; Tronick, 1989).

The scarcity of coordinated positive interactions between depressed mothers and their infants may lead to poor infant-mother relationships and to less sociable behaviors by these infants toward other adults. When you read later about family relationships (in chapter 11), you will learn much more about the powerful effects of family emotional climate on children's development.

## Emotional Information and Social Referencing

Under certain conditions, parents want their infants to recognize and respond emotionally to their expressions of negative emotions. Think of a 12-month-old girl crawling toward the stairs. The infant's mother calls out, "Stop!" and displays the facial expression of fear. This mother wants her daughter to take her facial and vocal expressions as signals of danger.

**Social referencing** is the use of another person's emotional expressions to interpret events that are ambiguous or difficult for individuals to interpret on their own (Sorce et al., 1985). In the example, the mother hoped that her infant daughter would engage in social referencing. That is, the mother hoped the daughter would look at her, recognize her expression of fear, interpret the expression as a sign of danger, and crawl away from the stairs. In short, the infant would use the mother's expression to judge her own situation.

The process of social referencing operates by 12 months of age. To study this process, researchers have not placed infants at the top of a staircase (which would be dangerous). Instead, one team of researchers placed infants on the shallow side of the visual-cliff apparatus (Sorce et al., 1985). They asked the infants' mothers to stand on the other side of the apparatus. Then they told mothers to pose expressions of either happiness or fear as their infants approached the deep side of the visual cliff. When their mothers looked happy, most 12-month-olds crawled across the deep side. When their mothers looked afraid, no 12-month-olds crawled across the deep side.

In other studies, mothers' emotional expressions affected how their infants reacted to new toys and unfamiliar adults (Klinnert et al., 1986; Nelson, 1987; Rosen, Adamson, & Bakeman,

**social referencing**
*The use of another person's emotional expressions to interpret events that are ambiguous or difficult for individuals to interpret on their own.*

1992). Infants also engage in social referencing with people other than their mothers. For example, infants in day care avoid a novel toy if one of their caregivers poses an expression of fear when looking at the toy. Infants most often engage in social referencing when interacting with caregivers who have been emotionally expressive in past interactions (Camras & Sachs, 1991).

The capacity for social referencing depends on early developments in perception and cognition. Before about 8 eight months of age, infants do not interpret others' emotions as signals about social situations. Only after that age is social referencing used by infants and children to learn about their environments (Campos et al., 1983).

## Patterns of Emotionality: Variations in Temperament

Infants differ in their emotional expressiveness and their emotional responses to events. Some infants are shy and afraid of new situations. Others are sociable, eager to begin a social interaction with people they meet. Some infants seem always on the move, involved in constant and intense activity. Others seem less active and more calm. These differences illustrate the variations in infants' temperaments.

Although definitions of temperament differ, Robert McCall identified several common elements in various theorists' definitions. He said that **temperament** refers to "relatively consistent, basic dispositions inherent in the person that underlie and modulate the expression of activity, reactivity, emotionality, and sociability" (in Goldsmith et al., 1987, p. 524).

*Activity* refers to the intensity and pace of a person's behavior and speech. *Reactivity* refers to the intensity of a person's responses to stimulation and the person's tendency to approach or withdraw from stimuli. *Emotionality* refers to the frequency and intensity of a person's emotions, both positive and negative. *Sociability* refers to a person's preferences for social interaction versus solitude and the person's willingness to initiate and respond to social contacts.

**temperament**
*The relatively consistent, basic dispositions inherent in the person that underlie and modulate the expression of activity, reactivity, emotionality, and sociability.*

### Biological Bases of Temperament

McCall described temperament as a basic disposition inherent in a person because he assumed that children's temperaments largely reflect their genotypes. Most theorists assume that children's genotypes have a strong influence on the various aspects of temperament, and many studies support this assumption. In infancy, monozygotic (MZ) twins, who have the same genotype, are more similar in their activity, sociability, and fearfulness than dizygotic (DZ) twins, who have different genotypes (Plomin, 1987).

By 14 months of age, MZ twins are more similar than DZ twins not only in the three aspects of temperament assessed in infancy but also in their shyness in social situations and their inhibition when shown novel objects (Emde et al., 1992). Between 14 and 24 months of age, MZ twins are also more similar than DZ twins in their behavioral inhibition, shown by their reluctance to approach an unfamiliar person or object (Robinson et al., 1992). In childhood, MZ twins are more similar in their irritability and shyness than DZ twins (Goldsmith & Gottesman, 1981).

Adoption studies suggest slightly different conclusions about genetic influences on temperament. During the first year of life, measures of adopted infants' temperament are not correlated with measures of their biological mothers' temperament. By 24 months of age, however, significant correlations are seen between temperament measures for adopted children and their biological mothers. For example, adopted children are more shy when their biological mothers are more introverted (Plomin, 1987). Genetic influences on temperament may be more obvious after infancy because measures of temperament are more reliable in older children than in infants (McDevitt, 1986).

If temperament reflects basic dispositions of a person, variations in temperament should be linked to distinctive patterns of brain activity. Differences in infants' inhibition have been linked to differences in the activity of the two brain hemispheres (Calkins & Fox, 1994). Differences in infants' distress when separated from their mothers have been linked to their brain activity, judged from evoked potentials, when seeing slides of unfamiliar women's faces (Gunnar & Nelson, 1994).

Nevertheless, research on the biological processes underlying temperamental differences is just beginning. The systems linking biology to behavioral differences are complex, involving many brain structures and many biochemical processes (Wachs & King, 1994). Much more research will be needed before these links are fully understood.

## Continuity in Temperament During Infancy and Childhood

McCall's definition of temperament as the "relatively consistent, basic dispositions" of a person implies that differences in temperament should be stable over time, or show high continuity. Jerome Kagan and his colleagues have examined the continuity in children's inhibition when faced with unfamiliar people and objects. In one series of studies, Kagan's team identified groups of extremely inhibited and extremely uninhibited 21-month-olds (Kagan, 1989; Kagan et al., 1984; Kagan et al., 1988). Each child was placed in a room with his or her mother and an unfamiliar child the same age. In this setting, the inhibited children often stayed close to their mothers and only stared at the other child. They were slow to initiate play both with that child and with unfamiliar objects. By contrast, uninhibited children rapidly approached the other child in the room and engaged in play. They also ran freely through the room, exploring the objects there.

When the two groups of children were 7½ years old, they were observed as they interacted with an unfamiliar adult who gave them various tests. They were also observed in a play group with 8 to 10 other children whom they had not met before. Children were judged as less inhibited if they talked more with the adult examiner and the other children and they stayed closer to the other children during their playtime.

Children with high levels of inhibition at 21 months often showed high levels at 7½ years, but the continuity in this aspect of temperament was only moderate. Some children who were highly inhibited at 21 months were fairly uninhibited at 7½ years and vice versa. When Kagan's team used similar procedures with toddlers, they found even less continuity in inhibition between 14 and 24 months of age than in the original studies with older children (Robinson et al., 1992).

Studies by other researchers also suggest that there is little continuity in temperament during infancy and between infancy and early childhood. For example, measures of infants' smiling, laughing, distress, and fear at 3 months of age are not correlated with similar measures of emotionality at 9 months of age (Rothbart, 1986). Measures of temperament at 6 months of age are not correlated with similar measures at 2 or 3 years of age (see McDevitt, 1986). Even when the degree of continuity in temperament is statistically significant, it is moderate or low (Pedlow et al., 1993; Plomin et al., 1993). Therefore, children's temperament cannot be accurately predicted from observing their behavior as infants.

Measures of temperament show greater continuity during childhood and adolescence. In one large Australian sample (Pedlow et al., 1993), 5- and 6-year-olds who were difficult to comfort and to control almost always showed the same characteristics at 7 and 8 years of age. The continuity in other facets of temperament such as persistence and shyness was lower but still substantial. Findings such as these show that continuity in temperament increases as children grow older.

Continuity in temperament is also greater when assessed over shorter periods. Between 21 months and 6 years of age, there is some continuity in children's inhibition in unfamiliar situations, but continuity between 21 months and the years beyond age 6 is nonsignificant (Kerr et al., 1994). Similarly, continuity in irritability and shyness is nonsignificant or low between 3 and 9 years of age (Caspi et al., 1995). Over several years, then, children's temperament can change greatly.

## Changes in Temperament During Infancy and Childhood

The changes in children's temperament result partly from genetic influence, the gradual unfolding of their genotypes. As children grow, different sets of genes affect their development. By examining changes in temperament for children who differ in genetic similarity, such as MZ and DZ twins, the effects of changes in gene expression on temperament can be measured.

Using this method, genetic influence on changes in inhibition, sociability, and other facets of temperament has been demonstrated (Plomin et al., 1993). A large twin study

showed that changes in behavioral inhibition, activity level, sociability, and other aspects of temperament were due partly to changes in genetic expression.

The characteristics of children's environments also influence the changes in their temperament. Indirect evidence of environmental influence comes from adoption studies, which show significant correlations between temperament measures for adopted children and their adoptive parents (Plomin, 1987). For example, 1- and 2-year-olds are higher in emotionality when their adoptive mothers are higher in emotionality. Because adopted children are not genetically related to their adoptive mothers, this similarity between mothers and children is likely to result from the mothers' interactions with their children.

More direct evidence of environmental influence comes from research in which both temperament and parent-child interaction were examined over time. For example, infants who decrease dramatically in crying and fussiness between 3 and 9 months of age have parents who are highly involved and sensitive when interacting with them. Infants who increase in smiling and other expressions of positive emotions also have parents high in involvement (Belsky, Fish, & Isabella, 1991).

## Responding to Children's Temperament: Goodness of Fit?

Suppose you accept the conclusion that temperament is partly under genetic control but can be influenced by parents' interactions with their children. How would you advise parents to respond to, or try to change, their children's temperament? One answer was suggested by Alexander Thomas and Stella Chess (1986), who collaborated with Herbert Birch on the first major study of children's temperament (Thomas, Chess, & Birch, 1968).

Thomas and Chess (1986) suggested that children benefit when their temperament matches the type that their parents value and are prepared to handle. Thomas and Chess described this hypothesis in terms of the "goodness of fit" between children and their parents. They argued, in particular, that temperamentally difficult children who are highly active and have trouble adapting to new situations are hard for most parents to rear successfully. However, if parents respond calmly or even positively to their children's distinctive traits, the children can develop normally. With proper guidance, they can even profit from their emotional intensity and high activity.

The goodness-of-fit hypothesis seems sensible but has been difficult to confirm (Windle & Lerner, 1986). Researchers looked first for evidence that temperamentally difficult infants cause problems for most parents. That is, they tried to see whether most parents interact less, and less successfully, with temperamentally difficult infants. A few researchers found evidence for this hypothesis, but other researchers found that parents were more engaged with and more sensitive to difficult infants (Crockenberg, 1986). Therefore, the implications of temperament for parent-infant interactions are uncertain. Moreover, some investigators have raised more general questions about the meaning of temperamental difficulty in infancy (see *Practical Applications of Research:* "Should Parents Worry About a Temperamentally Difficult Infant?").

Difficult temperaments during childhood are a greater source of concern. Temperamental difficulty at age 3 or later predicts behavioral problems in future years (Bates, 1987; Caspi et al., 1995). In particular, 3-year-olds who are unusually restless, negative, and prone to emotional overreactions have a high risk of attention problems and misbehavior in adolescence. By contrast, children with an easy, or "good," temperament are less likely to develop behavioral problems. In sum, more evidence shows benefits of a "good" (or easy) temperament than shows the importance of the goodness of fit between children's temperaments and their parents' childrearing styles.

What, then, can be done about children who seem to have difficult temperaments? Clinicians have offered several suggestions (Bates, 1989; Bates, Wachs, & Emde, 1994). First, parents should emphasize the positive side of their children's traits. For example, parents should label a child who is excitable as *enthusiastic* rather than out of control. Second, parents should try to predict their child's reactions to new situations and plan how they will respond. Third, parents should respect their child's individuality, remembering the old saying that "it takes all kinds to make a world." No temperament is ideal for all situations, and each child's temperament can prepare him or her for a special niche in society.

# SHOULD PARENTS WORRY ABOUT A TEMPERAMENTALLY DIFFICULT INFANT?

S ome infants make life difficult for their parents. They fuss and cry often. Their cries sound especially unpleasant to adults. These infants are easy to upset and difficult to soothe once they become upset (Bates, 1987; Daniels, Plomin, & Greenhalgh, 1984).

Why are some infants more difficult than others? Researchers have so far had little success in answering this question. Measures of infants' difficulty are not consistently related to measures of parents' emotionality or other aspects of parents' personalities. Infant difficulty is not related to measures of mothers' involvement and stimulation or other aspects of the home environment. Adoption studies do not suggest any genetic influence on temperamental difficulty in infancy (Daniels et al., 1984). So far, then, researchers have not traced infant difficulty to an obvious defect of nature or nurture.

What about the consequences of difficult temperament? Should parents expect serious problems if their infant is temperamentally difficult but otherwise normal? Recent research suggests that the answer is no. Difficult infants do not receive lower scores on tests of intellectual performance than infants with easy temperaments. Also, they do not seem to affect parents' attitudes toward them in important ways. In particular, parents' responsiveness is not greatly affected by their perceptions of their infants' difficulty (Bates, 1987).

Difficult infants are more likely to develop behavioral problems in the preschool years (Bates, 1987; Sanson et al., 1991), but infant difficulty by itself is only a weak predictor of later problems. Problems are only likely if a difficult temperament is accompanied by other problems such as prematurity. Moreover, the central component of infant difficulty—crying and fussiness—is largely unrelated to behavior problems in childhood (Daniels et al., 1984).

In sum, parents with a difficult infant might view themselves as unlucky because they must put up with more crying. However, they do not have serious cause for concern. Odds are that their difficult infant will grow into a child who is as intelligent, as well behaved, and as pleasant to interact with as other parents' easy infants.

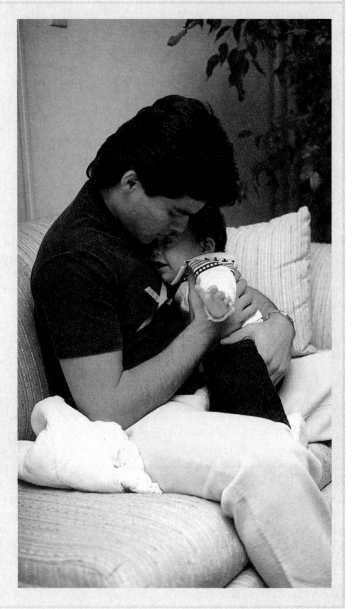

# INFANT-MOTHER ATTACHMENTS

Unlike the young of many other species, human beings form relationships with their parents that normally last for the parents' entire life. The importance of these relationships has not always been recognized. You read in chapter 1 that Plato (1942) argued for governmental control over mating and childrearing. He also thought that children should be reared in common, cared for by professional nurses rather than by their own parents.

How would Plato's experiment in childrearing have turned out? Research in the twentieth century has revealed the unfortunate answer. Correlational studies with children and experimental studies with monkeys have confirmed that alternatives to the typical pattern of

parental care in infancy can be harmful. Attempts to explain these harmful effects led John Bowlby (1969, 1988) to formulate the ethological theory of infant-parent attachments. This theory is central to current thinking about infant social development, so this chapter includes a detailed discussion of its assumptions and the research that it has generated.

## Origins and Principles of Attachment Theory

During and after World War II, several researchers studied infants placed in institutions because their parents had died or could not care for them (e.g., Goldfarb, 1943; Spitz, 1946). Often, these infants were severely retarded and their social behavior was abnormal. They were unresponsive to adults, seemed depressed, had poor appetites, and had a higher death rate than infants brought up by their own parents. Institutionalized children who survived infancy often engaged in undesirable behaviors like stealing and aggression. The better-adjusted of these children were friendly to adults, often unusually so, but they seemed unable to form close personal relationships.

Most researchers who studied institutionalized children accepted Freud's theory that children's relationships with their mothers are most important for their development, especially in infancy. They therefore assumed that the absence of mother-infant relationships was the primary cause of the abnormal behavior of institutionalized infants and children. They argued, in short, that the abnormal behavior was caused by maternal deprivation.

Later researchers pointed out that most children's institutions around World War II were poor environments for development in many ways (Rutter, 1972). The conditions in Iranian orphanages were described in the previous chapter, and those in European institutions were not much better. The development of the children in these institutions could have been impaired not by maternal deprivation but by a general lack of physical and social stimulation.

Conditions improved in children's institutions after World War II. Many institutionalized infants and children received appropriate environmental stimulation and responsive caregiving. Studies of these children rarely showed problems as severe as those found earlier, but some problems remained, especially in social development.

In one British study, 4-year-olds who had been reared in institutions were overly friendly with strangers but lacked close relationships with their caregivers (Tizard & Hodges, 1978; Tizard & Rees, 1975). At 8 years of age, after most of the children had been adopted or returned to their natural mothers, they still sought attention unusually often. At school they were more disobedient and unpopular than children reared by their parents at home. By contrast, the children received normal scores on measures of intelligence. Other studies also showed more social problems but not more cognitive problems in children reared in institutions (Rutter, 1979).

More evidence on the importance of the mother-infant relationship came from experiments on one of our evolutionary relatives, the rhesus monkey. Harry Harlow observed monkeys who were separated from their mothers and reared in isolation from birth to 1 year of age (Harlow & Mears, 1979). During the isolation period, monkeys were adequately fed but had no contact with other monkeys or with humans. The infant monkeys ate well during their months of isolation and grew normally, but their behavior was bizarre. They paced back and forth or held themselves in strange postures. They would suck on themselves, rock back and forth, or engage in other self-directed behaviors (see figure 6.3).

Monkeys who were isolated for six months or more never fully recovered. Even after they were released from isolation, these monkeys did not display normal patterns of play. Because their behavior was so abnormal, their cagemates often attacked them. Once they reached maturity, they rarely engaged successfully in sexual behavior.

The studies of children brought up in institutions and monkeys brought up in social isolation strongly suggest that relationships with warm, caring adults are necessary for healthy development. Human infants, in particular, need to establish a continuing relationship with a caregiver. In the institutions studied by Tizard (e.g., Tizard & Hodges, 1978), children had responsive caregivers, but their caregivers changed often. Between birth and age 4, children had more than 50 different caregivers. Therefore, they were never able to form lasting attachments like those that normally develop between infants and their own mothers.

## FIGURE 6.3

This monkey was separated from its mother and from other monkeys for the first year of life. Because of its abnormal experience, it shows extreme withdrawal and bizarre behavior.

**imprinting**
*The process by which birds and other animals become attached to other animals, people, or objects that they see shortly after birth.*

## Contributions of Ethology to Attachment Theory

The roots of attachment theory go back to the early 1950s, when Bowlby (1951) reviewed the research on institutionalized infants and children. At that time Bowlby agreed with the idea, derived from Freudian theory, that children reared in institutions show abnormal development because they suffer from maternal deprivation. Over the years, however, Bowlby expanded his theoretical perspective. He retained some ideas from Freudian theory, but he added ideas from the new discipline of ethology. Bowlby was especially intrigued by the observations of Konrad Lorenz on young birds.

Lorenz (1935/1957), one of the foremost ethologists of the twentieth century, did an amazing series of experiments on geese and other birds. He removed the birds' eggs from their nests before they hatched. Then he made sure that the birds saw him—and no adults of their own species—after they hatched. He found that these birds began to direct toward him all the behaviors that they would normally have directed toward their mothers. They came to Lorenz whenever they saw him. They followed him around, both on land and when he was swimming in a lake. The birds gave distress calls when he was absent and calls of contentment when he was present.

Lorenz concluded that the birds' visual exposure to him shortly after hatching made them *imprint* on him rather than on members of their own species. Lorenz defined **imprinting** as the process by which birds become attached to objects they see during a brief period after hatching. He suggested that imprinting is necessary for the survival of the young in many bird species. As stated in chapter 1, ethologists emphasize the evolutionary significance of behaviors. That is, they try to understand how specific behaviors contribute to an animal's survival and to the preservation of the animal's genes in the next generation.

Imprinting helps young birds survive because it makes them stay close to the first object they see after hatching, which would usually be their mother. By staying close to their mother, young birds get the benefit of her protection. She watches for danger and keeps them safe, safer than they would be if they wandered by themselves.

Of course, human infants do not develop in the same way as birds. Still, Bowlby (1969, 1988) argued that processes analogous to imprinting occur in human development.

Lorenz discovered the phenomenon of imprinting when he arranged for baby geese to imprint on *him*.

First, he argued that human infants form an **attachment,** an intimate emotional bond, to their natural parents or to other adults who substitute for the natural parents. Second, he defined **attachment behaviors** as any behaviors that help an infant gain or maintain proximity to an attachment figure. He assumed that the purpose of these behaviors is to ensure the safety and survival of the infant.

Bowlby also assumed that important differences exist between imprinting in birds and attachment in humans. Most important, human behavior is more flexible, less governed by fixed instincts, than the behavior of birds. To account for this flexibility, Bowlby adapted ideas from learning theories and theories of control in complex physical and biological systems. He used these ideas to explain both how attachments change with age and in which situations attachment behaviors will be activated.

**attachment**
*The intimate emotional bond that infants form during the first years of life to their mothers, fathers, and perhaps to other people with whom they interact often.*

**attachment behaviors**
*Behaviors that help an infant gain or maintain proximity to an attachment figure (i.e., crying, crawling to the attachment figure).*

## Principles of Contemporary Attachment Theory

Bowlby did not develop attachment theory independently. He collaborated for many years with Mary Ainsworth (Ainsworth & Bowlby, 1991), who also made important contributions to the theory (e.g., Ainsworth et al., 1978). In addition, many other researchers have added to the theoretical foundation of the theory and done important research to test its hypotheses (see Bretherton, 1992; Bretherton & Waters, 1985; Sroufe & Waters, 1977). The following summary of the theory's major principles derives partly from Bowlby's writings and partly from those of other researchers.

As you read these principles, you should be aware that some researchers question their validity. Some researchers also have questions about the methods used to measure infant-parent attachments, and the interpretation of findings based on these measures. Those questions will be considered later, but first you need to understand the central ideas of the theory.

1. *Attachment behaviors in human infants are evolutionarily programmed and instinctive. Their function is to enhance the survival of infants by keeping infants under their parents' protection.* The behaviors that keep human infants and parents close to each other are part of a biological program that is unlearned or instinctive, much like the program responsible for imprinting in birds. Human attachment behaviors also contribute to the survival of infants, just as imprinting contributes to the survival of birds.

FIGURE 6.4

Monkeys separated from their mothers shortly after birth prefer a soft terrycloth "mother" to a wire "mother," even if they are fed by the wire mother. (At feeding time, a bottle was placed in the holder on the "chest" of the wire mother.) Infant monkeys spent most of their time on the terrycloth mother, as the photograph shows, and spent almost no time in contact with the wire mother.

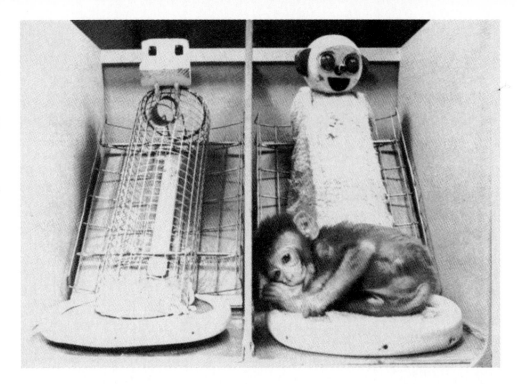

You may not think much about a human infant's need for protection. After all, few infants these days are eaten by lions or snatched away by wolves. But in the evolutionary history of our species, wild animals were a real threat to human infants. (They are still a threat to the Ache infants discussed in chapter 2.) Infants closer to their parents are safer from wild animals, so infants who formed attachments to their parents had a selective advantage. This advantage led, according to Bowlby, to the genetic programming of patterns of attachment behavior.

Attachment behaviors are adaptive today, even in modern societies. If you think for a moment, you can identify situations in which infants depend on the protection of their parents. Infants wandering on their own are prone to accidents that cause injury or death. News stories tell of infants or young children who fall into sewers, are attacked by aggressive dogs, or are run over by cars. When close to their parents, infants are unlikely to experience these dangers.

2. *Human attachments do not depend on an infant's need for food or the mother's providing milk.* Lorenz (1935/1957) proved that birds could imprint on objects from which they never received food. Birds became imprinted on Lorenz himself before they obtained any food from him. Some species of birds regularly imprint on their mothers despite never getting food from her. As soon as they hatch, the young birds begin to catch insects on their own.

Bowlby argued that these observations are inconsistent with both Freudian theory and traditional learning theories. Freud and his followers emphasized the importance of feeding during the earliest, oral stage of personality development. Some Freudian theorists argued that infants become attached to the mother's breast, the object from which they receive food. By contrast, Bowlby argued that attachments do not depend on feeding because the function of attachment behaviors is not to get food but to obtain protection from the mother.

Learning theorists had proposed that infants stay close to their mothers because they are rewarded for doing so, by getting food. To counter this argument, Bowlby referred not only to studies of imprinting but also to the classic studies of Harlow and Zimmerman (1959). These researchers separated monkeys from their mothers and gave them a choice between two substitute mothers. As figure 6.4 shows, one was made of wire and provided food—she had a bottle placed on her "chest." The other was made of soft terrycloth but did not have a bottle.

The infant monkeys spent almost all their time on the soft terrycloth mother and almost none on the wire mother. Most monkeys went to the wire mother only to get food. Most monkeys went to the cloth mother rather than the wire mother when they were frightened by a

large object placed in their cage. So, contrary to the hypotheses of learning theorists, the infant monkeys did not become attached to the wire mother who provided food. They became attached to the cloth mother who provided contact comfort.

3. *Human infants become attached to the one or few persons with whom they interact most frequently.* Bowlby did not reject all principles of learning theory. He assumed that some processes of learning are essential to the formation of attachments. These processes explain not only to whom human infants become attached but also why nearly all infants form attachments to one or more people during the first year of life (Waters et al., 1991).

According to Bowlby, infants become attached to the single person or small number of people with whom they interact most frequently. As just mentioned, attachment figures do not necessarily provide food. Infants often become attached to siblings who rarely or never feed them (Schaffer & Emerson, 1964). Feeding has some influence on the development of attachments, though. While feeding their infants, parents interact with them in ways that promote the development of infant-parent attachment.

4. *In the human species, the first year of life is a sensitive period for the development of attachments.* Young birds become imprinted on an object within a few days or weeks after birth. By contrast, the formation of attachments in human infants takes several months.

During the first weeks of life, human infants have a few signals that encourage adults to interact with them. Their cries can bring adults to relieve their pain or satisfy their hunger. After about two months, their social smiles can elicit positive interactions from adults. During the first few months of life, infants do not strongly prefer to interact with one adult over another. They have not formed the specific relationships that are defined as attachments.

After 3 months of age, infants show stronger preferences for their mothers and other familiar adults than for strangers, but they rarely react negatively to strangers. Although 3-month-olds will protest if their mother leaves them in a room by themselves, they rarely object to being left with someone else (Schaffer & Emerson, 1964).

Infants' behavior changes dramatically in the second half-year of life. Once infants begin to crawl, they often go to their mothers and ask to be held. Around 8 or 9 months of age, infants show heightened **separation protest,** or crying and distress, when their mothers leave them with someone else. Such a reaction to the mother's departure reflects infants' growing understanding of other people and events. Infants can now think of their mother when she is not present, and they feel uncertain about what might happen when she is gone. Because they lack the coping ability to resolve their uncertainty successfully, they experience distress (Kagan et al., 1978). Infants' special attempts to stay close to their mothers and their heightened reactions when separated from her indicate that they have formed an attachment to her.

After about 8 months of age, infants begin to express increased fear of strangers. Bowlby (1969) argued that infants' fear of strangers reduces the chances that they will form new attachments to other people. Therefore, the emergence of stranger fear limits the number of people to whom infants become attached and brings to a close the sensitive period for the formation of attachments. Since Bowlby (1969) presented this hypothesis, several studies have shown that stranger fear is neither as universal nor as closely related to attachment as Bowlby believed. Those studies are reviewed later in the chapter.

5. *Infants are strongly biased to direct their attachment behaviors toward one person, usually the mother. Although infants may become attached to several people, the attachment to the mother is most influential.* Remember that birds become imprinted on one animal or object, the first one they see regularly after they hatch. Bowlby (1969) knew that most human infants display attachment behaviors toward several people (see Schaffer & Emerson, 1964). Even so, he argued that the infant's attachment to the mother, or to a permanent mother-substitute, is primary. Bowlby felt that the existence of one primary attachment was implied by the studies of imprinting. He also wanted to emphasize the problem of having multiple caregivers for an infant. Remember that children raised in institutions by multiple caregivers often show abnormal social development (e.g., Tizard & Hodges, 1978).

**separation protest**
*The crying and distress that infants show after about 8 months of age when their mothers or other attachment figures leave them by themselves or with a person whom they don't know well.*

The family in this snapshot may seem commonplace, but examine it more carefully. The mother, not the father, holds their baby. The mother and baby look at each other while the father looks on. The snapshot illustrates Bowlby's assumption that infant's attachments to their mothers are stronger than to their fathers or anyone else.

In focusing on the relationship with the mother, Bowlby (1969) retained a key principle of Freudian theory. Freud suggested not only that the mother-infant relationship was critical for personality development but also that this relationship set the pattern for all later love relationships. Obviously, this hypothesis gives fathers a distinctly secondary role in children's development. The hypothesis also raises questions about the effects on infants of nonmaternal care (or day care). These implications of Bowlby's hypothesis, and the controversies surrounding them, are examined in greater detail later.

The hypothesis is mentioned now because it explains why the major heading for this section of the chapter is "infant-mother attachments." More important, it explains why nearly all studies of attachment have examined only infants' attachments to their mothers. You should assume, therefore, that the mother is an infant's primary attachment figure from this point on. Fathers and other attachment figures will come back into the picture later in the chapter.

6. *During the third year of life, attachments develop into goal-corrected partnerships between mothers and their infants.* This principle is the first that focuses on the flexibility of infant-parent attachments in humans. It also is the first that deals with the facet of Bowlby's theory concerned with control systems.

Remember that the goal of attachment behaviors is to ensure the protection of infants by keeping them close to their mothers. Of course, infants cannot stay close to their mothers forever. They must someday gain their independence. In preparation for that day, infants must learn about their environment through exploration.

Under certain conditions, infants can explore far from the mother and still be safe. Under other conditions, exploration is dangerous and infants must stay in contact with their mothers. How far an infant can explore safely will change from moment to moment and from month to month as the infant grows.

To provide for exploration and for safety, the system of attachment behaviors must be carefully controlled. In Bowlby's terms, the system must be goal-corrected. When an infant is too far away to be safe, the behavioral system should be activated to bring the infant closer. When the infant is closer than necessary, the behavioral system should be deactivated, and the infant should begin to explore more widely. Ainsworth (1967) described this balance between closeness and exploration by calling the mother a *haven of security* in times of danger and a *secure base* for exploration when danger is absent.

During an infant's first year, responsibility for maintaining the balance between closeness and exploration rests primarily with the mother, but a control system operates in the infant, too. By crying, infants can signal their insecurity or distress at being away from their mother. Still, young infants must rely on the mother to come to them when they cry. When infants can crawl or walk, the responsibility shifts somewhat. Then infants can move toward their mother when they feel insecure.

Responsibility shifts still further during infants' second and third years of life, as they begin to talk. Then they can tell their mothers about their needs and feelings. Their mothers, in turn, can tell them about their plans (Ainsworth, 1989). Mother and infant become partners in maintaining the balance between closeness and exploration. The achievement of this goal-corrected partnership is the final stage in the development of human attachments.

7. *When infants become attached to their mothers, they form internal working models of their mothers and, especially, of themselves.* Infants not only form an emotional bond with their mothers; they also develop ideas about their relationship. As their understanding increases, they form internal, cognitive models of their interactions with their mother. These models include images of previous interactions with the mother, expectations about the mother's future behavior, and plans for their behavior toward the mother. Also, infants construct models of themselves based on how their mothers treat them. Bowlby (1988) called these *working* models to emphasize that they can be modified when infants' interactions with their mothers change. Even so, Bowlby argued that models formed in the first year of life tend to persist and begin to operate on an unconscious level. They become resistant to change and part of a child's personality.

Notice that the idea of internal working models led Bowlby (1988) to the same conclusion that Freud reached decades earlier. Remember, Freud assumed that the early years of life were a sensitive period for the development of personality. A child's personality was largely molded, in Freud's view, by experiences during the first few years of life. Bowlby (1988) did not propose that a child's personality is fixed during infancy, but he attached special importance to the first years of life. This hypothesis is controversial, too, and you will read more about it later.

8. *Infants' attachments to their mothers differ in their security. Infants form secure attachments when their mothers are responsive to their needs.* Bowlby recognized that the attachment formed by each mother and infant is unique. Ainsworth (1967) suggested that the most important dimension of variations in attachments is that of security. Infants with secure attachments show a healthy balance between staying close to their mother and exploring their environment. In these infants' working models, mothers are seen as responsive and supportive, and infants view themselves as worthy of support (Bretherton, 1985).

Secure attachments form, according to the theory, when mothers have been sensitive to their infants' needs and desires. Insecure attachments are likely when mothers are overly intrusive or neglecting during their infants' first year of life (Ainsworth et al., 1978). This hypothesis does not consider an infant's potential contribution to the development of attachments. It suggests that influence goes from mother to infant and not vice versa. This is another controversial issue in attachment theory that will be evaluated shortly.

9. *Secure attachments have positive effects on the infants' later development.* The converse of this hypothesis should also be stated explicitly: Insecure attachments have negative effects on later development. According to the theory, infants with secure attachments should develop into competent, loving children who form mutually satisfying relationships with other children and with adults. In Erikson's (1963) terms, these infants leave life's first stage with a sense of basic trust in the world and in themselves.

By contrast, infants with insecure attachments should develop into children who distrust themselves and their world. As a result, their social behavior and personality development should be abnormal. Notice, again, that this hypothesis suggests experiences during infancy are especially important for later life. The early-experience hypothesis is just as hotly disputed with respect to social development as with other aspects of development. The dispute continues, as you will see, partly because the available data are inconclusive.

## Tests of Attachment Theory: Methods and Results

A theory as broad and provocative as the ethological theory of attachment is certain to be challenged. Since Bowlby (1969) presented the theory hundreds of studies of infant-mother attachments have been done. Those studies provide answers to some controversial questions about the theory. Before you can understand those studies fully, you need to know how researchers assess the security of infant-mother attachments.

## Measuring Infant-Mother Attachments: The Strange Situation

In the earliest studies of attachment, researchers recorded how intensely infants protested when separated from their mothers, how close infants stayed to their mothers, and how often infants smiled at their mothers (see Cohen, 1974). These measures proved inadequate because security of attachment can be judged only from organized patterns of behavior in specific situations (Sroufe & Waters, 1977). That is, a researcher needs to assess whether an infant treats the mother as a haven of security in frightening situations and whether the infant uses the mother as a secure base for the exploration of novel situations.

During the 1960s, Ainsworth (Ainsworth et al., 1978) devised a laboratory procedure called the **Strange Situation** that has become standard for measuring the security of infant-mother attachments. You got an abbreviated, infant's-eye view of the procedure in the earlier story of Tamaki and her mother. Now you'll see how it looks from a researcher's viewpoint.

**Strange Situation**
*A standard experimental procedure for measuring the security of infants' attachments to their mothers, their fathers, or other adults.*

## TABLE 6.2  *The Eight Episodes of Ainsworth's Strange Situation*

| NUMBER OF EPISODES | PERSONS PRESENT | DURATION | BRIEF DESCRIPTION OF ACTION |
|---|---|---|---|
| 1 | Mother, baby, and observer | 30 secs. | Observer introduces mother and baby to experimental room, then leaves. |
| 2 | Mother and baby | 3 min. | Mother is nonparticipant while baby explores; if necessary, play is stimulated after 2 minutes. |
| 3 | Stranger, mother, and baby | 3 min. | Stranger enters. First minute: Stranger silent. Second minute: Stranger converses with mother. Third minute: Stranger approaches baby. After 3 minutes mother leaves unobtrusively. |
| 4 | Stranger and baby | 3 min. or less[a] | First separation episode. Stranger's behavior is geared to that of baby. |
| 5 | Mother and baby | 3 min. or more[b] | First reunion episode. Mother greets and/or comforts baby, then tries to settle him again in play. Mother then leaves, saying "bye-bye." |
| 6 | Baby alone | 3 min. or less[a] | Second separation episode. |
| 7 | Stranger and baby | 3 min. or less[a] | Continuation of second separation. Stranger enters and gears her behavior to that of baby. |
| 8 | Mother and baby | 3 min. | Second reunion episode. Mother enters, greets baby, then picks him up. Meanwhile stranger leaves unobtrusively. |

Adapted from Ainsworth et al., "The eight episodes of Ainsworth's strange situation" in *Patterns of Attachment: A Psychological Study of the Strange Situation*, section: P37, table 3. copyright © 1978 Lawrence Erlbaum Associates, Inc., Mahwah, NJ. Reprinted by permission.
[a]Episode is curtailed if the baby is unduly distressed.
[b]Episode is prolonged if more time is required for the baby to become reinvolved in play.

The procedure involves the sequence of eight episodes shown in table 6.2. The first episode begins as an experimenter brings the mother into the laboratory playroom with her infant in her arms. After giving brief instructions to the mother, the experimenter leaves. To start the second episode, the mother places the infant on the floor next to a few toys. The mother then sits in a chair across the room and starts reading a magazine. An observer watching through a window records the infant's exploration of the toys and the room. The observer also watches to see if the infant moves close to the mother instead of exploring.

The third episode begins when an unfamiliar adult woman, the stranger, enters the room. She waits for a minute before interacting with the mother, and then she tries to interact with the infant. After 3 minutes, the mother leaves the room and the fourth episode begins. During this separation period, the stranger does not try to play with the infant, but she does try to distract or console infants who become distressed. The mother stays out of the room for 3 minutes. This period is shortened if the infant becomes highly distressed, as Tamaki did.

Then the mother returns to the room, and episode 5 begins. She pauses after opening the door to see whether her infant will approach her. Next, the stranger leaves and the mother tries to calm her infant. After the infant is comfortable, the mother tries to get him or her to play with the toys again.

Episode 6 begins after the mother again leaves the room, this time taking her purse and saying "bye-bye" as she goes out. The observer records how the infant reacts to the mother's departure and whether the infant plays with toys while she is gone. Then (episode 7), the strange woman enters the room and attempts to soothe the infant. If the infant calms down, the stranger tries to get him or her interested in the toys. In episode 8, the mother returns again. The observer again records how the infant responds to the mother's return.

Ainsworth and her coworkers (1978) observed the behavior in the Strange Situation of about 30 infants and mothers who were part of a longitudinal study. The researchers identified three patterns of mother-infant interaction that they initially labeled A, B, and C. As the research continued, the critical elements of these patterns and the quality of the infants' attachments to their mothers became clear.

Type B infants are defined as securely attached. In the two episodes (5 and 8) when infants are reunited with their mothers, type B infants greet their mother with a smile, a cry, or

This mother and infant are in the second episode of the Strange Situation. The mother is not interacting with her infant, but she is available if the infant feels afraid or upset. The infant is exploring the room. In Ainsworth's terms, the infant is using the mother as a secure base for exploration of a new setting.

an approach to her. They actively seek contact with the mother and are readily comforted by her. Eventually, they return to play. Recall that Tamaki showed this pattern of behavior in the opening vignette.

Type B infants may be friendly with the stranger and even seek comfort from her when their mother is absent, but they clearly prefer their mother to the stranger. Thus, they see their mother as a haven of security and a secure base for exploring the unfamiliar room and toys.

Type A and type C infants are insecurely or anxiously attached. The two groups differ in their pattern of attachment behaviors. Type A infants show an anxious-avoidant attachment. They do not take their mother as a haven of security. In the reunion episodes, they ignore their mother or look at her and then look away. They rarely approach their mother during reunion and they resist contact if she picks them up. Type A infants rarely react with outward displays of distress when left with the stranger. However, their heart rate increases dramatically, suggesting that they are upset by the mother's absence (Spangler & Grossman, 1993).

Type C infants have an anxious-resistant attachment. They seem not to trust the security that their mother offers them. They approach the mother when she returns after a separation, but they also resist contact and interaction with her. These behaviors suggest they are ambivalent toward their mother, so they are sometimes labeled as insecure-ambivalent. Even before separation, they seem unusually angry or unusually passive.

In the 1980s several researchers suggested that some infants show a pattern of behavior in the Strange Situation that is different from that of A, B, or C infants (Carlson et al., 1989; Main, Kaplan, & Cassidy, 1985). This new pattern, given the letter D, is characterized by disorganized, disoriented behavior. In the Strange Situation, D infants react with great increases in heart rate when separated from their mothers, suggesting that they are intensely alarmed (Spangler & Grossman, 1993). When reunited with their mothers, they seem confused, depressed, or dazed. They also show contradictory behaviors simultaneously, for example, approaching the mother but keeping their face averted from her.

## An Alternative Measure of Attachment: The Attachment Q-sort

Other procedures besides the Strange Situation have been used to assess infant-mother attachments. Everett Waters and Kathleen Deane (1985) devised a procedure based on observers' reports on an infant's behavior when interacting with the mother. Observers are given many items (90 or 100) describing behaviors relevant to attachment. For example, one item refers to mothers' and infants' sharing of emotions during play. Another deals with the infant's spontaneous approach to the mother after a period of exploration or independent play.

| TABLE 6.3 | *Four Types of Attachment* | |
|---|---|---|
| CLASSIFICATION | LABEL | BEHAVIOR IN THE STRANGE SITUATION |
| B | Secure | Approach the mother in reunion episodes and are readily comforted by her. Obviously prefer the mother to the stranger. |
| A | Anxious-avoidant | Ignore the mother in reunion episodes or look at her and look away. Show little outward distress when the mother leaves but have increased heart rate. |
| C | Anxious-resistant (or insecure-ambivalent) | Approach the mother but resist contact with her in reunion episodes. Seem unusually angry or unusually passive. |
| D | Disorganized-disoriented | Show great increases in heart rate when the mother leaves, suggesting intense alarm. Confused, depressed, or dazed at reunion, often showing contradictory behaviors. |

Observers sort these items, usually into nine groups, based on how characteristic each item is of a specific mother-infant pair. Observers are instructed to put only a few items into the extreme groups—those indicating behaviors most and least characteristic of a child. In fact, they are told exactly how many items to put into each of the nine groups. This kind of forced distribution is known as a Q-sort, so the measure is called the Attachment Q-sort.

An Attachment Q-sort can be done by parents as well as by outside observers. Researchers have probably used the Q-sort more often with parents than with anyone else (Vaughn et al., 1992). Regardless of whether mothers or trained observers do the sort, the next step is to compare their sort with a hypothetical Q-sort for an infant who is securely attached. Based on this comparison, infants are given a score for the security of their attachments to their mothers.

Use of the Strange Situation is far more common than use of the Attachment Q-sort or other procedures. Most of the research on infant-mother attachments deals with the differences between infants showing the A, B, C, and D patterns in the Strange Situation. To help you understand the following summary of this research, table 6.3 lists the usual labels for these patterns.

## Sources of Secure Attachments: Mothers' Contributions

According to ethological theorists, sensitive and responsive caregiving is critical for the development of secure attachments. To test this hypothesis, Ainsworth (Ainsworth et al., 1978) observed mothers' interactions with their infants every three weeks during the first year of life. The infants' attachments to their mothers were assessed in the Strange Situation when they were 12 months of age.

As expected, the mothers of infants who formed secure attachments (i.e., type B infants) were highly responsive to their infants' needs during their first three months of life. For example, they quickly comforted their infants when they were crying. These mothers also were affectionate when holding their infants and sensitive to their infants' signals. For example, they fed their infants when the infants seemed hungry rather than having them wait for food. Observers rated these mothers as accepting, sensitive, accessible (rather than ignoring), and cooperative (rather than interfering) toward their infants. The mothers of securely attached infants had similar characteristics in other studies (e.g., Belsky, Rovine, & Taylor, 1984; Egeland & Farber, 1984; Isabella, 1993).

Mothers of anxious-avoidant (A), anxious-resistant (C), and disorganized (D) infants also have distinctive patterns of interactions with their infants. Mothers of avoidant infants often are rejecting. They dislike physical contact with their infants. They treat feeding as a mechanical process rather than an opportunity for positive interactions. They often seem angry at their infants (Ainsworth et al., 1978; Egeland & Farber, 1984). When interacting with their infants, these mothers are likely to be intrusive and overstimulating. Their infants often act as if they want to get away from them (Belsky, Gilstrap, & Rovine, 1984). This negative pattern becomes more prominent near the end of the first year of life, when it is especially likely to provoke conflicts between mother and infant (Isabella, 1993).

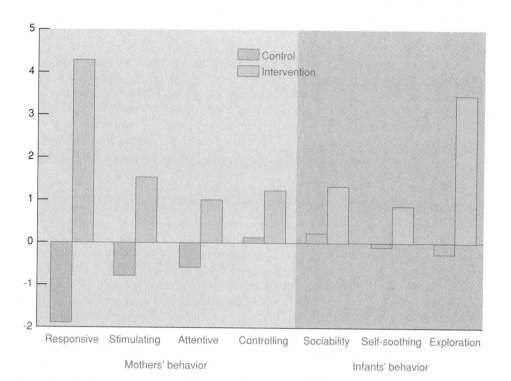

FIGURE 6.5

An intervention to enhance mothers' responsiveness not only made them more responsive but also had positive effects on other types of behavior. The infants of these mothers became more sociable, better at soothing themselves, and more eager to explore their environments. (Data from van den Boom, 1994.)

Mothers of resistant or ambivalent infants are not consistently negative or angry, but they spend little time with their infants (Cassidy & Berlin, 1994; Isabella, 1993). These mothers respond erratically to their infants' needs, or they rarely respond at all (Ainsworth et al., 1978; Belsky et al., 1984; Egeland & Farber, 1984). When their infants are playing happily on their own, these mothers often interrupt them and interfere with their exploration. Infants who experience neglect sometimes fall in the anxious-resistant group (Egeland & Sroufe, 1981).

Most severely neglected infants show the disorganized/disoriented type of attachment (Carlson et al., 1989; Main et al., 1985). This pattern is also common among infants who have been abused, infants whose mothers suffer from mental illness, and infants whose mothers lost their own parents in childhood or who were abused as children (Bowlby, 1988).

Do these differences in mothers' behavior cause their infants to form different types of attachments to them? Ethological theorists would answer yes, and the evidence certainly is consistent with that hypothesis. However, all the studies discussed so far had correlational designs, so conclusions about causality are open to challenge.

Recent experimental interventions have bolstered arguments that mothers' behavior affects the type of attachment their infants form (van IJzendoorn, Juffer, & Duyvesteyn, 1995). One experiment included 100 mother and infants from the Netherlands (van den Boom, 1994). The infants were assessed with the Neonatal Behavioral Assessment Scale mentioned in chapter 4 during their first two weeks of life. All those selected for the experiment received unusually high scores for their irritability. All the mothers were from families low in SES. These characteristics suggested that the mother-infant pairs might have a higher than average risk of forming a poor relationship.

At 6 months of age, mothers and infants were randomly assigned to the intervention condition or to a control condition. A psychologist visited the mothers in the intervention condition three times during the next three months. During each visit, the psychologist talked with mothers about interpreting infants' signals accurately, responding sensitively to those signals, and engaging in playful interactions with infants. The general goal of the intervention was to increase mothers' attentiveness and responsiveness to their infants.

The intervention proved highly effective. When their infants were 9 months of age, mothers who received the intervention were more responsive to their infants, both when the infants expressed positive emotions and when they were crying (see figure 6.5). These mothers also were more stimulating, playing more with their infants and giving them more

physical contact. In addition, they were more attentive to their infants and more controlling of their infant's behavior.

Not surprisingly, infants' behavior also differed in the two conditions. As figure 6.5 shows, infants whose mothers received the intervention showed more positive social behavior, soothed themselves more often, and engaged in more sophisticated exploration of their environment. These differences in mother-infant interaction were associated with dramatic differences in attachment security at age 1. Only 28 percent of infants in the control condition were securely attached, compared with 62 percent of the infants in the intervention. These data leave little doubt that a mother's behavior powerfully affects whether her infant forms a secure attachment to her.

## Sources of Secure Attachments: Infants' Contributions

Do infants also make a contribution to the type of attachment formed between them and their mothers? Several researchers have suggested that the innate characteristics of infants affect both the security of their attachments to their mothers and their mothers' behavior toward them (Campos et al., 1983; Fox, 1995; Goldsmith & Harman, 1994; Kagan, 1984). For example, two infants who are temperamentally different might behave differently in the Strange Situation and so appear to have different types of attachments. The differences in the infants' temperaments might also influence their behavior at home and, therefore, influence their interactions with their mothers.

Ethological theorists reject the hypothesis that temperament or other infant characteristics have a strong influence on attachment security. Bowlby (1969) assumed that all infants are biologically prepared to form a secure attachment to a mother who is sensitive and responsive. He and other ethological theorists argue that parents normally adjust their behavior to account for variations in infants' reactivity, irritability, or other temperamental characteristics (Sroufe, 1985). According to these theorists, insecure attachments arise only when mothers fail to provide the sensitive, responsive care that infants need and expect.

The evidence regarding the relation of temperament to attachment security is mixed. Many researchers have found no relation between measures of infants' temperaments and attachment classifications judged from the Strange Situation (Sroufe, 1985; Vaughn et al., 1989). When infants' security has been assessed with the Attachment Q-sort, relations to a dimension of temperament that involves negative emotionality (irritability, fussiness, and anger) have been found (Vaughn et al., 1992). The relations are weak in infancy, but they increase when temperament and attachment are measured at 2 and 3 years of age.

Instead of relying on standard temperament measures, some researchers have assessed infants' reactivity directly. Infants in one study were first observed when they were 2 days of age (Calkins & Fox, 1992). The observers recorded whether the infants cried when an adult took a pacifier out of their mouths. Fourteen months later, the infants and their mothers were seen in the Strange Situation. Infants who cried when the pacifier was taken away were more likely than those who did not cry to be classified as insecurely attached to their mothers. One possible interpretation of this result is that newborns with a low tolerance for frustration have a greater risk of forming insecure attachments. Still, most irritable newborns develop secure attachments to their mothers (Cassidy, 1994).

Finally, some studies suggest that variations in attachment security should be attributed neither to mothers alone nor to infants alone but to the interaction between the two (Cassidy, 1994; Rothbart & Ahadi, 1994). In other words, certain types of infants have difficulty forming secure attachments to certain types of mothers. For example, irritable and passive infants are more likely to develop resistant attachments when their mothers are under stress because of low income, little education, and other problems (Egeland & Farber, 1984). Irritable infants are more likely to develop insecure attachments if their mothers are socially isolated and have few people on whom they can rely for support (Crockenberg, 1981). Infants who tend to react more negatively in social situations often develop insecure attachments if their mothers are rigid and controlling (Mangelsdorf et al., 1990). These findings, taken together, imply that an infant's characteristics can influence the security of infant-mother attachments if a mother's life circumstances or her personality traits lessen her ability to adapt to her infant.

The conclusion that both mothers' behaviors and infants' characteristics affect the security of infant-mother attachments should not surprise you. That conclusion is consistent with the transactional approach mentioned in chapter 4 (Sameroff & Chandler, 1975). Remember, the central assumption of the transactional approach is that development depends on the characteristics of children and of their environments.

Nevertheless, the two types of characteristics may not be equally important. Current evidence suggests that the security of infant-mother attachments depends more heavily on mothers' responsiveness than on infants' characteristics (van IJzendoorn et al., 1992). That is, mothers have greater control than infants over the development of infant-mother attachments.

## Consequences of Secure Attachments

Why are researchers concerned about the security of infant-mother attachments? Bowlby (1951, 1969) proposed that insecure attachments lead to anxiety, an increased need for love, feelings of guilt and depression, antisocial behavior, and difficulties in forming social relationships later in life. Sroufe (1979) stated the same proposition in a more positive way. He argued that secure attachments are the foundation for healthy development. Infants who have formed a secure attachment to their mother should be more able to engage in effective, independent exploration as toddlers; as preschoolers, they should have especially positive relationships with peers. These hypotheses have been tested in longitudinal studies.

One study included toddlers who were seen with their mothers twice (Matas, Arend, and Sroufe, 1978). At 18 months of age, the toddlers' attachments to their mothers were assessed in the Strange Situation. At 24 months of age, the toddlers were given a brief time for play with toys. Then they were asked to do a few tasks. For example, they were given two sticks that they had to put together to get a toy out of a long tube.

The toddlers who were securely attached at 18 months of age were more imaginative when playing with the toys at 24 months of age than were insecurely attached toddlers. When working on the tasks, the securely attached toddlers were more enthusiastic, more persistent, and became less frustrated or angry. If their mothers made suggestions for solving the tasks, securely attached toddlers more often complied with the suggestions; insecurely attached toddlers more often ignored them. In other words, attachment security at 18 months was related to high-level play and obedience to the mother at 2 years of age.

In other studies, 3- and 4-year-olds who were securely attached as infants were better liked by their peers than those who were insecurely attached. Securely attached infants also showed fewer behavior problems during the preschool years than insecurely attached infants. Their preschool teachers rated them as more competent, less hostile toward peers, and less dependent on teachers (Erickson, Sroufe, & Egeland, 1985; Lafreniere & Sroufe, 1985; Suess, Grossmann, & Sroufe, 1992; Waters, Wippman, & Sroufe, 1979).

Differences among the groups of insecurely attached infants (A, C, and D) are smaller and less consistently found than those between the broader groups of secure and insecure infants. However, preschoolers who earlier had disorganized (type D) attachments are especially likely to show high levels of hostile behavior toward their peers (Lyons-Ruth, Alpern, & Repacholi, 1993). Preschoolers who earlier had anxious-resistant (type C) attachments to their mothers are especially likely to be hesitant or inhibited when exploring toys (Cassidy & Berlin, 1994). When interacting with peers, these children often seem withdrawn or submissive. At 5 to 7 years of age, they report greater loneliness than children who were securely attached or anxious-avoidant as infants (Berlin, Cassidy, & Belsky, 1995).

One especially provocative hypothesis is that infants' attachments to their mothers can affect their personality and behavior decades later, when they are adults with infants of their own. Remember that Bowlby (1969) accepted Freud's idea that the mother-infant relationship sets the pattern for later relationships. Remember, too, that this pattern is set because infants form internal working models of their mothers and themselves. Several researchers have assessed the working models of attachments that adults have, to explore the possible transmission of attachments across generations.

Researchers have found that a mother's "state of mind" about her experiences in childhood is highly consistent with the type of attachment her infant has to her (Benoit & Parker,

1994; Main & Hesse, 1990; van IJzendoorn, 1995). Infants who are securely attached usually have mothers who, when interviewed about their childhood, provide balanced and consistent reports of their attachment-related experiences. Often, these mothers report that they had loving parents, but they may report negative experiences, too. Most important is their ability to talk about their experiences coherently and, if necessary, with a sense of forgiveness for their parents. Mothers whose comments have these characteristics are labeled as *autonomous*.

Infants with an anxious-avoidant attachment usually have mothers who dismiss their childhood experiences as unimportant and often say they cannot remember them. When the mothers do provide information, it alternates between general positive statements and special details that contradict those statements. Mothers whose comments have these characteristics are labeled as *dismissing*.

Infants with an insecure-resistant attachment usually have mothers who seem obsessed with their attachment figures. They seem dependent on parents but have confusing and often angry relationships with them. They talk at length about these relationships in complex sentences that are difficult to follow and often ungrammatical. These mothers are labeled as *preoccupied* with their own attachment-related experiences.

Infants with a disorganized attachment usually have mothers whose state of mind about their attachment-related experiences seems unresolved. The mothers' comments have some characteristics like those of the other three groups, but their lapses of attention or reasoning during a conversation about their childhood are distinctive. Their confusion is especially evident when talking about the death of a loved one or their own experiences of child abuse. These mothers are labeled as *unresolved*.

In studies with hundreds of infants and parents, the correspondence between infants' attachment classifications and their parents' (mostly mothers') states of mind about attachment was greater than 60 percent (van IJzendoorn, 1995). These data are certainly consistent with Bowlby's hypothesis that "internal working models of attachment tend to be perpetuated across generations" (Benoit & Parker, 1994, p. 1454). However, the data do not prove the hypothesis, because no researchers have followed people from infancy into the parenting years. That is, no researchers have shown that infants with particular types of attachments become adults with corresponding states of mind about attachment. Evidence of this kind may be available in the future, however, as longitudinal studies of children first seen in infancy continue.

## Questions About the Consequences of Secure Attachments

Not all researchers have found differences during the preschool years between children who were securely and insecurely attached as infants (see Howes, Matheson, & Hamilton, 1994; Lamb & Nash, 1989). Some researchers have found differences between attachment groups for one sex but not the other (Lewis et al., 1984). Moreover, all researchers simply examined the relations between the security of infants' attachments and measures of their social behavior and personality during childhood. Because this kind of research has a correlational design, several explanations can be given for the differences that have been found.

Some researchers argue that children's nature, rather than their nurture, can explain the associations between attachment security in infancy and its correlates in the preschool years and later (Fox, 1995; Lamb & Nash, 1989). In this view, a child's genotype is a *third* variable that affects both the security of the child's attachment during infancy and the child's social behavior and personality during childhood. Some children, for example, may have a genetic propensity to interact sociably and positively with other people. These children are likely, as infants, to form secure attachments to their mothers; they are likely, as preschoolers, to form good relationships with their peers. They may also be likely to talk positively and coherently about their childhood experiences when interviewed in adulthood.

Another possibility is that continuities in parents' behavior serve as the third variable linking attachment security in infancy to preschool competence (Campos et al., 1983). Mothers who are sensitive and responsive in the first year of life help their infants form a secure attachment to them. Mothers who are responsive to their preschool children, but who also demand that their children behave appropriately, help their preschoolers become competent

in interacting with peers. Most important, mothers who interact more appropriately with infants often interact more appropriately with older children, too. This continuity in mothering could explain why securely attached infants often become competent preschoolers.

Advocates of the ethological theory of attachment do not reject this idea about continuity in mothering. Although Bowlby (1969) and other attachment theorists have emphasized the importance of experiences in infancy, they have not denied the importance of later experiences (van IJzendoorn, 1995). Indeed, advocates of the ethological theory have provided evidence that changes in mothers' behavior can change the relation between infant attachment security and later outcomes.

For one study, mothers and children were observed both in infancy and during the preschool years (Erickson et al., 1985). Some mothers were warm and responsive to their infants but were less successful in helping their children negotiate the transition to childhood. When their children were preschoolers, these mothers failed to set appropriate limits on their behavior, were relatively uninvolved with them, and gave them little support and encouragement. Their children were securely attached as infants but displayed many problem behaviors as preschoolers.

Other mothers seemed to interact more appropriately with their children as they grew older. When their children were infants, these mothers were not sensitive and responsive enough to allow their infants to form secure attachments to them. But when their children were preschoolers, these mothers were supportive while setting firm limits on the children's behavior. The mothers were involved with their children, provided appropriate materials for their play, and gave help to them without being intrusive. As a result, their children did not display serious behavior problems as preschoolers.

These patterns show that a secure attachment in infancy does not ensure the child's later development will be trouble free. Conversely, an insecure attachment in infancy does not always lead to abnormal behavior later. Children can change their path of development, particularly if their interactions with their mother and other significant people change.

Still, children are likely to develop best when their first social relationships give them a feeling of security. Erikson (1963) expressed the same idea when he discussed his first psychosocial stage: Life starts on a better footing with a sense of basic trust than with distrust.

## Using the Strange Situation in Other Cultures

The first research with the Strange Situation was done in the United States. About 70 percent of the U.S. infants in Ainsworth's sample were classified as securely attached (Ainsworth et al., 1978). About 20 percent were classified as anxious-avoidant. The remaining 10 percent were classified as anxious-resistant.

Soon researchers began to use the Strange Situation in other cultures. Several researchers studied samples of Japanese infants like Tamaki (Miyake, Chen, & Campos, 1985; Nakagawa, Lamb, & Miyaki, 1992; Takahashi, 1990). About the same percentage of Japanese infants as U.S. infants were classified as type B. The rest were classified as anxious-resistant (C). None was classified as anxious-avoidant (A).

The researchers argued that so many Japanese infants fell into type C because the Strange Situation was stranger—and more stressful—for them than for infants in the United States. As suggested in the Tamaki story, Japanese infants spend less time away from their mothers than do infants in the United States. The Strange Situation, then, may not have the same meaning for Japanese infants and U.S. infants. Stated more formally, the Strange Situation may not be a valid measure of attachment for infants and mothers in other cultures.

Other researchers disagree with this conclusion, arguing that the Strange Situation can give us valid measures of infant-mother attachments in other cultures (Sagi, van IJzendoorn, & Koren-Karie, 1991; van IJzendoorn & Kroonenberg, 1988). These researchers point out that the distribution of A, B, and C infants varies as much across samples *within* a single culture as *across* cultures. In one sample from northern Germany, more than 50 percent of infants were classified as anxious-avoidant (A). In another sample from southern Germany, tested by the same researchers, the distribution of A, B, and C infants was similar to that in Ainsworth's sample (Grossman & Grossman, 1990).

While this mother is at work, her 1-year-old will be at her child-care center. Growing numbers of infants and toddlers in the United States receive care in centers or day-care homes while their mothers work. There are conflicting opinions and mixed findings regarding the effects of such care on infants' development and their relationships to their mothers.

More important, within-culture variations in attachment are often related to variations in parenting. In northern Germany, for example, parents encourage their children's independence and worry about spoiling their infants by responding to them constantly. The demands of these mothers for early independence could account for their infants' unwillingness to rely on them for security in the Strange Situation.

Perhaps the strongest evidence for the cross-cultural validity of the Strange Situation comes from studies of Israeli infants (Aviezer et al., 1994; Sagi et al., 1994). As explained in *Cultural Perspectives:* "Attachment Security and the Kibbutz Experience," these studies show that infants' sleeping arrangements affect their chances of being classified as insecurely attached after being observed in the Strange Situation. The sleeping arrangements that heighten the risk of insecure attachments are exactly those that are assumed in attachment theory to reduce infants' sense of security. Therefore, these studies show the validity of the Strange Situation and provide evidence for hypotheses about the sources of secure attachments.

## Maternal Employment and Attachment

Arrangements for infant care are changing not only in Israel but also in the United States and many other countries. Increasing numbers of women are returning to work outside the home shortly after their infants are born. While these mothers are at work their infants receive some form of nonmaternal care. They may stay with a babysitter in their own home, go to the home of another babysitter who cares for several children, or go to a day-care center where several adults care for a group of children.

How do maternal employment and nonmaternal care during the working day affect infants' social development? Researchers and theorists differ sharply in their answers to this question. Some researchers who accept the ethological theory of attachment believe that infant day care increases the risk of insecure infant-mother attachments and so can have harmful effects on infants' development. These theorists regard infant day care as a form of institutional care.

As you remember, evidence on the retarded development and abnormal behavior of infants raised in institutions led Bowlby (1969) to formulate his theory of infant-mother attachments. Bowlby (1973) assumed that nonmaternal care during the work day has weaker effects than those of a residential institution. Still, he expressed concern about daily nonmaternal care for children under 3 years old. Similar concerns were expressed by Ainsworth (1973) and other researchers (Belsky, 1988; Vaughn, Gove, & Egeland, 1980).

Theorists and researchers not allied with the ethological theory of attachment often dismiss claims that infant day care is harmful (e.g., Clarke-Stewart, 1989; Scarr, Phillips, & McCartney, 1990). They argue that infants are adaptable and can adjust successfully when they

ATTACHMENT
SECURITY AND
THE KIBBUTZ
EXPERIENCE

S̲ome infants in Israel live in small, demo- cratically governed communities of 400 to 900 people. All the members of the community work cooperatively for the welfare of the entire group. Each community is called, in Hebrew, a **kibbutz** (the plural is *kibbutzim*).

Research on infants in kibbutzim is espe- cially significant because these infants are reared together, in groups under the care of several adults. All kibbutz infants receive care during the day in a child-care center supervised by sev- eral women. This day care frees the infants' mothers to work at various jobs and so allows women to fill the same roles in the community as men do. Such equality between men and women is a fundamental principle of kibbutz life (Aviezer et al., 1994).

On a few kibbutzim, group care for in- fants is also the norm during the night. Infants sleep in dormitories that house all children under 12. Two women monitor the dormitories from a central location by intercom. These women have the "night shift" for only about one week every six months. This means that infants are not likely to form an enduring relationship with them.

In addition, if infants become upset dur- ing the night, they are likely to receive comfort from a caregiver only after some delay, if at all. Moreover, some caregivers are likely to respond more often when monitoring at night than oth- ers, meaning that infants receive inconsistent care when they are distressed. These conditions should, according to ethological theory, lead to the formation of anxious-resistant attachments.

In other kibbutzim, infants sleep at home with their parents. Like the infants in communal sleeping arrangements, however, these infants spend most of the day with other infants while their mothers are at work. That is, the two types of kibbutzim differ primarily in infants' night- time sleeping arrangements.

This difference is critical. Figure 6.6 shows the attachment classifications for two samples of kibbutz infants, one in which in- fants slept communally and one in which in- fants slept at home. The percentage of infants who were securely attached was much higher for infants sleeping at home; the percentage who were anxious-resistant was much higher

for infants sleeping communally. No percent- ages are given for anxious-avoidant attach- ments because no infants in either group received this classification. The percentage of infants classified as disorganized was slightly but not significantly higher among those who had communal sleeping arrangements.

Fortunately, even before the negative ef- fects of communal sleeping on attachment were conclusively documented, kibbutz leaders had begun to abandon this practice. In 1994 only about 1 percent of Israeli kibbutzim still had communal sleeping arrangements for infants (Aviezer et al., 1994). One reason for the change is that the prosperity of kibbutzim had increased, making larger houses possible for each family. In addition, kibbutz leaders have reduced the emphasis on the community and increased the emphasis on family life. This change was due partly to the leaders' accep- tance of the ideas of Bowlby (1969) and other writers about the importance of parent-infant relationships. In other words, the changes in kibbutzim have many sources, but one is an ap- preciation of the practical implications of theo- ries of infant development.

**kibbutz**
*A small, democratically governed community in Israel in which groups of infants and children receive their daily care in community-run centers.*

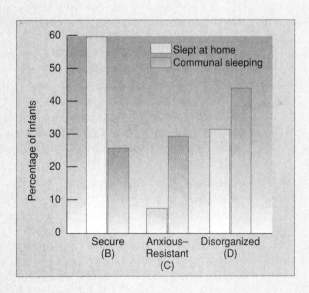

## FIGURE 6.6

Kibbutz infants who sleep in a dormitory for several infants, instead of at home with their mothers, less often have secure attachments to their mothers. (Data from Sagi et al., 1994.)

are not cared for exclusively by their mothers. Kathleen McCartney and Deborah Phillips (1988) also rejected the hypothesis in ethological theory that human infants are biologically prepared to form a primary attachment to a single caregiver. Instead, they suggested that human infants often had multiple caregivers during the evolutionary history of the species.

A pattern of multiple caregivers for infants is still the norm for some human groups. Among the Efe people who live in the African nation of Zaire, many adults and children share in infants' care. Infants spend only about half their time interacting with their mothers; they spend the other half interacting with their fathers, other adults, and, especially, older children (Tronick, Morelli, & Ivey, 1992).

Because of the theoretical and practical significance of this issue, many researchers have tried to resolve it. Unfortunately, they have had only limited success, because the results of different studies have often been contradictory. Several studies done during the 1980s suggested that infants receiving nonmaternal care for more than 20 hours a week have more insecure attachments to their mothers than do infants who spend less time or no time in nonmaternal care (Belsky & Rovine, 1988).

A more recent reanalysis of these and other studies also showed an increased risk of insecure infant-mother attachments for infants receiving nonmaternal care (Lamb, Sternberg, & Prodomidis, 1992). In the reanalysis, however, part-time care did not seem to eliminate the risks of insecure attachments. When infants' attachments were assessed after they were 15 months of age, part-time care was also associated with an increase in insecure attachments.

By contrast, another team of researchers found no evidence that nonmaternal care increases the risk of insecure attachments (Roggman et al., 1994). This team also discovered an important problem when they contacted other researchers in the United States who had studied infants' attachments. The other researchers often said that they had done studies that showed no effect of nonmaternal care on attachment security, but they had not published their results. Researchers hesitate to submit nonsignificant results for publication because the editors of scientific journals rarely accept such reports. These biases in submissions and in editors' decisions mean that published studies may exaggerate the relation between nonmaternal care and insecure attachments.

Nevertheless, the studies showing more insecure attachments among infants in nonmaternal care cannot be dismissed entirely. Under some conditions—that, unfortunately, cannot be specified precisely—infants apparently have trouble forming a secure attachment with mothers who work outside the home. Concern about these conditions is part of the impetus for laws allowing parents a paid or unpaid leave from work when they have a young infant. Such laws exist in most industrialized countries (Andersson, 1989; Gamble & Zigler, 1986).

In the United States, the Family and Medical Leave Act of 1993 provides 12 weeks of leave for employed mothers and fathers who have a newborn. Employees are not paid during the leave period, however, and the leave is available only for adults who work in businesses with more than 50 employees. Moreover, researchers do not agree about the age at which infants can most easily make the transition from home care to day care (Barglow, Vaughn, & Molitor, 1987; Brazelton, 1986; Lamb et al., 1992). From the perspective of ethological theory, the entire first year of life is important for the development of infant-parent attachments.

Still, all ethological theorists would agree that infants become attached to mothers who work outside the home. Furthermore, the kinds of maternal behavior that lead to secure attachments when a mother is not working outside the home also lead to secure attachments when she is working. In particular, working mothers who are more sensitive, warm, and accepting of their infants more often have infants who are securely attached to them (Belsky & Rovine, 1988; Benn, 1986). Most important, studies in the United States and other countries show that the majority of infants receiving nonmaternal care during the work week form secure attachments to their mothers (Belsky & Rovine, 1988; Clarke-Stewart, 1989; Sagi et al., 1994; Scarr et al., 1990).

Finally, most mothers who work when their children are infants continue to work as their children grow. Similarly, infants who are in day-care programs often remain in similar programs as they grow. In later chapters, you will learn about the effects of maternal

employment on broader aspects of child development. You will also learn about the effects of child care during the preschool years on cognitive and social development.

# BEYOND INFANT-MOTHER ATTACHMENTS: INFANTS' SOCIAL WORLDS

Focusing on the mother-infant relationship gives an incomplete picture of infants' social worlds. Focusing solely on attachment security and not on other aspects of infants' social relationships also gives an incomplete picture. To fill in the picture, information is needed about infants' relationships with their fathers, other caregivers, and strangers.

## Mothers and Fathers: Their Different (and Unequal) Roles

Most infants form attachments to their mother and to their father during the first year of life (Schaffer & Emerson, 1964). Infants typically form an attachment to their mother first, but many become attached to their mother and to their father at about the same time. A few become attached to their father before their mother.

### The Security of Infants' Attachments to Mothers and Fathers

Several researchers have used Ainsworth's Strange Situation to measure the security of infants' attachments to their mothers and to their fathers (Main & Weston, 1981; Sagi et al., 1985). Most researchers have found little consistency between infant-mother and infant-father attachments. Infants who have a secure attachment to their mother, for example, sometimes have an insecure attachment to their father, or vice versa. When researchers combined the data from several studies, however, they found more consistency between infant-mother and infant-father attachments than would be expected by chance (Fox, Kimmerly, & Schafer, 1991).

Ethological theorists would not necessarily expect infants to have the same type of attachment to both parents. Attachment security depends on the interactions that an infant has with a particular person. According to the theory, infant-mother and infant-father attachment should only be similar when fathers interact with their infants like mothers do.

As ethological theory predicts, the security of infant-father attachments is affected by a father's responsiveness toward his infant, just as is true for mothers (Campos et al. 1983; Cox et al., 1992). In addition, infants more often form secure attachment when their fathers are more positive and physically affectionate during play with them. A father's attitudes toward parenting are also related to the security of his infant's attachment to him. Infants have more secure attachments to fathers who believe they play an important role in their infant's life and who give a high priority to spending time with their infant.

Bowlby (1969, 1988) assumed that most infants take their mother rather than their father as their primary attachment figure, and several studies support this assumption. When infants are frightened by a surprising event or an unfamiliar setting, they can be comforted by their mother or their father. But when infants can choose between their parents, they often approach and seek to be held by their mother rather than by their father. The preference for the mother is most obvious between 12 and 18 months of age; it is less apparent in younger infants or older children (Campos et al., 1983).

Even when the mother is the primary attachment figure, infants' attachments to both parents are important. Mary Main and Donna Weston (1981) assessed the security of infants' attachments to their mothers and their fathers. Then these researchers evaluated how the infants reacted to an actor dressed in a clown costume who tried to play games and make friends with them. As figure 6.7 shows, infants who were securely attached to both parents responded most positively to the unfamiliar actor. Infants who were insecurely attached to both parents responded least positively to the actor. Infants with a secure attachment to one parent but not both were intermediate. Comparable results were obtained for ratings of the infants' distress or conflict when the unfamiliar actor was present.

Are infants' attachments to their mothers more important than their attachments to their fathers, as Bowlby (1988) proposed? They seemed to be in Main and Weston's study.

FIGURE 6.7
Observers rated how positively infants responded to a strange adult in a clown costume, and how much distress or conflict the infants showed. Infants with secure attachments to both their mothers and fathers responded more positively and were less distressed than infants with secure attachments to only one parent or neither parent. (Source: Main & Weston, 1981.)

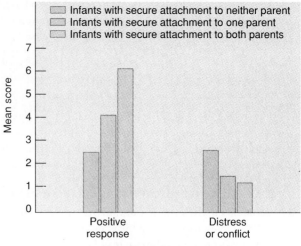

Another study looked at the relation between German children's attachments to parents at 12 months and their behavior toward peers at age 5 (Suess et al., 1992). Infants who were more securely attached to their mothers became 5-year-olds who played more positively with peers, resolved conflicts more effectively, and showed fewer problem behaviors. The security of the infants' attachments to their fathers was not significantly related to these indicators of their social competence at age 5.

Although these data are limited, they suggest that Bowlby was right about the relative importance of infants' attachments to their mothers and their fathers. The reasons for the difference are easy to understand, once you know more about mothers' and fathers' interactions with infants.

## Father- and Mother-Infant Interaction: Skill, Styles, and Amount

When they first see their newborn infants, most fathers feel intense joy and excitement (Greenberg & Morris, 1974). In the first few days after birth, they display a fascination with the appearance, behavior, and abilities of their new son or daughter. Fathers watch their newborns, and kiss and hold them, as much or more than mothers do. Fathers seem as skillful in caring for infants as mothers are. For example, if a young infant coughs or spits up when feeding, fathers respond as quickly and effectively to the infants' distress as mothers do (Parke & Tinsley, 1981).

Although fathers have the skills necessary for effective and responsive care of infants, their style of interaction differs from that of mothers. During the first year of life, fathers spend less time than mothers feeding their infants, changing their diapers, bathing them, or providing other kinds of routine care. Fathers spend more time than mothers in physical play with their infants. They throw infants up in the air and play games that involve vigorous movements of infants' arms, legs, and bodies. By contrast, mothers spend more of their play time reading to infants, showing them toys, and playing visual games like peek-a-boo (Parke & Tinsley, 1981). These differences in mother- and father-infant interaction have been found in both European American and African American families (Hossain & Roopnarine, 1994).

Infants seem to enjoy the vigorous play of fathers more than the quieter games of mothers. Thus they prefer fathers as play partners, although they prefer mothers as attachment figures. The different styles of interaction with mothers and fathers may have different effects on infants' development. The active style of play with fathers may have an especially strong influence on infants' sociability with strangers. That is, fathers may play a special role in helping infants learn to get along with people outside the family (Bridges, Connell, & Belsky, 1988).

Still, caution is needed in drawing conclusions about the different outcomes of mother-infant and father-infant interaction. The differences between mothers and fathers are matters of degree. Although the average behavior of mothers and fathers differs significantly, exceptions

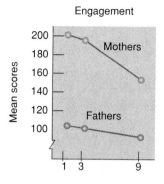

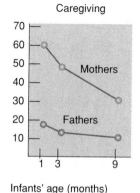

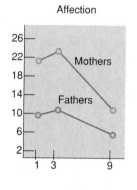

Infants' age (months)

FIGURE 6.8

Mothers usually spend more time engaged with their infants, caring for them and showing affection for them, than fathers do. In the study that found these results, the differences between mothers and fathers decreased as infants grew older, but only because mothers reduced the time they spent with their infants. (From Belsky, Gilstrap, & Rovine, 1984.)

abound. Some mothers engage in vigorous physical play with their infants more than most fathers do. Some fathers engage in quiet play with their infants more than most mothers do.

Also, the differences in fathers' and mothers' interaction styles may be less important than differences in their sheer amount of interaction with infants. Although most fathers seem fascinated with their newborn infants, they rarely take responsibility for infant care and feeding. Even when infants are being bottle-fed rather than breast-fed, mothers spend more time feeding them than fathers do (Hossain & Roopnarine, 1994; Parke & Tinsley, 1987).

After the newborn period, fathers spend less time in all types of interactions with their infants than mothers do. Some researchers estimate that fathers spend only about 15 minutes a day interacting with their infants (Campos et al., 1983). Other researchers (Belsky et al., 1984) looked carefully at how one sample of fathers and mothers used their time at home during their infants' first year. They observed families on weekday evenings when their infants were 1 month, 3 months, and 9 months of age. The researchers asked parents to go about their daily routines so that they could observe the infants under conditions as natural as possible.

Figure 6.8 shows the frequency of different types of mother-infant and father-infant interaction at each age. Notice that mothers were engaged with their infants much more often than were fathers. Mothers also spent more time caring for their infants than fathers did. More surprising, perhaps, is the last panel in the figure. Mothers spent far more time than fathers showing their affection for their infants by hugging and kissing them, smiling at them, and talking sweetly to them.

What were the fathers doing while their wives were interacting with their infants? During most of that time, fathers were reading (by themselves) or watching television. Reading and watching television were the only behaviors that fathers engaged in more than mothers did.

The differences between fathers' and mothers' behavior decreased as their infants grew older. This trend, when examined more closely, was not an especially encouraging one. As the figure shows, fathers did not increase their engagement with their infants over time. The differences between mothers and fathers decreased because mothers reduced the time they spent with their infant as the infant got older.

If interactions with fathers are important for infants' development, how can fathers be persuaded to spend more time with their infants? Ross Parke and Barbara Tinsley (1981, 1987) suggest that there are stereotypes in Western societies about the roles of fathers and mothers that discourage father-infant interaction. These stereotypes may make fathers believe that they lack the skills necessary for good care of infants. To counter the stereotypes, parent training programs should include explicit instruction about infant care and videotaped models of father-infant interaction. These programs may make fathers more confident about caring for their infants and increase their awareness of the importance of father-infant interactions.

Some fathers also accept stereotypes about male and female roles that limit their involvement in child care. Fathers who believe that mothers should not work outside the home, that fathers should be the primary breadwinners, and that men are better managers

than women usually interact less with their infants than fathers who reject these ideas (Deutsch, Lussier, & Servis, 1993). Therefore, countering these stereotypes and promoting more egalitarian sex roles may enhance fathers' involvement with infants. Their infants will, then, benefit more from their fathers' skills and their distinctive interaction style.

Finally, you might expect that husbands whose wives are employed would participate more in their infants' care than husbands of housewives. The evidence on this point is inconsistent. In one study fathers did more infant care when their wives worked more hours outside the home (Deutsch et al., 1993). In another study fathers interacted with infants about as often when their wives worked full-time as when they worked part-time (Hossain & Roopnarine, 1994). The division of family responsibilities seems to depend less on the sheer number of hours that a woman works than on the negotiations about family roles that occur between her and her husband (Ferree, 1994).

## Relationships with Caregivers Other Than Parents

Infants who regularly receive care from adults other than their parents often form close relationships with those adults. Infant-caregiver relationships function in many ways like the attachments that infants form to their parents (Barnas & Cummings, 1994; Goossens & van IJzendoorn, 1990). After infants have interacted regularly with caregivers for some time, they seek contact with those caregivers when they are distressed. During play, they intermittently approach and look at their caregivers or show things to them. These behaviors suggest that the infants view their caregivers, like other attachment figures, as a haven of security and as a secure base for exploration.

The security of infant-caregiver attachments has been assessed using both the Strange Situation and the Attachment Q-sort (Goossens & van IJzendoorn, 1990; Howes & Hamilton, 1992b; Howes et al., 1994). Infants in some samples seem as securely attached to the caregivers in their child-care setting as to their mothers. Infants in other samples seem less securely attached to other caregivers than to their mothers. These inconsistencies should not be surprising, because they can be explained by variations in infant-caregiver interaction.

Infants can only become attached to caregivers with whom they have interacted frequently for some time. In some child-care settings, however, caregivers often shift from one group of children to another, or they leave the field of child care entirely. One major U.S. study showed that employee turnover in child-care settings is greater than 40 percent per year (Whitebrook, Howes, & Phillips, 1990). When adults have cared for a group of infants for only one or two months, the infants rarely rely on them for comfort or approach them during play. Infants show these attachment behaviors much more often toward caregivers they have had for several months to a year (Barnas & Cummings, 1994).

The quality of infants' interactions with caregivers also affects their attachment to them (Goossens & van IJzendoorn, 1990; Howes & Hamilton, 1992a). Infants become securely attached to caregivers who are sensitive and responsive. Infants develop avoidant or resistant attachments to caregivers who are uninvolved or harsh. High levels of harshness and detachment are especially linked to insecure-avoidant attachments.

Finally, infants' relationships with caregivers are linked to their social competence at 4 or 5 years of age (Howes et al., 1994; Oppenheim, Sagi, & Lamb, 1988). Infants who have secure attachments to their caregivers are, as preschoolers, more empathic and sensitive toward peers. They are also more independent, achievement oriented, and goal directed in their behavior. By contrast, among preschoolers who have been in day care since infancy, the security of their attachments to their mothers is unrelated to their social competence when interacting with peers (Egeland & Hiester, 1995). Relationships with other caregivers may be especially important for this type of competence because the adults who care for groups of children have many chances to shape the children's interactions with peers.

## Infants' Reactions to Strangers: Fear and Liking

Infants do not spend all their time with their parents or regular caregivers. They meet many other people, ranging from relatives and neighbors to supermarket clerks and bank tellers. How infants respond to these people reveals more about their view of their social world.

Newborns show little reaction to strangers. Even when infants are several months old, they rarely react negatively when they meet a new person. Around 8 months of age, however, infants' behavior toward strangers changes. Most infants start to express wariness, or even fear, when they meet strangers. By 10 months of age, almost all infants show negative reactions to strangers. These reactions may or may not be intense. Some infants will start crying if a stranger approaches or tries to hold them. Other infants may simply look worried and avoid making eye contact with the stranger (Sroufe, 1977).

Why does wariness or fear of strangers emerge at around 8 months of age? You learned earlier that 8-month-olds protest when separated from their mother because they realize she is leaving and they don't know how to evaluate her absence. Similar cognitive processes lead to stranger fear or wariness (Sroufe, 1977). By 8 to 10 months of age, infants can construct the thought, "This is a face—and a person—that I don't know." Unfamiliarity in itself is arousing, but not necessarily distressing. Infants display fear or wariness if they evaluate their state of arousal as a sign of danger or unpleasantness. In short, they must view the stranger both as novel and as frightening.

Although separation protest and stranger fear depend on similar cognitive processes and emerge at roughly the same age, they are not closely linked to each other. Some infants begin to protest separation from their mother before they become afraid of strangers; others show the reverse sequence (Schaffer & Emerson, 1964). Also, separation protest is related to the development of attachment and stranger fear is not. The security of infants' attachments is not correlated with the intensity of their fear of strangers (Thompson & Lamb, 1983). Securely attached infants might not show much fear of strangers if their mother is present because they feel secure with their mother there. In the same situation, insecurely attached infants might not show much fear of strangers because they do not prefer their mother to the stranger (Sroufe, 1977).

Responses to strangers appear to involve a different behavioral system than attachment. When infants do not perceive strangers as threatening, they willingly approach them. Their behavior illustrates infants' sociability or the *affiliative* behavioral system. Infants can form an affiliation with, or come to like a stranger, if their first meeting with the stranger occurs under the right conditions.

What are the right conditions for friendly responses to strangers? This question is important, theoretically, because it indicates when an infant judges a new person as frightening or inviting. The question is practically significant to parents who want to know how best to introduce their infants to unfamiliar adults. Several studies help to answer the question (Bretherton, Stolberg, & Kreye, 1981; Feinman & Lewis, 1983; Kagan, 1989; Sroufe, 1977).

Infants respond more positively to strangers who keep their distance for a time and don't immediately try to touch or hold them. Infants respond somewhat negatively to strangers who make absolutely no effort to initiate interaction with them. They respond more positively to strangers who try to begin a conversation with them. Most infants also respond positively when a stranger approaches with a toy or tries to begin a game with them. They respond less positively to strangers who are more passive, waiting for them to make the first move.

Finally, infants differ in their wariness or, conversely, their friendliness toward strangers. Most infants will interact pleasantly with an unfamiliar person after being with them for an hour or less. Some infants need more time; others need less. As you read earlier, reactions to strangers are one indicator of an infant's tendency toward inhibited or uninhibited behavior in social situations. These reactions are, then, an important aspect of infant temperament. Adapting to their infants' usual response to strangers is one part of parents' accommodation to their infants' distinctive temperaments.

# THE SOPHISTICATED INFANT

Because this chapter focuses on infants' social interactions, an extended discussion of the significance of social relationships would be repetitive. Two points deserve further emphasis, however, because they show how sophisticated human social life is in infancy.

First, infants function in a complex world with many other people. Few human infants are like the young gosling that imprints on its mother and pays little attention to any other member of its species. The earliest research on human attachments shows that infants usually form special relationships with several other people (Schaffer & Emerson, 1964). Those other people certainly include their mothers and fathers, but they can also include regular caregivers and friends of their parents. In addition, they often include brothers, sisters, grandparents, and other relatives. Siblings, in particular, can function like attachment figures, providing infants with a haven of security in unfamiliar situations (Stewart, 1983). For most infants, the mother is the primary attachment figure, but infants get to know many people and will rely on them when in need. In other words, they will flexibly use whatever social resources are available in the circumstances they face.

Second, infants behave as if they have an extremely precise understanding of their social partners. If their mothers have been responsive to them, they seek comfort from their mothers in the Strange Situation. If their mothers have been rejecting, they avoid them even when distressed at being left alone in a strange setting. Similarly, most infants behave differently toward the mothers and fathers, because their history of interactions with each parent differs. Infants behave differently toward other caregivers, depending on how long they have known those caregivers and how responsive the caregivers have been. Infants also "size up" strangers quickly, deciding which ones they want to approach and which ones they should avoid.

Infants' social sophistication should not make you forget their dependence on their parents and other people. Although infants develop relationships with many other people, there is a limit to their flexibility. The studies of institutionalized infants proved that infants cannot develop normally unless they have a few people with whom they can form special relationships. The importance of these attachment figures has been confirmed by the research on kibbutz infants who have communal sleeping arrangements (Sagi et al., 1994).

Similarly, infants cannot adapt to any pattern of interaction with their attachment figures. When their atattachment figures are abusive, infants' behavior becomes disorganized and their later development is compromised. Only when infants receive sensitive, responsive care from the other people who interact with them can they develop the social sophistication that is one hallmark of normal development.

# SUMMARY

### Early Emotional Development
Infants' expressions of emotions organize their behavior and serve as signals to other people. Infants' ability to interpret others' emotions affects their social behavior and can enhance their safety. Typical patterns of emotional expression define an infant's temperament.

### Expressing and Interpreting Emotions
Newborns in all cultures express some discrete emotions, such as interest, with the same facial expressions. Other emotions, such as anger, are clearly recognizable from infants' facial expressions only after 6 months of age. By 12 months of age, infants become capable of social referencing.

### Patterns of Emotionality: Variations in Temperament
Infants differ in their activity, reactivity, emotionality, sociability, and inhibition when placed in novel situations. These differences are influenced by infants' genotypes and their environments. Temperamental differences show little continuity between infancy and childhood.

### Infant-Mother Attachments
Bowlby, Ainsworth, and other researchers formulated the ethological theory of attachment. Many studies have confirmed their hypothesis that responsive caregiving leads to secure attachments.

### Origins and Principles of Attachment Theory
Attachment theory derives from a combination of Freudian theory, ethology, learning theory, and theories of control systems. The central principles of attachment theory refers to the evolutionary significance of attachment behaviors, internal working models, and the causes and effects of secure attachments.

### Tests of Attachment Theory: Methods and Results
Infants' attachments are usually assessed with the Strange Situation or the Attachment Q-sort. Infants are classified as secure, anxious-avoidant, anxious-resistant, or disorganized-disoriented. Infants' classifications may depend both on their mothers' behavior and on their temperament. Variations in attachments may affect children's social competence and adults' states of mind about attachment.

### Maternal Employment and Attachment
Evidence on the relations of nonmaternal care to the security of infant-mother attachments is inconsistent. Whether a mother is employed or not, her infant is likely to be securely attached if she is sensitive and responsive to the infant's needs.

### Beyond Infant-Mother Attachments: Infants' Social Worlds
Most infants become attached to their fathers and other caregivers. Infants' development is affected by other facets of social interactions besides those that affect attachment security.

**Mothers and Fathers: Their Different (and Unequal) Roles**

Fathers interact skillfully with newborn infants. Fathers engage in more physical play with older infants than mothers do, but fathers interact less with infants than mothers do.

**Relationships with Caregivers Other Than Parents**

Infants develop secure attachments to stable and responsive caregivers. These attachments may also affect later social competence with peers.

**Infants' Reactions to Strangers: Fear and Liking**

Around 8 months of age, infants often begin to show wariness or fear of strangers. Their wariness or fear decreases when strangers approach them gradually, talk to them, and invite them to play.

**The Sophisticated Infant**

Infants often form distinctive relationships with many people. They also behave as if they have a sophisticated understanding of their social partners. Evaluations of their social understanding must be balanced by a recognition that they depend heavily on other people for protection and support.

# SUGGESTED READINGS

Bowlby, B. (1988). *A secure base: Parent-child attachment and healthy human development.* New York: Basic. This book includes a highly readable series of lectures by the foremost attachment theorist. Bowlby updates his earlier book on the development of attachment (Bowlby, 1969). He also discusses the research that influenced him most as he was formulating his attachment theory. In some chapters, he emphasizes the significance of attachment theory for traditional methods of psychoanalysis.

Ekman, P., & Davidson, R. J. (Eds.). (1994). *The nature of emotion: Fundamental questions.* Oxford, England: Oxford University Press. The editors of this book asked more than 20 researchers to answer 12 general questions about emotions. The researchers' answers reflect the diversity of ideas about the existence of basic emotions, the subjective experience of emotions, and the nature of emotional development.

Kamerman, S. B., & Kahn, A. J. (Eds.). (1991). *Child care, parental leave, and the under 3s: Policy innovation in Europe.* New York: Auburn House, 1991. As mentioned earlier, increases in maternal employment have occurred in many countries. This book describes how several European countries have tried to support mothers and fathers in parenting and in working to provide financial support for their families. Governments have adopted different policies to meet their societies' needs and to affirm their societies' values.

Parke, R. D. (1981). *Fathers.* Cambridge, MA: Harvard University Press. Parke describes his research and that of other people on father-infant interaction. He also talks about the father's role during other phases of children's development. He concludes with a discussion of social changes in fathers' roles, especially with the increase in dual-career families.

# LANGUAGE DEVELOPMENT

*L*anguages around the world present a fascinating combination of similarities and differences. When you look at the sentence above, you can tell immediately that it isn't in English. You might also guess that the sentence is in German. Perhaps you read German and can tell what the sentence means. (If not, you'll find out in a moment.)

If you were a young child, you wouldn't be able to read the sentence, but you might hear it spoken or actually say it yourself. Both are true of this sentence. It was spoken by a 2½-year-old boy, but he was repeating what his parents sometimes said to him (Mills, 1985). This one sentence illustrates four aspects of language—and the central problem of language development.

First, you might have realized the sentence was in German if you heard someone say it, even if you couldn't translate it. That is, you might have some knowledge of the sounds of German, or some idea of how German words are pronounced. The aspect of language that deals with the sounds of speech, both as produced by speakers and as heard by listeners, is called *phonology.*

Second, suppose someone told you that the sentence meant, "The man will come with big scissors and cut off my legs." With this translation, you easily understand the sentence. That means, of course, that the same concepts are expressed by the German words and by certain English words. Stated more simply, certain words in the two languages have the same meaning. The aspect of language that deals with the meaning of words is called *semantics.*

Third, the translation of the sentence tells you what it *means*, not exactly what it *says*. A very naive student of German might translate the sentence word for word, as follows: "Man will with the big scissors come and legs off-cut [ab-deschneidet]." Notice that the order of the German words does not match those in the good translation given earlier. The aspect of language that deals with the proper order of words in a sentence is called *grammar.*

Fourth, although you now know both what the sentence means and what it says, you won't fully understand it until you know the situation in which it was used. The 2½-year-old boy who said this sentence was imitating his parents. They often said the same thing to him when he put his feet on the table.

What is the sentence, then? It is a humorous form of a threat and an implied command: "Get your feet off the table!" The use of threats and commands involves the aspect of language called *pragmatics.* More generally, pragmatics deals with the appropriate use of language in social situations. It deals, for example, with who can say what to whom, how they can say it, and what effect their words should cause.

You might be surprised that a boy only 2½ years old could produce such a complex sentence, even in imitation. Your surprise is like that of a tourist in a foreign country who assumes that everyone he or she meets is very intelligent because they can speak a language the tourist finds incomprehensible! But when you were 2½ years old, you probably produced some English sentences that were just as complex as this boy's. You also know that you could have become a competent speaker of German, Chinese, or any other human language—if it had been your native language.

That obvious fact about language development is still amazing, and an important theoretical problem. Languages around the world differ greatly. People who speak only one language can understand little or nothing said by people speaking other languages. Yet children starting from birth can learn any language surprisingly quickly, without obviously trying. What's more, as you will see, the process of language learning is similar for children around the world.

How do children accomplish this feat? Do parents teach their children language, either explicitly or in more subtle ways? Do children acquire their native language largely by themselves because they are biologically prepared to do so? Various theorists have tried to answer these questions. Their theories are examined near the end of the chapter.

Before you can fully understand current theories of language development, you need to know more about what happens as children learn language. You will see that language development is related to other developments considered earlier. For example, the perception of speech sounds is linked to general processes of perceptual development. Learning to use words

**TABLE 7.1**    *Milestones of Four Aspects of Language Development*

| PHONOLOGY | SEMANTICS | GRAMMAR | PRAGMATICS |
|---|---|---|---|
| **Birth to Age 1** | | | |
| Categorical perception of phonemes at birth. Later, fine-tuning of speech perception to match the language being learned.<br><br>Reflexive sounds are followed by cooing, then by babbling and protowords. | Around age 1, most infants say their first word, but comprehension of words is apparent earlier. | No use of grammar is evident during this period. | Around 9 months, infants start using gestures for intentional communication. The gesture of reaching is earliest, followed by showing and pointing. |
| **Early Childhood (ages 1–5)** | | | |
| Use of phonological rules that may lead to temporary regression in pronunciation. | A vocabulary burst around 18–22 months increases the rate of vocabulary growth. Children use several principles and inferences from context to learn new words quickly. | Two-word utterances express semantic relations like agent and action. Children gradually learn to use morphemes such as *-ed* and the auxiliary verb *be*. | Children learn turn taking in conversations. Their ability to carry on a coherent conversation increases. |
| **Later Childhood and Adolescence** | | | |
| Increases in phonological awareness and its use in learning to read and spell. | Vocabulary growth accelerates during the elementary-school years, and children learn the figurative meaning of idioms and other literary devices. | English-speaking children master verbs in the passive voice, and linguistic awareness increases. | Children learn to switch linguistic codes so their language is socially appropriate, to give unambiguous messages, and to monitor their comprehension of messages. |

to express meaning is linked to participation in social interactions. Watch for these connections of language development to other facets of children's development as you read the chapter.

You will also see that language has distinctive features that make its development different from the development of perception or social interaction. Even the different aspects of language have different patterns of development. It's helpful, therefore, to begin by considering each aspect by itself. You will read about them in the order that they were introduced: phonology, semantics, grammar, and pragmatics.

Of course, the separation of different aspects of language is artificial. As the German sentence illustrated, all spoken language involves the four aspects simultaneously. During infancy and childhood, the four aspects are also related (Fenson et al., 1994). To help you keep these relations in mind, table 7.1 lists milestones of each aspect of language that are reached during specific phases of development. Some milestones described in the table may not make sense to you now, but you'll find out what they mean as you read the chapter. Then you can use the table to review some central points in the chapter.

# THE SOUNDS OF SPEECH: PERCEPTION AND PRODUCTION

When Superman was only a comic-book hero, not yet the star of prime-time television and movies, he faced some unusual adversaries. One villain was named Mr. Mxyzptlk. He was an alien who was not cruel but who was a nuisance because he played practical jokes on people. Superman could not defeat him outright, but he could force him to return to his own planet by making him say his name backward.

**TABLE 7.2** *The Phonemes of American English*

| VOWELS | | SEMIVOWELS | | FRICATIVES | | NASALS | | STOPS | | LIQUIDS | |
|---|---|---|---|---|---|---|---|---|---|---|---|
| /i/ | bead | /j/ | yet | /f/ | fie | /m/ | ram | /p/ | pill | /r/ | red |
| /ɪ/ | bid | /w/ | wet | /θ/ | thigh | /n/ | ran | /t/ | till | /l/ | led |
| /ej/ | bait | | | /s/ | sigh | /ŋ/ | rang | /k/ | kill | | |
| /ɛ/ | bet | | | /ʃ/ | shy | | | /tʃ/ | chill | | |
| /æ/ | bat | | | /v/ | vat | | | /b/ | bill | | |
| /a/ | tot | | | /ð/ | that | | | /d/ | dill | | |
| /ɔ/ | taught | | | /z/ | Caesar | | | /g/ | Gil(bert) | | |
| | | | | /ʒ/ | seizure | | | /dʒ/ | Jill | | |
| /ow/ | tote | | | | | | | | | | |
| /ʌ/ | putt | | | | | | | | | | |
| /ʊ/ | put | | | | | | | | | | |
| /uw/ | boot | | | | | | | | | | |
| /aj/ | bite | | | | | | | | | | |
| /æw/ | bout | | | | | | | | | | |

**phonology**
*The study of speech sounds themselves, the stress and intonation patterns that accompany speech sounds, and the rules for combining individual sounds into syllables.*

**phonemes**
*Distinctive categories of sounds recognized as meaningful in a specific language.*

You would probably have trouble saying Mr. Mxyzptlk's name *forward*. And even if no one had told you, you probably would have guessed he was an alien. You realize that no one on earth is likely to have the name *Mxyzptlk*. That is, you assume that neither English nor any other human language would have that combination of letter sounds.

Your hunches about the name *Mxyzptlk* reflect your understanding of **phonology.** Phonology is the study of speech sounds, the stress and intonation patterns that accompany speech sounds, and the rules for combining sounds into syllables. Every language has its own set of speech sounds. The distinctive categories of sounds recognized as meaningful in a specific language are called **phonemes.** Each phoneme describes a group of similar sounds that speakers of a particular language interpret as identical.

For example, one phoneme in English includes the group of sounds that speakers of English perceive as the consonant /b/. (Linguists represent phonemes by letters or other symbols with slashes on both sides.) When you say "b," you produce a sound different from that produced by a child saying "b." For one thing, the child's "b" will be higher in pitch than your "b." Despite this variation in the sound signal, you perceive the child's "b" as linguistically identical to your "b." That is, you treat the two sounds as the same phoneme, /b/.

People who speak the dialect of American English recognize about 40 different phonemes (see table 7.2). Other languages have different phonemes and, therefore, do not distinguish among speech sounds the way that English does. For example, the two sounds listed as liquids in table 7.2, /r/ and /l/, are not distinct phonemes in Japanese. Therefore, an adult Japanese speaker hearing English for the first time would be likely to perceive *rice* and *lice* as the same word.

Many languages distinguish sounds that in English are treated as identical, or the same phoneme. Czech, for example, has two phonemes for sounds that English speakers treat as one phoneme, /z/. One of the Czech phonemes occurs in the name of their most famous composer, Dvorak (dvor-zhak). For this reason, his name is hard for speakers of English to pronounce correctly.

Given the variations in phonemes across languages, how do children learn the specific phonemes in their native language? To answer this question, researchers have studied infants' perception of speech sounds.

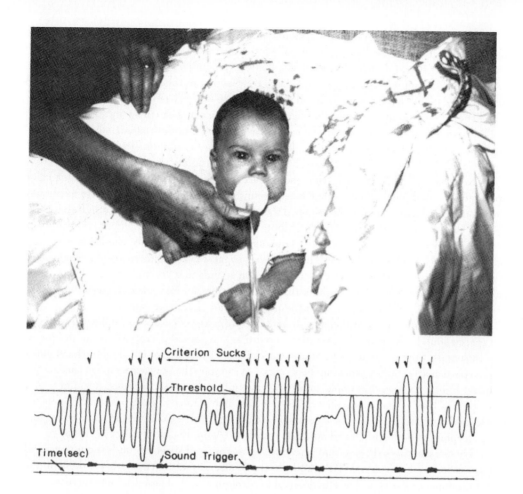

FIGURE 7.1

An infant in the high-amplitude sucking procedure. The graph shows that high-amplitude (or high-pressure) sucking responses trigger the playback of recorded speech sounds. When the pressure or amplitude of an infant's sucks falls below the criterion level, the infant does not hear any recorded sounds. (From Kuhl, 1987.)

## Speech Perception: Discrimination of Phonemes in Infancy

When people perceive different sounds as the same phoneme, they place those sounds in the same category and distinguish them from sounds falling in other categories. The perception of different sounds as falling in the same category, and so as representing the same phoneme, is known as **categorical perception.**

Is categorical perception present at birth? If so, infants would be prepared to begin learning language from the moment of birth. That is, they would be able to identify the distinctions among sounds that are critical for language learning.

### Linguistic Sophistication in Newborns?

In a classic study, Peter Eimas and his colleagues suggested that infants perceive speech sounds categorically by 1 month of age, if not before (Eimas et al., 1971). They drew this conclusion from research using a procedure called **high-amplitude sucking.** Infants sucked on a specially designed pacifier while they heard a sound like the syllable /ba/, which was produced by a speech synthesizer (see figure 7.1). Infants heard the sound whenever they gave an especially vigorous (or high-amplitude) suck on the pacifier. After listening for some time, infants habituated to the sound. (Remember the discussion of habituation in chapter 5.)

Then the researchers presented infants with a new sound. When displayed on a **sound spectrograph,** an instrument that gives a visual representation of sound waves, the new sound looked different from the original one. On some trials, the new sound was one that adults would place in the same phonemic category as the original sound. That is, adults would hear the new sound as another /ba/.

**categorical perception**
*The perception of different sounds as falling into the same category, that is, as representing the same phoneme.*

**high-amplitude sucking**
*A procedure for assessing young infants' speech perception by recording the vigor or intensity with which they suck a nipple when they hear specific sounds.*

**sound spectrograph**
*An instrument that provides a visual representation of sound waves.*

On other trials, the new sound was one that adults would place in a different phonemic category: They would hear it as a /pa/. Yet acoustically, or judged in terms of sound waves, the new sound that adults heard as a /pa/ was as similar to the original /ba/ sound as was the new /ba/ sound. Therefore, if infants were reacting to the sounds simply as acoustic stimuli, they should have responded as if both new sounds were new or neither was new.

The infants did not respond that way. To the researchers' surprise, infants responded as if they perceived the new sounds just as adults would. Infants showed little change in sucking when they heard a new sound that adults would call a /ba/. Infants dishabituated, or increased their sucking, when they heard a new sound that adults would call a /pa/.

To explain the infants' behavior, the researchers argued that infants are biologically prepared for categorical perception of speech sounds. That is, infants are sensitive to phonemic contrasts at birth. Later studies showed that infants discriminate among sounds that their parents hear as identical. For example, infants with English-speaking parents discriminate between the two phonemes in the Czech language that adult speakers of English treat as the single phoneme, /z/ (Trehub, 1976). These findings suggested that infants may be biologically prepared to recognize all distinctions among speech sounds that are important in any human language. In other words, researchers reasoned that infants may have a special ability to process the sounds of language so that they can learn any language rapidly.

Further studies weakened claims that infants are born with a special ability for perceiving speech sounds. Researchers first discovered that categorical perception is not unique to speech sounds. Suppose you are listening to a violin, and you are asked whether the violinist made a particular sound by plucking the string or by running the bow across it. By varying the acoustic signal, a researcher could influence your judgment about whether a sound was a "pluck" or a "bow." Moreover, you would show the same pattern of categorical judgments for plucks and bows as you show for speech sounds like /ba/ and /pa/. Infants, too, show categorical perception of both speech and nonspeech sounds (Aslin, Pisoni, & Jusczyk, 1983).

Then researchers showed that categorical perception of speech sounds is not restricted to human beings. Even chinchillas can be trained to discriminate between /ba/ and /pa/ in the way that human infants and adults do (Kuhl & Miller, 1978). These findings increased researchers' skepticism about the hypothesis that humans have unique and specialized abilities for processing speech sounds. After all, nearly all humans develop a spoken language, and no chinchillas do.

The new findings, taken together, have led many researchers to a theoretical aboutface. Rather than claiming that infants are biologically prepared to perceive speech sounds, they have argued that speech perception is no different from perception of other sounds (Aslin et al., 1983). Rather than having an innate knowledge of linguistically relevant sound variations, infants may process speech by drawing upon the considerable capabilities of their hearing system. Moreover, these capabilities may be shared with other mammals, such as chinchillas.

The case against the hypothesis of innate, language-specific perceptual abilities is not conclusive (Kuhl, 1987). Future research may reveal important ways in which infants' perception of speech sounds differs from their perception of other sounds. Currently, however, most researchers assume that general auditory analyzers—brain processes that allow humans to perceive all types of sounds—can explain the speech perception of newborns (Jusczyk, 1993; Kuhl, 1993). In other words, newborns' speech perception reflects not linguistic sophistication but well-developed general mechanisms for auditory perception.

One important function of those general mechanisms is allowing newborns to place sounds in phonemic categories. Once those placements are made, infants can begin to decipher the rest of the linguistic code. They can also begin to refine their perception of speech sounds to match the phonemic contrasts that are important in their native language.

## Tuning the System for Speech Perception

The fine-tuning of speech perception begins during the first year of life. Infants gradually learn to differentiate a continuous stream of speech sounds into distinct phonetic elements (Jusczyk, 1993; Werker, 1993). By 2 months of age, infants are sensitive to the typical

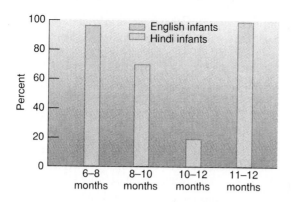

FIGURE 7.2

During the first months of life, English infants can easily distinguish between two Hindi phonemes. As English infants grow older, they are less able to distinguish between the two phonemes because they begin to ignore contrasts in speech sounds that are not important in their language. Hindi infants continue to distinguish between the phonemes because the contrast is important in their native language. (Source: Werker & Tees, 1984.)

intonation and phrase structure of sentences in their native language. Therefore, they remember words that are part of a sentence better than the same word heard as part of a simple list (Mandel, Jusczyk, & Kemler-Nelson, 1994).

By 6 months of age, infants recognize the characteristic sounds of words in their native language (Jusczyk et al., 1993). Infants with English-speaking parents therefore listen longer to unfamiliar words that have English sound patterns than to words with sound patterns more characteristic of Norwegian. In addition, 6-month-olds respond in the high-amplitude sucking procedure as if they have learned the phonemes for the vowels in their native language (Kuhl et al., 1992). Thus, infants with English-speaking parents respond to an English vowel sound differently than do infants whose parents speak Swedish.

Between 6 and 9 months, infants' sensitivity to the sound patterns of their native language increases still further (Jusczyk et al., 1993; Jusczyk, Luce, & Charles-Luce, 1994). This sensitivity should help infants begin to learn the meanings of words, because they can start to identify the combinations of phonemes that define individual words in a continuous stream of sound. For example, they can divide "L-OO-K-A-T-TH-E-D-O-G-E" into "Look at the doggie," rather than "Loo kat thed ogg ie" or something else.

The tuning of speech perception also means that infants gradually lose the ability to hear differences in speech sounds that are not important in their own language. For example, figure 7.2 shows that 6-month-olds with English-speaking parents can still distinguish between the phonemes in the Hindi language represented by /ta/ and /ṭa/. By 1 year of age, English-speaking infants can no longer discriminate between these Hindi morphemes (Werker & Lalonde, 1988; Werker & Tees, 1984). One-year-old Hindi infants can still discriminate between them because the variation is important in their own language.

Viewed more broadly, the fine-tuning of speech perception during infancy has costs as well as benefits. On one hand, infants gradually focus on the differences in sounds that are important in their native language. On the other hand, infants eventually fail to notice differences in sounds that are not important in their language. This loss of sensitivity to certain sound contrasts partly explains why adults have difficulty learning a foreign language. Adults have lost their initial ability to hear all the variations in sounds important in other languages.

Fortunately, the loss is not always permanent. With training, adults can become sensitive to phonemic contrasts in other languages (Eimas, Miller, & Jusczyk, 1987). Whether adults ever regain as much sensitivity to these contrasts as native speakers is uncertain (Hakuta, 1986; Werker & Polka, 1993). The answer depends partly on how different the phonemes in two languages are (Bialystok & Hakuta, 1994; Kuhl, 1993). Adults have no trouble when two languages use the same phonemes, and little trouble when the languages

use extremely different phonemes. They have the most trouble when the other language uses phonemes different from, but easily confused with, the phonemes in their native language.

## Speech Production: From Crying and Burping to First Words

Newborns have a very limited range of vocalizations. Their first sounds—cries, burps, and coughs—are reflexive, and none of them are speechlike (Menn & Stoel-Gammon, 1993). Between 2 and 4 months of age, infants enter the phase of *cooing* or *gooing* (Roug, Landberg, & Lundberg, 1989). At these ages, infants' vocalizations emphasize consonants such as /k/ (as in *kind*) and /g/ (as in *good*). Between 4 and 6 months of age, infants begin to master vowel-like sounds. They develop singing patterns with high-pitched trills and squeals, low-pitched growls, loud yells, and soft murmurs (Oller & Eilers, 1988).

**babbling**
*Reduplicated sounds like* ga-ga-ga *that represent the first true syllables.*

After 6 months of age, infants enter a new phase of **babbling.** They begin to use reduplicated sounds like *pa-pa-pa* or *ga-ga* (Sachs, 1989). These consonant-vowel sequences represent the first true syllables, the building blocks for actual words. Infants play with these sounds like they will later play with blocks, in ways that increase the precision and flexibility of their speech. Deaf children do not begin babbling as soon as hearing infants do, perhaps not until they are 1 to 2 years old (Oller & Eilers, 1988). This delay suggests that hearing speech sounds influences the development of babbling. Through babbling, infants give themselves feedback that apparently helps them learn to talk.

The early phases of infants' sound production are largely the same around the world, regardless of the language that infants hear around them. By 10 months of age, however, infants' babbling begins to reflect the sounds of their native language. The vowel sounds in 10-month-olds' babbling are more like those in their native language than in other languages (Boysson-Bardies et al., 1989). Infants with French-speaking parents sound more like French adults than do English infants. Infants with Arabic-speaking parents sound more like Arabic adults than do infants whose parents speak Cantonese.

After 10 months infants also begin to display complex sound sequences. Their babbling is not limited to duplicated consonants; they vary their consonants and produce sentencelike strings of consonant-vowel syllables. Often, infants add expressive intonation to their babbling, so they capture the melody of speech. Sometimes infants act as if they are talking earnestly to an adult when all their sounds are gibberish. Some infants "talk" to no one in particular, when alone in their cribs, in elaborate forms of language play. Some of their vocalizations sound like requests, others like emphatic "no's," and others like telling a story. At this age, however, infants rarely supply the words that would express these meanings clearly (Menn & Stoel-Gammon, 1993).

Most infants say their first true words when they are about 12 months old. Defining when an infant has said his or her first word is difficult, because the transition from babbling to speaking words is often gradual (Snow, 1988; Vihman & Miller, 1988). Researchers usually credit infants with knowing a word when they use it appropriately, in a context that suggests they understand its meaning. Also, researchers often count words only when they are pronounced in the conventional way. For example, saying "mama" for *mother* would count. Saying "gower" for *pacifier* (as did one child) would not count. Some researchers call utterances like "gower" **protowords.** Protowords are used like words but are not part of the adult language, so they do not have a conventional meaning.

**protowords**
*Sounds that infants use like words but that are not part of the adult language and, thus, do not have a conventional meaning.*

Some infants have few protowords. Apparently, they try to say only words that they can pronounce accurately. These infants are conservative about their language use, as if they were unwilling to be caught making a mistake in pronunciation (Menn & Stoel-Gammon, 1993). Other infants use language more freely, so more of their talk sounds to adults like gibberish.

Children's pronunciation improves as they gain greater control over the speech-production apparatus (vocal cords, lips, tongue, etc.). Because children's vocal control limits their speech production, they usually comprehend more words than they say (Fenson et al., 1994). The rule that comprehension exceeds production is a general one in language development that applies even in adulthood. You probably comprehend many words that you have never used in conversation (e.g., *picayune* or *torrential*).

Infants and young children often want to use words that are difficult for them to pronounce. To do so, they adopt various strategies. These strategies can be described as **phonological rules,** regular ways in which children change the pronunciation of conventional words (Menn & Stoel-Gammon, 1993). One child may regularly replace the phoneme /p/ with /b/, so that "pot" comes out as "bot." Another child may omit initial consonants, so that "school" comes out as "cool." Yet another child may take a sound at the end of a word and transfer it to the beginning, so that "dance" becomes "nance." Sometimes several rules are used together. For example, one young child for a time pronounced "cup" as "bupo," replacing the "c" with a "b" and adding a final "o."

**phonological rules**
*Regular ways that children change the pronunciation of conventional words, for example, by replacing the phoneme /p/ with /b/.*

For several reasons, it makes sense to assume that children's errors in pronunciation reflect rules rather than random mistakes (Menn & Stoel-Gammon, 1995). First, children usually are consistent in their pronunciation of a particular word. Second, children often mispronounce many words in a similar way. A child who says "pill" for "spill" will also say "tore" for "store."

Third, and most significant, children sometimes show regression in their pronunciation. When children begin to apply a new rule to certain words, they sometimes misapply it to other words that they previously had pronounced correctly. This temporary regression in pronunciation shows that children do not learn language simply by imitating what they hear other people say. Instead, they form hypotheses about how words should be pronounced and they refine these hypotheses over time (Macken, 1987). As you read further, you will see more evidence that children form and test hypotheses as they gradually master their native language.

## Later Phonological Development

A father walking through the zoo said to his 7-year-old son, "Look, there's a giant [SLOWTH]." His son replied, "Is that how you say it? I would pronounce it [SLAUTH]."

Phonological development continues into childhood, and even into adulthood, as people learn the accepted pronunciation of the words in their native language. For young children, some phonemes are often difficult to pronounce. In English, children often have trouble with the phonemes for the *th* in *thigh,* the *th* in *that,* and the *z* in *seizure* (see table 7.2). Most children do not consistently produce these phonemes correctly until 4 or 5 years of age (Reich, 1986).

Many children do not master correct pronunciation of all phonemes until around 7 years of age. If children still have problems in pronunciation after that age, some form of speech therapy may be given. Children may be taught, for example, exactly how to position their lips and tongue to produce a phoneme accurately.

As children gradually master the phonemes of their native language, they begin to speak with the distinctive accent of their language community (Grunwell, 1986). Children from the American South develop a Southern drawl; children from Brooklyn develop the pronunciation pattern that marks them as New Yorkers. In the movie *My Fair Lady,* Professor Higgins said that he could identify the origins of any person from the way he or she spoke. Of course, his special talents made it possible for Miss Eliza Doolittle *not* to betray her Cockney upbringing in her speech.

Children develop greater understanding of phonological rules as they grow, and they eventually learn to state these rules explicitly. They can tell you, for example, that you can change an English noun like *cat* from singular to plural by adding /z/ (so producing *cats*). They can make judgments about whether a large, slow-moving animal should be called a [SLOWTH] or a [SLAUTH]. Moreover, because they understand which sound combinations fit the rules for their own language, they can tell you that *Mxyzptlk* is not an acceptable English word!

Can children's learning of phonological rules be accelerated? Yes, it can, and doing so may be both highly enjoyable and very worthwhile. In particular, children's sensitivity to phonological variations can be enhanced by telling them nursery rhymes. These rhymes emphasize contrasting sounds, as in "Humpty Dumpty sat on a *wall*. Humpty Dumpty had

In the movie *My Fair Lady*, Professor Higgins trained Eliza Doolittle to speak "like a lady." That is, he trained her to pronounce words like a well-bred Englishwoman. In more technical terms, Professor Higgins changed the phonological rules Miss Doolittle used in speaking.

a great *fall*." Nursery rhymes also use devices like alliteration that make the initial sounds in words salient (e.g., *Tw*inkle, *tw*inkle, little star").

Sensitivity to phonological variations, in turn, facilitates such later skills as reading and spelling. One team of researchers assessed children's knowledge of nursery rhymes and their IQ scores at age 3 (Bryant et al., 1989). When the children were about 4½ years old, the researchers assessed their ability to tell whether two words rhymed or not. When the children were about 6 years old, the researchers assessed their reading ability.

Figure 7.3 outlines the results of the study. Children's knowledge of nursery rhymes and their IQ scores at age 3 were related to their rhyme detection at age 4½ and their reading ability at age 6. Children who knew more nursery rhymes and children who had higher IQs at age 3 became better rhyme detectors and better readers. Other analyses showed that knowledge of rhymes at age 3 was related to spelling ability at age 6. These findings suggest that learning nursery rhymes increases children's sensitivity to the sounds in words (i.e., to phonemes) and so prepares them for spelling and reading.

Should parents assume, then, that they can make their children better readers by teaching them lots of nursery rhymes? The answer is probably yes, but detection of rhymes and alliteration are only part of the broader construct of **phonological awareness** (McBride-Chang, 1995; Stahl & Murray, 1994). Also important is the ability to analyze whole words into phonemes. This ability can be assessed by asking children to say which sound begins the word *fancy* (/f/), which word you would have if you took the last sound off *bump* (bum), or which word you would have if you put together p-e-s-t (pest).

Children with greater phonological awareness typically read and spell better than other children, and training in phonological awareness improves children's reading ability (McBride-Chang, 1995; Wimmer, Landerl, & Schneider, 1994). You can guess, therefore, that the 7-year-old boy who was sensitive to the contrast between [SLOWTH] and [SLAUTH] is likely to be a good reader and a good speller. And, by the way, both he and his father passed that little test of phonology. Most dictionaries list both pronunciations for *sloth* as acceptable.

**phonological awareness**
*A broad construct that includes the detection of rhyme and alliteration, the ability to analyze the phonemes in a word, and other types of knowledge of speech sounds.*

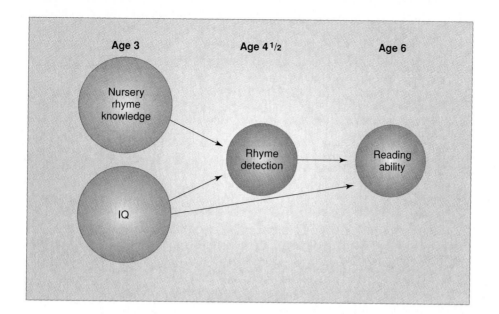

FIGURE 7.3

This figure describes the relations between knowledge of nursery rhymes and IQ, measured at age 3, detection of rhyming words at age 4½, and reading ability at age 6. IQ at age 3 is related both to rhyme detection at age 4½ and to reading ability at age 6. But nursery rhyme knowledge also contributes to detection of rhyme, and that contributes to reading. (Source: Bryant et al., 1989.)

# MEANING IN LANGUAGE: SEMANTIC DEVELOPMENT

The emergence of true words at around 1 year of age is an important milestone in development. In French, the word *infant* means "unable to speak." The ability to use words, or to "say what you mean," is, then, one marker of the transition from infancy to childhood.

Linguists regard the development of word meanings as part of **semantics.** The basic unit of word meaning is the **morpheme.** A word such as *happy* that can be used alone is a **free morpheme.** Letters or syllables that affect word meaning but that are not complete words are **bound morphemes.** The suffix *-ed* is one example. Rules of grammar govern the use of many bound morphemes, so those morphemes are considered in the section on grammatical development. This section focuses on children's understanding of free morphemes, or words.

**semantics**
*The study of word meanings.*

**morpheme**
*The basic unit of word meaning.*

**free morpheme**
*A morpheme that can be used by itself, as an entire word (e.g., happy).*

**bound morphemes**
*Letters or syllables that affect word meaning but that are not themselves complete words (e.g., the suffix -ed).*

## Early Vocabulary Growth and Word Meanings

Although most infants say their first word around 1 year of age, some do so at 8 months, and others delay until 18 months of age (Reich, 1986). The average child produces about 50 different words by 18 months of age (Nelson, 1973). Vocabulary growth increases rapidly after that point, along with changes in children's understanding of word meanings.

### Age Changes and Individual Differences in Vocabulary

The most extensive data on early vocabulary growth come from reports by more than 1,000 parents (Fenson et al., 1994). These parents completed questionnaires that included a list of several hundred words commonly produced by infants and young children. Parents checked every word that their child had used. Then the number of words used by infants and children between 8 and 16 months of age was tabulated. Next, vocabulary size was graphed for the child of each age who was at the median in the entire sample, and for children who were at the 10th, 25th, 75th, and 90th percentiles. Finally, these graphs were fitted, or "smoothed," to eliminate apparently random variations in scores. Figure 7.4 shows the results.

Vocabulary size increases as children grow older, but the variations among children also increase. At 16 months, children in the 90th percentile have produced more than 160 words; children in the 10th percentile have produced fewer than 10 words. Great differences in vocabulary size are also found among children between 16 and 30 months of age.

FIGURE 7.4

Vocabulary size increases between 8 and 16 months of age, but some children use many more new words than other children. The most-advanced children have already started their vocabulary burst. The average child shows the burst between 18 and 22 months. (Adapted from Fenson et al., 1994.)

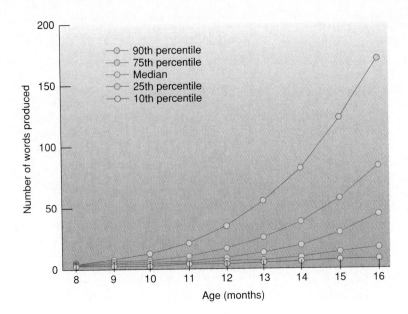

Also noticeable in figure 7.4 is a sharp increase, for the most-advanced children, in the rate of vocabulary growth after 12 months of age. This increase in rate has been called the "vocabulary burst" (Fenson et al., 1994) or the "naming explosion" (Gopnik & Meltzoff, 1987). It occurs in most children around 18 to 22 months of age, or after children have produced between 25 and 100 words (Fenson et al., 1994; Reznick & Goldfield, 1992).

One explanation for the vocabulary burst is that children for the first time realize that all objects have names that other people recognize. This "naming insight" (Reich, 1986) was described most dramatically by Helen Keller, a woman who became deaf and blind after an illness when she was 19 months old. When Helen was 6 years old, her family asked Anne Sullivan to become her teacher. Sullivan tried to teach Helen words like *water* by spelling them into her hand. She had little success at first. Then Sullivan tried an experiment. Helen later recalled what happened:

> We [she and Anne Sullivan] walked down the path to the well-house. . . . Someone was drawing water and my teacher placed my hand under the spout. As the cool stream gushed over one hand she spelled into the other the word *water,* first slowly, then rapidly. I stood still, my whole attention fixed upon the motions of her fingers. Suddenly I felt a misty consciousness as of something forgotten—a thrill of returning thought; and somehow the mystery of language was revealed to me. I knew then that "w-a-t-e-r" meant the wonderful and cool something that was flowing over my hand. That living word awakened my soul, gave it light, hope, joy, set it free! I left the well-house eager to learn. Everything had a name, and each name gave birth to a new thought (Keller, 1965, p. 21).

Helen Keller was 7 years old when she had the naming insight, much older than the typical seeing and hearing child. Consequently, the moment of insight was more dramatic than it often appears with younger children. Still, many children go through a phase around 18 to 22 months of age when they want to learn the names of all the objects they see (Gopnik & Meltzoff, 1986). Their rate of vocabulary development increases from a few words each month to several words each day. This rapid rate of vocabulary growth continues through the preschool years. By 6½ years of age, the average child knows more than 10,000 words (Anglin, 1993).

The naming insight and the burst in vocabulary growth are related to children's cognitive development. Some researchers attribute the vocabulary burst to a change in children's ability to classify objects into categories, which makes children want to learn the names for these categories (Gopnik & Meltzoff, 1987). Other researchers attribute the burst to an

When this girl first said "duck," she might have meant that this yellow rubber duck was floating in her bathtub. For her, the meaning of the word *duck* might have been tied not only to that specific toy duck but also to the specific context in which she was playing with the duck. The meanings of words become less context-specific as children grow older.

increase in children's memory capacity, an improvement in their ability to pronounce words, or a change in brain functioning (Bates & Carnevale, 1993; Fenson et al., 1994). The research necessary to decide between these explanations has not been done, and each may partly account for the acceleration in word learning after 18 to 22 months of age.

## Types and Meanings of Early Words

Many of children's early words are *nominals:* They are the names of people or things. General nominals refer to all members of a category. For example, children may say "ball" when talking about round objects that they play with. Specific nominals are names for specific persons, animals, or objects. A child may, for example, call the family dog by his name, "Bowser."

Other early words describe or accompany *actions.* A child may say "bye-bye" when someone leaves or "hi" when someone approaches. Occasionally, children use *modifiers* such as *all gone* or *there* that express absence or indicate location. Less often, children use *personal-social* words like *no, want,* and *please.* Children rarely use words that serve a purely grammatical function, such as the words that introduce questions (e.g., *where*).

A child's earliest nominals are often tied to a specific context (Barrett, 1986). One child first used the word *duck* only when he knocked one of his yellow rubber ducks off the edge of the bathtub. For this child at this early stage, *duck* was the name not of a single object but of a specific event in a specific setting. Thus, this child defined *duck* more narrowly than adults do. Such **underextensions** are common in early semantic development. Another child initially seemed to take *shoes* as referring only to his mother's shoes, not his father's or his own shoes (Reich, 1986).

Between 10 and 30 percent of young children's words are underextended at some point during their semantic development (Barrett, 1995). Often, underextensions disappear as word meanings become less context-specific. For example, the child who first said "duck" when knocking a rubber duck off the bathtub later said "duck" when playing with his rubber ducks out of the bath. A few weeks later, he used the word when he saw his rubber ducks lying on the floor. The child only said the word when looking at real ducks a few weeks after that. Still later, he said "duck" when looking at pictures of ducks. Thus, the meaning of *duck* broadened and became more adultlike over time.

Children may also attach meanings to words that are too broad rather than too narrow. Such **overextensions** often arise when children free their earliest words from the specific context in which they were first used. For example, the child who first said "duck" only when his rubber duck fell off the bathtub later said "duck" when he saw swans, geese, and quail (Barrett, 1986). Other children begin by using "daddy" to refer to their own father but then overextend the word by calling all men "daddy."

Young children seem to overextend between 10 and 30 percent of the words that they use (Barrett, 1995). However, these overextensions do not always reflect errors in word

**underextensions**
*The use of words to refer to narrower categories of objects or events than is conventional (e.g., the use of* duck *to refer only to a specific yellow toy duck).*

**overextensions**
*Use of words to refer to broader categories of objects or events than is conventional (e.g., using* Daddy *to refer to all men).*

Ask this toddler what that animal is, and he might say "duck." That is he might overextend the word *duck* and use it to refer to a goose as well.

| | |
|---|---|
| TABLE 7.3 | *Examples of Children's Word Inventions* |

| INVENTED WORDS | STANDARD ENGLISH WORDS |
|---|---|
| to broom | to sweep |
| to fire | to burn |
| to scale | to weigh |
| a fix-man | a mechanic |
| a tooth-guy | a dentist |
| a lessoner | a teacher |
| a locker | a lock |

Adapted from E. V. Clark, "The principle of contract: A constraint on language acquisition" in *Mechanisms of Language Acquisition*. Copyright © Lawrence Erlbaum Associates, Inc., Mahwah, NJ. Reprinted with permission.

learning (Pease, Berko Gleason, & Pan, 1993). They may sometimes reflect children's awareness of similarities. For example, a girl who says "daddy" when looking at a man who is not her father may mean to say—but be unable to say—"he looks like my daddy."

At other times, children may use the wrong word as a joke. When one boy's father showed him a toy helicopter and said "helicopter," the boy grinned and said "airplane." Incidents like these suggest that word play occurs in the earliest phases of language learning.

Some children for a time use words in ways that suggest both partial overextension and partial underextension. One child overextended the word *dog* by including calves as dogs, but underextended the word by not including small dogs (Kuczaj, 1986). This child, at this stage, apparently thought *dog* referred to a medium-sized, four-legged animal.

Finally, when children want to say something but don't know the correct words, they may invent their own words. These inventions are among the most charming and amusing by-products of language learning. One child reasoned that if a man who puts out fires is a fireman, a man who fixes cars must be a "fix-man." Table 7.3 includes other examples of children's invented words.

## Principles of Word Learning

The errors in children's word use should not be exaggerated. Even when children over- or underextend the meaning of a word, they are still likely to use the word appropriately most of the time. You might expect children to make errors more often than they do, especially during the toddler and preschool years when they are learning several new words each day.

Suppose, for example, that an 18-month-old girl was looking out her front window when she saw a red convertible pulling into her driveway. Her mother, standing beside her, said, "Here comes Aunt Mary." Why doesn't the girl draw the conclusion that "Aunt Mary" is a red convertible?

This example illustrates the ambiguity that often exists when children hear a new word. Yet children rarely make the kind of mistake suggested in the example. Many researchers assume that children avoid this kind of mistake because they follow certain principles for word learning. These principles allow **fast mapping,** an inference about the meaning of a word from an analysis of its linguistic and nonlinguistic context (Carey, 1978).

One simple principle is the **whole-object rule** (Markman, 1989). When children hear a new word applied to an object, they assume that the word refers to the entire object rather than to one of its parts or to its texture and shape. Children whose mothers say "deer" while pointing to a picture in a book typically guess that *deer* refers to the entire animal rather than to its antlers, its tail, or the color of its skin.

Another principle is that of **categorical scope** (Golinkoff et al., 1995). Children usually assume that a new word can be applied to objects in the same basic-level category as the object first labeled with that word. **Basic-level categories** include objects that are similar in shape and function, that are not context-specific, and that are labeled with common words. The category of *deer* is at the basic level. *Ungulate* (a mammal with hoofs) and the even more general *animal* represent superordinate rather than basic-level categories. *Buck, doe,* and *fawn* are more context-specific than the basic-level term because they refer to the animal's sex and age.

Toddlers and preschool children use the principle of categorical scope to guess the meaning of novel words (Golinkoff et al., 1995; Hall & Waxman, 1993; Waxman & Hall, 1993). That is, they usually assume that new words refer to basic-level categories. This assumption leads children to focus on the general characteristics of objects, rather than their individual features or the situation in which a novel word is used.

Other principles emphasize the linguistic context for word learning, especially the connections between new words and words already known. Eve Clark (1987) proposed the principle of **contrast,** which states that different words must have different meanings. A related principle is that of **mutual exclusivity,** which states that every object has only one category label (Liittschwager & Markman, 1994; Markman, 1987; Merriman & Bowman, 1989). For example, if an animal is called a *dog,* it cannot also be a *cat.*

Accepting the principles could help children correct overextensions of word meanings. A child who applies the word *duck* to both ducks and swans is likely, someday, to hear someone refer to a swan as "swan." The child must then decide whether *swan* is a synonym for *duck* or refers to a different category of animals. Because the principles of contrast and mutual exclusivity exclude synonyms, the child takes the latter option and narrows the definition of *duck* to exclude swans.

Accepting the principles could also help children replace their invented words with words in their native language. Consider a child who calls a mechanic a *fix-man.* Eventually, he or she is likely to hear someone refer to that person as a "mechanic." Then the child must either drop *fix-man* and use *mechanic* or vice versa. One corollary of the principle of contrast is that conventional words take priority over invented words (Clark, 1987). Therefore, when confronted with a choice, the child takes the conventional word *mechanic* and drops the invented word *fix-man* from his or her vocabulary.[1]

The principles of contrast and of mutual exclusivity are not always true: Some words are synonyms of other words. To allow for this possibility, researchers assume that children

**fast mapping**
*An inference about the meaning of a word heard for the first time, based on an analysis of its linguistic and nonlinguistic context.*

**whole-object rule**
*The assumption that a new word refers to an entire object rather than to one of its parts or to its texture or shape.*

**categorical scope**
*The assumption that a new word refers to objects in the same basic-level category as the object that was first labeled with that word.*

**basic-level categories**
*Categories that are labeled with common words, that are not context-specific, and that include objects similar in shape and function.*

**contrast**
*A principle of word learning, suggested by Clark, which states that different words must have different meanings.*

**mutual exclusivity**
*A principle of word learning that states that an object has only one category label (e.g., something called a dog cannot also be labeled as a cat).*

---

1. Of course, adults invent some words that become a standard part of the language. Think about words like *meltdown, dropout,* and *sideswipe* that were coined in the recent past. These inventions keep language alive and ever-changing.

can admit exceptions to the rules (Liittschwager & Markman, 1994). Perhaps the most important exception is the existence of both basic-level and superordinate terms for the same objects. For example, a chef in a restaurant may say "Get that *dog* (basic-level) out of here!" or "Get that *animal* (superordinate level) out of here!" By 4 years of age, children realize that words at both these levels can refer to the same object (Au & Glusman, 1990). Four-year-olds would know, then, that a chef could use either *dog* or *animal* to refer to their pet, Bowser.

The principles discussed so far could explain why an 18-month-old girl doesn't confuse her Aunt Mary with a red convertible. Most children that age already know the word *car* (Fenson et al., 1994), and the principles of contrast and mutual exclusivity rule out *Aunt Mary* as a synonym for *car*. Therefore, the girl knows that the car pulling into the driveway is not *Aunt Mary*. Most likely, the girl finds out who (or what) *Aunt Mary* is when her aunt walks in the door and her mother says, "Hello, Aunt Mary." Using the whole-object principle, the girl quickly concludes that *Aunt Mary* is not the red convertible but the person who drove it.

You might have noticed, however, that the principles already mentioned work best at explaining how children learn words for basic-level objects. They are less adequate for explaining how children guess the meanings of the many nouns that refer not to objects but to locations (*home*), actions (*drawing*), or events (a *bath*). They also leave open the question of how children learn the meaning of verbs, adjectives, and many other kinds of words. Most likely, children use many cues from others' speech and from observations of actual situations to infer what these types of words mean (Nelson, Hampson, & Shaw, 1993).

Suppose an adult is talking about an object's color. The linguistic context can help children learn the adult's words for color. If an adult says, "Bring me the beige one, not the blue one," children who know the word *blue* can infer that *beige*, like blue, is a color. If children can also recognize which "one" the *beige one* refers to, they can guess what color beige is. Even 2-year-olds use this form of fast mapping to learn terms for colors, textures, and shapes (Heibeck & Markman, 1987).

Close attention to actual events helps children learn verbs (Tomasello & Barton, 1994). Suppose an adult says, "I'm going to dunk this basketball." Then children see the adult run toward a basketball goal, jump high in the air, put the ball through the hoop, and say, "Yeah, DID it." Even 2-year-olds can use cues like these to guess the meaning of the verb *dunk*.

Finally, children can and do adopt different strategies for word learning. Some children focus on the learning of words that communicate feelings or desires. Nelson (1973) called these children **expressive.** Their early vocabularies include many personal-social words like *no, yes,* and *please.* They also include functional words like the *where* that begins a question. These words are often used in conventional social formulas such as "Please don't" and "Where are you going?"

Other children's early vocabularies include many general nominals. Nelson (1973) called these children **referential,** because they use language primarily for referring to objects. They also tend to have mothers who often name objects for them (Goldfield, 1993; Hampson & Nelson, 1993).

Although the terms *referential* and *expressive* suggest two distinct groups, no children have either a completely referential or a completely expressive style of word learning (Lieven, Pine, & Barnes, 1992; Nelson, 1981; Reich, 1986). Even relatively expressive children have many words for objects in their vocabularies; even relatively referential children learn social formulas. Also, the contrast between more referential and more expressive children is most apparent in the early phases of vocabulary growth. As children develop more complex speech, after 2 years of age, the contrasts between more expressive and more referential children decrease. Still, the contrast between the two styles shows that children can take different pathways when learning a language. There is not one universal pathway of semantic development.

## Later Semantic Development

Once children enter school, learning new words becomes part of their explicit curriculum. They are expected to learn words like *multiplication, punctuation, colonial,* and *atmosphere.* Children learn these words through oral instruction, and, once in first grade, through reading.

**expressive**
*A style of language learning that emphasizes the communication of feelings and desires with conventional formulas such as "Yes, please."*

**referential**
*A style of language learning that emphasizes the acquisition of vocabulary for referring to objects.*

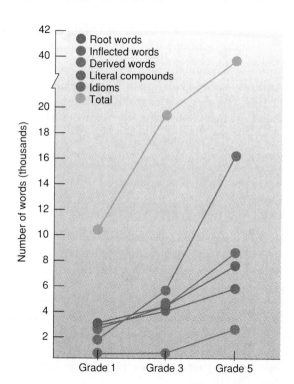

FIGURE 7.5
Vocabulary increases at an amazing rate during the elementary-school years. The most rapid increase is for derived words, one like *mucky* that have a root word (*muck*) and a prefix or suffix (*-y*) that changes the meaning of the root word. (Adapted from Anglin, 1993.)

The rate of vocabulary growth during the elementary grades is truly astonishing. Recall that children learn over 10,000 words between 1½ and 6½ years of age, or about 2,000 words in each of those five years. By Grade 5, however, the average child knows about 40,000 words (Anglin, 1993). Between Grade 1 and Grade 5, the average child learns almost 30,000 words. That means the child is learning about 7,500 words a year, more than three times the rate during the preschool years.

Figure 7.5 estimates the total vocabulary size for the average first, third, and fifth grader. The figure also shows the specific types of words known by children in these grades (Anglin, 1993). Root words such as *flop* and *closet* include a single free morpheme. Inflected words such as *soaking* and *changed* have one free morpheme and one bound morpheme as a suffix. Derived words such as *mucky* and *foundationless* usually have one free morpheme and prefixes or suffixes that create a different word. Literal compounds such as *payday* and *live-born* include two or more words whose meaning can be judged from the meaning of the separate words (e.g., *live + born*). An idiom consists of two or more words whose meaning cannot be understood by knowing the separate words. For example, *carrying on* is an idiom that refers to exciting, improper, or silly behavior (e.g., "They were really carrying on").

Children in the fifth grade know more words of all types than first and third graders. The improvement with age is greatest, however, for derived words. Jeremy Anglin (1993) asked children to define these types of words, and he concluded that children often figured out their meaning "on the spot," through analyzing their separate morphemes.

One child asked to define *foundationless* said, "I know what a foundation is. Like when you build a house you have a foundation, but if you don't have it, you're foundationless because you don't have it . . . it's -*less* . . . it's not there anymore" (p. 100).

Anglin argues that older children's ability to guess the meaning of words from analysis of their morphemes can partly explain their rapid vocabulary growth. Moreover, he suggests that this ability is important for reading comprehension during the school years.

Fifth graders also know many more idioms than first graders (see figure 7.5). Because idioms cannot be defined by combining the meanings of separate morphemes, their definitions cannot be figured out "on the spot." Therefore, improvements with age in understanding of idioms must involve the kinds of skills mentioned in the previous section, inferring meanings from the linguistic and nonlinguistic context.

Interpretation of idioms may be unusually difficult for young children because the literal meaning of the words is obvious but must be ignored. Suppose you heard the following story (from Cacciari & Levorato, 1989, p. 395):

> "One winter a little boy named Paul went to the mountains with his parents. They were staying at a hotel. The first day his mother told him that there were other children in the hotel and that he should try to meet them. He went to play on a frozen lake where there were other children, and he broke the ice."

Now answer the multiple-choice question: What did Paul do when he broke the ice?

    a.  he made friends with the other children;
    b.  he broke a piece of ice;
    c.  he told his mummy everything.

If you chose (a), you're right. You recognized that the phrase *broke the ice* has a figurative meaning that differs from the literal meaning of the words. Also, you connected Paul's mother's suggestion that he try to meet the other children with the idiomatic meaning of *breaking the ice* as beginning a social interaction.

When asked the same question, about three-fourths of a group of 9-year-olds interpreted *broke the ice* as an idiom, but only about half the 7-year-olds did so. The other 7-year-olds assumed that Paul literally broke a piece of ice. The younger children probably had more difficulty interpreting this idiom correctly because they had not heard it before. They may also have had difficulty using the context of the story to judge whether *breaking the ice* should be interpreted literally or figuratively.

Other literary devices that require children to go beyond the literal meaning of words are sarcasm, irony, and metaphor (Pease et al., 1993). However, not all literary devices are equally complex. Even 4- and 5-year-olds can understand certain types of metaphors, especially ones that involve similarities in physical features. If you say, "Hair is spaghetti," young children appreciate that both are long and stringy. Young children have more trouble with metaphors where physical similarity is lacking (e.g., "Your eyes are windows on the world" —because you see through both). Understanding of metaphors based on shared relations (such as seeing through eyes and through windows) improves during the school years (Gentner, 1988).

## Influences on Semantic Development

Children the same age differ in the number and complexity of the words that they know and use. Some children are advanced in their semantic development. Their vocabulary is large, and they use sophisticated words (like *sophisticated*!) appropriately. Other children have a small vocabulary made up of simple words.

These differences among children can have important consequences for their education and future achievement. Most intelligence tests include items that actually measure a child's vocabulary. Therefore, a child who has a small, simple vocabulary is likely to be judged as less intelligent than one who has a large, complex vocabulary. (Is such a judgment fair? You can answer that question after reading chapter 10.)

Theorists also want to understand how and why children differ in their vocabulary growth. By studying these differences, theorists can evaluate hypotheses about the specific experiences that influence semantic development. Thus far, researchers have identified several types of experiences that affect children's semantic development. The following points describe how the experiences of children advanced in semantic development are distinctive.

1. *Adults and, especially, parents talk to them frequently.* The sheer amount of speech that parents direct toward their children affects the children's vocabulary growth. On the average, twins develop language more slowly than children who are not twins (i.e., singletons). The contrast between twins and singletons is partly due to a difference in how much their mothers talk to them (Tomasello, Mannle, & Kruger, 1986). Because mothers of twins have

Children learn new words more rapidly when they and an adult share a focus of attention, as in this conversion about a picture book.

two young children to deal with simultaneously, they make fewer comments directly to each child than do mothers with only one young child. When mothers of twins spend more time talking to each child individually, the children develop language more rapidly.

2. *Adults name objects when they and the children with them are attending to the objects.* Adults' language has the greatest influence on children's word learning when the adults and the children share a focus of attention (Sachs, 1993). For example, if parents name a toy with which a 1-year-old is playing, the child becomes more attentive to the toy. One-year-olds also play more with toys that adults have labeled than with toys not labeled by adults (Baldwin & Markman, 1989). This effect is particularly striking because it occurs even when a 1-year-old has not yet learned the name used by the adult. If adults name a toy while a 1-year-old's attention is focused on it, the child is especially likely to learn the name of that toy (Dunham, Dunham, & Curwin, 1993).

3. *Adults often converse with children as they play together.* Adults can do more than name toys for children. They can join their children in play. During joint play, adults and children not only focus on the same objects but also give those objects a well-defined context. Children can use the context to figure out what the adults are talking about. Therefore, joint play is an especially favorable setting for vocabulary learning. Parents' language during play is also easy to understand because they use shorter sentences in play than in other activities. When playing, parents listen more to their children, so connected conversations last longer (Tomasello & Farrar, 1986).

Parent-child conversations can also affect children's style of word learning. Mothers in the United States more often name objects for their 6- to 19-month-old children than do Japanese mothers (Fernald & Morikawa, 1993). Consequently, U.S. children at these ages have larger noun vocabularies than do Japanese children. Japanese mothers, by contrast, more often use toys in ways that emphasize how to speak and act politely toward other people. The speech of Japanese mothers is also richer in the expression of affect and in sound play than that of U.S. mothers (Bornstein et al., 1992). These differences can bias children toward a more referential or more expressive style of word learning. More generally, these differences illustrate how early parent-child conversations reflect cultural values and preferences.

Reading books to children can contribute to their language development across a wide age range. Infants may learn the rules of turn taking in "conversations" with their parents about books. With toddlers, reading books can be an occasion for language games. Parents of older children can increase their children's vocabularies by reading books that teach children about things they would not see in their daily lives.

4. *Parents or other adults often read to children.* Even before infants produce their first words, parents often show them picture books and "converse" with them about the pictures (Ninio & Bruner, 1978). Parents comment on a picture and wait until the child replies with some vocalization. Such interactions train the child to take turns in a conversation.

Once children learn a few words, parents (especially in the United States) often turn a dialogue about picture books into a naming game. A parent points to a picture and names it, if the parent believes the child doesn't know the correct name. If the parent thinks the child does know the name, the parent asks, "What's that?" In this way parents not only help their children learn language; they also gauge their level of help to their children's current level of comprehension.

Picture-book reading may be especially valuable for vocabulary growth because books can teach children names for things that the children rarely see in their daily lives. Children reading an A-to-Z book, for example, will often encounter such exotic creatures as the armadillo and the zebra (Bridges, 1986).

The positive effects of reading books to children have been demonstrated in experimental studies. Parents in one study were instructed to ask questions while they read picture books to their 1- and 2-year-olds (Whitehurst et al., 1988). The parents were instructed to respond appropriately when their children tried to answer the questions. The parents in a control group received no special instructions. Tests after only one month showed that children in the experimental group spoke in longer, more complex sentences than the children in the control group. The differences between groups were smaller in a follow-up after nine months but were still apparent.

Asking questions during storybook reading is important for word learning (Sénéchal, Thomas, & Monker, 1995). Preschool children learn more new words from a storybook when they actively participate by answering questions than when they listen passively. Active participation may include labeling the pictures or simply pointing to pictures in response to adults' questions. Both forms of participation help children learn the new words that they encounter in a storybook.

5. *Adults reinforce children for correct word choices.* Many theorists discount the importance of positive reinforcement in language development. Obviously, children learn language even when they receive no explicit rewards for doing so. Yet researchers have found that positive reinforcement can affect the development of children's vocabulary.

In one experiment (Whitehurst & Valdez-Menchaca, 1988), 3-year-olds who spoke English were told the Spanish names for several toys. Then the experimenter allowed the children in one condition to play with the toys only when they used Spanish names to ask for them. These children learned the Spanish names more quickly than did children who received the toys regardless of whether they asked for them in Spanish or English. Thus, getting to play with toys was an effective reinforcement for learning Spanish.

Some reinforcement for appropriate language use probably occurs in natural settings, too. Parents more often give children what they want when they ask for it by name because such requests are easier to understand. Also, parents may encourage language use by praising their children for communicating with words rather than with the howls, grunts, or cries of an infant. This kind of reinforcement can affect semantic development.

6. *Children watch educational television programs.* Even watching television can have a positive influence on children's semantic development. In one experimental study (Rice & Woodsmall, 1988), 3- and 5-year-olds watched specially prepared cartoons about 12 minutes long. One cartoon was about a bug who broke his violin while playing hooky from his violin lesson. As table 7.4 shows, one version of the story included several words unfamiliar to most preschool children. The other version included only familiar words. Children saw the cartoons twice, a few days apart. After the second time, their comprehension of the unfamiliar words was tested by having them choose from a set of pictures the one that matched each word.

Children who saw the cartoons with the unfamiliar words comprehended those words better than did children who had seen the other cartoons. Each of the unfamiliar words

| TABLE 7.4 | Script for a Cartoon Used to Test Vocabulary Learning from Television[a] |
| --- | --- |

| VISUAL | NARRATION |
| --- | --- |
| 1. Billy in doorway with his mother. | His mother tells Billy Bug to go to his *viola* (violin) lesson. |
| 2. Billy looks down at the ground and walks down the road. | Billy is sad. He takes his *viola* (violin) and *trudges* (walks) down the road. He *trudges* (walks) until he sees a ball in the air. |
| 3. Billy stops to watch a ball being thrown into the air. | "What fun to play ball." Billy thinks. |
| 4. Billy looks down at the ground and walks down the road. | Billy keeps *trudging* (walking) down the road. He *trudges* (walks) and *trudges* (walks) until he reaches the stairs. |
| 5. Billy looks in a window and sees his viola lesson. | "My *viola* (violin) lesson has started," thinks Billy. |
| 6. Billy turns around and sees the ball. | "Oh, there's the ball again." Billy feels *jubilant* (happy). |
| 7. Billy kicks the ball and follows it over the hill. | "Oh boy, a soccer game!" |
| 8. The ball breaks Billy's viola. | "Uh, oh." |
| 9. A carpenter comes down the road. | An *artisan* (carpenter) comes down the road. |
| 10. The carpenter stops to listen to Billy and puts Billy on his wheelbarrow. | The *artisan* (carpenter) is a kind, *nurturant* (____) man. "Come with me," says the *nurturant* (kind) *artisan* (carpenter). "We must *fabricate* (make) a new *viola* (violin) for you." |
| 11. Billy smiles as he rides in the wheelbarrow. | Ah, Billy feels *jubilant* (happy) again. |
| 12. The carpenter stops the wheelbarrow and motions to Billy to wait. | "Wait here," says the *nurturant* (kind) *artisan* (carpenter). |
| 13. The carpenter returns with some tools and takes Billy's hand. | "Come with me," says the *nurturant* (kind) *artisan* (carpenter). |

© *The Society for Research in Child Development, Inc.*
[a]Italics indicate experimental words. Alternate control words are in parentheses. A (____) indicates an omission in the control script.

appeared about 5 times in each program, so children who saw the cartoon twice heard each word about 10 times. Despite this limited exposure, children gained enough information about some words to be able to recognize the appropriate picture for them.

What about real television programs? Can they improve children's vocabularies? When these programs are specially designed to teach language, they can do so effectively. Systematic evaluations of the most popular program for preschool children, "Sesame Street," have shown that it does promote the language development of preschoolers who watch regularly (Bogatz & Ball, 1972). In particular, watching "Sesame Street" helps children learn new vocabulary (Rice et al., 1990). However, children probably learn less from television than from talking to other people, because TV programs cannot give children direct, individualized feedback.

*7. Children read independently.* The ability to read may be critical for vocabulary development. When parents talk to young children, they use a fairly simple vocabulary. Even when talking to older children, parents rely on the same simple vocabulary (Hayes & Ahrens, 1988). Therefore, if children are to acquire the specialized vocabulary of well-educated adults, they must do so through reading. In particular, reading for school may account for a substantial fraction of the new words that children learn during the elementary grades (Anglin, 1993). Simply put, reading may be the best route to a high level of semantic development.

# FROM WORD TO SENTENCE: DEVELOPMENTAL CHANGES IN GRAMMAR

Think about a 1-year-old girl who is eating breakfast. If she wants more milk, she might say, "Milk!" and hold out her glass. Now imagine a similar scene, but this time the girl is 4 years old. If she wants more milk, she might say something like, "Could I have another glass of milk, please?" The most important difference between these two statements is not that the 4-year-old is more polite, because not all 4-year-olds are so polite. However, 4-year-olds

normally speak in complete sentences, and 1-year-olds normally use a single word to make a request or comment.

Four-year-olds speak in complete sentences because they have learned the basic grammar of their native language. For most of you, the word *grammar* probably recalls elementary-school classes in which you had to memorize rules of language. To a linguist, grammar also refers to language rules, but in a different sense. The **grammar** of a language describes the rules for producing and comprehending sequences of morphemes (Maratsos, 1983). Unlike a school grammar, these rules do not define what people should and should not say. Instead, they define what fluent speakers of a language actually do and do not say. They also define what statements fluent speakers of a language can understand and will judge as acceptable.

From a linguist's perspective, the grammar of a human language is a wondrous thing. Rather than constraining the users of the language, a grammar frees them. People who know the grammar of a language can produce an infinite variety of sentences that are immediately intelligible to other people. They can also interpret sentences by other speakers that they have never heard before. In short, a grammar gives the speakers of a language almost unlimited opportunity for creative expression that has meaning to other people.

Linguists divide grammatical rules into two sets, **syntax** and **morphology.** Syntax includes the rules for combining words into sentences. Morphology includes the rules for linking words, or free morphemes, to bound morphemes that modify their meaning. For example, in English, the bound morphemes *s* and *es* change singular nouns like *glass* to plural nouns like *glasses*.

Children do not know the grammar of any language at birth. Rather quickly, though, nearly all children learn the essential grammar of their native language. In this section you'll learn about the major steps in grammatical development, both during the preschool years and later. Then you'll see how adults' speech to children affects their progress through these steps.

## A Preschool Grammar

Children say their first words before they acquire any elements of grammar. Until children have learned about 50 words or reached roughly 18 months of age, they usually produce only one word at a time. They neither combine words nor add bound morphemes like the plural *s* to the base form of words. Stated more formally, they show no knowledge of syntax or morphology. They may, perhaps, comprehend more than they say, but evidence on this issue is limited.

Around 12 months of age, children sometimes say things that adults consider multi-word utterances. A 12-month-old may, for example, say "thank you." Yet to the child, this statement is a single word. Most 12-month-olds use "thank you" as much like a single word as do adults who say "pretzel."

At around 18 months of age, children begin to produce true two-word utterances. Researchers credit children with an understanding that they are linking separate words when they combine each word with several other words. A child may say "*more* cookie" and "*more* fish," or "water *off*" and "light *off*." The various combinations show that the children are putting together distinct words intentionally.

Children's first two-word utterances are often called **telegraphic speech** (Tager-Flusberg, 1993). When people send a telegram, they pay by the word. To save money, people omit words like *the* that can be eliminated without making the message unclear. Similarly, children's two-word utterances leave out words that are less essential for getting a message across.

Telegraphic speech is a negative description of children's earliest word combinations. The label suggests what children omit from their sentences but not what they include. Roger Brown (1973) offered a more positive description of early two-word speech. He proposed that these utterances express fundamental semantic relations like *agent* (someone who does something), *action*, and *object* (a thing to which something is done). Table 7.5 outlines the semantic relations that Brown identified in the two-word utterances of three U.S. children. Later research showed that children around the world express similar meanings in the two-word phase of language development. Children talk about agents who act on objects, or the location of objects, or the possessors of objects, when first learning all languages (Tager-Flusberg, 1993).

**grammar**
*The rules of a language for producing and comprehending sequences of morphemes.*

**syntax**
*Language rules for combining words into sentences.*

**morphology**
*Language rules for linking words, or free morphemes, to bound morphemes that modify their meaning.*

**telegraphic speech**
*Early utterances by young children that leave out words not essential for communicating meaning.*

| TABLE 7.5 | Some Semantic Relations in Children's Two-Word Utterances | |
| --- | --- | --- |

| SEMANTIC RELATION | EXAMPLES |
| --- | --- |
| Agent and action | mommy fix; car go |
| Action and object | drive car; hit ball |
| Agent and object | mommy sock; boy truck |
| Action and location | go park; put floor |
| Entity and location | baby table; toy floor |
| Possessor and possession | my daddy; mommy dress |
| Entity and attribute | box shiny; dog big |
| Demonstrative and entity | this doll; that Tommy |

In the earliest phases of two-word speech, children's rules for combining words may involve semantic relations less abstract than those in table 7.5. For example, instead of knowing the general rule for "possessor + possession" sequences, some children seem to use a more restricted rule, like "*my* + X." These children say things like "my doll" and "my truck" but not "Daddy car" or "Mommy hat." As children grow older, their rules for word combinations, or their grammars, become more general and more abstract (Maratsos, 1983).

Did you learn about semantic relations like *agent, action,* and *attribute* when you studied grammar? Probably not. Rather, you learned about grammatical categories such as *noun, verb,* and *adjective.* Semantic and grammatical categories sometimes correspond. Many verbs refer to actions, for example. Yet the correspondence is not always close. The standard grammatical categories include words with widely varying meanings—and varying semantic roles—that obey the same grammatical rules.

Think of the words *girl* and *idea.* Girls perform actions and, therefore, could easily fill the semantic role of an agent in a sentence. Ideas, by contrast, don't do things and so cannot be agents. You can sensibly say that "the girl hit the ball" but not that "the idea hit the ball." Yet both *girl* and *idea* are nouns and follow the grammatical rules for nouns. In particular, both can be changed from singular to plural by adding *s.* Both can be preceded by words like *a* (or *an*), *the,* or *that.*

Children will have trouble applying the grammatical rules for nouns if they do not understand that all nouns fall into the same grammatical category. However, children apparently do not understand grammatical categories in the earliest phase of two-word speech (Maratsos, 1983). Instead, as mentioned already, they use semantic relations to organize their word combinations. Children must at some point supplement or replace their grammars based on semantic relations with ones based on true grammatical categories.

When does the transition to grammatical categories occur? This question is somewhat misleading, because children do not develop an understanding of all grammatical categories simultaneously. By examining children's word combinations, researchers can judge which categories they understand at any specific age. They can look, in particular, for evidence that children consistently follow the rules that apply to a grammatical category when producing multiword utterances.

Table 7.6 summarizes four rules that apply to nouns in English. For example, English speakers use the word *a* before singular nouns but not plural nouns. They say "a cookie" but not "a cookies." Researchers judge whether children understand this rule and the other rules for nouns by analyzing what they say.

One researcher (Valian, 1986) examined thousands of utterances by six children who were 2 years old. The central question was whether the children followed the grammatical rules for nouns and for other grammatical categories when making these utterances. Table 7.7 shows the results for the noun category. Notice that all children distinguished singular from

**TABLE 7.6    Some Grammatical Rules That Apply to Nouns**

1. Singular nouns are distinguished from plural nouns. Singular nouns are preceded by *a* or *another* (e.g., *a* bell). Most plural nouns end in *s*, and words like *all* are used only with plural nouns (e.g., *all* cars).
2. Nouns that can be singular or plural (called *count* nouns, like *car*) are distinguished from nouns that have only a singular form (called *mass* nouns, like *spaghetti*).
3. Nouns are distinguished from pronouns (like *he* or *they*). Although a pronoun can take the place of a noun in a sentence, words like *a* and *the* can precede nouns but not pronouns.
4. All types of nouns can be preceded by *the* or a personal pronoun (e.g., *my*). Because this rule applies to all nouns, it establishes that the noun category encompasses singular and plural count nouns and singular mass nouns.

**TABLE 7.7    Two-Year-Olds' Understanding of the Grammatical Rules for Nouns**

| CHILD | USES SINGULAR/PLURAL DISTINCTION? | USES COUNT/MASS NOUN DISTINCTION? | USES NOUN/PRONOUN DISTINCTION? | USES *THE* WITH ALL TYPES OF NOUNS? |
|---|---|---|---|---|
| 1 | yes | no | yes | yes |
| 2 | yes | yes | yes | yes |
| 3 | yes | no | yes | yes |
| 4 | yes | no | yes | yes |
| 5 | yes | no | yes | no |
| 6 | yes | yes | yes | yes |

Data from Valian, 1986.)

plural nouns. All children distinguished nouns from pronouns. Most children used *the* or a personal pronoun with all types of nouns. Only two children clearly distinguished between count and mass nouns, but the children rarely used mass nouns. On the whole, the evidence suggests that these 2-year-olds understood the grammatical category of noun.

The 2-year-olds also showed an understanding of other grammatical categories such as adjective and preposition. Two-year-olds seemed to understand fewer grammatical categories than children who were 2½ years old, however. Even the older children appeared not to know all the rules for all grammatical categories. These results suggest that grammatical development is well advanced by 2½ years of age but is not completed until later.

Roger Brown (1973) provided the first detailed account of grammatical development in English. He recorded the speech of three children as they progressed from the one-word stage to that of complete sentences. He focused on children's use of morphemes that serve grammatical functions. For example, he documented children's acquisition of the morpheme *s* (or *es*) that converts singular to plural nouns.

Brown (1973) discovered that children learn the English grammatical morphemes in a highly consistent order (see also Fenson et al., 1994). This order is not dependent on a simple learning process. Children do not, for example, begin by learning the morphemes used most frequently by their parents. Rather, the order of acquisition seems to depend on children's gradual construction of increasingly complex grammatical rules.

One morpheme that children acquire early is the *s* that changes singular to plural nouns. One of the last morphemes that they acquire is the auxiliary verb *be*. In English, auxiliary *be* forms are used in sentences such as "He was drinking juice." In this sentence, *was* is the form of *be* that is appropriate for singular subjects in the third person and in the past tense.

Auxiliary verbs distinguish singular and plural, just as *s* does on nouns. Auxiliary verbs also differ for first-, second-, and third-person subjects and for verbs differing in tense. Because of the greater complexity of auxiliary forms, you would expect them to be acquired after the morpheme *s* —and they are.

Children learn about grammatical categories such as noun, verb, and adjective in school. But years before they enter school, they know how to produce sentences that depend on a knowledge of these categories.

Children's construction of grammatical rules is especially obvious from their errors in language use. (Remember the same point from the section on phonology.) One example that has been studied extensively concerns the past tense of regular and irregular verbs (Kuczaj, 1977; Marcus et al., 1992). Children first learn the past tense of irregular verbs like *run* (*ran*) and *see* (*saw*). They apparently learn these forms by rote memory, simply repeating words that they have heard adults use.

Next, children begin to produce the past tense for regular verbs like *walk* by adding *-ed* to the present-tense form. That is, children learn the grammatical rule in English for changing the tense of a verb.

Once they start to use past-tense regular verbs, children start to apply the *-ed* rule to some irregular verbs some of the time. They may say that another child *ranned* or *runned*, or that they *see-ed* or *saw-ed* a truck (Kuczaj, 1977). This error is known as **overregularization** because children overgeneralize the rule for the past tense of regular verbs.

Why do children make these errors? Children do not hear adults saying "runned" or "see-ed," so the emergence of these word forms at one stage in language development is strong evidence that children construct grammatical rules. Once children learn the new rule, they sometimes use it with verbs to which it does not apply.

If you listen to children, however, you should not expect to hear many overregularization errors. Most children overregularize irregular verbs less than 5 percent of the time (Marcus et al., 1992). Children are less likely to make these errors with irregular verbs that their parents use often, because often hearing an irregular verb strengthens children's memory for its correct form. Nevertheless, this phenomenon is still important in showing the rule-governed nature of children's speech.

Further evidence for the existence of grammatical rules comes from an unusual source—studies of deaf children. Deaf children rarely develop as much proficiency in spoken language as children who hear normally (Ratner, 1993). Deaf children who have deaf parents sometimes learn an alternative system for communication known as American Sign Language. The development of sign language corresponds in many respects to the first-language learning of hearing children (see *Cultural Perspectives:* "The Development of Sign Language in Deaf Children").

**overregularization**
*An error that children make when learning language in which they add the past-tense morpheme for regular verbs to irregular verbs (e.g.,* runned*).*

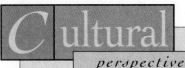
THE DEVELOPMENT
OF SIGN LANGUAGE
IN DEAF CHILDREN

Only a small fraction of deaf children have parents who are also deaf (Mayberry, Wodlinger-Cohen, & Goldin-Meadow, 1987). These few sometimes grow up learning American Sign Language (ASL) as their first language. ASL is a complex, conventional system of signs with its own syntax and morphology. For example, the verb *give* can be expressed in at least eight different ways by varying the details of the sign (as shown in figure 7.6). Learning ASL gives children access to a unique culture that is largely hidden from people with normal hearing (Padden & Humphries, 1988).

Deaf children learning ASL show a pattern of development surprisingly similar to that of children learning spoken English (Bellugi, 1988). The similarity is surprising because some

ASL signs seem so natural that researchers expected them to be acquired very early, earlier than the corresponding words are learned by children with normal hearing.

For example, in ASL a person says "I" by pointing to himself and says "you" by pointing to his or her listener. What could be simpler? Yet deaf children do not use such signs in the earliest phases of development. Instead of signing "I" and "you," they sign the names for themselves and their listener in their first sentences.

Even when deaf children start to use signs for pronouns, they make errors in signing like the errors that hearing children make in spoken language. If the mother says something like, "Do you want to go to the store?" the child may reply, in signs, "Yes, you want go store."

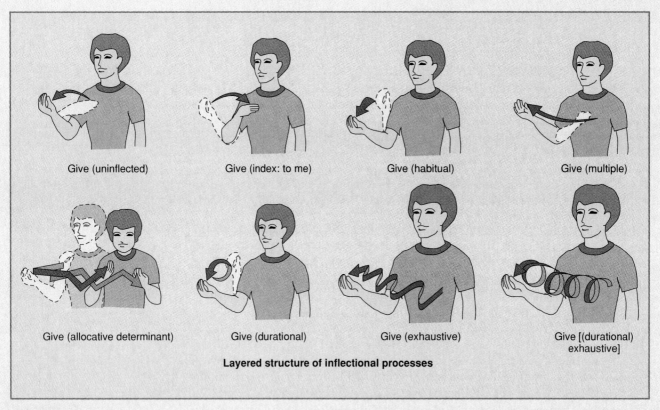

Give (uninflected)     Give (index: to me)     Give (habitual)     Give (multiple)

Give (allocative determinant)     Give (durational)     Give (exhaustive)     Give [(durational) exhaustive]

**Layered structure of inflectional processes**

## FIGURE 7.6

American Sign Language involves a complex system of signs. Here are, for example, eight different ways to say *give*.

From F. S. Kessel. *The Development of Language & Language Researchers,* section: pp. 153–186, fig. 7–5. Copyright © Lawrence Erlbaum Associates, Inc., Mahwah, N.J. Reprinted by permission.

Moreover, deaf children do not correctly use the signs for personal pronouns any earlier than hearing children correctly use the corresponding words (Petitto, 1988).

Children also invent forms in ASL, just as they do in spoken English (Bellugi, 1988). Nouns in ASL often have the same form as verbs, but hand movements are more restrained when signing nouns. When a 3-year-old signs the sentence, "You drive my (imaginary) car," the arm movements for the noun *car* are similar to those for the verb *drive,* but these movements are more vigorous for the verb than the noun. Similarly, figure 7.7 shows a child signing the noun *picnic* and then inventing a sign for a verb meaning *to have a picnic,* which is not a standard sign in ASL. So children learning ASL not only invent signs but also follow rules when they do so.

The research on ASL has contributed to a dramatic change in perspectives on deafness (Paul & Jackson, 1993). Deafness was long considered purely as a pathology, as a biological defect. The goal in working with deaf children was to make them as normal as possible, which usually meant teaching them to speak English. In this perspective, ASL was seen as an inferior mode of communication, so deaf children were often forbidden to use ASL in schools (Padden & Humphries, 1988).

In recent decades, many deaf and hearing adults have argued for the existence of a rich and distinctive culture of the deaf. These adults view the use of ASL as a central element of deaf culture. The concept of deaf culture is still controversial, and its implications for the education of deaf children are not entirely clear (see Turner, 1994). The concept is valuable, however, in replacing the totally negative view of deafness with a recognition of the many positive aspects of deaf people's lives.

Picnic

Child-invented
verb *to picnic*

**The acquisition of a spatial language**

## FIGURE 7.7

When children speak, they often invent words if they don't know the conventional word for what they want to say. Deaf children learning American Sign Language also invent words. One child invented a verb meaning "to picnic" by modifying the sign for *picnic.* The same kind of modification is used to change nouns like *car* into verbs like *drive.* Thus the deaf child was using a rule when he invented the sign for his verb *to picnic.*

From F. S. Kessel. *The Development of Language & Language Researchers,* section: pp. 153–186, fig. 7–6. Copyright © Lawrence Erlbaum Associates, Inc., Mahwah, N.J. Reprinted by permission.

Think back, now, to the 4-year-old girl's sentence, "Could I have another glass of milk, please?" To produce such a complex sentence, the girl had to learn the rules for grammatical categories such as the noun *glass* and the pronoun *I*. She had to learn the rule for the placement of auxiliary verbs, such as *could*, in a question. Finally, she needed to order the words of the sentence to make herself intelligible to people who know English. Although at 4 years of age she has not learned the entire grammar of English, her achievements are remarkable.

## Later Grammatical Development

One aspect of English grammar not fully mastered by 4-year-olds is the comprehension of passive sentences, those in which the noun phrase that begins the sentence is the object of the verb. In the passive sentence, "Batman was kicked by the Joker," *Batman* is the noun phrase that begins the sentence, but he receives (or is the object of) the kick. The true subject of the sentence, the Joker, is the one who does the kicking.

In active sentences, which are more common in English, the main verb follows the subject and precedes the object. That is, the normal word order in English is Subject-Verb-Object. When 4-year-olds hear passive sentences, they misinterpret them because they assume those sentences are also in Subject-Verb-Object order. So, if they hear that "Batman was kicked by the Joker," they think that Batman kicked the Joker (Bever, 1970).

Even after children correctly interpret passive sentences with action verbs like *kick*, they have trouble with other verbs. School-age children often misinterpret sentences such as "Goofy was liked by Donald" (Maratsos et al., 1985). These children know the rule for passive sentences, but they have difficulty applying the rule to verbs that do not refer to actions. Their difficulty illustrates a connection between grammar and semantics, or the application of grammatical rules to verbs that differ in meaning.

Mastery of passive sentences is not as delayed for children learning some languages other than English (Tager-Flusberg, 1993). Some languages mark the subject of a sentence with a special morpheme analogous to the *-ed* that marks regular past-tense verbs in English. Other languages allow most verbs to be expressed in the passive voice, so passive sentences are common. In these languages, preschool children understand and produce passive sentences correctly, because that aspect of grammar is critical for their communication with others.

During the school years, children also develop greater ability to judge whether sentences are grammatical. For example, 9-year-olds are more likely than 5-year-olds to recognize the grammatical error in the sentence "Tommy is more old than Sarah." Nine-year-olds are also more able than 5-year-olds to say how the sentence could be changed to make it grammatical (Bialystok, 1986). These abilities to judge and correct the grammar of sentences are components of children's **linguistic awareness.**

**linguistic awareness**
*Explicit, conscious knowledge of language rules as shown, for example, by the ability to judge the grammatical correctness of a sentence.*

Linguistic awareness does not depend solely on a child's age. Children who are bilingual have a heightened awareness of certain language distinctions. For example, the sentence, "If I am sick again tomorrow, I will have to see my fireman" is grammatical but nonsensical. If you're sick, you go to a doctor, not a fireman! Recognizing that a sentence is grammatically correct but makes no sense requires a separation of grammar from semantics. Children who are learning two languages can separate grammar from semantics more easily than monolingual (one-language) children, so they get higher scores on some measures of linguistic awareness (Bialystok, 1986).

Would you expect learning two languages to have more general effects on language or cognitive development? Read *Practical Applications of Research:* "Bilingualism and Children's Development" for a partial answer to this question.

## Adults' Contributions to Children's Grammatical Development

**child-directed speech (CDS)**
*A special pattern of speech to young children whose characteristics include high pitch, exaggerated intonation, and exaggerated facial expressions.*

Perhaps the most amazing feature of children's grammatical development is that it seems to occur spontaneously, without any explicit teaching. The only prerequisite for developing grammar seems to be exposure to people using language. Nevertheless, certain types of language exposure can lead to more rapid grammatical development. In particular, children may find it easier to learn language when people talk to them using the special pattern of language called **child-directed speech**, or **CDS.**

# BILINGUALISM AND CHILDREN'S DEVELOPMENT

About 10 percent of the U.S. population is bilingual, speaking both English and another language (Bialystok & Hakuta, 1994). The other language for most bilinguals in the United States is Spanish, but more than a million people speak German, Italian, French, and Chinese. Hundreds of thousands speak other languages ranging from Arabic to Vietnamese.

Public opinion and researchers' attitudes toward bilingualism are sharply divided (Hakuta, 1986). Some researchers have argued that learning two languages enhances children's intellectual development. Other researchers have argued that confusion between two languages retards children's development.

Until recently, few researchers designed studies that could adequately test these opposing hypotheses. Most early studies reflected the implicit assumption that exposure to two languages during childhood is a random event. However, in nearly all societies such exposure is not at all random. For example, many immigrant children in the United States are bilingual because they learn one language from their parents at home while learning English at school. These bilingual children often score lower on IQ tests than monolingual (one-language) children. The difference in IQ scores does not prove that learning two languages retards intellectual development. A more likely explanation is that immigrant parents often have low social status, limited education, and other problems that restrict their children's development.

By contrast, many English-speaking, middle-class parents in Canada encourage their children to learn French in school. In this social context, bilingual children often have higher IQ scores than monolingual children (Hakuta, 1986). Again, this difference may have nothing to do with bilingualism itself. The parents of these bilingual children may foster their development more, on the average, than do the parents of the comparison group of monolingual children. In the terminology of research design, the difference

in IQ scores is most likely caused by a confounding of bilingualism with social class. When this confounding does not exist, learning two languages seems to have little effect on children's intelligence.

Does learning two languages have positive or negative effects on *language* development? The best research suggests that bilingualism does not have lasting and general effects on language development. In the earliest phases of language acquisition, bilingual children often mix words and grammar from the two languages (Hakuta, 1986). By age 3 or so, bilingual children consistently separate the two languages. In middle childhood, knowing two languages can promote linguistic awareness (Bialystok, 1986; Yelland, Pollard, & Mercuri, 1993), but this effect may be small or temporary (Diaz, 1985; Hakuta, 1987).

The social effects of bilingualism are probably more significant than its effects on cognitive and language development (Hakuta, 1986). Some adults in the United States have argued that a common language holds society together. Therefore, they have opposed the education of immigrant children in their native language and argued that education in English will promote immigrants' assimilation into the larger society. These same adults often argue that learning foreign languages is important in elementary and secondary school, because it gives children a broader vision of themselves in the world.

Hakuta (1986) pointed out the contradiction in these arguments. He suggested that people in the United States should abandon "the paradoxical attitude of admiration and pride for school-attained bilingualism on the one hand and scorn and shame for home-brewed immigrant bilingualism on the other" (p. 229). He also proposed that educators set the goal of universal bilingualism. If all students become functional bilinguals, both greater acceptance of different ethnic groups and more effective participation in the global economy could be the result.

**B**ilingual children in the United States often learn to speak and then to read Spanish. Celebrations of Chinese New Year in U.S. cities are a reminder that many ethnic groups with many different languages raise their children as bilingual.

What is this mother saying to her daughter? We can't tell for certain, but we can guess that she is using child-directed speech. That is, she is speaking simply, slowly, and with exaggerated expression and intonation.

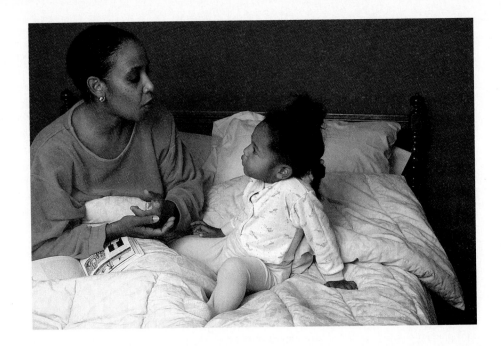

CDS is high pitched, with exaggerated intonation (e.g., "LOOK at the *pretty* baby!"), and exaggerated facial expressions (Bohannon, 1993). Adults speak slowly, with long pauses between their utterances. Their sentences are simple and grammatical. Sentences or parts of sentences are often repeated, especially if a child seems not to understand them. Vocabulary is simple, perhaps including invented words (e.g., *yucky*).

The topics of CDS are restricted to the here and now, what the adults and the child can both see or hear. When adults reply to a child's comment, they typically talk about the same topic as the child did. They sometimes repeat the child's comment exactly and sometimes ask a related question. Occasionally, they expand on the previous comment. If the child says, "Big truck," an adult may reply, "Yes, that's a big truck."

Child-directed speech was first called *motherese* because researchers assumed it was the special way mothers talked to their children. Then researchers discovered that fathers and adults who are not parents speak to young children in nearly the same way that mothers do. Fathers may use a larger vocabulary than mothers, but in other respects their speech to young children is like that of mothers (Reich, 1986). Even children often use CDS when talking to infants.

Nevertheless, CDS is not universal. Researchers observing adults and infants in diverse groups, including African Americans in North Carolina and Mayans in Guatemala (Sachs, 1993), have not seen adults talking to infants in high-pitched voices with exaggerated intonation. Still, these infants readily learn language. The special patterning of CDS is, therefore, not necessary for language development.

Even if not necessary, is CDS helpful for language development? Many researchers believe that it is, but they do not agree on why. One possibility is that children learn more from CDS than from typical speech among adults because they are more attentive to CDS. Even at 4 months of age, infants listen longer to CDS than to adult-directed speech (Fernald, 1985). Between 4 and 9 months of age, infants with English-speaking parents are more attentive to a woman using CDS, even when she is speaking in Cantonese (Werker, Pegg, & McLeod, 1994). The high pitch, exaggerated intonation, and long pauses in CDS obviously attract infants' attention even when they are listening to a language they have never heard before.

Another way that CDS might enhance language development is by providing obvious clues about the structure of a language. CDS makes the pauses between phrases within a sentence more distinct than they are in adult-directed speech. Also, infants listen longer to CDS when the pauses come at the natural boundaries between phrases rather than within a

phrase (Kemler Nelson et al., 1989). When adults separate phrases with pauses, they may help infants to analyze them. This help may be valuable for language learning because phrases are the building blocks of grammar.

Another way that adults might help children learn language is by giving them cues about the correctness of their grammar. Some years ago, Roger Brown and Camille Hanlon (1970) argued that parents do not provide feedback that would tell children whether their grammar is right or wrong. The parents in Brown and Hanlon's study rarely expressed disapproval of ungrammatical sentences that their children produced. The parents did not praise or reward their children when the children produced grammatical sentences.

Parents do give their children other kinds of cues about the adequacy of their language. Parents of 2- and 3-year-olds sometimes respond with an **expansion** of their child's previous statement. If the child says, "Car go," the parent may respond, "Yes, the car goes." Parents respond with expansions following ungrammatical utterances (such as "car go") more often than following grammatical utterances (Penner, 1987). These expansions could suggest to children that their own statements were incorrect. Also, the parent's expansions could show children how their ideas might be stated correctly.

Experimental studies have confirmed the effectiveness of expansions in promoting grammatical development (e.g., Nelson, 1977). For example, when adults regularly rephrase children's sentences to highlight specific grammatical rules, such as those for auxiliary verbs, children produce more sentences that reflect those rules. In natural settings, mothers who respond more consistently to their children's statements with expansions have children whose grammatical development is more rapid (Hoff-Ginsberg, 1986).

Parents also provide cues for language learning by asking questions after their children make ungrammatical statements. Parents may respond with a simple "What?" that functions as an implicit request for clarification. They may ask a question that includes an expansion of the child's previous statement (e.g., "Did the car go?"). Adults who are not parents also ask for a clarification or reply with expansion questions when children make ungrammatical statements (Bohannon & Stanowicz, 1988). Thus, children receive useful feedback about grammar from many people.

Many children interact daily, in a child-care center, with adults who are not their parents. The quality of the language environment in a center affects children's language development (McCartney, 1984). Children's language develops more rapidly in centers where caregivers often talk with them, but not all kinds of talk are beneficial. Children's language development may be delayed if their caregivers mainly give commands or use language only to direct their behavior.

In summary, adults influence the development of grammar by providing a rich language environment and by giving children cues about grammatical errors. Remember, though, that adults rarely teach language explicitly to children. Often, parents do little more than expose their children to correct language use (Pye, 1986). When parents expand on their young children's incorrect utterances, they only provide their children with clues about grammar. The children must still interpret these clues and construct language rules consistent with them (Maratsos, 1983; Marcus, 1993).

# LEARNING HOW TO COMMUNICATE: THE DEVELOPMENT OF PRAGMATICS

Language is not simply a system of sounds, words, and grammatical rules. Sounds, words, and grammar work together to make language a tool for communication among people. The aspect of language that focuses on its use for communication is **pragmatics.** Pragmatics includes children's ability to express their intentions and achieve their goals by using language. Pragmatics also includes children's ability to "say the right thing" in specific social situations. Finally, pragmatics includes children's ability to comprehend other people's language accurately. In short, pragmatics refers to accurate, effective, and appropriate comprehension and production of language.

**expansion**
*A complete, correct sentence said in response to a child's incomplete or ungrammatical utterance.*

**pragmatics**
*The aspect of language that focuses on its use for communication. More specifically, the branch of linguistics that focuses on the accurate, effective, and appropriate comprehension and production of language.*

# Preverbal Communication and Early Social Speech

Even before infants say their first word, they develop some skills needed for communication. In a conversation, people take turns speaking and listening. While one person speaks the other listens. The rhythm of turn taking is established very early in life. Only a few months after birth, infants exchange vocalizations with their parents that mimic conversations. After an infant makes a sound like "aaah" or "rrr," a parent responds by making similar sounds or by speaking to the infant.

When parents are interacting with their infants, they respond to almost all infant vocalizations (other than cries) by vocalizing to their infants (Keller & Scholmerich, 1987). In this way, parents give infants positive feedback on their vocalizations. They also help infants become accustomed to the rhythm of turn taking in conversations. In the first year of life, infants do little to produce the appearance of turn taking. They "talk" freely, starting and stopping whenever they wish. Parents tailor their speech to their infants' vocalizations. In other words, parents wait until their infants give them a turn to speak (Rutter & Durkin, 1987).

Between 1 and 2 years of age, the roles of parent and infant become more equal. Parents and children begin to work together to maintain uninterrupted turn taking in their conversations. They achieve this coordination by paying attention to each other's eye contact. Parents look away from their children during their speaking turns; they look at the children when just about to finish speaking. By 2 years of age, children adopt the same pattern of looking at their parents just as they finish speaking. Two-year-olds, then, engage in the nonverbal behaviors that allow smooth transitions between speaking turns.

Before infants begin to speak, they also develop an understanding of intentional communication. Infants discover that they can get what they want by communicating with other people. Moreover, this communication can occur without words. The following example shows how a 1-year-old got his message across without language (from Golinkoff, 1983, pp. 58–59):

**Jordan:** Vocalizes repeatedly until his mother turns around. Then he points to an object on the kitchen counter.
**Mother:** "Do you want this?" (Holds up a milk container).
**Jordan:** Shakes his head, signaling "no," and continues to point.
**Mother:** "Do you want this?" (Holds up a jelly jar).
**Jordan:** Again signals "no" and continues to point.
(Mother then offers two more objects to which Jordan signals "no." Finally,)
**Mother:** (picks up a sponge) "This?"
Jordan leans back in highchair, puts arm down, muscles relax. Mother hands Jordan the sponge.

Jordan gave several signals that he wanted the sponge and, more important, that he wanted his mother to get it for him. In other words, he showed that he expected to achieve his goal—getting the sponge—through communication with his mother. Intentional communication of this kind emerges around 9 months of age (Bates, 1979; Bates, O'Connell, & Shore, 1987; Bretherton, 1988). Like Jordan, 9-month-olds signal their intentions by gestures such as reaching for a toy while alternating between looking at it and looking at the mother. Like Jordan, 9-month-olds signal when they have gotten their message across by ending their gestures and relaxing as they wait for their mother to give them what they want.

The development of intentional communication depends on children's growing understanding of the relations between a means and a goal. Around 9 months of age, children acquire the ability to use tools. That is, they can use one object, the tool, as a means to a different goal. This achievement has a parallel in communication. When Jordan wanted the sponge, he treated his mother as a kind of "social tool," a means of getting the sponge. Of course, people are special kinds of tools. They have intentions, too. Around 9 months, infants seem to recognize that they can reach some of their goals by attracting other people's attention and directing other people's behavior. In other words, they try to make their own intentions comprehensible and relevant to other people's intentions (Bretherton, 1988).

Reaching for an object as a way of requesting help in getting it is one of the first gestures that infants display (Bates et al., 1987). Showing objects to adults often comes next, followed by giving objects to adults. Pointing, as used by Jordan, emerges near the end of the first year of life (Blake, O'Rourke, & Borzellino, 1994). Although younger infants extend their index finger as if pointing at something, this behavior does not regularly occur in circumstances where pointing would be anticipated. Moreover, infants younger than 10 to 12 months of age don't look where an adult is pointing; they are more likely to look at the adult's hand or index finger (Sachs, 1993).

The emergence of intentional, communicative gestures has also been studied experimentally (Goodwyn & Acredolo, 1993). Mothers of 11-month-olds were trained to use gestures such as arm flapping to symbolize *bird* and palms up to symbolize the question, "Where is it?" Mothers were asked to use these gestures daily, both with toys matched to each gesture and with storybooks that they read to their infants. For the next several months, mothers reported regularly on how often they modeled the gestures and whether their infants understood their gestures and used any gestures themselves.

Infants first used the trained gestures spontaneously around 12 months of age. The infants spoke their first words about a month later. Thus, use of symbols expressed through action (gestures) and expressed through speech (words) both appeared at the beginning of the second year of life. Gestures emerged a bit earlier than words, probably because they are more visible and so much easier to imitate than are the movements of the mouth, tongue, and other structures used in speech (Goodwyn & Acredolo, 1993).

After infants make the transition to social speech, they use language for several purposes. First, they continue to ask people to do things for them. The function of these verbal requests is *behavioral regulation,* the regulation of other people's behavior for the child's benefit. Second, children learn various social formulas, for example, for greeting people (e.g, "hello"). These formulas serve the function of accompanying and directing *social interaction.* Third, children learn to use phrases such as "look" or "see." The function of these statements is *directing attention,* or getting people to pay attention to their interests or actions (Bretherton, 1988; Sachs, 1993).

Children don't abandon the use of gestures when they learn to talk (Morford & Goldin-Meadow, 1992). One- and 2-year-olds often combine gestures with speech, for example, pointing to a toy and saying its name. Children at this age, whose sentences often include a single word, also use gestures as a substitute for speech. As mentioned earlier, these children have not learned the grammar necessary for well-formed requests such as, "Could I have another glass of milk, please?" They manage to communicate effectively by combining a gesture (holding out their glass) with a word ("Milk!").

Using gestures does not retard the development of speech. Children who use more gestures between 8 and 16 months of age also produce and comprehend more spoken words (Fenson et al., 1994). During the preschool years, gestures become more elaborate and flexible, serving as a foundation for pretend play with objects and imitation of adults' actions.

The developments in children's gestures and speech are accompanied by increases in their skill as conversational partners. In particular, children improve in their ability to "carry on a conversation." In a coherent conversation, each speaker makes a comment related to the previous speaker's comment but different from it. If one child says, "I like Batman," another child might reply, "I like Superman." Such a reply is a **contingent response.**

Sometimes young children imitate the previous comment rather than giving a contingent response. Sometimes young children make comments completely unrelated to the previous speaker's comment. If one child says, "I like Batman," the other child might say, "Look at my picture." The second comment has no relation to the first, so it is a **noncontingent response.**

When 21-month-olds are talking with their parents, they most often reply to their parents' comments with a noncontingent response (see figure 7.8). Contingent responses are less common, and imitation is least common. Between 21 and 36 months of age, the proportion of noncontingent responses decreases as the proportion of contingent responses increases. Imitative responses decline nearly to zero.

**contingent response**
*A response that depends on, or is logically related to, the previous speaker's comment.*

**noncontingent response**
*A response that has no relation to the previous speaker's comment.*

FIGURE 7.8

How 1- to 3-year-olds respond
to statements by adults. As
children grow older, their
responses to adults become
more contingent and are less
often noncontingent or an exact
imitation of what the adult said.
(Source: Bloom et al., 1976.)

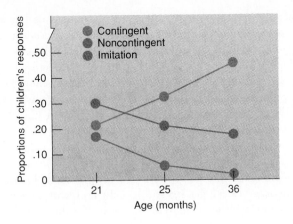

Figure 7.8 shows, however, that 36-month-olds give contingent responses to parents' comments less than half the time. You would not expect children to respond contingently to every comment by parents, because people do change topics during a conversation. It is still possible, though, to make these changes smoothly rather than abruptly.

As children move toward and into adolescence, they improve their ability to change topics without making a conversation disjointed or incoherent (Warren & McCloskey, 1993). One technique that they use is shifting from a specific topic to a related general topic or vice versa. Another technique is to use phrases that signal a change in topic, such as, "Let me tell you what happened to me." These techniques partly describe and partly explain the dramatic improvement with age in children's ability to carry on a coherent conversation.

## Egocentrism, Politeness, and Code Switching in Childhood

To communicate effectively with other people, children must not only relate their comments to the previous comments of others. Children must also recognize when their knowledge or their point of view is different from that of their listeners. That is, children must take account of differences between their perspective and their listeners' perspective.

Several decades ago, Piaget (1926/1971) suggested that this kind of perspective taking is beyond the cognitive ability of infants and preschool children. He argued that children under about 7 years of age are **egocentric,** unable to appreciate when someone else has a different viewpoint than they do. According to Piaget, this egocentrism leads to ineffective communication, because young children assume that other people can always understand what they are talking about.

Dozens of studies over the past few decades have disconfirmed Piaget's hypothesis. Even preschool children adjust their language for different listeners. When 4-year-olds are talking to 2-year-olds, they use shorter and less complex sentences than when talking to adults (Shatz & Gelman, 1973). Even 2-year-olds modify their speech when talking to more and less knowledgeable listeners (Shatz, 1983). Preschoolers are not always successful in communicating with other people, as you will see, but their communication failures are not due to complete egocentrism. Preschool children take account of some differences between themselves and their listeners, such as the difference in their ages (Shatz, 1983; Warren & McCloskey, 1993).

Children also take account of differences in the status or authority of their listeners. In particular, children speak more politely to adults than they do to their peers. When talking to an adult, children usually ask for things they want. When talking with peers, children often demand the things they want. When acting out different roles in play, children more often give commands in the parent role and more often make requests in the child role (Warren-Leubecker & Bohannon, 1989).

Understanding of polite forms of requests improves with age. Even 2-year-olds can vary the politeness of their requests (Bates, 1976), but older children use more techniques for adjusting

**egocentric**
*An inability to understand that other people can have perspectives different from one's own.*

TABLE 7.8    *Children's Judgments about the Politeness of Different Forms of Requests*

| REQUEST | AGE GROUP | |
| | 4-YEAR-OLDS | 5-YEAR-OLDS |
|---|---|---|
| GIVE ME A PENNY! (loud, negative tone) | .94 | 1.00 |
| Give me a penny. (soft, neutral tone) | | |
| I want a penny. (general verb form) | .81 | 1.00 |
| I would like a penny. (polite modal form) | | |
| Gimme a penny. (imperative) | .75 | .94 |
| I really like pennies. (hint) | | |
| I need a penny. (need statement) | .69 | 1.00 |
| May I have a penny? (permission directive) | | |
| Will you give me some pennies? (embedded imperative) | .69 | .81 |
| Do you have any pennies left? (question directive) | | |

Adapted from Judith A Becker, "Bossy and Nice Requests: Children's Production and Interpretation" in *Merrill-Palmer Quarterly*, 32:393–413, by permission of Wayne State University Press. Copyright © 1986 by Wayne State University Press, Detroit, MI.
Note: Values are the proportion of children at each age who matched adults' judgments about which form was more polite.

their degree of politeness. Table 7.8 lists some common techniques. The table also gives the proportion of 4- and 5-year-olds in one study (Becker, 1986) who understood each technique.

Almost all 4- and 5-year-olds recognized that the command "Give me a penny" was less polite when stated in a loud, negative tone than when stated in a soft, neutral tone. Almost all 4- and 5-year-olds knew that saying "I want a penny" was less polite than saying "I would like a penny."

By contrast, fewer 4-year-olds than 5-year-olds appreciated that people can make requests indirectly. If someone says to you, "I really like pennies," you might infer that the person wants one (or all!) of your pennies. Also, you probably view the indirect request "I really like pennies" as more polite than the direct request "Gimme a penny." Similarly, indirect requests such as "Do you have any pennies left?" are more polite than the direct request "Will you give me some pennies?" Most 4-year-olds make the same assumptions about the politeness of direct and indirect requests, but 5-year-olds agree more consistently with adults' judgments about politeness than 4-year-olds do (see table 7.8). Knowledge about how to ask politely increases further during the grade-school years (Wilkinson et al., 1984).

Parents often praise children when they speak politely and criticize them when they don't (Brown & Hanlon, 1970; Warren & McCloskey, 1993). Stated more generally, children do receive explicit training in this aspect of language development. Politeness and other facets of pragmatics are also important for children's social relationships with other people. Teachers form more negative impressions of children who are impolite in making requests or who fail to carry on a coherent conversation (Becker et al., 1991). Other children also tend to dislike peers who are impolite or lacking other pragmatic skills (Place & Becker, 1991).

When with their peers, Black children in the United States often speak a dialect of American English called (somewhat mistakenly) Black English. When speaking to a White teacher, Black children often switch to the standard dialect of American English.

**Black English**
*A dialect of American English with a somewhat different grammar.*

**code switching**
*Switching between Black English and standard English, or any other dialects, when such a switch is socially appropriate.*

Even when a child's language is conversationally appropriate, some people may judge it as the "wrong way to talk." Several groups of people in the United States speak a variant of American English that linguists call **Black English.** This label is not strictly accurate because many Blacks do not speak Black English and many non-Blacks (e.g., in the American South) do. Black English is a dialect of American English with a slightly different grammar. For example, a speaker of Black English might say, "She be working" when the most comparable sentence in standard American English would be, "She is working."

Laypeople often judge the grammar of Black English as primitive and incorrect. Linguists disagree. From a linguist's perspective, Black English is at least as complex as standard English. In certain respects, the grammar of Black English is even more precise than that of standard English. In Black English, the statement "He be working" has a slightly different meaning than the statement "He working." The first means that a man who is usually employed is now at work. The second means that a man who is usually unemployed is working now, on a temporary job (Warren & McCloskey, 1993). Standard English grammar does not make that grammatical (and semantic) distinction.

The prejudice against Black English can cause problems for children who learn this dialect. To avoid these problems, many children learn the grammars of both Black English and standard English. Then they switch linguistic codes when such a switch is socially appropriate. In school, they speak mostly in standard English, especially as they move to higher grades. In their neighborhoods, they speak mostly in Black English (Warren & McCloskey, 1993). These children's **code switching** is an impressive example of their pragmatic knowledge.

## Skills Children Need to Communicate Successfully

Children often face the pragmatic challenge of communicating information and interpreting other people's communications. Young children do not always meet this challenge successfully.

Their own messages are sometimes confusing or ambiguous, and they sometimes misunderstand messages they receive.

What could explain young children's difficulties in sending and receiving information? Conversely, what could account for the improvement with age in their ability to communicate information successfully? Researchers now believe that many skills are necessary for communicating information successfully. These skills can be classified into three types (Sonnenschein & Whitehurst, 1984).

First, the speaker and listener need to share relevant factual knowledge. If you tried to tell another person how a faucet works (which was one task that Piaget [1926/1971] gave young children), you might have trouble doing so. You might not know much about plumbing yourself. Your listener might know less than you do. Without a solid base of shared knowledge, successful communication between two people is difficult. Children's knowledge increases as they get older, so they can communicate more successfully in a wider range of situations.

Second, the speaker and listener need to have adequate perception, memory, and vocabulary. Suppose, again, that you wanted to tell someone about faucets. If you or your listener lacked the vocabulary necessary for precise descriptions of the handle, pipe, washer, and other parts of the faucet, you would have trouble communicating successfully. Children's vocabulary also increases with age, and this increase can partly account for their improved communication.

Third, effective communication depends on a knowledge of certain procedural rules and the skills necessary for applying these rules. One set of procedural rules requires speakers to adapt their messages to a particular listener's knowledge and abilities. Even preschool children understand some of these rules. For example, preschoolers know they should speak in short, simple sentences to younger children (Shatz & Gelman, 1973). Children's ability to adapt their messages to consider other variations in listeners' characteristics improves with age (Warren & McCloskey, 1993).

Another procedural rule that is especially important for communicating information is the **difference rule,** which states that a message referring to a particular object should distinguish that object from other objects with which it might be confused. To study children's understanding of this rule, researchers have used tasks for **referential communication** (e.g., Sonnenschein & Whitehurst, 1984). In these tasks, a speaker and a listener receive identical sets of objects. The objects may have unusual shapes, or they may all be the same shape (e.g., triangles) but differ in color, size, or other characteristics. The speaker must describe one object, called the *referent,* so that the listener sitting on the other side of a screen can choose that specific object from the entire set.

When preschool children are the speakers in referential communication tasks, they often construct ambiguous messages. For example, they tell the listener to pick "the blue one" when there are several blue objects. In other words, they fail to give messages that conform to the difference rule.

When preschool children take the listener role, they often act on ambiguous messages. That is, they immediately select one object when they hear a description that fits several objects. If asked later, they often say that they thought the ambiguous messages were perfectly adequate. When they fail to choose the right object after a speaker gives them an ambiguous message, they blame themselves for the failure instead of the speaker.

Even first graders are likely to judge ambiguous messages as adequate if the speaker is an adult, because they assume adults always send good messages (Sonnenschein, 1986). After first grade, though, children correctly judge when a message is ambiguous, whether the speaker was a peer or an adult. Usually, they ask speakers to clarify ambiguous messages. That is, first graders apply the difference rule when they are in the listener role.

Preschool and kindergarten children have difficulty identifying ambiguous messages because they are poor at **comprehension monitoring,** or judging whether they fully understand a message (Bonitatibus, 1988; Flavell, 1985). They have difficulties in comprehension monitoring because they seldom distinguish between the literal content of a message and the speaker's intentions. In other words, young children do not recognize that speakers sometimes fail to say exactly what they mean. And if the children know what a speaker meant to say, they are poor at judging whether the speaker's message was clear or ambiguous (Beal & Belgrad, 1990).

**difference rule**
*A rule of communication that specifies that a message referring to a particular object should distinguish that object from other objects with which it might be confused.*

**referential communication**
*A type of task in which a speaker and a listener sit on opposite sides of a screen and are given identical sets of objects. The speaker must describe one object, called the* referent, *so that the listener can pick it from the objects in front of him or her.*

**comprehension monitoring**
*The ability to judge one's understanding of a message.*

Another problem of preschool and kindergarten children is that their thinking doesn't fully control their action (Ackerman, 1993). If they take the listener role in a referential-communication task, they are likely to make a choice even when they know the speaker's message was ambiguous. If stopped before they make a choice, they can usually report accurately on whether a message was adequate. Thus, their comprehension monitoring doesn't regulate their behavior as effectively as it does in older children.

In addition, older children have a fuller appreciation that the words of a message may not accurately express what the speaker meant to say. Older children also remember the actual words of a message better, because they realize the importance of those words. And because their memory for a message is better than that of younger children, their ability to monitor their own comprehension and correctly identify ambiguous messages is greater.

The skills of comprehending messages and producing clear messages are critical for children, especially after they enter school. Children must be good listeners when their teachers give assignments or explain how to solve problems. Children must be good speakers when they participate in class discussions. They must be good at writing unambiguous answers when they take exams. Because good communication skills are so important, researchers have tried to find out how to improve children's skills.

One effective technique is to ask children to analyze and evaluate other people's communicative performance. That is, researchers train children to judge whether speakers and listeners followed the procedural rules for informative communications. In particular, children evaluate whether a speaker followed the difference rule in constructing his or her message. They evaluate whether a listener followed the same rule in deciding either to choose an object immediately or to ask first for clarification. When researchers train children in message evaluation, the children's communication improves (Sonnenschein & Whitehurst, 1984).

Even without explicit training, children become better at communicating information as they grow older. The age change may be due partly to children's learning to read and write. First graders identify ambiguous messages more successfully when the messages are written rather than spoken (Bonitatibus & Flavell, 1985). This suggests that the old maxim "Put it in writing" helps children as much as it does adults. Apparently, seeing a message in written form makes children more sensitive to its literal meaning. That sensitivity, in turn, helps children recognize both when the message may not say what the speaker meant and when their own comprehension may be incomplete.

Finally, as children learn to speak a language, they also learn to use language when engaged in play, when defending themselves, and when making promises (Opie & Opie, 1959). Children use standard phrases for expressing the rules in games, like "No touch-backs." They learn phrases for teasing or ridiculing others and replies to those phrases (e.g., "Takes one to know one"). They seal their promises with oaths such as, "Cross my heart and hope to die." These examples show other facets of pragmatics in childhood.

# EXPLANATIONS FOR LANGUAGE DEVELOPMENT

How are children able to learn language so quickly and apparently effortlessly? Every human language is highly complex, yet children around the world learn to use their native language effectively within a few years after birth. From the late 1950s through the 1960s, two contrasting theoretical perspectives on language development were popular. During the 1970s, several writers presented a new theoretical perspective that differed as much from the first two as they differed from each other.

Few current researchers ally themselves closely to any of the three theoretical perspectives popular a generation ago. Instead, researchers have proposed different explanations for different aspects of language development. Earlier you encountered some hypotheses about specific aspects of language development. Now it's time to consider issues important for a general understanding of language development. Advocates of the older theoretical

perspectives often stated the opposing positions on these issues clearly, so a brief review of those perspectives is helpful before a discussion of current evidence and issues.

## Three Theoretical Perspectives on Language Development

The most famous learning theorist, B. F. Skinner (1957), argued that children learn language in the same way as they learn anything else. Language, to Skinner, was simply another form of behavior. He called it *verbal behavior*. He believed that the principles of operant conditioning (described in chapter 1) could explain the learning of verbal behavior in the same way as they explain the learning of other behaviors.

More specifically, Skinner proposed that children learn to use words because they are reinforced for doing so. They learn to construct grammatical sentences because other people reward them for speaking grammatically and punish them for speaking ungrammatically. In short, Skinner assumed that language development depends on the consequences that children receive when they use language. As all learning theorists do, Skinner emphasized the role of nurture, or experience, in language development.

Skinner's (1957) theory was vigorously challenged by a linguist named Noam Chomsky (1959, 1968, 1988). Chomsky argued that children need no reinforcement for language learning. Children learn from mere exposure to language because they are born with considerable linguistic knowledge. Chomsky (1968) described this innate knowledge as a **universal grammar** that provides "a schema to which any particular grammar must conform," (p. 76). This schema includes principles of language, rules that provide a skeletal structure for a grammar, and a set of conditions for the elaboration of these principles and rules into the grammar of a specific language.

If children are born with knowledge of a universal grammar, the task of learning language is greatly simplified. The universal grammar constrains the rules children can form about the grammar of their own language. In a sense, children who innately possess a universal grammar do not have to learn grammatical rules. They need only to figure out which rules of the universal grammar are used in their native language. In Chomsky's words, the language learner needs only to "search among the possible grammars and select one that is not definitely rejected by the data available to him [or the speech the child has heard]" (p. 76).

Other theorists extended Chomsky's (1968) argument by proposing that children are born with a specific **Language Acquisition Device, or LAD** (McNeill, 1970). The LAD was described as a special mechanism in the brain that helps children see the connections between the universal grammar and the grammar of their own language. These ideas about an innate LAD and Chomsky's ideas about an innate universal grammar clearly represent extreme "nature" positions on the nature-nurture issue.

During the 1970s, several researchers proposed that Piaget's (1970) theory of cognitive development could better explain language development than did either Skinner's or Chomsky's theories. Piaget argued that language development does not depend on learning from experience, on innate linguistic knowledge, or on specialized brain mechanisms. Rather, general cognitive development explains the development of language. In particular, the emergence of productive language during the second year of life depends on developments in thinking during infancy.

Piaget did little research on language development, although he presented his views on the topic in a debate with Noam Chomsky that was later published (Piatelli-Palmerini, 1980). Several other researchers, however, have used Piaget's ideas when interpreting the findings of their studies. Most notably, Roger Brown (1973) drew on Piaget's theory when explaining children's early word combinations. Brown suggested that children express semantic relations such as agent–action in early two-word sentences because they gained an understanding of these relations during infancy. Remember from chapter 1 that Piaget assumed infants construct their view of the world by acting on it. According to Brown, the semantic relations that infants understand through *action* are later expressed by toddlers through *language*. Thus, Brown took Piaget's theory as the basis for the two-word phase in language acquisition.

As researchers continued to study language development, they found reasons to question some key assumptions in each of the three theoretical perspectives. Chomsky's (1959) critique convinced many researchers that Skinner's theory of language development was inadequate. And as mentioned earlier, several studies confirmed Chomsky's argument that direct reinforcement and explicit training are not necessary for language development (although they may be helpful).

The different versions of Chomsky's theory had their own problems, however. Many researchers were uncomfortable with hypotheses about an innate grammar or an innate language acquisition device. Nativist (or "nature"-oriented) theories did not offer satisfying answers to questions about why language development proceeds in the regular way that it does. On the contrary, they made the process of language acquisition seem rather mysterious (Maratsos, 1988; Pinker, 1988).

And what about Piaget? Although Piaget's ideas about infant development shed light on early two-word speech, they were less useful in explaining other aspects of language development. Also, researchers attracted to the information-processing approach to cognitive development argued that their approach provided a better basis for a theory of language development than did Piaget's theory (see MacWhinney, 1987).

These debates left researchers without a generally accepted theory of language development. Nevertheless, the issues raised by Skinner, Chomsky, Piaget, and their followers remain important. Decades of research have yielded valuable evidence on these issues.

## Evidence and Issues for Theories of Language Development

Some of the new evidence relates to the nature-nurture issue discussed most extensively by Skinner and Chomsky. Other evidence concerns the issues of how children acquire a language and how their growing language ability is related to their cognitive development. The evidence leads to five conclusions that must be taken into account in new theories of language development.

1. *Only human beings spontaneously learn and use language.* Chomsky (1968) proposed that the ability to learn and use language is uniquely human. Of course, other animals have ways to communicate with one another. However, Chomsky argued that only humans have a communication system as flexible and complex as any language. Chomsky regarded the uniqueness of human language as support for his hypothesis that children are born with innate linguistic competence. If only humans have language, the hypothesis that they are biologically prepared to learn language becomes more plausible.

Few researchers doubt Chomsky's claim that human languages are more complex than the communication systems of other animals. Even so, some researchers have claimed that other animals can learn language. During the 1970s, several teams of investigators tried to teach chimpanzees to use sign language or an artificial language based on abstract symbols (see Terrace, 1985). Early reports suggested that trained chimps used the signs or symbols much as young children use language. For example, the chimps sometimes used combinations of signs or symbols that seemed analogous to the two-word sentences of young children.

More careful analyses showed that chimps rarely combined words except when their trainers directly asked them to do so. Usually, the chimps' word combinations were partial imitations of their trainers' signs or were gibberish. In addition, despite years of effort, researchers were not able to teach chimpanzees to use signs or symbols as names for objects (Terrace, 1985). Although chimps learned the equivalence between symbols and objects that they see, touch, or smell (Savage-Rumbaugh, Sevcik, & Hopkins, 1988), no trained chimp showed an understanding of symbols as sophisticated as that of a 2-year-old child.

Greater success has been achieved with another species of primates, the bonobo (Savage-Rumbaugh et al., 1993). Wild bonobos live only in Zaire, and few have been caught and raised in zoos. However, some psychologists have concluded that they are more intelligent and communicative than chimpanzees.

One bonobo named Kanzi was raised in captivity from infancy, while researchers tried to teach his mother a simple language using geometric symbols for words. Although his

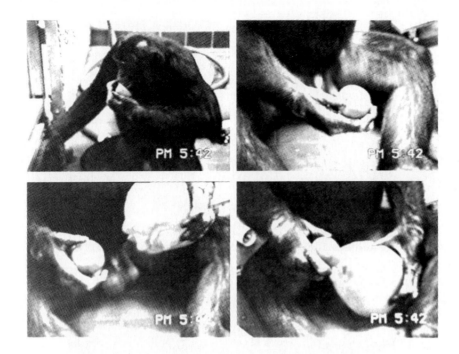

This figure illustrates Kanzi listening to the sentence "Feed your ball some tomato" (top left), selecting the tomato (top right), bringing a soft sponge ball with a "pumpkin" lace embedded within it into his lap (bottom left), and then placing the tomato into the mouth on the lace embedded in the ball (bottom right).

mother learned little, Kanzi began to show comprehension both of those symbols and of spoken language. Moreover, his comprehension seemed to grow without explicit teaching. He could also respond correctly when asked to "Put the ball on the pine needles" and to "Put the pine needles on the ball." These responses suggest that Kanzi understood the significance of word order, an important aspect of syntax. Indeed, his language comprehension was comparable to that of a 2-year-old boy whose mother was one of Kanzi's caretakers (Savage-Rumbaugh et al., 1993).

Nevertheless, after 2 years of age the boy's language development rapidly progressed beyond that of Kanzi. Also, wild bonobos do not seem to have anything like a human language. Further studies of wild bonobos might change this conclusion, but current data suggest that language use is restricted to the human species. In natural settings, only human beings develop a language that they use spontaneously for communication with others.

Although the uniqueness of human language is consistent with Chomsky's (1968) theory, it does not directly confirm his hypothesis that humans have an innate language-specific competence. An alternative view is that humans learn and use language because they have the high level of *general* cognitive ability necessary for doing so. In short, the uniqueness of human language could be viewed as evidence for cognitive theories of language development just as easily as for Chomsky's theory.

The question remains open because language development differs in important ways from other aspects of cognitive development. As you have seen, young children quickly learn complex rules of phonology, semantics, grammar, and pragmatics. They rarely show comparable learning ability or cognitive sophistication on nonlinguistic tasks. Unless cognitive theorists offer a plausible explanation for this rapid language learning, hypotheses about innate linguistic competence will remain attractive (Pinker, 1991).

2. *The ability to learn a first language is not highly related to general intelligence or IQ.* Another problem for cognitive theories is the absence of strong relationships between general intelligence and language development (Cromer, 1988; Ratner, 1993; Rice, 1989). Although language development is usually delayed in mentally retarded children, many children with low IQ scores have no difficulty learning the most complex grammatical rules. Conversely, some children with normal intelligence show marked delays in learning language. These findings suggest that language acquisition depends, at least partly, on language-specific abilities. If

Which group will learn more from their foreign-language class, the children or the adults? You might guess that children have a special ability to learn languages that adults have lost. However, researchers have found that adults often learn a second language as fast as children, or even faster.

learning language depended entirely on general cognitive abilities, then children with poor cognitive abilities should invariably have more trouble learning language.

3. *The brain is specialized for processing language, but the evidence for a sensitive period for language acquisition is weak.* Chomsky (1968) linked his hypotheses about innate linguistic competence to Lenneberg's (1967) theory of brain development. As discussed in chapter 5, Eric Lenneberg (1967) assumed that the left brain hemisphere becomes specialized for language during the first few years of life. He pointed out that language develops most quickly and naturally during this sensitive period. He also assumed that when brain damage disrupts language after this period, recovery of normal language is unlikely. Finally, Lenneberg assumed that learning a second language in adolescence or adulthood is more difficult than in childhood because the sensitive period covers childhood only.

These assumptions have been disconfirmed or greatly qualified by later research. As you recall from chapter 5, the left hemisphere is somewhat specialized for language, but this specialization exists at birth and changes little afterward. Brain damage to the left hemisphere does not always have less serious long-term effects when it occurs in childhood rather than in adulthood (Maratsos & Matheny, 1994; Snow, 1987).

New research has also disconfirmed Lenneberg's (1967) hypothesis about second-language learning. Adults can learn a second language as fast as young children, if they have equal exposure to the language and equal opportunity for practicing it (Bialystok & Hakuta, 1994). Under some conditions, adolescents and adults learn a second language even faster

than young children (Snow & Hoefnagel-Hohle, 1978). This evidence casts doubt on the hypothesis that a biological mechanism for language learning "kicks in" during the first years of life and "shuts off" later in childhood.

Chomsky might respond that his hypothesis about innate linguistic competence does not mean there must be a sensitive period for language development. An innate knowledge of universal grammar, for example, might simplify language learning throughout life, not only in early childhood. Nonetheless, the evidence against the sensitive-period hypothesis weakens claims for a special brain structure whose primary function is to help children learn their first language.

4. *Children construct rules about language that govern what they say and how they interpret what other people say.* This statement summarizes a vast amount of evidence that supports one of Chomsky's (1959) most central hypotheses about language development. Chomsky proposed that fluent speakers of a language understand rules that allow them to produce and interpret an infinite number of novel sentences. This proposal may seem obvious, but it is inconsistent with Skinner's (1957) theory of language acquisition. If children learn language through reinforcement, they should rarely produce, and have difficulty comprehending, sentences that they have not heard before — because these sentences have never been reinforced.

Children's language errors provide even more conclusive evidence against simple learning theories. Children never hear people say things like "He runned away" or "The cat drinked the milk," yet some children make these errors at one point in their language development. The most plausible explanation of these errors is that the children have constructed a rule that tells them how to convert a verb to the past tense.

On the other hand, the existence of grammatical rules is not conclusive evidence for Chomsky's (1968) universal grammar or an innate LAD. Cognitive theories of language acquisition also assume that children's errors in language are rule governed (Brown, 1973; MacWhinney, 1987). Moreover, cognitive theories may more easily explain why children acquire correct rules through a series of gradual approximations (e.g., when asking questions such as, "Could I have another glass of milk, please?"). In addition, cognitive theories may better explain why children often regress to incorrect language use (e.g., saying "runned" after previously saying "ran").

In addition, some type of learning must be involved in children's construction of language rules. After all, children cannot make up whatever rules they please. They must eventually use the rules that hold for their native language. Therefore, all theories of language development must include hypotheses about children's learning from experience.

5. *Some features of language development are universal, but patterns of development vary significantly among children.* If every human were born with the same universal grammar, then you might expect to find great similarity among children in their patterns of language development. Conversely, if language development depended entirely on learning from experience, then you might expect great variations in development, depending on a particular child's experience.

The true state of affairs differs from both these expectations. Yes, in some respects language development is similar around the world. Most children say their first word at around 1 year of age. Most children, regardless of their native language, express the same set of semantic relations during the two-word stage of language acquisition. In addition, most children learn to express semantic relations before they learn grammatical rules (Brown, 1973).

In other respects, however, individual children's patterns of development differ greatly. For example, some children pronounce many words incorrectly when learning to talk. Other children pronounce few words incorrectly, apparently because they don't try to say words that they cannot pronounce correctly. In addition, some children's early words reflect a mostly referential style of semantic development; other children's early words reflect a mostly expressive style (Nelson, 1981).

Additional evidence of differences in development comes from studies of children learning different languages. For example, children learning English normally begin by using word order to express meaning, putting agents (subjects) before actions (verbs). Only later do these children begin to add grammatical morphemes like the plural *-s* and the past-tense *-ed* to words.

By contrast, children who are learning languages in which word order is more flexible often reverse this sequence, using morphemes to mark agents and actions before they start using the word order that is most common in their language (Maratsos, 1988).

Children's flexibility in learning languages casts doubt on Chomsky's hypothesis of a universal grammar that children simply map onto their own language. Most researchers believe that children do not have an innate knowledge of specific linguistic rules, certainly not of the large number of rules originally suggested by Chomsky (1968). Instead, they may be biologically prepared to process language input in specific ways (Maratsos, 1988). In particular, children may have innate "operating principles" for generating linguistic rules after being exposed to language (Slobin, 1985). Stated more simply, children may know less about *language* and more about *learning language* than Chomsky believed.

Taken together, the five conclusions provide a basis for future theories of language development. However, a single theory may never explain all aspects of language development. Different theories may be needed to explain developments in phonology, semantics, grammar, and pragmatics. As you have seen, each aspect of language has a distinct course of development. Therefore, the development of each aspect will require its own explanation.

# LADs, LASSies, and Communication

Several researchers have argued that the behaviorist, linguistic, and cognitive theories of language development all underestimate the significance of social relationships. Remember from chapter 1 that Vygotsky (1962) described language as a tool for thought that children develop through social interaction. Language, for Vygotsky, begins in social interaction and is intimately connected with participation in a particular society and culture.

More recently, Bruner (1983) supplemented the idea of an innate Language Acquisition Device (LAD) with the idea of a **Language Acquisition Support System (LASS).** The LASS includes all the social interactions that, in infancy, provide a cognitive foundation for language development. It includes all the practices of parents, such as object naming and storybook reading, that contribute to semantic and grammatical development in early childhood. According to Bruner, just as "every laddie needs a lassie" (in the words of the old song), every LAD needs a LASS.

Many kinds of evidence suggest the importance of social interactions for all aspects of language development. The slow pace and exaggerated intonation of child-directed speech may make phonemes clearer and easier to discriminate, thereby enhancing speech perception (Bohannon, 1993). When adults talk face-to-face with young children, the children can do a form of lipreading, watching how the adults place their mouth and tongue when making different sounds. This lipreading may enhance the children's speech production (Studdert-Kennedy, 1993).

You have also read about the ways that social interactions may contribute to semantic, grammatical, and pragmatic development. For example, adults' naming of objects when playing with children may promote their vocabulary growth. Adults' use of child-directed speech may make the learning of syntax and morphology easier. Parents' feedback on ungrammatical speech may also guide children toward correct grammar (Bohannnon & Stanowicz, 1988). In addition, parents and other adults instruct children in correct speech and advise them in how to create messages that identify referents unambiguously.

However, much of the evidence supporting the social-interaction perspective is open to alternative interpretations. The reason is one with which you are already familiar: The evidence comes mainly from correlational studies. A correlational design leaves open the possibility that, instead of adults' language influencing children's language, how advanced children are in language use influences how adults talk to them.

Another problem for the social-interaction perspective is that many children acquire their native language without special help from adults. For example, many people throughout the world, and throughout history, learned to speak fluently without having adults read storybooks to them. These facts raise a question about what kind of LASS—or help from other people—is truly necessary for language development.

One central principle of the social-interaction perspective is less open to question. Stated most simply, the primary function of language is communication. Advocates of the behaviorist, linguistic, and cognitive perspectives sometimes ignore this point and so lose sight of why children acquire language at all. But each aspect of language aids in communication with other people.

Take phonology first. Even before they understand language, infants pay attention to the sounds of speech because those sounds help them understand other people's emotions. Perceptions of speech sounds also help infants identify the "voice signatures" of significant people in their lives, such as their parents (Studdert-Kennedy, 1993).

The functions of semantic and grammatical development are even more obvious. Children who want a specific toy for a birthday present are less likely to get it if they cannot tell adults its name. Children who want help dressing are less likely to get it if they say "sock" than if they say, "Help me put on my socks, please."

The functions of pragmatic development may be the most important of all. Recall that English-speaking adults interpret sentences such as "Can you get me a beer?" as indirect requests. In Japanese, however, these sentences are interpreted literally, so the correct response is not to give someone a beer but to say "yes" or "no" (Bialystok & Hakuta, 1994).

Speaking improperly can do much more than lead to misunderstanding. Recall that children who are impolite and who don't carry on a coherent conversation are judged more negatively by their peers and their teachers (Becker et al., 1991; Place & Becker, 1991). Among adults, misunderstood messages can have tragic consequences for millions of people. For example, a misunderstood—and partly distorted—telegram was the spark that led to war between France and Germany in 1870 (Crankshaw, 1981).

In short, "learning how to talk" is much more than putting words together. The development of language is an essential part of acquiring a culture and becoming a member of a specific society. Although the social-interaction perspective does not answer all questions about language development (Bohannon, 1993), its emphases on the social context of language learning and the social functions of language are a valuable complement to other theories.

# SUMMARY

### The Sounds of Speech: Perception and Production
Phonology is the study of speech sounds, the stress and intonation patterns that accompany speech sounds, and the rules for combining sounds into syllables. Phonemes are the distinctive categories of sounds recognized as meaningful in a language.

### Speech Perception: Discrimination of Phonemes in Infancy
Categorical perception of the phonemes in all language seems to be present at birth. Most researchers assume that this perception depends not on an innate knowledge of speech sounds but on general processes for analyzing sounds. During the first year of life, speech perception becomes tuned to the set of phonemes important in an infant's native language.

### Speech Production: From Crying and Burping to First Words
Before infants learn to talk, they go through regular phases of cooing and babbling. Most infants say their first true words around 1 year of age, but they cannot say all words correctly at that age. When words include phonemes that are difficult for children to pronounce, they substitute other phonemes in a systematic, rule-governed fashion.

### Later Phonological Development
Many children do not accurately pronounce all phonemes until age 7. Children also become aware of phonological rules that help them when learning to read and to spell. Improving children's phonological awareness can enhance their reading and spelling ability.

### Meaning in Language: Semantic Development
The first word can be viewed as the transition from infancy to childhood. The morpheme is the basic unit of word meaning.

### Early Vocabulary Growth and Word Meanings
The average child produces about 50 words by 18 months of age. Most children show a vocabulary burst, or increase in their rate of vocabulary growth, around 18 to 22 months of age. The vocabulary burst depends on the process of fast mapping, using principles such as contrast or mutual exclusivity to guess the meaning of novel words.

### Later Semantic Development
During the primary grades, the average child learns about 7,500 new words each year. Understanding of idioms is poorer in the early grades than later, because younger children usually interpret them literally rather than figuratively.

### Influences on Semantic Development
Semantic development is influenced by many experiences, including conversations with adults and storybook reading. Children may even learn new vocabulary from watching educational television.

### From Word to Sentence: Developmental Changes in Grammar
The grammar of a language describes the rules for producing and comprehending sequences of morphemes. Syntax includes the rules for combining words into sentences. Morphology includes the rules for linking words, or free morphemes, to bound morphemes that modify their meaning.

## A Preschool Grammar

Children show no understanding of syntax or morphology in the one-word phase of language development. In the two-word phase, children express semantic relations such as agent-action. Then morphology begins to appear and children acquire an understanding of grammatical categories like noun and adjective.

## Later Grammatical Development

Children learning English do not comprehend passive verbs fully until sometime during the school years. Linguistic awareness, or explicit knowledge of grammatical rules, also develops during the school years. Learning two languages may enhance linguistic awareness.

## Adults' Contributions to Children's Grammatical Development

Child-directed speech (or motherese) is high pitched, exaggerated in intonation, and simple in sentence structure. Child-directed speech may promote language development by increasing children's attention to adult language or by making the grammar of a language more salient. Adults may also help children develop a correct grammar by providing expansions of children's ungrammatical statements.

## Learning How to Communicate: The Development of Pragmatics

Pragmatics includes children's ability to express their intentions and achieve their goals by using language. It also includes children's ability to "say the right thing" in specific social situations.

## Preverbal Communication and Early Social Speech

Before infants learn to talk, they practice turn taking in exchanges of vocalizations with parents. By 9 months of age, infants communicate their intentions to others through gestures and vocalizations. During the preschool years, children gradually learn how to carry on a coherent conversation.

## Egocentrism, Politeness, and Code Switching in Childhood

Four-year-olds simplify their language when talking to younger children, showing that they are not completely egocentric. Understanding of techniques for varying the politeness of a request improves with age. So does understanding of the need to switch linguistic codes, for example, from Black English at home to standard English at school.

## Skills Children Need to Communicate Successfully

As children grow, their communication becomes more effective because their knowledge and vocabulary increase and they learn procedural rules for communication like the difference rule. Comprehension monitoring also improves with age.

## Explanations for Language Development

Although every human language is highly complex, all children around the world learn to speak their native language quickly and seemingly effortlessly. Three general explanations for this remarkable fact were offered during the 1950s, 1960s, and 1970s.

## Three Theoretical Perspectives on Language Development

B. F. Skinner suggested that children learn language through operant conditioning, just as they learn other behaviors. Noam Chomsky suggested that children have innate knowledge of a universal grammar, and language acquisition involves mapping a specific language onto that universal grammar. Jean Piaget argued that general cognitive development provides the foundation for language development.

## Evidence and Issues for Theories of Language Development

Some evidence about language development must be taken into account in any theory. For example, only human beings spontaneously learn and use language; language learning is not highly related to IQ; and children construct and modify rules about how to talk as they grow.

## LADs, LASSies, and Communication

Adults often support children's efforts to acquire language by using child-directed speech and by giving them feedback on their grammar. For all children, language is important in understanding others' emotions, communicating desires clearly, and being accepted as a competent, valued member of society.

# SUGGESTED READINGS

Berko Gleason, J. (Ed.). (1993). *The development of language* (3rd ed.). Columbus, OH: Merrill. This textbook includes chapters written by well-known researchers in the field of language development. The authors cover all the basic topics in the field. They also discuss such topics as writing, language change in adulthood, and language impairment.

Bialystok, E., & Hakuta, K. (1994). *In other words: The science and psychology of second-language acquisition.* New York: Basic Books. Although the focus of this book is on learning a second language, its coverage is far greater. The authors discuss the basic principles of first-language learning, the differences among languages, and the policy issues that arise in multilingual, multicultural societies. The book is written in a clear and engaging style.

Kessel, F. S. (Ed.). (1988). *The development of language and language researchers.* Hillsdale, NJ: Erlbaum. This book is a *festschrift,* a collection of essays written as a tribute to an esteemed scholar. In this case, the scholar is Roger Brown, a Harvard professor who trained the authors. The essays combine serious discussions of language development with both humorous and serious comments about graduate training in language development (or, "the development of language researchers").

Opie, I., & Opie, P. (1959). *The lore and language of schoolchildren.* New York: Oxford University Press. Iona and Peter Opie set themselves the delightful task of recording the language play and games of children. To accomplish this task, they traveled throughout England, Scotland, and Wales, observing or interviewing thousands of children. They summarize the vast array of language they recorded under headings such as "guile," "riddles," and "code of oral legislation." They also discuss the amazing continuity of children's language across generations and even centuries.

*C h a p t e r   E i g h t*

# Cognitive Development: Piaget, Vygotsky, and Their Followers

With Lucia A. French, University of Rochester

**Y**oung children's ideas about the world are often surprising. If asked whether a rabbit is alive, most kindergarten children say yes, just as you would. If asked whether a tree is alive, many kindergarten children say no. If asked whether a stone is alive, most kindergarten children say no, as you would, but they answer yes more often than adults do (Hatano et al., 1993).

Moreover, answers to these questions vary among children in different cultures. Children in Israel are less likely than those in the United States to say that a tree is alive. Children in Japan are more likely than those in the United States to say that a stone is alive and can feel warm or cold (Hatano et al., 1993).

Why do children have these inaccurate ideas about the concept of life? Why do their ideas become more accurate as they grow older? During the 1920s, Jean Piaget examined these questions in several classic studies. During a career that lasted for more than 60 years, Piaget did hundreds of studies of children's cognitive development. You will read in this chapter about some of his studies. You will also read about the descriptions and explanations of cognitive development that Piaget offered to account for his findings.

Along the way, you'll read about the work of other researchers who have followed Piaget. These researchers have sometimes found, as in the example of ideas about life, that children's thinking varies across cultures. In addition, later researchers have sometimes rejected Piaget's hypotheses about cognitive development—and you will learn why they have done so.

This chapter also includes a description of Vygotsky's theory of cognitive development. Like Piaget, Lev Vygotsky began his career in the early part of the twentieth century. Like Piaget, Vygotsky has had many followers. In recent years, acceptance of Piaget's ideas has decreased while acceptance of Vygotsky's ideas has increased. However, researchers today assume that each man's ideas were somewhat limited in scope and explanatory power. Furthermore, each was weak on points where the other was strong. Because the two theorists' ideas complement one another in this way, considering them in the same chapter makes sense.

The first section of this chapter focuses on Piagetian approaches to cognitive development. The second section focuses on Vygotsky's writings and the research of his followers. A final section includes a comparison of the two theories, with special emphasis on their differing assumptions about social relationships.

# PIAGET'S THEORIES

Jean Piaget wrote dozens of books and articles on the development of thinking and reasoning in infancy, childhood, and adolescence. Piaget examined children's understanding of many things, but especially their understanding of the physical world and of logical relations. As mentioned in chapter 1, Piaget was a *constructivist*, who believed that infants and children construct their knowledge of the world through their activity.

Piaget proposed that thought derives from actions. In infancy, actions are a form of thinking. According to Piaget, infants' actions depend on cognitive structures that become more complex as they grow older. As infants move into childhood, they become able to perform mental actions, actions not in the world but in the mind. As children move into adolescence, their mental actions become more abstract and less closely linked to physical actions. Thus, with increasing age, mental actions become more powerful tools for problem solving.

Piaget used many ingenious tasks to show the age changes in children's problem solving. Later researchers have been fascinated by these tasks and have tried to replicate Piaget's findings. Often, these attempts at replication have been successful. In addition, later researchers have created new tasks to test Piaget's hypotheses. When working on the new tasks, young children have often shown greater cognitive competence than Piaget assumed they had. The following sections include many examples of this progression in research.

The heading for this section refers to Piaget's *theories* because Piaget presented different sets of ideas about different aspects of cognitive development. The differences exist partly because Piaget changed his ideas somewhat during his long career. Piaget also emphasized different phenomena and processes of development when he wrote about children varying in age. Therefore, the following description of Piaget's work is divided into sections

All human beings explore their world by experimenting with objects. This infant is learning about the properties of objects by playing with pots that differ in size, weight, and materials. The adolescents are also learning about the properties of objects, but they do so more systematically than does an infant. In this chapter, we will examine the thinking and reasoning that underlie the experimenting and learning of infants, children, and adolescents.

| **TABLE 8.1** | *Piaget's Theories: General Features and Evaluations* | | |
|---|---|---|---|
| AGE RANGE (APPROX.) | STAGE OR CHARACTERISTICS | PIAGET'S DESCRIPTION OF FEATURES | EVALUATIONS BY LATER RESEARCHERS |
| Birth to 2 years | Sensorimotor intelligence | Beginning with reflexes, infants develop more complex and coordinated schemes. Infants gradually learn about the permanence of objects. | Piaget's stages of sensorimotor intelligence have been confirmed, but infants understand object permanence earlier than Piaget believed. |
| 2 to 6 years | Early work: animism, realism, and egocentrism | Young children think nonliving things are alive, dreams are physical events, and everyone sees things as they do. | Young children understand more about the physical and psychological worlds than Piaget believed, but their ideas differ qualitatively from adults. |
| | Later work: preoperational thought | Young children center on one dimension of objects, focus on states rather than transformations, and have trouble making relative judgments. | Young children can succeed on simplified versions of Piaget's tasks. Their performance is more affected by task variations than is older children's. |
| 7 to 11 years | Concrete-operational thought | Children succeed on conservation and other Piagetian tasks. Children are assumed to have logical operations that are interrelated and reversible. | Children's performance does not show the consistency that the idea of general stages implies. Piaget's conclusions about changes in children's logic are questioned. |
| 12+ years | Formal-operational thought | Adolescents are fully logical, can think about possibilities, and can engage in hypothetico-deductive reasoning. | Many researchers doubt that new forms of logic emerge in adolescence. Also, even adults often fail Piaget's formal-operational tasks. |

dealing with infancy, the preschool years, middle childhood, and adolescence. Each section includes a discussion of later researchers' evaluations of Piaget's ideas and research. For a preview of all the theories, see table 8.1.

## Infant Cognition and Sensorimotor Intelligence

During the 1920s and 1930s, Piaget (1936/1952) observed the behavior of his three children from their birth until they were about 2 years old. He assumed that their cognitive development would be apparent from their actions in response to sensations. He identified several stages of **sensorimotor intelligence** (where *sensorimotor* means "sensory and motor," or "sensation and action").

**sensorimotor intelligence**
*Piaget's label for the reasoning that is revealed, especially during infancy, in adaptive patterns of action (or motor skills) in response to sensations.*

| **TABLE 8.2** | *Piaget's Stages of Sensorimotor Intelligence* | |
|---|---|---|
| **STAGE (AND APPROXIMATE AGE RANGE)** | **DESCRIPTION** | **EXAMPLE** |
| 1 (birth–1 month) | Reflexes (the first schemes) | Sucking on the mother's breast |
| 2 (1–4 months) | The first acquired adaptations and the primary circular reaction | Thumb sucking |
| 3 (4–8 months) | Secondary circular reactions and procedures to make interesting sights last | Using leg kicks to make a crib mobile move |
| 4 (8–12 months) | The coordination of secondary schemes and their application to new situations | Pushing an obstacle away and then grabbing the toy behind it |
| 5 (12–18 months) | Tertiary circular reactions and the discovery of new means through active experimentation | Experimenting with dropping foods or other objects off a high-chair tray |
| 6 (above 18 months) | The invention of new means through mental combinations | Thinking of a way to get a watch chain out of a matchbox |

Piaget made his observations long ago, and only on his three children. It is a tribute to his genius that his outline of the development of sensorimotor intelligence has fared well over the years. Many investigators have successfully replicated his observations with larger samples (Harris, 1983). Other investigators have proposed different sequences of intellectual development during infancy (e.g., Fischer, 1987; McCall, Eichorn, & Hogarty, 1977). However, these alternative sequences are compatible in most respects with that defined by Piaget. Therefore, his description deserves careful study.

## The Six Stages of Sensorimotor Intelligence

Piaget defined six stages of sensorimotor intelligence between birth and 2 years of age (see table 8.2). *Stage 1* begins at birth and extends until roughly 1 month of age. The age ranges for this stage and for all later stages are approximate. Piaget assumed that some infants move through the stages faster than other infants, so some infants move to Stage 2 before 1 month of age, and others do so after that age. But according to Piaget, the stage sequence itself does not vary across infants. Only the infants' rate of development through the stages varies. When Piaget presented his cognitive stages for childhood and adolescence, he made the same assumption: Individual rates of development vary but the stage sequence does not. The research findings largely support this assumption (Weisz & Zigler, 1979).

Piaget (1936/1952) defined Stage 1 as that of reflexive activity. Reflexes are the first organized patterns of action. Piaget called such organized patterns **schemes.** A scheme is a cognitive structure that underlies consistent action patterns in certain situations or with certain objects.

One early scheme is the sucking reflex. When Piaget called this reflex a scheme, he was not trying to put his own label on a well-known phenomenon. Instead, he wanted to emphasize that reflexive behaviors are not fixed but are adapted through experience. Even reflexes illustrate one of the central principles in Piaget's theory, *adaptation*. As stated in chapter 1, adaptation depends on two cognitive functions, assimilation and accommodation. To see how these functions lead to changes in reflexive behaviors, consider the example of sucking.

A newborn's first sucks are often weak and inefficient. With practice, sucking becomes stronger and more efficient. Piaget described this change in terms of *assimilation*. As explained in chapter 1, Piaget defined assimilation as the integration of external elements into a cognitive structure. The sucking scheme is a cognitive structure for the young infant. When infants suck on the mother's nipple (an external element), they assimilate the nipple to the sucking scheme. Repeated assimilation, or practice in sucking, strengthens and consolidates the sucking scheme.

Infants also refine their sucking scheme during the first month. For example, they learn to suck differently on the mother's nipple and on a finger placed in their mouths. Piaget

**schemes**
*According to Piaget, the cognitive structures that underlie consistent action patterns in certain situations or with certain objects*

described this change in terms of *accommodation*, the modification of cognitive structures in response to external elements. The sucking scheme is gradually modified, or accommodated, to different objects. Through assimilation and accommodation, even reflexes become more intelligent actions—or more elaborated schemes—as infants grow older.

*Stage 2* (approximately 1 to 4 months of age) is the stage of "the first acquired adaptations and the primary circular reaction." A **circular reaction** is a process that leads to the preservation of behavior patterns. An infant may perform a certain action by chance. When the action leads to pleasing results, the infant tries to repeat it. This repetition sets up a circular reaction that helps the infant learn a new behavior pattern. In Piaget's terms, the repetition is a form of assimilation that leads to the formation of a new scheme.

At Stage 2, infants are limited to circular reactions that have no other goal than the action itself. For many infants, thumb sucking is one of the first acquired adaptations. By chance, infants get their thumbs into their mouths. Sucking the thumb is pleasing, so infants try to repeat this action. When they can do so consistently, they have acquired a new scheme that coordinates two separate schemes of moving the hand to the mouth and sucking. This coordination requires more than assimilation through repetition of the action. It also calls for the accommodation of each scheme, hand moving and sucking, to link with the other scheme. Thumb sucking is defined as a **primary circular reaction** because sucking describes both the infant's activity and the infant's goal.

*Stage 3* (approximately 4 to 8 months of age) is defined by "secondary circular reactions and procedures designed to make interesting sights last." The two parts of Piaget's label are connected. Stage 3 infants start to notice the effects of their actions on the world. They acquire action patterns, or form schemes, that produce interesting effects. The formation of these schemes reflects a **secondary circular reaction** because the schemes that are coordinated are more complex than at Stage 2. In particular, infants begin to distinguish between an action and its goal.

Piaget (1936/1952) described one secondary circular reaction that involved his daughter Lucienne. Lucienne was in her bassinet looking at some cloth dolls that hung from the hood of the bassinet. Then she shook the bassinet by kicking her legs. The dolls began to swing from the hood. Lucienne smiled as she looked at the dolls and kept kicking.

Piaget did not immediately assume that Lucienne had acquired a secondary circular reaction. He thought she might just be kicking because she was excited or happy. To settle the question, Piaget placed the dolls on the hood of the bassinet the next day. Lucienne shook her legs again, this time looking intently at the dolls without smiling. A week later, Lucienne started kicking her legs as soon as Piaget hung the dolls on the bassinet. She kicked with precise, rhythmic movements, as if she were studying how the dolls moved. Piaget was then convinced that her kicking was part of a secondary circular reaction, a procedure to make interesting sights last.

*Stage 4* (approximately 8 to 12 months of age) involves "the coordination of secondary schemes and their application to new situations." The "secondary" in the label refers to the secondary circular reactions that emerge at Stage 3. At Stage 4, these secondary schemes can be coordinated in means-ends relationships. One scheme serves as the means by arranging a situation that allows the infant to execute the second scheme.

Piaget gave many examples of Stage 4 coordination. Sometimes his infants pushed away obstacles that prevented them from grasping attractive toys. That is, the scheme of pushing away was coordinated with the scheme of grasping as *means* to *end*. His infants also learned to drop a toy they were holding in one hand to grab a more attractive toy he offered them. (Before this stage, the infants seemed puzzled by this situation, as if they couldn't figure out how to grab another toy when their hands were already full.) In short, the scheme of dropping was coordinated with that of grasping. The coordination of these schemes allowed the infants to solve problems that they faced. The use of new combinations to solve practical problems illustrates the "application to new situations" in Piaget's label for Stage 4.

Piaget also took the coordination among secondary schemes as the criterion for fully intentional behavior. When infants do one thing (like drop a toy) in order to do another (like grasp an object), they clearly differentiate between means and ends. This differentiation shows that they had the end (or goal) in mind before they began the sequence of actions. Therefore, they must have known what they were trying to do or must have acted intentionally.

**circular reaction**
*In Piaget's theory, a process that leads to the preservation (or learning) of behavior patterns through the repetition of these patterns and the assimilation that repetition promotes.*

**primary circular reaction**
*The earliest type of circular reaction in infancy, in which an infant's activity is equivalent to the infant's goal.*

**secondary circular reaction**
*According to Piaget, a type of circular reaction in which infants' actions (e.g., kicking their legs) can be distinguished from their goal (e.g., making toys on a crib mobile shake).*

*Stage 5* (12 to 18 months of age) is the stage of "tertiary circular reactions and the discovery of new means through active experimentation." You may think it strange to describe 1-year-olds as active experimenters, but they often do things just to see what will happen. They don't repeat an action over and over, looking for the same effect, as a Stage 3 infant would. They vary the action each time. Piaget described such repetition with variation as a **tertiary circular reaction.**

Did you ever watch a 1-year-old who was eating lunch while sitting in a high chair? Where did the lunch often end up? That's right—on the floor. Sometimes infants don't drop or spill food accidentally. They engage in Stage 5 experimentation. Try to imagine what infants might be saying to themselves during such an episode (if infants were able to mentally say things to themselves):

"Oh, here's a spoonful of applesauce. What would happen if I put the spoon over the edge of the high chair and turned it upside down?"
Splat!
"Now I'll try a piece of bread."
Flop!
"Now I'll throw down this cup of milk as hard as I can."
Bonk! Splash! (Let's hope the cup was plastic.)

Through their experimentation, 1-year-olds learn new ways to use schemes to reach goals. An infant girl may want a toy that is too far away to reach. By experimenting, she realizes that she can move the toy by pulling a string attached to it. Then she realizes that she can bring the toy within reach by pulling the string toward herself. This example illustrates the second part of Piaget's definition, learning new ways to solve problems by experimenting.

*Stage 6*, which begins at about 18 months of age, marks the end point of sensorimotor development and the start of a new period in cognitive development. Piaget defined Stage 6 as "the invention of new means through mental combinations." The key word in this definition is "mental." At Stage 6, toddlers can carry out actions mentally, thinking about what they might do and what might happen. The experimentation that the Stage 5 infant shows in action can be done by the Stage 6 infant in thought. In Piaget's terms, Stage 6 is the beginning of representational intelligence, because mental representation of objects and events first becomes possible at this stage. Representation is important not only for the development of intelligent action but also for symbolic play and language development.

Piaget's most dramatic example of Stage 6 action involved his daughter Lucienne. She was trying to get his watch chain out of a matchbox. The box was almost closed, so she couldn't directly grab the chain and pull it out. After pausing a few moments, she looked at the small opening in the box and then opened and shut her mouth several times. Immediately afterward, she put her finger into the matchbox and pulled its opening wider—just as she had opened her mouth wider.

In other words, Lucienne showed by her mouth movements that she was thinking about how to get the chain out of the box. She figured out what to do through mental combinations. She anticipated, in thought, how she would act.

Although the development of mental representation leads to a new cognitive stage with new possibilities, sensorimotor intelligence remains important throughout life. Suppose you want to get a book that fell behind the couch. You rely on sensorimotor intelligence when you use a broom handle to move the book beyond the end of the couch. You also rely on sensorimotor intelligence when you try to improve your golf swing, your score on a fast-action video game, or your handwriting. These intelligent actions do not represent the highest forms of cognition, but they are crucial to humans' adaptation to the world.

## The Concept of the Permanent Object

Along with his interest in infants' actions, Piaget (1937/1954) wanted to understand what infants know about their world. Piaget assumed that newborns have no sense of a reality outside themselves. Therefore, newborns believe that objects exist only when they themselves are paying attention to them. When the newborns stop paying attention, the objects

cease to exist. Piaget summarized this assumption about newborns' thinking by saying that they do not have a concept of the permanence of objects. In other words, newborns lack **object permanence.**

Piaget (1937/1954) described six stages in the development of object permanence that correspond to his six stages of intelligent action. Piaget concluded that the adult concept of permanent objects did not emerge until Stage 6, at around 18 months of age. This provocative claim has been the focus of much research. Two points in Piaget's six-stage sequence have received the greatest attention.

*Understanding of Objects' Continued Existence*    The first point concerns the earliest age (or stage) at which infants have any concept of objects as permanent. Piaget found that infants under 9 months of age rarely look for objects that move outside their field of vision. These young infants rarely search for objects that are out of sight. Piaget concluded that before 9 months, or his Stage 4, infants believe objects cease to exist when they go out of sight. That is, Piaget took infants' lack of visual search for hidden objects as proof that they believed objects have no permanent existence.

Later researchers have drawn different conclusions about infants' object concepts because they have set up different experimental situations and observed other kinds of behavior than Piaget did. Renee Baillargeon (1987, 1991, 1994; Baillargeon, Spelke, & Wasserman, 1985) devised an ingenious method for examining the object concepts of 3- and 4-month-old infants. She placed the infants in front of a silver screen about 1-foot square. The screen could rotate through 180 degrees, from a position flat against the floor with its top edge toward the infant to a position flat against the floor with its top edge away from the infant (see figure 8.1). After the infants saw the screen rotate back and forth a few times, Baillargeon placed a wooden box with a painted clown face on it in the path of the screen's rotation.

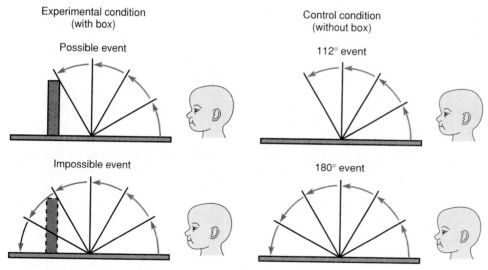

## FIGURE 8.1

In Baillargeon's (1987) studies of object permanence, 3- and 4-month-olds saw the events portrayed schematically here. Infants in the experimental condition sometimes saw a silver screen rotate backward until it apparently hit the top of a box behind it (possible event). On other trials, the infants saw the screen rotate backward a full 180 degrees, as if the box behind it had disappeared (impossible event). Infants in a control condition saw the screen rotate backward either 112 degrees of 180 degrees but were not shown a box behind the screen. Infants in the experimental condition looked longer at the impossible event, which suggests that they were surprised that the box—a permanent object—did not stop the movement of the screen. (Adapted from Baillargeon, 1987.)

On some trials, the infants then saw a possible event: The screen rotated backward 112 degrees, until it apparently was stopped by hitting the box. On other trials, the infant saw an (apparently) impossible event: The screen rotated backward 180 degrees, through the space that should have been occupied by the box. (The box seemed to disappear because it was on a platform that was lowered while the screen was moving. Sometimes psychologists borrow their experimental techniques from magicians!)

As figure 8.1 shows, the experiment also included a control condition. Infants in the control condition saw some trials like the possible event, in which the screen rotated backward 112 degrees and then rotated forward again. They saw other trials in which the screen rotated a full 180 degrees. But these infants never saw any trials in which the box was placed in the path of the screen.

If you saw the impossible event, you would be surprised and would try to figure out what happened. You know the box behind the screen should have stopped the screen's rotation. That is, you know that boxes, like other objects, are permanent (relatively speaking) and do not cease to exist just because they are hidden from view.

The 4-month-olds in this experiment seemed to share your concept of objects as permanent. In the experimental condition, they looked longer at the impossible event than at the possible event. In the control condition, they looked equally at the two events. Some 3-month-olds in the experimental condition also looked longer at the impossible event than the possible event. The 3-month-olds who were alert rather than fussy during the experiment were most likely to do so. In short, 3- and 4-month-olds who paid attention to the trials acted as if they were surprised by the impossible event.

The infants' behavior strongly suggests that they had a concept of object permanence. Their pattern of looking implies that they believe objects continue to exist when they are no longer in sight. Some theorists argue that even newborns understand that objects exist independently and continuously. That is, knowledge that objects exist continuously may be part of the innate cognitive capacities of humans (Spelke, 1994; Spelke et al., 1992).

Other researchers, including Baillargeon (1994), assume that infants are born not with innate knowledge about objects but with innate mechanisms that guide their early learning about objects. These mechanisms lead quickly, as infants experience the world, to judgments about many properties of objects, including their permanence.

Experiments by Baillargeon (1994) and her coworkers have shown that infants less than 4 months old know many things about objects. For example, they know that objects can't hang in space without support, that objects cannot move through other objects, and that an object is likely to move if hit by another object. However, 4-month-olds do not judge the properties of objects as precisely as older infants do.

For one experiment, infants saw an "impossible event" like that in figure 8.1, but the screen rotated backward 157 degrees, or only partway into the space where the box should have been. Four-month-olds seemed not to consider this new event as puzzling, but 6½-month-olds did. That is, infants more than 6 months old not only knew that the screen couldn't squash the box; they also had figured out at which point the rotating screen should have touched the box and stopped. Experiments on other types of events also show that infants' judgments about how objects affect one another become more accurate with increasing age.

In summary, researchers are not yet certain when infants first understand that objects exist even when the infants cannot see them. However, understanding of object permanence clearly exists several months earlier than Piaget believed. Whether this understanding is innate or develops in the first months of life is a controversial question. Experiments have shown that infants' knowledge about objects increases steadily as they grow older.

***The A-not-B Error***  The second controversy regarding Piaget's claims about object permanence concerns his Stage 4. Infants in Stage 4 will search for objects hidden behind a screen or under a cover. Yet they make a curious error when the search task is more complex. Figure 8.2 illustrates a more complex search task. The experimenter shows an attractive toy to an infant, and then hides the toy under a cloth at location A. The infant sees the object being hidden: The experimenter puts the toy under the cloth while the infant is watching.

## FIGURE 8.2

The experimental arrangements for the Stage 4 object-permanence task. Most 9-month-olds can find a set of keys hidden at location A. But if the keys are hidden a second time at location B, infants will often look for them at A rather than at B, thus committing the *A-not-B* error.

After a brief delay, the experimenter lets the infant search for the toy. Most 9-month-olds, but not younger infants, succeed in finding the toy under the cloth.

Then the task changes. The experimenter shows the infant the toy again but this time hides it under the cloth at location B. After a brief delay, the experimenter again lets the infant search for the toy. Most 9-month-olds do not search for the toy at B, where they just saw it hidden. Instead, they search at A, where they found the toy on the first trial. That is, they commit the *A-not-B* error.

Why would anyone, even a 9-month-old, not look for a toy where he or she just saw it hidden? Piaget (1937/1954) argued that infants initially link the scheme for finding an object with location A. The scheme remains linked to A even after the toy is hidden at B. So, when the toy is hidden, the infant executes the "finding scheme"—and looks for the object at A.

According to Piaget, the A-not-B error persists until the infant's scheme for finding hidden objects becomes more flexible, in Stage 5. The increase in flexibility results from a growing differentiation between the toy, or any permanent object, and the infant's actions on the toy. It therefore reflects another step toward a concept of objects as existing permanently and independent of a person's actions.

Further research on the A-not-B error has revealed some problems with Piaget's explanation (Wellman, Cross, & Bartsch, 1986). First, the error is uncommon, even among 9-month-olds, if they can search for the toy immediately after they see it hidden at B. Nine-month-olds typically make the error only if the experimenter imposes a delay of a few seconds between hiding and searching (Diamond, 1985). If the delay between hiding and searching is 10 seconds or more, even 12-month-olds often make the error. Piaget's theory does not explain why the timing of infants' search has such a powerful effect.

Second, Piaget's theory implies that the A-not-B error should be more likely when an infant's finding scheme links the toy more strongly to location A. You might expect this link to be stronger if infants have found the toy at location A several times, but research has not confirmed this expectation (Wellman et al., 1986). After finding the toy at A just once, infants search at A on B trials just as often as after finding it at A multiple times. Repeated A trials do not increase the likelihood of the A-not-B error.

Alternative explanations for the A-not-B error exist. One theory is that infants develop two procedures for finding objects (Wellman et al., 1986). With one procedure, infants search for the object where they last saw it and so do not make the error. With the other procedure, infants infer the object's current location from where they have found it before and so make the error. Another theory suggests that infants can base a search for an object either on a visual memory for the object's location or on associations in long-term memory between the object and its (various) locations (Harris, 1986). If infants do the latter, they commit the A-not-B error. Still a third theory is that infants accurately remember the location of objects, but they

have trouble coordinating information in memory with plans for action (Baillargeon & Graber, 1988). Each theory explains some evidence on the A-not-B error, but none fully explains the two findings troublesome for Piaget's theory: the effect of the delay between hiding and searching and the lack of effect of multiple trials in which infants find the object at location A.

The best explanation may involve two processes: memory and inhibition (Diamond, Cruttenden, & Neiderman, 1994). Infants do need to remember where the object was last hidden. This type of memory is weak in young infants and improves with brain development. In addition, infants need to inhibit their tendency to search for the toy where they have successfully found it before. The tendency to repeat actions that have been reinforced is a powerful one, and that tendency leads to searches at A. Only infants who remember the object's correct location and inhibit their tendency to repeat a reinforced action will avoid committing the A-not-B error.

Taken together, the many studies of the A-not-B error suggest that this error provides little information about infants' concepts of objects. Instead, the error shows how prior reinforcement, memory, and the ability to inhibit actions jointly affect infants' performance on what is, for them, a complex task.

## Other Aspects of Infant Cognition

Piaget (1937/1954) also proposed a sequence of developmental stages in infants' understanding of space, time, and causality. In addition, he described the developments in infants' imaginative play and their ability to imitate other people (Piaget, 1945/1962). Later researchers have focused on two questions about these developments.

The first question is whether young infants are as cognitively immature as Piaget assumed. Many researchers now assume that Piaget underestimated infants' competence in these other areas, just as he underestimated infants' knowledge of object permanence (Flavell et al., 1993). In chapter 9, for example, you will see that infants can imitate other people's actions far earlier than Piaget believed.

The second question that many researchers have asked is whether infants' performance is consistent across tasks, as the concept of a cognitive stage implies. For example, do infants who are scored at Stage 4 on their intelligent action also score at Stage 4 on their object concepts, play, and imitation?

**structured whole**
*Piaget's term for the organization of thinking and reasoning (which, in French, is structure d'ensemble). Often assumed to mean that a child's reasoning on all tasks should reflect the same stage of cognitive development.*

Remember that organization is, along with adaptation, a key principle in Piaget's theory. Piaget assumed that reasoning is organized even in infancy. He used the term *structure d'ensemble,* or **structured whole,** to express this assumption about the integration among the various facets of infants' reasoning.

Most researchers have interpreted the hypothesis of a structured whole as implying that an infant's responses to all tasks should reflect the same stage of sensorimotor intelligence (Flavell et al., 1993). Some researchers suggest that Piaget did not intend his hypothesis to be interpreted this way (Chapman, 1988), but most researchers assume that a theory of general stages makes little sense unless children's performance is consistent across tasks (Flavell, 1992; Kohlberg, 1976; Levin, 1986).

Researchers who have looked directly for the kind of consistency implied by the structured-whole assumption have found little (Harris, 1983). Infants who seem to be at a particular stage on one aspect of sensorimotor intelligence often seem to be at different stages on other aspects. This evidence suggests that the links between different aspects of infant cognition are weak. Apparently, each aspect of infant cognition develops fairly independently. Therefore, each aspect should be described separately. One general model, like Piaget's stage theory, does not fully explain all aspects of cognitive development in infancy.

Remember, however, that researchers still accept one aspect of Piaget's theory about infant cognition. As noted earlier, his stages of sensorimotor intelligence accurately describe the age changes in infants' actions. Moreover, researchers recognize the importance of Piaget's findings, for example, about the A-not-B error, even when they challenge his explanations of those findings.

# Preschool Children's Ideas About the World

Before Piaget started observing his infant son and daughters, he did years of research on thinking and reasoning in early childhood. In these studies, done during the 1920s, Piaget made his first attempts to describe how children think about the physical world and about thought itself. Piaget concluded that children's reasoning is qualitatively different from that of adults.

Many later researchers have criticized Piaget's methods and disputed his conclusions. These researchers have expressed doubts that young children's thinking is as different from that of adults as Piaget claimed. They have instead assumed that young children differ from adults mainly because these children have limited knowledge of the physical world and only partial insight into their own thinking.

The debate between Piaget and the researchers who followed him can be illustrated by examining three features of young children's thinking. Piaget labeled all three as "isms": *animism, realism,* and *egocentrism.* You will see that the theoretical disputes about these features of young children's thinking have been resolved in an intriguing way. Most researchers now agree that important differences exist between young children's thinking and adults' thinking, as Piaget claimed. The differences, however, are rarely as dramatic as Piaget suggested. Also, Piaget's description of the differences seems less accurate than alternative descriptions.

## Children's Animism, or What's Alive?

| Experimenter's Question | 8-Year-Old's Answer |
|---|---|
| Are you alive? | Yes, because I'm not dead. |
| Is a fly alive? | Yes, because it's not dead. |
| Is the sun alive? | Yes, because it makes daytime. |
| Is a candle alive? | Yes, because you can light it. |
| Is the wind alive? | Yes, because it makes it cold. |
| Are clouds alive? | Yes, because they make it rain. |

For one study, Piaget asked children which things are and are not alive. The preceding questions and answers are from one of these interviews (Piaget, 1929, p. 197). Piaget used such interviews as evidence that young children confuse the physical world with the psychological world. One indication of this confusion is the phenomenon of **animism.** Animism, for Piaget, meant the tendency to assume that nonliving (or inanimate) objects such as the sun or the wind have the properties of living things. In particular, these objects have motives, feelings, and intentions that affect their behavior.

**animism**
*According to Piaget, the tendency of young children to assume that nonliving (or inanimate) objects like the sun or the wind have the properties of living things (e.g., thoughts, motives, and feelings).*

Many researchers have tried to replicate Piaget's studies of children's animism. For one study, children were asked questions like those mentioned at the beginning of this chapter (Hatano et al., 1993). In particular, they were asked whether rabbits, trees, and stones were alive. They were also asked if each thing had various attributes of living things. For example, they were asked whether each one could feel cold or pain, and whether each one grows and dies.

The children in the study were in kindergarten, second grade, or fourth grade. They lived in the United States, Israel, or Japan. Piaget did not assume that children's ideas about life vary across cultures. As mentioned in chapter 1, Piaget assumed that the most important aspects of cognitive development are cultural universals. In this case, however, the evidence suggests otherwise.

Figure 8.3 shows how the kindergarten children answered the central questions in the study: Are animals (e.g., a rabbit), plants (e.g., a tree), and inanimate objects (e.g., a stone) alive? In response to these questions, almost all kindergartners in all three countries said that animals were alive. Only a few kindergartners in any country said that inanimate objects were alive. Although the differences in judgments about animals and inanimate objects were somewhat greater for older children, most kindergartners understood the distinction between living and nonliving things. Moreover, this distinction is understood even by preschool children (Bullock, 1985; Carey, 1985; Richards & Siegler, 1984).

FIGURE 8.3

Almost all kindergarten children say that animals like a rabbit are alive. Few children say that inanimate objects like a stone are alive. Kindergarten children disagree about whether plants are alive. Also, the judgments of children in the United States, Israel, and Japan sometimes differ because of differences in their language and culture.

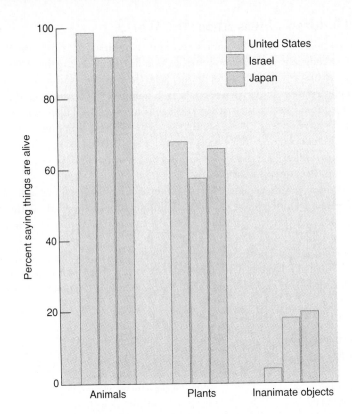

By contrast, only about 60 percent of the kindergarten children said that plants were alive. These judgments imply that preschoolers have a concept of living things, or a theory of biology, that is qualitatively different from that of adults (Carey, 1985; Hatano & Inagaki, 1994). In particular, preschoolers have little understanding of the biological processes that define living things.

For a preschooler, something is alive if it acts, moves, or shows other types of behavior. Because plants and trees don't move, preschoolers don't think of them as alive. For an adult, however, living things are biological organisms. All living things eat, grow, and reproduce; nonliving things do not. During the elementary school years, concepts of life are restructured. As children begin to understand biological processes and develop a biological theory, they move toward the adult concept of living things.

Figure 8.3 also shows small but intriguing differences among the children in the three countries. The Israeli children were least likely to say that a plant is alive. The responses of Israeli fourth graders are not shown in the figure, but they denied that plants were alive about as often as kindergartners did. In Hebrew, the word for *life* is closely related to the word for *animal* but unrelated to the word for *plant*. Also, some verses in the Bible refer to animals as living things but not to plants. Apparently, the influences of language and religion work together to delay Israeli children's recognition that plants are living, biological organisms.

Figure 8.3 also shows that Japanese children were most likely to say that inanimate objects such as a stone were alive. Even at fourth grade (not shown in the figure), a few Japanese children, but no U.S. or Israeli children, said that stones or other inanimate objects were alive. Again, cultural and religious traditions may explain these judgments. In Buddhism, even a tree may be assumed to have a mind. In Japanese culture, some inanimate objects such as a mountain are viewed as having feelings or other attributes of living things.

Of course, children who go to school are eventually taught about the actual attributes of living and nonliving things. This teaching leads to the replacement of their incorrect biological theories with scientific theories. Worth remembering, however, is that even

preschool children do not show the complete animism that Piaget described. In addition, exactly how young children think about life depends not only on their cognitive level but also on their language and culture.

## What's Real, and What's a Figment of Your Imagination?

| Experimenter's Question | 7-Year-Old's Answer |
|---|---|
| Where is the dream when you are dreaming? | Against the wall. |
| Should I see them if I was there? | Yes. |
| Where do they come from? | From outside. |
| What did you last dream of? | A man being run over. |
| Was he in front of you when you dreamed or inside you? | In front of me. |
| Where? | Under my window. |
| Should I have seen him if I was there? | Yes. |

Another confusion in preschoolers' thought, according to Piaget, is an inability to distinguish reality from imagination. This confusion is most striking when children are asked about their dreams. In the preceding exchange of questions and answers (Piaget, 1929, pp. 94–95), the 7-year-old said that his dreams are outside himself ("against the wall"). He also said his dream could be seen by another person in the room. According to Piaget, these answers illustrate young children's **realism.**

Piaget defined children as realists if they attribute the properties of physical objects to mental phenomena such as dreams. Such a child might say that things seen in a dream are different from real things, but the difference is not that between mental and physical things. The child believes things in a dream are as external and objective as things seen on a movie screen. Those things are outside the self, outside the mind.

When later researchers asked children the same kinds of questions as Piaget asked, they got the same kinds of answers (e.g., Broughton, 1978). Children did seem to confuse mental phenomena like dreams with real, physical objects. However, when researchers asked different questions, questions that may be less misleading, the evidence for realism in young children's thinking was much weaker.

The 3- to 5-year-olds in one study were asked about dreams and about three other mental phenomena: thinking, remembering, and pretending (Wellman & Estes, 1986). The children heard brief stories about two boys. One boy was dreaming of something (or thinking, or remembering, or pretending). For example, the boy was dreaming of a cookie because he was hungry. The other boy had a cookie that his mother had given him.

Then the experimenter asked the 3- to 5-year-olds which of the two boys could (a) see the cookie, (b) *not* touch the cookie, (c) eat the cookie, (d) let a friend eat the cookie, and (e) save the cookie to eat the next day. Children who understand the distinction between reality and imagination should choose the boy dreaming of the cookie for question (b). They should choose the boy who actually had the cookie for all the other questions.

Five-year-olds answered 92 percent of these questions correctly. Even 3-year-olds answered 72 percent of the questions correctly. No child consistently said that the boy dreaming of the cookie could see the cookie, eat the cookie, and so on. That is, no child said that dreams or other mental phenomena were real, external events. Younger children made more errors, but these errors were not systematic: They simply reflected preschoolers' tendency to respond more randomly than older children. These data strongly suggest that children understand the difference between reality and imagination by 3 years of age.

Suppose you want to know even more about young children's understanding of mental phenomena. For example, you might wonder what ideas they have about their own thoughts, their own minds? Adults have theories about their mental life, theories of how the mind operates. Preschoolers' ideas about dreams and other mental phenomena show that they have some notion of how the mind works (Flavell, 1988; Wellman, 1988; Wellman & Gelman, 1992). However, their notions differ from those of older children and adults.

**realism**
*According to Piaget, the tendency of young children to attribute the properties of physical objects to mental phenomena like dreams (e.g., they are visible to other people).*

FIGURE 8.4

An outline of Piaget and Inhelder's (1956) three-mountains task. Suppose you were sitting in chair number 1. How do you think the mountains would look to a person sitting in chair number 3? When young children were asked this question, they usually chose a picture that showed how the mountains looked to them, not how the mountains would look from the other person's position. In other words, they responded egocentrically.

Ask preschool or kindergarten children what kinds of things you need your mind to do (Johnson & Wellman, 1982). They will say you need your mind to think, dream, remember, and read. They will *not* say you need your mind to walk, grab something, or cough. Unlike older children and adults, they do not realize that our minds control walking, reaching, and coughing as well as purely mental acts.

More generally, young children correctly think of the mind as the location for thoughts, dreams, and other mental phenomena. They also recognize that the mind creates these phenomena. Older children understand, in addition, that the mind is the human information processor. The mind interprets input from the senses and directs all bodily functions. You see again that older children are not simply more knowledgeable than younger children. Older children have a qualitatively different view of mental life.

## What Do You See, and What Do I See?

Figure 8.4 shows a model of three mountains placed on a tabletop. A chair is on each of the table's four sides. Imagine that you are sitting in chair number 1. Now imagine that another person is sitting in chair number 3. If you saw photographs of the tabletop taken by people sitting in each of the four chairs, could you pick the photograph taken in chair 3?

Piaget and Barbël Inhelder (1956) used the three-mountains task to examine the *egocentrism* of young children. You first read about the concept of egocentrism in chapter 7. As you recall, Piaget (1926/1971) believed that young children cannot appreciate that other people may view things differently than they do. Therefore, according to Piaget, young children cannot communicate effectively with other people whose viewpoints differ from their own. But later researchers showed that even preschool children try to adjust their communication to fit the perspective of their listeners. Thus, preschoolers are not as egocentric as Piaget believed.

With the three-mountains task, Piaget and Inhelder tried to assess egocentrism in visual perspective taking rather than in communication. In their studies, most children under 7 or 8 years of age could not judge how the mountains would look to a person whose perspective differed from theirs. Moreover, young children's errors were systematic. If they were sitting at location 1 in figure 8.4, they usually said that people at any other location would see

mountains that looked like the mountains looked to them. Such a response certainly *seems* like evidence of egocentrism.

However, later researchers pointed out that the three-mountains task requires skills other than perspective taking. Children cannot succeed on the task simply by knowing that people sitting in different chairs would see the mountains differently. Children also need to create, in their minds, an accurate representation of the scene from each person's perspective. Next, they need to scan the available pictures and compare them to this mental representation. Even children who know that people in different chairs would see the scene differently might not be able to figure out exactly how it would look to each of them (Flavell, 1985).

Researchers tried to simplify the three-mountains task to distinguish the problem of egocentrism from the problem of accurately representing different perspectives. Studies with the simplified tasks suggested that Piaget exaggerated young children's difficulties in taking the visual perspective of another person (Borke, 1975; Donaldson, 1978). Still, the later studies confirmed that important developments occur in children's understanding of visual perspectives.

John Flavell (1978, 1985, 1988) provided evidence for two levels of knowledge about perspectives. At Level 1, children understand that another person may not see the same object that they currently see. In other words, what you see may not be what I see. Figure 8.5 shows a card with a dog's picture on one side and a cat's picture on the other. To test

A Level 1 perspective-taking task

What do I see? (dog)

What do you see? (cat)

A Level 2 perspective-taking task

Do I see the turtle right side up or upside down? (upside down)

Do you see the turtle right side up or upside down? (right side up)

FIGURE 8.5
What do you see and what do I see? Even 3-year-olds can give the right answer to such questions about a Level 1 task. They say that they see a dog and that the adult sees a cat. But 3-year-olds have trouble answering the following questions about a Level 2 task: "Do you see the turtle right side up or upside down? Do I see the turtle right side up or upside down?" Three-year-olds have trouble realizing that the same object may look different to people who have different perspectives on it.

Level 1 perspective taking, the card is placed between the child and the experimenter. The experimenter asks, "What do you see?" and "What do I see?"

Most 2- and 3-year-olds correctly answer that they see a cat and the experimenter sees a dog. That is, they demonstrate Level 1 knowledge of differences in perspectives. When nonverbal tasks are used, even children under 2 years of age seem to realize that other people do not always see what they see (Lempers, Flavell, & Flavell, 1977).

At Level 2, children understand that people may have different views of the same object. That is, *what* you see may be what I see, but it may look different to me than it does to you. Figure 8.5 also shows a simple Level 2 task involving a picture of a turtle. The picture is placed flat between the child and the experimenter in side view. The child then sees the turtle on its feet, or right side up; the experimenter sees the turtle on its back, or upside down.

Children are asked how they see the turtle, right side up or upside down, and how the experimenter sees the turtle. Most children above 4 years of age answer these questions correctly. Most 3-year-olds answer them incorrectly. Apparently, an understanding that two people can have different perspectives on the same object develops between 3 and 4 years of age.

Three-year-olds' difficulty with Level 2 tasks is one indication of a more general problem with the **appearance-reality distinction.** Suppose you see a rock that has been shaped and painted so that it looks very much like an egg. You hold the rock, and so know it's really a rock rather than an egg. Then I ask you two questions: "What does this look like right now?" and "What is it really?" You say it *looks* like an egg but *really* is a rock. You distinguish, then, between its appearance and reality (Flavell, 1988; Flavell, Green, & Flavell, 1986).

Few 3-year-olds make this distinction. Most give the same answer to both questions about the rock. They may say that the object looks like an egg and is an egg or that it looks like a rock and is a rock. Either way, they fail to acknowledge that objects may look different from what they are.

Children's answers to appearance-reality questions are related to their answers on Level 2 perspective-taking tasks (Flavell et al., 1986). Most children who know that appearances may differ from reality also know that an object may look different from different perspectives. The relation between children's answers on the two types of tasks suggests that they both assess the same developmental change.

Flavell (1988) suggested that this developmental change involves children's **theory of mind.** By 2 or 3 years of age, children understand that the mind makes connections between themselves and the world. They see something, or make a visual connection with it, by looking at it. They hear something, or make an auditory connection with it, by listening to it. These young children also realize that their cognitive connections may not be the same as those of other people, so what you see may not be what I see (Level 1 perspective taking). But such young children think all cognitive connections are direct, linking them with objects as they really are. Children at this level of understanding cannot appreciate that objects may be, in reality, different than they appear.

At about 4 years of age, children begin to realize that humans' cognitive connections to the world are not direct. Instead, humans form mental representations that serve as mediators between objects themselves and the experience of objects. Once children find out that experiences are mediated by mental representations, they also assume that there can be multiple representations of a single object. Two people may represent an object differently. It may look one way to you and another way to me (Level 2 perspective taking).

Also, a person may form different representations of an object at different times. Thus, the object may sometimes appear to be different from what it really is. The emergence of a representational theory of mind may have wide-ranging effects on children's social understanding (Flavell, 1988). Chapter 13 examines other implications of children's developing theories of mind.

## Logical Reasoning in Middle Childhood

During the late 1930s and the 1940s, Piaget greatly revised his theory of cognitive development during childhood and adolescence. He no longer focused on the three "isms" of early childhood—animism, realism, and egocentrism. Instead, he formulated the theory of stages

**appearance-reality distinction**
*The ability to distinguish between the way something looks (e.g., like an egg) and what it actually is (e.g., a rock).*

**theory of mind**
*Ideas about mental states like thoughts, beliefs, or dreams, and about the relations among these mental states.*

of logical reasoning for which he is most famous. He argued that each stage is defined by a different kind of logic, different rules for drawing conclusions from evidence and observation.

Piaget used the revised theory to account for an astonishing number of new discoveries about young children's thinking. He made these discoveries when he examined children's responses to several unusual tasks.

## Conservation and Other Piagetian Tasks

Look at the two rows of pennies in the column labeled "Initial state" in figure 8.6. If you were asked whether each row has the same number of pennies, you would say yes. Then suppose that an experimenter stretched out the top row of pennies as you watched. The experimenter also pushed together the pennies in the bottom row. Now the rows look like those in the column labeled "Final state" in figure 8.6. You are asked again: Does each row have the

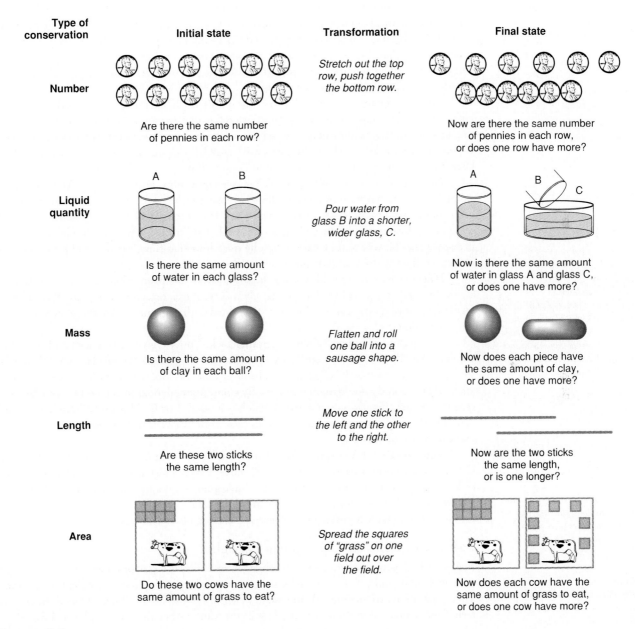

### FIGURE 8.6
Some of Piaget's conservation tasks. For each task, children must realize that some property (e.g., quantity or area) is conserved or is not changed by the experimenter's transformation.

same number of pennies, or does one row have more? Of course, you say the two rows have the same number. If asked why, you say something like "Because no pennies were added or taken away. They were just moved around."

Piaget discovered that preschool children do not give that simple, commonsense answer. They usually say that the longer row has more "because it's longer." Sometimes they say that the shorter row has more "because they're all packed together." Either way, they don't believe that the number of pennies in the two rows remains the same after the rows are moved. In Piaget's terms, preschool children fail to *conserve* number. More specifically, they do not believe that number remains constant when the spatial arrangement of objects changes.

Preschool children also fail other **conservation tasks,** other tasks that assess children's understanding that some transformations leave important properties of objects unchanged. Figure 8.6 shows five types of conservation that Piaget explored: number, liquid quantity, continuous quantity (or mass), length, and area.

The procedures for all these tasks are similar. To begin (the "initial state"), children are shown two identical objects or arrays and asked to agree that they are identical. Next, one or both of the objects or arrays is transformed. As in the pennies' example, the transformation is always one that does not change the property whose conservation is being tested. Then children are asked whether the objects or arrays are still identical. Finally, children are asked to justify or explain their response.

The easiest conservation task is that for number. Children usually succeed on that task before age 7. The most difficult task in figure 8.6 is that for area. Most children succeed on that task several years after they succeed on number conservation. The other tasks fall in between, but the order in which the tasks are passed varies among children. As you will see later, that variability has led to criticism of Piaget's theory.

Next, look at the top of figure 8.7. You see eight tulips and four roses. The question is simple: Are there more tulips or more flowers? You may be a bit puzzled by the question, but you would answer (correctly), "More flowers." All preschoolers and many school-age children say "More tulips." These children know that tulips are flowers. (Previous questions proved that.) However, they cannot handle questions that force them to compare a class of objects (tulips) with its superordinate class (flowers).

Piaget called this a problem with **class inclusion.** Children cannot think of *tulip* both as a class by itself and as included in a larger class. Therefore, instead of answering the question, "Are there more tulips or more flowers?" they answer the question, "Are there more tulips or more *other* flowers?"

The bottom of figure 8.7 shows another task. You are given two sticks and are asked whether A or B is longer. The sticks are very similar in length, so you need to stand them next to each other to see which is longer. You discover that A is longer than B. Then you are given sticks B and C and asked which is longer. By standing them next to each other, you discover that B is longer. Finally, you are asked which is longer, A or C. This time, though, you can't compare the sticks directly. You are told to base your answer on what you know already, to make a logical deduction.

You infer that if A is longer than B, and B is longer than C, then A must be longer than C. In logic, this is known as a transitive inference. Piaget's task assesses transitive inference, or knowledge of **transitivity.** As you might have guessed, young children often fail the transitivity task. They sometimes say they can't tell whether A is longer or shorter than C. Alternatively, they take a guess but are correct no more often than chance.

## Features of Concrete-Operational Thought

Piaget (1983) proposed that the age changes in children's performance on conservation, class inclusion, and transitivity tasks are a result of the development of **logical operations.** These operations are the mental equivalent of actions in the world. Piaget defined them as internalized actions because they take place in the mind rather than in the physical world.

Each operation is connected with other operations in a logical structure. In each logical structure, every operation is matched with another operation that reverses its effect. For example, in the number conservation task, the operation (in thought) of stretching out a row

---

**conservation tasks**
*Tasks devised by Piaget to find out whether children understand that some transformations of objects leave some of their properties unchanged (or conserved). For example, changing the spatial arrangement of a set of objects does not change the number of objects in the set.*

**class inclusion**
*Piaget's term for children's understanding that objects falling in one class (e.g., tulips) may also fall into a superordinate class (e.g., flowers). Also used to refer to tasks designed to assess children's understanding of this characteristic of classes.*

**transitivity**
*An understanding of transitive inference. For example, an understanding that if one object is taller than a second and the second is taller than the third, the first is also taller than the third.*

**logical operations**
*Defined by Piaget as internalized actions that are reversible and that are connected with other operations in logical structures.*

Piaget's class-inclusion task

Are there more tulips or more flowers?

Piaget's transitivity task

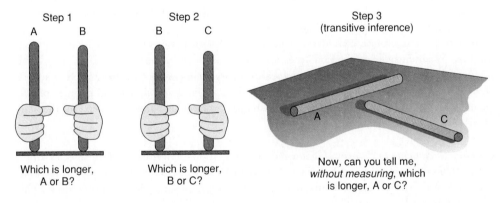

Step 1

A    B

Which is longer,
A or B?

Step 2

B    C

Which is longer,
B or C?

Step 3
(transitive inference)

A    C

Now, can you tell me,
*without measuring*, which
is longer, A or C?

FIGURE 8.7
Piaget's class-inclusion and
transitivity tasks. To answer the
class-inclusion question
correctly, children must
understand that the class,
flowers, includes both
subclasses, tulips and roses. To
succeed on the transitivity task,
children must realize that if one
stick is longer than a second,
and the second is longer than a
third, the first must logically be
longer than the third.

of pennies is matched by the operation (in thought) of shortening the row by pushing the pennies together.

The reversibility of operations and their interlocking in structures are essential to their role in reasoning. According to Piaget, structures of reversible operations allow children to make logical deductions. For example, they allow children to deduce that changes in the length of a row of pennies could easily be undone, so changes in the row's appearance do not mean that the number of pennies has changed.

Piaget assumed that children construct their first logical operations at around 7 years of age. These operations are limited because they can be applied only to mental representations of physical objects and current events. Children are thinking about things, rather than simply acting in the world as they did in the sensorimotor period, but their thoughts stay on a concrete level.

Piaget defined the logical operations that exist at this stage as **concrete operations.** The period after their emergence is the **concrete-operational stage.** Younger children who lack this type of logical operations are preoperational, or in the **preoperational stage.** Piaget assumed that children who lacked concrete operations were incapable of the logical reasoning necessary to succeed on the tasks discussed earlier. Conversely, he viewed success on the

**concrete operations**
*According to Piaget, the first logical operations that children construct, around 7 years of age. These operations can be applied only to concrete objects and current events.*

**concrete-operational stage**
*The stage of cognitive development, in Piaget's theory, in which children are capable only of concrete operations.*

**preoperational stage**
*The stage of cognitive development, in Piaget's theory, before children have constructed any logical operations.*

tasks for conservation, class inclusion, and transitivity as evidence that a child has reached the concrete-operational stage.

Many researchers view Piaget's hypotheses about the development of logical operations as the centerpiece of his theory of cognitive development, and with good reason. Piaget did more research over a longer period on logical operations than on sensorimotor development, egocentrism, or other topics.

Piaget not only presented hypotheses about the logical operations that explain children's responses on his tasks. He also described the general features of preoperational and concrete-operational thought. Many researchers believe that Piaget's descriptions capture important truths about cognitive development (Flavell et al., 1993; Ginsburg & Opper, 1988). Three of these truths are especially well accepted by later researchers.

***Centration to Decentration*** Preoperational children center their attention on one aspect of a task. On the number conservation task, they typically pay attention only to the length of the rows. Piaget defined this single-minded focus on length as **centration.** Concrete-operational children broaden their focus, giving equal attention to the length of the rows and to their density. Piaget described this broadening of focus as **decentration.** With the shift from centration to decentration, children become aware of more relevant information. On number conservation and other tasks, this shift leads to improved performance.

***States to Transformations*** Preoperational children base their judgments about a situation on the current state of affairs, what they see at the moment. On the number conservation task, preoperational children act as if they have forgotten what the rows looked like originally and how the experimenter changed their appearance. After the rows are transformed, preoperational children base their judgments solely on the final state of the rows—how they look to them when the key question is asked.

Concrete-operational children focus on the transformations that change one state into another. When answering the final question on the number conservation task, they take account of both the initial state of the rows and the experimenter's transformation. They say that "the two rows were the same before [initial state], and you didn't add pennies or take pennies away [the transformation did not change number], so the rows are still the same [final state]."

***Absolute Judgments to Relative Judgments*** Preoperational children tend to think of an object's attributes as absolutes. On the transitivity task, they begin by labeling stick A as "long" and stick B as "short." They are in trouble, then, when they start comparing B with C. They already labeled B as "short," but they find it looks "long" compared with C. Because they think of length in absolute rather than relative terms, they cannot integrate their observations about B and C with their observations about A and B.

Concrete-operational children tend to think of the attributes of one object relative to those of other objects, so they label stick A as "longer" than B. Then they label stick B as "longer" than C. They have no problem thinking of stick B as both shorter than A and longer than C. Therefore, they have no difficulty making a transitive inference.

The three features of preoperational thought—centration, a focus on states rather than transformations, and a tendency to judge objects in absolute rather than relative terms—apply across a variety of tasks. Similarly, the three features of concrete-operational thought—decentration, a focus on transformations as well as states, and an ability to judge one object relative to another—help explain the superior performance of older children on a variety of tasks (Flavell, 1985). By highlighting these features of cognitive development, Piaget's theory has been valuable.

## Later Research on Concrete Operations

The researchers who have followed Piaget agree that he identified surprising and consistent limitations in young children's reasoning. If you know some 5-year-old children, you might try giving them Piaget's conservation, class inclusion, and transitivity tasks. If you present the

**centration**
*Piaget's term for young children's tendency to focus their attention on one element of a task or one dimension of an object.*

**decentration**
*Piaget's term for the broadening of attention that occurs as children develop concrete operations, which allows them to pay attention to more than one element of a task or more than one dimension of an object.*

tasks as Piaget did, the 5-year-olds will probably fail the tasks just as the young children tested by Piaget did.

Researchers have also tested Piaget's hypothesis that a transition from preoperational to concrete-operational thought occurs in all cultures. Results have varied across studies, but most studies suggest that conservation is achieved at about the same age in traditional cultures and in modern societies (e.g., Nyiti, 1976). The cross-cultural research also has shown age changes in children's performance on other Piagetian tasks used to assess the concrete-operational stage (Rogoff & Chavajay, 1995).

However, young children can give more correct answers, or seem more "logical," if tested on different tasks. In the 1970s many researchers argued that Piaget's tasks were unnecessarily difficult. Some tasks seemed to require children to keep track of more information than is essential. For other tasks, such as class inclusion, children are asked questions that seem confusing and potentially misleading. Therefore, young children might have failed the tasks even when they understood the concepts being assessed. (Remember that Piaget's three-mountains task for measuring egocentrism was criticized for the same reason.)

When researchers simplified Piaget's tasks and eliminated misleading questions, they found that young children's performance was much better than on the original tasks (e.g., Donaldson, 1978; Rose & Blank, 1974). Especially dramatic evidence of young children's competence was obtained in a classic experiment by Rochel Gelman (1972) on children's concepts of number. You could easily replicate Gelman's experiment using the following procedure.

First, put three green plastic mice in a row on one small plate. Put two mice in a row on another plate (see figure 8.8). Next, show both plates to a 3-year-old girl. Tell her that the plate with three mice is the "winner." Tell her that the plate with two mice is the "loser."

Cover the plates with cans and move the cans around, like the old shell game. Then stop and ask her to find the winner. But unlike the old shell game, reward her whenever she finds the can with three mice, whether she picks that can first or second. In this way, you help her learn the difference between the "winner" and "loser" plates.

Now play a little trick. After she has found the plate with three mice several times, remove the middle mouse from that plate when she is not looking. At other times, leave all three mice on the plate, but push the mice together so their row is the same length as the row of two mice on the old "loser" plate (see figure 8.8).

What do you think the girl would do when she discovered your trick? Which plate would she indicate as the winner? Piaget's studies of number conservation imply that a 3-year-old would not notice the removal of one mouse as long as the entire row remains the same length. Three-year-olds would notice when the three mice were pushed together because they pay attention to row length when judging number.

Exactly the opposite happened in this experiment. Three-year-olds were surprised when a mouse disappeared from the winning plate. They often looked for the missing mouse or asked where it had gone. When the row on the "winner" plate was shortened, children rarely expressed surprise and still considered that plate as the winner. In short, they defined the winning plate by its number of mice, not by the length of its row. These responses suggest that the children understood the concept of number.

Some understanding of number may exist even in infancy. Newborn infants in one study discriminated between slides with two dots on them and slides with three dots, regardless of the placement of the dots on the slides (Antell & Keating, 1983). The 7-month-olds in another study heard two or three drumbeats while they watched slides with either two or three objects on them. When the infants heard two drumbeats, they looked longer at the slide with two objects on it and vice versa (Starkey, Spelke, & Gelman, 1983). That is, the infants were sensitive to the sheer number of visual or auditory stimuli that they experienced. Perhaps 3-year-olds' appreciation that number is important in the "magic mice" experiment (Gelman, 1972) has its origins in infancy.

## Innate Competence Versus Gradual Development

In later studies, Gelman (1982; Gelman & Gallistel, 1978; Gelman & Meck, 1986) examined other facets of young children's understanding of number. She felt the ability to count accurately

## FIGURE 8.8

The materials Gelman (1972) used to find out whether young children realize that changing the spatial arrangement of objects does not change their number. After learning which plate was the winner and which was the loser, children were surprised when the experimenter removed a mouse from the winning plate but left the length of its row constant. Children were not surprised and assumed that the three-mice plate was still the winner if the experimenter changed the length of the row of mice.

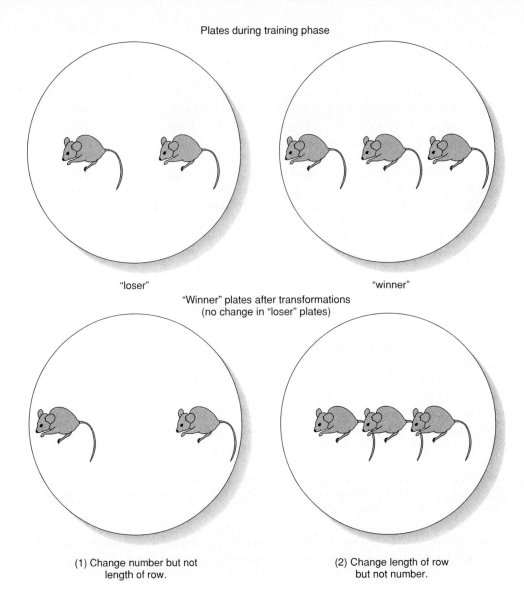

Plates during training phase

"loser"

"winner"

"Winner" plates after transformations
(no change in "loser" plates)

(1) Change number but not
length of row.

(2) Change length of row
but not number.

was especially important for the development of number concepts, so she studied children's knowledge of counting principles. For example, one principle of counting is that order does not matter. You can count objects from left to right or right to left and still get the correct number.

Gelman (1982) argued that children understand the principles of counting by 3 years of age, if not earlier. She also argued that these principles reflect an innate competence for learning about number. Remember that Piaget, by contrast, felt that children construct their knowledge of number as they act on objects. Gelman and some other cognitive-developmental theorists have argued, instead, that children are born with certain cognitive capacities. In this view, some understanding of basic concepts like number is part of the human genetic endowment (see Carey & Gelman, 1991).

The issue of innate cognitive competence is highly controversial. Even children's understanding of simple counting principles seems more limited than the hypothesis of innate competence implies. Suppose you count a dozen pennies as a 3-year-old watches. You make an error in counting, by skipping one penny, so you count the last penny as "11" and say you have 11 pennies.

Suppose, also, that the 3-year-old noticed that you counted wrong by skipping a penny and told you so. Then you ask the child how many pennies there are. Although the child

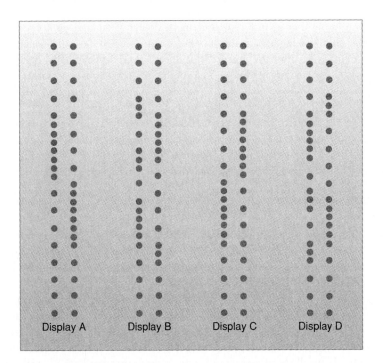

FIGURE 8.9
The displays used to assess conservation of number in Halford and Boyle's (1985) experiment. Children saw one of the displays, A, B, C, or D. Without counting, they guessed which of the two rows in the display had more beads. Next the experimenter moved the beads so that the rows looked like those in another of the displays. Then the experimenter again asked children to guess which row had more beads. Most 3- and 4-year-olds changed their guesses, which implies that they thought moving the beads around could change their number.
©The Society for Research in Child Development, Inc.

knows you counted wrong, he or she is likely to answer "11." The 3-year-old does not appreciate that your error in counting makes your total incorrect.

Full understanding of the counting principles seems to develop during the preschool years (Briars & Siegler, 1984; Frye et al., 1989; Fuson et al., 1985; Sophian, 1988). This understanding may be acquired partly as a result of practice in counting objects. If so, the development of counting principles would provide more support for a constructivist theory than for a theory of innate competence.

Also troublesome for a theory of innate competence is evidence on children's reasoning about number. In the "magic mice" experiment (Gelman, 1972), 3-year-olds demonstrated implicit knowledge of two principles for numerical reasoning: (1) Taking an object away from a set changes the number in the set, and (2) rearranging the objects in a set does not change their number.

However, 3-year-olds' grasp of these principles must be shaky. If they firmly grasped the principles, they would not fail Piaget's number conservation task. The "magic mice" task might be fairly easy for young children because they are asked to compare rows of two and three mice. In Piaget's experiments, rows had at least six objects (as in figure 8.6), and often more than six (Ginsburg & Opper, 1988). If children can only answer questions about number correctly when two or three objects are involved, their understanding of number is highly limited.

Also, children who were given the "magic mice" task did not see the transformation of the rows and so could not be distracted by it. By contrast, the experimenter's transformation is the most dramatic event in the number conservation task. Children need a firm grasp of numerical reasoning principles to judge the two rows as equal after they have seen an experimenter change the rows' appearances so much.

Such a firm grasp of numerical reasoning principles is rare before 6 or 7 years of age. In one experiment (Halford & Boyle, 1985), 3- to 7-year-olds were shown one of the displays in figure 8.9. (Notice how many beads are in each row.) Then they were asked to point to the row with more beads. If they started to count the objects, as a few of the older children did, they were asked to decide without counting.

Then the experimenter changed the display so that it looked like another display in the figure. The experimenter pushed the beads in a row together or moved them apart, but did not move any beads from one row to the other. Then the children were asked again to say which row had more beads.

If children know that spatial rearrangement does not change number, their answers after the change should match their answers beforehand. Most 6- and 7-year-olds gave the same answers before and after the change. Very few 3- and 4-year-olds showed this consistency. If the 3- and 4-year-olds made two judgments in a row, however, without any change in the beads, their answers were consistent. Therefore, they were not simply responding more randomly. They seemed to believe that rearrangements *can* change number.

Taken together, these studies indicate that children's ability to reason logically about numbers improves gradually during childhood. Children may still have some innate numerical competence, but this competence must be limited. Children must increase their competence greatly as they gain more practice in counting, grouping, and using numbers in other ways.

## General Stages Versus Specific Cognitive Domains

The examples in the previous sections focused on children's understanding of number for several reasons. First, Piaget's hypotheses about number concepts have often been tested by later researchers. Second, alternatives to Piaget's theory have been specified and studied extensively. Third, understanding of number concepts has obvious significance for later performance in school and in everyday life.

The focus on number concepts raises a question, however. Do conclusions about the development of number concepts hold for other Piagetian tasks such as class inclusion? Piaget believed that the answer was yes. In his view, all the tasks illustrated in figures 8.5 and 8.6 capture the difference between preoperational and concrete-operational thought. Children's reasoning about all these tasks (and many others that he devised) reflects the same structured whole of thinking and reasoning, or the same type of logic.

Other researchers reject this argument. They assume that each of Piaget's tasks has its own developmental story. Even tasks that seem generally similar may show different patterns of development. For example, all conservation tasks deal with children's ability to realize that some transformations do not change some quantities. However, the ways children can establish that two quantities are equal differ for different tasks. In the number conservation task, children can see whether the rows are equal or unequal by putting the objects in one-to-one correspondence (as shown on the left in figure 8.6). Nothing analogous to one-to-one correspondence exists in the task for conservation of liquid quantity, so how children develop an understanding of conservation may differ for the two tasks (Gelman & Baillargeon, 1983).

The tasks for transitivity and class inclusion differ even more greatly from number conservation. Transitive inference seems to depend on the ability to keep both premises in mind (A > B and B > C) when drawing the conclusion (A > C). "Keeping them in mind" does not simply mean remembering them. It means keeping them in focus, at the center of attention, when trying to answer the experimenter's question (Case, 1985; Chapman & Lindenberger, 1988).

Class inclusion is special because the experimenter's question, "Are there more tulips or more flowers?" is an odd one (Winer, 1980). Most people use the connective *or* to refer to mutually exclusive classes, such as dogs *or* cats, apples *or* oranges, hamburgers *or* hot dogs. Even adults have difficulty with questions in which *or* does not refer to mutually exclusive classes.

Other evidence strengthens the argument for important differences between tasks. As mentioned earlier, children do not succeed on all Piagetian tasks at the same time. Also, children more advanced on one task are not necessarily more advanced on the other tasks (Flavell et al., 1993). This evidence suggests that different tasks require different sets of competencies, principles, strategies, and skills.

What conclusions should you draw, then, about Piaget's hypothesis of general cognitive stages? John Flavell, a prominent cognitive-developmental researcher, summarized current views this way: "Most contemporary developmentalists seem either to ignore or to doubt the existence of such general, transdomain developmental similarities and synchronisms, focusing instead on more specific developments within a single content area or knowledge domain" (1992, p. 1000). In short, few researchers today try to test hypotheses about general cognitive stages. Instead, their primary goal is to understand the age changes in children's reasoning about specific types of tasks.

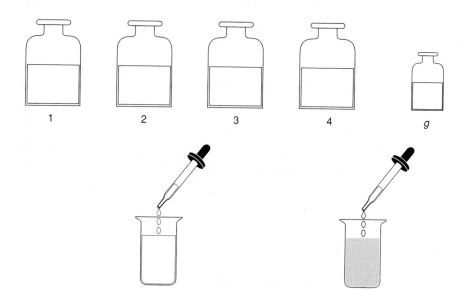

FIGURE 8.10
A diagram of Piaget's task for colored and colorless chemicals. Adding drops from *g* to the first glass has no apparent effect. Adding drops from *g* to the second glass turns the liquid in that glass yellow. If you could use liquids from the four numbered bottles and from *g*, how would you try to reproduce this effect?

## Scientific Reasoning in Adolescence

Thinking and reasoning change dramatically between childhood and adolescence. According to Piaget (1983), children begin to move into a new stage of cognitive development around 11 or 12 years of age. This new stage is fully developed or well established by 16 or 17 years of age.

Piaget called the new stage **formal-operational thought.** Formal operations are more complex and integrated than concrete operations. Although Piaget did not believe that adolescents consciously employ the logic taught in philosophy courses, he assumed that adolescents' thinking is consistent with formal logic. Formal-operational thought is, then, equivalent to mature logical reasoning. The achievement of formal operations is the end point of cognitive development.

Formal operations also allow more abstract reasoning than is possible in middle childhood. Remember that the concrete-operational thinker is limited to reasoning about physical objects and current events. Formal-operational adolescents can also reason logically about verbal statements and about hypotheses. They can generate hypotheses, make deductions based on those hypotheses, and systematically test their deductions. Those tests can lead to revisions in the hypotheses and a repetition of the cycle.

### Tasks for Assessing Formal-Operational Thought

You can better appreciate the characteristics of formal-operational thought if you understand how Piaget assessed this type of reasoning. Most often, Piaget used tasks that deal with problems in chemistry and physics. Figure 8.10 shows the materials used in a task for "colored and colorless chemical bodies" (Inhelder & Piaget, 1958).

Imagine that you were faced with this task. You see four large bottles, one smaller bottle, two small glasses, and an eyedropper. All the bottles and glasses contain colorless liquids. The experimenter takes a few drops of liquid from the small bottle labeled *g* in the figure and puts the drops in one of the glasses. Nothing happens.

Then the experimenter puts a few drops of liquid from *g* in the other glass. The liquid in that glass turns yellow. The experimenter asks you to reproduce this effect in a new glass, using liquids from the four bottles and from *g*. What would you do?

When preoperational children are given this task, they pour water from bottles into glasses randomly. They rarely reproduce the yellow color and, if they do, they cannot explain why. Concrete-operational children may combine *g* with the liquid in each of the other bottles, but they do not test more complex combinations or they do not use a system for testing all possible combinations.

Piaget credited adolescents with formal operations if they systematically tested all possible combinations while forming hypotheses about which combination caused the yellow

**formal-operational thought**
*According to Piaget, the final stage of cognitive development, which begins in adolescence. The logical operations of this stage are abstract and are consistent with formal logic.*

color to appear. Usually, formal-operational adolescents start by adding $g$ to the liquid from bottle 1 ($1 \times g$). Then they test $2 \times g$, $3 \times g$, and $4 \times g$. None of these combinations produces the yellow color, so they begin testing $1 \times 2 \times g$, and so on. They find that the color appears when they test the combination $1 \times 3 \times g$ (because of the particular chemicals dissolved in those liquids). Formal-operational thinkers do not stop there, however. They evaluate the remaining combinations to test their hypothesis that only $1 \times 3 \times g$ yields a yellow liquid.

## Features of Formal-Operational Thought

According to Piaget, the formation of a plan for systematically testing all possible combinations depends on a logic more complex than concrete operations. Therefore, Piaget assumed adolescents had entered the formal-operational stage if they succeeded on the task for colored and colorless chemicals. Piaget also described some general contrasts between concrete- and formal-operational thought. Other researchers agree that two of Piaget's contrasts portray important differences between children's and adolescents' reasoning (Flavell et al., 1993; Keating, 1990).

***Data Collection Versus Hypothesis Testing***   Concrete-operational children try to solve problems by collecting facts. When given the chemicals' task, they try a few combinations of the liquid in $g$ with a liquid in one of the numbered bottles. When asked to explain what's happening, they simply report the results of each combination.

By contrast, formal-operational adolescents test combinations systematically while searching for a general explanation that accounts for all their observations. This search involves three steps: (a) forming a hypothesis about how the yellow color is produced; (b) making a deduction about what should happen with specific combinations of liquids if the hypothesis is true; and (c) testing the hypothesis by seeing whether the deduction proves correct.

**hypothetico-deductive**
*One term that Piaget used for formal-operational thought, because adolescents in this stage of cognitive development form hypotheses and test deductions from the hypotheses.*

This description of formal-operational thought should remind you of the discussion of scientific theories in chapter 1. According to Piaget, adolescents are like scientists in their reasoning about events. Piaget described formal-operational thought as **hypothetico-deductive** because the formation of hypotheses and the test of deductions from these hypotheses are central to thinking at this stage.

In high-school science classes, adolescents regularly engage in the hypothetico-deductive reasoning that Piaget viewed as the hallmark of formal-operational thought.

***Emphasis on the Real Versus the Possible*** Concrete-operational children focus on the here and now, on what is both concrete and in the present. Formal-operational adolescents spend much more time thinking about possibilities, about what might be but is not yet. When working with the chemicals' task, concrete-operational children merely observe what happens with different combinations of liquids. Formal-operational adolescents instead think about what might happen with new combinations. Adolescents also think about possibilities in other realms, like politics and philosophy. They devise plans for ideal societies or ponder the deep questions of the universe. (According to Chapman [1988], Piaget's description of adolescent thought contains more than a touch of autobiography.) The broader scope of adolescents' thought means a broader consideration of options for themselves, for society, and for reality itself.

## Later Research on Formal Operations

Consider a different kind of cognitive problem. Figure 8.11 shows four cards. Each card has information about a person sitting at a table in a campus bar. One side of each card gives the person's age. The other side tells the beverage that the person is drinking, beer or cola.

Now think about the following rule: "If a person is drinking beer, then the person must be over 21 years of age." You must decide which card or cards you would need to turn over to figure out whether the rule is being *broken*. Before reading further, decide which card or cards you would choose and why.

You certainly need to turn over the card, "drinking beer," to see whether the age printed on the other side is over 21. If the person drinking beer was younger than 21, you would know that the rule is being broken. You also need to turn over the card, "16 years of age," to see whether that person, although underage, was drinking beer and so violating the rule. You need not turn over the "22 years of age" card because that person could be drinking beer or cola without breaking the rule. You need not turn over the "drinking cola" card because the rule does not apply to drinking cola.

This simple task involves reasoning about a statement, or verbal reasoning. Piaget assumed that verbal reasoning did not become fully logical until adolescence, with the development of formal operations. Figure 8.12 shows the data from four studies that tested Piaget's hypothesis (Overton et al., 1987; Ward & Overton, 1990).

The subjects in each study had to solve reasoning problems like the one you just did. The figure shows the percentage of students at each grade who seemed to be capable of formal-operational reasoning, because they answered most problems correctly. That is, they chose only the critical two cards on each problem.

Verbal reasoning improved with age, and few students below the eighth or ninth grade got more than half the problems correct. These age trends and those in other experiments

FIGURE 8.12

Percentage of students in various grades whose answers to verbal reasoning problems suggested that they were formal reasoners. (Adapted from Ward & Overton, 1990.)

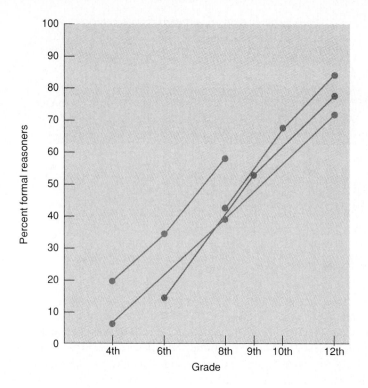

(e.g., Byrnes & Overton, 1988) imply that the development of logical competence is not completed during childhood and may be completed only in late adolescence. If so, Piaget would be correct in arguing that a new form of logical reasoning emerges in adolescence.

Yet even the oldest adolescents did not do well on all problems of verbal reasoning. Besides problems with familiar content, like the example of drinking beer, adolescents were given more abstract problems. For example, they had to evaluate the rule, "If there is a vowel on one side, there is an odd number on the other." The older adolescents who solved the problems with familiar content often failed the abstract problems.

## The Growth of Logical Competence in Adolescence?

At least three explanations can be given for older adolescents' poor performance on abstract reasoning problems. One is to argue that Piaget overestimated the reasoning ability of adolescents (Kuhn, 1989). In some sense, this argument may be correct. Cognitive development may extend for a longer period than Piaget assumed, and may not be completed in adolescence (Flavell, 1992). However, adults' performance on many types of cognitive problems is not much better than that of late adolescents (Siegler, 1991). (How well would *you* have done on the colorless-chemicals' problem?) If performance on cognitive problems doesn't improve greatly between late adolescence and adulthood, the argument that cognitive development continues into adulthood is greatly weakened.

A second explanation rests on a distinction between competence and performance (Overton et al., 1987). On verbal-reasoning problems, children rarely give the correct answers. Their poor performance might be attributed to their lack of the necessary logical competence. But when that competence exists, correct answers are not assured. Adolescents and adults who give incorrect answers to abstract problems seem to have difficulty *encoding* the information given. That is, they have trouble forming a mental representation of the problem and keeping that representation in mind. When encoding or representation is difficult, performance is poor. Therefore, the gap between competence and performance is greater for abstract problems than for familiar problems.

The third explanation for the age changes in performance is more radical. Many information-processing theorists argue that no important changes occur in logical competence.

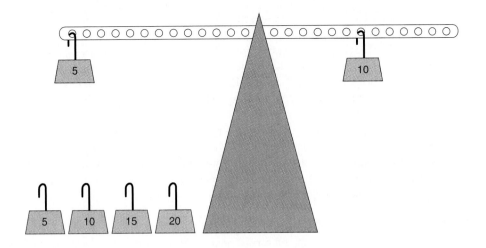

Changes in performance are due entirely to changes in information processing (see Klahr, 1992; Flavell et al., 1993). To understand this type of explanation better, consider another of Piaget's tasks.

Figure 8.13 shows a simple balance scale that Piaget used to assess formal-operational thought (Inhelder & Piaget, 1958). When Piaget asked young children to figure out how the scale worked, they were unable to do so. They sometimes put more weight on one side than on the other and then made the scale "balance" by holding it level with their hands! Older children could make the scale balance by itself, but could not explain why it did so.

Adolescents usually discovered the general principle or law of the balance scale. The scale balances, they said, when the ratio of the weights on the left and right sides of the balance matches the inverse ratio of their distances from the midpoint. That is, they referred to the equality of two proportions:

$$\frac{Weight_{Left}}{Weight_{Right}} = \frac{Distance_{Right}}{Distance_{Left}}$$

According to Piaget, an understanding of proportions requires the complex logic that defines formal-operational thought. Therefore, he viewed adolescents who could explain how a balance worked as in the formal-operational stage.

Robert Siegler (1976, 1978) proposed an alternative, information-processing analysis of the age changes in understanding of the balance. Siegler argued that reasoning about the balance depends on (a) the information a person considers when working with the balance, and (b) how the person uses this information.

Siegler (1976) defined several rules that people might use when making predictions about the balance. For example, the simplest rule is to consider only the amount of weight on the two sides of the balance, ignoring the distance of the weights from the midpoint. The most complex rule is the correct one, which corresponds to the equality of the proportions described by Piaget. To use more complex rules, people must consider more information about the weights and distances. The additional information must also be coordinated properly, to fit the law of the balance scale.

Using carefully selected problems, Siegler showed that children were using the rules he had defined. He also showed that adolescents used more complex rules than children did. Most important, Siegler (1978) found that adolescents could easily discover the correct rule if they received a little training. In particular, they needed to keep a record of their tests with different combinations of weights and distances. They also needed to express these combinations in quantitative form (e.g., how much weight was placed how far from the center). When adolescents were encouraged to think quantitatively about the balance, they usually discovered the correct relation between weight, distance, and the movement of the balance. The success of the training supported Siegler's hypothesis that most adolescents do poorly on

formal-operational tasks not because they lack logical competence but because they lack experience with the tasks.

Evidence like Siegler's has greatly reduced researchers' acceptance of Piaget's hypotheses about logical competence. Piaget referred explicitly to the "growth of logic" in the titles of two major books (Inhelder & Piaget, 1958, 1964). Today, however, few researchers assume that the basic structure of children's logic changes with age. On this issue, Piaget's critics now dominate the field.

You should recognize, however, that Piaget's critics do not discount the value of his research. On the contrary, many later researchers (like Siegler) have used Piaget's tasks in their own research. Many later researchers accept the statements that you read earlier about the distinctive features of adolescent thought. In summary, several aspects of Piaget's work on adolescent reasoning remain important today.

## Explaining and Accelerating Development

Piaget's (1983) theories of concrete and formal operations include both a description of cognitive stages and an explanation of development through the stages. His explanation has important practical implications. If researchers know what normally causes the age changes in children's thinking, they can use that information to accelerate children's development.

Piaget (1983) believed that explicit training could accelerate cognitive development to a modest degree under certain conditions. First, training could succeed only if children were cognitively ready for it. Piaget assumed that children could only develop, through training, logical structures for which they already had the prerequisite structures.

Second, training could succeed only if it caused children to engage in the processes of assimilation, accommodation, and equilibration. Earlier you saw how Piaget used assimilation and accommodation to explain infants' progress through the stages of sensorimotor intelligence. Piaget assumed that assimilation and accommodation are also important for improvements in reasoning during childhood and adolescence. However, when talking about cognitive development beyond infancy, Piaget emphasized the process of equilibration.

*Equilibration* was defined in chapter 1 as a process of self-regulation that results from a sense of cognitive conflict or disequilibrium. When children experience cognitive conflict because their reasoning about some situation doesn't match their observations, they search for a new way of thinking about the situation that will remove the sense of conflict. In other words, they try to reach a new state of equilibrium.

The concept of equilibration can best be explained by example. In one study (Ames & Murray, 1982), first and second graders were tested on the tasks for conservation of length, liquid, and mass. Children who failed the tasks were paired with other children who had also given wrong, but different, answers. For example, a child who answered the conservation of liquids question by saying that the taller beaker had more liquid was paired with a child who said that the wider beaker had more liquid.

Then the two children discussed the tasks on which they disagreed. Four weeks later, the children were again tested on the conservation tasks they had discussed with a partner and on other tasks. First and second graders in a control condition took the pretests and posttests but did not discuss the tasks with another child.

As figure 8.14 shows, the children in both conditions had low scores on the pretests. The posttest scores of the children in the control group were nearly as low as their pretest scores. The posttest scores of children who discussed the tasks with a classmate were significantly higher than their pretest scores.

To explain this change, the researchers proposed that the children's discussions with a classmate started a process of equilibration that led to advances in their own reasoning. The children were placed in cognitive conflict when they heard a classmate disagree with their answers. As the two children tried to resolve the conflict and reach a new equilibrium, they developed a better understanding of the tasks and of conservation.

The experiment also provided modest support for Piaget's hypothesis about children's readiness for training. Second graders did better on the pretest than first graders, which suggests that they more often had the prerequisite logical structures for conservation. In

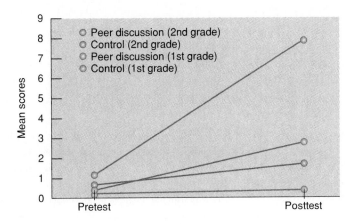

## FIGURE 8.14

Children who give incorrect answers on Piaget's conservation tasks can gain a more correct understanding of the tasks if they discuss them with a peer. The improvement occurs even if the peer also gave incorrect answers, provided that the peer's answers differed from the child's. The peer discussions may provoke cognitive conflict that causes children to question their own reasoning and move toward a better understanding of the tasks. (Source: Ames & Murray, 1982.)

addition, the improvement between the pretest and the posttest was somewhat greater for second graders than for first graders. Several other experiments, although not all, have shown that training on Piagetian tasks is more effective with older children (Brainerd, 1983; Brown et al., 1983).

However, a different explanation could be given for the greater improvement shown by second graders. Older children have several abilities that might explain why they respond more positively to training. Information-processing theorists would point to older children's better encoding abilities, their better memories, or their greater experience in problem solving (Gelman & Baillargeon, 1983; Siegler, 1983).

A different explanation could also be given for the overall effect of discussing conservation tasks with a classmate. Although this effect might be partly due to a process of conflict resolution, that process need not be linked to Piaget's construct of equilibration. Many neo- (or new-) Piagetians have accepted some of Piaget's basic assumptions while they have suggested revisions in his theory. Without using the construct of equilibration, neo-Piagetians often argue that cognitive conflicts can lead to the restructuring of thinking (see Sternberg, 1987). Information-processing theorists also consider the recognition and resolution of cognitive conflicts as one mechanism for cognitive change (Klahr, 1989, 1992).

Moreover, techniques that are not intended to induce cognitive conflict can be effective in changing children's reasoning (Brainerd, 1983). Children's performance on Piagetian tasks can be improved by showing them peer or adult models who answer the experimenter's questions correctly. Their performance can be improved by directly telling them the correct answers on a task. Even giving positive reinforcement for correct answers can improve children's reasoning.

You've heard people say, "There's more than one way to skin a cat." That saying captures some of the current understanding of cognitive development. There's more than one way that children move from immature reasoning to the complex reasoning of adolescents and adults. Many types of experiences that affect many cognitive processes influence cognitive development (Flavell, 1985).

Finally, because Piaget set conditions on the acceleration of cognitive development, you might assume that he was pessimistic about educators' ability to change their students' reasoning. That assumption is not entirely correct. Piaget wrote frequently about the educational implications of his theories (see Flavell, 1963; Piaget, 1970). Some of his followers created

# PIAGETIAN AND POST-PIAGETIAN PERSPECTIVES ON EDUCATION

During the 1960s and 1970s, several writers discussed the implications of Piaget's theory for education (e.g., Elkind, 1976; Flavell, 1963; Ginsburg & Opper, 1969). These writers emphasized the following points.

First, educators should understand how children think. In particular, educators should understand children's reasoning about specific concepts. For example, when trying to teach arithmetic, educators should consider young children's ideas about number.

Second, educators should realize that children learn best through acting on objects. According to Piaget, logical thinking depends on internalized actions. Piagetian educators assume that children can only internalize actions that they have practiced with physical objects. Therefore, these educators argue for giving children experiences playing and working with objects.

Third, educators should encourage actions that are linked to logical operations. Figures 8.5 and 8.6 give examples of these actions. They include adding and removing objects, reversing transformations, and grouping objects into categories. Practicing these actions is expected to promote the development of the corresponding logical operations.

Fourth, educators should allow small groups of children to work together. While working together children hear different perspectives on cognitive problems, which should provoke the cognitive conflicts that lead to equilibration. In addition, hearing other perspectives should promote the perspective taking and decentration that Piaget described as important for young children's advances in reasoning.

Several educators quickly translated these principles into curricula for students. Greatest emphasis was given to curricula for preschool children (Forman & Kuschner, 1977; Kamii & DeVries, 1978; Lavatelli, 1970). However, curricula were also created for students in elementary school and in high school (Kamii & Joseph, 1989; Shayer & Adey, 1993).

The criticisms of Piaget's stage theories have lessened enthusiasm for Piagetian curricula. Some researchers continue to defend Piaget's theories as the only scientific basis for education (Kamii & Clark, 1993). Other researchers have pointed out that some elements of Piagetian education, such as the emphasis on children's activity, are common to other models of education such as discovery learning (Ginsburg & Opper, 1988). Still other researchers have argued that educators need to do more than provide an environment for children's activity (Inagaki, 1992; O'Loughlin, 1992). Educators also need to guide and direct children's learning. This view of education is often linked to Vygotsky's sociocultural theory, about which you will read next.

In summary, few researchers now believe that Piaget's theories provide a completely adequate basis for educational practice. Because Piaget's hypotheses about logical operations have been criticized most heavily, the value of teaching actions related to those operations is most doubtful. By contrast, researchers continue to endorse the value of understanding how children think, using activities during instruction, and allowing small groups to work together. Piaget's theories (and most others) imply that these practices can enhance children's cognitive development.

educational programs consistent with his principles. *Practical Applications for Research: "Piagetian and Post-Piagetian Perspectives on Education"* describes the initial enthusiasm for those programs and their changing status as Piaget's theories were reevaluated.

# VYGOTSKY'S SOCIOCULTURAL THEORY

As mentioned in chapter 1, Lev Vygotsky had a short but amazingly productive career in psychology. He gave his first important speech at a Russian psychological convention in 1924. He died of tuberculosis 10 years later. During those 10 years, Vygotsky was a major figure in Russian psychology. He gave lectures, conducted research with children, handled administrative duties, and wrote more than 100 books and papers. Shortly after his death, however, his work was banned by the Communist party. Only in the 1970s and 1980s did most of his writings become available to researchers throughout the world (e.g., Vygotsky, 1978; see Wertsch & Tulviste, 1992).

Because you have read so much about Piaget's theory, you can best understand Vygotsky's theory by seeing how his central assumptions and emphases contrast with Piaget's. One obvious contrast is in research methods. Unlike Piaget, Vygotsky did not try to devise tasks that would assess different stages of cognitive development. Indeed, Vygotsky rarely used standardized tasks to assess children's thinking. He preferred instead to observe

children's thinking in context, in the settings where children normally spend their time. The researchers who have followed Vygotsky have sometimes observed children in laboratory settings, but they have always used tasks, such as completing puzzles, like those children do in natural settings (Wertsch, 1979).

Vygotsky never tried to devise tasks to assess stages of cognitive development because he did not assume that there *were* general stages. Indeed, one weakness of Vygotsky's theory is that he said little about how children's thinking normally changes with age (Wertsch & Tulviste, 1992). By contrast, Piaget's theories and research focused on the age changes in children's thinking.

Nevertheless, as mentioned earlier, Vygotsky's theory is strong where Piaget's theory is weak. Vygotsky offered an explanation of cognitive development that many researchers regard as superior to Piaget's. Unlike Piaget, Vygotsky emphasized the crucial contributions of social relationships and of language to cognitive development. As you will see, this emphasis gives Vygotsky's theory special relevance for the education of children.

## The Social Origins of Cognition

Vygotsky (1978) proposed that human thinking and reasoning are products of social activity (Rogoff & Morelli, 1989). As children interact with adults or more capable peers, they not only gain new information but also learn *how* to think. For Vygotsky, thinking itself is a product of social interaction.

Consider a simple task, that of completing a puzzle of a truck (Wertsch, 1979; Wertsch & Hickmann, 1987). Preschool children and their mothers are shown two completed puzzles that are identical (figure 8.15). Then the experimenter takes the pieces out of one puzzle frame and asks the child to put that puzzle back together. The child's mother is asked to help the child whenever she feels the child needs help.

Some 2-year-olds have no experience with puzzles, so their mothers' first task is to help them understand what they are supposed to do. The mother may say something such as, "See the pieces (taken out of the puzzle frame)? We're going to put them back where they go."

Children who have more experience may need less direct help. These children know what the task is all about, but they may need a reminder to pay attention to the details of the original puzzle so they can copy it correctly. For example, if a child is holding a purple triangle, the mother may say, "Where does the purple one go?"

If the child doesn't appreciate that the purple triangle has to go in the upper left corner of the truck's cargo area (see figure 8.15), the mother may be more explicit. She may say, "Look at this puzzle? Where is the purple one?" This kind of question not only helps children complete the puzzle correctly; it also tells children that they should pay close attention to a

**FIGURE 8.15**
To explore Vygotsky's hypothesis about the social origins of cognition, researchers observed mothers as they taught their preschool children how to complete this puzzle. (From Wertsch & Hickmann, 1987.)

model when they are copying something. Attention to detail and systematic comparison with a model are cognitive skills that can be used on many types of cognitive activities, from copying a drawing to copying letters and words.

When children fully understand the task, their mothers help them less and encourage them to do more independently. If a child says, "Where should I put this one [triangle]?" the mother may reply, "Do you see one like it on the model?" With this response, the mother directs the child's attention, as in the previous example, and indirectly refuses to answer the child's question. The mother is saying, implicitly, "I think you know pretty much how to do this now, so I'll let you figure the rest out for yourself."

The mother's role in this type of interaction can be described as **scaffolding** (Wood, Bruner, & Ross, 1976). A scaffold provides temporary support during the construction of a building or other structure. The scaffold is moved and altered as the building nears completion. When the building is done, and ready to stand on its own, the scaffold is taken away.

Similarly, when adults provide scaffolding for children who are working on cognitive tasks, they provide the amount and kind of assistance that children need at the moment. That assistance may involve explaining the task to the child, directing the child's attention to important objects or events, modeling the proper behavior for the child, offering suggestions, and providing other kinds of guidance. Exactly what adults do when interacting with specific children depends on the task the children are doing and the kinds of assistance they need.

During these types of interactions, the adults' goal is always to transfer responsibility for the task to the children themselves. As children learn how to do the task, adults give them less assistance. The adults, in a sense, remove the scaffold when it is no longer needed.

You might wonder whether children who often receive assistance from adults ever learn to do things on their own. If you are concerned about that possibility, you are not alone. Piaget (1983) felt that young children only have a full understanding of things they discover, or construct, themselves. Can children really learn to do things independently by working with adults?

Increasing evidence from systematic research not only suggests that they can, but they do so very effectively. For one study (Rogoff, Ellis, & Gardner, 1984), mothers of 6- and 8-year-olds taught their children how to do two tasks. The tasks were done in a psychology laboratory but they were like those children do at home and at school. For the first task, children had to put various snacks, fruits, and other grocery items on shelves in a model kitchen. For the second task, children had to sort photographs of objects into categories such as machines (e.g., a typewriter), cleaning tools (e.g., a broom), and utensils (e.g., a wooden spoon).

Mothers were told that they could use any form of instruction they wanted for as long as they wanted. Once the mothers were finished with their instructions, their children were tested on their ability to place grocery items and sort photographs independently.

The researchers predicted that mothers would give the most instruction on tasks that they perceived as unfamiliar to their children. Mothers were expected to view the homelike task as familiar to both older and younger children. Mothers were expected to view the school-like task as more familiar to 8-year-olds than to 6-year-olds. Therefore, mothers should have judged their instruction as most needed for 6-year-olds on the school task.

Figure 8.16 shows that these predictions were largely confirmed. Mothers gave the most **directives** to 6-year-olds on the school task. The category of directives included specific statements about the materials and commands to follow instructions. Mothers also asked more questions, gave more nonverbal instructions, and spent more time reviewing the school task with 6-year-olds. Moreover, the mothers' extra effort paid off. Performance on the independent test was highest for 6-year-olds on the school task.

For Vygotsky, this example shows much more than the effectiveness of intensive instruction. Vygotsky and his followers assume that this example shows the social nature of many cognitive activities. Mothers and their children were learning the tasks together. The processes necessary to complete the tasks were practiced by a mother and her child before the child carried them out individually.

Vygotsky (1981) proposed that the cognitive benefits of social interactions reflect a general law of development. According to Vygotsky, every cognitive process appears first on the social plane, as part of a collaborative activity. The process later appears on the psychological

**scaffolding**
*An informal term for the support and assistance that parents or other adults provide for children's learning. Support and assistance are reduced as children become more capable of completing cognitive tasks independently.*

**directives**
*Specific commands or instructions.*

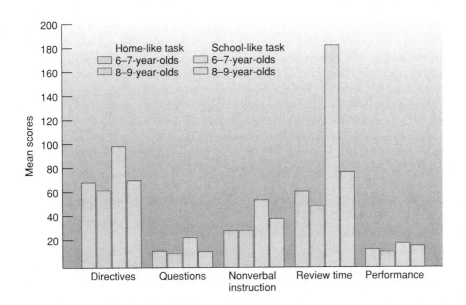

FIGURE 8.16
Mothers give the most instructions (e.g., directives) when they think their children need the most help, so they give more on school-like tasks than on home-like tasks. They also give more to younger children. Their instruction pays off, as the good performance of 6- to 7-year-olds on the school-like task shows.

plane, after it is internalized by a child. Vygotsky argued that this general law applied equally to simple cognitive processes such as attention and to complex processes such as the formation of concepts.

## The Zone of Proximal Development

The idea of scaffolding emphasizes the functions of adults' assistance to children who are working on cognitive tasks. Vygotsky's (1978) theory includes another construct that emphasizes children's perspectives during this type of collaborative activity. This construct, introduced in chapter 1, is the *zone of proximal development*. Most people assume that children's level of cognitive development should be judged from their success in solving cognitive problems independently. Vygotsky argued that it is equally important to know how successfully children can solve problems if they receive guidance from adults or more capable peers. Most children perform at a higher level with this kind of guidance than they do on their own. The difference between children's levels of performance under the two conditions defines their zone of proximal development.

When working with children on cognitive tasks, adults try to stay within the children's zone of proximal development. Adults can go outside this zone in two directions. First, adults can do too much for children, so the task is completed but the children don't learn any more than they knew initially. Second, adults can do too little for children, so children do not complete the task and, therefore, do not learn how to do it. But when adults stay within the children's zone of proximal development, the children are always being challenged to increase their understanding of the problem while never being asked to do more than they can do.

Often children work on cognitive tasks with peers. After working on tasks with peers, children may show poorer independent performance than after working on the same task with an adult (Radziszewska & Rogoff, 1988, 1991). Pairs that include a child and a peer usually plan their work less thoroughly and use less efficient strategies for problem solving than pairs that include an adult and a child. These differences suggest that adults are more successful than peers at working within a child's zone of proximal development.

Of course, not all adults are equally good at working with children. On some tasks, mothers who are mildly depressed show less sensitivity to their children's knowledge and a more limited range of teaching strategies than mothers with better emotional adjustment (Goldsmith & Rogoff, 1995). The other influences on parenting discussed in chapter 11 may also be related to parents' ability to stay within their children's zone of proximal development.

The characteristics of collaborative problem solving do not depend entirely on adults. Children also influence the course of collaborative activities (Laboratory of Comparative Human Cognition, 1983; Wertsch & Hickmann, 1987). On the puzzle task, children

eventually say things such as, "Don't tell me. I know where it goes." On other tasks, children eventually say things such as, "Okay, I can do the rest myself." These comments illustrate children's knowledge of what is and is not within their competence. They also illustrate the continual shifts in the zone of proximal development.

As children gain more experience with tasks, they internalize the cognitive processes that have been carried out in collaboration with others. Therefore, their level of independent performance increases. Simultaneously, their level of performance when provided with guidance by an adult or more capable child becomes greater.

## Private Speech

How does a child make the transition from doing a task with assistance to doing the task independently? In other words, how does the child move from other-regulation to self-regulation? The transition depends partly on the specific task, but Vygotsky viewed language as the key to successful completion of many tasks.

Vygotsky assumed that language, or, more precisely, speech, is the prototypical example of his general law of development. Speech is first used by children during social interaction, as adults regulate children's activities and respond to children's questions. Eventually, this social dialogue is transformed into an inner dialogue. According to Vygotsky, social speech becomes inner speech, or thought. This inner speech is essential throughout life for what Vygotsky called the higher mental processes: planning, evaluating, remembering, and reasoning.

As support for this hypothesis, Vygotsky reinterpreted evidence obtained earlier by Piaget. During the 1920s, Piaget (1926/1971) observed young children in a nursery school. These children often made statements that were not directed to other children and that were phrased in ways that other children were not likely to understand. Piaget considered these statements as evidence for his hypothesis that young children's thought is egocentric.

Vygotsky (1962) made similar observations of young children's speech, but he explained them differently. He argued that speech not directed to other children is **private speech** rather than egocentric speech. Private speech is spoken aloud but is directed to oneself rather than to a specific listener. Vygotsky argued that private speech is an intermediate phase between purely social speech and inner speech or thought.

Many later studies have confirmed Vygotsky's account of private speech (Berk, 1994). When working on difficult problems, children ask themselves what to do next, tell themselves what they need to remember, and make other comments that direct their actions. Moreover, the statements that they make while engaged in these dialogues with themselves are like those that adults have used with them.

Recall the task in which children and their mothers were completing a puzzle of a truck (figure 8.15). Children who needed little help from their mothers, but who still found the task challenging, often talked aloud to themselves as they worked on the puzzle (Wertsch, 1979). This private speech was a form of self-regulation comparable to the regulation that less-advanced children received from their mothers.

So children who talk to themselves should be better on cognitive tasks, right? No, neither Vygotsky's hypothesis nor the research findings can be stated so simply (Berk, 1994). First, not all private speech regulates cognitive activity. Some talking aloud is word play, some may be simply an expression of feelings, and some may accompany daydreaming. These types of private speech do not improve performance on cognitive tasks.

Second, children do not talk to themselves forever. When children can easily complete a cognitive task, they no longer use private speech to regulate their activity. When speech has become fully internalized, it becomes thought. Rather than talking themselves through a problem, children think through it.

Suppose that two children are working on the same task. While working, one child is engaged in private speech that is relevant to the task. The other child is silent, relying on inner speech to complete the task. The second child is likely to be more advanced in cognitive development and, therefore, to do better on the task. For example, 10-year-olds from low-income families usually do less well on cognitive tasks than middle-class children, and they also use more private speech than middle-class children (Berk & Garvin, 1984). Similarly, children

**private speech**
*Vygotsky's term for speech that is spoken aloud but that is directed to oneself rather than other people. Viewed by Vygotsky as an intermediate phase between purely social speech and inner speech or thought.*

with learning disabilities engage in more private speech than other children the same age (Berk & Landau, 1993). In short, the use of private speech at certain ages on certain tasks may be a sign of cognitive delays or disabilities rather than cognitive competence.

Third, children sometimes are given tasks so difficult for them that private speech does not help. Remember that private speech is assumed to follow social speech. When children have little understanding of a task, they may need to talk it through with a more knowledgeable person, rather than doing it alone.

The benefits of task-related private speech can be shown if children work at tasks that are challenging but not too difficult for them. The 5-year-olds in one study were asked to use small building blocks to copy a structure like a model (Azmitia, 1992). Children did the task four times, with the same or different models. The children who made the most accurate models on the first trial also used the most task-related private speech. Moreover, these children used progressively less private speech on the later trials. By talking to themselves, these children not only gave themselves the guidance necessary to do well on the first trial; they also reduced their need for private speech on later trials. In Vygotsky's terms, their initial private speech speeded their movement toward self-regulating inner speech.

In summary, many experiments suggest that private speech can be a valuable accompaniment to cognitive activity. Therefore, children who engage in task-related private speech should not be discouraged from doing so (Berk, 1994). Private speech is not a substitute for instruction: Children often need to work on tasks with more capable partners before they can use private speech effectively. But when children are trying to guide themselves, adults should not make it harder by telling them to "close your mouth" or to keep quiet. Instead, adults should provide settings that allow children to engage in private speech without becoming embarrassed or interfering with classmates.

## Implications for Education

Because Vygotsky stressed the importance of social interactions for cognitive development, his theory has great relevance to education (Davydov, 1995; Wood, 1988). Vygotsky emphasized that humans have invented many aids to thought that are transmitted to children with the rest of a culture. Children learn to use these inventions as part of formal instruction. For example, you probably learned how to use a protractor in a junior-high-school math class. You may have learned how to prepare an outline or use reference cards in an English class. These cultural inventions help children develop their minds as instruments for planning, reasoning, and regulating their behavior.

Vygotsky's theory also contains hypotheses about teaching methods that will most effectively encourage children's development. In chapter 1 you read about reciprocal teaching (Brown et al., 1991). This method involves the use of discussion groups with a teacher and several students. These groups are designed to provide children with instruction beyond their independent level of competence but in their zone of proximal development (Brown & Palincsar, 1982; Brown et al., 1991).

The discussion groups are led by students, with each student taking a turn. The student leader is responsible for making sure that all group members practice the activities that contribute to reading comprehension. Those activities include summarizing the main idea of a passage, generating questions about the passage, clarifying parts of the passage that were misunderstood, and predicting the content of the next passage. Skilled readers do these things automatically, but beginning readers do not. Vygotsky would describe these activities as the aids to thought that children need to learn while learning to read.

Reciprocal teaching makes reading comprehension skills explicit and provides a dialogue that gradually allows the student members of the group to internalize the skills. Children's progress toward internalization can be seen in the interactions of the discussion groups. Initially, children need a great deal of assistance from the adult as they work together to understand what they have read. Over time, students become competent in formulating appropriate questions about the text, summarizing the main idea, and making intelligent predictions about what will come next.

## GUIDED PARTICIPATION IN MOTHER-CHILD INTERACTION

**guided participation**
*A variety of adult practices that contribute to children's cognitive development. These practices include explicit instruction, allowing children to watch as competent adults do tasks, and allowing children to work with other people who have more competence on a task.*

Cognitive development may be especially encouraged by children's participation in activities under adult guidance. The idea of **guided participation** includes both explicit instruction and learning by observing other people. This idea is similar to but broader than Vygotsky's principle of social interaction within a child's zone of proximal development. Guided participation includes not only the instructional dialogues emphasized by Vygotsky but also less structured interactions in which children work with others or simply watch other people at work.

To explore cultural variations in guided participation, Barbara Rogoff and her coworkers interviewed mothers and their 1-year-olds in the United States, Guatemala, Turkey, and India (Rogoff et al., 1993). During the interviews, mothers and children were shown novel objects such as a jumping-jack doll that danced when a string was pulled. Then mothers were asked to invite their children to explore the objects. The social interactions that followed were videotaped and later analyzed.

The analyses showed some similarities among the mother-toddler pairs in all countries, but the differences between countries were even more striking. These differences suggested two contrasting patterns of guided participation. One pattern was clearly shown by the U.S. mothers and children from middle-class families in Salt Lake City. The other pattern was clearly shown by Mayan families from the small town of San Pedro in Guatemala. Table 8.3 summarizes the two patterns.

First, parents' goals for their children's development differed in Salt Lake and San Pedro. Parents in Salt Lake had already begun preparing their children for school. Most mothers had tried to teach their children how to walk and talk; one mother was trying to teach her toddler to read and count. Few of the San Pedro mothers had tried to teach these skills, but more of the San Pedro toddlers had already begun doing simple chores and errands. Mothers seemed to be preparing these children for the activities of maintaining a household.

Second, modes of communication differed in the two groups. Mothers and children in Salt Lake talked more during their social interactions than did mothers and children in San Pedro. By contrast, San Pedro mothers emphasized communication by touch, gesture, or other nonverbal means. Their children, in turn, sought assistance more often by a touch, gesture, or look than U.S. children did.

Third, mothers and children in the two groups seemed to have different assumptions about who was responsible for the children's learning. Salt Lake mothers often structured their exploration of the novel objects as mini-vocabulary lessons. These mothers often labeled the objects or asked their children to label them. Mothers in Salt Lake also tried to motivate their children by showing mock excitement as they introduced each novel object to their toddler.

As Vygotsky's theory predicts, the skills learned and practiced in group discussions transfer to independent reading activities. More than a dozen studies of reciprocal teaching have confirmed the effectiveness of this method (Rosenshine & Meister, 1994). Students whose teachers use the method receive higher scores on standardized tests of reading ability than children in regular classrooms. These students also receive higher scores on special tests of ability to summarize information. Furthermore, the method is effective with students who vary greatly in age and ability.

You should realize that the method of reciprocal teaching is designed specifically for improving reading comprehension. Teachers who are trying to develop other cognitive skills may need to use different methods. Still, Vygotsky's theory suggests that a teacher's primary role is to help students internalize the tools for thought applicable to a specific subject.

## The Cultural Context of Development

Vygotsky's theory is often described as taking a *sociocultural* perspective on cognitive development (Forman, Minick, & Stone, 1993; Rogoff & Chavajay, 1995). Vygotsky proposed that all cognitive activities reflect the cultural context in which people live. He argued that each culture provides its members (children and adults) with a distinctive set of tools for

These behaviors suggest that mothers viewed themselves as their children's teachers, who needed to give information and increase the children's desire to learn.

San Pedro mothers rarely taught vocabulary and rarely showed mock excitement. But more often than Salt Lake mothers, those in San Pedro first showed their children what they could do with the novel objects and then told their child to do the same. In other words, they modeled a behavior and expected their children to observe them carefully. Afterward, they did not directly test their children. Instead, they simply remained ready to respond to any requests for help.

Rogoff and her coworkers (1993) did not argue that one pattern of guided participation was better than the other. On the contrary, they argued that both patterns have value. In communities where children can often see adults engaged in important cultural activities, training children to observe carefully is especially valuable. In communities where adult occupations are achieved after a long period of schooling, an emphasis on verbal communication is especially valuable. Moreover, the two patterns are not mutually exclusive. Children benefit from dialogues with adults and from careful observation of adults engaged in important activities. Cross-cultural research on these two routes of competence can, therefore, contribute to a broader view of parenting and education.

| **TABLE 8.3** | *Patterns of Guided Participation in Two Communities* | |
|---|---|---|
| | SALT LAKE (U.S.) | SAN PEDRO (GUATEMALA) |
| Goals of development | Emphasis on preparation for schooling | Emphasis on preparation for adult activities (e.g., through household chores) |
| Modes of communication | Emphasis on verbal interaction | Emphasis on nonverbal cues (e.g., gaze, posture, touch) |
| Responsibilities for learning | Emphasis on adult teaching, with parents' motivating children through conversation and play as a peer | Emphasis on child observation, with caregivers available to provide assistance |

thought, including not only a specific language but also a mathematical system and strategies for solving cognitive problems.

Only a few later researchers have focused on Vygotsky's assumptions about the cultural context for learning (Tudge & Winterhoff, 1993). One reason is that his ideas about the role of culture varied over time, and some of those ideas are not widely accepted today (Wertsch & Tulviste, 1992). In his early work, Vygotsky argued that cultures differ in their evolutionary level. He suggested that "primitive" cultures do not provide their members with tools for thought as complex as modern cultures do. In his last writings, Vygotsky instead suggested that each culture provides its members with tools that match the activities and challenges in their own environment.

The validity of Vygotsky's final position is suggested by studies of cultural differences in how parents and children jointly arrange for the children's learning. Several of these studies are linked to a new perspective on culture and cognition that emerged during the 1980s and 1990s (Rogoff & Chavajay, 1995). Some of the most important cross-cultural research has been done by Barbara Rogoff and her coworkers. *Cultural Perspectives:* "Guided Participation in Mother-Child Interaction" describes her work on early patterns of mother-child interaction.

# ARE CHILDREN SOLITARY OR SOCIAL THINKERS?

At first glance, Piaget's and Vygotsky's ideas about social relationships and cognitive development could hardly look more different (Flavell, 1992). Piaget seemed to regard young children as little scientists, constructing not only theories about the world but their actual experience of the world through their own actions. According to Piaget, children learn about the existence of objects, about living things, about numbers, and about abstract systems of thought as they first reflect on their actions and later reflect on their logical operations.

By contrast, Vygotsky seemed to regard young children as social beings whose minds are formed by social interactions with other people. Children learn about the world and about themselves as they interact with adults and older children who talk with them and direct their activities. Most important, children develop language, an essential tool for reasoning, as social dialogues are transformed into the inner speech that constitutes thought.

These views of young children are linked to the two theorists' ideas about social and cultural influences (Glassman, 1994). Piaget believed that his cognitive stages represented the basic steps in the development of reasoning. Because these steps are so basic, social experiences and cultural pressures can only speed up or slow down children's progress. Neither the characteristics nor the sequence of the steps themselves can be changed.

Vygotsky believed that social experiences and cultural practices mold children's minds. In cultures that emphasize reading, for example, the mind is molded in one way. In cultures that emphasize learning through observation, the mind is molded in a different way.

Why did the two theorists come to such different conclusions? The answer becomes clear when you think about what they studied. Think again about Piaget's task for number conservation. He wanted to know when and why children discover that the number of objects in a row does not change if the row is stretched or shortened. This discovery tells children something about the world (of numbers) that is true in all cultures.

By contrast, think about children learning language, which for Vygotsky was the preeminent tool for thought. Children cannot learn language on their own. They must learn language through interactions with other people. Only after they have mastered social speech can they internalize that speech as a tool for thought.

These examples illustrate that Piaget and Vygotsky's perspectives on cognitive development complement rather than contradict each other. Both theorists explored children's relations to the world. However, Piaget focused on children's relations to the physical world; Vygotsky focused on children's relations to the world of social relationships and culture. Together, the two theorists offer a wealth of information about cognitive development.

# SUMMARY

**Piaget's Theories**
Piaget was a constructivist, who believed that infants and children construct their knowledge of the world through their activity. During his career Piaget presented many theories, many sets of ideas about how and why children's thinking and reasoning improve with age.

**Infant Cognition and Sensorimotor Intelligence**
Piaget described six stages of sensorimotor intelligence between birth and 2 years of age. He also discussed infants' understanding of the permanence of objects. Later research has shown that Piaget

underestimated the cognitive competence of young infants.

**Preschool Children's Ideas About the World**
In early studies Piaget defined animism, realism, and egocentrism as three errors in preschoolers' thinking. Later research has shown that Piaget exaggerated the contrasts between children's and adults' ideas about the world. Still, preschoolers' ideas are often qualitatively different from those of adults.

**Logical Reasoning in Middle Childhood**
According to Piaget, most children over 7 years of age are concrete-operational

thinkers. Most later researchers question Piaget's hypotheses about the logic underlying the concrete-operational stage. Later researchers agree with Piaget that thinking in middle childhood has several characteristics (e.g., the ability to make relative judgments) not found in the preschool years.

**Scientific Reasoning in Adolescence**
For Piaget, the highest stage of cognitive development was that of formal-operational thought. Like scientists, formal-operational adolescents think about abstract possibilities and solve problems using the hypothetico-deductive method. Later researchers have

disputed whether these new cognitive achievements reflect the emergence in adolescence of new forms of logic.

### Explaining and Accelerating Development
Piaget assumed that cognitive development could be accelerated only if children had prerequisite cognitive structures and the process of equilibration was activated by provoking cognitive conflict. Later research has shown that many techniques are effective in improving children's performance on Piaget's tasks.

### Vygotsky's Sociocultural Theory
Unlike Piaget, Vygotsky did not propose general stages of cognitive development. Instead, Vygotsky emphasized the influence of social experiences on the development of children's minds.

### The Social Origins of Cognition
Vygotsky argued that thinking itself was a product of social activity. His general law of development was that every cognitive process appears first on the social plane, during collaborative cognitive activity, and later is internalized.

### The Zone of Proximal Development
The zone of proximal development is the difference between children's level of performance when working independently and their level when working under the guidance of an adult or more capable peer. Adults help children develop when their guidance stays within this zone.

### Private Speech
Private speech is talking aloud that is not directed to a particular listener. Children use task-related private speech when making the transition from social speech to inner speech or thought. This kind of speech can improve children's problem solving.

### Implications for Education
Vygotsky regarded education primarily as training in the use of tools for thought. Reciprocal teaching is one method that is consistent with Vygotsky's theory and that improves children's reading comprehension.

### The Cultural Context of Development
Children in every culture acquire the tools for thought that are important in their culture. Rogoff's research on guided participation has shown that adults differ in whether they emphasize learning through verbal interaction or learning through adult demonstration and child observation.

### Are Children Solitary or Social Thinkers?
Piaget seemed to regard children as little scientists, making discoveries by themselves as they act on the world. Vygotsky seemed to regard children as social beings whose minds are formed to fit their social and cultural context. The two theorists' ideas most often complement rather than contradict each other.

# SUGGESTED READINGS

**Flavell, J. H., Miller, P. H., & Miller, S. A. (1993).** *Cognitive development* (3rd ed.). Englewood Cliffs, NJ: Prentice-Hall. In the 1960s John Flavell wrote a comprehensive book on Piaget's developmental theories. At the end of that decade, Patricia and Scott Miller were Flavell's students at the University of Minnesota. This team of researchers provides a balanced, readable account of Piagetian research and the broader theories and research that have followed it.

**Piaget, J. (1981).** *The psychology of intelligence.* Totowa, NJ: Littlefield Adams. You cannot understand Piaget's ideas fully until you read his own writings. But which of his scores of books should you read? Although this book was first published in English in 1950, it is based on lectures Piaget gave in 1942. The lectures are easier to read than many of Piaget's other writings. They provide a summary of Piaget's theories of cognitive stages.

**Rogoff, B. (1990).** *Apprenticeship in thinking.* New York: Oxford University Press. You have already read about Rogoff's research on guided participation. This book provides more information about her extension of Vygotsky's theory. She also draws connections between her research and studies of communication, social psychology, education, and anthropology.

**Vygotsky, L. S. (1978).** *Mind in society: The development of higher psychological processes* (M. Cole, V. John-Steiner, S. Scribner, & E. Souberman, Eds.). Cambridge, MA: Harvard University Press. This book is not a simple translation of Vygotsky's writings. Instead, it is a collection of his work that was carefully edited by a team that included prominent U.S. researchers. Publication of the book partly coincided with, and partly sparked, the revival of interest in Vygotsky's theory.

### Chapter Nine

# COGNITIVE DEVELOPMENT: INFORMATION-PROCESSING COMPONENTS

## WITH LUCIA A. FRENCH, UNIVERSITY OF ROCHESTER

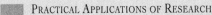

A ge changes in children's thinking can be examined from many perspectives. Chapter 8 focused on the perspectives of Piaget, Vygotsky, and the researchers who have accepted or criticized their theories. This chapter offers complementary perspectives by focusing on research that deals with the components of the information-processing system. To illustrate how this research differs from that associated with Piaget's and Vygotsky's theories, an example is useful. The following story, based on research by Saxe (1988a, 1988b), tells about the experiences and the cognitive competence of a boy who rarely attends school.

Child candy vendors in Brazil must develop a number of mathematical skills to perform their task successfully.

Jose, who is 10 years old, lives in the city of Recife, Brazil. Jose's family is poor, and he spends almost every day trying to make money for himself and his family. At 6 years of age, Jose started selling candy and other small items on the streets of Recife. He is now 10 years old, but he still spends most of his time selling candy rather than going to school. Jose is getting his education mostly in the streets, not in the classroom.

Jose's unusual education has given him an unusual profile of cognitive abilities. Suppose you show him two cards. Each card has a number printed on it. For example, one card might say 847 and the other card might say 1,000. If you ask Jose to tell you which of these numbers is larger, he gives you the correct answer less than half the time. He seems to have only a limited understanding of the basic math skills of reading and comparing numbers.

Then you give Jose a math problem that seems more difficult. You show him a bag of small candies and ask him to think about the price for which he would sell them. You suggest that he could sell one piece of candy for Cr$200 (200 cruzeiros, the Brazilian currency) or seven pieces for Cr$1,000. You ask him which method of pricing, one for Cr$200 or seven for Cr$1,000, would give him a bigger profit. You're surprised to find that Jose gets problems like these correct about three-fourths of the time. Indeed, he does much better on these problems than do children the same age who attend school regularly.

Then you realize what's happening. Every day while selling candy, Jose works with ratio problems like the ones you gave him. By contrast, he never needs to compare numbers out of context, as in the first problem. Therefore, he does less well on such problems.

The powerful effects of children's familiarity with specific types of problems may seem obvious, but these effects were long ignored by researchers (Laboratory of Comparative Human Cognition, 1983). Attention to these effects increased partly because of the emergence of the information-processing approaches mentioned in chapter 1 (Klahr, 1992). Researchers who advocate these approaches assume that children's thinking can be understood only if the elements of cognitive problems and the steps necessary to solve those problems are analyzed in detail.

Information-processing researchers emphasize the careful analysis of specific problems because they are impressed by the variations in children's performance on different types of problems. Notice, for example, that the performance of children like Jose varies greatly on number-comparison and ratio problems. Such variations make information-processing researchers unwilling to accept Piaget's hypotheses about general stages of cognitive development. Therefore, in contrast to chapter 8, you will not read in this chapter about any models of cognitive stages.

In another respect, traditional information-processing approaches are similar to Piaget in focusing on an individual problem solver confronted with a specific task (Bruer, 1994). Like Piaget, information-processing researchers have usually adopted the commonsense view that thinking goes on inside one person's head. By contrast, Vygotsky (1978) emphasized children's problem solving when working with other people. As you read in chapter 8, Vygotsky was particularly interested in children's problem solving when they were guided by adults or more-experienced peers.

In the early sections of this chapter, you will not read much about collaborative problem solving or about social influences on children's information processing. In the later

section on learning, however, you will see examples of researchers' attempts to improve children's performance on various cognitive tasks. These attempts involve instruction by adults, and so overlap with Vygotsky's focus. This overlap between information-processing approaches and Vygotsky's theory is discussed in the final section of the chapter.

You also should be aware that the story about Jose reflects only one kind of information-processing research. In chapter 1 you read that some information-processing researchers study the operation of the entire information-processing system as children think about cognitive problems. This approach was used in the research with candy sellers. Many other examples of research using the same approach are described later in the chapter.

An alternative approach is to study a single component of the information-processing system. The processes of perception and attention provide input to the system, and many researchers have examined how these processes change with age. The major findings of this research are reviewed in the next section.

Often, problem solving depends on linking new information obtained through perception with information already in the system. Research on mental representation deals with the organization of stored information about objects, places, and events. Research on world knowledge deals with the effects of children's knowledge about subjects like soccer on their solution of problems related to those subjects. Both types of research are examined in the second section of the chapter.

The retrieval of information stored in the system is the focus of research on remembering. Many cognitive problems can be solved by simply remembering relevant information. For example, you could use the phone book every time you want the number for a pizza delivery service. Memorizing the number would be much faster, though. How and why remembering improves during childhood is examined in the third section of the chapter.

The fourth section deals not with a single component of information processing but with the collection of processes that allows learning from experience. Basic processes of learning in infancy are examined first. Then the more complex forms of learning that occur in childhood, especially in classrooms, are examined.

Finally, you might wonder why the subtitle of this chapter is "information-processing components" rather than "information-processing theories." The distinction is important. Many researchers who study specific components of information processing would ally themselves with information-processing theories, broadly defined, but some would not. You will read, for example, about several learning theories with basic assumptions quite different from those of the information-processing approaches defined in chapter 1. Despite these theoretical differences, the general idea of information-processing components can serve as a framework for describing how specific facets of thinking and problem solving change with age.

# PERCEPTION AND ATTENTION

Information must be perceived before it can be processed further, so perception is a crucial component of information processing. Closely linked to perception is **attention,** which refers to the selective focusing of perception. Through perception and attention, children gain information about the world that affects other cognitive processes and the behaviors that result from them.

In chapter 5 you learned about the perceptual abilities of the newborn infant and the changes in perception during infancy. Most of that chapter dealt with **sensory primitives,** the simple reception of sensory input (Aslin & Smith, 1988). Some examples would be how well infants can distinguish between shades of gray, and whether they distinguish between sweet- and sour-tasting liquids.

By contrast, this chapter deals with the higher level of **perceptual representation,** how sensory input is interpreted or given meaning. The representation of input from the senses becomes more complex as children gain more experience in the world. In addition, improvements in perception contribute to improved performance on many cognitive tasks. The term **perceptual learning** refers to the improvements in perception as children grow older and to the improvements in cognitive performance that result from changes in perception (Pick, 1992).

**attention**
*The selective focusing of perception.*

**sensory primitives**
*The lowest level of perception, which deals with the reception of sensory input (e.g., the ability to distinguish shades of gray).*

**perceptual representation**
*The level of perception above that of sensory primitives. This higher level deals with the interpretation of sensory input (e.g., judgments of the functions of objects).*

**perceptual learning**
*The improvements in perception as children grow older, and the improvements in cognitive performance that result from changes in perception.*

The most important theory of perceptual learning was proposed by Eleanor Gibson (1969, 1992; Gibson & Radner, 1979; Gibson & Spelke, 1983). Gibson developed her theory before the information-processing perspective became prominent in cognitive development. She has described her approach as ecological, because she emphasizes the fit between organisms and their environments. However, other researchers who have studied Gibson's theory have often placed their work within the framework of information processing, so considering the theory in this chapter is appropriate.

Gibson argued that perception is always active and purposeful. Children (and adults) explore and monitor their environment in search of cues that will guide their behavior. Gibson stated this hypothesis more formally by introducing the concept of affordances. The **affordances** of an object are "what it offers that has utility and provides support for [a person's] actions" (Gibson, 1992, p. 218). In Gibson's terms, a floor affords support, water affords drinking, and an electrical outlet affords electrical connections—or a shock!

The most general goal of perception is to discover the affordances of the environment. Children discover what an environment affords by exploring the environment, attending selectively to objects and events, and learning to differentiate between objects with different affordances. Five conclusions about perceptual learning derive from Gibson's theory and later research (Gibson & Spelke, 1983; Miller, 1993; Pick, 1992).

1. *As children explore the world, they continually increase their knowledge of affordances in their environment.* If you watch children for long, you will see that they are learning constantly about the properties of objects, the meaning of events, and the characteristics of places. This learning may be most obvious in young children because they so quickly act upon what they have learned.

Before my youngest son was 2 years old, he learned a great deal about the operation of our home computer. He first learned that you can see interesting pictures on the computer's monitor and hear funny beeping sounds if you bang your hands on the keyboard. Then he learned that flat, square objects fit in a slot in the computer (as shown by his attempts to put a diskette into the disk drive). Shortly afterward, he learned that the button on the metal strip behind the computer would make the screen light up and start the computer beeping. In technical terms, he learned that a keyboard affords banging, a diskette affords insertion into the drive, and a switch on a power strip affords starting the computer.

My son's attempt to become computer literate was a bit backward. If you use a computer, you probably begin by turning on the power. If necessary, you then insert a diskette in the drive. Shortly afterward, you start banging on the keyboard. Although your sequence of actions differs from my son's, you had to learn about the affordances of a computer just as he did. That is, you had to engage in some kind of perceptual exploration. This aspect of perceptual development is important throughout life.

2. *Perceptual exploration becomes more systematic with increasing age.* Although young children explore their environment constantly, they explore more randomly than older children and adults do. Look at the pair of houses at the top of figure 9.1. Are the two houses the same or different? To answer this question, you would probably compare each window in one house with the corresponding window in the other house. After looking at all six pairs of windows, you would say that the two houses are the same because all the windows are the same.

Now, what about the pair of houses at the bottom of figure 9.1? Are they the same or different? If you start comparing windows at the top, you quickly notice that the windows on the top right are different in the two houses. Thus, you can give the correct answer, "different," after looking at no more than four windows.

How well do young children do on the same task? The accuracy of children's judgments about the identity of the two houses increases greatly between 4 and 8 years of age (Vurpillot, 1976). When researchers used a camera to record children's eye movements,

What will this boy learn by playing on the computer? He'll learn how to change the pictures on the screen, how to make the computer beep, and perhaps how to make lights on the keyboard turn on or off. In Gibson's terms, he will learn something about the affordances of the computer.

**FIGURE 9.1**
Are the two houses in the top row exactly the same, or are they different? What about the two houses in the bottom row? To answer these questions, you systematically scan each window of each house. Children only gradually develop such a systematic process of perceptual exploration. (From Vurpillot, 1968.)

they quickly found out why accuracy improves. As figure 9.2 shows, the average 8-year-old looks at nearly all the windows before judging two identical houses as the same, just as you would. The average 8-year-old looks at fewer windows when several pairs of windows differ in the two houses. In that case, 8-year-olds know they don't need to look at all the windows. They say "different" as soon as they find one pair of windows that is different, just as you would.

By contrast, 4-year-olds say "same" or "different" after viewing only about half the windows in the two houses. They also look at roughly the same number of windows when the two houses are identical and when they differ in three pairs of windows. In short, their visual exploration of the houses is unsystematic. Therefore, they are not often successful on the task.

Young children also have trouble with the house-comparison task because they rarely devise a plan for their perceptual exploration that fits the task they face. In one experiment (Vlietstra, 1982), children ranging from 5 to 11 years of age compared a standard house with six other houses. Each house had three doors. Behind each door was a picture.

FIGURE 9.2

The number of windows at which children looked when comparing pictures of two houses. Older children looked at almost all the windows when the two houses were identical to be certain that no windows differed. Older children looked at fewer windows when three windows differed, because they gave an answer as soon as they saw one pair of windows that was different. Younger children looked at roughly the same number of windows in both cases. (Source: Vurpillot, 1976.)

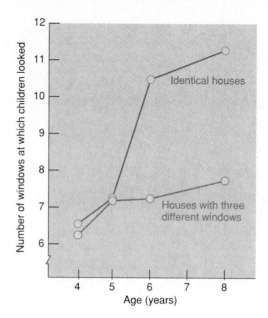

Five-year-olds explored the houses haphazardly, opening doors almost at random, as if they were playing a game. By 11 years of age, children not only explored systematically but also adjusted their behavior to the specific instructions for the task. When told to find *one* house that was different from the standard, they opened doors until they found one. When told to find *all* houses that were different from the standard, they looked at all of them. By contrast, 5-year-olds behaved similarly, no matter what instructions they received. The age change in reactions to instructions suggests that the older children, but not the younger, devised a plan for exploration that matched the instructions. The match between plans and instructions illustrates a third conclusion about perceptual learning.

3. *Perceptual exploration becomes more efficient with increasing age.* People explore more efficiently when they focus on the information needed in a specific situation. Of course, people need different kinds of information in different situations. Therefore, efficient exploration is flexible, adapted to particular tasks. Young children's exploration shows this flexibility less often than does that of older children.

Imagine that you are looking at a rectangular box. On the front of the box are two rows of doors with six doors in each row. When you open each door, you see a picture of an animal or a household object. Your task is to decide whether the pictures in the two rows are the same.

What do you do? You open the first door in the top and bottom rows. If the two pictures match, you open the second door in each row. You continue until you find two pictures that are different or until you have opened all the doors. Even 6-year-olds use this strategy most of the time (Miller et al., 1986). Thus, 6-year-olds explore more systematically than the 4- and 5-year-olds who compared houses in the earlier experiments.

Now the instructions change. Your new task is to find pictures of animals and then remember which animal is behind each door. You also get a hint: All the animals are behind the doors that have pictures of a cage on them. Household objects are behind the doors that have a picture of a house on them. So what do you do? You open the doors with cage pictures and ignore the doors with house pictures.

Few 6-year-olds adopt such a selective and efficient strategy. Even if they are told only to remember where the animals are, they often look behind the doors with houses on them. Many 6-year-olds do an exhaustive (or systematic) but inefficient search. They open corresponding doors in the two rows, or they open all the doors in one row and then all those in the other row. In short, they fail to match their exploration to the features of the task.

Age changes in the efficiency of children's exploration are found on other types of tasks (Gibson & Spelke, 1983). When comparing strings of letters, older children look longer at the

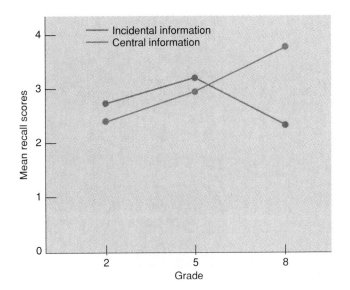

FIGURE 9.3

Because older children focus their attention more selectively, they learn information that is central to a task better than younger children do. Yet this focusing may also result in older children's learning less incidental information than younger children do. (Source: Miller & Weiss, 1981.)

critical letters in a string and less at irrelevant letters than younger children do. When comparing objects they can touch but not see, older children identify the information necessary for making comparisons more rapidly than younger children do. Older children are also more flexible in following instructions for attending to auditory stimuli, such as spoken words. In all perceptual modalities, then, efficient attention to stimuli increases with age.

4. *Perception of incidental information about a task sometimes decreases with age.* Selective attention to the information relevant for completing a task can have costs. In one study (Miller & Weiss, 1981), children again saw doors with pictures of animals or household objects on them. They again were told that they should find out where specific animals were. But this time the experimenter opened all the doors for the children and showed them which kind of object was behind each door. Then the experimenter asked children two types of questions.

For one type of question, the experimenter showed children a picture of an animal and asked which door that animal was behind. This question deals with *central* information, information to which children were instructed to attend. For the other type of question, the experimenter showed children a picture of a household object and asked which door that object was behind. This question deals with *incidental* information, information made available to the children (the experimenter *had* opened all the doors) when the children were prompted to attend to something else.

Figure 9.3 shows how accurately children in different grades answered the two types of questions. Accurate reports on central information increased steadily from second to eighth grade. Accurate reports on incidental information increased from second to fifth grade and then decreased slightly.

In other words, older children were more successful at the task defined by the experimenter's original instructions. They focused their attention more selectively and learned more about the pictures mentioned in the instructions. Younger children learned more about pictures not mentioned in the instructions. Their less selective attention paid off when the experimenter changed the task and asked for information not mentioned in the instructions.

The decrease with age in perception of incidental information was smaller in some earlier studies than in this one (see Hagen & Hale, 1973), which is why the conclusion states that older children *sometimes* perceive less incidental information than younger children do. Even so, all studies show a comparable developmental trend. The trend is even more obvious when elementary-school children are compared with college students (Lane, 1980).

Outside the psychology laboratory, the young child's strategy of *not* focusing so selectively on task-relevant information may be adaptive. When learning about the world, young

FIGURE 9.4

An item from the Matching
Familiar Figures Test. Look
carefully at the bear on top.
Then find which of the six bears
on the bottom exactly matches
the one on top.

From J. Kagan et al., "Information
processing in the child" in *Psychological
Monographs*, (Whole No. 578). Copyright
© 1964 by The American Psychological
Association. Adapted with permission.

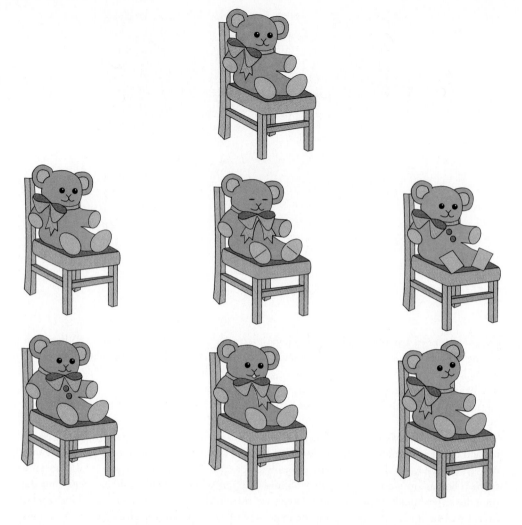

**differentiation**
*In perception, the process of analyzing
the component parts or properties of
objects so as to distinguish them.*

children may profit from taking a broad view. If these children focused only on information relevant for a specific task, they might have more difficulty adjusting to new tasks or instructions. Thus, wide-ranging exploration can have advantages for young children. By increasing their perceptual experience, this exploration prepares young children for the full range of tasks they will face as they grow (Vlietstra, 1982).

5. *Perception becomes more specific and more differentiated with increasing age.* When looking at a complex object, older children analyze it in its specific parts more readily than younger children do. In particular, older children perceive more details about the object's structure and form. The growing ability to make fine distinctions among the aspects or properties of objects reflects **differentiation** in perception.

Look for a moment at figure 9.4. If young children see these pictures, they are likely to say that they are all the same. Older children are more likely to pay attention to the distinct parts of each picture. They are more likely to notice that only one bear at the bottom exactly matches the bear at the top. (Try to pick which one it is.) The other bears differ in their bows, their chairs, or other details of their figures. Young children pay less attention to these details than to the overall similarity of the figures.

Even with simpler visual displays, younger children attend more to global similarity than older children and adults do. If 3-year-olds see circles that differ in both diameter and shade of green, they group together circles that are most similar in both size and color. By 5 years of age, children focus on a single dimension, either size or color, and put together

circles that are most similar on that dimension (Smith, 1989). The shift in perceptual focus from overall similarity to specific details and individual dimensions affects children's responses on a wide range of tasks (Aslin & Smith, 1988).

Perceptual differentiation also varies among children the same age. Figure 9.4 is an item from a widely used measure called the Matching Familiar Figures Test, or MFFT (Kagan et al., 1964). How fast and how accurately children respond to such items indicates their **cognitive style,** or the way they approach cognitive tasks (Zelniker & Jeffrey, 1976). *Reflective* children respond slowly to the MFFT items and are usually correct because they prefer to process information analytically, with attention to small differences. *Impulsive* children respond quickly and are often incorrect because they prefer to process information globally, in terms of overall similarity.

As you might guess, analytic processing of stimuli leads to greater success on many academic tasks than does global processing. Consider the printed letters *c* and *e*. The outside contours of these two letters are the same, but children must learn to differentiate between their interior parts in order to read. That differentiation is far from the last one children are asked to make. As they grow older, children must also learn to differentiate among many other symbols (e.g., $, @, &) that have special meanings in particular contexts.

Finally, you should recognize that the age changes described in this section involve not only perception and attention but other cognitive processes, too (Aslin & Smith, 1988). For example, efficient perceptual exploration requires several higher-order skills. Children must first understand the verbal instructions for a task. They must consider the instructions while planning a strategy for the task. Their plan must include a method of attending to stimuli that fits the task instructions.

In this example, as in "real life," perception and attention work in combination with language comprehension, strategy choice, and other cognitive processes. Therefore, perceptual learning is not a function of perception alone. It is influenced by developments in many other components of the information-processing system.

**cognitive style**
*The way that children approach cognitive tasks. Most researchers have focused on two contrasting styles, labeled reflective and impulsive.*

# MENTAL REPRESENTATION AND WORLD KNOWLEDGE

Differentiation in perception is closely related to changes in the mental representation of objects. When you first looked at figure 9.4, you probably perceived it—or mentally represented it—as a set of teddy bears on chairs. However, as you tried to find the two identical bears, you probably changed your mental representation of each bear.

Your final representation of the bear in the top row, if you had stated it in words, might have been something like "a teddy bear with eyes open and mouth closed who is looking straight ahead (not upward or sideways), who has a bow tied at the right side of the neck, no buttons on the front, and oval feet." Notice how many details about the bear have become part of your mental representation. In other words, your knowledge of the bear's features increased as you compared that bear with the others.

How children represent information is critical to their information processing. The information that they currently have, which defines their knowledge of the world, also affects their processing of new information. Moreover, mental representations and world knowledge change dramatically as children grow older and receive instruction in schools. The changes in children's concepts, in specific domains of their knowledge, and in their representation of places and events have been most thoroughly explored.

## Concepts and Categories

In common usage, the term *concept* means almost the same thing as *idea*. Within one area of cognitive-developmental research, however, this term is defined more narrowly. A **concept** is "a mental grouping of different entities into a single category on the basis of some underlying similarity—some way in which all the entities are alike, some common core that makes them all, in some sense, the 'same thing'" (Flavell et al., 1993, p. 88).

**concept**
*A mental grouping of different entities into a single category on the basis of some underlying similarity—some way in which all the entities are alike.*

Most common nouns such as *lion* and *tool* define concepts. Notice that the things categorized as the "same thing" may look similar: All lions have four legs, a tawny color, and a tail. Other concepts group together things that do not look at all alike: A knife does not look like a pair of pliers but both are tools.

To understand children's concepts, researchers have often asked them to classify objects. This task seems appropriate, because it seems only to require children to convert their mental groups into physical groups. But as you read, you will discover that a classification task is not the only way, and may not be the best way, to assess children's concepts.

Suppose that you give children some plastic toy figures—cowboys, horses, cows, barns, and houses. Some figures of each type are yellow, some are red, and some are blue. You ask the children to put together the toys that go together. You also ask them to explain why they put particular toys together.

Children's responses to such a task vary consistently with age (Bjorklund, 1995). Most 2-year-olds group the figures in a way that seems random to adults. When asked to explain their groups, they often make comments such as, "Those (e.g., a cow and a house) go together because I like cows and I like houses."

Most 3- and 4-year-olds group the figures that look alike. For example, they may put all the yellow figures in one group, all the red ones in a second group, and all the blue ones in a third group. They may also explain their groups with comments such as, "These all look the same."

In the early elementary-school years, children often group objects that have functional relations to each other. These children may put figures of cowboys together with horses and cows. If asked why, the children say that cowboys use horses to round up cows.

Finally, by 10 years of age children usually form groups that are consistent with the earlier definition of a concept. That is, they put all the cows in one group, the horses in another, and so on. Alternatively, they may form larger groups that fit more general concepts. For example, they may group the cows and horses because they are both animals.

Do these patterns show that children only form true concepts around 10 years of age? Other research shows that the answer to this question is a definite no. In cultures where no formal school system exists, even adults often group together objects that have functional relations to each other (Cole et al., 1971). So do elderly adults in our culture who have been out of school for many years (Smiley & Brown, 1979). In short, these adults form groups like those of young elementary-school children.

One researcher, puzzled by these findings, asked unschooled adults in the African country of Liberia to explain their groupings (Glick, 1975). They readily did so. For example, they said that they put a knife with an orange because "you use the knife to cut the orange." They also said that was how a wise man would group the objects.

Then the researcher asked one adult how a *fool* would group the objects. The man immediately put all the tools in one group, all the fruits in another, and so on. For this man, putting together objects that fit in the same general category made less sense than putting together objects that would be used together.

This evidence, and evidence from other studies, shows that the standard classification task does not always reveal the structure of people's concepts (Bjorklund, 1995). Instead, people's responses may show what they have been taught. In schools, children are often taught to put together things that have no functional relation to one another. For example, children may be asked to name the months of the year or the different types of governments. These experiences, and not their basic representation of concepts, may account for their grouping by conceptual relations when tested by an adult experimenter.

Researchers who have used alternatives to the classification task have found that young children have a surprisingly sophisticated understanding of concepts. For one alternative task, children judge the properties of unfamiliar objects (Gelman & Coley, 1990).

Suppose that you see a picture of a bluebird. You are told that it is a bird and that it lives in a nest. Then you see a picture of the extinct dodo bird, which had very short wings and could not fly. You are told that this is a bird and then asked if you think it lives in a nest. If you answer like most adults, you will say yes. Thus, you infer that the dodo lives in a nest because it belongs to the same category, *bird*, as the bluebird does.

**FIGURE 9.5**
Some of the birds on the top are more similar in shading to the airplanes at the bottom than they are to the other birds. Despite this perceptual similarity, even 9-month-old infants recognize the distinction between the global category of *bird* and the global category of *airplane*. (From Mandler & McDonough, 1993.)

Placed in the same situation, even 2-year-olds are likely to say that a dodo lives in a nest, although they do not say so as often as adults do. But if shown a picture of an extinct flying reptile, the pterodactyl, and told it is a dinosaur, most 2-year-olds say it does not live in a nest.

Although the pterodactyl looks more like the bluebird than the dodo, 2-year-olds ignore this type of similarity when judging where these animals live. Instead, the 2-year-olds seem to say that "Animals in the *bird* category live in nests. The dodo is a bird and the pterodactyl is not, so only the dodo lives in a nest." More generally, 2-year-olds' inferences seem to be based on conceptual similarity (what's common to birds) rather than perceptual similarity (which pictures look alike).

Attention to conceptual similarities has been demonstrated with even younger children. Figure 9.5 shows models of birds and of airplanes. The difference between the birds and the airplanes is obvious to you, but notice how similar the two sets of objects are in size, shape, and shading. The objects were also similar in texture because they had all been sprayed with the same plastic coating.

Would you expect 9-month-old infants to distinguish between the birds and the airplanes? Ingenious experiments have shown that they do (Mandler & McDonough, 1993). If these infants are given time to look at and touch several birds in succession, they express little interest in another bird. However, if they see an airplane after seeing several birds, they respond with renewed interest. The change in their behavior suggests that they place airplanes in a different category than birds, despite their perceptual similarity.

How infants make this distinction is currently controversial (e.g., Jones & Smith, 1993; Mandler, 1993). One possibility is that infants continually engage in a form of perceptual analysis that allows them to create concepts. For example, think about objects that you see in the sky. If you watch an object for a very short time, you can tell whether it is a bird or a plane. Birds can move in circles and change direction quickly. Planes move in a straight or slightly curved path and usually move at a constant speed. Your analysis of patterns of movement tells you whether an object is an example of the concept *bird* or the concept *plane.* Moreover, the same form of perceptual analysis may be available to infants (Mandler, 1992).

On the other hand, you learned in the previous section that the processing of perceptual information changes as children grow older. Along with these changes, children gain more knowledge about the relations among things. Changes in their concepts are therefore likely.

Frank Keil (1989) has argued that concepts reflect simple theories about the causes of similarities and differences between things. For example, you distinguish between cats and dogs (both four-legged house pets) because cats are members of the cat family (with lions, tigers, and so on) while dogs are members of a different family that includes wolves. In making these distinctions, you are aided by your knowledge of language, which includes words that distinguish objects and partly show relations among objects.

As children's theories about objects in the world change, so do their concepts. Perceptual analysis, knowledge acquisition, and language learning work in combination to change children's concepts as they move from infancy through childhood.

During the preschool years, children start to differentiate among different types of animals (Mandler, Bauer, & McDonough, 1991). During the elementary-school years, children increasingly make judgments about objects based not on their perceptual similarity but on theories about their essential characteristics (Farrar, Raney, & Boyer, 1992). In short, age changes in children's concepts reflect changes in their knowledge of the world.

## Knowledge in Specific Domains

Children who have different experiences acquire different knowledge about the world. For example, some children acquire more knowledge about the game of soccer than other children do. Some children acquire more knowledge about the game of chess than other children do. Researchers describe knowledge about soccer as falling in one domain and knowledge about chess as falling in a different domain.

Researchers describe children as *experts* when their knowledge in a particular domain is unusually extensive. Researchers describe children as *novices* when they know little about a particular domain. Experts and novices differ not only in how much they know about a domain but also in how their knowledge is represented and organized (Bjorklund, 1995; Larkin, 1979). Experts see more connections among concepts within the domain than novices do. Experts also think about problems in the domain at a deeper level. A novice on physics may think that a certain problem simply involves coiled springs. To a physics expert, the same problem may illustrate the principle of conservation of energy.

Differences in knowledge can strongly influence information processing. For one experiment, German children took a test on their knowledge about soccer rules and events during games (Schneider, Korkel, & Weinert, 1989). Children with high scores on the test were considered experts; those with low scores were considered novices.

Then the children listened to a tape-recorded story about a younger soccer player's experiences during an important game. After hearing the story, the children were asked to recall the story as fully and accurately as possible. Figure 9.6 shows that experts recalled the story better than novices at every grade level. Moreover, third-grade experts recalled slightly more than seventh-grade novices who were four years older.

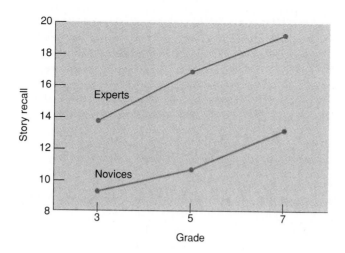

FIGURE 9.6
German children who know a great deal about soccer (experts) can recall more ideas from a story about a soccer game than children with less soccer knowledge (novices). Third-grade experts even recall the story better than fifth- and seventh-grade novices. (Data from Schneider et al., 1989.)

Given sufficient contrasts in expertise, children may even exceed adults in their cognitive performance. One study included a group of 10-year-olds who were experts in chess and a group of adults who were chess novices (Chi, 1978). Each child or adult saw a picture of a chessboard with pieces arranged as they might be arranged in the middle of a game. After viewing the chessboard for 10 seconds, the child or adult was asked to place actual chess pieces in the same positions on a blank board. Although the chess experts were only 10 years old, their performance on this task was superior to that of the adults.

The effects of domain-specific knowledge are not always so great (Schneider & Bjorklund, 1992). Sometimes expertise in a domain boosts young children's performance without making their performance equal to that of older children. Also, the effects of expertise vary with the task children are asked to perform. Expertise affects performance on simple recall tasks more than on tasks where children have an opportunity to organize information before they must recall it.

Still, domain-specific knowledge enhances problem solving on most tasks (Chi & Glaser, 1980; Glaser & Chi, 1988). Experts in a domain are more likely than novices to analyze a problem carefully before trying to solve it. Often, experts solve problems almost automatically by remembering how they solved similar problems before. Finally, experts have more accurate and abstract mental representations of problems than novices do, so their information processing more often leads them to the correct solution.

In school and in other settings, children gain expertise in many domains as they grow older. This expertise can partly explain why performance on most cognitive tasks improves with age. Cognitive development involves more than increases in children's knowledge in specific domains, however. Older children also develop skills that allow them to learn more, and so to move more quickly from novice to expert status, than younger children do (Flavell et al., 1993). Those skills are discussed in later sections of this chapter.

## Representations of Places and Events

So far you've learned about children's representations of things (concepts), and about children's knowledge of specific domains like soccer. Those kinds of representation do not capture two important aspects of the world. Things exist in space, and their placement is often meaningful. Things also exist in time. Changes in the relations among things, over time, define events. Children's world knowledge also includes representations of places and events.

### Spatial Representations

Stop reading for a moment and think about where you are. Think about an exit from your building that you cannot see right now. From your location, could you accurately point in the direction of that exit? Could you accurately point in the direction of the nearest bathroom? If so, you have a mental representation of your environment.

***Mental Maps: Indoors and Outdoors*** Children form a fairly accurate mental representation of their own home before they reach 5 years of age (Lockman & Pick, 1984). While standing in the kitchen with the door closed, they can point in the direction of their living room. They can also point in the direction of their bedroom on the second floor. However, their accuracy in pointing to rooms on another floor is lower than that in pointing to rooms on the same floor. Accuracy in pointing to objects on another floor increases after early childhood. That is, this type of spatial representation improves as children grow older (Rider & Rieser, 1988).

Of course, children's homes are relatively small and highly familiar environments. How accurately can children represent a large and novel environment like a college campus? Such a task can be difficult even for adults.

Do you remember the first time you stepped onto your college campus? Did you know where your classes met, where the library was, or even where to find a public telephone? Probably not at first. Gradually, though, you formed a mental map, a spatial representation of your environment. That map allowed you to move confidently from place to place and to find new routes from one point to another.

Now think of a young child visiting your college campus for the first time. Do you think the child could form an accurate mental map of such a large environment? To answer this question, researchers invited 6- and 12-year-old children to come to a college campus they had never visited before (Cornell, Heth, & Broda, 1989). Then each child was taken on a short walk across the campus. The walk followed the route shown in figure 9.7.

At the other end of the campus, the child was asked by the woman who accompanied the child to lead the way back to the starting point. The woman promised the child that they would not get lost. She also said she would give the child hints about which way to go if the child asked for them.

As expected, 12-year-olds were more successful in leading the way back than 6-year-olds. The 12-year-olds spent more time on the correct route and needed fewer hints from the adult because they had lost their way than 6-year-olds did. When children had to choose which path to take (the numbers in figure 9.7 show the choice points), 12-year-olds more often made the right choices than did 6-year-olds. The age differences suggest that older children constructed a more accurate spatial representation of the campus after a brief walk through it than younger children did.

Twelve-year-olds are as successful as adults at retracing their route across an unfamiliar college campus (Cornell, Heth, & Rowat, 1992). Their success does not mean that they have constructed a mental map exactly like the one in the figure. Even adults would probably need many trips on many routes before they could draw a map like that in the figure.

Moreover, such a detailed map is not necessary for retracing a single route. A simpler strategy for retracing the route is to identify landmarks at choice points and remember how those landmarks looked from the route. Older children and adults retrace a route across a campus more successfully if they are encouraged to look back several times during the first trip (Cornell et al., 1992). Looking back helps them represent how the landmarks will look on the return trip.

When given the same instructions to look back periodically, 6-year-olds do not retrace the route more successfully. Children this age also have special difficulty telling when they have strayed from the original route. When they stray, they have difficulty judging which way leads back to the correct route (Cornell, Heth, & Alberts, 1994). These findings suggest that mental representations of large-scale environments are more sketchy and less organized in younger children.

***Understanding Models of Environments*** If young children have trouble forming a spatial representation of an environment, why not give them a map to use? Better yet, make it a three-dimensional model made exactly to scale. Even preschool children should have no trouble representing an environment if they have a scale model before them, right?

Wrong. Using a scale model requires specific knowledge that preschool children develop only gradually. In fascinating experiments, Judy DeLoache, Nancy Burns, and their coworkers identified the kinds of knowledge required (DeLoache & Burns, 1993, 1994).

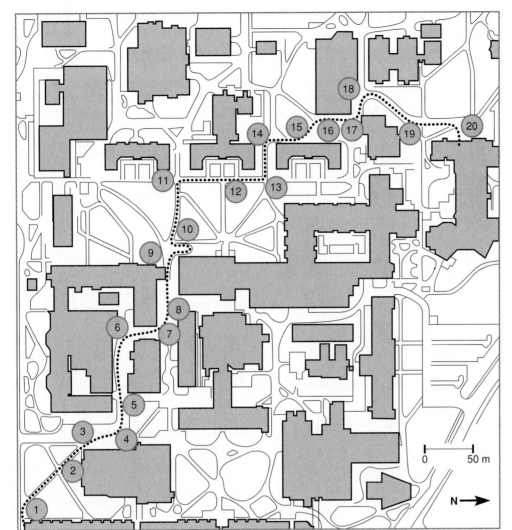

FIGURE 9.7

A map of the college campus on which children were tested for their ability to remember a path through an unfamiliar environment. The dotted line shows the path that children took from one end of the campus to the other. The numbered circles show choice points on that path. Circles are numbered in the order in which choice points were encountered on the return trip.

From E. H. Cornell et al., "Children's wayfinding: Response in instructions to use environmental landmarks" in *Developmental Psychology*, 25: 755–756. Copyright © 1989 by The American Psychological Association. Reprinted with permission.

The experiments also revealed a curious pattern of errors among young children who lack that knowledge.

In the standard experimental procedure, children see a room furnished like a typical living room with a couch, coffee table, armchair, and other living-room furniture. Children also see a scale model of the room that is about 2 feet square. In the model are miniature pieces of furniture that match those in the living room and that are in the same relative locations.

The experimenter shows children "Little Snoopy," a small toy dog, and explains that "Big Snoopy" is hidden in the living room. Then the experimenter puts the small toy dog behind the small couch in the model and says the big dog is hidden in the *same place* in the big room. Finally, the experimenter asks the child to find the big dog.

Most children who are at least 36 months of age can find the big dog in the living room. Most children who are only 30 months of age cannot find the big dog. The 30-month-olds can find the big dog if they see the experimenter hide Big Snoopy in the big room, so their problem is not in finding a hidden object. The problem is in using a scale model to judge where a full-size object is hidden.

Additional experiments showed that 30-month-olds lack **representational insight,** which is the understanding that a thing in a model stands for a corresponding larger object in a real-life setting. In particular, 30-month-olds do not appreciate that the little dog is a symbol for the big dog in the living room.

**representational insight**
*The understanding that an object in a model stands for a corresponding object in a real-life setting.*

**dual representation**
*The ability to think simultaneously about a symbol and the thing to which it refers.*

Understanding of this type of symbol requires **dual representation,** the ability to think simultaneously about a symbol and the thing to which it refers. To use the scale model, children need to consider Little Snoopy both as a toy that they could play with and as a symbol of Big Snoopy that can help them find Big Snoopy.

The importance of dual representation was shown by experiments in which 36-month-olds spent extra time looking at and playing with the scale model before they used it to find Big Snoopy. Recall that children this age normally do well on the standard task. However, when 36-month-olds were more familiar with the model, they did worse on the task of finding Big Snoopy. The extra familiarity apparently made them think of Little Snoopy more as a toy than as a symbol that could show them where Big Snoopy was.

Representational insight and an appreciation of dual representation are also needed to use other models of reality. For example, a photograph is a two-dimensional model of reality. If 30-month-olds are shown a photograph of Big Snoopy's hiding place in the living room, they usually can find Big Snoopy successfully. But few 24-month-olds succeed on the same task.

When children have just turned 2, they seem to view pictures only as things in themselves. They have not achieved an understanding of dual representation with respect to pictures. The same point can be stated less formally. To you, "one picture may be worth a thousand words"—but not to a child only 24 months old.

## Scripts and Special Events

Many events have a typical or standard order. As children participate in events, they quickly form a mental representation of them. In the following interview, a 4-year-old describes the typical order of events during a meal at a restaurant (French & Nelson, 1985, p. 15).

| Experimenter's Question | 4-Year-Old's Answer |
|---|---|
| Tell me what you do at a restaurant. | You come in and sit down. |
| | And a waiter comes along. |
| | And you order your food. |
| What else happens? | And then the waiter comes back |
| | with the food and you eat it. |
| What else happens? | You pay and then you go out. |

**script**
*A mental representation of a sequence of events that typically occur in a specific context.*

This 4-year-old, like most 4-year-olds, understood the normal sequence of events at a restaurant. Stated differently, the 4-year-old understood the restaurant script. A **script** is a mental representation of a sequence of events that typically occur in a specific context. The representation indicates which events occur first, last, and in between. It often includes information about the causal links between events (e.g., a waiter comes *to get your order*) and about optional elements (e.g., you might pay at the table or at the cash register).

When narrating a script, children use language appropriate for representing a routine event. They refer to individuals or groups of people with the nonspecific "you" (e.g., "you come in"). They use a "timeless" verb form, as in "you order," and "you pay." They also refer to people not by name but by their roles (e.g., "the waiter").

Katherine Nelson and her coworkers have argued that scripts are among the earliest and most stable forms of mental representation (Nelson, 1986, 1993a; Nelson & Gruendel, 1981; Nelson & Hudson, 1988). Preschool children often describe general representations of events more readily than they can describe specific events (Farrar & Goodman, 1992). For example, 3-year-olds can say a great deal about what generally happens when people go to the grocery store, but they may not be able to say what happened when they went to the store yesterday.

Children's knowledge of scripts is useful to them in understanding events, interpreting others' behavior, and planning their own behavior. For example, when children know the restaurant script, they can anticipate what will happen when their parents say they are going to a restaurant. They also can predict what the waiter and other customers will do. Finally, they know what they should do before, during, and after they eat.

Scripts may provide building blocks for more abstract forms of knowledge. Think about the concept *silverware.* This concept probably derives from scripts for eating meals.

Spoons, forks, knives, and other types of silverware are "things you use to eat with." (Notice the switch to "you" and the "timeless" verb.) In scripts for eating, all kinds of silverware belong in approximately the same "slot." Things that fill the same slot in a script can then be classified together as instances of the same concept (Lucariello, Kyratzis, & Nelson, 1992).

Not every event can be fitted into a script. Some events are truly special. Even young children can form a mental representation of such special events. For example, when 3-year-olds visit Disney World, they keep in mind whom they saw and what they did there. If interviewed 18 months later, they can report accurately on their visit. Moreover, they can give as much information about the visit as do children who were 4 years old when they went to Disney World (Hamond & Fivush, 1991).

You might also expect event representations to change with age, and they do. After a Disney World trip, older children can give more information about the event spontaneously, without prompting, than younger children can. Older children can also give more details about single events (Hamond & Fivush, 1991).

Similar changes occur in scripts (Nelson, 1986). Younger children's scripts rarely contain inaccurate information, statements about events that are not part of the typical sequence. However, older children provide more details about scripts. Older children also say more about how one event affects another, and about optional elements in the script. In short, both the amount of knowledge that children have about routine events, and the organization of that knowledge, increase with age.

# REMEMBERING

**Memory** refers to the cognitive processes that allow people to store, retain, and recall their experiences. People also use the word *memory* to describe what a person knows about past events. For example, people say things like, "We have fond memories of our trip." The heading for this section is *remembering*, because the emphasis is on memory as a process. Special attention is given to the developmental changes in remembering, starting in infancy.

**memory**
*The cognitive processes that allow people to store, retain, and recall their experiences.*

## Infant Memory

Do newborn infants have any memory at all? If *you* remember what you read in chapter 5, you know that the answer to this question is yes. Think, for example, about the research on a newborn's sense of smell. When only a few days old, breast-feeding infants will turn toward a nursing pad their mother had used rather than toward another mother's pad (Cernoch & Porter, 1985). Infants could behave this way only if they recognized—that is, remembered—the smell of their mothers' nursing pads.

Memory is functional even earlier than the first week of life. You also read about the phenomenon of habituation in chapter 5. If newborns are shown the same picture several times, they look less at the picture each successive time. The decrease in looking implies that the infants remember the picture from one time to the next. They act as if they said to themselves, "Oh, I've seen that picture before, and I'm bored with it."

Newborns habituate to visual stimuli, to buzzers or other sounds, and to the touch of various objects (Rovee-Collier, 1987). Even a fetus in the womb will show habituation. If a vibrating object is placed on a mother's abdomen when her fetus is about 7 months old, the fetus will start to jump around. If the object is removed for a short time and then placed again on the mother's abdomen, the fetus will again move. But if this sequence is repeated several times, the fetus will gradually quit reacting to the vibrations. That is, the fetus will habituate to the stimulus. This habituation shows that the fetus remembers something about its previous experiences. Also, a fetus who more rapidly habituates to a vibrating object is, after birth, more responsive to people and events than is a fetus who habituates slowly (Madison, Madison, & Adubato, 1986).

Still, if you considered only studies of habituation, you would think that young infants have very poor memories. Typically, infants behave as if they remember visual stimuli to which they have habituated for only a few minutes. If a short delay occurs between the habituation trials and the next stimulus presentation, infants respond to the stimulus they saw

before as much as to a novel stimulus (Rovee-Collier, 1989). After only a few minutes, infants act as if they forgot that they had ever seen the original stimulus.

More impressive memory performance has been demonstrated with a different procedure (Swain, Zelazo, & Clifton, 1993). Two-day-old infants will turn their head toward a novel sound, such as someone saying the word *beagle*. After hearing the word for a short time, they will habituate and stop turning toward the sound. If the same procedure is used 24 hours later, infants will turn toward the sound of a new word but not toward the sound of the same word. This difference in their behavior shows that they remember the word they heard a full day (one-third of their life!) before.

Beyond the newborn period, infants' memory has been assessed with other procedures. In a variant of the visual habituation procedure, infants see one stimulus repeatedly until they habituate to it. Then a delay occurs in which they don't see any stimuli. The delay period may range from a few seconds to days or weeks. After the delay, infants are shown not just one stimulus (the original one or a new one) but the original stimulus and a novel one.

By 2 or 3 months of age, infants prefer to look at novel stimuli rather than familiar stimuli. Therefore, they will look less at the original stimulus than at the novel stimulus—if they remember that they saw the original stimulus before. To test infants' memories, researchers see how long the delay can be before infants show no preference for the novel stimulus. Because this test involves infants' recognition of visual stimuli, it is called a test of **visual recognition memory** (Fagan, 1984).

By 5 months of age, infants can recognize visual stimuli after a delay of two weeks. Recognition memory is enhanced when infants have more time to look at the original stimulus. With more time to study the original stimulus, infants can more easily recognize that stimulus when it is paired with a novel one. Also, recognition is enhanced when the novel stimulus differs to a greater extent from the original stimulus. When the two stimuli differ greatly, infants more easily recognize the original stimulus.

By varying the experimental conditions, researchers have discovered how infants' recognition memory improves with age. As infants grow older, they recognize stimuli after longer delay intervals, with shorter study times, and with smaller differences between the original and novel stimuli (Fagan, 1984). The results are so consistent, and the resulting measures so reliable, that researchers have begun to use this procedure to examine topics other than memory.

Some researchers have used tests of visual recognition memory as measures of infant intelligence. These tests are discussed in chapter 10. Other researchers have adapted the visual recognition memory procedure to study the age changes in infants' categorization of visual stimuli (Younger, 1993; Younger & Gotlieb, 1988). One finding in these studies is that even 3-month-olds can judge when two or more stimuli represent variations on a simple pattern. In other words, even three-month-olds can detect the category into which several stimuli fall. As infants grow older, they can judge when two or more stimuli represent variations on complex patterns. Thus, the procedure for assessing infants' visual recognition memory has also provided information about other aspects of cognitive development in infancy.

Another experimental procedure yields even more impressive estimates of young infants' memory ability (Rovee-Collier, 1989, 1995). Figure 9.8 shows a 2-month-old girl in a crib with a ribbon tied to her ankle. The other end of the ribbon is tied to a mobile above her crib. When the infant kicks her legs, the ribbon moves and jiggles the mobile. For infants, seeing the mobile jiggling is rewarding, so they kick more often. In the language of operant conditioning, the mobile's movement is a reinforcement for kicking.

Now the memory question. How long do infants remember that they can make the mobile move by kicking their legs? Suppose you wait a few days and then put infants back in the crib with the mobile overhead. For this repeat performance, disconnect the ribbon from the mobile. Then you can see whether infants kick as much on their second time in the crib as they did the first time, after they learned that kicking moved the mobile. If they do, you can infer that they remember their kicking leads to an enjoyable visual display.

**visual recognition memory**
*An experimental paradigm that allows researchers to determine how long infants can remember specific visual stimuli.*

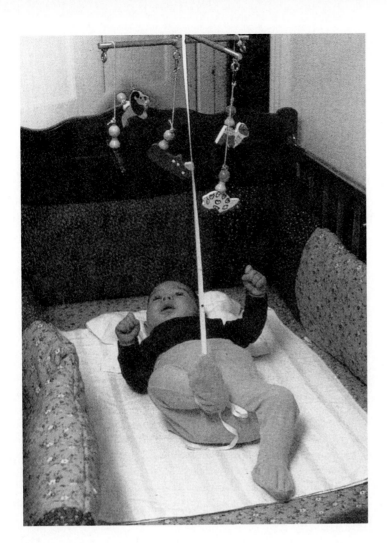

FIGURE **9.8**
This infant is learning to move the mobile by kicking her legs. Days or weeks later, researchers will place the infant in the same situation again and see whether she remembers the association between kicking and mobile movement. (From Rovee-Collier, 1989.)

Figure 9.9 shows the results for 2- and 3-month-olds tested after different delay intervals. Average "retention ratios" are shown on the y axis. Infants have a retention ratio of 1.0 if they kick as much at the beginning of the second session as they did at the end of the first session. That is, they act as if they are starting just where they left off. They seem not to have forgotten anything about their prior experience.

Retention ratios of around 0.5 mean that infants kick during the second session only half as much as they did at the end of the first session. This rate is no higher than that of infants who never moved the mobile by kicking their legs. Therefore, a ratio of around 0.5 implies that infants forgot what happened during the first session. The stars in the figure mark retention ratios that are significantly greater than 0.5, or high enough to draw the conclusion that infants remembered their first session.

The figure shows that 3-month-olds remember their first session in the crib almost perfectly for several days. Even after eight days, 3-month-olds who learn that their kicking makes the mobile move kick more during the second session than infants who never did so.

Memory is poorer in 2-month-olds. After only three days, these infants seem to have forgotten what happened during the first session. However, 2-month-olds' performance was more impressive in a later experiment. When 2-month-olds began with three sessions of reinforced kicking instead of one, they remembered the association of kicking with the jiggling of the mobile for two weeks. In addition, their performance matched that of the 3-month-olds who were in the same experiment (Rovee-Collier, 1989).

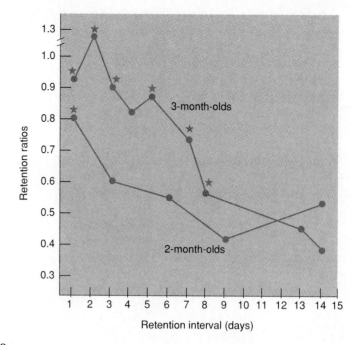

## FIGURE 9.9

Two- and 3-month-olds were tested for their memory of the association between kicking and movement of a crib mobile. Retention ratios of 1.0 indicate that infants kicked as often on a day after the original training as on the day they were trained, which suggests that the infants remembered the association between kicking and mobile movement. Retention ratios of 0.5 or less suggest that infants forgot the association between kicking and mobile movement because infants kicked that often before any training. The stars indicate ratios significantly higher than expected by chance.

Source: From Rovee-Collier, *Memory: Interdisciplinary Approaches.* Copyright © 1989 by Springer-Verlag New York, Inc. Reprinted by permission.

Under the right conditions, young infants can remember experiences far longer than two weeks. Suppose that you wait a month before placing a 3-month-old girl back in the crib with the mobile above her. But this time you don't measure her kicking. You just let the infant watch as *you* jiggle the mobile for a few minutes. Your jiggling serves as a reminder of her original experience.

A day later, you bring the infant back to the lab. To test her memory, you observe how much she kicks when placed in the crib again. With the benefit of a reminder the day before, 3-month-olds show retention ratios of around 1.0, even after one month. Two-month-olds show high retention ratios after three weeks but not after a full month. In each case, reminders seem to reactivate or reinstate a memory that would otherwise be inaccessible.

Most surprising are the effects of variations in the time between the reminder and the memory test. When infants get the reminder right before the memory test, it is ineffective. When they get the reminder an hour before the test, it doesn't help. Memory does improve if the reminder is given 8 hours before the memory test. A reminder is even more effective if given 24 hours in advance. It is most effective if given three days in advance!

Comparable results have been found in studies with animals, children, and adults (see Rovee-Collier, 1995). Apparently, reactivating a memory of an experience can take considerable time. In infancy, some cognitive processes must operate for hours or even days before infants reestablish the mental connection between their leg kicks and the mobile's movements (Rovee-Collier, 1989).

Other variations in this experimental procedure have led to more discoveries (Rovee-Collier, 1995). First, reminders only work if infants receive two sessions of training initially, and those sessions are less than four days apart. If only one session is given at first, infants' memories apparently are not strong enough to be reactivated by a reminder. If the first two sessions are too far apart (four days or more), infants seem to view them as separate events, and so have weak memories for each.

Second, infants' memories can be modified by changing the characteristics and the timing of their experiences after training. Suppose 3-month-olds receive two days of training with a mobile that has yellow blocks with the number "2" written on them. Either one day or three days after those training sessions, infants are shown a new mobile that has stylized wire butterflies hanging from its arms. Infants see this mobile for three minutes but cannot kick their legs to move it (the ribbon is not attached). A day later, infants' memory for their experiences is tested.

During the test, infants who saw the novel mobile one day after training respond strongly both to that mobile and to the original mobile, showing that they remember both of them. Infants who saw the novel mobile three days after training respond strongly to the novel mobile but not to the original one. Apparently, seeing the novel mobile three days after training makes it difficult for infants to retrieve a memory of their original experience: Infants only remember what happened the previous day.

In summary, remembering in infancy is surprisingly complex. How long infants remember an experience depends on how extensive their experience was, whether they receive a reminder about the experience, when the reminder is given, and other variables. Moreover, infants' memories can be reactivated, updated, and modified in other ways. Remembering improves during and after infancy, but many intriguing features of human memory can be seen and studied in infants only 2 or 3 months old (Rovee-Collier, 1995).

## Remembering in Childhood

To assess children's memory, researchers normally use tests much more direct than the procedures used with infants. Try taking a simple test. First read the following numbers, one second at a time:

4-6-3-1-5-7-2

Now look away from this page for a few seconds and then try to repeat the numbers aloud. If you are successful in doing so, your **digit span** is at least seven. Digit span equals the number of digits (or numbers) you can remember long enough to repeat them correctly after hearing them once.

**digit span**
*The number of digits (or numbers) that a person can remember long enough to repeat correctly after hearing them once.*

The average adult has a span of roughly seven digits. Span increases regularly with age. The average 2-year-old can repeat either two or three digits accurately; the average 5-year-old can repeat between four and five digits; the average 9-year-old can repeat about six digits. Less dramatic changes occur in the number of words and letters that children can repeat accurately (see figure 9.10). That is, word span and letter span also increase regularly with age (Dempster, 1981).

The age changes in span show that performance on typical memory tasks improves with age. You are probably not surprised by this result. The more interesting question is why the improvement occurs. Researchers have offered four types of explanations for age changes in remembering. As you will see, systematic research has yielded some evidence consistent with all four.

### Processing Capacity or Speed of Processing

One possible explanation for the age changes in memory span is that memory capacity increases with age. Stated figuratively, older children have more slots in which to hold information temporarily. In this view, younger children have smaller memory spans because they forget information that they receive when their few slots are already full. The increase with age in memory slots is usually attributed to maturation. That is, normal biological changes in the brain are assumed to produce an increase in memory capacity.

FIGURE 9.10

As children grow older, they can remember longer lists of numbers (or digits), words, and letters. In short, memory span increases with age. Why do you think this increase occurs? As you continue reading, you'll see some answers that researchers have proposed. (Source: Dempster, 1981.)

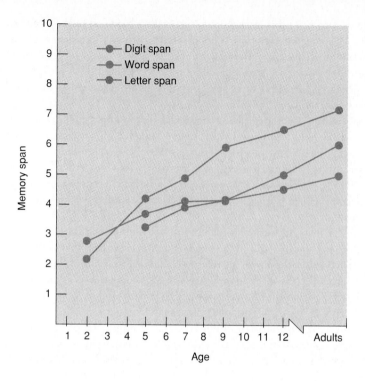

**working memory**
*The memory available for current cognitive processes.*

A few theorists have suggested that age changes in memory span are due to biological changes in memory capacity (e.g., Pascual-Leone, 1970), but some data are difficult for these theorists to explain. Apparent memory span varies for different tasks (see, e.g., the different lines in figure 9.10), and the reasons for these variations are not clear. If children had a certain number of memory slots and adults had more, the differences between children's and adults' performance should be more consistent across tasks (Siegler, 1983).

Still, the hypothesis of age changes in memory capacity is difficult to test, and therefore difficult to disconfirm. Some researchers judge the current evidence as showing that memory capacity does not increase with age (Bjorklund, 1995; Dempster, 1981). Other researchers tentatively draw the same conclusion but consider the issue still debatable (Flavell et al., 1993; Siegler, 1991).

Robbie Case (1984) has argued that total memory capacity does not increase as children get older, but the proportion of total capacity that can be used for storing information does increase. Figure 9.11 shows the contrast between these two hypotheses. In the figure, the amount of mental space that a given child has for processing information is shown by a circle. This space can be defined as the child's **working memory,** the memory available for current cognitive processes. Notice that total processing space is divided in two parts, one for operating space and one for storage space. Operating space is devoted to perception, attention, monitoring body functions, and so on. Storage space is used for holding information temporarily.

Now notice how the two models explain the developmental change in storage space, or memory span. In Model I, the entire circle representing working memory is larger at 10 than at 5 years of age. In other words, the 10-year-old is assumed to have a larger memory capacity than the 5-year-old. As mentioned, current evidence casts doubt on this model but does not clearly show that it is false. Therefore, an increase in memory capacity might be one reason for the improvement with age in children's memory.

In Model II, the total capacity of working memory does not increase between 5 and 10 years, but storage space increases because operating space decreases. According to Case (1984), operating space decreases because older children execute cognitive processes more efficiently or more automatically than younger children. The increasing efficiency of perceptual exploration was mentioned earlier in the chapter. Other cognitive processes also become

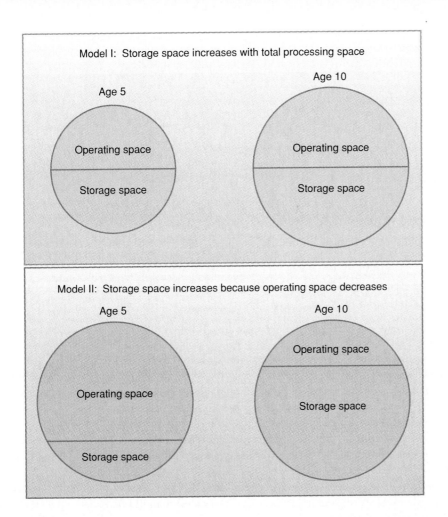

FIGURE 9.11
Two models of the developmental changes in working memory. Model I suggests that the total space available for processing information increases with age. Model II suggests that information processing becomes more efficient, so the operating space needed for solving problems decreases. This change leaves more space for storing information. (Adapted from Case, 1984.)

more efficient with increasing age. Even an act as simple as counting objects can be done more quickly by older children than by younger children (Case, Kurland, & Goldberg, 1982). Improvements in scientific and social reasoning can also be explained by increases with age in operating space (Marini & Case, 1994). Therefore, most researchers agree that Model II partly explains the increase with age in memory span (Bjorklund, 1995; Flavell et al., 1993).

What, then, explains the increase with age in the efficiency of cognitive operations? This question is controversial, but some theorists argue that basic biological changes in the brain are responsible. For example, Case (1985) suggested that **myelinization,** the coating of nerve fibers with an insulating tissue called *myelin,* may account for the increase in processing efficiency.

Robert Kail (1988, 1991, 1993) has not tried to specify exactly which aspect of brain development leads to the age changes in processing efficiency. He argues strongly, however, that the age changes must be linked to a basic change in brain functioning because similar age changes are found on very different tasks.

Kail studied children's performance on memory tasks, on the mental rotation task described in chapter 2, and on other tasks. Children responded more quickly on all these tasks as they grew older. Kail (1991) also reexamined the data from dozens of other studies involving thousands of children and adults.

Figure 9.12 shows how children's reaction times compare with those of adults doing the same tasks. Six-year-olds take almost three times as long to react as adults do. Twelve-year-olds take between one and two times as long as adults do. The age changes in reaction times are greater between 6 and 12 years of age than between ages 12 and 20.

**myelinization**
*The coating of nerve fibers with insulating tissue (myelin).*

FIGURE 9.12

Speed of processing increases with age on many cognitive tasks. The age change is most dramatic in the first decade of life. (Adapted from Kail, 1991.)

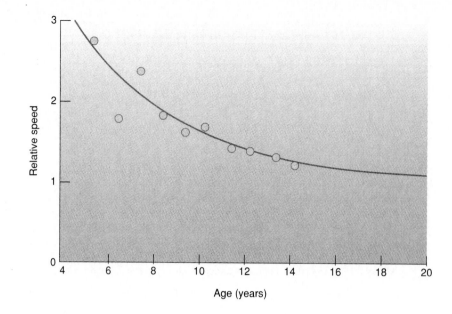

Most important, the age changes in speed of processing are virtually identical for different tasks (Hale, 1990; Kail, 1993; Kail & Park, 1994). Whether children are working with letters, numbers, or other types of visual stimuli, the curve in figure 9.12 accurately describes how their speed increases with age. The curve applies to tasks as varied as repeating lists of words, doing mental addition, or mentally rotating letters or numbers.

You might assume that speed of processing is only important for tasks where reaction time is measured directly—but you would be wrong. Most cognitive tasks are affected by processing speed in some way.

Think, for example, about reading (Kail & Hall, 1994). To read fluently, you must recognize individual words and hold those words in memory until you have read all the words in a sentence. If you are slower in recognizing words, you may take so long to read a sentence that you've forgotten the beginning before you get to the end. Because children process information more slowly than you do, they cannot comprehend sentences as long and complex as you can.

In summary, speed of processing increases greatly during childhood and adolescence. The age change in processing speed affects performance on memory tasks and so can partly explain why remembering is better in older children. In addition, similar increases with age in processing speed are found across a wide range of tasks. This similarity suggests that the increases depend more on brain maturation than on children's experience with specific tasks.

## Memory Strategies

One important exception to the general rule about age changes in processing speed must be mentioned (Kail, 1993). The age changes are similar across tasks only when children and adults solve tasks in the same way. For example, adults and children use the same cognitive process when working on a task like mental rotation. On certain tasks, however, adults use cognitive strategies that children do not use. By using appropriate strategies, adults multiply the benefits of their greater processing speed. Age changes in strategy use provide a second explanation for the improvements with age in remembering.

Think back to the example of the digit-span task. What did you do after you read the numbers, while you were looking away from the page? Many adults repeat the numbers "in their heads" during that time. In psychologists' terms, adults use the memory strategy of re-hearsal. **Rehearsal** involves repeating the information to be remembered, aloud or silently, during the interval between receiving that information and being asked to recall it. Rehearsal is one of several strategies that adults use more often and more efficiently than children do.

**rehearsal**

*A memory strategy that involves repeating the words or information to be remembered either aloud or mentally.*

***Rehearsal: When Children Do It, and Why They Don't*** Rehearsal seems like an obvious strategy for remembering lists of items. It is not obvious to preschool children, though. Few preschool children rehearse aloud or mentally when they have a list to remember. In a classic study (Flavell, Beach, & Chinsky, 1966), only 10 percent of 5-year-olds rehearsed the names of objects they were asked to remember, but 85 percent of 10-year-olds did so.

Older children also use rehearsal more effectively than younger children (Pressley & Van Meter, 1993). When 7-year-olds rehearse a list of words, they usually repeat one word several times in a row. Older children and adults repeat several words in order, thus connecting the words in memory.

With increasing age, children more precisely match their rehearsal strategy to the specific requirements of a task. If adults know that they will receive extra points for remembering certain words, they rehearse those words more than the rest of the list. Children are less likely to change their rehearsal strategy in this way (Kail, 1990). This example shows that flexibility in rehearsal improves for several years after this strategy is first used spontaneously.

One puzzling question is why most 5-year-olds and younger children don't use rehearsal spontaneously when given a memory task. Children who do not rehearse spontaneously can be trained to do so (Keeney, Cannizzo, & Flavell, 1967). And when these children rehearse, they remember more items on a list. So they *can* use the strategy, and they benefit from doing so.

Children have a **production deficiency** when they do not spontaneously use strategies that would improve their performance. One reason for production deficiencies is young children's lack of cognitive planning. Often, young children don't think of using any strategy for remembering lists. They don't try to devise a plan that will make remembering easier. You read about young children's lack of planning in the earlier section on perceptual learning. Age changes in tendencies to plan ahead also influence children's remembering.

Another possible reason for production deficiencies focuses on the effort needed to carry out a strategy. Imagine that you had to tap a telegraph key as fast as possible, but you also had to repeat a list of words while you tapped. (Does this remind you of the old joke about the man who couldn't walk and chew gum at the same time?) You would tap more slowly when rehearsing the words than when simply tapping. The same is true for children, but adding rehearsal has a greater effect on younger children's tapping rate (Guttentag, 1984). Apparently, rehearsing a list of words takes more effort for younger children and so conflicts to a greater extent with tapping on a key.

Because rehearsal takes so much effort, young children sometimes forgo use of this strategy. Instead, they rely on simpler strategies such as listening carefully to a list of words (Flavell, 1985). But with practice, rehearsal becomes easier, more automatic, and more efficient. Then children often use the strategy spontaneously.

A third reason for production deficiencies is that children do not always know that using a strategy would be valuable. Children's remembering improves when they are trained to use rehearsal, as mentioned earlier (Keeney et al., 1967). But young children may not notice the improvement. If they don't notice it, they may not continue to rehearse after the training ends. Later, you'll read more about how children's knowledge of memory strategies affects their remembering.

***Other Memory Strategies*** Sometimes rehearsal is less effective than other strategies for remembering. Organizing information is another strategy that is suitable for certain memory tasks. For example, a grocery list might include various meats, vegetables, and paper products. By mentally organizing the specific items into these categories, memory can be improved. Once this mental organization is complete, recall of the category label is likely to trigger recall of the specific items in the category.

Occasionally, adults use a memory strategy called **elaboration,** which involves linking items to be remembered in a vivid image or a novel sentence. Suppose you were learning Spanish and wanted to remember that the Spanish word *carta* means *letter* in English. You could link *carta* and *letter* in a mental picture of a letter in a grocery cart. Or you could

**production deficiency**
*A failure to spontaneously use memory strategies (or strategies for completing other cognitive tasks) that would improve performance.*

**elaboration**
*A memory strategy based on linking items to be remembered in a vivid image or a novel sentence.*

remember the sentence, "The letter was in the mailman's cart." Either technique of elaboration would improve your recall of the Spanish word (Pressley, 1982; Pressley & Van Meter, 1993).

The age changes in the organization and elaboration strategies largely mirror those for rehearsal. Young children use these strategies less than older children and adults do. The organization strategy is more complex than rehearsal, and its spontaneous use emerges somewhat later in development (Flavell et al., 1993). Spontaneous use of the elaboration strategy emerges even later. The most advanced thinkers studied by memory researchers—college students—do not always use elaboration when doing so would improve their remembering (Pressley & Van Meter, 1993).

However, even young children are not completely lacking in effective memory strategies. True, they rarely rehearse, rarely organize information, and rarely use elaboration. Still, young children seem much more competent at remembering if the focus shifts to a different set of strategies for different kinds of tasks. More specifically, young children often successfully handle the memory tasks they face in their daily lives.

Think about one task that all children face, that of remembering where they put their toys. Now think about an experimentally controlled version of that task. An adult shows a 1½-year-old a stuffed toy that resembles Big Bird (from the TV show "Sesame Street"). Then the adult hides the toy under a pillow while the child watches. Once the toy is hidden, the adult asks the child to remember where the toy is. Next, the adult invites the child to play with other toys in the room. Four minutes later, a bell rings, and the adult asks the child to find the toy.

When given this task, nearly all children between 1½ and 2 years of age succeed in finding the toy. Over repeated trials, these toddlers find the toy almost 90 percent of the time (DeLoache, Cassidy, & Brown, 1985). To remember the toy's location, toddlers use several strategies. They talk to the adult or to themselves about the toy and its hiding place. They look toward the hiding place and point at it. They often move toward the hiding place during the interval before the bell rings.

All these behaviors occur more often after the toy is hidden than in a comparison condition in which the toy is visible. The contrasts between the toddlers' behaviors in the two conditions imply that their talking, looking, and other behaviors toward the hidden toy are not only signs of attention. They are also strategies toddlers use for remembering where the toy is.

By 3 or 4 years of age, children can use a primitive form of the organization strategy. They do not mentally categorize words or objects, but they will put objects in groups that make it easier to remember their distinctive characteristics (DeLoache & Todd, 1988). Preschoolers do not use the grouping strategy consistently, though. They sometimes make mistakes when putting objects into groups; they sometimes fail to group all the objects once they have started to use a grouping strategy.

For these reasons, young children do not always remember better when they use a strategy than when they don't. Strategies are most likely to improve performance when children have fully mastered them (Ornstein, Baker-Ward, & Naus, 1988). Until children reach the point of mastery, they may put so much mental effort into using a strategy that they have little left to do the task. Indeed, performance on many types of tasks often does not change or even deteriorates when children first use a new strategy (Flavell et al., 1993; Miller, 1990). Using the strategy takes mental effort that reduces the amount of processing capacity available for other cognitive processes and so impairs overall performance.

As children gain more practice with a cognitive strategy, use of the strategy becomes more automatic. Automatically activated strategies put little or no load on processing capacity. Therefore, the benefits of the strategy become apparent. In short, children's performance improves.

***Cultural Influences on Strategy Use***   The development of memory strategies is strongly influenced by children's experience. Children often learn strategies such as rehearsal and organization from their parents or their teachers (Carr et al., 1989; Pressley & Van Meter, 1993). In schools especially, children are often expected to remember lists of items (e.g., all the U.S. presidents). They are also expected to know the categories in which different pieces of information belong (e.g., the one-celled organisms that are classified into larger groups).

Not surprisingly, children receive direct or indirect instruction in strategies that make remembering this information easier.

Sometimes strategies learned for school are inappropriate for other kinds of tasks. Suppose that you must remember the location of objects in a three-dimensional panorama. The panorama includes models of a mountain or volcano, a lake, a road, trees, and buildings. While you watch, an examiner places 20 small objects like toy cars, toy animals, and household items in the panorama. Your task is to remember which objects are in which locations.

After you have studied the panorama for as long as you want, the examiner asks you to take a break. During the break, when you are not watching, the experimenter removes the 20 objects and places them in a larger set of 80 objects. After the break, the experimenter asks you to place the 20 objects in the panorama where they were before.

What would you do to improve your memory on this task? What strategies would you use? When given this task, 9-year-olds in the United States and in a small town in Guatemala used different strategies (Rogoff & Waddell, 1982). About one-third of the 9-year-olds from the United States used a rehearsal strategy. That is, they repeated the names of the objects during the study time. That strategy is not especially appropriate for the panorama task. The greatest problem on that task is not remembering the names of the objects but remembering their locations.

Almost none of the Guatemalan children used the rehearsal strategy. Instead, they looked closely at the panorama, trying to fix a picture of it in their minds. Similar strategies have been reported in other studies of children in traditional cultures, such as aborigine children in Australia (Kearins, 1981). Close visual attention to the surrounding world and the objects in it may be adaptive for people who hunt or gather food in an open, changing environment. This strategy also seems adaptive for memory tasks in which spatial arrangement is important. On the panorama task, Guatemalan children did better than U.S. children, although the difference was small.

Few researchers have studied the development of this visual strategy for remembering. Why not? Perhaps because this strategy is not very effective for remembering the lists that are important for schoolchildren in modern societies. Thus, the cultural context affects not only which strategies develop in childhood but also how researchers design their studies of strategies.

## Remembering and World Knowledge

A third explanation for age changes in remembering emphasizes the benefits of increases in relevant knowledge. Think about that seven-digit number that you read earlier. Suppose that, by chance, the number matched your telephone number. Then you would have had no trouble remembering the number. You might have said to yourself, "I don't need to try to *remember* that number; I *know* it."

This example suggests a general hypothesis about memory development: Memory improves with age because older children have a more extensive **knowledge base,** or greater knowledge about the world, than younger children do. Children add to their knowledge base each day, so they should more often find that their knowledge helps in solving specific memory tasks. In short, they should remember things more easily as they become more knowledgeable.

**knowledge base**
*A person's knowledge of the world, especially the knowledge that is helpful for remembering new information or solving cognitive problems.*

In the section on mental representation, you read about research in which children's knowledge base affected their remembering. One example dealt with children's memory for a short story about a soccer player (Schneider et al., 1989). Another example dealt with children's and adults' memory for the position of chess pieces on a chessboard (Chi, 1978). In both studies, children who had more knowledge about the relevant domain—who were experts on soccer or chess—did better on the memory test.

Children's knowledge can have more basic effects on remembering (Bjorklund, 1995). Suppose that the numbers in the earlier digit-span example were the following:

neli-kuus-kolm-üks-viis-seitse-kaks

These *are* the same numbers as in the early example—but they are written in Estonian. Unless you understand the Estonian language, you would have more difficulty remembering

these numbers than those given earlier. Even with numbers written (or spoken) in English, children would have more difficulty remembering the numbers than adults, partly because children are less familiar with the numbers. This kind of familiarity affects remembering and partly accounts for the age changes in memory span (Henry & Millar, 1991).

Other effects of the knowledge base on remembering are more subtle (Bjorklund, 1995). Suppose that you had to remember several items from a list of groceries. Although the items are presented randomly, you recall them in groups that correspond to meats, produce, and so on. Your pattern of recall suggests that you used the strategy of organization, but you may not have done so deliberately. Because you know general categories of groceries, recall of one item in a category could simply have triggered recall of other items. Of course, children who have done little grocery shopping would not have the same knowledge. The age change toward a more organized knowledge base can partly explain why memory for items in the knowledge base improves with age (Bjorklund & de Marchena, 1984).

Children's knowledge also influences their interpretation of new information. In the process of **constructive memory,** children form a mental representation of new information that depends partly on what they saw or heard and partly on what they add from their knowledge base (Flavell et al., 1993). For one study of constructive memory, children heard sentences like, "My brother fell down on the playground" (Paris, Lindauer, & Cox, 1977). After a brief delay, they were asked to repeat the sentences. First, though, they received a recall cue.

In one condition, the recall cue was a word in the original sentence (e.g., *playground*). In another condition, the cue was a phrase that stated the most likely outcome of the event (i.e., "and he skinned his knee"). This outcome was not stated in the original sentence, but children who thought about the event could easily infer the outcome. Through the process of constructive memory, children could have formed a mental representation that linked the event in the original sentence to its outcome. After they made this link, hearing the outcome, "and he skinned his knee," would trigger recall of the original sentence, "My brother fell down on the playground."

Apparently, young children are less active in making inferences when they hear a sentence than adults are. Second graders who received outcome cues recalled the original sentences much less often than did sixth graders and college students (see figure 9.13). So information about outcomes that were not stated explicitly did not improve second-graders' remembering.

By contrast, second-graders' recall improved greatly—reaching the level found for adults—if the cues were words from the original sentences. In short, second graders benefited from cues that matched information explicitly given but did not benefit from cues that were inferences from the information given. This contrast implies that remembering is a less constructive process for second graders than for sixth graders and adults.

On the other hand, young children do not always limit themselves to the information given. If that information is relevant to their own experiences, they often relate it to their prior knowledge. Even during the preschool years, the knowledge that children have gained from their life experiences influences their memory for new information.

Suppose that you ask preschoolers to remember lists of animals' names. Preschoolers remember lists that include animals typically found in a single setting, such as a zoo, better than lists that include animals typically found in several settings. For example, they would remember the list *elephant, tiger, monkey,* and *bear* better than the list *elephant, dog, cow,* and *rabbit.* Children often see the animals in the first list during the same event, a trip to the zoo. Using terms defined earlier, we can say that all the animals in the first list belong to a zoo script. Because the animals are part of the same script or event representation, they are easier to remember when they are listed together (Lucariello & Nelson, 1985).

Constructive memory and script-based processing can lead to inaccurate recall. If new information is inconsistent with a script, preschool children often forget it or distort it so that it fits the script. Older children use scripts more flexibly than preschoolers, so they can more accurately recall new information that deviates from a script (Farrar & Goodman, 1992).

**constructive memory**
*An automatic process of forming a mental representation of new information that depends partly on the new information received and partly on information added from a person's knowledge base.*

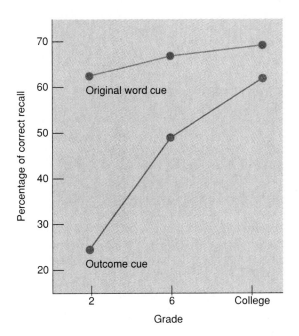

**FIGURE 9.13**
Children's recall of sentences is about as good as that of college students if the cues to recall are nouns from the original sentences. Children do much less well than college students if the cues to recall are statements about the likely outcomes of actions mentioned in the original sentences. The contrast between children's performance in the two conditions suggests that remembering is less of an active, constructive process for children than for adults. (Source: Paris et al., 1977.)

Prior knowledge can lead to errors in remembering even among older children. The process of linking new information with information in the knowledge base is so automatic that children and adults have difficulty noticing when it occurs. Therefore, children and adults sometimes assume that they heard things, or were told things, that they only inferred (Brown et al., 1977).

Fortunately, these errors are less common when people's knowledge is greater and better organized. One implication of this conclusion is that even preschoolers can accurately recall novel information that is inconsistent with a fully understood script. As with other aspects of memory development (Pressley & Van Meter, 1993), age changes are strongly affected by the knowledge children have and the task with which they are faced.

## Metamemory, or Knowledge about Memory

Along with processing speed, world knowledge, and memory strategies, a fourth type of explanation for age changes in remembering can be given. This type of explanation involves **metamemory,** people's thoughts and ideas about memory. In elementary-school children, metamemory can be surprisingly complex. The following example illustrates one third-grader's ideas about how to remember a phone number:

> Say the number is 633-8854. Then what I'd do is—say that my number [or exchange] is 633, so I won't have to remember that, really. And then I would think, now I've got to remember 88. Now I'm 8 years old, so I can remember, say, my age two times. And then I say how old my brother is, and how old he was last year. And that's how I'd usually remember that phone number. (Kreutzer, Leonard, & Flavell, 1975, p. 11)

Such complicated strategies are unusual for a third grader, so the adult who interviewed this child asked whether the child often used strategies like those for remembering a phone number. The child replied, "Well, usually I write it down." Taken together, the third-grader's comments refer to several aspects of metamemory.

***Aspects of Metamemory***   One aspect of metamemory involves judgments about how much information can be held in memory at one time. In several experiments, college students and

**metamemory**
*People's ideas about the amount of information they can hold in working memory, the difficulty of particular memory tasks, the effectiveness of specific memory strategies, and the content of their memories.*

FIGURE 9.14

Predicted and actual memory spans for nursery-school children (N), kindergarten children (K), grade-school children, and college students. Young children think they can remember several more items of information than they actually do. By fourth grade, children's predictions about their memory span are close to their actual span. The change reflects developments in metamemory, or knowledge about memory. (From Kail, 1990.)

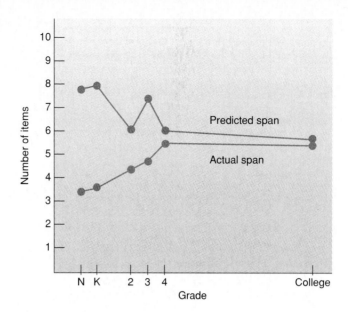

children of various ages predicted how many pictures of objects they could remember (Flavell, Friedrichs, & Hoyt, 1970; Yussen & Levy, 1975). Then their actual memory was assessed. Figure 9.14 shows the results. Preschool and kindergarten children predicted that they could remember many more pictures than they actually remembered. As children grew older, their predictions became more accurate.

The increase in accuracy was a result of two changes in metamemory. First, some young children responded as if they thought their memory was unlimited. They were asked if they could recall one picture, two pictures, and so on, up to a maximum of 10 pictures. Some young children said that they could recall all 10 pictures. Moreover, these children seemed to feel they could recall any number of pictures if they tried. Older children rarely gave such unrealistic answers; they acknowledged that their memory was limited.

Second, even the preschool children who recognized the limits on their memory were less accurate in their predictions than were older children and adults. As children gain more experience with memory tasks and think more about their experience, they gradually bring their predictions in line with their performance.

During the preschool years, knowledge about forgetting also increases (Lyon & Flavell, 1993, 1994). If you wait a long time before trying to find something that you saw only once, you are likely to forget where you saw it. You know this fact about forgetting, but most 3-year-olds do not. Most 3-year-olds do not recognize that forgetting becomes more likely as the interval between getting information and trying to remember it increases. By contrast, most 4-year-olds understand that the chances of forgetting increase over time. The age change reflects 4-year-olds' greater knowledge of how the mind works, both in gaining information and in retrieving information from memory.

Another aspect of metamemory is knowledge about the difficulty of particular memory tasks. In one study (Kreutzer et al., 1975), children heard about a girl who listened to a story on a record so that she could tell it to someone else. The children were asked whether this memory task would be easier if the girl had to tell the story "word for word, just like on the record," or if she could tell it in her own words. Kindergarten children did not appreciate the difference between the two options: They chose each option about as often. By fifth grade, all children said (correctly) that word-for-word remembering is more difficult than telling a story in your own words.

Yet another aspect of metamemory is knowledge about memory strategies. The third-grader's explanation of how to remember a phone number illustrates several strategies. The comment that the first three digits are easy to remember because they match his number shows the strategic use of world knowledge. The comment that the next two digits match his

age shows the use of the elaboration strategy. The comments about ways to remember the last two digits are other examples of elaboration.

You should be surprised to learn that a third grader was so knowledgeable about the elaboration strategy. As mentioned earlier, use of this strategy is rare before adolescence. When school-age children are asked about strategies that may be helpful in remembering information, they rarely discuss elaboration. Thus, the exemplary third grader was precocious as well as creative.

Conscious knowledge of sophisticated memory strategies is more characteristic of adolescents than of elementary-school children. When school-age children are asked what they could do to improve their memory for a list of items, they usually mention some form of rehearsal (Kreutzer et al., 1975). When given the task of remembering pairs of words, adolescents say that elaboration would be the best strategy more often than school-age children do (Kail, 1990). When remembering could be improved by classifying items into general categories, older children say they prefer this organization strategy more often than younger children do (Justice, 1985). Older children, therefore, not only know more strategies for simplifying memory tasks. They also are better at judging the best strategy for a specific task.

The previous aspects of metamemory deal with knowledge about remembering and forgetting. The broad category of metamemory also includes thoughts and feelings about actual memory experiences. Do you ever feel that you know something but you can't quite remember it? Have you ever said that you can't recall a person's name but, "I'd recognize it if you said it"?

Even preschool children have some idea about the information that is in their memories. In one study (Cultice, Somerville, & Wellman, 1983), 4- and 5-year-olds saw pictures of people who were either in their school or were total strangers. Then the children were asked to name the person in each picture. When they said they couldn't name a person, they were asked whether they thought they could pick the person's name from a list of names. Then they were given several names and asked to point to the pictures of the persons named.

These preschool children did significantly better than chance at judging the content of their memories. When they predicted they could recognize a person if they heard his or her name, they were correct slightly more than half the time. When they predicted they could not pick out a person's picture, even if they heard the person's name, they guessed the right picture less than one-third of the time. This difference in accuracy implies that the preschoolers had information in memory that they could not recall immediately. Moreover, they often knew that they had this information.

Finally, consider the third-grader's last comment about remembering a phone number, "Well, usually I write it down." This is another aspect of metamemory, knowing how to use external aids to reduce the mental effort of remembering. Using these aids is not as simple as the third-grader's comment might suggest.

To be effective, external aids to remembering must be informative and must be placed where they will be noticed at the right time. Have you ever written a note with someone's phone number and then forgotten whose number it was? If so, you've experienced the problem of uninformative memory aids. Have you ever written a phone number and then lost the paper on which you wrote it? If so, you should appreciate that memory aids are useless if they cannot be found when needed.

The ability to create effective external aids to remembering improves with age (Beal, 1985; Flavell, 1985). This improvement is related to the developments in communication discussed in chapter 7. Children get better at preparing informative messages for other people as they grow older. Children also get better at preparing informative messages for themselves, messages that help them remember the right information at the right time. Knowing how to prepare an effective external aid for remembering is another aspect of metamemory.

*Relations of Metamemory to Remembering*   Now you understand the many ways in which metamemory improves with age. Do the improvements in metamemory affect remembering itself?

This boy is using a calendar as a memory aid. To make the calendar an effective aid, though, some conditions must be met. The boy must use a reminder that is unambiguous. A cue like "Big Day" or "Don't Forget" will be less effective than one like "Party at 4:00, Steve's." Also, the boy must look at the calendar regularly to see the cues he placed there earlier. Younger children have more trouble creating unambiguous cues, and they more often fail to notice those cues, so they have less success with memory aids.

In answering this question, it's helpful to distinguish between "knowing how" and "knowing that" (Bruner, 1972). A person who "knows how" can actually complete a task. A person who "knows that" can describe how a task should be done. The two types of knowledge do not always go together. Many great athletes have said something like, "I can't explain what I do; I just do it." Conversely, many sports commentators can say exactly what the players on the field should be doing, but they couldn't come close to following their instructions themselves.

To a large degree, metamemory is "knowing that" rather than "knowing how," so you might be skeptical about whether sophisticated knowledge about memory will enhance actual remembering. This skepticism seemed justified when researchers first looked at the correlations between children's metamemory and their performance on memory tasks. The correlations were modest at best and often nonsignificant (see Brown, Day, & Jones, 1983).

By contrast, the results were much more positive when researchers began to examine the match between specific aspects of metamemory and specific memory tasks (Borkowski, Milstead, & Hale, 1988). For example, preschoolers who know that rehearsal keeps information in mind more often use rehearsal when they have a list to remember (Fabricius & Cavalier, 1989). These children also remember more than preschoolers who know less about how rehearsal aids memory.

The strongest effects of metamemory on remembering have been found in experimental interventions. Often, increasing children's knowledge about remembering was only one of the techniques used in these interventions. Moreover, the goal of the interventions was not to improve remembering itself but to enhance children's learning. Therefore, these interventions are discussed in the later section of the chapter on learning.

### Chapter Nine

# Autobiographical Memory

Can you remember what you did on your first birthday? How about on your second birthday? If you are like most people, your answers to these questions are no. **Infantile amnesia** is the inability to remember personal experiences from the first few years of life. Infantile amnesia also shows the absence of **autobiographical memory,** memory for the events of one's own life (Bauer, 1993; Nelson, 1993b).

As the questions about birthdays imply, a lack of autobiographical memory is not usually limited to infancy. Most people cannot remember events that occurred before they were 3 years old (Howe & Courage, 1993). Although *early childhood amnesia* would be a more accurate term for this phenomenon, most researchers continue to refer to infantile amnesia.

Infantile amnesia lasts longer for certain types of events than for others. In one study college students were asked about four types of events in childhood (Usher & Neisser, 1993). Students who experienced the birth of a new sibling when they were 2 years old accurately recalled some information about that event. Students who were hospitalized when age 2 recalled some information about that experience. However, students did not accurately recall two other types of events, a death in the family and a family move, unless those events occurred after they reached age 3 or 4.

Infantile amnesia is puzzling because infants and young children can remember information for long periods. For example, 1-year-olds can imitate novel sequences of actions that they first imitated several months earlier (Bauer, 1993). Their imitation is evidence that they remember the actions they performed months before.

Other experiments suggest that young children can remember experiences they had in psychology laboratories when they were infants (Howe & Courage, 1993). In all these experiments, however, memory was judged from differences in the behavior of children who did and did not have the earlier experiences. That is, memory was assessed nonverbally, rather than from statements by children. Indeed, children whose behavior suggested they had a memory for their earlier experiences often said that they didn't remember being in the laboratory before (e.g., Perris, Myers, & Clifton, 1990).

The contrast between the nonverbal and the verbal measures of memory suggests one explanation for infantile amnesia. Perhaps children only develop autobiographical memory after they have learned to construct narratives about events, to talk about events in terms of who, what, when, where, and why. The ability to construct narratives may depend on experiences talking about events with adults (Nelson, 1993b).

Another possible explanation for infantile amnesia is that children's autobiographical memory takes shape only when they develop a definite self-concept (Howe & Courage, 1993). As you will read in chapter 13, that development occurs around 2 years of age.

A third possibility is that age changes occur in the types of memories that children form. One theory of cognitive development, called **fuzzy-trace theory,** suggests that memory traces or mental representations of experience differ in their exactness (Brainerd & Reyna, 1993). Some representations include many specific details, or are like verbatim copies of experience. Other representations are "fuzzy traces," which capture only the gist of experiences. Fuzzy-trace theory has been used to explain many findings about cognitive development, ranging from performance on Piagetian tasks to language development.

Fuzzy-trace theory can also explain infantile amnesia if infants and young children typically form exact or verbatim representations of experience. Researchers have found that verbatim representations fade faster, or are forgotten more quickly, than fuzzy representations. Other data suggest that children may shift toward more fuzzy representations of experience as they grow older. Such a shift would contribute to the emergence of a stable autobiographical memory, because fuzzy representations are more durable (Leichtman & Ceci, 1993).

Not enough research has been done to tell which of these hypotheses, or which combination of them, best explains infantile amnesia. The question is practically important because adults often want to know about young children's experiences. In particular, young children are sometimes required to testify in court about events they have witnessed or personally experienced. Whether they can report these events accurately is an extremely controversial issue. *Practical Applications of Research:* "Children as Witnesses" describes some research findings on this issue.

**infantile amnesia**
*The inability to remember personal experiences from the first few years of life.*

**autobiographical memory**
*People's memory for the events of their own lives.*

**fuzzy-trace theory**
*A theory that suggests some mental representations of experience are fuzzy, capturing only the gist of experiences, while other mental representations are like verbatim copies of experiences.*

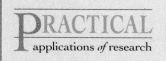

## CHILDREN AS WITNESSES: ACCURATE TESTIMONY OR RESPONSES TO SUGGESTION?

Sensational news stories have described cases in which child-care workers were accused of sexually abusing the children in their care. Some forms of sexual abuse leave no physical signs, and no other adults were present when the abuse was alleged to occur. Therefore, the cases against the child-care workers depended almost entirely on the testimony of the children involved. Because of the time needed to prepare the legal cases, children sometimes took the witness stand months or years after the abusive acts were believed to have occurred.

Whether children can provide accurate testimony under these conditions has been vigorously debated. Stephen Ceci and Maggie Bruck (1993) carefully reviewed nearly 100 years of research on this question. They concluded that preschool children can recall events that occurred months or years before, especially if they participated in those events. Preschoolers' recall is less complete than that of older children, however. As you've read often in this chapter, remembering improves with age.

However, recalling an event is very different from testifying to that event in a legal case. Before a case is tried, children may be required to talk to many adults about what happened, and some adults may be hostile. Ceci and Bruck (1993) illustrated the types of questioning to which children are subjected by quoting from an interview in a case involving a child-care worker named Kelly. A boy given the code number 8C was interviewed by a social worker named Fonolleras and a police detective named Mastrangelo. After the boy said he forgot what he told Fonolleras in a previous interview, the following exchange occurred:

**Fonolleras:** Oh, come on. We talked to a few more of your buddies. And everyone told me about the nap room, and the bathroom stuff, and the music room stuff, and the choir stuff, and the peanut butter stuff, and everything [other circumstances surrounding the alleged abuse]. . . . All your buddies [talked]. . . . Come on, do you want to help us out? Do you want to keep her in jail? I'll let you hear your voice and play with the tape recorder; I need your help again. . . .

**Child:** I forgot.

**Mastrangelo:** No listen, you have to behave.

**Fonolleras:** Do you want me to tell him to behave? Are you going to be a good boy, huh? While you are here, did he [the detective] show you his badge and his handcuffs? . . . Back to what happened to you with the wooden spoon. If you don't remember words, maybe you can show me [with anatomical dolls present].

In this part of a longer interview, the child receives several types of encouragement to tell about alleged abuse. The adults use appeals to conformity ("All your buddies . . ."), hints of rewards ("I'll let you hear your voice"), and implied threats (the badge and handcuffs). Such tactics are used not only by prosecutors. Ceci and Bruck quote from another interview in which a lawyer for a man accused of sexual abuse repeatedly and vehemently accused a 6-year-old boy of lying. Under this kind of hostile questioning, even adults might yield and testify falsely.

Many studies reviewed by Ceci and Bruck show that young children are susceptible to these kinds of pressure. In addition, young children are more suggestible than adults. Even without direct pressure, their testimony can be swayed by leading questions, hints, or other cues. In particular, giving preschoolers anatomical dolls (as mentioned in the interview) can lead preschoolers to report falsely that an adult previously touched their genitals (Bruck et al., 1995).

Does this mean that preschool children should not be allowed to testify in court? Ceci and Bruck (1993) say no, that children's testimony can be valuable and reliable. However, they strongly advise that judges and juries should have many types of information about the conditions in which children testified. Judges and juries should know the circumstances in which children first mentioned abusive acts, the number and kinds of interviews that the children had, whether interviewers were motivated to bias the children's reports, and whether the children gave consistent reports over time. Only with this information can adults make good judgments about the likely accuracy of the children's testimony.

## LEARNING

In chapter 1, *learning* was defined as a change in behavior in a specific situation due to experience in that situation (Stevenson, 1983). This definition makes it impossible to draw a sharp distinction between learning and remembering, because changes in behavior must depend on some kind of memory for experiences. Consequently, some topics discussed in this section overlap with those discussed in the previous one.

The two sections differ in their focus, however. For example, in the previous section you read about the effects of children's strategies (e.g., rehearsal) on their remembering. In this section you will read about how children learn to use those strategies. But before

exploring such complex types of learning, you should know more about the basic learning processes that allow even newborns to respond adaptively to their environments.

## Learning in Infancy

Chapter 1 included descriptions of three processes of learning: classical conditioning, operant conditioning, and observational learning. All three processes operate in newborns.

Stated most generally, classical conditioning involves learning the relations between events (Rescorla, 1988). If 2-week-old infants feel a puff of air near their eyes, they display the eyeblink reflex. If they consistently hear a tone 1.5 seconds before the air puff, their behavior changes. After several pairings of the tone with the puff, the infants start blinking just before they would normally feel the puff. This anticipatory blink indicates that infants have learned the relation between the tone and the puff. In terms of classical conditioning, the tone has become a conditioned stimulus. Because of its association with the air puff (the unconditioned stimulus), the tone elicits the conditioned response of blinking.

Infants show less efficient conditioning than older children or adults (Little, Lipsitt, & Rovee-Collier, 1984). With adults, conditioning of an eye blink is most effective when the interval between the tone and the puff is less than 1 second. Infants under 1 month old need an interval of more than a second to learn the association between the tone and the puff. Also, younger infants forget the association of the tone with the puff more rapidly than older infants or adults do. Even this simple process of learning the relations between events becomes more efficient with increasing age.

Operant conditioning has also been demonstrated with newborns. You read in chapter 5 that newborns change their sucking pattern if they hear a tape of their mother reading a familiar story when they do so (DeCasper & Spence, 1986). You also read that newborns increase their rate of sucking if they receive sweetened water as a reinforcement for sucking (Maurer & Maurer, 1988). In this chapter, you learned that researchers have used the movement of a mobile as a reinforcement for infants' kicking.

The examples show that researchers have relied on principles of operant conditioning when devising techniques for studying what infants perceive and remember. The ability to learn through operant conditioning is even more important for infants themselves. As Skinner (1974) noted, operant conditioning is "a process through which a person comes to deal effectively with a new environment" (p. 39). In short, operant conditioning contributes to infants' adaptation.

Whether observational learning occurs during the newborn period is more controversial. The most common criterion for observational learning is imitation. Researchers first arrange for infants to watch another person model some behavior. Then the researchers watch the infants to see whether they imitate the behavior.

Piaget (1962) argued that true imitation is not possible until infants are more than 6 months old. According to Piaget, imitation of another's behavior calls for a level of cognitive sophistication that newborns lack. However, several researchers have shown that infants can imitate some behaviors in the first days or weeks of life.

In one of the first studies (Meltzoff & Moore, 1977), 2- to 3-week-old infants watched adults who stuck out their tongues, opened their mouths wide, or pursed their lips. As figure 9.15 shows, infants often matched the adults' gestures. Moreover, these matches did not occur by chance. Infants usually made matching gestures immediately after seeing an adult model them; infants rarely made the gestures at other times during the experiment. The infants were, therefore, clearly imitating the adults.

In another study (Reissland, 1988), infants imitated an adult's gestures before they were 1 hour old. The study took place in the delivery room of a hospital in Nepal. In that hospital, newborns were not given to their mothers until the newborns had been cleaned and the mothers had expelled the placenta. During this interval, the experiment was done.

An adult put her face close to a newborn and modeled the facial gestures of pursed lips or lips widened in a broad smile. As she did so, a camera videotaped the facial expressions of the newborn. When the adult pursed her lips, the babies tended to purse their lips. When she widened her lips, the babies tended to widen their lips.

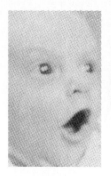

## FIGURE 9.15

When this adult opened her mouth wide, stuck out her lower lip, or gave a broad smile, 2- to 3-week-old infants imitated those gestures.

How do infants achieve such early imitation of body movements? One possibility is that they innately recognize the parallels between body movements they see and body movements they could perform themselves (Meltzoff & Moore, 1989). In other words, infants' perceptions of body movements and their execution of body movements may depend on the same internal code. Using this internal code, infants can directly map movements that they perceive into a plan for their own movements. Imitative behaviors occur when infants carry out this movement plan.

By 6 weeks of age, infants can both form and remember an internal code for body movements (Meltzoff & Moore, 1994). If infants see an experimenter stick out his or her tongue, they imitate the behavior immediately and imitate it again if brought back to the laboratory the next day. Their delayed imitation occurs even when the experimenter looks at them without making any mouth or tongue movements. Piaget (1962) did not expect infants to be capable of such delayed imitation until about 18 months of age. Obviously, infants have more advanced capabilities for learning than Piaget assumed.

The existence of a code that links the perception and the production of body movements could have a major influence on infants' development. Language acquisition, for example, depends on infants' ability to imitate sounds made by other people. The development of social interaction may also be enhanced by infants' ability to imitate the emotional expressions and movements of other people.

The processes of classical conditioning, operant conditioning, and observational learning are not fully mature at birth. These processes become more efficient during infancy and childhood. Imitation, in particular, becomes more consistent and more general during the second year of life. After 1 year of age, children improve in their ability to imitate sounds, actions, and words (Masur, 1993). These improvements mark the emergence of a new capacity for mental representation that may enhance children's ability to learn many types of information.

## Principles of Learning in Childhood

Traditional learning theories were the starting points for research on children's learning (Stevenson, 1983). However, many studies suggested that new models were needed to explain how children learn the vast amount of information to which they are exposed in schools and other settings. Most current models are based on the following principles (Brown & Campione, 1994; Brown et al., 1983; Bruer, 1994).

First, children are active and strategic when engaged in learning. Children do not simply absorb facts given to them. Instead, they interpret what they see, hear, or read. They also try to figure out ways to solve the cognitive problems that they confront. You read earlier about children's strategies for remembering information. You also read about constructive memory, the integration of new information with prior knowledge. Other illustrations of children's active, strategic behavior when engaged in learning are presented later.

Second, learning is more than the process of acquiring new information. As children grow, they learn more about *how* to learn new information. **Learning to learn** refers to the acquisition of strategies, skills, and knowledge that improve a person's ability to understand and retain new information. Interventions that can promote the development of learning to learn are discussed in the next section.

Third, learning to learn is closely related to **metacognition,** people's ability to think about their thoughts and control their cognitive processes. Because memory is one component of cognition, metamemory is a part of metacognition. Metacognition goes beyond metamemory to include planning, monitoring progress in problem solving, and evaluating the solutions reached. As you will see, learning is more efficient when children explicitly recognize the strategies that they might use to accomplish cognitive tasks. In other words, when cognitive work is guided by metacognitive processes, performance improves.

Fourth, children's learning is influenced by their general level of cognitive development. A 2-year-old does not learn in the same way as a 10-year-old does. Moreover, interventions to improve children's learning are usually less effective with younger children (Brown et al., 1983). Younger children benefit less from training partly because of age differences in metacognition. In particular, younger children less often reflect on their past performance and strategy choices. Also, younger children are less sensitive to the "rules of the game," or the features of a problem that match a general class of problems (Brown & Kane, 1988). Besides reflecting metacognitive differences, these age differences seem partly to reflect the changes in processing resources discussed earlier (Pressley & Van Meter, 1993).

Fifth, learning does not involve either a single cognitive process or a small set of processes. Learning depends on all the information-processing components discussed earlier in the chapter—perception, attention, mental representation, remembering—and more. Learning also depends on motivation and social interaction. You'll see in a moment how researchers have tried to capture the complexity of learning in their models and interventions.

Sixth, much of learning is **domain-specific,** linked to specific types of information, specific skills, or specific kinds of tasks. You read earlier that some children gain unusual expertise in domains such as soccer or chess. Similarly, some children gain unusual expertise in mathematics; other children gain unusual expertise in other academic subjects. To help children learn, researchers need to know which types of information and which skills lead to expertise in a specific domain. In the following section, you will read about research on several cognitive domains that are important for children's academic success.

## Understanding and Enhancing Children's Learning

The new models of learning derived partly from research on memory strategies. The models also derived from research on traditional academic skills. One focus of research was on reading; another focus was on arithmetic. As you read about the two research areas, think about how they illustrate the general principles and what they reveal about learning in each domain.

### Training Memory Strategies

During the 1960s and 1970s, many researchers tried to improve children's remembering by teaching them specific memory strategies (e.g., Keeney et al., 1967). These studies showed that children could be trained to use memory strategies, and use of the strategies improved their recall. But after the training ended, children usually stopped using the strategies and their recall dropped to its original level. In addition, children rarely used the trained strategy on new tasks where it would have been appropriate. In short, strategy training had only temporary and task-specific effects (Brown et al., 1983).

To increase the effectiveness of strategy training, researchers enlisted children's metacognition. In particular, researchers tried to make children aware of the value of the strategy being trained (Belmont, Butterfield, & Borkowski, 1978; Brown et al., 1983). For example, children were told directly that their memory would improve if they used strategies such as rehearsal. Children also received feedback about how much more they remembered when they used strategies. Adding these components to experimental interventions increased

**learning to learn**
*The acquisition of strategies, skills, and knowledge that improve a person's ability to understand and retain information.*

**metacognition**
*People's ability to think about their thoughts and control their cognitive processes.*

**domain-specific**
*Knowledge or learning that is linked to specific types of information, skills, or tasks.*

children's use of memory strategies after training ended. It also increased children's transfer of memory strategies to new tasks.

Besides knowing that a strategy is valuable, children must be able to use the strategy well. Using strategies takes effort, especially before they are fully mastered (Guttentag, 1984). Before children have mastered a strategy, they sometimes put so much mental effort into using it that they have little left for doing the specified task. Therefore, task performance may not improve immediately after strategy training (Kail, 1990; Woody-Ramsey & Miller, 1988). Moreover, when children exert great effort with little apparent payoff, they may decide that the new strategy is ineffective and stop using it.

The importance of training memory strategies to the point of mastery was shown in a study of first and third graders (Borkowski et al., 1983). The children were pretested on their ability to recall 15 pictures. Then an adult trained children in an experimental condition to sort the pictures into categories such as food, animals, and tools. After children sorted the pictures, the experimenter asked them to rehearse the names of the pictures, one category at a time. In other words, the experimenter trained children to use a combination of the organization and rehearsal strategies.

Next, the experimenter told children that this combination of strategies would improve their memory. The experimenter also told children to use the same strategies the next time they faced a similar task. In this way, the experimenter tried to change children's metacognition about tasks involving remembering.

In another setting two weeks later, the children did the same task again, with no additional strategy instruction. In a third session, held about three months after the second one, the children received more instruction about the use and value of strategies. About a month later, they again were tested on their use of organization and rehearsal when given a memory task. Children in a control condition received no training but took the same tests at the same times as the children in the experimental condition.

This intervention led to lasting improvements in strategy use (see figure 9.16). After training, children in the experimental condition used strategies more consistently than did children in the control condition. The difference between groups increased with additional training, which suggests that children more often used the memory strategies after they had mastered them.

Figure 9.16 also shows that strategy training improved children's recall. After one training session, children in the strategy-training group had better recall than children in the other group. After two training sessions, the group differences increased. Greater mastery, then, made the strategies both easier to use and more effective.

Moreover, the children who received strategy training did better on a novel memory task than the children in the control group. They did better because they more often used strategies to remember the novel information. That is, the children learned the strategies well enough to transfer them to a new task.

Training in memory strategies can be effective even with preschool children (Lange & Pierce, 1992). Like older children, preschoolers must be told that use of strategies will improve their remembering. Preschoolers also need demonstrations of the benefits of strategies. They need enough practice with a strategy so that they can master it.

In addition, increasing children's motivation to learn can enhance the effectiveness of strategy training. Preschoolers are more likely to use memory strategies when they are given incentives for working hard on a task (Lange & Pierce, 1992). Elementary-school children are more likely to use strategies when they are praised for using them and for improving their performance (Pressley & Van Meter, 1993).

Finally, strategy training is more effective when it is part of the regular school curriculum (Moely et al., 1992; Pressley & Van Meter, 1993). Elementary-school teachers occasionally encourage children to use rehearsal, elaboration, or other strategies to remember information. Teachers occasionally ask children to think about what they could do to remember something, thus encouraging the development of metamemory. When children's classes include these types of instruction, improvements in their learning are likely.

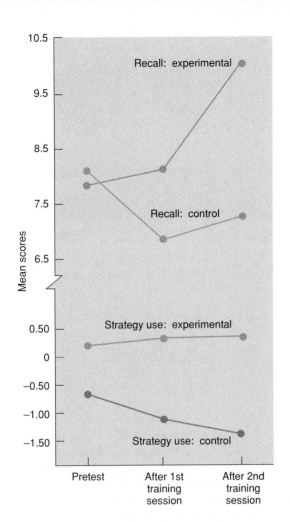

**Figure 9.16**

After training in memory strategies, children in the experimental condition used those strategies more than did children in a control condition. Children in the experimental condition also had more correct answers on memory tasks than did children in the control condition. Notice that the differences between conditions were larger after two sessions of training than after one. (Source: Borkowski et al., 1983.)

## Learning to Read, and Reading to Learn

When you first learned to read, you probably read each word and every sentence in order. Now that you are a skilled reader, you probably treat the task of reading very differently. You may not be aware of the differences, however, because you apply your reading strategies automatically.

Think about the last time you picked up a newspaper. Did you start by reading the title, the date, and the other information at the very top of the page? More likely, you scanned the headlines and selected certain stories to read because of their interest or importance to you. Once you started reading a story, you probably focused on the first paragraph and, perhaps, skimmed the rest of the story. If you used these strategies, would your comprehension of the main points of the story be lower than that of a beginning reader? Definitely not. Your strategies make you both a rapid reader and an effective reader.

Scott Paris and Janis Jacobs (1984) identified a variety of strategies that define the transition from beginning reader to skilled reader. Certain strategies involve the evaluation of a reading task itself. Skilled readers know that the first few sentences in a story are especially important. Those sentences establish the setting for the story and may introduce the main characters. By contrast, beginning readers often assume that there is nothing special about the first sentences in a story.

A second set of reading strategies involves planning. If you don't have much time, you know you should focus on the important parts of the story rather than on the details. In newspaper stories, the most important parts tell you "who did what to whom, when, and where."

## FIGURE 9.17

Third- and fifth-graders' knowledge of reading strategies improved when they received instruction in types of strategies, how to use the strategies, and when and why strategy use is appropriate. Some improvement in knowledge of reading strategies occurred even in the control condition, due to regular classroom instruction, but the improvement was greater with specially designed instruction. (Adapted from Paris & Jacobs, 1984.)

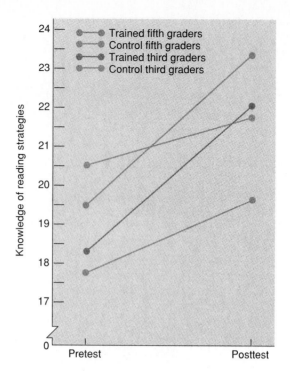

Skilled readers emphasize important parts of a story when their reading time is limited. Beginning readers simply read all the words in the story as fast as they can.

A third set of strategies involves the regulation of reading as it occurs. Skilled readers monitor themselves, making certain that they understand what they are reading. If they don't understand a sentence, they reread it or see whether they can relate it to the sentences that come before and after it. Beginning readers are less likely to check themselves in this way and are less aware of what to do when they don't understand something.

After Paris and Jacobs (1984) identified the differences between beginning and skilled readers, they decided to see whether they could teach schoolchildren the strategies for skilled reading. In addition, these researchers wanted to see whether strategy instruction improved children's reading comprehension. The instruction had three components.

First, children were taught which strategies are appropriate for evaluating, planning, and regulating reading. This component relates to one aspect of metacognition in the domain of reading. Second, children were taught how to use the strategies. That is, they received the practice necessary to make later, spontaneous use of a strategy possible. Third, children were taught when the use of particular strategies was appropriate and why these strategies were helpful. This component relates to another aspect of metacognition about reading.

Several classrooms of third and fifth graders received training in reading strategies from a special teacher. The strategy lessons lasted about 30 minutes and occurred twice weekly for 14 weeks. Other classrooms of third and fifth graders were in a control condition that received no special training. Before and after the lessons, the students in both groups were tested on their knowledge of reading strategies and their reading comprehension. To evaluate the effectiveness of the training, the researchers examined the changes in students' scores between these pretests and posttests.

Figure 9.17 shows that the training was effective in boosting students' knowledge of reading strategies. Reading strategies improved slightly between the pretest and the posttest, even in the control group. This slight change is not surprising because the regular curriculum of reading instruction would be expected to have some effect. However, the students receiving strategy lessons improved significantly more than those in the control group. Strategy instruction was equally effective among third graders and fifth graders. Thus, fifth graders who had been reading for several years still benefited from training in the deliberate use of reading strategies.

| TABLE 9.1 | Children's Strategies for Solving Addition Problems | |
|---|---|

| STRATEGY | TYPICAL USE OF STRATEGY TO SOLVE 3 + 5 |
|---|---|
| Sum | Put up 3 fingers, put up 5 fingers, count fingers by saying "1,2,3,4,5,6,7,8." |
| Finger recognition | Put up 3 fingers, put up 5 fingers, say "8" without counting. |
| Shortcut sum | Say "1,2,3,4,5,6,7,8," perhaps simultaneously putting up one finger on each count. |
| Min | Say "5,6,7,8" or "6,7,8," perhaps simultaneously putting up one finger on each count beyond 5. |
| Count-from-first-addend | Say "3,4,5,6,7,8" or "4,5,6,7,8," perhaps simultaneously putting up one finger on each count. |
| Retrieval | Say an answer and explain it by saying "I just knew it." |
| Guessing | Say an answer and explain it by saying "I guessed." |
| Decomposition | Say "3+5 is like 4+4, so it's 8." |

From R. S. Siegler and E. Jenkins, *How Children Discover New Strategies.* Copyright © 1989 Lawrence Erlbaum Associates, Inc., Mahwah, N.J. Reprinted by permission.

Strategy instruction also improved students' scores on two tests of reading comprehension. Again, the improvement was equally great at each grade. Even fairly skilled readers benefited from more conscious evaluation of reading tasks, planning for comprehension, and regulation or self-checking during reading.

As with memory strategies, instruction in reading strategies should have especially powerful effects when it is part of the regular curriculum. Many teachers mention strategies helpful in learning to read and in reading to learn (Moely et al., 1992). For example, they mention looking for root words when trying to decode an unfamiliar word. They mention using the context, or accompanying pictures, when trying to understand paragraphs or text. When teachers give these types of strategy instruction, their teaching is consistent with the principle that children are active, strategic learners. That consistency increases the learning that occurs in their classrooms.

## Strategies for Doing Arithmetic

One domain in which you might *not* expect to find active, strategic learning is that of arithmetic. After all, don't children start by simply memorizing their "math facts"?

In fact, they don't. Before children have mastered math facts completely, they use various strategies to solve arithmetic problems (Griffin, Case, & Siegler, 1994; Siegler, 1987; Siegler & Jenkins, 1989). Table 9.1 shows the most common strategies. The "min" strategy, also called "counting up," is to take the larger number and count from that. The "shortcut sum," also called "counting all," is to count up the two addends in order. Of course, if children know a math fact, they simply retrieve the answer from memory. And if all else fails, they may just guess.

Few children in the early school grades rely on only one strategy. By observing individual children's responses to many arithmetic problems, researchers have found that most children use several strategies (Siegler, 1994; Siegler & Crowley, 1991). Moreover, children progress toward the fast retrieval strategy by different routes.

Some regularities exist, however. As children grow older, they use the guessing strategy and the inefficient "shortcut-sum" strategy less often. As they grow older, they use the retrieval strategy more often. That is, they rely on their memory for addition facts.

Children do not often choose a specific strategy consciously (Siegler, 1988a). When given a simple math problem, children apparently try automatically to retrieve the necessary fact from memory. If their knowledge of math facts is weak, their attempt at retrieval may be unsuccessful. Alternatively, these children may retrieve an answer but not give that answer because they are not confident that it is correct.

If the retrieval strategy fails, children switch, usually without conscious awareness, to a backup strategy that involves computing the answer. With addition problems, for example, they may switch to the "min" strategy. When children get the right answer with the backup strategy, their memory for that arithmetic fact is strengthened. Therefore, they are more

likely to retrieve the answer the next time they need to recall the same fact. In this way, children's procedures for strategy choice help them shift toward the fast, efficient solution of arithmetic problems by retrieving facts.

Children's strategy choices are not entirely determined by their knowledge of math facts (Griffin et al., 1994; Siegler, 1988b). First graders who are good students know math facts well and often use the retrieval strategy. First graders who are poor students do not know their math facts well, but they still use the retrieval strategy frequently. Of course, they often retrieve the wrong answer.

Students in a third group are perfectionists. When they use retrieval, they are correct nearly 100 percent of the time. Even so, they use retrieval on less than half the problems they are given. Apparently, they often retrieve the correct answer but, to be absolutely sure, they check that answer with a backup strategy. Why these students become perfectionists is not yet known.

A more important question is how to help poor students. These students receive low scores on standardized tests and are often kept in first grade for another year. One technique to help these students might be to encourage their use of backup strategies for solving arithmetic problems. Although adults often assume that backup strategies like counting on fingers lessen children's learning of math facts, the opposite may be true. As mentioned earlier, accurate use of backup strategies should strengthen the associations between problems and their correct answers. When children later try to retrieve the answer, they will be more confident and more often correct.

Finally, what happens to children who don't go to elementary school and so are not given assignments to help them learn math facts? The chapter began with a description of one of these children, Jose, who sold candy on the streets of Recife, Brazil. *Cultural Perspectives:* "Street Math and School Math" describes how unschooled candy sellers' math performance compares with that of children who regularly attend school.

# CLASSROOM LEARNING THROUGH SOCIAL INTERACTION

In the early studies of information-processing components, researchers often focused on individual children dealing with specific tasks. Over time, however, some information-processing researchers started to explore children's thinking about academic subjects as varied as first-grade math and high-school physics (McGilly, 1994). When these researchers entered actual classrooms, they began to appreciate the broad range of influences on children's learning. Several researchers then devised intervention programs in which social interactions among students and between teachers and students were crucial.

John Bruer (1994) suggested five hypotheses to explain why these interventions have been effective. The first hypothesis relates to the contrast between novices and experts. During social interactions in classrooms, individuals with more expertise may convey their knowledge and strategies to novices. Teachers certainly have more expertise than most students, but some students also have more expertise in certain domains than other students do. Encouraging social interactions both with teachers and among classmates may enhance learning by providing more channels for the transfer of this expertise to novices.

Bruer's second hypothesis focuses on collaboration among students. When working on cognitive problems, a collaborative group may be more successful than an individual because the mental effort can be shared. For example, a single student does not need to hold in memory all the information required to solve the problem. By sharing this information, students can solve more problems and gain more practice in successful problem solving. Over time, the added practice may reduce the mental effort that students must exert to solve similar problems, and so improve individual students' performance.

The third hypothesis focuses on the verbal component of social interactions in classrooms. Students discuss problems with one another and with their teacher. During these discussions, students must try to state facts and express ideas in a coherent, integrated form. Transforming knowledge into coherent language can be done successfully only if that knowledge is

STREET MATH AND
SCHOOL MATH

andy sellers like Jose were invited to participate in a study of their mathematical understanding (Saxe, 1988a, 1988b). The study included a second group of children who were not candy sellers but who, unlike the sellers, were currently enrolled in school.

Both groups of children were given problems that involved comparing two numbers, like 345 and 721, and saying which was larger. They were also given problems that required estimating the profit they could earn by selling different numbers of candies for different prices. For these problems, the children had to compare ratios. Children were given a third set of problems that involved arithmetic with actual money.

For example, they had to make change from large bills or add bills with different denominations (e.g., Cr$500 and Cr$10,000).

Figure 9.18 shows the percentage of each type of problem that children in each group answered correctly. Candy sellers did very well on the ratio comparisons and currency arithmetic that were directly related to candy selling. The children who attended school did very well on the task of comparing numbers in standard form. These findings show that children learn, through formal schooling or the informal instruction available on the street, the arithmetic skills important for their everyday activities.

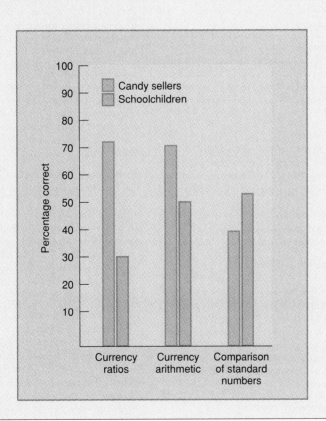

**FIGURE 9.18**
How Brazilian children performed on three types of arithmetic problems. Notice that children who regularly sold candy on the streets did better on problems involving Brazilian currency than did other children of the same age. But urban children who attended school did better than the candy sellers on comparisons of standard numbers.

well understood. Therefore, students may gain a deeper understanding of information if they discuss it with others than if they merely listen to a lecture or read a textbook.

The fourth hypothesis is that social interactions in classrooms may increase students' belief that thinking, problem solving, and careful analysis of intellectual issues are valued activities. In addition, these interactions may convince students that they can participate fully in intellectual discussions. Participating in classroom discussions may, therefore, increase students' motivation to learn.

The fifth hypothesis is that social interactions do not simply influence cognitive processes but are the basis for all thinking. As you read in chapter 8, Vygotsky (1978) was

the originator of this hypothesis. According to Vygotsky, social interactions are not the "icing on the cake," something that makes learning more palatable. Social interactions are the cake itself, the essential ingredient by which an individual's thoughts are transformed.

The first three of Bruer's (1994) hypotheses fall within the broad framework of information-processing theories. The fourth hypothesis, dealing with motivation, falls within the expanded information-processing framework discussed earlier in connection with memory strategies (e.g., Pressley & Van Meter, 1993). By contrast, the final hypothesis crosses the boundary between information-processing approaches and a sociocultural theory of cognitive development.

Which of these hypotheses are correct? Only future research will tell. One possibility is that all are correct or contain a kernel of truth. This possibility deserves more careful study, because advances in understanding of children's learning could set the stage for dramatic changes in children's schooling.

# Summary

### Perception and Attention
Eleanor Gibson's theory of perceptual learning emphasizes children's exploration, selective attention, and perceptual differentiation. The goal of perception is to discover the affordances of objects in the environment. With increasing age, children's perceptual exploration becomes more systematic, efficient, and selective.

### Mental Representation and World Knowledge
How children mentally represent information is critical to their information processing. The information that they currently have, which defines their knowledge of the world, also affects their processing of new information.

### Concepts and Categories
In a free classification task, whether children put together objects that belong to the same conceptual category (e.g., tools) depends on their age and their schooling. Yet, even infants recognize global categories such as birds and planes. The concepts of children seem to reflect simple theories about the causes of similarities and differences between things.

### Knowledge in Specific Domains
Children with extensive knowledge in a specific domain such as soccer can be defined as experts in that domain. Children with little knowledge in a domain can be defined as novices. Experts are superior to novices in their ability to solve most cognitive problems in their domain of expertise.

### Representations of Places and Events
Children form mental representations of familiar places like their own homes. Children can also form representations of large-scale environments like a college campus. Between 2 and 3 years of age, children begin to appreciate that pictures and scale models correspond to real places.

Young children also form scripts, mental representations of routine events like a trip to a restaurant.

### Remembering
Memory—the ability to store, retain, and recall experiences—is critical to thinking, reasoning, and action. Memory is functional in infancy but improves and becomes more planful during childhood.

### Infant Memory
Memory in infants can be studied with the habituation procedure, tests of visual recognition memory, and a procedure in which infants' kicking is reinforced by seeing a mobile move. Experiments on infants and mobiles have shown that infants only a few months old can remember their experiences for several weeks.

### Remembering in Childhood
Improvements in remembering during childhood are caused partly by increases in children's speed of processing information. On many tasks, older children also use memory strategies such as rehearsal that improve their remembering. In addition, remembering is affected by increases in children's knowledge base and their metamemory.

### Autobiographical Memory
Infantile amnesia is the inability to remember personal experiences from the first few years of life. Infantile amnesia reflects the absence of autobiographical memory, memory for the events of one's own life. Possible explanations for infantile amnesia include a lack of ability to construct narratives, the lack of a definite self-concept, and a tendency to form verbatim rather than fuzzy traces of events.

### Learning
Learning is a change in behavior in a specific situation due to experience in that situation.

Learning involves remembering, because changes in behavior must depend on some kind of memory for experiences. Learning occurs even before birth, but its complexity and precision increase with age.

### Learning in Infancy
Traditional learning theories focus on three learning processes: classical conditioning, operant conditioning, and observational learning. All three processes operate at birth. These processes become more efficient during infancy.

### Principles of Learning in Childhood
All children are active and strategic when engaged in learning. With increasing age, children learn more about *how* to learn new information. Learning to learn is closely related to metacognition, children's ability to think about their thoughts and control their cognitive processes. Much of learning is domain-specific, linked to specific types of information, skills, and tasks.

### Understanding and Enhancing Children's Learning
Children learn to use strategies for remembering information, comprehending material they read, and solving math problems. Training children to use strategies is most effective when the children are told explicitly why a strategy is useful, and they see that using the strategy improves their performance. Training should continue until children have fully mastered the strategy.

### Classroom Learning Through Social Interaction
Social interactions with teachers and other students are a central element in many interventions to improve classroom learning. The effectiveness of these interventions may be explained by information-processing approaches, by a sociocultural theory of cognitive development, or by a combination of these ideas.

# Suggested Readings

**Bjorklund, D. F. (1995).** *Children's thinking: Developmental function and individual differences* **(2nd ed.). Pacific Grove, CA: Brooks/Cole.** This textbook on cognitive development is unusually comprehensive. Besides chapters on Piaget's theory and information-processing approaches, the book includes chapters on reading and number concepts, intelligence testing, and biological bases of cognitive development.

**Kail, R. (1990).** *The development of memory in children* **(3rd ed.). New York: W. H. Freeman.** This clearly written book includes information about the relation of remembering to other cognitive processes and to social behavior. Kail also talks about applications of memory research to improve the performance of mentally retarded children. In the same chapter, he discusses the accuracy of children's legal testimony about events.

**McGilly, K. (Ed.). (1994).** *Classroom lessons: Integrating cognitive theory and classroom practice.* **Cambridge, MA: MIT Press.** This book describes the work of cognitive scientists who have tried to test their theories and models in children's schools. The title, "classroom lessons," has a double meaning. It refers not only to the use of cognitive theories to develop lessons (curricula and teaching methods) but also to what cognitive theorists have learned from working in classrooms.

**Siegler, R. S., & Jenkins, E. (1989).** *How children discover new strategies.* **Hillsdale, NJ: Erlbaum.** This brief book (140 pages) reports the authors' research on strategies children use to solve arithmetic problems. The research was unusual because the authors assessed how individual children's strategies changed across problems and over time. One chapter describes how each of five children discovered more efficient strategies for arithmetic.

### Chapter Ten

# INTELLIGENCE AND ACADEMIC ACHIEVEMENT

**psychometric approach**
*The research tradition that focuses on the nature and assessment of human intelligence, most often by using standardized tests to assess general intelligence and specific cognitive abilities.*

*T*hree perspectives on cognitive development were discussed in chapters 8 and 9, those of Piaget, Vygotsky, and information-processing theorists. None of these perspectives is as old—or as controversial—as the one discussed in this chapter. The **psychometric approach** to the study of cognitive development focuses on the nature and assessment of human intelligence. The adjective *psychometric* can be applied to any form of psychological measurement. In the field of cognitive development, however, the psychometric approach refers to the research tradition in which standardized tests are used to assess general intelligence and specific cognitive abilities.

The first intelligence tests were created early in the twentieth century, and they soon were linked to contentious political issues (Gould, 1981). During World War I, a new intelligence test was given to more than a million men who enlisted in the United States Army. Recent immigrants, especially those from southern and eastern Europe, usually received lower scores on the test than did men who were born in the United States.

How would you explain this difference? Probably not the way some psychologists did. They argued that the immigrants were genetically inferior to the men born in the United States. Furthermore, they recommended that the federal government limit immigration from southern and eastern Europe to avoid lowering the intelligence of the U.S. population.

Of course, the psychologists' negative judgments about these immigrants soon proved false. Most of them not only became productive citizens; either these immigrants or their children often became leaders in business, the professions, academia, and other fields. So much for their genetic inferiority!

Now for a contrasting story. During the 1980s, a team of psychologists did another cross-national comparison, this time between people in the United States and people in Japan and Taiwan. Instead of Army recruits, however, the participants in this research were schoolchildren. Also, the researchers compared the children's scores not on a presumed intelligence test but on tests of academic achievement.

You may be able to guess the results of the study. The children in Japan and Taiwan received higher scores on tests of mathematics achievement than did the U.S. children (Stevenson, Lee, & Stigler, 1986). Do you think the psychologists concluded that U.S. children are genetically inferior to those in Japan and Taiwan? No, they did not. They argued instead that differences in the children's environments, especially in their education, were the source of the differences in their achievement-test scores. The researchers also documented differences between the educational systems in the United States and in the other countries that could explain the difference in the children's math scores.

The child with the small colored blocks is taking an intelligence test under the guidance of the adult examiner. The students in the classroom are trying to improve their academic achievement. The two photographs are related because intelligence tests were first devised to help educators choose the most appropriate education for children. That is still the purpose for which the tests are most often given.

A third story brings this look at history into the 1990s. A book titled *The Bell Curve: Intelligence and Class Structure in American Life* (Herrnstein & Murray, 1994) was a best-seller in 1994. The book created a major stir because the authors discussed racial differences in intelligence. They also raised the question of whether those differences are genetically based. Their answer was stated tentatively: "It seems highly likely to us that both genes and environment have something to do with racial differences. What might the mix be? We are resolutely agnostic on that issue: as far as we can determine, the evidence does not yet justify an estimate" (p. 311). But for raising the issue and for other reasons, many reviewers vehemently criticized the book, calling it dishonest, racist, and neo-Nazi (Fraser, 1995).

These three (true) stories relate to a central issue in this chapter, the influence of heredity versus environment on intelligence-test scores and academic achievement. You will learn that the variations in children's intelligence are due partly to their experience and partly to their genotypes. You will also learn more about racial differences in intelligence, and about the controversy over *The Bell Curve*. However, several issues need to be addressed before you can fully understand how genes and experiences influence intelligence.

# DEFINING AND MEASURING INTELLIGENCE

Before researchers could study the influences on children's intelligence, they needed to decide how intelligence should be defined. Once they settled on a definition of intelligence, they needed to create tests that would measure intelligence accurately.

## Multiple Definitions of Intelligence

Dictionaries list several definitions of intelligence. Most generally, **intelligence** is the human faculty of thought and reason. That is, intelligence refers to cognitive processes. A second definition of intelligence is the ability to acquire knowledge and use that knowledge to anticipate and solve problems. This definition takes intelligence out of the realm of abstract thought and links it to practical activities and real-life challenges.

A third definition of intelligence is mental acuteness, or superior mental powers. This definition implies that people differ in their understanding, reasoning, and ability to acquire and use knowledge. People are considered intelligent when their thinking, reasoning, and problem solving are greater than those of the average person. People are considered unintelligent when their intellectual ability is lower than that of the average person.

Most studies of intelligence focus on the differences among people in their intellectual abilities. In this respect, research on intelligence contrasts with the research examined in chapters 8 and 9. The focus in those chapters was on age changes in reasoning and information processing. This chapter focuses, instead, on cognitive (or intellectual) differences among children who are the same age.

The dictionary definition of intelligence does not capture all the meaning that the average person (the person of average intelligence!) gives to the term. Researchers have asked both children and adults what intelligence means to them (e.g., Nicholls, Patashnick, & Mettetal, 1986; Sternberg & Wagner, 1986). In one study (Sternberg et al., 1981), groups of undergraduates, commuters waiting at a train station, and supermarket shoppers were asked to list behaviors that they considered intelligent. They listed a total of 170 behaviors. Then a new group of adults rated how much each behavior was characteristic of their ideal of an intelligent person.

Table 10.1 shows some of the major results. Three dimensions seemed to underlie the adults' ratings of an ideally intelligent person. The researchers labeled the strongest dimension as practical problem-solving ability. Several behaviors associated with this dimension refer to problem solving explicitly. For example, people believe that an intelligent person "poses problems in an optimal way" and "deals with problems resourcefully." Other behaviors seem, despite the label for the dimension, to deal with abstract reasoning ability. Some examples are "reasons logically and well," "interprets information accurately," and "perceives implied assumptions and conclusions." This dimension, then, deals both with the application of knowledge and with the general qualities of thinking and reasoning that are part of the dictionary definition of intelligence.

**intelligence**
*The human faculty of thought and reason; the ability to acquire and use knowledge in problem solving; mental acuteness.*

| TABLE 10.1 | *Dimensions Underlying Adults' Ratings of an Ideally Intelligent Person* | |
|---|---|---|
| **PRACTICAL PROBLEM-SOLVING ABILITY** | **VERBAL ABILITY** | **SOCIAL COMPETENCE** |
| Reasons logically and well | Speaks clearly and articulately | Accepts others for what they are |
| Identifies connections among ideas | Is verbally fluent | Admits mistakes |
| Sees all aspects of a problem | Converses well | Displays interest in the world at large |
| Keeps an open mind | Reads with high comprehension | Is on time for appointments |
| Responds thoughtfully to others' ideas | Reads widely | Thinks before speaking and doing |
| Interprets information accurately | Writes without difficulty | Makes fair judgments |
| Poses problems in an optimal way | | |
| Perceives implied assumptions and conclusions | | |
| Deals with problems resourcefully | | |

From R. J. Sternberg, et al., "People's conceptions of intelligence; in *Journal of Personality and Social Psychology*, 41:37–55. Copyright © 1981 by The American Psychological Association. Adapted with permission.

The second dimension underlying people's ratings is for verbal ability. People assume that intelligent people show their verbal ability in speaking, reading, and writing. The ideally intelligent person "converses well," "reads widely," and "writes without difficulty." Verbal ability is not explicitly mentioned in most dictionary definitions of intelligence, but the average adult assumes that high verbal ability is a sign of superior intelligence.

The third dimension shown in table 10.1 is for social competence. Some behaviors related to this dimension involve thinking and reasoning, such as "thinks before speaking and doing." Other behaviors reflect social skill and positive social attitudes like "makes fair judgments" and "accepts others for what they are." Notice that this dimension of people's ratings is not reflected in the usual dictionary definitions of intelligence.

A group of psychologists who were viewed as experts on intelligence rated the same behaviors as the lay adults. The first dimension underlying the experts' ratings was for problem-solving ability. A second dimension was for verbal intelligence. A third dimension, which partly overlapped with the other adults' dimension of social competence, was for practical or social adaptation. However, the experts viewed verbal ability as more central to intelligence, and social adaptation or social competence as less central to intelligence, than the lay adults did. As you will see, these differences are relevant to the history and interpretation of IQ tests.

Even so, the similarities between the experts' ratings and those of the other adults were more striking than the differences. Both assumed that problem-solving ability is critical to the definition of intelligence. Both viewed verbal ability as one sign of intelligence. And both treated social skill or adaptation as one characteristic of the intelligent person (Sternberg et al., 1981).

Adults include still other characteristics in their definitions of an intelligent child. When the parents of elementary-school children were asked to describe an intelligent first grader, they mentioned problem-solving skills, verbal ability, and social skills (Okagaki & Sternberg, 1993). For example, they said an intelligent first grader understands complex information, has a good vocabulary, and shows respect for others. In addition, they mentioned characteristics specific to the school context, including behaviors that reflect high academic achievement and achievement motivation. For example, they said an intelligent first grader gets good grades, likes school, and attends school regularly.

Parents from different ethnic groups varied in the importance they attached to achievement motivation and actual achievement (Okagaki & Sternberg, 1993). Anglo-American parents placed less emphasis on these characteristics than did parents who came to the United States from Mexico, Cambodia, Vietnam, and the Philippines. Unlike the immigrant parents, the Anglo-American parents considered verbal ability and creativity as more central to intelligence than motivation and achievement in school. As you will see later, this difference may partly explain why the math achievement of U.S. students lags behind that of students in many other countries.

# The First Successful Intelligence Test and the IQ Paradigm

For psychologists, defining intelligence is only the first step in research. The next step is to devise measures of individual differences in intelligence. The first successful intelligence test was created in France early in the twentieth century.

In 1904 the Minister of Public Instruction in Paris appointed a commission to study the educational needs of mentally retarded children. The commission concluded that children should be removed from regular classes and taught in special classes only if an examination showed that they could not learn in regular classes. The commissioners did not say what kind of examination should be given. When they presented their report, no examinations seemed adequate for this purpose.

Alfred Binet, a member of the commission, set himself the task of devising such an exam. With Theodore Simon, he began to construct a scale of intelligence. Binet and Simon devised many short, simple tests of visual coordination, word definition, memory, and other cognitive processes. In 1905 they published their first intelligence scale with 30 tests (see table 10.2). In 1908 and 1911 they presented revised versions of the scale.

Binet and Simon did not use cognitive theories as a basis for their intelligence scale. When they did their work, no widely accepted cognitive theories existed. Even so, Binet and Simon made one important, theoretically relevant decision. They decided to measure complex, or high-level, mental processes. Earlier researchers had tried to devise intelligence tests with measures of reflex response, reactions to sensations, and speed of movement. However, scores on these measures seemed not to relate strongly to other indicators of intellectual ability. Binet and Simon assumed that intelligence, the "faculty of thought and reason," could best be measured by getting samples of children's reasoning. In defending their approach, Binet and Simon argued that "to judge well, to comprehend well, to reason well, these are the essential activities of intelligence" (1916/1973, p. 42).

The next step for Binet and Simon was to prove that their intelligence scale accurately measured differences in children's intelligence. They offered two kinds of evidence. First, normal children received higher scores on the scale than did children judged by teachers or physicians as retarded. Thus, the scale yielded results consistent with the judgments of

Around the turn of the century, when Binet and Simon began work on their intelligence test, French classrooms often looked like this one. Intelligence testing should, ideally, help teachers choose the most effective instruction for particular children.

## TABLE 10.2 Sample Tests on Binet and Simon's First Intelligence Scale

| | |
|---|---|
| 1. *Visual Coordination* | The experimenter watches to see whether children follow with their head and eyes when a lighted match is moved back and forth before them. |
| 2. *Verbal Knowledge* | Children are asked to touch their head, nose, and other parts of their body on command. They are asked to give the examiner a key when shown a cup, a string, and a key. |
| 3. *Knowledge of Objects in a Picture* | Children are shown a picture with several common objects in it and asked to point to specific objects when the examiner names them. |
| 4. *Visual Discrimination* | Children are shown two lines and asked to say which is longer. |
| 5. *Definitions* | Children are asked to define a house and other familiar objects. |
| 6. *Visual Memory* | Children are shown 13 pictures of objects pasted on pieces of cardboard for 30 seconds. Then the objects are taken away and the children try to recall them. |
| 7. *Weight Seriation* | Children must put five weights of 3, 6, 9, 12, and 15 grams in order (or in a series). The weights are equal in size. |
| 8. *Sentence Completion* | Children must complete simple sentences. For example, "The weather is clear, and the sky is . . . (blue)." |
| 9. *Comprehension* | Children must answer questions like "Why is it better to continue until you have finished what you started instead of quitting and starting something else?" |
| 10. *Word Comparisons* | Children must explain the difference between related words like *sad* and *bored*. |

**mental age**
*An index of a child's intellectual ability relative to that of other children the same age. Mental age is judged by comparing the intelligence-test items that a child answers correctly with the average age at which children answer those items correctly.*

knowledgeable adults. Second, beginning with the 1908 scale, Binet and Simon reported the average age at which children passed each test. They also grouped the tests by the age at which most children passed them.

The attention to age norms was critical for the later history of IQ testing. With the 1908 scale, Binet and Simon introduced the concept of **mental age.** Children's mental age was defined by the tests that they passed. For example, a child who passed all tests passed by an average 7-year-old but no tests passed by an average 8-year-old had a mental age of 7 years. Of course, the concept of mental age implies that intelligence develops or increases as children grow. Children are, then, retarded if their mental age is below their actual or chronological age.

With the introduction of the concept of mental age, the model for intelligence testing was nearly set. The final piece was supplied by Lewis Terman in the United States. Terman revised the tests on the Binet-Simon scales, added new tests, and dropped others. He also measured the average age at which children passed each test more precisely than had Binet and Simon. Terman gave the final version of each item on his new scale to more than 1,000 children and adults before setting the mental age for the item.

Terman made an even more important change in the scoring of intelligence tests. He adopted the suggestion of a German psychologist that children's final scores should be the ratio of their mental age (MA) to their chronological age (CA). Because this ratio is obtained by dividing MA by CA, the resulting number is a quotient. (Remember that term from grade-school mathematics?) To simplify the final score, Terman multiplied the quotient by 100, devising the formula: $MA/CA \times 100 = IQ$. That is, multiplying the ratio of children's MA to their CA by 100 yields their IQ, or **intelligence quotient.**

**intelligence quotient**
*Originally, the ratio of children's mental age to their chronological age multiplied by 100. Now calculated differently (see deviation IQ on page 385) but still an index of how much children's measured intellectual abilities exceed or fall below those of an average child their age.*

Terman was at Stanford University when he completed his revision of the Binet scales. In 1916 he published the first edition of the new intelligence scale, which he called the Stanford-Binet. With the publication of this scale, the basic procedures for measuring children's intelligence were set.

The approach to intelligence testing started by Binet and Simon and refined by Terman might be called the IQ paradigm. The central features of this paradigm can be stated in four points. You have encountered the first two already. The next two are more controversial.

1. *Children show their intelligence by their success in solving problems.* To judge a child's intelligence, psychologists see whether the child can solve a standard set of problems. This point relates to Binet and Simon's emphasis on high-level cognitive processes rather than basic processes. Notice that this emphasis is consistent with commonsense definitions of intelligence.

2. *Intelligence increases with age, so children's intelligence can be estimated by comparing their performance with that of other children the same age.* This statement summarizes the key ideas behind the mental age (MA) and the IQ.

3. *Children's intelligence can be accurately described by a single score, their IQ.* This statement implies that intellectual ability is a single thing and that some people have more of it than others. In more formal terms, intellectual ability is one-dimensional, and some people are higher on the dimension than are others. In the early 1900s researchers investigated the correlations between children's scores on the many types of items that are part of an IQ test. Each type of item was somewhat distinct from the other types. Still, each type seemed partly to measure the same ability, or the same dimension, as the other types.

Charles Spearman (1927) described the ability that all items measure as general intelligence, or *g*. He assumed that *g* involves the ability to infer and use knowledge about the relations among objects or ideas. He further assumed that an IQ score is a measure of *g*.

The hypothesis of general intelligence, or *g*, is controversial because people often seem to have special talent in certain types of reasoning. Some people have high verbal ability, for example, but lower mathematical ability. And as you recall, when people define intelligence they treat verbal ability, problem-solving ability, and social competence as distinct dimensions (Sternberg et al., 1981).

A few psychologists rejected Spearman's hypothesis that intellectual ability is one-dimensional. Louis Thurstone (1938) argued that there are several basic mental abilities. For example, he separated verbal comprehension from inductive reasoning.

Some psychologists have argued that both Spearman's and Thurstone's ideas were partly correct. In this view, intellectual abilities are structured hierarchically, with *g* at the top and various special abilities below it (Carroll, 1992; Neisser et al., 1996). The correlations among measures of cognitive abilities suggest that they are all related to *g*. In addition, some kinds of measures are more strongly related to one another than they are to other measures. Groups that include the same kinds of measures can be taken as defining special abilities.

Nevertheless, ideas about specific cognitive abilities did not become part of the IQ paradigm (Thorndike, 1994). In research and in practice, children's intelligence was most often reported as a single score, their IQ.

4. *Children's scores on IQ tests show their intellectual potential, or learning ability.* Binet and Simon wanted to identify children who could not learn in a regular school classroom. They assumed that children's scores on their intelligence scale would show how much children could learn, or their intellectual potential. Binet and Simon did not believe that children's scores would be influenced by how much they had already learned, the information they had already acquired. Indeed, they boldly claimed that "we have succeeded in completely disregarding the acquired information of the subject. We give him nothing to read, nothing to write, and submit him to no test in which he might succeed by rote learning. It is simply the level of his natural intelligence that is taken into account" (1916/1973, p. 42).

It was not long before theorists and researchers took the next, apparently simple step in reasoning. If IQ scores are measures of intellectual potential, and they are not influenced by acquired knowledge, they must reflect the innate intellectual capacity of the child. Although Binet and Simon did not take a stand on the question of innate intelligence, by the 1920s most psychologists assumed that IQ tests measured innate intellectual capacity (Carroll, 1982). That is, most people who studied and used IQ tests assumed that differences in children's IQ scores were determined by heredity rather than by environment. So when Army recruits who were recent immigrants from eastern and southern Europe received lower IQ scores than recruits born in the United States, many psychologists jumped to the conclusion that the immigrants were lower in innate intelligence.

**g**
*General intelligence, or what Spearman and other theorists assumed was the single dimension that all items on an IQ test measure to some degree.*

## On Verbal Scale

### Information

How many fingers do you have?
Who discovered America?

### Arithmetic

If I have three pieces of gum and get another one, how many pieces will I have?

If a shirt sells for $^1/_3$ off the price marked, what is the actual cost of a $27 shirt?

### Comprehension

Why do we wear socks?

Why do we have courts?

## On Performance Scale

### Picture completion

The task is to identify the essential missing part of the picture.

An example is shown at right.
What is missing from this picture?

### Picture arrangement

The task is to arrange a series of pictures into a meaningful sequence.
An example is shown below.

These pictures tell a story, but they are in the wrong order.
Put them in the right order so that they tell a story.

### Block design

The task is to reproduce stimulus designs using blocks.
An example is shown below.

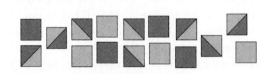

Put the blocks together to make this picture.

FIGURE 10.1

Six subtests and sample items like those on the Wechsler Intelligence Scale for Children. (Source: The Psychological Corporation.)

Great controversy surrounds the assumption that there is a single dimension of general intelligence, *g*, which is determined by children's heredity and not by their environment (Fraser, 1995; Herrnstein & Murray, 1994; "Mainstream science," 1994; Slater, 1995; Sternberg, 1994; Thorndike, 1994). This assumption continues to be debated explicitly, as you will see later in the chapter. The continuing controversy has also influenced the changes in IQ testing since Terman devised the Stanford-Binet in 1916.

## Current IQ Tests: A Review and Status Report

For several decades the Stanford-Binet was the preeminent IQ test in the United States. Even so, some features of the test were a focus of criticism. Some critics suggested that the test relied too heavily on verbal items and paid too little attention to problem-solving ability. Also, critics noted that little rationale existed for the selection of test items. Any item that discriminated among children of different ages might be included. The cognitive processes assessed by different items received little attention.

To avoid the problems with the Stanford-Binet, David Wechsler devised new procedures for the construction of IQ tests. He first created an intelligence test for adults called the Wechsler-Bellevue Intelligence Scale. Then he created tests appropriate for school-age children and preschool children. The current version of the test for schoolchildren is the Wechsler Intelligence Scale for Children-Third Edition, or WISC-III (Wechsler, 1991).

### The WISC-III

Figure 10.1 gives the labels of 6 of the 13 subtests on the WISC-III, along with sample items like those on the actual tests. The Information, Arithmetic, and Comprehension subtests are part of a larger, Verbal Scale. The Picture Completion, Picture Arrangement, and Block Design subtests are part of a larger, Performance Scale. All tests on the Performance Scale are timed. For example, children have 20 seconds to answer each item on the Picture Completion test. By including both verbal and performance subtests, Wechsler created an IQ test that is less heavily influenced by verbal ability than were the early editions of the Stanford-Binet.

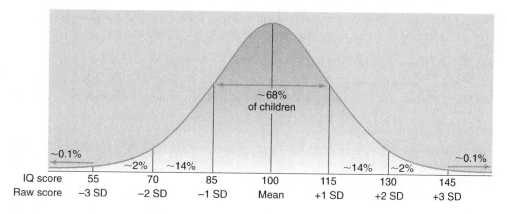

| IQ score | 55 | 70 | 85 | 100 | 115 | 130 | 145 |
| Raw score | −3 SD | −2 SD | −1 SD | Mean | +1 SD | +2 SD | +3 SD |

## FIGURE 10.2

A normal distribution of IQ scores. Children are defined as having an IQ of 100 if their raw score on the IQ test equals the mean score for children their age in the standardization sample. Children have an IQ of 115 if their raw score falls one standard deviation (SD) above the mean for children their age. IQ scores for children with other raw scores are assigned in a comparable way. The figure shows that IQ scores are normally distributed: Most children's scores fall between 85 and 115, or within one standard deviation of the mean. Very few children have scores more than three standard deviations from the mean.

Children who take the WISC-III may be given both a Verbal IQ score and a Performance IQ score. The manual for the WISC-III also suggests that the 13 subtests may be grouped into sets that assess four facets of intelligence (or four specific abilities). However, other researchers have suggested that the various subtests measure only three facets of intelligence (Kamphaus et al., 1994). Thus, how best to summarize WISC-III scores is debatable (Sattler, 1994).

Wechsler also changed the calculation of IQ scores when he created his new intelligence tests. He pointed out that the original formula for the IQ, MA/CA × 100, can yield misleading scores. Intellectual growth is more rapid in younger children, so a one-year difference in MA does not correspond to the same change in cognitive performance at younger and older ages. In addition, MA scores are not equivalent for children who differ in age. A precocious 5-year-old and an average 8-year-old who both have an MA of 8 years do not reason in exactly the same way.

To avoid these problems, Wechsler devised a new procedure called the **deviation IQ** score. Children who take the WISC-III get a score for each item. Their total score for all items is their *raw score* for the entire test. (For simplicity, assume the goal is to calculate total IQ, instead of separate scores for Verbal and Performance IQ.) A child's raw score is then compared with the scores of other children the same age who were in the **standardization sample.**

The standardization sample included thousands of children varying in age who took the WISC-III before its official publication. The raw scores of these children were converted to IQ scores using the procedure outlined in figure 10.2. At each age children's raw scores formed a nearly normal distribution, or bell-shaped curve. Children whose raw scores were at the mean for their age were credited with an IQ of 100.

When children's raw scores differed from the mean, the size of the difference was expressed in terms of standard deviations (a measure of variability). Then a difference of one standard deviation was treated as equivalent to 15 IQ points. A child whose raw score was one standard deviation above the mean received an IQ score of 115. A child whose raw score was two standard deviations below the mean received an IQ of 70, and so on.

The distribution of scores in the original, standardization sample determines the IQ scores given to students who later take the published version of the test. For example, a 7-year-old with the same raw score as the average 7-year-old in the original sample is credited with an IQ of 100. A 7-year-old with a raw score two standard deviations above the

**deviation IQ**
*An IQ score computed by determining how much a child's score on an intelligence test differs from the mean score for children the same age. The difference between the child's raw score and the mean score is transformed into standard deviation units, and then these units are translated into IQ points (with one standard deviation = 15 points).*

**standardization sample**
*The group of children whose responses define the norms and establish the scoring for tests later given to other children.*

**1. Memory for digits**
The task is to recall a series of digits (e.g., 5-8-9-4).

**2. Memory for objects**
The task is to recall pictured objects in the exact sequence in which they were presented. The examinee points to the pictured items on a card that contains both the stimulus items and distractor items. For example, the examinee is first shown a picture of a knife and a dog and then shown a card containing the pictures of a knife, dog, spoon, cat, and house.

**3. Vocabulary**
The task is to name a pictured object (e.g., a train) or define words given orally (e.g., *taut*).

**4. Comprehension**
The task is to point to body parts (e.g., a doll's foot) or to answer questions dealing with social comprehension (e.g., Why do we have a Congress?).

**5. Pattern analysis**
The task is like that of Block Design on the WISC-R.

**6. Matrices**
The task is to select the object, design, or letter that best completes a matrix. An example is shown below.

Answers:  Y  A  X  11

*Note:* These items are similar to those on the Stanford-Binet: Fourth Edition, but they are not actually from the test.

FIGURE 10.3

Six subtests and sample items like those on the Stanford-Binet: Fourth Edition. (Source: Sattler, 1988.)

**crystallized intelligence**
*Intellectual abilities that, in theory, are heavily influenced by education and socialization in a culture. Tests of vocabulary and comprehension are usually viewed as measures of crystallized intelligence.*

mean of the 7-year-olds in the original sample is credited with an IQ of 130. Nearly all modern intelligence tests use some variant of this deviation-IQ scoring method.

## Stanford-Binet: Fourth Edition

The Stanford-Binet was revised by Terman and his associates in 1937. Terman died in 1956, but Maud Merrill, one of his long-time colleagues, completed another revision of the scale in 1960. During the 1980s, the scale was revised much more extensively. The newest version is the Stanford-Binet Intelligence Scale: Fourth Edition (Thorndike, Hagen, & Sattler, 1986). In contrast to the earlier versions, the tests in the fourth edition are not grouped by age. Instead, children at every age take most of the 15 subtests on the scale. In this respect, the fourth edition is similar to the WISC-III.

As with most IQ tests, the total score on the newest Stanford-Binet is viewed as an estimate of general intelligence, or *g*. Smaller sets of tests are assumed to measure different facets of intelligence.

Figure 10.3 shows tests intended to measure three facets of intelligence. The tests of memory for digits and objects are designed to assess children's short-term memory. The vocabulary and comprehension tests can be viewed as measures of **crystallized intelligence,** which is assumed to be heavily influenced by education and socialization in a culture (Cattell, 1971; Horn & Cattell, 1982). Success on the vocabulary and comprehension tests depends on mastery of a specific language, which comes through education and cultural learning.

The tests of pattern analysis and matrices can be viewed as measures of **fluid intelligence,** which is assumed to be heavily influenced by speed and flexibility in manipulating abstract symbols. R. B. Cattell (1982) argued that fluid intelligence depends little on education or socialization. In his view, therefore, performance on the quantitative and pattern-analysis items should not be affected by formal instruction or informal learning.

Many researchers do not accept the distinction between fluid and crystallized intelligence (see Brody, 1992; Lohman, 1989; Sternberg & Powell, 1983). John Horn, one of the original advocates of the distinction, has more recently argued that intelligence has not two facets but at least nine (Horn & Hofer, 1992). Some of these facets are assessed by subtests on scales like the Stanford-Binet. Other facets, such as one for perceptions of sound patterns, are not assessed on IQ tests.

In addition, children's scores on the Stanford-Binet subtests do not show the specific pattern of correlations that is implied by the distinction between fluid and crystallized intelligence (Sattler, 1988). A contrast between verbal comprehension and nonverbal reasoning may describe these correlations more accurately than the fluid-crystallized distinction does.

Nevertheless, the distinction is important. The fourth edition of the Stanford-Binet is one of several new IQ tests that are based on explicit theories of cognitive development (see also Kaufman & Kaufman, 1983). A large gap still exists between psychometric approaches to cognitive development and the other approaches discussed in chapters 8 and 9 (Sternberg & Powell, 1983). This gap may become narrower as researchers try to devise an integrated picture of developmental changes and individual differences in intelligence.

## Special Tests for Infants and Older Children

Traditional IQ tests cannot be used with infants. If you ask a 6-month-old to repeat digits or define the word *house*, you will get a blank stare at best. Traditional tests also may be inappropriate for children who must be tested in a language different from their native language. In addition, the best-known tests take an hour or longer to administer. Researchers often want measures of intelligence that can be obtained more quickly. Special tests have been devised to deal with each of these cases.

***Bayley Scales of Infant Development***   Nancy Bayley (1969) created scales for measuring the mental and motor development of infants and children between 2 and 30 months of age. The simplest items on the mental scale measure attention to sensations. On one item for 4-month-olds, the examiner shakes a rattle and watches to see whether the infant turns toward it. For older infants and children, the items are more complex. They assess abilities to manipulate

The simplest items on intelligence tests for infants deal with perceptual abilities like that of following objects. More difficult items, for toddlers, often involve skills like building a tower of blocks.

objects, follow directions, remember the locations of objects, and understand the meanings of simple words. At 16 months, toddlers are expected to build a tower with three blocks. At 22 months, they are expected to name objects shown in pictures. These and the other items for older toddlers are similar to the easiest items on IQ tests for preschool children.

Scores on the mental scale are transformed into a Mental Development Index (or MDI) with a mean of 100 and a standard deviation of 16. Several researchers have used infants' MDI scores as the first measure of their intelligence and then used longitudinal designs to examine the stability of intelligence from infancy to childhood. Their findings are considered in the next section of the chapter.

During the 1990s, the Bayley Scales were extensively revised (Bayley, 1993). Items were added so that the scale could assess mental and motor development between 1 and 42 months of age. Many new items assess abilities about which you have read in previous chapters, including habituation (chapter 5), social referencing (chapter 6), and infant memory (chapter 9). With these revisions, the Bayley is likely to be used well into the twenty-first century.

*Raven's Progressive Matrices*   As noted earlier, many psychologists viewed the early versions of the Stanford-Binet as biased toward verbal intelligence. To avoid this bias, some psychologists created IQ tests that are almost completely nonverbal. The Raven's is the best known of the nonverbal tests (Raven, Court, & Raven, 1986).

The standard form of the Raven's test is for 6- to 17-year-olds. Each item shows an incomplete matrix of symbols (see figure 10.4). Children must complete the matrix by choosing the correct option from six choices.

The Raven's is often described as a culture-fair or culture-reduced test (Sattler, 1988). Because performance on the Raven's depends little on children's knowledge of English, it seems fairer for children who do not grow up in the mainstream culture. Consequently, some researchers expected that the scores of White children and children from minority ethnic groups would be more similar on the Raven's than on traditional IQ tests. This expectation has not been confirmed. The scores of children from different ethnic groups differ at least as much on culture-reduced tests as on standard IQ tests (Herrnstein & Murray, 1994; Mackenzie, 1984).

*Peabody Picture Vocabulary Test-Revised*   How about going to the opposite extreme from the Raven's and creating a completely verbal test? The Peabody includes only one type of item (Dunn & Dunn, 1981). The examiner shows a child four pictures of animals or objects. Then the examiner says a word and asks the child to point to the picture that best represents that word. The test begins with easy items, like the word *bed*. The items gradually become more difficult, and some (e.g., *rhombus*) are not accurately named by most adults.

**fluid intelligence**
*Intellectual abilities that, in theory, are heavily influenced by speed and flexibility in manipulating abstract symbols. They are assumed to depend little on education or socialization. Most nonverbal tests of intelligence are viewed as measures of fluid intelligence.*

FIGURE 10.4

An item like those on the
Raven's Progressive Matrices.
Which circle is the right one to
fill the hole in the matrix?
Notice that this item places
minimal demands on your
verbal ability or your
knowledge of a specific culture.

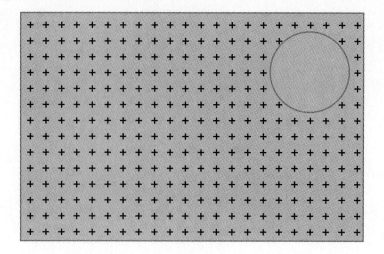

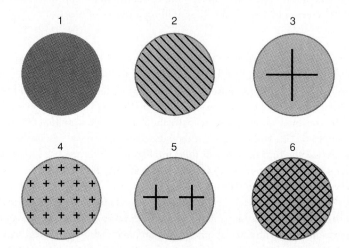

The PPVT-R has several features that make it a popular choice for researchers. For example, no sophisticated technical apparatus is needed to give the test, and the procedure is easy for children to understand. The PPVT-R is especially attractive to researchers and practitioners because it can be given in 15 minutes or less. By contrast, the latest version of the Stanford-Binet may take hours to administer (Sattler, 1988).

In this case, though, "more is better." The Stanford-Binet, the WISC-III, and other comprehensive intelligence tests assess many aspects of children's thinking and reasoning. Consequently, they provide better measures of general intellectual ability than short tests like the PPVT-R. Although some researchers have used the PPVT-R as a quick measure of general intelligence, this practice is unwise (Sattler, 1988). You should interpret research data derived from quick measures or abbreviated tests more cautiously than data derived from the complete version of a comprehensive IQ test.

## Evaluating IQ Tests

Now that you know what IQ tests are like, you can ask a more important question: How well do IQ tests do the job for which they were constructed? In other words, how well do they measure children's intelligence? To answer this question, you need to consider the basic principles of measurement discussed in chapter 2. More specifically, you need to know the reliability and validity of the IQ scores derived from these tests.

***Reliability*** Remember that *reliability* refers to the precision of a measure or the consistency with which a particular attribute is measured. Test makers typically evaluate the

reliability of their measures in two ways. First, they see whether children who receive higher scores on one item receive higher scores on other items. If all items are measuring the same attribute (general intelligence), then children's performance should be consistent across items. As mentioned in chapter 2, this type of reliability is called *internal consistency*.

Internal consistency is estimated on a scale from .00 to 1.0, where higher scores reflect greater internal consistency. The best IQ tests, like the WISC-III and the Stanford-Binet, have internal consistencies near or above .90, which indicates a high degree of reliability.

Second, test makers judge reliability by giving children the same test twice. The correlation between children's scores on the original test and on the retest is an index of test-retest reliability. When children's scores are consistent over time, the test-retest correlations are high. On the Stanford-Binet, Fourth Edition, the correlation between children's scores on two tests taken several months apart is above .90, which shows excellent reliability (Sattler, 1988).

*Validity*    Measures that are more accurate are defined as more valid. In intelligence testing, *validity* means the extent to which differences in children's IQ scores accurately reflect differences in their intelligence. But how can test makers judge the validity of IQ scores as measures of intelligence? As you learned in chapter 2, they must use an indirect approach. They must show that IQ scores relate to other measures in a way that is consistent with well-accepted ideas about intelligence.

Recall that Binet showed children's IQ scores are correlated with their success in school. He judged academic success from teachers' ratings of children's academic performance. Since Binet's time many standardized measures of academic achievement have been created. Across studies, the correlations between IQ scores and achievement measures range from .50 to .60 (Brody, 1985; Ceci, 1991). These correlations are not perfect (i.e., not equal to 1.0), so many children with high IQs do not get high scores on achievement tests, and vice versa. Still, a moderate relation exists between the two types of measures. As Binet hoped, IQ tests are valuable in judging a child's success in school.

In adulthood, people's IQs are correlated with their performance on their jobs (Brody, 1992; Neisser et al., 1996). Managers with higher IQs receive higher ratings from their supervisors. Even sales clerks tend to perform better on the job when their IQs are higher.

Moreover, adults with higher IQ scores are less likely to be on welfare, to commit criminal acts, or to be abusive parents (Brody, 1992; Herrnstein & Murray, 1994; Scarr, 1995; Stattin & Klackenberg-Larsson, 1993; White et al., 1994). You should know, though, that the correlations of IQ with these characteristics and behaviors are weaker than those with academic achievement. The weak correlations indicate that many other characteristics besides IQ affect adults' performance as employees, citizens, and parents. From another perspective, the weak correlations show that IQ is not a measure of everything good about a person. IQ tests measure cognitive functioning specifically—as they were intended to do.

Perhaps the major criticism of IQ tests is that they are biased in favor of White children from middle-class families. The critics claim that the tests are biased against children who belong to ethnic minority groups or who are from lower-class families. Because of this cultural bias in the tests, the critics say, the IQ scores of ethnic minority and lower-class children are not valid measures of their intelligence.

IQ testing might be culturally biased in several ways. First, the content of the test items might be more familiar to children in one ethnic group than in another. The difference in familiarity could give an advantage to children in the first group. This kind of bias was certainly a problem when the Army gave an early, flawed intelligence test to men who were recent immigrants to the United States (Gould, 1981).

By contrast, there is little evidence for this kind of bias when modern IQ tests are given to children from different ethnic groups in the United States. When adults choose items on IQ tests that they believe are biased against some ethnic groups, they rarely agree on which items are biased against which groups. Also, when children's IQ scores are recalculated with the supposedly biased items omitted, the mean scores of various ethnic groups are similar to their scores on the original tests. These data suggest that item content is not an important source of cultural bias in the most common IQ tests (Kaplan, 1985; Reynolds, 1994; Sattler, 1988).

Second, a cultural bias in IQ testing might derive from the conditions of testing rather than from the content of the test. Taking an IQ test might arouse more anxiety in children from ethnic minority groups or lower-class families than in White middle-class children. Children who are more test-anxious might respond more hesitantly to test questions and so get lower scores. In one study (Zigler et al., 1982), lower-class preschool children took the Stanford-Binet twice. If test anxiety lowered these children's scores on the first test, they would be expected to receive higher scores on the second test.

The mean scores of the lower-class children did increase by several points between the first and second test. Unfortunately, the study did not include a group of middle-class children. Middle-class children might have gained as much on the retest as did the lower-class children, because most children's scores improve if they retake the test after a few weeks (Sattler, 1988). Therefore, the improvement shown by lower-class children does not prove that the conditions of IQ testing are biased against them.

Third, a cultural bias in IQ testing might be shown by the correlations of IQ scores with other measures. For example, researchers could examine the correlations of IQ with academic achievement separately for ethnic minority or lower-class children and for White middle-class children. If the correlations were weaker for ethnic minorities and lower-class children, the argument for cultural bias would be supported.

Little evidence for this type of cultural bias exists. In most studies, the correlations of IQ scores with academic achievement are comparable for children in all ethnic groups (Kaplan, 1985; Neisser et al., 1996; Sattler, 1988). In this sense, IQ scores appear to be equally valid measures of intelligence for all groups.

Nevertheless, the conclusion that IQ scores are valid measures of intelligence is somewhat ambiguous. The ambiguity relates, first, to the definition of intelligence and, second, to the interpretation of IQ scores. Even if you were willing to grant that IQ scores are valid (or accurate) measures of something, you would still have to ask what that "something" is. Is it a child's innate, fixed, intellectual potential? Or is it the child's level of cognitive functioning at the time of testing? Might that level change over time with changes in the child's experiences?

Of course, these questions are specific forms of the general question about the roles of nature and nurture in development. The specific questions address two, somewhat separate, issues. One issue, considered in the next section, is the degree to which IQ scores are stable (fixed) or changeable. The second issue, considered in the following section, is how much children's genes and their environments affect their IQ scores.

# STABILITY AND CHANGE IN IQ SCORES

Early psychologists who argued for the genetic inferiority of immigrants from southern and eastern Europe assumed that IQ tests measure a person's innate intelligence. This assumption implies that IQ scores should be stable from birth through childhood into adulthood because they are "written in a person's genes." Evidence on the amount of stability and change in IQ scores was not available, however, until longitudinal research on children's IQs was completed.

To evaluate the stability of IQ scores, researchers correlated the scores that children received at one age with their scores at later ages. To examine the changes in IQ scores, researchers charted the variations in individual children's scores as they grew. Because questions about stability and questions about change call for different methods of data analysis, they are not like two sides of the same coin. After you read about the stability of IQ scores, you will probably be surprised to learn how much children's scores can change between birth and adulthood.

## How Stable Are Individual Differences in IQ Scores?

For a quick but partly misleading answer to the question in the heading, look at figure 10.5. The figure shows the correlations between children's IQ scores at age 15, when mental age comes close to its adult level, and their IQ scores at earlier ages. The data come from a longitudinal study by Nancy Bayley (1949). To make these data more reliable, Bayley correlated

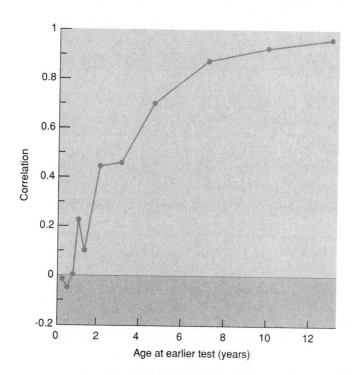

FIGURE 10.5

Correlations of individuals' IQ scores at age 15 with their IQ scores at earlier ages. Each value is the average correlation for the age plotted and for the two adjacent ages. For example, the value at age 13 is for IQ tests given when individuals were 12, 13, and 14 years of age. The correlations are near zero in infancy, but they increase rapidly during early and middle childhood. (Data from Bayley, 1949.)

the average scores that children received on three IQ tests. For example, the correlation at age 7 indicates how strongly the average of children's IQ scores at 6, 7, and 8 years of age was related to the average of their IQ scores at 14, 15, and 16 years.

The figure shows that IQ scores in middle childhood and early adolescence are very strongly correlated with those at age 15. For example, the correlation of IQ scores around age 10 with those around age 15 is above .90, close to a perfect correlation of 1.0. This high correlation means that children with high IQs in the elementary grades are very likely to have high IQs in high school. Conversely, children with low scores in the elementary grades are very likely to have low IQs in high school. In short, IQ scores show high stability in later childhood and adolescence.

Earlier in life, stability is much lower. The figure shows that IQ scores between birth and 1 year of age have a zero correlation with those at age 15. Therefore, people's IQ scores at age 15 cannot be predicted from their scores on IQ tests given in the first year of life. Good prediction of age-15 IQ becomes possible only during the elementary-school years.

Later studies confirmed the pattern in Bayley's (1949) early study and added new information (Vandenberg & Vogler, 1985). First, the studies showed that the stability of IQ scores increases with age. As figure 10.5 suggests, children's IQ scores vary less from one year to the next as they grow older.

Second, the later studies established that the stability of IQ scores decreases as the interval between tests increases. Figure 10.5 shows that the correlation of age-15 IQ scores with those around age 10 is lower than that of age-15 IQ scores with those around age 13. This difference is not entirely due to the difference in the children's ages at the earlier test (10 years old vs. 13 years old). It is partly due to the time between tests (five years vs. two years). Even in older children, stability decreases as the interval between tests increases (Schuerger & Witt, 1989). This decrease implies that some change in IQ scores occurs throughout childhood and adolescence.

Third, later researchers replicated Bayley's (1949) finding that IQ scores show little stability from infancy to childhood (McCall, 1979). Does this mean that intelligence shows little stability from infancy to childhood? In other words, is intellectual development marked by more discontinuity than continuity between infancy and childhood?

Until the 1980s many researchers assumed the answers to these questions were yes. However, several researchers have argued that the discontinuity exists only in IQ *tests,* not

in intelligence itself (e.g., Bornstein & Sigman, 1986; Rose et al., 1989). These researchers have suggested that traditional measures of infant intelligence, such as the original Bayley (1969) Mental Development Index, are poor measures of infants' cognitive functioning. Most items for young infants assess motor ability (e.g., building a tower of blocks) and orienting to stimuli (e.g., turning toward a rattle). These items may depend on cognitive processes very different from those that influence performance on IQ tests for children and adults. If similar cognitive processes were assessed in infancy and childhood, scores on infant measures might be more strongly correlated with IQ scores in childhood.

New measures of infant cognition have proved this prediction to be accurate. One well-known measure focuses on the phenomenon of visual recognition memory described in chapter 9 (Fagan, 1984; Fagan & Detterman, 1992). As you recall, infants are shown a picture of a face, an object, or a geometric form until they habituate, or lose interest in it. Then they are shown the picture that they saw before and a novel picture. Infants who remember the old picture show a preference for the novel one. Infants with a stronger novelty preference are better able to encode and remember the original stimulus; that is, their information processing is more efficient. If individual differences in information processing are stable from infancy to childhood, then infants with better visual recognition memory should, as children, get higher scores on IQ tests.

One team of researchers (Rose et al., 1989) tested this hypothesis with samples of full-term and preterm infants who were followed from birth until 5 years of age. At 7 months of age, the infants were given the test of visual recognition memory. They were given the Bayley (1969) Mental Development Scale at 7, 12, 18, and 24 months of age. They were given traditional IQ tests at 3, 4, and 5 years of age.

Table 10.3 shows the correlations between the infants' scores for visual recognition memory and their later IQ scores. For comparison, the table shows the correlations between the Bayley Mental Development Index (or MDI) at 7 months and later MDI and IQ scores.

For the full-term infants, MDI scores at 7 months were not significantly correlated with later IQ scores, replicating the results shown in figure 10.5. By contrast, scores for visual recognition memory were correlated with MDI scores at 24 months and with IQ scores during the preschool years. These correlations support the hypothesis that there is continuity in cognitive functioning from infancy to childhood.

For preterm infants, the pattern of correlations was different. The infants' MDI scores at 7 months were correlated with some measures of later IQ. Other studies have also shown that traditional tests such as the Bayley are useful in predicting the later IQ scores of preterm infants and other infants with a heightened risk of delayed development (Siegel, 1989). However, table 10.3 shows that prediction was even better for visual recognition memory, because those scores were significantly correlated with all measures of later IQ.

The same sample of children was followed until they reached 11 years of age (Rose & Feldman, 1995). Visual recognition memory assessed at 7 months of age was still significantly

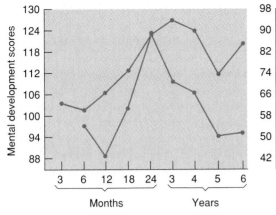
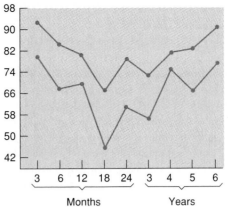

FIGURE 10.6

Age changes in the IQ scores of two pairs of dizygotic (DZ) twins between 3 months and 6 years of age. Notice that the age trends for the two children in each pair show only a loose correspondence. (Adapted from Wilson, 1983.)

correlated with IQ at age 11. The correlation was equally strong for full-term and preterm infants and was similar in magnitude (.41) to the correlations found several years earlier. Unlike the correlations between IQ tests, the correlations between infant cognitive measures and later IQ scores do not decrease regularly as the interval between tests increases (McCall & Carriger, 1993).

In other research, stability in cognitive functioning from infancy to childhood has been shown for simple measures of habituation and dishabituation. Infants who habituate more quickly to repeated stimuli and infants whose attention recovers more fully when a new stimulus is presented have higher IQ scores in childhood (Bornstein & Sigman, 1986; McCall & Carriger, 1993; Slater, 1995).

Why should measures of infants' habituation and visual recognition memory predict their IQ scores in childhood? One possible explanation is that infants' scores on these measures reflect an aspect of their information processing, perhaps speed of processing, that remains stable with age (Rose & Feldman, 1995). Another possibility is that the control of attention is the critical factor (McCall, 1994). In tests of habituation and visual recognition memory, infants need to inhibit attention to salient, familiar stimuli. When taking an IQ test, children need to inhibit attention to distracting stimuli and, instead, focus on the specific questions and tasks they are given. Additional research will be needed to determine whether speed of processing, control of attention, or something else is responsible for the continuity between infant cognitive functioning and childhood IQ scores.

## How Much Do IQ Scores Change as Children Grow?

After reading about the continuity in cognitive functioning from infancy to childhood, you might think that you could predict a child's IQ, within a few points, by assessing the child's cognitive functioning as an infant. If you really think so, you need to think again. Despite the moderate correlations in cognitive scores between infancy and childhood, the scores of individual children can and do fluctuate greatly.

Figure 10.6 shows the IQ scores of two pairs of dizygotic (DZ, or fraternal) twins on tests given between 3 months and 6 years of age. The scores for these pairs are representative of those for a large sample of DZ twins (Wilson, 1983). Notice how much these children's scores varied in their first six years of life. In the pair shown on the left, the scores of the child with a higher average score ranged from less than 106 to more than 124. The range for the twin was even greater, from roughly 88 to 124, or almost 40 points. The IQ scores of the pair on the right were below average at all ages. Even so, the variations in the children's scores between 3 months and 6 years were large, between 25 and 40 points.

Large changes in IQ scores during childhood are not unusual. In the California longitudinal studies, variations in children's IQs of more than 20 points were typical (McCall, 1983). The children took IQ tests more than a dozen times between 2 and 17 years of age. On the average, the range of variation in their IQ scores was more than 30 points. About 20

percent of the children had IQ scores that varied more than 40 points. One child's score varied more than 70 points!

Of course, some of these variations in scores may reflect random error. One source of random error is misinterpretation of children's answers or outright mistakes in scoring children's responses. Other sources of random error include illness, fatigue, or other temporary disruptions in children's physical or mental health. In a large New Zealand study (Moffitt et al., 1993), most fluctuations in children's IQ scores between 7 and 13 years of age seemed to reflect these types of random error. Moreover, few children showed either a steady increase or a steady decrease in IQ across that age range.

In summary, children's IQ scores show considerable stability but can change greatly as they grow older. Dramatic changes are more likely during infancy and early childhood than during middle childhood and adolescence.

# GENETIC AND ENVIRONMENTAL INFLUENCES ON THE DEVELOPMENT OF IQ

Why do IQ scores change, when they do? How much can they be changed, if special efforts are made? Answers to these questions have almost always been phrased in terms of the nature-nurture issue. That is, researchers have taken positions on the relative contributions of genes and environments to the development of IQ.

Unfortunately, most researchers who have studied genetic influences have included little information about the environments in which children live. Conversely, most researchers who have studied environmental influences have included little information about possible genetic differences among children. Because of this separation in the research, each topic requires separate consideration. Let's begin with questions about genetic influences on IQ scores.

## Genes, IQ, and Changes in IQ

Recall from chapter 3 that monozygotic (MZ) twins are more similar genetically, and more similar in IQ, than are dizygotic (DZ) twins. One implication of these findings is that children's genes affect their IQ scores. The data from twin studies suggest that about half the variation in children's IQs is due to variations in their genes (Neisser et al., 1996; Plomin et al., 1996).

### Estimating Genetic Influence

Other types of behavior-genetic designs lead to different estimates of genetic influence on IQ. In several studies, researchers collected data on the IQ scores of adopted children, their biological parents, and their adoptive parents (Horn, 1983; Scarr & Weinberg, 1976, 1978, 1983). The correlations between adopted children's IQs and the IQ scores of their biological parents allow researchers to estimate the genetic influence on IQ. Because the biological parents passed their genes to their children but did not control the environments in which the children were reared, any similarity between the parents and their children can reasonably be attributed to heredity.

Conversely, the correlations between adopted children's IQs and the IQ scores of their adoptive parents allow researchers to estimate the environmental influence on IQ. The adoptive parents do not affect their adopted children's genotypes, of course, but they do control their home environments. Moreover, you would expect parents with higher IQs to provide more enriched environments for their adopted children and so to enhance their intellectual development.

Figure 10.7 shows the correlations between mothers' and children's IQ scores from two longitudinal adoption studies (Loehlin, Horn, & Willerman, 1989; Scarr, Weinberg, & Waldman, 1993). In both studies, children first took an IQ test at a mean age around 7 years. In both studies the children were tested again about 10 years later. At both times, the correlations for birth mothers and their children were stronger than those for adoptive mothers and children. In other words, mothers and children who only shared genes were more similar in

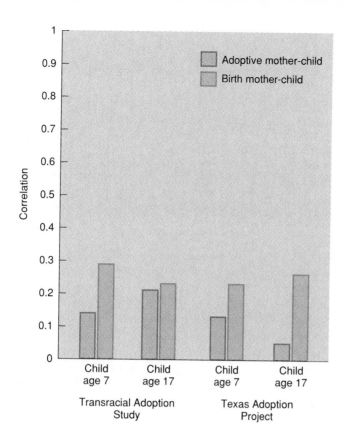

**FIGURE 10.7**

The IQ scores of adopted children are correlated with their biological or birth mothers' IQ scores. Adopted children's IQs are also correlated, although more weakly, with their adoptive mothers' IQs. The correlations suggest that children's IQs are influenced by their genes and by their home environments. (Data from Loehlin et al., 1989; Scarr, Weinberg, & Waldman, 1993.)

IQ than mothers and children who only shared a family environment. This difference suggests that children's heredity has more influence on their IQ scores than their family environment does. Still, both sets of parent-child correlations are greater than zero, which implies that both genotypes and environments affect IQ.

## Racial Differences in Intelligence: What's the Evidence?

Figure 10.7 includes correlations from a study by Sandra Scarr and Richard Weinberg (1976) called the Transracial Adoption Study. This study included White parents who had adopted children of other races. Most of the adopted children were Black. The results of the study have been extensively discussed by researchers concerned with racial differences in intelligence.

In *The Bell Curve* (Herrnstein & Murray, 1994), the controversial book mentioned at the beginning of the chapter, the Transracial Adoption Study was described as "the most comprehensive attempt yet to separate the effects of genes and of family environments on the cognitive development of American blacks and whites" (p. 309). Genetic differences between racial groups was only one topic of *The Bell Curve*, as *Practical Applications of Research:* "The Science and Politics of *The Bell Curve* Debate" explains, but this topic is largely responsible for the intensity of the debate surrounding the book. Partly for that reason, a careful examination of the results of the study is needed.

About 100 families participated in the study. Many of these families included both adopted Black children and White children who were the biological offspring of the White parents. Most of the Black children were placed in their adoptive homes during the first year of life. From adoption records, the researchers obtained information about the education of the Black children's biological mothers. When the Black children had a mean age of 7 years (the range was from 4 and 18 years), they, their adoptive parents, and their White siblings were given IQ tests.

Adoption records provided information about the level of education of the adopted children's biological mothers. This information was used to estimate their IQs. On the average,

# THE SCIENCE AND POLITICS OF
## *THE BELL CURVE* DEBATE

hroughout the twentieth century, IQ tests have been at the center of debates about ethnic groups, education, and public policies (Carroll, 1982; Gould, 1981). These debates were revived by the publication of *The Bell Curve*. The following statements illustrate the variety of issues examined in the book. The statements reflect the conclusions of Richard Herrnstein and Charles Murray, the authors of the book. Many critics of the book strongly reject some or all of these conclusions.

- People differ in their general cognitive ability, and IQ tests measure these differences with reasonable accuracy.
- In recent decades the salaries of adults in occupations that call for a high IQ (e.g., lawyers) have increased much more than those of adults in occupations that do not call for a high IQ (e.g., construction workers). This discrepancy is increasing the separation between a small cognitive elite and the rest of society.
- Women with low IQs have illegitimate children and become dependent on welfare more often than women with high IQs. Women with low IQs create poorer environments for rearing children than women with high IQs.
- The level of cognitive ability in the U.S. population is decreasing because women with low IQs have more children than those with high IQs, and because most immigrants have low IQs.
- Minority students who are admitted to college through affirmative-action programs often do poorly in college. These programs should be modified to give preference

to students from any ethnic group who are economically disadvantaged.

These statements show why the publication of *The Bell Curve* created such a furor. Herrnstein and Murray drew conclusions about some issues, such as the existence of *g*, that scientists have debated for decades. They drew conclusions about other issues, such as affirmative action, about which political leaders have argued for equally long.

Some reviewers praised the book, for example, calling it "superbly written and exceedingly well-documented (Bouchard, 1995, p. 418). Other reviewers attacked it in even stronger terms, for example, as a "frequently careless and incompetent assemblage of good science, bad science, and pseudo-science that is likely to do great damage" (Hauser, 1995, p. 149). Only months after the book was published, two books filled mostly with chapters by its critics appeared (Fraser, 1995; Jacoby & Glauberman, 1995).

Who's right, Herrnstein and Murray or their critics? This question does not have a simple answer because the book has so many facets. Deciding who's right is also difficult because few reviews of the book were written by impartial scholars. Many positive reviews came from researchers whose main interest is the study of IQ (e.g., Bouchard, 1995; "Mainstream science," 1994). Many negative reviews came from researchers who had earlier attacked studies of human intelligence as unscientific or racist (e.g., Dorfman, 1995; Gould, 1995; Kamin, 1995). Under the circumstances, whether the debate over *The Bell Curve* will generate some light—or only heat—is uncertain. Still, the debate shows that research on IQ can have significant implications for education and government policy.

the biological mothers of the Black children had completed fewer than 11 years of school. By contrast, the adoptive mothers had an average of 15 years of schooling. Not surprisingly, the IQ scores of the adoptive mothers were high, averaging about 120. These mothers could be expected to provide a highly stimulating, educationally enriched environment for both their adopted and biological children.

The Black adopted children had a mean IQ of 106. The White biological children had a mean IQ of 116. The 10-point difference cannot be viewed as a measure of genetic differences between Blacks and Whites because the environments of the two groups of children were not identical. Remember that the Black and White children were not reared in the same home from birth. About one-third of the Black adopted children were not placed in their adoptive home until after their first birthday. The Black children who were adopted earlier had a mean IQ of 110, which was 12 points above the mean IQ of those adopted later. This difference suggests that earlier and longer exposure to an enriched home environment leads to greater improvements in adopted children's IQs.

On the follow-up, about 10 years later, the mean IQ of the Black children adopted early in life was about 99. That of their White siblings was about 109. Both groups' scores were lower than on the original tests, probably because the IQ tests that they took the second time were scored against more recent (and more stringent) age norms than on the original tests.

Black children who are adopted by White, middle-class parents have IQ scores about the same as those of the parents' biological children, especially if the Black children are adopted shortly after their birth.

The decline in IQ was not significantly greater for the Black adopted children than for their White siblings (Weinberg, Scarr, & Waldman, 1992).

Again, the difference between Whites and Blacks cannot be attributed entirely to genetic differences because their early experiences were different. For example, the prenatal environment of the early-adopted Black children may not have been very good. Their biological mothers probably had poorer nutrition during pregnancy, and poorer prenatal care, than the mothers of their White brothers or sisters. Moreover, you read in chapter 4 about many kinds of prenatal experiences (e.g., maternal alcohol use) that can powerfully affect intellectual development after birth. These experiences could certainly have differed for the adopted Black children and their White siblings.

The mean difference between the adopted and biological children might also have a genetic basis. Recall that the biological parents of the White children in these families were more highly educated than the biological parents of the Black adopted children. This difference in educational level is probably related to differences in the genotypes that each group of biological parents passed to their children. The correlations in adoption studies between the IQ scores of biological parents and their adopted children, shown in figure 10.7, suggest that parents' genotypes affect children's IQs. Still, differences in parents' genotypes need not be linked to the parents' *race*.

Regardless of their race, parents who place their children for adoption often have lower IQs than parents who bring up their own children. So even when their children are raised in a good adoptive home, these children may not attain the same IQ as the biological children of their adoptive parents. White adopted children, for example, have lower IQ scores than White children reared by their own parents (see Scarr & Weinberg, 1978, 1983). In short, the results of the Transracial Adoption Study may provide more information about IQ differences between adopted and nonadopted children than about IQ differences between Blacks and Whites.

Other kinds of evidence suggest that differences in the IQ scores of Blacks and Whites should not be explained by racial differences in genetic potential (Crane, 1994; Neisser et al., 1996; Nisbett, 1995; Scarr et al., 1977). Many Black children in the United States have some White ancestors. Their degree of White ancestry can be estimated from their self-reports or from analyses of their blood types. Contrary to hypotheses of racial differences in genetic potential, Black children with several White ancestors do not have higher IQ scores than those with exclusively Black ancestors.

Also encouraging is evidence on the historical changes in children's IQ scores. In past decades the mean IQ score for Black adults was about 15 points lower than the mean IQ score for White adults (Herrnstein & Murray, 1994). The Black-White gap was smaller, however, in recent standardization samples for several IQ tests given to children (Vincent, 1991). On one test the mean difference between Blacks and Whites was only about 7 points. When differences in the SES of the children's families were statistically controlled, the Black-White difference was as little as 1 point on some tests at some ages.

Other evidence for a narrowing gap between Blacks and Whites has come from standardized achievement tests. These tests are viewed by many researchers as indirect measures of intellectual ability. During the 1970s and 1980s, the Black-White differences in achievement-test scores decreased (Hauser, 1995; Jones, 1984). The reasons for the improving achievement of Black students are not clear, but changes in education seem partly responsible. For example, more Black students are enrolling in advanced math classes in high school.

Will the gap between Blacks' and Whites' IQ and achievement-test scores continue to shrink? The question is difficult to answer. On tests of achievement in some academic subjects at some ages, the differences between Blacks' and Whites' scores remained stable during the early 1990s or even increased slightly (U.S. Department of Education, 1994, 1995).

Nevertheless, the historical changes in the Black-White differences in IQ and achievement imply that these differences are not caused by genetic differences between the two racial groups. Instead, differences in Black and White children's schools and in other aspects of their environments may better explain why their IQ and achievement-test scores differ. If equal opportunity in education and in other arenas of life became a reality for Blacks and Whites in the United States, equality in their IQs and achievement could also be expected.

## Genetic Influence on Changes in IQ

You learned in the previous section that children's IQ scores can change dramatically between birth and adulthood. Are these changes in IQ influenced by children's genotypes?

The answer is definitely yes. Figure 10.8 should look familiar to you because you saw the bottom half earlier (as figure 10.6). That half shows the changes in IQ scores between 3 months and 6 years of age for two pairs of DZ twins. This time, the panel for each pair of twins includes the value of the twins' DSI, or Developmental Synchronies Index. This index reflects the degree of match between the age changes for the two children in a pair of twins. If the twins' graphs matched perfectly, their DSI would equal 1.0.

The new data in the figure, shown in the top half, are the IQ scores from 3 months to 6 years for two pairs of MZ twins. Notice that the peaks and valleys in the graphs for these pairs correspond more closely than they do for the DZ twins. The DSI for each pair of MZ twins is around .90, considerably higher than the values for the pairs of DZ twins.

The patterns shown in the figure are typical of those in large samples of MZ and DZ twins (Wilson, 1983). MZ twins not only are more similar than DZ twins in their adult IQ scores, they also are more similar in their pattern of age changes in IQ. Ronald Wilson (1983) concluded that "there is a strong developmental thrust in the growth of intelligence that continues through adolescence and is guided by an intrinsic template or ground plan. The template is rooted in genetic processes that act throughout childhood and adolescence" (p. 311).

The influence of children's genotypes on the changes in their IQs has also been shown in adoption studies. Figure 10.7 showed some results from the Texas Adoption Project (Loehlin et al., 1989). Other data from that study were used to estimate how much children's genotypes and their family environments affected the changes in their IQs over 10 years.

The variations in children's IQ scores on their first test, around age 7, were explained partly by differences in their genotypes and partly by differences in their family environments. By contrast, only the differences in children's genotypes seemed to explain the changes in their IQ scores between 7 and 17 years of age. Sharing a family environment with more intelligent or less intelligent parents seemed to have little effect on the changes in children's IQs.

These results imply that the full impact of children's genotypes on their IQ scores is not evident at birth, during infancy, or even during early childhood. Changes occur in IQ scores

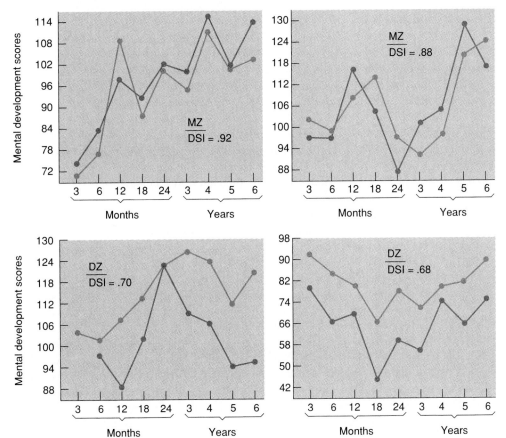

FIGURE 10.8
The correspondence in age trends for the IQ scores of two pairs of MZ twins and two pairs of DZ twins. In these pairs, the developmental synchronies index (or DSI) is higher for the MZ twins than for the DZ twins. In a larger sample of twins, the DSI was generally higher for MZ than for DZ twins. This suggests that children's genotypes influence the changes in their IQ during childhood. (Adapted from Wilson, 1983.)

during middle childhood and adolescence that reflect the gradual expression of children's genotypes. As Wilson (1983) said, the growth of intelligence is rooted in genetic processes that act throughout childhood and adolescence, and perhaps even later in life.

The conclusion that family environments do not affect the changes in children's IQ scores cannot be accepted so confidently, for two reasons. First, the family environment was not measured directly in the Texas Adoption Project. Instead, the researchers used the adoptive parents' intelligence, education, and income as indicators of the environment they were likely to provide for their children. These indicators do not adequately assess the features of children's environments that influence their intellectual growth (Wachs, 1983). To understand how children are affected by their environments, researchers need to assess the features of these environments directly.

Second, in the Texas study the correlation between the IQ scores of adoptive mothers and their adopted children decreased between 7 and 17 years of age (see figure 10.7). This decrease may explain why the data analyses showed no apparent effect of the family environment on IQ changes during that period. However, a comparable decrease has not been found in all adoption studies. For example, figure 10.7 shows a slight increase with age in the adoptive mother-child correlation in the Transracial Adoption Study. Again, you see that research findings need to be replicated before firm conclusions are drawn.

In summary, behavior-genetics research leaves no doubt that children's genotypes influence the changes in their IQs as they grow. The same research has yielded inconsistent answers to the question of whether children's environments influence the changes in the IQs. Yet in most behavior-genetics studies, the important features of children's environments have not been measured directly. You will see, next, that researchers who have directly measured these features have identified powerful effects of children's environments on their IQ scores.

## Family and School Environments, IQ, and Changes in IQ

In 1969 Arthur Jensen asked the provocative question, "How much can we boost IQ?" In other words, how much can we increase children's IQ scores if we provide them with the most intellectually stimulating environments? Jensen's answer was "not much." He felt that children's genotypes largely determined their intelligence. The effects of children's environments, in Jensen's view, were small.

In the 1990s this question remains controversial (e.g., Herrnstein & Murray, 1994; Hauser, 1995; Nisbett, 1995), but several kinds of research suggest that Jensen was wrong. Rearing children in more stimulating environments can greatly affect their IQ scores at maturity. This optimistic conclusion is suggested by research on the two environments most important for children's intellectual development, the family and the school.

### IQ Scores and the Home Environment

Two methods have been used to examine family influences on the development of IQ. One method is to see how children's IQ scores vary with their family structure and their position in the family. Robert Zajonc (1976, 1983, 1993) tried to summarize the effects of these variations in the **confluence model.** He proposed that a child's IQ depends on the combined influence, or confluence, of every other family member's contributions to the child's intellectual development.

The confluence model includes specific predictions about the effects on children's IQs of their birth order, the spacing between them and their siblings, and the size of their families. Many of these predictions were confirmed in one early study (Zajonc & Markus, 1975). In later and better-controlled studies, however, few of the predictions were confirmed (e.g., Galbraith, 1982; Retherford & Sewell, 1991; Rodgers, 1984). Even the model's successful predictions explained little of the variability in children's IQ scores (Bouchard & Segal, 1985).

These findings indicate that children's birth order, family size, and spacing from siblings do not have strong or consistent effects on their IQs (Rodgers & Rowe, 1994). More generally, the findings suggest that measures of family structure and position do not adequately capture the differences in family environments that affect children's IQs. To find out how family environments affect children, researchers must observe exactly what happens in families.

**confluence model**
*A model devised by Zajonc that is intended to explain the effects on a child's IQ of the child's family structure and position in a family.*

The confluence model predicts a low level of intellectual achievement for later-born children in large families. But take a look at the young boy sitting on his father's lap in this photograph. You can see that he is the last-born in a large family. He may also look familiar because he is Senator Edward Kennedy, photographed with his family in 1938. The Kennedy family illustrates that family size and birth order do not have strong and consistent effects on intellectual achievement. Other aspects of the family environment are more critical.

| TABLE 10.4 | *Subscales of the Home Observation for the Measurement of the Environment (HOME)* |
|---|---|
| 1. Emotion and Verbal RESPONSIVITY of Mother | Example: Mother caresses or kisses child at least once during visit. |
| 2. ACCEPTANCE of child | Example: Mother does not interfere with child's actions or restrict child's movements more than three times during visit. |
| 3. ORGANIZATION of Physical and Temporal Environment | Example: Child's play environment appears safe and free of hazards. |
| 4. Provision of Appropriate PLAY MATERIALS | Example: Mother provides toys or interesting activities for child during interview. |
| 5. Maternal INVOLVEMENT with Child | Example: Mother tends to keep child within visual range and to look at the child often. |
| 6. Opportunities for VARIETY in Daily Stimulation | Example: Child eats at least one meal per day with mother and father. |

From R. Elardo and R. Bradley, "The home observation for measurement of environment: A review of research" in *Developmental Review*, 1:113–145. Copyright 1981 by Academic Press, Orlando, FL. Reprinted by permission of the publisher.

Direct observation of family environments is the second method that researchers have used to assess family influences on children's IQs. One assessment procedure is aptly named the HOME, which stands for Home Observation for Measurement of the Environment (Caldwell & Bradley, 1984; Elardo & Bradley, 1981). An adult visits the child's home for roughly one hour. During that time, the adult observes and records the number of toys or other learning materials available to the child. The adult also observes how the mother or another regular caregiver interacts with the child. To obtain more information, the adult interviews the mother. Then the adult completes the HOME inventory. The questions on the inventory deal with several aspects of the family environment, from the mother's responsivity to the variety in the child's daily stimulation (table 10.4).

Many researchers have used the HOME inventory in large-scale longitudinal studies. The data from six studies in the United States and Canada were combined and analyzed (Bradley et al., 1989). The combined sample included nearly 1,000 children. Researchers visited the children when they were 12 months of age. At 12 and 24 months of age, the children were tested on the Bayley Mental Development Scale. They were tested on the Stanford-Binet (third edition) at 36 months.

Children with higher scores on the HOME inventory had higher IQ scores at 12, 24, and 36 months of age. Two subscales on the HOME had especially strong relations to the measures of children's IQ. These subscales were for provision of appropriate play materials and maternal involvement (see table 10.4). Apparently, children's intellectual development is more rapid when their environment is rich in stimulating objects (toys) and in social stimulation. In other words, children profit intellectually from chances to explore interesting objects and to interact with adults.

The quality of children's early environments is related not only to their later IQ scores but also to the changes in their IQs over time. Figure 10.9 shows the mean IQ scores at 12, 24, and 36 months for children with low HOME scores at 12 months (i.e., HOME scores one or more standard deviations below the mean). Stated more generally, the figure shows how the IQs of children in unstimulating environments change between 1 and 3 years of age. The figure also shows the comparable scores for children with high HOME scores and average HOME scores at 12 months of age.

The IQ scores of children with low HOME scores, who lived in unstimulating environments, dropped sharply between 12 and 36 months of age. By 36 months their mean IQ was only 88. Children with high HOME scores increased slightly in IQ. By 36 months they had a mean IQ of 116. Children with average HOME scores declined in IQ after 12 months and by 36 months had a mean IQ of 103.

Another study showed that decreases in children's IQ between 2 and 4 years of age were associated with low HOME scores (Pianta & Egeland, 1994). Between 6 and 9 years of age, children's scores on the Peabody Picture Vocabulary Test (PPVT) are higher when their HOME scores are higher (Luster & McAdoo, 1994). Taken together, these studies

FIGURE 10.9

The changes in children's IQ during the first three years of life can be affected by the quality of their home environments. The IQ scores of children in better environments, ones with higher scores on the HOME inventory, were less likely to decrease between 12 and 36 months of age.

Adapted from R. H. Bradley et al., "Home environment and cognitive development in the first 3 years of life: A collaborative study involving six sites and three ethnic groups in North America," in *Developmental Psychology*, 25:217–235. Copyright © 1989 by The American Psychological Association. Adapted with permission.

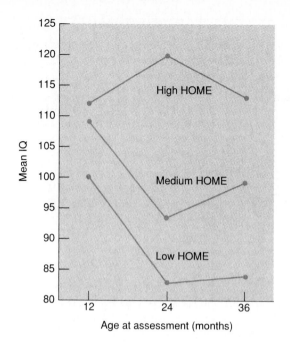

strongly suggest that children's environments influence their intellectual development during infancy and childhood.

Still, a skeptic could dispute this conclusion. The skeptic could argue that parents with high intelligence pass genes to their children that cause them to be high in intelligence. These same parents create intellectually stimulating environments for their children. The correlations between children's environments and their IQ scores might, therefore, reflect the passive genotype-environment correlation discussed in chapter 3 (Scarr & McCartney, 1983). More specifically, scores on the HOME inventory might be correlated with children's IQ scores because HOME scores and IQ scores both depend on parents' genotypes.

This argument might be valid for some environment-IQ correlations, but it does not fully explain the correlations between HOME scores and children's IQs. First, the correlation between HOME scores and children's scores on the PPVT remains significant when their mothers' IQs are taken into account (Luster & McAdoo, 1994).

Second, if the correlations were due entirely to the effects of parents' genotypes, then they should be near zero in families with adopted children. If the correlations were due partly to genetic influence, then they should be smaller in families with adopted children (where parents and children share environments but not genes) than in families with only biologically related children (where parents and children share both genes and environments). However, the correlations of children's IQs with the involvement and variety-of-experience subscales of the HOME are statistically significant and nearly equal for families with and without adopted children (Plomin, Loehlin, & DeFries, 1985).

Finally, tracing differences in HOME scores to genetic differences in parents' scores does not prove that the home environment is unimportant. A plausible alternative is that the HOME environment mediates the relation between mothers' IQ scores and their children's IQ scores. In other words, more intelligent mothers have children with higher IQs partly because those mothers provide their children with more stimulating environments. If the mothers failed to do so, their children's intellectual development would suffer.

In summary, many kinds of data suggest that children's home environments affect the development of their IQ. The data illustrated in figure 10.9 suggest that environmental effects can be large. Still, before trying to answer Jensen's question, "How much can we boost IQ?" you should consider the effects of another environment in which children spend their time, the school.

## IQ and Schooling

Jensen's (1969) original question focused on the effects of the school rather than the home environment. In addition, he was less concerned with traditional schools than with special educational interventions for preschool children. During the 1960s, many researchers started experimental programs that provided educational enrichment to disadvantaged children. The U.S. government began its own program, called Head Start, to offer educational experiences to preschoolers. Each program had unique features, but one goal of every program was to foster the intellectual development of the preschool children who participated.

Did the programs meet that goal? Jensen (1969) said that they did not, because early evaluations suggested that the programs did not produce a large and sustained increase in children's IQ scores. Many researchers disputed Jensen's conclusion. One large-scale study (Lazar & Darlington, 1982) combined the data from 11 preschool programs. These data showed that the experimental programs affected preschoolers' IQ scores. A year or two after the programs ended, the preschool children who had participated in them had higher IQ scores than did comparable children who had not participated.

Unfortunately, the differences between the two groups of children decreased as they grew older. The children's IQs were assessed for the last time when they were between 10 and 17 years of age. At that time, few significant differences were found between the IQ scores of children who did and did not participate in the programs. Careful studies of Head Start programs have also shown that their positive effects on children's intellectual abilities decrease over time (Lee et al., 1990).

Other effects of the experimental interventions were more lasting (Lazar & Darlington, 1982). Almost 30 percent of the students in the comparison groups were placed in special-education classes sometime during their school years. Less than 15 percent of the program participants were placed in special education. In addition, the participants were less often retained (kept back a grade) during their school years.

Why, then, didn't the participants in these programs show a lasting improvement in their IQ scores? The best way to answer this question is to look at the effects of traditional elementary and secondary schools.

Experiments on the effects of schooling are difficult to do. Children cannot be assigned randomly to two groups, one group that attends school and one group that does not. It is possible to identify groups of students who differ in years of schooling, but they usually differ in

Well-run and stimulating preschool programs like this one can produce improvements in children's IQ scores. The improvements may not be maintained, however, if children later go to elementary schools that provide less adequate instruction.

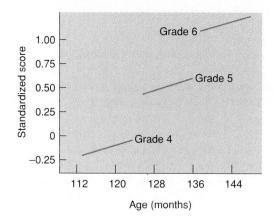

## FIGURE 10.10

How much does children's performance on arithmetic story problems improve as they grow older? How much does an additional year of schooling improve their performance? This graph suggests that a year of schooling has a larger effect than does simply growing older. The same is true for many other tests of intellectual and academic ability. (Source: Cahan & Cohen, 1989.)

age as well. For example, students in the fifth grade are usually a year older than students in the fourth grade.

Still, with a little ingenuity the effects of age and schooling can be disentangled. Consider a school district in which children must be 5 years old by December 1 to enroll in kindergarten. Now think of two children, one born on November 30 and one born on December 2. The first child enrolls in kindergarten at age 5; the second child can't enroll until the following year. If these two children pass each grade, the first one will always have one more year of school than the second. And if schooling affects children's IQ scores, the first child should have a higher IQ than the second.

Now compare the first child, born on November 30, with another child born on the previous December 2. The two children will be in the same grade, but the second will be nearly a year older than the first. If age itself influences IQ scores, the second child should have a higher IQ than the first.

By extending the same logic, researchers can make comparisons among all children differing in age and in grade. Then they can estimate the effect of an additional year in school, or an additional year of age, on children's IQs. In one study (Cahan & Cohen, 1989), these effects were estimated with data from thousands of Israeli students. Figure 10.10 shows the results for a test of arithmetic story problems from a group-administered IQ test.

The lines for each grade slope upward, indicating that children in the same grade get higher scores as their age increases. In addition, there are large gaps between the lines for different grades. The gaps show that an added year of schooling improves children's performance considerably. On this arithmetic test, an added year of schooling improved children's scores three times as much as an added year of age. On nearly all the tests that children took, schooling had a greater effect than age. Even on a culture-reduced test like the Raven's Progressive Matrices, a year of school improved scores twice as much as a year of age.

Many other kinds of evidence show the effects of schooling on children's IQ scores (Ceci, 1991). For example, children's IQ scores decrease during the summer when they are not attending school. Children's IQ scores decrease when they are prevented from attending school by war or school closings. Adolescents' IQs decrease after they drop out of school. Moreover, these effects can be large, ranging from .25 to 6 IQ points per year of schooling.

The research on elementary schools helps to explain why the experimental preschool programs did not permanently affect children's IQs. The effects probably diminished over time because the children who participated in the programs went to the same schools and received the same instruction as the children who did not. This instruction led to improvements

in the reasoning of both groups of students. The similarity in their instruction also led, gradually, to similarity in their IQ scores (Ramey, 1982).

This research implies that lasting improvements in disadvantaged children's IQ scores cannot be expected unless educational enrichment continues into the school years (Lee et al., 1990). Enrichment should start early, with a high-quality program for preschool children that provides comprehensive services to ensure children's health and promote their development (Zigler & Muenchow, 1992). Enrichment should continue during elementary school, with continued comprehensive services, an emphasis on parental involvement, and innovative programming that meets the needs of the children who participate (Zigler & Styfco, 1993).

## How Much Can IQ Be Raised?

Taken together, the results of the many experimental interventions provide an answer to Jensen's (1969) question. That is, they make it possible to estimate how much improving children's environments can raise their IQ scores. Chapter 3 introduced the concept of the reaction range for various characteristics. Questions about how much improvements in children's environments can raise their IQ scores are questions about the size of the reaction range for IQ.

You read in chapter 2 about the Abecedarian Project, an intensive intervention in infancy and the preschool years (Campbell & Ramey, 1994; Ramey, 1994). Children who participated in that intervention had IQ scores at age 12 that were 5 points higher than those of children randomly assigned to the control group. Therefore, the reaction range for IQ must be at least 5 points.

Another early intervention program included more than 700 children who were randomly assigned to the intervention or to a control group before they were 1 year old (Liaw & Brooks-Gunn, 1994). The children assigned to the intervention attended childcare centers, beginning at age 1, with a curriculum designed to promote their development. At age 3, these children had mean IQ scores 9 points higher than those in the control group.

Earlier in this chapter, you read about the Transracial Adoption Study. When the mean age of the children adopted into middle-class families was 7 years, their IQ scores were about 20 points higher than would have been expected if they had been reared by their biological mothers. Therefore, the reaction range for IQ may exceed 20 points (Weinberg, 1989).

Historical research can also furnish estimates of the reaction range for IQ. In some countries, generations of young adults have taken the same IQ test, for example, when registering for military service. These data can reveal how IQ scores in a population have changed over time. Such changes can also be measured when IQ tests are revised, and both the old and new tests are given to the same children.

These kinds of historical data have yielded a surprisingly consistent picture (Flynn, 1987, 1994; Lynn & Pagliari, 1994). IQ scores in many countries have increased steadily during the twentieth century. Moreover, the increases have been large, equal in some countries to more than 25 IQ points in 25 years. Changes of this magnitude can hardly be attributed to improvements in genetic potential; they must be attributed to some change in human environments. The cause of the changes has not yet been identified, but these findings further raise the estimate of the reaction range for IQ.

Even these estimates of IQ's reaction range may be too low. In most studies of family and school influences on IQ, researchers examine the effects of the **shared environment.** As mentioned in chapter 3, these are effects experienced by all children in the same family, all preschoolers in the same experimental program, or all students in the same grade.

Many facets of the environment that could affect children's IQs are not shared by all children in the same setting. Chapter 3 also introduced the concept of *nonshared environmental influences.* Table 10.5 lists several sources of influence that may not be shared by children in the same family or educational setting. These influences may be more difficult to measure than influences of the shared environment. Still, behavior-genetics studies suggest that the nonshared environment affects children's IQs as much or more than does the environment shared by children in the same family or school (Luo, Petrill, & Thompson, 1994; Rodgers, Rowe, & May, 1994; Rowe & Plomin, 1981). Careful studies of nonshared influences could raise the estimate of the reaction range for IQ still further.

**shared environment**
*The environment experienced by all children in the same family, the same preschool, or the same classroom in a school.*

| TABLE 10.5 | *Specific Sources of Nonshared Environmental Influences* |
| --- | --- |
| **SOURCES** | |
| *Accidental Factors* | Physical illness |
| | Prenatal and postnatal trauma |
| *Sibling Interaction* | Differential treatment |
| *Family Structure* | Birth order |
| | Sibling spacing |
| *Parental Treatment* | Differential treatment of children |
| | Interactions of parent and child characteristics |
| *Extrafamilial Networks* | Peer group members not shared by siblings |
| | Teachers |
| | Television |

From D. C. Rowe and R. Plomin, "The importance of nonshared (E1) environmental influences in behavioral development" in *Developmental Psychology*, 17:517:531. Copyright © 1981 by The American Psychological Association. Adapted with permission.

# IS INTELLIGENCE MORE THAN IQ?

Up to this point, you've read mostly about research on children's IQ scores. However, one controversy that has surfaced repeatedly during the twentieth century is whether important facets of intelligence are not captured by IQ tests. Recall that laypeople assume intelligence involves more than the kinds of reasoning assessed by IQ tests. Laypeople view intelligence not as a single ability but as multiple, partly independent abilities. The view that intelligence involves several abilities has also been proposed by some researchers (e.g., Horn, 1985; Horn & Hofer, 1992), but this view remains highly controversial (Brody, 1992; Lohman, 1989).

The evidence that IQ scores have increased greatly during the twentieth century has also raised questions about whether IQ tests accurately measure people's intelligence (Flynn, 1987, 1994). The increases in IQ scores have not been accompanied by any other evidence that children or adults are becoming more intelligent. Indeed, some evidence suggests the contrary. Between 1960 and 1990, when IQ scores were increasing, students' scores on the SAT were decreasing (Flynn, 1987). If IQ is an accurate measure of intelligence, the opposing trends for IQ scores and SAT scores are difficult to explain.

Robert Sternberg (1985, 1988, 1994) rejects the idea that intelligence is a single, general ability that can be measured by traditional IQ tests. He argues that intelligence has three parts. Each part corresponds to a subtheory of intelligence. When the three subtheories are united, they form a **triarchic theory** of intelligence.

The *componential* subtheory specifies the information-processing components responsible for intelligent behavior. At the highest level, these components help intelligent children decide the problem to be solved and the best strategies to be used. For example, students who are writing a term paper must choose a topic that will best meet their course requirements within the time they have available. At lower levels, information-processing components do the mental work of encoding information, combining new and old information, and sifting relevant from irrelevant information. As students do research for a term paper, they must accomplish all these tasks. A person's skill in using these information-processing components is defined as their *analytical intelligence.*

The *experiential* subtheory focuses on the familiarity of a task for a child. According to Sternberg, children most clearly show their intelligence at two times. First, when children are given a totally novel task, their ability to cope with this novelty is a good sign of their intelligence. For example, children show their coping ability each school year when they move to a new grade with a new teacher. Sternberg defined this ability as part of *creative intelligence.*

**triarchic theory**
*Sternberg's theory of three parts of intelligence. Includes a componential subtheory, an experiential subtheory, and a contextual subtheory.*

Natives of the Pacific Islands learn to navigate on the ocean far from land. They do so not only during the day but also at night, using the stars. Howard Gardner defines this skill as an indication of their spatial intelligence.

Second, when children have highly familiar tasks to do, how automatically they can do these tasks without exerting much mental effort is another sign of their intelligence. For instance, halfway through a school year students should have devised a strategy for doing homework and studying that is effective and takes little thought.

The *contextual* subtheory considers differences in the behavior that is intelligent in different cultural contexts. Intelligent children usually vary their behavior so that it is appropriate to their current context. For example, they respond flexibly when they have several teachers who make different demands and use different criteria for evaluation. Intelligent children may also try to change the context in which they work so that it better fits their skills and preferences. Sternberg calls this kind of thinking *practical intelligence.*

Sternberg argues that traditional IQ tests assess children's information-processing components most directly. Even here, the tests are not ideal. For example, items on IQ tests often measure what children have already learned, not how well they can learn new information. In addition, IQ tests do not consider children's familiarity with the test problems, thus ignoring the experiential part of the triarchic theory. Finally, IQ tests ignore the contextual nature of intelligent behavior. To take context into account, Sternberg suggests that IQ tests be supplemented by evidence on children's ability to adapt to the problems they face daily.

Sternberg has devised tests for students and for business executives that assess the abilities linked to each subtheory (Miele, 1995). He has also devised programs for improving these abilities. His goal is not primarily to remedy people's weaknesses but to help them capitalize on their strengths. In other words, he does not feel people should aim to be equally good at everything but instead should concentrate on developing their special talents.

Howard Gardner (1983; 1993) has taken the idea of multiple intelligences even further than Sternberg. Gardner defines an *intelligence* as the capacity to solve problems or create things that are valued in a culture. Thus, people can be intelligent in any domain or area that is culturally valued. However, Gardner limits the definition of intelligence to skills universal to the human species. He also limits the definition to skills rooted in biology that can be encoded in a symbol system. For example, the skills involved in counting and calculation are encoded in mathematics.

Gardner has argued that there are at least seven types of intelligence. One is logical-mathematical, as illustrated by the scientist who devises and tests hypotheses. A second is linguistic, as illustrated by writers like Shakespeare. A third is musical, illustrated by a concert pianist. A fourth is bodily-kinesthetic, which means related to the use of muscles and limbs, as shown by an athlete or a dancer. Fifth is spatial, illustrated by a native of the Pacific Islands who can navigate on the ocean using the stars. Sixth is interpersonal, illustrated by the ability to notice people's moods, intentions, or temperaments. This intelligence was unusually developed in Helen Keller's teacher, Anne Sullivan. Seventh is intrapersonal, having full

awareness of one's emotions and being able to discriminate among emotions. This intelligence is most obvious in introspective writers such as Virginia Woolf.

According to Gardner (1983, 1993), traditional IQ tests mostly assess logical-mathematical and linguistic intelligence. They provide little information about the other intelligences. Consequently, the tests are good at predicting success on school-related tasks and less good at predicting success outside school. Gardner believes that adults should assess all of children's intelligences when planning their education. He believes levels of each intelligence should be assessed not by standardized tests but by interviewing children and observing their work in their everyday environment.

Gardner links his theory of multiple intelligences to proposals for school reform. He argues that schools should help to develop all the intelligences of children. He believes education should be individualized, with teachers trying to understand and promote each child's cognitive profile. Rather than putting all children through a standard curriculum, each child should be offered activities and experiences that will help him or her reach appropriate educational and occupational goals. These activities and experiences would often be integrated into multidisciplinary projects completed by students.

Gardner (1993) has described a few schools in the United States that have adopted the school reforms he advocates. Some schools are for preschool and elementary-school children; others are for middle- and senior-high-school students. Some schools are based on ideas both from Gardner's theory and from Sternberg's triarchic theory of intelligence. Evaluating the effectiveness of these schools will not be easy, however. Because advocates of multiple-intelligences theory discount the validity of standardized tests, they do not want to measure the success of their school reforms using such tests.

In summary, both Sternberg's triarchic theory and Gardner's theory of multiple intelligences are based on the assumption that intelligence is far more than IQ. Both theories are intended to offer a more complete description of intellectual abilities. Both theories include the assumption that IQ is only one of many predictors of significant achievements.

# ACADEMIC ACHIEVEMENT AND ACHIEVEMENT MOTIVATION

Even in the domain for which IQ tests were created, that of academic achievement, the significance of IQ can be exaggerated. As noted earlier, the correlation between children's IQ scores and their achievement in school is only about .50 (Ceci, 1991; Neisser et al., 1996). Although this correlation is substantial, it leaves most of the variations in achievement unexplained. These variations must depend partly on children's motivation, or their drive to succeed in school.

## Elements of Achievement Motivation

Imagine that a fifth-grade girl is starting a new unit on psychology in her social-studies textbook. As she begins reading the unit, she runs across sentences that are very difficult to understand. A section on imitation, for example, includes this question: "How can one best describe the nature of the people who will most of all be that way which will make the imitating of others happen most often?" (Got that?) The other sentences in the section are equally confusing.

How will the girl react to such confusing sentences? Will she conclude that the new unit is too difficult for her? Will she decide, then, not to even try to understand the rest of it? Will she instead take the unit as a challenge, and try harder to master it? In other words, will she respond as if she were helpless, or will she respond in a mastery-oriented fashion?

### Helpless and Mastery Orientations

The questions about how the girl will respond to the new unit are related to important differences in children's achievement motivation. These differences were illustrated in a study of fifth graders who faced a situation like the one described (Licht & Dweck, 1984).

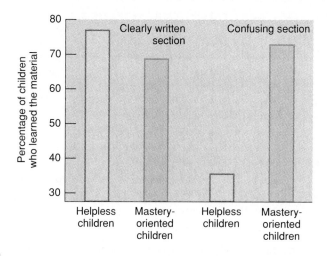

## FIGURE 10.11

When the initial material that students had to read was clearly written or not confusing, helpless and mastery-oriented students learned the rest of the material equally well. But when the initial material was confusing, helpless students seemed to give up, and few ever learned the rest of the material, even though the rest was clearly written. Most mastery-oriented students learned the rest of the material even when the initial material was confusing. (Source: Licht & Dweck, 1984.)

The students first read a brief booklet on psychology and then answered questions about what they had read. Half the students read a section on imitation that was highly confusing. This section included the sentence quoted earlier and other complex sentences. The rest of the students read a section on imitation that was clearly written. Then all students read additional sections of the booklet that were clearly written. The central question in the study was how students who first encountered either a confusing or a clearly written section would react to the later sections.

Several weeks earlier, the students had completed a brief questionnaire that assessed their **causal attributions** for academic failures. That is, students were asked about occasions on which they did poorly at school. They could attribute this poor performance either to a lack of effort or to external causes not under their control (e.g., poor instruction). Students who attributed most academic failures to a lack of effort were viewed as **mastery-oriented** because their responses implied that they could succeed if they tried harder. Students who attributed most failures to external causes were viewed as **helpless** because they seemed to believe that they could do nothing to improve their performance (see Weiner, 1985).

How did the helpless and mastery-oriented students react after they read a confusing section of a textbook? The confusing section did not disrupt the learning of the mastery-oriented students. They learned as much from the later sections of the book when they first read the confusing section as when they first read the clearly written section (see figure 10.11). Students with the helpless attributional style also learned the material well when they did not encounter a confusing section. However, when the section on imitation was confusing, few helpless students learned the material in the later sections. Apparently, they felt they could not understand the unit, so they didn't even try.

Symptoms of helplessness can be seen in some children even in kindergarten (Heyman, Dweck, & Cain, 1992). When pictures that kindergartners have painted are criticized by an adult, some but not all of them evaluate their own work more negatively. The children who give lower evaluations of their work are also less willing to paint another picture, are more likely to report they feel sad, and are more likely to rate themselves as unintelligent. These kinds of responses reflect low self-esteem and suggest that the children will avoid challenging tasks in the future.

**causal attributions**
*People's explanations for various outcomes of their actions or other people's actions.*

**mastery-oriented**
*A characteristic of students who attribute their academic failures to a lack of effort and so believe they could succeed if they tried harder.*

**helpless**
*A characteristic of students who attribute their academic failures to causes not under their control and so believe they cannot improve their performance.*

| TABLE 10.6 | *Three Types of Academic Achievement Goals* |
|---|---|
| TYPE OF GOAL | STATEMENTS TYPICAL OF STUDENTS WHO HAVE THAT GOAL |
| Task mastery | I want to learn as much as possible. |
| | I want to find out something new. |
| Ego-social | I want other people to think I am smart. |
| | Doing better than other students is important to me. |
| Work-avoidant | I want to do as little work as possible. |
| | I want to do things as easily as possible, so I don't have to work. |

Source: From information in Meece et al., 1988; Meece & Holt, 1993.

During the elementary-school years, a tendency toward helplessness when faced with difficult tasks can lower academic achievement. Some children are underachievers, showing academic performance lower than would be expected given their IQ. These students differ from their classmates in their causal attributions for success at school. Underachievers less often attribute their successes to effort and more often attribute them to luck, ability, help from others, or an easy test (Carr, Borkowski, & Maxwell, 1991). In short, helpless and mastery-oriented students differ in their causal attributions for academic failures and successes.

## Achievement Goals

The distinction between a helpless and a mastery orientation is related not only to causal attributions but also to children's goals in achievement situations. That is, achievement orientations are related to another element of achievement motivation, the goal that children set for themselves when faced with a task.

Students prone to helplessness when faced with a difficult task often set a *performance goal*, the goal of showing their competence (Dweck & Elliott, 1983; Dweck & Leggett, 1988). They want to be sure that they will "look smart." They want to avoid making errors that would make them "look dumb."

By contrast, mastery-oriented students often approach tasks with a *learning goal*, the goal of increasing their competence. They view problems as challenging and want to learn how to solve them. Therefore, they take failures as useful feedback, showing them which strategies for solving a problem are incorrect. For them, errors are an expected and valuable part of the learning process.

In schools, more than two achievement goals can be distinguished. Judith Meece and her colleagues asked fifth and sixth graders to report the goals they had during each of six science lessons (Meece, Blumenfeld, & Hoyle, 1988; Meece & Holt, 1993). As table 10.6 shows, one type of goal on which students reported was task mastery. This goal is achieved when students learn new things about science. Another type of goal, called *ego-social*, is comparable to the performance goal described previously. This goal is achieved when other people think a student is smart. A third goal is that of avoiding academic work. This goal is achieved when students go through a class while doing very little work.

Meece and her colleagues discovered one group of students who rated task mastery higher than the other two types of goals. Another group rated ego-social goals higher than other students but also gave high ratings to task mastery. A third group rated the goal of avoiding work more highly than did students in the first two groups.

The students in the third group, who placed the strongest emphasis on avoiding work, had the lowest grades in science. The students who emphasized task mastery above other goals had the highest science grades. The grades of students who wanted to achieve both task mastery and ego-social goals were intermediate, but not significantly higher than those of the work-avoidant students.

Apparently, children achieve most at school when their motive for learning is not weakened by the competing goal of looking smart. When that competing goal is present,

students may reduce their involvement. For example, students may put less effort into academic tasks on which they are not sure they can do better than their classmates. As a result, they actually learn less at school and so get poorer grades.

Even with preschool children, differences in achievement goals can be measured (Smiley & Dweck, 1994). When completing simple wooden puzzles, some preschoolers set the goal of performing well in front of an adult, so they choose easy puzzles to do. Other preschoolers set the goal of learning, so they are motivated to try again on a puzzle that at first they could not solve.

Preschoolers with the performance goal often show helplessness after failing to solve a puzzle: They express negative feelings and disengage from the task. These reactions are exaggerated among preschoolers who also lack confidence in their puzzle-solving ability. In other words, the combination of performance goals and a lack of confidence in one's ability creates the greatest risk of helplessness in the face of failure.

## Theories of Intelligence

Another element of children's achievement motivation is their set of ideas about intelligence. Different sets of ideas can be described as different theories of intelligence (Dweck & Elliott, 1983). Children's theories of intelligence are systematically related to the other elements of achievement motivation, especially to the contrast between the helpless and mastery orientations.

Helpless students often assume that intelligence is a global and stable characteristic. Because they view intelligence as global, they assume they are generally smarter than some people and dumber than other people. To judge how smart they are, they compare their performance with others' performance. In addition, because they view intelligence as a stable characteristic, they assume that they cannot raise their intelligence. They view intelligence as a thing, an entity, that they possess in a certain, unchangeable amount. According to this **entity theory of intelligence,** people can increase their knowledge but cannot increase their intelligence.

**entity theory of intelligence**
*The idea that a person's intelligence is a stable characteristic that cannot be improved by effort or training.*

Mastery-oriented students often define intelligence as the repertoire of abilities and skills that a person has at a specific time. These students assume that the size of the repertoire can be increased through effort and practice. Moreover, they judge their intelligence against personal norms, considering how much they can add to their abilities and skills as they master new problems. According to this **incremental theory of intelligence,** people can increase their basic intellectual ability, not merely their knowledge of specific skills or information (Dweck & Elliott, 1983).

**incremental theory of intelligence**
*The idea that a person's intelligence can be increased through training, effort, and practice.*

A relation between children's theories of intelligence and their tendencies toward helplessness is evident by fifth grade (Cain & Dweck, 1995). Fifth graders who view intelligence as a stable entity are likely to express negative feelings and to avoid challenging tasks after they have experienced an initial failure. Among younger children, views of intelligence are not consistently related to helplessness.

The best explanation for this developmental change is not yet clear. One explanation might focus on children's experiences at school, where achievement is regularly evaluated. Another explanation might focus on broader changes in cognitive functioning, or cognitive development itself. In a later section, you'll learn more about how schools and cognitive development affect children's ideas about achievement.

## Expectancies and Values

Another theory of achievement motivation refers to elements that only partly overlap with the elements discussed already. This theory emphasizes the importance of people's expectancies for success and the value that they attach to success. It is called the **expectancy-value theory** of achievement motivation (Atkinson & Feather, 1966; Berndt & Miller, 1990; Eccles, 1983; Wigfield, 1994; Wigfield & Eccles, 1992).

**expectancy-value theory**
*A theory of achievement motivation that emphasizes the importance of people's expectancies for success and the value that they attach to success.*

Students with a high expectancy for success are usually motivated to achieve. Students who believe they are likely to fail are often unmotivated, because they see no point in putting effort into a task on which they cannot succeed. The difference between high and low expectancies parallels that between mastery-oriented and helpless children.

Mastery-oriented students have a high expectancy for eventual success, so they are persistent in trying to learn new information even if they encounter difficulties. Helpless students are less persistent because they view any difficulty as proof that they can never learn the information. Their expectancies for success are either low or are easily disrupted by failure. Moreover, a low expectancy for success is closely associated with a lack of confidence in one's ability. This association explains why children who not only set performance goals but also have little confidence in their ability are highly likely to display helplessness (Smiley & Dweck, 1994).

Students' expectancies usually have a basis in reality. That is, students who have been academically successful typically have high expectancies for continued success (Berndt & Miller, 1990; Eccles, 1983). Exceptions occur, though. Some high-achieving students have low expectancies for success and do not believe they are as academically competent as their high grades suggest (Phillips, 1984). Their perception of incompetence may eventually lower their achievement, if they avoid advanced classes because they fear the classes will be too difficult (Meece, Wigfield, & Eccles, 1990).

Also crucial to students' achievement motivation is the value they place on achievement. Even students who believe they can succeed at a task show little motivation unless they regard success at the task as valuable. For example, you might think that you could raise your score on a video game by 50,000 points if you played the game for five hours straight. But if you don't value success on video games that much, you won't spend the five hours trying to improve your score.

Academically successful students typically value achievement more than do students who are less successful (Berndt & Miller, 1990). As mentioned earlier, academically successful students also have higher expectancies for success, so their expectancies and values are related. However, expectancies and values are sometimes unrelated or only weakly related to each other.

In the early 1980s adolescent girls in the United States received grades in math courses that were as high as those of adolescent boys. Consequently, boys and girls differed little in their expectancies for success in math. But girls valued math achievement less than boys did, so fewer girls than boys enrolled in advanced math classes (Eccles, Adler, & Meece, 1984).

By the early 1990s these sex differences disappeared. Adolescent boys and girls no longer differed significantly in the math courses that they took (Hoffer, Rasinski, & Moore, 1995). Still, both expectancies and values continue to affect math achievement. Among both boys and girls, having high expectancies for math success is a predictor of high grades in math. Among both boys and girls, placing a high value on math is a predictor of enrollment in advanced math classes (Meece et al., 1990). These findings confirm that both expectancies and values are important for understanding students' motivation and achievement.

## Influences on Motivation and Achievement

Why do some children have higher motivation to achieve than others? Why do some children reach a higher level of achievement in school than others? Of the many possible influences on students' motivation and achievement, the most powerful are likely to come from parents and from experiences at school.

### Effects of Parents

Parents affect their children's achievement motivation and actual achievement in many ways. The following statements describe how the parents of highly motivated and high-achieving students behave. The statements can also be taken as guidelines for improving the motivation and achievement of alienated or low-achieving students.

1. *Parents have high expectations for their children's performance and express these expectations clearly to them.* Parents' comments to their children can strongly affect the children's expectancies for achievement. When children do well in school, parents may say that they knew their children would be successful or that they assume the children will continue to do well. When children do poorly on a test or assignment, parents may express concern, say they are sure the children can do better, or comment directly on the children's abilities.

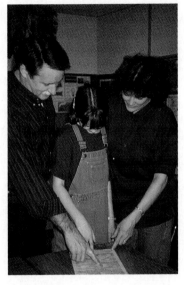

Parents can help their children achieve at school in many ways. For example, they can show that they are interested in and value their children's achievement. They can monitor their children's schoolwork or help them directly with homework. They can also play word games that give children practice in academic skills like vocabulary and spelling.

However parents' beliefs are communicated, they appear to influence their children's beliefs. For example, when parents view their adolescents as high in math ability, the adolescents rate their ability highly and have high expectancies for success in math. Conversely, when parents view math as difficult for their adolescents, the adolescents view math as difficult and have low expectancies for success (Parsons, Adler, & Kaczala, 1982).

Can parents set expectations that are too high? Can parents put too much pressure on their children? Third graders who suffer from the illusion of incompetence—who perceive their ability as low despite getting high grades—may suffer from excessive parental pressure (Phillips, 1987). These students report greater parental pressure than do equally able students with more positive perceptions of their competence.

The problem goes deeper, though. Parents of third graders with the illusion of incompetence have high standards for achievement despite having a low opinion of their children's ability. Apparently, they send a harmful double message to their children: "You have to do well in school, but you are not really very smart." This double message is likely to have negative effects that do not occur when parents' expectations match their perceptions of their children's ability.

2. *Parents show their children that they value the children's academic success.* In the 1980s, when girls valued math achievement less than boys did, their parents also viewed math achievement as less important to the future success of girls than boys (Parsons et al., 1982). Parents' attitudes may partly explain why their children either do or do not judge academic success in a specific subject—or academic success in general—as valuable.

3. *Parents are warm, accepting, and responsive to their children.* One team of researchers (Estrada et al., 1987) used interviews and observations to assess the emotional quality of mothers' relationships with their 4-year-old children. Eight years later, the researchers assessed the children's academic achievement. The 12-year-olds who were higher achievers had

mothers who were warmer, more accepting, and more responsive to their interests and activities at 4 years of age.

Positive relationships between parents and children may affect children's achievement in several ways. At age 4, the children who had better relationships with their mothers were more willing to accept their mothers' help when they were playing a game together. Children who have learned to get help from their mothers may be more willing and able to get help from teachers or other adults at school. As a result, they may learn more from their social interactions at home and at school.

Also, the 4-year-olds who had more positive relationships with their mothers were more persistent when working on tasks. Their mothers' support may have fostered the development of a mastery orientation rather than a helpless orientation.

During the school years, parents' warmth may be expressed in ways that directly contribute to a mastery orientation. While their children are working on a difficult task parents can either express positive comments or make negative and critical comments. Moreover, parents can encourage their children to continue working on a difficult task while trying new ways to solve it, or say little to keep their children working. Not surprising, parents who are more positive and encouraging have children who are more mastery-oriented than helpless. These children work longer on difficult tasks and show more enthusiasm while working (Nolen-Hoeksema et al., 1995).

4. *Parents help children learn at home.* You read in chapter 7 that parents can increase their children's reading ability by reading to them or playing verbal games with them. Children also benefit when books and other reading materials are available at home (Hess & Holloway, 1984; Rodgers et al., 1994).

Even before their children learn to read, parents can provide materials that promote learning. Remember the discussion of the HOME scale. Higher scores on this scale are related not only to higher IQ scores but also to better academic achievement during the elementary-school years (Bradley, 1993; Bradley, Caldwell, & Rock, 1988). Two-year-olds who have more appropriate toys and whose parents interact more often with them become 10-year-olds with higher achievement-test scores. Parents who provide an educationally rich environment for their 2-year-olds often continue to provide a rich educational environment as their children grow. Stimulation in the toddler years and in middle childhood both contribute to children's academic achievement at age 10.

5. *Parents make academic work into play—and then build a commitment to excellence.* Fostering academic achievement is similar in important respects to fostering any kind of talent. Benjamin Bloom (1985) tried to identify the family experiences that contribute to exceptional talent in six fields: music, art, swimming, tennis, mathematics, and science. He and his colleagues interviewed about two dozen adults who were unusually successful in each field. For example, they interviewed swimmers who had won many national and international competitions.

The researchers found some common elements in the early experiences of the talented individuals in all fields. When these individuals started in the field, as children, parents and teachers made their learning enjoyable and rewarding. They encouraged the children to think of the activity as play. As the children gained greater knowledge and skill, they began to think of themselves as talented. Then they were ready to commit themselves to increasing their talent.

Parents responded to this new level of commitment by emphasizing high standards and sustained effort. Parents began to require their children to do their work (e.g., practicing the piano) before play. They also encouraged their children to do their best always, or to make a commitment to excellence. In this way, parents helped their children take the step from having fun to striving for world-class achievement. In addition, these parents often looked for teachers or schools that would give their children the special training needed for world-class achievement in their chosen field.

6. *Parents tell children that effort will lead to success.* Sustained effort over many years is necessary for world-class achievement, but some effort is needed to reach any goal. When par-

ents encourage their children to keep working on difficult tasks, they are indirectly telling their children that continued effort will have good results. This message is critical, because children may otherwise make different—and less desirable—attributions for their successes and failures. Recall that helpless children are more likely to attribute their failures to external causes than to lack of effort. Helpless children are more likely to attribute their successes to high ability or to external causes than to their effort.

Children have higher achievement motivation and higher academic achievement when their parents emphasize that effort is the primary cause of outcomes (Gottfried, Fleming, & Gottfried, 1994). These parents encourage children to complete their school work independently, and to try harder when they have a problem that seems difficult to solve.

Of course, children cannot achieve at a high level if they never receive help from their parents and other adults. Children cannot take full responsibility for their own education. Still, children benefit when their parents make clear that trying harder, on one's own, is a good first response to a difficult problem. Such an emphasis on individual effort leads to an orientation toward task mastery and independent learning.

## Effects of Schools

You read earlier that some educational programs for disadvantaged preschool children did not have a lasting effect on the children's IQs but did affect their educational success. The participants in these programs were less often placed in special-education classes and less often retained in a grade than were comparable children not in the programs (Lazar & Darlington, 1982). With no lasting differences in IQ scores, how can these differences in educational success be explained?

The most likely explanation is that the programs increased the children's achievement motivation (Lazar & Darlington, 1982). The graduates of the programs tended to rate their school competence more highly than did the children who did not participate. Because they felt more competent, they probably had higher expectancies for academic success. Also, program graduates had more positive attitudes toward school than did the nonparticipating children. This difference in attitudes suggests that the graduates placed a higher value on school achievement. In short, participation in the special preschool programs had positive effects on some critical elements of achievement motivation. More motivated students then had greater educational success.

***Effects of School Organization and Climate*** Children's motivation to achieve is certainly not fixed when they enter elementary school. The organization of a school and a student's place in that organization can raise or lower achievement motivation (Ames, 1987; Nicholls, 1989). For example, students are often grouped by ability within classes or assigned to academic tracks that include only students similar in ability. The usual argument for ability grouping or tracking is that students learn the most when they are placed with other students at the same level.

The available research does not strongly support this argument (Kulik & Kulik, 1982; Oakes, 1985). When high-ability students take classes with equally able peers, they sometimes benefit from the faster pace of instruction that they receive (Rogers, 1993). Low-ability students, by contrast, sometimes learn less in classes that include only other low-ability students than in classes with a more mixed group of students. The net effect is that academic achievement does not differ significantly in classes that are ability grouped and those that are not (Slavin, 1993).

This net effect may be less important, however, than the negative effects of ability grouping on students placed in the low-ability track (Ball, 1981; Oakes, 1985). These students sometimes lower their expectancies for success and devalue the academic success that is denied them. Whether these negative effects occur, and how large they are, varies greatly across schools (Hallinan, 1994). Negative effects are reduced when students' placements depend on their ability in specific subjects rather than on their general ability. Negative effects are less likely when competent, experienced, and energetic adults teach in the low-ability track (Rutter, 1983). The continued use in the lower tracks of a strong academic curriculum, rather than watered-down courses, is also important (Gamoran, 1993).

Students' achievement motivation is also affected by the mood or emotional climate of a school (Rutter, 1983). Students learn more in school when their teachers emphasize the purpose of learning. Students learn more when their teachers are effective and interesting, and when student participation is encouraged. Schools with these characteristics foster more positive attitudes toward learning and, therefore, increase students' motivation.

*Effects of Cooperative Learning*   Finally, students' achievement is affected by the instructional techniques that their teachers use. A collection of the research literature on effective techniques of instruction would fill a small library, and several comprehensive handbooks on the subject are available (e.g., Wittrock, 1985). Only two points can be considered here.

First, children can benefit from working cooperatively with other students rather than individually or in competition with others (Stevens & Slavin, 1995). Cooperative learning methods are most effective when students are rewarded as a group and when these rewards depend on the performance of every member of their group (Slavin, 1983). If no reward is offered, children have no incentive to work together and are likely to "goof off." If the group's reward does not depend explicitly on how much each individual has learned, one child may do all the work while the others loaf. Then the child who does the work learns something, and the loafers do not.

To avoid this problem, a group's rewards can be based on the average performance of each child in the group, or each child can be given a unique task. Then the group cannot be successful unless each child contributes fully. When cooperative learning is central to classroom organization and instruction, students have higher academic achievement than do similar students in comparison schools. Social relationships among students are also better (Stevens & Slavin, 1995).

Why does cooperative learning work when these conditions are met? Apparently because students who are working together set high standards for their performance. They also encourage the other students in their group to set high standards. You see, then, that the benefits of cooperative learning depend partly on peer influence. Children are more motivated to achieve when their classes are structured to maximize the positive influence of peers on their attitudes toward schoolwork.

*Effects of Time on Task and Beliefs About Achievement*   Children learn more when their teachers spend more time teaching. Children learn less when their teachers spend more time disciplining students, taking attendance, or performing other management and administrative duties (Rutter, 1983). On these counts, classrooms in the United States do not score very well.

You read at the beginning of the chapter about a study that included school-age children in the United States, Taiwan, and Japan. For one part of the study, the researchers observed how much school time was actually spent on mathematics instruction. They concluded that children in the United States did not receive sufficient instruction. Compared with Japanese and Taiwanese children, U.S. children spent less time each year in school, less time each day in mathematics classes, and less time in each class receiving instruction. In U.S. classrooms, students often worked alone at their seats on material that they did not understand very well. Students also spent large amounts of time in transition from one activity or classroom to another (Stigler, Lee, & Stevenson, 1987, pp. 1284–1285).

Is it surprising, then, that American children had lower scores on tests of math achievement than did children in Taiwan and Japan? "Time on task" is not all that's important in learning, but its influence is far from trivial.

Other differences, both in the school and in the family, may help to explain why math achievement differs so greatly in the United States, Taiwan, and Japan. Some of these differences are described in *Cultural Perspectives:* "Why Do U.S. Students Do So Poorly in Math?" The information in the box illustrates and adds to what you have already learned about achievement motivation and achievement.

Children in Japan have higher scores on some academic tests than do children in the United States. Two likely reasons for this difference are that Japanese children spend more time in school and their teachers spend more time directly instructing them. By contrast, Japanese children spend less time than U.S. children working on their own or moving between classes.

## The Development of Achievement Motivation

Achievement motivation has its roots in infancy. Beginning soon after birth, infants are motivated to learn about and to gain control over their environment. Infants' behavior is not usually measured against standards of achievement, so the motive that explains their behavior is often called **mastery motivation** rather than achievement motivation (White, 1959; Yarrow et al., 1983). To assess infants' mastery motivation, researchers watch them as they explore toys or try to solve problems such as getting a toy from behind a barrier.

**mastery motivation**
*Motivation to learn about and gain control over one's environment.*

Young infants show their mastery motivation by their attention to novel objects. Around 9 months of age, infants' behavior becomes clearly intentional. As discussed in chapter 7, infants at that age begin using gestures to communicate what they want others to do. Nine-month-olds also enter the sensorimotor stage that Piaget defined by the use of means to reach a goal. Nine-month-olds express their mastery motivation by their persistence in attempts to reach a goal or control the environment (Barrett, Morgan, & Maslin-Cole, 1993; Jennings, 1993).

After about 18 months of age, toddlers start to pay attention to how others react to their accomplishments (Stipek, Recchia, & McClintic, 1992). For example, toddlers call their mothers when they finish putting together a puzzle. Toddlers also recognize that other people might evaluate them for not accomplishing some task. They show their concern about negative evaluations by looking away from an adult who is watching when they fail on a task.

Between 18 months and 3 years of age, children begin to link chains of actions to reach more complex goals (Jennings, 1993). They may, for example, set themselves the goal of putting all their blocks into a storage box—or out of the box onto the floor! When they complete such a task, they smile and pause to let others see that they have mastered it.

After age 3 the relation between mastery motivation and achievement motivation becomes harder to define. Some researchers have argued that mastery motivation is transformed into achievement motivation when children try to reach certain goals and evaluate their success in doing so. That is, children begin to evaluate themselves based on their judgments about their ability to achieve their goals (Dweck & Elliott, 1983). The influence of reaching or not reaching a goal on children's self-evaluations is apparent by age 3 (Stipek et al., 1992).

## WHY DO U.S. STUDENTS DO SO POORLY IN MATH?

Figure 10.12 shows the scores of fifth graders in the United States, Taiwan, and Japan who were tested on their reading and math achievement (Stevenson & Lee, 1990). The reading test had separate parts for vocabulary and comprehension; the math test had parts for operations (computation) and problem solving. To make comparisons easier, the mean scores for students in each country on each test have been divided by the U.S. students' mean and then multiplied by 100.

U.S. students did less well than students in Taiwan and Japan on both math operations and math problem solving. The differences were especially great on the test of problem solving. On the reading tests, however, U.S. students' scores were not significantly different from those of Asian students.

Other cross-national studies have yielded similar results. Statistics reported by the U.S. Department of Education continue to show poorer math performance by United States students than by Asian students (U.S. Department of Education, 1994). By contrast, U.S. students' scores in reading are higher than those of students in most other countries. In short, academic achievement is not lower on all subjects in the United States than in other countries.

U.S. students do not do poorly in math because their IQs are lower than those of Asian students. When Harold Stevenson, Chuansheng Chen, and Shin-ying Lee (1993) gave a test of general information to students in the United States, Japan, and Taiwan, students in all three countries received similar scores. Researchers who have given IQ tests to U.S. and Asian children have not found consistent differences in the scores obtained by U.S. and Asian children (Neisser et al., 1996).

Why, then, do U.S. students do so poorly in math? One reason was mentioned in the text: U.S. students spend less time studying math than do students in Japan and Taiwan. For example, Taiwanese students spend about 8 hours each week in math classes, compared with only about 3½ hours in the United States (Stevenson & Lee, 1990).

Other reasons relate more directly to achievement motivation. When asked about likely reasons for high achievement, U.S. teachers and parents say that innate intelligence is most important (Stevenson et al., 1993). By contrast, Japanese teachers and parents say that studying hard is most important. Thus, U.S. teachers and parents attribute academic success to ability, and so adopt the entity theory of intelligence. Asian teachers and parents attribute academic success to effort, and so adopt the incremental theory of intelligence.

In addition, U.S. parents express greater satisfaction with their children's academic performance than do Asian parents (Stevenson & Lee, 1990). Parents who are satisfied are unlikely to set higher expectations for their children's future performance than for their current performance. Their children, then, are unlikely to try to improve their performance.

Extreme pessimism is not warranted, however. As the message about the poor performance of U.S. students has reached more educators and policymakers, efforts have been made to increase the emphasis on math achievement. This increased emphasis may have already started to pay off (U.S. Department of Education, 1994). Between 1980 and 1992 the math achievement of U.S. students rose significantly. If educators in the United States keep trying to motivate students to do well in math, the trend toward improved math achievement may continue.

## FIGURE 10.12

On math tests, fifth graders in the United States do less well than students in Taiwan and Japan. By contrast, the reading achievement of students in the three countries is similar. The U.S. students' poor performance in math may be the result of limited time for math instruction, the belief of U.S. adults that math achievement reflects innate ability, and the failure of U.S. adults to set high standards for students' math achievement.

Suppose you learned that these two children did equally well on the test for which they are studying. Which one would you think was smarter? You might guess it was the boy who also spent some of his time watching TV because he could do well on the test even while wasting some of his study time. Young children say the opposite. They assume that children who work harder are smarter.

Achievement motivation changes dramatically after age 3. Weiner (1985) argued that most adults attribute variations in achievement to ability, effort, task difficulty, or luck. Adults distinguish each cause of achievement from the others. They recognize, for example, that ability and effort are both internal causes of performance but that ability is relatively stable and effort is relatively unstable. Preschoolers and young children do not make the same distinctions.

Suppose you watched two boys working on arithmetic problems. One worked steadily for the entire time you were watching. The other spent some time working on the problems and some time looking around the room and playing with a pencil. Later, you find out that the two boys did equally well and got the same score on their work. Which boy would you think was smarter?

Most adults say that the boy who didn't work the whole time is smarter (Nicholls, 1978, 1989). Why? Because he did just as well as the other boy, even though he didn't work as hard. Adults accept the view of ability as capacity (see table 10.7). In this view, ability is like the power of an automobile engine. A car with a big engine (or more capacity) doesn't have to work as hard to get up a steep hill as a car with a small engine. Similarly, a child high in ability doesn't have to work as hard to get good test scores as does a child low in ability.

Children under 7 years of age do not view ability and effort in the same way as adults do. These children often say that the boy who worked the whole time was smarter because "he was working and not playing." They assume that smarter children always work harder. Stated more formally, children under age 7 show little differentiation between ability and effort and so are at Level 1 of table 10.7.

As children grow, they begin to reason at a higher level (Level 2) and assume that only effort affects achievement. Children at Level 2 do not have a separate concept of ability. These children believe that people who work harder must always be more successful. Exceptions to this rule are hard for Level 2 children to explain.

Older children begin to suggest that the boy who doesn't work as hard but still does as well may be smarter. That is, they start to recognize the separate effects of ability and effort on performance, and thus they fit the description of Level 3 in table 10.7. Not until 11 or 12 years of age do most children differentiate fully between ability and effort. Only then do most children accept the adult concept of ability as capacity (Level 4).

Is it desirable for children to develop adultlike concepts of ability and effort as they approach adolescence? Is it helpful for them to outgrow their obviously mistaken belief that hard-working students are always smarter than students who work less? There are two reasons to hesitate before answering yes.

| **TABLE 10.7** | *Levels of Differentiation of Ability and Effort* |
|---|---|
| *Level 1* | Effort or outcome is defined as ability. Effort, ability, and performance outcomes are imperfectly differentiated as cause and effect. Explanations of outcomes are circular. Children center on effort (people who try harder than others are seen as smarter even if they get a lower score) or on outcome (people who get a higher score are said to work harder even if they do not and are seen as smarter). |
| *Level 2* | Effort is defined as the cause of outcomes. Effort and outcome are differentiated as cause and effect. Effort is the prime cause of outcomes: Equal effort is expected to lead to equal outcomes. When attainment is equal but effort varies, this is seen as either inexplicable, or due to compensatory effort (the apparently lazier student must have worked really hard for a while), or to misapplied effort (the one who worked harder went too quickly and made mistakes). |
| *Level 3* | Effort and ability are partially differentiated. Effort is not the only cause of outcomes. Explanations of equal outcomes following different effort involve suggestions that imply the conception of ability as capacity (the person working less hard is faster or brighter). These implications are not, however, systematically followed through; children may still assert that individuals would achieve equally if they applied equal effort. |
| *Level 4* | Ability is defined as capacity. Ability and effort are clearly differentiated. Ability is conceived as capacity, which (if low) may limit or (if high) may increase the effect of effort on performance. Conversely, the effect of effort is constrained by ability. When achievement is equal, lower effort implies higher ability. |

Reprinted by permission of the publisher from *The Competitive Ethos and Democratic Education* by John G. Nicholls, Cambridge, Mass.: Harvard University Press, Copyright © 1989 by the President and Fellows of Harvard College.

First, think back to the discussion of the entity and incremental theories of intelligence. Young children who confuse the notions of ability and effort often think that they can improve their intelligence by reading books or getting more information (Nicholls et al., 1986). These responses are consistent with the incremental theory of intelligence. Remember that children who accept this theory are more likely to show mastery-oriented responses to academic failures and difficult tasks.

By contrast, most adolescents and adults who think of ability as capacity accept something like the entity view of intelligence. They regard intelligence as a capacity for problem solving that does not change with experience. Recall that this view of intelligence is associated, by fifth grade, with a helpless rather than a mastery-oriented response to failure. Therefore, becoming more sophisticated about the causes of performance may mean becoming more susceptible to helplessness (Miller, 1985).

Second, the mature conception of ability as capacity can change children's ideas about the kinds of people they would like to be. Suppose you watched the two boys work on their arithmetic problems, and then I asked you which boy you would prefer to be. Most adolescents and college students say they would prefer to be the boy who didn't work as hard but still got a good score. Most children with immature ideas about ability and effort say they would prefer to be the boy who worked the entire time (Nicholls et al., 1986).

Adolescents and adults are not generally more lazy than younger children. Their preference for the boy who didn't work as hard is almost demanded by their ideas about ability and intelligence. How often have you heard someone say, "I aced the test without even studying!" The clear implication is, "I'm really smart!" When people think of ability as capacity and of intelligence as a stable entity, they think they can demonstrate their high intelligence by getting a good score without working hard.

But what about students who don't ace the test? For them, studying or working hard on academic tasks can be threatening (Covington & Omelich, 1981). If the effort doesn't pay off, their egos can be severely bruised. They can only say, "I studied for days and I still flunked the test." The clear implication is, "I must be really dumb."

How can children avoid these negative consequences of growing older and wiser—or developing more sophisticated ideas about ability and intelligence? Researchers have offered several suggestions.

First, children should be encouraged to attribute academic difficulties to a lack of effort rather than a lack of ability (Forsterling, 1985). Second, children should be encouraged to value learning for its own sake, for self-improvement, and not to always compare their

performance with that of other children (Gottfried et al., 1994; Nicholls, 1989). Finally, children should be told when they are young—and reminded when they are adolescents—that intellectual abilities can always be improved with effort and sustained involvement in learning (Dweck & Elliott, 1983).

# SOCIAL INTELLIGENCE?

You read earlier that the average adult assumes intelligent people have many desirable characteristics (Sternberg et al., 1981). Among these characteristics are the tendencies to accept others for who they are, to admit mistakes, and to make fair judgments. You also read about the characteristics that parents attribute to an intelligent first grader (Okagaki & Sternberg, 1993). Among these characteristics were several that involve social behavior, including "plays well with other children," "has good manners," and "is happy and well adjusted."

Now think about the rest of the chapter. Have you read about any items on IQ tests that assess a person's tendencies to accept others for what they are? Have you read about any items that assess how well a child plays with other children? No, because social competence and social adaptation are not assessed on standard IQ tests.

**Social intelligence** can be defined as the collection of abilities that underlie social competence and social adaptation. Many people assume that social intelligence is not closely linked to the abilities assessed on IQ tests. Some people go further, assuming that children with very high IQs will be social misfits and not get along well with their peers. These people also assume that adults with high IQs often have problems in psychological adjustment.

Are these assumptions correct? The best evidence on this issue comes from a unique longitudinal study begun by Lewis Terman. The study included more than 1,500 California children who received scores above 135 on an IQ test given in 1921, when they were about 11 years old. The children were studied for the rest of their lives. Many books and articles have been written about their occupations, their families, and even when and why they died (Goleman, 1980, 1995; Sears, 1977; Terman, 1925; Terman & Oden, 1959; Tomlinson-Keasey & Little, 1990).

On tests of emotional stability, the children with high IQs received better scores than a comparison group of randomly selected children. The children's teachers judged them as more self-confident, cheerful, and truthful than their classmates, but they were neither more nor less popular than average. Similar results have been found in more recent studies (Schneider, 1987).

As adults, these gifted individuals did not show any special problems in adjustment. Nearly all the men were in professional or managerial occupations. Most of the women were not employed during their childrearing years, but when they were, they were more successful than average.

However, these adults were not immune to life's problems. They were hospitalized for mental illness about as often as individuals in the general population. They got married and divorced as often as other adults in the United States. Finally, they rated their happiness as highly but no more highly than did adults with average IQs.

These findings can be interpreted in several ways. Robert Sternberg (1985), the creator of the triarchic theory of intelligence, might argue that the findings show the deficiencies of standard IQ tests. If tests were defined to assess practical intelligence, the facet linked to his contextual subtheory, they might show stronger relations to social success and psychological adjustment.

Howard Gardner, the creator of the theory of multiple intelligences, might take the findings as proof that interpersonal (or social) intelligence is different from the types of intelligence assessed on IQ tests. Several researchers have tried to create measures of social intelligence (e.g., Wong et al., 1995), but so far these measures have been used mostly with adults.

A third alternative is to argue that IQ tests should not be expected to assess children's social competence. The tests assess cognitive functioning, and are reasonably good predictors of academic achievement, so they serve the purpose for which they were originally created. However, children's social competence depends on far more than their level of cognitive functioning. Social competence also reflects aspects of children's personality or character that cannot be captured by an IQ score.

**social intelligence**
*The cognitive abilities that underlie social competence and social adaptation.*

# Summary

## Defining and Measuring Intelligence

Most researchers who focus on intelligence have adopted the **psychometric approach** to the study of cognitive development. These researchers have tried first to define intelligence and then to devise standardized tests for measuring children's intelligence.

## Multiple Definitions of Intelligence

**Intelligence** is the human faculty of thought and reason. Adults assume that an intelligent person is good at solving practical problems, high in verbal ability, and competent in social situations. Adults assume that intelligent children get good grades in school and are motivated to achieve in school. Immigrant parents in the United States believe achievement motivation is more closely related to high intelligence than do Anglo-American parents.

## The First Successful Intelligence Test and the IQ Paradigm

Alfred Binet and Theodore Simon devised the first successful intelligence test early in the twentieth century. They also proposed the construct of **mental age.** Lewis Terman devised the Stanford-Binet and proposed that children's scores should be reported as an **intelligence quotient,** or IQ. Other researchers argued that IQ scores reflect *g*, children's general intelligence or learning potential.

## Current IQ Tests: A Review and Status Report

The best-known IQ tests were devised by Terman and by David Wechsler. Other researchers devised tests for infants and toddlers or tried to develop less verbal and more culture-fair tests. The best IQ tests yield scores that are highly reliable (e.g., stable over short periods of time). The scores also correlate substantially with academic achievement, which suggests that the tests are reasonably valid.

## Stability and Change in IQ Scores

Many people have assumed that IQ scores should be stable throughout childhood and adulthood because they are "written in a person's genes." This assumption has been partly disconfirmed by evidence from longitudinal research.

## How Stable Are Individual Differences in IQ Scores?

During middle childhood, IQ scores are highly stable across one- or two-year intervals. IQ scores are less stable in younger children and with longer intervals between tests. Measures of infants' visual recognition memory and habituation are significantly correlated with their IQ scores in early and middle childhood.

## How Much Do IQ Scores Change as Children Grow?

Most children show some change in IQ after infancy. Many children show changes of 30 points or more. However, some of these changes seem to reflect random error, temporary fluctuations in scores due to illness or other causes, rather than lasting change.

## Genetic and Environmental Influences on the Development of IQ

Variations in children's genes and in their environments contribute to the variations in their IQ scores. Researchers have used different methods to examine the effects of changes in gene expression and changes in environments on children's IQs.

## Genes, IQ, and Changes in IQ

Twin studies and adoption studies confirm that the genes parents pass to their children affect the children's IQs. Several kinds of evidence cast doubt on hypotheses that racial differences in children's mean IQ scores are due to genetic differences among racial groups.

## Family and School Environments, IQ, and Changes in IQ

The IQ scores of infants with stimulating home environments often increase between 1 and 3 years of age. Schooling, either in special programs for preschool children or in regular elementary schools, also influences children's IQ scores.

## Is Intelligence More Than IQ?

IQ scores are imperfect measures of intelligence. Sternberg's triarchic theory describes other abilities that could be included in the definition of intelligence but that are not measured by IQ tests. Gardner's theory of multiple intelligences emphasizes that people display problem-solving ability in areas as diverse as athletics and music.

## Academic Achievement and Achievement Motivation

Children's IQs are related to their academic achievement, but most of the variation in achievement is not explained by variations in IQ. Children's achievement also depends on their motivation, their drive to succeed in school.

## Elements of Achievement Motivation

Children differ in whether they adopt a helpless or a mastery orientation when faced with a difficult academic task. Children also differ in their causal attributions for academic successes and failures, their goals when working on academic tasks, and their ideas of intelligence. Moreover, children's achievement motivation is affected by their expectancies for success and the value they attach to academic success.

## Influences on Motivation and Achievement

Parents set expectations for their children's performance; they can also encourage children to exert the effort needed for success. In school, students are influenced by the instructional techniques that teachers use (e.g., cooperative learning) and by the amount of time devoted to instruction.

## The Development of Achievement Motivation

Infants are motivated to master their environments. Around 3 years of age, children begin to evaluate themselves based on their success in reaching their goals. Full understanding of the contributions of ability and effort to achievement is not attained until 11 or 12 years of age.

## Social Intelligence?

Children with high IQs are not generally more or less socially successful than children with average IQs. These findings can be used to bolster arguments that IQ tests should be expanded to assess social intelligence. An alternative, however, is to argue that IQ scores are designed to assess cognitive functioning, not all aspects of personality or character.

# SUGGESTED READINGS

Fraser, S. (Ed.). (1995). *The bell curve wars: Race, intelligence, and the future of America.* New York: Basic.

Herrnstein, R. J., & Murray, C. (1994). *The bell curve.* New York: Free Press.

Jacoby, R., & Glauberman, N. (Eds.). (1995). *The bell curve debate: History, documents, opinions.* New York: Times Book. These three books are listed together because you can better judge the arguments in *The Bell Curve* if you also read the commentaries by other experts. Although the books are not concerned only with children's intelligence, issues concerning the stability of children's IQs and the effectiveness of programs to improve children's intelligence are discussed.

Stevenson, H. W., & Stigler, J. W. (1992). *The learning gap.* New York: Summit. For more than a decade, Stevenson and Stigler have been involved in research comparing U.S. elementary schools with those in Japan and Taiwan. Their major findings are presented in this book. The book also discusses reforms in the U.S. educational system that could improve children's academic achievement.

Sternberg, R. J. (Ed.). (1994). *Encyclopedia of human intelligence.* New York: Macmillan. If you want to know more about intelligence and IQ, this book is an excellent place to look. Its two volumes include more than 1,200 pages of brief articles. The articles range from biographies of scholars like Alfred Binet to descriptions of specific IQ tests and discussions of ethnic differences in IQ scores.

Zigler, E., & Muenchow, S. (1992). *Head Start: The inside story of America's most successful educational experiment.* New York: Basic Books. Edward Zigler served on the committee that planned the Head Start program. In 1972 he became the first director of the Office of Child Development, the federal agency responsible for Head Start. This book describes the program's origins as part of President Johnson's War on Poverty, its uncertain fortunes in the 1970s, and its favored political status in 1990.

11

# PARENTING AND FAMILY RELATIONSHIPS

*N*early all children grow up in a family with one or both of their parents. Children's development is profoundly influenced by their interactions with family members. To examine these influences, researchers compare variations in family interactions to variations in children's behavior. The following paragraphs describe a particularly dramatic interaction between a mother and her young son. As you read, think about how this interaction might affect the son's development.

When Manyara was 2 years old, his mother planned a visit to a neighbor's house. She decided to take Manyara's baby sister with her, but she told Manyara to stay with his father's other wife and that woman's daughter. However, Manyara tried to follow his mother, so she grabbed a stick and chased him back to the homestead. Then she rapped him across the legs several times and began to leave again.

Manyara continued crying, so his mother called him to her and then rapped him again on the legs with the stick. After that, his father's other wife picked him up, carried him into his mother's hut, and locked the door. She didn't let him out until he stopped crying (LeVine & LeVine, 1963).

Manyara was one of the Gusii people of western Kenya. He lived in the community of Nyansongo, a collection of 18 homesteads on the hills of the western highlands, about 30 miles east of Lake Victoria. Most of the households in Nyansongo were polygynous, with one husband who had two or more wives. Manyara and his mother were observed during the 1950s by researchers who were studying children in six cultures around the world (Whiting, 1963).

Manyara's mother reacted so strongly—and violently—to his protests when she left because she thought he was jealous of the baby she was taking with her. She also thought that his crying meant that he wanted to hurt or kill his baby sister. But among the Gusii, physical punishment of children was common even in other cases. Gusii mothers often hit children with sticks when they were disobedient, neglected their chores, or engaged in some type of sex play.

As Gusii children grew older, their mothers hit them less, partly because they relied on other punishments like deprivation of food. Mothers also had less success in applying physical punishments, because older children often ran away when their mothers tried to hit them. To deal with this problem, a mother sometimes called the father or an older brother to beat a child who was disobedient.

One reason Gusii mothers might not have hesitated to use physical punishment is because they were themselves the victims of it. Their husbands sometimes beat them if they didn't obey orders. Husbands, in turn, were subservient to their fathers, who had authority over the entire family. Even when a son was an adult with a wife (or wives) and children of his own, his father could attack him or punish him in other ways if he went against his father's wishes.

This portrait of the Gusii people obviously is an unbalanced one. It focuses on only one aspect of their social interactions and not on the more positive aspects of their social life. Later in the chapter, you will learn that Gusii people also trained their children to be generous, helpful, and supportive of other people. In the six-cultures study, Gusii children showed more of this **prosocial behavior** (i.e., positive social behavior) than the children in several other cultures, including the United States.

In addition, the preceding description of the Gusii does not say why they used physical punishment so often. Beatrice and John Whiting (1975) suggested that the Gusii emphasized obedience to authority and handed out severe punishments for disobedience because their social structure demanded these practices. To solve conflicts within the extended Gusii family, the family head needed authority over his sons and their families. To keep this authority, he sometimes had to use force. Similarly, husbands may have needed to use force and keep some emotional distance from their wives and children to maintain peace within a polygynous household.

Notice, though, that the description of Gusii childrearing and culture is stated in the past tense. Like other cultures around the world, traditional Gusii culture has been affected by historical change. In the 1970s Gusii parents still showed many elements of the childrearing patterns first observed in the 1950s (Levine, 1994). However, men had begun mi-

**prosocial behavior**
*Positive social behaviors, including sharing, helping, and comforting.*

grating to the cities for work, rather than working near their homes. Over time, this change in adults' occupations is likely to have changed family roles and childrearing patterns.

Still, you might wonder how Gusii childrearing during the 1950s affected the development of children like Manyara. Whiting and Whiting (1975) provide part of the answer. Observers of 3- to 10-year-old Gusii children found that these children were more aggressive and domineering when interacting with other people than were the children in the other five cultures studied. These data imply that Gusii parents' punitive behavior toward their children had undesirable effects on the children's social development.

The effect of parents' behavior on their children's development is the first topic of this chapter. You will see how researchers have described variations in parenting, and how these variations are related to variations in children's behavior.

The second topic of the chapter is sibling relationships, like those between Manyara and his baby sister. The analysis of sibling relationships will help you understand a complete family system of parents and children who influence each other.

The third topic is the changing American family. In recent decades, family roles have changed not only in traditional cultures like the Gusii but also in modern societies like the United States. Rates of maternal employment, divorce, and single parenting have all increased. The increase in the divorce rate has brought an increase in the number of children living in remarried families. You will learn how parenting patterns and children's behaviors differ in these contrasting family forms.

The final topic of the chapter is child maltreatment, the infrequent but tragic cases in which parenting goes awry. You will read about the kinds of child maltreatment and their causes. You will also read about interventions for victims of maltreatment and programs to prevent it.

# PARENTING AS SOCIALIZATION

In chapter 6 you read about the special relationships, or attachments, that infants form to their parents. As you recall, the development of attachments depends most heavily on parents' responsiveness. Infants are most likely to form secure attachments when their parents respond quickly and sensitively to their needs.

Once infants reach their first birthday, most parents try to do more than simply respond to their needs. As infants grow into toddlers, parents increasingly try to control and direct their behavior. This change in parenting reflects an important shift in parents' goals. When children are roughly 1 year of age, most parents adopt the goal of teaching them to behave appropriately in social situations. In more psychological terms, they begin to socialize their children (Maccoby & Martin, 1983).

**Socialization** is the process by which children acquire the beliefs, values, and behavior considered appropriate for people in their society and culture. Children in our culture are socialized to eat with a spoon, fork, and knife. Children in other cultures may be socialized to eat with chopsticks or with their hands. Children in our culture are socialized to wear clothes when they are in public places. Children in other cultures may be socialized to go without clothes until they reach adolescence or even later.

Parents have the primary responsibility for socializing their children. That is, parents are the most important agents of socialization. Implicitly or explicitly, parents teach their children how to behave, what to value, and what to believe. They may teach by example, by direct instruction, or by encouraging certain behaviors and discouraging others. The different modes of teaching are linked to different processes of socialization.

For decades, child development researchers have studied the contributions of parents to children's socialization. For most of this time, researchers emphasized parents' effects on children and ignored the possible effects of children on parents. This omission has been corrected in recent years, as researchers have emphasized that influence may go in both directions. Children may, in a sense, socialize their parents while their parents are trying to socialize them. Before finishing this section, you will read about research aimed at answering the question "Who is socializing whom?"

**socialization**
*The process by which children acquire the beliefs, values, and behavior considered appropriate for people in their society and culture.*

Still, it makes sense to begin by examining the role of parents in the socialization process. Researchers have used various approaches to study the effects of parents on their children. You will learn first about the oldest and best-known approach, the analysis of broad dimensions of parenting.

## Dimensions of Parenting

The general characteristics of parent-child interactions are often defined in terms of three dimensions of parenting. Two of the dimensions, warmth and control, were identified by researchers several decades ago (e.g, Becker, 1964). The third dimension, involvement, began to receive attention in the 1980s (e.g., Maccoby & Martin, 1983). The features of parents' interactions with their children define their positions on these dimensions. Parents' positions are, in turn, related to their children's behaviors. These relations provide clues about the kinds of parenting that lead to successful socialization.

### Warmth

The dimension of parenting that has the strongest and most consistent effects on children's development is **warmth.** Parents high on the dimension are accepting of their children and nurturant. Parents low on the dimension are cold or rejecting and low in nurturance (Maccoby, 1980).

The warmth dimension is extremely broad, including many types of parental behavior. What it means to be a warm parent can be stated more precisely by defining three separate but overlapping facets of parental warmth:

1. *Responsiveness.* Warm parents respond to their children's needs and desires rather than ignoring or frustrating them. For example, if their infant is crying, they pick up the infant rather than letting him or her cry. Warm parents comfort a preschooler who is hurt or upset rather than telling the child to "get over it." Warm parents help school-age children who are having trouble with schoolwork, rather than saying they are too busy.

These examples illustrate that the behaviors indicating a parent's warmth change with age because their children's needs and desires change. This flexibility is implied by the word *responsiveness.* The same kinds of adaptations to a child's developmental status hold for other facets of warmth, too. As a result, parental warmth has a powerful influence on children of all ages.

2. *Praise.* Warm parents praise their children when their behavior is especially good or they are successful at a difficult task. Warm parents praise their toddlers when they obey a command. Warm parents smile and applaud their preschoolers when they draw their first self-portrait with crayons. They do the same when their older children hit their first home run or show their accomplishments in another arena. Recall from chapter 10 that warm parents praise their children for their academic achievement.

This facet of the warmth dimension obviously overlaps with the idea of positive reinforcement. As mentioned in chapter 1, positive reinforcement is an important principle of all learning theories. However, researchers who focus on warmth in parenting view praise as an indication of how positively parents interact with their children, not how well parents apply learning principles.

3. *Expressions of positive emotions.* Warm parents often express their love for their children both physically and verbally. The importance of this facet of warmth is reflected by public-service messages and questions such as, "Have you hugged your child today?" These expressions of positive emotions differ from the signs of responsiveness because they do not come only when children are upset or in need. They also differ from praise because they are not limited to occasions when the child has done something good. Instead, they reflect the general emotional climate of parent-child interactions.

Warm parents not only express positive emotions *toward* their children; they also express positive emotions when *around* their children, thereby making their home a happy and

cheerful place. Every family is a miniature social system, and children are affected by the relationships among all the members of that system. Thus, parental warmth is compromised when fathers and mothers have many conflicts with each other (Erel & Burman, 1995). Parental warmth is also compromised when siblings are continually involved in arguments, because parents become entangled in those arguments. The inevitable result is that negative emotions begin to displace positive emotions in the home.

The effects of parental warmth are easily summarized: Warm parents are more successful in socializing their children than are cold or rejecting parents. As you know, one facet of warmth, responsiveness to an infant's needs, relates to the formation of secure attachments. In addition, children are more responsive to the needs of other people when their mothers are more responsive to their needs.

For one study (Zahn-Waxler, Radke-Yarrow, & King, 1979), mothers of toddlers kept records of their children's behavior when they saw someone in distress. For example, mothers noted whether their toddler tried to comfort a playmate who fell down and got hurt. Figure 11.1 shows that the children who gave more comfort to playmates in these cases had mothers who were more responsive to their needs when they were hurt or upset.

The toddlers in this study sometimes caused distress to other people. Occasionally, they bit another child or did something else that hurt another person. The toddlers who more often tried to make reparation for the hurt they had caused (tried to make the other child feel better) had mothers who had been more responsive to them (see figure 11.1). Even by 1 or 2 years of age, then, parents' warmth is associated with the desirable behavior of their children.

Warm parenting also relates to the psychological adjustment of preschool and school-age children. When their parents are more warm, preschool children are more happy, self-reliant, and self-controlled (Baumrind, 1967). School-age children with warmer parents are higher in self-esteem (Coopersmith, 1967) and better behaved at school (Bradley, 1989). Adolescents whose parents are more warm are more likely to confess when they have done something wrong. They are more likely to base their moral decisions on principles than on fear of punishment or hope of rewards (Hoffman & Saltzstein, 1967).

A lack of warmth has negative effects on children, even at a young age. As mentioned in chapter 6, even 2-year-olds were upset when the emotional climate around them was disturbed by an angry conflict between two adults (Cummings et al., 1985). Two-year-olds showed emotional distress during the conflicts and an increase in aggression toward peers afterward. Slightly older children showed emotional distress in another study when they witnessed an angry argument between their mother and another adult (Cummings et al., 1989).

Outside the laboratory, conflicts between parents or other family members may also contribute to distress, anxiety, and aggression in children. As you read, husbands in Nyansongo sometimes beat their wives. In addition, children in Nyansongo sometimes saw their mothers beat their siblings. Witnessing these conflicts probably contributed to the high level of aggression that these children showed.

Research in the United States confirms that conflicts between spouses are related to poorer child development. When interactions between husbands and wives involve more hostility, rejection, and antisocial behavior, their adolescent children have poorer relationships with peers and a poorer adjustment to school. In addition, these adolescents report lower self-confidence (Conger, Conger et al., 1992, 1993).

Moreover, a lack of parental warmth in early childhood is related to social adjustment measured decades later. A large study in the 1950s showed that 5-year-old children were more aggressive and less advanced in moral development when their parents were less warm toward them (Sears, Maccoby, & Levin, 1957). Some children in this study were assessed as adults, an average of 36 years later. Those with warmer parents in early childhood had better social relationships during adulthood. In particular, they had happier marriages, had been married a longer time, and had better relationships with their close friends (Franz, McClelland, & Weinberger, 1991).

Why is the expression of positive emotions, or the presence of warmth, so valuable for children's socialization? Different theorists would answer these questions differently

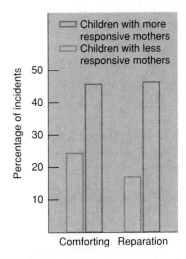

**FIGURE 11.1**

One- and 2-year-olds whose mothers are more responsive to them more often try to comfort a playmate who is hurt and more often make reparation when they have hurt a playmate. (Source: Zahn-Waxler et al., 1979.)

(Maccoby & Martin, 1983; MacDonald, 1992). A Freudian theorist might answer that children most readily identify with warm parents and so accept their standards for behavior. A social learning theorist might say that warm parents model sensitivity to others' needs and that children imitate the behavior of their parents. A theorist who emphasizes operant conditioning might say that warm parents are likely to praise their children for their desirable behavior, thus positively reinforcing it. Another theorist might argue that warm parents create a home environment that enhances children's emotional security and so contributes to good socioemotional development (Davies & Cummings, 1994). Because warmth is such a broad dimension of parenting, all these explanations may be part of the answer. That is, the positive effects of parental warmth probably result from many processes linked to many theories.

## Control: The Controversial Dimension

**control**
*The dimension of parenting that focuses on parents' expectations for their children's behavior, their training of children to meet these expectations, their enforcement of rules, the openness of their communication with their children, their situational management, and their reliance on physical punishment or power assertive discipline.*

The second dimension of parenting, **control,** is more complex than warmth, because neither of the extreme points on the dimension is desirable. If parents exert too little control, they are likely to end up with a child who is "out of control." If parents exert too much control, they may prevent children from developing self-control and individuality.

Popular writers on childrearing often encourage parents to be firm but flexible. They say that parents should not try to "run their children's lives for them" but that they should not let their children "get away with murder." This advice contains a kernel of truth: Parental control can be too restrictive or too permissive. But the advice may be hard to follow because parents cannot easily judge the happy medium between restrictiveness and permissiveness.

The solution to this problem is to distinguish forms of control that have good effects on children from forms that have bad effects. In other words, the solution is to decide which forms are generally effective in socializing children and which are not.

***Effective Forms of Parental Control*** There is no consensus among child development researchers about how forms of parental control should be classified. More consensus exists about whether specific forms of control are effective or ineffective in socialization. Researchers agree that the following four forms of control are likely to have positive effects on children's behavior and development.

1. *Set high expectations for children's behavior and train children to meet those expectations.* Parents who do not expect their children to behave in socially desirable ways should expect their children to be troublesome. For example, parents who assume that 3-year-olds are too young to share their toys with other children are likely to have 3-year-olds who don't share. Children are not likely to exceed the standards their parents set for them, so setting high standards for behavior is a step toward effective socialization (Maccoby, 1980).

The next step after setting high standards is training children to meet them. In this sense, standards must be realistic, or age-appropriate. Parents should not expect the average 2-year-old to sit still for an hour in a doctor's office with nothing to do. Parents can expect 2-year-olds not to run around the doctor's office if they can instead look at books or play with toys.

The value of setting high expectations for children's behavior was shown in the six-cultures study mentioned earlier (Whiting & Whiting, 1975). For the study, researchers observed children's behavior in Kenya (in Nyansongo), India, Okinawa, the Philippines, Mexico, and the United States. In each country, observers spent several months recording the behavior of 24 children from 3 to 11 years of age. The observers paid special attention to prosocial behaviors such as helping, supporting, and giving advice to another person.

Prosocial behavior was most frequent in Nyansongo, Kenya, and least frequent in the United States (see figure 11.2). Why would Gusii children so often behave prosocially toward other people? A closer analysis of all six cultures suggested the answer. Children showed the most prosocial behavior in cultures like that of the Gusii where families were large, mothers had many duties outside the home, and children often took care of their younger siblings or helped prepare food. In these cultures, children formed habits of helping because their parents expected them to do so and the family's welfare depended on their help.

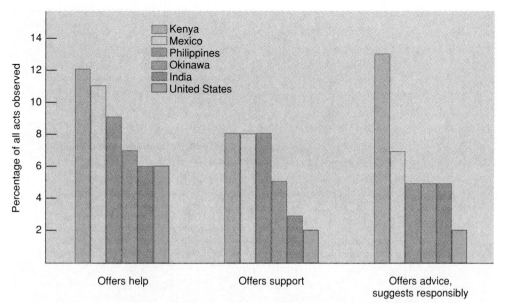

FIGURE 11.2

Prosocial behaviors by children in six cultures. Notice the high proportion of prosocial behaviors in Nyansongo, Kenya and the low proportion in the United States. In Nyansongo, parents expected children to be helpful, and the family's welfare depended on the children's help. This is less often true in the United States.

By contrast, the conditions that foster prosocial behavior (e.g., large families) were less common in the middle-class U.S. families that were observed.

Setting high but age-appropriate expectations does not make children feel anxious or inadequate. In one study (Baumrind, 1967), parents were rated on their maturity demands, the degree to which they insisted that their children be both socially responsible and independent. Parents who made more maturity demands had children who were more cheerful and more competent in their interactions with teachers and classmates at nursery school. In another study (Coopersmith, 1967), school-age boys whose parents had many rules for their behavior had higher self-esteem than boys with more permissive parents.

2. *Enforce rules consistently.* Parents who have given their children rules for behavior must then enforce these rules consistently (Maccoby, 1980). Even 2- to 3-year-old children more often obey their mothers' rules when those rules are consistently enforced. Also, mothers who are more consistent in enforcing rules have children who show more self-control. For example, the children more often stop themselves before violating a rule (Lytton, 1980).

Consistent enforcement of rules is equally important in middle childhood and adolescence. Jack Block (1971) examined the records of participants in the California longitudinal studies mentioned in chapter 2. Some participants, as adolescents, were highly impulsive. When they wanted something, they demanded it immediately. They rarely showed concentrated attention to any task. They expressed their emotions freely, and often explosively. Block labeled these adolescents as *undercontrolled.* He concluded that their parents' inconsistency in rule enforcement led to their lack of control. In his words:

> It is troublesome, interrupting, and onerous to have to discipline a child; it is far easier—immediately—to ignore the occasion for instruction or punishment. The parents of the undercontrollers, by virtue of their own impulsivity and self-absorption, simply did not invest the time nor exhibit the constancy needed to deliver the precepts of self-regulation to their child. Controlling the world of their child for the good of their child was not felt or acted on as a responsibility. (1971, p. 264)

And when parents did not take this responsibility, their children were not adequately socialized.

3. *Keep lines of communication open between parent and child.* Parents who value **open communication** explain the reasons for rules and then allow their children to express their opinions about them. These parents are eager to learn how their children feel and ready to take

**open communication**
*A positive aspect of parental control that involves frequent discussions between parents and their children. Parents explain the reasons for their rules and allow children to express their opinions about the rules.*

Is this mother going to buy more than she intended just to keep her daughter from causing a scene in the store? She might have avoided potential problems by bringing things for her daughter to read or play with during the shopping trip. Such planning would show a kind of situational management, which is a positive aspect of parental control.

their children's reasoning into account. Nevertheless, they do not "give in" when children complain about rules. Instead, the parents maintain control by reserving the right to make the final decision.

Parents who communicate openly with their children have preschoolers who behave competently rather than immaturely in social situations (Baumrind, 1967). These preschoolers are independent, cheerful, and self-controlled. Open communication with school-age children contributes to high self-esteem (Coopersmith, 1967). When parents are willing to explain their point of view to their children and willing to listen to their children's point of view, the process of socialization goes more smoothly (Maccoby, 1980).

4. *Practice situational management.* Often, parents can anticipate problematic situations and arrange them so that appropriate behavior by children is more likely. This form of **situational management** is easiest to define by example.

**situational management**
*A positive aspect of parental control that involves anticipating problematic situations and trying to structure them so that appropriate behavior by children is more likely.*

Suppose you are with a 2-year-old in a supermarket. Your goal is to get your week's grocery shopping done without buying all the junk food your child sees and without having the child cause a scene if you don't get everything he or she wants. How can you achieve this goal?

For one study, mothers were observed as they shopped with their 2-year-olds (Holden, 1983). During these shopping trips, the 2-year-olds asked for things at a rate of nearly one request per minute. Mothers refused these requests 86 percent of the time, either with an explanation or with a simple no. Most often, children did not repeat the request—at least for the next 20 seconds. Sometimes, though, the children persisted, and more extended conflicts occurred between mothers and children.

One tactic that some mothers used to avoid conflicts with their 2-year-olds was to divert their attention from things in the store. These mothers prepared for the shopping trip by packing food, books, or toys for their children. Then they gave their children something to eat, a book to read, or a toy to play with while they shopped. Children made fewer requests when their mothers used these tactics, and fewer conflicts arose between mothers and children.

One mother explained her use of these tactics by saying, "I try to anticipate [a problem] and therefore fix it so we don't run into a lot of confrontations. I guess I'm an environmental-structural person. I try to structure the environment so we don't run into problems" (Holden, 1983, p. 238). Such situational management is an especially important form of parental control. Through situational management, parents keep control without provoking conflicts.

***Ineffective Parental Control, and Power Assertion***   The ineffective forms of parental control are, in part, the opposite of the effective forms. For example, setting high expectations for children's behavior but not giving them the training necessary to meet these expectations does not contribute to successful socialization. High expectations without adequate training leads to harsh but pointless punishment, because punishment by itself will not teach children how to do what their parents expect.

One form of punishment deserves special attention because it is both commonly used and often ineffective. Power assertive discipline, or **power assertion,** is the use of physical punishment, force, or deprivation of privileges to control behavior and punish misbehavior (Hoffman, 1970). The way Manyara's mother treated him is an example of power-assertive discipline. So are spanking, slapping, and threatening to do these things.

When parents use power assertion, they rely on their ability to punish their child and on the child's fear of punishment. They explain neither the reasons for rules nor the reasons for punishment. Therefore, they miss opportunities to increase their child's understanding of rules and to promote the development of self-control based on that understanding. By choosing power-assertive discipline, parents say, in effect, "You have to obey this rule because I said so, and you'll be punished if you don't."

Parents often use power assertion because they want to express their anger toward their children in a physical way. They may also believe they should hit or spank a child whose misbehavior has angered them. Moreover, they may believe that power assertion is an effective technique of socialization (Patterson, 1982).

Parents can, on occasion, get more immediate obedience from children when they use power assertion than when they reason with their children (Lytton & Zwirner, 1975), so power assertion can be effective, in the short term. Even its short-term effectiveness is not guaranteed, however. In one study, 2-year-olds were more defiant toward their mothers when their mothers used power-assertive discipline than when they made suggestions or attempted to persuade them to do something (Crockenberg & Litman, 1990). The defiant 2-year-olds either said no when asked to do something or did exactly the opposite of what they were asked to do.

In the long term, power assertion has consistently negative effects. Children whose parents rely on power assertion as the primary mode of discipline are relatively lacking in internal standards for behavior. They obey rules if they think they will be punished if they don't; they break rules when they think they won't get caught (Hoffman & Saltzstein, 1967). These children are under control only when a powerful adult is present.

Children whose parents rely on power assertion are often low in self-esteem and high in aggressive behavior (Maccoby, 1980; Whiting & Whiting, 1975). In particular, parents who more often use physical punishment have elementary-school children who are more often aggressive toward peers and who more often misbehave in the classroom (Dodge, Pettit, & Bates, 1994). The parents' punishment does not reduce these problems: These children become more aggressive over time (Weiss et al., 1992).

Why does power-assertive discipline have such negative effects on children's development? Many answers to these questions can be given (Hoffman, 1970; Patterson, 1982). One answer derives from **attribution theory** (Lepper, 1983), which suggests that people's attributions about the causes of their behavior strongly affect their later behavior. Two people who behave similarly at one time will differ in their later behavior if they make different attributions about—or adopt different explanations for—their initial behavior.

Power-assertive discipline encourages children to attribute their good behavior to external causes. When parents use power-assertive discipline, children make the attribution, "I will obey my parents' rules in the future because I will get punished if I don't." Children who make such external attributions are likely to disobey their parents' rules whenever they think they won't get punished.

Children attribute their good behavior to internal causes when their parents avoid power-assertive discipline and, instead, explain how obeying the rules helps the child or other people. Children then make an attribution like, "I will obey my parents' rules in the future because I would hurt myself or other people if I didn't." Children who make such internal

**power assertion**
*The use of physical punishment, force, or deprivation of privileges to control behavior and punish misbehavior. A negative aspect of parental control.*

**attribution theory**
*A social-psychological theory that emphasizes the effects of people's attributions about the causes of their behavior on their later behavior.*

attributions often follow the rules even when their parents are absent because they know why the rules exist.

A second explanation for the negative effects of power assertion derives from social learning theory (Bandura, 1986; Grusec & Goodnow, 1994). Children subjected to this kind of discipline see that their parents hit other people (i.e., themselves or their siblings) when they are angry. Children who use their parents as models for their own behavior will conclude that they, too, can hit other people when those people make them angry. Not surprisingly, using physical punishment when children are aggressive does not reduce their aggression and may increase it (Parke & Slaby, 1983).

A third explanation refers to the balance of power in families. Several researchers have suggested that children are most willing to obey their parents when they view their parents as sharing control with them (Lewis, 1981; Maccoby & Martin, 1983). Parents have more power than their children, so parents usually give commands to children, while children usually address requests to parents. Yet children may be most ready to comply with parents' commands when their parents most often comply with their requests. This shared control — you give a little, I give a little — is associated with harmony in family life. Shared control also increases young children's obedience to their parents (Crockenberg & Litman, 1990).

Of course, even the best-behaved children are not always obedient. In all families, parents must occasionally exert control over their children. Children normally benefit from such firm parental control (Baumrind, 1983). They benefit most when parents use the alternative to power-assertive discipline about which you will read next.

***Effective Discipline Through Induction or Reasoning***   Martin Hoffman (1970) defined **inductive discipline** as that in which parents give explanations or reasons for requiring children to change their behavior. According to Hoffman, reasons that point out the harmful effects of children's behaviors on other people are especially effective. Hoffman also defined a form of discipline called **love withdrawal,** in which parents directly express their anger or disapproval of children's behavior by refusing to speak with them, threatening to leave them, or otherwise showing a lack of affection. However, few researchers have examined the effects of love withdrawal, because early studies suggested that it has only weak and inconsistent relations to children's behavior (Maccoby & Martin, 1983).

Inductive discipline, on the other hand, has often been linked to obedience and positive behaviors by children (Grusec & Goodnow, 1994; Hoffman, 1970; Maccoby & Martin, 1983). The links are stronger for middle-class than for working-class children, although the explanation for this difference is unknown. The types of reasoning included in the category of inductive discipline also vary greatly. At one extreme, parents may explain in detail how a child's misbehavior has hurt or could hurt another person. At the other extreme, parents may simply say that the child's misbehavior violated a rule (e.g., "Don't take things that belong to someone else").

Variations in types of reasoning are crucial to the effectiveness of inductive discipline. Socialization proceeds most successfully when two conditions are met (Grusec & Goodnow, 1994). First, children must accurately perceive parents' messages about how they should behave. Accurate perception depends on many factors, starting with whether parents state their messages in terms their children can understand. For example, a message adequate for a 5-year-old would rarely be adequate for a 2-year-old. In addition, messages cannot be perceived accurately unless they are delivered when children are paying attention and parents show that the message is important to them.

Second, having perceived the parents' message, children must accept it. Children are more likely to accept messages that they view as appropriate to a specific situation. Also, children are more motivated to accept parents' messages when they have a highly positive relationship with their parents. Acceptance is even more likely when a message increases children's feelings that they are *not* obeying because of external pressure. Such a message increases the chances that children will attribute their obedience to internal causes.

Finally, you should realize that different types of discipline are not mutually exclusive. Sometimes the effectiveness of inductive discipline can be enhanced by combining it with

**inductive discipline**
*The use of reasons when disciplining children, especially reasons that point out the harmful effects of the children's actions on other people.*

**love withdrawal**
*Parents directly express their anger or disapproval of children's behavior by refusing to speak with them, threatening to leave them, or otherwise showing a lack of affection.*

small amounts of power assertion (Grusec & Goodnow, 1994; Hoffman, 1970). Induction makes the parents' message easy to perceive accurately; a small amount of power assertion makes children more attentive to, and more motivated to accept, the message. These goals may also be achieved, however, by the calculated use of irony, humor, or drama when disciplining children. Parents who think carefully about how best to discipline their children are most likely to have control and to accelerate their children's progress toward self-control.

## Involvement

More attention has been given to the dimensions of warmth and control than to the dimension of parental involvement (Maccoby & Martin, 1983). **Involvement** can be defined in terms of parents' attitudes and behavior. In attitudes, highly involved parents are child centered. They are interested in their children's lives and unwilling to put their own needs and desires ahead of their children's. Highly involved parents also take time to interact with their children. These frequent interactions are a behavioral sign of their involvement.

In theory, involvement does not overlap with the other two dimensions of parenting. Highly involved parents could be warm and accepting or cold and rejecting when they interact with their children. These parents could be high or low in control (Maccoby & Martin, 1983).

In reality, high involvement is usually linked to warmth and the positive aspects of control (Conger, Conger, et al., 1992, 1993; Franz et al., 1991). One important facet of warmth is a parent's responsiveness to a child's needs. Parents who are uninvolved, who spend little time with their children, cannot be highly responsive because they are often absent when their children are in need. Similarly, one positive aspect of control, consistent enforcement of rules, depends on frequent monitoring of a child's behavior. Uninvolved parents cannot do this monitoring.

Children suffer when their parents are not involved. Parents who spend little time with their children, who place their desires ahead of their children's needs, often have children who are impulsive and aggressive. Adolescents with uninvolved parents are often delinquent, prone to alcohol abuse, and lacking in long-term goals (Maccoby & Martin, 1983; Patterson, 1982). Gerald Patterson (1982) suggested that uninvolved parents seem unattached to their children because they *are* parents but do not *want* to be parents. He also noted that children develop less successfully when their parents are unwilling to make a commitment to parenting.

## Other Theoretical Perspectives on Parenting

Most researchers who study children's socialization have relied on some form of the dimensional approach. That is, they have examined the effects on children of variations in parents' warmth, control, and involvement. However, alternative approaches exist that derive from important theoretical perspectives. As you read about the alternative approaches, think about how they add to, or complement, the dimensional approach.

## Baumrind's Patterns of Parental Authority

Diana Baumrind (1971, 1973, 1991) has argued for a focus not on single dimensions of parenting but on patterns of parent-child interactions. Her special emphasis is on how parents exert their control or authority over their children. She began by identifying parents who are highly controlling or demanding. Among this group, parents differ in how much they encourage their children's independence and individuality. They also differ in their level of warmth or responsiveness.

**Authoritative** parents exert firm control and encourage their children's independence. These parents are consistent in their enforcement of rules and value obedience by their children. They expect mature behavior from their children, but they also recognize their children's rights. Therefore, they allow their children some independence and are willing to reason with them about rules and demands. In addition, they are high in warmth or responsiveness.

**Authoritarian** parents are highly controlling but do not encourage their children's independence. Like authoritative parents, they are consistent in enforcing rules, but they value order and obedience as ends in themselves. Authoritarian parents are unwilling to discuss

**involvement**
*The dimension of parenting that focuses on the amount of time that parents spend in interaction with their children and the degree to which their attitudes are child centered.*

**authoritative**
*A parenting style that includes firm control with high warmth and encouragement of children's independence. Authoritative parents value obedience and expect mature behavior from their children, but they are also willing to reason with them about rules.*

**authoritarian**
*A parenting style that includes firm control, low warmth, and little encouragement of children's independence. Authoritarian parents value unquestioning obedience. They assume that children should just do what they are told.*

FIGURE 11.3
A classification of parenting patterns in terms of the dimensions of warmth and control. (Adapted from Maccoby & Martin, 1983.)

| | | Responsiveness (warmth) | |
|---|---|---|---|
| | | High | Low |
| Demandingness | High | Authoritative | Authoritarian |
| (control) | Low | Permissive | Rejecting-neglecting |

**permissive**
*A parenting style marked by low parental control and lax enforcement of rules but high warmth.*

**rejecting-neglecting**
*A parenting style marked by low parental control and low warmth or responsiveness.*

rules with their children. They assume that children should just do what they are told. In addition, they are low in warmth or responsiveness.

Differences also exist among parents who are low in control. **Permissive** parents set few restrictions on their children's behavior. These parents are lax in enforcing rules, rarely expect their children to help in household chores, and rarely direct their children's behavior. However, they are high in warmth or responsiveness.

**Rejecting-neglecting** parents exert little control over their children and are low in warmth or responsiveness. This combination reflects low involvement in childrearing. Some parents in this group are so lacking in involvement that their children suffer from neglect.

As figure 11.3 shows, Baumrind's four parenting patterns can be defined in terms of the warmth and control dimensions. To examine the effects of these patterns, Baumrind did a longitudinal study with more than 100 children and their parents. When the children were 4 years of age, they and their parents were interviewed and observed at nursery school and at home. The full assessment took about 50 hours for each family. Similar assessments were done when the children were 9 years old, and again when they were 15.

At all ages, children with authoritative parents showed the most desirable behavior. They had good relationships with peers and adults. They were usually cheerful and self-reliant. In adolescence, they showed a high level of social competence and rarely had problems with drug abuse. Other researchers have confirmed that adolescents with authoritative parents are higher in competence, achievement, and psychological adjustment than those who experience other patterns of parenting (Lamborn et al., 1991).

The preschoolers in Baumrind's study who had authoritarian parents were less well adjusted and showed less independence than those with authoritative parents. At age 4, boys with authoritarian parents were somewhat hostile and resistant to authority. Adolescents with authoritarian parents tend to be high in obedience to adults but low in self-esteem (Lamborn et al., 1991). In addition, they have lower academic achievement than adolescents with authoritative parents (Steinberg et al., 1994).

The preschoolers with permissive parents also showed poorer psychological adjustment than those with authoritative parents. Adolescents with permissive parents have high self-esteem but are also high in drug use and misconduct at school (Lamborn et al., 1991). Moreover, their misconduct increases during the high school years (Steinberg et al., 1994).

Finally, both Baumrind and other researchers have reported the poorest psychological profile for children with rejecting-neglecting parents. These children are low in social competence. In adolescence, they are likely to have problems with drug use and to engage often in delinquent behavior (Baumrind, 1991; Lamborn et al., 1991; Steinberg et al., 1994).

Some researchers have found that Asian American parents seem more authoritarian than European American parents (Dornbusch et al., 1987). Ruth Chao (1994) suggests that this cultural difference exists because Baumrind's parenting patterns ignore important differences between Asian and Western culture. She suggests that Asian parents view firm control and careful training as a reflection of their concern and love for their children. For Asians, then, a high level of firm control may not reflect the demand for unquestioning obedience and the rigid rules that are part of Baumrind's definition of authoritarian parenting.

Nevertheless, findings from several large samples suggest that the effects of the four parenting patterns are similar for Asian American and European American children and adolescents (Rowe, Vazsonyi, & Flannery, 1994; Steinberg et al., 1994). Asian Americans with authoritative parents are higher in achievement and in psychological adjustment than Asian Americans with authoritarian parents. The same is true for African American and Hispanic American groups. In other words, the effects of parenting patterns do not vary greatly across ethnic groups. Likewise, these effects do not vary greatly with age or for boys and girls.

You might ask, though, why parenting patterns are examined at all. If each pattern is defined by positions on the warmth and control dimensions, why not focus only on these dimensions? The analysis of two separate dimensions is often simpler than an analysis of four patterns. Nevertheless, the description of parenting patterns is valuable. Baumrind's patterns make salient the combination of behaviors that is most strongly linked to effective socialization. That combination, found in the authoritative pattern, includes the exercise of firm but appropriate control by warm and responsive parents.

## Social Learning Theories of Parenting

One drawback of the approaches to parenting discussed so far is their generality. When researchers say a parent is warm, for example, they don't say exactly how the parent behaves in specific situations. Social learning theorists look at parenting much more specifically (Bandura, 1977b, 1986; Patterson, 1982). They would not ask how warm parents are, but which behaviors parents positively reinforce. They would not ask how controlling parents are, but which behaviors parents punish and which kinds of punishment parents use. They would not ask how involved parents are, but which behaviors parents model for their children. These theorists emphasize the influence of positive reinforcement, punishment, and observational learning on children's socialization.

*Positive Reinforcement*    The effects of positive reinforcement are most obvious when parents reinforce behaviors not considered desirable in the larger society. For example, some parents actively encourage their children to behave aggressively toward their peers (Dodge et al., 1994). In a classic study (Bandura & Walters, 1959), the father of one aggressive boy was asked whether he ever urged his son to use his fists to defend himself. He replied, "Yes, if necessary. I told him many times that if someone wanted to fight with him and started the old idea of the chip on the shoulder, 'Don't hit the chip, hit his jaw, and get it over with.'" Then the father was asked whether his son ever complained that another boy was giving him a rough time. The father said, "Yes," and reported his advice to his son: "I told him to hit him" (p. 115).

When the same boy's mother was asked whether she ever urged her son to use his fists to defend himself, she replied, "Oh yes. Oh yes. He knows how to fight." In answer to the question about another boy giving him a rough time, the mother said, "I told him, 'Go on out and fight it out yourself'" (pp. 115–116). Other mothers of aggressive boys said they told their sons they would spank them if they didn't fight to defend themselves. Parents of nonaggressive adolescents rarely encouraged their sons to be aggressive. These differences in parents' reinforcement of aggression partly explain the differences in their children's aggressive behavior.

Of course, reinforcement can also be used to increase the rate of desirable behaviors. One component of most behavior-modification programs is the systematic use of reinforcement for positive behaviors (e.g., Bank et al., 1991; O'Leary & Wilson, 1987). Before beginning such a program, therapists talk with children and their parents about which behaviors they would like to encourage and discourage. Then the therapists write a formal contract with parents and children, specifying the rewards children will receive for changing their behavior in the desired ways. This form of **contracting** is an essential element of the social learning approach to behavior change.

**contracting**
*The process of writing a formal agreement between parents and children that specifies the rewards the children will receive if they change their behavior in desired ways.*

*Punishment: Effects and Side Effects*    To reduce the frequency of undesirable behaviors, punishment is often necessary and effective. Experimental studies in laboratory settings have shown that children learn not to play with attractive toys if they are punished with a loud

The little girl in this picture is getting an early lesson in social action from her mother. From their parents, children learn—or don't learn—that they can take part in political campaigns and work to improve society.

buzzer when they touch the toys (Parke, 1977). Even after the punishment phase of the experiment is over, children are likely to avoid toys that they have been punished for touching.

Unfortunately, laboratory studies suggest more positive effects of punishment than are found outside the laboratory. Parents who more often punish their children do not necessarily have better-behaved children. In some studies, more punitive parents have children who are more antisocial, more aggressive, or more delinquent than other children (Patterson, 1982). That was certainly true with the Gusii parents in Nyansongo. What's going wrong?

You learned earlier that power-assertive discipline can make children focus on whether they will be punished, not why an act is wrong. Experimental studies may not show this negative side effect of punishment because children in a laboratory probably assume any misbehavior will be caught and punished.

Remember, too, that inductive discipline is more effective than power assertion. Experimental studies confirm this conclusion. Children in laboratory experiments are less likely to touch forbidden toys when they are told why they should not touch those toys (Parke, 1977). Like anyone else, children are more likely to do what is right and avoid what is wrong when they know why one is right and the other is wrong. Because highly punitive parents often fail to explain why they punish, their punishments are often ineffective.

Highly punitive parents often break other "rules" for effective punishment. They may be highly inconsistent, sometimes ignoring misbehavior altogether and sometimes severely punishing mild forms of misbehavior (Patterson, 1982; Vuchinich, Bank, & Patterson, 1992). Again, laboratory studies suggest that inconsistent punishment is ineffective or even counterproductive. Undesirable behavior is likely to increase if punishment is delivered inconsistently (Parke, 1977).

What should a parent do? Social learning theorists agree that misbehavior must be punished. However, the type and conditions of punishment must be carefully chosen. Gerald Patterson (1982) said: "If I were allowed to select only one concept to use in training parents of antisocial children, I would teach them how to punish more effectively" (p. 111). Patterson's recommendations for effective punishment are presented later, along with the discussion of coercive behavior in families.

***Observational Learning from Parent Models***    Children's behavior can be strongly affected by watching someone else's behavior. In a classic experiment (Bandura et al., 1963), young

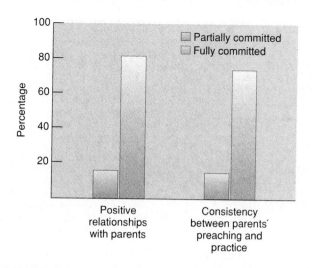

## FIGURE 11.4

When are children and adults most likely to make a full commitment to prosocial behavior? A full commitment is most likely when a person has positive relationships with parents who model prosocial behavior. Children and adults who lack positive relationships with parents, or whose parents' preaching is not consistent with their practice, often commit themselves only partially to prosocial behavior toward others. (Source: Rosenhan, 1970.)

children watched a short film in which an adult attacked a large, inflated "Bobo" clown. When the children were placed in a room with the same toy, they behaved more aggressively toward the Bobo clown than did children who had not seen the film.

Throughout childhood and adolescence, parents are important models for their children. Observational learning from parents was demonstrated most vividly in a study of civil rights workers during the 1960s (Rosenhan, 1970). The adults interviewed for the study differed in their level of commitment to the civil rights movement. The "partially committed" had gone on only one or two freedom rides. The "fully committed" had been continuously active for a year or more on projects such as voter registration and the education of poor children.

The two groups of adults differed in their relationships to their parents and their perceptions of their parents' behavior, as figure 11.4 shows. Most of the fully committed civil rights workers viewed their parents positively. They had a warm relationship with their parents based on mutual respect. Few of the partially committed workers had such positive relationships with parents. They described these relationships as hostile, avoidant, or ambivalent.

Both groups of adults said that their parents often expressed concern about social justice and other moral issues. However, the two groups differed in the match between the parents' talk and their action. The parents of the fully committed adolescents were models of prosocial behavior. They had devoted their lives to activities that contributed to people's welfare or justice in society (see figure 11.4). The parents of the partially committed were, by contrast, models of hypocrisy. They talked about how people should treat other people but did not act in the same way. Their preaching was not consistent with their practice.

So what did the two groups of adults learn from their parents' example? The fully committed learned from their parents' words and deeds that they should respond to the needs of other people and act to protect people's rights. Because they had such positive relationships with their parents, they willingly chose their parents' lives as models for their own. The partially committed learned to "talk a good line," that is, to discuss the value of working for civil rights but not to change their lives to match their words. They showed the inconsistency between words and deeds that their parents modeled.

**Negative Reinforcement and the Coercive Cycle**   Parents do not always notice how they influence their children's behavior. Parents often fall into what Gerald Patterson (1980) called the **negative reinforcement trap,** illustrated in figure 11.5.

**negative reinforcement trap**
*Interactions between a parent and a child that end when each person provides negative reinforcement for the other's behavior. The interactions are described as a trap because each person inadvertently promotes the aversive behavior of the other.*

**FIGURE 11.5**

The negative reinforcement trap. A son's coercive behavior may have positive effects in the short term, but its long-term effects on family interaction are negative for all concerned. (From Patterson, 1980.)

**Negative reinforcement arrangement**

| | Time frame 1 | Time frame 2 | Time frame 3 |
|---|---|---|---|
| Behavior: | Mother ("clean your room") | Child (whine) | Mother (stops asking) |

| | Short-term effect | Long-term effect |
|---|---|---|
| Mother | The pain (child's whine) stops | Mother will be more likely to give in when child whines |
| Child | The pain (mother's nag) stops | Given a messy room, mother less likely to ask him to clean it up in the future |
| Overall | The room was not cleaned | Child more likely to use whine to turn off future requests to clean room |

**negative reinforcement**
*The removal (or termination) of a negative stimulus, which leads to an increase in the frequency of the preceding behavior.*

**coercive cycle**
*Interactions between a parent and a child in which each person uses coercive behavior, or negative reinforcement, to control the other's behavior. Called a cycle because the negative reinforcement contributes to an increase in coercive interactions.*

The top part of the figure is a schematic representation of an interaction between a mother and her son. The interaction begins when the mother asks her son to clean his room. Time Frame 2 shows the son's response: He argues, complains that she is picking on him, and, in short, whines. In Time Frame 3, the mother gives in and stops asking the child to clean the room.

There is nothing extraordinary about this interaction. Many children complain when their parents ask them to do chores. On occasion, the parents give in. But such interactions can have harmful effects on the children's future behavior and on parent-child relationships. The second part of the figure describes these effects.

Look first at the short-term effects. For the mother, the short-term effect is positive. She no longer has to listen to her son's whining because he stops whining when she stops asking him to clean the room. For the son, the short-term effect is also positive. His mother is no longer nagging him to clean his room. In the figure, both effects are labeled the same: The pain stops. This label is theoretically important. Both mother and son are trying to control the other by administering a painful or negative stimulus, nagging by the mother and whining by the son. The interaction ends with the removal of the negative stimulus.

Following B. F. Skinner, Patterson (1980) defined the removal of a negative stimulus as **negative reinforcement.** Negative reinforcement is different from punishment. It is, in a sense, the opposite of punishment. When you punish someone, you *deliver* a negative stimulus. In episodes of negative reinforcement, the interaction ends with the *removal* of a negative stimulus. Even more important, punishment reduces the frequency of the behavior it follows: People are less likely to do what they are punished for doing. Negative reinforcement, like its better-known counterpart, positive reinforcement, increases the frequency of the behavior it follows.

Look at the long-term effects of negative reinforcement on the mother's behavior. Because she stopped the child's whining by giving in, she is more likely to give in when the child whines in the future. Similarly, the son stopped the mother's nagging by whining, so he is more likely to whine in the future.

Figure 11.5 illustrates a negative reinforcement trap because the mother does not realize the trouble she is creating for herself when she surrenders to her son's whining. Of course, the son doesn't appreciate that he will become a more whiny, obnoxious child because his mother gave in to him this time. Both mother and son are involved in a **coercive cycle.** The son's use of whining to avoid chores is a form of coercion. By giving in, the mother strengthens the child's use of coercion to control her behavior.

Mothers are not willing to give in every time, however. If they really want their children to obey them, they increase the force they use. Thus, mothers of coercive children alternate between giving in and using extreme force (Dumas, Lafreniere, & Serketich, 1995).

This analysis of the coercive cycle illustrates the subtlety and precision of the social learning approach to parenting. The cycle was illustrated by a mother-son interaction because more coercion occurs between mothers and sons than between other family members. As a child's behavior becomes more coercive, fathers reduce their frequency of interaction with the child. Then the mother's role expands to include that of crisis manager (Patterson, 1980).

Fathers do not escape entirely, though. Coercive children direct high levels of negative behavior toward fathers and toward siblings as well as toward their mothers. The environment in these families is unpleasant for everyone.

### Family Management Skills

What can be done to prevent or reverse the coercive cycle? How can parents avoid the negative reinforcement trap? Four kinds of family management skills that parents need have been suggested (Patterson 1982; Patterson & Stouthamer-Loeber, 1984).

The first skill is being able to punish children's misbehavior consistently and effectively. As stated earlier, many parents of out-of-control children punish often and use severe physical punishment. However, their punishments are ineffective or counterproductive.

Parents can be trained in effective alternatives to physical punishment. One alternative is the **time-out.** Children who misbehave are told to sit by themselves in a quiet place, usually the bathroom, for three to five minutes. This is a punishment because the child must stop whatever he or she was doing.

The bathroom is often a suitable place for a time out because it seldom contains toys, books, television, or other reinforcers. The three- to five-minute interval is long enough to be unpleasant without being so long that parents will not enforce it consistently. Moreover, during that interval the parent's and the child's level of anger decline, so they can interact more positively when the time is up.

With adolescents, a time-out is less appropriate than other punishments (Bank et al., 1991). Some options include restriction of free time, assignments of chores, or the loss of points earned as part of a systematic contracting program. The purpose of these punishments is the same as with a time-out. Parents want to remove the adolescent from a reinforcing situation without doing something that has negative effects in the long term.

The second skill that parents need is being able to positively reinforce children's good behavior. Parents of coercive children rarely give praise or approval to their children. Because the children receive little positive reinforcement from parents, they have little motivation to comply with their parents' requests. Parents can be trained to reinforce good behavior systematically, and all behavior-modification programs include this kind of training.

The third skill is being able to monitor children's behavior. Parents must keep track of where their children are, who they are with, and what they are doing. Parents who don't monitor their children's behavior are not aware of the children's misbehavior and cannot reinforce their good behavior. As mentioned in chapter 2, poor monitoring by parents is a good predictor of the delinquent behavior of adolescent boys (Patterson & Stouthamer-Loeber, 1984). Thus monitoring is necessary not only in childhood but in adolescence, too.

The fourth skill is being able to resolve the problems that arise in family interaction. Parents of coercive children often have trouble talking about family problems in a calm, rational way. They must be trained to state the problem that needs to be solved in neutral rather than hostile terms. They must specify the behavior that they want their children to change, and negotiate with their children about different ways to solve the problem.

Social learning theorists focus on parent training because they assume that parents unintentionally create the conditions that lead to their children's problem behavior. Therefore, the children's behavior cannot be changed without the involvement and participation of parents. Parents often need guidance because they cannot always recognize subtle problems such as the negative reinforcement trap. With proper training, parents can be successful in dealing with problems as difficult as chronic delinquency (Banks et al., 1991).

**time-out**
*A form of punishment recommended by social learning theorists in which children are given a time away from all reinforcing activities and interactions for three to five minutes.*

Where is this girl going? What is she going to do? When will she be back? Adolescents are not always pleased to have their parents monitor their activities. But if monitoring is part of a pattern of warm, involved parenting, it can contribute to desirable behavior by adolescents.

This training does not always need to be done during individual meetings with a therapist. Several researchers have written books for parents that describe the social learning approach. One example, a book by Patterson, is listed with the suggested readings for this chapter.

## The Family Grows Up: Developments in Parent-Child Relationships

Parents do not treat infants in the same way as they treat preschool children. Parents do not treat elementary-school children in the same way as they treat adolescents. Parent-child interactions change as children grow, and so do the goals that their parents set for them (Maccoby, 1984).

In chapter 1 you read about Erikson's psychosocial stages. His stages for infancy, childhood, and adolescence can be matched with corresponding goals for parenting. These matches are shown in table 11.1. Like any description of developmental stages, this one cannot be taken too literally, but it does capture some important changes in the salient themes of parenting.

Parents of infants try mainly to respond to their needs, feeding and clothing them, trying to keep them safe from harm, and beginning to build a relationship with them. Infants' sense of basic trust is affected by the responsiveness their parents show toward them. Recall from chapter 6 that parents' responsiveness affects the security of infant-parent attachments.

During the second year of life, parents increase their attempts to control their children's behavior (Gralinski & Kopp, 1993). At first parents try to teach their toddlers which behaviors are safe and unsafe. For example, they tell toddlers not to put their hands near electrical sockets. Parents also teach their toddlers which social behaviors are acceptable and unacceptable. For example, they tell toddlers not to bite other children. Toddlers who are successfully socialized at this stage gain a sense of autonomy, in Erikson's terms. Toddlers who are not successfully socialized are likely to express shame and doubt about their own worth.

The gradual transition between infancy and early childhood is accompanied by gradually increasing demands for self-control (Gralinski & Kopp, 1993). Parents encourage children to share their toys freely, without being told. Parents encourage children to put away toys when they are finished playing, to walk instead of being carried, and to make their beds. Self-control that leads to greater independence can result, according to Erikson, in a sense of initiative. Lack of self-control can lead to guilt.

## TABLE 11.1    *Changes in Psychosocial Stages and in Parenting*

| AGE PERIOD | ERIKSON'S PSYCHOSOCIAL STAGE | A MAJOR GOAL OF PARENTING |
|---|---|---|
| Infancy | Basic trust vs. mistrust | Responsiveness to infants' needs |
| Toddlerhood | Autonomy vs. shame and doubt | Controlling children's behavior |
| Early childhood | Initiative vs. guilt | Fostering self-control |
| Middle childhood | Industry vs. inferiority | Promoting achievement (e.g., in school) |
| Adolescence | Identity vs. role confusion | Encouraging individuality with continuing connections |

The emphasis of parents on fostering self-control is also shown by changes in their techniques for controlling their children (Kuczynski et al., 1987). Mothers of 1-year-olds often take control with a simple act. Instead of saying, "wash your face," they simply wash the toddler's face themselves.

By contrast, mothers of 3-year-olds act less and talk more. They tell children what they want them to do. They may also give children reasons for their commands (e.g., "You can't play with this because it will break too easily"). Sometimes mothers will bargain with their children ("Eat two more bites and then you can leave"). These behaviors show that mothers recognize their children's growing cognitive sophistication. They also suggest that mothers want to build self-control by getting children to agree to do something rather than forcing them.

Middle childhood brings a transition to school life and a new concern with academic achievement. As discussed in chapter 10, most parents try to promote their children's achievement by monitoring the children's work and helping on difficult assignments. Children's success on their schoolwork affects whether they view themselves positively, in Erikson's sense of *industry*, or they start to believe in their inferiority.

In two-parent families, mothers interact more with school-age children than fathers do, just as was true in infancy and early childhood (Collins & Russell, 1991; Russell & Russell, 1987). Fathers show special concern with their children's achievement. Fathers also spend time in play or recreation with their children. Mothers' interactions with their children may involve the same kinds of work and play, but more than fathers, mothers also talk with their children about problems in social relationships. In addition, mothers talk more with children about the chores they should be doing around the house.

As children move into adolescence, family relationships change dramatically. Many adolescents want more independence and earlier independence than their parents think is good for them. Many parents want more control over their adolescents than their adolescents want to give them. Disagreements between adolescents and parents about the proper balance of independence and control often create conflicts.

Imagine that you are watching an adolescent boy, his mother, and his father plan a weekend trip to a nearby city (Steinberg, 1981). They are trying to decide what to do during the afternoon and where to have dinner. As you watch, you notice that the boy has not yet gone through puberty. He still has the round face of a young boy instead of the more squared-off face of an adult.

Several months later, you observe the same family again. Now the boy has started to go through puberty. His face has changed, and he has the awkward gait of a pubertal adolescent. After several more months, you return for a third time. Now the boy is nearly through puberty. He has some facial hair, a coordinated and adultlike gait, and the fully defined muscles of an adult male.

If you watch carefully, you will also see that the family's conversations change as the boy moves through puberty. In particular, conflicts between the adolescent and his parents increase. For example, the adolescent and his parents start to interrupt each other more often. Conflicts decline, to a degree, as the adolescent moves through the peak of puberty to its end (Steinberg, 1988).

"Dad, can I have the keys to the car tonight?" As adolescents move through puberty, their power in the family increases. They also expect their parents to give them more privileges, like driving the family car. Adolescents gain power partly at the expense of their mothers. Notice how father and son take center stage in this photograph, with the mother in the background looking on.

Don't assume, though, that the decline in conflicts means a return to the family system that existed before puberty. The decline coincides with an important shift in family power. As adolescent boys move through puberty, they gain greater influence over family decisions—at the expense of their mothers. For example, adolescent boys continue to interrupt their mothers as they move toward maturity. Their mothers, by contrast, begin to defer to them.

The changes in parent-daughter relationships around puberty are similar but not identical to those for sons. As mentioned in chapter 5, the central pubertal event for adolescent girls is menarche. Figure 11.6 shows that disagreements with mothers increase until about one year after menarche (Holmbeck & Hill, 1991). One reason for the increase may be mothers' concern about their daughters' sexuality and, perhaps, the threat that the daughters' sexuality poses to their own sexual identity. One consequence of these disagreements is an increase in the daughters' influence on family decisions. As for sons, this increase seems to be linked to a decrease in mothers' influence (Steinberg, 1988). Once this change has occurred, mother-daughter disagreements decrease.

Another shift after puberty is toward greater emotional distancing between parents and their adolescents (Collins & Russell, 1991; Holmbeck & Hill, 1991). As adolescents become more physically mature, they report less closeness to parents. The decline in closeness may be a consequence of the conflicts that occur during the pubertal period. To avoid these conflicts, adolescents and parents may decide to draw apart from each other.

Drawing apart may not be entirely a bad thing. Adolescents should begin to prepare for independent living, away from their parents. Several researchers have suggested that the growing distance between adolescents and parents is a healthy response to adolescents' growing maturity that makes it easier for them to move toward independent living (Holmbeck & Hill, 1991; Steinberg, 1988).

Other researchers have a different view of the changes in adolescent-parent relationships (Grotevant & Cooper, 1985; Youniss, 1980; Youniss & Smollar, 1985). They agree that adolescents must begin to think of themselves as independent individuals rather than as their parents' children, but they argue that becoming an individual does not mean cutting the bonds between adolescents and parents. In the most healthy pattern of development, growing independence is balanced by connectedness, continued feelings of closeness between adolescents and parents.

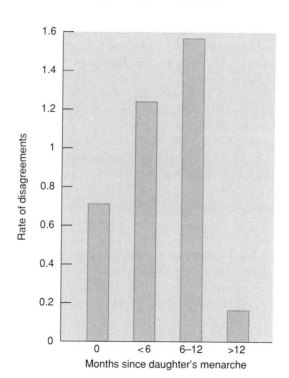

FIGURE 11.6

The rate of disagreements between mothers and daughters increases during the year after menarche. After that year, disagreements become less frequent, apparently because daughters have gained—and their mothers have lost—influence on family decisions. (Data from Holmbeck & Hill, 1991.)

Remember that infants form attachments to their parents during the first year of life. These attachments do not fade away. They remain important during childhood, adolescence, and adulthood (Ainsworth, 1989; Main et al., 1985). In infancy, a secure attachment involves a balance between physical closeness that provides security and physical distance that allows exploration. As children grow, this balance shifts further toward independent exploration. From one theoretical perspective, this shift reflects the process of individuation. Still, even adolescents rely on their parents for advice and support (Youniss & Smollar, 1985). Their development continues to depend on their family relationships.

Too much independence early in adolescence can be risky. In one longitudinal study (Feldman & Wood, 1994) the fathers of 11-year-olds were asked when they expected their sons to begin doing things like going to rock concerts and drinking beer. Fathers who expected to grant this kind of independence at younger ages had sons who, at age 15, put less effort into their schoolwork, received lower grades, and more often reported having had multiple sex partners. Perhaps these boys would have been better off if their fathers had slowed their progress toward adult activities.

As table 11.1 shows, Erikson viewed the task of adolescence as the achievement of identity. He assumed that the primary risk in adolescence was role confusion, uncertainty about current and future positions in society. Parents make their most positive contribution to identity achievement when they encourage their adolescents' striving for identity while maintaining close relationships with them.

## Parents and Children: Who Is Socializing Whom?

In the previous sections, a few experimental studies of socialization were given special attention. Those studies were emphasized because their experimental design is unusual. Most researchers have used correlational designs to assess parents' contributions to their children's socialization. That is, researchers have assessed some aspect of parenting, measured children's attitudes or behaviors, and then examined the relations between the two.

At several points in this book, but most directly in chapter 2, you read that firm conclusions about cause and effect cannot be drawn from correlational studies. Strictly speaking, a correlational design can only show whether two variables are related. Such a design cannot conclusively show which variable is the cause and which is the effect.

For many years, researchers assumed that they knew the causal direction in studies of socialization. They assumed that variations in parents' behavior cause variations in their children's behavior. For example, they assumed that children are more prosocial when their parents are warmer toward them.

Could the causal arrow go in the opposite direction? Could children's behavior affect their parents' behavior? Indeed, it could, and it does (Bell & Chapman, 1986; Dumas et al., 1995). Researchers have used several experimental designs to show the effects of children on parents. For example, one team of researchers identified a group of 6- to 11-year-old boys with serious conduct problems (Anderson, Lytton, & Romney, 1986). The boys were truants, set fires, were highly aggressive, or often threw temper tantrums. The researchers identified another group of boys with only a normal level of behavior problems.

Both groups were observed as they interacted in a laboratory playroom with their mothers and with the mother of a boy from the other group. The boys with conduct problems were more disobedient during these interactions, whether they were interacting with their mother or another boy's mother. By contrast, the mothers of boys with conduct problems interacted as positively with normal boys as did the mothers of normal boys. Thus, mothers adapted to the behavior of their partners and boys did not. These findings suggest that the boys influenced the behavior of their mothers and other boys' mothers more than vice versa.

Findings like these have suggested to some researchers that conduct problems in childhood are due more to children's genetic predisposition than to their parents' treatment of them (Lytton, 1990). In chapter 3 you learned that other researchers have drawn the same conclusion about most of children's social behaviors and personality traits, suggesting that these behaviors and traits are influenced more by children's nature than by their nurture (Scarr, 1992, 1993). More specifically, these researchers have concluded that parents have little influence on their children's socialization.

You may recall from chapter 3 that other researchers strongly reject this conclusion (Baumrind, 1993; Hoffman, 1983; Jackson, 1993). These researchers argue that children typically have limited control over their parents' behavior. Parents often try to change their children's behavior, and they are usually successful when they do. Children less often try to change their parents' behavior, and they often fail when they do. Moreover, parents vary in their reactions to the same behavior by a child. Some parents tolerate behaviors that other parents find unacceptable and try to change (Baumrind, 1993; Hoffman, 1991; Maccoby & Martin, 1983). In short, children do not totally determine how their parents treat them. Therefore, it makes sense to assume that differences between children are partly due to differences in parenting (Dodge, 1990; Wahler, 1990).

In summary, the most reasonable resolution of this controversy is to accept the transactional model mentioned in chapter 4. That model allows for the effects of both nature and nurture. More specifically, children's behavior is influenced by their genotypes and by their parents' interactions with them. Stated differently, a family with parents and children involves a system of relationships, and children's socialization depends on the reciprocal influences of each person in the system on every other person (Rothbaum & Weisz, 1994).

# SISTERS AND BROTHERS

Most families include not just one child but two or more. These children often interact with one another. Parents also direct, and respond to, the siblings' interactions. All these interactions have a profound influence on the entire family system. Consequently, they can have a great impact on each child's development.

By 1 year of age, infants spend more time with their siblings than with their fathers. Once they enter the preschool years, children spend more time with their siblings than with either parent (Dunn, 1983). The many hours that siblings spend together suggest that these relationships are highly significant. To understand how sibling relationships might affect children, you need to know more about the features of these relationships.

# Developments in Sibling Relationships

Siblings love each other. Siblings hate each other. Both these statements are true, to varying degrees, in all sibling relationships. Ambivalence, or a mixture of positive and negative feelings, is typical of sibling relationships throughout life. This ambivalence is apparent very early, in older siblings' initial reactions to their newborn brothers and sisters. Judy Dunn (1985, p. 10) observed a young child who caressed her new brother while saying in a comforting voice, "All right, baby." In the next breath, the child told her mother, "Smack him."

## Infants and Preschool-Age Siblings

The ambivalence in sibling relationships is obvious very early. On the one hand, older siblings often react positively toward a new baby brother or sister. They try to feed and comfort the new baby. They also watch how their parents care for their new brother or sister, and they try to act like their parents do. New babies, in turn, become attached to their older brothers and sisters just as they become attached to their parents.

To measure sibling attachments, some researchers have used the Strange Situation described in chapter 6 (e.g., Stewart, 1983). When their mother leaves the room during the Strange Situation, most older siblings try to calm a 1-year-old brother or sister. Most 1-year-olds are reassured by their siblings and resume their play with toys until their mother returns to the room.

On the other hand, older siblings sometimes react negatively to a new baby brother or sister. Often, these negative reactions seem to spring from jealousy, as Manyara's mother in Nyansongo suspected. Older siblings resent no longer being the sole focus of their parents' attention. Therefore, problem behaviors most often occur when a mother is showing affection for her newborn baby. For example, one young boy saw his mother gazing at his baby sister in an especially loving way. The boy then took his cup of milk to the sofa and, while looking at his mother, began to sprinkle the milk on the sofa (Dunn, 1985).

How much jealousy older siblings show toward a new baby in the family is not strongly related to the siblings' age. Although children over 5 years of age seem less jealous than do children under 5, siblings in most families are less than five years apart. Popular writings for parents often include advice about the ideal spacing of siblings, but the research data do not support any specific recommendation. Behavior problems after the birth of a new sibling occur about as often when siblings are spaced two, three, or four years apart (Dunn, 1985; Stewart et al., 1987).

As a new sibling grows older, the negative reactions of older brothers and sisters change in intensity. During the first month after a sibling's birth, older brothers and sisters often show increased crying and clinging. If the older siblings were toilet-trained before the baby's birth, they may begin to have toilet accidents. These behaviors could be seen as regression, the older siblings' return to a more immature phase of development. Another possibility is that the older siblings are trying to get their mothers' attention. Most mothers greatly decrease their interactions with their firstborn children when they have a new baby. Older siblings may try to get their mothers to interact with them by showing that they are upset and in need of comfort (Stewart et al., 1987).

Older siblings' anxiety over the loss of their mothers' attention, and their imitation of infant behaviors such as crying and clinging, decrease during their younger sibling's first year of life. However, as the younger sibling starts to move about independently, conflicts between younger and older siblings become more frequent. These conflicts reach a peak when the younger sibling is about 8 months of age and then begin to decline (Stewart et al., 1987).

Preschool children's adjustment after the birth of a younger sibling is affected by their parents' behavior (Dunn, 1985). Older siblings have fewer behavior problems when their mothers give them more attention after the baby's birth. Mothers can also encourage their older children to help with the baby, thus including the older children in mother-infant interactions. When mothers must give all their attention to the baby, they can reduce conflicts by giving their older child things to do. For example, when some mothers are preparing to breast-feed their babies, they give their older child drinks, snacks, books, or

crayons and paper before they start. (This example should remind you of the earlier discussion of situational management.)

In addition, fathers can help to improve a preschooler's adjustment to a new sibling. Fathers can offset the reduction in mother-child interaction by maintaining a high rate of interaction with their preschooler (Stewart et al., 1987). Fathers' involvement with the preschooler may have lasting positive effects on sibling relationships. Their affection toward firstborns at age 3 is related to the frequency of positive interactions between firstborns and their younger siblings at age 6 (Volling & Belsky, 1992).

In summary, parents who are responsive to an older sibling's needs for attention and stimulation not only reduce behavior problems by that child but also help the child form a better relationship with a new brother or sister. Again, you see that families are systems in which each relationship affects all other relationships.

## Sibling Relationships in Childhood and Adolescence

As children grow older, the mixture of positive and negative interactions between siblings continues. Differences in the maturity of older and younger siblings also continue to affect their interactions. Older brothers and sisters have more power and greater competence than their younger siblings. This inequality in sibling relationships is obvious in both positive and negative interactions.

One team of researchers studied pairs of siblings longitudinally (Abramovitch et al., 1986). They first observed the sibling pairs when the younger one was 1½ years old and the older one was either 3 or 4½ years old. Eighteen months later, they observed the sibling pairs again. After another 24 months, they observed the pairs for a third time. By this time, the younger siblings were 5 years old and the older ones were either 6½ or 8 years old.

At each time observers recorded the siblings' interactions at home for one or two hours. The observers recorded all prosocial behaviors such as sharing, helping, and comforting. They also recorded all conflicts and aggressive behaviors such as hitting, teasing, and fighting over toys. Finally, they noted cases in which one sibling imitated the other's behavior.

Figure 11.7 shows that prosocial behavior by each sibling was more common at Time 2 than at Time 1, and more common at Time 3 than earlier. That is, siblings had more positive interactions as they grew older. The age change is one sign of the siblings' growth in social maturity.

At each time, older siblings showed more prosocial behavior than younger siblings. The difference is not surprising when you think about the relative competence of the siblings. Older siblings could help their younger siblings more than vice versa because the older siblings were stronger and knew more than their younger siblings did.

Also obvious in figure 11.7 is a difference in the siblings' conflicts and aggression. Older siblings started more fights and were more aggressive toward their younger siblings than vice versa. In other words, older siblings used their greater power to hurt as well as to help their younger brothers and sisters. Worth noting explicitly, though, is that conflicts and aggression were less frequent than prosocial behavior between siblings.

Finally, figure 11.7 shows that younger siblings imitated their older siblings more than vice versa. Imitation declined with age, but older siblings rarely imitated their younger siblings at any age. Younger siblings often view an older brother or sister as an expert, someone who can teach them how to do things. Older siblings do spend considerable time teaching their younger brothers and sisters (Brody, Stoneman, & MacKinnon, 1982; Dunn, 1983). In the process, younger siblings learn about the world. Older siblings, in turn, benefit by increasing their own understanding of what they teach.

Sibling relationships continue to change during middle childhood and adolescence. These changes can be documented by asking children and adolescents to report on their relationships. In one study (Buhrmester & Furman, 1990), third, sixth, ninth, and twelfth graders answered questions about their relationship with either an older or a younger sibling. With increasing age, adolescents reported both less dominance and less nurturance (or prosocial behavior) by older siblings (see figure 11.8). In other words, both the negative and the positive aspects of older siblings' power became less salient as children moved through

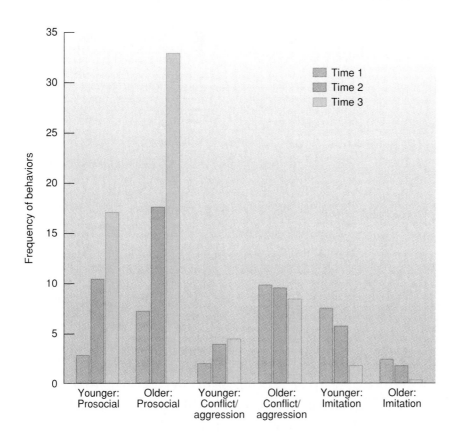

FIGURE 11.7

Results of a longitudinal study of siblings' behavior toward each other. At Time 1, the younger sibling was 1½ years old and the older one was either 3 or 4½ years old. Time 2 was 18 months later. Time 3 was two years after Time 2. At all times, older siblings displayed more prosocial behavior and more conflict/aggression. At all times, younger siblings imitated their older siblings more than vice versa. (Source: Abramovitch et al., 1986.)

adolescence. Reports of quarrels and competition with older siblings also decreased between third and twelfth grade. In short, siblings saw themselves as more equal and had fewer conflicts with each other as they got older.

In addition, sibling relationships decrease in their closeness as children move into adolescence. Figure 11.8 shows that older adolescents less often reported that they and their siblings were companions in activities. The decrease in companionship was similar whether the adolescents reported on relationships with older or with younger siblings. In addition, older adolescents reported less affection and less intimacy in their relationships with siblings.

Sibling relationships become less close partly because adolescents become more involved in other relationships. Friendships, especially, increase in importance and lessen the frequency of sibling interactions (Dunn, Slomkowski, & Beardsall, 1994). However, sibling relationships that are closer and more positive in childhood tend to remain closer and more positive in adolescence (Brody, Stoneman, & McCoy, 1994; Dunn et al., 1994). In other words, sibling relationships show considerable continuity across years.

To some degree, the quality of sibling relationships depends on how much siblings differ in age and whether they are the same sex. In one study, dominance by older siblings and quarreling and competition between siblings were greater when siblings were less than four years apart (Buhrmester & Furman, 1990). Remember, though, that other studies suggest variations in spacing of less than four years have little effect on sibling relationships (Abramovitch et al., 1986).

Finally, intimacy and companionship are greater between same-sex than other-sex siblings; that is, girls feel closer to their sisters, and boys feel closer to their brothers (Buhrmester & Furman, 1990). During adolescence, relationships between brothers weaken more than relationships between sisters (Dunn et al., 1994). These effects are small, though, and being the same sex does not increase or decrease reported conflicts between siblings. Often, relationships between other-sex siblings are as positive as those between same-sex siblings (Abramovitch et al., 1986; Dunn, 1983).

FIGURE 11.8

As children move into and through adolescence, they change their views of their sibling relationships. Older siblings are less often perceived as dominant and nurturant. Also, reports of quarrels and competition with older siblings decrease. Companionship, affection, and intimacy between siblings become less common. (Data from Buhrmester & Furman, 1990.)

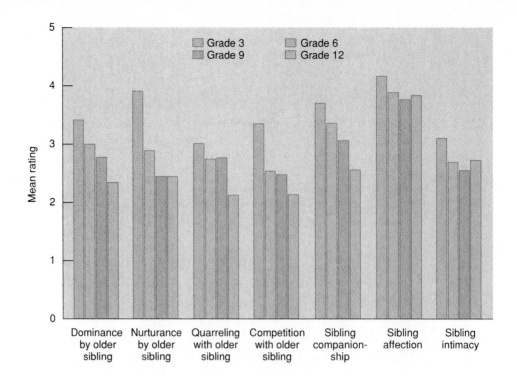

## Influences of Parents on Siblings and Siblings on Each Other

Earlier you read that older siblings have fewer conflicts with a baby brother or sister when their mothers give equal attention to them and to the newborn. Similar effects are found with preschool and school-age children (Brody, Stoneman, & McCoy, 1992, 1994; Stocker, Dunn, & Plomin, 1989). At these ages, children are less competitive with siblings and play more positively with them when their parents give equal attention and affection to all of them.

When parents do not treat all their children equally, their favoritism can affect the children's psychological adjustment. Eight- and 10-year-olds are more satisfied with their relationships to parents and are higher in self-esteem when their parents treat them and their siblings equally (McHale et al., 1995). Adolescents who feel less close to their parents than their siblings do also report more emotional distress and more delinquent behavior than their siblings (Daniels et al., 1985).

Nevertheless, you should recognize that "Treat them equally" is not the most important rule for parents' interactions with their children. "Treat them warmly, and use effective forms of control" are more important rules. Brothers and sisters are not likely to have good relationships or to develop normally if their parents are equally rejecting and equally permissive or authoritarian toward all of them!

When the home environment is less warm because of frequent conflicts between husbands and wives, conflicts between siblings are more frequent (Brody et al., 1992, 1994). Conversely, harmony in sibling relationships is more common when husbands and wives have harmonious relationships. When mothers are highly intrusive, seeking to control their children's behavior rather than develop the children's self-control, aggression between siblings is more common (Volling & Belsky, 1992).

Siblings also influence each other. To document this influence, researchers first compared children who differed in their birth order or in the sex of their siblings. Many popular writers adopted the same approach and tried to describe the characteristics of firstborns, laterborns, or boys with brothers but no sisters. Some writers even tried to describe the typical characteristics of younger brothers, or firstborn girls who had several younger sisters but no younger brothers.

These descriptions are not based on systematic, replicated research. They belong more in the realm of fantasy or astrology than science. Researchers have found few consistent effects of children's birth order or of their siblings' sex (Dunn & Plomin, 1990;

Wagner, Schubert, & Schubert, 1979). One reason for the inconsistent findings is the variability in sibling relationships. One younger brother, for example, may have a very different relationship with his older sister than another one does. These differences are ignored by popular writers who consider only a child's position in the family structure. Therefore, such family-structure variables shed little light on questions about how sibling relationships affect children's development.

A better way to evaluate the effects of sibling relationships is to look closely at what happens during children's interactions with siblings. Consider the following interaction between a 15-year-old girl and her 2-year-old brother. The children lived in the South Pacific on the Solomon Islands. The girl was teaching her brother how to refuse food politely (Watson-Gegeo & Gegeo, 1989, p. 73).

**Girl:** Then when you're full you just speak like this, "I don't want any more now."
**Boy:** mumbles something.
**Girl:** "Just put _____."
**Boy:** "Uh?"
**Girl:** "I don't want to eat any more now."
**Boy:** "I don't want?"
**Girl:** Then you just speak as I said like this, "I don't want any more now."

The interaction continued until the boy repeated what his sister said. Through interactions like these, older siblings help to socialize their younger brothers and sisters. Conversely, younger siblings give their older brothers and sisters many opportunities for prosocial behavior. As mentioned in connection with figure 11.2, cultural differences in how much children care for younger siblings partly explain the cultural differences in prosocial behavior. From an even broader perspective, sibling interactions teach children that people depend on one another, within families and in larger social groups. This kind of learning also contributes to children's socialization.

The features of sibling relationships make older siblings especially effective teachers (Azmitia & Hesser, 1993). Compared with unrelated children the same age, older siblings provide more guidance, explanations, and positive feedback to a younger brother or sister. Younger siblings, in turn, pay more attention to and request more help from an older brother or sister than from an unrelated child. Younger siblings also are willing to challenge an older sibling's control of a teaching situation. When working with an older sibling, they feel free to say, "Okay, I'm ready to try that by myself." In this way, sibling interactions enhance children's independent mastery of tasks.

Finally, what about children who have no siblings? For many years, psychologists assumed that only children suffer from not having siblings. However, systematic data do not support this assumption. On measures of intelligence, academic achievement, and personality, only children do not differ consistently from firstborn children or children in two-child families (Falbo & Polit, 1986).

In one study of Chinese children (Jiao, Ji, & Jing, 1986), the classmates of only children rated them as less cooperative, more self-centered, less persistent in completing tasks, and as less likable than children with siblings. By contrast, a more recent study of 4,000 Chinese children showed few differences in the academic achievement or social development of children with and without siblings (Falbo & Poston, 1993). The safest conclusion, therefore, is that being an only child does not radically change children's normal path of development. Although only children are not influenced by siblings, they must be influenced in similar ways by playmates and classmates.

# THE CHANGING AMERICAN FAMILY

During the 1960s, many television programs portrayed the typical American family as having two or more children, a father who had a job outside the home, and a mother who was a homemaker. Those television programs accurately depicted the most common family type of their time, but families have changed dramatically since then.

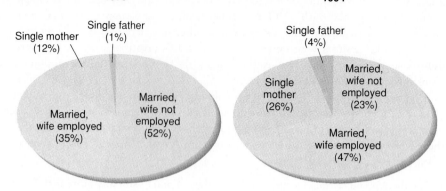

**1970**

Single mother (12%)

Single father (1%)

Married, wife employed (35%)

Married, wife not employed (52%)

**1994**

Single father (4%)

Single mother (26%)

Married, wife not employed (23%)

Married, wife employed (47%)

## FIGURE 11.9

U.S. families with children have changed greatly in the last generation. Two-parent families in which only the father is employed have decreased greatly. Two-parent families in which both the father and mother are employed, and families with a single father or a single mother, have increased. (Data from the U.S. Bureau of the Census, 1994c, 1995a.)

Figure 11.9 shows some of the changes in U.S. families between 1970 and 1994. Three aspects of these changes are worth noting.

First, in 1970 a majority of U.S. families with children did have two parents with a wife who was not employed outside the home. In 1994 only about one quarter of families were of this type. The increase in the rate of maternal employment is one of the most obvious changes in families during the last generation.

Second, in 1970 about 13 percent of U.S. children were in families with a single parent. Almost all these children lived with their mothers. By 1994 about 30 percent of children were in single-parent families. Most still lived with their mothers, but about 4 percent lived with their fathers. The increase in single-parent families was due partly to an increase in the divorce rate and partly to an increase in births to women who never married.

Third, the figure does not show all the important changes in U.S. families during recent decades. After a divorce, many parents remarry. Until recently, the Census Bureau did not ask married adults whether they were in the first marriage or a remarriage. However, the increase in the divorce rate has been accompanied by a high remarriage rate, and about one-fifth of two-parent families in 1990 included a parent who had had a divorce (U.S. Bureau of the Census, 1992). The children in these families are growing up with a stepmother or stepfather.

How have these changes in families affected children? Are some children more affected than others? Which types of parenting, and which interventions by other adults, help children adapt most successfully to these new family forms? Those questions will come up repeatedly as you read about the changes in families that accompany maternal employment, parental divorce, single parenting, and remarriage.

## Maternal Employment and Children's Development

In chapter 6 you read about the research on maternal employment and the security of infant-mother attachments. In this chapter the focus is on how maternal employment might affect children and adolescents. During the early 1990s, about 60 percent of married women in the United States with children under 6 years of age worked outside the home (U.S. Bureau of the Census, 1994c). About 75 percent of married women with children from 6 to 17 years of age worked outside the home. Rates of maternal employment vary greatly in other countries, ranging from almost all mothers in Sweden to a small minority of mothers in Japan ("Child Care Around the World," 1989).

What differences exist between children whose mothers do and do not work outside the home? How can these differences be explained? The available data only partly answer these questions.

## Differences in Children's Development

On most measures of personality, social behavior, and cognitive development, children with employed mothers receive scores similar to those of children with mothers who are not employed (Gottfried & Gottfried, 1988; Greenstein, 1995; Hoffman, 1989; Scarr, Phillips, & McCartney, 1989). However, differences related to maternal employment have been found on three types of measures (Hoffman, 1979, 1989).

First, daughters of employed women have higher educational and occupational aspirations than daughters of homemakers. Daughters of employed women more often plan to go to college; they more often aim for careers that yield a high income and are high in prestige. Maternal employment is not consistently associated with higher or lower aspirations in sons.

Second, daughters of employed women often see male and female roles in society as more equal than do daughters of homemakers. For example, employed women's daughters are more likely to say that either a man or a woman can be a doctor or an engineer. Sons of employed women also view male and female roles in a more egalitarian way than do sons of homemakers, but the difference is smaller than that for daughters. The evidence on this issue is not entirely consistent, however. One large Canadian study did not show a significant effect of maternal employment on children's ideas about male and female roles (Serbin, Powlishta, & Gulko, 1993).

Third, maternal employment may be associated with differences in children's academic achievement. In one study, low-income second graders had higher math scores when their mothers were employed than when they were not (Vandell & Ramanan, 1992). In another study, preschool children from families varying in income had lower scores on the Peabody Picture Vocabulary Test when their mothers had worked during their infancy than when their mothers had not been employed (Baydar & Brooks-Gunn, 1991).

With older children and adolescents, more consistent results have been found. In middle-class families, the sons of women employed outside the home often have poorer academic achievement than the sons of women who are homemakers (Gottfried & Gottfried, 1988; Hoffman, 1974, 1989). The effect is strongest when mothers work full-time. One estimate of the magnitude of the difference is between one-fifth and one-third of a letter grade (Bogenschneider & Steinberg, 1994). By contrast, maternal employment seems not to affect girls' academic achievement. Although girls have higher aspirations when their mothers are employed, their academic achievement is typically no higher and no lower than that of girls whose mothers are homemakers.

## Explaining the Effects of Maternal Employment

Why is maternal employment associated with differences in children's aspirations, attitudes, and achievement? Why does it seem to have such different effects on boys and girls? One reason is that girls model themselves after their mothers to a greater extent than boys do. A girl who sees her mother succeed in the world of work is likely to set the same goal for herself. A boy is less likely to base his occupational goals on his mother's example. Therefore, daughters learn more about future work roles by observing mothers who are employed outside the home than sons do.

Observational learning also affects children's attitudes about male and female roles. When children see their mothers holding a job, just as their fathers do, they believe women can fill the same roles in society that men do. Yet again, the effect of the mother's example is greater for daughters than for sons because daughters identify more with their mothers.

The relation of maternal employment to middle-class boys' academic achievement is harder to explain. One possibility is that working full-time has an indirect effect on mothers' warmth toward their sons. Working mothers sometimes have difficulty coping with the combined demands of their jobs and their families (Hoffman, 1989; Scarr et al., 1989). The mothers' difficulty may especially affect their relationships with their sons because, as you read earlier, mother-son relationships are typically less harmonious and more coercive than mother-daughter relationships. However, the available data regarding the effects of maternal employment on mothers' warmth are inconsistent (Bronfenbrenner, Alvarez, & Henderson, 1984; Greenberger & O'Neil, 1992).

Another possibility is that maternal employment reduces a mother's involvement with her children. Mothers typically spend less time in the primary care of their children when they are employed than when they are not. Primary-care activities include feeding children, taking them places, talking with them, helping them with homework, and so on. In one survey (Robinson, 1989), mothers who were not employed spent roughly 13 hours each week in primary child-care activities. Mothers working 40 or more hours a week spent roughly 5 hours a week in primary child care.

If mothers have less time to spend with their children when they are employed, why is academic achievement sometimes lower for their sons but not for their daughters? Perhaps working mothers reduce their involvement with their sons more than with their daughters (Hoffman, 1989). Perhaps the decrease in maternal involvement affects boys more than girls. Perhaps both these explanations are partly correct.

The working mothers in one study allowed their sons more unsupervised time after school than did mothers who were not employed (Muller, 1995). Moreover, this difference in supervision was significantly related to a difference in the sons' academic achievement. In another study, mothers monitored their children's behavior about as much when they were and were not employed (Crouter et al., 1990). However, lower monitoring by mothers was related to poorer academic achievement by boys but not by girls. In sum, when working mothers do not adequately monitor their sons' behavior, the sons' academic achievement is likely to suffer.

## Maternal Employment and Family Systems

Neither the positive effects of maternal employment on girls nor its occasionally negative effects on boys are inevitable. Strictly speaking, maternal employment has no *direct* effects on children. Maternal employment affects children's development only when it leads to significant changes—positive or negative—in family systems.

Suppose you observe two middle-class mothers who work in the same company for the same hours. The two women adapt differently to their work, however, so their families function differently. One mother is unhappy about her job and negative toward her children because of the stress and unhappiness she feels. This woman's daughter is unlikely to take her as a role model and unlikely to have positive attitudes toward working mothers.

The other mother is committed to doing well at work but is also committed to being a good parent (Greenberger & Goldberg, 1989). This woman's son should do well in school because his mother, after work, helps with homework and encourages his efforts to achieve. In other words, children's development depends less on maternal employment itself than on how mothers and families adapt to it.

In two-parent families, the other adult member of the family system, the father, should also be considered. Fathers can ease the strain on their spouses by taking some child-care and household responsibilities. Children benefit if fathers do so willingly; they suffer if fathers lend little support to their wives or resent the time they must take away from their own pursuits (Hoffman, 1989). This resentment may explain why, in one study, fathers with employed wives perceived their 5- or 6-year-old daughters as more disobedient and aggressive than fathers with wives who were homemakers (Greenberger & O'Neil, 1992).

Maternal employment may have more serious consequences for family systems. In two-parent families, maternal employment is associated with an increased rate of parental divorce (Carver & Teachman, 1993; Greenstein, 1990; U.S. Bureau of the Census, 1993b). The reasons for this effect are unclear. Researchers speculate that the greater financial independence of working women makes them more willing to leave a bad marriage, that these women have greater exposure to alternative partners in the work environment, or that working increases women's concern with sources of fulfillment outside the family. These are only speculations, though, because few researchers have examined the processes by which maternal employment affects family systems (Greenberger & O'Neil, 1992).

Finally, an examination of family systems may not tell the whole story about maternal employment and children's development. Also important to consider is what happens to children when their parents are working. Often, children spend this time in child-care

settings with other children and adults. In chapter 10 you learned how child-care programs can affect preschoolers' intellectual development. In chapter 12 you will learn how peer groups in child-care settings influence children's social behavior.

## Parental Divorce and Children's Development

Between 1950 and 1981 the rate of parental divorce increased greatly in the United States. Since 1981 the U.S. divorce rate has decreased somewhat, but it is among the highest in the world (Burns & Scott, 1994). Current estimates are that 4 in 10 first marriages will end in divorce (U.S. Bureau of the Census, 1993b). About 35 percent of children are likely to experience their parents' divorce before they reach age 18 (Stevenson & Black, 1995).

Divorce can dramatically affect children's experiences and life circumstances. Before the divorce, frequent and intense conflicts among family members are common. Once the parents separate, the children spend less time with the parent, usually the father, who does not have custody of them. Many children gradually lose contact with their fathers altogether. In addition, a divorce often decreases the money available for children's needs. Noncustodial parents may be legally required to pay for their children's support, but these payments are not always made. In 1991 about one-fourth of fathers did not make the required payments to mothers who had custody. About one-third of mothers did not make the required payments to fathers who had custody (U.S. Bureau of the Census, 1995d). Taken together, all these experiences and life circumstances can have negative effects on children whose parents divorce.

### A Profile of the Children of Divorce

One major study of the effects of divorce involved more than 100 families of 4-year-old children (Hetherington, 1988, 1989; Hetherington, Cox, & Cox, 1982). The researchers assessed children's characteristics and their relationships to parents at four times. In about half the families, the parents had divorced roughly two months before the first assessment. Mothers had custody of the children in all these families. The families were assessed again one, two, and six years later. The other half of the sample included families whose parents had not divorced. The same measures were obtained for these families at the same times.

When the researchers first observed the families, two months after the parents' divorce, they found less adequate parenting in divorced families than in nondivorced families (Hetherington, Cox, & Cox, 1982). Divorced mothers were less affectionate toward their children, less demanding of mature behavior, and less able to control their children's behavior than mothers in nondivorced families. Divorced mothers and their sons, in particular, were involved in many coercive interactions. Noncustodial fathers were extremely indulgent when they did interact with their children. Like their former spouses, these fathers had trouble getting their children to obey them, but their trouble occurred because of their general permissiveness.

The interactions of divorced parents and their children improved over time. Two years after the divorce, mothers were more affectionate toward their children and more often used reasoning to control the children's behavior. Fathers became more demanding of mature behavior, but they also became more detached and less nurturant over time. When their former wives had custody, most divorced fathers gradually decreased their involvement with their children.

Six years after the divorce, mothers and daughters typically had reestablished a positive relationship with each other. Divorced mothers continued to have problems with their sons. E. Mavis Hetherington (1988) classified mothers' styles of parenting as authoritative, authoritarian, permissive, or disengaged. The disengaged type corresponds to that labeled *rejecting-neglecting* in figure 11.3.

About half the mothers in nondivorced families were authoritative with their sons and their daughters (see figure 11.10). Half the divorced mothers were authoritative with their daughters, but less than one-fourth were authoritative with their sons. The most common parenting style for divorced mothers with sons was authoritarian. These mothers tried to control their sons' behavior by force rather than reasoning. Other divorced mothers with sons were permissive. They seemed to have given up trying to control their sons' behavior.

FIGURE 11.10

Percentages of mothers with various parenting styles in Hetherington's (1988) study. Divorced mothers with sons were least authoritative.

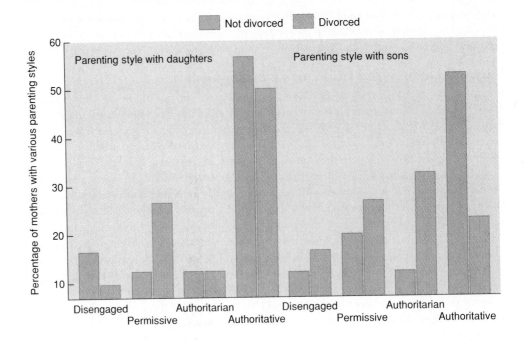

With daughters, divorced mothers were somewhat less authoritative and somewhat more permissive than mothers who were not divorced. These differences may contribute to the behavioral problems sometimes shown by adolescent girls whose mothers are divorced. These girls sometimes have a high rate of conflicts with their mothers when they begin dating and start to engage in sexual behavior with boyfriends (Hetherington, 1972; Hetherington, 1989).

The high rate of conflicts reflects the difficulties that many divorced mothers face, whether they have sons or daughters, in monitoring their children's behavior. Compared with mothers who are not divorced, divorced mothers less often know where their sons and daughters are, who they are with, and what they are doing (Hetherington, 1989). As you learned earlier in the chapter, a lack of parental monitoring often leads to undesirable behavior, especially in adolescence.

E. Mavis Hetherington and Glenn Clingempeel (1992) did another longitudinal study of divorced parents with children between 9 and 13 years old. The evidence from this study matched that from the earlier study in some respects. Children whose parents were divorced received lower ratings for social and scholastic competence from their parents and from their teachers than did children from nondivorced families. Divorced mothers who had custody of their children had more negative interactions with them and less control over them than nondivorced mothers.

The results of the two longitudinal studies differed in other respects. In the second study neither patterns of parenting nor the effects of divorce on children differed greatly for sons and daughters. Moreover, little improvement in parenting or in children's behavior was found over the two years of the study.

Other studies have confirmed the negative profile of children whose parents have divorced. One meta-analysis of 92 studies involving more than 13,000 children showed that children from divorced families had poorer school achievement, conduct, psychological adjustment, self-concepts, and social adjustment than children from nondivorced families (Amato & Keith, 1991). Moreover, both mother-child and father-child relationships were significantly less positive in divorced than nondivorced families. The negative effects of divorce were similar for boys and girls, and they did not decrease markedly with the number of years since the parents' divorce.

Long-term studies show that divorce often alters children's life paths by affecting their educational opportunities. When the children in one study reached age 18, their noncustodial

fathers stopped sending money for their financial support, and their mothers often could not pay their college costs (Wallerstein, Corbin, & Lewis, 1988). The fathers' unwillingness to pay is not surprising, because noncustodial fathers often reduce contact with their children, especially if they remarry (Seltzer, 1994). Consequently, children with divorced parents more often drop out of high school and less often graduate from college than those from non-divorced families.

Adults whose parents divorced when they were children continue to have poorer relationships with their parents than adults whose parents never divorced (Aquilino, 1994; White, 1994). Relationships are poorer with both mothers and fathers, no matter which one has custody. Moreover, adults whose parents divorced have a higher risk of ending their own marriages by divorce (Stevenson & Black, 1995). Women with divorced parents have a higher risk of bearing children outside marriage (White, 1994).

## Interpreting the Data on Children of Divorce

As you think about the data on parental divorce, you need to keep several issues in mind. One issue concerns the magnitude of the apparent effects of divorce. Knowing how children's characteristics differ when their parents are and are not divorced is important, but knowing how much their characteristics differ is equally important. For example, you read in the preceding section that children from divorced families have poorer self-concepts than those from nondivorced families (Amato & Keith, 1991). The difference is small, however, and usually nonsignificant in samples of elementary-school children.

Not all differences between children with divorced and nondivorced parents are small. Eleanor Maccoby (1992) carefully reviewed the data presented in Hetherington and Clingempeel's (1992) study of parental divorce. She pointed out that more children in divorced families than in nondivorced families were described by their parents as having behavioral problems serious enough to warrant counseling or treatment. Although most children of divorce were still functioning within the normal range, the differences between the children with divorced and nondivorced parents were, in Maccoby's opinion, "large enough to be consequential" (1992, p. 232). Meta-analyses suggest that the differences between children with divorced and nondivorced parents are largest in behavioral problems and in relationships with fathers (Amato & Keith, 1991). Differences in school achievement, mother-child relationships, and other characteristics are smaller.

A second issue that arises when interpreting data on parental divorce relates to research design. Like most studies of parenting, studies of parental divorce and children's development are correlational. Therefore, judgments about cause and effect cannot be made with absolute confidence. In a few longitudinal studies, children's behavioral problems were assessed years before their parents divorced (Block, Block, & Gjerde, 1986; Cherlin et al., 1991). Even before the divorce, boys whose parents would later divorce showed more behavioral problems than those whose parents would stay married. Some writers have taken these findings as evidence that divorce itself may not have important effects on children.

However, the longitudinal studies did not show that girls' behavioral problems after parental divorce were apparent before the divorce occurred. These studies did not show whether boys' problems, although present early, increased after their parents divorced. More generally, the argument that parental divorce does not affect children's development is difficult to defend. As noted earlier, children's interactions with their parents change dramatically when the parents divorce. All theories of development suggest that these changes should affect children's behavior and adjustment.

The controversy over the effects of divorce raises a third issue that should be mentioned explicitly. All researchers who have studied divorce and its aftermath agree that some children benefit when their parents divorce. Divorce can improve children's lives if it removes them from the influence of an alcoholic or abusive parent (Wallerstein & Kelly, 1980). Divorce can improve children's lives if it reduces the level of family conflict that they witness or in which they are involved (Amato & Keith, 1991; Cherlin et al., 1991). In short, divorce may be the best option that children in some families have.

# IMPROVING CHILDREN'S ADJUSTMENT AFTER PARENTAL DIVORCE

When a divorce involves children, a decision must be made about which parent should have physical custody of them. In the United States in 1990, mothers were awarded physical custody of their children in about three-fourths of divorces. Joint custody, in which children divide their time between their mother and their father, was ordered by courts about one-sixth of the time. Fathers were awarded custody less than 10 percent of the time (Clarke, 1995).

A few researchers have suggested that children develop best when they are in the custody of their same-sex parent, girls with their mother and boys with their father (Camara & Resnick, 1988; Lee et al., 1994; Zimiles & Lee, 1991). In most studies, however, no definite benefits of same-sex custody have been found (Downey & Powell, 1993; Seltzer, 1994; Stevenson & Black, 1995).

The same conclusion holds for the currently popular arrangement of joint physical custody (Grych & Fincham, 1992). Although children in joint custody have more contact with both parents than children in single custody, they do not show better psychological adjustment (Kline et al., 1989). After studying California families in which joint physical custody was arranged, Eleanor Maccoby and Robert Mnookin (1992) concluded that it often increases stress on children. Many parents who get a divorce remain hostile to each other. Children are drawn into the parents' conflicts when regular shifts between the mother's house and the father's house are required. Therefore, joint custody is unwise unless parents are able to cooperate with each other.

More generally, children benefit when the father and mother have a less hostile relationship with each other after the divorce occurs. When conflict between ex-spouses is lower, children have fewer behavior problems and are better accepted by peers (Kline et al., 1989). When divorced parents can be cordial toward each other, children's behavior is also more desirable.

To improve relationships among ex-spouses, counseling can be helpful. Counseling can begin before the divorce is final.

With effective counseling, some divorces can even be prevented (Katzman & Karoly, 1988). Once parents have filed for divorce, a mediator may be consulted to resolve issues of finances and custody. Mediation usually increases the parents' satisfaction with the divorce settlement (Grych & Fincham, 1992). After the divorce is final, parents' and children's adjustment can be improved by carefully planned intervention programs (Grych & Fincham, 1992).

The focus of some interventions is on parenting skills, such as setting limits on children's behavior, that newly divorced parents may have stopped using or never learned before (Stolberg & Walsh, 1988). These programs also include information to help parents understand their children and their role as a parent. Programs of this kind seem more effective in helping children of divorce than programs that focus on helping parents deal with their feelings about the divorce and rebuild their relationships with other adults.

Other programs target children whose parents have recently divorced. Sometimes groups of children with divorced parents meet at school. During these meetings, children share their experiences, provide one another with emotional support, and learn skills for solving family problems. Child counseling programs can be effective in reducing behavior problems and improving children's communication with parents (Emery, 1988; Stolberg & Walsh, 1988).

Programs may be most effective when they target not only the children of divorce but also parent-child relationships and the relationship between ex-spouses. A divorce changes the entire family system. Improvements in children's adjustment after divorce are more likely when professionals help them and their parents to create a new family system that provides a positive emotional climate, adequate monitoring of children's behavior, and the other elements of successful parenting.

A final issue concerns the practical implications of the evidence on parental divorce. The evidence shows that divorced parents typically use less effective parenting styles than parents who are not divorced. In addition, children whose parents have divorced typically show less desirable social behavior and poorer psychological adjustment than children whose parents are not divorced. Faced with this evidence, many professionals have suggested policies and established programs to help families that have experienced divorce. *Practical Applications of Research:* "Improving Children's Adjustment After Parental Divorce" describes these policies and programs.

## Single-Parent Families

You have already learned about one type of single-parent family, that formed after parental divorce. Several other types of single-parent families exist. In the United States in 1994, about 5 percent of children lived with a single parent because their other parent had died. About 20 percent had married parents who were separated (perhaps later to be reunited, or

to divorce). About 38 percent were headed by a parent who had never married, leaving 37 percent headed by a parent who was divorced (U.S. Bureau of the Census, 1995c).

The rates of different types of single-parent families differ across ethnic groups. More White single parents have been divorced than have never married. More Black single parents have never married than have been divorced. About equal numbers of Hispanic single parents have been divorced and have never married (U.S. Bureau of the Census, 1993a).

Few researchers have directly compared the various types of single-parent families. Usually, all children in single-parent families have been compared with all children in two-parent families. The results of these comparisons have been both consistent and discouraging. Children living with a single parent are more aggressive and misbehave more in elementary school than children with two parents (Dodge et al., 1994). Children and adolescents from single-parent families are lower in academic achievement than their classmates from two-parent families (Downey, 1994; Downey & Powell, 1993; Dronkers, 1994; Gringlas & Weinraub, 1995). Adolescents from single-parent families are more delinquent and drop out of high school more often than those in nondivorced two-parent families (National Commission on America's Urban Families, 1993). Adolescents with single parents are more likely than their peers to bear children themselves (Astone & Washington, 1994).

These differences in children's and adolescents' behavior are linked to differences in the parenting they receive. Single mothers, the group studied most often, are less affectionate toward their children and use more harsh, physical punishment than mothers in nondivorced two-parent families (Dodge et al., 1994; McLoyd, 1990b). Single mothers provide their children with less cognitive stimulation, do less to discourage their children's aggressive behavior, and use reasoning or inductive discipline less than do mothers in two-parent families. The rate of mother-child and sibling conflict is also higher in single-mother families (Laursen, 1995).

The quality of parenting suffers in single-parent families partly because of the many stressors that single parents face (Gringlas & Weinraub, 1995; McLoyd, 1990b). Single parents are often poor, so they must worry about how to pay the rent, buy their children clothes, and provide the other necessities of life for their children. Poor single parents move often and so do not build up a network of supportive friends and neighbors as easily as married parents do.

Nevertheless, the financial stress on single-parent families does not completely explain their children's negative profile. For example, adolescents from single-parent families show an increased rate of delinquency even when their low income is taken into account (National Commission on America's Urban Families, 1993).

Another difference between one- and two-parent families is that many single parents remain embroiled in conflicts with their former partners. As mentioned earlier, marital conflicts often have negative effects on children's development. You might, therefore, expect children whose mothers never married to be better off than those whose mothers divorced.

Think again, though, about the experiences of adults who never married but who are rearing children. Many of these adults live together for a time with the father or mother of their children. However, these relationships often break up (Burns & Scott, 1994; Seltzer, 1994). The conflicts surrounding these breakups may be as intense as those surrounding the breakup of a marriage.

It is not surprising, then, that the few studies of never-married parents have yielded results similar to those for all single parents. The children of never-married parents misbehave more at school and are lower in academic achievement than children from two-parent families. The differences exist among middle-class, White families in the United States (Gringlas & Weinraub, 1995) and among Dutch families in the Netherlands (Dronkers, 1994).

The school achievement of Dutch children with never-married mothers decreased during the 1980s. The decrease occurred at the same time that funding for welfare programs was reduced in the Netherlands (Dronkers, 1994). The two historical trends imply that one way to help children in single-parent families might be to increase government funding of child-support programs, including child care and national health insurance (Wong, Garfinkel, & McLanahan, 1993).

Scholars and public officials have sometimes suggested another alternative, which is to reduce the number of single-parent families. The members of one U.S. commission adopted

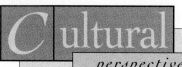

CHILDREARING IN
EXTENDED BLACK
FAMILIES

Extended families are uncommon among both Blacks and Whites, but in 1993 about 12 percent of Black children and only 4 percent of White children lived in their grandparents' home (U.S. Bureau of the Census, 1994b). Most extended Black families include one or more children, their mother, and their grandmother.

Living in an extended family can have benefits for mothers. A grandmother who does some child care can relieve the mother from being "on call" 24 hours a day. If the grandmother is not employed, the mother also can attend school or be employed while the grandmother is with the children. Adolescent mothers in extended families more often finish high school and less often depend on public assistance than do adolescent mothers who live with their children alone (Wilson, 1989).

In addition, a grandmother may model appropriate parenting and advise her daughter on how to raise children (Tolson & Wilson, 1990). However, the extent to which grandmothers typically encourage and model good parenting is uncertain. Some studies suggest that grandmothers are more responsive and less punitive toward children than are adolescent mothers, but other studies suggest the reverse (McLoyd, 1990b).

A recent study included about 100 African American mothers, some of whom lived with their grandmothers and some of whom did not (Chase-Lansdale, Brooks-Gunn, & Zamsky, 1994). The mothers and grandmothers were similar in parenting style, but mothers who lived with their grandmothers did not show higher-quality parenting. On the contrary, these mothers were less supportive and more disengaged when interacting with their children than mothers who lived alone. Grandmothers' parenting was also less positive when they lived with their daughters than when they did not, unless their daughters had their first child as a young teenager.

These data imply that extended families can have costs as well as benefits. Grandmothers may experience overload as they balance their other responsibilities with caring for their daughter's children. If a mother and grandmother disagree about who is in charge of the children, neither may take responsibility for them.

In addition, the relationship between a mother and grandmother may conflict with that between a mother and the father of her children. Few extended Black families include fathers (Pearson et al., 1990). A mother may decide not to marry her children's father or not to pick a new marital partner because her mother opposes the marriage (Wilson, 1986).

Unfortunately, evidence on the development of children in extended Black families is rare. One large survey of adolescents included Black families with a mother and another adult who was either a grandmother or another relative or friend (Dornbusch et al., 1985). Adolescents in these extended families were better behaved at school and less delinquent than those in single-mother families. These differences could be attributed to the greater control that mothers in extended families exerted over their adolescents' behavior. But more research is needed before firm conclusions can be drawn about when, or for which children, living in an extended family is beneficial.

the explicit goal of increasing the number of children who are raised in a "stable, loving, two-parent home" (National Commission on America's Urban Families, 1993). To achieve this goal, the commission recommended many changes in the legal system, education, and government programs. For example, they argued that tax laws should be changed to give bigger tax breaks to married couples with children.

Finally, comparisons of single-parent and two-parent families ignore other family types. Mothers who are divorced or who never married sometimes live with their own mothers or other relatives. How growing up in such an extended family might affect children's development is discussed in *Cultural Perspectives: "Childrearing in Extended Black Families."*

## Remarriage and Stepfamilies

Most parents remarry if their first marriage ends in divorce. Children then become part of a stepfamily with one biological parent and one stepparent. About one-fifth of the children in

the United States lived in stepfamilies in 1990 (U.S. Bureau of the Census, 1992). Perhaps twice that many will spend some time in a stepfamily before they reach age 18 (Glick, 1988).

On the average, children in stepfamilies are not as well adjusted as children in never-divorced two-parent families (Allison & Furstenberg, 1989; Amato & Keith, 1991; Hetherington & Clingempeel, 1992; Steinberg, 1987; Zill, 1988). Children in stepfamilies have more behavioral problems and do less well in school than children in families with two biological parents. They also report more emotional distress and greater willingness to engage in antisocial behavior with peers.

Children in stepfamilies typically have about as many behavioral and academic problems as children in single-parent families with a divorced parent (Amato & Keith, 1991). These findings are surprising because stepparents can share responsibility for rearing their children. In addition, household income is usually higher in stepfamilies than in single-parent families. However, the additional adult in the home and the additional income do not regularly translate into better psychological adjustment in children. What's going on?

The answer, again, involves the quality of parenting. A new marriage for a divorced mother or father brings changes in the family system that was established after the divorce. These changes are often disturbing to children. Some problems in parent-child relationships that emerged after the parents' divorce may reemerge (Hetherington, 1989). Children may become difficult to control, and hostile interactions between parents and their children may become more common.

On a closer look, parenting problems in stepfamilies differ from those in single-parent families formed after divorce (Hetherington, 1989; Hetherington & Arasteh, 1988; Hetherington & Clingempeel, 1992). The intensity of conflicts in stepfamilies depends on children's age. Family conflicts are most intense in remarriages involving elementary- and junior-high-school children. Younger children may take a new stepparent in stride. They value having another adult to help and play with them. Older adolescents, in the high-school years, may express little concern about a parent's remarriage because they spend more time with friends than at home. Also, older adolescents realize that their stepparent will be a companion for their mother or father after they leave home for college or a job elsewhere.

Children approaching adolescence are usually most negative toward stepparents. These children are not happy to have a new adult trying to control their behavior or "boss them around." In addition, they may be jealous of the relationship between the stepparent and their mother or father. This new relationship may disrupt the close relationship they had established with their custodial parent after their parents' divorce.

In mother-stepfather families, you might expect girls to be more jealous and to react more negatively after a remarriage than boys do. Although some evidence consistent with this hypothesis has been found (Hetherington, 1991), other studies have suggested that remarriage has similar effects on boys' and girls' relationships to their parents (Hetherington & Clingempeel, 1992). The effects of a remarriage on children's behavior and adjustment also seem similar for boys and girls.

Conflicts between children and parents are not the most serious parenting problem in stepfamilies. To avoid these conflicts, some parents and stepparents lessen their control over their children's behavior. In particular, they less often work toward an authoritative parenting style (Hetherington & Clingempeel, 1992).

When the mother is the biological parent, she monitors her children's behavior less carefully than do mothers in first marriages. The stepfather, rather than compensating for the mother's lack of monitoring, compounds the problem. He responds to children's negative behavior by reducing his involvement with them. He may even justify his low involvement by asserting that the children are his wife's responsibility. Some stepfathers express this view of their role in statements like "I married her [their new spouse], not her kids."

Avoiding conflicts by treating children permissively is, to use an old proverb, like jumping out of the frying pan into the fire. When stepfathers disengage and mothers don't take control over children's behavior, misbehavior by the children is almost inevitable. Moreover, the situation is not likely to improve with the passage of time.

A better strategy for parents in a remarriage involves two phases (Hetherington, 1988). In the first phase, new stepparents try to establish positive relationships with stepchildren

while supporting their spouse's efforts at parenting. Establishing such positive relationships takes time—several months at least, and perhaps years. In the second phase, once positive relationships exist, stepparents try more directly to influence their children's behavior. That is, they gradually shift from a hands-off, secondary role to authoritative parenting.

What can be said, then, about the changing American family? Although children differ, on the average, in different types of families, these average differences are often small (Amato & Keith, 1991). Therefore, an individual child's characteristics cannot be predicted accurately from information about whether the child lives with one parent, two biological parents, or a parent and a stepparent. Moreover, the negative profile of children in certain types of families does not apply to all children in those families. After decades of research, E. Mavis Hetherington (1989) concluded that "depending on the characteristics of the child, particularly the age and gender of the child, available resources, subsequent life experiences, and especially interpersonal relationships, children in the long run may be survivors, losers, or winners of their parents' divorce and remarriage" (p. 13).

# WHEN PARENTING GOES AWRY: CHILD MALTREATMENT

Children's dependence on their families is most obvious when their parents' behavior is grossly abnormal. Some parents are so angered by mild forms of child misbehavior that they physically abuse their children. Some parents sexually abuse their children or allow sexual abuse by other people. Some so seriously neglect their children's needs that the children's health and development are threatened.

In U.S. law, child maltreatment is defined as the "physical or mental injury, sexual abuse, negligent treatment, or maltreatment of a child under the age of 18 by a person who is responsible for the child's welfare under circumstances which would indicate that the child's health or welfare is harmed or threatened thereby" (Fryer, 1993, p. 80). Three aspects of this definition are important.

First, the definition refers to four kinds of maltreatment (National Research Council, 1993). Physical abuse includes actions that leave a child disfigured, that disrupt bodily functioning, or that cause other forms of serious physical injury. Sexual abuse includes acts such as incest, fondling of the genitals, and involvement in child pornography. Negligent treatment can include abandonment, lack of caretaking, and lack of needed medical treatment or other kinds of help. Emotional maltreatment includes verbal abuse, acts intended to terrorize a child, and gross inattention to a child's emotional needs.

Second, the definition specifies that the person who maltreats the child is responsible for the child's welfare. Acts done by complete strangers or by a child's peers are not classified in the law as child maltreatment. In the vast majority of cases, the perpetrators of child maltreatment are the child's parents (Fryer, 1993). Only a small percentage of cases involve other relatives, babysitters, or staff in child-care centers as perpetrators.

Third, the definition indicates that it is illegal to perform acts that harm or threaten a child's health or welfare, but it does not specify which acts do so. Some researchers have defined physical abuse as including acts such as spanking, even when the spanking does not cause physical injury. Other researchers, especially medical professionals, pay more attention to the effects of acts on children than to the definition of the acts themselves. In other words, they look for evidence of harm or threat to the child's health or welfare.

The ambiguity in the definition of child maltreatment makes it difficult to assess its frequency, but it undoubtedly is a serious problem (National Research Council, 1993). About 2,000 children in the United States die each year because of maltreatment. More than 2 million reports of suspected maltreatment are filed with state agencies each year. In 1992, more than 900,000 of these reports were substantiated after investigation (U.S. Bureau of the Census, 1994c). Although the rate of child maltreatment varies across cultures (Korbin, 1987),

countries such as England and Sweden have rates comparable to the U.S. rate (Browne, Davies, & Stratton, 1988; National Research Council, 1993).

The most common form of child maltreatment is neglect. Of the substantiated U.S. cases in 1992, the majority were for child neglect. About one-fourth were for physical abuse and about one-eighth were for sexual abuse. Only about 5 percent of the cases involved emotional maltreatment (U.S. Bureau of the Census, 1994c).

The victims of child maltreatment can be any age. About 40 percent of the substantiated cases in 1992 involved children under 5. Another 25 percent involved children 6 to 9 years of age. The remainder involved 10- to 17-year-olds (U.S. Bureau of the Census, 1994c). Clearly, child maltreatment is not limited to infancy and early childhood.

Why would anyone, especially a parent, maltreat a child? What causes parents to act this way?

## Causes of Child Maltreatment: An Ecological-Transactional Model

The problem of child maltreatment was largely ignored until the early 1960s, when a few physicians began writing about "the battered-child syndrome" (Kempe et al., 1962). Initially, most researchers assumed that only parents who were mentally ill would severely abuse their children. Unfortunately, this assumption is false.

Currently, researchers acknowledge that child maltreatment has many causes of several types. These types can be classified using a variant of Urie Bronfenbrenner's (1979) ecological model, which was outlined in chapter 1. In addition, conditions that increase the risk of child abuse can be distinguished from conditions that lower risk by compensating for weaknesses in the ecological systems related to child maltreatment. Stated differently, maltreatment is the result of complex transactions between parents' characteristics, children's characteristics, and the environments in which families are located (National Research Council, 1993).

An ecological-transactional model can encompass many influences on child maltreatment, as table 11.2 shows (Belsky, 1993; Bronfenbrenner, 1986; Kaufman & Zigler, 1989; National Research Council, 1993). The table does not include all the conditions related to child maltreatment, only the most important and extensively investigated ones. Also, the conditions leading to different kinds of maltreatment (e.g., neglect versus sexual abuse) are not listed separately. The main reason for not separating them is that they often occur together (Belsky, 1993). For example, a child who is sexually abused is also likely to be neglected or a victim of emotional maltreatment. Therefore, the table is useful in understanding the causes of all kinds of maltreatment.

### Parents' Characteristics

Two of the most widely accepted—and false—assumptions about the causes of child abuse relate to the first level in the model. One of these assumptions has been mentioned already, but it bears repeating. Many people believe that only parents who are "crazy"—mentally ill or psychologically disturbed—would abuse their children. The evidence does not support this assumption. A very small proportion of the parents who abuse their children are suffering from serious mental illness (National Research Council, 1993; Zigler & Hall, 1989).

Although abusive parents are rarely psychotic or mentally disturbed, they differ in personality from parents who are not abusive. Abusive parents are often low in self-esteem, depressed, and anxious. They are high in antisocial behavior, partly because their skills for dealing with social conflicts are poor. Most important, abusive parents have a simplistic view of parent-child relationships. They have little understanding of how situations affect children's behavior or which behaviors are appropriate for children at different ages (Pianta, Egeland, & Erickson, 1989). These characteristics are associated with limited education. Conversely, parents with good interpersonal skills are unlikely to maltreat their children.

The other false assumption about causes of child maltreatment is that all people who were abused as children become abusive parents. As table 11.2 indicates, people who were maltreated as children are somewhat more likely to maltreat their own children, but this generalization is more often false than true. Some researchers have estimated that only about 30

| | | | |
|---|---|---|---|
| **TABLE 11.2** | *An Ecological-Transactional Model of the Causes of Child Maltreatment* | | |

| PARENTS' CHARACTERISTICS | CHILDREN'S CHARACTERISTICS AND THE FAMILY ENVIRONMENT | EXOSYSTEM CHARACTERISTICS | MACROSYSTEM CHARACTERISTICS |
|---|---|---|---|
| ***Conditions Increasing Risk*** | | | |
| Low self-esteem, depression, and anxiety | In infancy, prematurity and low birth weight | Poverty | High rate of criminal violence |
| Antisocial behavior | Difficult temperament in childhood | Unemployment or underemployment | Frequent displays of violence in the media |
| Poor understanding of children | Family violence and marital discord | Stressful life events | |
| Limited education | Extremely authoritarian or rejecting-neglecting parenting | Social isolation | |
| Abused as children | Single parents and stepfamilies | | |
| | | | |
| ***Conditions Compensating for Risks*** | | | |
| Good interpersonal skills | Positive and supportive relationships between spouses | Supportive relationships with relatives, friends, or neighbors | Cultural norms opposing violence against children |
| A positive relationship with one adult during childhood | | Strong religious affiliation | |
| Therapy after past abuse | | | |

percent of abused children become abusive parents (Kaufman & Zigler, 1989). Although other researchers argue that the available data are too limited to justify precise estimates (Belsky, 1993), it seems fair to conclude that most people who were victims of maltreatment do not maltreat their own children.

Other experiences can reduce the chances that victims of child abuse will become abusive parents (Belsky, 1993; Egeland, Jacobvitz, & Sroufe, 1988). Child victims who had a positive relationship with one adult during their childhood are less likely as adults to abuse their children. Adults who receive psychotherapy to help them overcome their memories of childhood abuse are less likely to succumb to the cycle of abuse. Talking with a skilled therapist can allow adults to work through their past experiences and reject their parents' model.

Finally, an ecological-transactional model implies that a history of past abuse is only one influence on parents' treatment of their children. This history is unlikely to result in child maltreatment if other ecological systems are functioning well. Conversely, when other ecological systems include many conditions that increase risk, parents are more likely to fall into the cycle of abuse (Belsky, 1993).

## Children's Characteristics and the Family Environment

Children who are more difficult to interact with are more likely to be abused. Premature and low-birth-weight infants are more difficult to care for and have more aversive cries than full-term, normal-weight babies (Browne, 1988; Zigler & Hall, 1989). Premature and low-birth-weight infants are also more likely to be abused by their parents (see table 11.2). However, some researchers question whether these infant characteristics actually are causes of child maltreatment. The alternative position is that these characteristics are merely correlated with other risks such as low parental education (National Research Council, 1993).

Children who have a difficult temperament have a higher risk of being abused by their parents. Their chances of being abused depend partly on their parents' beliefs about the reasons for their behavior and partly on the parents' assumptions about whether the children's behavior can be controlled (Bugental, Blue, & Lewis, 1990). Parents respond most negatively to difficult children when they view the children's inappropriate behavior as willful or deliberate and they view themselves as unable to control it. Again, you see that child abuse is the outcome of a transactional process that is affected by children's and parents' characteristics.

One contributor to child abuse is social isolation. In Western societies, families often live in houses separated from those of their neighbors by roads and fences. There may also be little contact between neighbors and little community support for troubled families. By contrast, in the small villages of traditional cultures, contact and support may be easily obtained from parents in huts only a few feet away, so there is less of the isolation that can lead to the abuse of children.

The physical abuse of children is often part of a pattern of family violence. Parents who physically abuse their children often report that they approve of slapping a spouse under certain conditions. These parents are more likely to report episodes of violence between parents and a lack of marital satisfaction (National Research Council, 1993; Straus & Kantor, 1987). This pattern should remind you of the earlier description of Manyara's family. By contrast, child abuse is less likely when marital relationships are positive, stable, and supportive (Belsky, 1993; Crnic et al., 1983; Egeland et al., 1988).

Some parenting styles lead to or may be defined as child maltreatment (National Research Council, 1993). When parents are extreme in their adherence to Baumrind's (1991) rejecting-neglecting style, their children are certain to suffer from neglect. When parents are extreme in their use of an authoritarian style, their children may become victims of physical abuse.

Finally, you know that the less desirable parenting styles are more common in single-parent families and in stepfamilies than in never-divorced two-parent families. The incidence of child abuse is also higher in single-parent families and stepfamilies than in families with two nondivorced parents (National Research Council, 1993). Remember, though, that life circumstances also differ across family types. These life circumstances, seen now as characteristics of their exosystem, can greatly affect the risk of child maltreatment.

## Exosystem Level: Stress and Support

Many abusive parents have difficult lives outside the home (McLoyd, 1990b; National Research Council, 1993; Straus & Kantor, 1987). They are often under great financial stress. They may be unemployed or underemployed. They may have health problems, troubles with relatives, or other stressful life events. When stress is great, parents interact less positively with their children and have a heightened risk of child maltreatment (Crnic et al., 1983; Kaufman & Zigler, 1989).

In addition, abusive parents are often socially isolated. They lack strong relationships with relatives and seldom live near relatives. They belong to few community organizations, such as clubs or business groups. They rarely attend a church or socialize with church members (Zigler & Hall, 1989).

In other cultures, parents more often abuse their children when they are less involved in kinship networks. Social isolation means that parents cannot call on another adult for help in times of stress. In addition, other adults cannot monitor the parents' behavior and intervene when parents are extremely harsh or abusive (Korbin, 1987).

Support from relatives, neighbors, and friends lowers the probability that parents will abuse their children, partly because it reduces the parents' isolation (Belsky, 1993). Having supportive relationships with other people can also lessen the stress on parents. Parents can get help from others with childrearing, financial problems, or other difficult conditions. A strong religious affiliation, linked to regular church participation, can also compensate for other negative conditions and lower the risk of child maltreatment.

## Macrosystem Characteristics

In the United States, violent behavior is seen everywhere and is even institutionalized. More murders occur in the United States than in other industrialized countries, but gun-control legislation is opposed by many citizens and groups. Television stations broadcast a steady diet of shootings, fistfights, and other violent acts. One consequence of these cultural messages is an acceptance of violence for handling problems with other people (Zigler & Hall, 1989).

In particular, most adults in the United States condone violence toward children. Nearly all parents use some form of physical punishment. Some mothers spank infants younger than 6 months old, who have little ability to control their behavior. In addition, the U.S. Supreme Court ruled in 1977 that spanking was an acceptable form of discipline in schools. By contrast, in Sweden, physical punishment of children is a criminal act.

It is not clear, however, whether abusive violence against children is less common in Sweden than in the United States (Korbin, 1987; National Research Council, 1993). More generally, documenting causes of child maltreatment at the macrosystem level is difficult. Still, when cultural norms strongly oppose violence against children, maltreatment of children should be less common.

# Effects of Child Maltreatment, Intervention, and Prevention

Being a victim of maltreatment has serious and long-lasting effects on children. Abused children rarely form secure attachments to their parents. In the Strange Situation, they seem afraid of their parents, show dazed facial expressions, or alternate between approaching their parents and avoiding them (Carlson et al., 1989).

Children and adolescents who were physically abused are unusually aggressive themselves, thus modeling the violent behavior their parents directed toward them (Malinosky-Rummell & Hansen, 1993). Modeling does not completely account for the increased aggression, though, because children severely neglected by parents are also more aggressive toward peers (Widom, 1989). Abused children are often rejected by peers and tend to withdraw from interactions with peers. These children have lower IQ scores and slower language development than nonabused children. They do less well in school and suffer from depression and drug abuse more often than their peers (Cicchetti & Carlson, 1989; Malinosky-Rummell & Hansen, 1993). Adolescents who have been abused are more often delinquent and more often run away from home (National Research Council, 1993).

In adulthood, victims of child maltreatment continue to show a high rate of emotional problems, including suicide attempts (Malinosky-Rummell & Hansen, 1993; National Research Council, 1993). Compared with other adults, they more often are drug abusers and have serious psychological problems. Women who were victims of incest or other forms of sexual abuse are more likely than other women to have multiple short-term sexual relationships. Men who were victims of physical abuse are more violent than other men toward their wives.

Accurately judging the effects of child maltreatment is not easy, however, because it is associated with so many other problems. Remember that maltreatment is more common when parents are high in antisocial behavior, marital discord is high, and parenting styles are undesirable (see table 11.2). Maltreatment is more common when families are poor, parents are unemployed, and the life stress on parents is high. That maltreatment has its own effects on children seems unquestionable, but separating the effects of maltreatment from those of other negative conditions is difficult.

Unfortunately, children's problems do not end once their maltreatment is recognized by adults (Spaccarelli, 1994). Sometimes children's trust in adults is destroyed because they do not receive help when they expect it. For example, some mothers react negatively when their daughters report that they have been sexually abused by their fathers. These mothers deny the girls' reports, get angry at them, or tell them not to say anything to anyone else. If parents' maltreatment becomes publicly known, children may be placed in the traumatic situation of disclosing the criminal behavior of a parent in court. Children then face the prospect of leaving their family for an uncertain future in the child welfare system.

Nevertheless, children's lives are sometimes so threatened that their removal from their home is necessary. When little hope of improving the home situation exists, parents' rights over their children are terminated and the children are placed with other relatives, in foster care, or in an adoptive home. In less extreme cases, children may be removed from their parents' care temporarily while their parents participate in an intervention program. If the intervention is successful, bringing the parents and children back together may be in the children's best interests (Goldstein, Freud, & Solnit, 1973, 1979).

The goal of some interventions is to train abusive parents both in controlling their children's behavior and in increasing their self-control. The best programs include components targeting all types of maltreatment. For example, parents of neglected children may be trained in nutrition and given instructions about their children's physical needs. Unfortunately, few systematic evaluations of these programs have been done. Significant improvements in family functioning have been found over a few weeks or months, but longer-term evaluations have not been done or have yielded discouraging results (National Research Council, 1993; Nicol, 1988).

The goal of other intervention programs is to preserve the family and so eliminate possible negative effects of family disruption. Rather than taking a maltreated child from the home, professionals move into the home for up to 30 hours a week. During this time the professionals try to protect the children, strengthen family bonds, increase parents' skills in child-rearing, and help parents learn to call upon community resources when under stress. The intensive phase of work with a family lasts only a month or two, during what is presumed to be the crisis period after an episode of maltreatment. However, the effects of the program fade over time, and whether their benefits outweigh their high cost is not yet known (National Research Council, 1993).

Nearly all intervention programs for child maltreatment are still in the preliminary stages of development. These programs reach a very small fraction of maltreated children. Many children receive no services focused on their needs. Even when reports of child abuse are substantiated, perhaps one-third of U.S. children receive no supportive or therapeutic services (National Research Council, 1993). Services are unavailable because funds for child protective services, the state agencies responsible for investigating and dealing with child maltreatment, are inadequate.

Of course, researchers and practitioners would like to prevent child abuse, not simply intervene after it has occurred. To be effective, prevention programs must target each of the ecological levels that affect the risk of abuse (National Research Council, 1993; Nicol, 1988; Olds & Henderson, 1989; Zigler & Hall, 1989).

## Parents' Characteristics

Many parents need education in parenting. They need to know what behavior is normal for children of different ages; they need to be trained in effective techniques of controlling children's behavior without using excessive force. The family-management skills mentioned earlier are good targets for training.

## Child Characteristics and the Family Environment

Some characteristics of children that increase their risk of being abused can be altered. For example, mothers who receive adequate prenatal care less often give birth to premature and low-birth-weight infants. Parents who are trained to use an authoritative parenting style are less likely to have children who are unpleasant to interact with.

Another outcome of parent-training programs might be to improve marital relationships. In one program to prevent child abuse, nurses visit the homes of young infants to provide instruction in infant care (Olds & Henderson, 1989). The nurses especially invite fathers to participate with their wives. Participation in the program is intended to increase fathers' involvement in parenting and fathers' support for their wives.

## Exosystem Characteristics

Exosystem influences on the risk of child abuse cannot be completely controlled. Although government programs can reduce the proportion of children in poor families, unemployment and underemployment would be hard to eliminate. Still, parents' employment opportunities could be increased by vocational training programs. Special emphasis might be given to programs for unmarried young mothers, because they have an elevated rate of child maltreatment (Fryer, 1993).

Similarly, stress will always be part of life, but the amount of support that parents receive to help them cope with stress could be increased. Instead of dealing only with children's physical health, physicians and nurses could try to offer support to parents. Home visits by nurses could reduce the social isolation that many mothers experience. Home visitors could also inform parents about their eligibility for social services that they are not receiving. Self-help groups such as Parents Anonymous make it easier for parents to talk with someone else when they are angry or depressed. In all these ways, parents can become part of a supportive social network.

## The Macrosystem

Public awareness of child abuse as a social problem has increased greatly during recent decades. The media campaigns of the National Committee for the Prevention of Child Abuse (Cohn, 1987) are partly responsible for this increase. The media have also presented brief public-service messages about good parenting (e.g., "Have you hugged your child today?").

Media campaigns are not enough, though, because they do not reach the isolated parents who have the highest risk of child maltreatment. To reach these parents, government agencies charged with protecting children's welfare must receive adequate funding. Many of these agencies have a staff so small that they cannot respond in any meaningful way to reports of child maltreatment. The conditions of work are so poor that turnover sometimes exceeds 70 percent per year (National Research Council, 1993).

Despite public outcry over the most sensational cases of child maltreatment, citizens and legislators have never allocated enough money to investigate and then intervene in all cases of child maltreatment. After completing an extensive survey, George Fryer (1993) argued that "The current public investment in child protection is at best symbolic. Given the present scale of the problem, it may no longer purchase peace of mind" (p. 96).

Other writers admit that the child-protection system must be improved, but they also suggest a need for changes in society. The U.S. Advisory Board on Child Abuse and Neglect has proposed "a rebuilding of our society," with "new policies, programs, and grass-roots action that build or rebuild connections among and within families" (Melton & Barry, 1994, p. 11). These experts affirm that only a concerted attack on all the contributors to child maltreatment, at all ecological levels, can eliminate this tragic form of parenting gone awry.

# RELATIONSHIPS IN FAMILY SYSTEMS

**family systems perspective**
*A theoretical perspective that assumes the family is a system whose members influence and are influenced by one another.*

When studying the effects of parental divorce and remarriage, Hetherington and Clingempeel (1992) adopted a **family systems perspective.** In this perspective, each member of a family is assumed to have a distinctive relationship with every other member, and each relationship influences every other relationship. The family systems perspective originated in clinical psychology, where it provides the theoretical foundation for one form of family

therapy. Patricia Minuchin (1985) described six principles of family systems theory that are important for understanding all families.

1. *Systems are organized wholes, and all parts of the system are interdependent.* The family is a system whose members influence and are influenced by one another. Thus, the behavior of any member of the family can be understood only in the context of the other members' behavior. For example, the behavior of a child with a newborn sibling can only be understood by knowing about the mother's and the father's interactions with the newborn (Dunn, 1985).

2. *Interactions in family systems involve feedback loops, not chains of causes and effects.* In a family, one member does not directly cause the behavior of another. For example, children's whining does not directly cause their parents to give in to their coercion. However, parents and children can together create a pattern of interaction, a coercive cycle, that has negative consequences for all (Patterson, 1980, 1982). The cycle is maintained by the feedback that each person provides to others.

3. *Systems operate to maintain the stability of their patterns.* This statement expresses the principle of **homeostasis.** Families have typical patterns of interaction that define their equilibrium position. When the behavior of a family member deviates from the typical pattern, other family members act to restore the equilibrium by changing that member's behavior. The negative response that mothers sometimes give to daughters who report sexual abuse by the father may be an example of this principle (Spaccarelli, 1994). Mothers may be trying to preserve the current family pattern, despite its cost to their daughters.

**homeostasis**
*The principle in family systems theory that systems operate to maintain the stability of their patterns.*

4. *Open systems evolve and change.* Families cannot keep the same pattern of interaction forever. Changes come, in part, because each family member is growing older, and growth forces changes in the family system. Earlier you read about the changes in families that occur after the birth of a new child. You also read about the changes in families as children move through adolescence. Most families cope with these changes adaptively, but some need help from a therapist or another person who can guide their evolution.

5. *Complex systems include subsystems.* The family is a system with multiple subsystems. In different subsystems, the same person has different roles. A woman may have the role of mother in the parent-child subsystem and the role of wife in the spouse system. The importance of these subsystems is suggested by the final principle.

6. *Subsystems have boundaries, and implicit rules govern interactions across boundaries.* In most families, parents share information with their spouses that they wouldn't share with their children, and vice versa. Such boundaries between subsystems are often functional. For example, children might be excessively troubled if their parents shared all their worries and fears with them.

Changes in subsystems may disrupt the entire family system and so provoke conflicts. For example, children in single-parent families sometimes have especially close relationships with their mothers. Relationships in this parent-child subsystem can be disrupted if the mother remarries, and this disruption may partly account for the conflicts often found between children and stepparents (Hetherington & Clingempeel, 1992).

You can see that the family systems perspective is more complex than the view of parenting with which this chapter began. You learned at the beginning that parents need to maintain a high level of warmth, appropriate forms of control, and a high level of involvement. But as the examples in this section show, family relationships involve more than these dimensions of parenting. Relationships among family members can only be fully understood if the principles of the family systems perspective are also taken into account.

# Summary

## Parenting as Socialization

The family is the primary context in which the socialization of children takes place. Socialization is the process by which children acquire the beliefs, values, and behavior considered appropriate for people in their society and culture.

## Dimensions of Parenting

Warmth, control, and involvement are broad dimensions of parenting that help to explain parents' success in socializing their children. The most successful parents are high in warmth, use effective forms of control, and are highly involved with their children. Enforcing rules consistently is one effective form of control. Using power-assertive discipline is generally an ineffective form of control.

## Other Theoretical Perspectives on Parenting

Baumrind identified four parenting styles that differ on the dimensions of warmth and control. The most successful parents are high in both warmth and control, or authoritative. Social learning theorists focus less on dimensions or styles of parenting than on parents' reactions to specific behaviors by a child. Patterson emphasized the problem of coercive cycles in parent-child interaction.

## The Family Grows Up: Developments in Parent-Child Relationships

As children move out of infancy, parents begin to try to control their behavior. In early childhood, parents increase their emphasis on fostering their children's self-control. The goals of promoting achievement and encouraging individuality but continuing family connections become important in middle childhood and adolescence.

## Parents and Children: Who Is Socializing Whom?

Parents influence their children's behavior, but children also influence their parents' behavior. Families are systems in which every person affects every other member of the family. During childhood, however, parents have more power over their children than vice versa.

## Sisters and Brothers

Most families include siblings who influence each other. Older siblings sometimes help and sometimes hurt their younger brothers or sisters. Younger siblings often imitate their older brothers or sisters.

## Developments in Sibling Relationships

Sibling interaction increases in early childhood as children's social skill and competence increase. Closeness and companionship between siblings decrease in adolescence as older siblings spend more time with friends. Age spacing of less than four years has few consistent effects on sibling relationships.

## Influences of Parents on Siblings and Siblings on Each Other

The quality of sibling relationships is influenced by how their parents treat them. Siblings have fewest conflicts when their parents treat them equally and give them equal attention. Siblings also have more positive relationships when their parents treat them with warmth and respect. Older siblings influence younger siblings by teaching them social norms and cognitive skills.

## The Changing American Family

During the last generation, the traditional family with an employed father and a mother who is not employed has become less common in the United States and several other countries. Rates of maternal employment, parental divorce, single-parent families, and remarriage have all increased.

## Maternal Employment and Children's Development

Girls with employed mothers have higher aspirations for themselves than do girls whose mothers are not employed. Children's beliefs about male and female roles, and the academic achievement of middle-class boys, are also related to their mothers' employment.

## Parental Divorce and Children's Development

On the average, children whose parents have divorced show more behavioral and emotional problems and poorer academic achievement than children whose parents are not divorced. Also, authoritative parenting is less common in divorced families than in nondivorced families. The long-term effects of parental divorce depend on many features of children's families and their lives.

## Single-Parent Families

The number of children living in single-parent families has increased not only because of parental divorce but also because more never-married women are having children. The behavioral profile of children with never-married single parents is much like that of children whose parents have divorced.

## Remarriage and Stepfamilies

Children often react negatively when a divorced parent remarries and they become part of a stepfamily. Problems in stepfamilies are most severe when the children are approaching adolescence and when parents and stepparents do not carefully monitor their children's behavior.

## When Parenting Goes Awry: Child Maltreatment

Child maltreatment includes the physical abuse, neglect, sexual abuse, or emotional maltreatment of children by people—usually their parents—who are responsible for their welfare. In the United States in 1992 about 900,000 reports of suspected abuse were substantiated.

## Causes of Child Maltreatment: An Ecological-Transactional Model

Parents' characteristics, characteristics of children and the family environment, and characteristics of the exosystem and macrosystem all affect the risk of child maltreatment. Conditions increasing risk and those compensating for increased risk act together through a transactional process.

## Effects of Child Maltreatment, Intervention, and Prevention

Child maltreatment is associated with psychological problems ranging from insecure attachments in infancy to violent behavior in adulthood. Professionals have devised intervention programs for abusive parents, but few evaluations of these programs have been done. Preventing child maltreatment is difficult but possible, if programs focus on all its causes, from parents' ignorance about child development to inadequate funding for agencies charged with protecting children.

## Relationships in Family Systems

Families form systems in which each relationship influences all other relationships. These systems normally operate to maintain their stability, but they also evolve and change as each member grows older. They also change when family composition changes, for example, with a remarriage or the birth of a sibling.

# SUGGESTED READINGS

**Dunn, J., & Plomin, R. (1990).** *Separate lives: Why siblings are so different.* **New York: Basic Books.** This brief book (172 pages) weaves the biographies of famous people and the data from empirical research into an explanation of the differences between siblings. Judy Dunn has done some of the most important research on sibling relationships. Robert Plomin is a central figure in research on developmental behavior genetics. The book concludes with implications for researchers, clinicians, and parents.

**National Research Council (1993).** *Understanding child abuse and neglect.* **Washington, DC: National Academy Press.** In 1991 the National Research Council convened a panel of experts to review the existing research on child maltreatment. This book is the panel's major report. Chapters focus on the definition of child maltreatment, its frequency in the United States, its causes and consequences, and options for its prevention and intervention. Although the book deals primarily with research needs and issues, the chapters provide valuable information about maltreatment itself.

**Patterson, G. R. (1975).** *Families: Applications of social learning to family life.* **Champaign, IL: Research Press.** As you know by now, Gerald Patterson has studied problems in families from a social learning perspective. He has also worked to solve the problems that many parents have with their children. This book provides guidance for parents about how to handle misbehavior and encourage good behavior. For a more in-depth analysis of families and their problems, try his 1982 book, *Coercive Family Processes.*

**Stevenson, M. R., & Black, K. N. (1995).** *How divorce affects offspring: A research approach.* **Madison, WI: Brown & Benchmark.** Some books about divorce seem either too anecdotal, telling about the author's friends and acquaintances, or too abstract, mostly reviewing statistics. By contrast, Stevenson and Black balance accurate and current information from research with case studies based on the authors' teaching and clinical work with families. This book provides a valuable supplement to the information in this chapter.

*Chapter Twelve*

# PEER RELATIONSHIPS

A child's **peers** include all other children who are similar to the child in age. These peers usually include the child's best friends, although some children have best friends who are older or younger than they are. In the typical age-graded school, children's classmates also belong in the category of peers. Because children may like or dislike their classmates—and may be liked or disliked in return—children often have positive relationships with some of their peers and negative relationships with others.

Peer relationships can have many and varied influences on children's development. One type of influence is the focus of the following story. Strictly speaking, the story is fictional, but it is based on research done in the 1960s, before the breakup of the Soviet Union.

One Monday morning, Ivanov arrived early at his fifth-grade classroom because he was a class monitor for the week. That meant his unit, the group of classmates in his row, had chosen him to prepare the room for classes by opening the windows, watering the flowers, and making sure that each blackboard had enough chalk and erasers. Ivanov was pleased, even honored, to have this responsibility, and he wanted to make sure that his unit received high marks from their teacher.

When classes started for the day, something unusual happened. The teacher introduced a researcher from the Academy of Pedagogical Sciences in Moscow. The researcher told them that he wanted them to answer a brief questionnaire. After the questionnaires were distributed, Ivanov started reading the first item. It read as follows:

*You and your friends accidentally find a sheet of paper that the teacher must have lost. On this sheet are the questions and answers for a quiz that you are going to have tomorrow. Some of the kids suggest that you not say anything to the teacher about it so that all of you can get better marks. What would you **really do?** Suppose your friends decide to go ahead. Would you go along with them or refuse?*

| Refuse to Go Along with My Friends | | | | Go Along with My Friends | |
|---|---|---|---|---|---|
| *absolutely certain* | *fairly certain* | *I guess so* | *I guess so* | *fairly certain* | *absolutely certain* |

Ivanov hesitated for a moment, but not because he wasn't sure what he would do. He was amazed that anyone would even think of cheating on a quiz this way. Ivanov definitely would not have thought of doing that. On the questionnaire, he checked that he was "absolutely certain" he would refuse to go along with friends who urged him to cheat.

The other questionnaire items also posed situations where friends supposedly encouraged him to neglect homework, disobey parents, or do other antisocial actions. Ivanov was sometimes tempted to do what friends suggested, but most often he finally checked that he would do what he knew was right, despite pressure from friends.

Ivanov's questionnaire was part of a unique cross-national study (Bronfenbrenner, 1970). The study involved students like Ivanov from several schools in the Union of Soviet Socialist Republics (USSR), and students the same age from schools in the United States. Most students in the USSR behaved like Ivanov, rarely agreeing to comply with friends who supposedly encouraged them to engage in antisocial behavior. Students in the United States responded differently. Much more than those in the USSR, they said they were willing to go along with friends who pressured them to do some antisocial behavior.

Why this difference between the two countries? Urie Bronfenbrenner (1970), the researcher who designed this unique cross-national study, proposed that it resulted from important differences in children's socialization. He emphasized the scope of these differences in a book about the research, *Two Worlds of Childhood: U.S. and U.S.S.R.*

Bronfenbrenner's book became a best-seller, partly because his thesis was highly provocative. The book was published in 1970, when many people in the United States

regarded the USSR as an "evil empire," and many aspects of the Communist system were regarded as inhumane or unjust. Yet Bronfenbrenner argued that children were socialized much more successfully in the USSR than in the United States. Moreover, the evidence seemed to support this argument.

What, then, was wrong with the socialization of children in the United States? Bronfenbrenner proposed that in recent decades, peer influence in the United States had increased and parent influence had decreased. He also proposed that this change was bad for children because peer influence is largely negative. In his words,

> If the institutions of our society continue to remove parents, other adults, and older youth from active participation in the lives of children, and if the resulting vacuum is filled by the age-segregated peer group, *we can anticipate increased alienation, indifference, antagonism, and violence on the part of the younger generation in all segments of our society* (p. 121).

Bronfenbrenner further argued that peers do not encourage socially desirable behaviors. Therefore, "If children have contact only with their own age-mates, there is no possibility for learning culturally-established patterns of cooperation and mutual concern" (p. 121). In short, Bronfenbrenner assumed that when peers have an important influence on the socialization of children and parents do not, the effects on children's socialization are disastrous.

Bronfenbrenner's hypothesis presents one position on a central issue in the chapter, whether peers have a positive or negative effect on children's development. As you might guess, other theorists have taken the opposite position on this issue. They have argued that peer relationships have largely positive influences on social development in general, and cooperation and concern for others in particular (Piaget, 1965; Sullivan, 1953; Youniss, 1980).

In addition, Bronfenbrenner's hypothesis deals with the link between peer relationships and relationships with parents. Although he emphasized the opposition between parent-child and peer relationships, this hypothesis is controversial, too. Many theorists assume that little opposition exists between parents and peers. Indeed, they assume that good relationships with parents give children the skills they need to interact successfully with peers. You will read about the evidence on this issue throughout the chapter.

Finally, you should realize that the peer social world has many facets, and its structure can be examined either at simple or at more complex levels (Hartup, 1984; Hinde, 1987). To understand the approaches that different researchers have chosen, you need to understand these levels of complexity. Then you will be ready to explore the developmental changes that occur at each level.

# LEVELS OF COMPLEXITY IN THE PEER SOCIAL WORLD

At the simplest level, the peer social world is defined by interactions among children who are similar in age (see table 12.1). Among preschool children, peer interactions usually occur in the context of play. Therefore, play is listed in table 12.1 as the prototypical example of this level.

Some researchers who focus on the level of peer interactions are concerned with the social skills that these interactions reveal. As you will see, children can manage longer and more coordinated sequences of interactions as they grow older. Other researchers who focus on this level examine the quality of children's peer interactions. For example, they observe how often children show positive behaviors such as cooperation and negative behaviors such as aggression when interacting with peers.

Interactions define the basic level of the peer social world throughout childhood, adolescence, and adulthood. But as children grow older, the second level of the social world, that of relationships, becomes more important (see table 12.1). A **relationship** involves a series of interactions between two people who know each other. It also involves the expectations and emotions that the two people associate with their history of interaction (Hartup, 1984; Hinde, 1987).

**relationship**
*A tie between two people who have had several interactions over time. Also involves the expectations and emotions that the two people associate with their history of interactions.*

| TABLE 12.1 | *Levels of Complexity in the Peer Social World* |
|---|---|
| LEVEL | PROTOTYPICAL EXAMPLE |
| 1. Interactions | Play |
| 2. Relationships | Friendship |
| 3. Position in a group | Social status |
| 4. Group membership and reputation | Cliques and crowds |

**social status**
*A child's position or popularity in a group, defined by how much the peers in the group like or dislike them.*

**clique**
*A small group of close friends.*

**crowd**
*A large group of adolescents who have similar reputations for behavior and who may be identified with the same label (e.g., "jocks").*

The most important of children's relationships with peers are those with their best friends, so friendship is listed in the table as the prototypical example at the relationships level. Friendships emerge during the preschool years but attain their full significance during later childhood and adolescence.

The third level of the peer social world is that of a child's position in a group. This level is more complex than the preceding ones because it reflects children's relationships with several peers. Many researchers have examined one indicator of these relationships, children's **social status.** Children are high in status, or popular, when most of their peers like them. Children are low in status, or unpopular, when few of their peers like them or many of their peers dislike them. More generally, children's social status is defined by how much the peers in a particular group like or dislike them.

The social structure of the peer world is still more complex than a measure of social status implies. The group of peers in the same classroom or the same grade at school is usually divided into small groups of children who are close friends. The members of a single friendship group define a **clique.**

Friendship groups are especially important in theories of peer influence. Remember that Bronfenbrenner (1970) asked students like Ivanov to say how they would react to pressure from their group of friends. Later research has shown, as Bronfenbrenner assumed, that the peers who influence children and adolescents most are the members of their friendship group or clique (Berndt, 1992; Cohen, 1983).

As children move into adolescence, they may belong not only to a clique but also to a **crowd,** a group of students who have similar reputations (Brown, 1989). For example, students who belong to athletic teams and are heavily involved in athletics are sometimes called "jocks." That is, they are regarded as part of the jock crowd.

In a large high school, a single crowd may include dozens of adolescents, so crowds are much larger than cliques. Adolescents in the same crowd may not be close friends and may not even interact with one another. In other words, they may be part of different cliques. Conversely, adolescents in the same clique often belong to different crowds (Urberg et al., 1995).

Nevertheless, crowd members are assigned the same label because their peers view them as behaving in similar ways or as enjoying similar activities. Also, both cliques and crowds represent subgroups of the larger peer group. Therefore, both can be placed at the same level of social complexity.

You should keep these levels of social complexity in mind as you read the sections of this chapter. The next section focuses on the level of interactions, beginning with the first interactions between infants and their peers. The following section focuses on friendships, beginning with their origins in early childhood and continuing to their full flowering in adolescence. The third section focuses on the definition of social status and the reasons that children differ in their status. A fourth section focuses on the functioning of cliques and crowds, especially in adolescence.

In each section, you will read about the potential effects of peer relationships. Be forewarned, though, that these effects differ at different levels of social complexity. Therefore, you should not expect to receive one general answer to the question about whether peer

The features of peer relationships change greatly as children grow. In the preschool years, pretend play is an especially important form of peer interaction. During the elementary-school years, friendships like those between the three girls in school set the stage for enjoyable interactions and support. In adolescence, cliques or crowds structure the social world and define who goes to which parties with whom.

relationships are good or bad for children. Still, after reading the chapter you will know more about when and why each facet of peer relationships has positive effects and negative effects on children's development.

# PEER INTERACTIONS IN INFANCY AND EARLY CHILDHOOD

If you spend some time watching children in a preschool or nursery school, you'll see many interactions like the following.

> Jane, who is 4 years old, is playing with dolls, dressing them in various outfits. Linda, who is also 4 years old, is playing with pots, pans, and utensils at a toy stove, pretending to cook. Linda asks Jane whether she wants to play house. Jane says, "Okay, sure."

One-year-olds are interested in their peers and often watch as their peers play with toys. But they don't initiate interactions with peers as much as older children do, and most of their interactions focus on toy play.

Linda replies, "Then I'll be the mommy and you be the baby."

"No," Jane says, "I don't want to be the baby."

They continue talking and finally agree that they will both be mommies and use dolls as their babies. They play together happily for the next 15 minutes.

This sequence of interactions may seem simple and unsophisticated, but you would not expect to see such play in newborns, or even in toddlers. A long period of development of social skills prepared Jane and Linda for their cooperative play with dolls. Let's see where they began and how they gradually moved to their 4-year-old competence.

## Infants' and Toddlers' Behavior Toward Peers

Newborns and young infants rarely direct social behavior toward peers. Six-month-olds sometimes respond to peers by staring at them, reaching for them, and touching them. Between 6 and 12 months of age, social behavior toward peers becomes more frequent and more complex. Infants smile at peers, gesture to them, and begin to synchronize their looks at peers with attempts to touch or show them things (Hartup, 1983; Vandell, Wilson, & Buchanan, 1980).

By 12 months of age, infants can engage in simple social interactions with a peer. They can draw a peer's attention to a toy by pointing to it. They can imitate simple actions that a peer does with a toy (Eckerman & Stein, 1982). Yet these interactions do not occur very often. When infants are in the same room, they engage in social behavior toward each other less than once a minute (Hartup, 1983). Social contact is more frequent when no toys are around and the infants' mothers are not paying attention to them. At 1 year, infants seem to enjoy playing with toys or interacting with their mothers more than with a social partner as immature as themselves.

When 1-year-olds interact, they are more positive than negative toward each other. On occasion, 1-year-olds push down a peer or hurt the peer in another way. Often, though, these acts seem aimed at exploration rather than injury. One-year-olds seem to view peers as interesting toys—you push them to see what happens—not as other people like themselves (Bronson, 1975).

During the second and third years of life, expressions of positive emotions become more frequent during peer interactions (Brownell, 1990). In addition, gestures and talking

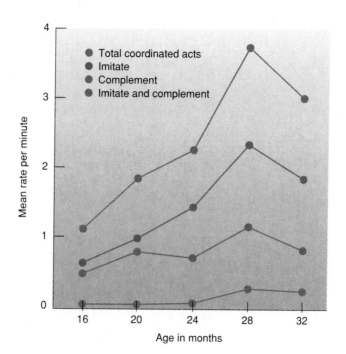

FIGURE 12.1
Between 16 and 32 months of age, the frequency of coordinated acts between peers increases. The type of coordinated act that increases most during this period is imitation. (Source: Eckerman et al., 1989.)

increase. Children's growing social skill is also shown by an increase in interactions that involve several sequences of actions by one child and responses by the other.

Other important changes in peer interactions were identified in a longitudinal study of preschool children (Eckerman, Davis, & Didow, 1989). When the children were 16 months old, and every four months after that, they were observed interacting with a peer in a laboratory playroom equipped with toys. As figure 12.1 shows, between 16 and 32 months of age children increased from about one to more than three coordinated acts per minute. Acts were considered as coordinated when they related to the partner's previous activity but expanded the activity to include both children. These acts could range from giving the other child a toy to imitating the other child's previous action.

Figure 12.1 also shows the rates for three types of coordinated acts. Imitative acts were most common and increased most sharply with age. In a related experimental study (Eckerman & Stein, 1990), preschoolers who were imitated by another person often looked at their partner and repeated the action that was imitated. In that study and in the longitudinal study, imitation by a social partner often led to an imitative game.

Children were judged to be playing a game when they did the same acts repeatedly and both children seemed to enjoy the interaction. For example, children might take turns jumping off a box or throwing a beanbag at a target. In this way, the act of imitation fostered extended social contact and contributed to the development of a relationship between partners.

Imitative games might seem very simple, but they involve more elements than you might imagine. Suppose 2-year-old Mary wants to play a throwing game with her playmate, Susan. Mary must first signal to Susan that she wants her to play the game. Susan must signal that she is willing to play. Mary must take her turn, indicate when her turn is over, and signal that Susan now should take her turn. After Susan takes her turn, she must signal Mary that she's done (Eckerman & Stein, 1982).

The task for children gets even more complex when the two children do not do the same thing. In complementary acts, playmates take different roles. If your playmate is chasing you, for example, you might do your part by running away, not by chasing him or her. In complementary games, children must manage their different roles across a series of interactions. Even apparently simple roles like Mommy and Daddy can be difficult for young children to coordinate because they must agree on what the child in each role should do. Perhaps this complexity explains why complementary acts and games were more rare than imitative ones and only increased slightly between 16 and 32 months of age (see figure 12.1).

FIGURE 12.2

More than 60 years ago, Parten (1932) showed that cooperative play occurs more frequently among 4-year-olds than among 2-year-olds. Yet throughout this age range, cooperative play is less common than parallel and associative play. (Adapted from Parten, 1932.)

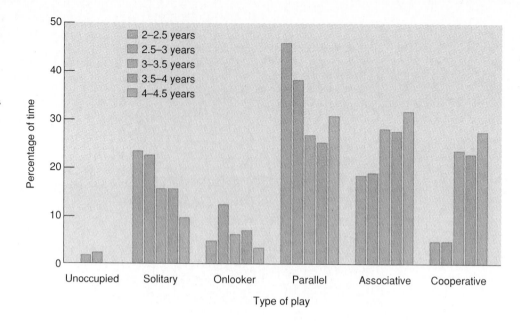

Finally, the figure shows that some acts involved both imitative and complementary elements, for example, picking up a ball thrown by the partner (complementary) and throwing it back (imitation). Although these mixed acts were not common, they increased with age. They may provide a bridge between the imitative games of toddlers and the "pretend" play of preschool children (Eckerman et al., 1989).

Still, the strategy of imitation is a significant achievement in itself. By imitating another, children send an obvious signal that they are ready for joint play. They also show that they see the other person as like themselves. When children can signal their intentions and recognize that peers are similar to themselves, they have the potential for complex forms of social interaction. This potential flowers during the preschool years, in social play.

## Types of Play in Preschool Children

In a classic study, Mildred Parten (1932) observed children in nursery-school classrooms during free-play periods, when the children could do what they wanted with little direction by teachers. She defined six types of play and assessed how often 2- to 4-year-olds engaged in each type. Figure 12.2 shows her results.

Parten (1932) ordered the six play types in the figure by their assumed complexity. She judged **cooperative play** as most complex. Cooperative play includes social pretend play like the mommy-baby play mentioned earlier. It also includes constructive play, for example, when children are making a castle and one child builds the palace while another builds the outer walls. In addition, Parten included formal games in the category of cooperative play. The figure shows that cooperative play was rare before 3 years of age and was more common among 4-year-olds than among 3-year-olds.

The most common play type among 4-year-olds was **associative play.** Children engaged in associative play use the same materials and talk together. They may also share toys or imitate each other. Unlike in cooperative play, however, children do not take different roles or work on different parts of a joint construction.

**Parallel play** was almost as common among 4-year-olds as associative play. Among 2-year-olds, parallel play was most common. Parten defined parallel play as independent play with the same toys or materials as other children. In her words, a child "plays with toys that are like those which the children around him are using, but he plays with the toys as he sees fit, and does not try to influence or modify the activity of the children near him. He plays *beside* rather than *with* other children" (1932, p. 250). Parten viewed parallel play as less socially mature than associative or cooperative play.

**cooperative play**
*The most socially complex of Parten's play types, which includes social pretend play, constructive play in which children work on different parts of a structure, and formal games.*

**associative play**
*Defined by Parten as the play type in which children use the same materials and talk together, or share toys and imitate each other, but do not take different roles or work on different parts of a construction.*

**parallel play**
*According to Parten, the play type in which a child plays with the same toys or materials as other children but does not try to influence or interact with the other children.*

These two preschoolers are engaged in *parallel play*. They are playing with similar toys but they are not talking to each other. They are playing beside rather than with each other.

The remaining play types shown in the figure—onlooker, solitary, and unoccupied—reflect nonsocial activities. In a strict sense, the onlooker and unoccupied categories reflect the absence of play. A child is engaged in **onlooker play** when he or she is watching or listening to other children at play but is not playing with them. A child is engaged in **unoccupied play** when he or she is not playing with anyone or anything, just looking around the classroom at whatever seems interesting. **Solitary play** involves play, but children play with toys different from those of the children around them, and they ignore what the other children are doing. In Parten's study, these three types of behavior decreased with age.

Later researchers have replicated many of Parten's findings but have refined or qualified her conclusions (see Hartup, 1983; Howes, 1987; Rubin, Fein, & Vandenberg, 1983). Parten focused on the complexity of children's social interactions during play, but play also varies in its cognitive complexity. When researchers focused on the cognitive skills that children reveal in their play, they identified four distinct types of play (Piaget, 1962; Smilansky, 1968).

The type of play lowest in cognitive complexity is **functional, or practice, play** with objects. In this type of play, children practice sensorimotor skills by repeating an action many times. For example, they slide down a slide over and over.

More cognitively complex is **constructive play.** Children are not only exercising motor skills but also creating a product. They may build with blocks or make a landscape in the sandbox.

Still more complex, from this theoretical perspective, is **dramatic play.** The 4-year-old girls' mommy-baby play is one example. Most complex are **games with rules.** Some games played by children, like baseball and soccer, mimic the sports of adults. Other games like tag and marbles are played mostly by children.

Researchers sometimes code children's play simultaneously for its social and cognitive complexity. For example, they describe a child on a slide by himself as engaged in solitary functional play. They define the 4-year-olds' mommy-baby play as cooperative-dramatic play. When researchers began to code children's play in this way, they made three discoveries about the development of play.

One discovery was that only some types of solitary play reflect a lack of social maturity. In particular, solitary-functional play can be a sign of immaturity. Preschoolers who often engage in repetitive motor activities by themselves usually are younger than their classmates and have lower scores on the Peabody Picture Vocabulary Test, or PPVT (Rubin, 1982). By contrast, solitary-constructive play is not related to age or PPVT scores. Therefore,

**onlooker play**
*Parten's category for times in which a child is watching or listening to other children but not playing with them.*

**unoccupied play**
*Parten's label for episodes in which a child is only looking around the classroom, not playing with anyone or anything.*

**solitary play**
*Children are playing alone, with toys different from those of other children, and are paying no attention to the other children.*

**functional (practice) play**
*The type of play lowest in cognitive complexity, in which children practice sensorimotor skills by repeating an action like sliding down a slide many times.*

**constructive play**
*Play in which children create something, like a building made of blocks.*

**dramatic play**
*Play in which children take on imaginary roles like Mommy and baby. Also known as pretend play.*

**games with rules**
*A category for children's play that includes sports such as baseball and children's games such as tag.*

| TABLE 12.2 | *Howes's Levels of Peer Play* |
|---|---|
| TYPE OF PLAY | DEFINITION |
| Parallel | Children are near one another and engaged in the same activity but have no contact. |
| Parallel aware | In addition to the requirements for parallel play, children make eye contact. |
| Simple social | In addition to previous requirements, children talk, smile, exchange toys, or interact in another way. |
| Complementary and reciprocal | Children play games such as peekaboo in which they switch roles. |
| Cooperative social pretend | Children take complementary roles while pretending to be other people (e.g., doctor and patient). |
| Complex social pretend | While engaged in social pretend play, children name their roles, explicitly assign roles, or engage in other organizing and directing of their joint play. |

preschoolers who spend more time building things by themselves cannot be judged as immature. They may simply prefer working with objects to interacting with peers. When they do choose to interact with peers, they may do so as successfully as do more sociable children (Hartup, 1983).

The second discovery relates to Parten's categories for time spent unoccupied or as an onlooker. Preschoolers who are more often unoccupied or onlookers are not only socially immature. Many of these preschoolers have other problems that limit their ability to join in play with other children (Berndt & Bulleit, 1985; Putallaz & Wasserman, 1990; Roper & Hinde, 1978). They may be shy, withdrawn, or engage in behavior that other children dislike. You'll learn more about these children's problems in the section of this chapter on social status.

The third discovery concerns Parten's category of cooperative play. Some types of cooperative play are more cognitively complex than others. Distinguishing these types makes it easier to assess preschoolers' social competence.

After observing many preschoolers in many settings, Carollee Howes (1980; Howes & Matheson, 1992; Howes, Unger, & Seidner, 1989) devised a new scale for assessing peer play. Table 12.2 shows that the new scale has three levels of cooperative play. The "complementary and reciprocal" level includes simple games such as peekaboo that can be seen even in 18- to 24-month-olds. The "cooperative social pretend" level adds an element of make-believe, or taking on another's role, to the simpler forms of cooperative play.

The highest level of Howes's scale, "complex social pretend" play, is characterized by explicit organizing and directing of the play. Children state which roles they are taking on, they tell other actors what they can and can't do when "in role," and so on. This type of play is not shown by most children until after 4 years of age.

The Howes Peer Play Scale also subdivides Parten's category for parallel play. Parallel play in which children are attending to each other, by making eye contact, is distinguished from parallel play that involves simply using the same activities. The former type of "parallel aware" play is found among older children and suggests more social competence than simple parallel play does.

No ages are listed for the different types of play in table 12.2 because their frequency does not depend solely on children's age. The setting in which children are playing also affects the level of play that they regularly show. In lower-quality child-care centers, which have fewer teachers for each group of children and fewer activities appropriate for the children's age, children usually show lower levels of play (Howes & Matheson, 1992).

Finally, the Howes scale is designed for preschool children, so it does not include games with rules, the most cognitively complex form of play (Piaget, 1962). Games like

When rhesus monkeys are separated from their mothers at birth and reared together, they develop abnormal patterns of behavior. They become highly attached to one another and spend most of their time clinging together. Thus they do not learn normal patterns of play.

hopscotch, tag, or King of the Mountain call for greater social skill than do the other types of cooperative play. To organize and play these games, children must take others' perspectives (Piaget, 1965).

As you saw in chapter 7, perspective-taking ability is one requirement for successful communication with a peer. For group games, children must communicate effectively to a group, not just to one other child. Few preschool children have this degree of communication skill (Hartup, 1983). Consequently, games with rules are played more often by elementary-school children than by preschoolers (Eiferman, 1971; Smilansky, 1968). Stated differently, children spend less time in pretend play, and more time playing games with rules, as they move from the preschool to the school years.

In summary, Parten's (1932) categories do not capture all the important variations in children's play, but they illustrate a significant change in peer interaction during the preschool years. They capture the shift from largely independent play to long sequences of social play in which children adopt distinct and complementary roles.

## Effects of Young Children's Interactions with Peers: Good or Bad?

During infancy and early childhood, the frequency of interactions with peers increases. During the same period, children's social skills increase. Many researchers have proposed that these two developments are related, because peer interactions contribute to the learning and refinement of social skills. This hypothesis has been tested in four kinds of research.

### Peer Deprivation in Monkeys

The importance of peer interactions was shown most dramatically in studies done not with children but with young rhesus monkeys. You read in chapter 6 about Harlow's studies of monkeys that were separated from their mothers shortly after birth and raised with cloth or wire surrogate mothers. In other experiments, monkeys were reared by their mothers but without any peer contact (see Suomi, 1979; Suomi & Harlow, 1975). These experiments showed the negative effects of peer deprivation.

Play between an infant monkey who was reared in social isolation (center) and a younger "therapist" monkey (right).
(From Suomi & Harlow, 1975.)

The peer-deprived monkeys were not as abnormal in their behavior as were monkeys separated from their mothers. Even so, peer-deprived monkeys had problems when they were finally allowed to interact with peers. They rarely engaged in the playful interactions typical of young monkeys. When they did interact with peers, they were highly aggressive. In short, they had not learned the social skills necessary for playful, friendly interaction. These social skills apparently are learned from peers rather than parents.

Interactions with peers are not sufficient by themselves, however, to ensure normal development. Monkeys also develop abnormally if they are reared only with peers and not with their mothers or other adults. Groups of infant monkeys who are separated from their mothers become highly attached to one another. Their attachment is excessive, though. They spend great amounts of time clinging to each other and little time in play. When introduced to a strange environment, they give more distress calls and are less active than monkeys reared only by their mothers (Higley et al., 1992). In adulthood, they are highly aggressive toward monkeys who were not reared with them. This evidence confirms that monkeys—and, most likely, humans—need to interact with both peers and adults to develop normally.

The experiments with monkeys raise another question. The experiments show that early experiences of peer deprivation or maternal deprivation have effects that last into adulthood. You might wonder whether these effects are unchangeable or can be counteracted by later experience. Is there, in other words, some therapy that can make peer- or mother-deprived monkeys normal?

The answer is yes, but the form of the therapy may seem surprising (Novak & Harlow, 1975). The therapy was first tested with monkeys who were both peer- and mother-deprived. These monkeys were reared in total social isolation, away from all members of their species, for six months after birth. Then they were paired with "therapist" monkeys several months younger than themselves.

When the pairs of monkeys were together, the younger monkeys tried to engage the isolate-reared monkeys in play. At first, these efforts were unsuccessful, but the younger monkeys persisted. Eventually, the isolate monkeys responded positively to the "therapists" and began to play. As the younger monkeys grew older, they showed increasingly complex play that the isolate monkeys also learned. In short, the behavior of the isolate-reared monkeys became more normal, and the negative effects of their early experiences were reduced.

The younger therapists were successful partly because their behavior—unlike that of the isolated-reared monkeys—was normal for their age. But why was their behavior normal? The answer: They were reared in a normal environment with their parents and other monkeys. Indirectly, then, these monkeys' effectiveness as therapists depended on their relationships with

their parents. This experiment shows that parents influence the peer interactions of their off-spring even when the parents are not present during those interactions. You will see more examples of the influence of parents on peer relationships later.

## Effects of Peer Experience Among (Human) Toddlers

Experiments on monkeys are relevant for an understanding of human behavior because monkeys and humans are evolutionary relatives. However, few researchers assume that studies of monkeys and of humans would yield exactly the same results. Whether peer experience has beneficial effects on children as well as on monkeys must be examined directly.

Researchers cannot do peer-deprivation studies with children because depriving young children of a potentially valuable experience would be unethical. However, researchers can examine the differences among children who differ in their peer experience. These studies suggest that toddlers who have greater peer experience are more socially skilled (Vandell & Wilson, 1982). Toddlers who have interacted more frequently with peers are more sociable toward unfamiliar peers and show more coordinated social behavior toward those peers.

Because these findings come from studies with correlational designs, they do not prove that greater peer experience actually makes children more sociable and more socially skilled. To test this causal hypothesis, experimental studies are needed. These experiments involve not peer deprivation but increasing children's experience with peers.

In one experimental study (Vandell, 1979), six toddlers were given extra experience with peers in a special playgroup. The playgroup met five mornings a week for six weeks. Another six toddlers who were similar to the first group in age, sex, and family characteristics served as a control group. The two groups did not differ in their interactions with parents before the playgroup began. Parent-child interactions were assessed again a few weeks after the playgroup ended. At that time, the playgroup toddlers were more responsive to their parents and participated more equally in their interactions with parents than did those in the control group. Interacting with peers, then, increased the toddlers' skills in interacting with their parents.

## Effects of Preschool Play

Other theorists have focused not on the amount of peer experience that children have but on the characteristics of their play with peers. These theorists have proposed that social pretend play, in particular, has positive effects on children (see Rubin et al., 1983). When 4-year-old Jane pretends to be a mommy, for example, she explores new ways of thinking about herself, other people, and their relationships to one another. When she uses a wagon as a baby carriage or pretends to serve food to her baby, she practices thinking about objects in unconventional ways. These exercises in imagination may enhance both her cognitive and her social development.

Findings regarding the effects of social pretend play are mixed (Connolly & Doyle, 1984; Rubin et al., 1983). In several correlational studies, children who spent more time in social pretend play were better at taking other people's perspectives, more creative, and more popular with their peers. Their teachers viewed them as more competent than children who less often engaged in social pretend play.

In several experimental studies, children received explicit training in social pretend play. Sometimes children were provided with materials for pretend play (e.g., a stethoscope for doctor and nurse play). Sometimes children were given props and encouraged to act out fairy tales. Sometimes children were given a field trip and then encouraged to reenact what they saw in play (Rubin et al., 1983). In a few studies, play training increased children's perspective-taking ability, creativity, and social competence.

Other experimental studies yielded less positive results. Either the children given play training did not differ from children in a control group, or they differed on only a few of the dependent variables in a study (Rubin et al., 1983). The reasons for the contrasting results are not clear. The play-training procedures differed across studies, and some procedures may have been more effective than others. Also, the training in some cases may not have added greatly to the play skills that children already had.

However, nearly all studies show that training in social pretend play increases children's tendency to engage in pretend play in their regular preschool classroom. That is, the training affects both children's sociability toward peers and the specific social skills needed for pretend play. In addition, preschoolers are happier and act more positively toward other children during social pretend play than when they are doing other activities. Preschoolers also interact with larger groups of peers for longer periods when engaged in social pretend play (Connolly, Doyle, & Reznick, 1988).

Taken together, the evidence shows that social pretend play allows children to practice desirable skills for peer interaction. Practice does not always "make perfect," but it is usually a step in the right direction.

## Effects of Experience in Child-Care Centers

In 1993 almost 3 million preschool children in the United States were enrolled in organized child-care centers (U.S. Bureau of the Census, 1995b). The children who attend these centers have more peer experience than do children who spend their preschool years mostly at home. Would you expect the two groups of children to differ in their behavior? If so, how would they differ?

These questions have long been controversial, and recent studies have yielded inconsistent results (Andersson, 1992; Clarke-Stewart, 1989; Clarke-Stewart & Fein, 1983; Scarr, Phillips, & McCartney, 1990). In some studies, children enrolled in child-care centers were more self-confident and socially competent than children reared solely at home. These studies appear to confirm the hypothesis that peer experience increases children's social skills. In other studies, children in child-care centers and children reared at home differed little in their social behavior and social competence.

Several researchers have found that preschoolers with extensive experience in child-care centers are more aggressive toward peers than are children reared at home (Clarke-Stewart, 1989). The research data are not completely consistent, but greater aggression among children in day care has been reported often enough to be a source of concern. The effect of child-care centers on children's aggressive behavior can persist into the elementary-school years, although the effect becomes weaker as children grow older (Bates et al., 1994; Haskins, 1985).

Why do children attending child-care centers sometimes show increased aggressive behavior? You can make an educated guess by considering the characteristics of preschoolers' aggression.

Preschoolers fight most often over toys (Hartup, 1983; Parke & Slaby, 1983). Their fights usually are brief, and few provoke any reaction by teachers. Often teachers don't even notice that an aggressive act has occurred. Partly for this reason, aggressors are often successful. A child who grabs a toy usually gets to keep it. In theoretical terms, aggressive behavior is positively reinforced. This reinforcement leads, over time, to increases in preschoolers' aggressive behavior (Patterson, Littman, & Bricker, 1967).

Does this description of aggression in preschoolers' groups sound familiar? Some of you may be reminded of the novel by William Golding, *Lord of the Flies.* In Golding's novel, several boys whose plane crashed on an island were highly aggressive, partly because they were not restrained by adults. (Their pilot was wounded in the crash and could not lead them.) The lack of adult restraint is also critical to aggressive behavior among preschoolers.

The solution is simple. If the adults in child-care centers monitor children's behavior carefully and prevent children from being reinforced for aggression, aggressive behavior should decline—and it does (Clarke-Stewart, 1989). This means that the ability and willingness of adult caregivers to monitor children's behavior and punish aggression is one indicator of the quality of a child-care center. Of course, monitoring preschoolers' behavior is more difficult when caregivers have many children to watch. Therefore, the quality of child care is typically higher when the ratio of caregivers to children is high.

Caregivers can do more than prevent children from being reinforced for aggression. They can also encourage desirable behaviors with praise, other types of rewards, or modeling.

What ratio of adults to children is shown in this picture? One adult seems to be in charge of seven preschoolers. Although the children seem happy, they are unlikely to receive high-quality care if that ratio holds throughout the day. The adult is unlikely to provide individual children with much verbal or cognitive stimulation. In addition, she cannot adequately monitor the children's behavior toward their peers.

Caregivers with training in child development are more likely to provide such encouragement. Caregiver training is another indicator of child-care quality that relates positively to children's development (Scarr et al., 1990).

Trained caregivers who are not overwhelmed by large numbers of children can engage in more verbal interaction with their children. When caregivers talk more with children, not just to give orders but to converse with them, children are more sociable and more considerate of others (Phillips, McCartney, & Scarr, 1987).

In summary, experiences with peers in child-care centers can have positive or negative effects on children's development. When children attend centers with a good teacher-child ratio, well-trained teachers, and an educationally stimulating curriculum, they are likely to be high in social and academic competence when they enter elementary school. In particular, they are likely to be emotionally mature, popular, and leaders in their class (Field, 1991).

Unfortunately, recent surveys suggest that the typical day-care center in the United States does not provide high-quality care (Phillips et al., 1994). For example, an average classroom for toddlers has one teacher and seven children, when experts recommend a 1:5 ratio at most. More than one-quarter of child-care staff have a high-school degree or less. Moreover, centers that mostly serve middle-class families typically provide the lowest-quality care. These centers do not receive the government subsidies available to low-income centers and cannot charge as much as centers serving upper-class families.

Finally, not all preschoolers who receive daily care from people other than their parents are in child-care centers. In the United States in 1993, more than 1.6 million of these children were in family day-care homes (U.S. Bureau of the Census, 1995b). In these homes, one or more adults care for several children.

The criteria for a high-quality family day-care home are similar to those for a high-quality center. Homes offer higher-quality care when the caregivers schedule, organize, and monitor the children's activities. The care is higher in quality when there are fewer children per caregiver and when the caregivers spend more time in conversation with children. Also, high-quality homes have enough space for children either to play together or to be alone.

When children are in better family day-care homes, they have more positive interactions with peers and show more complex social play (Howes & Stewart, 1987). Stated more generally, adults partly control the characteristics of peer interactions. In both child-care centers and family day-care homes, caregivers structure children's experiences in ways that can either foster positive peer relationships or elicit aggressive and other negative behaviors. Consequently, adults have a powerful influence on how children's interactions with peers affect their development.

# How Do Parents Influence Their Children's Interactions with Peers?

The adults who have the most influence on children's peer interactions are their parents. Parents have both direct and indirect influences on their children's behavior toward peers (Ladd & Le Sieur, 1995; Parke & Bhavnagri, 1989).

## Modes of Direct Influence

Parents can directly influence their children's peer interactions in many ways. For example, parents choose where their family will live. On one hand, they can choose a neighborhood with playgrounds, parks, and other children as playmates. On the other hand, they can choose a neighborhood where houses are far apart, children are few, and most peer interactions must be prearranged (Medrich et al., 1982).

Parents can also enroll their children in organized activities such as sports, Scouting, 4-H, or other youth organizations. They can take their young children to the library for group story time, to the pool for group swimming lessons, or to church for Sunday School. Preschool children who participate in more of these community activities are less anxious when they enter kindergarten (Ladd & Price, 1987).

In addition, parents can arrange less formal interactions with peers. They can invite other children to visit, thereby increasing their children's chances to interact with peers. When their children are playing at home, parents can monitor those interactions to be sure the children enjoy their time together and resolve their conflicts quickly (Parke & Bhavnagri, 1989).

You may wonder whether it is good for parents to interfere with their children's peer interactions in these ways. Much of the time, the world of peers is separate from that of parent-child relationships. Wouldn't it be good for parents to respect this separation and let their children handle all their contacts with peers by themselves?

The answer to this question is not as simple as you might think. Parents' *initiations* of peer interactions may have different effects, and be done for different reasons, than parents' *monitoring* of peer interactions.

***Effects of Parents' Initiations*** In chapter 2 you read about a study by Gary Ladd and Beckie Golter (1988) in which parents reported on their children's interactions with peers. During evening telephone interviews, parents told whether their preschool- or kindergarten-age child had any interactions with peers that day, and who had initiated the interactions. Most often, the children had asked to play with another child or another child had asked them to play. The parents had rarely arranged playmates for their children, but about half of them did so at least once.

How were children affected by their parents' initiations? The data in figure 12.3 suggest that the children benefited from their parents' involvement. Preschool and kindergarten children had more contacts with peers when their parents sometimes arranged interactions for them. Children had more consistent playmates when their parents sometimes arranged interactions. Moreover, boys were better liked by their classmates when their parents sometimes arranged interactions, but this effect was not found for girls.

In a later study (Ladd & Hart, 1992), similar methods were used to examine the relations of parents' initiations to preschoolers' emotions and behavior at school. When their parents initiated more peer interactions, preschoolers were less anxious and engaged in more cooperative play and conversation in the preschool. As in the original study, boys but not girls were better liked by their classmates when their parents initiated more interactions for them. The gender difference may exist because boys typically have a larger group of peers with whom they interact frequently than girls do. Parents' initiations may help boys to form and manage such a large group.

Parents' initiations of peer interaction may be valuable even with school-age children and adolescents. Sometimes children run out of ideas for activities, and parents can suggest an activity that would be enjoyable to do with peers. Sometimes children need parents to facilitate peer interactions by driving them to another child's house or serving as hosts for other children. Parents who volunteer to take on these roles help their children to build relationships

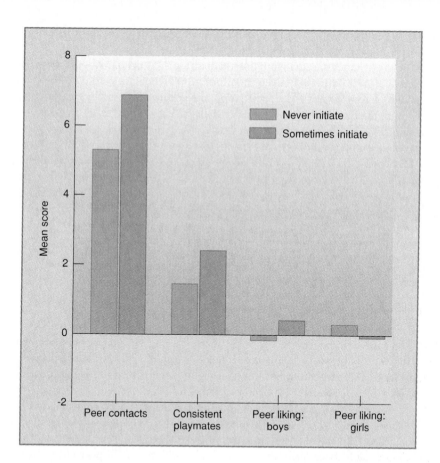

FIGURE 12.3
Parents' initiations of peer interactions are related to their preschoolers' success in peer relationships. Preschoolers seem to benefit when their parents sometimes arrange a peer playmate for them. (Source: Ladd & Golter, 1988.)

with peers. Moreover, children can learn how to arrange an activity with peers by observing their parents' example. When parents initiate more peer interactions for their preschool children, the children themselves initiate more interactions with peers (Ladd & Hart, 1992).

*Effects of Parents' Monitoring*   Whether young children benefit from their parents' monitoring of their peer interactions is difficult to say. In Ladd and Golter's (1988) study, parents were asked whether they monitored their child's interactions with peers by staying with the children or participating in their play. Some parents reported that they rarely monitored directly but that they did indirect monitoring. That is, they checked on the children occasionally and kept aware of what they were doing but did not get involved in the play themselves. Few parents said that they left children completely unsupervised. They probably assumed (rightly) that leaving preschool or kindergarten children completely by themselves is not safe.

The children whose parents monitored their play more directly were less socially competent than those whose parents did more indirect monitoring. The children whose parents used direct monitoring were less well liked and more often disliked by classmates than those whose parents monitored indirectly. Teachers rated the children whose parents used direct monitoring as more aggressive than children whose parents were more indirect.

A second study clarified why parents of young children monitor peer interactions directly (Mize, Pettit, & Brown, 1995). Mothers supervised their children's play more closely when they perceived their children as having poor social skills. Mothers' ratings of their children's social skills were strongly correlated with the ratings of the children's preschool teachers, suggesting that mothers judged their children's social competence accurately.

These findings come from a correlational study, so they can be explained in at least two ways (Ladd & Golter, 1988; Mize et al., 1995). On one hand, direct monitoring by parents may hinder the development of children's social skills. Preschoolers whose play is always monitored at home may show more out-of-control behavior in preschool classrooms where

monitoring is less frequent. Moreover, parents' monitoring may be so intrusive and inappropriate that it lowers children's social competence.

On the other hand, parents who directly monitor their preschoolers' interactions may have preschoolers who especially need monitoring. Preschoolers who tend to be more aggressive or out of control may force their parents to supervise them closely. As you learned in the previous chapter, children can socialize their parents as well as vice versa.

Most likely, both these explanations are partly correct. From a practical perspective, neither explanation suggests that parents should avoid monitoring their children's play (Ladd & Le Sieur, 1995). As you recall, preschoolers in child-care centers tend to become aggressive if no adults monitor their peer interactions. Even in adolescence, monitoring of peer interactions is needed to ensure that adolescents do not drift into deviant behaviors with peers (Patterson & Stouthamer-Loeber, 1984; Steinberg, 1986). Some parents may need to monitor their children more closely than other parents do, but all parents should pay attention to their children's behavior toward peers. In short, parents' greatest concern should be not that they will do too much but that they will do too little to foster positive peer interactions.

## Modes of Indirect Influence

Children's interactions with peers can also be influenced, indirectly, by the quality of parent-child relationships. For example, attachment theorists suggest that peer interactions are affected by the security of infant-mother attachments (Sroufe, 1983). Infants who are securely attached to their mothers tend to become preschoolers who are well accepted by peers and socially skilled (e.g., Lafreniere & Sroufe, 1985; Ladd & Le Sieur, 1995). Insecurely attached infants are less successful in peer interactions as preschoolers. Compared with securely attached infants, those insecurely attached are likely to become less popular and less socially competent 10-year-olds (Elicker, Englund, & Sroufe, 1992).

It is not possible to say definitively that children differ in their peer interactions *because* they, as infants, differed in their attachments to their mothers. Remember from chapter 6 that genetic differences among children may affect their ability to form secure attachments to their mothers. These genetic differences may also affect the development of social skills for interacting with peers. Therefore, children's genotypes could be a third variable that explains the correlations between attachment security in infancy and peer competence in childhood (Lamb & Nash, 1989).

Other researchers have compared older children's interactions with parents to their interactions with peers. Baumrind's (1967, 1971) research on parenting styles, discussed in chapter 11, is a good example. Preschoolers with authoritative parents were cheerful and friendly when interacting with peers. Preschoolers with authoritarian or permissive parents were either hostile toward peers, highly withdrawn, or too dependent on adults to interact well with peers. Later studies have confirmed that preschoolers whose parents express more warmth and use more consistent discipline have more positive interactions with peers (Ladd & Le Sieur, 1995).

The studies of parenting had correlational designs, so the findings do not prove that variations in parenting caused the variations in preschoolers' behavior toward peers. But as you recall from chapter 11, other research strengthens the case for a causal influence of parents on their children's behavior. The same research strengthens the case for an indirect influence of parents on children's peer interactions.

Finally, parents who use some form of child care have another way to influence their children's peer relationships. When parents choose a child-care program, they can and often do magnify the effects of their own parenting pattern (Howes & Olenick, 1986; Howes & Stewart, 1987). Parents who are warm toward their children typically choose high-quality child-care programs. Their children's competence with peers is enhanced not only by the parents themselves but also by involved and supportive caregivers. Parents who are less warm toward their children typically choose lower-quality child-care programs. Their children's competence with peers is impaired both at home and in the child-care setting. In terms of development, the rich get richer and the poor get poorer.

# CHILDREN'S FRIENDSHIPS

Although children interact with many peers, they most enjoy their interactions with their best friends. As noted earlier, friendships represent a higher level of social complexity than simple interactions. Friendships are relationships that are based on a history of interactions. Some preschool children form friendships that can be significant for their emotional adjustment and development. But more often, friendships become truly intimate relationships only in adolescence. Such close and intimate friendships may have positive effects on children's development.

## Origins of Friendship in Early Childhood

Even a toddler can have a history of interactions with a peer. Toddlers do not call their playmates "friends," but some of their relationships satisfy at least part of the definition of friendship (Howes, 1983, 1988). Some pairs of 1- and 2-year-olds interact often with each other. They display highly positive emotions when they interact, suggesting that they like each other. They also coordinate their behavior as they interact. For example, they play the games with complementary roles described earlier.

The features of friends' interactions change as children move from the simple games of toddlers to the complex social pretend play of preschoolers. John Gottman (1986) described coordinated play as the central activity for friends during early childhood. To play together, friends must first find some common ground; that is, they must agree on what to play. A willingness to agree with each other also helps children move toward play in which their behavior is highly responsive to the previous behavior of their social partners. Consequently, how often preschoolers agree with each other during play is strongly related to how well they "hit it off" and progress toward friendship (Gottman, 1983, 1986).

Children's agreements with each other are important not only when friendships are forming. They remain important in established friendships. Preschool children who are friends give more help, praise, and gifts to each other than do those who are not friends (Masters & Furman, 1981). They also have more neutral interactions with each other, and most of these interactions involve play (see Howes, 1988).

Friendships have a less positive side. Conflicts often arise when one friend acts negatively toward another. Negative behaviors such as teasing or attacking another are more common between preschoolers who are friends than between those who are not (Masters & Furman, 1981). Therefore, the ability to manage conflicts is also essential in preschoolers' friendships.

Conflict management operates differently between preschoolers who are friends than between nonfriends (Hartup et al., 1988). Friends have less emotionally intense conflicts than nonfriends do. Compared with nonfriends, friends more often break off an argument rather than insist on their rights, and more often continue playing together after conflicts. Staying together after a conflict may be important for the stability of preschoolers' friendships, because it keeps them talking and playing together.

Friendships can be highly stable during the preschool years. When children attend the same child-care center for several years, they often keep the same friends for more than a year (Howes, 1988). Preschoolers with stable friendships are higher in social competence than those with unstable friendships. Those with stable friendships spend more time in social pretend play, are better liked by their classmates, and are rated by their teachers as more sociable.

In addition, the qualities of preschool children's friendships are moderately stable over time (Park, Lay, & Ramsay, 1993). Friends who play more happily and share more with each other at about 4 years of age tend to have similarly positive interactions at about 5 years of age. That is, the positive features of their relationship show substantial continuity over one year.

Losing a close friend, perhaps because the friend moves away, can be distressing for preschool children and disrupt their social behavior (Field, 1984; Howes, 1988). When a friend moves, children may also lose an important source of social support. Preschoolers have more difficulty joining a group of classmates who are already playing together when they have no friends in the group.

Prescholers who are close friends often argue with each other, but their arguments are less intense than those between nonfriends. Friends continue playing together after an argument more often than nonfriends.

More dramatic evidence of the value of peers' support comes from a unique case study (Freud & Dann, 1951). During World War II, many Jewish children were orphaned because their parents were killed in Nazi concentration camps. Six of these children were separated from their mothers at birth or during the first year of life. Until they were 3 years of age, these six children lived together in a ward for orphans in a concentration camp. When the war ended and the camp's survivors were released, the children were flown to England. They spent the next year in a special home with trained nurses and staff.

The children did not behave normally when they first arrived in England. They broke toys and furniture; they were either indifferent or hostile to adults. By contrast, the children were very attached to one another and strongly protested even brief separations from one another. They showed almost no rivalry or competition. They helped and comforted one another rather than seeking help and comfort from adults.

The children's friendships with one another probably helped them survive in the concentration camp. These friendships also may have helped them adjust to the new world of England. When they grew up, they became normal and competent adults (Hartup, 1983).

The experiences of these six children suggest that friendships can partly substitute, in early childhood, for relationships with parents. Remember, though, that the children's behavior was not normal when they first arrived in England. They suffered to some extent from their lack of parenting early in life. To develop most successfully, children need close and supportive relationships both with parents and with peers.

## Features of Friendships in Childhood and Adolescence

As children grow older, peer relationships may play a unique role in their development, a role that cannot be filled by parents or other adults. Piaget (1965) argued that peer relationships, unlike relationships with parents, are based on equality. The equality between peers promotes a sense of fairness that involves a concern for other people's needs. According to Piaget, fairness and concern for others are by-products of the cooperation that occurs among peers who view one another as equals.

Piaget assumed that peer relationships based on equality first become apparent during the elementary-school years. Harry Stack Sullivan (1953), a psychiatrist who devised a highly original adaptation of Freudian theory, also argued that friendships change

dramatically during the elementary-school years. Sullivan focused not on the equality between peers but on the intimacy of children's friendships. He proposed that friends first share their most private thoughts and feelings as children approach adolescence. He argued that such intimate friendships enhance adolescents' self-esteem and their understanding of other people.

Researchers have used two methods to examine these hypotheses about the developments in friendships. First, they have asked children to talk about their ideas of friendships or their actual friendships. Second, they have observed friends' behavior as the friends work together on specially designed tasks. This research has partly supported, but also qualified, Piaget's and Sullivan's hypotheses.

## What Children Say About Friends and Their Friendships

Ask a kindergarten boy how he can tell someone is his best friend. He'll give you answers like these (Berndt, 1986):

- I play with him all the time.
- He's nice to me.
- He doesn't get into fights with me.
- He likes me and I like him, too.

Now compare the kindergarten boy's answers with these answers by a sixth-grade girl:

- She asks me over to her house.
- She does good things for me, helps me.
- She doesn't fight with me all the time, and if we get in an argument, afterwards we say we're sorry.
- You can tell her things and she won't tell anyone else. If you're in trouble, she talks to you and tells you not to worry about it.

Do you see any similarities between the two sets of answers? The younger boy and the older girl both say that friends interact frequently with each other. Friends play together or go to each other's houses. In short, friends are companions for each other. Both children say that friends are nice or helpful to each other. In psychological terms, friends behave prosocially toward each other. Both children say that friends don't have too many conflicts with each other. In summary, both children and adolescents know that friendship demands frequent interaction, prosocial behavior, and a lack of serious or prolonged conflicts.

Notice, too, the important differences between the kindergartner's answers and those by the sixth grader. The kindergarten boy says that friendship is based on mutual liking: He likes me and I like him. Sixth graders and older adolescents realize that mutual liking is part of the definition of friendship, but they seldom mention it explicitly. They view other features of friendship as more important.

Even more important is the older girl's emphasis on intimacy in friendship. The girl refers to intimacy when she says friends will talk with you about your troubles and won't tell your secrets to anyone else. Adolescents also refer to intimacy when they say that friends understand your feelings, make you feel better when you're "down," and know almost everything there is to know about you. The kindergarten boy made no comments of this type. Kindergarten children rarely refer to the intimacy of their friendships. They rarely say even that they share secrets with friends. So, consistent with Sullivan's (1953) hypothesis, comments about the intimacy of friendship increase greatly between childhood and adolescence (Berndt, 1986; Youniss, 1980).

Adolescents also report higher levels of intimacy in their actual friendships than do younger children (Berndt, 1994; Hartup, 1992). Figure 12.4 illustrates this age change with data from second- to eighth-grade students (Berndt & Perry, 1986). The students were interviewed about the relationships with one classmate who was a close friend and another classmate who was merely an acquaintance. One question about the intimacy of these relationships was, "When you have a problem at home or at school, how often do you talk to [name of friend or acquaintance] about it?"

Intimacy becomes an important feature of friendship in adolescence, especially among girls. Best friends like these girls can talk about their most personal fears and joys with each other. They know they can trust their friend to respond with support and encouragement.

Eighth graders described their friendships as more intimate than did younger students. The intimacy of friendships increases still further during the years of senior high school (Furman & Buhrmester, 1992; Sharabany, Gershoni, & Hofman, 1981). By contrast, reports of play or association with friends, prosocial behavior by friends, and conflicts with friends did not show consistent changes with age (see figure 12.4a). Conflicts with friends decreased somewhat, however, and other studies suggest the decrease continues into middle and late adolescence (Furman & Buhrmester, 1992).

At all ages, students described their relationships with acquaintances as less intimate than their relationships with friends (see figure 12.4b). In addition, students said they spent less time in play or association with acquaintances and they expected less prosocial behavior from acquaintances than from friends. In the lower grades, students reported fewer conflicts with friends than with acquaintances. However, eighth graders reported few conflicts with either friends or acquaintances. Unlike younger students, eighth graders viewed acquaintances simply as peers with whom they rarely interacted, rather than as peers with whom they didn't get along (Berndt & Perry, 1986).

If you compare the two panels of figure 12.4, you'll see that the differences between friends and acquaintances increased with age (see also Furman & Bierman, 1984; Selman, 1980). As children move into adolescence and form more intimate friendships, they also view their friendships as more distinct from other relationships. Young children will call almost anyone they like a "best friend." Older children and adolescents reserve the term "best friend" for people with whom they have an especially close relationship.

Adolescent girls describe their friendships as more intimate than do adolescent boys (Berndt, 1994; Youniss & Smollar, 1985). Also, more boys than girls say they would not disclose personal information to a best friend because the friend might tease or laugh at them. Boys without an intimate friendship may miss the benefits of sharing problems with friends and be forced to deal with these problems by themselves.

Still, intimate friendships have risks. Compared with boys, girls worry more about the unfaithfulness of friends (Berndt, 1986). That is, more girls than boys say that they fear a close friend will leave them for someone else. After a girl has shared so much of herself with a friend, she may feel that losing the friendship is losing part of herself.

In addition, a girl's intimate disclosures to a friend may, if the friendship ends, be told to other people. During their conversations, friends not only talk about their problems but also gossip about other people (Gottman & Mettetal, 1986). Some of this gossip is negative and could cause hurt feelings if the targets of the gossip hear it. Even so, most theorists agree with Sullivan (1953) that intimate friendships have more positive than negative effects on social development.

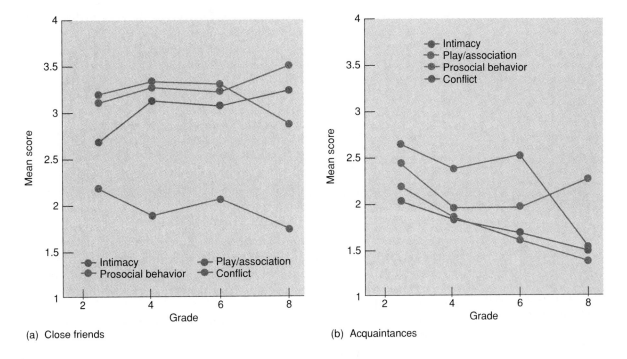

(a) Close friends

(b) Acquaintances

## FIGURE 12.4

Students describe their friendships as involving more prosocial behavior, more intimacy, and more play or association than their relationships with acquaintances. Below eighth grade, students also report fewer conflicts with friends than acquaintances. The reported intimacy of friendships increases between second and eighth grade. (Source: Berndt & Perry, 1986.)

## How Children Behave Toward Their Friends

Children and adolescents say that friends are nice and helpful toward each other, but are they really? Do friends actually behave more prosocially toward each other than nonfriends do? Suppose you decide to find out. In the fall of a school year, you identify fourth graders and eighth graders who are close friends. Then you pair each fourth grader and each eighth grader with one of his or her close friends.

You ask each pair of friends to play a simple game. Each child must draw the same design, but they must share a single drawing tool. You tell them they will get a prize based on how well they do. To let them know how they are doing on each trial, you will give them nickels. The child who gets more done on each trial will get two nickels; the other child will get one nickel.

The rewards give the children a reason to try hard on the task. More important, the rule for distributing rewards makes sharing the drawing tool costly for each child. The more that children share the tool, the more likely they are to get less done and get fewer nickels than their partners.

You return in the spring and ask the same pairs of students to do the task again. By this time, some of the students' friendships have changed. Some pairs are still close friends. Other pairs are no longer close friends, but they have drifted apart rather than become enemies. Now how much do students in the two types of pairs share with each other?

Figure 12.5 shows the results (Berndt, Hawkins, & Hoyle, 1986). The fourth graders who were still friends shared less with their partners than did the fourth graders paired with former friends. By contrast, eighth graders who were still close friends shared more with their partners than did eighth graders paired with former friends.

To understand the fourth- and eighth-graders' behavior, consider some implications of Piaget's (1965) hypothesis about equality in peer relationships. In the game, children's equality with their partners was threatened. If children let their partner use the drawing tool for

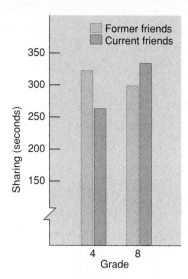

**FIGURE 12.5**

How much do fourth and eighth graders share with friends and nonfriends—or former friends—when given a choice between sharing and competition? Fourth graders share less with current friends than former friends; eighth graders do the reverse. The contrast reflects changes in how friends try to maintain the equality between themselves. (Source: Berndt, Hawkins, & Hoyle, 1986.)

a long time, they increased the chances that they would lose the game to their partner by getting fewer nickels. This outcome could make them look inferior to the partner rather than equal to him or her. To reduce the chances that this would happen, children sometimes chose to compete with their partners rather than to share with them.

A sense of equality is important in all peer relationships, as Piaget said, but it is especially critical in friendships (Rawlins, 1992; Tesser, 1984). Because children assume that they are similar to friends, they often compare themselves with friends. Children less often compare themselves with nonfriends, so they care less about whether they perform better or worse than nonfriends.

The process of comparison with friends begins early in life and is well established by fourth grade. So, when faced with the threat of looking inferior to their partner, fourth graders competed more intensely and shared the drawing tool less when their partner was still a close friend rather than a former friend.

Eighth graders also cared more about the outcome of a game played with a close friend than with a former friend. But the eighth graders devised a strategy for achieving equality over the several trials in the game without competing with a close friend. They tried to ensure equality in rewards, and a tie in the game, by sharing the drawing tool equally. This strategy would lead to a tie if one player won on the first trial, the other player won on the second trial, and so on.

Of course, this strategy works only if each player can trust the other to follow it. Trust between friends increases between childhood and adolescence (Hestenes, Berndt, & Gruen, 1995). Differences in ability to think of a strategy for achieving equality without competition, and differences in trust between friends, can explain the differences between fourth- and eighth-graders' behavior.

Don't exaggerate how much friends' behavior changes with age, though. Young children often behave more positively toward their friends than toward other peers. When young children do not risk looking inferior to a friend, they show more positive behavior toward friends than toward nonfriends.

The distinctive characteristics of friends' behavior were revealed by a meta-analysis of 82 studies published during the last 60 years (Newcomb & Bagwell, 1995). The behaviors examined in these studies were classified into four general categories. Then how much friends' behavior differed from that of nonfriends (i.e., the effect size for this difference) was calculated.

Figure 12.6 shows that friends and nonfriends differ most in behaviors classified as positive engagement. Compared with nonfriends, friends engage in more frequent interactions, conversations, cooperation, and smiling or other expressions of positive emotions. Friends and nonfriends also differ in relationship properties, with friends higher on such features as mutual liking, closeness, loyalty, and equality. Friends and nonfriends differ in task activity, with friends having better performance than nonfriends.

Finally, friends and nonfriends differ in their conflict management. As mentioned earlier, friends resolve conflicts more successfully than nonfriends (Hartup et al., 1988). However, friends become involved in conflicts about as often as nonfriends. Under certain conditions, friends even have more conflicts with each other than nonfriends do (Berndt, 1987; Hartup, 1993).

Chapter 2 included a brief description of a study in which third and fourth graders played a board game with either a best friend or another classmate (Hartup et al., 1993). The experimenters increased the likelihood of conflicts between the children by telling them different rules for the game. Most conflicts were very low in intensity, but friends had more and longer conflicts than nonfriends. These conflicts may have arisen because the game created a competitive situation that threatened the equality between the friends. Another possibility is that friends feel more free than nonfriends to disagree with each other because friends understand each other so well.

Finally, you should not assume that conflicts between friends are common only during childhood. Although some adolescents have intimate, trusting relationships with their friends, others have ambivalent or troubled relationships with friends (Dishion, Andrews, & Crosby,

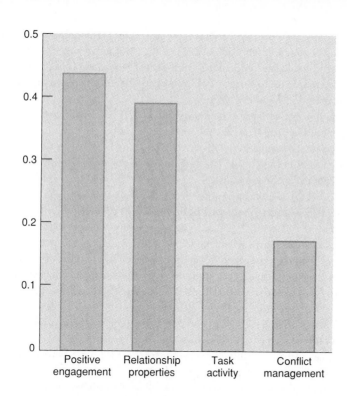

FIGURE 12.6
The mean effect size from many studies for the differences between friends' and nonfriends' behavior. All the effect sizes are positive, showing that friends display more positive engagement in their interactions, have relationships higher on properties such as mutual liking, do better on joint tasks, and manage their conflicts better than nonfriends do. (Data from Newcomb & Bagwell, 1995.)

1995; Savin-Williams & Berndt, 1990; Windle, 1995). Throughout childhood and adolescence, friendships can be marked by high levels of positive and negative emotions, by agreements and by disagreements.

## Effects of Friendships, and Parents' Influence on Friendships

Now you know that Piaget (1965) and Sullivan (1953) were correct in emphasizing the intimacy and equality of friendships during early adolescence. Were they also right in arguing that intimate friendships based on equality have positive effects on children's development? The evidence is limited and only partly consistent with their hypotheses.

Elementary-school children who have a close, mutual friendship report less loneliness than those who do not (Parker & Asher, 1993). When elementary-school children are followed over time, those who lose friends become more lonely (Renshaw & Brown, 1993). Having friendships is, then, important for children's emotional well-being.

Instead of simply asking whether children have a best friend, many researchers have examined the intimacy, equality, or other characteristics of best friendships. The characteristics of children's best friendships are related to many indicators of their emotional, social, and academic adjustment in childhood and adolescence (Berndt & Keefe, 1995; Dishion et al., 1995; East & Rook, 1992; McGuire & Weisz, 1982; Parker & Asher, 1993). Children and adolescents whose friendships are more intimate and supportive, and those whose friendships are lower in hostility and conflicts, are less lonely and depressed and have higher self-esteem. Children and adolescents with high-quality friendships are less likely to be socially isolated at school and more likely to be popular, generous, and high in social skills. They are also less likely to be disruptive at school and more likely to have high grades.

These correlations are consistent with hypotheses about the effects of friendship, but they have the usual limitations of correlational data. A skeptic could argue that high self-esteem, good social skills, and other desirable characteristics help children form good friendships rather than vice versa. Evidence from longitudinal studies is often more convincing, because longitudinal designs make it possible to see whether having good friendships predicts increases in adjustment over time.

Surprisingly, longitudinal studies have often failed to show an effect of friendship quality on children's and adolescents' adjustment (DuBois et al., 1992; Dubow et al., 1991;

Keefe & Berndt, 1996; Windle, 1992). Having high-quality friendships at one time is not related to the changes over time in depression, self-esteem, grades in school, and drug use in adolescence. Instead, children's and adolescents' adjustment seem to affect the quality of their friendships. For example, in one study delinquent adolescents showed an increase over time in conflicts with friends (Windle, 1995).

Other studies suggest that friendship quality does affect certain aspects of children's and adolescents' social adjustment. The preschoolers in one study liked kindergarten more when their kindergarten classroom included many children they knew from their preschool or their neighborhood (Ladd & Price, 1987). The early adolescents in another study increased in their positive involvement at school when they had better friendships early in the school year (Berndt & Keefe, 1995). The adolescents' best friends usually attended the same school, so having good friendships probably gave a positive tone to their entire school experiences.

In another study (Berndt, 1989), adolescents with more supportive friendships during the first semester of seventh grade became more popular and were viewed more positively by their classmates as the year continued. The first-semester friendships of these adolescents apparently were central to a circle of peer relationships that widened during the year. In other words, the supportive friendships that these adolescents had early in the year helped them find a satisfying place in the social world of junior high.

And what about the other social world in which children and adolescents live, that of the family? As you might expect, friendships and family relationships are often comparable in quality. More specifically, children and adolescents who have better friendships usually have better relationships with their parents, too.

For example, 4-year-olds with secure attachments to their mothers have more harmonious interactions with friends than do 4-year-olds with insecure attachments (Park & Waters, 1989). Similarly, adolescent girls who express more affection for their mothers have more intimate friendships (Gold & Yanof, 1985). Of course, some children have close relationships with parents but not friends or vice versa. Nevertheless, the more general pattern is one of continuity between parent-child relationships and best friendships.

# STATUS IN THE PEER GROUP

The next level of social complexity above that of relationships involves a person's position in a social group. In the realm of peer relationships, the prototypical example of this level, as mentioned earlier, is a child's social status. Since the 1930s many researchers have explored the variations in children's social status (see Newcomb et al., 1993; Renshaw, 1981). Researchers first assumed that these positions were located on a single dimension, ranging from popular to unpopular. Often this dimension has been defined as that of **sociometric status,** a term that derives from the most common technique for assessing a child's social position.

## Sociometric Techniques, Dimensions, and Groups

**Sociometric techniques** are methods for assessing a person's position in the social structure of a group. The term *sociometric* is short for measurement of social relationships. Although sociometric techniques have been used with people of all ages in various groups, the most research has been done in children in classroom groups.

To measure children's sociometric status, a researcher asks all children in a classroom to name the other children they like most or would choose as play partners. Usually, children are told to name three other children. These names are defined more formally as *positive nominations.* Usually, the same children are asked to make *negative nominations,* that is, to name the three other children whom they like least or would not want as play partners.

Children receive scores based on the number of positive nominations and negative nominations they receive from classmates. Then these scores are transformed. One set of transformations locates each child in a two-dimensional space for social status (see figure 12.7). First, a child's score for positive nominations is subtracted from that for negative nominations. The result (positive – negative) defines the child's location on the dimension of **social preference,** or **peer acceptance.** A child nearer the "plus" end on this dimension is

**sociometric status**
*Another term for social status that derives from the most common technique for assessing a child's social position.*

**sociometric techniques**
*Methods for assessing the social status of specific persons in the social structure of a group.*

**social preference (peer acceptance)**
*How much other children like a particular child, judged by the difference between the number of positive nominations and the number of negative nominations that the child receives from other children when all children in a group complete sociometric questionnaires.*

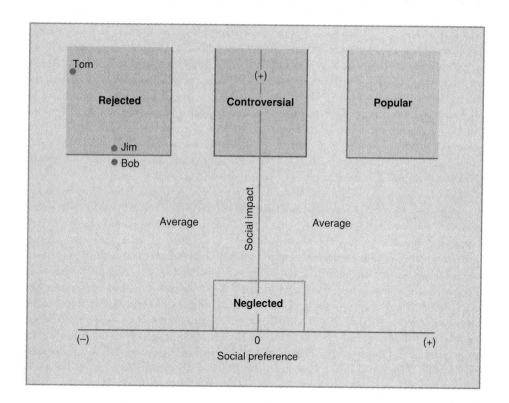

**FIGURE 12.7**

This graph illustrates the two approaches to the measurement of children's social status. One approach is to assess children's scores on the social preference and social impact dimensions. The other is to classify children into social status groups based on how often their peers say they like and dislike them. The usual names for these groups are shown. Data points for three hypothetical children, Jim, Bob, and Tom, are also shown.

more popular, that is, better liked by classmates. Notice that popularity is judged not by which children are believed to be popular, but by which children are actually liked by most of their classmates.

Next, a child's scores for positive and negative nominations are added. The result (positive + negative) defines the child's location on the **social impact** dimension. A child nearer the high end on this dimension gets more nominations and so stands out in the peer group. The preference and impact dimensions are treated as orthogonal, or at right angles to each other, as figure 12.7 shows.

A few researchers have examined the characteristics of children who differ either in their social preference or their social impact (e.g., Newcomb & Bukowski, 1984). More often, researchers who take this dimensional approach look only at variations in children's social preference or peer acceptance. Later you will read about how children high or low in peer acceptance differ in their social understanding and social behavior.

Another set of transformations of the scores for positive and negative nominations is more complicated (Coie, Dodge, & Coppotelli, 1982; Newcomb & Bukowski, 1984). Without going into details, the purpose of these transformations is to classify children into groups differing in social status. In other words, the groups have different positions in the two-dimensional space shown in the figure.

Children who receive many positive nominations and few negative nominations are high in social preference and in social impact. They are classified as **popular.** Children who receive many negative nominations and few positive nominations are low in social preference but high in social impact. They are classified as **rejected.** Children who receive few positive or negative nominations are near the zero points on both the preference and impact dimensions. They are classified as **neglected.** Children who receive many positive nominations and many negative nominations are near the zero point on the preference dimension but are high in social impact. They are classified as **controversial.** Finally, children who don't fit any of the previous groups because they have moderate numbers of positive and negative nominations are usually classified as **average status.**

**social impact**
*How much a child stands out in a peer group, judged by the total number of positive nominations and negative nominations that the child receives from other children when all children in a group complete sociometric questionnaires.*

**popular**
*The social status group that includes children who receive many positive nominations and few negative nominations on sociometric questionnaires.*

**rejected**
*The social status group that includes children who receive many negative nominations and few positive nominations on sociometric questionnaires.*

**neglected**
*The social status group that includes children who receive few positive or negative nominations on sociometric questionnaires.*

**controversial**
*The social status group that includes children who receive many positive and many negative nominations on sociometric questionnaires.*

**average status**
*The social status group that includes children who receive a moderate number of positive and negative nominations on sociometric questionnaires.*

Most researchers focus on popular, rejected, and neglected children. Little research has been done on controversial children because only about 5 percent of the children in most peer groups fit this category (Newcomb & Bukowski, 1983). Researchers often include the average-status group, but usually only to clarify the special characteristics of the three more extreme groups.

The classification of children into groups has one major advantage over the use of preference and impact dimensions. With the classification approach, rejected and neglected children are clearly distinguished. Both groups are relatively unpopular, but rejected children are disliked and neglected children are not. The two groups are more difficult to distinguish when a researcher looks separately at the preference and impact dimensions.

One disadvantage of the classification approach is that differences among children within a group are ignored. Look at the dot in figure 12.7 that marks the position of a hypothetical boy named Jim. Jim just meets the criteria for the rejected group, so his dot is inside the boundary for that group. Look now at the dot that marks the position of another boy named Bob. Bob's scores on the preference and impact dimensions are nearly the same as Jim's, but because Bob is outside the boundary, he falls in the average-status group.

Tom, by contrast, is highly rejected. Because most of his peers dislike him, the dot for his scores falls at the extremes on the preference and impact dimensions. In the classification approach, however, Jim and Tom are treated as more similar—by being put in the same category—than Jim and Bob. In this respect, the classification approach is somewhat arbitrary and artificial (Bukowski & Hoza, 1989). These problems with the classification approach should be kept in mind as you read about the causes of variations in social status.

## Why Are Some Children More Popular Than Others?

Think back to elementary school and high school. You probably remember some students who were highly popular and others who were highly unpopular. If asked why, you might give one or more of the following explanations:

1. Popular boys are handsome. Popular girls are beautiful. Most children want to be friends with boys and girls who are good looking.

2. Popular children are friendly and easy to get along with. Unpopular children are either obnoxious or socially withdrawn.

3. Popular children fit in well. They like to do what most other children like. Unpopular children are different from the other children. Their behavior is socially acceptable, but they are from a different ethnic group or social class than their classmates, or they have interests different from everyone else's.

Each of these explanations captures part of the truth, but the second one explains the variations in children's social status better than the other two do. Let's review them in order.

### Popularity and Physical Attractiveness

Children higher in peer acceptance usually are more physically attractive than their classmates (Hartup, 1983). Very strong correlations between physical attractiveness and peer acceptance have been found in some groups of children (Cavior & Dokecki, 1973), but weaker correlations (ranging from .30 to .50) are found in most groups. When children are familiar with each other, physical attractiveness relates more strongly to girls' popularity than to boys' (Vaughn & Langlois, 1983), but the reason for this gender difference is unclear.

Other data suggest that physically attractive children are not popular just because they are attractive. Their behavior is also more desirable than that of unattractive children. More attractive 5-year-olds are less aggressive toward peers (Langlois & Downs, 1979). More attractive elementary-school children interact more positively with teachers and are higher in academic achievement (Hartup, 1983). In addition, careful analyses suggest that children's social behavior affects their popularity more than their physical attractiveness does (Dodge, 1983).

In summary, physically attractive children display more desirable behavior partly because they are treated more positively by adults and peers. This positive treatment evokes

Popular children are often, literally, the center of attention, so we might guess that the girl in the center of this photograph is more popular than the children clustered around her. Popular children are sociable and have a good sense of humor, so other children enjoy spending time with them. Popular children also have good ideas for play activities, so it is fun to be around them.

positive responses from children, like a self-fulfilling prophecy. The available data suggest, however, that children's popularity is caused more by their desirable social behavior than by their good looks.

## Popularity and Social Behavior: The Dimensional Approach

Researchers using the dimensional approach have documented many differences between the behavior of children high and low in peer acceptance (Bukowski et al., 1993; Eisenberg et al., 1993; Hartup, 1983; Renshaw & Brown, 1993). More popular children are more outgoing, friendly, helpful, and socially skilled than their classmates. They also have better friendships than their classmates, not only because of their social skill but also because they can select compatible friends from among the many classmates who like them.

Less popular children cooperate less with their peers, engage in more disruptive behavior, and often show immature behavior. Less popular children often display intense emotional reactions to frustrating or anxiety-provoking situations. Their emotional intensity often contributes to undesirable behaviors because they are relatively lacking in strategies for coping constructively with social problems. Sometimes children low in peer acceptance are aggressive, but aggressive behavior seems to affect girls' popularity more than that of boys (Bukowski et al., 1993).

Not all children low in peer acceptance have the same behavioral profile (Hymel, Bowker, & Woody, 1993). Children who are unpopular because they are shy and prefer

solitary play often have good relationships with adults and are well behaved in school. Children who are unpopular because they are aggressive often remain involved in peer activities but misbehave in school and do poorly on their schoolwork. Children who have multiple problems—low social acceptance, aggression, and social isolation—have the worst behavioral profile. They have poor relationships with adults and peers. They also perform poorly in sports and in schoolwork. They do not have a good sense of humor, are not cooperative, and often get into trouble at school.

## Popularity and Social Behavior: The Classification Approach

Researchers who classify children into social-status groups have also found significant differences among children differing in popularity (Coie, Dodge, & Kupersmidt, 1990; Newcomb et al., 1993; Wentzel & Asher, 1995). The differences suggest that children earn their social position by behaving in a specific way. Each status group has a distinctive behavioral pattern.

Children who are classified in the popular group have many positive characteristics. They are helpful, friendly, considerate of others, cheerful, and sociable. Not surprisingly, they rarely feel lonely. Popular children have a good sense of humor and are good at sports. They have above-average intelligence, are good students, and are skilled in solving social problems. They usually obey the rules in their school and other settings. As a result, they have good relationships with their teachers and other adults. They also have high-quality friendships that are unusually stable over time (Howes, 1990).

Popular children do not refrain from all forms of socially undesirable behavior. They are physically aggressive toward peers about as often as children average in status. However, popular children avoid disruptive behavior and hostile verbal aggression. In this sense, they seem assertive—not the kind of kids you'd try to push around—rather than antisocial.

Children who fall in the rejected group have many negative characteristics. They are physically aggressive, disruptive at school, and hostile toward peers. In addition, their aggression is often unprovoked or socially inappropriate (Dodge et al., 1990). Rejected children are often inattentive at school; they often have low grades and test scores.

Even in a school setting, rejected children are alone much of the time because their peers ignore or exclude them. In addition, they lack effective strategies for joining groups of peers already engaged in activities (Putallaz & Wasserman, 1990). Rejected children report high anxiety and depression. Their relationships with adults are poor. Their friendships are relatively lacking in positive qualities and are high in conflicts and rivalry. Some rejected children also have unpleasant personal habits (e.g., they may wear dirty or worn-out clothes). All these characteristics suggest that peers have good reasons for disliking rejected children.

Although neglected children are not popular, their psychological portrait is far more positive than that of rejected children. On the negative side, neglected children are less sociable than children of average status. Neglected children spend more time in solitary play or schoolwork than average-status children do, but they do not describe themselves as lonely. They also report less depression than average.

Neglected children show few deficits in social skills (Rubin & Krasnor, 1986). They are as competent in solving social problems as average-status children, and their friendships are no different from the average. They are also less aggressive and disruptive than is average. Taken together, their behavior and psychological adjustment suggest that they are not at risk of any serious psychological problems. Although few of their peers know them well, they do not lack either social skills or a sense of emotional well-being. They may simply be more independent of peers than is typical and more motivated to succeed in school than in the social world (Wentzel & Asher, 1995).

Controversial children display a mixed behavioral pattern. Children classified as controversial are even more aggressive, disruptive, and hot-tempered than rejected children. However, they are as highly sociable as popular children. Their level of social interaction is extremely high, bolstered by positive traits such as athletic ability, physical attractiveness, or a good sense of humor. Researchers do not yet know whether the positive qualities of these children outweigh their negative qualities.

Of course, children in the same status group do not always behave the same way. For example, not all popular children have good relationships with their teachers, and not all

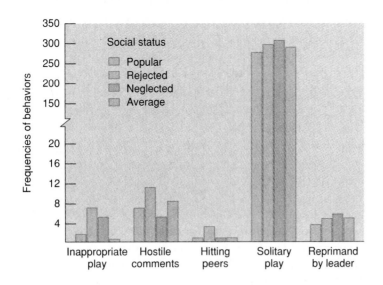

FIGURE 12.8

The social status that boys have in a new peer group depends on their behavior toward the other members of the group. Boys who are eventually rejected by the rest of the group show more inappropriate play, hostile comments, and aggression. Boys who eventually fall into the neglected group spend more time in solitary play and inappropriate play. Popular boys receive fewer reprimands from the adult leader. (Source: Dodge, 1983.)

rejected children are aggressive. Because of concern about the long-term consequences of peer rejection, variations within the rejected group have been most fully explored.

Perhaps half the children rejected by peers are not highly aggressive and disruptive (Bierman, Smoot, & Aumiller, 1993). Instead, they seem often to be withdrawn, passive, and socially awkward. They may also be immature and rude or selfish. Some rejected children are also submissive, judged by their peers as "easy to push around" (Parkhurst & Asher, 1992; Wentzel & Asher, 1995). Although these children are low in aggressive behavior and average in school adjustment, they are often lonely and worried about peer rejection. Their peers view them as uncooperative and untrustworthy. With these characteristics, their peers' dislike for them is easy to understand.

You should also realize that evidence on the behavior of children in different status groups comes largely from correlational studies. However, a few innovative experimental studies have verified that children's behavior affects their social status. Kenneth Dodge (1983) recruited 48 second-grade boys for special playgroups. Each group included eight boys who did not know each other before their playgroup met. The groups met for one hour a day for eight days. During each hour, the boys did a structured task and then had free play while observers coded their social behavior. After the last group meeting, each boy was interviewed and asked to name the other two boys in the group he liked most and the two he liked least. Based on these nominations, boys were classified as popular, rejected, neglected, controversial, or average in social status.

The boys' final status was significantly related to their behavior in the playgroup (see figure 12.8). (The data for controversial boys are not shown because only three boys were in that group.) Boys who were eventually rejected by their playmates played more inappropriately, doing such things as standing on the tables or disrupting the other boys' games. Compared with average-status boys, the rejected boys also made more hostile comments and more often hit other boys.

The boys who finally landed in the neglected-status group had a mixed behavioral profile. They spent more time in solitary play than the average-status boys and made fewer hostile comments, but they also engaged in inappropriate play more than the average boys. Boys who became popular tended to be more sociable than average, but they only differed significantly from their average playmates in reprimands from the adult leader. The leader needed to reprimand popular boys less than the boys in any other status group.

In another experimental study (Coie & Kupersmidt, 1983), researchers assessed the social status of fourth-grade boys in their regular elementary-school classrooms. Then boys from different schools who differed in their social status were assigned to the same playgroup. Each playgroup met once a week for six weeks.

After only three weeks, the boys' status in their new playgroup was similar to their status in their regular classroom. Boys who were popular at school were usually popular in their

playgroup. Boys unpopular at school usually became unpopular with their new playmates, too. Moreover, boys' popularity in their playgroups depended on how sociable and cooperative they were and on how appropriate their behavior was. A later study with first- and third-grade boys yielded similar results (Dodge et al., 1990). Taken together, these experimental studies establish that children's social behavior affects whether their peers like or dislike them and so affects their social status.

## Popularity and Children's Fit with a Group

The third explanation for the variations in children's popularity remains to be considered. Even if children's behavior has a major influence on their social status, how well children's characteristics fit those of most peers in their group could also have some influence.

The question of fit may be most important when new children enter a group. Children rapidly form impressions about newcomers based on their race, their clothes, and the way they talk (Eckert, 1989; Hymel, Wagner, & Butler, 1990). These impressions can affect the children's behavior toward the newcomers and so affect the newcomers' behavior. The early interactions between newcomers and old members of the group can set the pattern for future interactions and give new children reputations that are difficult to change. Other children may begin to react to the children's reputations as much as to their behavior.

Surprisingly little research has been done on the relations of children's status to their fit with a specific group. In studies done several decades ago, children from a minority ethnic group were less popular in a mixed peer group than were children from the majority group (Hartup, 1970). More recent data are limited, but two methods have been used to examine this issue.

One method is to see how family background affects the social status of children who live in different neighborhoods. Consider, for example, children from low-income families who attend neighborhood schools with children from mostly middle-income families. Will the low-income children not fit in and so be rejected by classmates?

Some data suggest that such children will be rejected if they are also White children from single-parent families (Kupersmidt et al., 1995). Nearly 50 percent of White children from low-income single-parent families were classified as rejected when they attended schools in middle-income neighborhoods. Only about 20 percent were rejected when they attended schools in low-income neighborhoods.

However, other "mismatches" between children's family backgrounds and those of their classmates were not associated with an increased risk of peer rejection. For example, Black children from low-income single-parent families did not have an above-average rate of rejection when they attended schools in middle-income neighborhoods. Therefore, these findings provide only weak or qualified evidence for the importance of children's fit with their peer group.

A second method of examining the effects of group fit is to study children in other cultures. Social behaviors that are not valued in one culture may be valued in another. If so, the behaviors that are associated with high social status would also vary across cultures. *Cultural Perspectives:* "Shyness and Peer Acceptance in Shanghai" describes one behavioral pattern that is valued differently, at certain ages, in Western and in Chinese culture.

## Stability and Change in Social Status

Being rejected by classmates can be a highly unpleasant experience. You might wonder, though, whether children who have been rejected by one set of classmates will be rejected by a new set of classmates. In other words, how stable is peer rejection, or social status in general? If social status is stable, what are its long-term consequences? If the long-term consequences of low social status are negative, as you might expect, what interventions are effective in improving children's social status? Research findings provide at least partial answers to each of these questions.

### Social Status in Short-Term and Long-Term Perspective

One longitudinal study of social status began with a large group of third and fifth graders (Coie & Dodge, 1983). Each year for five years, the students were assigned to one of the standard status groups. Then the researchers identified students who did and did not remain in the same groups across time.

In the philosophy of Confucius, which still permeates Chinese culture, self-restraint and inhibition are highly valued (Chen, Rubin, & Sun, 1992). Children who are shy, quiet, and sensitive to criticism are praised. In Western culture, by contrast, shyness and sensitivity to criticism are negatively valued. Shy and sensitive children are often considered as lacking in self-confidence, fearful, and immature.

Do these differences in cultural values affect children's acceptance by peers? Are shy and sensitive children more popular in China than in Western countries because these children's personalities fit the larger cultural environment better in China than in the West?

To answer these questions, researchers used sociometric techniques with children in Shanghai, China, and in southern Ontario, Canada (Chen et al., 1992). Instead of transforming children's scores in the ways described earlier, the researchers simply scored the number of positive nominations and negative nominations that children received. In addition, the researchers asked children to evaluate their peers' social behavior on the Revised Class Play discussed in chapter 2. With the Chinese children, these assessments were repeated after two years, when the children were 8, 10, and 12 years of age (Chen, Rubin, & Li, 1995).

Children in both countries gave more positive nominations to classmates whom they viewed as sociable, as good leaders, and as helpful and fair. Children gave more negative nominations to children who often got into fights, teased others, and were hot-tempered and bossy. As you know, these findings match those in many other studies.

By contrast, the peer acceptance of shy and sensitive children differed in the two countries. In the first assessment, Chinese children gave *more* positive nominations to children whom they viewed as shy and sensitive than to an average child. Canadian children gave *fewer* positive nominations to shy-sensitive children than to an average child. However, the results changed somewhat in the follow-up of the Chinese children (Chen et al., 1995). As figure 12.9 shows, children judged as more shy and sensitive were better liked at 8 and 10 years of age. But by 12 years of age, shy-sensitive Chinese children were disliked by more classmates than the average child was.

Other findings suggested an explanation for this age change. At 12 years but not earlier, shy-sensitive children were assumed to have trouble making friends and trouble getting other children to listen to them. Perhaps shy children are unwilling to talk freely with friends, so they less often have intimate friendships in early adolescence. Perhaps shy children are so unassertive that their peers see them as lacking in independence. In short, shy-sensitive children may be unprepared for the new forms of adolescent peer relationships.

More generally, this research shows that cultural values can partly determine which children are popular and unpopular with peers. Remember, though, that sociability and leadership were linked to popularity, and aggressive-disruptive behavior to unpopularity, in both China and Canada. These characteristics may have similar effects on children's peer status in all cultures.

## SHYNESS AND PEER ACCEPTANCE IN SHANGHAI

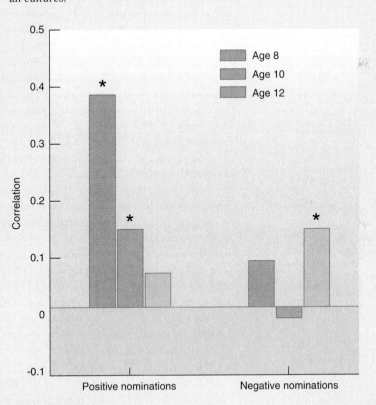

### FIGURE 12.9

At ages 8 and 10, Chinese children who are more shy and sensitive receive more positive nominations from their peers. By age 12 more shy and sensitive children receive more negative nominations from their peers. The asterisks above bars indicate significant correlations.

| TABLE 12.3 | Percentage of Students in Each Social Status Group Who Have the Same Status One and Four Years After a First Assessment | |
|---|---|---|
| SOCIAL STATUS | TIME INTERVAL | |
| | PERCENTAGE STABLE OVER ONE YEAR | PERCENTAGE STABLE OVER FOUR YEARS |
| Popular | 36 | 21 |
| Rejected | 45 | 30 |
| Neglected | 25 | 24 |
| Controversial | 31 | 14 |

*Source:* Coie & Dodge, 1983.

Table 12.3 shows the stability of classification into different groups across one year and four years (Coie & Dodge, 1983). Notice that rejected status was more stable over time than neglected status. About 45 percent of the children in the rejected group one year were in the same group the next year. For neglected children, stability over the same period was only 25 percent.

You could read the same figures differently. Even in the rejected-status group, over half the children changed their status after one year. In another study (Newcomb & Bukowski, 1984), the stability of social status groups was even lower. These studies show that children whose classmates reject them during one school year are not doomed to be rejected throughout their school years. When these children move to a new grade, they have a good chance to improve their status.

Still, many rejected children do not succeed in improving their status. The table shows that nearly one-third of the children rejected in one year were still in the rejected group four years later. Among children who are also high in aggression, the stability of rejected status is even higher than for the rejected group as a whole (Cillessen et al., 1992). Such children often need psychological help. Without that help, they may be headed for more serious problems in adolescence and adulthood.

In dozens of studies, researchers have examined the relations of low social status in childhood to psychological problems later in life (Kupersmidt, Coie, & Dodge, 1990; Parker & Asher, 1987). Most studies show that low-status children are several times more likely to have problems in later life than are children with average or high status. Children who are less popular with peers more often drop out of high school before graduation. Less popular children more often engage in criminal acts during adolescence and adulthood. When they become adults, less popular children more often suffer from mental illness.

When researchers distinguish between children who are rejected versus neglected by their peers, they find sharply different outcomes in later life (Parker & Asher, 1987). Neglected children are no more likely than average-status children to drop out of high school or commit criminal acts during adolescence. Also, the shyness and withdrawal associated with neglected status are not consistently related to social or psychological problems in adulthood. More research is needed to find out whether neglected children have any special risks in later life (see Rubin, LeMare, & Lollis, 1990), but current data suggest that they do not (Newcomb et al., 1993).

Rejected children are at risk for several kinds of negative outcomes. For one longitudinal study, researchers followed children from age 11 to age 18 (Kupersmidt & Coie, 1990). Compared with average students, rejected students were more likely to be truant from school, suspended from school, school dropouts, and have a police record. More than 60 percent of the rejected students had one or more of these problems. Only about 35 percent of the average students in the low-income, rural sample had one or more of the problems.

Poor developmental outcomes are especially likely when children's status in the rejected group is stable over time. Elementary-school children who are classified in the rejected-status group for more than one year are more aggressive at school than those rejected for only one year. Those never in the rejected-status group are least aggressive (DeRosier, Kupersmidt, & Patterson, 1995).

## Interventions to Raise Children's Social Status

Can the problems of rejected children be solved? Are any interventions effective in changing the behaviors that contribute to their rejection by peers? Many researchers believe the answers to these questions are yes, and several kinds of interventions have been tested (Coie & Koeppl, 1990; LaGreca, 1993).

One common goal of these interventions is to improve children's social skills. For example, Sherri Oden and Steven Asher (1977) taught low-status children how to begin a social interaction, cooperate with peers, communicate effectively, and act in a friendly, helpful way. The intervention led to immediate improvements in children's status with peers. These improvements were still apparent in a follow-up a year later.

Social-skills training is most effective in improving children's status when researchers first confirm that the children to be trained are deficient in the skills targeted for training (Ladd, 1981; Mize & Ladd, 1990). Then the researchers do not waste time teaching children social skills that they have already mastered. The social skills most often targeted for training are positive ones such as cooperating with peers. Unfortunately, these interventions often change children's behavior without changing their social acceptance by peers.

To change peer acceptance, it may be necessary not only to increase positive social behaviors but also to decrease negative behaviors. Remember that rejected children's status results partly from their high frequency of aggression and disruption. One study evaluated an intervention aimed both at increasing positive behaviors and at reducing negative behaviors (Bierman, Miller, & Stabb, 1987). Researchers identified 32 boys in the first to third grades who were rejected by their classmates. One-fourth of the boys were trained in the positive social skills of sharing, cooperating, and using questions to get information or invite others to play. These boys were rewarded with a token when they showed these positive behaviors toward peers.

Another fourth of the boys were given rules prohibiting negative behaviors. They were told that they could not fight, yell, whine, or be mean to their playmates. The boys were not instructed in positive social skills, but they were rewarded when they interacted positively with peers. If they did any prohibited, negative behaviors, they lost the chance to earn rewards for one minute.

One-fourth of the boys got both types of training. They were instructed in positive social skills and told about negative behaviors that were prohibited. They also received tokens as rewards for positive behavior. The remaining boys received no training. All the boys were observed before and after the training as they interacted with 5 to 12 classmates.

The three groups of boys who received some training showed less negative behavior toward classmates after training than before. However, none of the trained groups improved in their social status in their regular classroom. Training did have positive effects on the boys' relationships with the classmates who were in their playgroup. These classmates viewed the boys who received both types of training most positively after the training than before. Apparently, these classmates realized that the boys given training were behaving less negatively. Therefore, they changed their views of those boys.

Why didn't the rejected boys' status improve in the regular classroom? The most likely explanation is that their negative reputations with classmates were hard to change. To make interventions for rejected children more effective, it may be necessary to involve more of their peers in the intervention. If most of a child's peers participate in a social-skills intervention, they are more likely to notice when the child's behavior improves and more likely to change their opinion of the child (Bierman & Furman, 1984; LaGreca, 1993).

## Should Interventions Begin at Home?

Other strategies for improving the social status of rejected children exist. Chapter 11 described Gerald Patterson's (1982) social learning approach to reducing coercive or aggressive behavior in children. Patterson's approach differs from the interventions considered so far because he focuses on children's behavioral problems, not their social status. Still, the two are closely related. Remember that rejected children, in particular, often show high levels of aggressive or coercive behavior.

In addition, Patterson (1982) assumes that behavioral problems begin in the family. He tries to reduce these problems by changing parent-child interactions. The interventions discussed so far try to improve rejected children's status by changing their interactions with peers. The two approaches ultimately come together because parents' behavior toward their children affects the children's behavior toward peers, which, in turn, affects the children's social status.

Researchers have identified several aspects of parenting that appear to lead to high or low status in the peer group (Ladd & Le Sieur, 1995). These patterns can be described in terms of the dimensions introduced in chapter 11.

1. *Parents who express more warmth have children who are higher in peer status.* Parents of popular children are warm and sensitive to their children's feelings. Parents of rejected children often are cold or rejecting. In one study (Putallaz, 1987), first graders and their mothers played a word game. The mothers of popular first graders often agreed with their children and directed positive behaviors toward them. The mothers of unpopular first graders often made negative comments to their children during the game. In another study, parents and their elementary-school children worked on puzzles together. The parents of more popular children made more positive comments and fewer negative comments while working together than did the parents of rejected children (Dekovic & Janssens, 1992).

2. *Parents who are more involved with their children have children higher in peer status.* In one study of preschoolers (MacDonald & Parke, 1984), the parents of more popular children spent more time in play with them. Fathers, especially, were physically playful with their children. More popular children's parents also talked more with them. All these behaviors reflect parents' involvement.

3. *Parents who are more authoritative and democratic have children higher in peer status. Parents who are more authoritarian and punitive have children lower in peer status.* The parents of popular children usually control their children's behavior through suggestions, explanations, and information rather than commands and prohibitions. This contrast partly defines the difference between authoritative and authoritarian parenting (Dekovic & Janssens, 1992). The parents of popular children show a moderate level of directiveness that expresses their respect for their children's independence (MacDonald & Parke, 1984).

Parents of unpopular children are sometimes highly controlling, particularly in a play situation (Putallaz, 1987). They are restrictive and rely on power assertion when disciplining their children (Dekovic & Janssens, 1992; Ladd & Le Sieur, 1995). Sometimes, however, the parents of unpopular children are extremely permissive. These parents are neither consistent nor effective in disciplining their children (Dishion, 1990).

The parenting pattern that most regularly leads to high peer status, and the reasons it does so, were summarized by Martha Putallaz and Anne Heflin (1990):

> Parental involvement, warmth, and moderate control appear to be important in terms of children's social competence. Within the social context of the family, children appear to learn certain interactional skills and behaviors that then transfer to their interactions with peers. (p. 204)

Of course, variations in parenting patterns do not completely explain the variations in children's social status. In all studies the correlations of parenting measures with social status are modest. Nevertheless, the correlations imply that interventions that involve parents may be most effective in raising the social status of unpopular children.

# CLIQUES, CROWDS, AND PEER GROUP INFLUENCE

The peer social world becomes most complex in adolescence. The increase in complexity is reflected in two ways. First, friendship groups become more precisely defined and develop more distinctive norms or standards of conduct. In their deviant forms, these groups are called *gangs*. The more neutral term for such groups, as mentioned earlier, is *cliques*. The central issue concerning these cliques is how they influence the behavior of adolescents.

Second, adolescents may be associated with a group of peers by reputation. Earlier, these reputation-based groups were defined as *crowds*, groups of adolescents who are expected to behave similarly even when not part of the same clique. Crowds often get slang names like the "jocks," "druggies," or "burnouts" (Brown, 1989; Eckert, 1989). Belonging to a crowd can also influence adolescents' behavior and development.

## Processes of Influence in Adolescents' Cliques

The following anecdote illustrates how many popular writers, and some scholars, view peer influence:

> A tenth-grade girl goes with a group of her friends to a party after a high-school football game. The party is at the home of a tenth-grade boy who is a friend of a friend. A stereo is blaring at full volume in the living room, but no one seems to mind because the boy's parents are not at home.
>
> The girl and her friends go into the kitchen. The boy who lives there offers them a beer from the refrigerator. Her friends take one, but she hesitates. One of her friends says, "Go ahead. It won't kill you!" After pausing for a few seconds, she says, "No thanks. I'll have a Coke." She stays a few minutes longer but decides the party is not her type and goes home.

This anecdote dramatizes many parents' fears about how adolescents might be influenced by their peers. Some researchers share these fears (e.g., Bronfenbrenner, 1970; Dinges & Oetting, 1993; Steinberg, 1986). They assume that peer groups or cliques have a powerful influence on adolescents' attitudes and behavior. They also assume that this influence is largely negative. That is, groups of friends usually pressure adolescents to act in undesirable or antisocial ways.

The earliest research on these hypotheses was not done with actual situations. (Few ethical-review boards would approve a research project in which groups of peers offered beer to adolescent subjects!) Instead, researchers asked adolescents to respond to hypothetical situations like the one in the story at the beginning of the chapter. As you remember, when Bronfenbrenner (1970) used similar dilemmas with adolescents from the United States and the Soviet Union, he found that U.S. adolescents agreed more with friends' suggestions to engage in antisocial behavior than did adolescents in the Soviet Union.

More recent studies suggest that Bronfenbrenner was correct in emphasizing the influence of friendship groups or cliques on adolescents' behavior (Berndt, 1992; Berndt & Keefe, 1995). However, he exaggerated the degree to which friends' influence leads to antisocial behavior. In one study (Berndt, 1979a), third to twelfth graders responded to several antisocial dilemmas like those used by Bronfenbrenner (1970). The students also responded to dilemmas involving conformity to friends on neutral behavior. For example, they reported what they would do if their friends invited them to go bowling when they had planned to go to a movie. Figure 12.10 shows how often students in each grade said they would go along with the friends' suggestions on the antisocial and neutral dilemmas.

Conformity to friends on antisocial behavior increased sharply between third and ninth grade. After ninth grade, antisocial conformity to friends decreased. Similar trends have been found in other samples (Brown, Clasen, & Eicher, 1986; Steinberg & Silverberg, 1986). Conformity on the neutral dilemmas showed a similar age trend, but the age changes were smaller than those for antisocial conformity.

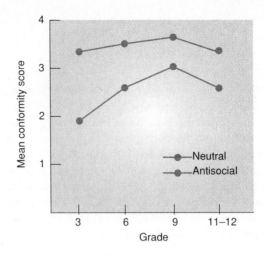

**FIGURE 12.10**

Conformity to peers on antisocial and neutral dilemmas. Higher scores indicate greater conformity. The neutral point on the scale is 3.5, so the mean scores indicate that students at all grades are more likely to reject peers' suggestions than to conform to them. This is especially true for antisocial dilemmas. But conformity on both types of dilemmas is greater at ninth grade than at other grades. (Adapted from Berndt, 1979a.)

In natural settings, friends' influence also rises until midadolescence, or around ninth grade, and then starts to fall. The age changes partly reflect changes in the significance of friendship groups. As adolescents move through the junior-high years, they more often say that they belong to a close friendship group or clique (Crockett, Losoff, & Petersen, 1984). Between fifth and ninth grade, the amount of time that adolescents spend with friends increases (Raffaelli & Duckett, 1989).

In addition, a classic study done more than 60 years ago showed that midadolescence is the peak age for membership in gangs (Thrasher, 1927). More recent studies suggest the same conclusion (Brown, 1989; Horowitz & Schwartz, 1974). Midadolescence, around age 15, also is the peak age for acts of minor delinquency, most of which are committed with one or two friends (Gold & Petronio, 1980).

After its midadolescent peak, friends' influence decreases. Adolescents begin to spend less time with friends and more time in dating and romantic relationships (Dunphy, 1963; Horowitz & Schwartz, 1974). You may have heard the old refrain, "Wedding bells are breaking up that old gang of mine." Like most songs, it contains a kernel of truth. The growing importance of opposite-sex relationships lessens the influence of same-sex friends.

Is Bronfenbrenner (1970) also right when he claims that friends' influence is largely negative, at least up to ninth grade? At first glance, the data graphed in figure 12.10 seem to support that hypothesis. However, a more careful analysis of that study and other research suggests a different answer. That analysis suggests four reasons for doubting that peer influence is either as negative, or as opposed to parental influence, as Bronfenbrenner argued.

First, notice the values of the mean scores for antisocial conformity in figure 12.10. Those values are below 3.5 at all ages. On the response scale, 3.5 was the neutral point between the answers, "Go along with my friends" and "Refuse to go along." Scores below 3.5 indicate that most students said they would *not* agree with friends who encouraged them to cheat on a quiz or do other antisocial acts. That's why the earlier story of the tenth-grade girl ends with the girl's refusal to drink the beer offered to her. Other studies confirm that adolescents are more independent, and friends' influence is weaker, than Bronfenbrenner and other researchers have suggested (Berndt & Keefe, 1995; Sebald, 1986).

Second, the age changes in antisocial conformity were due partly to changes in evaluations of antisocial behavior. Adolescents judge many antisocial behaviors as less wrong

than younger children do. For example, most third graders believe that cheating on a quiz is very bad. Most ninth graders say that cheating is not good but not terrible. Some say that cheating is okay. When these ninth graders say they would go along with friends who suggest cheating, they are not conforming to friends' pressure. They are saying what they would do even if their friends put no pressure on them. When age changes in evaluations are taken into account, the age changes in antisocial conformity are small, much like those for neutral behavior.

Third, research with hypothetical dilemmas does not reveal what friends actually pressure adolescents to do. When large samples of adolescents were asked this question (Brown et al., 1986), they said they received less pressure from friends toward antisocial behavior than toward desirable behavior. Adolescents said friends most often discouraged drug use, vandalism, and theft, and most often encouraged studying hard and avoiding fights. Even alcohol use is discouraged more than encouraged by friends during adolescence (Keefe, 1994).

Fourth, large-scale surveys show that adolescents usually choose friends whose norms and standards are similar to their own (Hartup, 1983; Kandel & Lesser, 1972). These friends are more likely to strengthen an adolescent's views than to influence him or her in a negative direction. Also, the norms of adolescents' friends often match the norms of their parents. The clash between parent and peer influence has been overrated by many popular writers and some social scientists.

Yet surely some adolescents are negatively influenced by their friends. Some adolescents have friends who, as in the earlier anecdote, regularly serve as models of alcohol use. These friends may reward adolescents who use alcohol with praise and approval. They may punish adolescents who refrain from drinking alcohol by teasing or laughing at them. Besides alcohol use, friends can influence many other behaviors from risky driving and sexual activity to violence (Millstein, Petersen, & Nightingale, 1993).

To counter the possibly negative influences of peers, many interventions have been devised. Probably the best known is the "Just Say No" approach to prevention of drug use. Careful evaluations of these intervention programs have shown that they are partly based on faulty assumptions about the processes of peer influence. *Practical Applications of Research:* "'Just Say No' versus 'Not *Everybody's* Doing It'" outlines these faulty assumptions and describes one element of effective programs.

One final question concerns which adolescents are most negatively influenced by friends. Adolescents are most likely to belong to cliques that negatively influence their behavior when their parents have not filled their roles adequately. Adolescents turn to friends, and often to antisocial friends, when their parents either show little interest in them or are actively hostile toward them (Condry & Siman, 1974; Conger, Lorenz, et al., 1992; Hartup, 1983). Adolescents also join cliques with antisocial friends when their parents fail to monitor their behavior adequately (Steinberg, 1986).

These findings should remind you of Bronfenbrenner's (1970) original hypothesis about peer influence. He argued, correctly, that the most negative effects of peer relationships occur when parents do not participate actively in the lives of their children. In other words, children suffer when their parents are uninvolved or rejecting. Often, these children become friends with other children who also suffer from a lack of effective parenting. When several of these children are in the same clique, they will negatively influence one another.

## Part of the Crowd: Mixed Results of Belonging to a Group

Q:     What makes somebody a burnout?
A:     You know, maybe somebody who smokes all the time, you know, smokes marijuana and stuff, but you know, everybody does that. You could call me a Burnout. You know, I've did that . . . maybe, maybe it's the way they dress. It's a lot of things, I think. Your look, you can wear these leather—and these wallets with chains and look really bad, you know—lot of people say, "Oh, that guy's got to be a Burnout." (Eckert, 1989, p. 49)

---

# "JUST SAY NO" VERSUS "NOT *EVERYBODY'S* DOING IT"

If peer pressure leads to drug use in adolescence, then teaching adolescents to resist peer pressure should reduce their use of alcohol, marijuana, and other illegal drugs. That is, teaching adolescents to "just say no" should solve the problem of adolescent drug abuse. Do you think it really would?

If *you* (just) say no, you are at least partly right. Teaching adolescents to "just say no" was one component of a drug-abuse prevention program conducted in hundreds of California schools (Donaldson, Graham, & Hansen, 1994; Donaldson et al., 1995). In the fifth grade, many students in the program received training in resistance skills, techniques for refusing drug offers from peers. In the seventh grade, a shorter version of the same training program was given. In the eighth grade, the students' use of alcohol and marijuana was assessed.

In one sense, resistance-skills training was effective. Assessments showed that students did learn how to resist explicit drug offers from peers. However, this training did not generally reduce the drug use of eighth graders. Some eighth graders who received the training actually used drugs more than those who did not.

One negative side effect of resistance-skills training was that it often made students believe that many of their peers used drugs. Students seemed to say, "If adults spend so much effort telling me to say no to drug-using peers, then lots of my peers must use drugs." These beliefs about peers' drug use can strongly influence adolescents who think that drug use is acceptable. Their reasoning might go like this: "If most of my peers are using drugs, and that's okay, I might as well do it, too."

Fortunately, another intervention that was part of the larger drug-abuse prevention program was more effective. This intervention directly targeted students' beliefs that most of their peers used drugs. In fifth and seventh grade, adults presented information that showed those beliefs were false. That is, most students do not use drugs, and few drug-using students offer drugs to nonusing peers. In addition, the adult leaders gave special attention to students who felt drug use was unacceptable. This attention helped to set a peer-group norm opposing drug use.

Correcting false beliefs about drug use and reinforcing antidrug norms reduced students' drug use in eighth grade. Evaluations of other intervention programs have also shown that changing adolescents' perceptions of peer-group norms has powerful effects on their behavior (Cook, Anson, & Walchli, 1993).

Taken together, the evaluations of these programs confirm conclusions reached in more basic research. Direct pressure is not the primary source of friends' influence, so teaching adolescents to "just say no" to peer pressure often fails to affect their behavior. Friends' influence more often depends on an adolescent's belief that "everybody's doing it." Changing this belief about peer-group norms changes adolescents' behavior.

**T**elling adolescents to "just say no" to peer pressure to use drugs does not work with adolescents who think drug use is acceptable. Also, these programs can make adolescents believe more of their peers use drugs than is actually true.

Q:  So what is a jock then?
A:  Someone who gets into school, who does her homework, who, uh, goes to all the activities, who's in Concert Choir, who has her whole day surrounded by school. You know, "Tonight I'm gonna go to Concert Choir practice and today maybe I'll go watch track, and then early this morning maybe, oh, I'll go help a teacher or something." (Eckert, 1989, p. 1)

Adolescents who belong to the same crowd tend to be similar in their self-esteem. These boys belong to the athletic crowd that is high in social status in most high schools. The boys, in turn, are high in self-esteem.

During the 1980s, some students in high schools near Detroit were described by others, and sometimes described themselves, as burnouts. Other high-school students were described by themselves and others as jocks. As you know already, these labels refer to reputation-based groups or crowds (Brown, 1989, 1990). Sometimes the "jock" label refers to athletes, not to the broader category of school-oriented students in the definition above. Students who recognize this ambiguity may qualify the labels they attach to others. They may call someone a "jock-jock," meaning they are positively oriented toward school and involved in sports. They may describe themselves as not fitting any crowd exactly but as between two crowds (Eckert, 1989).

Well-defined crowds are most obvious in adolescence. With increasing age, adolescents offer more elaborate definitions of the crowds in their school (O'Brien & Bierman, 1988). They also become more accurate in identifying the crowd to which most of their peers think they belong.

The categories of high-school crowds partly reflect divisions in adult society. Often a crowd will include many students from one social class. In the high school near Detroit, jocks came mostly from middle-class families. Burnouts came mostly from working-class families (Eckert, 1989). In schools with several ethnic groups, crowd labels may refer to these groups. Blacks, for example, may be treated as a distinct crowd in schools with few Black students (Brown, 1989). The emphasis that a community places on athletics or academics may also affect the visibility and size of crowds like the "jocks" or "brains."

Crowds vary in their prestige or social standing. In one community, junior- and senior-high-school students named five crowds in their schools (Brown & Lohr, 1987). The jock (or athlete) crowd had the highest prestige. The populars, who led social activities, came next. The normals, who were seen as middle-of-the-road students, came third. Druggies and toughs, who were known for drug use and delinquent acts, were fourth. Nobodies, students who had poor social or academic skills, came last.

Adolescents' self-esteem was related to the prestige of the crowds to which they belonged. Adolescents whose peers classified them as jocks were highest in self-esteem, with populars close behind. Adolescents classified as nobodies were lowest in self-esteem. The same rankings for self-esteem held when adolescents reported the crowd they thought they belonged to, so adolescents' evaluations of themselves were consistent with their crowd's social standing.

A tug-of-war between the Rattlers and the Eagles during the stage of greatest conflict between the groups. The Eagles first sat down and dug in while the Rattlers exhausted themselves pulling. Then the Rattlers tried the same strategy, but the Eagles still won the contest.

About one-third of the adolescents in these schools did not belong to any crowd. The self-esteem of these outsiders depended on their satisfaction with their social position. Outsiders who knew they were not part of a crowd but didn't care had average self-esteem. Outsiders who knew they didn't belong to a crowd but who wanted to belong to one had low self-esteem.

The relations between self-esteem and crowd membership do not necessarily mean that being in a popular crowd, for example, raises adolescents' self-esteem. Another possibility is that having a positive self-image and high self-confidence is a requirement for membership in a high-prestige crowd. Conversely, having low self-esteem may increase the chances that an adolescent will be viewed by peers as a nobody.

Adolescents' crowd membership is related to more than their self-esteem. Crowd membership is also related to adolescents' social behavior and school achievement (Brown, 1990; Brown et al., 1993). For example, adolescents in the druggie crowd use drugs more than average. Adolescents in the brain crowd found in some high schools have higher grades than average.

As discussed in earlier chapters, parents' expectations, values, and behaviors affect their children's social behavior, personality, and school adjustment. Indirectly, then, parents also affect the crowd to which their children are assigned in adolescence (Brown et al., 1993). Parents who emphasize academic achievement are likely to have adolescents with high grades who are part of the brain crowd. Parents who are permissive and fail to monitor their adolescents' behavior are likely to have adolescents who use drugs and are part of the drug crowd. Other emphases in parenting may partly explain why adolescents become part of the populars, jocks, normals, and nobodies. That is, research on crowd membership reveals yet another way in which parents influence their children's peer relationships.

Crowd memberships may, in turn, influence adolescents' adjustment, especially to school. Think for a moment about those adolescents called burnouts. Most burnouts are hostile toward school and alienated from it (Eckert, 1989). They want an education but do not believe that their high-school classes teach them what they will need to know for their future jobs. They also think teachers are biased against them. Burnouts rarely participate in school sports because they don't want to be associated with the school and they don't want to spend time with students in the jock crowd.

Eckert (1989) suggests that burnouts don't just have a bad experience at school. They learn lessons that limit them in their later life. In particular, they learn how to be marginal

Cooperative efforts by the Rattlers and Eagles to start a supposedly stalled truck began to break down the barriers between the groups. Gradually, the groups became friendly toward each other.

members of a social organization. They learn to do what is necessary to stay in school but not to succeed there.

Can the problems of adolescents in low-ranking crowds be solved? Can the relationships between crowds like the burnouts and the jocks be improved? In one classic experiment, a team of researchers was successful in reducing the hostility between two groups of adolescents. Although the experiment was not done in a school, it suggests ways to improve relationships between school crowds.

The Robbers Cave experiment took place during the early 1950s in Robbers Cave State Park in southeastern Oklahoma (Sherif et al., 1961). To begin, 11-year-old boys who were strangers to one another were recruited for a special summer camp. Eleven of the boys met each other for the first time when they took a bus from their homes to a campsite in the state park. Another 11 boys took a different bus to a different campsite.

During the first week of camp, the boys in each group got to know each other well. As the boys worked and played together, leaders emerged in each group. In addition, one group decided to name themselves the Rattlers. The other group decided to name themselves the Eagles.

During the second week of camp, the two groups of boys were allowed to meet. They decided to arrange a tournament involving several types of games. One day the boys had a tug-of-war. The Eagles tricked the Rattlers by sitting down and digging in rather than standing and pulling. After the Rattlers got tired, the Eagles gradually pulled them across the line.

Losing the tug-of-war angered the Rattlers, so they decided to raid the Eagles' cabin that night. They turned beds over, ripped mosquito netting, and stole the jeans of the Eagles' leader. The Eagles retaliated with a raid the next day. Hostility between the groups increased, and each group began to collect rocks for a fight with the other group.

Then the researchers tried to defuse the conflict between groups. They first arranged times for both groups to get together for enjoyable events like a movie. However, these occasions only gave the boys in each group more chances to hurl insults, threats, and accusations at the other group.

Then the staff arranged situations in which both groups of boys had to cooperate to reach goals valuable to both. For example, the boys were taken on a trip away from camp. The truck that was to get their food wouldn't start. To get the truck started, the boys pulled it with their tug-of-war rope. Both groups of boys pulled together. Once they got the truck started, they shouted for joy and congratulated each other.

Quickly, the separation between groups began to break down. With more opportunities for working together, some Rattlers became friends with Eagles. When camp ended, all the boys rode back to their homes on the same bus, laughing and singing together.

Could happy endings like these be duplicated with naturally existing groups? Could better relationships be established between crowds like the jocks and burnouts? The answer is yes, if adolescents in both crowds can be persuaded to adopt goals that they can only reach by working together. Working together in pursuit of common goals can reduce conflicts between groups at any age level. The trick, of course, is finding realistic goals that would be adopted by students in different crowds.

# BEYOND THE PEER SOCIAL WORLD: MIXED-AGE INTERACTIONS

You have read so far about two of children's social worlds. Chapter 11 focused on children's relationships with family members. This chapter focuses on children's relationships with peers. However, another social world is also important in children's lives. That world involves mixed-age interactions, interactions among children who differ in age.

Some information about mixed-age interactions and their effects was presented earlier in this chapter. Recall the experiments in which infant monkeys served as "therapists" for monkeys several months older who had been reared in social isolation. After interacting for a long period with the infant monkeys, the isolate-reared monkeys developed more normal patterns of social behavior. By contrast, interacting with other monkeys the same age was not helpful in improving the social behavior of isolate-reared monkeys. One implication of these results is that mixed-age interactions can make unique contributions to social development.

Children, too, often interact with other children who are not their peers (Ellis, Rogoff, & Cromer, 1981). In schools and, especially, in their own neighborhoods, children spend time with other children older or younger than themselves. Such mixed-age interactions were probably more common than same-age interactions during most of the evolutionary history of the human species (Konner, 1975). The earliest human groups were so small that few children had same-age playmates.

The characteristics of mixed-age interactions are much like those of the interactions among siblings discussed in chapter 11. Older peers and siblings usually dominate younger children. Most often, this dominance takes positive forms. Older peers and siblings exercise leadership, keep activities organized, and even seek the opinions of younger children (French et al., 1986; Hartup, 1983). Older peers and siblings give help and instruction to younger children.

Conversely, younger children assume they can ask older peers or siblings for help or instructions (French, 1984; Whiting & Whiting, 1975). Younger children, especially those under 3 years of age, enjoy interacting with more competent social partners (Brownell, 1990).

Elementary-school children, by contrast, seem to prefer same-age interactions. When these children can choose their partners, they interact more with other children the same age than with younger or older children (Roopnarine & Johnson, 1984). Apparently, elementary-school children prefer to interact with other children whose abilities are roughly equal to their own. In addition, children may get messages from peers or adults that they are now too old to be playing with infants and toddlers (Lederberg et al., 1986).

Jean Piaget (1932/1965) argued that same-age interactions are important in helping children learn to interact with their equals, and that is certainly true. However, learning to interact with older and younger people is also important (Hartup, 1983). Most adults work not only with colleagues but also with superiors and subordinates. A balance of same- and mixed-age interactions during childhood and adolescence may be the best preparation for success with the full range of adult relationships.

# SUMMARY

## Levels of Complexity in the Peer Social World

The social world of peer relationships is complex and multifaceted. Its simplest level involves interactions between peers. A higher level deals with relationships such as friendships. Still higher levels involve a child's position in a group and the type of group to which a child belongs.

## Peer Interactions in Infancy and Early Childhood

Social behavior toward peers emerges within a few months after birth. With increasing age, peer interactions become more complex and coordinated.

## Infants' and Toddlers' Behavior Toward Peers

The frequency of peer interactions increases during the second and third years of life. Imitative acts and simple games help toddlers practice the skills needed for long sequences of social play.

## Types of Play in Preschool Children

Preschoolers gradually develop the skills necessary for cooperative play involving complementary dramatic roles. Sequences of types of play have been defined by Parten, Piaget, Howes, and other researchers.

## Effects of Young Children's Interactions with Peers: Good or Bad?

Experiments with rhesus monkeys suggest that peer interactions are critical for normal development. Experiments with children suggest that peer experience promotes the learning of social skills. Studies of child-care centers suggest that adult supervision is necessary to ensure that children do not learn aggressive styles of interaction.

## How Do Parents Influence Their Children's Interactions with Peers?

Parents can directly influence their children's interactions with peers when they choose a neighborhood or initiate peer interactions for their young children. Parenting patterns and parents' disciplinary techniques indirectly influence children's interactions with peers.

## Children's Friendships

Friendships are relationships that are based on a history of interactions. The features of children's friendships can have important effects on their development.

## Origins of Friendship in Early Childhood

During the preschool years, friendships center on play. Preschoolers resolve conflicts with friends more successfully than those with nonfriends. Even in early childhood, friends' support can enhance children's social development.

## Features of Friendships in Childhood and Adolescence

Friendships become more intimate relationships during middle childhood and adolescence. During adolescence, girls typically have more intimate friendships than boys do. More than younger children, adolescents try to maintain their equality with friends by sharing rather than competing with them.

## Effects of Friendship, and Parents' Influence on Friendships

Although intimate friendships are often assumed to enhance children's self-esteem, longitudinal studies suggest that friendship may only affect certain aspects of social adjustment. Children who have good relationships with their parents usually form good relationships with friends.

## Status in the Peer Group

Children differ in their social status, the degree to which other children in their peer group like or dislike them. Other terms used to describe these differences in children's social position are popularity and sociometric status.

## Sociometric Techniques, Dimensions, and Groups

Social status can be assessed with dimensions of social preference and social impact. Alternatively, children can be classified as popular, rejected, neglected, controversial, or average.

## Why Are Some Children More Popular Than Others?

Popular children usually are physically attractive, but physical attractiveness is not the primary reason for their popularity. Variations in popularity are largely a consequence of variations in children's social behavior. Popularity may depend partly on the fit between children's characteristics and their peers' characteristics.

## Stability and Change in Social Status

Social status is moderately stable over time. Rejected children have an increased risk of social and psychological problems in adulthood. To prevent these problems, researchers have tried to change the behavior of rejected children and to raise their social status. Improving their parents' skill in childrearing may also improve these children's status with peers.

## Cliques, Crowds, and Peer Group Influence

As children move into adolescence, friendship groups become more cohesive and influential. Adolescents also become part of reputation-based groups called crowds.

## Processes of Influence in Adolescents' Cliques

Peer influence reaches a peak in midadolescence. For most adolescents, this influence promotes desirable rather than undesirable behaviors. The most important influence process is not overt pressure but change triggered by perceptions of peer-group norms.

## Part of the Crowd: Mixed Results of Belonging to a Group

Adolescent crowds such as the jocks and the burnouts are defined by their reputations for specific values and behavior. Crowds differ in their social standing, and adolescents' self-esteem is related to the ranking of their crowd in the social hierarchy. Crowd membership reflects adolescents' behavior, which is influenced by the parenting they have received.

## Beyond the Peer Social World: Mixed-Age Interactions

Children often interact with other children who are older or younger than they are. Mixed-age interactions are comparable in many respects to interactions with older or younger siblings. Mixed-age interactions may prepare children for the full range of social relationships in adulthood.

# Suggested Readings

Asher, S. R., & Coie, J. D. (Eds.). (1990). *Peer rejection in childhood.* Cambridge, England: Cambridge University Press. This book includes thorough and precise summaries of the most important research on low-status children. Much of this research was done by the editors and the authors of specific chapters. The book shows why some children are rejected by peers, what the long-term effects of peer rejection might be, and how rejected children's status might be improved.

Bronfenbrenner, U. (1970). *Two worlds of childhood: U.S. and U.S.S.R.* New York: Russell Sage Foundation. Not all of Bronfenbrenner's conclusions can be accepted, and not all his predictions about the United States have come true. Still, this book remains fascinating. He vividly portrays a society that no longer exists, a society in which peers were organized to inculcate political ideas and enhance social control over individuals.

Bukowski, W. M., Newcomb, A. F., & Hartup, W. W. (Eds.). (1996). *The company they keep: Friendship during childhood and adolescence.* New York: Cambridge University Press. More than any other, this book reviews current efforts to understand children's friendships. Some authors review what is known about friendships in early childhood, whereas others focus on middle-childhood and adolescent friendships. Some authors present intriguing theoretical perspectives on the development of friendship; others explore the issues that arise when studying friendships.

Parke, R. D., & Ladd, G. W. (Eds.). (1992). *Family-peer relationships: Modes of linkage.* Hillsdale, NJ: Erlbaum. In earlier decades, studies of family relationships and studies of peer relationships were completely separate. During the 1990s, however, more attention has been given to the connections between families and peers. The chapters in the book cover a wide range, from attachment in infancy to cross-cultural differences. Many prominent scholars discuss the processes by which parent-child relationships affect peer relationships and vice versa.

*Chapter Thirteen*

# Social Cognition: Understanding of Self and Other People

*A*s children develop, they form ideas about themselves and other people. In their spontaneous comments they most clearly reveal their thoughts about self and others. The following examples illustrate how varied (and how amusing) these comments can be. The examples come from anthropologists' observations of children and families in the small village of Taira on the island of Okinawa (Maretzki & Maretzki, 1963).

Hitoshi, a 4-year-old boy, carefully examines the head of his new baby sister. Then he hugs her and whispers, "You have two cowlicks just like me! You and I are 'naughty'." He turns next to the adults in the room and, with great glee, tells them the same thing.

Hitoshi had heard his parents say that children with two cowlicks, rather than just one, become naughty children. He didn't mind being called naughty because he knew that his parents, like all parents in Taira, were very indulgent toward children his age. He did not have to worry about being "naughty." He could, for a few years at least, relax and enjoy it. Notice, though, that he had already formed some idea of the kind of person he was by 4 years of age.

Susumu is 6 years old and has just entered the first grade. Several preschool children stand around him as he proudly says, "You don't know how to write your name . . . see, this is how you write." Then he begins to make the syllables of written Japanese in the sand with his fingers as the younger children look on in admiration.

Besides forming ideas about the kind of person they are, children evaluate their worth or competence. Susumu, like most children his age, felt proud to be a first grader and felt superior to younger children who did not go to school. As you will see, children's evaluations of themselves change as they move through the elementary-school years and into adolescence.

Hanako, a first-grade girl, cries out, "Fool ones!" when she sees the boys in the bushes above the road. The boys are picking and eating wild berries from the bushes. In doing so, they are disregarding a safety rule they learned as young children. They are supposed to stay on the road to avoid getting bitten by poisonous snakes.

Hanako and the girls with her frown at the boys. When the boys see them, they mimic the girls' frowns and keep eating berries. Then a truck rolls down the road and a man in the truck yells at the boys to get out of the bushes. The embarrassed boys come down the hill toward the road that the girls are on. The girls start laughing and telling stories, loud enough so the boys can hear, about children who have been bitten by snakes.

This incident reveals a great deal about the social world of children in Taira and their social understanding. In her first comment, Hanako shows what she thinks about boys who risk danger just to collect berries. The boys' reaction is a mocking show of disdain for the girls. But the girls get the last laugh (literally), as the boys obey the man's order to get out of the bushes.

All three incidents are related to the topic of this chapter, the development of social cognition. **Social cognition** refers to thinking about human beings and human affairs. It includes thoughts about the self and other people (Flavell et al., 1993; Shantz, 1983).

The first section of the chapter explores the age changes in children's understanding of self. The next section examines children's **self-esteem,** their evaluations of their worth, value, and competence. A third section focuses on the sense of identity that is elaborated in adolescence and early adulthood.

Then the focus turns from understanding of self to understanding of other people. You will see how children like Hanako learn to interpret other people's emotional expressions, and when children begin to make inferences about the personality of other people. In a final section, you will learn about the links between children's social cognition and their social behavior.

The chapter deals both with self-understanding and with understanding of other people because the two show a similar course of development. The similarity is not surprising

**social cognition**
*Thinking that relates to human beings and human affairs; includes thoughts related to the self and to other people.*

**self-esteem**
*People's evaluations of their worth, value, and competence.*

because children must use the same head to understand both (Flavell, 1985). Watch for the similarities as you read the chapter.

Watch, also, for overlap between this chapter and the earlier ones on cognitive development. The development of social cognition is related to broader trends in cognitive development. Even so, social-cognitive development differs from other aspects of cognitive development because people are different from the other things that you might think about. Indeed, people are not *things* at all. Other people have motives and feelings, they act voluntarily, and they interact with others who are thinking about them.

Finally, be aware that this chapter covers only part of the domain of social cognition. Defined most broadly, the social-cognitive domain includes understanding of all aspects of the social world. This broad definition includes children's understanding of social relationships, social norms, and social institutions.

Some topics not addressed in this chapter will be covered in later chapters. The next chapter, on sex-role development, examines social norms that limit and direct the behavior of boys and girls. It also describes girls' ideas about boys and vice versa.

Chapter 15, on moral development, examines children's understanding of norms for behavior in close relationships and in entire societies. You will see how children's views about obedience to adults change as they move into adolescence and then become adults themselves. In addition, you will learn why boys in Taira who disobey adults by picking berries in the bushes often become adults who yell at boys who pick berries!

# WHO AM I? THE DEVELOPMENT OF SELF-UNDERSTANDING

One important difference between self-understanding and understanding of other people is that, literally and figuratively, we do not see ourselves as we see other people. We see ourselves only through a process of reflection, as if in a mirror. Infants may actually recognize themselves for the first time in a mirror. To begin the exploration of self-understanding, let's look at infants looking at themselves in mirrors.

## Self-Recognition in Infancy

You learned in chapter 5 that young infants are fascinated by the human face. However, when newborns see their face in a mirror, they do not act as if they know it is their face. Self-recognition develops gradually during the first two years of life. The following outline of phases in the development of self-recognition is based on studies by several researchers (Asendorpf & Baudonniere, 1993; Damon & Hart, 1982; Lewis, 1987; Lewis & Brooks-Gunn, 1979).

During the first three months of life, infants may look with interest at their face in a mirror, but they look just as long at another infant's face. Between 3 and 8 months, infants begin to notice that their mirror image does exactly what they do. Then they begin to wave at the mirror image, or smile at it, or bounce along with it. However, they do not show any clear recognition that the face in the mirror is their face.

Between 8 and 12 months, infants become more responsive to the match between their actions and the actions of their mirror image. They respond even more positively to a live television image of themselves. If a TV camera is focused on their face, they will make faces at their image on a TV screen because they are attracted to images that mimic their actions.

By contrast, if infants this age see TV images of themselves that were made earlier, they are much less responsive. If they see themselves and another baby on videotape when neither image is live, they respond as positively to the other baby as to their own image. These reactions suggest that the infants still do not recognize their own facial features.

Around 18 months of age, recognition of self emerges. Researchers have obtained the strongest evidence for self-recognition by adapting a technique first used with chimpanzees. When a toddler is not paying close attention, a researcher pats a spot of rouge on the toddler's nose. Then the toddler is placed in front of a mirror and asked, "Who's that?" Toddlers in this

This girl didn't notice when someone put a red spot on her nose. But when she saw herself in a mirror, she knew the spot was on *her* nose, so she touched her nose. Infants under 1 year of age, who lack this kind of self-recognition, touch the mirror rather than their nose when they see a spot on the mirror image of themselves.

age range are surprised to see the red spot on their nose. They often touch their nose, rather than the mirror, which shows that they know the face in the mirror is their own.

Between 18 and 24 months of age, toddlers learn more about themselves. They can say their name, their age, and whether they are a boy or a girl. That is, they begin to recognize not just who they are, but the important social categories in which they fall.

The emergence of self-recognition in a mirror is a prerequisite for embarrassment, the emotion linked to self-consciousness. Toddlers who touch their noses when they see the red spot in the mirror sometimes act embarrassed when they are lavishly praised or asked to dance for an audience. Toddlers who don't touch their noses rarely show embarrassment under any circumstances (Lewis et al., 1989).

Self-recognition is also related to what might seem like selfish behavior. One researcher (Levine, 1983) tested 2-year-olds for self-recognition with the mirror-and-rouge procedure. She also tested them for appropriate use of personal pronouns like *I, my,* and *your.* The 2-year-olds who showed self-recognition most clearly were most likely to claim toys as "mine" when playing with a peer. These claims did not lead to more negative interactions with the peer. On the contrary, toddlers with greater self-recognition had more positive conversations with their peers. Claiming toys as "mine" was not a sign of selfishness; rather, it showed the toddlers' emerging self-awareness.

Self-awareness and awareness of other people normally emerge around the same time. Toddlers who show self-recognition in a mirror also show more immediate imitation of peers during play (Asendorpf & Baudonniere, 1993). Immediate imitation is defined by toddlers' use of the same objects in the same way as a playmate is using them. This result suggests that toddlers with greater self-awareness are more aware of other people and their actions. In addition, self-aware toddlers show their understanding of other people through prosocial behaviors such as sharing and comforting (Zahn-Waxler et al., 1992).

The emergence of self-recognition seems to depend more on infants' cognitive development than on their social experience. Even the experience of maltreatment by parents does not retard the development of self-recognition in a mirror (Schneider-Rosen & Cicchetti, 1991). However, maltreated infants show less positive emotional expressions when they see themselves in a mirror than other infants do. These emotional expressions may reflect a less positive evaluation of self, which is the topic of the later section on self-esteem.

## TABLE 13.1    Age Changes in Self-Concepts

| AGE PERIOD | EMPHASIS OF SELF-DESCRIPTIONS | EXAMPLES |
|---|---|---|
| *Early Childhood (2–5)* | Physical appearance | I have blue eyes. |
| | Typical actions | I go to school. |
| | Possessions | I have a dog. |
| | Competence | I wash my hair myself. |
| *Middle Childhood (6–11)* | Physical appearance | I have brown hair. |
| | Activities | I play Hockey! |
| | Preferences (likes and dislikes) | I LOVE Sports! |
| | Social comparison | I'm almost the smartest boy in my class. |
| *Adolescence (12–17)* | Political ideology | I am a liberal. |
| | Personality traits | I am ambitious. |
| | Self-awareness | I don't know who I am. |
| | Future orientation | I want to be a psychologist. |

## Self-Concepts in Childhood and Adolescence

Although toddlers can recognize themselves in a mirror and tell you their name, age, and sex, they don't know much more about themselves. They have few ideas about their physical skills, mental abilities, or personality traits. In psychological terms, they have a limited **self-concept.** As children grow older, their self-concepts, their ideas about themselves, become richer and more complex.

The most direct way to assess children's self-concepts is to ask them to describe themselves. One procedure for doing so is to have them write 20 answers to the question, "Who am I?" A boy named Bruce gave the following answers to this question (Montemayor & Eisen, 1977, p. 317):

> My name is Bruce C. I have brown eyes. I have brown hair. I have brown eyebrows. I'm 9 years old. I LOVE! Sports. I have seven people in my family. I have great! eye site. I have lots! of friends. I live on 1923 Pinecrest Dr. I'm going on 10 in September. I'm a boy. I have an uncle that is almost 7 feet tall. My school is Pinecrest. My teacher is Mrs. V. I play Hockey! I'am almost the smartest boy in the class. I LOVE! food. I love freash air. I LOVE SCHOOL. [Spelling is Bruce's.]

Notice that several of Bruce's answers refer to his physical appearance. In particular, he says he has brown eyes, hair, and eyebrows. Descriptions of the "physical self" are common in the "Who am I?" responses of children Bruce's age (Harter, 1983).

Table 13.1 shows other categories of self-descriptions that are common in middle childhood. Children Bruce's age often mention their activities. For example, Bruce says he plays hockey. Thus, besides referring to the physical self children refer to the "active self" (Damon & Hart, 1982).

Also common in middle childhood are descriptions of preferences, or likes and dislikes. Bruce says that he "LOVEs" sports, food, fresh air, and school. These comments reflect not the physical self or the active self but the inner, psychological self (Damon & Hart, 1982). They tell us something about Bruce that cannot be seen from the outside, either by looking at him or by watching his behavior.

In addition, self-descriptions involving social comparison are frequent in middle childhood. Bruce says he is "almost the smartest boy in my class." This comment shows that Bruce

**self-concept**
*People's ideas about their physical skills, mental abilities, personality traits, and other characteristics.*

can distinguish between his talents and those of his peers. He can also integrate his judgments about self and others.

Preschool children's self-descriptions have characteristics partly similar to, and partly different from, those of older children (Keller, Ford, & Meacham, 1978). Comments about physical appearance are even more common among preschool children than among older children (see table 13.1). So are comments about activities, including routine actions like going to school. These comments show that the physical self and the active self are especially salient to preschoolers.

Another important category of preschoolers' self-descriptions includes comments about possessions. To an adult, a statement like "I have a dog" is strange as a self-description. However, the boundary between what I *am* and what I *own* is less distinct to preschoolers than to older children and adults.

Preschoolers also comment frequently on their competence. As table 13.1 suggests, preschoolers don't hesitate to brag when describing themselves. But notice the difference between a comment like "I wash my hair myself" and "I'm the smartest child in my class." Preschool children rarely compare themselves with others when talking about their talents and abilities. Instead, they talk simply about what they can do. In this and other ways, preschoolers' self-descriptions are less complex than those of older children.

The self-concepts of preschool children are just as distinctive for what they lack as for what they include. When describing themselves, preschoolers say little about their preferences for activities, foods, or anything else. In other words, preschoolers say little about their psychological self, even aspects of the psychological self as simple as what they like and dislike (Keller et al., 1978). Instead of talking about their feelings, motives, or ideas, preschoolers talk about characteristics that are concrete and readily observed.

Still, preschoolers' lack of self-understanding should not be exaggerated. When asked specific questions that are stated in concrete terms, preschoolers can report their usual behaviors and their attitudes (Eder, 1990). For example, they can report their preferences for social interaction if asked whether they think it's more fun to do things alone or with other people. However, preschoolers rarely make such comments spontaneously. They know a lot about themselves, but they are not fully aware of all that they know. Their self-descriptions lack even the level of psychological depth found in Bruce's "Who am I?" responses.

Even in middle childhood, self-descriptions rarely have much psychological depth. Bruce does not talk about his beliefs, his personality traits, or the way he thinks. The psychological dimension of the self-concept becomes much fuller in adolescence. The "Who am I?" answers of a 17-year-old girl illustrate this change (Montemayor & Eisen, 1977, p. 318):

> I am a human being. I am a girl. I am an individual. I don't know who I am. I am a Pisces. I am a moody person. I am an indecisive person. I am an ambitious person. I am a very curious person. I am not an individual. I am a loner. I am an American (God help me). I am a Democrat. I am a liberal person. I am a radical. I am a conservative. I am a pseudoliberal. I am an atheist. I am not a classifiable person (i.e., I don't want to be).

Most obvious in the girl's answers are the many, often contradictory comments about her political ideology (see table 13.1). She says she is a Democrat, a liberal, a radical, a conservative, and a pseudoliberal. Leave aside, for the moment, the contradictions among these labels. The labels themselves show a concern with systems of beliefs far more complex than Bruce or other 9-year-olds can comprehend. The concern with political ideology is one facet of the psychological depth of adolescents' self-concepts.

In addition, psychological depth is shown by the girl's references to personality traits. The girl says she is moody, indecisive, ambitious, curious, and a loner. Lists of personality traits are common in the self-descriptions of late adolescents and adults, but they are rare in children's self-descriptions. Personality traits are more abstract than preferences or physical characteristics, and abstract attributes of the self are recognized more by adolescents than by children (Harter, 1990).

This girl is typical of other late adolescents in a third way: She has reached a new level of self-awareness or self-consciousness. When she says, "I don't know who I am," she turns

the self on itself. William James (1890/1963), the most famous American psychologist of the nineteenth century, said that people talk about two aspects of the self. First, the self is the controlling agent of mental life, the "I" who knows, thinks, remembers, and guides a person's behavior. Second, the self can be an object of thought, the "me" who is known. When the 17-year-old says, "I don't know who I am," she integrates the "I" and the "me." Her statement could be translated into James's terms by saying, "*I* don't know *me*." Integration of the two aspects of the self is a new achievement of adolescence.

The "Who am I?" answers of the 17-year-old girl do not illustrate a fourth feature of adolescents' self-concepts. As table 13.1 indicates, many adolescents describe themselves by talking about their orientation toward the future. In particular, adolescents often mention their career plans (e.g., "I want to be an electrical engineer"). Children's self-descriptions focus mostly on the present, the here and now. Adolescents increasingly think about what they will or might be, not merely what they are now. The future orientation of adolescents is linked to a growing concern about their options in life, about possible selves that differ from their actual self today (Harter, 1990).

Finally, what about the most obvious feature of the 17-year-old girl's self-description? Too much can be read into a person's responses to a brief test like the "Who am I?" but the girl certainly listed more negative personality traits (e.g., moody, indecisive, a loner) than positive ones (e.g., ambitious). Is such a negative view of self typical in late adolescence? You'll learn the answer to this question in the next section.

# HOW GOOD AM I? VARIATIONS IN SELF-ESTEEM

Earlier, *self-esteem* was defined as a person's feelings of self-worth, value, and competence. Children with high self-esteem feel positively about who they are and what they are like. Children with low self-esteem dislike themselves and want to be a different kind of person. Although several definitions of self-esteem exist (see Harter, 1983), central to most definitions is a person's positive or negative evaluation of himself or herself.

## General and Specific Aspects of Self-Evaluation

Self-evaluations can be highly specific or very general. For decades, researchers tried to measure children's general self-esteem, their overall sense of self-worth. Measures of general self-esteem have been useful (e.g., Coopersmith, 1967; Rosenberg, 1979), but more recent research has shown that they are incomplete. Children also evaluate themselves in specific domains important to them. For example, they evaluate how good they are at schoolwork, how physically attractive they are, and how much their classmates like them. During the 1980s, several researchers created measures that assess both general self-esteem and self-evaluations in specific domains.

A self-esteem measure devised by Susan Harter (1985), the Self-Perception Profile for Children (SPPC), was described briefly in chapter 2. The SPPC assesses children's global self-worth (or general self-esteem) and their self-perceptions in five domains: scholastic competence, social acceptance, athletic competence, physical appearance, and behavioral conduct.

Table 13.2 lists sample items for each subscale on the SPPC. The table also shows the format of the items. Children first decide whether they are more like the kids described in the sentence on the left side or more like those described in the sentence on the right side. Then they decide whether the sentence is "sort of true" or "really true" for them. Children with higher self-esteem more often choose the more positive sentences as "really true" for them.

Herbert Marsh and Richard Shavelson (Marsh, 1989; Marsh & Shavelson, 1985) devised a self-esteem scale called the Self-Description Questionnaire I (or SDQI). Like Harter's measure, the SDQI includes a subscale for general self-esteem. Other subscales are for self-evaluations of physical or athletic ability, physical appearance, and peer relations or social acceptance. Rather than having one subscale for scholastic competence, the SDQI has subscales for perceived competence in reading, mathematics, and other subjects. Marsh and

## TABLE 13.2 Sample Items from Harter's (1985) Self-Perception Profile for Children

| | Really true for me | Sort of true for me | | | | | Sort of true for me | Really true for me |
|---|---|---|---|---|---|---|---|---|
| **Global Self-Worth** | ☐ | ☐ | Some kids are often *unhappy* with themselves | but | Other kids are pretty *pleased* with themselves. | | ☐ | ☐ |
| **Scholastic Competence** | ☐ | ☐ | Some kids feel that they are very *good* at their school work | but | Other kids *worry* about whether they can do the school work assigned to them. | | ☐ | ☐ |
| **Social Acceptance** | ☐ | ☐ | Some kids find it *hard* to make friends | but | Other kids find it's pretty *easy* to make friends. | | ☐ | ☐ |
| **Athletic Competence** | ☐ | ☐ | Some kids do very *well* at all kinds of sports | but | Other kids *don't* feel that they are very good when it comes to sports. | | ☐ | ☐ |
| **Physical Appearance** | ☐ | ☐ | Some kids are *happy* with the way they look | but | Other kids are *not* happy with the way they look. | | ☐ | ☐ |
| **Behavioral Conduct** | ☐ | ☐ | Some kids often do *not* like the way they *behave* | but | Other kids usually *like* the way they behave. | | ☐ | ☐ |

Shavelson subdivided the domain of scholastic competence because they found that many students did not view their competence as equal in all subjects. Some students who thought they were good in reading, for example, did not think they were good in math, and vice versa.

Both Harter's SPPC and Marsh and Shavelson's SDQI are intended for students in elementary and junior high school. Harter (1990) created another scale for adolescents that includes eight subscales. Five of the subscales are similar to those on the SPPC. The other three are for adolescents' perceptions of their job competence, close friendships, and romantic appeal. Marsh also created self-description questionnaires with additional subscales for adolescents and for adults (see Marsh, 1989). Both Harter and Marsh assumed that additional subscales are needed because adolescents and adults evaluate themselves in more domains than children do.

Only a few researchers have tried to measure the self-esteem of preschool children, and these measures are somewhat controversial. Susan Harter and Robin Pike (1984) created a scale for 4- to 7-year-olds that includes subscales for perceived cognitive competence and perceived physical competence. It also includes subscales for preschoolers' perceptions of their acceptance by their mother and their peers.

Harter and Pike's scale does not include a subscale for general self-esteem because they felt that 4- to 7-year-olds have not yet developed a sense of their overall worth. Other researchers have questioned this conclusion. Attachment theorists have proposed that the security of young children's attachments to their parents affects their general self-esteem (Cassidy, 1990). This hypothesis implies, of course, that young children do form some idea of their overall worth. More recent studies with the SPPC and the SDQI have confirmed that variations in general self-esteem can be reliably measured in children as young as 6 (Cassidy, 1988; Marsh & Craven, 1991).

## Age Changes in Self-Esteem

The creation of improved measures led to a surge in self-esteem research during the 1980s and 1990s. One focus was on the changes in self-esteem during childhood and adolescence. Although the evidence is not entirely consistent, five conclusions can be drawn.

1. *Self-evaluations become more differentiated during the elementary-school years.* When Harter and Pike (1984) used their self-esteem scale with 4- to 7-year-olds, they found that children

who rated their cognitive competence highly usually rated their physical competence highly. Conversely, children who gave low ratings for cognitive competence often gave low ratings for their physical competence. In their self-perceptions, these young children differentiated little between their competence in the cognitive and physical domains. Similarly, the children differentiated little between their acceptance by their mothers and their acceptance by peers.

More differentiated responding was shown by kindergarten children who responded to the SDQI during an individual interview (Marsh & Craven, 1991). In particular, analyses of the kindergartners' responses suggested that they could differentiate between their physical ability and their school performance. Even so, the correlations among these subscales were stronger than those found for first and second graders.

The differentiation among self-esteem subscales increases steadily during the elementary-school grades (Boivin, Vitaro, & Gagnon, 1992; Eccles et al., 1993; Marsh, 1989). Children become more able to say that they are very good readers but not as good in math, or only average at sports but very popular with peers. One practical implication of this age change is that older children can better comprehend adults' messages that no one can excel at everything. Children can, then, be encouraged to base their general self-esteem, their overall sense of self-worth, on their competence or standing in domains where they do well.

2. *Self-evaluations become less positive during the elementary-school years.* Most preschoolers have very positive impressions of their competence in all domains (Harter & Pike, 1984). Even after they enter school, children retain these positive impressions of themselves. At the beginning of the chapter, you read about Susumu, who proudly told some younger children about how he was learning to write. Many first graders have similar views of themselves. For example, many first graders say they are among the smartest children in their class (Stipek & Tannatt, 1984).

As children move through the elementary grades, they more often compare themselves with their classmates. Remember Bruce's comment (and spelling): "I'am almost the smartest boy in my class." Bruce probably exaggerated a bit but not as much as he would have in first grade. Older children more often engage in social comparison, evaluating their performance relative to that of their classmates when making judgments about themselves (Ruble et al., 1980). Because of this increase in social comparison, older children make more accurate judgments about where they stand in their class. This growing accuracy leads to a modest decrease in children's self-esteem (Eccles et al., 1993).

Whether growing accuracy is the only reason for the decrease in self-esteem during the elementary-school years is uncertain (Eccles et al., 1993). Another possibility is that children have experiences that lead to more negative self-evaluations. In the upper elementary grades, teachers may use more stringent standards for academic work, so fewer children get feedback that they are doing "really well" on their schoolwork. At home, parents may increase their demands for responsible behavior or high achievement. In other words, children's school and home environments may become less conducive to high self-esteem as children get older. Currently, however, evidence on this possibility is scarce.

3. *Self-esteem levels off during the middle-school or junior-high years.* In a well-known longitudinal study, girls' general self-esteem dropped after the move from sixth grade in elementary school to seventh grade in junior high school (Simmons & Blyth, 1987). Other researchers have replicated this result or found decreases in self-esteem after the move from fifth grade in elementary school to sixth grade in middle school (Seidman et al., 1994; Wigfield et al., 1991). These findings have led some writers to claim that early adolescence is a poor time, developmentally, to move students to a new school environment (Entwistle, 1990). Other writers have argued that the problem is not the school transition but a poor match between adolescents' characteristics and the characteristics of a typical junior high school (Eccles et al., 1993).

A more complete review of the available data suggests that these conclusions are premature. Adolescents in several studies did not show any significant change in self-esteem

after the transition to junior high (Fenzel & Blyth, 1986; Harter, Whitesell, & Kowalski, 1992; Hirsch & Rapkin, 1987). Adolescents in some studies increased in self-esteem after the transition (Nottelmann, 1987). Moreover, even when decreases in self-esteem have been found, a rebound has sometimes been found during the first year in the new school (Wigfield et al., 1991).

Several researchers have ignored the issue of school transitions and simply looked at the changes in general self-esteem during the early adolescent years (Marsh, 1989). The evidence is mixed, but the safest general conclusion is that self-esteem neither increases nor decreases consistently during early adolescence. Adolescents' self-esteem may be affected by the characteristics of their school environments (Eccles et al., 1993), but these effects do not consistently lead to a drop in self-esteem after a school transition.

4. *General self-esteem increases during middle and late adolescence.* The average 18-year-old has higher self-esteem than the average 13-year-old (McCarthy & Hoge, 1982; Savin-Williams & Demo, 1984). In addition, self-esteem typically increases between 18 and 23 years of age (O'Malley & Bachman, 1983). The reasons for the increase have not been conclusively identified. One likely contributor is an increase in adolescents' actual competence. For example, adolescents often have more skill in using computers than their parents do. Another likely contributor is the achievement of adult status in many domains. Driving a car, for example, is an important marker of social maturity and independence.

5. *Age changes in general self-esteem may differ little across ethnic groups.* You might expect children from minority ethnic groups to have lower self-esteem than those in the majority group, but such a difference is not often found. Since 1980 several researchers have assessed the general self-esteem of large numbers of adolescents from various ethnic groups (Dukes & Martinez, 1994; Tashakkori, 1993; Tashakkori & Thompson, 1991). In these studies, African American adolescents usually had higher self-esteem than White adolescents. Asian adolescents usually had lower self-esteem than White adolescents. Most often, however, the differences between groups were small. Unfortunately, no firm conclusions can yet be drawn about the reasons for these small differences or their possible consequences.

Groups of African American, Hispanic, and White adolescents have been included in a few longitudinal studies (e.g., Hirsch & Rapkin, 1987; Seidman et al., 1994). The adolescents in all ethnic groups showed similar changes in self-esteem as they grew older and experienced transitions to new schools. Although these data are limited, they suggest that developmental changes in self-esteem may be comparable for different ethnic groups.

With these five conclusions in mind, think again about the 17-year-old girl whose self-description you read earlier. If she truly had low self-esteem, as her "Who Am I?" comments suggest, then she was not a typical adolescent. Most adolescents have high and increasing self-esteem. Only a minority have low self-esteem.

Many adolescents with low self-esteem also had low self-esteem during childhood. More generally, self-esteem shows a significant degree of continuity between childhood and adolescence (Coopersmith, 1967; O'Malley & Bachman, 1983). Continuity in self-esteem also exists during adolescence, although self-esteem can change dramatically over a period of two or three years (Alsaker & Olweus, 1992).

On the other hand, some children who have average or high self-esteem suffer a drop in self-esteem when they enter adolescence. These cases fit the stereotype that adolescence is a time of emotional turmoil, or storm and stress. Yet this stereotype applies to only a small fraction of adolescents, probably about 10 to 20 percent (Offer & Offer, 1975; Rutter, 1980).

For most children, the move into adolescence does not lead to psychological turmoil, self-doubt, and declining self-esteem (Savin-Williams & Demo, 1984). Therefore, when a particular adolescent has low self-esteem, it should most often be attributed not to the adolescent's age but to his or her experiences. An investigation of adolescents' experiences often reveals the origins of the variations in their self-esteem.

# In the Looking Glass: Origins of Self-Esteem

Few social scientists are known for their poetry, but one couplet is justifiably famous. Charles Cooley (1922) wrote that

> Each to each a looking glass
> Reflects the other that doth pass.

As you know, *looking glass* is an old term for a mirror. Cooley explained his couplet this way: "As we see our face, figure, and dress in the glass [or mirror], and are interested in them because they are ours . . . so in imagination we perceive in another's mind some thought of our appearance, manners, aims, deeds, character, friends, and so on, and are variously affected by it" (p. 184). In this quotation, Cooley drew a parallel between the self-recognition in a mirror that begins in infancy and the processes that lead to self-understanding in childhood and adulthood. He assumed that other people are the mirrors in which we see ourselves. Our thoughts about ourselves are affected by how other people react to us. Later writers like George Mead (1934) also emphasized the social origins of self-understanding and self-concepts.

The process of social reflection affects self-esteem as well as self-concepts. Cooley argued that children evaluate themselves as they think other people evaluate them. For example, the looking-glass metaphor implies that popular children should be high in perceived social acceptance because their classmates show their liking for them. Classmates, then, should be the looking glass in which popular children see themselves. As the metaphor suggests, children's perception of their social acceptance is related to their popularity (Cauce, 1987; Harter, 1982).

Similarly, students whose academic performance is superior should have more positive perceptions of their scholastic competence, and they do. Students with higher scores on standardized achievement tests are higher in perceived scholastic competence (Harter, 1982). Students with higher math grades have higher scores on the SDQI subscale for self-evaluations in math. Students with higher English grades have higher scores on the SDQI subscale for self-evaluations in English (Marsh & Holmes, 1990).

The looking-glass metaphor implies more than a relation between others' evaluations and self-evaluations. It implies that the first causes the second. For example, the feedback that students receive on their academic achievement, from grades and test scores, should directly affect their self-evaluations. The data from a few longitudinal studies are consistent with this hypothesis (Bachman & O'Malley, 1977; Hoge, Smit, & Hanson, 1990; Skaalvik & Hagtvet, 1990).

An equally popular hypothesis is that high self-esteem leads to improvements in academic achievement (Marsh, 1990). Students who feel more positively about themselves, especially if they feel positively about their academic ability, should be more motivated to work hard at school. Their perceptions of their competence should lead to high expectancies of academic success. Those expectancies, as noted in chapter 10, should enhance achievement motivation.

Effects of students' self-esteem on their academic achievement have been found in some studies (Marsh, 1987, 1990; Skaalvik & Hagtvet, 1990) but not in others (Maruyama, Rubin, & Kingsbury, 1981). The inconsistent results make it risky to draw conclusions, but two possibilities are worth suggesting. First, academic achievement and self-esteem may influence each other. Getting good grades may raise students' self-esteem and having high self-esteem may motivate children to work hard and so attain a high level of achievement.

Second, the effects of self-esteem on achievement have been shown more often with adolescents than with elementary-school children (Marsh, 1990; Skaalvik & Hagtvet, 1990). As mentioned earlier, the stability of self-esteem increases with age (Alsaker & Olweus, 1992), so it may have a greater influence on adolescents' behavior than on children's. If so, the self-esteem enhancement programs that are often used with young children (e.g., Bean, 1992) may have even greater benefits if adapted for adolescents. More generally, parents and

# THE SELF-ESTEEM OF THE BIG FISH IN THE LITTLE POND

Have you heard the saying, "It is better to be a big fish in a little pond than to be a little fish in a big pond"? Stated less figuratively, this saying means that people usually compare themselves with the other people closest to them.

In particular, academically talented students who are in regular classes with average- and low-ability classmates are like big fish in a little pond. By contrast, academically talented students who are in gifted and talented classes composed entirely of talented students are like little fish in a big pond. They are surrounded by classmates whose academic talents are equal or superior to their own. The saying implies that academically talented students will have lower self-esteem when they attend gifted and talented classes than when they attend regular classes.

A careful analysis of Cooley's looking-glass metaphor makes it possible to specify this big-fish-little-pond effect (Marsh et al., 1995). Being in a gifted and talented class should lower students' perceptions of their academic competence but should not necessarily affect other domains of self-evaluation. This hypothesis follows from evidence that gifted students rate their academic competence more highly than do average students. By contrast, gifted students do not consistently rate their peer acceptance or their success in other nonacademic domains as higher (or lower) than average students do (Berndt & Burgy, 1996; Hoge & Renzulli, 1993). In short, gifted students differ from average students only in academic self-esteem, so the effects of gifted and talented classes should be limited to the academic domain.

To test these hypotheses, Herbert Marsh and his colleagues (1995) identified elementary-school students who were selected for a gifted and talented class. The researchers identified a comparison group of high-achieving students who were not selected for the special class. The students in both groups completed Marsh's self-esteem questionnaire, the SDQI, in the beginning, the middle, and the end of a school year. Students' scores on the various subscales of the SDQI were combined into two measures. The measure of academic self-esteem assessed students' evaluations of their ability in math, reading, and other school subjects. The measure of nonacademic self-esteem assessed students' evaluations of their peer acceptance, athletic ability, physical appearance, and relationships with parents.

The crucial question in the study was how the self-esteem of students in each group changed during the year. As figure 13.1 shows, students' nonacademic self-esteem improved during the year, and the improvement was similar for the students in gifted and talented and in regular classes. Academic self-esteem also improved for students in regular classes, but it decreased for students in gifted and talented classes. Apparently, becoming a little fish in a big pond did make gifted students perceive their academic ability less positively.

These findings do not necessarily mean that gifted and talented classes are bad for children. If these classes positively affect students' academic achievement, which they may (Marsh et al.,

1995), educators and parents may be willing to accept a modest negative effect on students' academic self-esteem. Some adults might even argue that these students benefit from seeing that other students are equal or superior to them in academic ability.

However, lower academic self-concepts could potentially lead to lower achievement motivation and lower educational aspirations. To avoid these outcomes, educators and parents need to think more carefully about which students are invited to participate in gifted and talented classes and how these classes are structured. Students who are more concerned about their own learning than about their performance relative to classmates should be less affected by their placement in a gifted class. Classes in which competition receives little emphasis, and gifted students work mostly on individual projects, should have less negative effects on students' self-esteem. These classroom practices can help all students see themselves as big fish in their own ponds.

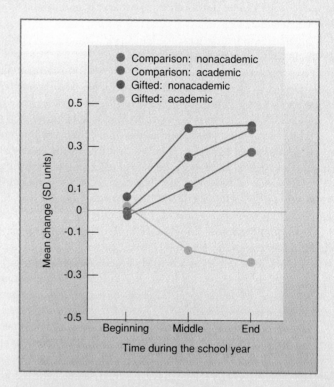

## FIGURE 13.1

The academic self-esteem of gifted students who were placed in a special class dropped during the school year. By contrast, the academic self-esteem of a comparison group of high-achieving students rose during the year. Both groups showed an increase in nonacademic self-esteem. Apparently, gifted students evaluated their academic ability less positively when they had daily opportunities to compare themselves with other gifted students. However, this result may not occur if classes for gifted students are appropriately structured.

teachers who want adolescents to achieve more in school may need to boost the adolescents' feelings of competence at schoolwork.

Another question suggested by the looking-glass metaphor is *which* mirror children look into when evaluating themselves. Consider a fourth-grade girl who is high in academic achievement. Suppose that this girl's academic talents are recognized by her teachers, so she is placed in a special program for gifted and talented students. Once in the program, will this girl compare her achievement with that of all the other children in her grade, and so have high self-esteem? Will she, instead, compare her achievement with that of the other talented students in her special program, and so have somewhat lower self-esteem? *Practical Applications of Research:* "The Self-Esteem of the Big Fish in the Little Pond" answers these questions and considers the implications of the answers for educational programs.

Finally, the looking-glass metaphor can explain the origins of general self-esteem in childhood. To some extent, general self-esteem must be the sum or the product of self-evaluations in specific domains. Children who are academically successful, popular, and physically attractive should have higher general self-esteem than children who perceive themselves as failing in these domains—and they do (Harter, 1990; Marsh, 1993).

Other researchers extend the looking-glass metaphor in a different direction. They explore how children are treated by the other people most important in their lives. Those people, defined as **significant others,** affect evaluations of self in many domains. For children, parents are significant others. Parents' behavior is likely to have strong effects on children's general self-esteem.

Only a few researchers have explored how parents' behavior might affect their children's self-esteem. Still, the findings of this research should not surprise you. High self-esteem seems to be fostered by the types of parenting described earlier as most desirable (Johnson, Shulman, & Collins, 1991).

In one study (Cassidy, 1988), 6-year-old children and their mothers participated in a procedure analogous to the Strange Situation for measuring infants' attachment security. The children were separated from their mother for about an hour. Observers recorded how the children responded to the mother when she returned. Then the observers rated the security of the children's attachments to the mother. Children who were more securely attached had higher scores on a measure of general self-esteem. In other words, children who had learned to trust in their mothers' acceptance and responsiveness had also learned to value themselves.

Chapter 11 briefly mentioned another, classic study of the origins of self-esteem. Stanley Coopersmith (1967) assessed the general self-esteem of 10- to 12-year-old boys. He also assessed their parents' behavior toward them. The parents of boys with higher self-esteem were more affectionate and more involved with their sons. These parents made decisions democratically, thus showing their respect for their sons' views. They tended to avoid physical punishment and to rely on reasoning with their sons. In these ways, the parents showed that they valued their sons and respected their judgment. When parents provide such a "looking glass" for their children, the children have high self-esteem.

The parents of boys with high self-esteem were also strict. They set rules for their sons' behavior and enforced them consistently. Such strictness, combined with democratic decision making, probably helped these boys develop self-control. In addition, these boys probably developed patterns of behavior that earned them the approval of other people. By contrast, boys with permissive parents probably showed more out-of-control behavior that led to disapproval by other people and low self-esteem. In a looking glass, children can see their vices as clearly as their virtues.

In summary, what conclusions can be drawn about the minority of adolescents with low self-esteem? They may have received negative evaluations of their performance or skills in important domains. They may get poor grades, be unpopular with peers, have little skill at sports, or do poorly in other domains. They may not have secure, trusting relationships with parents. Their parents' behavior may not exemplify the warmth, involvement, and appropriate control that define an authoritative parenting style (Johnson et al., 1991). All these experiences can contribute to low self-esteem.

**significant others**
*The other people most important in a person's life, who have the greatest effect on the person's self-esteem.*

# IDENTITY DEVELOPMENT IN ADOLESCENCE

**identity**
*According to Erikson, the sense of continuity that gives people a link to the past and a direction for the future.*

Understanding of self takes another step forward during late adolescence with the formation of an identity. Erik Erikson (1963) defined **identity** as a sense of continuity that gives adolescents a link to their past and a direction for their future. In Erikson's stage theory of personality development, identity formation is the critical developmental task of adolescence. As children enter adolescence, they experience all the changes associated with puberty and the achievement of sexual maturity. These changes cause them to question who they are. Adolescents also realize that they must soon choose a career. That is, they need to set a direction for their future. Adolescents form an identity when they decide who they are and where they want to go in life.

Most studies of identity development have been based on James Marcia's (1966, 1980) extension of Erikson's theory. Like Erikson, Marcia assumed that identity formation occurs during a period of personal crisis. Adolescents must reduce their ties to parents, give up fantasies about "what I'll be when I grow up," and make realistic plans for their future. Marcia admitted that this identity crisis is not always dramatic or personally troubling, yet it always involves important decisions about a vocation and a personal ideology.

To judge adolescents' identity status, researchers use a long, semistructured interview (Marcia et al., 1993). The questions used with adolescents differ from those used with college students and with adults not in college. The main topics on the adolescent interview are vocational plans, plans for marriage and a family, religious beliefs, political beliefs, and sex-role attitudes. However, researchers may include questions about other facets of identity, depending on the purpose of the interview.

For each aspect of identity, interviewers try to find out whether an adolescent has explored alternatives. Regarding vocational plans, the interviewer will ask what the adolescent wants to do after high school and whether the adolescent has considered other options. Responses to these questions show whether the adolescent has experienced an identity crisis, a struggle to define personal goals, values, beliefs, and plans.

Another goal of the interview is to find out whether an adolescent has made a commitment to a certain direction in life. To judge an adolescent's commitment, the interview includes questions about plans and steps taken to achieve them. For example, when adolescents say they plan to work after high school, the interviewer asks what kind of work they have chosen, if any. If they have not chosen some kind of work, the interviewer asks whether they are trying to make that decision or just waiting to see what might happen.

Both adolescents' exploration of alternatives and their commitment to life plans are considered when judging their identity status. Four identity-status groups are distinguished. Table 13.3 defines the groups and illustrates their responses during an identity-status interview.

**identity diffusion**
*The identity status of people who may or may not have experienced a personal crisis but who have not made any commitments to life plans.*

**foreclosure**
*The identity status of people who have made a commitment to important life goals but who have neither chosen their goals themselves nor experienced a period of crisis. Usually, they have simply accepted goals their parents set for them.*

**moratorium**
*The identity status of people who are currently in an identity crisis and who have delayed or deferred making a commitment to life goals.*

**identity achievement**
*The identity status of people who have experienced a personal crisis or decision-making period that ended with a commitment to self-chosen life goals.*

The least desirable status is **identity diffusion.** Some adolescents in this group began to explore alternatives at one time but then failed to reach any definite life decisions. Other adolescents in this group have not tried to set goals for themselves or chart a life direction. Therefore, the central characteristic of this group is their lack of commitment.

The status of identity **foreclosure** is more desirable than that of diffusion, because adolescents in the foreclosure group have made commitments to life goals. However, these commitments have been made without much exploration of alternatives. Often, individuals in this group have accepted their parents' goals for them instead of choosing goals themselves. That is, the central characteristic of this group is commitment without exploration.

Adolescents in the **moratorium** status are currently in an identity crisis. The word *moratorium* means a delay or deferment. These adolescents have delayed or deferred making commitments to self-chosen goals. They are currently exploring alternatives, though, so the outlook for them is positive. Their identity crisis should lead eventually to the commitments that define the final identity-status group.

**Identity achievement** comes after a period of questioning and exploration. Adolescents who have experienced a crisis or decision-making period, but who have now made commitments

## TABLE 13.3  *Marcia's Identity-Status Groups*

| STATUS | DEFINING FEATURES | EXAMPLES OF AN INTERVIEW RESPONSE |
|---|---|---|
| *Identity Diffusion* | Individuals in this group have not made a commitment to definite values or goals. They either have not tried to explore alternatives or have given up on the effort. | When asked about religious beliefs, an individual in this group might say, "I believe in God but I haven't given much thought to why. I don't think much about religion." |
| *Foreclosure* | Individuals in this group have made a commitment to personal goals and values, but they did so without considering their options fully. Often, they simply chose to do what their parents wanted them to do. | When asked about career plans, a person in this group might say, "I want to be a concert pianist. My mother has been teaching me piano for 10 years, and she thinks I can do it." |
| *Moratorium* | Individuals in this group have not made commitments to personal goals and values. They are currently exploring alternatives, trying to decide who they are and what they want to become. | When asked about family plans, a person in this group might say, "I want to have children and have a career, but I can't decide when to have children or what kind of career would be best." |
| *Identity Achievement* | Individuals in this group have made commitments to personal goals and values after exploring alternatives thoroughly. | When asked about political beliefs, a person in this group might say, "My parents are Republicans and my friends are mostly Democrats. I've talked a lot to all of them, and I consider myself a conservative Democrat." |

*Source:* Archer, 1993; Marcia, 1993; Waterman, 1993.

to self-chosen goals, fit into this group. In Erikson's (1963) and Marcia's (1980; Marcia et al., 1993) theories, this status represents the normal end point of identity development.

Junior- and senior-high-school students are typically in the foreclosure or identity-diffusion statuses (Archer, 1982; Waterman, 1982, 1993). As these students move through the high-school years, they may achieve an identity in some areas, most often in the area of occupational choice. Even greater progress toward identity achievement occurs during the years immediately after high school. Many people reach the status of identity achievement around age 21.

However, patterns of movement through the identity statuses can be highly irregular (Waterman, 1993). During adolescence, some individuals stay in the foreclosure or moratorium groups for several years. During college, some students shift to the status of identity diffusion while others shift into the moratorium group. During adulthood, shifts into and out of the foreclosure, moratorium, and achievement groups can occur. These patterns suggest that, as life circumstances change, adolescents and adults often change their views of themselves and so move to different identity-status groups.

Adolescents whose interview responses place them in the identity-achievement group have higher grades than those in the other groups (Marcia, 1993). In some studies, but not all, high self-esteem is also characteristic of adolescents who are identity achieved (Waterman, 1992). Adolescents in the moratorium status report the most anxiety, perhaps partly because they are more honest about their feelings than those in the other groups. Adolescents in the foreclosure status are most authoritarian, favoring strong leaders over democratic

To achieve an identity, adolescents must set goals for their education, occupation, and other important parts of their lives. Parents can best promote their adolescent's progress toward an identity by being warm and accepting but also respecting their adolescent's individuality. Therefore, parents must be willing to accept some situations in which their adolescent disagrees with them.

groups. Identity-diffused adolescents are low in self-esteem, self-direction, and intimacy with others. They use drugs more often than adolescents in the other groups.

Gender differences in identity status are uncommon (Waterman, 1993). At any given age, the proportions of males and females in the different status groups are similar. The course of development through the status groups is also similar for males and females. Sometimes, however, males and females emphasize different issues when talking about their identity. In the area of vocational choice, males often emphasize the prestige and financial rewards associated with a career choice. Females, by contrast, emphasize the choice of a career that helps others and is personally satisfying (Archer, 1993).

Adolescents in different identity-status groups differ in their relationships with parents (Marcia, 1980, 1993). Identity-diffused adolescents often view their parents as rejecting and uninvolved with them. Foreclosed adolescents often have closer relationships with parents than do other adolescents. Foreclosed adolescents see their parents as child centered but also as possessive and demanding of conformity.

Adolescents in the moratorium status often have ambivalent relationships with parents. They have conflicts with parents because of their struggles for independence. At the same time, they want to please their parents but feel their parents are disappointed in them. Adolescents who have achieved an identity also tend to have ambivalent relationships with parents, but these relationships are more positive than those of moratorium adolescents. The tension found in the moratorium phase seems to be transformed into a balanced view of the positive and negative features of parent-child relationships.

A few researchers have tried to define more precisely how parents promote the identity development of their adolescents. In one model (Grotevant, 1992; Grotevant & Cooper, 1985), parent-adolescent interactions are defined in terms of individuality and connectedness. Individuality is greater when parents and adolescents feel more free to state their views, even when they differ from others' views. Connectedness is greater when parents and adolescents show more respect for one another's views and greater responsiveness to one another.

A first test of this theory suggested that individuality is most critical for identity exploration. High-school seniors were rated as higher in identity exploration if they had considered many options for careers and other life decisions and examined most options in depth. Those higher in identity exploration were more likely, in a family discussion, to state their opinions about family plans, even when that meant disagreeing with someone else.

Other research suggests that parents can support their adolescent's progress toward independence and self-understanding by being warm and accepting (Hauser et al., 1984). Most adolescents receive enough warmth and acceptance from parents to form a positive identity and so develop a healthy, mature sense of self.

# UNDERSTANDING OTHER PEOPLE

As children develop greater understanding of themselves, they also develop greater understanding of other people. In particular, children gradually realize that other people may have different perceptions, knowledge, and beliefs than they do. You read a bit about children's awareness of the differences between themselves and other people in earlier chapters, in connection with Piaget's construct of egocentrism.

However, one important aspect of childhood egocentrism that was not discussed in earlier chapters is children's inability to figure out what other people might be thinking. The corresponding ability can be described as **role taking** because it involves adopting, in thought, the perspective or role of other people. The best way to describe the process of role taking is to examine a few tasks that researchers have used to measure it.

**role taking**
*The ability to adopt, in thought, the perspective or role of another person.*

## Do You Know What I Know? Egocentrism and Role Taking

The cartoons in figure 13.2 tell a simple story (Chandler, 1973). A girl is unhappy to see her father leave on an airplane trip. After she gets home from the airport, she receives a package from the mail carrier. She is happy to be getting a present but starts to cry when she sees it is an airplane. The mail carrier is puzzled by her reaction to the present. Can you guess why he is puzzled?

Now consider a second story (Selman, 1980).

> Holly is an 8-year-old girl who likes to climb trees. She is the best tree climber in the neighborhood. One day while climbing down from a tall tree she falls off the bottom branch but does not hurt herself. Her father sees her fall. He is upset and asks her to promise not to climb trees anymore. Holly promises.
>
> Later that day, Holly and her friends meet Shawn. Shawn's kitten is caught up in a tree and cannot get down. Something has to be done right away or the kitten may fall. Holly is the only one who climbs trees well enough to reach the kitten and get it down, but she remembers her promise to her father.

What are your ideas about this story? Does Holly know how Shawn feels about the kitten? Does Shawn know why Holly can't decide whether to climb the tree? How would Holly's father feel if he found out she decided to climb the tree to get the kitten?

Consider one more task, which is a game rather than a story. An experimenter shows you two cups turned upside down. Glued on the bottom of one cup is a nickel, or 5 cents. The experimenter lifts the cup and shows you that it also has a nickel under it. Glued on the bottom of the other cup are two nickels, or 10 cents. The experimenter lifts that cup and shows you that it also has two nickels under it. Then the experimenter tells you that another person named Morton will be coming to play the game with you. Morton will pick one cup. If money is under the cup, Morton gets it. Your job is to trick Morton by taking the money that is under the cup you think Morton will pick (Flavell et al., 1968).

What would you do, and why? Would you (1) pick a cup randomly, because you have no idea what Morton might be thinking? Would you (2) take the money under the 10-cent cup because you guess Morton would pick the cup with more money? Would you (3) take the money under the 5-cent cup because you recognize that Morton might be trying to second-guess *your* strategy? He might think that you think he will pick the 10-cent cup, so he'll switch to the 5-cent cup, but you think he's going to do that, so you switch, too.

Or would you (4) know that Morton could follow your entire line of reasoning? You think that Morton thinks that you think that he would like to get the most money by picking the 10-cent cup, so he thinks of switching to the 5-cent cup. But you think that Morton also thinks that you might try to outwit him by picking the 5-cent cup, so he will try to

## Figure 13.2

What does the mail carrier think about the little girl who is crying? The mail carrier didn't see the girl go to the airport and start crying when her father left on a trip, so he should not be able to figure out why she's crying. Yet young children often say the mail carrier would know why the girl is crying because *they* know why. That is, young children often fail to take the role of other people whose knowledge differs from theirs.

outwit you by picking the 10-cent cup. There you have him (you think) because you take the money under the 10-cent cup!

Your reasoning during the game reflects your ability to take the role of another person. Consider the more-sophisticated strategies, (3) and (4). They depend on an understanding not only that other people's thoughts may be different from yours but also that other people can think about what you are thinking.

Many games require children to take the role of the other players. As these children play chess, they must try to guess what their opponent is planning, what his or her strategy is, and where he or she will move next. Children who are better at role taking, who have greater social understanding, should do better in games as well as in the more serious activities of life.

Reasoning about the mail carrier cartoons and the Holly story also requires role-taking ability. To interpret the cartoons correctly, children must realize that the toy airplane reminds the girl of her father's trip but that the mail carrier does not know about that trip. To interpret the Holly story correctly, children must realize that Holly, Shawn, and her father differ in their knowledge of the story's events. Therefore, each of them has different ideas about why Holly might or might not decide to climb the tree to get the kitten.

## The Hypothesis of Egocentrism and the Analysis of Role Taking

Preschool children often do poorly on role-taking tasks. They show little ability to take account of what people with different roles in the cartoons, the story, and the game might be thinking. Instead, they often suggest that everyone has the same knowledge of the situation, the knowledge they themselves have. Responses of this kind led Piaget (1926/1971) to describe young children as egocentric, unable to appreciate that other people's knowledge, emotions, or motives might differ from their own.

Piaget's hypothesis about childhood egocentrism was first mentioned in chapter 7, on language development. The discussion in that chapter focused on the age changes in children's ability to take account of another's perspective when communicating with that person. Piaget's hypothesis was mentioned again in chapter 8. The discussion in that chapter focused on the age changes in children's understanding of another's visual perspective. In both chapters, you learned about the criticisms of Piaget's hypothesis. You also learned about alternative explanations for the better performance of older children.

The role-taking tasks described in this chapter involve neither communication nor inferences about visual perspectives. Instead, the tasks assess children's ability to recognize differences between their own knowledge or motives and those of other people. Still, Piaget's hypothesis about childhood egocentrism is as controversial here as in the other cases.

Some researchers see no need for the construct of egocentrism (e.g., Ford, 1979, 1985). Children's performance on role-taking tasks improves as they get older, but this improvement need not be attributed to a decrease in egocentrism. The improvement could, instead, be due to developments in language comprehension, perception, or general intelligence.

Other researchers take a more positive stance toward Piaget's theory (Waters & Tinsley, 1985). They point out that children's errors on role-taking tasks are often the kind

## TABLE 13.4  Selman's Levels of Social Perspective Taking

**Level 0:**

Egocentric or undifferentiated perspectives (about ages 3 to 7)

Children cannot clearly differentiate between one person's thoughts or feelings and those of another person. Therefore, they don't realize that another person's perspective on some event or situation may differ from their own.

**Level 1:**

Subjective or differentiated perspectives (about ages 4 to 9)

Children appreciate that two people may interpret the same situation differently. They also understand that two people may have different ideas about a third person's motives for doing something.

**Level 2:**

Self-reflective or reciprocal perspectives (about ages 6 to 12)

Children can, in thought, put themselves in another person's place and understand how the other person might view their actions. In this way, children can reflect on their own thoughts and feelings. They also assume other people can understand their thoughts and feelings.

**Level 3:**

Third-person or mutual perspectives (about ages 9 to 15)

Children or adolescents recognize that a person can mentally step outside of a social interaction and think about the perspectives of the two people who are interacting. This ability is the basis for an understanding of interpersonal relationships in which people appreciate their mutual or shared perspectives.

**Level 4:**

Societal or in-depth perspectives (about age 12 to adulthood)

Adolescents or adults appreciate that a social situation can be viewed from the perspective of commonly accepted social norms. They also appreciate that two people's interactions can be understood in terms of their social behavior, their likes and dislikes, and their deeper, unstated motives and feelings.

Based on information in Selman, 1981; Selman & Byrne, 1974.

implied by the egocentrism hypothesis. For example, when shown the mail carrier cartoons, young children often say that the mail carrier will know what they know: The girl is sad because the toy airplane reminds her of her father's departure.

Robert Selman (1980, 1981) agreed with Piaget (1926/1971) that young children are egocentric in their thinking. Selman also connected Piaget's early ideas about egocentrism with his later stage theory of cognitive development. Selman described five levels of role taking between approximately 3 years of age and adulthood. He has often called these levels of social perspective taking because they reflect children's growing ability to take the perspective of other people. Table 13.4 describes each level.

Level 0 is egocentric. Children at this level do not recognize the differing perspectives implicit in the Holly story. For example, children at Level 0 are likely to say that Holly will save the kitten because she likes kittens. The children believe that Holly's father will be happy when he finds out because he likes kittens, too.

Children at Level 1 often assume that Holly's father would be angry if he found out she climbed the tree. This assumption shows that the children distinguish between Holly's perspective and her father's. However, children at Level 1 sometimes assume that Holly's father would change his mind if she told him she was trying to save the kitten.

Children at Level 2 assume that Holly would know, before she climbed the tree, that her father would understand why she did so and not punish her. In other words, these

children can think about Holly's thoughts about her father's thoughts about her reasons for disobeying his order. These children appreciate that Holly's thinking may have this self-reflective and reciprocal quality.

Adolescents at Level 3 can also judge what Holly and her father might decide together if the two of them discussed the situation. Adolescents or adults at Level 4 can consider Holly's dilemma in terms of broader social norms or the history of the relationship between Holly and her father.

Selman (1980) and his colleagues have shown that children's level of role taking can be reliably judged from their answers to the Holly story and similar stories. They have shown that older children score at higher levels, consistent with the basic hypothesis about the development of role taking. In longitudinal studies, children's scores improve as they grow older, and little regression or skipping of stages occurs. This evidence suggests that the levels of role taking form a cognitive-developmental sequence.

Selman's levels of perspective taking are a good example of a Piagetian, cognitive-developmental approach to the analysis of social-cognitive development. Selman and other researchers have used similar approaches to examine the age changes in children's ideas about friendship, adult authority, and social institutions (see Damon, 1977; Selman, 1981).

Other researchers describe the development of role taking differently than Selman does. Rather than assessing a child's level of role taking, these researchers assess the cognitive abilities required for success on specific role-taking tasks (e.g., LeMare & Rubin, 1987). For example, to answer the questions about the mail carrier cartoons correctly, children must first interpret the pictures presented. Then they must decide how the girl felt in the two parts of the story, or make inferences about her emotions. Then they must figure out why she was unhappy to get the toy plane. Only then are they ready to answer the question that focuses directly on their role-taking ability: "What did the mail carrier think when he saw the girl crying?"

Some children give the wrong answer to the role-taking question because they misinterpret the pictures or they draw the wrong inferences about how the girl felt and why. Yet even when children have all the necessary information, some fail to answer the role-taking question correctly. In one study (LeMare & Rubin, 1987), third graders more often answered the role-taking question incorrectly when they were more isolated or socially withdrawn at school. This finding is consistent with Piaget's (1926/1971) hypothesis that experiences with peers are important for the development of role-taking ability. Therefore, children who have less peer experience because they withdraw from social interaction do less well on role-taking tasks.

Still other researchers have used role-taking tasks without trying to judge whether children's performance depends specifically on role-taking or on other cognitive abilities. This strategy makes sense because most real-world tasks also call for several abilities. Role-taking tasks would prove their value for these researchers if the tasks help to explain the variations in children's social behavior.

## Role Taking and Social Behavior

For several years researchers tried to test the hypothesis that children better at role taking are more generous and helpful to classmates. These researchers assumed that better role takers can better judge when such prosocial behavior is needed and appropriate. The research findings, however, were mixed (Radke-Yarrow, Zahn-Waxler, & Chapman, 1983). Sometimes children with higher scores on role-taking tasks were less generous and helpful to classmates (Iannotti, 1985).

A closer look at the findings and a more careful consideration of role taking clarified what was happening. As stated earlier, role-taking tasks do not measure role-taking ability alone. The cups' game described earlier also evokes competitive motivation. Children who are more competitive will get higher scores in the game but will often ignore opportunities to be generous and helpful to classmates (Iannotti, 1985). This example illustrates that being able to take another person's role, in thought, does not always go with wanting to help the other person. Skilled charlatans and swindlers are also good at taking the role—or recognizing the weaknesses—of their victims.

**FIGURE 13.3**

Second graders high in role-taking ability are better tutors of kindergarten children than are second graders low in role-taking ability. Those low in role taking more often fail to answer questions and lend a hand when needed because they don't pick up the younger children's subtle cues that they need help. Low role takers less often solve the social problems that arise during tutoring sessions. High and low role takers do not differ significantly, though, in how often they smile and comfort the children they are tutoring. (Source: Hudson et al., 1982.)

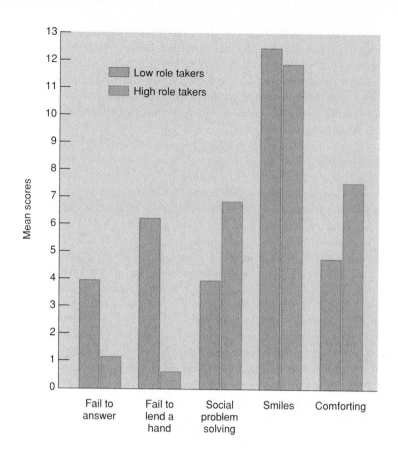

Variations in children's role-taking ability should have more consistent effects on their social behavior when all children have the same motives or are trying to reach the same goal. In one study (Hudson, Forman, & Brion-Meisels, 1982), second graders did three role-taking tasks. Then the children with the highest and lowest scores were asked to tutor kindergarten children. Each second grader taught a pair of kindergartners to make caterpillars with construction paper, scissors, glue, and crayons.

You can assume that all the second graders wanted to be good tutors; that is, they all had the same goal. Even so, the second graders with greater role-taking ability more often achieved that goal. They were better tutors than their classmates low in role-taking ability (see figure 13.3). Compared with the high role takers, low role takers more often failed to answer the kindergartners' questions. Also, the low role takers more often failed to lend a hand when it was needed. Despite these lapses, the low role takers were trying to be helpful. As the figure shows, they made about as many comforting comments and smiled as often as high role takers.

The low role takers had good intentions but were often unhelpful because they misunderstood the kindergartners' questions or they ignored the kindergartners' subtle requests for help. For example, if a kindergarten girl was straining with scissors and glancing at her second-grade tutor without saying anything, the low role takers often did nothing. By contrast, high role takers asked whether the girl needed help. High role takers were also better at anticipating problems such as the need to take turns with scissors. In other words, they were better at social problem solving (see figure 13.3).

Can anything be done to help children with deficits in role-taking ability? Two provocative experiments suggest that training can reduce these deficits. What's more, the experiments suggest that this training has benefits both for the children and for other people.

In the first experiment, Michael Chandler (1973) used police records to identify delinquent adolescent boys. Chandler arranged for groups of these boys to receive 10 sessions of training in role taking. The training was highly enjoyable. The boys acted out the roles of different characters as they made films together.

As expected, the training improved the boys' scores on role-taking tasks such as the mail carrier cartoons. More important, the training affected the boys' social behavior. Juvenile court records for all the boys were examined 18 months after the training program ended. The records showed that boys in the training groups had fewer encounters with the juvenile court than did boys in a control group.

In discussing this finding, Chandler (1973) was appropriately cautious. He pointed out that fewer court contacts may not mean fewer delinquent acts. Perhaps the role-taking training improved the boys' skills in taking the perspective of the police so they could commit delinquent acts without getting caught. In short, the training may have made the boys "smarter" without making them less delinquent.

The second experiment strengthened the case for an effect of role-taking training on delinquent behavior (Chalmers & Townsend, 1990). This experiment involved adolescent girls in a minimum-security prison. The girls received role-taking training like that in the first experiment. The girls were also trained in specific social skills such as apologizing when you are wrong and behaving in a way that shows respect for others. (Remember the discussion of social-skills training from chapter 12.)

As in Chandler's (1973) study, training led to an increase in these adolescents' role-taking ability. The training program also led to improvements in their classroom behavior in the prison school. After training, girls showed more positive behaviors in their classes than before. The behavior of girls in a control group showed little change. Because all girls were observed in the same setting under standard conditions, it is safe to assume that a real change occurred in the trained girls' behavior, not simply a change in the behavior "caught" by other people. In short, the girls who received training became not only "smarter" but also better behaved.

Again, remember that the girls were trained in more than role taking. They were also taught social skills related to desirable social behavior. The social-skills emphasis may have guaranteed that the girls' greater role-taking ability was channeled in positive directions. When channeled in this way, improvements in role taking contribute to improved social behavior.

## Inferring Others' Emotions, Intentions, Beliefs, and Traits

Social cognition involves more than role taking. Remember the example of Hanako and the boys eating berries. When Hanako called out, "Fool ones!" she not only wanted the girls with her to notice the boys. She also wanted her friends to infer that she believed the boys were doing something foolish and thus showing themselves to be fools.

A moment later, when Hanako and her friends frowned at the boys, they recognized her emotional expression and inferred that she disapproved of their behavior. When they mimicked her frown, they wanted her to infer that they intended to continue eating berries despite what she thought.

Beliefs, emotions, and intentions are part of the content of the psychological world. Judgments about other people's characteristics—for example, that boys are foolish—are related to another part of the psychological world, personality traits. Defined most precisely, **personality traits** are characteristics of people that are fairly stable over time and obvious in a variety of situations. Some examples are sociability, impatience, ambition, and, yes, foolishness.

How much do young children know about the psychological world? Even during the preschool years, children understand some parts of the psychological world (Shantz, 1983). As children grow, their inferences about the psychological world become more complex, more abstract, and less tied to immediate events. Because of these changes, children gain greater skill in describing and explaining human behavior.

### How Do You Feel? Inferring Others' Emotions

Learning about the psychological world begins in infancy. You read in chapter 6 that infants can figure out when other people are experiencing certain emotions by observing the people's facial expressions. You also read that infants respond appropriately to other people's

**personality traits**
*Characteristics of people that are fairly stable over time and obvious in a variety of situations (e.g., sociability and impatience).*

FIGURE 13.4

How 2-year-olds and adults judge the similarity between emotions: the pleasure and arousal dimensions. (Source: Russell & Bullock, 1986.)

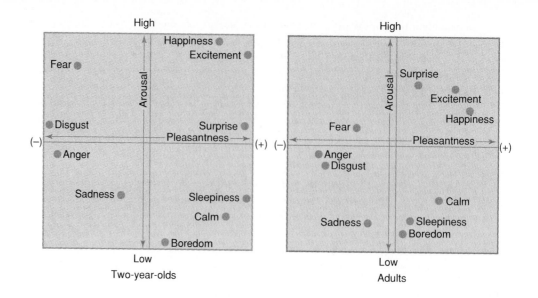

emotional expressions. When other people smile, infants often show happiness and seek to interact with them. When other people frown, infants often withdraw or express negative emotions themselves. Moreover, infants treat others' emotional expressions as cues about their own safety, in the process of social referencing.

During the second year of life, toddlers learn more about emotions during conversations with their mothers (Dunn, Bretherton, & Munn, 1987). They talk about being angry with other people, being afraid of monsters in picture books, or being sad because they can't get what they want. With older siblings, 2-year-olds may also play with emotional expressions, for example, pretending to be afraid or angry. Interactions with parents and siblings increase young children's understanding of other people's emotional experience and add to their knowledge about specific emotions.

Two-year-olds have a surprisingly adultlike understanding of many emotions. The 2-year-olds in one study saw pictures of women posing 10 emotions such as happiness, anger, and boredom (Russell & Bullock, 1986). Then the 2-year-olds sorted the pictures into groups. They were told to put the "mommies" who felt alike in one pile and the mommies who felt differently in different piles. Their groupings of the pictures were analyzed to find out which emotions they viewed as similar and which they viewed as different. In the data analysis, emotions placed in the same group by most children were positioned close to each other in what can be called a conceptual space. Emotions placed in different groups by most children were positioned far from one another in the space.

The resulting conceptual space can be shown in a two-dimensional graph (see figure 13.4). The first dimension, running from left to right, contrasts unpleasant emotions with pleasant ones. For example, disgust and anger are unpleasant. Happiness and excitement are pleasant. The second dimension, running from top to bottom, contrasts emotions that are high and low in arousal. Happiness is highly arousing; boredom is, well, boring.

The figure also shows the results for adults given the same task. The correspondence between the adults' graph and the 2-year-olds' graph is striking. Like toddlers, adults view emotions as differing in pleasantness and in arousal. The match between the adults' and toddlers' judgments is easy to understand. It implies that when adults talk with 2-year-olds about these emotions, as they often do (Dunn et al., 1987), they have little difficulty comprehending one another. They are, in emotional terms, speaking the same language.

Children can infer other people's emotions without seeing their faces if they know enough about the social situation. Suppose you hear that Mary, who is 3 years old, left her favorite toy at a playmate's house. Mary couldn't get the toy for a long time. How would you think Mary felt? You answer, of course, that she felt sad. Preschool children often give the same answer (Reichenbach & Masters, 1983).

Preschoolers can also judge which situations will make another child feel happy or angry and which will not provoke any strong emotional reaction. By kindergarten age, children can even judge which situations will evoke specific negative emotions (Levine, 1995). Kindergartners assume that sadness often follows an experience of loss such as wanting to play baseball but being injured and unable to play. Kindergartners assume that anger often accompanies an aversive situation such as having to stay inside on a warm summer day.

Still, kindergartners' judgments about which situations will lead to which emotions are not perfectly accurate, if accuracy is measured by agreement with adults' judgments. As children grow older, their inferences about emotions gradually become closer to those of adults. The age change shows that children learn more about emotions as their reasoning ability and their social experience increase (Reichenbach & Masters, 1983).

The task of inferring a person's emotions is sometimes complicated because the person's facial expression differs from that expected in the situation. Look at figure 13.5. Would you say that the girl in the picture is happy or afraid? Her facial expression, a smile, suggests that she is happy, but she is in a situation that would frighten most children: She is just about to get a shot from her doctor.

Most preschool children ignore the conflict between the facial expression and the situation. They simply say that the girl is happy because she looks happy (Gnepp, 1983, 1989). If they are asked to explain why a girl who is about to get a shot would be happy, they seldom give a clear answer. By contrast, if 6-year-olds are asked the same question, they often make a reasonable guess about why the girl is smiling. For example, they may say that the girl has been sick and is happy because she expects to feel better after getting the shot.

By 12 years of age, children not only guess why a girl might be happy to get a shot; they also guess why the girl might look happy when she's not. For example, one 12-year-old said the girl in the picture is "hanging onto the chair, smiling, trying to hide her fear from the doctor" (Gnepp, 1989, p. 162). Older children increasingly recognize that people can mask their emotions and express emotions different from the ones they feel (Saarni, 1979, 1989).

Often, you can do more than guess about why someone's emotions are different from what you would expect in the situation. Suppose you hear that a boy is invited by a friend to go horseback riding. You would probably guess that the boy would be happy. Then you learn that the boy's father took him horseback riding last week. The boy couldn't control his horse and he fell off and got hurt.

## TABLE 13.5 Children's Spontaneous Comments About the Causes of Emotions

| EMOTION | CAUSE |
|---------|-------|
| Happy | "I give a hug. Baby be happy." |
| Cry | "Me fall down. Me cry." |
| Sad | "You sad Mommy. What Daddy do?" |
| Hurt feelings | "I'm hurting your feelings, 'cause I was mean to you." |
| Scared | "It's dark. I'm scared."<br>"The firecracker scared me."<br>"I see tiger. That too scary." |
| Mad | "Grandma mad. I wrote on wall." |
| Bad, naughty | "I bad girl. I wet my pants." |

Adapted from Bretherton et al., 1986.

Now if you were asked how the boy would react to a friend's invitation, you would probably say he would be afraid or unhappy. You use information about the boy's personal history to judge how he will react in a later situation. *You* do—but most kindergarten children do not (Gnepp, 1989). They predict that the invitation will make the boy happy whether or not they know about his last experience with horses.

Consider another type of personal information. If you are familiar with a person, you know something about his or her personality traits. You may know, for example, that a person is scrupulously honest. Adults and older children use their knowledge of a person's personality when making inferences about the person's emotions. For example, they assume that an honest child would be happy to return the money in a lost wallet to its owner. Kindergarten children often ignore information they receive about an actor's personality when inferring the actor's emotional reactions. They only take account of the emotional reactions most people would have in a particular situation (Gnepp & Chilamkurti, 1988).

When older children and adolescents pay attention to an actor's history and personality, they go beyond the immediate situation. Young children are less able to do so. This does not mean that young children cannot understand why people feel the way they do. Even toddlers understand the causes of some emotions (Bretherton et al., 1986). As table 13.5 shows, some toddlers understand that loud noises scare people, that hugging people makes them happy, and that their writing on the walls makes people angry. In these cases, however, the emotion is closely linked to the event or action. They occur at nearly the same time.

The causes of emotions sometimes lie farther back in time, outside the immediate situation. Suppose you got a poor grade on a test. You might feel guilty if you did poorly because you didn't study. You might feel angry if you found out that a classmate who studied with you gave you lots of wrong answers. Adults assume actors would feel guilty and angry, respectively, if their poor grades resulted from these causes.

Second graders, by contrast, simply say that the actors would feel sad (Thompson, 1987). The second graders focus only on the outcome for the actor, a poor test grade. When inferring the actors' emotions, second graders rarely consider the causes of these outcomes. Therefore, another reason that older children and adults are better at inferring others' emotions is that they look beyond the immediate situation for the causes of events.

Finally, you might ask why children or adults bother making inferences about other people's emotions. The answer, in short, is that satisfying, skillful social interaction depends on accurate inferences about other people's emotions (Bretherton et al., 1986). If 2-year-olds can recognize when another person is happy, angry, or sad, they can figure out when their behavior causes these emotional reactions. Thus, they can judge which of their behaviors are desirable and undesirable.

As children grow, they gradually learn how they can change other people's emotions. They learn to give other children a hug if those children are sad. They learn to give other children toys to play with if someone has taken those children's toys (Fabes et al., 1988).

Children also learn to disguise and to exaggerate their emotional expressions to avoid embarrassment, get help, or attract attention (Saarni, 1989). Children learn to exaggerate negative emotions to express disapproval, as Hanako and the other girls did. Children learn to mimic emotional expressions to indicate mockery, as the boys did when they saw Hanako and her friends. You see, then, that accurate inferences about other people's emotional expressions and skilled control over emotional expressions are necessary for competent behavior in social situations.

## What Are You Trying to Do? Inferring Others' Intentions

Suppose that you show preschoolers a short film (Smith, 1978). As the film begins, a young woman walks across a room and sits in a chair. Then she does some exercises and chews a piece of gum. Next, she sneezes, yawns, gets up from her chair, and trips over a box while walking back across the room. Finally, she slips on a rug and falls into an easy chair.

This film may seem simple, even boring. What preschoolers say about the film is more intriguing. Four-year-olds, like adults, say that the woman was trying to walk across the room when she did so. She was trying, they say, to sit in the chair, do exercises, and chew gum when she did those things. Most 4-year-olds also say the woman was trying to sneeze, trying to yawn, and even trying to trip over the box and slip on the rug. At 4 years of age, children seem to think that people are trying to do everything they do. That is, 4-year-olds think all human acts are intentional.

Other research suggests that 4-year-olds partly understand the distinction between intentional and unintentional acts. Suppose two 4-year-old boys are shooting at targets with a toy gun. If one boy says he's aiming at a red target and then shoots a green one, the other boy will not say that his pal intentionally shot the green one (Shultz & Wells, 1985). Preschoolers understand that the outcome of an act is unintentional when it does not match what the actor said he or she would do.

Of course, people rarely announce what they are trying to do before they do it, even when shooting at targets with a toy gun! Lacking such an announcement, children must infer whether an outcome was intentional or not. Preschoolers accurately make such judgments when actors express great surprise or obvious sadness at the outcomes of their acts (Moses, 1993). In other words, preschoolers can use inferences about actors' emotions to decide whether their actions were intended or accidental.

When actors' emotional expressions are more restrained, preschoolers' accuracy in judging intentionality is low. The errors in preschoolers' judgments are systematic: They usually assume that involuntary acts are intentional rather than vice versa. Only as children move into the elementary-school years do they recognize that many acts such as sneezing and tripping are involuntary, not intentional (Miller & Aloise, 1989).

Suppose that you judge that a specific act was intentional. Could you say what the actor was trying to do? Not necessarily, or, not entirely. You would also need to infer the actor's *motives*. You could say, for example, that the woman in the film intentionally walked across the room, but why did she do so? You might say she walked across the room to get to the chair. Why did she want to get to the chair (i.e., what was her motive for that)? The answer: so she could sit down. That's an incomplete answer, though. Why did she want to sit down? These questions could be extended indefinitely. The answers would provide a progressively deeper understanding of the woman's motives.

Young children have difficulty inferring motives that are not obvious from the current situation. You should not be surprised—you just learned that young children have trouble inferring emotions whose causes are not immediately obvious. When the chain of motives leading to an act is long, young children often understand only the final links in the chain. When the motives are subtle, like the unconscious motives or defense mechanisms described by Sigmund Freud, they are especially hard for young children to understand (Miller & Aloise, 1989; Whiteman, 1967). For example, young children find it hard to understand why

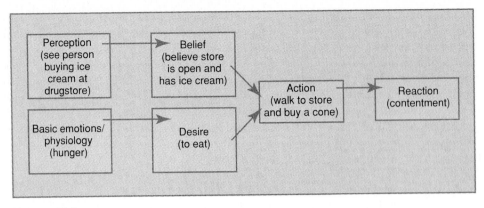

## FIGURE 13.6

A model of the relations between beliefs, desires, actions, and other constructs. Hunger may lead to a desire to eat. Seeing a person buying ice cream at a drugstore may lead to a belief that a person can buy ice cream there during the day, when the store is open. The combination of desire and belief leads to action, and then a reaction. (Source: Bartsch & Wellman, 1989.)

a child who is spanked by his mother might then yell at his younger sister. As children grow older, they are more able to explain such complex, hidden motives.

## What Do You Believe? First Steps Toward a Theory of Mind

Motives and emotions are mental states: They exist in the mind. Adults have definite ideas about how these mental states relate to others, like beliefs and desires. Many researchers assume that adults' ideas about all mental states are part of a **theory of mind** (Astington, Harris, & Olson, 1988; Wellman, 1988; Wellman & Gelman, 1992). The theory is not fully explicit, like some scientific theories, but it has three features of scientific theories.

First, the central concepts in scientific theories are defined in relation to one another. In adults' theories of mind, concepts like beliefs are related to, but distinguished from, other mental entities like memories and dreams. Second, every scientific theory has its own domain, the range of phenomena it describes. The domain of theories of mind is the mental world, which is distinguished from the world of actions and objects. Third, as you learned in chapter 1, theories are used to explain phenomena and are tested by their ability to predict phenomena. Adults rely on their theories of mind to explain and predict people's behavior. That is, adults explain what other people do in terms of their beliefs, desires, emotions, motives, and traits. Adults refer to the same mental entities when they predict what people will do.

If adults have a theory of mind, where does it come from? How does it develop? Currently, these questions are highly controversial (see Astington et al., 1988; Sullivan & Winner, 1993). Some researchers argue that 3-year-olds or even younger children have a true theory of mind. Other researchers argue that a theory of mind does not emerge until 4 or 5 years of age or even later. The argument depends on what counts as evidence for a theory of mind. Let's look at some evidence for each side.

Consider the simplified model in figure 13.6 for reasoning about beliefs and desires. Suppose you were hungry, which is a physiological state classified with *basic emotions/physiology*. Hunger leads to a *desire* to eat, perhaps to get an ice cream cone. Yesterday, you saw a person buying an ice cream cone at the drugstore a block from your home (*perception*). You believe that the store is open now and has ice cream cones (*belief*). Your belief coupled with your desire leads to *action*. You walk to the store and buy a cone. Your *reaction?* Contentment, as the tasty ice cream reduces your hunger.

Now suppose you told young children about an actor's behavior and asked them to explain the behavior. If they referred to beliefs and desires in their explanation, you could assume that they understand at least part of the model for belief-desire reasoning. That is, they have

the essential elements of a theory of mind. When studies of this type were done, even 3-year-olds seemed to understand that actions spring from beliefs and desires (Bartsch & Wellman, 1989). Three-year-olds say, for example, that Susie might go to a drugstore because she's hungry (*physiology*), wants ice cream (*desire*), and thinks the store sells ice cream (*belief*).

With such simple stories, 3-year-olds explain the actors' behavior in much the same way as adults do. Adults more often refer to the actor's beliefs without being prompted, and they give more explicit explanations. Still, adults and children appear to share a set of concepts for explaining human action, those shown in the figure. Both children and adults assume that actions in the real world spring from beliefs and desires in the mental world. In short, 3-year-olds, like adults, seem to have a coherent theory of mind.

But if 3-year-olds have a theory of mind, they make some curious errors in applying that theory (Hogrefe, Wimmer, & Perner, 1986). Suppose you show Willy, a 3-year-old boy, a matchbox. You ask Willy what's inside. He answers, "Matches." Then you show him that the box really contains a piece of chocolate, not matches. You ask, "Now, what's really in the matchbox?" He answers, "Chocolate."

Now the crucial step. You tell Willy that another boy is coming to the room. You ask him what the other boy will say is in the box. If Willy is a typical 3-year-old, he will say, "Chocolate." He thinks the other boy will say that the matchbox contains chocolate because *he* knows it contains chocolate. The typical 5-year-old gives the correct answer, "Matches." Five-year-olds recognize that the appearance of the matchbox is deceiving. Because most matchboxes contain matches, another boy without their knowledge would believe, falsely, that matches are in this matchbox.

Three-year-olds seldom attribute a false belief to another person (Wimmer, Hogrefe, & Sodian, 1988; Wimmer & Perner, 1983). Instead, they assume that what they know, everyone knows. One possible explanation for this mistaken assumption is that 3-year-olds do not understand the origins of beliefs about the world (Wimmer et al., 1988). Like other children and adults, 3-year-olds get information about the world through their senses. However, 3-year-olds are not aware that this sensory information is the source of their beliefs. They simply accept what they believe as true. Because children this age do not link their beliefs to their origins in perception, they cannot imagine that other people—with different perceptions— would hold beliefs different from theirs.

With increasing age, children realize that beliefs depend on perceptions, so people with different perceptions may have different beliefs. That is, older children recognize that people's beliefs derive from their representation of the environment, not from direct knowledge of the environment (Keenan, Ruffman, & Olson, 1994; Perner, Ruffman, & Leekam, 1994). Stated less formally, older children understand that the mind provides a picture of the world, not the world itself. When children first appreciate that another person's beliefs may be false, they take an important step toward this kind of representational theory of the mind.

What helps children take this step in social cognition? A partial answer to this question was given in an article with the engaging title, "Theory of Mind Is Contagious: You Catch It from Your Sibs" (Perner et al., 1994). The article reported two studies of the relation between family size and understanding of false beliefs. Children with more siblings "passed" the false-belief task more often than only children. Apparently, interacting with siblings encourages children to develop the representational theory of mind that is tested by the false-belief task. Especially beneficial may be social pretend play with siblings. This type of play involves acting as if one thing (e.g., a doll) is another thing (e.g., a live infant). Such "acting as if" may help children appreciate that what a person *thinks* may differ from what really *is*.

Of course, only children eventually pass false-belief tasks, too. Interactions with peers may help them form a representational theory of mind. Also important may be interactions with adults. Adults may provoke an understanding of the influence of perceptions on beliefs by asking questions such as, "How do you know that?" or "Why do you think so?" Children may also learn about the shaky connection between beliefs and reality through games like hide-and-seek. These games emphasize the contrast between what the hider knows and what the seeker knows. They increase children's understanding that beliefs can be false if based on incomplete or misleading perceptions.

Exactly how much 3-year-olds understand about false beliefs is still a topic of debate. On one hand, some researchers argue that the questions children are asked in the false-belief task are unclear (Lewis & Osborne, 1990). Thus, most 3-year-olds give the wrong answer to the standard question, "What will the other boy think is inside the box?" Most 3-year-olds give the correct answer if asked the more precise question, "What will the other boy think is in the box before I take the top off?" Also, when playing a game, 3-year-olds will sometimes try to deceive the person playing against them or make that person believe something that is false (Chandler, Fritz, & Hala, 1989; Sullivan & Winner, 1993). Both types of experiments suggest that the standard procedure for judging 3-year-olds' understanding of false beliefs may underestimate how much they know.

On the other hand, if 3-year-olds have a knowledge that beliefs can be false, this knowledge must be very shaky. In several experiments with simplified versions of the false-belief task, 3-year-olds rarely performed well (Flavell et al., 1990; Moses & Flavell,1990). In one experiment, 3-year-olds were explicitly told that another person didn't know that some cat food was under a dishcloth on the table. But when these children knew the cloth concealed some cat food, they usually said that the other person would think cat food was there, too.

In other experiments, children saw a movie in which someone played a trick on a girl, so she found some rocks in a bag where she had placed crayons. Even after hearing the girl say, in surprise, "Hey, there are rocks in here!" most 3-year-olds said the girl had expected the bag to have rocks rather than crayons in it. The 3-year-olds said this, apparently, because they knew the bag contained rocks.

The researchers argued that the only reasonable explanation for the 3-year-olds' incorrect answers is that the children did not understand that people can have false beliefs. In the various experiments, children received many kinds of obvious cues that other people had different beliefs than they did. Yet they persisted in reporting that the other people would believe what they themselves knew was true. They seemed to say, "If I *know* what's really in the box [or under the cloth, or in the bag], then everyone else must *think* so, too."

Taken together, the evidence suggests important differences between 3-year-olds and older children in their ideas about beliefs. Only after 3 years of age do children show plainly and consistently that they accept a representational theory of mind that can account for false beliefs. That acceptance does not, however, mean that 4- or 5-year-olds have a theory of mind similar to that of adults.

Suppose that someone explains why they got the wrong answer on a test by saying, "My mind tricked me." You would probably assume that this metaphor, translated into less figurative language, means something like, "I thought I remembered the correct answer, but my memory was wrong." A child in the early elementary grades is, instead, likely to say the metaphor means something like, "I was thinking a lot."

Understanding of metaphors about the mind increases greatly between 6 and 10 years of age (Wellman & Hickling, 1994). Other examples of these metaphors include, "My mind was racing" and "My mind wandered." In metaphors like these, the mind is viewed as a separate entity that can partly act on its own. The understanding that the human mind has this sort of semi-independence is another step in children's development toward a mature theory of mind.

## What Are You Like? Inferring Others' Traits

When a 7-year-old girl was asked to describe someone she disliked, she gave the following response (Livesley & Bromley, 1973, pp. 213–214):

> He is six feet tall. He isn't very well dressed. He has two sons, Peter and William. They can afford a car. Peter and William got a tractor each for Christmas. William has two bicycles. Their dad has blue eyes, black trousers, green jumper. They have hens and a cat and dog and a budgie [parakeet]. Their telephone is. . . .

Contrast that description with a 14-year-old girl's description of a boy she disliked (Livesley & Bromley, 1973, pp. 220–221):

> I dislike this boy because he is very rude, ignorant, cheeky, and thinks he is the best. Although he can sometimes be very nice, his poorer qualities outnumber his better

qualities which are not very good to start with. He is very rude to his friend who is nice and this leads to an argument. . . . He is exceptionally cheeky to his mother when his friends are there especially.

Does the younger girl's description remind you of something? Earlier, you read a 9-year-old boy's description of himself. Remember that the boy's self-description focused on physical appearance and on the people around him, such as his family and his teacher. Similarly, this 7-year-old girl gives a physical description of the man she dislikes. We learn his height, eye color, and even what clothes he has. We also learn about his family and their possessions. Such parallels between self-descriptions and descriptions of others are evident throughout childhood and adolescence.

Notice, too, that the younger girl does not say anything about the man's personality traits, his characteristic behavior toward other people, or his usual habits. She doesn't even say what made her dislike him! By contrast, the older girl tells us nothing about the physical appearance of the boy she dislikes. She tells us a great deal about his personality traits, starting with her first comments that he is rude, ignorant, and cheeky. (In case you're wondering, both girls were from England, where *cheeky* is a common term for impudent or brash.)

The two girls' comments reflect developmental changes found in many later studies (see Shantz, 1983). The emphasis on physical characteristics found in young children is replaced in later childhood and adolescence by an emphasis on personality traits. One conclusion you might draw from these findings is that young children do not realize that people have traits that make their behavior consistent across times and situations.

You should pause before drawing that conclusion, though. What children say when they describe another person tells us only part of what they know about the person. You could use another procedure to find out whether young children attribute personality traits to other people. You could give children information about a person and see what inferences they make about the person. In particular, do they assume that the person has traits that will lead to consistent behavior in other situations?

In one study (Rholes & Ruble, 1984), children saw videotaped episodes in which actors behaved either generously or selfishly. For example, in one episode an actor shared part of his lunch with a classmate who had none. In another, an actor refused to share his lunch. Other episodes showed actors who behaved either bravely or fearfully.

After the children saw each videotaped episode, they heard pairs of stories. Then they picked the story in each pair that they thought was about the same actor as in the previous videotape. The actor in one story behaved in a manner consistent with the videotaped actor's behavior. For example, after seeing an actor share his lunch, children heard a story about an actor who helped another child rake leaves. In the other story, the actor behaved in a manner inconsistent with the videotaped actor's behavior.

The key question was whether young children would assume that an actor's behavior was consistent across situations. For example, would they assume that actors who shared their lunch would also help another child rake leaves? If they did, you could conclude that they inferred a personality trait, kindness toward others, held across situations.

Figure 13.7 shows that 9- to 10-year-olds inferred that the actors' behavior would be consistent across situations. Almost always, they said that an actor who was kind toward others in one situation would be kind in other situations. They said that an actor who was brave in one situation would be brave in other situations. And if they saw actors behave in a selfish or fearful way in one situation, they said these actors would behave similarly in other situations.

By contrast, 5- to 6-year-olds seldom inferred that the actors' behavior would be consistent across situations. When these children had to choose between one story that described behavior consistent with that on the videotape and another story that described inconsistent behavior, their choices seemed random. As the figure shows, 5- to 6-year-olds chose the consistent story only about 50 percent of the time. Given a choice between two stories, 50 percent choice of the consistent story would be expected by chance.

The 5- to 6-year-olds could understand terms like *nice, kind,* and *brave* that refer to personality traits. They used these terms to describe the behavior of the actors in the videotapes.

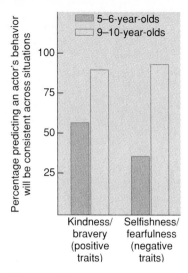

FIGURE 13.7

Children 9 and 10 years of age are more likely than 5- and 6-year-olds to assume that an actor's behavior will be consistent across situations. After hearing about one situation in which an actor behaved in a kind, brave, selfish, or fearful way, older children are more likely to assume that the actor will behave the same way in a later situation. (Source: Rholes & Ruble, 1984.)

Even younger children may use similar terms. Remember that Hitoshi, the 4-year-old mentioned at the beginning of the chapter, described himself as "naughty." But such terms may not have the same meaning for young children as for older children and adults. They may not mean that the young children expect a person to behave similarly in other situations.

Still, young children have some understanding of personality traits. By 5 years of age, if not earlier, children assume that a person's behavior in the same setting will be consistent over time (Eder, 1989; Rholes & Ruble, 1984). For example, they expect a classmate who shares his lunch on one day to share his lunch on other days, too. As you recall, such consistency over time is one part of the definition of a personality trait.

In addition, 5-year-olds are more likely to make inferences about another child's personality traits if they assume they will later interact with the other child (Feldman & Ruble, 1988). Apparently, these young children realize that they can better predict the behavior of a social-interaction partner when they know something about the partner's personality. Therefore, when given some information about another child's past behavior, they more often draw conclusions about the child's traits if they expect a future interaction with the child.

Five-year-olds will also make predictions about an actor's behavior in new situations if they have enough information about the actor's past behavior. In the study described earlier (Rholes & Ruble, 1984), children heard about only one behavior before making predictions about an actor's future behavior. When 5-year-olds hear about several of an actor's behaviors, they more often infer the actor's traits and predict consistent behavior by the actor in the future (Gnepp & Chilamkurti, 1988; Heller & Berndt, 1981). For example, if 5-year-olds hear that a boy was helpful to elderly people, to new kids at school, and to his mother, they usually assume that he will help his younger sister clean her room.

Yet even under the most favorable conditions, young children less often base their predictions of people's future behavior on their past behavior than do older children and adults. Older children and adults are more likely, when making predictions about others' behavior, to use information that goes beyond the immediate situation. You read earlier about a similar developmental trend in children's inferences about others' emotions. The tendency to use information outside the immediate situation can also account for the increase with age in children's inferences about personality traits.

Finally, you should not regard the ability to infer personality traits as the high point in social-cognitive development. Trait inferences can be misleading or inaccurate, because no one's behavior is entirely consistent across situations. Adolescents and adults recognize this lack of consistency. Adolescents, for example, are aware that traits may only be expressed under certain conditions. Remember the comments of the 14-year-old girl. She said the boy she disliked was "exceptionally cheeky to his mother when his friends are there especially." In this brief phrase, the girl mentions a trait (cheeky) directed toward a specific person (his mother) in a specific situation (when his friends are there).

Adolescents regularly and flexibly qualify their trait inferences (Barenboim, 1977). They say exactly when an actor shows certain characteristics ("He's shy when he's around girls"). They point out when one trait does not go with another that you might expect ("She is curious about people but naive"). Occasionally, they tell you how people's traits have changed over time, or they make guesses about why people have the traits they do. In short, they use personality traits as part of a larger vocabulary for describing and explaining people's behavior.

# LINKING SOCIAL COGNITION TO SOCIAL BEHAVIOR

Children's thoughts about themselves and other people should affect their behavior. Many researchers would also assert that children with greater social understanding should show more desirable and competent social behavior. However, researchers disagree about how to define the

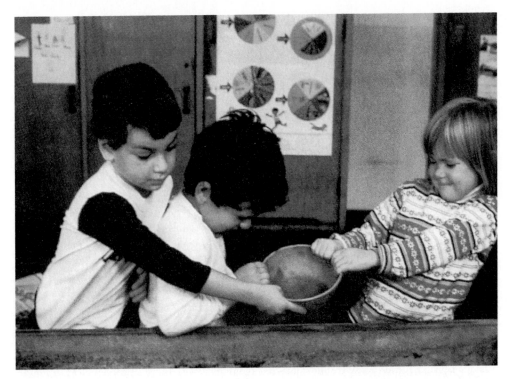

Why are these children fighting? What were they thinking when they started tugging over the bowl? Did they consider other ways of getting it or holding onto it? Did they think about the other children's feelings or the possibility that the fight would escalate to punches? As we continue to examine the relation of social cognition to social behavior, you will see that the answers to these questions help explain why some children are more aggressive than others.

variations in social cognition that are linked to variations in social behavior. The contrasting positions that are most prominent today can be described in terms of two general approaches.

## Interpersonal Cognitive Problem Solving

One approach emphasizes children's ability to think of many strategies for solving social problems. More than two decades ago, George Spivack and Myrna Shure (1974; Shure & Spivack, 1978) proposed that children who know more strategies for solving social problems are higher in social competence and less likely to engage in aggressive or impulsive behaviors. According to Spivack and Shure, five skills are crucial to thinking about social problems. In other words, these five skills define the components of interpersonal cognitive problem solving.

The first skill is sensitivity to social problems, the ability to recognize them when they arise. The second skill is figuring out not just one solution to a social problem but many alternative solutions. The third skill is thinking about how to carry out these solutions, or identifying the possible means to reach a social goal. The fourth skill is considering the consequences of possible actions, especially how other people might react to those actions. The fifth skill is considering the many possible causes of other people's behavior.

Greatest attention has been given to the three intermediate skills: figuring out alternative solutions, identifying means of reaching goals, and considering consequences (Denham & Almeida, 1987). Spivack and Shure devised measures of these skills that assess the number of responses children can generate. For example, if asked about a conflict between two preschoolers who want the same toy, how many ways of resolving the conflict can a child suggest? Measures like these assess the degree to which children think about what to do before acting. They also assess the flexibility in children's thinking.

Spivack and Shure (1974, 1978) showed that impulsive and withdrawn children receive lower scores on their measures of interpersonal cognitive problem solving than do children whose behavior is more desirable. In other studies, children with lower scores on the measures were rated by peers and teachers as having poorer psychological and social adjustment (Denham & Almeida, 1987). Moreover, significant relations of problem-solving skill to competent social behavior have been found even with variations in the children's IQs

taken into account (Pellegrini, 1985). This evidence shows that skill in solving interpersonal problems is different from general intellectual ability.

The next step for Spivack and Shure was to devise a program to teach children problem-solving skills (Shure, 1992). Different versions of the program have been used with preschool and elementary-school children. Similar programs have been used as one component of large-scale interventions to prevent delinquency and drug abuse (Hawkins et al., 1992).

In Spivack and Shure's first studies (1974, 1978), the training program significantly improved the interpersonal cognitive problem-solving skills of impulsive and withdrawn children. The children's teachers also reported that the training improved the children's social behavior. Improvements in children's social behavior after this type of training have not been found in all studies (see Rubin & Krasnor, 1986). Still, successful training programs outnumber unsuccessful ones (Pellegrini & Urbain, 1985; Shure, 1993; Weissberg & Allen, 1986). Moreover, when training improves children's social behavior, the improvement can be linked to increases in children's cognitive problem-solving skills (Denham & Almeida, 1987).

The most common criticism of the interpersonal cognitive problem-solving approach deals not with the effectiveness of training but with more basic assumptions about social-cognitive maturity. Remember that social-cognitive skill is assessed, in this general approach, by the sheer number of responses children give. When scoring children's skills, coders ignore the quality or appropriateness of the children's responses. This means that children could receive high scores if they suggest many aggressive or otherwise undesirable solutions to social problems.

An advocate of this approach might argue that this criticism is disproved by the facts. Yes, it's possible for aggressive children to receive high scores, but it's unlikely. Recall that in many studies the children with better social adjustment received higher scores for problem-solving skills. In no studies did children with poor social adjustment receive the highest scores for their problem solving.

Finally, a distinctive feature of this approach is its emphasis on *how* children think instead of *what* they think. Training programs are designed to teach children to plan their behavior and to adapt their behavior to specific social situations. The success of these programs confirms the benefits of the general approach.

Of course, an alternative approach that focuses explicitly on *what* children think might also be beneficial. Such a focus is part of the second model for linking social cognition to social behavior.

## A Social Information-Processing Model

For a moment, imagine yourself back in elementary school. You are sitting in the school lunchroom, eating lunch with your friends. Suddenly, you feel something bump on your back. Immediately afterward, you feel a cold liquid dripping down your shirt. When you turn around, you see a classmate behind you holding a lunch tray. There is no milk carton on the classmate's tray, and an empty carton is lying on the floor behind you. You quickly realize that the liquid on the back of your shirt is milk from the carton. What would you think, and what would you do?

When aggressive children are asked about this situation, they often say that the classmate intentionally dropped the milk carton on their back (Dodge, 1980; Dodge & Frame, 1982). They are also likely to say that they would retaliate against the classmate. Nonaggressive children more often assume that the milk carton dropped accidentally, and they less often say they would retaliate. In short, the two groups of children differ in their inferences about the classmate's intentions and in their decisions about how they would react.

Children's responses after hearing about such hypothetical situations are one basis for a comprehensive model of the links between social cognition and social behavior. Nicki Crick and Kenneth Dodge (1994) have defined it as a social information-processing model because its basic elements overlap with those of the information-processing models described in chapter 9.

Figure 13.8 outlines the elements of social information processing and their presumed sequence. The central circle in the figure refers to children's database or memories, the store of

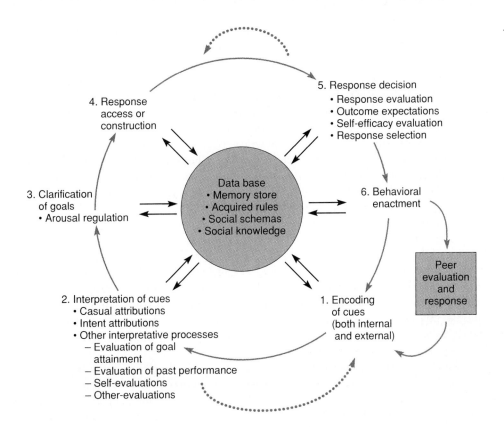

FIGURE 13.8

A model of the information processing that underlies children's social behavior. Processing begins with the encoding of cues in social situations (Step 1). Additional steps in information processing lead finally to behavior (Step 6). Then peers respond to the children's behavior, which creates a new situation that children must encode and interpret.

From N. R. Crick & K. A. Dodge, "A review and reformulation of social information-processing mechanisms in children's social adjustment" in *Psychological Bulletin*, 115:74–101. Copyright © 1994 by The American Psychological Association. Reprinted with permission.

information that they have gained from their experiences. This database includes memories of specific events, such as past interactions with particular classmates. It also includes rules for behavior that either were given to children by adults or have been formed by children after reflecting on events. Children's reflections on events may also have led to the formation of **social schemas,** memory structures that organize information. For example, aggressive children may have schemas that predispose them to interpret their peers' behavior toward them as aggressive.

Memories for specific events, rules, and schemas can be described collectively as children's social knowledge. As the arrows from the central circle to the other elements in the figure imply, this knowledge affects how children process information in a specific situation. Conversely, their inferences about a specific situation add to their social knowledge, altering the database for later interactions.

Processing of information in a specific situation begins with Step 1 in the figure, encoding of cues. As children perceive and attend to the many cues in the situation, they decide what has happened so far. If children do not encode social cues effectively, their behavior is likely to be inappropriate. For example, aggressive children pick up fewer cues from a social situation before drawing inferences about other people than do nonaggressive children (Slaby & Guerra, 1988). Aggressive children pay more attention to aggressive cues in a situation than do other children (Gouze, 1987). More than other children, aggressive children base their inferences about a social situation on the most recent cues, ignoring relevant cues presented earlier (Dodge, 1986). As a result, their encoding is less complete and more biased than that of nonaggressive children.

Step 2, interpretation of cues, can involve many types of inferences (see figure 13.8). Children may make attributions about the causes of, or reasons for, another person's behavior. They may make attributions about another person's intentions, especially whether the person intended to affect them positively or negatively. In addition, children may evaluate whether the current situation matches a goal that they had set after previous interactions with the same person. Finally, children may use situational cues to evaluate their own behavior and competence or those of another person in the situation.

**social schemas**
*Information about social events or social situations that is part of memory structures, and which therefore affects interpretation of new events and interactions.*

Figure 13.8 shows a feedback loop from Step 2 to Step 1. If children have difficulty interpreting situational cues, they may return to the first step and try to get more cues. This process may be repeated until children think they understand a situation well.

Many researchers have examined the variations in children's interpretation of social cues (Crick & Dodge, 1994). For example, many studies have confirmed that aggressive children often interpret ambiguous acts as hostile when the acts affect them (e.g., they get the milk on their back). But if another boy is the target of an ambiguous act, aggressive boys do not interpret the act as hostile more often than do nonaggressive boys (Dodge & Frame, 1982).

In natural settings, aggressive children are often the targets of other children's aggression (Dodge, 1980; Parke & Slaby, 1983). In other words, they not only attack more often but are attacked more often. Consequently, their bias to interpret ambiguous acts directed toward them as hostile has a basis in reality. Stated differently, this bias relates to a difference in their social knowledge derived from experience.

If biased interpretations of social situations can lead to aggressive behavior, maybe changing children's interpretations can change their social behavior. For one intervention program, researchers set the goal of reducing aggressive boys' tendency to view ambiguous acts as hostile (Hudley & Graham, 1993). That is, the intervention was designed to change the boys' attributions about the intentions of their interaction partners. Another distinctive feature of this intervention was its sample, which included only African American boys. *Cultural Perspectives:* "Changing the Social Cognition of Aggressive African American Boys" includes a description of the intervention and its results.

Step 3 in processing social information is clarifying goals. Suppose two boys are playing basketball, and they have a contest to see who is better at foul shots. After one boy makes a shot, the other boy claims the shot shouldn't count because the boy stepped on the foul line while shooting. A boy whose only goal is to win the contest might reply, "I did not," and insist on counting that shot. A boy whose only goal is to avoid an argument might say, "OK, I won't count that one." Another response that might allow the boy to achieve both goals is to say, "I don't think I did, but I'll do the shot over if you want."

When aggressive boys are asked about situations like these, they are less likely than their classmates to respond in ways that might achieve both goals (Rabiner & Gordon, 1992). Instead, their responses are ones likely to achieve self-focused goals such as winning the foul-shooting contest.

Other studies indicate that poor social adjustment in children stems partly from a lack of emphasis on relationship goals (Crick & Dodge, 1994). Poorly adjusted children often express little interest in helping their peers or avoiding arguments with peers. Instead, they want to show their superiority to peers or get material objects (e.g., toys) for themselves. Sometimes this lack of emphasis on building relationships is coupled with a strong interest in being liked by peers. Poorly adjusted children seem not to realize the truth of the saying, "If you want to have friends, be a friend."

Step 4 in the model can be executed in two ways. First, children may access possible responses to the current social situation from memory; that is, they may recall strategies they have used in similar situations. Second, children confronted with a novel situation may construct a response they have never tried before. Variations in the responses children access or construct are related to their typical patterns of social behavior. In situations like that of the spilled milk carton, aggressive children suggest the response of attacking another person more often than do nonaggressive children. Aggressive children less often think of competent, socially desirable responses (Dodge, Murphy, & Buchsbaum, 1984; Dorsch & Keane, 1994; Slaby & Guerra, 1988). In other types of situations, such as that of initiating an interaction with an unfamiliar peer, aggressive children often seem uncertain about what they might do. Their uncertainty reflects the social-cognitive deficits mentioned in the section on the interpersonal cognitive problem-solving approach. Similar deficits are shown by rejected children.

Step 5 in the model, response decision, involves several processes. The processes listed in figure 13.8 can be illustrated by questions you might ask yourself about the lunchroom situation mentioned earlier. First, would hitting the classmate who dropped the milk carton on your back be a good thing to do (response evaluation)? Second, would the classmate hit you

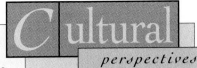

"Shoot first and ask questions afterward" may be a good rule for soldiers on sentry duty but not for daily life. Children who are interacting with peers would be better advised to follow the rule, "Don't go off half-cocked." Aggressive boys, in particular, need to interpret social cues more carefully before they lash out at someone.

One part of the interpretation of social cues is making accurate attributions about whether another person's behavior was hostile. Cynthia Hudley and Sandra Graham (1993) assumed that many boys are aggressive partly because they make inaccurate attributions. For example, if a classmate bumps them so that they drop their books, they assume the classmate did so deliberately rather than by accident. These researchers assumed that they could reduce boys' aggressive behavior by training them to make accurate attributions about others' intent.

To test this assumption, Hudley and Graham first used teacher ratings and peer nominations to identify a group of aggressive African American boys. These boys attended schools in which the great majority of students were African American. The aggressive boys were randomly assigned to one of three groups.

The first group had 12 lessons of attribution training. During the lessons, boys were taught how to judge whether an action was intentional. They also were taught to recognize when information about others' intent was ambiguous. Finally, they were taught to link their attributions to their behavior. That is, they were taught not to react aggressively when they were unsure whether another's action was intended to harm them. The lessons involved not lectures by the adults but role playing, conversations about the boys' own experiences, and other activities.

The second group of boys was assigned to a condition called attention training. This group received the same amount of attention from the adult leaders as the first group (which explains the label, *attention* training), but they were not trained in social-cognitive skills. Instead, their program dealt with skills for classifying information or following directions. The last group of boys was assigned to a control condition.

The boys' teachers rated their aggressive behavior on a pretest two weeks before training began. Teachers rated the boys' behavior again on a posttest two weeks after training ended.

The scores of the three groups on reactive aggression (i.e., reactions to a provocation by a peer) are shown in figure 13.9. Boys' aggressive behavior decreased only in the group given attribution training. Thus, changing the boys' social cognition did change their social behavior.

Hudley and Graham cautioned, however, that inaccurate attributions may not completely explain these boys' aggression. All the boys attended schools in economically depressed areas. One boy whose aggression did not decrease after training commented that his local park was occupied by gang members who often victimized elementary-school children. To change the behavior of such boys, more than changes in social information processing are necessary. Changes are also needed in the social environments where many African American boys grow up. If these boys think they live in a war zone where it's safest to "shoot first and ask questions afterward," adults may reduce their aggression only by reducing the violence surrounding them.

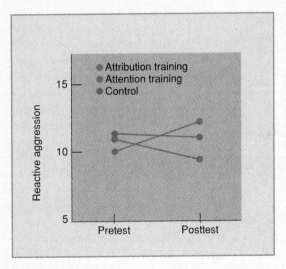

## FIGURE 13.9

Training aggressive boys to make accurate attributions about their peers' intentions decreased their reactive aggression toward peers. Training involving adult attention but no instruction in social-cognitive skills did not decrease boys' aggression. Boys in a control condition, who received no training, also changed little in their reactive aggression. (Source: Hudley & Graham, 1993.)

back if you hit him or her (outcome expectations)? Third, would you have the guts, and the strength, to hit him or her (self-efficacy evaluation)? The answers to these questions determine how favorably you are likely to feel toward each response generated in Step 4. You should choose the response for which the answers to the three questions are most positive (response selection).

When asked about hypothetical situations, aggressive and rejected children evaluate aggressive responses more positively than other children do (Crick & Dodge, 1994). Aggressive children also have greater self-efficacy or greater confidence about their ability to attack or insult another person than do nonaggressive children.

Whether aggressive children expect more positive outcomes of aggressive behavior is less clear. That is, aggressive children do not always expect physical aggression to lead to more positive outcomes than nonaggressive children do (Quiggle et al., 1992). These children may still behave aggressively, though, if they cannot think of another response or they evaluate aggression positively for other reasons.

Step 6, behavioral enactment, means that children do what they chose to do in the previous step. Then their behavior is evaluated by the peers who are in the same situation. As figure 13.8 shows, that evaluation is followed by the peers' response. Strictly speaking, these elements in the figure are not part of the social information-processing model. After Step 5, information processing is done. Step 6 and the next step to peer evaluation and response are included in the figure to show how information processing is linked to children's behavior and social interactions. In addition, the peer response creates a new social situation with new cues. Children's encoding of those cues begins the cycle of information processing again.

One purpose of the social information-processing model is to integrate the findings from many studies of social cognition and social behavior (Crick & Dodge, 1994). Another purpose is to demonstrate that measuring all the information-processing steps allows more accurate predictions of behavior than can be achieved with measures of one step (Dodge & Price, 1994). A third purpose is to provide a basis for interventions to improve the social behavior of children low in social adjustment. No intervention based on the full model has been reported yet, but part of the model was tested in an intervention with aggressive adolescents (Guerra & Slaby, 1990).

The adolescents were in a maximum-security institution in California. They had committed one or more violent criminal acts such as battery, robbery, rape, or murder. They were randomly assigned to one of three groups. The training group focused on improving the adolescents' social-cognitive skills and changing their beliefs that aggression is acceptable. An attention-control group received instruction in basic skills like math and reading when the training group was meeting. A control group only took pretests and posttests when the other groups did.

The adolescents in the training group met weekly for about an hour. They discussed social problems commonly experienced by institutionalized adolescents. For example, the adolescents had to share a TV with many other people, so they couldn't always watch their favorite programs. The adolescents were trained to think before reacting to such problems, to interpret the problems accurately, to consider several possible actions, and to evaluate the likely consequences of their actions before doing anything.

As they considered the consequences of possible actions, the adolescents also discussed their beliefs about aggression. Adult leaders invited the adolescents to counter beliefs that encourage aggression. For example, they asked adolescents to argue against the idea that you can show people how tough you are by being a good fighter.

The training was effective not only in improving the adolescents' social information processing but also in changing their beliefs about the acceptability of aggression. Most important, the training affected the adolescents' behavior in their residential cottages, outside the classrooms where the training took place. As figure 13.10 shows, adolescents in the training group became less aggressive, impulsive, and inflexible. The behavior of the other adolescents changed little. These results show the practical value of research on the social cognition of children and adolescents.

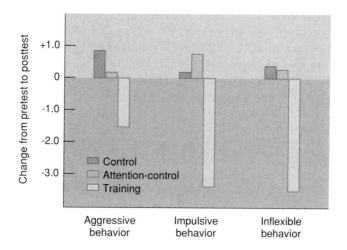

**FIGURE 13.10**
The behavior of adolescents in a prison improved when they received training designed to increase their social-cognitive skills and decrease their acceptance of beliefs that aggression is acceptable. The behavior of adolescents in the attention-control and no-treatment control conditions changed little between the pretest and the posttest. (Source: Guerra & Slaby, 1990.)

Finally, you might wonder how this training program compares with the role-taking training discussed earlier in the chapter (Chalmers & Townsend, 1990; Chandler, 1973). Many features of the programs differ, but one difference is especially critical. Training in role taking is often based on the premise that aggressive and delinquent adolescents are developmentally delayed. In this view, most aggressive and delinquent adolescents are assumed not to have reached the level of role-taking ability shown by their normal peers. The goal of training, then, is to accelerate this facet of their social-cognitive development.

By contrast, the social information-processing model and the training programs based on it emphasize the differences between aggressive and nonaggressive (or delinquent and nondelinquent) adolescents in their social cognition. The goal of training, in this view, is not to accelerate social-cognitive development but to make these groups of adolescents similar in their social information-processing. Stated more generally, the goal is to make aggressive or delinquent adolescents think more like their normal peers.

Both perspectives capture part of the truth. On one hand, viewing delinquent and aggressive behavior only as a sign of developmental delay is too optimistic. If this view were correct, adolescents would inevitably grow out of these problem behaviors, but they often do not (Kazdin, 1987). On the other hand, a focus on group differences in information processing that does not include some attention to developmental norms is incomplete and potentially misleading. Delinquent and aggressive behaviors are, in part, a consequence of social-cognitive immaturity (Selman & Schultz, 1989; Selman et al., 1983).

The issue of delays in social-cognitive development versus differences in social information processing is complex and currently unresolved. Because of its practical implications, more research on the issue is needed. Perhaps you will choose this topic of research for your career. Your findings could be valuable in designing programs to reduce problem behaviors in childhood and adolescence.

# THINKING ABOUT RELATIONSHIPS AND MULTIPLE SELVES

Children's relationships with other people were not mentioned often in this chapter. You read in a few places about how children's relationships affect their social-cognitive development. For example, children's self-esteem is affected by the kind of parenting they receive, which is one facet of parent-child relationships. Similarly, parent-child relationships affect identity development in adolescence.

You also read in a few places about how children's social cognition affects their social relationships. For example, children's ability to infer other people's emotions can help them learn how to behave appropriately in social situations, which is essential for having good

relationships. Also, Crick and Dodge's (1994) social information-processing model includes a step for clarifying goals, and these researchers mentioned relationship goals explicitly. Children who do not consider the goal of building relationships when planning their social behavior are unlikely to have good relationships.

One topic missing from this chapter is children's thinking about relationships themselves. The main reason for the omission is that this topic was discussed extensively in previous chapters. Chapter 6 included information about infants' and children's internal working models of their attachments to parents. Ideas about parent-child relationships are part of those working models. Chapter 11 included information about parenting and its effects. Often, variations in parenting have been judged from children's reports on—or their ideas about—their relationships with parents. Chapter 12 on peer relationships included information on children's views of—or their ideas about—their friendships. In short, you learned how children think about specific relationships when you learned about the other features of these relationships.

Not examined in previous chapters was the connection between children's thoughts about relationships and their thoughts about themselves. In several intriguing studies, Susan Harter and Ann Monsour (1992) examined the changes in this connection during adolescence. They found that adolescents' self-descriptions increasingly referred to multiple selves, distinct self-concepts that are linked to different social roles. For example, one adolescent described herself as helpful when with parents and as fun-loving when with friends.

Adolescents' growing appreciation of their multiple selves was sometimes associated with negative feelings, especially if the adolescents perceived their differing self-concepts as in conflict. For example, one ninth grader said, "I really think of myself as a happy person, and I want to be that way with everyone because I think that's my true self, but I get depressed with my family and that bugs me because that's not what I want to be like" (Harter & Monsour, 1992, p. 253).

As mentioned earlier, self-awareness increases during adolescence, so increases in adolescents' recognition of conflicting elements in their self-concepts would be expected. However, reports of such conflicting elements reached a peak around ninth grade and then decreased. Older adolescents resolved the conflicts by thinking of themselves as complex individuals. By eleventh grade, adolescents made statements like, "I'm sometimes happy and sometimes depressed, but that's normal for most people so that's okay."

Adolescent girls typically reported more conflicting elements in their self-concepts than adolescent boys. Harter and Monsour (1992) suggested that girls may be more concerned than boys about their multiple relationships to parents, siblings, and friends of the same and opposite sex. More than boys, girls may feel that they must try to bring these relationships into harmony with one another. Boys may treat different relationships as largely independent.

Nevertheless, both boys and girls live in complex social worlds that involve many relationships. To maintain these relationships and form new ones, boys and girls must think about their roles in these many relationships. Gaining an understanding of the multiple selves that are linked to multiple social relationships is an important facet of social-cognitive development.

# Summary

### Who Am I? The Development of Self-Understanding

Children increase in their understanding of self as they increase in understanding of other people. Self-understanding is distinctive, however, because children can only see themselves through a process of reflection analogous to looking in a mirror.

### Self-Recognition in Infancy

During the first year of life, infants begin to recognize when their image in a mirror matches their actions. During the second year, infants recognize their facial features. This self-recognition is accompanied by changes in emotional expressions and in social behavior.

### Self-Concepts in Childhood and Adolescence

When preschool children describe themselves, they focus on their physical appearance and their activities. Elementary-school children add a focus on comparisons of self and others. In adolescence, self-descriptions include many comments about personality traits.

## How Good Am I? Variations in Self-Esteem

Self-esteem is a person's evaluation of his or her worth, value, and competence. Children with high self-esteem feel positively about who they are and what they are like.

## General and Specific Aspects of Self-Evaluation

Children not only have a general sense of their worth; they also evaluate themselves in specific domains like academics and athletics. Modern measures of self-evaluation like Harter's SPPC and Marsh's SDQI provide information about children's general self-esteem and their self-evaluations in specific domains.

## Age Changes in Self-Esteem

Self-esteem in highly positive during early childhood and becomes less positive during the elementary-school years. Self-esteem does not change consistently after the transition to middle or junior high school but it increases during adolescence.

## In the Looking Glass: Origins of Self-Esteem

Children's self-esteem partly reflects reality. For example, popular children perceive their social acceptance as high. Self-esteem also depends on children's relationships with significant others. Parents, especially, can promote high self-esteem in their children by using an authoritative parenting style.

## Identity Development in Adolescence

Erikson first suggested the importance of identity formation, but most researchers have adopted Marcia's extension of Erikson's theory. Marcia defined four types of identity status: achievement, moratorium, foreclosure, and diffusion. Adolescents' identity status is related to their personality, social behavior, and relationships with parents.

## Understanding Other People

Children's understanding of other people increases with age. Children gradually realize that other people's thoughts and feelings may differ from their own. Children also become better at inferring other people's thoughts and feelings.

## Do You Know What I Know? Egocentrism and Role Taking

Role taking is the ability to adopt, in thought, the perspective of another person. Selman proposed a developmental sequence of levels of perspective taking. Other researchers have examined the specific abilities required for success on specific role-taking tasks.

## Inferring Others' Emotions, Intentions, Beliefs, and Traits

Preschool children often infer emotions accurately from an actor's facial expression or from information about the actor's situation. Older children more often look beyond the immediate situation when drawing inferences about an actor's emotions. Children's ability to judge when a behavior is intentional or accidental and their ability to infer an actor's motives improve with age. Three-year-olds' responses to questions about false beliefs suggest they have not yet developed a representational theory of mind. The age changes in children's descriptions of other people parallel the age changes in self-descriptions.

## Linking Social Cognition to Social Behavior

Children's thoughts about themselves and other people affect their behavior. Many researchers have suggested how children's social cognition is linked to social behavior. The most important suggestions are encompassed by two general approaches.

## Interpersonal Cognitive Problem Solving

In one approach, social interaction is considered as a type of problem solving. Socially competent children are assumed to have several problem-solving skills, including the ability to think of alternative solutions to problems and the ability to anticipate the consequences of behaviors.

## A Social Information-Processing Model

In the other general approach, social behavior is assumed to result from a series of information-processing steps that involve encoding social cues, interpreting the cues, clarifying goals, thinking of possible responses, and selecting one response. Both this approach and the previous one have been the basis for intervention programs that have improved children's social behavior.

## Thinking About Relationships and Multiple Selves

Adolescents increasingly recognize that somewhat differing self-concepts can be linked to their different social roles. Recognition of conflicting elements in self-descriptions peaks around ninth grade. Older adolescents appreciate that they have multiple selves related to their multiple social relationships.

# SUGGESTED READINGS

Bartsch, K., & Wellman, H. M. (1995). *Children talk about the mind.* Oxford, England: Oxford University Press. Karen Bartsch and Henry Wellman have done some of the most important research on the child's theory of mind. The focus of this book is on children's spontaneous comments about their thoughts, beliefs, desires, and ideas. What these comments suggest about the developing theory of mind is summarized in the final chapters. Earlier chapters present the details of specific studies.

Bracken, B. A. (Ed.). (1996). *Handbook of self-concept: Developmental, social, and clinical considerations.* New York: Wiley. Despite its title, this handbook is about self-esteem as well as self-concepts. Separate chapters focus on global self-esteem and on specific domains of self-evaluation such as academic ability and physical appearance. The authors are well-known researchers, and their chapters are easier to read than in many handbooks.

Marcia, J. E., Waterman, A. S., Matteson, D. R., Archer, S. L., & Orlofsky, J. L. (1993). *Ego identity: A handbook for psychosocial research.* New York: Springer-Verlag. When reading this chapter, did you think about your own identity status? This book can help to answer your questions. It includes a list of the questions on an identity-status interview, and information on the criteria for scoring people's responses. Also included are summaries of research on age changes, sex differences, and personality correlates of identity status.

Saarni, C., & Harris, P. H. (Eds.). (1991). *Children's understanding of emotions.* Cambridge, England: Cambridge University Press. The chapters in this book summarize the most significant recent research on children's understanding of emotions. Besides describing the normal course of "emotion cognition," the authors consider how children's thinking about emotions is affected by circumstances like entering the hospital.

### Chapter Fourteen

# Sex-Role Development

**sex roles**
*Behaviors and other characteristics that are expected or considered appropriate for males and females in a specific culture.*

F rom an early age, boys and girls differ in their patterns of social activity. Even when boys and girls are involved in the same activity, their behavior often differs dramatically. These differences partly reflect **sex roles,** behaviors and other characteristics that are expected or considered appropriate for males and females in a specific culture. The following examples show how much boys' and girls' behavior can differ when they are supposedly doing the same thing, caring for a younger sibling.

Marina, a 10-year-old girl who lives in a small village in the Philippines, is taking care of her baby sister, Leonida. First she puts the baby's face next to hers and rubs noses with her. Then another girl, who is also carrying a baby, walks by and talks to Leonida. A third girl, again holding a baby, smiles at Leonida and asks Marina, "Has she teeth already?" Marina proudly answered, "Yes, two." Then she looks at Leonida, jiggles her, and laughs, "Hee, hee, hee."

Crescencio, a 7-year-old boy in the same barrio, has been told to take care of his baby brother, Pico. However, he is spending most of his time watching other children play tag. When Pico drops a stick that he was playing with and starts fussing, Crescencio picks it up and gives it back to him. When Pico drops it again, Crescencio says, "Stupid! You keep dropping it! And then you let me pick it up!" Crescencio gives the stick to Pico, but Pico throws it down. Crescencio says, "You want me to put you in the manure pile? I'll slap you, huh?" and he slaps Pico lightly on the bottom. When Pico starts to cry, Crescencio imitates his whimpering. Pico cries louder, so Crescencio picks him up and tries to comfort him (Whiting & Edwards, 1988).

These observations from the Philippines could be duplicated in many cultures. Throughout the world, girls spend more time caring for younger children than boys do (Whiting & Edwards, 1988). Girls also seem to enjoy caring for children more than boys do (Berman, 1980). Sometimes, as in the examples, girls are more responsive and affectionate when caring for children than boys are.

The differences in boys' and girls' behavior toward their younger siblings probably don't surprise you. You might be saying, "I knew that already." That is, the differences match your beliefs about how the sexes differ. But where did your beliefs come from? The formation of those beliefs is part of the process of sex-role development. Defined fully, **sex-role development** is the process by which children acquire the beliefs, behaviors, and other characteristics expected or considered appropriate for individuals of their sex in their culture. Another name for this process is **sex typing.** To understand the process of sex-role development, you need to understand the many components of sex typing itself. The first section of the chapter includes a description of these components.

**sex-role development**
*The process by which children acquire the beliefs, behaviors, and other characteristics expected or considered appropriate for individuals of their sex in their culture.*

**sex typing**
*A synonym for sex-role development.*

Before beginning that section, you should know about one issue of terminology. Where the word *sex* is used in the preceding paragraphs, some researchers would substitute the word *gender*. For example, they would describe the roles of males and females not as sex roles but as gender roles.

Several researchers argue strongly that the word *sex* should only be used to refer to the biological differences between males and females that are caused by genetic differences (Geis, 1993; Lott & Maluso, 1993). These researchers argue that *gender* is a social construction, defined by the attributes that are assigned to males and females in a particular culture. For these researchers, differences in preschool boys' and girls' chromosomes would be *sex differences;* differences in boys' and girls' choices of toys would be *gender differences*.

Other researchers disagree with this distinction. Eleanor Maccoby (1988) argues that the attempt to distinguish between differences that are genetically based and those that are a social construction is difficult, because many psychological differences are likely to have both genetic and social causes. Moreover, she argues that questions about the causes of differences between boys and girls should be answered by careful research, not "assumed at the outset through the choice of terminology" (p. 755).

One way to resolve (or evade) this controversy is not to make an explicit distinction between *sex* and *gender,* but to take research reports and other scholarly writings as a guide to

Throughout the world, girls spend more time caring for infants and young children than boys do. This difference between boys and girls is one of many aspects of sex-role development.

the appropriate use of these terms (Ruble, 1988). In these writings, some constructs are typically prefaced by the word *gender* (e.g., gender identity). Other constructs are typically prefaced by the word *sex* or *sex-role* (e.g., sex typing). The terms in this chapter match those commonly found in the scientific literature. This match will make it easier for you to understand what researchers mean if you do additional reading yourself.

# THE MANY COMPONENTS OF SEX TYPING

The psychological makeup and social lives of boys and girls differ in many ways. These differences can be classified into sets that refer to separate components of sex typing. Aletha Huston (1983; Mussen et al., 1990) defined the most important sets by crossing four content areas with four constructs. Table 14.1, which is adapted from Huston's writings, shows the 16 components of sex typing that result from these combinations.

The content areas that define the rows of the table reflect types of differences between the sexes. Boys and girls differ in their (1) biological category, that is, whether they are male or female; (2) activities, interests, and cognitive abilities; (3) personality traits and social behavior; and (4) gender-based social relationships.

The constructs that define the columns of the table reflect ways in which sex differences are represented in people's thinking and behavior. As you read the chapter, you will also see that the columns refer to different types of research on sex-role development.

The first column includes people's beliefs about the differences between the sexes. For the moment, skip the first row in that column, labeled "Gender constancy," and look at the other rows. These rows focus on **sex stereotypes,** beliefs about how the sexes differ. Defined more precisely, sex stereotypes are assumptions or expectations about how males and females differ in their activities, personality traits, or other characteristics. Your belief that interest in babies is greater among girls than among boys falls into the second row of the table. Most children and adults also believe that boys and girls differ in their social behaviors, like aggression, and in their choices of friends. In the next section of the chapter, you will read about the development of sex stereotypes and the age changes in children's interpretations of the stereotypes.

You might think that stereotypes refer to false beliefs, ideas that have no basis in reality. However, the example of boys' and girls' interest in babies suggests that some stereotypes reflect reality. The third section of the chapter reviews some evidence on the actual differences between boys and girls. Most of the evidence falls into column 2 in table 14.1, differences in boys' and girls' behavior. Somewhat less research deals with the sex differences in preferences (column 3) and self-perceptions (column 4). For example, researchers have asked children which toys they like most or which personality traits they think they have. Sex differences in behavior, preferences, and self-perceptions are all part of sex-role development.

**sex stereotypes**
*Assumptions or expectations about how males and females differ in their activities, personality traits, or other characteristics.*

## TABLE 14.1  Components of Sex Typing

| | CONSTRUCT | | | |
|---|---|---|---|---|
| CONTENT AREA | BELIEFS (KNOWLEDGE ABOUT GENDER AND SEX STEREOTYPES) | BEHAVIOR (WHAT A PERSON DOES) | PREFERENCES (WHAT A PERSON LIKES) | SELF-PERCEPTION (HOW PEOPLE SEE THEMSELVES) |
| Biological category | Gender constancy | Displaying bodily attributes of one's gender (e.g., male or female clothing) | Wish to be male or female | Gender identity |
| Activities, interests, and cognitive abilities | Beliefs about sex typing of interests, activities, toys, and abilities | Spending time with toys, games, interests, and cognitive skills | Preferred toys, games, interests, and academic tasks | Perception of own interests and abilities |
| Personality traits and social behavior | Beliefs about sex typing of aggression, kindness, and other traits and behaviors | Observed aggression, kindness, and other behaviors | Attributes people value, would like to have | Perception of own personality |
| Gender-based social relationships | Beliefs about norms for same-sex friends, opposite-sex friends, opposite-sex lovers, and the like | Selecting others for social or sexual contact on the basis of gender (e.g., same-sex peer choices) | Preference for male or female friends, lovers, models to emulate | Perception of own patterns of friendship, sexual orientation |

*Source:* Adapted from Huston, 1983.

Researchers have to find out how the sexes differ before they can understand why these differences exist. That is, researchers need to describe sex-role development before they can fully explain it. In some respects, though, the task of explaining sex-role development is more important and more difficult than describing it. Controversies about sex-role development often involve questions about *why* the sexes differ in abilities, traits, social behaviors, or other characteristics. For this reason, the section on explanations of sex-role development is the longest one in the chapter. But even before you reach that section, you should have some idea of the major theories.

Some theorists assume that important differences between males' and females' behavior are due at least partly to the biological differences between the two sexes (e.g., Halpern, 1992; Money, 1987). Of course, the genotypes of males and females differ, and these differences lead to differences in physical features, hormones, and biological processes. But are biological differences responsible for sex differences in the other content areas in table 14.1, such as activities, personality traits, and social relationships? The arguments and evidence on this question are reviewed later in the chapter.

Other theorists emphasize the differences in the socialization of males and females (e.g., Block, 1983; Eagly, 1987; Lott & Maluso, 1993). From infancy, boys and girls are treated differently by parents, peers, and other socialization agents. Think about the opening examples. Girls and boys differ in the time they spend caring for children partly because their parents (usually their mothers) assign child care more to daughters than to sons. This case is fairly obvious, but it is not easy to decide how well differences in socialization account for the many differences between boys' and girls' behavior. Researchers also need to find the content areas in which differences in socialization are most and least important, and the socialization processes that are involved in each area.

Still other theorists emphasize the impact of children's cognitive development on their sex-role development (e.g., Kohlberg, 1966; Martin & Halverson, 1981). The discussion of cognitive-developmental theories will focus on two constructs in table 14.1 that were ignored earlier. The first is **gender identity**, children's perceptions of themselves as male or female. The second is **gender constancy**, children's knowledge that a person's sex is stable over time and cannot be changed by a change in clothes, hairstyle, or activities. Cognitive-developmental

**gender identity**
*Children's perceptions of themselves as male or female.*

**gender constancy**
*Children's knowledge that a person's sex is stable over time and cannot be changed by a change in clothes, hair style, or activities.*

theorists emphasize that children form ideas about the biological category in which they fall. These ideas, in turn, affect other aspects of sex typing.

To avoid misunderstanding, one point should be stated explicitly. In this chapter you will not read a specific "developmental story" about each of the 16 boxes (4 constructs × 4 content areas) in table 14.1. Because of gaps in research, a full set of such developmental stories could not be written. Table 14.1 is still useful in suggesting that the developmental story for one component of sex typing may differ from that for other components.

For example, you will find out that children with greater knowledge of sex stereotypes do not consistently show more stereotyped behavior themselves. Similarly, children who show more stereotyped behavior do not necessarily have a stronger preference for same-sex playmates. These contrasts make the explanation of sex-role development more complicated—and more fascinating.

The contrasts between the different components of sex typing have important implications for social judgments. Because these components are often only weakly related, judgments about a child's general level of sex typing are likely to be imprecise. No children or adults are completely sex typed in the sense that they have only the stereotypical characteristics of their own sex. Some boys who are not interested in babies may love to cook. Some girls who like playing with dolls may also enjoy competitive sports. Several theorists suggest that such combinations of masculine and feminine characteristics are the ideal end points for sex-role development (see Huston, 1983; Ruble, 1988). The evidence on this issue is examined near the end of the chapter.

# WHAT ARE GIRLS AND BOYS MADE OF? A LOOK AT CHILDREN'S STEREOTYPES

Many children learn the nursery rhyme that says girls are made of "sugar and spice and everything nice." The rhyme continues by saying that boys are made of "snips and snails and puppy dogs' tails." Children don't take those statements literally, but they do believe that boys and girls are different. That is, they accept many stereotypes about the differences between boys and girls. As they grow older, they form more sex stereotypes and change their ideas about the stereotypes.

The most evidence on developmental changes in children's stereotypes is available for two content areas in table 14.1. One is the area of personality traits and social behaviors; the other is the area of activities, interests, and abilities. Let's look first at children's knowledge of sex stereotypes in those areas.

## Developmental Changes in Stereotypes

Suppose someone asked you whether a boy or a girl would be more likely to get into fights. You would probably say a boy. Suppose someone asked you whether a boy or a girl would be more emotional, or cry a lot. You would probably say a girl. Questions like these have been used by many researchers to find out whether children know the stereotypes applied to males and females in their society. In short, the questions assess **stereotype knowledge.**

### Stereotype Knowledge Increases with Age

One major study of stereotype knowledge included children between 5 and 11 years of age (Best et al., 1977). The study focused on children's knowledge about the stereotypical traits and behaviors of boys and girls. Table 14.2 summarizes the age changes found.

At each age, children were credited with knowledge of a stereotype if two-thirds of them gave the same answer to the boy-or-girl question that adults gave. Notice that 5-year-olds already knew (or assumed) that boys are more likely than girls to be strong, aggressive, messy, cruel, coarse, ambitious, and dominant. Five-year-olds also knew (or assumed) that girls are more likely than boys to be emotional, gentle, softhearted, and affectionate.

As you would expect, 8-year-olds had more knowledge of sex-role stereotypes than 5-year-olds did, and 11-year-olds had more knowledge of stereotypes than 8-year-olds did.

**stereotype knowledge**
*Awareness of commonly accepted stereotypes about males and females, assessed from a person's judgments about whether a behavior or other characteristic is more typical for males or for females.*

## TABLE 14.2  Sex-Role Stereotypes of 5-, 8-, and 11-Year-Olds

| 5-YEAR-OLDS EXPECT BOYS TO . . . | 8-YEAR-OLDS ALSO EXPECT BOYS TO . . . | 11-YEAR-OLDS ALSO EXPECT BOYS TO . . . |
|---|---|---|
| • Be the strong person (robust)<br>• Get into a fight (aggressive, tough)<br>• Be a messy person (disorderly)<br>• Say bad words (coarse)<br>• Own a big store (ambitious)<br>• Make most of the rules (dominant) | • Be adventurous<br>• Get along by themselves (independent)<br>• Talk loudly (excitable)<br>• Brag about the things they have done | • Be sure of themselves (confident)<br>• Be the steady person (stable, unemotional)<br>• Be the jolly person |

| 5-YEAR-OLDS EXPECT GIRLS TO . . . | 8-YEAR-OLDS ALSO EXPECT GIRLS TO . . . | 11-YEAR-OLDS ALSO EXPECT GIRLS TO . . . |
|---|---|---|
| • Cry a lot (emotional)<br>• Be a gentle person<br>• Be softhearted (sensitive)<br>• Hug and kiss a lot (affectionate) | • Be a weak person<br>• Always say "thank you" (appreciative)<br>• Be excitable<br>• Always change her mind (fickle)<br>• Be the shy person (meek)<br>• Be dependent on someone else to make the rules (submissive)<br>• Be the complaining person (whiny) | • Be talkative<br>• Buy silly things (frivolous) |

*Source:* Best et al., 1977.

Other investigators have confirmed that knowledge of sex stereotypes about personality traits and social behaviors increases steadily with age (Huston, 1983; Ruble, 1988; Signorella, Bigler, & Liben, 1993). The age change was confirmed yet again in the 1990s with a sample of more than 500 Canadian children (Serbin et al., 1993).

Table 14.2 also shows that children believe both sexes have some good and some bad qualities. Children say that boys have some positive characteristics such as strength and ambition. Children also say that boys have negative characteristics such as messiness and cruelty. Girls, too, are believed to have a combination of positive and negative characteristics. Children believe that girls are more gentle and affectionate than boys but that girls are also more weak and fickle. These beliefs do not suggest a definite advantage—in stereotypic traits and behaviors—to being masculine rather than feminine or vice versa.

Many researchers have argued that though positive and negative traits are assigned to both sexes, masculine traits are generally evaluated more positively than feminine traits (Golombok & Fivush, 1994). However, the research consistent with this argument included an incomplete, and biased, set of personality traits. If the stereotypic characteristics of men and women are assessed more systematically, adults judge the female stereotype more favorably than the male stereotype (Eagly, Mladinic, & Otto, 1991). Again, though, this overall evaluation can obscure a more important fact, that sex stereotypes portray both males and females as having both desirable and undesirable traits.

Developmental research has also revealed that children know the stereotypes applicable to their own sex as well as those applicable to the opposite sex. Boys mostly agree with girls about the typical behaviors and traits of girls. Girls mostly agree with boys about the typical behaviors and traits of boys. These findings suggest that children learn about the roles of both sexes. They learn the stereotypes for the opposite sex about as quickly as they learn those for their own sex (Huston, 1983; Intons-Peterson, 1988).

One qualification to this conclusion needs to be made. In the large Canadian study mentioned earlier (Serbin et al., 1993), children between 5 and 10 years of age seemed to know more about positive traits stereotypical for their sex than about positive traits stereotypical for the opposite sex. Conversely, children in this age range seemed to know more about negative traits stereotypical for the opposite sex than about negative traits stereotypical for their sex.

These results are best interpreted not as a strictly cognitive phenomenon but as an illustration of a self-serving bias. For example, more boys than girls say that a boy is more likely than a girl to be confident. More girls than boys say that a girl is more likely than a boy to be affectionate. The opposite tendencies hold for negative masculine traits (e.g., "messy") and negative feminine traits (e.g., "weak"). In short, children show favoritism toward their own sex when they answer standard questions about their stereotype knowledge (Powlishta, 1995).

Own-sex favoritism is even more obvious in preschool children's judgments about social behaviors and personality traits (Kuhn, Nash, & Brucken, 1978). This bias in judgments, coupled with actual ignorance about sex stereotypes, can explain why preschoolers receive lower scores than older children on measures of stereotype knowledge. For example, preschoolers do not consistently say that boys are stronger than girls, or that girls are more kind than boys.

Preschoolers' lack of knowledge about stereotypical traits contrasts sharply with their wealth of information about the typical activities and interests of boys and girls (Kuhn et al., 1978). In particular, they know that girls play with dolls and like to cook more than boys do. They know that boys play with cars and like to build things more than girls do. These findings illustrate a more general principle: Sex stereotypes about activities and interests are often learned earlier than those about personality traits and social behaviors (Huston, 1983).

Preschool children also have stereotypes about the activities and interests of men and women. One boy, only 2 years of age, saw a woman with short hair who was working in a park. The woman was wearing pants and driving a small tractor around the park, mowing the grass. The boy's father noticed that he called the driver "that man." The father tried to tell the boy that the driver was a woman. The boy replied, "No, it's not. Womans [sic] don't drive that [tractor-mower]."

Even 2-year-olds believe a man is more likely than a woman to mow the grass, drive a truck, or be a firefighter (Kuhn et al., 1978; Weinraub et al., 1984). Two-year-olds believe a woman is more likely than a man to clean the house, be a nurse, sew, and wash clothes. Children gain more knowledge of sex stereotypes for adults' activities and interests as they grow, just as they gain more knowledge of sex-stereotyped traits and behaviors.

## Stereotype Flexibility Increases with Age

Remember the question about whether a boy or a girl would be more likely to get into fights? Suppose that you rephrased the question slightly and asked, "Who can get into fights: boys, girls, or both boys and girls?" Answers to questions of this sort have been used to assess children's **stereotype flexibility.** Children are assumed to have more flexible stereotypes when they answer such questions by saying "both." That is, they assume that most behaviors can be shown by boys and girls. They also assume that boys and girls can play with dolls or play with cars. They assume that men and women can mow the grass or be firefighters.

Children's stereotype flexibility increases during their same years as their stereotype knowledge increases (Signorella et al., 1993). The age changes were directly compared in a few studies that assessed both aspects of sex-role development. Figure 14.1 shows the results of one of these studies (Carter & Patterson, 1982).

When kindergarten children were asked whether boys or girls usually play with cars, dolls, or other stereotypical toys, they gave the expected answers about 85 percent of the time. When asked whether a man or a woman is more likely to be a doctor, a nurse, or have other stereotypical occupations, they gave the expected answer about 75 percent of the time. Such stereotype knowledge, especially of adult occupations, increased further by eighth grade.

**stereotype flexibility**
*Willingness to assert that males and females can engage in the same behaviors, choose the same activities, and show similarities on other characteristics.*

FIGURE 14.1

Children's knowledge of sex stereotypes that apply to children's toys and adults' occupations increases between kindergarten and eighth grade. Children's stereotype flexibility, their understanding that males and females may like the same toys or choose the same occupations, also increases between kindergarten and eighth grade. (Source: Carter & Patterson, 1982.)

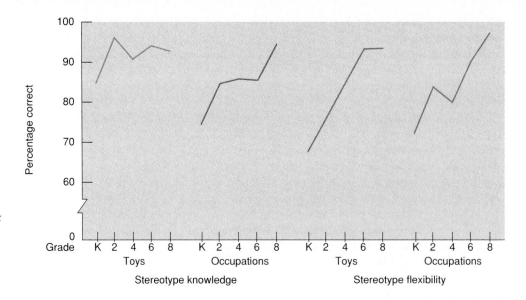

Stereotype flexibility also increased between kindergarten and eighth grade. Nearly all eighth graders, but only two-thirds of kindergarten children, said that both boys and girls can play with cars and other stereotypical toys. Nearly all eighth graders, but less than three-fourths of kindergarten children, said that both men and women can be doctors or have other stereotypical occupations.

A meta-analysis of the many studies on children's sex stereotypes showed that boys usually have less flexible stereotypes than girls (Signorella et al., 1993). In other research mentioned later, boys' behavior also seemed more constrained by sex stereotypes than girls' behavior was (Maccoby, 1980). Also, the flexibility of children's stereotypes is not related to their intelligence, but stereotype flexibility is greater when children's mothers are employed outside the home.

By contrast, children's knowledge of sex stereotypes is related to their intelligence and is not related to their mothers' employment (Signorella et al., 1993). This pattern suggests that stereotype knowledge comes from observing how male and female roles actually differ in a society. Stereotype flexibility reflects, instead, children's attitudes toward equal roles for the two sexes.

## The Persistence of Stereotypes

Does the increase in stereotype flexibility mean that children begin to ignore sex stereotypes as they grow older? Do children form less sexist attitudes as they become more mature? In one study adolescents expressed more tolerance of other people whose activities do not fit traditional stereotypes than children did (Katz & Ksansnak, 1994). However, other studies have suggested a more complex picture of the age changes in sex stereotypes.

One study included students in kindergarten, third grade, sixth grade, and college (Berndt & Heller, 1986). Each student heard brief stories about the activities of boys and girls. In one condition, these activities were consistent with sex stereotypes. For example, a girl chose to bake brownies rather than fix a bicycle, and a boy chose the reverse. In another condition, the boys' and girls' activity choices were inconsistent with sex stereotypes.

After hearing the stories, the children and adults predicted the future activity choices of the actors in the stories. The actors had to choose between masculine activities such as mowing the lawn and feminine activities such as washing dishes. Children and adults in a third condition predicted the choices of boy and girl actors without hearing any stories beforehand. That is, they made predictions knowing only the actors' sex. This condition was included to see how much knowing the actor's past activity choices affected the predictions in the other two conditions.

This boy is helping his mother make burritos, an activity that fits the stereotypes for girls better than those for boys. Do you think other children would expect this boy to choose to make burritos in the future? If he did make that choice, do you think other children would expect him to be popular with peers? As you read, you'll see that the answers to these questions vary with children's age.

As figure 14.2 shows, third-graders' predictions differed sharply from those of sixth graders and college students. (Kindergartners' predictions were difficult to interpret because their knowledge of the stereotypes tested in the study was poorer than that of older subjects.) The rather flat lines in the figure for third graders show that they made similar predictions in all conditions. Most third graders expected boys and girls to choose stereotypical activities, regardless of their past activity choices. For example, they expected that boys who had chosen to bake brownies would choose masculine activities in the future. They expected that girls who had chosen to fix a bicycle would choose feminine activities in the future. Third graders seemed to say, "She is a girl, so despite what she did before, she will act like a girl," or, "He is a boy, so despite what he did before, he will act like a boy."

College students responded very differently. The results for girl actors are most striking. College students predicted that a girl who had chosen masculine activities in the past would choose masculine activities in the future. Indeed, college students expected such a girl to choose masculine activities as often as a boy in the actor's-sex-only condition, whose past choices were unknown. College students' predictions about a boy who had chosen feminine activities showed the same pattern but were not as extreme.

What were these college students thinking? Were they ignoring sex stereotypes when they predicted that a girl might choose masculine activities and a boy might choose feminine activities? Are their predictions a sign of stereotype flexibility? Not exactly.

A popular book a few years ago had the title *Real Men Don't Eat Quiche*. The title was intended to be humorous, of course, but let's take it seriously. It implies that eating quiche is inconsistent with the stereotypes for men. As you know (with your vast stereotype knowledge), men are supposed to eat steak and potatoes. So what inference should be made about a man who eats quiche? Perhaps that he is not a "real" man—or not stereotypically masculine. College students often make inferences about people's masculinity and femininity from information about their activities, occupations, social behavior, and maybe even what they like to eat (Deaux & Lewis, 1984).

Similar inferences are involved in college students' predictions about boys' and girls' activity choices. After hearing that a girl chose masculine activities such as fixing a bike, college students apparently inferred that the girl usually preferred masculine activities, or was a tomboy. Therefore, they predicted she would choose masculine activities in the future, too.

So what do college students say to themselves to explain their predictions? They might say something like this: "She is a girl, but not all girls prefer feminine activities. I can judge

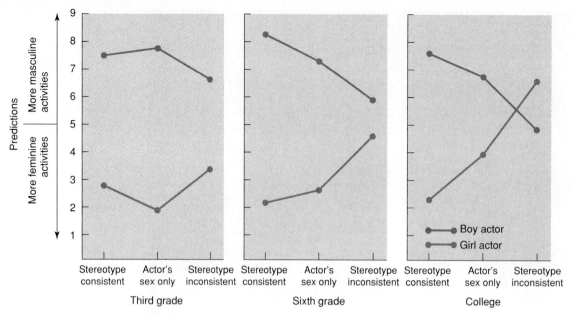

## FIGURE 14.2

College students predict that actors who previously chose activities inconsistent with sex stereotypes will choose similar activities in the future. Third graders predict that an actor's activity choices will be consistent with sex stereotypes, regardless of the actor's previous choices. Sixth-graders' predictions are intermediate. In short, as children grow older they increasingly acknowledge that not all people act in accordance with sex stereotypes.

Adapted from T. J. Berndt & K. A. Heller, "Gender stereotypes and social inferences: A developmental study" in *Journal of Personality and Social Psychology*, 50:889–898. Copyright © 1986 by The American Psychological Association. Adapted by permission.

how feminine this girl is, and predict how feminine her future activities will be, if I pay attention to her past activity choices." Similarly, they might say, "He is a boy, but not all boys prefer masculine activities. I can judge how masculine this boy is, and predict how masculine his future activities will be, if I pay attention to his past activity choices."

Notice that these students are not ignoring sex stereotypes. Rather, they are applying the stereotypes in a more sophisticated fashion than younger children do. They are, in short, predicting from the masculinity or femininity of previous choices to that of future choices.

As children grow, they more often make inferences like those of adults (Biernat, 1991). Notice in figure 14.2 that the pattern of sixth-graders' responses is intermediate between that of third graders and college students. Even third graders sometimes consider an actor's past behavior when judging the actor's future behavior (Martin, 1989). They do so when the past behavior is inconsistent with strong stereotypes. For example, third graders expect a boy who likes to play with dolls to choose other feminine toys more often than a boy who likes to play with trucks. Below third grade, children largely ignore an actor's past choices even when those choices are extremely different from the ones typical for their sex. That is, preschool and kindergarten children always predict that "boys will be boys" and "girls will be girls."

What, then, do children think about those boys who do not behave like most boys, or those girls who do not behave like most girls? In other words, how do children react to other children whose behavior is inconsistent with sex stereotypes? Do positive reactions to such children increase with age, with the increase in stereotype flexibility?

During the elementary-school years, behavior inconsistent with sex stereotypes is not viewed as wrong, but children often report that they would dislike peers who behave in that way. Children probably are most attracted to peers whose behavior is stereotypical because they perceive their own behavior as stereotypical (Carter & McCloskey, 1983–1984).

Positive reactions to behavior inconsistent with sex stereotypes do not increase between childhood and adolescence (Berndt & Heller, 1986; Carter & McCloskey, 1983–1984). Reactions differ greatly, however, for boys and girls. Adolescents expect girls with masculine

interests (or tomboys) to be more accepted than boys with feminine interests (or sissies) (Berndt & Heller, 1986; Huston, 1983). Similarly, adolescents expect boys who play games with girls to be less popular than girls who play games with boys (Lobel et al., 1993). These differences are another indication that the stereotypes for girls' behavior are weaker or less confining than those for boys' behavior (Maccoby, 1980).

Nevertheless, certain violations of sex stereotypes may be taboo for both boys and girls. The actual popularity of children whose behavior is inconsistent with sex stereotypes has rarely been assessed. For one study, however, 10- and 11-year-olds were observed repeatedly during summer camps that lasted four weeks (Sroufe et al., 1993). Children who interacted more often with the opposite sex were less popular, whether they were boys or girls. These findings suggest that choosing same-sex peers as social partners is an especially important element of sex roles in middle childhood.

Finally, you might have expected to have heard more, by this point, about historical changes in sex stereotypes. In the United States and many other countries, the social roles of men and women have changed dramatically during recent decades. You read about some of these changes in earlier chapters. However, these changes would not necessarily affect people's judgments about the typical traits, social behaviors, and interests of males and females.

To understand what has changed over time, think again about the distinction between stereotype knowledge and stereotype flexibility. Judgments about which personality traits and behaviors are more typical of males than females have changed little in recent decades, whether those judgments have been made by children, or adults (Golombok & Fivush, 1994; Ruble, 1988; Signorella et al., 1993). In other words, major changes have not occurred in those types of stereotype knowledge, because changing social roles do not automatically change personality traits and social behavior. Boys are, probably, still more messy than girls; girls are, probably, still more gentle than boys (see table 14.2).

By contrast, changes have occurred in some facets of stereotype flexibility (Signorella et al., 1993). More children today than 20 years ago think that both men and women can be firefighters. More children today than 20 years ago think that boys and girls can learn to sew. In sum, changes in society have led to changes in children's and adolescents' beliefs about which social roles and activities are open to both men and women.

# DIFFERENCES BETWEEN BOYS AND GIRLS: SAMPLING THE EVIDENCE

As stated earlier, stereotypes sometimes have a basis in reality. In many of the components of sex typing outlined in table 14.1, the average boy does differ from the average girl. No attempt is made in this chapter to describe all the differences. Such a description would take up the entire chapter, and more. (One review of the literature [Maccoby & Jacklin, 1974] had an annotated bibliography more than 200 pages long, but other researchers criticized that review for excluding relevant studies [Block, 1976].)

This section provides only a sampling of the evidence, as the heading suggests. Examples of sex differences from each content area in table 14.1 are considered. As you read about these differences, you will probably find yourself asking why they exist. You'll need to wait for a full answer to that question until the next section, which examines theories of sex-role development. Before you learn about those theories, you should know the evidence they are intended to explain.

Two general points should be kept in mind as you read about the evidence on sex differences. First, many conclusions about sex differences are controversial (Buss, 1995; Eagly, 1995; Hyde & Plant, 1995; Marecek, 1995). Even when two researchers review the same studies, they may summarize the findings differently. One researcher may conclude that a sex difference exists for a particular type of behavior. The other may conclude that the difference is not consistently found or is so small that it has no theoretical or practical significance. In this section, you will hear about both sides of these controversies. You will also find references to the relevant research so you can, if you want, explore questions in more depth and draw your own conclusions.

Second, even when statistically significant differences between males and females exist, the distributions of the scores for males and females often overlap greatly. Consider the example of height. On the average, men are taller than women, yet you probably know men who are shorter than most women and women who are taller than most men. Sex differences in psychological characteristics are usually smaller than the sex difference in height (Pool, 1994).

Still, not all sex differences in psychological characteristics are small (Eagly, 1995). In the next few pages, you will read about some sex differences that are small and others that are large. Stated differently, you will read about some components of sex typing where boys and girls are more similar than different. You will read about other components of sex typing where most boys differ from most girls. Pay careful attention, therefore, to information not only about how boys differ from girls, on the average, but about how big these average differences are.

## Biological and Physical Characteristics

Important biological differences exist between males and females. The two sexes differ in chromosomes, internal organs, genitals or external sex organs, and secondary sex characteristics. They also differ in size and strength. For example, chapter 5 included figures showing that, except in early adolescence, the average boy is taller than the average girl. Those figures also showed that the average boy is heavier than the average girl after puberty but not before. Differences in boys' and girls' height also increase after puberty.

On many tests of physical abilities, boys perform better than girls (Thomas & French, 1985). For example, boys have a stronger grip, can jump farther, and can throw a ball farther, faster, and more accurately than girls. The difference in the speed with which boys and girls can throw a ball is especially large. Robert Pool (1994) illustrated the size of this difference using the example of a hypothetical contest.

Suppose that you randomly selected a hundred 11-year-olds, half of whom were boys and half were girls. You asked all the children to throw a ball as fast as they could. Then you picked the 50 children who threw the ball the fastest; that is, you identified which children threw faster than the average for the group as a whole. How many would be boys? Given the effect size found in previous research, the 50 "winners" of this contest would typically include 48 boys and 2 girls.

On measures of activity level that involve large-muscle or whole-body movements, girls also receive lower scores than boys (Eaton & Enns, 1986; Eaton & Yu, 1989). By contrast, girls' performance is superior to that of boys on fine motor tasks (Pool, 1994; Thomas & French, 1985). Girls are better than boys at tasks such as tracing, sewing, and other tasks requiring manual dexterity. Moreover, the sex differences in activity level and physical abilities often increase with age. Like the sex differences in height and weight, sex differences in physical abilities are often largest after puberty.

In basic biological health, girls and women also are superior to boys and men. Researchers estimate that male embryos outnumber female embryos by at least 20 percent, but only about 5 percent more males than females are born (Pool, 1994). This means that fewer males than females survive the prenatal period. Even those males who do live until birth suffer from birth complications more than females do. In addition, males more often have developmental problems such as bed-wetting. Throughout life, males seem more vulnerable than females to disease or injury (Jacklin, 1989; Maccoby & Jacklin, 1974).

Females also live longer than males. Suppose you thought of life itself as a contest, and asked how many men and women live at least to age 85. You pick 50 "winners" of this contest at random, and then see how many are women. According to U.S. Census Bureau (1995a) statistics, about 36 would be women and only 14 would be men. These statistics and those mentioned earlier illustrate that the biological differences between males and females are large and significant.

## Personality Traits and Social Behavior

You read earlier that young children assume boys are more aggressive than girls. Research data confirm this assumption. Janet Hyde (1984) identified 143 studies of boys' and girls'

aggressive behavior that were done between 1935 and 1981. Then she did a meta-analysis of these studies. As mentioned in chapter 2, a meta-analysis summarizes the evidence from several studies. Differences between groups are expressed with a score, $\partial$, which is a measure of effect size. In meta-analyses of sex differences, $\partial$ is the difference between the means for males and females in standard deviation units. A $\partial$ of .50, for example, indicates that the mean scores for males and females are half a standard deviation apart.

For studies of aggressive behavior, Hyde (1984) found that the median value of $\partial$, across all studies, was .50, with males higher. On the average, males are more aggressive than females, and the average scores of males and females differ by half a standard deviation. The meta-analysis also showed that males were both more physically aggressive and more verbally aggressive than females. The sex difference was found in studies done in both laboratory and natural settings. The difference existed throughout childhood and adolescence, as early as 2 years of age.

Some stereotypes about girls' traits and behaviors are also valid. The chapter began with examples of how girls and boys in one Philippine community cared for babies. Some researchers in the United States observed boys' and girls' interactions with babies under standard conditions (Berman & Goodman, 1984). Children who attended a child-care center were asked to take care of a baby for a few minutes. Observers recorded what the children did during that time, paying special attention to how much the children interacted with the baby.

As figure 14.3 shows, girls from 2½ to 5½ years of age interacted with the baby no more than did boys the same ages. Girls from 5½ to 7½ years of age, by contrast, interacted with the baby far more than same-age boys did. Older girls often gave toys to the baby, talked to the baby, and touched or held the baby. Boys less often gave the baby toys or talked with the baby. None of the boys in the study, in either age group, ever touched or held the baby—even accidentally!

Konrad Lorenz (1943, cited in Berman, 1980), an ethologist mentioned in earlier chapters, assumed that young girls are innately programmed to respond to infants with nurturant behavior. He assumed that these responses would be evident by 2 years of age. The data from this study and others suggest that Lorenz was wrong. Before 5 years of age, boys respond to babies as much as girls do. Boys' styles of interaction are less physical and more verbal than those of girls, but young boys are as responsive to babies as young girls are. Only after 5 years of age do girls become more responsive to babies than boys are. This age change is not unusual. Sex differences on many characteristics increase during childhood and adolescence (Block, 1976).

Sex differences in some behaviors are apparent very early. As infants, girls are more responsive to other infants' cries than boys are (Hoffman, 1977). Female infants more often start to cry when they hear another infant crying than male infants do. Some researchers view these data as showing that girls are more empathic than boys, more likely to react emotionally to expressions of emotions by other people. A sex difference in empathy would fit the stereotype that girls are more emotional and sensitive than boys.

During childhood and adolescence, girls report more empathic feelings than boys. That is, girls say that they feel bad when other people are in trouble more often than boys do (Eisenberg & Lennon, 1983). However, when researchers have observed children's facial or gestural expressions of empathy, they have found little difference between boys and girls. For example, when watching a sad movie or listening to a tape recording of a crying infant, girls do not show more intense emotional reactions than boys. Apparently, girls and boys perceive themselves as differing in empathy more than they actually do.

If girls were more empathic than boys, you might expect them to show more active concern for others by helping people in need. However, when researchers have used comparable procedures to assess helping by boys and girls, they have not found consistent differences between the two sexes (Radke-Yarrow et al., 1983). Sometimes girls are more helpful than boys; sometimes boys are more helpful than girls; often there is no difference between the two sexes.

The reason for the mixed results became clear when researchers considered the types of helping that are associated with the male and female roles (Eagly, 1987). Males are expected to

FIGURE 14.3

After 5½ years of age, but not before, girls spend more time interacting with a baby than boys do. (Source: Berman & Goodman, 1984.)

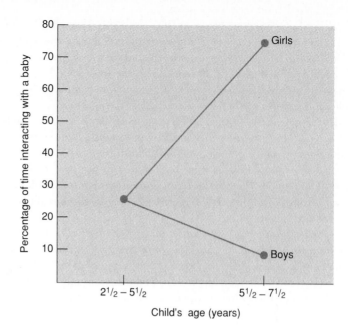

**instrumental traits**
*Aspects of personality such as independence that are related both to getting things done in the world and to judgments of masculinity.*

**expressive traits**
*Aspects of personality such as kindness that are related to emotionality, concern for others, and judgments of femininity.*

be helpful in situations where chivalry or heroism is required, and they are. For example, men are likely to volunteer to carry a woman's heavy boxes or to try to stop a thief from stealing someone's belongings. Women are expected to be helpful when care or nurturance is required, and they are. For example, women are likely to volunteer to work with retarded children.

Several researchers have defined broad dimensions of personality that are associated with male and female roles. Janet Spence and Robert Helmreich (1978) proposed that **instrumental traits,** those linked to getting things done in the world, are most closely related to masculinity. Aggressiveness, ambition, and independence are examples. **Expressive traits,** those linked to emotionality and concern for others, are most closely related to femininity. Gentleness, kindness, and tact are examples.

Spence and Helmreich devised the Personal Attributes Questionnaire (or PAQ) for measuring adults' perceptions of these personality dimensions. Judith Hall and Amy Halberstadt (1980) created a version for children called the Children's PAQ (or CPAQ). Table 14.3 lists some items on this measure. Children respond to each item by saying how true it is for them, so the scale deals with the component of sex typing defined in table 14.1 as self-perceptions of personality.

The masculine scale on the CPAQ includes items related to the instrumental dimension of personality and the male sex role. No item mentions aggressive behavior because the scale measures only neutral or desirable aspects of masculinity. Similarly, the feminine scale includes neutral or desirable aspects of the expressive dimension of personality and the female sex role.

When children respond to the CPAQ items, girls usually have higher scores than boys on the feminine scale; boys usually have higher scores than girls on the masculine scale. The differences in boys' and girls' self-descriptions are not always significant (e.g., Mitchell, Baker, & Jacklin, 1989). However, the differences are very consistent across samples.

Meta-analyses of more than a hundred studies that included more than a hundred thousand children and adults have revealed sex differences in instrumental and expressive traits (Feingold, 1994). Males report greater assertiveness and less anxiety than females. Females report greater tender-mindedness, or empathy and nurturance, than males. The effect sizes for these differences are similar to those for aggressive behavior, around .50.

**gender intensification**
*The hypothesis that differences in the personalities of boys and girls increase after puberty.*

Do the sex differences in personality increase after puberty, as those in biological features and physical abilities do? John Hill and Mary Lynch (1983) proposed such a **gender intensification** hypothesis, but the data on the hypothesis are inconsistent.

For one longitudinal study, boys and girls reported on their masculinity and femininity when they were in the sixth, seventh, and eighth grades (Galambos, Almeida, & Petersen,

| TABLE 14.3 | Sample Items on the Masculine and Feminine Scales of the Children's Personal Attributes Questionnaire (CPAQ) |
|---|---|
| *Masculine Scale* | I really want to get ahead in life. |
| | I hate to lose a game or have other kids do better than me. |
| | When I meet someone, I am always the first to try and make friends. |
| | In most ways, I am better than most of the other kids my age. |
| | I would rather do things for myself than ask grown-ups and other kids for help. |
| | I am more busy and active than most of the other kids my age. |
| *Feminine Scale* | My feelings get stirred up easily. |
| | I am a very considerate person. |
| | I am kind to other people almost all of the time. |
| | I try to do everything I can for the people I care about. |
| | I am a gentle person. |
| | I almost always notice how other people are feeling. |

Adapted from J. A. Hall & A. G. Halberstadt, "Masculinity and femininity in children: Development of the children's personal attributes questionnaire," in *Developmental Psychology*, 16:270–280. Copyright © 1980 by The American Psychological Association. Adapted with permission.

1990). The sex difference in boys' and girls' masculinity increased with age, as the gender intensification hypothesis suggests. The sex difference in boys' and girls' femininity did not change as they grew older. Other data suggest that sex differences in masculine and feminine traits do not increase between the high school and college years (Feingold, 1994).

You might also have heard people say that girls are more psychologically mature than boys. This belief was confirmed, in part, by another meta-analysis (Cohn, 1991). On a measure of ego development devised by Jane Loevinger (1976), the complexity of people's psychological insight into themselves and other people is defined by a sequence of stages. Adolescent girls score at higher stages on this measure than adolescent boys. The effect size for this sex difference is between .50 and .70. The difference does not exist before adolescence and it disappears during adulthood. That is, girls truly are precocious: They reach their adult level of ego development sooner than boys do.

## Activities, Interests, and Cognitive Abilities

If you were reading carefully, you probably noticed that the sex differences in personality traits and social behavior are smaller than many sex differences in physical abilities. Sex differences in personality traits and social behaviors also are smaller than many sex differences in activities, interests, and cognitive abilities (Huston, 1983).

Boys and girls choose different activities and express different interests very early, before 2 years of age. To chart the emergence of these differences, researchers gave 1- and 2-year-olds opportunities to play with various toys (O'Brien & Huston, 1985). Some toys were traditionally masculine, like a set of tools and a truck. Other toys were traditionally feminine, like a doll and a tea set. Neutral toys were also provided, so the children were not forced to choose between masculine and feminine toys.

Even at 15 months of age, boys played with the tools, truck, and other masculine toys more than girls did (see figure 14.4). This sex difference increased with age because girls played less with the masculine toys as they grew older. A sex difference in play with feminine toys was not apparent as early. Between 15 and 18 months of age, girls played with the doll, the tea set, and other feminine toys no more often than boys did. After that age, girls played with the feminine toys more often than boys did. By 20 months of age, then, children of both sexes obviously preferred sex-typed toys.

The activities and interests of boys and girls diverge even more in middle childhood (Zill, 1985). For example, young boys often like playing with guns, but most girls don't. Young girls often like dancing, but most boys don't. As they grow older, many boys but few

FIGURE 14.4

Even at 15 months of age, boys
spend more time playing with
masculine toys than girls do.
The preference of girls for
feminine toys is not apparent
until later, at around 19 or 20
months of age.

From M. O'Brien & A. C. Huston,
"Development of sex-typed play behavior in
toddlers" in *Developmental Psychology*,
21:866–871. Copyright © 1985 by The
American Psychological Association.
Reprinted by permission.

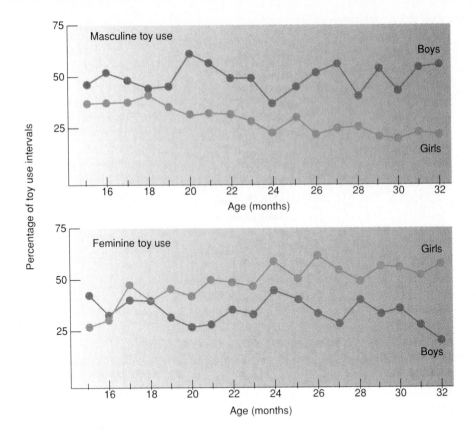

girls enjoy aggressive sports like boxing. These differences in activities and interests are often
extremely large, leaving little overlap between the two sexes. You could probably name girls
whom you consider fairly aggressive or boys whom you consider fairly gentle. You would
have a harder time naming any female quarterbacks or any men who do needlepoint.

Sex differences in activities and interests have often been dismissed as obvious and
unimportant, but they may affect the skills that children develop and the careers that they
choose (Huston, 1983). These effects are considered later, along with a discussion of the possible implications of traditional sex-role development.

Most adults have assumed that children's cognitive abilities are more important for
their future lives than their activities and interests. Commonly held stereotypes suggest that
verbal ability is greater in girls and mathematical ability is greater in boys. These stereotypes
also seem to be accepted by adolescents themselves (Bornholt, Goodnow, & Cooney, 1994).

After a thorough review of the available research, Eleanor Maccoby and Carol Jacklin
(1974) concluded that the stereotypes were valid. However, since Maccoby and Jacklin published their conclusions, many other researchers have reexamined the question of sex differences in abilities. The current state of affairs is more complicated than the stereotypes suggest.

One widely used measure of cognitive abilities is the Preliminary Scholastic Aptitude
Test, or PSAT. You may have taken this test as a high-school junior. The PSAT yields two
scores, one for verbal ability and one for mathematical ability. The test was first standardized
on more than 10,000 high-school juniors in 1960. It was standardized again in 1966, 1974,
and 1983. The total number of students in these standardization samples was nearly 100,000.

In the 1966 standardization sample, females had higher average scores on the verbal
scale, and males had higher average scores on the math scale (Feingold, 1988). Figure 14.5
shows the differences between the mean scores for males and females expressed as effect
sizes. Note that a negative $\partial$ indicates a difference favoring females; a positive $\partial$ indicates a
difference favoring males. So far, the data support common stereotypes and Maccoby and
Jacklin's (1974) conclusions.

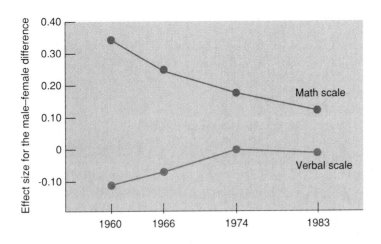

FIGURE 14.5
The effect size (∂) for the sex difference in scores on the verbal portion of the Preliminary Scholastic Aptitude Test (or PSAT) decreased to nearly zero between 1960 and 1983. The effect size for the sex difference in scores on the math portion of the test also decreased during that period. Positive effect sizes indicate higher mean scores for males. (Source: Feingold, 1988.)

Look, though, at what happened to the ∂s on these scales in later years. The mean differences between males and females decreased dramatically. On the verbal scale, the mean difference dropped to only two-hundredths of a standard deviation by 1983. On the math scale, the mean difference dropped from about one-third to about one-tenth of a standard deviation.

Other researchers have also found that sex differences in adolescents' verbal and mathematical abilities have decreased within the past few decades (Feingold, 1988; Friedman, 1989; Hyde & Linn, 1988). Some researchers argue that the best conclusion, now, is that sex differences in verbal ability are absent and sex differences in math ability are unimportant. Other researchers have written articles with titles proclaiming, "Cognitive Gender Differences Are Disappearing" (Feingold, 1988).

This conclusion is probably premature (Halpern, 1992). On some measures of verbal ability, girls continue to receive higher scores than boys. Girls are better than boys at spelling (Feingold, 1988); girls are better than boys in reading (Feingold, 1993). Moreover, you should note that the PSAT results illustrated in figure 14.5 are for samples of adolescents. More recent studies suggest that the sex differences in cognitive abilities have decreased in recent decades *only* for adolescents. When test scores have been compared for children and for adults, little change over time has been found in the magnitude of sex differences (Feingold, 1993).

Similarly, boys are better than girls in mechanical reasoning (Feingold, 1988); boys are also better than girls on most tests of spatial ability (Voyer et al., 1995). The male superiority is especially great on the mental rotation task described in chapter 2. On some versions of the task, the effect size for the sex difference is greater than .90. Moreover, the difference has increased rather than decreased in recent years (Voyer et al., 1995).

On measures of mathematical ability, the pattern of sex differences is more complex (Feingold, 1993; Hyde, Fennema, & Lamon, 1990). During the elementary-school grades, girls' math scores are often higher than those of boys, because girls excel at the computation that is emphasized in those grades. During the secondary-school grades, boys' math scores are often higher than those of girls, because boys excel in the abstract problem solving that is emphasized in those grades. The male advantage has been shown not only in U.S. samples but also in other countries such as Japan and Taiwan (Lummis & Stevenson, 1990).

Has the male advantage decreased in recent decades, as the data in figure 14.5 on the PSAT imply? The evidence on this issue is mixed (Feingold, 1993; Hyde et al., 1990). Some evidence against significant changes has come from research on a special group, seventh graders with exceptional mathematical talent. *Practical Applications of Research:* "Mathematical Reasoning Ability in Boys and Girls" describes an important research program on that group of adolescents, which includes far more boys than girls.

# MATHEMATICAL REASONING ABILITY
# IN BOYS AND GIRLS

In 1972 Camilla Benbow and Julian Stanley (1980) identified seventh graders who scored among the top 5 percent of U.S. students on a standardized math achievement test. Then these students, who were 12 or 13 years old, took the Scholastic Aptitude Test (SAT). On the SAT math scale, the talented boys received scores substantially higher than the talented girls. The boys' mean score was 460; the girls' mean score was 423.

Benbow and Stanley repeated their talent search in the following years. Boys always had higher mean scores on the SAT math scale than girls. Moreover, the size of the sex difference changed little during the next 15 years (Benbow, 1988).

Figure 14.6 shows the distribution of SAT math scores for the students who participated in the talent search from 1980 through 1983. More girls than boys scored below 400 on the scale; more boys than girls scored above 500. The mean difference between boys and girls was just over 30 points, but the imbalance of boys and girls was greatest for extremely high scores, those over 600.

These findings are extremely controversial. When Benbow (1988) reviewed this research and presented her explanation for the sex difference, 42 other researchers wrote commentaries in which they agreed with or, more often, disputed her conclusions. Most researchers granted that the SAT math scores of talented boys and girls differ. They did not agree on why the differences exist or what their consequences are.

The sources of these sex differences are discussed later, along with explanations of sex-role development. The consequences—or lack of consequences—of these differences may surprise you. During high school, the talented girls took as many advanced math classes as the boys did. In college, the talented females majored in mathematics as often as the talented males did. However, more males than females majored in engineering, computer science, and the physical sciences. More males than females entered graduate programs in math or science after college.

Marcia Linn and Janet Hyde (1989) have suggested that the sex difference in SAT math scores is only one contributor to sex differences in college majors and career choices—and it may not be a major one. They argue that girls have less confidence in their math ability than boys do, even

when their grades match those of boys. Girls may also be less assertive in math classes, deferring often to males. Finally, girls who are aiming for stereotypically feminine occupations may not view math skills as important.

Other researchers, including Camilla Benbow, suggest that sex differences in college majors and career choices are not necessarily a source of concern (Pool, 1994). If these differences reflect males' and females' interests and choices, rather than differences in educational opportunities, they need not be the target of special interventions.

What do you think? Should educators always assume there is a problem when boys and girls differ in their performance on cognitive tests? If you think there is a problem, how would you solve it?

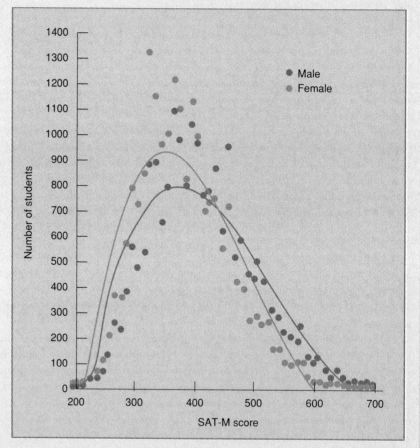

## FIGURE 14.6

Among the intellectually talented seventh graders who participated in Benbow and Stanley's studies, the mean score of girls on the SAT math scale was lower than the mean score of boys. Also, more boys than girls had scores above 600 on the scale. (Source: Benbow, 1988.)

# Gender-Based Social Relationships

When school-age children name their best friends, they almost always name peers of the same sex (Berndt, 1988). The few children who name an opposite-sex peer as a best friend are rarely named by the peer in return. The separation between the sexes in close peer relationships is almost total.

Children also interact most frequently with same-sex peers. The bias toward same-sex interaction increases with age. Eighteen-month-olds interact with opposite-sex peers about as often as with same-sex peers. Girls initiate interactions with other girls more than with boys by 27 months of age; boys do not show a similar bias until 36 months of age (Lafreniere, Strayer, & Gauthier, 1984). By 4 years of age, children interact three times as often with same-sex peers as with opposite-sex peers. By 6 years of age, the ratio of same-sex to opposite-sex peer interaction is 11 to 1 (Maccoby, 1990).

Preferences for same-sex friends and same-sex interaction may be related to differences in boys' and girls' styles of play. You learned earlier that boys are more aggressive than girls are. Boys also spend more time in **rough-and-tumble play** with peers than girls do (Maccoby, 1990). Rough-and-tumble play refers to wrestling, pretend fighting, and jumping on one another. In addition, when boys want to get something or do something, they express their desires assertively. They will order their peers around instead of relying on persuasion. If a child is blocking their way, they may simply push the child aside (Charlesworth & Dzur, 1987). No wonder girls stay away from them when they can!

In adolescence and adulthood, gender-based social relationships change dramatically in nature and significance. Most males and females report sexual arousal by, and sexual behavior with, members of the opposite sex. However, some males and females report sexual arousal by and sexual behavior with members of the same sex. In short, the sexual orientation of adolescents and adults can be either heterosexual or homosexual.

Differences in adults' sexual orientations are related to their reports of sex-typed behavior in childhood (Bailey & Zucker, 1995). Homosexual men and women more often report dressing in opposite-sex clothing when they were children than heterosexual adults do. Homosexual adults report greater preferences in childhood for toys and activities stereotyped as appropriate for the opposite sex. In addition, these adults report having had more opposite-sex playmates in childhood. The effect sizes for these differences vary, but most are greater than .50 and some are greater than 1.0.

Adults' reports could be questioned because their memory for childhood experiences might be biased by their current sexual orientation (Baumrind, 1995). This problem does not exist with longitudinal studies. About 100 boys who visited clinics because they showed extreme patterns of opposite-sex behavior have been followed in longitudinal studies (Bailey & Zucker, 1995). Many of these boys became homosexual adults. This result implies that sex-typed activities and interests in childhood are linked to gender-based social relationships in adulthood.

You should be aware, though, that studies with representative samples of children show weak or nonsignificant relationships among the different components of sex typing (Maccoby, 1988; Powlishta, Serbin, & Moller, 1993; Serbin et al., 1993). In these samples, preferences for sex-typed activities are not related to children's frequency of interaction with same-sex playmates. Similarly, preferences for same-sex playmates are not related to the flexibility of children's stereotypes about child activities, adult occupations, and personality traits. Children's preferences for sex-typed activities are related to their interest in sex-typed adult occupations, but this relation is weak.

The same point can be stated in terms of the sex-typing components in table 14.1. A child who seems highly sex-typed on one component (e.g., personality traits and social behavior) may not be sex-typed on another component (e.g., preferences for adult occupations). The patterning of sex-role development is not that simple. You should expect, therefore, that several types of theories will be needed to explain the many components of sex typing.

**rough-and-tumble play**
*A style of play in which children wrestle, pretend to fight with each other, and jump on each other.*

# EXPLANATIONS OF SEX-ROLE DEVELOPMENT

Some theories of sex-role development emphasize biological influences. These theories take the *nature* side of the nature-nurture issue and argue that sex differences in genotypes and in biological development affect children's activities, behaviors, and personality. Other theorists emphasize the effects of *nurture*. They argue that differences in the socialization of boys and girls can account for the psychological differences between them. Still other theorists emphasize the impact of children's thinking, or *cognitive development*, on sex typing. Early in life, children learn whether they are boys or girls. Once they know which sex they are, they may try to act as they think children of their sex typically act.

No single theory is likely to explain all components of sex typing. In the following sections, you'll read about some evidence consistent with each of the three types of theories mentioned.

## Biological Theories, or the Nature of Boys and Girls

The first step in sex differentiation occurs at conception. As you recall, a normal girl receives X chromosomes from her mother and her father. A normal boy receives an X chromosome from his mother and a Y chromosome from his father. Boys and girls receive another 22 pairs of chromosomes that don't differ for the two sexes. In their genetic material, therefore, boys and girls are more alike than different.

The next step in sex differentiation takes place around the seventh week after conception (Moore, 1988). As you read in chapter 4, genes on the Y chromosome send a chemical signal to change the primitive sex organs of the embryo into testes. Once the testes develop, they release hormones called **androgens** that lead to the differentiation of the genitals, the external sex organs. The most important of these hormones is **testosterone.**

If the embryo has no Y chromosome, it develops as a female. Ovaries become apparent by the 10th week after fertilization. Development of the genital organs continues after that time but is largely completed during the first trimester. Later in the prenatal period, sex hormones affect the development of the brain. For example, they affect the area of the hypothalamus that influences sexual behavior in adulthood (Hood et al., 1987).

## Sex Chromosome Defects and Sex Typing

In chapter 3, you learned that some children are born with more or fewer sex chromosomes than normal. Children with Turner syndrome have only one sex chromosome, an X. They have the internal organs and the genitals of a female because, as just mentioned, female development occurs when embryos lack a Y chromosome. As you may recall, girls with Turner syndrome are short in stature and tend to receive low scores on tests of visual and spatial ability. The question for this chapter, however, is whether these girls differ in sex typing from girls who have the normal complement of two X chromosomes.

The answer to this question seems to be no. When girls with Turner syndrome are evaluated on measures of sex typing, they sometimes appear to be more feminine than average (Downey et al., 1987). More often, however, their scores do not differ from those of girls with normal chromosomes (Hines, 1982; Hood et al., 1987). Thus, having only one X chromosome does not make girls with Turner syndrome consistently less feminine or more feminine than is normal.

In rare cases, children are born with one X and two Y chromosomes. Their Y chromosomes ensure that they develop as males. Early studies suggested that XYY males are more aggressive than normal, XY males. More recent studies have not replicated this finding. Instead, the recent studies suggest that having two Y chromosomes is linked not to greater aggressive behavior but to slightly lower intelligence (Schiavi et al., 1988; Theilgaard, 1984). There is no evidence that XYY males are either more or less masculine than normal males.

Taken together, the studies of Turner syndrome females and XYY males suggest that sex-chromosome defects do not directly affect sex typing. These defects can cause a variety of problems, but they do not shed much light on the process of sex-role development.

---

**androgens**
*Hormones that normally have higher levels in males and that lead to the differentiation of the genitals during the prenatal period.*

**testosterone**
*The most important of the androgens, which contributes to masculinization during the prenatal period.*

---

## Hormonal Influences on Sex Typing

Children with normal sex chromosomes are occasionally exposed to abnormal levels of sex hormones during the prenatal period. Sometimes the adrenal glands of a fetus malfunction and produce excessive amounts of androgens. Boys with this problem show accelerated masculine development. They go through puberty during childhood, as early as 18 months of age (Money, 1987). But if the hormonal problem is detected early, their level of androgens can be regulated with cortisone so that they develop normally.

Females are more seriously affected by excessive androgen production during the prenatal period. The excess hormones can make a female's genitals look like those of a male. In extreme cases, a girl may be born with a clitoris that looks and functions like a penis. In less extreme cases, the clitoris may simply be enlarged. If doctors detect the hormonal problem shortly after birth, they can prevent the girl's further masculinization with regular doses of cortisone, just as with boys. Of course, cortisone given after birth cannot counter any effects of prenatal androgens on brain development.

Girls with a high level of prenatal androgen exposure seem, in childhood, more masculine in their activities and behavior than other girls (Berenbaum & Snyder, 1995; Collaer & Hines, 1995; Hines & Kaufman, 1994; Money & Ehrhardt, 1972). These girls prefer to play with cars more than and with dolls less than other girls do. Some of these girls prefer boys as playmates more often than is typical. However, they do not show an increased rate of the vigorous physical play typical of boys. Again, you see that the different components of sex typing are not always related. Prenatal hormones may affect some of these components but not others.

The sexual orientation of females with high prenatal androgen exposure may also differ from that of females with normal prenatal hormones. John Money (1987) studied 30 adult women with high prenatal androgen exposure. Eleven of these women said their sexual orientation was bisexual or lesbian. This proportion was higher than in a control group. Money concluded that the women's early androgen exposure had altered their brain development and predisposed them to a bisexual or lesbian orientation as adults.

Money cautioned that prenatal androgens alone do not determine whether a person will be masculine in interests and sexual orientation. Many girls exposed to prenatal androgens still develop feminine interests and a heterosexual orientation. In Money's study of 30 women, 12 were exclusively heterosexual as adults. (The rest of the women were noncommittal about their sexual orientation.) Other studies with larger samples indicate that prenatal androgens increase the chances of homosexuality but still leave most females with a heterosexual orientation (Collaer & Hines, 1995). This result suggests that prenatal hormones and socialization after birth both influence this component of sex typing.

Other researchers are skeptical of Money's conclusions about the effects of prenatal hormones. They point out that androgen-exposed girls whose genital organs look like those of males may receive different treatment from parents and other adults than normal girls. Although surgery after birth can make the girls' genitals look more normal, their parents may still see them as different. The behavior of these girls may also be affected by the cortisone given to regulate their hormonal levels. Cortisone can increase children's activity levels and so make girls seem more like tomboys (Huston, 1983; Hood et al., 1987).

Arguments for the effects of hormones are bolstered by evidence on other biological conditions. Prenatal exposure to some hormones seems to affect sex-role development without affecting the appearance of the genitals (Collaer & Hines, 1995; Meyer-Bahlburg et al., 1995). Recall from chapter 4 that DES is an artificial estrogen that, when given to pregnant women, increases the risk of one type of vaginal and cervical cancer in their daughters. The genitals of these daughters are not obviously abnormal. However, the daughters were exposed to estrogens prenatally, and normal girls are not. Prenatal estrogen exposure does not consistently lead to homosexuality in adulthood, but it is related to an above-average rate of bisexual or homosexual dreams and imagery.

Keep in mind, however, that the discussion so far has focused on *abnormal* exposure to sex hormones. You might ask whether normal variations in prenatal hormones are also related to variations in sex typing. Unfortunately, evidence on this question is limited and

inconclusive (Collaer & Hines, 1995). Levels of sex hormones in newborns' umbilical cords are related to certain characteristics at age 6 (e.g., spatial ability and timidity), but the relations are complex and sometimes vary with sex (Jacklin, 1989).

At puberty, hormones contribute to the development of secondary sex characteristics and the activation of new behaviors. During adolescence, boys with higher levels of the male hormone, testosterone, engage in more sexual behavior (Udry, 1988). Hormonal levels are also related to the sexual behavior of adolescent girls, but the effects are weaker and are complicated by other variables. In addition, adolescents with more testosterone or other androgens show more aggressive behavior (Olweus et al., 1980; Susman et al., 1987).

Does this mean, as many popular writers suggest, that hormones drive adolescents to sex and aggression? Not necessarily. A relation exists between hormonal levels and those behaviors, but relations can go in two directions. One recent study suggested that increases in testosterone levels do make adolescent boys more likely to respond aggressively to provocations or threats (Olweus et al., 1988). Another study with male rhesus monkeys suggested that increases in testosterone levels are often caused by a monkey's participation in a fight or aggressive encounter (Rose, Bernstein, & Gordon, 1975). These studies suggest that hormonal levels affect behavior and behavior affects hormonal levels in an interactive process.

## Strengthening the Case for Genetic Differences

Only a few researchers check children's chromosomes or measure their hormonal levels to explore biological influences on sex typing. Most researchers rely on other types of evidence that suggest, but do not prove, that sex differences in behavior or other characteristics have a genetic basis. In other words, they strengthen the case for "nature" as the source of sex differences in behavior but are not conclusive. You have read about some of these types before, so only one example of each is given.

***Evidence from Nonhuman Primates***    The nonhuman primates, monkeys and apes, are the evolutionary and biological relatives of humans. Of course, monkeys and apes do not have a language or the social institutions of human cultures. Therefore, when sex differences in the behavior of nonhuman primates match sex differences in human behavior, our common genetic heritage is often the most plausible explanation.

For example, males are more aggressive than females in most species of monkeys and apes. The primate species that is closest, biologically, to human beings is the chimpanzee. Male chimpanzees are 4 to 10 times as aggressive as females. This difference strengthens arguments that sex differences in children's aggressive behavior are partly due to genetic differences between boys and girls (Maccoby & Jacklin, 1980).

On the other hand, human behavior is less instinctive and more influenced by learning than is the behavior of other primates. Consequently, researchers hesitate to apply findings about nonhuman primates directly to the human species. Yet, as Maccoby and Jacklin (1980) state, "There are similarities that reflect our evolutionary history, and animal studies can sometimes guide us to important discoveries at the human level" (p. 972). They can, in particular, suggest a genetic basis for sex differences in human behavior.

***Evidence from Cross-Cultural Studies***    If the sex difference in some behavior is strongly influenced by socialization pressures, cross-cultural variations in the sex difference might be expected. After all, cultures differ greatly in the behaviors they allow and prohibit. However, if comparable differences between the sexes are found in all cultures, sex differences in the human genotype are likely to be the reason.

Researchers have observed children's aggressive behavior in more than a dozen cultures around the world. In no culture were girls generally more aggressive than boys. In almost all cultures, boys were generally more aggressive than girls (Maccoby & Jacklin, 1980; Whiting & Edwards, 1988). Because researchers have not studied children's development in all human cultures, they cannot say that the sex difference in aggressive behavior is universal. Still, you would expect more variation across cultures if the difference had no genetic basis.

These two male chimpanzees are making threat gestures toward another male chimp who is not in the picture. In primates like the chimpanzees, just as in humans, males generally are more aggressive than females are.

*Evidence from Newborn Infants*    Sex differences in the behavior of newborn infants are usually attributed to their nature rather than their nurture. Newborns have not been shaped by interacting with people, so researchers who find sex differences in their behavior often suggest that the differences reflect differences in boys' and girls' genotypes.

You read earlier that infant girls, only a few hours old, often start to cry when they hear another infant crying. Infant boys less often display such contagious crying. Hoffman (1977) argued that this contagious crying "is not true empathy, but it does suggest the possibility of a constitutional precursor that together with differences in socialization may account for later sex differences in empathy" (p. 720).

Hoffman is appropriately cautious in his conclusion. Even as newborns, boys and girls may be treated differently (e.g., in the newborn nursery). It is difficult to prove that no experiences during the first few hours of life contribute to the sex difference in contagious crying. Hoffman also argues for the joint influence of children's genotypes (or constitution) and their later socialization. Probably no differences in boys' and girls' behavior depend entirely on the differences in their genotypes.

*Evidence from Behavior-Genetics Research*    To study genetic influences on IQ, researchers often examine whether people who are more genetically similar have more similar IQs. The same strategy can be used to study genetic influences on sex-role development. For example, monozygotic (MZ) twins who have the same genotypes should be more similar in their masculinity and femininity than dizygotic (DZ) twins who are the same sex but have different genotypes.

Several studies support this assumption. In one study (Mitchell et al., 1989), 8- to 14-year-old MZ and DZ twins completed two questionnaire measures of masculinity and femininity, one of which was the CPAQ. As figure 14.7 shows, MZ twins were more similar in their masculinity and in their femininity than were same-sex DZ twins. These findings imply that children's genotypes affect masculinity and femininity of their personalities.

Why, you might ask, is such data treated only as strengthening the case for genetic differences, rather than proving the case conclusively? Consider the correlations in figure 14.7 carefully. The correlations show that differences in *individual* children's scores on the masculinity and femininity scales were related to differences in their genotypes. They do not show that differences in the *average* scores of boys and girls were due to an average difference between boys' and girls' genotypes.

In other words, the correlations provide information about the origins of differences between individuals; they do not provide information, directly, about the origins of differences between groups (i.e., boys vs. girls). Moreover, the information not provided by the correlations is more important when the goal is to explain why the average boy differs from the average girl.

Most surprising, the boys and girls in this twin study did not differ significantly in their average scores on the scales of the CPAQ (Mitchell et al., 1989). The absence of significant differences was mentioned earlier, with the comment that males and females differ less in their personality traits than in their activities and interests.

Nevertheless, suppose that researchers found significant sex differences in certain traits or behaviors. In addition, suppose that studies of twins or other genetically related persons showed that individual differences in genotypes were linked to the individual differences in these traits or behaviors. Then researchers would have evidence, but not completely conclusive evidence, that the average difference between the sexes may depend partly on genetic differences between them.

*No Evidence for Sex Differences in Socialization*    If a difference in boys' and girls' behavior cannot be linked to differences in socialization, the case for genetic contributions to the sex difference is strengthened. As you will see shortly, many sex differences in behavior are strongly linked to differences in socialization. However, this may not be true of the sex difference in exceptional mathematical ability.

Remember Camilla Benbow and Julian Stanley's (1980) research on academically talented adolescents (See *Practical Applications of Research:* Mathematical Reasoning Ability in Boys

FIGURE 14.7

Similarity correlations for
monozygotic (MZ) and
dizygotic (DZ) twins on the
masculinity and femininity
scales of the Children's Personal
Attributes Questionnaire. The
correlations show that MZ
twins perceive themselves as
more similar in masculinity and
femininity than DZ twins. This
difference suggests there is
some genetic influence on sex
typing. (Source: Mitchell
et al., 1989.)

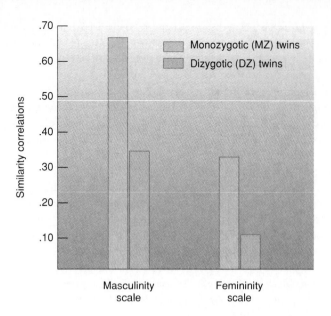

and Girls on p. 580). When seventh graders are given the SAT, far more boys than girls receive math scores above 600. After this sex difference was discovered, Camilla Benbow (1988) tried strenuously to identify differences in boys' and girls' social experiences that might account for it. Did the boys take more advanced math classes than the girls? No, they did not. Did the boys receive more encouragement to continue in math than the girls did? Not to any measurable degree. Did the girls like math less than the boys or think math ability was less important for their future careers? Among this group of talented adolescents, the answers to these questions were also no. In 1991 Benbow told one reporter, "After 15 years of looking for an environmental explanation and getting zero results, I just gave up" (quoted in Pool, 1994, p. 19).

Reasoning from negative evidence—it isn't *this* (environmental influence), so it must be *that* (genes)—is always risky. Researchers cannot assess all the possible differences in the social experience of boys and girls that might affect their mathematical ability. Even so, when researchers look carefully for sex differences in socialization and fail to find them, they must consider the possibility that behavioral differences have a genetic basis. Again, this type of evidence is not conclusive, but when combined with other types, it can make a strong case for genetic influences on sex-role development.

## Socialization Theories and the Agents of Sex-Typing

The absence of firm evidence for sex differences in the socialization of exceptional mathematical ability is worth noting because it is unusual. Often, researchers who have looked for sex differences in children's socialization have found them. Children receive messages from many agents of socialization about how they should behave, and the messages given to boys and girls often differ. Let's see what messages children receive from the most important socialization agents, starting with their parents.

### What Boys and Girls Learn from Parents

Parents who are told that their newborn baby is a girl may judge the baby as weaker than if told it is a boy. Conversely, parents who are told that their newborn baby is a boy may judge the baby as better coordinated than if told it is a girl. These differences are fairly weak, however, and often nonsignificant (Stern & Karraker, 1989).

To judge parents' stereotypes about boys and girls more precisely, you might label a male infant shown in a videotape as female. Similarly, you might label a female infant shown in a videotape as a male. Then you might recruit mothers—not including the mothers of those infants—and ask the mothers to watch the videotapes and rate the infants' characteristics.

In one study using this procedure, mothers' ratings were not affected by whether the infants seen in videotapes were labeled as boys or as girls (Vogel et al., 1991). In another

study with a similar procedure, labeling infants as boys or as girls did not affect college students' ratings of the infants' characteristics (Karraker & Stern, 1990). These results suggest that adults do not always view children in sex-stereotyped ways. In other words, sex stereotypes do not have as powerful effects as some people assume.

Nevertheless, parents interacting with their own children often treat sons differently from daughters. The differences in parents' treatment can be classified into four types.

***Structuring Children's Environments***   Parents give their sons and daughters different environments in which to play and live. Starting in infancy, parents choose different clothes for sons and for daughters. Boys wear blue; girls wear pink. Parents also decorate boys' and girls' rooms differently. Boys may have sheets with cars, spaceships, or super heroes printed on them. Girls' sheets have flowers, gentle animals, or designs in pastel colors (Fagot & Leinbach, 1987).

Parents also buy different toys for girls and boys. Even before their children are 2 years old, parents expect them to prefer sex-typed toys (Eisenberg et al., 1985). Parents assume that toddler girls will want to play with dolls, stuffed toys, and kitchen toys. They assume that toddler boys will want to play with trucks, hammers, and blocks. If these assumptions are wrong, and children want toys that are not stereotypical for their sex, they are not likely to receive them. Children who want specific toys for Christmas less often get what they ask for if those toys are not stereotypical for their sex (Etaugh & Liss, 1992).

By giving children sex-typed toys, parents channel them toward sex-typed play. As children grow older, parents also attempt to foster different talents in boys and girls, thus contributing to sex differences in their children's activities, interests, and behaviors.

***Reinforcing Stereotypical Behavior***   After parents set the stage for children's activities by structuring their environments, they often reinforce sex-typed behaviors and punish other behaviors. Before children are 2 years old, parents begin shaping sex-typed behaviors.

In one study (Fagot, 1978), undergraduates observed 20- to 24-month-olds in their homes. The observers recorded what the children did and how their parents reacted to their behavior. As figure 14.8 shows, parents reacted more positively to sons than to daughters who were playing with blocks. In particular, parents often praised their sons, guided their behavior, or joined them in play. Parents reacted more negatively to sons than to daughters who were playing with dolls, for example, criticizing their sons or preventing them from playing with dolls. As you might expect, boys played with blocks more than girls did, and girls played with dolls more than boys did.

Not all differences in parents' reinforcement were matched by differences in children's behavior. Parents responded more negatively to daughters than to sons who were running, jumping, or climbing on things in the house (as the figure shows). As mentioned earlier, boys often show more of such high-activity behavior than girls do (Eaton & Enns, 1986). However, in this group of toddlers, girls engaged in such behavior about as often as boys did.

Conversely, parents responded as positively to girls as to boys when they played with cars and trucks. Parents seldom responded negatively to either girls or boys, yet boys played with cars and trucks more than three times as often as girls did. The sex difference in this activity may depend on socialization processes other than parents' reinforcement and punishment.

Figure 14.8 is somewhat misleading because it combines the reactions of mothers and fathers. In this study, fathers encouraged sex-typed behavior more than mothers did. For example, fathers reacted more negatively than mothers when their sons played with dolls. In another study with preschool children (Langlois & Downs, 1980), mothers sometimes showed affection for their sons when they played with feminine toys like a doll house. Fathers usually criticized their sons and daughters or stopped their play when they used toys typical for the opposite sex.

Fathers' pressure for sex-typed behavior is directed especially at sons. In one study (Snow, Jacklin, & Maccoby, 1983), fathers gave toy trucks to their 1-year-old daughters as often as to their sons. Fathers also gave dolls to their daughters, but they did not give dolls to their sons, and they discouraged sons from playing with dolls.

---

FIGURE 14.8

Parents encourage sex-typed play in 1- and 2-year-olds by reacting positively to behavior consistent with sex stereotypes and reacting negatively to behavior inconsistent with the stereotypes. For example, parents respond positively to their sons but not to their daughters when the children play with blocks. Yet some differences in parents' reactions to boys and girls, like those for running and jumping, are not matched by sex differences in young children's behavior. (Source: Fagot, 1978.)

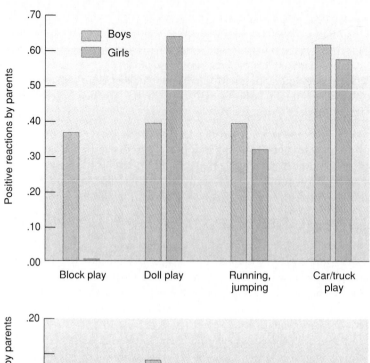

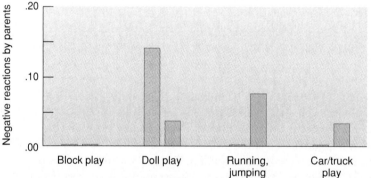

Throughout childhood, boys receive more punishment for behavior counter to sex stereotypes than girls do. The punishment comes mostly from fathers, but even mothers discourage feminine activities by sons more than they discourage masculine activities by daughters (Langlois & Downs, 1980; Maccoby & Jacklin, 1974). These data are another indication that the stereotypes for boys are more rigid or allow fewer exceptions than do those for girls. That is, girls who are viewed as tomboys receive less socialization pressure to change their behavior than do boys who are viewed as sissies.

***Setting Rules for Children's Behavior***   Many parents are more concerned about the physical safety of their daughters than their sons, so they make rules that keep daughters closer to home than sons (Huston, 1983). Many parents let their sons go places with friends after school but tell their daughters to come directly home. In addition, most boys are allowed to roam farther from home than most girls are.

When they are at home, girls do more chores and different chores than boys do (Goodnow, 1988). Girls clean bathrooms, wash dishes, and cook. Boys mow lawns, shovel snow, and take out the garbage. For their work, boys are more often paid extra than girls are. Goodnow described what children learn from their chores by saying that "mothers do not get paid in money, and their daughters seem to be socialized into a similar pattern of work that is 'for love.' The messages contained in children's work have to do not only with what work belongs to what people but also with its appropriate reward" (p. 15).

***Serving as Models for Observational Learning***   Does a girl learn to be a "little lady," just like her mom? Does a boy learn to be a "little man," just like his dad? Researchers have had a

This father and son are planting a tree. Fathers encourage their sons to engage in such stereotypically masculine activities more than mothers do. Fathers discourage stereotypically feminine activities by sons more than mothers do.

hard time proving it. More feminine women do not consistently have more feminine daughters. More masculine men do not consistently have more masculine sons (Maccoby & Jacklin, 1974).

These findings are easier to understand if you think about what masculinity and femininity mean in childhood and in adulthood. A masculine man does not build towers out of blocks or play with toy trucks in his spare time. A feminine girl does not wear low-cut black dresses, expensive perfumes, and high heels. Children do not directly imitate their parents in all their behaviors because such imitation would be impossible or inappropriate. The sex stereotypes for children's behavior differ from those for adults' behavior.

In a broader sense, parents do serve as models for their children. As you read in chapter 11, maternal employment affects children's sex stereotypes. In most studies, children whose mothers were employed outside the home viewed occupations as less strictly "for men" and "for women" than did children whose mothers were not employed. Also, daughters in most studies expressed higher aspirations for their future lives and less traditionally feminine aspirations when their mothers were employed (Hoffman, 1989; Huston, 1983).

Many children cannot take a parent as a model because the parent is absent. Although few children grow up in homes without a mother, many grow up in homes without a father. Several theorists have suggested that father-absent boys suffer from the lack of a male role model and do not develop an appropriately masculine identity.

A meta-analysis of 67 studies casts doubt on this hypothesis (Stevenson & Black, 1988). On various measures, father-absent boys were less stereotypically masculine than boys who grew up with their fathers at home. Overall, though, the mean difference between father-absent and father-present boys was small. Significant differences were found for some measures of sex typing but not others. Whether there was a significant difference also depended on the age of the boys tested and the reason for the father's absence (e.g., death, divorce, or military service). Moreover, any differences found between father-present and father-absent boys cannot be attributed solely to having or not having a male role model in the home. Mothers, too, take on different roles in single-parent and in two-parent families (as you read in chapter 11).

The meta-analysis further suggested that father absence has little effect on girls' sex-role development. In a few studies, adolescent and young adult females were less stereotypically

feminine when their father was absent from the home. However, the differences were small and could be due to single mothers taking on more masculine roles and so providing a different model for their daughters.

In a classic study, E. Mavis Hetherington (1972) found larger and more important differences between girls who did and did not have fathers at home. She studied adolescent girls whose fathers were absent because of either divorce or death. She found few differences between father-present and father-absent girls on standard measures of femininity or sex typing, just as in the later meta-analysis. However, the girls differed greatly in their interactions with males.

Daughters whose fathers had died were shy, withdrawn, and anxious around males. Daughters of fathers absent because of divorce were uninhibited and sexually precocious. Hetherington suggested that fathers help girls learn to interact skillfully and appropriately with males. Father-absent girls lack these opportunities for learning, but how they react to father absence depends on whether their fathers died or were divorced from their mothers. The father-absent girls in Hetherington's study were an extreme group. None had male siblings. Most had lost their father due to death or divorce before they were 5 years old. None of their mothers had remarried; none had had any males living in the home since their separation from the father. The effects of father absence would be more extreme for this group than for girls who have a brother or stepfather.

***How Much Influence Do Parents Have?*** So far, you've read about the various processes by which parents affect children's sex typing. The processes themselves are not controversial, but some researchers question how much influence parents have on the many components of sex typing.

Hugh Lytton and David Romney (1991) reviewed more than 100 studies that provided information on whether parents treated their sons differently from their daughters. They looked for differences in many areas, ranging from parental warmth to specific behaviors such as parents' encouragement of aggression. Their conclusion: Parents' treatment of their sons and daughters generally varies little.

The only important exception to this conclusion was for parents' encouragement of sex-typed activities and their perceptions of sex-stereotyped characteristics. This category includes such things as encouraging girls to play with dolls and expecting boys to shovel the sidewalk when it snows. Notice that most of the examples discussed earlier would fall into this category (e.g., giving children sex-typed toys and assigning them sex-typed chores).

Lytton and Romney could not link many other differences in boys' and girls' behavior to differences in parents' treatment. For example, parents discouraged boys' aggression about as much as girls' aggression. Parents provided as much motor stimulation, which might contribute to the development of physical abilities, to sons as to daughters. Parents encouraged sons' and daughters' achievement in mathematics equally, confirming Benbow's conclusion that sex differences in exceptional math ability are not easy to explain by differences in parents' behavior.

Other researchers suggest that conclusions about limited parental influence should not be accepted too quickly. The influence of parents may be obscured if researchers do not focus on the age periods when patterns of behavior are first established. For example, when their children are only 1 year old, but not later, parents express more positive reactions to the negative behaviors of sons than daughters (Fagot & Hagan, 1991). These positive reactions may contribute to the sex difference in aggressive behavior, even if parents later react similarly to boys' and girls' aggression. In other words, parents' treatment may be particularly influential when children are first learning about their own sex and about social behavior (Fagot, Leinbach, & O'Boyle, 1992).

Moreover, few researchers have assessed parents' attitudes toward traditional sex roles. Some parents in these studies probably gave little thought to the pattern of sex typing they wanted to promote in their children. Therefore, these studies provide more information about what parents *are* doing than about what parents *could* do to affect their children's sex-role development.

Assume that you wanted your children not to accept traditional sex roles. Instead, you wanted your sons and daughters to view the two sexes as equal in all important respects. If you adopted this socialization goal, could you achieve it?

One longitudinal study included 23 "avant-garde" families in which parents were highly committed to equality in sex roles (Weisner & Wilson-Mitchell, 1990). These parents were mostly college educated, mostly two-parent dual-career families in which parents shared child care and household tasks. When the children in these families were about 6 years old, they were interviewed about various components of their sex typing. The children's responses were compared with those of children in other families, including families whose lifestyle was generally traditional or conventional.

When compared with the children in conventional families, those in the avant-garde families had more flexible stereotypes about activities for children and occupations for adults. The girls in avant-garde families, but not the boys, also gave less stereotyped answers when asked what they wanted to be when they grew up. By contrast, children in the avant garde and conventional families did not differ in their preferences for sex-typed play or for same-sex friends. The children's mothers did not rate them as differing significantly on masculine traits (e.g., adventurous) or feminine traits (e.g., gentle).

These findings suggest that parents can affect some components of sex typing. They can, in particular, affect the degree to which children believe certain activities and roles are for males, for females, or open to both sexes. Parents may have less influence on their children's play behavior, preference for friends, or development of sex-typed personality traits.

Why don't parents have more influence? One answer is that they are not the only agents of sex-role socialization (Perry & Bussey, 1979). Children are also influenced by other people, and perhaps especially by their peers.

## Peer Influences: "But All the Other Girls (Boys) Are . . ."

The processes by which peers contribute to sex-role development are similar but not identical to those involving parents. Peers model and reward sex-typed behavior. In subtle ways, peers structure children's environments. Yet unlike parents, peers do not set rules for children's behavior, at least not explicitly.

That peers serve as models for children's behavior is obvious in natural settings. Parents often hear their children say, "I've got to have these shoes [or jeans, or jacket]. All the other girls [or boys] are wearing them." Children pay attention to what their peers have and do, and they often want to have and do the same things.

The influence of peer models on sex-typed behavior has been demonstrated in experimental studies. The preschool children in one study were shown a few balloons and toy xylophones (Masters et al., 1979). Some of these toys were labeled "for boys" and others were labeled "for girls." Then the children saw either a boy or a girl playing with the toys. Afterward the children spent the most time playing with the toys labeled for their sex. But if children had seen a same-sex peer playing with toys labeled for the opposite sex, their preference for those toys increased. Thus, a same-sex peer's behavior affected children's toy preferences.

Children pay attention to peer models partly because their peers can, and do, reward them for sex-typed behavior and punish them for behavior that is not sex-typed. Preschool children who play with toys typically chosen by the opposite sex are often ignored or teased by their peers (Langlois & Downs, 1980). Preschoolers who engage in sex-typed play get positive comments from peers and are often imitated by their peers. Among older children and adolescents, too, sex-typed behavior is usually rewarded. Behavior not consistent with sex stereotypes is often punished by ridicule or rejection (Carter, 1987).

Occasionally, researchers have directly shown that peers' reinforcements and punishments change children's behavior (Lamb, Easterbrooks, & Holden, 1980). When peers punish preschool children's behavior with disapproval or criticism, the children usually shift to another behavior. When the children's initial behavior was not stereotypical for their sex, the shift to another behavior occurs very quickly. Conversely, when peers reward children's behavior with praise or imitation, the children usually continue the behavior, especially if it was sex-stereotypical.

Modeling and reinforcement often work together. That is, children see their peers engage in certain behaviors and then see how those children are treated by peers. Children in one experiment watched a videotape in which a child actor did an activity stereotypical for the opposite sex (e.g., a boy acted as if he was a cooking instructor). The videotape then showed a peer giving positive comments to the child actor. Seeing a videotape of this kind increased elementary-school children's willingness to do nonstereotypical activities themselves (Katz & Walsh, 1991).

Finally, peers structure children's environments by engaging them in distinctive styles of interaction. As mentioned earlier, a rough-and-tumble play style is more common among boys than among girls. A style of influencing others by persuasion rather than by direct orders or force is more common among girls than among boys (Maccoby, 1988). Because children interact mostly with same-sex peers, boys and girls learn and practice different interaction styles.

Even when boys and girls are supposedly playing the same game, their style of play differs. *Foursquare* is a game that schoolchildren often play at recess or lunchtime. The object of the game is to get the other players "out" by bouncing a ball into their square so that they can't return it. However, when girls play the game they don't try to get all the other players "out." Instead, they try to keep their friends in the game and get other girls who are not their friends "out" (Hughes, 1988). In short, girls value winning the game less than being nice to friends.

How do boys play the game? Although good evidence is lacking, boys often compete vigorously, even with friends. They don't think games are fun unless every player is intensely competitive (Lever, 1978). What happens, then, when boys play foursquare with girls? In such (rare) cases, boys modify their goals. They try first to get all the girls "out" so that they can have a competitive game in which all the other players are boys (Hughes, 1988). No wonder boys and girls seldom play together!

Maccoby (1990) suggested that boys and girls live in different cultures throughout most of childhood. In their distinctive cultures, boys and girls learn how persons of their sex are expected to behave. They also develop styles of interaction that affect their future interactions with other people of the same and opposite sex.

## Teachers: Not Always in Favor of Stereotypical Behavior

Besides their parents and other close relatives, teachers are the most important adults in children's lives. Teachers affect children's sex typing, but their effects are more complex than you might think.

Look into a typical preschool classroom. You might want to see, first, whether teachers reward sex-typed behavior. The usual answer is "not always." Many teachers reward preschool boys and girls for stereotypically feminine behaviors such as drawing and cutting. Experienced teachers more often encourage such behaviors, whether these teachers are male or female. They do so not because they want boys and girls to become more feminine, but because they view these fine motor skills as important for the children's success in school (Fagot, 1978; Huston, 1983).

If teachers make the effort, they can alter children's patterns of sex-typed behavior. For example, if a teacher moves into the block corner, a typically male area, more preschool girls begin to play with blocks. If a teacher moves to a drawing table, more preschool boys begin to draw (Serbin, Connor, & Citron, 1981). Teachers can also increase the rate of preschoolers' cross-sex play by reinforcing it. Chapter 2 described an experiment in which teachers' praise of boys and girls who were playing together increased the rate of cross-sex play (Serbin et al., 1977).

You may recall, though, that the teachers' influence on children's play patterns was temporary. Preschoolers engaged in cross-sex play as long as teachers rewarded them for doing so. Once the rewards ended, children quickly returned to sex-segregated play (Serbin et al., 1977, 1981).

Similarly, teachers' physical presence has limited effects on children's play. Girls will readily follow a teacher who moves into a typically masculine area such as the block corner. Boys are less willing to shift their behavior when a teacher shifts her position in the room,

especially if they would end up in a typically feminine area. Again, you see that boys are more rigidly sex-typed than girls are.

In elementary schools and junior high schools, teachers often interact more with boys than with girls (Huston, 1983). Some boys receive more praise from teachers. Other boys, who are more disruptive, receive more criticism (Parsons, Kaczala, & Meece, 1982). Thus, teachers interact differently with boys and girls partly because those boys and girls behave differently in class. How much teachers' behavior affects their students' behavior is unclear.

Myra and David Sadker (1994) wrote a book with the provocative title *Failing at Fairness: How America's Schools Cheat Girls*. They argue that "girls are the majority of our nation's schoolchildren, yet they are second-class educational citizens. The problems they face—loss of self-esteem, decline in achievement, and elimination of career options—are at the heart of the educational process" (p. 1).

This assessment is difficult to square with the facts. Recall from chapter 12 that most studies show no difference between girls' and boys' self-esteem. As for the decline in girls' achievement, the Sadkers admit that boys receive lower grades than girls and that boys more often drop out of school. Concerning career options, some researchers have suggested that sex differences derive from the social roles available to adults, not from sexism in schools (Eagly, 1987). In other words, women may be second-class citizens in the United States and many other societies, but this situation may not be due to their earlier being second-class educational citizens.

Some reviewers of the Sadkers' book expressed concern about the heavy reliance on anecdotes rather than systematic evidence to make the case (Rayman, 1995). Other reviewers suggested that boys and girls may be treated differently in school because they act differently (Tanenbaum, 1994). For example, boys may be suspended more often because their aggressive and disruptive behavior creates conflicts with peers and teachers.

These reviewers point to important gaps in research on teachers and schools. Few studies of teacher-student interaction have been done. Few of those studies had research designs that allow an assessment of teachers' influence on students and students' influence on teachers. Because sex stereotypes are so pervasive in society, sex biases in education are likely. Nevertheless, more research will be needed to find the extent of these biases and their consequences.

## Stereotyping in the Media

The content of most television programs is highly sex-stereotyped (Huston et al., 1992; Vande-Berg & Streckfuss, 1992). The major characters in most programs are men rather than women. Men typically are the authorities; women are often homemakers. In most programs, men take active roles, while women are onlookers or followers. During the 1980s, prime-time television programs increasingly showed women who were employed outside the home, but children's programs still showed males and females in stereotyped roles.

Stereotyped portrayals of males and females are especially common in television commercials and in music videos. Toy commercials portray many toys as strictly for boys or strictly for girls (Rajecki et al., 1993). Commercials on weekend sports programs portray men as dominant and in positions of authority; they portray women in subordinate roles and as sex objects (Craig, 1992). In music videos, females are shown less often than males; females wear revealing clothing far more often than males; and many females are targets of explicit or implicit sexual advances, often ones tinged with aggression (Seidman, 1992; Signorielli, McLeod, & Healy, 1994; Sommers-Flanagan, Sommers-Flanagan, & Davis, 1993).

Children who watch more television have more stereotypical preferences and attitudes. For example, children who watch more television are more convinced that certain household chores should be done by girls and others should be done by boys (Signorielli & Lears, 1992). These correlations could, however, reflect an effect of children's stereotypes on their TV viewing rather than vice versa. Whether television has important effects on children's sex stereotypes can be better judged from longitudinal studies.

Adolescents in one study reported how much television they watched (Morgan, 1982). They also reported their attitudes about the proper roles of men and women. A year later, the

same adolescents reported again on their TV viewing and sex-role attitudes. Boys' attitudes became less sexist over time, but the change occurred no matter how much TV they watched. And even at the end of the study, boys had more sexist attitudes than girls did.

The changes in girls' attitudes were affected by how much television they watched. Girls who were heavy viewers formed more sexist attitudes. Girls who watched little television formed less sexist attitudes. By the end of the study, girls who were heavy viewers had attitudes about the roles of men and women that were as sexist as the average boy's. In short, seeing many stereotypical portrayals of men and women on TV did not strengthen the already sexist attitudes of boys, but it increased girls' acceptance of sexist attitudes.

The effects of TV viewing on adolescents' attitudes toward household chores were examined in another longitudinal study (Morgan, 1987). Boys and girls who watched more television formed increasingly stereotyped attitudes about who should do specific chores. However, adolescents' TV viewing did not affect the chores that they actually did. That is, TV viewing had a noticeable effect on adolescents' attitudes but not their behavior.

In a few experiments, researchers have exposed children to nonsexist media content and examined the effects on children's stereotypes. For example, preschool children were read books or shown films in which boys and girls had similar roles (Flerx, Fidler, & Rogers, 1976). Exposure to these books and films reduced the children's tendency to sex-type children's activities and adults' occupations. Viewing a series of nonsexist television programs can also weaken children's stereotypes about what persons of each sex can do (Huston et al., 1992). These experiments show that the mass media can not only reinforce traditional stereotypes; they can also counter these stereotypes by showing males and females in similar roles.

## Cognitive Theories: Gender Constancy and Gender Schemas

Children are not passive recipients of messages from socialization agents. They may accept or reject these messages, depending on their own ideas about boys and girls, men and women. Several cognitive-developmental theorists have emphasized the impact on sex typing of children's ideas about gender and sex stereotypes. The first major theorist to present a cognitive explanation for sex-role development was Lawrence Kohlberg (1966).

### Kohlberg on Gender Constancy and Sex Typing

In Kohlberg's (1966) theory, *gender* refers specifically to the biological categories of male and female. Kohlberg argued that children's *gender identity*, their sense of themselves as male or female, is critical for sex-role development. Kohlberg also proposed that the development of gender identity is related to Piagetian stages of cognitive development.

By 2 or 3 years of age, children can correctly say whether they are boys or girls. That is, they show accurate **gender labeling,** which is the first step in the development of gender identity.

Young children who can accurately label their gender may not assume that they have always been, and will always be, the same gender. Preschool boys sometimes say they were girls when they were little babies. Preschool girls sometimes say they could grow up to be a daddy (Slaby & Frey, 1975). Full awareness of **gender stability** is the second step in the development of gender identity.

Young children who know that gender is stable over time often think that people can change their gender. Most preschoolers think they could—and would—change their gender if they changed their clothing, hairstyle, or activities. These children do not yet realize that gender is not defined by these superficial attributes and is constant across situations. An understanding of *gender constancy* is the last step in the development of a mature gender identity.

The age at which children appear to attain an understanding of gender constancy depends on the exact questions that they are asked (Frey & Ruble, 1992). Children are convinced of the constancy of their own gender, for example, before they are convinced that other people cannot change their gender (Wehren & De Lisi, 1983). Most researchers agree that an understanding of gender constancy normally develops between 4 and 8 years of age. Around these ages, children also develop an understanding of what Piaget called conservation of number and quantity. As Kohlberg assumed, children with a better understanding of

**gender labeling**
*The first step in the development of gender identity, when children can correctly say whether they are boys or girls.*

**gender stability**
*The second step in the development of gender identity, when children know they always were and always will be the same gender.*

conservation also have a better understanding of gender constancy (De Lisi & Gallagher, 1991; Marcus & Overton, 1978).

By contrast, Sandra Bem (1989) has suggested that gender constancy depends not on Piagetian stages but on a knowledge of the sex difference in genital organs. She found that most preschoolers who knew a child with a penis was a boy and a child with a vagina was a girl also knew that gender is unchangeable. Bem's data suggest that young children fail tests of gender constancy because they don't realize that the genitals are the defining features of gender. However, some children in Bem's study who knew the difference between the male and female genitals still failed the test of gender constancy. Therefore, the cognitive prerequisites for gender constancy are open to debate.

Kohlberg was not interested in gender constancy merely as an important cognitive achievement. He assumed that gender constancy and the steps leading to it affect children's preferences for sex-typed behavior. He outlined this hypothesis with statements children might make to themselves. Children might say, "I am a girl (or boy). Therefore, I want to do girl (boy) things. Therefore, the chance to do those things—and be praised for doing them—is rewarding."

You can see why Maccoby and Jacklin (1974) called Kohlberg's theory one of *self-socialization*. According to Kohlberg, children's ideas about gender guide their behavior. Children first figure out which gender they are. Then they try to make their behavior consistent with their view of themselves. They value "things"—objects and behaviors—that they believe are appropriate for their gender.

Kohlberg's theory implies two specific hypotheses. First, children should not show sex-typed behavior before they know whether they are boys or girls. Sex differences in behavior should not appear before children make that first self-statement: "I am a girl (or boy)." Second, as children gain greater understanding of gender constancy, their behavior should become more sex-typed. As they begin to realize that "I am a boy (or girl) and will always be one," they should try more regularly to do boy (or girl) things.

Kohlberg's first hypothesis has turned out to be wrong (Frey & Ruble, 1992). Before boys and girls can label their gender accurately, their behavior differs. As you learned earlier, boys prefer masculine toys like trucks and girls prefer feminine toys like dolls before they are 2 years old. These early sex differences seem to depend not on children's ideas about gender but on the rewards that parents and other socialization agents provide for sex-typed play. That is, the differences depend less on cognitive development than on social learning.

Kohlberg's second hypothesis—that a growing understanding of gender constancy leads to more sex-typed behavior—has received mixed support. Contrary to the hypothesis, children's understanding of gender constancy is not closely related to other aspects of sex-role development. Boys in one study with a greater understanding of gender constancy also played for a longer time with an unattractive toy that other boys had said they liked (Frey & Ruble, 1992). These boys apparently felt they should play with the toy "for boys" whether it was attractive or not. However, the comparable effect for girls was not significant. Moreover, in several other studies children with a better understanding of gender constancy showed neither more nor less sex-typed preferences and behavior (Bussey & Bandura, 1992; Carter & Levy, 1988; Marcus & Overton, 1978; Martin & Little, 1990).

Kohlberg's second hypothesis also implies that children's understanding of gender constancy should affect their observational learning. In particular, children who know their gender is unchangeable should pay more attention to same-sex models. A girl, for example, should say to herself, "I will always be a girl, so I want to do girl things. I will *watch* other girls to see what they do and then imitate them." Some researchers have found a correlation between measures of gender constancy and observation or imitation of same-sex models (e.g., Ruble, Balaban, & Cooper, 1981). Other researchers have found no relation between the two (e.g., Bussey & Bandura, 1984).

These mixed results suggest that children's ideas about gender may be related to their sex-typed behavior, but Kohlberg's theory may not describe the relation correctly. During the 1980s, an alternative theory was proposed that derives from information-processing approaches to cognitive development.

## Gender Schemas: Structure and Functioning

Carol Martin and Charles Halverson (1981) proposed that children develop cognitive structures that organize their information about gender and sex-role stereotypes. These structures influence children's perceptions of other people, affect other cognitive processes like memory, and guide children's behavior. Martin and Halverson (1987; Martin, 1993) called such structures **gender schemas.** They took the term *schema* not from Piagetian theory but from social-psychological theories of information processing.

The best way to describe gender schemas is to state their primary functions and give examples of how they work. Martin and Halverson (1981, 1987) emphasized three functions of the schemas:

1. *Schemas affect attention to, and organization of, information.* Gender schemas control the processing of new information. They can, for example, improve the encoding of new information that is consistent with previously organized structures. They can cause children to distort new information that doesn't fit the schemas.

Suppose you show young children pictures of adults in sex-typed activities. One picture shows a woman sewing. Another picture shows a male police officer directing traffic. With these pictures are other ones showing adults in activities not consistent with sex stereotypes. For example, one picture shows a female police officer directing traffic. After children see the pictures, you ask them to do a distracting task for a few minutes. Then you ask them to tell you which pictures they saw.

Children typically have the most accurate recall of pictures in which actors were doing sex-typed activities. For example, they remember the woman sewing better than the woman directing traffic. Thus, the stereotypes that are part of their gender schemas bias their encoding and recall of the pictures (Carter & Levy, 1988; Martin & Halverson, 1983). The bias is greater when children have less flexible stereotypes or more rigid and structured schemas for male and female behavior (Signorella & Liben, 1984).

Children sometimes recall pictures as consistent with sex stereotypes when they were not. Children who see a woman directing traffic will often say that the person was a man. These distortions are important because they make stereotypes hard to change. When children meet other people whose behavior doesn't match the stereotypes, they may not even realize it. Even a young child whose mother is a doctor may say that "only men are doctors." For a while, at least, these children pay no attention to information that conflicts with their gender schemas, perhaps because they never encode the information accurately.

Fortunately, children do not misinterpret all information inconsistent with sex stereotypes. Information that sharply conflicts with gender schemas may be remembered better than information consistent with them (Martin & Halverson, 1983). In addition, children can be trained to process information about gender more accurately.

Children in one summer-school program were taught not to use gender stereotypes as a basis for judgments about who could choose which occupations (Bigler & Liben, 1990). Instead, the children were taught that two important criteria for occupations are people's liking for the work and their learning the skills needed. So, for example, women can be construction workers if they like to build things and they learn how to use big machines.

When children given this training heard stories in which adults had nonstereotypical occupations (e.g., a dentist was a woman), they remembered the adults' sex better than untrained children. This effect held only for children at least 8 years of age, which suggests that cognitive immaturity may limit children's processing of information about nontraditional sex roles. Even among 6- and 7-year-olds, however, training led to more flexible stereotypes about adult occupations.

The success of this training program highlights an important facet of gender-schema theory. Although gender schemas are cognitive structures, their content is strongly influenced by children's social experience. Parents, teachers, and other socialization agents greatly affect the ideas about gender that children form. These ideas do far more than influence children's interpretation of new information, as functions 2 and 3 demonstrate.

**gender schemas**
*Cognitive structures that organize children's knowledge about gender and sex-role stereotypes.*

2. *Schemas affect inferences drawn from information.* Because gender schemas link different ideas into a structure, children can use them to draw inferences from partial information. In the simplest case, children infer which toys another child will like from knowledge of the child's sex and of the sex stereotypes for toys.

Children can also make more complex inferences. If children get information about one boy's characteristics, they often assume that other boys have the same characteristics. If preschoolers hear that a boy has something called *andro* (referring to the androgens) in his blood, they assume that other boys also have *andro* in their blood (Gelman, Collman, & Maccoby, 1986).

Earlier, you learned about still more complex inferences that older children and adults make. Adults, adolescents, and sometimes children will predict an actor's future behavior using two types of information: the actor's sex and the actor's past behavior (Berndt & Heller, 1986; Biernat, 1991; Martin, 1989). Before making these predictions, children and adults make several inferences.

They first infer whether the actor's past behavior was or was not stereotypical for his or her sex. If the actor's past behavior was not stereotypical, they infer that the actor does not prefer stereotypical behavior. Then they infer that the actor's future behavior will not be stereotypical. All these inferences are guided by gender schemas.

3. *Schemas affect children's behavior.* The third function of gender schemas is to help children plan their own behavior and their reactions to other people's behavior. Here gender schema theory overlaps with Kohlberg's (1966) cognitive-developmental theory. Both theories suggest that children must know their gender before they can deliberately choose to behave in sex-typed ways. However, unlike Kohlberg, gender-schema theorists do not regard the development of gender constancy as critical. Children take the first step toward gender schemas when they label themselves as boys or girls. They take the next step when they consider what is appropriate for one sex or the other as they process new information.

Accurate gender labeling is related to some measures of sex-typed behavior in young children (Martin, 1993). Toddlers who know whether they are boys or girls choose more same-sex playmates (Fagot, Leinbach, & Hagan, 1986) and, in some studies, prefer more sex-typed toys (Weinraub et al., 1984). In addition, preschoolers with stronger gender schemas, who often think about what is appropriate for their sex versus the opposite sex, more often prefer sex-typed toys (Carter & Levy, 1988).

Experimental studies show even more clearly how gender schemas affect children's behavior (e.g., Bradbard et al., 1986). If children are shown unusual objects such as a garlic press or a shoe stretcher and told that the objects are for girls, girls examine the objects more than boys do. If girls and boys are told that the objects are for boys, boys examine them more than girls do. Thus, the gender labels attached to objects affect whether children think of them as "for me" or "not for me."

Because children examine objects more carefully when they view the objects as "for me," they learn more about them (Martin, 1993). Children remember more information about objects labeled for their own sex than about those labeled for the opposite sex. Such learning helps children to elaborate their "my sex" schema. By contrast, when children label objects as "not for me" and spend little time examining them, they learn little about them. In this way, gender schemas lead to differences in what boys and girls learn about their world.

# MASCULINE, FEMININE, OR ANDROGYNOUS: WHAT'S BEST FOR CHILDREN?

Perhaps the main message of the chapter, so far, is that biology, socialization, and cognition all contribute to sex differences in children's physical characteristics, activities, interests, abilities, traits, behaviors, and social relationships. You might wonder whether this is good news or bad news. Is it good for children to learn so many stereotypes about males and females? Is it good for children to conform to the stereotypes, as so many do?

**androgyny**
*A combination of desirable masculine and feminine characteristics.*

Many theorists believe that traditional patterns of sex typing are not good for children (Bem, 1981; Bigler & Liben, 1990; Block, 1983). Some theorists believe that feminine girls and masculine boys are not as healthy, psychologically, as androgynous children. **Androgyny** refers to a combination of masculine and feminine characteristics. Children are considered androgynous if they have many of the desirable characteristics of both males and females. When children describe themselves on questionnaires like the CPAQ, they are seen as androgynous if they have high scores for both masculine and feminine traits.

Androgynous children usually have higher self-esteem than highly feminine children, but they do not always have higher self-esteem than highly masculine children (Alpert-Gillis & Connell, 1989; Hall & Halberstadt, 1980; Rose & Montemayor, 1994). With adults, too, high masculinity is most strongly related to high self-esteem and healthy psychological adjustment. Femininity may also contribute to self-esteem and adjustment, but not as much as masculinity does (Taylor & Hall, 1982; Whitley, 1983).

These findings suggest that traditional sex typing is most problematic for girls. Suppose that a girl is highly and traditionally sex typed. Her self-esteem and adjustment are likely to be noticeably lower than those of girls who have a combination of feminine and masculine traits. Now consider a boy who is highly and traditionally sex typed. His self-esteem and adjustment are not likely to be noticeably lower than those of boys who have a combination of masculine and feminine traits. In short, girls benefit from having an androgynous personality far more than boys do (Lau, 1989; Markstrom-Adams, 1989).

Some researchers argue that fostering androgynous personalities is less important than changing other aspects of traditional sex typing. Sandra Bem was one of the first theorists to propose androgyny as the ideal end point of development, but she later rejected this position. She said that the concept of androgyny

> appeared to provide a liberated and more humane alternative to the traditional, sex-biased standards of mental health. . . . But the concept of androgyny can also be seen as replacing a prescription to be masculine *or* feminine with the doubly incarcerating prescription to be masculine *and* feminine. The individual now has not one but two potential sources of inadequacy to contend with. (1981, pp. 362–363)

Bem (1981, 1989) argued that instead of trying to rear androgynous children, parents and other adults should try to change children's gender schemas. According to Bem, the scope of these schemas should be very narrow or restricted. Children should get the message from parents and other adults that a person's sex matters only for reproduction. Children should not think that a person's sex has important consequences for nonreproductive behaviors or social roles. Yet in all societies, a person's sex does have important consequences far beyond the domain of reproduction. Getting children to accept a different message would probably be difficult.

Alice Eagly (1987) argued that sex differences in behavior are due mainly to the differences between males' and females' roles in society. She suggested that greater attention should be given to the roles open to males and females as adults than to their socialization as children. For example, parents should not be concerned if their sons play with trucks or their daughters play with dolls. Parents should be concerned about whether their sons and daughters, when they grow up, have equal opportunities to become doctors, nurses, truck drivers, or anything else.

Jeanne Block (1983) presented a counterargument. She suggested that socialization during childhood can affect the adult roles that boys and girls are prepared to fill. For example, boys' toys and games may give them more experience in acting on the world and showing their competence than do girls' toys and games. Girls may also have fewer chances to explore the world and solve problems independently because they are more closely supervised than are boys. In Block's view, the sex roles of men and women can be made more equal only if the activities and opportunities of boys and girls become more equal.

Which position is correct? The evidence needed to answer this question is not yet available, but you can gain a broader perspective by looking at societies different from your own. This chapter began with a glimpse of a Philippine culture in which boys' and girls' roles were unequal. In particular, girls had more responsibility for the care of younger children than boys did.

In other countries, systematic efforts are being made to eliminate the traditional differences in the roles of boys and girls, men and women. The government of Sweden decided in 1968 to adopt the goal of gender equality both in the larger society and in the family. *Cultural Perspectives:* "Social Policy and Sex Roles: Sweden's Bold Experiment" describes the steps taken by the government, and the apparent effects of government policies on children's attitudes. As you will see, Sweden has not yet reached its goal, but the society has moved toward a new model of sex-role development.

# EXPLAINING WHY BOYS AND GIRLS SELDOM PLAY TOGETHER

Of the many components of sex typing outlined in table 14.1, one that has received little attention so far—especially in terms of its explanation—deals with behaviors that reflect gender-based social relationships. Recall that boys almost always play with boys and girls almost always play with girls (Maccoby, 1990). By age 6, more than 90 percent of children's social interactions are exclusively with other children of the same sex.

Eleanor Maccoby (1988) argues that the sex segregation in children's social interactions can be best explained by integrating hypotheses from the three types of theories of sex-role development. Consider biological influences first. The strong preference for same-sex playmates is likely to be due, in part, to differences in boys' and girls' genotypes and corresponding hormones. Evidence for this conclusion comes from studies of girls who were prenatally exposed to high levels of male sex hormones. Some of these girls did become tomboys who preferred play with boys (Berenbaum & Snyder, 1995). In addition, the importance of biological influences is suggested by studies of nonhuman primates, who also show patterns of same-sex play.

Consider social influences next. Parents often encourage their children to play with same-sex peers. Classmates often tease children who play with opposite-sex peers. This teasing is one sign of the unpopularity of children who often interact with opposite-sex peers (Sroufe et al., 1993).

On the other hand, same-sex play is less common in societies where few playmates of the same age and sex are available (Harkness & Super, 1985). Thus, boys and girls will play together if same-sex playmates are unavailable. But when playmate choices are possible, parents and peers encourage children to choose same-sex playmates.

Finally, consider cognitive influences. Maccoby argues that the pattern of same-sex interaction must be due partly to self-socialization, to the effects of children's ideas about who they are and where they belong. To paraphrase Kohlberg (1966), children probably say to themselves, "I am a girl [or boy], so I want to play with other girls [or boys]." Same-sex play does become more common when children are accurate at gender labeling (Fagot et al., 1986). Also, preferences for same-sex playmates are stronger when children know that their sex will not change as they grow (Martin & Little, 1990).

Currently, researchers cannot say whether biology, socialization pressure, or children's own cognition has the greatest influence on the sex segregation of their social interactions. However, the three types of influences are more likely to work together than to counteract one another. Moreover, the same conclusion may hold for other components of sex typing. All sorts of differences between boys and girls may depend on the joint influences of children's biology, socialization, and cognition. Explaining how these influences work together will be an essential part of a future, integrated theory of sex-role development.

Do you see any girls in this picture? No, the group includes only boys. During the elementary-school years, children have an overwhelming preference for same-sex play. Girls rarely join boys' groups, and vice versa. Maccoby suggests that hypotheses from several theories of sex-role development can be used to explain this strong same-sex preference.

SOCIAL POLICY
AND SEX ROLES:
SWEDEN'S BOLD
EXPERIMENT

The Swedish government realized that equality in male and female roles could not be achieved without major changes in society and in family roles. Government officials announced in 1968 that both parents are responsible for the emotional and the financial well-being of their children. They encouraged both mothers and fathers to participate actively in caring for children.

The government also encouraged employment for men and women. During the mid-1980s, more than 85 percent of Swedish mothers with preschool children were employed outside the home (Calasanti & Bailey, 1991). The comparable figure in the United States was only about 55 percent (U.S. Census Bureau, 1994c). In both Sweden and the United States, women's salaries are lower than those of men doing comparable work, but the difference is smaller in Sweden (Intons-Peterson, 1988).

Both the differences between Sweden and the United States, and the lack of complete gender equality in Sweden, are evident in children's attitudes toward sex roles. Margaret Intons-Peterson (1988) assessed the sex-role attitudes of Swedish and American adolescents. Especially revealing were the adolescents' responses to what Intons-Peterson called the "change-sex story."

Suppose that when you wake up one morning, you discover that you have become the opposite sex. What do you think your life would be like? Some adolescents, mostly boys, thought that such a change would be devastat-

ing. One boy answered, "Catastrophe! Hopeless! My life would be ruined." Another boy said, "I would have to commit suicide."

Other adolescents, often girls, welcomed such a change. One girl said, "Oh good, now I can go to college." Another girl said, "It would be what I have always wanted." Many males and females gave neutral answers or mentioned some advantages to changing their sex and some advantages to staying the same sex.

Excluding the neutral answers and focusing on the proportion of answers that were positive rather than negative gives the results in figure 14.9. Notice that very few boys in either country gave positive answers to the change-sex story. They saw few advantages to becoming a girl.

Most American girls responded more positively than negatively to the change-sex story. They thought they could do more things and have more freedom as a boy. Eighteen-year-old American girls felt less positively about changing sex than younger American girls. The older girls apparently recognized some disadvantages as well as advantages to becoming a boy.

The results for Swedish females were striking. The 11- and 14-year-old Swedish girls gave more negative than positive answers to the change-sex story. Unlike American girls the same age, these Swedish girls said they were happier as a girl than they would be as a boy. The difference between the girls in Sweden and

# SUMMARY

**The Many Components of Sex Typing**
Sex-role development is the process by which children acquire the beliefs, behaviors, and other characteristics expected of persons of their sex in their culture. The many components of sex typing involve various constructs (e.g., self-perceptions) in various content areas (e.g., personality traits).

**What Are Girls and Boys Made Of?**
**A Look at Children's Stereotypes**
Children accept many stereotypes about how boys and girls differ. Their knowledge of stereotypes increases as they grow older,

but changes also occur in their interpretations of the stereotypes.

**Developmental Changes in Stereotypes**
Children learn sex stereotypes about activities and interests earlier than those about personality traits. Older children have more flexible stereotypes, if flexibility is defined by a belief that boys and girls can do the same activities and have the same social roles.

**The Persistence of Stereotypes**
Although sex stereotypes become more flexible, they continue to affect adolescents'

and adults' judgments about other people. For example, adolescents and adults consider whether an actor's past behavior was sex-typed when they judge how masculine or feminine the actor is. Behaving in ways inconsistent with sex stereotypes can lower children's popularity, especially if they are boys.

**Differences Between Boys and Girls: Sampling the Evidence**
Some sex stereotypes reflect actual differences between an average boy and an average girl. Some sex differences are small but others are large, with mean scores for

in the United States suggests that Swedish governmental policies had affected the girls' sex-role attitudes. Swedish girls were not eager to become boys because they saw girls' and women's roles as desirable and valuable.

The pattern differed at age 18. A slight majority of Swedish females (52 percent) felt positively about changing their sex. Intons-Peterson suggested that these females, as they approached adulthood, believed that they had fewer opportunities than males. These females believed that males could get jobs more easily than they could. They also recognized that most females in Sweden still do not prepare for the kinds of jobs that most men have. In school, females choose the secretarial and social-service courses more than males do. Males choose the technical and scientific courses more than females do (Bron-Wojciechowska, 1995).

Both official statistics and the results of the change-sex stories indicate that Sweden has not achieved full gender equality. Still, the responses of younger Swedish females imply that governmental policies have affected the sex-role attitudes of children and adolescents. Societies change slowly, but social policies that equalize the opportunities of men and women can make boys and girls view their own sex more positively.

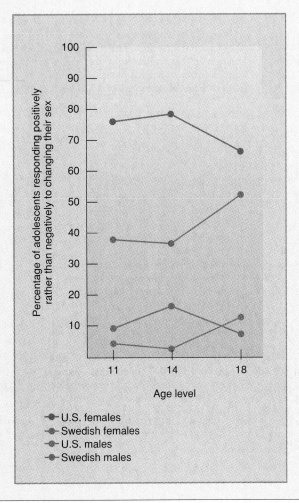

FIGURE 14.9
Percentages of adolescent males and females in the United States and in Sweden who responded positively rather than negatively to the thought of changing their sex. Few males in either country thought they would like being the opposite sex. Fewer females in Sweden than in the United States responded positively, suggesting that Swedish females were more happy with their sex than were females in the United States. But the responses of females in the two countries also changed with age. (Source: Intons-Peterson, 1988.)

boys and girls differing by more than a standard deviation.

**Biological and Physical Characteristics**
Especially after puberty, boys exceed girls in height, weight, and gross motor abilities like throwing a ball. Girls exceed boys in fine motor abilities, resistance to disease or injury, and life expectancy.

**Personality Traits and Social Behavior**
On the average, boys are more aggressive than girls and have more instrumental traits. Girls are more interested in babies and more emotionally expressive than boys. In adolescence, girls' ego development is more advanced than boys'.

**Activities, Interests, and Cognitive Abilities**
Before they are 2 years old, boys and girls differ in their activities and interests. Boys and girls also differ in their average performance on tests of certain verbal and math abilities.

**Gender-Based Social Relationships**
A bias toward same-sex peer interactions increases during early and middle childhood. Nearly all children name best friends of the same sex. Extreme preferences for opposite-sex playmates and for activities typical for the opposite sex have been linked to homosexuality in adulthood.

**Explanations of Sex-Role Development**
Sex differences in children's characteristics can be attributed to differences in their biology, their social experiences, and their cognition. All three types of influences must be considered when trying to explain the many components of sex typing.

**Biological Theories, or the Nature of Boys and Girls**
Abnormal exposure to sex hormones during the prenatal period is related to variations in sex typing during childhood and adulthood. Genetic influences on sex typing are also suggested by studies of nonhuman primates, children in other cultures, newborn infants, and twins.

### Socialization Theories and the Agents of Sex Typing

Boys and girls receive different messages about how they should behave from most parents, peers, teachers, and the mass media. These socialization agents structure children's environments, reward some behaviors and punish others, set rules for children, and serve as models for them.

### Cognitive Theories: Gender Constancy and Gender Schemas

Kohlberg emphasized the importance for sex-role development of children's understanding of gender constancy. By contrast, gender-schema theorists suggest that children organize their information about gender and about sex stereotypes into structures that affect their behavior and their perceptions of other people.

### Masculine, Feminine, or Androgynous: What's Best for Children?

Some theorists suggest that children develop best when they are androgynous, or have a combination of masculine and feminine characteristics. Others suggest that children are more affected by the restrictions on the social roles of boys and girls, men and women. Sweden is one society that has tried, with some success, to move toward gender equality.

### Explaining Why Boys and Girls Seldom Play Together

Eleanor Maccoby has argued that the sex segregation in children's social interactions is caused partly by biological influences, partly by socialization, and partly by children's ideas about what's appropriate for individuals of their sex. The three types of influences may also be important to consider jointly when explaining other differences between boys and girls.

# SUGGESTED READINGS

Beall, A. E., & Sternberg, R. J. (Eds.). (1993). *The psychology of gender.* New York: Guilford. The 10 chapters in this book explore both biological and social influences on males and females. Some of the chapters focus on adults, but several examine the development of gender differences in childhood. The chapters are clearly written and directly address the possible consequences of gender differences for individual and societies.

Golombok, S., & Fivush, R. (1994). *Gender development.* Cambridge, England: Cambridge University Press. If you want more information about any topic discussed in this chapter, you can find it in this book. The book also includes information about the psychoanalytic approach to gender development, gender differences in mental health, and gender differences in adult employment.

Pool, R. (1994). *Eve's rib: The biological roots of sex differences.* New York: Crown. The style of the book is entertaining, but the book is also carefully documented. Although no research citations are included in the text, 37 pages of footnotes give the sources of all factual statements. The author interviewed many researchers who have studied biological influences on sex-role development. The comments about their motives and careers are fascinating.

Whiting, B. B., & Edwards, C. P. (1988). *Children of different worlds: The formation of social behavior.* Cambridge, MA: Harvard University Press. Although the title of this book is general, the authors focused on a more specific question. They wanted to know what cross-cultural data could tell us about the origins of sex differences in behavior. A key observation from the book—that girls spend more time caring for younger children in all cultures than boys do—introduced this chapter. The authors also looked at dominant or assertive behaviors and examined cultural influences on the sex differences in these behaviors.

# MORAL DEVELOPMENT

*T*he following story describes a moral dilemma. Although the dilemma is hypothetical, it is more famous than many moral dilemmas people have faced in real life. Tens of thousands of children and adults around the world have considered this dilemma and made judgments about what the main actor, Heinz, should do. After you read it, think about what you feel Heinz should do and why he should do it.

In Europe, a woman was near death from a special kind of cancer. There was a drug that the doctors thought might save her. It was a form of radium that a druggist in the same town had recently discovered. The drug was expensive to make, but the druggist was charging ten times what the drug cost him to make. He paid $400 for the radium and charged $4,000 for a small dose of the drug. The sick woman's husband, Heinz, went to everyone he knew to borrow the money, but he could only get together about $2,000, which is half of what it cost. He told the druggist that his wife was dying, and asked him to sell it cheaper or let him pay later. But the druggist said, "No, I discovered the drug and I'm going to make money from it." So having tried every legal means, Heinz gets desperate and considers breaking into the man's store to steal the drug for his wife (Colby & Kohlberg, 1987, vol. 2, p .1).

Should Heinz steal the drug? Why or why not? Most children, like most adults, say that Heinz should steal the drug. But children give different reasons for this judgment than adults do. Here are examples of reasons given by children in the United States and two other cultures (Colby & Kohlberg, 1987; Snarey, 1985):

**U.S.:** "Because his wife might return the favor some day."
**Alaskan native (Eskimo):** "Because otherwise nobody will cut fish for him."
**Taiwan (Chinese):** "Because if she dies, he'll have to pay for the funeral, and that costs a lot."

Each child's answer reflects the circumstances of his or her culture, yet all the answers focus on how Heinz would benefit from saving his wife's life or what he would lose if he didn't. All the children seem to be asking the question, "What's in it for Heinz?" In this general sense, all three children thought about the Heinz dilemma in the same way—a way that you and most other adults have abandoned. By the time people reach adulthood, they no longer think the issue "What's in it for Heinz?" is crucial in judging what Heinz should do. One facet of moral development is this kind of change in thinking about moral issues.

Morality involves more than thinking; it involves behavior, too. Consider how children from two cultures played a simple game (Kagan & Madsen, 1971). A group of Mexican children was from a village in Baja California. A group of Anglo-American children was from Los Angeles. The children in both groups were 7 to 9 years old. Pairs of children played the game shown in figure 15.1.

To begin the game, a marker was placed in the center of the board, on the circle in row D and column 4. Children took turns moving the marker. On each turn, one player moved the marker one circle in any direction. If the marker reached the circle labeled A4, on one side of the board, the child on that side got a toy. If the marker reached the circle labeled G4, on the other side, the child on that side got a toy. If the marker did not reach either circle in 20 moves, neither child got a toy.

When Mexican children played the game, they usually got the toy quickly by cooperating with each other. One child began by moving the marker toward one side of the board. The other child moved the marker farther in the same direction. The first child moved in the same direction again, and so reached a winning circle in only three moves.

When Anglo-American children played the game, they rarely got the toy at all. Sometimes they competed for all 20 moves. One child would move the marker toward himself or herself; the other child would move it back. They continued to move the marker back and forth until the game ended. They were unable to work together to win toys.

Were the Anglo-American children behaving immorally? Strictly speaking, no. They didn't cheat or break the rules of the game. They "played fair." Yet, besides being self-defeating, their competitive behavior was not consistent with a broad definition of morality.

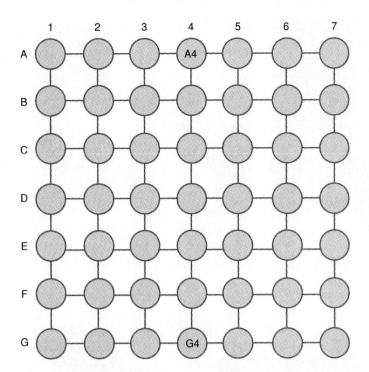

FIGURE 15.1

A diagram of the game used to study the cooperative and competitive behavior of Anglo-American and Mexican American children. The letters for the rows and the numbers for the columns were not on the game board, but they are included in the diagram to make it easier to describe the game.

From S. Kagan & M. C. Madsen, "Cooperation and competition of Mexican, Mexican-American, and Anglo-American children of two ages under four instructional sets" in *Developmental Psychology*. 5:32–39. Copyright © 1971 by The American Psychological Association. Reprinted by permission.

Scholars disagree about the best definition of morality, but most assume that acts affecting the rights, duties, and welfare of other people belong in the moral domain (Rest, 1983; Turiel, 1983). When the Anglo-American children competed in the game, they did not violate their partner's rights, but they showed little regard for the partner's welfare. Therefore, their behavior falls within the moral domain and is one indicator of their moral development.

Moral development involves still more than thinking and behavior. Long ago, Freud (1920/1965) emphasized the significance of moral emotions. He suggested that the anticipation of guilt is a motivation for moral behavior. More recently, other theorists suggested that children may improve another person's welfare not because they would feel guilty if they didn't but because they feel empathy for the other person (Eisenberg, 1989). Moral behavior also may be motivated by positive emotions. Children may do what they think is right because they feel good when they do so. Age changes in children's experience of these emotions relate to yet a third facet of moral development.

Historically, the three facets of moral development were linked to different theories. Theorists influenced by Freud focused on guilt and other moral emotions. Cognitive-developmental theorists focused on moral judgments and the reasoning that led to them. Social learning theorists focused on moral behavior.

During the 1970s and 1980s, these theories changed. Social learning theorists gave greater attention to the thinking that underlies children's behavior (Bandura, 1986; Mischel, 1973). Cognitive-developmental theorists gave greater attention to the links between moral reasoning and behavior (Rest, 1983; Kohlberg & Candee, 1984). Freud's hypotheses about moral emotions were reevaluated by theorists who examined the relations of children's emotions to their thinking and behavior (e.g., Eisenberg, 1986).

Yet even today most researchers focus on a single facet of moral development, either reasoning or emotions or behavior. This strategy is sensible because the three facets cannot be integrated until each facet has been analyzed by itself. For the same reason, this chapter has separate sections for the three major facets of morality. As you read, however, you will notice comments about the relations among these facets. Those comments will be most explicit in the sections of the chapter on moral behavior and promoting moral development.

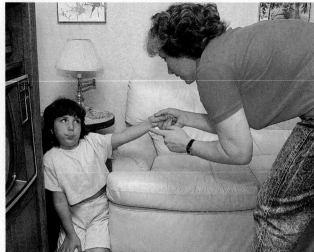

Morality and moral development have three facets. One facet involves judgments and reasoning. Children learn, for example, to judge what is right by using the Golden Rule, "Do unto others as you would have them do unto you." The second facet involves emotions. The girl in the top right photograph looks somewhat guilty as she is scolded by her mother. Her guilt may motivate her to behave more morally in the future. The third facet involves behavior. Collecting food for the needy is one example of moral behavior that children show. This chapter examines the three facets of morality as they develop from infancy through adolescence.

# THINKING ABOUT MORALITY

To explore children's thinking about morality, researchers have usually told them brief stories and then asked them questions. The story of Heinz and the drug that began this chapter was written by Lawrence Kohlberg, the most important theorist who has studied the development of moral judgment. Kohlberg built upon the work of previous theorists, particularly Jean Piaget (1932/1965). Because Piaget's work inspired many later researchers, his ideas and findings are examined first.

## Piaget on Moral Evaluations and Social Relationships

Piaget's typical method was to tell children pairs of stories and then ask the children to compare them. The best known of these story pairs follows:

> I. A little boy who is called John is in his room. He is called to dinner. He goes into the dining room. But behind the door there was a chair, and on the chair there was a tray with fifteen cups on it. John couldn't have known that there was all this behind

the door. He goes in, the door knocks against the tray, bang go the fifteen cups and they all get broken!

II. Once there was a little boy whose name was Henry. One day when his mother was out he tried to get some jam out of the cupboard. He climbed up on a chair and stretched out his arm. But the jam was too high up and he couldn't reach it and have any. But while he was trying to get it he knocked over a cup. The cup fell down and broke. (p. 122)

After telling children the stories, Piaget asked them which boy was the naughtiest. In other words, he asked them for their moral evaluations of the actors in the stories. These evaluations changed dramatically at around 8 years of age. Children above that age said Henry was the naughtiest because he wanted to take the jam without asking. They said John wasn't naughty because he didn't break the cups on purpose. Children under 8 years old said John was the naughtiest because he broke 15 cups. Henry wasn't as naughty because he broke only 1 cup.

Piaget assumed that the age changes in moral evaluations were due to changes in children's social understanding and in their relationships with parents and peers. However, most later researchers were more interested in the findings themselves than in Piaget's general explanation for them. These researchers first attempted to replicate the age changes in children's responses to the cup stories. These attempts were successful not only when European and European American children were interviewed, but also when interviews were done with Asian and Native American children (Lickona, 1976). The next step, then, was to extend Piaget's work and define more precisely which criteria children use for their moral evaluations at which ages.

## Children's Criteria for Moral Evaluations

When evaluating the actors in the cup stories, young children seem to consider only one criterion, the consequences of the actors' behavior. They judge an actor who causes more negative consequences as more naughty. Therefore, the boy who broke 15 cups is worse than the boy who broke 1 cup.

By contrast, older children use a different criterion for moral evaluations. Piaget said the older children judge actors by their intentions. In defining an actor's intentions, Piaget usually referred to the distinction between behavior that is accidental and behavior that is intentional. According to Piaget, older children do not blame actors for the consequences of unintentional behavior. In their view, John is not naughty because he didn't break the cups on purpose.

Yet strictly speaking, Henry did not intentionally break a cup either. He broke the cup because he was careless. In legal terms, he was negligent. John was not negligent because, as the story says, he "couldn't have known that there was all this behind the door." When adults evaluate actors who have caused damage, they consider more than whether the damage was accidental or intentional. They also consider whether the damage resulted from carelessness or negligence (Grueneich, 1982).

Young children also distinguish among actors who cause damage intentionally, accidentally, or through negligence (Karniol, 1978). The children in one study heard stories about a child who lent a model airplane to another child (Shultz, Wright, & Schleifer, 1986). In one of the stories, the other child damaged the plane intentionally by deliberately crashing it into a tree. In another story, the child damaged the plane accidentally. In a third story, the child damaged the plane through negligence, by not being careful.

After they heard the stories, children were asked how bad the child was for damaging the airplane. Figure 15.2 shows that children evaluated the child as very bad when he or she intentionally damaged the plane. The child was less bad if he or she damaged the plane through negligence, and least bad if he or she did so accidentally. The differences in evaluations were apparent by 5 years of age. So, contrary to Piaget's hypothesis, 5-year-olds do not focus solely on the damage caused by a person. Even 3- and 4-year-olds give different evaluations to actors who cause damage intentionally or unintentionally, if the children hear stories in which this distinction is clear (Nelson-Le Gall, 1985).

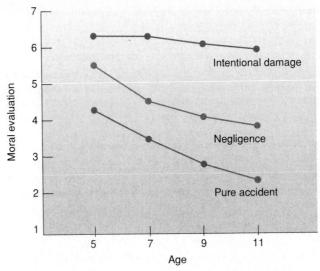

## FIGURE 15.2

How bad is it to damage another child's airplane intentionally, accidentally, or through negligence? In this figure, higher scores indicate more negative evaluations of a child who damages another child's plane. The mean scores indicate that even 5-year-olds evaluate a child who causes damage intentionally as worse than one who caused damage through negligence. Five-year-olds evaluate a negligent child as worse than one who causes damage accidentally. These differences in evaluations increase as children get older, however. (Adapted from Shultz et al., 1986.)

Thus far, though, one important detail of Piaget's stories has not been mentioned. John and Henry differed not only in how they broke the cups (accidentally or negligently) but also in what they were trying to do. The word *intentions* captures this difference, too, when people speak of actors with "good intentions" or "bad intentions." Used in this way, *intention* is a synonym for *motive*. In the cup stories, Henry's motive was bad. He wanted to get some jam without asking. John's motive was good. He wanted to obey his parents by coming to dinner when he was called.

Piaget did not make a clear distinction between the two meanings of the word *intention*: as intentionality and as motive. When later researchers made this distinction, they found that even preschool children recognize the difference between actors with good motives and those with bad motives. Preschoolers also evaluate actors with good motives more positively than those with bad motives (Keasey, 1978). Contrary to Piaget's claim, then, young children do use an actor's motives as a criterion for moral evaluations.

By now you should be puzzled. You have read that Piaget was wrong when he concluded that young children don't consider intentionality as a criterion for moral evaluation. You have read that Piaget was wrong when he concluded that young children don't consider motives when evaluating actors. But you have also read that later researchers replicated the age changes that Piaget found. How can this be?

This question has a three-part answer. First, Piaget asked children to choose between stories that differed in several ways (Karniol, 1978). In the cup stories, for example, John and Henry differed in their motives, the intentionality of their behavior, and the consequences of their acts. The later researchers who replicated Piaget's results used the same stories as he did, or similar stories.

Researchers then began to examine each criterion for moral evaluations separately. For example, in the research with stories about a child who damaged another child's airplane (Shultz et al., 1986), only the intentionality of the actor's behavior varied across stories. The consequences of the actor's behavior, or the amount of damage to the airplane, was the same in all stories. Therefore, children could not use differences in consequences as a criterion for

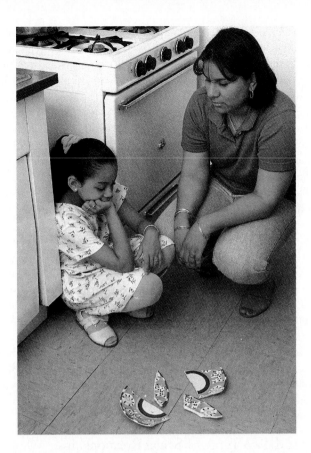

Will this mother punish her daughter for breaking the dish? Will she decide not to punish her daughter if the daughter tells her it was an accident? Will she excuse her daughter if the daughter says she was trying to help by putting the dishes in the dishwasher? The judgments that the mother makes about when to punish her daughter will affect the daughter's moral judgments, too.

their moral evaluations. If the youngest children in that study had heard stories in which the consequences of the actors' behavior differed, they probably would have weighed consequences heavily when evaluating the actors. That is, they would have based their moral evaluations on consequences to a greater extent than on intentionality.

Second, young children may place a great emphasis on consequences when making moral evaluations because these consequences are stated directly and are easy to understand. By contrast, children must often infer what an actor's motives were and how intentional his or her actions were. (Remember how you inferred the actors' motives and intentionality in the cup stories.) As mentioned in chapter 13, young children's understanding of motives and intentionality is limited or fragile. These children should find it more difficult to make inferences about motives and intentionality than older children do.

It's not surprising, then, that young children do not rely heavily on motives and intentionality as moral criteria. Figure 15.2 shows that the differences between children's evaluations of actors who caused damage intentionally, through negligence, and accidentally increased with age. Five-year-olds evaluated the various actors differently, but 11-year-olds made sharper distinctions between them. As children gain more understanding of the causes of people's actions, they treat these causes as more important criteria for moral evaluations.

Third, some young children may focus on consequences because adults do the same when evaluating them. One researcher examined how 6- to 7-year-olds and their mothers evaluated actors who caused various amounts of damage (Leon, 1984). Some mothers based their evaluations on the damage caused by the actors rather than on the actors' intentions — and their children did the same.

These mothers probably evaluated their children in the same way as they evaluated the actors in stories. Their children, in turn, modeled their moral evaluations on those of their mothers. Age changes in children's evaluations can be given a similar explanation. As they grow older, children may place less emphasis on consequences and more on intentionality and motives partly because their parents change their criteria for evaluating them.

In everyday life, parents have many opportunities for moral evaluations of their children. In response to these evaluations, children gradually learn to explain, excuse, or justify their actions. For example, they say they should not be punished for hurting their baby brother because "I didn't do it on purpose." When they break moral rules intentionally, they learn to minimize the damage ("She's not really hurt") or to assert their good motives ("I was trying to make her do what you told her to").

Children's experiences also help them learn to use other criteria for moral evaluations besides intentionality, consequences, and motives (Bersoff & Miller, 1993; Rest, 1983). For example, children consider whether an actor was provoked by something another person had done. They consider whether the actor caused damage to other people or only to property. Once a misdeed has occurred, children consider whether the actor apologizes for it. Indeed, most of the criteria involved in legal judgments of crime and punishment eventually become part of children's criteria for moral evaluations.

The word *eventually* in the previous sentence is important. Children only gradually develop adultlike use of the many criteria for moral evaluations. Even preschoolers, for example, judge a child who breaks a flower pot and lies about it as worse than a child who breaks the pot but confesses (Bussey, 1992). However, preschoolers distinguish less sharply between the liar and the child who confesses than elementary-school children do. The age difference exists partly because older children more accurately distinguish between a lie and a truthful statement.

Adults do not view children as morally mature until they use all the relevant criteria for making moral evaluations of their behavior and other people's behavior. As children gain greater knowledge of social situations and social norms, their evaluations become more sophisticated. The development of sophisticated moral evaluations is a critical aspect of moral development.

## Two Moralities and Two Types of Social Relationships

Although Piaget (1932/1965) tried to specify the criteria for children's moral evaluations, that was not the main goal of his research. Instead, he wanted to document a change with age in the basis of children's morality. He argued that children younger than about 8 define right and wrong by what adults tell them. Their morality is one of **heteronomy,** which comes from the Greek words meaning "rule by others." Young children do not judge for themselves which behaviors are moral and immoral; they merely accept whatever adults say.

Piaget said that young children accept adults' rules because they have an attitude of **unilateral respect** for adults. They see adults, correctly, as wiser and more powerful than themselves. They respect adults for those reasons. Their respect, however, is unilateral, or one-sided, because they are egocentric and cannot understand why adults make certain rules. They cannot take the adults' perspective.

Piaget argued that children move gradually, after 8 years of age, toward a different basis for morality. As they grow older and less egocentric, they spend more time interacting with peers. They also see their peers as equal to themselves. Because no child in a peer group is superior to any other, all children in the group must work together, cooperatively, to devise rules for their social interactions. As children discuss possible rules or resolve conflicts over violations of rules, they must adopt the attitude of **mutual respect.** Each child expects the others to listen to what he or she says. Each child must, in turn, listen to what the other children say. Only in such an atmosphere of mutual respect can peers reach agreement on rules to govern their interactions.

Peer interactions based on mutual respect lead gradually to a new morality. Piaget called this morality one of *cooperation.* He claimed that its result would be moral rules based on principles of fairness and justice. And because each child has participated in making the rules, each child accepts them as a guide for his or her behavior. Thus, the new morality is one of autonomy, or self-government.

Table 15.1 summarizes Piaget's theory in terms of the two moralities, the social understanding that is their basis, and the features of social relationships that lead to them. But what do these two moralities have to do with intentions, consequences, or the cup stories?

**heteronomy**
*Piaget's term for the basis of young children's morality, when they accept whatever adults say rather than judging for themselves which behaviors are moral and immoral.*

**unilateral respect**
*According to Piaget, young children's attitude toward adult authority. Young children respect adults' power and wisdom but cannot take the adults' perspective and so cannot understand the reasons for adults' rules.*

**mutual respect**
*Piaget's term for the attitude that prevails in children's interactions with peers. Each child expects the other to listen to him or her and, in turn, listens to the others.*

| TABLE 15.1 | *Piaget's Two Moralities* | | |
|---|---|---|---|
| AGE (APPROX.) | BASIS OF MORALITY | ATTITUDE TOWARD SOCIAL RELATIONSHIPS | MOST IMPORTANT RELATIONSHIPS |
| Under 8 years | Heteronomy, authority | Unilateral respect for more powerful adults | Unequal relationships with parents and other adults |
| Over 8 years | Autonomy, cooperation, justice | Mutual respect among peers | Egalitarian relationships with peers |

Probably not much. The two moralities have more to do with children's thoughts about stories like the following:

> One Thursday afternoon, a mother asked her little girl and boy to help her around the house, because she was tired. The girl was to dry the plates and the boy was to fetch in some wood. But the little boy went and played in the street. So the mother asked the other one to do all the work. Was that fair? (p. 277)

Most 6- and 7-year-olds said it was fair "because the mother had told her to." According to Piaget, this answer shows that young children have a heteronomous morality in which adults define what is morally right.

Most children over 7 years of age said the mother's request wasn't fair. Some older children said the little girl should refuse to do all the work. Others said the girl should do the work not because it was fair but simply to help her mother. These children recognized that parents may order them to do things that are not fair or just. Some of the older children, however, had a sense of justice that called for helpfulness because of love for parents.

Other researchers have partly replicated Piaget's findings regarding the age changes in respect for parents' authority (e.g., Damon, 1977; Youniss, 1980), so Piaget's proposal about the two moralities accurately describes part of moral development. However, Piaget exaggerated the unilateral respect of children for parents. Suppose parents tell children they must steal something. Children do not believe they must obey a parent's order to commit immoral acts (Damon, 1977).

Moreover, even 6-year-olds believe parents' authority is limited. Six-year-olds do not believe that parents can simply forbid them to play with one of their classmates (Tisak, 1986). These children accept such orders only if the parents provide a reasonable justification, such as concern about the classmate's negative behaviors (Tisak & Tisak, 1990).

Elementary-school children are pragmatic, though. They usually advise compliance with parents, teachers, lifeguards, and other adult authorities (Braine et al., 1991). One reason they give for compliance is simply to avoid punishment. Another reason that applies in certain situations is that children believe the orders are fair or are for the children's protection. In addition, some children give reasons consistent with Piaget's idea of unilateral respect, that people in positions of authority should be obeyed.

The variety of reasons indicates that elementary-school children have a highly differentiated idea of authority. When judging whether they should obey, children consider what an authority is telling them to do, whether the command falls within the authority's limits, and whether the command is fair. Children are still likely to obey when they have doubts about these issues, but contrary to Piaget's assertions, the children don't always think their obedience is morally required.

On the other hand, Piaget was not completely inaccurate when he emphasized young children's respect for authority. Indeed, Piaget in some ways exaggerated the age changes in children's ideas about morality. Other researchers have found that certain types of heteronomy, or acceptance of others' rules, are characteristic of children whom Piaget expected to be

more mature. These researchers have also shown that a truly autonomous morality does not develop as early as Piaget believed. Most of this new research has been linked to Kohlberg's theory of moral judgment.

## Kohlberg's Theory of Moral Judgment

The three major parts of Kohlberg's theory are (1) a description of six stages of moral judgment, (2) assumptions about how development through the stages occurs, and (3) hypotheses about the processes and experiences that contribute to moral development. Before considering these three parts, a brief look at Kohlberg's method for measuring people's moral judgments is useful.

### The Moral-Judgment Interview

To measure people's moral judgments, Kohlberg used the Heinz dilemma and other dilemmas. In the standard procedure, an interviewer reads each dilemma to a child or adult and then asks questions about it. The questions are designed to reveal how the person being interviewed thinks about moral issues. Therefore, the person's decision on each dilemma is less important than the reasons given for that decision. For example, whether you think Heinz should steal the drug does not affect your stage of moral judgment. Your stage depends on why you think Heinz should or should not steal it.

The standard moral-judgment interview includes questions about three dilemmas (Colby & Kohlberg, 1987). The interview takes about 45 minutes. Scoring the responses for a person's stage of moral reasoning is a complex, 17-step process. Its complexity is suggested by the length of the standard scoring manual: more than 1,000 pages.

Several researchers have devised simpler procedures for measuring people's stage of moral reasoning. For the Defining Issues Test (DIT), people read several moral dilemmas (Rest, 1986). After reading each dilemma, people read a series of questions that are relevant for making a decision on the dilemma. For example, one question about the Heinz dilemma is, "Isn't it natural for a loving husband to care so much for his wife that he'd steal?"

Each question is phrased so that it represents an issue important at a specific stage of moral judgment. People rate the importance of each question for making a decision on the dilemma. Then they rank the four questions that they consider most important. People who rank questions representing higher stages as more important are assumed to be at higher stages themselves. Although scores on the DIT are not equivalent to those on Kohlberg's interview, they are moderately correlated with them. Therefore, research using this test can and has provided evidence on Kohlberg's theory.

People's moral judgment can also be assessed with the Sociomoral Reflection Measure-Short Form (SRM-SF; Gibbs, Basinger, & Fuller, 1992). This measure is shorter partly because people are not asked to read moral dilemmas. Instead, they are asked to respond to 11 brief items. For example, one item reads, "Think about when you've made a promise to a friend of yours. How important is it for people to keep promises, if they can, to friends?" After rating the importance of keeping promises, people write a few sentences to explain their rating.

People's scores on the SRM-SF are correlated with their scores on Kohlberg's moral-judgment interview (Gibbs et al., 1992). However, the SRM-SF is based on a stage theory somewhat different from that proposed by Kohlberg. John Gibbs, a creator of the SRM-SF, worked with Kohlberg for several years. During this period, Gibbs (1977, 1979) concluded that only the first four of Kohlberg's six stages are part of a true developmental sequence. Therefore, only those four stages are considered in the scoring of the SRM-SF.

Few people score above Stage 4 on Kohlberg's moral-judgment interview, so the difference between Kohlberg's and Gibbs's theories is rarely crucial to the measurement of moral judgment. For Kohlberg, however, the last two stages define moral maturity. In the next sections, you'll see why those stages are crucial to the theory and why they are the focus of criticism.

### Stages of Moral Judgment

Kohlberg proposed six stages of moral judgment that are analogous to, and dependent on, Piaget's stages of cognitive development. The stages are also related to the levels of perspective

## TABLE 15.2  Kohlberg's Stages of Moral Judgment

| LEVEL AND STAGE | TYPE OF MORALITY | EXAMPLE: "HEINZ SHOULD STEAL THE DRUG . . . |
|---|---|---|
| **Preconventional Level** | | |
| Stage 1 | Heteronomous (others' norms) | . . . because his wife might be a very important person." |
| Stage 2 | Individualistic, instrumental | . . . if he thinks it is worth the trouble or risk." |
| **Conventional Level** | | |
| Stage 3 | Interpersonally normative | . . . because he should care about his wife." |
| Stage 4 | Social system | . . . because people must be willing to save others if society is to survive." |
| **Postconventional Level** | | |
| Stage 5 | Human rights and social welfare | . . . because certain rights have been agreed upon or defined by people through a kind of social contract." |
| Stage 6 | Universalizable, reversible, and prescriptive general ethical principles | . . . because, when faced with a conflict between stealing and protecting the life of another person, protection of human life is more important." |

*Source:* Adapted from Colby & Kohlberg, 1987.

taking defined by Selman (1980), which you read about in chapter 13. As table 15.2 illustrates, Kohlberg grouped the six stages into three levels, each with two stages. The following sections clarify Kohlberg's definitions of each level and stage.

*I. The Preconventional Level*    Most children under age 9, and some adolescents and adults, reason about moral dilemmas at the preconventional level. Children at this level are preconventional because they do not consider social conventions or social norms when making moral decisions (Colby & Kohlberg, 1987). Preconventional reasoning may reflect complete egocentrism, an inability to understand another person's perspective. Alternatively, preconventional children may take the perspective of an isolated individual who has no enduring relationships with anyone else.

*Stage 1. Heteronomous Morality.* Children at Stage 1 are heteronomous in Piaget's sense. They assume that adult authorities define what is right and wrong. These children judge acts prohibited by authorities as wrong without considering the actors' motives. They also think a person's power, wealth, and size determine the person's importance.

In response to the Heinz dilemma, a Stage 1 child might say Heinz should not steal the drug because stealing is against the law. A Stage 1 child might argue, instead, that Heinz should steal the drug because his wife might be a very important person. Notice that children's decisions on the dilemma do not determine their stage. Their reasons for their decisions are critical.

*Stage 2. Individualistic, Instrumental Morality.* Children or adolescents at Stage 2 can consider more than one perspective on a situation and can recognize conflicts between two people's perspectives. As a result, they reject the total respect for authority that typifies the responses of children at Stage 1. However, they can only think of two people's perspectives at once. Therefore, they assume that the best way to resolve conflicts between people is to let each do what he or she wants or to have them make a deal. The emphasis that individuals at this stage place on letting people do what they want explains why their moral judgments are called individualistic.

In this chapter's introduction, you read the responses of three children who gave Stage 2 reasons. These children suggested that Heinz should do whatever had the most benefits and fewest costs for him personally. Their guiding rule for making moral decisions is stated by the question, "What's in it for me?" Children at Stage 2 base their moral judgment on what is instrumental in meeting their own needs or desires, which explains the second label for this stage.

**II. The Conventional Level**   Most adolescents and adults in the United States and other countries reason at the conventional level. They are conventional because they understand and accept the social norms for their behavior. When making moral decisions, they focus on these norms. In other words, they adopt the perspective of a loyal member of their society. This member-of-society perspective takes different forms at the two stages on this level.

*Stage 3. Interpersonally Normative Morality.* Stage 3 is sometimes called the "good boy–good girl" morality. Adolescents and adults at this stage assume that people should act as other people expect them to. Stage 3 individuals also say that people should do what's expected of people with their role in society. For example, a person should behave like a good husband or a responsible druggist.

A person at Stage 3 might say that Heinz should steal the drug for his wife because he should care about her. Even if he doesn't love her, he should steal the drug because he's still her husband. Alternatively, a Stage 3 person might say that Heinz should not steal the drug because he wants people to think he is an honest, law-abiding citizen.

*Stage 4. Social System Morality.* Adults at Stage 4 take the perspective not of a specific member of society but of an impartial individual who wants to maintain the social system. Stage 4 individuals usually emphasize the importance of abiding by laws that maintain order and promote the common good. However, they may emphasize either the laws of their society or the moral codes of their religion. In the latter case, they may express their moral decisions in terms of the demands of conscience.

Stage 4 individuals might say that Heinz should steal the drug because people must be willing to save others if society is to survive. They might, instead, say that Heinz should not steal the drug because the druggist's right to his property must be respected. Whatever their choice, they emphasize the smooth functioning of a social system rather than the needs or rights of individuals.

**III. The Postconventional Level**   According to Kohlberg, only a few adults reach the postconventional level, and most do so after they are 25 years of age. Adults at this level understand and usually accept the rules of their society, but they do so because they recognize the moral principles that underlie those rules. If they view any rules in their own society as inconsistent with moral principles, they feel obliged to act according to their principles rather than society's rules. Consequently, this level of moral reasoning is also called the principled level.

Principled moral reasoning depends on a prior-to-society perspective. Postconventional adults do not base their moral decisions on the norms or laws of their own society, as conventional thinkers do. Instead, they take the perspective of a person who makes decisions, before any society exists, about what the society's norms should be.

*Stage 5. Human Rights and Social Welfare Morality.* Adults at Stage 5 accept certain rights and values as necessary for a moral society. They believe societies exist to ensure these rights and promote the welfare of all.

When discussing the Heinz dilemma, a Stage 5 adult might say that Heinz should steal the drug because the right to life takes precedence over any person's right to property. Kohlberg assumed that all adults at Stage 5 should say that Heinz should steal the drug (Kohlberg & Candee, 1984). That is, at Stage 5 (but not at the lower stages), only one moral decision is possible in the Heinz dilemma. Kohlberg made this assumption because he

viewed the right to life as the moral principle most relevant to the Heinz dilemma, and that principle allows only one decision.

*Stage 6. Morality of Universalizable, Reversible, and Prescriptive General Ethical Principles.* It's best to unpack the long label for this stage one word at a time. First, Stage 6 adults consider their moral principles as universalizable. That is, they would want everyone to act in the way they think is most moral. A common alternative position is that of relativism. Moral relativists assume that they cannot judge what would be morally right or wrong for other people, only for themselves. According to Kohlberg, Stage 6 individuals reject this kind of moral relativism.

Second, adults at Stage 6 view their moral principles as reversible, or acceptable from all possible positions. They decide what Heinz should do after putting themselves in Heinz's place, the druggist's place, and the place of Heinz's wife. Only through this process of "moral musical chairs" (Colby & Kohlberg, 1987) can they fully consider the viewpoints of each person involved in a dilemma.

Third, Stage 6 adults view their principles as prescriptive: They define what people should and must do. Adults at this stage think not only of what is immoral, or what they should not do, but also of what their moral principles oblige them to do.

Fourth, the ethical principles accepted at Stage 6 are general, or apply in all situations. Notice, particularly, that "ethical principles" is plural. Kohlberg (1976) once suggested that justice was the only universal ethical principle. Near the end of his life, he argued that Stage 6 individuals place highest value on respect for other people. This respect for human dignity leads to a concern with at least two moral principles, justice and benevolence toward others (Colby & Kohlberg, 1987; Kohlberg, Boyd, & Levine, 1990).

What does the Stage 6 person say about the Heinz dilemma? The standard scoring manual does not answer this question (Colby & Kohlberg, 1987). No one in Kohlberg's longitudinal study clearly showed reasoning higher than Stage 5, so he and his coworkers did not try to devise rules for identifying Stage 6 reasoning. In other words, people's responses to the standard moral-judgment interview are classified at one of Kohlberg's first five stages. No person can be scored as higher than a "pure" Stage 5.

Stage 6 is still important in Kohlberg's theory because it defines the theoretical end point of the development of moral judgment (Kohlberg et al., 1990). For Kohlberg, Stage 6 describes the structure of moral reasoning that is ideal. In contrast to the lower stages, reasoning at Stage 6 focuses exclusively on moral principles rather than on beliefs about the law, social norms, or other nonmoral issues. Moreover, Kohlberg argued that Stage 6 reasoning is morally superior to that at Stage 5, in part because of the type of role taking ("moral musical chairs") found only at Stage 6.

Anne Colby and Lawrence Kohlberg (1987) gave a few examples of moral reasoning that they considered "illustrative of Stage 6." The examples came from a moral-judgment interview with a woman who had graduate training in philosophy. The following excerpt is from an answer explaining when and why Heinz should steal the drug.

> . . . if it came to a point where nothing else could be done, I think that in consultation with his wife, if he and his wife decided that that would be an acceptable alternative for Heinz, then yes he should. Because I think that ultimately it comes down to a conflict of duties . . . breaking into a store and stealing is not an action that can be prescribed for humanity, for our societal group as a whole. On the other hand, Heinz, I think has, just by virtue of being a member of the human race, has an obligation, a duty to protect other people . . . when it comes down to a conflict between those two, I think that the protection of human life is more important (Colby & Kohlberg, 1987, pp. 33–34).

This comment expresses a universalizable, reciprocal, prescription for action. The prescription derives from an ethical principle of protection of human life. Those elements define, for Kohlberg, the highest stage of moral judgment.

FIGURE 15.3

The mean scores for the percentage of moral reasoning at each stage for the participants in Kohlberg's longitudinal study. Reasoning at Stages 1 and 2 decreased as the subjects grew older. Reasoning at Stage 4 increased greatly from 10 to 36 years of age. (From Colby & Kohlberg, 1987.)

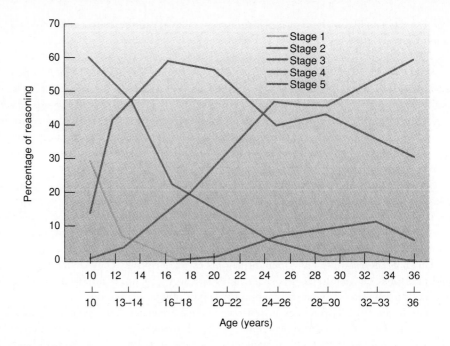

## Moral Development: Assumptions and Evidence

Kohlberg made the same assumptions about development through his moral-judgment stages that Piaget made about cognitive development (Colby & Kohlberg, 1987; Kohlberg, 1976). Four assumptions are most important.

*1. Children move to higher stages as they grow older.* This assumption may seem self-evident, but it is basic to Kohlberg's claim that the six stages represent a developmental sequence. Dozens of studies support the assumption. Perhaps the best known is Kohlberg's own longitudinal study, begun during the 1950s. The study included more than 50 boys who were first interviewed when they were between 10 and 16 years of age. The boys were interviewed again at three- or four-year intervals for 20 years. Figure 15.3 shows the percentage of moral reasoning at each stage that the boys showed at different ages.

At age 10, almost 60 percent of the boys' reasoning was at Stage 2. About 25 percent of their reasoning was at Stage 1, and the remainder was at Stage 3. By age 16–18, however, Stage 3 reasoning was most common. Only about 25 percent of the boys' reasoning was at Stage 2, and Stage 1 reasoning had disappeared.

Stage 4 reasoning was virtually absent at age 10, but it accounted for the largest percentage of the participants' reasoning at ages 24–26. It became even more common as the boys grew older. Stage 5 reasoning also became more common after age 20, but it never accounted for much more than 10 percent of the participants' moral reasoning.

Figure 15.3 clearly shows that lower stages of reasoning become less common and higher stages become more common with increasing age. Many other studies in the United States and other countries have shown the same age trends (Rest, 1983). When responding to interviews about moral dilemmas, people do give answers consistent with higher stages of moral reasoning as they grow older.

*2. Movement to higher stages occurs in an invariant sequence.* According to Kohlberg, the development of moral judgment is highly constrained. Children should move through the stages in order, without skipping any. Once children have reached some stage, they should never go back to lower stages. Both the absence of skipping and the absence of regression are implied by the assumption that movement to higher stages occurs in an invariant sequence.

The invariant-sequence assumption is critical to Kohlberg's claim that the moral-judgment stages depend on cognitive development rather than on specific social influences. Kohlberg argued that each higher stage is a logical extension of the previous stage. Children cannot skip

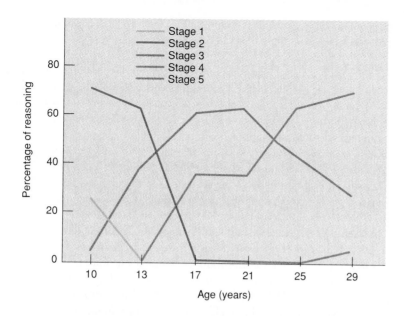

FIGURE 15.4
The percentage of moral reasoning at each stage for one boy in Kohlberg's longitudinal study. Notice the gradual decrease in lower-stage reasoning and the gradual increase in higher-stage reasoning. Notice, also, that most of the boy's reasoning at each age was at one stage of moral judgment. For example, the boy showed mostly Stage 2 reasoning at age 10. This pattern is consistent with Kohlberg's assumption that each stage forms a structured whole. (From Colby & Kohlberg, 1987.)

stages because they cannot make the jump in logical reasoning that such a skip would require. Children's logic for thinking about moral issues must develop in an orderly fashion, with each improvement in logic building on the previous understanding of morality.

Also, children should move to higher stages when they have discovered the problems or deficiencies in lower-stage reasoning. Once having done so, they should never regress to the lower stages. They should not return to modes of reasoning they know are inadequate.

Research data largely support the assumption that development occurs in an invariant sequence (Colby & Kohlberg, 1987; Rest, 1983). Children do not move from low to high stages without passing through the intermediate stages. A few children show decreases in moral stage scores when retested on the moral-judgment interview, but this regression may be more apparent than real. The measurement of moral stages is not perfect. Because of errors in measurement, a person's stage scores can go up or down a little, even if no change occurs in the person's basic pattern of moral reasoning. The occasional decreases over time in children's stage scores seem more likely to reflect this sort of measurement error than true regression (Colby & Kohlberg, 1987).

*3. Each stage forms a "structured whole."* According to Kohlberg, moral-judgment stages describe the organization of a person's thinking about moral issues. No matter what issue a person is considering, that organization should be apparent in the person's answers. Interpreted most strictly, this assumption would imply that every statement a person makes about any moral dilemma should be coded at the same stage. A Stage 3 person, for example, should express Stage 3 reasoning 100 percent of the time.

Such a strict interpretation of the structured-whole assumption is inappropriate because it conflicts with more general assumptions about developmental change. A child (or an adult) does not change overnight from one moral-judgment stage to the next. Researchers expect to find children reasoning mostly at one stage but partly at the stages they have moved from or are moving toward. Most children scored with the current scoring manual show this pattern (Colby & Kohlberg, 1987).

Figure 15.4 looks like the previous one, but it shows the percentage of reasoning at each stage for one boy in Kohlberg's longitudinal sample. About 70 percent of the boy's reasoning on several moral dilemmas was at Stage 2 when he was 10 years old. About 60 percent of his reasoning was at Stage 3 when he was 17 years old. About 70 percent of his reasoning was at Stage 4 when he was 29 years old.

In the entire longitudinal sample, about two-thirds of the boys' reasoning at each age was at a single stage. Other research has shown that children reason at roughly the same stage on Kohlberg's hypothetical dilemmas and on moral dilemmas that they personally

experienced (Walker, DeVries, & Trevethan, 1987). Therefore, the moral-judgment stages seem to reflect the basic structure of people's thinking about morality.

*4. Kohlberg's moral-judgment stages are universal.* The boldest assumption that Kohlberg made is that his stages apply to all people around the world. In 1976 he wrote, "The claim we make is that anyone who interviewed children about moral dilemmas and who followed them longitudinally in time would come to our six stages and no others" (p. 47). Do the research data support this bold assumption?

Yes and no. Researchers have studied the development of moral reasoning in more than 20 cultures (Snarey, 1985). The moral reasoning of most children and adults in every culture can be scored with minor adaptations of the standard scoring manual. Remember the earlier examples of reasoning by children in three cultures. Each child's reasoning could be readily recognized as Stage 2. In addition, a handful of longitudinal studies in other cultures showed an invariant sequence of development to higher stages, just as in the United States.

On the other hand, adults in some cultures answered questions about moral dilemmas in ways that seemed to reflect postconventional reasoning but that are not treated as post-conventional in the standard scoring manual (Snarey, 1985). For example, adults in India often bring ideas from ancient Indian philosophies into their discussion of the Heinz dilemma. One central idea is that of *dharma*, which refers to a complex combination of duty, obligation, and religion. Notice how this idea determined one Hindu man's response to the Heinz dilemma, when the main character was given the name Ashok:

*Should Ashok steal the drug?*
No. He's feeling desperate because his wife is going to die and that's why he is [thinking of] stealing the drug. But people don't live forever and providing her the drug does not necessarily mean that she will live long. How long you live is not in our hands but in God's hands. And there are other ways to get money like selling his landed property or even he can sell himself to someone and can save his wife's life . . . There is no way within Hindu dharma [religion, duty, obligation, law] to steal even if a man is going to die (Shweder & Much, 1987, p. 235).

Notice that this Hindu man does not question the assumption that human life is important. Instead, the man questions whether stealing the drug will be an effective and acceptable way for Ashok to save his wife's life. Richard Shweder and Nancy Much (1987) argued that this man's reasoning is postconventional in structure. The man refers to basic ethical principles that define what Ashok should do. The man does not attribute these principles to the social consensus of his group or to the law of his country, as would a person at the conventional level. He views the principles as flowing from dharma, a universal law.

Dharma is not the only postconventional principle that is part of the Indian cultural tradition. In Buddhism, both dharma and compassion for others can be phrased as ethical principles (Huebner & Garrod, 1993). Indian children and adults also give moral force to the obligations to help family members and friends who are in need (Miller & Bersoff, 1992). Some Indians apparently view these social obligations as springing from ethical principles as basic as the principle of justice emphasized by Kohlberg.

Taken together, the cross-cultural data imply that Kohlberg's first four stages are found universally and reflect most if not all features of children's and adults' moral judgments (Gibbs & Schnell, 1985; Snarey, 1985). By contrast, Kohlberg's original description of post-conventional moral reasoning seems most valid for Western cultures. Kohlberg's description probably does not provide an accurate account of postconventional reasoning in cultures whose philosophical or religious traditions differ greatly from the Western tradition. In his final statements on moral development, Kohlberg accepted these conclusions (Colby & Kohlberg, 1987).

### Gender Differences in Moral Judgment?

In 1982 Carol Gilligan argued that researchers need not look to other cultures to find biases and omissions in Kohlberg's theory of moral judgment. She suggested that Kohlberg's early reliance on samples of boys and men led him

to ignore important elements of moral reasoning in girls and women. In particular, Gilligan suggested that girls and women emphasize caring for others when responding to moral dilemmas. She asserted that such an emphasis is devalued in Kohlberg's system, so women are scored as lower in their moral-judgment stages than men.

Studies with more than 100 samples of children and adults have proved that Gilligan's (1982) argument is incorrect (Walker, 1984, 1986). Sex differences in stages of moral reasoning are usually nonsignificant. When differences are found, females are scored at higher stages than males about as often as the reverse.

Responding to this evidence, Carol Gilligan and Jane Attanucci (1988) modified their claims of gender bias in Kohlberg's theory. They proposed that women's emphasis on caring may not affect their stage of moral judgment but does represent a distinctive orientation toward morality. Gilligan and Attanucci contrasted a caring orientation with an orientation toward justice, or treating people fairly.

A few studies have provided evidence for such a sex difference in orientations toward caring and justice (e.g., Donenberg & Hoffman, 1988). More often, however, children and adults of both sexes give answers to moral dilemmas that reflect both a justice and a caring orientation (Galotti, Kozberg, & Farmer, 1991; Jadack et al., 1995; Kahn, 1992; Walker, 1989). In these studies, few differences have been found between males and females in the emphasis given to caring versus justice.

You should be cautious, however, about drawing the conclusion that moral reasoning does not differ for the two sexes. Some studies suggest that males and females differ in the kinds of moral issues that they consider most significant and confront most often in daily life (Golombok & Fivush, 1994; Walker et al., 1987). Differences of this sort would be expected, given the sex differences in social roles and in close relationships that were reviewed in chapter 14. Yet, currently, few statements about these differences can be made with confidence.

## Explaining and Promoting the Development of Moral Judgment

If you agree that higher stages of moral reasoning are "better," as most researchers do (Kurtines & Gewirtz, 1991; Rest, 1983), you might ask how to encourage the development of higher-stage thinking. Kohlberg (1976) offered three answers: (a) provoke cognitive-moral conflict, (b) provide opportunities for role taking, and (c) give people a social environment in which justice and a sense of community prevail.

***Cognitive-Moral Conflict*** Like Piaget (see chapter 8), Kohlberg assumed that children move to higher stages when they feel a sense of cognitive disequilibrium. Moral-judgment stages give people a structure that they can use to interpret and resolve moral dilemmas. If they think that their current structure is inadequate because it leads to contradictions or leaves some dilemmas unresolved, they search for a new structure. Stated differently, when they experience cognitive-moral conflict, they try to reach a higher stage of reasoning about morality.

How, then, do you provoke cognitive-moral conflict? One way is to expose people to moral reasoning at stages higher than their own. When people hear someone reasoning at a higher stage than they do, they may reconsider their mode of making moral decisions. Often, children are likely to hear higher-stage reasoning from parents. Children whose parents are at higher stages of moral judgment also tend to be at higher stages themselves (Speicher, 1994).

To show more conclusively that exposure to higher-stage reasoning leads to moral advance, researchers have conducted experimental studies (Kohlberg, 1976; Walker, 1980). In these experiments, adolescents increased their use of higher-stage reasoning after being exposed to arguments about moral dilemmas that represented higher stages. Researchers cannot say for certain that the rise in stage scores was caused by cognitive-moral conflict: They cannot directly observe conflicts inside adolescents' heads. Still, these findings are easiest to explain by assuming that cognitive-moral conflict fosters the development of moral judgment.

Moral discussions can also provoke cognitive-moral conflict. They are most likely to do so when they bring together people with different opinions on moral issues and different ways of reasoning about them. In several studies, discussions of moral dilemmas led, as expected, to movement toward higher stages of moral reasoning (Rest, 1983). Discussions most

often led to moral advances when people directly challenged one another's reasoning during the discussions (Berkowitz & Gibbs, 1985). Such challenges are more common in children's discussions with peers than with parents, which makes peer discussions especially effective in promoting advances in moral reasoning (Kruger, 1992).

Parents can also challenge their children's ideas, and such challenges sometimes lead to progress in moral reasoning (Kruger, 1992). Parents must be careful, however. Comments challenging children's ideas may be perceived as hostile. They may also be perceived as a form of lecturing, which can cause children to "turn off" instead of seriously considering parents' views (Walker & Taylor, 1991).

To be effective in enhancing children's moral development, parents need to provide supportive comments during moral discussions. Advice to children needs to be supplemented by careful listening to the children's comments, encouragement to participate, and humor. This combination creates a positive atmosphere that increases the impact of parents' reasoning (Speicher, 1992; Walker & Taylor, 1991).

***Opportunities for Taking Other People's Perspectives***   Remember that Selman's (1980) levels of perspective taking are the foundation for levels of moral judgment. Therefore, improving people's perspective taking should make them more able to move to higher stages of moral judgment. How do you improve people's perspective taking? One strategy, according to Kohlberg (1976), is to give them opportunities for taking different perspectives or seeing different viewpoints on social and moral issues.

Techniques that provoke cognitive-moral conflict also give people opportunities for perspective taking. During a moral discussion, people hear viewpoints on moral issues that differ from their viewpoint. To understand the other viewpoints fully, people must take the others' perspectives. Similarly, when people are exposed to moral reasoning at stages higher than their own, they must take the perspective of other people. Thus, moral discussions and exposure to higher-stage reasoning engage both processes that contribute to moral development.

Of course, role-taking opportunities are part of everyday life. All social interactions demand some accommodation to other people and some ability to take their perspectives. Perspective taking is especially necessary for leaders in social organizations. To be effective, leaders must recognize the views of other people and other groups. They must set rules or make decisions that help the organization function harmoniously.

In the United States, adolescents who are leaders at school, in clubs, and in other social organizations reason at higher moral stages than their peers (Keasey, 1971). In other cultures, adult leaders reason at higher stages than adults similar in age and education who are not leaders (Harkness, Edwards, & Super, 1981).

Among the Maisin people of Papua New Guinea, some men are heads of clans, others serve on official village councils, and others lead religious organizations. All Maisin leaders score higher on moral judgment stages than do nonleaders in the same villages (Tietjen & Walker, 1985). The mean score for leaders is above 250, which indicates that their reasoning is closer to Stage 3 than to Stage 2. The mean score for nonleaders is around 210, which indicates that nearly all their reasoning is at Stage 2.

Researchers cannot prove that the Maisin leaders' experience raised their stage of moral judgment, because the data are correlational. The leaders might have been chosen because other people recognized their high level of moral reasoning rather than vice versa. Still, experience in solving interpersonal problems while leading an organization probably accounts for part of the difference in moral reasoning between leaders and nonleaders. Stated in practical terms, giving people opportunities for taking others' perspectives may be one effective technique for promoting development in moral judgment.

***Living in a Just Community***   Kohlberg (1976) argued that development in moral judgment is difficult for people whose environments reflect low stages of morality. Kohlberg worked in prisons that seemed to operate according to a Stage 2 morality. As one inmate said, "If a guy messes up in a certain way or doesn't brown-nose as much as he should, the counselor won't do a job for him. It's all favoritism" (p. 51). In other words, people help only the people who help them, which fits the Stage 2 idea of justice.

Kohlberg proposed that moral development is most rapid when people live in environments where more mature ideas of justice are upheld. To test this hypothesis, he tried to create such environments. He worked longest in public high schools, where he and his coworkers established Just Communities (Higgins, 1991; Power, Higgins, & Kohlberg, 1989).

The Just Communities established by Kohlberg included about 100 students and five teachers in a special school, or a "school within a school." All students and teachers met each week to plan activities, make rules for members' behavior, and decide how to discipline rule breakers. In these meetings, decisions were made democratically, by majority vote. When voting, teachers had no veto power: Each had one vote, just like each student. Teachers had a special role, though, which was to encourage students to think about the moral implications of the group's decisions. Teachers also worked to build a sense of community, a sense that every person's welfare was important.

The Just Community approach represents a significant extension of cognitive-developmental theory. During community meetings, members of Just Communities discuss not hypothetical moral dilemmas, but dilemmas that arise in everyday life. In Just Communities, people do not merely consider the philosophical question, "What is justice?" They consider the harder question, "How can we live justly with one another?" But justice is not enough by itself. The focus on building a sense of community complements Kohlberg's original focus on individual rights and duties.

Students in Just Communities often showed advances in moral reasoning greater than those in traditional schools (Power et al., 1989). Only a few Just Communities were set up in schools, however, so evidence on their effects is limited. More evidence exists on the effects of living in another kind of community, the family.

In one study of families in India (Parikh, 1980), adolescents scored at higher moral stages when their parents encouraged their participation in moral discussions. Adolescents also scored at higher stages when their parents used reasoning when disciplining them instead of relying on power assertion. This study and similar studies of U.S. families (Hoffman, 1988) counter Piaget's claim that the unequal relationship between parents and children can only lead to a morality of obedience to authority.

Moreover, you read earlier that moral discussions with parents can promote children's moral reasoning if parents are supportive and encouraging. In addition, parents' warmth is related to their children's moral development (Hart, 1988; Speicher, 1992). Parents can, then, promote the development of their children's moral reasoning by talking with them about moral issues and by creating a positive emotional climate. In this way, parents create a family atmosphere like that of the Just Communities that Kohlberg created in schools.

## Morality, Social Conventions, and Personal Issues

While eating dinner, a 6-year-old girl begins to pick up a green bean with her fingers. Her father tells her, "Don't eat with your fingers! Use your fork." She drops the green bean, picks up her fork, and continues to eat.

What does this girl think about her father's order? After reading about Piaget's and Kohlberg's theories, you might assume that she thinks eating with your fingers is morally wrong. After all, she is supposed to have a heteronomous morality, in which adult authorities define what is right and wrong.

According to Elliot Turiel (1983), you would be incorrect if you made that assumption. He argued that children distinguish between moral rules and other kinds of rules long before age 6. Children view rules as falling in the domain of morality when they affect the rights, duties, or welfare of other people. Stealing, lying, and hitting are examples.

Children view other rules as social conventions. **Social conventions** are "behavioral uniformities that coordinate interactions of individuals within social systems" (p. 34). Conventions ensure that organizations run smoothly, or they symbolize important elements of the social order. According to Turiel, eating with a fork instead of your fingers is a social convention. So is addressing teachers by their title and last name (e.g., Mrs. Morelli) instead of by their first name (e.g., Gina).

Do not confuse Turiel's (1983) definition of social conventions with Kohlberg's definition of conventional moral reasoning. Turiel described social conventions as a category of

**social conventions**
*Behavioral uniformities that coordinate interactions of individuals within social systems (e.g., the rule that teachers are addressed by their title and last name rather than by their first name).*

**TABLE 15.3** *Percentage of Incidents in Which the Peers and Mothers of 2- and 3-Year-Olds Showed Specific Types of Reactions to Violations of Moral Rules and Social Conventions*

| | TYPE OF VIOLATION | |
| --- | --- | --- |
| | MORAL RULE | SOCIAL CONVENTION |
| ***Peers' Response*** | | |
| Emotional reaction | 8 | 1 |
| Physical retaliation | 5 | 1 |
| Commands | 6 | 0 |
| Injury/loss statements | 6 | 0 |
| ***Mothers' Response*** | | |
| Commands | 11 | 26 |
| Rules statements | 1 | 4 |
| Disorder statements | 0 | 3 |
| Rights statements | 6 | 0 |

rules that are distinct from moral rules. What Kohlberg called conventional moral reasoning is reasoning about *moral* issues (or moral rules) that focuses on social norms or beliefs about how people must behave to ensure a society's survival (Colby & Kohlberg, 1987). In other words, Turiel used *convention* to describe a type of rule, and Kohlberg used the same term to describe one basis for people's moral judgments.

Turiel (1983) also proposed a third domain, the personal domain, besides those of morality and social conventions (see Nucci, 1981). Acts that fall in the personal domain do not involve the rights or welfare of other people and do not directly affect the functioning of social systems. They are "just personal," and so not subject to rules. Some examples are watching TV, keeping a private diary, and choosing anyone you like as a friend.

Suppose, then, that a parent makes a rule about a personal issue. Suppose a 6-year-old boy's mother says he can't play with one of his friends. From Piaget's and Kohlberg's descriptions of young children's moral reasoning, you might expect the boy to accept his mother's order and think the order is fair. But children don't think that way (Nucci, 1981; Tisak, 1986). As mentioned earlier, even 6-year-olds say their parents do not have the authority to tell them who their friends can be. Definite limits exist on young children's heteronomy, or their unilateral respect for adults. One important limit, recognized even by young children, is that personal issues are not under parents' control.

Children also distinguish between the moral and conventional domains (Turiel, 1983). By 3 years of age, children say that acts such as hitting and stealing, which violate moral rules, would be wrong even if there were no rules against them (Smetana, 1981). Three-year-olds say that acts such as not participating in "show and tell" at nursery school, which violate social conventions, would not be wrong if there were no rules against them.

Children distinguish between moral and conventional rules because their parents and peers respond differently to violations of the two types of rules. In one study (Smetana, 1989), 2- and 3-year-olds were observed as they interacted at home with their mother or a peer. During these interactions, the children sometimes broke moral rules. For example, they took toys from the peers or hit them. Also, the children sometimes violated social conventions. For example, they did not say "please" when they asked for things, or they ate with their fingers.

Table 15.3 shows that peers more often responded to violations of moral rules than to violations of social conventions. After moral violations, children showed emotional reactions such as crying or anger. They also responded with physical retaliation, commands not to do that, and statements that the other person had hurt them or taken something from them. These responses are not surprising because aggression was the most common moral violation.

What's important, though, is that peers almost never cried, got angry, or did anything else when a child violated a convention like eating with fingers.

Mothers responded to violations of social conventions more often than peers did. Mothers issued commands, restated the rule that the child had broken, or talked about the disorder the child caused. Mothers responded differently to violations of moral rules. They gave commands, but not as often as for violations of conventions. They also told their child that he or she had violated another person's rights. These reactions of mothers and of peers show children that moral rules are different from social conventions (Nucci, 1985; Smetana, 1984).

Of course, parents do not always agree with their children about how a particular rule should be classified. Often, parent-child conflicts are caused by differences in beliefs about whether an act is a personal issue, a social convention, or a moral rule (Smetana & Asquith, 1994). The prototypical example of these differences concerns a parent's request that adolescents keep their bedrooms clean.

To many parents, such a request is reasonable because house-cleaning is a responsibility of all family members and all are expected to abide by the same standards of cleanliness. In short, most parents treat keeping rooms clean as a legitimate social convention. By contrast, many adolescents say, "It's my room, so I can have it the way I want." That is, they treat the appearance of their room as a personal issue. Fortunately, conflicts over these types of issues decrease as adolescents approach adulthood and parents grant them more autonomy (Smetana & Asquith, 1994).

What counts as a social convention may differ across cultures. Moslem Arab children in one study said that addressing teachers by their first name was wrong and should be prohibited by law (Nisan, 1987). One interpretation of this finding is that the children treated a violation of a social convention as morally wrong. But these data are controversial (Nisan, 1988; Turiel, Nucci, & Smetana, 1988). Another study suggested that Korean children distinguish between moral rules and conventions as U.S. children do (Song, Smetana, & Kim, 1987).

Some cultural differences in evaluations of actions may result from different beliefs about the consequences of actions (Shweder, Mahapatra, & Miller, 1987; Wainryb, 1993). For example, people in northern India think that a widow who eats fish will become sexually aroused, have intercourse with men, and thereby offend the spirit of her deceased husband. People in the United States do not think that eating fish has those consequences. Therefore, a widow who eats fish is viewed as immoral in India but not in the United States.

## IS IT IMMORAL TO EAT YOUR DOG?

The following stories were told to 10- to 12-year-olds in Philadelphia and in the city of Recife, Brazil. The children were part of a study of cultural differences in moral judgments (Haidt, Koller, & Dias, 1993).

> Imagine that a family had a dog, and one day the dog was killed by a car in front of the family's house. The family had heard that dog meat is delicious, so they took the dead dog, skinned it, and ate it for dinner. Was it wrong for them to do that?

> Imagine that a woman was cleaning out her closet and found an old American flag. She didn't want the flag anymore, so she cut it into pieces and used the pieces as rags when cleaning her bathroom. Do you think it was wrong to do that?

Earlier you read that most scholars define the moral domain as including acts that affect the rights, duties, and welfare of other people. Neither eating the family dog or using pieces of a flag to clean toilets affects other people's rights, duties, or welfare. Are these acts, therefore, not immoral?

To answer this question, other criteria for defining an immoral act are helpful. One criterion is whether other people can legitimately interfere with the person doing the act. In particular, can they stop or punish a person for doing the act? If other people have no right to interfere, then the act probably falls within the personal domain rather than the moral domain.

Another criterion for an immoral act is that it would be unacceptable in all human societies. When people judge an act as immoral, they assume the act should be universally prohibited. This criterion distinguishes immoral acts from acts that merely violate the social conventions in a specific country.

These criteria were used to judge whether children in Philadelphia and Recife, Brazil, considered it immoral to do the acts described in the earlier stories. These acts harm no one but may offend people, so they were called harmless-offensive acts. Children also heard a story involving an immoral and aggressive act, about a girl pushing a boy off a swing. The aggression story was included to be certain that the questions given to children differentiated between immoral and other types of acts.

Figure 15.5 shows how children in each city answered the question about whether a person who did each specific act should be stopped or punished. The responses are shown separately for children from high-SES and low-SES families. The same pattern of responses was found on a question about whether the acts should be prohibited in all countries.

Almost all children felt that a person who commits an act of aggression should be stopped or punished. Thus, children in every group agreed that aggression was immoral. Most or all the children in three of the groups also agreed that persons who commit harmless-offensive acts such as eating the family dog should be stopped or punished. The only exception was the group of high-SES children from Philadelphia. In response to another question, most of these children admitted that it would bother them to see people eating their dog or cleaning a bathroom with the flag. However, their unwillingness to stop or punish these people implies that they did not consider these acts immoral.

Other cultural differences in evaluations of actions are less easy to explain by differences in beliefs. A few cross-cultural studies suggest that well-educated people in the United States—a group that includes moral development researchers—define morality more narrowly than many other people do. One of those studies is described in *Cultural Perspectives:* "Is It Immoral to Eat Your Dog?"

Even in the United States, people differ in the behaviors they consider as moral, conventional, and personal. According to Turiel (1989), these differences show not that the distinctions among domains are invalid but that people must often coordinate different domains of judgment. This coordination is often difficult to achieve and, thus, is difficult for researchers to describe.

Think about your own opinions regarding abortion, one issue studied by Elliot Turiel, Carolyn Hildebrandt, and Cecilia Wainryb (1991). These researchers asked adolescents and adults many questions about abortion. For example, they asked whether it was right or wrong, whether it should be prohibited by law, and whether all countries should have laws

The differences in the children's answers cannot be attributed to differences in their maturity, because a similar pattern held for groups of adults from each city. The best explanation of the differences is in terms of different moral codes (Shweder, 1990). High-SES children and adults in the United States define morality like the scholars mentioned earlier. In this *ethics of autonomy*, morality serves only to protect each individual's freedom, so acts that do not harm other people cannot be judged as immoral.

However, at least two other moral codes exist. In the *ethics of community*, individuals belonging to any community are obliged to show respect to the symbols of that community and to its leaders. Using the national flag as a rag can, therefore, be viewed as an immoral act.

In the *ethics of divinity*, individuals are viewed as having a spiritual nature that must be kept pure. Acts that are disgusting or degrading can be viewed, then, as polluting the individual's spiritual nature. Eating the family dog is such an act and so is immoral.

Research on these three moral codes has barely begun. However, current evidence suggests that moral development researchers have defined morality more narrowly than most children and adults do. Definitions that do not include all three moral codes are likely to miss part of what morality means to most people in most cultures.

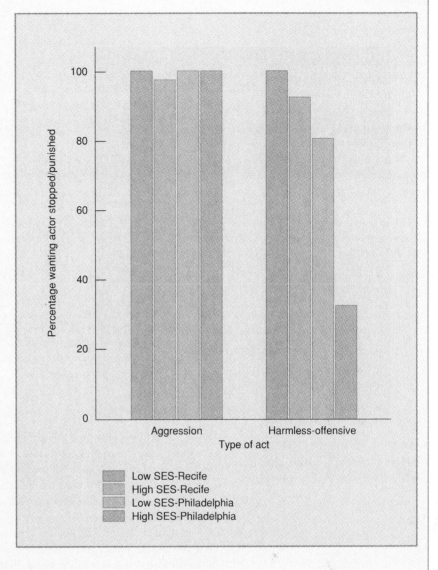

## FIGURE 15.5

Children from Philadelphia and from Recife, Brazil, think that people who act aggressively should be stopped or punished. But what about people who commit harmless but offensive acts like eating the family's dog after it has been accidentally killed? Fewer than half the Philadelphia children from high-SES families—but most children in other groups—said that such people should be stopped or punished. The contrast implies that different groups of children adopt different definitions of morality.

against it. Some students said that abortion was wrong, implying that they considered it immoral, but they still said it should not be illegal. Even among students who felt abortion was not wrong, ambivalence in responses was common. Issues like this one are difficult to classify neatly into the moral, conventional, or personal domain.

Finally, Larry Nucci and Elliot Turiel (1993) are among the few researchers who have examined the relations of children's moral judgments to their religious beliefs. These researchers interviewed one group of children who were Amish-Mennonite. Members of this religious denomination do not have radios or televisions in their homes, and they are required to dress in simple, often homemade clothing. Women are also expected to wear a specific bonnet or head covering after they are baptized, which usually occurs during adolescence. Another group of children in the study were Orthodox Jews. Members of this religious denomination follow strict rules about acceptable foods and observe many rituals during religious holidays. Boys and men also wear a special head covering (the yarmulke or skullcap).

**FIGURE 15.6**

Amish-Mennonite and Orthodox Jewish children consider stealing as unacceptable under all circumstances. However, these children believe that the rules of their religions about proper head coverings do not apply to people of other religions and would not hold if the Bible said nothing about them. The children thus distinguish between universal moral rules and nonmoral rules binding only for people of their religions.

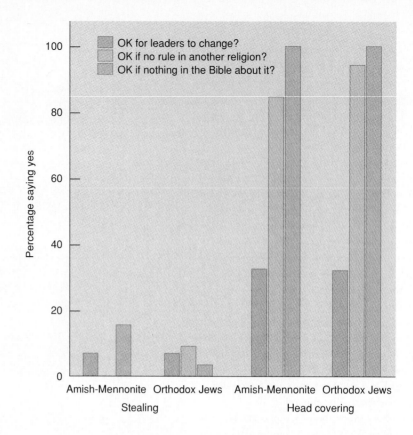

Nucci and Turiel expected children in these groups to distinguish between moral rules that apply universally and nonmoral rules that apply only to members of their denomination. Children's responses were largely consistent with these expectations. As figure 15.6 shows, very few Amish-Mennonite or Orthodox Jewish children believed that it would be okay for their religious leaders to change or eliminate the rule against stealing. Very few children thought stealing would be okay for people in another religion that had no rule about stealing. Very few children thought stealing would be okay even if the Bible contained no commands against stealing. In short, the children viewed the rule against stealing as a universal moral rule.

The children responded differently about the rules specific to their own denomination. In particular, most Amish-Mennonite children thought it would be okay for women who belonged to another religion not to wear the bonnet that Amish-Mennonite women wore. Most Orthodox Jewish children thought it would be okay for men who belonged to another religion not to wear the yarmulke that Orthodox Jewish men wore. All the children agreed that no special head covering would be required if the Bible did not contain a rule commanding one.

Figure 15.6 also shows that less than half the children in each group thought that their respective rules about head covering could be changed by their religious leaders. These children did not view such religious rules as comparable to social conventions like eating with a fork, which can be changed by social consensus or legitimate authorities. Instead, the children thought that the authority to change these rules rested with God, and God's word (the Bible) indicated that these rules should not be changed by any religious leader.

Most intriguing were the responses to a final question, asked only of the Orthodox Jewish children: "Suppose God had commanded that Jews should steal. Would it then be right for a Jew to steal?" Only 16 percent of the children said yes. Most children said that stealing would still be wrong because it was unjust and would harm people. Moreover, most children said that God could not give such a command, because it would be wrong and God is perfect and cannot do wrong. In other words, these children held that the rules of morality apply not only to all humans but also to God.

# Moral Emotions: Guilt, Empathy, and Good Feelings

Once children have decided what is morally right and what is morally wrong, what makes them do what's right—when they do? Freud's answer was that they know they'll feel guilty if they don't. Freud's hypotheses about guilt inspired much of the early research on moral emotions in children.

## Guilt: Its Adaptive and Maladaptive Forms

For Freud (1920/1965, 1930/1961), guilt was a necessary evil. He believed that guilt derives from parent/child relationships early in life. As children move into the phallic stage at around 3 years of age, they feel sexually attracted to their opposite-sex parent and hostile toward their same-sex parent. Remember from chapter 1 that Freud regarded these feelings as symptoms of an Oedipal crisis in boys and an Electra complex in girls. Young boys and girls realize that they cannot express their sexual and hostile impulses overtly. They must repress them. The repressed impulses provide the energy or motivation for moral behavior.

In the process of repression, the superego is formed. The contents of the superego, its "shoulds" and "should nots," also come from parents. Children identify with their parents and internalize their rules. When children are tempted to violate a rule, they feel anxious about doing so because they anticipate feelings of guilt. This guilt is "bad," in Freud's view, because it prevents children from freely expressing their natural impulses. Even so, Freud believed the development of guilt was necessary for the socialization of children and, therefore, necessary for the survival of civilization. This explains the title of one of his final books, *Civilization and Its Discontents*.

Child development researchers accept some aspects of Freud's analysis of guilt. They agree with Freud on the definition of **guilt**, "thoughts and feelings of remorse and responsibility that accompany real or imagined wrongdoings" (Zahn-Waxler et al., 1990). They also agree that guilt is one source of motivation for moral behavior that emerges during early childhood. One reason children do what's right, when they do, is that they would feel guilty if they didn't (Hoffman, 1988; Rest, 1983).

However, most researchers disagree with Freud about how guilt arises. Rather than attributing guilt to the repression of sexual and hostile impulses, they point out that parents often hold children responsible for their actions. Parents tell children, clearly and forcefully, when they have done something wrong. The parents' disapproval of immoral behavior is likely to be internalized as self-blame, or guilt.

Also, many parents explicitly tell their children why their immoral behavior is wrong. That is, they rely on inductive discipline. As defined in chapter 11, inductive discipline is the use of reasons when disciplining children, especially reasons that point out the harmful effects of certain behaviors on other people. Children most fully internalize moral rules and feel guilty if they violate them when their parents rely on this type of discipline (Hoffman, 1988).

Children's feelings of guilt are first evident around age 2, after the emergence of the self-recognition discussed in chapter 13 (Kochanska, 1991; Kochanska, Casey, & Fukumoto, 1995; Kochanska et al., 1994). When 2- and 3-year-olds have broken a toy or violated a parent's rule, they sometimes hang their heads, blush, look sad, or look away when people look at them. They may also apologize, blame themselves for what happened, or attempt to repair damage they caused. All these reactions suggest that they recognize they have done wrong and feel guilty.

By 5 years of age, guilt may take different forms in different children. Adaptive guilt contributes to moral behavior without being excessive. Another form of guilt is maladaptive because it is excessive, dysfunctional, or inappropriate. The two forms of guilt were contrasted in a study of 5- to 9-year-olds (Zahn-Waxler et al., 1990).

The children heard stories about incidents in which boys or girls interacted with their mothers or with a peer. The stories were written so that they were likely to elicit expressions

**guilt**
*Thoughts and feelings of remorse and responsibility that accompany real or imagined wrongdoings.*

FIGURE 15.7

When children whose mothers are not depressed hear a story about a mother who is angry at her child, they more often talk about the child's guilt as they grow older. This age change does not occur for children with depressed mothers. Also, at 5 to 6 years of age, children with depressed mothers talk more about the child's guilt than do children whose mothers are not depressed. These results suggest that guilt may take a more maladaptive form among children with depressed mothers. (Source: Zahn-Waxler et al., 1990.)

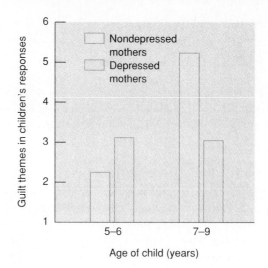

of guilt. For example, one story portrayed a mother with her son in the kitchen. The mother said she was leaving the house for a while because she was very angry. Her son watched her go out the door and then continued watching her through the kitchen window.

After the children heard each story, they were asked a few questions about it. Children were asked how the boy in the story felt, whether he thought he did anything to make his mother angry, and whether he could do anything to make her feel better.

Children sometimes said that the child characters in the stories felt guilty. For example, they said that the boy with an angry mother felt sorry for doing something, wanted to punish himself, or tried to make up for what he did. How much children talked about the guilt of the story characters varied with their age and the mental health of their mothers. Some children had mothers who had been diagnosed as clinically depressed. Other children had mothers who were not depressed.

Children with nondepressed mothers expressed more guilt when answering questions about the stories at 7 to 9 years of age than at 5 to 6 years of age (see figure 15.7). In other research, normal children acknowledged and expressed more guilt as they grew older because they took more responsibility for their actions. The data for children with nondepressed mothers reflect this developmental trend.

Five- and 6-year-olds with depressed mothers talked more about the story characters' guilt than did children the same age with nondepressed mothers. In other research, depressed mothers spoke more negatively about their children when interacting with them than nondepressed mothers. Depressed mothers often said they tried to make their children feel guilty when they punished them (Susman et al., 1985). These mothers may have believed, erroneously, that increasing their children's guilt or anxiety was an effective technique of socialization.

These disciplinary techniques may not have been chosen so deliberately, though. Another possibility is that these forms of discipline reflect the mothers' poor emotional regulation, resulting in negative emotions expressed toward the child as well as toward themselves. Such disciplinary techniques apparently make young children feel more responsibility for their behavior than is appropriate or make children blame themselves for things that are not their fault. The mothers' discipline leads, in short, to maladaptive guilt.

Seven- to 9-year-olds with depressed mothers talked less about the story characters' guilt than did those with nondepressed mothers. Yet when responding to a standard psychiatric interview, the children with depressed mothers blamed themselves as much for negative events they experienced as did those with nondepressed mothers. Both groups of children with depressed mothers gave bizarre responses to the stories more often than did the other children. They made comments like, "The mom's leaving home because the boy wouldn't eat his peas." For another story, one child said, "They had the dog put to sleep and now the mother is calling the vet to see if they can make it come alive again." These comments also suggest a maladaptive form of guilt.

Not all children with depressed mothers made such bizarre comments. Indeed, many children with depressed parents show normal moral and social development. Many cope constructively with their parents' emotional problems, and some may develop unusual interpersonal maturity. But such positive outcomes cannot always be expected. A parent's depression is often hard for children to understand and can lead to abnormal feelings of guilt.

By contrast, adaptive guilt has positive effects on children's moral behavior (Baumeister, Stillwell, & Heatherton, 1994). Because they feel guilty, children apologize when they do something wrong and they try to repair any damage they caused. Gradually, feelings of adaptive guilt may be transformed into a general sense of responsibility for others and concern for their welfare. Children who talk more openly about the guilt that story characters might feel also are more helpful when they see others in distress (Chapman et al., 1987). Thus, the development of guilt feelings makes children more sensitive to other people in need.

More generally, children who express more negative feelings about behaviors such as taking others' toys have better relationships with their siblings during the preschool years (Dunn, Brown, & Maguire, 1995). These findings suggest that the experience of guilt may have important social functions in promoting close and positive social relationships (Baumeister et al., 1994).

The reasons that children feel guilty change as they grow older (Williams & Bybee, 1994). For example, more 5th graders than older children say they have felt guilty about fighting with peers. More 11th graders than younger children say they have felt guilty about inconsiderate behaviors such as forgetting someone's birthday. In addition, 11th graders also mention more situations in which they felt guilty because they neglected their responsibilities and failed to attain their ideals.

These differences partly reflect the changes in social understanding described in chapter 13. As adolescents become more able to think about the psychological world, they become more aware of behavior that does not cause physical injury but may hurt another's feelings. As adolescents become more able to think about possibilities, they better understand when they haven't done what they should or might have done. Through processes like these, developments in moral feelings are influenced by developments in moral reasoning.

## Empathy and Positive Feelings

Another emotion that can motivate children to help other people is **empathy**. Definitions of empathy vary, but most researchers consider empathy as (a) an emotional response to the perceptions of another person's emotional state (b) that is congruent with the other's emotional state (Eisenberg & Miller, 1987). For example, an empathic person is distressed when he or she sees another person in distress. Young children describe the experience of empathy in comments like, "He's sad because she's sad" (Chapman et al., 1987, p. 142).

Many theorists have suggested that empathy can lead to prosocial behaviors such as sharing, helping, and comforting people who are hurt or upset (Eisenberg & Miller, 1987; Hoffman, 1988). Children or adults who empathize with people in distress should, in theory, want to help those people so that they can reduce their own empathic distress. That is, they should try to make the other people feel better so that they themselves can feel better.

Researchers have not found strong or consistent correlations between measures of empathy and prosocial behavior. The research findings make more sense when different measures of empathy are distinguished (Eisenberg, 1992; Eisenberg & Miller, 1987).

Empathy is sometimes judged from children's responses to questionnaires. For example, children may be asked to agree or disagree with statements like "Seeing a girl who is crying makes me feel like crying" (Bryant, 1982). Alternatively, children may be observed as they watch films that portray children or adults in distress. Children who express more negative emotions as they watch these films are assumed to empathize more with the characters. Still a third method of assessing empathy is to tell children stories about people in distress and see how often they comment on one character's empathy for another character. They might say, "He feels sad because she's sad." These three types of empathy measures usually are positively related to measures of prosocial behavior. Children who are scored as more empathic tend to be more helpful to children or adults in need.

**empathy**
*An emotional response to the perceptions of another person's emotional state that is congruent with the other's emotional state (e.g., feeling distressed when another person is in distress).*

The method of assessing empathy that seems most straightforward, at first glance, does not yield empathy measures that are consistently related to prosocial behavior. Researchers have often told children stories about children who are unhappy or upset. Then the researchers ask children how they feel. Children who express more empathy, who say they feel unhappy when a story character is unhappy, do not always give more help when they see actual people in need. These findings seem to reflect problems in the empathy measure. After hearing a few stories, children may guess what the researcher wants them to say and respond accordingly (Eisenberg & Miller, 1987). Other types of empathy measures seem to yield more reliable and valid findings.

You should not expect empathy to lead always to helping, though. Some people who respond empathically to others may be so upset at another's plight that they want to escape rather than help (Eisenberg, 1992; Hoffman, 1988). For these people, empathy leads to personal distress rather than to sympathy for the other person. Measures of empathy are more strongly related to prosocial behavior for older children and adults than for young children. The relation may become stronger with increasing age because, as children grow older, empathy less often leads to personal distress and more often evokes a sympathetic concern for others.

Even in the early elementary grades, children differ in whether their emotional response to other people in need is one of sympathy or personal distress. Kindergarten and second-grade children in one study heard through a speaker what they thought was a crying infant in another room (Fabes et al., 1994). (Actually, the children heard only tape-recorded cries.) Children who had difficulty controlling their level of emotional arousal in this situation were less likely to respond with sympathy and more likely to express irritation at the infant. Control of emotions is, then, critical to the distinction between becoming distressed and reacting sympathetically to other people.

Prosocial behavior also occurs when people are not in distress. Preschool children in one study were observed during free play in their nursery school classrooms (Lennon & Eisenberg, 1987). These children usually expressed positive emotions when they shared toys with each other. Both the giver and the recipient of a toy seemed happy when they shared. The children's positive emotions are easy to understand because sharing usually occurred during friendly, cooperative play.

Preschool and school-age children may also express positive emotions when they help other people. Children smile and look happy when they give a bottle of milk to a hungry baby (Chapman et al., 1987). Helping can, therefore, be a rewarding experience in two senses of the word. Helping makes people feel good. Helping can also promote more helping, or be positively reinforcing (Cialdini, Kenrick, & Baumann, 1982).

By themselves, neither empathy nor positive emotions are an adequate basis for morality because they may not motivate children to treat all people fairly and equally (Baumeister et al., 1994; Hoffman, 1988; Rest, 1983). Like adults, children probably interact most positively with other children who share their attitudes and interests. They less often interact with children who have different attitudes and interests. This bias in interactions can produce a bias in behavior, too. Children may be more generous and helpful toward their friends and toward other peers whom they like than toward strangers or peers whom they don't like.

Similarly, children probably empathize most readily with their friends and with other children whom they like. Therefore, they may most often provide help and comfort when the others in need are peers with whom they already have a close relationship. Yet, if children behave prosocially only, or mostly, toward friends and liked peers, you would probably accuse them of favoritism rather than say they behaved morally.

Martin Hoffman (1988) proposed that empathy may be transformed as children grow so that it becomes less biased and more just. Children may begin to empathize not only with their friends but with groups of people who are chronically in need. Eventually, the scope of empathy may be broadened to include all people. The positive emotions that enhance prosocial behavior may also be transformed and broadened in scope. These transformations would make empathy and positive emotions operate partly like the moral principle of concern for others' welfare. But unlike an abstract principle, empathy and positive emotions would still have a motivational force that encourages children to behave morally when doing so conflicts with their self-interest.

Another perspective on the moral emotions, offered by Grazyna Kochanska (1991, 1993, 1995; Kochanska et al., 1994), is that their roles in moral development may vary with children's temperament. For children who are temperamentally low in fearfulness and anxiety, moral development may be heavily influenced by the positive emotions in parent-child interactions. When children have positive relationships with parents, they may be especially motivated to comply with parents' commands.

For children who are temperamentally high in fearfulness and anxiety, moral development may be heavily influenced by parents' disciplinary techniques. Parents who use power-assertive discipline may so frighten these children that they cannot pay proper attention to their parents' message and so do not internalize the parents' rules. By contrast, parents who rely on firm but gentle guidance and reasoning may, when disciplining, create a moderate level of arousal that leads to guilty feelings and to internalization.

Results consistent with these hypotheses were obtained in one study of preschoolers and toddlers (Kochanska, 1995). Measures of these children's internalization of parents' rules were obtained from mothers' reports and laboratory observations. For children low in fearfulness, internalization was most strongly related to the security of the children's attachment to the mother. This relation is consistent with the idea that positive emotions and positive relationships are the optimal route to internalization for these children. Among children high in fearfulness, internalization was most strongly related to their mothers' use of gentle discipline. This relation is consistent with the idea that moderate arousal leading to guilt is the optimal route to internalization for these children.

Of course, data from one study must be viewed as tentative until replicated. Kochanska's perspective is important, however, in suggesting that children differ in the types of emotions that most influence their moral behavior. Moral development may not be a process where "one size fits all," one pathway to moral maturity is the best for all children. Instead, children's characteristics and, especially, their temperament may affect which types of discipline will most effectively develop their moral emotions.

# MORAL BEHAVIOR

Many types of behavior fall in the moral domain. In this section you will read about three types that have often been studied: cheating (or, conversely, honest behavior), prosocial behavior, and aggression. Some aspects of prosocial and aggressive behavior were discussed earlier in this chapter and in other chapters. The focus in this section is on the age changes in these behaviors. In addition, you will learn about several models of the relations between these behaviors, the moral emotions, and moral reasoning.

## Cheating, Honesty, and Self-Control

Cheating is an important moral issue for school-age children who take academic tests individually. It is less an issue for preschool children. However, one prerequisite for honest behavior in testing situations is self-control, and self-control emerges during the preschool period. Self-control is a prerequisite for most moral behaviors, so it makes sense to begin this section by examining the development of self-control.

### Age Changes

Infants have some control over their behavior immediately after birth, but this control is largely reflexive (Kopp, 1982). For example, newborns will close their eyes in bright sunlight. As they grow older, infants gain greater control over their perception and motor movements (see chapter 5).

Near the end of their first year, infants take a major step toward self-control. They start to comply with commands from adults to inhibit an activity. If a mother says, "Don't touch that!" infants sometimes will draw back their hands. The infants' compliance with the mother's command is a step toward self-control because the mother does not need to restrain her infant physically. Infants modify their behavior in response to their mother's order.

Between 18 and 24 months of age, children develop what Claire Kopp (1982) describes as true self-control. By 24 months of age, children will often do what parents tell them even

FIGURE 15.8

How long would you expect a child to obey an adult's request not to touch an attractive toy telephone? As this figure shows, the answer depends on the child's age. Dramatic increases in self-control occur between 18 and 30 months of age. The increases make older children more able to obey a request not to touch a toy telephone. They also make older children more able to wait before taking a raisin from under a cup or opening an attractively wrapped gift. (Source: Vaughn et al., 1984.)

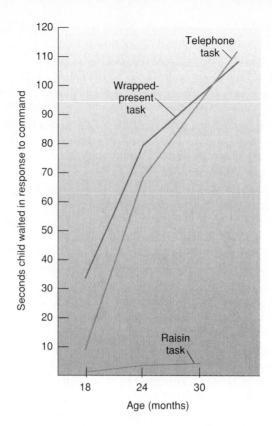

if the parents gave the command some time earlier. An ingenious study showed that this type of self-control emerges at around 24 months (Vaughn, Kopp, & Krakow, 1984).

Children who were 18, 24, or 30 months of age came to a psychology laboratory with their mothers. An experimenter showed each child a telephone with some unusual features, like having the dial on the bottom. Then the experimenter said she had to leave to get more toys. She told the child not to touch the phone while she was gone. An observer recorded whether the child followed the instruction and, if not, how soon the child touched the phone after the experimenter left.

For another task, the experimenter hid a raisin under one of three cups. The experimenter told the child to "wait until I tell you" before getting the raisin. For a third task, the experimenter showed the child a brightly wrapped package and said, "It's a present, and it's for you." Then the experimenter said she had to do some work and asked the child not to touch the present until she was finished. Again, observers recorded whether the child followed instructions and, if not, how long the child waited before violating them.

Children's ability to wait in response to an adult's order changed dramatically with age (see figure 15.8). With the attractive telephone nearby, the average 18-month-old waited only 10 seconds before touching it. By contrast, 24-month-olds waited about 70 seconds, on the average; 30-month-olds waited more than 100 seconds. Older children also waited longer for the raisin and the present. Not shown in the figure are the correlations between children's scores on the three tasks. These correlations increased steadily with age, which suggests that self-control became a moderately stable characteristic of children during this age range.

By 4 years of age, self-control has become a personality trait with predictive value. The 4-year-olds in one study were asked to wait before opening a wrapped present (Olson & Hoza, 1993). A year later, when the children were in kindergarten, their teachers rated their impulsive and aggressive behavior. Four-year-old boys with less ability to wait for a present were rated more negatively by their kindergarten teachers.

Even longer-term prediction from variations in children's self-control was obtained when children were tested for their **delay of gratification.** Four-year-olds were given a choice between two rewards: They could have one marshmallow immediately or two marshmallows in

**delay of gratification**
*An experimental procedure in which children can choose between a small reward available immediately and a larger reward that will be given only after some delay.*

Will the girl with the blindfold play the game fairly, or will she cheat by peeking under the blindfold? Long ago, Hartshorne and May discovered that children's tendencies to cheat in games depend both on their moral rules regarding honesty and on their interpretation of specific situations.

15 minutes. (Notice that the delay is measured in minutes now, not in seconds as in the earlier study.) Children who decided to wait for the larger reward and who actually waited for a longer time got higher scores for delay of gratification.

For one study, preschoolers who were tested for delay of gratification at age 4 were assessed again in middle and late adolescence (Mischel, Shoda, & Rodriguez, 1989; Shoda, Mischel, & Peake, 1990). Four-year-olds who could delay gratification longer, especially with marshmallows in plain sight, had more positive self-concepts and higher academic competence between 15 and 18 years of age. The preschoolers with greater self-control became adolescents who were described by their parents as more persistent, better able to cope with frustrations and temptations, and less distractible.

Moreover, the adolescents with greater self-control had higher SAT scores than their peers. These findings suggest that self-control shows considerable continuity over time. They also suggest that self-control is important both for moral development and for other aspects of psychological development.

Most children can delay gratification for a longer time as they grow older (Mischel et al., 1989). Should we expect, then, more moral behavior from older children? In particular, should we expect older children to be more honest in situations in which they are tempted to cheat?

Unfortunately, no. Hugh Hartshorne and Mark May (1928–1930) did a comprehensive series of studies on children's cheating more than 60 years ago. Their studies included many different tests with children ranging from the 3rd to the 12th grade. The testing program involved more than 10,000 students and took five years to complete.

Some tests were for cheating on school exams. Other tests were for cheating in athletic contests and in games like Pin the Tail on the Donkey. Children's behavior varied across tests, but their level of cheating did not consistently increase or decrease with age. Girls did not consistently cheat less or more than boys did. However, later analyses of the data showed that cheating was moderately consistent across tasks (Burton, 1963, 1976); that is, children who cheated on one test were likely to cheat on others.

Later researchers have occasionally found a slight decrease in cheating as children grow older, but the explanation for this decrease is uncertain. Older children might have been less tempted to cheat because they could more easily succeed on the tasks without cheating. Also, older children might have been more aware that they could get caught (Burton, 1976).

Cheating obviously does not disappear as children move into adolescence and adulthood. Cheating on academic tests remains a problem throughout the high-school and college

years, and news reports all too often describe the cheating or dishonest behavior of adults. From this perspective, the typical end point of moral development is discouraging.

## Moral Judgments and Honesty

Moral development can be examined from another perspective, though. Consider the relations of cheating or honest behavior to the other facets of morality, moral emotions and moral reasoning. Very little evidence exists on the relations of the moral emotions to honesty, and that evidence is inconsistent. Children who express more guilt about cheating may cheat less (Hoffman, 1970), but they don't always do so.

However, moral emotions can be assessed in a more indirect way. Suppose you ask children how a boy would feel if he stole some candy from a store. Then you ask them how a girl would feel if she shared her lunch with a classmate. Some children will mention moral emotions: The boy would feel bad because he stole and the girl would feel good because she was kind to someone else. Other children mention selfish emotions: The boy would feel good because he has some candy and the girl would feel bad because she has less lunch for herself. Children who answer these questions by mentioning the moral emotions are less likely to cheat when playing a game than those who mention the selfish emotions (Asendorpf & Nunner-Winkler, 1992).

What about the relations of honesty to moral reasoning? Many researchers have examined the relations of children's or adults' cheating to their stage of moral judgment. In most studies, individuals at higher Kohlberg stages cheated less. A few studies, though, showed no relation of moral-judgment stages to cheating. Occasionally, subjects at higher stages cheated more (Blasi, 1980).

Lawrence Kohlberg and Daniel Candee (1984) tried to explain these mixed results with a model of the relation between moral reasoning and moral behavior. The model has four major elements. The first, not surprisingly, is a person's stage of moral reasoning.

Kohlberg and Candee noted that people at low stages of moral reasoning will sometimes decide that they should behave morally. Stage 2 adolescents, for example, will decide not to cheat on tests when the probability of getting caught is high. Still, as people move to higher stages they more often decide to behave morally simply because it's the right thing to do. This makes the behavior of higher-stage people more consistently moral than is the behavior of lower-stage people.

The second element in the model is a person's sense of moral responsibility. Even when people know what should be done in a situation, they may not feel obliged to do that. That is, people may not accept any personal responsibility to do what is right. According to Kohlberg and Candee (1984), people at higher moral-judgment stages more often feel this sense of responsibility, which is another reason they more often behave morally.

The third element in the model is a person's type of moral reasoning. Kohlberg and Candee (1984) suggested that people at each stage show mainly Type A or mainly Type B reasoning. Type A reasoning is less prescriptive than Type B reasoning, which means that it does not always give people clear directions about what they are obliged to do. On the Heinz dilemma, for example, a person with Type A reasoning might say that Heinz should steal the drug if he wants to but not if he doesn't. A person with Type B reasoning might say that Heinz must steal the drug because his wife would do the same for him if he were in need.

Type A reasoning is also less universalistic than Type B reasoning. On the Heinz dilemma, a person with Type A reasoning might say that Heinz should steal the drug if he loves his wife, but that not every husband has the same duty. A person with Type B reasoning might say, instead, that all people should help one another.

As these examples suggest, people with Type B reasoning intuitively understand the morally correct solution to moral dilemmas. They may receive low stage scores because they cannot express their understanding in terms of moral principles, but their reasoning leads to the right decisions and to moral behavior. When proposing this model, therefore, Kohlberg and Candee (1984) acknowledged that a person need not be a moral philosopher to do what is right.

The fourth element in the model is the collection of nonmoral skills that allow a person to follow through on a decision. After people have decided what to do when faced with a

Why is the boy on the left cheating by copying his classmate's answers? Is it because he is at a low stage in his moral reasoning? According to Kohlberg and Candee, that may be part of the answer, but even children at low stages of moral reasoning often have an intuitive understanding of right and wrong.

moral choice, they must carry out their decision. For effective follow-through, people must have self-control, perseverance, and the intelligence to figure out how to do what should be done. People who make the right decision and feel responsible for acting on it may still not behave morally if they lack this follow-through.

Kohlberg and Candee's model for moral behavior is like that proposed by several other theorists (Blasi, 1983; Hoffman, 1988; Rest, 1983). So far the models have not been thoroughly tested in research. Nevertheless, they are highly plausible, and they help to explain why people don't always behave the way they know they should.

## Prosocial Behavior

Prosocial behavior is intriguing because it is rarely obligatory. This point was mentioned earlier, in the description of Anglo-American children playing the circles' game. Their failure to cooperate with their partner in the game is not immoral, in a narrow definition of the term. But in a broader view, morality includes a concern for others' welfare that often calls for cooperative, generous, and helpful behavior. How does this type of behavior develop, and how does it relate to moral emotions and reasoning?

### Age Changes

Infants behave prosocially as soon as they can engage in any coordinated social interactions (Eisenberg, 1992). By 12 months of age, infants give objects to their mothers and participate in cooperative interactions with them (Hay, 1979). By 18 months of age, toddlers begin to help their parents with household tasks (Rheingold, 1982). Toddlers pick up things on the floor, put away laundry, or try to set the table for meals. As they grow older and more competent, they help with more tasks.

Another type of prosocial behavior, comforting people in distress, also occurs in very young children. At around 1 year of age, infants show empathic distress when they see another person who is crying or in pain. At around 18 months of age, toddlers try to comfort people in distress by touching or patting them. Two-year-olds call adults to help a person in distress, and they tell the person they are sorry that he or she is hurt (Radke-Yarrow et al., 1983).

All these behaviors show that young children are inclined to act prosocially toward other people. As children gain more skill in social interaction, more knowledge about the world, and more understanding of other people's emotions, their prosocial behavior becomes more frequent and more effective. But even while they are very young, children show concern for other people and act on that concern.

How prosocial behavior changes as children grow older is less clear. Researchers have often asked children in laboratory studies to donate money or prizes to hypothetical needy children. Under these conditions, older children usually are more generous than younger children (Eisenberg, 1992; Radke-Yarrow et al., 1983). The data are difficult to interpret, though, because older children may also be more sensitive to an experimenter's expectations that they will donate to the needy.

Children in one study were explicitly told by an experimenter that it's good to give to poor children (Zarbatany, Hartmann, & Gelfand, 1985). Fifth graders who heard this message were more generous to hypothetical needy children than were first and third graders. When students in the same grades were not given that message, first and third graders were as generous as fifth graders.

Under some conditions, older children behave less prosocially toward others than younger children do. In the circles' game described earlier (Kagan & Madsen, 1971), 7- to 9-year-olds in the United States typically are less cooperative than 4- to 5-year-olds. Even Mexican children, who usually are more cooperative than Anglo-Americans, become less cooperative and more competitive as they grow older (Kagan & Madsen, 1972).

On tasks similar to the circles' game, age changes toward more competitive and less cooperative behavior have been found in countries from Greece to Japan (Toda et al., 1978). These changes can be attributed at least partly to children's social experience. Children from middle-SES families are less cooperative than those from lower-SES families (Knight & Kagan, 1977). Children from urban areas usually are less cooperative than children from rural areas (Eisenberg, 1992; Thomas, 1975). Urban-rural differences have been found not only in Mexico, but also in Israel, Colombia, Korea, and New Zealand. Moreover, attending Western-style schools that provide many opportunities for social comparison among classmates is also related to more competitive and less cooperative behavior.

In summary, no general conclusion about the age changes in prosocial behavior would be accurate. Age changes vary with the type of prosocial behavior, the method of assessment, and the age range under consideration (Radke-Yarrow et al., 1983). This evidence adds to that already mentioned about honesty, strengthening the conclusion that moral development does not involve a steady increase in moral behavior as children grow older.

## Moral Reasoning and Prosocial Behavior

Just as with honesty, it is possible to examine the development of prosocial behavior from another perspective. In particular, you might expect age changes in prosocial behavior to be linked to the age changes in moral emotions or moral reasoning. You learned earlier about the relations of prosocial behavior to emotions such as guilt and empathy. The focus in this section is on the relations of prosocial behavior to moral reasoning.

Nancy Eisenberg (1986) wanted to study children's reasoning not about all moral issues but about prosocial behavior in particular. She wrote dilemmas involving prosocial behavior that have the same format but simpler language than Kohlberg's moral dilemmas. The following dilemma was used with girls (Eisenberg, 1986, p. 135).

> One day a girl named Mary was going to a friend's birthday party. On her way she saw a girl who had fallen down and hurt her leg. The girl asked Mary to go to her house and get her parents so the parents could come and take her to the doctor. But if Mary did run and get the child's parents, she would be late for the birthday party and miss the ice cream, cake, and all the games. What should Mary do? Why?

Eisenberg was interested in children's reasons for their decisions, but she did not try to define stages of prosocial reasoning that match Piaget's or Kohlberg's stages. Instead, she tried to identify categories of reasons and order the categories in a plausible developmental sequence. Table 15.4 lists the categories and the five developmental levels in which Eisenberg placed them. The table also shows the ages at which each level is most common, based on data from longitudinal studies (Eisenberg , Lennon, & Roth, 1983; Eisenberg et al., 1987; Eisenberg et al. 1991).

| | | |
|---|---|---|
| **TABLE 15.4** | *Eisenberg's Levels of Prosocial Reasoning* | |

| ORIENTATION | AGE RANGE | DESCRIPTION |
|---|---|---|
| 1. Hedonistic | Most preschoolers and many elementary-school children | Hedonists pursue their own pleasure. Children who reason this way focus on how they might gain or lose from their actions, or whether they like another person enough to help them. |
| 2. Needs-oriented | Some preschoolers and many older children | These children are concerned about the needs of others but they show little role taking, don't directly express their sympathy, and don't mention feelings such as guilt that would suggest they have internalized prosocial norms. |
| 3. Approval, interpersonal, or stereotyped | Some elementary- and high-school students | Reasoning focuses on what a good person would do or what action would bring social approval. |
| 4a. Self-reflecting empathy | Many high-school students | These adolescents express sympathy, explicitly take the perspective of the other, or say how their action or inaction would lead to positive feelings or to guilt. |
| 4b. Transitional | A few high-school students and adults | Reasoning focuses on internalized values, social conditions, or the need to protect other people's rights, but these ideas are not clearly stated. |
| 5. Strongly internalized | A small minority of high-school students and adults | Reasoning emphasizes internalized values and responsibilities, a desire to improve society, or a belief in the dignity of all people. Concerns with maintaining self-respect by living up to one's values are also expressed. |

*Sources:* Eisenberg, 1986, 1992; Eisenberg et al., 1991.

Preschool children often use hedonistic reasoning, reasoning that focuses on what is pleasant for them. Some preschoolers say that Mary doesn't want to miss the party, so she won't help the girl who hurt her leg. On the other hand, many preschool children express concern for other people's needs. Some preschoolers say that Mary would help the girl because she can see that the girl is hurt and needs help. The early appearance of concern for others, expressed in these simple terms, is consistent with the data on young children's prosocial behavior. Notice, too, that needs-oriented reasoning does not disappear as children grow older. It increases until 7 or 8 years of age and remains common after that age.

Eisenberg's Level 3 is analogous to Kohlberg's Stage 3. Children at Level 3 might say that Mary should help because "the girl would like Mary if she helped her." Level 4 is more complex because children must explicitly take the perspective of other people or say how helping would affect a person who gave help. A child at Level 4 might say that "Mary would help because it would make her feel good."

Finally, Eisenberg's Level 5 is analogous to Kohlberg's postconventional level. Adolescents or adults at this level might say that "Mary would think badly of herself if she didn't live up to her principles." Because Eisenberg's levels partly parallel Kohlberg's stages, children at higher levels on her dilemmas usually are at higher stages on Kohlberg's dilemmas.

How do levels of prosocial reasoning relate to prosocial behavior? An accurate but somewhat unsatisfying answer is, "it depends." Children who express more hedonistic reasoning on prosocial dilemmas are less generous to other people than children who express more needs-oriented reasoning (Eisenberg, 1986, 1992; Eisenberg et al., 1991). But prosocial reasoning rarely relates significantly to children's helpfulness toward others. Moreover, the relations of reasoning to generosity are seldom strong.

Eisenberg (1986, 1992) has suggested that prosocial reasoning is only one influence on children's prosocial behavior. She proposed that several processes affect prosocial behavior. Children must first pay attention to another's needs. To do so, they must interpret social situations accurately, take the other's perspective, and avoid preoccupation with their own affairs.

Once children have interpreted the situation, they must decide whether to help. This decision depends partly on whether they feel empathic toward the person in need and partly on their beliefs about the costs and benefits of help. In addition, the decision depends on children's values regarding prosocial behavior, which are reflected in their prosocial reasoning. If children decide to help the other person, they must be able to help and know they are able to do so. Finally, children who are willing and able to help need self-control to follow through on their decision to do so.

You can see that Eisenberg's model includes elements similar to those in Kohlberg and Candee's (1984) model. Other researchers have presented comparable models of the links between reasoning, emotion, and prosocial behavior (Krebs & Van Hesteren, 1994). Although Eisenberg's model has not been tested extensively, it does fit the data now available. Furthermore, most researchers agree with Eisenberg that children's reasoning, emotions, and other aspects of their personalities must all be considered to predict their prosocial behavior accurately.

## Aggressive Behavior

**Aggression** is behavior that is intended to harm or hurt another person (Crick & Grotpeter, 1995; Parke & Slaby, 1983). Unlike honesty and prosocial behavior, aggression changes consistently in form and in frequency as children grow.

### Age Changes

You may recall from chapter 12 that 1-year-olds sometimes hurt peer playmates by hitting or pushing them. However, when children so young hit or push a peer, they seem as if they are just exploring an interesting object. If that is the children's purpose, their actions don't fit the definition of aggression, because they are not trying to harm or injure the peer.

As toddlers approach 2 years of age, they begin to act in ways that are more clearly aggressive. Most often, these aggressive acts occur during struggles over toys. Toddlers will grab a toy from a peer or push the peer away from a toy. Before this aggression occurs, toddlers may tell their playmate that they want the toy, and the playmate may refuse to give it. This verbal exchange shows that the toddlers recognize their playmates as human beings like themselves (Hay & Ross, 1982). Therefore, toddlers must realize that they are harming another person when they act this way, indicating that they have the motive required for truly aggressive behavior.

Between 2 and 5 years of age, physical aggression decreases (Cummings, Iannotti, & Zahn-Waxler, 1989). As children grow older, they less often hit, kick, bite each other, and grab each other's toys. But as children's language competence increases, they show more verbal aggression. In particular, they begin to tease or ridicule one another.

By 4 years of age, observers can reliably judge the purpose of a child's aggression. Some aggression is **instrumental.** Its goal is to get an object or to protect a territory or play space. Other aggression is **hostile.** Its goal is to hurt another person. Between 4 and 7 years of age, the frequency of instrumental aggression decreases. Because of this decrease, the percentage of aggression that is hostile increases with age (Hartup, 1974).

Moreover, among older children, teasing and ridicule often provoke a verbal response. Among younger children, teasing and ridicule may provoke either a physical or verbal response. That is, older children often trade insults; younger children sometimes counter an insult with a punch or a kick.

aggression
*Behavior that is intended to harm or hurt another person.*

instrumental aggression
*Aggression whose purpose is to get an object or to protect a territory or play space.*

hostile aggression
*Aggression whose only purpose is to hurt another person.*

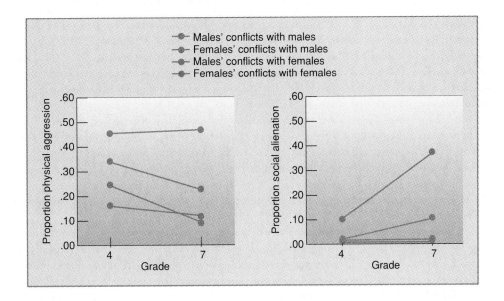

FIGURE 15.9

Two salient themes in the conflicts reported by children and adolescents are physical aggression and social alienation. These data from a longitudinal study show that physical aggression is especially common in males' conflicts with other males. Between fourth and seventh grade, social alienation becomes a major theme in females' conflicts with other females. (Source: Cairns et al., 1989.)

Between childhood and adolescence, further changes in the form and frequency of aggression occur. The most detailed evidence on these changes comes from a 6-year longitudinal study (Cairns et al., 1989). The study began with more than 200 boys and girls in the fourth grade. Each year from the fourth to the ninth grade, the students reported how often they got into trouble at school, got into fights, and got into arguments.

As the students grew older, they said they less often got into trouble at school and less often got into fights. They reported about as many arguments in the ninth grade as in the fourth grade. The decrease in reported fights is surprising because official crime statistics show an increase in assaults and other violent crimes during adolescence. Violent crimes apparently increase, despite the general decline in aggression, because adolescents are stronger than young children and so can inflict more serious harm. Also, more adolescents than children use deadly weapons (guns or knives) during fights.

Many adolescent males view aggressive behavior as an acceptable technique for solving problems with other males. As part of the longitudinal study, students were interviewed about recent conflicts with peers of the same and opposite sex. The interviews took place when the students were in the fourth and seventh grades. The themes of the students' conflicts varied with their grade, their sex, and the sex of their opponent. Figure 15.9 shows that males often reported conflicts with other males that involved physical aggression. Females sometimes reported physical aggression in conflicts with males, but neither males nor females reported much physical aggression in conflicts with females. As long as males accept physical aggression as a way of resolving conflicts, assaults and other violent crimes are likely.

Figure 15.9 also shows the distinctive feature of conflicts among females. Many females reported conflicts with other females that involved social alienation. For example, girls described how other girls were rejected by an established clique or how girls spread malicious gossip intended to damage another girl's reputation. Notice that these forms of aggression (or intentional harm to another) increased dramatically in females' conflicts between fourth and seventh grade. Amazingly, boys never mentioned conflicts with such themes.

Other studies confirm that girls are more likely than boys to try to hurt classmates by ruining their social relationships (Crick & Grotpeter, 1995). Examples of this sort of **relational aggression** include excluding classmates from a group at recess and, when angry at classmates, telling other children not to be friends with them. Even elementary-school children recognize this form of aggression when it is used by their peers. They also report that more girls than boys engage in relational aggression.

Finally, despite the changes in the form and frequency of aggression, more aggressive children tend to remain more aggressive than their peers. Two-year-olds who engage in more physical aggression toward peers tend to become 5-year-olds who are more physically

**relational aggression**
*Harming other people by ruining their social relationships, for example, excluding them from a group.*

aggressive (Cummings et al., 1989). More aggressive schoolchildren tend to become more aggressive adolescents and adults (Parke & Slaby, 1983; Stattin & Magnusson, 1989). Eight-year-old boys who are described by their peers as highly aggressive tend at age 30 to abuse their wives, have more crime convictions, and rate themselves as more aggressive. Eight-year-old girls who are described by peers as highly aggressive tend at age 30 to be more punitive toward their children (Huesmann et al., 1984).

As always, you should interpret evidence on the continuity of behavior cautiously. Do not assume that all aggressive 2-year-olds, or even all aggressive schoolchildren, will have problems with excessive aggression in adulthood. The correlations between early and later aggression are moderate and do not allow accurate predictions about which children will become highly aggressive adults. Research has shown that these correlations usually exaggerate the risk of long-term problems. Aggressive children can and often do become well-adjusted and relatively nonaggressive adults (Parke & Slaby, 1983; Parker & Asher, 1987).

Moreover, evidence on the continuity of aggressive behavior does not imply that programs to change the behavior of highly aggressive children will be ineffective. Children's aggression can be reduced by altering the variables controlling it. You learned in earlier chapters that many variables control children's aggression. For example, aggressive behavior is affected by children's exposure to aggressive models and the frequency with which their aggression is reinforced. In addition, children's aggression is influenced by their norms or standards for behavior. Children behave aggressively partly because they think it is the right thing to do.

## Moral Bases for Aggression?

Most people view aggression as the right thing to do under certain conditions (Feshbach, 1971). One rule that justifies aggressive behavior is "an eye for an eye and a tooth for a tooth." In other words, when someone strikes you, you have the right to strike back. Children accept this norm of retaliation as early as age 6, and most adults also accept it (Berndt, 1979b).

Many other rules excuse or justify aggressive behavior. A boxer is paid to behave aggressively toward other people, in the ring at least. Adults often justify their aggression by saying they were acting in self-defense. You should not be surprised, then, that some children have difficulty sorting out when aggression is and is not acceptable. Stated differently, you can expect some children to judge their aggression as morally right.

This expectation was confirmed in a study of aggressive and nonaggressive children (Astor, 1994). When asked about acts of unprovoked aggression, both aggressive and nonaggressive children said such acts were wrong. However, the two groups of children differed in their judgments about hitting another person after being provoked verbally (e.g., by being called names). The nonaggressive children said hitting was wrong because it caused physical harm. The aggressive children said hitting was justified because of the psychological harm caused by name calling. In other words, the aggressive children thought they were entitled to respond with a physical attack when they were attacked verbally.

Cognitive social-learning theorists have also examined how children's judgments about aggression are related to their behavior (Bandura, 1986; Perry, Perry, & Rasmussen, 1986). One study included third through sixth graders whose classmates described them as aggressive or nonaggressive (Boldizar, Perry, & Perry, 1989). The children were asked how they felt about various consequences of aggression. For example, they were asked how concerned they were that their aggression might hurt another child. Figure 15.10 shows the results.

Compared with nonaggressive children, aggressive children said they would care less about the suffering of their victims. Aggressive children also said they would care less about being rejected by peers or facing retaliation from the victim if they behaved aggressively. In addition, these children had relatively little concern about evaluating themselves negatively or blaming themselves for having done the wrong thing if they were aggressive toward another person. Finally, aggressive children valued having control over their victims more than did nonaggressive children. In sum, aggressive children viewed the potential costs of aggression less negatively and the potential benefits more positively than did nonaggressive children.

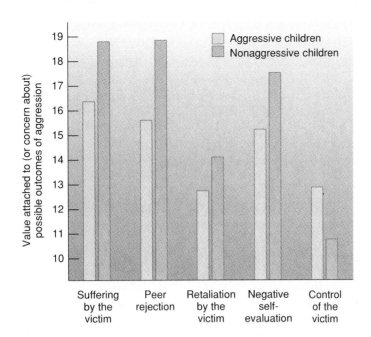

FIGURE 15.10
Aggressive children evaluate
possible outcomes of aggressive
behavior differently from
nonaggressive children.
Aggressive children are less
concerned about the potential
costs of aggression, like peer
rejection or retaliation, than are
nonaggressive children.
Aggressive children value
control over the victim more
than do nonaggressive children.
(Source: Boldizar et al., 1989.)

Furthermore, aggressive and nonaggressive children differ in their beliefs about the consequences of aggression (Perry et al., 1986). Most aggressive children think they can get what they want by acting aggressively. They think that attacking a peer who is bothering them will make the peer stop it. Nonaggressive children doubt that aggressive behavior will be effective in achieving these results.

Why do aggressive children believe aggression has such positive consequences? You learned some answers to this question in earlier chapters. For example, parents of aggressive children sometimes reward them for behaving aggressively. Peers sometimes give in to bullies who attack them. There are, however, other reasons for aggressive children's beliefs.

Aggressive children often watch television programs that portray successful aggressors. Of course, the "bad guys" don't win when they act aggressively, but the "good guys" often use aggression to defeat their foes. In short, aggression is portrayed as justified and as effective (Bandura, 1986). Aggressive children also think violent television programs are realistic, that they show what life is really like (Eron et al., 1983). It is no wonder that watching violent television programs often increases children's aggressive behavior (Huston et al., 1992).

Fortunately, the beliefs that contribute to aggressive behavior can be unlearned. Recall one experimental study described in chapter 13 (Guerra & Slaby, 1990). The study evaluated a program to reduce the aggressive behavior of delinquent adolescents. Before the program began, the delinquent adolescents believed that aggression is legitimate (e.g., "It's okay to hit someone if you just go crazy with anger"). They also believed that aggression improves an adolescent's reputation with peers (e.g., "It's important to show everyone how tough you are by being a good fighter") and that aggression helps to avoid a negative reputation (e.g., "If you back down from a fight, everyone will think you're a coward"). After going through the program, the delinquent adolescents less often accepted these statements about aggression. As mentioned earlier, their aggressive behavior also decreased.

The success of this program implies that judgments about the legitimacy of aggression and about its consequences for self and others affect adolescents' aggression. More generally, the program's success implies that moral judgments influence moral behavior. Cognitive social learning theorists assume that moral judgments are only one influence on behavior (Bandura, 1986). Moral behavior is also influenced by children's interpretation of social situations, by their capacity for self-control, and by other factors. Still, changing moral judgments can be one means of changing moral behavior.

# PROMOTING MORAL DEVELOPMENT

How, specifically, can moral judgments be changed? In the program for delinquent adolescents, the main technique was group discussion of hypothetical dilemmas that included temptations to behave aggressively. You read earlier that group discussions of moral dilemmas can accelerate development to higher stages of moral reasoning. Now you see that the same technique can improve behavior. Every technique discussed earlier in connection with moral reasoning can promote moral behavior as well.

In addition, you should not think of moral development as separate from other aspects of development. You read in earlier chapters about other desirable outcomes for children such as high self-esteem, competence in peer relationships, and the formation of close, trusting relationships with parents. Earlier chapters also included information about practices by parents, other adults, and peers that promote these desirable outcomes. The same practices generally have positive effects on moral development, too.

Moral development is special, though, because it involves a unique integration of reasoning, emotion, and behavior. One intriguing study by Carolyn Zahn-Waxler, Marian Radke-Yarrow, and Robert King (1979) that was described briefly in chapter 11 illustrates this integration. As you may recall, these researchers trained mothers of 1- and 2-year-olds to report incidents of distress—pain, sorrow, fear, or anger—that their child witnessed. The mothers also reported what caused the distress, how their child reacted, and how they themselves responded.

Mothers often reported incidents in which their children had caused distress to another child. One mother reported the following incident between her 21-month-old son, Todd, and a 4-year-old girl, Susan, who was visiting their home.

> Todd and Susan were in the bedroom playing and all of a sudden Susan started to cry and ran to her mother. Todd slowly followed after and watched. I said, "What happened?" and she said, "He hit me." I said, "Well, tell him not to hit you," and I said, "Todd." He didn't seem particularly upset; he was watching her cry. I said, "Did you hit Susan? Why would you hit Susan? You don't want to hurt people."

Then Todd and Susan went back into the bedroom. Soon, he hit her again. This time his mother said sternly, "No, Todd. You mustn't hit people." Todd then took a flower from a table nearby and handed it to Susan with a smile. His mother felt that he was trying to make up with her or give her something to stop her crying.

At other times, toddlers who had not caused another person's distress responded to signs of distress with sympathy, help, or assistance. That is, they behaved prosocially toward the other person. The central questions in the study were (a) why some toddlers often tried to make up for distress they had caused while others rarely did; and (b) why some toddlers often acted prosocially toward people in distress while others rarely did. The results showed that certain behaviors by mothers were related to how often their toddlers helped people in distress, whether their toddlers had caused the distress or not.

How did the mothers of helpful toddlers behave? The answer can be stated as guidelines for promoting moral development. Although the study of mothers and toddlers is used to illustrate the guidelines, they are consistent with many other studies of children's honesty, prosocial behavior, and aggression (Burton, 1976; Eisenberg, 1992; Parke & Slaby, 1983; Radke-Yarrow et al., 1983).

1. *State the rules for moral behavior clearly and forcefully.* Todd's mother told him sternly, "You mustn't hit people." Other mothers said, equally forcefully, "It's not nice to bite" and "You must *never* poke anyone's eyes." These mothers explained exactly what the rules were and how their children had violated them. By contrast, some mothers relied on simple prohibitions like "Stop that!" These mothers did not clearly tell their children what they had done wrong, and their children less often tried to help people in distress.

By itself, clearly stating moral rules is not enough. Children need to be convinced that abiding by these rules is important. Toddlers' behavior was related to their mothers'

explanations of rules only if those explanations were delivered in an emotionally intense way. Apparently, explanations delivered in a neutral tone were ignored.

When mothers were emotionally expressive as they explained why their toddlers' behavior was wrong, the toddlers probably paid more attention. Also, these toddlers probably were more motivated to do what their mothers said. As you learned earlier, emotions can provide the motivational force that makes moral reasoning effective.

2. *Explain how children's behavior affects other people.* After the first time Todd hit Susan, Todd's mother told him, "You don't want to hurt people." Other mothers said, "You made Doug cry," and "Can't you see Al's hurt?" These comments encourage children to take the perspective of their victim. They imply that children should not act without considering how their actions affect other people.

Remember that taking others' perspectives is important in Kohlberg's (1976) theory of moral judgment. Emphasizing the effects of children's behavior on other people is also part of the desirable technique of inductive discipline. In addition, Eisenberg (1986, 1992) has argued that attention to other people and their needs is the first step toward prosocial behavior. Cognitive social learning theorists also assume that children who care about the effects of their behavior on other people are less likely to behave aggressively.

You see, then, that theorists who take different perspectives on moral development all stress the importance of explaining how moral rules protect the welfare of other people. Of course, these explanations must be stated in age-appropriate ways. Young children may benefit little from a philosophical discourse about the rights and duties of human beings. Yet the study of Todd and the other toddlers suggests that age-appropriate explanations can affect the behavior of very young children.

3. *Model warmth and empathy.* During the months that mothers were recording their toddlers' behavior, researchers occasionally visited their homes to observe how they interacted with their children. As mentioned in chapter 11, when mothers were more warm or responsive to their toddlers, the toddlers themselves gave more help to people in distress. The mothers' behavior probably served as a model for their children's behavior. In addition, a mother's warmth may have made her toddler more receptive to her commands and explanations.

Many other studies show that greater warmth in parents is associated with more prosocial and less aggressive behavior in their children (Parke & Slaby, 1983; Radke-Yarrow et al., 1983). Still, one note of caution about the effects of parents' warmth is necessary. In some studies, children cheated more in games and on tests when their parents responded more warmly to their successes (Burton, 1976). In school settings, "the desire for good marks seems to be the most common motive leading to deceit [or cheating]" (Hartshorne & May, 1928, p. 398). Therefore, parents who reward their children for high achievement may indirectly foster dishonesty. To avoid this outcome, one more guideline for promoting moral development must be stated.

4. *Place the highest value on moral behavior, and help children recognize conflicting norms.* A strong emphasis on achievement can lead not only to dishonesty; it can also reduce prosocial behavior. Remember that Anglo-American children become much more competitive in the circles' game between 5 and 7 years of age. That is, they change their behavior around the time that they enter school. This change may be related to the emphasis in most elementary schools on individual achievement judged in comparison with peers.

Do schools place too much emphasis on individual achievement measured by performance relative to classmates? Are many children under excessive pressure to follow the social norm of getting the best score they can on every test and every game? Do parents too often give kids that famous message: "Winning isn't the most important thing. It's the only thing!"

Child development researchers cannot provide the final answer to questions like these. Such questions involve social and moral values as much as, or more than, research data. Even so, research data can contribute to the debate over values (Kurtines, Alvarez, & Azmitia, 1990). Think, again, about children's behavior in the circles' game. Instead of telling these

In the intensity of a game, strong emotions are often expressed, and great efforts are made to win. But is winning everything? If too high a value is placed on winning the game, players may be tempted to sacrifice other values, like the moral rules that are the foundation of good sportsmanship.

children to try less hard to achieve, adults might help them recognize when cooperation is more adaptive and, perhaps, more moral than competition. The ability to recognize situations in which there are conflicting norms and then select behaviors consistent with the highest moral values is another critical part of moral development.

Finally, you might wonder whether the four guidelines for promoting moral development are valid only for young children. Earlier, you learned that development in moral reasoning continues long into adulthood. Do other aspects of moral development also continue into adulthood? *Practical Applications of Research*: "Keys to an Exemplary Moral Life" summarizes a unique study of adults whose moral development was exceptional. The study also provided hints about how these adults reached their unusual level of moral commitment and action.

# THE MORALITY OF SOCIAL RELATIONSHIPS

This chapter includes many examples of children's reasoning about hypothetical moral dilemmas. The following dilemma illustrates one final issue concerning moral development, and moral development research, that deserves your attention.

> Bob brings candy to share with everyone. His close friend George does not want Bob to give candy to Tim. George and Tim do not get along and Tim has been picking on George. What should Bob do?

This dilemma was given to students in the third, sixth, and ninth grades (Smetana, Killen, & Turiel, 1991). More than 85 percent of these students said that Bob should share his candy with everyone, including Tim. These responses were taken as evidence that the students favored justice over expectations tied to social relationships. In other words, the students decided to act morally rather than to comply with a friend's request.

You might wonder why the researchers chose to present friendship in such a negative light. Why did they write a dilemma in which a friend encouraged Bob to distribute his candy unequally, and unfairly? In short, why did they portray friendship as in conflict with morality?

Such negative portrayals of social relationships are common in moral development research. Remember Piaget's story about the mother who had a son and a daughter. When her son didn't do the chores that she had given him, the mother asked her daughter to do all the chores. Why did Piaget write a dilemma in which a mother treated her children so unfairly?

The answer, stated most generally, is that many moral development researchers view social relationships as likely contributors to immoral behavior. This view reflects a distrust of social relationships that is common in European American culture. Hazel Markus and Shinobu Kitayama (1994) argued that European American culture is profoundly individualistic. Partly

# KEYS TO AN EXEMPLARY MORAL LIFE

For three decades, Susie Valadez has spent her life working for poor Mexican children and adults. She has built medical centers, provided funds for schools, and provided food for thousands of people. She did not start her work with a big organization. While living in California, she received what she and her pastor regarded as a call from God to move to Mexico to help poor children. She and her family made the move and started the work that has grown in scope over the year.

Anne Colby and William Damon described the life of Susie Valadez in their book on *moral exemplars*, people whose lives illustrate unusual moral commitment. In *Some Do Care: Contemporary Lives of Moral Commitment*, Colby and Damon defined moral exemplars by several characteristics: (a) a life that reflects a long-term commitment to moral principles, including respect for all human beings; (b) actions consistent with those principles; (c) a willingness to put moral values above self-interest; (d) an ability to inspire others to moral action; and (e) humility about their own importance.

The moral exemplars profiled in the book range greatly in age, education, religion, and in the focus of their work. However, Colby and Damon identified some common elements in their experiences and personalities. One striking finding was the exemplars' openness to social influence. Although they were chosen partly because they had inspired others, they relied heavily on other people for direction. For example, Susie Valadez was guided by her pastor in interpreting God's call to go to Mexico. Other exemplars received guidance from coworkers and others who were already engaged in similar work.

Colby and Damon describe the influences of other people by saying that they "challenged, prodded, supplied information, asked questions, gave feedback, and otherwise supported the exemplar's movement toward an expanded moral vision" (p. 295). This process is similar to the development that occurs in childhood through moral discussions that provoke cognitive conflict. What was distinctive about the moral exemplars, however, was their willingness to think deeply about their discussions with others. The exemplars regularly reevaluated their own ideals, and their goals, as they considered the advice of others.

Equally important was the exemplars' drive to make their lives consistent with their ideals and goals. Colby and Damon point out that some people change their ideas without changing their actions. The moral exemplars did not accept such a split between thoughts and deeds. They felt a personal responsibility to make their identity and their work an expression of their moral ideals. Recall that personal responsibility was also emphasized in Kohlberg and Candee's (1984) models of the links between moral reasoning and behavior.

In addition, the lives of these moral exemplars illustrate the force of continuity in development. Actions consistent with moral ideals became habits of daily life. The most courageous decisions were made without much hesitation because the exemplars were immersed in work that gave them a sense of total involvement and unquestioned purpose. The sense of total involvement was fostered by the correspondence between their sense of self and their goals.

Finally, the exemplars often had problems and frustrations during their work. Like Susie Valadez, many of them were sustained by a deep spiritual faith. Even the few exemplars who did not identify themselves as religious had a sense that they were working toward something greater and more important than themselves.

Because Colby and Damon did what might be called "developmental psychology through biography," their book vividly shows how the exemplars' thoughts, feelings, beliefs, and actions combined to create lives of moral excellence. However, Colby and Damon argue that similar processes are at work in the moral development of every person. These processes, when better understood, may be applied to enhance moral development at any age.

## WHERE YOU HAVE MADE A DIFFERENCE

Sister Suzie & The Staff Of Christ For Mexico Mission

God's call to Susie Valadez came in a vision of poor children holding a banner saying "Cuidad Juarez." Her pastor said that the vision meant God wanted her to help poor children in that city. This picture comes from a greeting card sent to people who have helped her Mexico Mission. In Susie's original vision, the children had no shoes and were more ragged. What made Susie Valadez a moral exemplar was her willingness to accept guidance from her pastor and then commit herself to a life of unusual moral action.

for this reason, European Americans often assume that social relationships lead to undesirable behaviors such as irrational conformity and unthinking obedience to authority. People are seen as more mature—and more moral—when they refuse to conform to friends and they resist pressure from parents or other authorities (Bukowski & Sippola, 1996; La Follette, 1991).

Markus and Kitayama argued that very different ideas about social relationships prevail in most Asian cultures. In these cultures, people define themselves by their social roles and relationships. Instead of focusing on their individual rights, Asian people focus on their responsibilities as members of social groups. Moreover, as mentioned earlier, Asian adults and children attach moral force to their obligations to help friends, family, and members of other important groups (Miller & Bersoff, 1992). Asian people thus see social obligations not as opposed to morality but as essential to their moral code.

Why do Asians and European Americans differ so dramatically in their ideas about morality and social relationships? From birth, children in these cultures receive different messages about themselves and the world. Recall from chapter 1 that most European American infants in the United States sleep in a separate room from their mothers (Morelli et al., 1992). By contrast, in Mayan families in Guatemala, most infants sleep in the same bed with their mothers. In Japan, most children sleep in the same bed or the same room with their parents not only in infancy but also in childhood and early adolescence (Shweder, Jensen, & Goldstein, 1995). In this way, sleeping arrangements reinforce the idea of the independent individual in European American culture; they reinforce the idea of interdependence in Asian culture.

These contrasting ideas are further reinforced by schooling, the legal system, and other social institutions (Markus & Kitayama, 1994). For example, U.S. students usually leave the lunch room for the playground whenever they are finished with lunch. Japanese students leave the lunch room only when everyone is finished, and then they exit as a group. In addition, the U.S. government is founded on the Declaration of Independence and the Bill of Rights, both of which emphasize individual rights. In Asian countries, laws and customs instead emphasize people's duties to their nation and to smaller social groups.

These differences between cultures are not absolute. Asian history is filled with examples of men who overthrew the established authorities while pursuing their individual ambition. Recent history is filled with examples of Asian people who have given their lives while fighting for individual rights.

Similarly, European Americans are not completely individualistic. When U.S. adults describe themselves, they often say that they are *caring, responsible,* and *loved* (Markus & Kitayama, 1994). These attributes reflect not independence but involvement in social relationships. Also, many U.S. scholars have rejected the emphasis on individual rights that is prominent in many theories of morality and moral development (Gilligan, 1982; La Follette, 1991; Youniss, 1992). These scholars argue that children begin to accept moral principles only after they have participated in social relationships based on mutual trust and help.

Nevertheless, individualism is definitely valued more in European American culture than in Asian culture. Markus and Kitayama (1994) suggest that more attention should be given to such cultural differences. Recognition of the differences would increase people's understanding of human possibilities. Acknowledging this type of cultural diversity would also lead to a more comprehensive theory of moral development. Such a theory would explain how children learn about their moral obligations both as individuals and as partners in social relationships.

# SUMMARY

**Thinking About Morality**
The moral domain is usually defined as including behaviors that affect the rights, duties, and welfare of other people. Age changes occur in children's evaluations of specific actions and in their reasoning about moral dilemmas.

**Piaget on Moral Evaluations and Social Relationships**
Piaget found that young children weigh consequences more heavily than intentions when evaluating actors. Later researchers have shown that young children can consider many criteria for moral

evaluations when these criteria are easy to comprehend. Piaget and other researchers have also examined the degree to which young children have unilateral respect for adults.

## Kohlberg's Theory of Moral Judgment

Kohlberg's six stages of moral judgment describe distinct structures of reasoning about moral issues. Kohlberg made several assumptions about development through the stages (e.g., it occurs in an invariant sequence). He also stated hypotheses about the processes that cause progress through the stages (e.g., cognitive-moral conflict).

## Morality, Social Conventions, and Personal Issues

Turiel argued that children and adults distinguish moral rules from social conventions, and that children view some actions as falling in a personal domain with which others should not interfere.

## Moral Emotions: Guilt, Empathy, and Good Feelings

Freud proposed that the anticipation of guilt is the motivation for moral behavior. Later researchers have shown that moral behavior can also be motivated by empathy and by the positive feelings that good behavior arouses.

## Guilt: Its Adaptive and Maladaptive Forms

Depending on parents' disciplinary techniques and psychological adjustment, children may develop either adaptive or maladaptive forms of guilt. The events that arouse feelings of guilt also change as children grow older and gain greater psychological and social understanding.

## Empathy and Positive Feelings

Children most often act prosocially when their empathy for others is transformed into sympathy rather than a sense of personal distress. Children also behave prosocially because they feel good when they do so. Kochanska has proposed that the socialization of the moral emotions varies with children's temperament.

## Moral Behavior

As children grow older, they do not consistently show either more moral behavior or less moral behavior. The development of morality can be better understood in terms of models that link moral reasoning, moral emotions, and other processes to moral behavior.

## Cheating, Honesty, and Self-Control

Self-control is a prerequisite for honesty and other types of moral behavior. Self-control emerges during the preschool years and increases during childhood. Honesty in testing situations does not change regularly with age, but people at higher stages of moral reasoning usually are more honest.

## Prosocial Behavior

Very young children sometimes are generous and helpful to other people. The frequency of prosocial behavior does not change consistently during childhood. Children who talk more about other people's needs when reasoning about prosocial dilemmas also

share more with other people, but many processes besides reasoning influence prosocial behavior.

## Aggressive Behavior

Aggressive behavior increases in early childhood and declines in early adolescence. Children who believe that aggression has fewer costs and more benefits are more aggressive. Changing children's beliefs about aggression can reduce their aggressive behavior.

## Promoting Moral Development

Adults can encourage children's moral development by stating moral rules clearly and forcefully, by explaining how children's behavior affects other people, and by modeling warmth and empathy for others. Adults can also encourage children to give higher priority to moral rules than to other norms for behavior.

## The Morality of Social Relationships

Moral development theorists have sometimes portrayed social relationships negatively. These portrayals reflect a distrust of social relationships that is common in individualistic cultures. Moral obligations to friends, family, and members of other important groups are emphasized in Asian cultures. Attention to such cultural differences should lead to a better understanding of human possibilities and a more comprehensive theory of moral development.

# SUGGESTED READINGS

**Colby, A., & Damon, W. (1992).** *Some do care: Contemporary lives of moral commitment.* **New York: Free Press.** Some features of this book were discussed in this chapter's *Practical Applications of Research* box. The authors are researchers who have devoted their careers to the study of moral development. The book does more than any other to explore the psychological world of people who have faced and surmounted difficult moral challenges.

**Colby, A., & Kohlberg, L. (1987).** *The measurement of moral judgment.* **Cambridge, England: Cambridge University Press.** If you want to know more about Kohlberg's theory, this is

the definitive source. The title actually refers to two volumes. The first volume presents the philosophical foundations of the theory and the data from Kohlberg's longitudinal study. The second volume is the coding manual for the moral-judgment interview.

**Eisenberg, N. (1992).** *The caring child.* **Cambridge, MA: Harvard University Press.** During the 1970s, Nancy Eisenberg was one of few researchers who emphasized the morality of good deeds such as sharing and helping. Most other researchers focused on immoral acts such as aggression, cheating, and stealing. Since the 1970s Eisenberg has studied all aspects of

prosocial behavior from its biological to its cognitive bases. This book provides a brief (149 pages of text) review of the evidence to date.

**Kurtines, W., & Gewirtz, J. L. (Eds.). (1991).** *Handbook of moral behavior and development.* **Hillsdale, NJ: Erlbaum.** Handbooks tend to be massive, and this is no exception. Its nearly 1,000 pages are divided into three volumes. The first, on theory, concentrates on Kohlberg's theory and recent alternatives to it. The second, on research, includes chapters on many topics in the broad arena of morality. The third, on applications, deals with ideas and programs related to moral education.

# GLOSSARY

## A

**accelerated longitudinal design**   Use of a cohort-sequential design to examine changes over a greater age span than that for which any specific child is assessed.  *67*

**accommodation**   A cognitive function that, in Piaget's theory, describes the modification of existing cognitive structures by new elements.  *26*

**active genotype-environment correlation**   A relation between children's genotypes and their environments that results from children's efforts to seek environments compatible with their genotypes.  *103*

**adolescent growth spurt**   A sharp increase in the rate of growth in height and weight early in the second decade of life.  *159*

**affordances**   In Gibson's theory of perception, what an object offers a person, or what it provides or furnishes. For example, a floor affords support.  *334*

**age norms**   The average ages at which children master specific developmental tasks, such as learning to walk.  *60*

**aggression**   Behavior that is intended to harm or hurt another person.  *640*

**allele**   The genetic information, or the form of a gene, encoded at a particular locus on a chromosome.  *92*

**amniocentesis**   A procedure for examining the genetic makeup of a fetus. Amniotic fluid that contains cells shed by the fetus is extracted and cultured to obtain a karyotype of the fetus.  *99*

**amnion**   The inner of two membranes that surround the embryo or fetus.  *118*

**androgens**   Hormones that normally have higher levels in males and that lead to the differentiation of the genitals during the prenatal period.  *582*

**androgyny**   A combination of desirable masculine and feminine characteristics.  *598*

**animism**   According to Piaget, the tendency of young children to assume that nonliving (or inanimate) objects like the sun or the wind have the properties of living things (e.g., thoughts, motives, and feelings).  *299*

**appearance-reality distinction**   The ability to distinguish between the way something looks (e.g., like an egg) and what it actually is (e.g., a rock).  *304*

**assimilation**   A cognitive function defined by Piaget as the integration of external elements into existing cognitive structures.  *26*

**associative play**   Defined by Parten as the play type in which children use the same materials and talk together, or share toys and imitate each other, but do not take different roles or work on different parts of a construction.  *480*

**attachment**   The intimate emotional bond that infants form during the first years of life to their mothers, fathers, and perhaps to other people with whom they interact often.  *217*

**attachment behaviors**   Behaviors that help an infant gain or maintain proximity to an attachment figure (i.e., crying, crawling to the attachment figure).  *217*

**attention**   The selective focusing of perception.  *333*

**attribution theory**   A social-psychological theory that emphasizes the effects of people's attributions about the causes of their behavior on their later behavior.  *433*

**authoritarian**   A parenting style that includes firm control, low warmth, and little encouragement of children's independence. Authoritarian parents value unquestioning obedience. They assume that children should just do what they are told.  *435*

**authoritative**   A parenting style that includes firm control with high warmth and encouragement of children's independence. Authoritative parents value obedience and expect mature behavior from their children, but they are also willing to reason with them about rules.  *435*

**autism**   A pervasive developmental disorder whose symptoms include an absence or impairment of social relationships and ritual or self-stimulating behavior.  *91*

**autobiographical memory**   People's memory for the events of their own lives.  *363*

**autosomes**   The 44 human chromosomes that can be grouped into pairs of chromosomes similar in size and gene sequence.  *81*

**average status**   The social status group that includes children who receive a moderate number of positive and negative nominations on sociometric questionnaires.  *499*

## B

**babbling**   Reduplicated sounds like *ga-ga-ga* that represent the first true syllables.  *248*

**Babinski reflex**   A reflex elicited by stroking the sole of a newborn's foot, moving from the heel toward the toe. In response, normal newborns extend and spread their toes.  *179*

**banding pattern**   The pattern of lighter and darker regions on a chromosome after the chromosome has absorbed specific dyes.  *81*

**baseline**   In experiments testing the effects of reinforcement, the initial phase before any change in reinforcement patterns is made.  *66*

**basic-level categories**   Categories that are labeled with common words, that are not context-specific, and that include objects similar in shape and function.  *255*

**behavioral state**   A general description of an infant's (or adult's) position on the dimension from intense activity to quiet sleep.  *175*

**behavior genetics**   A subfield of science whose goal is the exploration of the genetic contribution to variations among individuals.  *104*

**Black English**   A dialect of American English with a somewhat different grammar.  *276*

**bonding**   The development of a relationship between a mother and her newborn infant after sustained contact early in the neonatal period. *145*

**bound morphemes**   Letters or syllables that affect word meaning but that are not themselves complete words (e.g., the suffix *-ed*). *251*

**brain plasticity**   The degree to which the brain is modifiable or open to change. *174*

**brain stem**   The lowest portion of the brain, just above the spinal cord, which regulates bodily functions such as breathing. *172*

# C

**canalization**   A theoretical principle that states that an organism tends to return to its hereditarily determined path of development (or its own "canal") after being pushed off that path by a temporary disturbance. *163*

**catch-up growth**   A period of rapid growth that follows a period of abnormally reduced growth. *162*

**categorical perception**   The perception of different sounds as falling into the same category, that is, as representing the same phoneme. *245*

**categorical scope**   The assumption that a new word refers to objects in the same basic-level category as the object that was first labeled with that word. *255*

**causal attributions**   People's explanations for various outcomes of their actions or other people's actions. *409*

**centration**   Piaget's term for young children's tendency to focus their attention on one element of a task or one dimension of an object. *308*

**cephalocaudal principle**   The principle that development generally proceeds from the head to the foot. Body parts closer to the head develop earlier than those closer to the feet. *120*

**cerebral cortex**   The highest level of the brain, consisting of several thin layers of neurons that cover the cerebrum. *172*

**cerebrum**   The top and largest part of the human brain. Neurons in the cerebrum control voluntary motor movements, perception, and more complex psychological processes. *172*

**cesarean section**   A method of delivery that involves cutting through the mother's abdominal wall and lifting the baby out of the uterus. *148*

**child development**   Age changes in children's characteristics that are systematic rather than haphazard, and successive rather than independent of earlier conditions; also, the scientific discipline that focuses on these age changes. *5*

**child-directed speech (CDS)**   A special pattern of speech to young children whose characteristics include high pitch, exaggerated intonation, and exaggerated facial expressions. *268*

**chorion**   The outer of two membranes that surround the embryo or fetus. *99, 118*

**chorionic villus sampling (CVS)**   A procedure done in early pregnancy to examine the genetic makeup of a fetus. Hairlike projections (villi) from a membrane that surrounds the fetus (the chorion) have cells genetically identical to those of the fetus, so those cells can be used to make a karyotype of the fetus. *99*

**chromosomes**   Threadlike structures within the nucleus of every cell that contain the DNA or genetic material of an organism. *78*

**chronosystem**   In Bronfenbrenner's model, the patterns of stability and change in children's environments over time. *34*

**circular reaction**   In Piaget's theory, a process that leads to the preservation (or learning) of behavior patterns through the repetition of these patterns and the assimilation that repetition promotes. *293*

**classical conditioning**   A type of learning that results from the repeated pairing of two stimuli. The response that naturally follows one stimulus (e.g., the presentation of food) begins to occur following the other stimulus (e.g., a bell), after the two stimuli are repeatedly paired. *12*

**class inclusion**   Piaget's term for children's understanding that objects falling in one class (e.g., tulips) may also fall into a superordinate class (e.g., flowers). Also used to refer to tasks designed to assess children's understanding of this characteristic of classes. *306*

**clique**   A small group of close friends. *476*

**code switching**   Switching between Black English and standard English, or any other dialects, when such a switch is socially appropriate. *276*

**codominance**   A pattern of gene expression in which both alleles on homologous chromosomes contribute to the phenotype. *97*

**coercive cycle**   Interactions between a parent and a child in which each person uses coercive behavior, or negative reinforcement, to control the other's behavior. Called a cycle because the negative reinforcement contributes to an increase in coercive interactions. *440*

**cognition**   The processes of thinking and reasoning. *24*

**cognitive style**   The way that children approach cognitive tasks. Most researchers have focused on two contrasting styles, labeled reflective and impulsive. *339*

**cohort**   In research design, the term used to refer to all children born during the same year. *61*

**cohort-sequential design**   A research design in which the characteristics of multiple cohorts of children are measured on more than one occasion. *67*

**comprehension monitoring**   The ability to judge one's understanding of a message. *277*

**concept**   A mental grouping of different entities into a single category on the basis of some underlying similarity—some way in which all the entities are alike. *339*

**concordance**   In genetics, the percentage of genetically related persons who show similar characteristics (e.g., the percentage of twins who are either both schizophrenic or both nonschizophrenic). *108*

**concrete-operational stage**   The stage of cognitive development, in Piaget's theory, in which children are capable only of concrete operations. *307*

**concrete operations**   According to Piaget, the first logical operations that children construct, around 7 years of age. These operations can be applied only to concrete objects and current events. *307*

**conditioned response**   The term in classical conditioning for an organism's reaction to a conditioned stimulus. *12*

**conditioned stimulus**   The term in classical conditioning for the stimulus that begins to elicit a response after it is repeatedly paired with another stimulus that spontaneously elicits the same response (see **classical conditioning**). *12*

**confluence model**   A model devised by Zajonc that is intended to explain the effects on a child's IQ of the child's family structure and position in a family. *400*

**conscience**   Defined by Freud as the part of the superego that represents the punitive side of norms, telling children what they should not do and making them feel guilty if they do so. *21*

**conservation of liquid quantity**   Piaget's term for one property of liquids, which is that their amount does not change if you pour them from one container into another. Also refers to Piaget's task for testing children's understanding of this property. *52*

**conservation tasks**   Tasks devised by Piaget to find out whether children understand that some transformations of objects leave some of their properties unchanged (or conserved). For example, changing the spatial arrangement of a set of objects does not change the number of objects in the set. *306*

**constructive memory** An automatic process of forming a mental representation of new information that depends partly on the new information received and partly on information added from a person's knowledge base. *358*

**constructive play** Play in which children create something, like a building made of blocks. *481*

**constructivist** A theorist who believes, as Piaget did, that children actively construct their knowledge of the world, and build their cognitive structures, through their activity. *27*

**constructs** Entities that are part of some psychological theory but that cannot be observed directly (e.g., intelligence and hyperactivity). *16*

**construct validity** The degree to which a measure provides an accurate assessment of the psychological construct it is supposed to measure. *58*

**context** The social relationships in which children are involved, the features of their culture that influence how they are reared, and the social institutions that affect the beliefs and behaviors of parents and other caregivers. *31*

**contextualists** Theorists who emphasize the importance of children's social and cultural context. *31*

**contingent response** A response that depends on, or is logically related to, the previous speaker's comment. *273*

**continuity** Stability over time, or the degree to which a child follows the same path of development from birth to maturity. More precisely, the degree to which differences between children present at one point in development are preserved as the children grow to maturity. *7*

**continuous real-time measurement** Recording every occurrence of a behavior during a set period of observation. *43*

**contracting** The process of writing a formal agreement between parents and children that specifies the rewards the children will receive if they change their behavior in desired ways. *437*

**contrast** A principle of word learning, suggested by Clark, which states that different words must have different meanings. *255*

**control** The dimension of parenting that focuses on parents' expectations for their children's behavior, their training of children to meet these expectations, their enforcement of rules, the openness of their communication with their children, their situational management, and their reliance on physical punishment or power assertive discipline. *430*

**control condition** In experimental designs, the condition in which children are not exposed to the independent variable. *66*

**controversial** The social status group that includes children who receive many positive and many negative nominations on sociometric questionnaires. *499*

**convergent validity** A type of validity that is high when a measure is strongly correlated with other measures that are presumed to assess the same construct. *58*

**cooperative play** The most socially complex of Parten's play types, which includes social pretend play, constructive play in which children work on different parts of a structure, and formal games. *480*

**corpus callosum** A bundle of nerve fibers that links the left and right hemispheres of the brain. *173*

**correlational design** A design in which a researcher examines the relation between the scores of children (or adults) on two or more measures. *63*

**correlation coefficient** A statistic that indicates the strength of the relation between two measures. *63*

**critical period** A time when a specific part of a developing organism is affected by environmental influences that have little or no effect at other times. *125*

**cross-cultural research** The study of children in two or more human groups that are geographically separated and part of distinct societies or nations. *14*

**crossing over** An exchange of genetic material during meiosis that occurs when segments of homologous chromosomes break off and reattach to the other chromosome in the pair. *83*

**cross-sectional design** A research design in which two or more groups of children who differ in age are assessed at roughly the same time. *59*

**crowd** A large group of adolescents who have similar reputations for behavior and who may be identified with the same label (e.g., "jocks"). *476*

**crystallized intelligence** Intellectual abilities that, in theory, are heavily influenced by education and socialization in a culture. Tests of vocabulary and comprehension are usually viewed as measures of crystallized intelligence. *386*

**cultural specificity** An assumption that descriptions and explanations of children's development are specific to a culture and vary across cultures. *13*

**culture** A pattern of behaviors, beliefs, arts, language use, values, ideas, and social institutions that is characteristic of a human group and that is transmitted from one generation to the next. *13*

# D

**decentration** Piaget's term for the broadening of attention that occurs as children develop concrete operations, which allows them to pay attention to more than one element of a task or more than one dimension of an object. *308*

**delay of gratification** An experimental procedure in which children can choose between a small reward available immediately and a larger reward that will be given only after some delay. *634*

**deoxyribonucleic acid (DNA)** The substance on the chromosomes that carries the genetic information for the production and regulation of proteins that, in turn, affect the observable characteristics of an organism. *79*

**dependent variable** In experimental designs, a measure that a researcher expects to be affected by the independent variable or treatment. *66*

**developmental niche** The cultural context in which children are reared and to which they are adapted. *13*

**developmental universals** Descriptions or explanations of children's development that are assumed to hold in every culture. *13*

**deviation IQ** An IQ score computed by determining how much a child's score on an intelligence test differs from the mean score for children the same age. The difference between the child's raw score and the mean score is transformed into standard deviation units, and then these units are translated into IQ points (with one standard deviation = 15 points). *385*

**diethylstilbesterol (DES)** A drug once given to pregnant women to decrease the risk of spontaneous abortions that, unfortunately, increased the risk their adolescent daughters would develop a specific type of vaginal and cervical cancer. *130*

**difference rule** A rule of communication that specifies that a message referring to a particular object should distinguish that object from other objects with which it might be confused. *277*

**differentiation** In perception, the process of analyzing the component parts or properties of objects so as to distinguish them. *338*

**digit span** The number of digits (or numbers) that a person can remember long enough to repeat correctly after hearing them once. *351*

**directives** Specific commands or instructions. *322*

**discontinuity** Instability over time, or substantial changes in children's developmental paths between birth and

maturity. More precisely, the degree to which differences between children present at one point in development are altered as the children grow to maturity (see **continuity**). *8*

**discriminant validity**    A type of validity that is high when a measure of one construct is not correlated with measures of different constructs. *58*

**dizygotic twins**    Twins that result from the fertilization of two egg cells by two sperm cells at roughly the same time; also called fraternal twins. *84*

**domain-specific**    Knowledge or learning that is linked to specific types of information, skills, or tasks. *367*

**dominant**    The allele for a characteristic (e.g., hair color) that is expressed even if a person has a different allele for the same characteristic on the homologous chromosome. *92*

**Down syndrome**    A chromosomal abnormality that leads to unusual physical features (e.g., relatively flat faces and almond-shaped eyes), an increased likelihood of medical problems, and severe mental retardation. *86*

**dramatic play**    Play in which children take on imaginary roles like Mommy and baby. Also known as pretend play. *481*

**dual representation**    The ability to think simultaneously about a symbol and the thing to which it refers. *346*

**dynamic-systems approach**    A theoretical perspective in which patterns of behavior are assumed to be the product of self-organizing systems involving many component processes. Changes in these processes over time lead to the emergence of new behavioral patterns. *183*

# E

**ecological validity**    A type of validity that is high when participants in research perceive the research setting as having the properties that the researcher assumes it has. *58*

**ecology**    The science of the relationships between organisms and their environments. *34*

**effect size**    The difference between the means for two groups expressed in standard deviation units. *70*

**ego**    In Freud's theory, the component of personality that tries to resolve the conflicts that arise between instinctive desires and reality. *21*

**egocentric**    An inability to understand that other people can have perspectives different from one's own. *274*

**ego ideal**    Defined by Freud as the part of the superego that represents the positive side of norms, which encourages children

to model desirable behavior and achievement. *21*

**ego integrity**    Erikson's term for the ideal end point of personality development, when people look back on their experiences and accomplishments with a sense of pride or, at least, acceptance. *23*

**elaboration**    A memory strategy based on linking items to be remembered in a vivid image or a novel sentence. *355*

**Electra complex**    According to Freud, a stage between 3 and 6 years of age when girls are sexually attracted to their fathers and hostile to their mothers. *20*

**embryo**    The name given to the developing human from two to eight weeks after conception. *119*

**empathy**    An emotional response to the perceptions of another person's emotional state that is congruent with the other's emotional state (e.g., feeling distressed when another person is in distress). *631*

**entity theory of intelligence**    The idea that a person's intelligence is a stable characteristic that cannot be improved by effort or training. *411*

**equilibration**    According to Piaget, the process of self-regulation by which children change their cognitive structures in response to events. *27*

**ethnographic research**    A collection of methods designed to provide a comprehensive and objective account of all aspects of a culture. *54*

**ethology**    The study of an organism's behavior in its natural habitat, with special attention to behavioral patterns that contribute to the survival of a species. *30*

**evocative genotype-environment correlation**    A relation between children's genes and the reactions they evoke from other people. Those reactions partly define the environments in which the children grow up. *103*

**exosystem**    In Bronfenbrenner's model, the level of the environment that includes settings that children do not enter but that affect them indirectly (e.g., their parents' workplace). *34*

**expansion**    A complete, correct sentence said in response to a child's incomplete or ungrammatical utterance. *271*

**expectancy-value theory**    A theory of achievement motivation that emphasizes the importance of people's expectancies for success and the value that they attach to success. *411*

**experience-dependent information storage**    A process that facilitates learning about specific (nonuniversal) aspects of an environment (e.g., how to play with specific toys). *171*

**experience-expectant information storage**    A process especially important early in development that facilitates learning

about aspects of the environment that exist everywhere and remain constant across times. *170*

**experimental condition**    In experimental designs, the condition in which children are exposed to the independent variable. *66*

**experimental designs**    Designs that allow conclusive tests of hypotheses about cause and effect because the presumed cause is under the researcher's control. *65*

**expressive**    A style of language learning that emphasizes the communication of feelings and desires with conventional formulas such as "Yes, please." *256*

**expressive traits**    Aspects of personality such as kindness that are related to emotionality, concern for others, and judgments of femininity. *576*

**eyeblink reflex**    People's tendency to blink when they see a bright light or feel a puff of air near the eye. *179*

# F

**failure to thrive**    A medical condition defined by severely retarded growth. *198*

**falsifiable**    A property of a good theory, indicating that experiments can be designed to show conclusively whether the theory is right or wrong. A falsifiable theory contains one or more hypotheses whose disconfirmation would lead to a rejection of the entire theory. *17*

**family systems perspective**    A theoretical perspective that assumes the family is a system whose members influence and are influenced by one another. *468*

**fast mapping**    An inference about the meaning of a word heard for the first time, based on an analysis of its linguistic and nonlinguistic context. *255*

**fetal alcohol syndrome**    A pattern of birth defects caused by regular and heavy drinking of alcoholic beverages during pregnancy. It includes physical abnormalities of the face and internal organs, and problems in intellectual functioning and social behavior. *134*

**fetoscopy**    The insertion into the uterus of a tube containing a small light so that a physician can see the fetus. A sample of fetal blood may also be obtained during this procedure. *99*

**fetus**    The name of the developing human from eight weeks after conception, when it has begun to take human form, until birth. *121*

**fine motor behavior**    Behavior that depends primarily on control of the hands and fingers, or eye-hand coordination. *180*

**fluid intelligence**    Intellectual abilities that, in theory, are heavily influenced by speed

and flexibility in manipulating abstract symbols. They are assumed to depend little on education or socialization. Most nonverbal tests of intelligence are viewed as measures of fluid intelligence. *387*

**foreclosure**   The identity status of people who have made a commitment to important life goals but who have neither chosen their goals themselves nor experienced a period of crisis. Usually, they have simply accepted goals their parents set for them. *554*

**formal-operational thought**   According to Piaget, the final stage of cognitive development, which begins in adolescence. The logical operations of this stage are abstract and are consistent with formal logic. *313*

**fragile X syndrome**   A chromosomal abnormality in which one region on the X chromosome is pinched in. Children with the syndrome are often mentally retarded. *90*

**free morpheme**   A morpheme that can be used by itself, as an entire word (e.g., *happy*). *251*

**functional (practice) play**   The type of play lowest in cognitive complexity, in which children practice sensorimotor skills by repeating an action like sliding down a slide many times. *481*

**fuzzy-trace theory**   A theory that suggests some mental representations of experience are fuzzy, capturing only the gist of experiences, while other mental representations are like verbatim copies of experiences. *363*

# G

*g*   General intelligence, or what Spearman and other theorists assumed was the single dimension that all items on an IQ test measure to some degree. *383*

**games with rules**   A category for children's play that includes sports such as baseball and children's games such as tag. *481*

**gametes**   Cells with only 23 chromosomes that are created during the process of meiosis. The gametes created in the male testes are called sperm; those created in the female ovaries are called ova or egg cells. *84*

**gender constancy**   Children's knowledge that a person's sex is stable over time and cannot be changed by a change in clothes, hairstyle, or activities. *566*

**gender identity**   Children's perceptions of themselves as male or female. *566*

**gender intensification**   The hypothesis that differences in the personalities of boys and girls increase after puberty. *576*

**gender labeling**   The first step in the development of gender identity, when children can correctly say whether they are boys or girls. *594*

**gender schemas**   Cognitive structures that organize children's knowledge about gender and sex-role stereotypes. *596*

**gender stability**   The second step in the development of gender identity, when children know they always were and always will be the same gender. *594*

**gene**   A segment of the DNA that carries instructions for the production of a particular protein. Also, the units of heredity that determine specific characteristics such as hair color. *81*

**generativity**   Erikson's term for the trait of producing and giving to others, which ideally develops in adulthood. *22*

**genetic engineering**   The placement of normal genes into the cells of people with genetic disorders in order to cure those disorders. *81*

**genetic epistemology**   Piaget's term for the study of the development of children's knowledge of their own thoughts and the external world. *25*

**genome**   The total genetic material on all the chromosomes of an organism. *81*

**genotype**   The genetic makeup of an individual. *85*

**genotype-environment correlation**   A systematic relation between variations in children's genotypes and variations in their rearing environments. *102*

**germ disc**   The part of the cell mass during the germinal period of prenatal development that eventually becomes the fetus. *118*

**germinal period**   The earliest phase in prenatal development, the period from fertilization to two weeks after conception. *116*

**grammar**   The rules of a language for producing and comprehending sequences of morphemes. *262*

**gross motor behavior**   Behavior that involves the movement of the entire body or major parts of the body (e.g., head, arms, legs). *180*

**guided participation**   A variety of adult practices that contribute to children's cognitive development. These practices include explicit instruction, allowing children to watch as competent adults do tasks, and allowing children to work with other people who have more competence on a task. *326*

**guilt**   Thoughts and feelings of remorse and responsibility that accompany real or imagined wrongdoings. *629*

# H

**habituation**   A decrease in responding to stimuli presented repeatedly. *188*

**helpless**   A characteristic of students who attribute their academic failures to causes not under their control and so believe

they cannot improve their performance. *409*

**hemophilia**   A serious X-linked disorder in which people lack a substance that leads to normal clotting of blood. *96*

**heritability**   An estimate of the amount of genetic influence on a characteristic, or the proportion of the variation in an observable characteristic that is due to variations in genotypes. *104*

**heteronomy**   Piaget's term for the basis of young children's morality, when they accept whatever adults say rather than judging for themselves which behaviors are moral and immoral. *612*

**heterozygous**   In genetics, having two different alleles at the corresponding locations on homologous chromosomes. *92*

**heuristic value**   One criterion for the evaluation of a theory. A theory is of great heuristic value when it provokes a great deal of research designed to evaluate, expand, or even to disconfirm the theory. *18*

**high-amplitude sucking**   A procedure for assessing young infants' speech perception by recording the vigor or intensity with which they suck a nipple when they hear specific sounds. *245*

**homeostasis**   The principle in family systems theory that systems operate to maintain the stability of their patterns. *469*

**homologous**   A term for pairs of chromosomes that are similar in size, banding patterns, and genetic makeup. *81*

**homozygous**   In genetics, the condition of having two alleles of the same type on homologous chromosomes. *92*

**hostile aggression**   Aggression whose only purpose is to hurt another person. *640*

**Huntington's disease**   A rare, autosomal dominant disorder that does not affect early development but does lead to physical and mental problems and early death in adulthood. *95*

**hypotheses**   Statements that have not yet been proved, which are derived from the assumptions and principles of a theory. *16*

**hypothetico-deductive**   One term that Piaget used for formal-operational thought, because adolescents in this stage of cognitive development form hypotheses and test deductions from the hypotheses. *314*

# I

**id**   In Freud's theory, the component of personality that always seeks the immediate gratification of instinctive desires. *21*

**identification**   According to Freud, the process that motivates children to try to

---

become like their same-sex parent in all important respects. *20*

**identity**   According to Erikson, the sense of continuity that gives people a link to the past and a direction for the future. *534*

**identity achievement**   The identity status of people who have experienced a personal crisis or decision-making period that ended with a commitment to self-chosen life goals. *534*

**identity diffusion**   The identity status of people who may or may not have experienced a personal crisis but who have not made any commitments to life plans. *534*

**implantation**   During prenatal development, the process by which the small ball of cells that will become the embryo lodges itself in a hole in the lining of the uterus. *117*

**imprinting**   The process by which birds and other animals become attached to other animals, people, or objects that they see shortly after birth. *216*

**incremental theory of intelligence**   The idea that a person's intelligence can be increased through training, effort, and practice. *411*

**independent variable**   In experimental designs, a manipulation or treatment by the experimenter that is the presumed cause of some behavior or event. *65*

**inductive discipline**   The use of reasons when disciplining children, especially reasons that point out the harmful effects of the children's actions on other people. *434*

**infantile amnesia**   The inability to remember personal experiences from the first few years of life. *363*

**informed consent**   Children's agreement to participate in a research project after they have been fully informed about its procedures. *70*

**instrumental aggression**   Aggression whose purpose is to get an object or to protect a territory or play space. *640*

**instrumental traits**   Aspects of personality such as independence that are related both to getting things done in the world and to judgments of masculinity. *576*

**intelligence**   The human faculty of thought and reason; the ability to acquire and use knowledge in problem solving; mental acuteness. *379*

**intelligence quotient**   Originally, the ratio of children's mental age to their chronological age multiplied by 100. Now calculated differently (see **deviation IQ**) but still an index of how much children's measured intellectual abilities exceed or fall below those of an average child their age. *382*

**intermodal perception**   The integration of information from two or more sensory modalities (e.g., vision and touch). *197*

**internal consistency**   An index of the reliability of multiitem measures based on the correlations between items, or the degree to which all items yield similar scores for particular children. *57*

**interobserver agreement**   An index of reliability based on the correspondence between the scores that two observers assign to specific children when they observe the children simultaneously. *56*

**intervention**   An experimental manipulation that is intended to enhance children's development. *68*

**involvement**   The dimension of parenting that focuses on the amount of time that parents spend in interaction with their children and the degree to which their attitudes are child centered. *435*

# K

**karyotypes**   Photographs of individuals' chromosomes in which the chromosomes are arranged in order of their size and labeled according to a standard procedure. *81*

**kibbutz**   A small, democratically governed community in Israel in which groups of infants and children receive their daily care in community-run centers. *231*

**Klinefelter syndrome**   A chromosomal abnormality that usually results from the presence of two X chromosomes and one Y chromosome. Children with the syndrome are phenotypically male but never produce sperm. *90*

**knowledge base**   A person's knowledge of the world, especially the knowledge that is helpful for remembering new information or solving cognitive problems. *357*

**kwashiorkor**   A disease resulting from diets very low in protein but with adequate calories. The abdomen, face, and legs swell with water, the hair falls out, and sores develop on the skin. *163*

# L

**Language Acquisition Device (LAD)**   A hypothetical mechanism in the brain that helps children see the connections between their innate universal grammar and the grammar of their own language. *279*

**Language Acquisition Support System (LASS)**   A general term for all the social interactions with parents and other people that contribute to children's language development. *284*

**lateralization**   The process by which brain functions become specialized either in the left or in the right hemisphere. *173*

**learning**   A change in behavior in a specific situation due to experience rather than to fatigue or other causes. *23*

**learning to learn**   The acquisition of strategies, skills, and knowledge that improve a person's ability to understand and retain information. *367*

**libido**   Freud's term for a fund of sexual energy that is focused on different bodily organs during different periods in development. *20*

**linguistic awareness**   Explicit, conscious knowledge of language rules as shown, for example, by the ability to judge the grammatical correctness of a sentence. *268*

**locus**   The term in genetics for the position of a specific gene on a chromosome. *92*

**logical operations**   Defined by Piaget as internalized actions that are reversible and that are connected with other operations in logical structures. *306*

**longitudinal design**   A research design in which children are assessed on multiple occasions over periods of months or years. *61*

**love withdrawal**   Parents directly express their anger or disapproval of children's behavior by refusing to speak with them, threatening to leave them, or otherwise showing a lack of affection. *434*

# M

**macrosystem**   In Bronfenbrenner's model, the most global level of the environment, which describes the consistencies in lower-level systems across a society or culture. *34*

**major depression**   A serious impairment in psychological functioning with some combination of depressed mood, suicidal ideas, sleep disturbances, and social withdrawal. *108*

**marasmus**   A disease caused by severe protein-energy undernutrition. Growth stops, the skin wrinkles, and the tissues begin to waste away. *163*

**mastery motivation**   Motivation to learn about and gain control over one's environment. *417*

**mastery-oriented**   A characteristic of students who attribute their academic failures to a lack of effort and so believe they could succeed if they tried harder. *409*

**maturation**   The process by which children's genes control the course of their development. *11*

**measurement**   A set of rules for assigning numbers to objects in such a way as to represent quantities of attributes. *41*

**meiosis**   A process of cell division that prepares the way for sexual reproduction by producing new cells that have only half the number of chromosomes in normal body cells. *83*

**memory**   The cognitive processes that allow people to store, retain, and recall their experiences. *347*

**menarche** The first occurrence of menstruation and the onset of regular menstrual cycles. *168*

**mental age** An index of a child's intellectual ability relative to that of other children the same age. Mental age is judged by comparing the intelligence-test items that a child answers correctly with the average age at which children answer those items correctly. *382*

**mesosystem** In Bronfenbrenner's ecological model, the level of the environment that reflects the connections among microsystems (e.g., between a child's home and school). *34*

**meta-analysis** The statistical analysis of a large collection of analysis results from separate studies. *68*

**metacognition** People's ability to think about their thoughts and control their cognitive processes. *367*

**metamemory** People's ideas about the amount of information they can hold in working memory, the difficulty of particular memory tasks, the effectiveness of specific memory strategies, and the content of their memories. *359*

**microsystem** In Bronfenbrenner's model, the lowest level of the environment, which includes the setting for a child's behavior and the activities, participants, and roles in that setting. *34*

**mitosis** A process of cell division in which two new cells with exactly the same DNA are formed from a single cell. *80*

**modifier genes** Genes that affect the expression or functioning of genes at other loci on the chromosomes. *97*

**monozygotic twins** Twins that develop from a single zygote that separates into two zygotes shortly after fertilization; also known as identical twins. *84*

**moratorium** The identity status of people who are currently in an identity crisis and who have delayed or deferred making a commitment to life goals. *554*

**Moro reflex** A reflex elicited by placing infants on their backs and abruptly reducing their support. In response, infants arch their back, extend their legs, and throw their arms outward and then pull them back toward each other. *179*

**morpheme** The basic unit of word meaning. *251*

**morphology** Language rules for linking words, or free morphemes, to bound morphemes that modify their meaning. *262*

**multiculturalism** Concerned with the cultural diversity, or the differences among cultural groups, within a single nation. *14*

**multifactorial inheritance** Patterns of genetic inheritance involving the action of multiple genes that do not follow the principle of dominance; also allows for interactions or correlations between children's genotypes and the environments in which they grow up. *97*

**mutations** Permanent changes in the DNA that lead to changes in the observable characteristics of an organism. *97*

**mutual exclusivity** A principle of word learning that states that an object has only one category label (e.g., something called a *dog* cannot also be labeled as a *cat*). *255*

**mutual respect** Piaget's term for the attitude that prevails in children's interactions with peers. Each child expects the other to listen to him or her and, in turn, listens to the others. *612*

**myelinization** The coating of nerve fibers with insulating tissue (myelin). *353*

# N

**naturalistic observation** A technique for measuring children's typical behavior by observing them in their homes, classrooms, playgrounds, or other natural settings. *42*

**nature** A general term that refers to the effects of heredity or genetic influence on children's development. *9*

**negative reinforcement** The removal (or termination) of a negative stimulus, which leads to an increase in the frequency of the preceding behavior. *440*

**negative reinforcement trap** Interactions between a parent and a child that end when each person provides negative reinforcement for the other's behavior. The interactions are described as a trap because each person inadvertently promotes the aversive behavior of the other. *439*

**neglected** The social status group that includes children who receive few positive or negative nominations on sociometric questionnaires. *499*

**neonate** The name for human infants during the first four weeks of life. *145*

**neurons** Nerve cells. *145, 169*

**niche picking** A term used by Scarr and McCartney to describe children's attempts to find an environment—a niche—that matches their talents and interests. *103*

**noncontingent response** A response that has no relation to the previous speaker's comment. *273*

**nonshared environmental influences** Effects of features of the environment that are unique to a specific child, not shared by the child and his or her siblings. *106*

**nurture** A general term that refers to the effects of learning, training, education, and other environmental influences on children's development. *9*

# O

**object permanence** Piaget's term for infants' understanding that objects do not cease to exist when they go out of sight; the concept that objects exist independent of our own actions. *295*

**observational learning** The principle in social learning theory that refers to learning from observing other people's behavior. *24*

**Oedipal crisis** According to Freud, a stage between 3 and 6 years of age when boys are sexually attracted to their mothers, and are hostile to their fathers, but are not fully conscious of their feelings. *20*

**onlooker play** Parten's category for times in which a child is watching or listening to other children but not playing with them. *481*

**open communication** A positive aspect of parental control that involves frequent discussions between parents and their children. Parents explain the reasons for their rules and allow children to express their opinions about the rules. *431*

**operant conditioning** Defined by Skinner as the type of learning that reflects the control of behavior by rewards and punishments. *24*

**operants** Skinner's term for behaviors that are emitted spontaneously by an organism. *24*

**overextensions** Use of words to refer to broader categories of objects or events than is conventional (e.g., using *Daddy* to refer to all men). *253*

**overregularization** An error that children make when learning language in which they add the past-tense morpheme for regular verbs to irregular verbs (e.g., *runned*). *265*

# P

**palmar grasp reflex** Newborns' tendency to grab and hold onto a stick pressed against their palms. *179*

**parallel play** According to Parten, the play type in which a child plays with the same toys or materials as other children but does not try to influence or interact with the other children. *480*

**passive genotype-environment correlation** A relation between the genes that parents give to their children and the environments that they provide for their children. *102*

**peers** Other children who are similar to a child in age. *474*

**perceptual learning** The improvements in perception as children grow older, and the improvements in cognitive performance that result from changes in perception. *353*

**perceptual representation** The level of perception above that of sensory primitives. This higher level deals with the interpretation of sensory input (e.g., judgments of the functions of objects). *335*

**permissive** A parenting style marked by low parental control and lax enforcement of rules but high warmth. *436*

**personality traits** Characteristics of people that are fairly stable over time and obvious in a variety of situations (e.g., sociability and impatience). *543*

**phenotype** The observable characteristics of an individual. *85*

**phenylketonuria (PKU)** An autosomal recessive disorder that makes children unable to break down the amino acid phenylalanine. Unless placed on a restricted diet early in life, children with the disorder suffer severe mental retardation. *93*

**phonemes** Distinctive categories of sounds recognized as meaningful in a specific language. *244*

**phonological awareness** A broad construct that includes the detection of rhyme and alliteration, the ability to analyze the phonemes in a word, and other types of knowledge of speech sounds. *250*

**phonological rules** Regular ways that children change the pronunciation of conventional words, for example, by replacing the phoneme /p/ with /b/. *249*

**phonology** The study of speech sounds themselves, the stress and intonation patterns that accompany speech sounds, and the rules for combining individual sounds into syllables. *244*

**pictorial cues** Cues to depth that can be interpreted with visual input from just one eye. *193*

**placenta** An organ that links the life-support systems of a pregnant woman and her embryo or fetus. It is attached both to the lining of the woman's uterus and to the umbilical cord that transfers oxygen and other substances to and from the embryo or fetus. *118*

**polygenic inheritance** A pattern of gene expression in which multiple genes that affect the phenotype combine in a simple, additive fashion. *97*

**popular** The social status group that includes children who receive many positive nominations and few negative nominations on sociometric questionnaires. *499*

**power assertion** The use of physical punishment, force, or deprivation of privileges to control behavior and punish misbehavior. A negative aspect of parental control. *433*

**pragmatics** The aspect of language that focuses on its use for communication. More specifically, the branch of

linguistics that focuses on the accurate, effective, and appropriate comprehension and production of language. *271*

**precedence effect** The tendency to hear only the first sound if two identical sounds come from different directions a few milliseconds apart. *194*

**preeclampsia** A syndrome of pregnancy that involves elevated blood pressure, swelling of the hands and feet, and the abnormal excretion of protein into the urine. *130*

**preferential looking technique** Testing an infant's ability to distinguish between two visual stimuli by showing the stimuli simultaneously and observing whether the infant looks longer at one stimulus than the other. *188*

**preoperational stage** The stage of cognitive development, in Piaget's theory, before children have constructed any logical operations. *307*

**preterm** Infants born before they have completed the 37th week of prenatal development. *149*

**primary circular reaction** The earliest type of circular reaction in infancy, in which an infant's activity is equivalent to the infant's goal. *293*

**private speech** Vygotsky's term for speech that is spoken aloud but that is directed to oneself rather than other people. Viewed by Vygotsky as an intermediate phase between purely social speech and inner speech or thought. *324*

**production deficiency** A failure to use spontaneously memory strategies ( or strategies for completing other cognitive tasks) that would improve performance. *355*

**prosocial behavior** Positive social behaviors, including sharing, helping, and comforting. *426*

**protein-energy malnutrition (PEM)** A lack of protein, a lack of other foods that provide the body with energy, or both. *164*

**protowords** Sounds that infants use like words but that are not part of the adult language and, thus, do not have a conventional meaning. *248*

**proximodistal principle** The principle that development usually proceeds from the center of the body outward. In particular, the arms develop earlier than the hands and fingers. *120*

**psychoanalysis** A treatment for mental illness devised by Sigmund Freud in which patients talk at great length and with virtually no interruptions about their past experiences and their current thoughts, wishes, and emotions. *19*

**psychometric approach** The research tradition that focuses on the nature and assessment of human intelligence, most often by using standardized tests to

assess general intelligence and specific cognitive abilities. *378*

**psychosexual stages** Developmental phases proposed by Freud that reflect changes in the focus of sexual energy on different bodily organs. The stages describe the psychological consequences of transformations in sexuality. *20*

**psychosocial stages** Erikson's description of the distinct phases of development that are consequences of the social experiences and major events of the human life cycle. *21*

**puberty** The onset of the capability for sexual reproduction or childbearing. More generally, the physical and physiological changes that accompany adolescence and the development of reproductive ability. *159*

# R

**random assignment** A procedure in which chance determines in which condition children in an experimental study are placed. *66*

**random error** Errors of measurement that reduce the consistency of scores and therefore lower the reliability of measures. *56*

**reaction range** The degree to which variations in environments can affect the development of individuals with a particular genotype and, thus, affect their mature phenotypes. *101*

**reactivity** Children's responses to observers or to conditions of observation. *45*

**realism** According to Piaget, the tendency of young children to attribute the properties of physical objects to mental phenomena like dreams (e.g., they are visible to other people). *301*

**recessive** The allele for a characteristic (e.g., hair color) that is expressed only if a person does not have a different allele for the same characteristic on the homologous chromosome. *92*

**reciprocal determinism** The mutual influence of people's thoughts, behaviors, and environments on each other, which implies both that people can shape their destiny and that self-direction has limits. *25*

**reciprocal teaching** A method of classroom learning in which students and an adult teacher take turns leading a group discussion of some topic or material. *32*

**referential** A style of language learning that emphasizes the acquisition of vocabulary for referring to objects. *256*

**referential communication** A type of task in which a speaker and a listener sit on opposite sides of a screen and are given identical sets of objects. The speaker must describe one object, called the

referent, so that the listener can pick it from the objects in front of him or her. *277*

**reflexes** Distinct and regular patterns of involuntary activity that are elicited by specific stimuli. *178*

**rehearsal** A memory strategy that involves repeating the words or information to be remembered either aloud or mentally. *354*

**rejected** The social status group that includes children who receive many negative nominations and few positive nominations on sociometric questionnaires. *499*

**rejecting-neglecting** A parenting style marked by low parental control and low warmth or responsiveness. *436*

**relational aggression** Harming other people by ruining their social relationships, for example, excluding them from a group. *641*

**relationship** A tie between two people who have had several interactions over time. Also involves the expectations and emotions that the two people associate with their history of interactions. *475*

**relationships** Ties between individuals who know each other that are defined by their multiple interactions over time. *36*

**reliability** The precision of a measure, or the consistency with which a particular characteristic is measured. *56*

**replication** The test of a hypothesis or the investigation of a research question with multiple samples of subjects and, often, with different but parallel methods. *41*

**representational insight** The understanding that an object in a model stands for a corresponding object in a real-life setting. *345*

**representative sample** A sample of children's behavior that reflects all of the children's experiences, not a biased selection of them. *45*

**representative samples** Samples that include children from all segments or subgroups of the population under study. *59*

**research design** The structure of a research project, including the characteristics of the participants, the participants' experiences, and the schedule of measurements and treatments. *58*

**retinal disparity** The difference in the images of the same scene in the two eyes. This difference is a binocular cue to the distance of objects from the viewer. *193*

**reversal** In experiments testing the effects of reinforcement, the phase in which the pattern of reinforcements is returned to that of the baseline phase. *66*

**reverse causation** A hypothesis that the true cause-effect relation between two variables is in the direction opposite to that assumed by a researcher. *65*

**role taking** The ability to adopt, in thought, the perspective or role of another person. *557*

**rooting reflex** A newborn's response to a touch on the cheek—turning the head toward the object—opening the mouth, and closing it on the object. *179*

**rough-and-tumble play** A style of play in which children wrestle, pretend to fight with each other, and jump on each other. *581*

# S

**scaffolding** An informal term for the support and assistance that parents or other adults provide for children's learning. Support and assistance are reduced as children become more capable of completing cognitive tasks independently. *322*

**schemes** According to Piaget, the cognitive structures that underlie consistent action patterns in certain situations or with certain objects. *292*

**schizophrenia** A broad category of psychological disorders that include such symptoms as delusions, hallucination, bizarre behavior, disturbances of thought, and a relative absence of emotional expression. *108*

**script** A mental representation of a sequence of events that typically occur in a specific context. *346*

**secondary circular reaction** According to Piaget, a type of circular reaction in which infants' actions (e.g., kicking their legs) can be distinguished from their goal (e.g., making toys on a crib mobile shake). *293*

**secular trends** Changes in human populations over generations or long time periods. *167*

**self-concept** People's ideas about their physical skills, mental abilities, personality traits, and other characteristics. *525*

**self-efficacy** Beliefs about one's ability to behave in a way that produces desired outcomes. *24*

**self-esteem** People's evaluations of their worth, value, and competence. *522*

**semantics** The study of word meanings. *251*

**sensitive periods** A time interval, usually early in development, during which organisms are strongly affected by experiences that have weaker effects at other periods. *125*

**sensorimotor intelligence** Piaget's label for the reasoning that is revealed, especially during infancy, in adaptive patterns of action (or motor skills) in response to sensations. *291*

**sensory primitives** The lowest level of perception, which deals with the reception of sensory input (e.g., the ability to distinguish shades of gray). *333*

**separation protest** The crying and distress that infants show after about 8 months of age when their mothers or other attachment figures leave them by themselves or with a person whom they don't know well. *219*

**sequential analysis** A procedure for judging the antecedents and consequences of behavior that is based on the analysis of sequences of behaviors by one or more people. *44*

**sex chromosomes** The pair of chromosomes in human beings that is responsible for sex differentiation. *82*

**sex-role development** The process by which children acquire the beliefs, behaviors, and other characteristics expected or considered appropriate for individuals of their sex in their culture. *564*

**sex roles** Behaviors and other characteristics that are expected or considered appropriate for males and females in a specific culture. *564*

**sex stereotypes** Assumptions or expectations about how males and females differ in their activities, personality traits, or other characteristics. *565*

**sex typing** A synonym for sex-role development. *564*

**shaping** In Skinner's theory, the process of reinforcing spontaneous behaviors that more and more closely match a desired new behavior. *24*

**shared environment** The environment experienced by all children in the same family, the same preschool, or the same classroom in a school. *405*

**sickle-cell anemia** A genetic disorder of which one symptom is that blood cells are curved like a sickle rather than having the rounded shape of normal red blood cells. Other symptoms can include increased bacterial infections, episodes of blocked circulation, and problems of organ degeneration. *100*

**significant others** The other people most important in a person's life, who have the greatest effect on the person's self-esteem. *533*

**sister chromatids** Two copies of a single chromosome that are formed during the first step in mitosis. *80*

**situational management** A positive aspect of parental control that involves anticipating problematic situations and trying to structure them so that appropriate behavior by children is more likely. *432*

**social cognition** Thinking that relates to human beings and human affairs; includes thoughts related to the self and to other people. *522*

**social conventions** Behavioral uniformities that coordinate interactions of individuals within social systems (e.g.,

the rule that teachers are addressed by their title and last name rather than by their first name). *625*

**social-desirability bias** A bias to give responses that are perceived as socially acceptable. *49*

**social impact** How much a child stands out in a peer group, judged by the total number of positive nominations and negative nominations that the child receives from other children when all children in a group complete sociometric questionnaires. *499*

**social intelligence** The cognitive abilities that underlie social competence and social adaptation. *421*

**socialization** The process by which children acquire the beliefs, attitudes, and behaviors expected of members of their society and culture. *208, 427*

**social learning theory** A theory of learning that emphasizes not only the control of behavior by rewards and punishments but also learning by observation of other people. *24*

**social preference (peer acceptance)** How much other children like a particular child, judged by the difference between the number of positive nominations and the number of negative nominations that the child receives from other children when all children in a group complete sociometric questionnaires. *498*

**social referencing** The use of another person's emotional expressions to interpret events that are ambiguous or difficult for individuals to interpret on their own. *210*

**social schemas** Information about social events or social situations that is part of memory structures, and which therefore affects interpretation of new events and interactions. *555*

**social status** A child's position or popularity in a group, defined by how much the peers in the group like or dislike them. *476*

**socioeconomic status (SES)** A composite measure of the wealth of a family and the prestige of the parents' occupations or roles in society. *164*

**sociometric status** Another term for social status that derives from the most common technique for assessing a child's social position. *498*

**sociometric techniques** Methods for assessing the social status of specific persons in the social structure of a group. *498*

**solitary play** Children are playing alone, with toys different from those of other children, and are paying no attention to the other children. *481*

**sound spectrograph** An instrument that provides a visual representation of sound waves. *245*

**standard deviation** An index of the variability of the scores in a group. *70*

**standardization sample** The group of children whose responses define the norms and establish the scoring for tests later given to other children. *385*

**statistically significant** A relation between two measures that is stronger than would be expected by chance. *63*

**stepping reflex** Newborns' tendency to make alternating movements of their two legs and feet if they are held, standing, and tilted slowly left and right. *179*

**stereotype flexibility** Willingness to assert that males and females can engage in the same behaviors, choose the same activities, and show similarities on other characteristics. *569*

**stereotype knowledge** Awareness of commonly accepted stereotypes about males and females, assessed from a person's judgments about whether a behavior or other characteristic is more typical for males or for females. *567*

**Strange Situation** A standard experimental procedure for measuring the security of infants' attachments to their mothers, their fathers, or other adults. *221*

**structured whole** Piaget's term for the organization of thinking and reasoning (which, in French, is *structure d'ensemble*). Often assumed to mean that a child's reasoning on all tasks should reflect the same stage of cognitive development. *298*

**Sudden Infant Death Syndrome (SIDS)** The sudden death of an infant or young child that is unexpected by history and for which no adequate cause is revealed by a thorough postmortem examination. *176*

**superego** In Freud's theory, the component of personality that represents cultural norms and standards as internalized by the child. *21*

**syntax** Language rules for combining words into sentences. *262*

# T

**telegraphic speech** Early utterances by young children that leave out words not essential for communicating meaning. *262*

**temperament** The relatively consistent, basic dispositions inherent in the person that underlie and modulate the expression of activity, reactivity, emotionality, and sociability. *211*

**teratogens** Known causes of birth defects. *124*

**teratology** The field of study concerned with the causes and distribution of birth defects. *124*

**tertiary circular reaction** According to Piaget, a type of circular reaction that involves the repetition of behavior patterns with deliberate variations. The variations reflect a kind of experimenting, to see how the effects of a behavior change when the behavior is changed slightly. *294*

**testosterone** The most important of the androgens, which contributes to masculinization during the prenatal period. *582*

**test-retest reliability** The correlation between the scores for some sample of children on a first test and a later test (or retest). *56*

**thalidomide** A drug that is a mild sedative for adults, but that causes severe birth defects if taken by pregnant women during the first trimester of pregnancy. *128*

**theory** A system of assumptions, accepted principles, and rules of procedure devised to analyze, predict, or otherwise explain a set of phenomena. *16*

**theory of mind** Ideas about mental states like thoughts, beliefs, or dreams, and about the relations among these states. *304, 548*

**third variable** In correlational designs, an unmeasured variable that accounts for the relation between two variables that are measured. *65*

**time-out** A form of punishment recommended by social learning theorists in which children are given a time away from all reinforcing activities and interactions for three to five minutes. *441*

**time sampling** A procedure in which an observer watches a specific child for a set time that is divided into smaller intervals. The observer records whether the child displays a specific behavior (or behaviors) during each interval. *44*

**transactional approach** A theoretical perspective that assumes children's development depends on the transactions (or interchanges) between the children and their environments. These transactions depend jointly on the children's characteristics and the characteristics of their environments. *127*

**transitivity** An understanding of transitive inference. For example, an understanding that if one object is taller than a second and the second is taller than the third, the first is also taller than the third. *306*

**treatment** The phase in some experiments in which reinforcement patterns are changed. More generally, the independent variable to which participants in an experiment are exposed. *66*

**triarchic theory** Sternberg's theory of three parts of intelligence. Includes a componential subtheory, an experiential subtheory, and a contextual subtheory. *406*

**trisomy-21** The chromosomal abnormality that most often causes Down syndrome, which is the presence of three rather than the normal two chromosomes of type 21. *86*

**Turner syndrome** A chromosomal abnormality that results from the presence of only one sex chromosome, an X. Children with this syndrome are phenotypically female but sterile. *89*

## U

**umbilical cord** A long cord containing two arteries and one vein that carries oxygen, nutrients, and other substances between the placenta and the fetus. *121*

**unconditioned response** In classical conditioning, the natural, spontaneous, or unlearned response to an unconditioned stimulus. *12*

**unconditioned stimulus** In classical conditioning, the term for the signal or event that elicits the unconditioned response. *12*

**underextensions** The use of words to refer to narrower categories of objects or events than is conventional (e.g., the use of duck to refer only to a specific yellow toy *duck*). *253*

**unilateral respect** According to Piaget, young children's attitude toward adult authority. Young children respect adults' power and wisdom but cannot take the adults' perspective and so cannot understand the reasons for adults' rules. *612*

**universal grammar** According to Chomsky, a schema for all human languages that includes language principles, rules that provide structure for a grammar, and conditions for the elaboration of the principles and rules into the grammar of a specific language. *279*

**unoccupied play** Parten's label for episodes in which a child is only looking around the classroom, not playing with anyone or anything. *481*

## V

**validity** The accuracy of a measure, or the extent to which differences in scores on the measure match differences in children's actual characteristics. *57*

**variable** Anything that varies or can be varied. *65*

**vernix caseosa** A cheesy coating of dead cells and oils that protects the skin of a fetus from chapping in the amniotic fluid. *122*

**visual accommodation** The process by which eye muscles change the shape of the lens to bring objects at different distances into focus. *187*

**visual acuity** An index of the sharpness of a person's vision, or how well they can see objects. *186*

**visual recognition memory** An experimental paradigm that allows researchers to determine how long infants can remember specific visual stimuli. *348*

## W

**warmth** The dimension of parenting that focuses on the emotional tone of parent-child interactions. Important aspects of parental warmth include responsiveness to children's needs, praise for good behavior, and expressions of positive emotions toward and around children. *428*

**whole-object rule** The assumption that a new word refers to an entire object rather than to one of its parts or to its texture or shape. *255*

**withdrawal reflex** Newborns' tendency to flex their knee and move their foot away if they feel a pinprick on the sole of their foot. *179*

**working memory** The memory available for current cognitive processes. *352*

## X

**X-linked** A term for genetic disorders that can be traced to genes on the X chromosome. *96*

## Z

**zone of proximal development** The distance between children's apparent level of cognitive development when working independently and their level when solving problems under adult guidance or working with more capable peers. *52*

**zygote** The new cell formed when a sperm cell with 23 chromosomes fertilizes an egg cell with 23 chromosomes. The new cell has the 46 chromosomes that are normal for a human being. *84*

# REFERENCES

Abramovitch, R., Corter, C., Pepler, D. J., & Stanhope, L. (1986). Sibling and peer interaction: A final follow-up and a comparison. *Child Development, 57,* 217–229.

Achenbach, T. M. (1991). *Manual for the Child Behavior Checklist and 1991 Profile.* Burlington, VT: University of Vermont, Department of Psychiatry.

Ackerman, B. P. (1993). Children's understanding of the relation between referential knowledge and referential behavior. *Journal of Experimental Psychology, 56,* 385–411.

Ainsworth, M. D. S. (1967). *Infancy in Uganda.* Baltimore: Johns Hopkins.

Ainsworth, M. D. S. (1973). The develop-ment of infant-mother attachment. In B. Caldwell & H. Riccuiti (Eds.), *Review of child development research, Vol. 3* (pp. 1–94). Chicago: University of Chicago Press.

Ainsworth, M. D. S. (1989). Attachments beyond infancy. *American Psychologist, 44,* 709–716.

Ainsworth, M. D. S., Blehar, M. C., Waters, E., & Wall, S. (1978). *Patterns of attachment: A psychological study of the strange situation.* Hillsdale, NJ: Erlbaum.

Ainsworth, M. D. S., & Bowlby, J. (1991). An ethological approach to personality development. *American Psychologist, 46,* 333–341.

Allison, P. D., & Furstenberg, F. F., Jr. (1989). How marital dissolution affects children: Variations by age and sex. *Developmental Psychology, 25,* 540–549.

Almli, C. R., & Finger, F. (1987). Neural insult and critical period concepts. In M. H. Bornstein (Ed.), *Sensitive periods in development. Interdisciplinary perspectives* (pp. 123–144). Hillsdale, NJ: Erlbaum.

Alpert-Gillis, L. J., & Connell, J. P. (1989). Gender and sex-role influences on children's self-esteem. *Journal of Personality, 57,* 97–114.

Alsaker, F. D., & Olweus, D. (1992). Stability of global self-evaluations in early adolescence: A cohort longitudinal study. *Journal of Research on Adolescence, 2,* 123–146.

Amato, P. R., & Keith, B. (1991). Parental divorce and the well-being of children: A meta-analysis. *Psychological Bulletin, 110,* 26–46.

American Psychological Association. (1992). Ethical principles of psychologists and code of conduct. *American Psychologist, 47,* 1597–1611.

Ames, C. (1987). The enhancement of student motivation. In M. L. Maehr & D. A. Kleiber (Eds.), *Advances in motivation and achievement, Vol. 5* (pp. 123–149). Greenwich, CT: JAI Press.

Ames, G. J., & Murray, F. B. (1982). When two wrongs make a right: Promoting cognitive change by social conflict. *Developmental Psychology, 18,* 894–897.

Amiel Tison, C., Reynolds, F., & Cabral, C. (1994). Letter: The effects of maternal epidural anesthesia on neonatal behavior during the first month. *Developmental Medicine and Child Neurology, 36,* 91–92.

Ammala, P., Hiilesmaa, V. K., Liukkonen, S., Saisto, T., Teramo, K., & von Koskull, H. (1993). Randomized trial comparing first-trimester transcervical chorionic villus sampling and second-trimester amniocentesis. *Prenatal Diagnosis, 13,* 919–927.

Anderson, K. E., Lytton, H., & Romney, D. M. (1986). Mothers' interactions with normal and conduct-disordered boys: Who affects whom? *Developmental Psychology, 22,* 604–609.

Andersson, B. E. (1989). Effects of public day-care: A longitudinal study. *Child Development, 60,* 857–866.

Andersson, B. E. (1992). Effects of day-care on cognitive and socioemotional competence of thirteen-year-old Swedish schoolchildren. *Child Development, 63,* 20–36.

Anglin, J. M. (1993). Vocabulary development: A morphological analysis. *Monographs of the Society for Research in Child Development, 58* (10, Serial No. 238).

Antell, S. E., & Keating, D. P. (1983). Perception of numerical invariance in neonates. *Child Development, 54,* 695–701.

Apgar, V. (1953). A proposal for a new method of evaluation in the newborn infant. *Current Research in Anesthesia and Analgesia, 32,* 260–267.

Aquilino, W. S. (1994). Impact of childhood family disruption on young adults' relationships with parents. *Journal of Marriage and the Family, 56,* 295–313.

Archer, S. L. (1982). The lower age boundaries of identity development. *Child Development, 53,* 1551–1556.

Archer, S. L. (1993). Identity status in early and middle adolescents: Scoring criteria. In J. E. Marcia, A. S. Waterman, D. R. Matteson, S. L. Archer, & J. L. Orlofsky (Eds.), *Ego identity: A handbook for psychosocial research* (pp. 177–204). New York: Springer-Verlag.

Aries, P. (1962). *Centuries of childhood* (R. Baldick, Trans.). New York: Knopf.

Asendorpf, J. B., & Baudonniere, P. M. (1993). Self-awareness and other-awareness: Mirror self-recognition and synchronic imitation among unfamiliar peers. *Developmental Psychology, 29,* 88–95.

Asendorpf, J. B., & Nunner-Winkler, G. (1992). Children's moral motive strength and temperamental inhibition reduce their immoral behavior in real moral conflicts. *Child Development, 63,* 1223–1235.

Asher, S. R., & Coie, J. D. (Eds.). (1990). *Peer rejection in childhood.* Cambridge, England: Cambridge University Press.

Ashley, C. T., Wilkinson, K. D., Reines, D., & Warren, S. T. (1993). FMR1 protein: Conserved RNP family domains and selective RNA binding. *Science, 262,* 563–566.

Aslin, R. N. (1987). Visual and auditory development in infancy. In J. D. Osofsky (Ed.), *Handbook of infant development* (pp. 5–97). New York: Wiley.

Aslin, R. N. (1993). Commentary: The strange attractiveness of dynamic systems to development. In L. B. Smith & E. Thelen (Eds.), *A dynamic systems approach to development: Applications* (pp. 385–399). Cambridge, MA: MIT Press.

Aslin, R. N., Pisoni, D. B., & Jusczyk, P. W. (1983). Auditory development and speech perception in infancy. In M. M. Haith & J. J. Campos (Eds.), *Handbook of child psychology: Vol. II. Infancy and developmental psychobiology* (pp. 573–687). New York: Wiley.

Aslin, R. N., & Smith, L. B. (1988). Perceptual development. *Annual Review of Psychology, 39,* 435–473.

Astington, J. W., Harris, P. L., & Olson, D. R. (Eds.). (1988). *Developing theories of mind.* New York: Cambridge University Press.

Astone, N. M., & Washington, M. L. (1994). The association between grandparental coresidence and adolescent childbearing. *Journal of Family Issues, 15,* 574–589.

Astor, R. A. (1994). Children's moral reasoning about family and peer violence: The role of provocation and retribution. *Child Development, 65,* 1054–1067.

Atkinson, J. W., & Feather, N. T. (Eds.). (1966). *A theory of achievement motivation.* New York: Wiley.

Au, T. K., & Glusman, M. (1990). The principle of mutual exclusivity in word learning: To honor or not to honor? *Child Development, 61,* 1474–1490.

Aviezer, O., van IJzendoorn, M. H., Sagi, A., & Schuengel, C. (1994). "Children of the dream" revisited: 70 years of collective early child care in Israeli kibbutzim. *Psychological Bulletin, 116,* 99–116.

Azmitia, M. (1992). Expertise, private speech, and the development of self-regulation. In R. M. Diaz & L. E. Berk (Eds.), *Private speech: From social interaction to self-regulation* (pp. 101–122). Hillsdale, NJ: Erlbaum.

Azmitia, M., & Hesser, J. (1993). Why siblings are important agents of cognitive development: A comparison of siblings and peers. *Child Development, 64,* 430–444.

Bachman, J. G., & O'Malley, P. M. (1977). Self-esteem in young men: A longitudinal analysis of the impact of educational and occupational attainment. *Journal of Personality and Social Psychology, 35,* 365–380.

Bailey, J. M., & Zucker, K. J. (1995). Childhood sex-typed behavior and sexual orientation: A conceptual analysis and quantitative review. *Developmental Psychology, 51,* 31–42.

Baillargeon, R. (1987). Object permanence in 3½- and 4½-month-old infants. *Developmental Psychology, 23,* 655–664.

Baillargeon, R. (1991). Reasoning about the height and location of a hidden object in 4.5- and 6.5-month-old infants. *Cognition, 38,* 13–42.

Baillargeon, R. (1994). How do infants learn about the physical world? *Current Directions in Psychological Science, 3,* 133–140.

Baillargeon, R., & Graber, M. (1988). Evidence of location memory in 8-month-old infants in a nonsearch AB task. *Developmental Psychology, 24,* 502–511.

Baillargeon, R., Spelke, E. S., & Wasserman, S. (1985). Object permanence in five-month-old infants. *Cognition, 20,* 191–208.

Baldwin, D. A., & Markman, E. M. (1989). Establishing word-object relations: A first step. *Child Development, 60,* 381–398.

Ball, S. J. (1981). *Beachside comprehensive.* Cambridge, England: Cambridge University Press.

Baltes, P. B., Reese, H. W., & Nesselroade, J. R. (1977). *Life-span developmental psychology: Introduction to research methods.* Monterey, CA: Brooks/Cole.

Bandura, A. (1977a). Self-efficacy: Toward a unifying theory of behavioral change. *Psychological Review, 84,* 191–215.

Bandura, A. (1977b). *Social learning theory.* Englewood Cliffs, NJ: Prentice-Hall.

Bandura, A. (1978). The self system in reciprocal determinism. *American Psychologist, 33,* 344–358.

Bandura, A. (1986). *Social foundations of thought and action.* Englewood Cliffs, NJ: Prentice-Hall.

Bandura, A. (1992). Social cognitive theory. In R. Vasta (Ed.), *Six theories of child development: Revised formulations and current issues* (pp. 1–60). London: Jessica Kingsley.

Bandura, A., Ross, D., & Ross, S. A. (1963). Imitation of film-mediated aggressive models. *Journal of Abnormal and Social Psychology, 66,* 3–11.

Bandura, A., & Walters, R. H. (1959). *Adolescent aggression.* New York: Ronald.

Bank, L., Marlowe, J. H., Reid, J. B., & Patterson, G. R. (1991). A comparative evaluation of parent-training interventions for families of chronic delinquents. *Journal of Abnormal Child Psychology, 19,* 15–33.

Banks, M. S., & Dannemiller, J. L. (1987). Infant visual psychophysics. In P. Salapatek & L. Cohen (Eds.), *Handbook of infant perception. Vol. 1. From sensation to perception* (pp. 115–184). Orlando, FL: Academic.

Banks, M. S., & Ginsburg, A. P. (1985). Early visual preferences: A review and new theoretical treatment. In H. W. Reese (Ed.), *Advances in child development and behavior* (Vol. 19, pp. 207–246). New York: Academic.

Banks, M. S., & Salapatek, P. (1983). Infant visual perception. In M. M. Haith & J. J. Campos (Eds.), *Handbook of child psychology: Vol. II. Infancy and developmental psychobiology* (pp. 435–571). New York: Wiley.

Barclay, A., & Walton, O. (1988). Phenylketonuria: Implications of initial serum phenylalanine levels on cognitive development. *Psychological Reports, 63,* 135–142.

Barenboim, C. (1977). Developmental changes in the interpersonal cognitive system from middle childhood to adolescence. *Child Development, 48,* 1467–1474.

Barglow, P., Vaughn, B. E., & Molitor, N. (1987). Effects of maternal absence due to employment on the quality of infant-mother attachment in a low-risk sample. *Child Development, 58,* 945–954.

Barnas, M. V., & Cummings, E. M. (1994). Caregiver stability and toddlers' attachment-related behavior towards caregivers in day-care. *Infant Behavior and Development, 17,* 141–147.

Barness, L. A. (1994). The pediatric history and physical examination. In F. A. Oski, C. D. DeAngelis, R. D. Feigin, J. A. McMillan, & J. B. Warshaw (Eds.), *Principles and practices of pediatrics* (2nd ed., pp. 29–44). Philadelphia: Lippincott.

Barr, H. M., Streissguth, A. P., Darby, B. L., & Sampson, P. D. (1990). Prenatal exposure to alcohol, caffeine, tobacco, and aspirin: Effects on fine and gross motor performance in 4-year-old children. *Developmental Psychology, 26,* 339–348.

Barrera, M., & Maurer, D. (1981). The perception of facial expressions by the three-month-old. *Child Development, 52,* 203–206.

Barrett, K. C., & Campos, J. J. (1987). Perspectives on emotional development II: A functionalist approach to emotions. In J. D. Osofsky (Ed.), *Handbook of infant development* (pp. 555–578). New York: Wiley.

Barrett, K. C., Morgan, G. A., & Maslin-Cole, C. (1993). Three studies on the development of mastery motivation in infancy and toddlerhood. In D. Messer (Ed.), *Mastery motivation in early childhood: Development, measurement and social processes* (pp. 83–108). New York: Routledge.

Barrett, M. (1995). Early lexical development. In P. Fletcher & B. MacWhinney (Eds.), *The handbook of child language* (pp. 362–392). Oxford, England: Blackwell.

Barrett, M. D. (1986). Early semantic representations and early word usage. In S. A. Kuczaj, II, & M. D. Barrett (Eds.), *The development of word meaning* (pp. 39–68). New York: Springer-Verlag.

Barry, H., III. (1981). Uses and limitations of ethnographic descriptions. In R. H. Munroe, R. L. Munroe, & B. B. Whiting (Eds.), *Handbook of cross-cultural human development* (pp. 91–111). New York: Garland.

Bartsch, K., & Wellman, H. (1989). Young children's attribution of action to beliefs and desires. *Child Development, 60,* 946–964.

Bass, M., Kravath, R. E., & Glass, L. (1986). Death scene investigation in sudden infant death. *New England Journal of Medicine, 315,* 100–105.

Bates, E. (1976). *Language and context: The development of pragmatics.* New York: Academic.

Bates, E. (1979). *The emergence of symbols: Cognition and communication in infancy.* New York: Academic.

Bates, E., & Carnevale, G. F. (1993). New directions in research on language development. *Developmental Review, 13,* 436–470.

Bates, E., O'Connell, B., & Shore, C. (1987). Language and communication in infancy. In J. D. Osofsky (Ed.), *Handbook of infant development* (2nd ed., pp. 149–203). New York: Wiley.

Bates, J. E. (1987). Temperament in infancy. In J. D. Osofsky (Ed.), *Handbook of infant development* (pp. 1101–1149). New York: Wiley.

Bates, J. E. (1989). Applications of temperament concepts. In G. A. Kohnstamm, J. E. Bates, & M. K. Rothbart (Eds.), *Temperament in childhood* (pp. 321–355). New York: Wiley.

Bates, J. E., Marvinney, D., Kelly, T., Dodge, K. A., Bennett, D. S., & Pettit, G. S. (1994). Child-care history and kindergarten adjustment. *Developmental Psychology, 30,* 690–700.

Bates, J. E., Wachs, T. D., & Emde, R. N. (1994). Toward practical uses for biological concepts of temperament. In J. E. Bates & T. D. Wachs (Eds.), *Temperament: Individual differences at the interface of biology and behavior* (pp. 1–14). Washington, DC: APA.

Bauer, P. J. (1993). Identifying subsystems of autobiographical memory: Commentary on Nelson. In C. A. Nelson (Ed.), *Memory and affect in development— The Minnesota Symposia on Child Psychology, Vol. 26* (pp. 25–37). Hillsdale, NJ: Erlbaum.

Baumeister, R. F., Stillwell, A. M., & Heatherton, T. F. (1994). Guilt: An interpersonal approach. *Psychological Bulletin, 115,* 243–267.

Baumrind, D. (1967). Child care practices anteceding three patterns of preschool behavior. *Genetic Psychology Monographs, 75,* 43–88.

Baumrind, D. (1971). Current patterns of parental authority. *Developmental Psychology Monographs, 4* (1, Pt. 2).

Baumrind, D. (1973). The development of instrumental competence through socialization. In A. D. Pick (Ed.), *Minnesota Symposium on Child Psychology* (Vol. 7). Minneapolis: University of Minnesota Press.

Baumrind, D. (1983). Rejoinder to Lewis's reinterpretation of parental firm control effects: Are authoritative families really harmonious? *Psychological Bulletin, 94,* 132–142.

Baumrind, D. (1991). The influence of parenting style on adolescent competence and substance use. *Journal of Early Adolescence, 11,* 56–95.

Baumrind, D. (1993). The average expectable environment is not good enough: A response to Scarr. *Child Development, 64,* 1299–1317.

Baumrind, D. (1995). Commentary on sexual orientation: Research and social policy implications. *Developmental Psychology, 31,* 130–136.

Baydar, N., & Brooks-Gunn, J. (1991). Effects of maternal employment and child-care arrangements on preschoolers' cognitive and behavioral outcomes: Evidence from the children of the National Longitudinal Survey of Youth. *Developmental Psychology, 27,* 932–945.

Bayley, N. (1949). Consistency and variability in the growth of intelligence from birth to eighteen years. *Journal of Genetic Psychology, 75,* 165–196.

Bayley, N. (1969). *Manual for the Bayley scales of infant development.* New York: Psychological Corporation.

Bayley, N. (1993). *Bayley scales of infant development: Birth to two years* (2nd ed.). San Antonio, TX: Psychological Corporation.

Beal, C. R. (1985). Development of knowledge about the use of cues to aid prospective retrieval. *Child Development, 56,* 631–642.

Beal, C. R., & Belgrad, S. L. (1990). The development of message evaluation skills in young children. *Child Development, 61,* 705–712.

Bean, R. (1992). *The four conditions of self-esteem: A new approach for elementary and middle schools.* Santa Cruz, CA: ETR Associates.

Becker, J. (1986). Bossy and nice requests: Children's production and interpretation. *Merrill-Palmer Quarterly, 32,* 393–413.

Becker, J. A., Place, K. S., Tenzer, S. A., & Frueh, B. C. (1991). Teachers' impressions of children varying in pragmatic skills. *Journal of Applied Developmental Psychology, 12,* 397–412.

Becker, W. C. (1964). Consequences of different kinds of parental discipline. In

M. L. Hoffman & L. W. Hoffman (Eds.), *Review of child development research* (Vol. 1). New York: Russell Sage.

Bell, R. Q., & Chapman, M. (1986). Child effects in studies using experimental or brief longitudinal approaches to socialization. *Developmental Psychology, 22,* 595–603.

Bell, S. M., & Ainsworth, M. D. S. (1972). Infant crying and maternal responsiveness. *Child Development, 43,* 1171–1190.

Bellinger, D., & Needleman, H. L. (1994). The neurotoxicity of prenatal exposure to lead: Kinetics, mechanisms, and expressions. In H. L. Needleman & D. Bellinger (Eds.), *Prenatal exposure to toxicants* (pp. 89–111). Baltimore, MD: Johns Hopkins University Press.

Bellugi, U. (1988). The acquisition of a spatial language. In F. S. Kessel (Ed.), *The development of language and language researchers: Essays in honor of Roger Brown* (pp. 153–186). Hillsdale, NJ: Erlbaum.

Belmont, J. M., Butterfield, E. C., & Borkowski, J. G. (1978). Training retarded people to generalize memory methods across memory tasks. In M. M. Gruneberg, P. E. Morris, & R. N. Sykes (Eds.), *Practical aspects of memory* (pp. 418–425). New York: Academic.

Belsky, J. (1988). The "effects" of infant day care reconsidered. *Early Childhood Research Quarterly, 3,* 235–272.

Belsky, J. (1993). Etiology of child maltreatment: A developmental-ecological analysis. *Psychological Bulletin, 114,* 413–434.

Belsky, J., Fish, M., & Isabella, R. A. (1991). Continuity and discontinuity in infant negative and positive emotionality: Family antecedents and attachment consequences. *Developmental Psychology, 27,* 421–431.

Belsky, J., Gilstrap, B., & Rovine, M. (1984). The Pennsylvania Infant and Family Development Project, I: Stability and change in mother-infant and father-infant interaction in a family setting at one, three, and nine months. *Child Development, 55,* 692–705.

Belsky, J., & Rovine, M. (1988). Nonmaternal care in the first year of life and the security of infant-parent attachment. *Child Development, 59,* 157–167.

Belsky, J., Rovine, M., & Taylor, D. G. (1984). The Pennsylvania Infant and Family Development Project, III: The origins of individual differences in infant-mother attachment: Maternal and infant contributions. *Child Development, 55,* 718–728.

Bem, S. L. (1981). Gender schema theory: A cognitive account of sex typing. *Psychological Review, 88,* 354–364.

Bem, S. L. (1989). Genital knowledge and gender constancy in preschool children. *Child Development, 60,* 649–662.

Benbow, C. P. (1988). Sex differences in mathematical reasoning ability in intellectually talented preadolescents: Their nature, effects, and possible causes. *Behavioral and Brain Sciences,* 11, 169–232.

Benbow, C. P., & Stanley, J. C. (1980). Sex differences in mathematical ability: Fact or artifact? *Science, 210,* 1262–1264.

Benn, R. K. (1986). Factors promoting secure attachment relationships between employed mothers and their sons. *Child Development, 57,* 1224–1231.

Benoit, D., & Parker, K. C. H. (1994). Stability and transmission of attachment across three generations. *Child Development, 65,* 1444–1456.

Berenbaum, S. A., & Snyder, E. (1995). Early hormonal influences on childhood sex-typed activity and playmate preferences: Implications for the development of sexual orientation. *Developmental Psychology, 31,* 31–42.

Berg, W. K., & Berg, K. M. (1987). Psychophysiological development in infancy: State, startle, and attention. In J. D. Osofsky (Ed.), *Handbook of infant development* (pp. 238–317). New York: Wiley.

Bergeman, C. S., & Plomin, R. (1989). Genotype-environment interaction. In J. S. Bruner & M. C. Bornstein (Eds.), *Interaction in human development* (pp. 157–171). Hillsdale, NJ: Erlbaum.

Berk, L. E. (1994, November). Why children talk to themselves. *Scientific American,* 78–83.

Berk, L. E., & Garvin, R. A. (1984). Development of private speech among low-income Appalachian children. *Developmental Psychology, 20,* 271–286.

Berk, L. E., & Landau, S. (1993). Private speech of learning disabled and normally achieving children in classroom academic and laboratory contexts. *Child Development, 64,* 556–571.

Berkowitz, L., & Donnerstein, E. (1982). External validity is more than skin deep: Some answers to criticisms of laboratory experiments. *American Psychologist, 37,* 245–257.

Berkowitz, M. W., & Gibbs, J. C. (1985). The process of moral conflict resolution and moral development. In M. W. Berkowitz (Ed.), *Peer conflict and psychological growth* (pp. 71–84). San Francisco: Jossey-Bass.

Berlin, L. J., Cassidy, J., & Belsky, J. (1995). Loneliness in young children and infant-mother attachment: A longitudinal study. *Merrill-Palmer Quarterly, 41,* 91–103.

Berman, P. W. (1980). Are women more responsive than men to the young? A review of developmental and situational variables. *Psychological Bulletin, 88,* 668–695.

Berman, P. W., & Goodman, V. (1984). Age and sex differences in children's responsiveness to babies: Effects of adults' caretaking requests and instructions. *Child Development, 55,* 1071–1077.

Berndt, T. J. (1979a). Developmental changes in conformity to peers and parents. *Developmental Psychology, 15,* 608–616.

Berndt, T. J. (1979b). Lack of acceptance of reciprocity norms in preschool children. *Developmental Psychology, 15,* 662–663.

Berndt, T. J. (1986). Children's comments about their friendships. In M. Perlmutter (Ed.), *Cognitive perspectives on children's social and behavioral development: The Minnesota Symposia on Child Psychology* (Vol. 18, pp. 189–212). Hillsdale, NJ: Erlbaum.

Berndt, T. J. (1987). Conversations between friends: Theories, research, and implications for sociomoral development. In W. M. Kurtines & J. L. Gewirtz (Eds.), *Moral development through social interaction* (pp. 281–300). New York: Wiley.

Berndt, T. J. (1988). The nature and significance of children's friendships. In R. Vasta (Ed.), *Annals of child development* (Vol. 5, pp. 155–186). Greenwich, CT: JAI Press.

Berndt, T. J. (1989). Obtaining support from friends in childhood and adolescence. In D. Belle (Ed.), *Children's social networks and social supports* (pp. 308–331). New York: Wiley.

Berndt, T. J. (1992). Friendship and friends' influence in adolescence. *Current Directions in Psychological Science, 1,* 156–159.

Berndt, T. J. (1994). Intimacy and competition in the friendships of adolescent boys and girls. In M. R. Stevenson (Ed.), *Gender roles through the life span* (pp. 89–110). Muncie, IN: Ball State University Press.

Berndt, T. J., & Bulleit, T. N. (1985). The effects of sibling relationships on preschoolers' behavior at home and at school. *Developmental Psychology, 21,* 761–767.

Berndt, T. J., & Burgy, L. (1996). The social self-concept. In B. A. Bracken (Ed.), *Handbook of self-concept* (pp. 171–209). New York: Wiley.

Berndt, T. J., Hawkins, J. A., & Hoyle, S. G. (1986). Changes in friendship during a school year: Effects on children's and adolescents' impression of friendship and sharing with friends. *Child Development, 57,* 1284–1297.

Berndt, T. J., & Heller, K. A. (1986). Gender stereotypes and social inferences: A developmental study. *Journal of Personality and Social Psychology, 50,* 889–898.

Berndt, T. J., & Keefe, K. (1995). Friends' influence on adolescents' adjustment to school. *Child Development, 66,* 1312–1329.

Berndt, T. J., & Miller, K. E. (1990). Expectancies, values, and achievement in junior high school. *Journal of Educational Psychology, 82,* 319–326.

Berndt, T. J., & Perry, T. B. (1986). Children's perceptions of friendships as supportive relationships. *Developmental Psychology, 22,* 640–648.

Bersoff, D. M., & Miller, J. G. (1993). Culture, context, and the development of moral accountability judgments. *Developmental Psychology, 29,* 664–676.

Bertenthal, B. I., & Campos, J. J. (1987). New directions in the study of early experience. *Child Development, 58,* 560–567.

Bertenthal, B. I., Proffitt, D. R., Kramer, S. J., & Spetner, N. B. (1987). Infants' encoding of kinetic displays varying in relative coherence. *Developmental Psychology, 23,* 171–178.

Best, D. L., Williams, J. E., Cloud, J. M., Davis, S. W., Robertson, L. S., Edwards, J. R., Giles, H., & Fowles, J. (1977). Development of sex-trait stereotypes among young children in the United States, England, and Ireland. *Child Development, 48,* 1375–1384.

Bever, T. G. (1970). The cognitive basis for linguistic structures. In J. R. Hayes (Ed.), *Cognition and the development of language* (pp. 279–362). New York: Wiley.

Bialystok, E. (1986). Factors in the growth of linguistic awareness. *Child Development, 57,* 498–510.

Bialystok, E., & Hakuta, K. (1994). *In other words: The science and psychology of second-language acquisition.* New York: Basic Books.

Bierman, K. L., & Furman, W. (1984). The effects of social skills training and peer involvement on the social adjustment of preadolescents. *Child Development, 55,* 151–162.

Bierman, K. L., Miller, C. L., & Stabb, S. D. (1987). Improving the social behavior and peer acceptance of rejected boys: Effects of social skill training with instructions and prohibitions. *Journal of Consulting and Clinical Psychology, 55,* 194–200.

Bierman, K. L., Smoot, D. L., & Aumiller, K. (1993). Characteristics of aggressive-rejected, aggressive (nonrejected), and rejected (nonaggressive) boys. *Child Development, 64,* 139–151.

Biernat, M. (1991). Gender stereotypes and the relationship between masculinity and

femininity: A developmental analysis. *Journal of Personality and Social Psychology, 61,* 351–365.

Bigler, R. S., & Liben, L. S. (1990). The role of attitudes and interventions in gender-schematic processing. *Child Development, 61,* 1440–1452.

Binet, A., & Simon, T. (1916/1973). *The development of intelligence in children.* (Elizabeth S. Kite, Trans.). New York: Arno Press.

Bithoney, W. G., & Newberger, A. H. (1987). Child and family attributes of failure-to-thrive. *Journal of Developmental and Behavioral Pediatrics, 8,* 32–36.

Bjorklund, D. F. (1995). *Children's thinking: Developmental function and individual differences* (2nd ed.). Pacific Grove, CA: Brooks/Cole.

Bjorklund, D. F., & de Marchena, M. R. (1984). Developmental shifts in the basis of organization in memory: The role of associative versus categorical relatedness in children's free recall. *Child Development, 55,* 952–962.

Blake, J., O'Rourke, P., & Borzellino, G. (1994). Form and function in the development of pointing and reaching gestures. *Infant Behavior and Development, 17,* 195–203.

Blasi, A. (1980). Bridging moral cognition and moral action: A critical review of the literature. *Psychological Bulletin, 88,* 1–45.

Blasi, A. (1983). Moral cognition and moral action: A theoretical perspective. *Developmental Review, 3,* 178–210.

Blass, E. M., & Ciaramitaro, V. (1994). A new look at some old mechanisms in human newborns: Taste and tactile determinants of state, affect, and action. *Monographs of the Society for Research in Child Development, 59* (1, Serial No. 239).

Block, J. (1971). *Lives through time.* Berkeley, CA: Bancroft Books.

Block, J. H. (1976). Issues, problems, and pitfalls in assessing sex differences: A critical review of "The Psychology of Sex Differences." *Merrill-Palmer Quarterly, 22,* 283–308.

Block, J. H. (1983). Differential premises arising from differential socialization of the sexes: Some conjectures. *Child Development, 54,* 1335–1354.

Block, J. H., Block, J., & Gjerde, P. F. (1986). The personality of children prior to divorce: A prospective study. *Child Development, 57,* 827–840.

Bloom, B. S. (Ed.). (1985). *Developing talent in young people.* San Francisco: Jossey-Bass.

Blurton Jones, N. (Ed.). (1972). *Ethological studies of child behavior.* Cambridge, England: Cambridge University Press.

Bogatz, G. A., & Ball, S. (1972). *The second year of Sesame Street: A continuing evaluation.* Princeton, NJ: Educational Testing Service.

Bogenschneider, K., & Steinberg, L. (1994). Maternal employment and adolescents' academic achievement: A developmental analysis. *Sociology of Education, 67,* 60–67.

Bogin, B., & MacVean, R. B. (1983). The relationship of socioeconomic status and sex to body size, skeletal maturation, and cognitive status of Guatemala City schoolchildren. *Child Development, 54,* 115–128.

Bohannon, J. N., III. (1993). Theoretical approaches to language acquisition. In J. Berko Gleason (Ed.), *The development of language* (3rd ed., pp. 239–298). New York: Macmillan.

Bohannon, J. N., III, & Stanowicz, L. (1988). The issue of negative evidence: Adult responses to children's language errors. *Developmental Psychology, 24,* 684–689.

Boivin, M., Vitaro, F., & Gagnon, C. (1992). A reassessment of the self-perception profile for children: Factor structure, reliability, and convergent validity of a French version among second through sixth grade children. *International Journal of Behavioral Development, 15,* 275–290.

Boldizar, J. P., Perry, D. G., & Perry, L. C. (1989). Outcome values and aggression. *Child Development, 60,* 571–579.

Bolton, P., Macdonald, H., Pickles, A., Rios, P., Goode, S., Crowson, M., Bailey, A., & Rutter, M. (1994). A case-control family history study of autism. *Journal of Child Psychology and Psychiatry, 35,* 877–900.

Bonitatibus, G. (1988). Comprehension monitoring and the apprehension of literal meaning. *Child Development, 59,* 60–70.

Bonitatibus, G. J., & Flavell, J. H. (1985). Effect of presenting a message in written form on young children's ability to evaluate its communication adequacy. *Developmental Psychology, 21,* 455–461.

Borke, H. (1975). Piaget's mountains revisited: Changes in the egocentric landscape. *Developmental Psychology, 11,* 240–243.

Borkowski, J. G., Milstead, M., & Hale, C. (1988). Components of children's metamemory: Implications for strategy generalization. In F. E. Weinert & M. Perlmutter (Eds.), *Memory development: Universal changes and individual changes* (pp. 73–100). Hillsdale, NJ: Erlbaum.

Borkowski, J. G., Peck, V. A., Reid, M. K., & Kurtz, B. E. (1983). Impulsivity and strategy transfer: Metamemory as mediator. *Child Development, 54,* 459–474.

Bornholt, L. J., Goodnow, J. J., & Cooney, G. H. (1994). Influences of gender stereotypes on adolescents' perceptions of their own achievement. *American Educational Research Journal, 31,* 675–692.

Bornstein, M. H. (1987). Sensitive periods in development: Structural characteristics and causal interpretations. *Psychological Bulletin, 105,* 179–197.

Bornstein, M. H., & Sigman, M. D. (1986). Continuity in mental development from infancy. *Child Development, 57,* 251–274.

Bornstein, M. H., Tal, J., Rahn, C., Galperín, C. Z., Pêcheux, M. G., Lamour, M., Toda, S., Azuma, H., Ogino, M., & Tamis-LeMonda, C. S. (1992). Functional analysis of the contents of maternal speech to infants of 5 and 13 months in four cultures: Argentina, France, Japan, and the United States. *Developmental Psychology, 28,* 593–603.

Borstelmann, L. J. (1983). Children before psychology: Ideas about children from antiquity to the late 1800s. In P. H. Mussen (Series Ed.) & W. Kessen (Vol. Ed.), *Handbook of child psychology: Vol. 1. History, theory, and methods* (pp. 1–40). New York: Wiley.

Bouchard, T. J., Jr. (1995). Breaking the last taboo [Review of the book *The bell curve*]. *Contemporary Psychology, 40,* 415–418.

Bouchard, T. J., Jr., & Segal, N. L. (1985). Environment and IQ. In B. B. Wolman (Ed.), *Handbook of intelligence* (pp. 391–464). New York: Wiley.

Bowlby, J. (1951). *Maternal care and mental health.* Geneva: World Health Organization.

Bowlby, J. (1969). *Attachment and loss. Vol. 1. Attachment.* New York: Basic.

Bowlby, J. (1973). *Separation: Anxiety and anger.* New York: Basic.

Bowlby, J. (1988). *A secure base: Parent-child attachment and healthy human development.* New York: Basic.

Boysson-Bardies, B., de Halle, P., Sagart, L., & Durand, C. (1989). A cross-linguistic investigation of vowel formats in babbling. *Journal of Child Language, 16,* 1–17.

Bradbard, M. R., Martin, C. L., Endsley, R. C., & Halverson, C. F. (1986). Influence of sex stereotypes on children's exploration and memory: A competence versus performance distinction. *Developmental Psychology, 22,* 481–486.

Bradley, R. H. (1989). HOME measurement of maternal responsiveness. In M. H. Bornstein (Ed.), *Maternal responsiveness: Characteristics and consequences* (pp. 63–74). *(New Directions for Child Development, 43).* San Francisco: Jossey-Bass.

Bradley, R. H. (1993). Children's home environments, health, behavior, and intervention efforts: A review using the

HOME Inventory as a marker measure. *Genetic, Social, and General Psychology Monographs, 119*, 437–490.

Bradley, R. H., Caldwell., B. M., & Rock, S. L. (1988). Home environment and school performance: A ten-year follow-up and examination of three models of environmental action. *Child Development, 59*, 852–867.

Bradley, R. H., Caldwell, B. M., Rock, S. L., Ramey, C., Barnard, K. E., Gray, C., Hammond, M. A., Mitchell, S., Gottfried, A. W., Siegel, L., & Johnson, D. L. (1989). Home environment and cognitive development in the first 3 years of life: A collaborative study involving six sites and three ethnic groups in North America. *Developmental Psychology, 25*, 217–235.

Bradley, R. H., Casey, P. H., & Wortham, B. (1984). Home environments of low SES non-organic failure-to-thrive infants. *Merrill-Palmer Quarterly, 30*, 393–402.

Bradley, R. H., Whiteside, L., Mundfrom, D. J., Casey, P. H., Caldwell, B. M., & Barrett, K. (1994). Impact of the Infant Health and Development Program (IHDP) on the home environments of infants born prematurely and with low birth weight. *Journal of Educational Psychology, 86*, 531–541.

Braine, L. G., Pomerantz, E., Lorber, D., & Krantz, D. H. (1991). Conflicts with authority: Children's feelings, actions, and justifications. *Developmental Psychology, 27*, 829–840.

Brainerd, C. J. (1983). Varieties of strategy training in Piagetian concept learning. In M. Pressley & J. L. Levin (Eds.), *Cognitive strategy research: Educational applications* (pp. 3–28). New York: Springer-Verlag.

Brainerd, C. J., & Reyna, V. F. (1993). Domains of fuzzy-trace theory. In M. L. Howe & R. Pasnak (Eds.), *Emerging themes in cognitive development* (Vol. I, pp. 50–93). New York: Springer-Verlag.

Brazelton, T. B. (1986). Issues for working parents. *American Journal of Orthopsychiatry, 56*, 14–25.

Brazelton, T. B., Nugent, J. K., & Lester, B. M. (1987). Neonatal behavioral assessment scale. In J. D. Osofsky (Ed.), *Handbook of infant development* (2nd ed., pp. 780–817). New York: Wiley.

Bremner, J. G. (1994). *Infancy* (2nd ed.). Oxford, England: Blackwell.

Bretherton, I. (1985). Attachment theory: Retrospect and prospect. In I. Bretherton & E. Waters (Eds.), *Monographs of the Society for Research in Child Development, 50* (1–2, Serial No. 209).

Bretherton, I. (1988). How to do things with one word: The ontogenesis of intentional message making in infancy. In M. D. Smith & J. L. Locke (Eds.), *The emergent lexicon: The child's development of a linguistic vocabulary.* New York: Academic.

Bretherton, I. (1992). The origins of attachment theory: John Bowlby and Mary Ainsworth. *Developmental Psychology, 28*, 759–775.

Bretherton, I., Fritz, J., Zahn-Waxler, C., & Ridgeway, D. (1986). Learning to talk about emotions: A functionalist perspective. *Child Development, 57*, 529–548.

Bretherton, I., Stolberg, U., & Kreye, M. (1981). Engaging strangers in proximal interaction: Infants' social initiative. *Developmental Psychology, 17*, 746–755.

Bretherton, I., & Waters, E. (Eds.). (1985). Growing points of attachment theory and research. *Monographs of the Society for Research in Child Development, 50* (1–2, Serial No. 109).

Briars, D., & Siegler, R. (1984). A featural analysis of preschoolers' counting knowledge. *Developmental Psychology, 20*, 607–618.

Bridges, A. (1986). Actions and things: What adults talk about to 1-year-olds. In S. A. Kuczaj, II, & M. D. Barrett (Eds.), *The development of word meaning* (pp. 225–256). New York: Springer-Verlag.

Bridges, L. J., Connell, J. P., & Belsky, J. (1988). Similarities and differences in infant-mother and infant-father interaction in the strange situation: A component process analysis. *Developmental Psychology, 24*, 92–100.

Briggs, G. G., Freeman, R. K., & Yaffe, S. J. (1994). *Drugs in pregnancy and lactation* (4th ed.). Baltimore: Williams & Wilkins.

Brody, G. H., Stoneman, Z., & Mackinnon, C. W. (1982). Role asymmetries in interactions among school-aged children, their younger siblings, and their friends. *Child Development, 53*, 1364–1370.

Brody, G. H., Stoneman, Z., & McCoy, J. K. (1992). Associations of maternal and paternal direct and differential behavior with sibling relationships: Contemporaneous and longitudinal analyses. *Child Development, 63*, 82–92.

Brody, G. H., Stoneman, Z., & McCoy, J. K. (1994). Forecasting sibling relationships in early adolescence from child temperaments and family processes in middle childhood. *Child Development, 65*, 771–784.

Brody, N. (1985). The validity of tests of intelligence. In B. B. Wolman (Ed.), *Handbook of intelligence* (pp. 353–389). New York: Wiley.

Brody, N. (1992). *Intelligence* (2nd ed.). San Diego, CA: Academic.

Bronfenbrenner, U. (1970). *Two worlds of childhood: U.S. and U.S.S.R.* New York: Russell Sage.

Bronfenbrenner, U. (1977). Toward an experimental ecology of human development. *American Psychologist, 32*, 513–531.

Bronfenbrenner, U. (1979). *The ecology of human development.* Cambridge, MA: Harvard University Press.

Bronfenbrenner, U. (1986). Ecology of the family as a context for human development: Research perspectives. *Developmental Psychology, 22*, 723–742.

Bronfenbrenner, U. (1992). Ecological systems theory. In R. Vasta (Ed.), *Six theories of child development: Revised formulations and current issues* (pp. 187–249). London: Jessica Kingsley.

Bronfenbrenner, U., Alvarez, W. F., & Henderson, C. R., Jr. (1984). Working and watching: Maternal employment status and parents' perceptions of their three-year-old children. *Child Development, 55*, 1362–1378.

Bronfenbrenner, U., & Crouter, A. C. (1983). The evolution of environmental models in developmental research. In P. H. Mussen (Series Ed.) & W. Kessen (Vol. Ed.), *Handbook of child psychology: Vol. I. History, theory, and methods* (pp. 357–414). New York: Wiley.

Bronson, W. C. (1975). Developments in behavior with age-mates during the second year of life. In M. Lewis & L. A. Rosenblum (Eds.), *Friendship and peer relations* (pp. 131–152). New York: Wiley.

Bron-Wojciechowska, A. (1995). Education and gender in Sweden: Is there any equality? *Women's Studies International Forum, 18*, 51–60.

Broome, M. E., & Koehler, C. (1986). Childbirth education: A review of effects on the woman and her family. *Family and Community Health, 9*, 33–44.

Broughton, J. (1978). Development of concepts of self, mind, reality, and knowledge. *New Directions for Child Development, 1*, 75–100.

Brown, A. L. (1982). Learning and development: The problem of compatibility, access, and induction. *Human Development, 25*, 89–115.

Brown, A. L., Bransford, J. D., Ferrara, R. A., & Campione, J. C. (1983). Learning, remembering, and understanding. In J. H. Flavell & E. M. Markman (Eds.), *Handbook of child psychology: Vol. 3. Cognitive development* (4th ed., pp. 77–166). New York: Wiley.

Brown, A. L., & Campione, J. C. (1994). Guided discovery in a community of learners. In K. McGilly (Ed.), *Classroom lessons: Integrating cognitive theory and classroom practice* (pp. 229–270). Cambridge, MA: Bradford.

Brown, A. L., Campione, J. C., Reeve, R. A., Ferrara, R. A., & Palincsar, A. S.

(1991). Interactive learning, individual understanding: The case of reading and mathematics. In L. T. Landsmann (Ed.), *Culture, schooling and psychological development* (pp. 136–170). Hillsdale, NJ: Erlbaum.

Brown, A. L., Day, J. D., & Jones, R. S. (1983). The development of plans for summarizing texts. *Child Development, 54,* 968–979.

Brown, A. L., & Kane, M. J. (1988). Preschool children can learn to transfer: Learning to learn and learning from example. *Cognitive Psychology, 20,* 493–523.

Brown, A. L., & Palincsar, A. S. (1982). Inducing strategic learning from texts by means of informed, self-control training. *Topics in Learning and Learning Disabilities, 2,* 1–17.

Brown, A. L., Smiley, S. S., Day, J. D., Townsend, M. A. R., & Lawton, S. C. (1977). Intrusion of a thematic idea in children's comprehension and retention of stories. *Child Development, 48,* 1454–1466.

Brown, B. B. (1989). The role of peer groups in adolescents' adjustment to secondary school. In T. J. Berndt & G. W. Ladd (Eds.), *Peer relationships in child development* (pp. 188–215). New York: Wiley.

Brown, B. B. (1990). Peer groups and peer cultures. In S. S. Feldman & G. R. Elliott (Eds.), *At the threshold: The developing adolescent* (pp. 171–196). Cambridge, MA: Harvard University Press.

Brown, B. B., Clasen, D. R., & Eicher, S. A. (1986). Perceptions of peer pressure, peer conformity dispositions, and self-reported behavior among adolescents. *Developmental Psychology, 22,* 521–530.

Brown, B. B., & Lohr, M. J. (1987). Peer-group affiliation and adolescent self-esteem: An integration of ego-identity and symbolic-interaction theories. *Journal of Personality and Social Psychology, 52,* 47–55.

Brown, B. B., Mounts, N., Lamborn, S. D., & Steinberg, L. (1993). Parenting practices and peer group affiliation in adolescence. *Child Development, 64,* 467–482.

Brown, R. (1973). *A first language: The early stages.* Cambridge, MA: Harvard University Press.

Brown, R., & Hanlon, C. (1970). Derivational complexity and the order of acquisition in child speech. In R. Brown (Ed.), *Psycholinguistics* (pp. 155–207). New York: Free Press.

Browne, K. (1988). The nature of child abuse and neglect: An overview. In K. Browne, C. Davies, & P. Stratton (Eds.), *Early prediction and prevention of child abuse* (pp. 15–30). New York: Wiley.

Browne, K., Davies, C., & Stratton, P. (Eds.). (1988). *Early prediction and prevention of child abuse.* New York: Wiley.

Brownell, C. A. (1990). Peer social skills in toddlers: Competencies and constraints illustrated by same-age and mixed-age interaction. *Child Development, 61,* 838–848.

Bruck, M., Ceci, S. J., Francouer, E., & Renick, A. (1995). Anatomically detailed dolls do not facilitate preschoolers' reports of a pediatric examination involving genital touching. *Journal of Experimental Psychology Applied, 1,* 95–109.

Bruer, J. T. (1994). Classroom problems, school culture, and cognitive research. In K. McGilly (Ed.), *Classroom lessons: Integrating cognitive theory and classroom practice* (pp. 273–290). Cambridge, MA: MIT Press.

Bruner, J. S. (1972). Nature and uses of immaturity. *American Psychologist, 27,* 687–708.

Bruner, J. S. (1983). *Child's talk: Learning to use language.* New York: W. W. Norton.

Bryant, B. (1982). An index of empathy for children and adolescents. *Child Development, 53,* 413–425.

Bryant, P. E., Bradley, L., Maclean, M., & Crossland, J. (1989). Nursery rhymes, phonological skills, and reading. *Journal of Child Language, 16,* 407–428.

Bryson, Y. J., Pang, S., Wei, L. S., Dickover, R., Diagne, A., & Chen, I. S. (1995). Clearance of HIV infection in perinatally infected infant. *New England Journal of Medicine, 332,* 833–838.

Bugental, D. B., Blue, J., & Lewis, J. (1990). Caregiver beliefs and dysphoric affect directed to difficult children. *Developmental Psychology, 26,* 631–638.

Buhrmester, D., & Furman, W. (1990). Perceptions of sibling relationships during middle childhood and adolescence. *Child Development, 61,* 1387–1398.

Bukowski, W. M., Gauze, C., Hoza, B., & Newcomb, A. F. (1993). Differences and consistency between same-sex and other-sex peer relationships during early adolescence. *Developmental Psychology, 29,* 255–263.

Bukowski, W. M., & Hoza, B. (1989). Popularity and friendship: Issues in theory, measurement, and outcome. In T. J. Berndt & G. W. Ladd (Eds.), *Peer relationships in child development* (pp. 15–45). New York: Wiley.

Bukowski, W. M., Newcomb, A. F., & Hartup, W. W. (Eds.). (1996). *The company they keep: Friendship during childhood and adolescence* (pp. 238-261). Cambridge, England: Cambridge University Press.

Bukowski, W. M., & Sippola, L. (1996). Friendship and morality: (How) Are they related? In W. M. Bukowski, A. F. Newcomb, & W. W. Hartup (Eds.), *The company they keep: Friendship during childhood and adolescence* (pp. 238–261). Cambridge, England: Cambridge University Press.

Bullock, M. (1985). Animism in childhood thinking: A new look at an old question. *Developmental Psychology, 21,* 217–225.

Burns, A., & Scott, C. (1994). *Mother-headed families and why they have increased.* Hillsdale, NJ: Erlbaum.

Burton, R. V. (1963). Generality of honesty reconsidered. *Psychological Review, 70,* 481–499.

Burton, R. V. (1976). Honesty and dishonesty. In T. Lickona (Ed.), *Moral development and behavior: Theory, research, and social issues* (pp. 173–197). New York: Holt, Rinehart & Winston.

Bushnell, E. W. (1985). The decline of visually guided reaching during infancy. *Infant Behavior and Development, 8,* 139–155.

Bushnell, E. W. (1994). A dual-processing approach to cross-modal matching: Implications for development. In D. J. Lewkowicz & R. Lickliter (Eds.), *The development of intersensory perception: Comparative perspectives* (pp. 19–38). Hillsdale, NJ: Erlbaum.

Bushnell, E. W., Shaw, L., & Strauss, D. (1985). Relationship between visual and tactual exploration in 6-month-olds. *Developmental Psychology, 21,* 591–600.

Buss, D. (1995). Psychological sex differences: Origins through sexual selection. *American Psychologist, 50,* 164–168.

Bussey, K. (1992). Lying and truthfulness: Children's definitions, standards, and evaluative reactions. *Child Development, 63,* 129–137.

Bussey, K., & Bandura, A. (1984). Influence of gender constancy and social power on sex-linked modeling. *Journal of Personality and Social Psychology, 47,* 1292–1323.

Bussey, K., & Bandura, A. (1992). Self-regulatory mechanisms governing gender development. *Child Development, 63,* 1236–1250.

Byrnes, J. P., & Overton, W. F. (1988). Reasoning about logical connectives: A developmental analysis. *Journal of Experimental Child Psychology, 46,* 194–218.

Cacciari, C., & Levorato, M. C. (1989). How children understand idioms in discourse. *Journal of Child Language, 16,* 387–405.

Cahan, S., & Cohen, N. (1989). Age versus schooling effects on intelligence development. *Child Development, 60,* 1239–1249.

Cain, K. M., & Dweck, C. S. (1995). The relation between motivational patterns

and achievement cognitions through the elementary school years. *Merrill-Palmer Quarterly, 41,* 25–52.

Cairns, R. B., Cairns, B. D., Neckerman, H. J., Ferguson, L. L., & Gariepy, J.-L. (1989). Growth and aggression: 1. Childhood to early adolescence. *Developmental Psychology, 25,* 320–330.

Calasanti, T. M., & Bailey, C. A. (1991). Gender inequality and the division of household labor in the United States and Sweden: A socialist-feminist approach. *Social Problems, 38,* 34–53.

Caldwell, B., & Bradley, R. (1984). *Home observation for measurement of the environment.* Unpublished manuscript. Little Rock: University of Arkansas at Little Rock.

Calkins, S. D., & Fox, N. A. (1992). The relations among infant temperament, security of attachment, and behavioral inhibition at twenty-four months. *Child Development, 63,* 1456–1472.

Calkins, S. D., & Fox, N. A. (1994). Individual differences in the biological aspects of temperament. In J. E. Bates & T. D. Wachs (Eds.), *Temperament: Individual differences at the interface of biology and behavior* (pp. 199–217). Washington, DC: American Psychological Association.

Camara, K. A., & Resnick, G. (1988). Interparental conflict and cooperation: Factors moderating children's post-divorce adjustment. In E. M. Hetherington & J. D. Arasteh (Eds.), *Impact of divorce, single parenting, and stepparenting on children* (pp. 197–214). Hillsdale, NJ: Erlbaum.

Campbell, F. A., & Ramey, C. T. (1994). Effects of early intervention on intellectual and academic achievement: A follow-up study of children from low-income families. *Child Development, 65,* 684–698.

Campos, J. J., Barrett, K. C., Lamb, M. E., Goldsmith, H. H., & Stenberg, C. (1983). Socioemotional development. In P. H. Mussen (Ed.), *Handbook of child psychology: Vol. II. Infancy and developmental psychobiology* (pp. 783–916). New York: Wiley.

Campos, J. J., Langer, A., & Krowitz, A. (1970). Cardiac responses on the visual cliff in prelocomotor human infants. *Science, 170,* 196–197.

Camras, L. A. (1994). Two aspects of emotional development: Expression and elicitation. In P. Ekman & R. J. Davidson (Eds.), *The nature of emotion: Fundamental questions* (pp. 347–351). New York: Oxford.

Camras, L. A., Oster, H., Campos, J. J., Miyake, K., & Bradshaw, D. (1992). Japanese and American infants' responses to arm restraint. *Developmental Psychology, 28,* 578–583.

Camras, L. A., & Sachs, V. B. (1991). Social referencing and caretaker expressive behavior in a day care setting. *Infant Behavior and Development, 14,* 27–36.

Camras, L. A., Sullivan, J., & Michel, G. (1993). Do infants express discrete emotions? Adult judgments of facial, vocal, and body actions. *Journal of Nonverbal Behavior, 17,* 171–186.

Capute, A. J., & Shapiro, B. K. (1985). The motor quotient: A method for the early detection of motor delay. *American Journal of Diseases of Children, 139,* 940–942.

Carey, S. (1978). The child as word learner. In M. Halle, G. Miller, & J. Bresnan (Eds.), *Linguistic theory and psychological reality* (pp. 264–293). Cambridge, MA: MIT Press.

Carey, S. (1985). *Conceptual change in childhood.* Cambridge, MA: Bradford Book.

Carey, S., & Gelman, R. (Eds.). (1991). *The epigenesis of mind: Essays on biology and cognition.* Hillsdale, NJ: Erlbaum.

Carlson, V., Cicchetti, D., Barnett, D., & Braunwald, K. (1989). Disorganized/disoriented attachment relationships in maltreated infants. *Developmental Psychology, 25,* 525–531.

Carlsson, G., Uvebrant, P., Hugdahl, K., Arvidsson, J., Wiklund, L. M., & von Wendt, L. (1994). Verbal and nonverbal function of children with right- versus left-hemiplegic cerebral palsy of pre- and perinatal origin. *Developmental Medicine and Child Neurology, 36,* 503–512.

Carr, J. (1994). Long term outcome for people with Down's syndrome. *Journal of Child Psychology and Psychiatry, 35,* 425–439.

Carr, M., Borkowski, J. G., & Maxwell, S. E. (1991). Motivational components of underachievement. *Developmental Psychology, 27,* 108–118.

Carr, M., Kurtz, B. E., Schneider, W., Turner, L. A., & Borkowski, J. G. (1989). Strategy acquisition and transfer among American and German children: Environmental influences on metacognitive development. *Developmental Psychology, 25,* 765–771.

Carroll, J. B. (1982). The measurement of intelligence. In R. J. Sternberg (Ed.), *Handbook of human intelligence* (pp. 29–120). Cambridge, England: Cambridge University Press.

Carroll, J. B. (1992). Cognitive abilities: The state of the art. *Psychological Science, 3,* 266–270.

Carroll, J. L., & Loughlin, G. M. (1994). Sudden infant death syndrome. In F. A. Oski, C. D. DeAngelis, R. D. Feigin, J. A. McMillan, & J. B. Warshaw (Eds.), *Principles and practice of pediatrics* (2nd ed., pp. 1051–1057). Philadelphia: Lippincott.

Carter, D. B. (1987). The role of peers in sex role socialization. In D. B. Carter (Ed.), *Current conceptions of sex roles and sex typing* (pp. 101–121). New York: Praeger.

Carter, D. B., & Levy, G. D. (1988). Development of androgyny: Parental influences. *Psychology of Women Quarterly, 11,* 311–326.

Carter, D. B., & McCloskey, L. A. (1983–1984). Peers and the maintenance of sex-typed behavior: The development of children's conceptions of cross-gender behavior in their peers. *Social Cognition, 2,* 294–314.

Carter, D. B., & Patterson, C. J. (1982). Sex roles as social conventions: The development of children's conceptions of sex-role stereotypes. *Developmental Psychology, 18,* 812–824.

Carver, K. P., & Teachman, J. D. (1993). Female employment and first union dissolution in Puerto Rico. *Journal of Marriage and the Family, 55,* 686–698.

Case, R. (1984). The process of stage transition: A Neo-Piagetian view. In R. J. Sternberg (Ed.), *Mechanisms of cognitive development* (pp. 19–44). New York: W. H. Freeman.

Case, R. (1985). *Intellectual development: A systematic reinterpretation.* New York: Academic Press.

Case, R., Kurland, D. M., & Goldberg, J. (1982). Operational efficiency and the growth of short-term memory span. *Journal of Experimental Child Psychology, 33,* 386–404.

Casey, P. H. (1992). Failure to thrive. In M. D. Levine, W. B. Carey, & A. C. Crocker, (Eds.), *Developmental-behavioral pediatrics* (pp. 375–383). Philadelphia: W. B. Saunders.

Caskey, C. T., Pizzuti, A., Fu, Y-H., Fenwick, R. G., Jr., & Nelson, D. L. (1992). Triplet repeat mutations in human disease. *Science, 256,* 784–788.

Caspi, A., Henry, B., McGee, R. O., Moffitt, T. E., & Silva, P. A. (1995). Temperamental origins of child and adolescent behavior problems: From age three to age fifteen. *Child Development, 66,* 55–68.

Cassidy, J. (1988). Child-mother attachment and the self in six-year-olds. *Child Development, 59,* 121–134.

Cassidy, J. (1990). Theoretical and methodological considerations in the study of attachment and the self in young children. In M. T. Greenberg, D. Cicchetti, & E. M. Cummings (Eds.), *Attachment in the preschool years: Theory, research, and intervention* (pp. 87–120). Chicago: University of Chicago Press.

Cassidy, J. (1994). Emotion regulation: Influences of attachment relationships. *Monographs of the Society for Research in*

*Child Development, 59* (Serial No. 2–3), 228–283.

Cassidy, J., & Berlin, L. J. (1994). The insecure/ambivalent pattern of attachment: Theory and research. *Child Development, 65,* 971–981.

Cattell, R. B. (1971). *Abilities: Their structure, growth and action.* Boston: Houghton Mifflin.

Cattell, R. B. (1982). *The inheritance of personality and ability: Research methods and findings.* New York: Academic.

Cauce, A. M. (1987). School and peer competence in early adolescence: A test of domain-specific self-perceived competence. *Developmental Psychology, 23,* 287–291.

Cavior, N., & Dokecki, P. R. (1973). Physical attractiveness, perceived attitude similarity, and academic achievement as contributors to interpersonal attraction among adolescents. *Developmental Psychology, 9,* 44–54.

Ceci, S. J. (1991). How much does schooling influence general intelligence and its cognitive components? A reassessment of the evidence. *Developmental Psychology, 27,* 703–722.

Ceci, S. J., & Bruck, M. (1993). Suggestibility of the child witness: A historical review and synthesis. *Psychological Bulletin, 113,* 403–439.

Cernoch, J. M., & Porter, R. H. (1985). Recognition of maternal axillary odors by infants. *Child Development, 56,* 1593–1598.

Chalmers, J. B., & Townsend, M. A. R. (1990). The effects of training in social perspective taking on socially maladjusted girls. *Child Development, 61,* 178–190.

Chandler, M., Fritz, A. S., & Hala, S. (1989). Small-scale deceit: Deception as a marker of two-, three-, and four-year-olds' early theories of mind. *Child Development, 60,* 1263–1277.

Chandler, M. J. (1973). Egocentrism and antisocial behavior: The assessment and training of social perspective taking skills. *Developmental Psychology, 9,* 326–332.

Chao, R. K. (1994). Beyond parental control and authoritarian parenting style: Understanding Chinese parenting through the cultural notion of training. *Child Development, 65,* 1111–1119.

Chapman, M. (1988). *Constructive evolution: Origins and development of Piaget's thought.* New York: Cambridge University Press.

Chapman, M., & Lindenberger, U. (1988). Functions, operations, and decalage in the development of transitivity. *Developmental Psychology, 24,* 542–551.

Chapman, M., Zahn-Waxler, C., Cooperman, G., & Iannotti, R. (1987).

Empathy and responsibility in the motivation of children's helping. *Developmental Psychology, 23,* 140–145.

Charlesworth, W. R., & Dzur, C. (1987). Gender comparisons of preschoolers' behavior and resource utilization in group problem solving. *Child Development, 58,* 191–200.

Chase-Lansdale, P. L., Brooks-Gunn, J., & Zamsky, E. S. (1994). Young African-American multigenerational families in poverty: Quality of mothering and grandmothering. *Child Development, 65,* 373–393.

Chasnoff, I. J. (1986). Perinatal addiction: Consequences of intrauterine exposure to opiate and nonopiate drugs. In I. J. Chasnoff (Ed.), *Drug use in pregnancy* (pp. 52–63). Lancaster, England: MTP Press.

Chasnoff, I. J., Hatcher, R., & Burns, W. J. (1982). Polydrug- and methadone-addicted newborns: A continuum of impairment? *Pediatrics, 63,* 279–285.

Chassin. L., Presson, C. C., Sherman, S. J., & McGrew, J. (1987). The changing smoking environment for middle and high school students: 1980–1983. *Journal of Behavioral Medicine, 10,* 581–593.

Chen, X., Rubin, K. H., & Li, Z. (1995). Social functioning and adjustment in Chinese children. *Developmental Psychology, 31,* 531–539.

Chen, X., Rubin, K. H., & Sun, Y. (1992). Social reputation and peer relationships in Chinese and Canadian children: A cross-cultural study. *Child Development, 63,* 1336–1343.

Cherlin, A. J., Furstenberg, F. T., Chase-Lansdale, P. L., & Kiernan, K. E. (1991). Longitudinal studies of effects of divorce on children in Great Britain and the United States. *Science, 252,* 1386–1389.

Chestnut, D. H., & Gibbs, C. P. (1991). Obstetric anesthesia. In S. G. Gabbe, J. R. Niebyl, & J. L. Simpson (Eds.), *Obstetrics: Normal & problem pregnancies* (2nd ed., pp. 493–538). New York: Churchill Livingstone.

Chi, M. T. H. (1978). Knowledge structures and memory development. In R. S. Siegler (Ed.), *Children's thinking: What develops* (pp. 73–105). Hillsdale, NJ: Erlbaum.

Chi, M. T. H., & Glaser, R. (1980). The measurement of expertise: Analysis of the development of knowledge and skill as a basis for assessing achievement. In E. L. Baker & E. S. Quellmalz (Eds.), *Educational testing and evaluation: Design, analysis and policy.* Beverly Hills, CA: Sage.

"Child Care Around the World." (1989). *Newsletter of the International Society for the Study of Behavioral Development, 2* (Serial No. 16), 4–8.

Children's Defense Fund. (1994). *Wasting America's future: The Children's Defense Fund report on the costs of child poverty.* Boston: Beacon.

Chomsky, N. (1959). Review of B. F. Skinner's Verbal Behavior. *Language, 35,* 26–129.

Chomsky, N. (1968). *Language and mind.* New York: Harcourt, Brace & World.

Chomsky, N. (1988). *Language and problems of knowledge: The Managua lectures.* Cambridge, MA: MIT Press.

Cialdini, R. B., Kenrick, D. T., & Baumann, D. J. (1982). Effects of mood on prosocial behavior in children and adults. In N. Eisenberg (Ed.), *The development of prosocial behavior* (pp. 339–359). New York: Academic Press.

Cicchetti, D., & Carlson, V. (Eds.). (1989). *Child maltreatment: Theory and research on the causes and consequences of child abuse and neglect.* New York: Cambridge University Press.

Cillessen, A. H. N., van IJzendoorn, H. W., van Lieshout, C. F. M., & Hartup, W. W. (1992). Heterogeneity among peer-rejected boys: Subtypes and stabilities. *Child Development, 63,* 893–905.

Clark, E. V. (1987). The principle of contrast: A constraint on language acquisition. In B. MacWhinney (Ed.), *Mechanisms of language acquisition* (pp. 1–33). Hillsdale, NJ: Erlbaum.

Clarke, A. M., & Clarke, A. O. B. (1976). *Early experience: Myth and evidence.* London: Open Books.

Clarke, S. C. (1995). Advance report of final divorce statistics, 1989 and 1990. *Monthly vital statistics report, 439* (supplement). Hyattsville, MD: National Center for Health Statistics.

Clarke-Stewart, K. A. (1989). Infant day care: Maligned or malignant? *American Psychologist, 44,* 266–273.

Clarke-Stewart, K. A., & Fein, G. G. (1983). Early childhood programs. In P. H. Mussen (Ed.), *Handbook of child psychology Vol. II: Infancy and developmental psychobiology* (pp. 917–1000). New York: Wiley.

Clausen, J. A. (1975). The social meaning of differential physical and sexual maturation. In S. E. Dragastin & G. H. Elder (Eds.), *Adolescence in the life cycle* (pp. 25–47). New York: Halsted.

Clifton, R. K., Morrongiello, B. A., & Dowd, J. M. (1984). A developmental look at an auditory illusion: The precedence effect. *Developmental Psychobiology, 17,* 519–536.

Clifton, R. K., Morrongiello, B. A., Kulig, J. W., & Dowd, J. M. (1981). Newborns' orientation toward sound: Possible implications for cortical development. *Child Development, 52,* 833–838.

Clifton, R. K., Muir, D. W., Ashmead, D. H., & Clarkson, M. G. (1993). Is

visually guided reaching in early infancy a myth? *Child Development, 64,* 1099–1110.

Cochran, W. D. (1994). Management of the normal newborn. In F. A. Oski, C. D. DeAngelis, R. D. Feigin, J. A. McMillan, & J. B. Warshaw (Eds.), *Principles and practice of pediatrics* (2nd ed., pp. 303–308). Philadelphia: Lippincott.

Cohen, J. (1983). Commentary: The relationship between friendship selection and peer influence. In J. L. Epstein & N. Karweit (Eds.), *Friends in school* (pp. 163–176). New York: Academic.

Cohen, L. J. (1974). The operational definition of human attachment. *Psychological Bulletin, 81,* 207–217.

Cohn, A. H. (1987). Our national priorities for prevention. In. R. E. Helfer & R. S. Kempe (Eds.), *The battered child* (4th ed., pp. 444–456). Chicago: The University of Chicago Press.

Cohn, L. D. (1991). Sex differences in the course of personality development: A meta-analysis. *Psychological Bulletin, 109,* 252–266.

Coie, J. D., & Dodge, K. A. (1983). Continuities and changes in children's social status: A five-year longitudinal study. *Merrill-Palmer Quarterly, 29,* 261–282.

Coie, J. D., Dodge, K. A., & Coppotelli, H. (1982). Dimensions and types of social status: A cross-age perspective. *Developmental Psychology, 18,* 557–570.

Coie, J. D., Dodge, K. A., & Kupersmidt, J. B. (1990). Peer group behavior and social status. In S. R. Asher & J. D. Coie (Eds.), *Peer rejection in childhood* (pp. 17–59). Cambridge, England: Cambridge University Press.

Coie, J. D., & Koeppl, G. K. (1990). Adapting intervention to the problems of aggressive and disruptive rejected children. In S. R. Asher & J. D. Coie (Eds.), *Peer rejection in childhood* (pp. 309–337). Cambridge, England: Cambridge University Press.

Coie, J. D., & Kupersmidt, G. K. (1983). A behavioral analysis of emerging social status in boys' groups. *Child Development, 54,* 1400–1416.

Colby, A., & Kohlberg, L. (1987). *The measurement of moral judgment (Vol. 1). Theoretical foundations and research validation. Standard issue scoring manual (Vol. 2).* Cambridge, England: Cambridge University Press.

Cole, M., Gay, J., Glick, J. A., & Sharp, D. W. (1971). *The cultural context of learning and thinking: An exploration in experimental anthropology.* New York: Basic Books.

Colgrove, R. W., & Huntzinger, R. M. (1994). Academic, behavioral, and social adaptation of boys with hemophilia/HIV

disease. *Journal of Pediatric Psychology, 19,* 457–473.

Collaer, M. L., & Hines, M. (1995). Human behavioral sex differences: A role for gonadal hormones during early development? *Psychological Bulletin, 118,* 55–107.

Collins, N. L., Dunkel-Schetter, C., Lobel, M., & Scrimshaw, S. C. (1993). Social support in pregnancy: Psychosocial correlates of birth outcomes and postpartum depression. *Journal of Personality and Social Psychology, 65,* 1243–1258.

Collins, W. A., & Russell, G. (1991). Mother-child and father-child relationships in middle childhood and adolescence: A developmental analysis. *Developmental Review, 11,* 99–136.

Condry, J., & Siman, M. L. (1974). Characteristics of peer- and adult-oriented children. *Journal of Marriage and the Family, 36,* 543–554.

Conel, J. L. (1939–1963). *The postnatal development of the human cerebral cortex* (Vol. 1–6). Cambridge, MA: Harvard University Press.

Conger, R. D., Conger, K. J., Elder, G. H., Jr., Lorenz, F. O., Simons, R. L., & Whitbeck, L. B. (1992). A family process model of economic hardship and adjustment of early adolescent boys. *Child Development, 63,* 526–541.

Conger, R. D., Conger, K. J., Elder, G. H., Jr., Lorenz, F. O., Simons, R. L., & Whitbeck, L. B. (1993). Family economic stress and adjustment of early adolescent girls. *Developmental Psychology, 29,* 206–219.

Conger, R. D., Lorenz, F. O., Elder, G. H., Jr., Melby, J. N., Simons, R. L., & Conger, K. J. (1992). A process model of family economic pressure and early adolescent alcohol use. *Journal of Early Adolescence, 11,* 430–449.

Connolly, J. A., & Doyle, A. B. (1984). Relation of social fantasy play to social competence in preschoolers. *Developmental Psychology, 20,* 797–806.

Connolly, J. A., Doyle, A. B., & Reznick, E. (1988). Social pretend play and social interaction in preschoolers. *Journal of Applied Developmental Psychology, 9,* 301–313.

Connor, E. M., Sperling, R. S., Gelber, R., Kiselev, P., Scott, G., O'Sullivan, M. J., VanDyke, R., Bey, M., Shearer, W., Jacobson, R. L., Jimenez, E., O'Neill, E., Bazin, B., Delfraissy, J-F., Culnane, M., Coombs, R., Elkins, M., Moye, J., Stratton, P., & Balsley, J. (1994). Reduction of maternal-infant transmission of human immunodeficiency virus type 1 with zidovudine treatment. *New England Journal of Medicine, 331,* 1173–1180.

Cook, T. D., Anson, A. R., & Walchli, S. B. (1993). From causal description to causal explanation: Improving three already good evaluations of adolescent health program. In S. G. Millstein, A. C. Petersen, & E. O. Nightingale (Eds.), *Promoting the health of adolescents* (pp. 339–374). New York: Oxford University Press.

Cooley, C. H. (1922). *Human nature and the social order* (Rev. ed.). New York: Scribner.

Cooper, H. M., & Hedges, L. V. (Eds.). (1994). *The handbook of research synthesis.* New York: Russell Sage.

Coopersmith, S. (1967). *The antecedents of self-esteem.* San Francisco: W. H. Freeman.

Cornell, E. H., Heth, C. D., & Alberts, D. M. (1994). Place recognition and way finding by children and adults. *Memory and Cognition, 22,* 633–643.

Cornell, E. H., Heth, C. D., & Broda, L. S. (1989). Children's wayfinding: Response to instructions to use environmental landmarks. *Developmental Psychology, 25,* 755–764.

Cornell, E. H., Heth, C. D., & Rowat, W. L. (1992). Way finding by children and adults: Response to instructions to use look-back and retrace strategies. *Developmental Psychology, 28,* 328–336.

Costanzo, P. R., & Schiffman, S. S. (1989). Thinness—not obesity—has a genetic component. *Neuroscience and Biobehavioral Reviews, 13,* 55–58.

Covington, M. V., & Omelich, C. L. (1981). As failures mount: Affective and cognitive consequences of ability demotion in the classroom. *Journal of Educational Psychology, 73,* 796–808.

Cox, M. J., Owen, M. T., Henderson, V. K., & Margand, N. A. (1992). Prediction of infant-father and infant-mother attachment. *Developmental Psychology, 28,* 474–483.

Craig, R. S. (1992). The effect of television day part on gender portrayals in television commercials: A content analysis. *Sex Roles, 26,* 197–211.

Crane, J. (1994). Exploding the myth of scientific support for the theory of black intellectual inferiority. *Journal of Black Psychology, 20,* 189–209.

Crankshaw, E. (1981). *Bismarck.* New York: Viking.

Crick, N. R., & Dodge, K. A. (1994). A review and reformulation of social information-processing mechanisms in children's social adjustment. *Psychological Bulletin, 115,* 74–101.

Crick, N. R., & Grotpeter, J. K. (1995). Relational aggression, gender, and social-psychological adjustment. *Child Development, 66,* 710–722.

Crnic, K. A., Ragozin, A. S., Greenberg, M. T., Robinson, N. M., & Basham, R. B. (1983). Social interaction and

developmental competence of preterm and full-term infants during the first year of life. *Child Development, 54,* 1199–1210.

Crockenberg, S. (1981). Infant irritability, mother responsiveness, and social support influences on the security of infant-mother attachment. *Child Development, 52,* 857–865.

Crockenberg, S. (1986). Are temperamental differences in babies associated with predictable differences in care-giving? In J. V. Lerner & R. M. Lerner (Eds.), *Temperament and social interaction in infants and children* (pp. 53–74). San Francisco: Jossey-Bass.

Crockenberg, S., & Litman, C. (1990). Autonomy as competence in 2-year-olds: Maternal correlates of child defiance, compliance, and self-assertion. *Developmental Psychology, 26,* 961–971.

Crockett, L., Losoff, M., & Petersen, A. C. (1984). Perceptions of the peer group and friendship in early adolescence. *Journal of Early Adolescence, 4,* 155–181.

Cromer, R. F. (1988). The cognition hypothesis revisited. In F. S. Kessel (Ed.), *The development of language and language researchers* (pp. 223–248). Hillsdale, NJ: Erlbaum.

Crook, C. (1987). Taste and olfaction. In P. Salapatek & L. Cohen (Ed.), *Handbook of infant perception. Vol. 1. From sensation to perception* (pp. 237–264). Orlando, FL: Academic.

Crouter, A. C., MacDermid, S. M., McHale, S. M., & Perry-Jenkins, M. (1990). Parental monitoring and perceptions of children's school performance and conduct in dual- and single-earner families. *Developmental Psychology, 26,* 649–657.

Cruikshank, D. P., & Hays, P. M. (1991). Maternal physiology in pregnancy. In S. G. Gabbe, J. R. Niebyl, & J. L. Simpson (Eds.), *Obstetrics: Normal & problem pregnancies* (2nd ed., pp. 59–91). New York: Churchill Livingstone.

Cultice, J. C., Somerville, S. C., & Wellman, H. M. (1983). Preschoolers' memory monitoring: Feeling of knowing judgments. *Child Development, 54,* 1480–1486.

Cummings, E. M., Iannotti, R. J., & Zahn-Waxler, C. (1985). Influence of conflict between adults on the emotions and aggression of young children. *Developmental Psychology, 21,* 494–507.

Cummings, E. M., Iannotti, R. J., & Zahn-Waxler, C. (1989). Aggression between peers in early childhood: Individual continuity and developmental change. *Child Development, 60,* 887–895.

Cummings, E. M., Pellegrini, D. S., Notarius, C. I., & Cummings, E. M. (1989). Children's responses to angry adult behavior as a function of marital distress and history of interparent hostility. *Child Development, 60,* 1035–1043.

Cummings, E. M., Zahn-Waxler, C., & Radke-Yarrow, M. (1981). Young children's responses to expressions of anger and affection by others in the family. *Child Development, 52,* 1274–1282.

Cunningham, F. G., MacDonald, P. C., Leveno, K. J., Gant, N. F., & Gilstrap, L. C., III. (1993). *Williams obstetrics.* Norwalk, CT: Appleton and Lange.

Damon, W. (1977). *The social world of the child.* San Francisco: Jossey-Bass.

Damon, W., & Hart, D. (1982). The development of self-understanding from infancy through adolescence. *Child Development, 53,* 841–864.

Daniels, D., Dunn, J., Furstenberg, F. F., Jr., & Plomin, R. (1985). Environmental differences within the family and adjustment differences within pairs of adolescent siblings. *Child Development, 56,* 764–774.

Daniels, D., Plomin, R., & Greenhalgh, J. (1984). Correlates of difficult temperament in infancy. *Child Development, 55,* 1184–1194.

Dannemiller, J. L., & Stephens, B. R. (1988). A critical test of infant pattern preference models. *Child Development, 59,* 210–216.

Darwin, C. (1859). *The origin of species.* New York: Modern Library.

Darwin, C. (1871). *The descent of man.* New York: Modern Library.

Darwin, C. (1872). *The expression of emotions in man and animals.* London: John Murray.

Dasen, P. R. (1977). *Piagetian psychology: Cross cultural contributions.* New York: Gardner Press.

Davies, P. T., & Cummings, E. M. (1994). Marital conflict and child adjustment: An emotional security hypothesis. *Psychological Bulletin, 116,* 387–411.

Davydov, V. V. (1995). The influence of L. S. Vygotsky on education theory, research, and practice. (S. T. Kerr, Trans.) *Educational Researcher, 24* (3), 12–21.

Day, N. L, Richardson, G. A., & McGauhey, P. J. (1994). The effects of prenatal exposure to marijuana, cocaine, heroin, and methadone. In H. L. Needleman & D. Bellinger (Eds.), *Prenatal exposure to toxicants: Developmental consequences* (pp. 184–209). Baltimore: Johns Hopkins University Press.

Deaux, K., & Lewis, L. L. (1984). Structure of gender stereotypes: Interrelationships among components and gender label. *Journal of Personality and Social Psychology, 46,* 991–1004.

DeCasper, A. J., & Fifer, W. P. (1980). Of human bonding: Newborns prefer their mothers' voices. *Science, 208,* 1174–1176.

DeCasper, A. J., & Spence, M. J. (1986). Prenatal maternal speech influences newborns' perception of speech sounds. *Infant Behavior & Development, 9,* 133–150.

Dehner, L. P., & Gersell, D. J. (1994). Congenital syphilis: A reminder about the return of an old scourge. *Missouri Medicine, 91,* 630–635.

Dekovic, M., & Janssens, J. M. A. M. (1992). Parents' child-rearing style and child's sociometric status. *Developmental Psychology, 28,* 925–932.

De Lisi, R., & Gallagher, A. M. (1991). Understanding of gender stability and constancy in Argentinean children. *Merrill-Palmer Quarterly, 37,* 483–502.

DeLoache, J. S., & Burns, N. M. (1993). Symbolic development in young children: Understanding models and pictures. In C. Pratt & A. F. Garton (Eds.), *Systems of representation in children: Development and use* (pp. 91–112). Chichester, England: Wiley.

DeLoache, J. S., & Burns, N. M. (1994). Symbolic functioning in preschool children. *Journal of Applied Developmental Psychology, 15,* 513–527.

DeLoache, J. S., Cassidy, D. J., & Brown, A. L. (1985). Precursors of mnemonic strategies in very young children's memory. *Child Development, 56,* 125–137.

DeLoache, J. S., & Todd, C. M. (1988). Young children's use of spatial categorization as a mnemonic strategy. *Journal of Experimental Child Psychology, 46,* 1–20.

Dempster, F. N. (1981). Memory span: Sources of individual and developmental differences. *Psychological Bulletin, 89,* 63–100.

Denham, S. A., & Almeida, M. C. (1987). Children's social problem-solving skills, behavioral adjustment, and interventions: A meta-analysis evaluating theory and practice. *Journal of Applied Developmental Psychology, 8,* 391–409.

Dennis, W. (1960). Causes of retardation among institutionalized children: Iran. *Journal of Genetic Psychology, 96,* 47–59.

Depp, R. (1991). Cesarean delivery and other surgical procedures. In S. G. Gabbe, J. R. Niebyl, & J. L. Simpson (Eds.), *Obstetrics: Normal & problem pregnancies* (2nd ed., pp. 635–693). New York: Churchill Livingstone.

DeRosier, M. E., Kupersmidt, J. B., & Patterson, C. J. (1995). Children's academic and behavioral adjustment as a function of the chronicity and proximity of peer rejection. *Child Development, 65,* 1799–1813.

Deutsch, F. M., Lussier, J. B., & Servis, L. J. (1993). Husbands at home: Predictors of paternal participation in childcare and housework. *Journal of Personality and Social Psychology, 65,* 1154–1166.

deVries, L. B. A., Halley, D. J. J., Oostra, B. A., & Niermeijer, M. F. (1994). The fragile X syndrome: A growing gene causing familial intellectual disability. *Journal of Intellectual Disability Research, 38,* 1–8.

Diamond, A. (1985). Development of the ability to use recall to guide action, as indicated by infants' performance on AB. *Child Development, 56,* 868–883.

Diamond, A., Cruttenden, L., & Neiderman, D. (1994). AB with multiple wells: I. Why are multiple wells sometimes easier than two wells? II. Memory or memory + inhibition? *Developmental Psychology, 30,* 192–205.

Diamond, J. (1989, February). Blood, genes, and malaria. *Natural History,* 8–18.

Diaz, R. M. (1985). Bilingual cognitive development: Addressing three gaps in current research. *Child Development, 56,* 1376–1388.

Dick-Read, G. (1933). *Natural childbirth.* London: W. Heineman.

Dinges, Martin M., & Oetting, E. R. (1993). Similarity in drug use patterns between adolescents and their friends. *Adolescence, 28* (110), 253–266.

Dishion, T. J. (1990). The family ecology of boys' peer relations in middle childhood. *Child Development, 61,* 874–892.

Dishion, T. J., Andrews, D. W., & Crosby, L. (1995). Antisocial boys and their friends in early adolescence: Relationship characteristics, quality, and interactional process. *Child Development, 66,* 139–151.

Dodge, K. A. (1980). Social cognition and children's aggressive behavior. *Child Development, 51,* 162–170.

Dodge, K. A. (1983). Behavioral antecedents of peer social status. *Child Development, 54,* 1386–1399.

Dodge, K. A. (1986). A social information processing model of social competence in children. In M. Perlmutter (Ed.), *Minnesota Symposia on Child Psychology* (Vol. 18, pp. 77–125). Hillsdale, NJ: Erlbaum.

Dodge, K. A. (1990). Nature versus nurture in childhood conduct disorder: It is time to ask a different question. *Developmental Psychology, 26,* 698–701.

Dodge, K. A., Coie, J. D., Pettit, G. S., & Price, J. M. (1990). Peer status and aggression in boys' groups: Developmental and contextual analyses. *Child Development, 61,* 1289–1309.

Dodge, K. A., & Frame, C. L. (1982). Social cognitive biases and deficits in aggressive boys. *Child Development, 53,* 620–635.

Dodge, K. A., Murphy, R. R., & Buchsbaum, K. (1984). The assessment of intention-cue detection skills in children: Implications for developmental psychopathology. *Child Development, 55,* 163–173.

Dodge, K. A., Pettit, G. S., & Bates, J. E. (1994). Socialization mediators of the relation between socioeconomic status and child conduct problems. *Child Development, 65,* 649–665.

Dodge, K. A., & Price, J. M. (1994). On the relation between social information processing and socially competent behavior in early school-aged children. *Child Development, 65,* 1385–1397.

Donaldson, M. (1978). *Children's minds.* New York: W. W. Norton.

Donaldson, S. I., Graham, J. W., & Hansen, W. B. (1994). Testing the generalizability of intervening mechanism theories: Understanding the effects of adolescent drug use prevention interventions. *Journal of Behavioral Medicine, 17,* 195–216.

Donaldson, S. I., Graham, J. W., Piccinin, A. M., & Hansen, W. B. (1995). Resistance-skills training and onset of alcohol use: Evidence for beneficial and harmful effects in public schools and in private Catholic schools. *Health Psychology, 14,* 291–300.

Donenberg, G. R., & Hoffman, L. W. (1988). Gender differences in moral development. *Sex Roles, 18,* 701–717.

Dorfman, D. D. (1995). Soft science with a neoconservative agenda [Review of the book *The bell curve*]. *Contemporary Psychology, 40,* 418–421.

Dornbusch, S., Carlsmith, J., Bushwall, S., Ritter, P., Leiderman, H., Hastorf, A., & Gross, R. (1985). Single parents, extended households, and the control of adolescents. *Child Development, 56,* 326–341.

Dornbusch, S. M., Ritter, P. L., Leiderman, P. H., Roberts, D. F., & Fraleigh, M. J. (1987). The relation of parenting style to adolescent school performance. *Child Development, 58,* 1244–1257.

Dorsch, A., & Keane, S. P. (1994). Contextual factors in children's social information processing. *Developmental Psychology, 30,* 611–616.

Downey, D. B. (1994). The school performance of children from single-mother and single-father families: Economic or interpersonal deprivation? *Journal of Family Issues, 15,* 129–147.

Downey, D. B., & Powell, B. (1993). Do children in single-parent households fare better living with same-sex parents? *Journal of Marriage and the Family, 55,* 55–71.

Downey, J., Ehrhardt, A. A., Morishima, A., Bell, J. J., & Gruen, R. (1987). Gender role development in two clinical syndromes: Turner syndrome versus constitutional short stature. *Journal of the American Academy of Child and Adolescent Psychiatry, 26,* 566–573.

Dronkers, J. (1994). The changing effects of lone parent families on the educational attainment of their children in a European welfare state. *Sociology, 28,* 171–191.

Drotar, D. (1988). Failure to thrive. In D. K. Routh (Ed.), *Handbook of pediatric psychology* (pp. 71–100). New York: Guilford.

DuBois, D. L., Felner, R. D., Brand, S., Adan, A. M., & Evans, E. G. (1992). A prospective study of life stress, social support, and adaptation in early adolescence. *Child Development, 63,* 542–557.

Dubow, E. F., Tisak, J., Causey, D., Hryshko, A., & Reid, G. (1991). A two-year longitudinal study of stressful life events, social support, and social problem-solving skills: Contributions to children's behavioral and academic adjustment. *Child Development, 62,* 583–599.

Dukes, R. L., & Martinez, R. (1994). The impact of ethgender on self-esteem among adolescents. *Adolescence, 29,* 105–115.

Dumas, J. E., LaFreniere, P. J., & Serketich, W. J. (1995). "Balance of power": A transactional analysis of control in mother-child dyads involving socially competent, aggressive, and anxious children. *Journal of Abnormal Psychology, 104,* 104–113.

Dunham, P. J., Dunham, F., & Curwin, A. (1993). Joint-attentional states and lexical acquisition at 18 months. *Developmental Psychology, 29,* 827–831.

Dunn, J. (1983). Sibling relationships in early childhood. *Child Development, 54,* 787–811.

Dunn, J. (1985). *Sisters and brothers.* Cambridge, MA: Harvard University Press.

Dunn, J., Bretherton, I., & Munn, P. (1987). Conversations about feeling states between mothers and their young children. *Developmental Psychology, 3,* 132–139.

Dunn, J., Brown, J. R., & Maguire, M. (1995). The development of children's moral sensibility: Individual differences and emotion understanding. *Developmental Psychology, 31,* 649–659.

Dunn, J., & Plomin, R. (1990). *Separate lives: Why siblings are so different.* New York: Basic Books.

Dunn, J., Slomkowski, C., & Beardsall, L. (1994). Sibling relationships from the preschool period through middle childhood and early adolescence. *Developmental Psychology, 30,* 315–324.

Dunn, L. M., & Dunn, L. M. (1981). *Peabody Picture Vocabulary Test Revised.* Circle Pines, MN: American Guidance Service.

Dunphy, D. C. (1963). The social structure of urban adolescent peer groups. *Sociometry, 26,* 230–246.

Dweck, C. S., & Elliott, E. S. (1983). Achievement motivation. In E. M. Hetherington (Ed.), *Handbook of child psychology: Vol. 4* (pp. 643–691). New York: Wiley.

Dweck, C. S., & Leggett, E. L. (1988). A social-cognitive approach to motivation and personality. *Psychological Review, 95,* 256–273.

Eagly, A. H. (1987). *Sex differences in social behavior: A social-role interpretation.* Hillsdale, NJ: Erlbaum.

Eagly, A. H. (1995). The science and politics of comparing women and men. *American Psychologist, 50,* 145–158.

Eagly, A. H., Mladinic, A., & Otto, S. (1991). Are women evaluated more favorably than men? An analysis of attitudes, beliefs, and emotions. *Psychology of Women Quarterly, 15,* 203–216.

East, P. L., & Rook, K. S. (1992). Compensatory patterns of support among children's peer relationships: A test using school friends, nonschool friends, and siblings. *Developmental Psychology, 28,* 163–172.

Eaton, W. O., & Enns, L. R. (1986). Sex differences in human motor activity level. *Psychological Bulletin, 100,* 19–28.

Eaton, W. O., & Yu, A. P. (1989). Are sex differences in child motor activity level a function of sex differences in maturational status? *Child Development, 60,* 1005–1011.

Eccles, J. (1983). Expectancies, values, and academic behaviors. In J. T. Spence (Ed.), *Achievement and achievement motives* (pp. 75–146). San Francisco: W. H. Freeman.

Eccles, J. P., Adler, T., & Meece, J. L. (1984). Sex differences in achievement: A test of alternate theories. *Journal of Personality and Social Psychology, 46,* 26–43.

Eccles, J., Wigfield, A., Harold, R. D., & Blumenfeld, P. (1993). Age and gender differences in children's self- and task perceptions during elementary school. *Child Development, 64,* 830–847.

Eckerman, C. O., Davis, C. C., & Didow, S. M. (1989). Toddlers' emerging ways of achieving social coordinations with a peer. *Child Development, 60,* 440–453.

Eckerman, C. O., & Stein, M. R. (1982). The toddler's emerging interactive skills. In K. H. Rubin & H. S. Ross (Eds.), *Peer relationships and social skills in childhood* (pp. 41–71). New York: Springer-Verlag.

Eckerman, C. O., & Stein, M. R. (1990). How imitation begets imitation and toddlers' generation of games. *Developmental Psychology, 26,* 370–378.

Eckert, P. (1989). *Jocks and burnouts: Social categories and identity in the high school.* New York: Teachers College, Columbia University.

Eder, R. A. (1989). The emergent personologist: The structure and content of 3½-, 5½-, and 7½-year-olds' concepts of themselves and other persons. *Child Development, 60,* 1218–1228.

Eder, R. A. (1990). Uncovering young children's psychological selves: Individual and developmental differences. *Child Development, 61,* 849–863.

Edge, V., & Laros, R. K., Jr. (1993). Pregnancy outcome in nulliparous women aged 35 or older. *American Journal of Obstetrics and Gynecology, 168,* 1881–1884.

Egeland, B., & Farber, E. A. (1984). Infant-mother attachment: Factors related to its development and changes over time. *Child Development, 55,* 753–771.

Egeland, B., & Hiester, M. (1995). The long-term consequences of infant day-care and mother-infant attachment. *Child Development, 66,* 474–485.

Egeland, B., Jacobvitz, D., & Sroufe, L. A. (1988). Breaking the cycle of abuse. *Child Development, 59,* 1080–1088.

Egeland, B., & Sroufe, L. A. (1981). Attachment and early maltreatment. *Child Development, 52,* 44–52.

Eiferman, R. R. (1971). Social play in childhood. In R. E. Herron & B. Sutton-Smith (Eds.), *Child's play* (pp. 270–297). New York: Wiley.

Eimas, P. D., Miller, J. L., & Jusczyk, P. W. (1987). On infant speech perception and the acquisition of language. In S. Harnad (Ed.), *Categorical perception: The groundwork of cognition* (pp. 161–198). Cambridge, MA: Cambridge University Press.

Eimas, P. D., Siqueland, E. R., Jusczyk, P., & Vigorito, J. (1971). Speech perception in infants. *Science, 171,* 303–306.

Eisenberg, N. (1986). *Altruistic emotion, cognition, and behavior.* Hillsdale, NJ: Erlbaum.

Eisenberg, N. (Ed.). (1989). *Empathy and related emotional responses. New Directions for Child Development, No. 44.* San Francisco: Jossey-Bass.

Eisenberg, N. (1992). *The caring child.* Cambridge, MA: Harvard University Press.

Eisenberg, N., Fabes, R. A., Bernzweig, J., Karbon, M., Poulin, R., & Hanish, L. (1993). The relations of emotionality and regulation to preschoolers' social skills and sociometric status. *Child Development, 64,* 1418–1438.

Eisenberg, N., & Lennon, R. (1983). Sex differences in empathy and related capacities. *Psychological Bulletin, 94,* 100–131.

Eisenberg, N., Lennon, R., & Roth, K. (1983). Prosocial development: A longitudinal study. *Developmental Psychology, 19,* 846–855.

Eisenberg, N., & Miller, P. A. (1987). The relation of empathy to prosocial and related behaviors. *Psychological Bulletin, 101,* 91–119.

Eisenberg, N., Miller, P. A., Shell, R., McNalley, S., & Shea, C. (1991). Prosocial development in adolescence: A longitudinal study. *Developmental Psychology, 27,* 849–857.

Eisenberg, N., Shell, R., Pasternack, J., Lennon, R., Beller, R., & Mathy, R. M. (1987). Prosocial development in middle childhood: A longitudinal study. *Developmental Psychology, 23,* 712–718.

Eisenberg, N., Wolchik, S. A., Hernandez, R., & Pasternack, J. F. (1985). Parental socialization of young children's play: A short-term longitudinal study. *Child Development, 56,* 1506–1513.

Ekman, P. (1994). Strong evidence for universals in facial expressions: A reply to Russell's mistaken critique. *Psychological Bulletin, 115,* 268–287.

Ekman, P., Friesen, W. V., & Ellsworth, P. (1982). What are the similarities and differences in facial behavior across cultures. In P. Ekman (Ed.), *Emotion in the human face* (pp. 128–144). Cambridge, England: Cambridge University Press.

Elardo, R., & Bradley, R. (1981). The Home Observation for Measurement of the Environment: A review of research. *Developmental Review, 1,* 113–145.

Elicker, J., Englund, M., & Sroufe, L. A. (1992). Predicting peer competence and peer relationships in childhood from early parent-child relationships. In R. D. Parke & G. W. Ladd (Eds.), *Family-peer relationships: Modes of linkage* (pp. 77–106). Hillsdale, NJ: Erlbaum.

Elkind, D. (1976). *Child development and education: A Piagetian perspective.* Oxford, England: Oxford University Press.

Ellis, S., Rogoff, B., & Cromer, C. C. (1981). Age segregation in children's social interactions. *Developmental Psychology, 17,* 399–407.

Ellsworth, C. P., Muir, D. W., & Hains, S. M. (1993). Social competence and person-object differentiation: An analysis of the still-face effect. *Developmental Psychology, 29,* 63–73.

Emde, R. N. (1992). Individual meaning and increasing complexity: Contributions of Sigmund Freud and Rene Spitz to developmental psychology. *Developmental Psychology, 28,* 347–359.

Emde, R. N., Plomin, R., Robinson, J., Corley, R., DeFries, J., Fulker, D. W., Reznick, J. S., Campos, J., Kagan, J., & Zahn-Waxler, C. (1992). Temperament, emotion, and cognition at fourteen months: The MacArthur longitudinal twin study. *Child Development, 63,* 1437–1455.

Emery, R. E. (1988). *Marriage, divorce, and children's adjustment.* Newbury Park, CA: Sage.

Entwistle, D. R. (1990). School and the adolescent. In S. S. Feldman & G. Elliott (Eds.), *At the threshold: The developing adolescent* (pp. 197–224). Cambridge, MA: Harvard University Press.

Epstein, L. H., & Cluss, P. A. (1986). Behavioral genetics of childhood obesity. *Behavior Therapy, 17,* 324–334.

Epstein, L. H., & Wing, R. R. (1987). Behavioral treatment of childhood obesity. *Psychological Bulletin, 101,* 331–342.

Erel, O., & Burman, B. (1995). Interrelatedness of marital relations and parent-child relations: A meta-analytic review. *Psychological Bulletin, 188,* 108–132.

Erickson, M. F., Sroufe, L. A., & Egeland, B. (1985). The relationship between quality of attachment and behavior in preschool in a high-risk sample. *Monographs of the Society for Research in Child Development, 50* (1-2, Serial No. 209).

Erikson, E. H. (1963). *Childhood and society* (2nd ed.). New York: Norton.

Eron, L. D., Huesmann, L. R., Brice, P., Fischer, P., & Mermelstein, R. (1983). Age trends in the development of aggression, sex typing, and related television habits. *Developmental Psychology, 19,* 71–77.

Estrada, P., Arsenio, W. F., Hess, R. D., & Holloway, S. D. (1987). Affective quality of the mother-child relationship: Longitudinal consequences for children's school-relevant cognitive functioning. *Developmental Psychology, 23,* 210–215.

Etaugh, C., & Liss, M. B. (1992). Home, school, and playroom: Training grounds for adult gender roles. *Sex Roles, 26,* 129–147.

Eveleth, P. B., & Tanner, J. M. (1990). *Worldwide variation in human growth.* New York: Cambridge University Press.

Ewart, D. P., Frederick, P. D., & Mascola, L. (1992). Resurgence of congenital rubella syndrome in the 1990s. *Journal of American Medical Association, 267,* 2616–2620.

Fabes, R. A., Eisenberg, N., Karbon, M., Troyer, D., & Switzer, G. (1994). The relations of children's emotion regulation to their vicarious emotional responses and comforting behaviors. *Child Development, 65,* 1678–1693.

Fabes, R. A., Eisenberg, N., McCormick, S. E., & Wilson, M. S. (1988). Preschoolers' attributions of the situational determinants of others' naturally occurring emotions. *Developmental Psychology, 24,* 376–385.

Fabricius, W. V., & Cavalier, L. (1989). The role of causal theories about memory in young children's memory strategy choice. *Child Development, 60,* 298–308.

Fagan, J. F. (1984). Infant memory: History, current trends, relations to cognitive psychology. In M. Moscovitch (Ed.), *Infant memory: Its relation to normal and pathological memory in humans and other animals* (pp. 1–28). New York: Plenum.

Fagan, J. F., & Detterman, D. K. (1992). The Fagan test of infant intelligence: A technical summary. *Journal of Applied Developmental Psychology, 13,* 173–193.

Fagot, B. I. (1978). The influence of sex of child on parental reactions to toddler children. *Child Development, 49,* 459–465.

Fagot, B. I., & Hagan, R. (1991). Observations of parent reactions to sex-stereotyped behaviors: Age and sex effects. *Child Development, 62,* 617–628.

Fagot, B. I., & Leinbach, M. D. (1987). Socialization of sex roles within the family. In D. B. Carter (Ed.), *Current conceptions of sex roles and sex typing* (pp. 89–100). New York: Praeger.

Fagot, B. I., Leinbach, M. D., & Hagan, R. (1986). Gender labeling and the adoption of sex-typed behaviors. *Developmental Psychology, 22,* 440–443.

Fagot, B. I., Leinbach, M. D., & O'Boyle, C. (1992). Gender labeling, gender stereotyping, and parenting behavior. *Developmental Psychology, 28,* 225–230.

Falbo, T., & Polit, D. F. (1986). Quantitative review of the only child literature: Research evidence and theory development. *Psychological Bulletin, 100,* 176–189.

Falbo, T., & Poston, D. L. (1993). The academic, personality, and physical outcomes of only children in China. *Child Development, 64,* 18–35.

Family and Medical Leave Act of 1993, 29 U.S.C. § 2611 *et. seq.*

Fantz, R. L. (1966). Pattern discrimination and selective attention as determinants of perceptual development from birth. In A. H. Kidd & J. L. Rivoire (Eds.), *Perceptual development in children.* New York: International University Press.

Farrar, M. J., & Goodman, G. S. (1992). Developmental changes in event memory. *Child Development, 63,* 173–187.

Farrar, M. J., Raney, G. E., & Boyer, M. E. (1992). Knowledge, concepts, and inferences in childhood. *Child Development, 63,* 673–691.

Feingold, A. (1988). Cognitive gender differences are disappearing. *American Psychologist, 43,* 95–103.

Feingold, A. (1993). Cognitive gender differences: A developmental perspective. *Sex Roles, 29,* 91–112.

Feingold, A. (1994). Gender differences in personality: A meta-analysis. *Psychological Bulletin, 116,* 429–456.

Feinkind, L., & Minkoff, H. L. (1988). HIV in pregnancy. *Clinics in Perinatology, 15,* 189–202.

Feinman, S., & Lewis, M. (1983). Social referencing at ten months: A second-order effect on infants' responses to strangers. *Child Development, 54,* 878–887.

Feldman, N. S., & Ruble, D. N. (1988). The effect of personal relevance on psychological inference: A developmental analysis. *Child Development, 59,* 1339–1352.

Feldman, S. S., & Wood, D. N. (1994). Parents' expectations for preadolescent sons' behavioral autonomy: A longitudinal study of correlates and outcomes. *Journal of Research on Adolescence, 4,* 45–70.

Fenson, L., Dale, P. S., Reznick, J. S., Bates, E., Thal, D., & Pethick, S. J. (1994). Variability in early communicative development. *Monographs of the Society for Research in Child Development, 59* (Serial No. 242).

Fenzel, L. M., & Blyth, D. A. (1986). Individual adjustment to school transitions: An exploration of the role of supportive peer relations. *Journal of Early Adolescence, 6,* 315–329.

Fernald, A. (1985). Four-month-old infants prefer to listen to motherese. *Infant Behavior and Development, 8,* 181–195.

Fernald, A., & Morikawa, H. (1993). Common themes and cultural variations in Japanese and American mothers' speech to infants. *Child Development, 64,* 637–656.

Ferree, M. M. (1994). Negotiating household roles and responsibilities: Resistance, conflict and change. In M. R. Stevenson (Ed.), *Gender roles through the life span* (pp. 203–222). Muncie, IN: Ball State University Press.

Feshbach, S. (1971). Dynamics and morality of violence and aggression: Some psychological considerations. *American Psychologist, 26,* 281–292.

Field, T. (1984). Separation stress of young children transferring to new schools. *Developmental Psychology, 20,* 786–792.

Field, T. (1991). Quality infant day-care and grade school behavior and performance. *Child Development, 62,* 863–870.

Figueroa-Colon, R., von Almen, T. K., & Suskind, R. M. (1992). The genetics of childhood obesity. In P. L. Giorgi, R. M. Suskind, & C. Catassi (Eds.), *The obese child* (pp. 1–20). New York: Karger.

Fischer, K. W. (1987). Relations between brain and cognitive development. *Child Development, 58,* 623–632.

Flavell, J. H. (1963). *The developmental psychology of Jean Piaget.* New York: Van Nostrand.

Flavell, J. H. (1978). The development of knowledge about visual perception. In C. B. Keasey (Ed.), *Nebraska Symposium*

on *Motivation* (Vol. 25). Lincoln: University of Nebraska Press.

Flavell, J. H. (1984). Discussion. In R. J. Sternberg (Ed.), *Mechanisms of cognitive development* (pp. 188–209). New York: W. H. Freeman.

Flavell, J. H. (1985). *Cognitive development* (2nd ed.). Englewood Cliffs, NJ: Prentice-Hall.

Flavell, J. H. (1988). The development of children's knowledge about the mind: From cognitive connections to mental representations. In J. W. Astington, P. L. Harris, & D. R. Olson (Eds.), *Developing theories of mind* (pp. 244–267). New York: Cambridge University Press.

Flavell, J. H. (1992). Cognitive development: Past, present, and future. *Developmental Psychology, 28*, 998–1005.

Flavell, J. H., Beach, D. H., & Chinsky, J. M. (1966). Spontaneous verbal rehearsal in a memory task as a function of age. *Child Development, 37*, 283–299.

Flavell, J. H., Botkin, P. T., Fry, C. L., Jr., Wright, J. W., & Jarvis, P. E. (1968). *The development of role-taking and communication skills in children*. New York: Wiley.

Flavell, J. H., Flavell, E. R., Green, F. L., & Moses, L. J. (1990). Young children's understanding of fact beliefs versus value beliefs. *Child Development, 61*, 915–928.

Flavell, J. H., Friedrichs, A. G., & Hoyt, J. D. (1970). Developmental changes in memorization processes. *Cognitive Psychology, 1*, 324–340.

Flavell, J. H., Green, F. L., & Flavell, E. R. (1986). Development of knowledge about the appearance-reality distinction. *Monographs of the Society for Research in Child Development, 51* (1, Serial No. 212).

Flavell, J. H., Miller, P. H., & Miller, S. A. (1993). *Cognitive development* (3rd ed.). Englewood Cliffs, NJ: Prentice-Hall.

Flerx, V. C., Fidler, D. S., & Roger, R. W. (1976). Sex-role stereotypes: Developmental aspects and early intervention. *Child Development, 47*, 998–1007.

Flynn, J. R. (1987). Massive IQ gains in 14 nations: What IQ tests really measure. *Psychological Bulletin, 101*, 171–191.

Flynn, J. R. (1994). IQ gains and intelligence. In R. J. Sternberg (Ed.), *Encyclopedia of human intelligence* (pp. 619–622). New York: Macmillan.

Fogel, A., & Thelen, E. (1987). Development of early expressive and communicative action: Reinterpreting the evidence from a dynamic systems perspective. *Developmental Psychology, 23*, 747–761.

Ford, M. E. (1979). The construct validity of egocentrism. *Psychological Bulletin, 86*, 1169–1188.

Ford, M. E. (1985). Two perspectives on the validation of developmental constructs: Psychometric and theoretical limitations in research on egocentrism. *Psychological Bulletin, 97*, 497–501.

Forman, E. A., Minick, N., & Stone, C. A. (1993). *Contexts for learning*. New York: Oxford University Press.

Forman, G. E., & Kuschner, D. S. (1977). *The child's construction of knowledge: Piaget for teaching children*. Monterey, CA: Brooks/Cole.

Forsterling, F. (1985). Attributional retraining: A review. *Psychological Bulletin, 98*, 495–512.

Fox, N. A. (1995). Of the way we were: Adult memories about attachment experiences and their role in determining infant-parent relationships: A commentary on van IJzendoorn. *Psychological Bulletin, 117*, 404–410.

Fox, N. A., Kimmerly, N. L., & Schafer, W. D. (1991). Attachment to mother/attachment to father: A meta-analysis. *Child Development, 62*, 210–225.

Frankenburg, W. K., & Dodds, J. B. (1967). The Denver Developmental Screening Test. *Journal of Pediatrics, 71*, 181–191.

Frankenburg, W. K., Fandal, A. W., Sciarillo, W., & Burgess, D. (1981). The newly abbreviated and revised Denver Developmental Screening Test. *Journal of Pediatrics, 99*, 995–999.

Franz, C. E., McClelland, D. C., & Weinberger, J. (1991). Childhood antecedents of conventional social accomplishment in midlife adults: A 36-year prospective study. *Journal of Personality and Social Psychology, 60*, 586–595.

Fraser, A. M., Brockert, J. E., & Ward, R. H. (1995). Association of young maternal age with adverse reproductive outcomes. *New England Journal of Medicine, 332*, 1113–1117.

Fraser, S. (Ed.). (1995). *The bell curve wars: Race, intelligence, and the future of America*. New York: Basic.

Freij, B. J., & Sever, J. L. (1988). Herpes virus infections in pregnancy: Risks to embryo, fetus, and neonate. *Clinics in Perinatology, 15*, 203–231.

Freij, B. J., South, M. A., & Sever, J. L. (1988). Maternal rubella and the congenital rubella syndrome. *Clinics in Perinatology, 15*, 247–258.

French, D. C. (1984). Children's knowledge of the social functions of younger, older, and same-age peers. *Child Development, 55*, 1429–1433.

French, D. C., Waas, G. A., Stright, A. L., & Baker, J. A. (1986). Leadership asymmetries in mixed-age children's groups. *Child Development, 57*, 1277–1283.

French, L. A., & Nelson, K. (1985). *Young children's knowledge of relational terms: Some ifs, ors, and buts*. New York: Springer-Verlag.

French, V. (1977). History of the child's influence: Ancient Mediterranean civilizations. In R. Q. Bell & L. V. Harper (Eds.), *Child effects on adults*. Hillsdale, NJ: Erlbaum.

Freud, A., & Dann, S. (1951). An experiment in group upbringing. In R. S. Eissler, H. Hartmann, A. Freud, & E. Kris (Eds.), *The psychoanalytic study of the child* (Vol. 6, pp. 127–168). New York: International Universities Press.

Freud, S. (1930/1961). *Civilization and its discontents* (J. Strachey, Trans. and Ed.). New York: Norton.

Freud, S. (1920/1965). *A general introduction to psychoanalysis* (J. Riviere, Trans.). New York: Washington Square Press.

Frey, K. S., & Ruble, D. N. (1992). Gender constancy and the "cost" of sex-typed behavior: A test of the conflict hypothesis. *Developmental Psychology, 28*, 714–721.

Fried, P. A. (1986). Marijuana and human pregnancy. In I. J. Chasnoff (Ed.), *Drug use in pregnancy: Mother and child* (pp. 64–74). Lancaster, England: MTP Press.

Fried, P. A., Watkinson, B., Dillon, R. F., & Dulberg, C. S. (1987). Neonatal neurological status in a low-risk population after prenatal exposure to cigarettes, marijuana, and alcohol. *Journal of Developmental and Behavioral Pediatrics, 8*, 318–326.

Friedman, L. (1989). Mathematics and the gender gap: A meta-analysis of recent studies on sex differences in mathematical tasks. *Review of Educational Research, 59*, 185–214.

Frodi, A. M., Lamb, M. E., Leavitt, L. A., Donovan, W. L., Neff, C., & Sherry, D. (1978). Fathers' and mothers' responses to the faces and cries of normal and premature infants. *Developmental Psychology, 14*, 490–498.

Fry, D. P. (1992). Respect for the rights of others is peace: Learning aggression versus nonaggression among the Zapotec. *American Anthropologist, 94*, 621–639.

Frye, D., Braisby, N., Lowe, J., Maroudas, C., & Nicholls, J. (1989). Young children's understanding of counting and cardinality. *Child Development, 60*, 1158–1171.

Fryer, G. E., Jr. (1993). *Child abuse and the social environment*. Boulder, CO: Westview.

Furman, W., & Bierman, K. L. (1984). Children's conceptions of friendship: A multidimensional study of developmental changes. *Developmental Psychology, 20*, 925–931.

Furman, W., & Buhrmester, D. (1992). Age and sex differences in perceptions of

networks of personal relationships. *Child Development, 63,* 103–115.

Fuson, K., Pergament, G., Lyons, B., & Hall, J. (1985). Children's conformity to the cardinality rule as a function of set size and counting accuracy. *Child Development, 56,* 1429–1436.

Gabbe, S. G., Niebyl, J. R., & Simpson, J. L. (1991). *Obstetrics: Normal & problem pregnancies* (2nd ed.). New York: Churchill Livingstone.

Galambos, N. L., Almeida, D. M., & Petersen, A. C. (1990). Masculinity, femininity, and sex role attitudes in early adolescence: Exploring gender intensification. *Child Development, 61,* 1905–1914.

Galbraith, R. C. (1982). Sibling spacing and intellectual development: A closer look at the confluence model. *Developmental Psychology, 18,* 151–173.

Gall, C., Ivy, G., & Lynch, G. (1986). Neuroanatomical plasticity: Its role in organizing and reorganizing the central nervous system. In F. Falkner & J. M. Tanner (Eds.), *Human growth: A comprehensive treatise* (pp. 411–436). New York: Plenum.

Galotti, K. M., Kozberg, S. F., & Farmer, M. C. (1991). Gender and developmental differences in adolescents' conceptions of moral reasoning. *Journal of Youth and Adolescence, 20,* 13–30.

Gamble, T., & Zigler, E. (1986). Effects of infant day care: Another look at the evidence. *American Journal of Orthopsychiatry, 56,* 26–41.

Gamoran, A. (1993). Alternative uses of ability grouping in secondary schools: Can we bring high-quality instruction to low-ability classes? *American Journal of Education, 102,* 1–22.

Gardner, H. (1983). *Frames of mind.* New York: Basic Books.

Gardner, H. (1993). *Multiple intelligences: The theory in practice.* New York: Basic Books.

Geis, F. L. (1993). Self-fulfilling prophecies: A social psychological view of gender. In A. E. Beall & R. J. Sternberg (Eds.), *The psychology of gender* (pp. 9–54). New York: Guilford.

Gelman, R. (1972). Logical capacity of very young children: Number invariance rules. *Child Development, 43,* 75–90.

Gelman, R. (1982). Basic numerical abilities. In R. J. Sternberg (Ed.), *Advances in the psychology of human intelligence* (Vol. 1). Hillsdale, NJ: Erlbaum.

Gelman, R., & Baillargeon, R. (1983). A review of Piagetian concepts. In J. H. Flavell & E. M. Markman (Eds.), *Handbook of child psychology: (Vol. 3.) Cognitive development.* New York: Wiley.

Gelman, R., & Gallistel, C. (1978). *The child's understanding of number.* Cambridge, MA: Harvard University Press.

Gelman, R., & Meck, E. (1986). The notion of principle: The case of counting. In J. Hiebert (Ed.), *Conceptual and procedural knowledge: The case of mathematics* (pp. 29–57). Hillsdale, NJ: Erlbaum.

Gelman, S. A., & Coley, J. D. (1990). The importance of knowing a dodo is a bird: Categories and inferences in 2-year-old children. *Developmental Psychology, 26,* 796–804.

Gelman, S. A., Collman, P., & Maccoby, E. E. (1986). Inferring properties from categories versus inferring categories from properties: The case of gender. *Child Development, 57,* 396–404.

Gentner, D. (1988). Metaphor as structure mapping: The relational shift. *Child Development, 59,* 47–59.

Gesell, A. (1954). The ontogenesis of infant behavior. In L. Carmichael (Ed.), *Manual of child psychology* (pp. 335–373). New York: Wiley.

Gesell, A., & Thompson, H. (1929). Learning and growth in identical twins: An experimental study by the method of co-twin control. *Genetics Psychology Monographs, 6,* 1–124.

Gibbs, J. C. (1977). Kohlberg's stages of moral judgment: A constructive critique. *Harvard Educational Review, 47,* 43–71.

Gibbs, J. C. (1979). Kohlberg's moral stage theory: A Piagetian revision. *Human Development, 22,* 89–112.

Gibbs, J. C., Basinger, K. S., & Fuller, D. (1992). *Moral maturity: Measuring the development of sociomoral reflection.* Hillsdale, NJ: Erlbaum.

Gibbs, J. C., & Schnell, S. V. (1985). Moral development "versus" socialization: A critique. *American Psychologist, 40,* 1071–1080.

Gibson, D., & Harris, A. (1988). Aggregated early intervention effects for Down's syndrome persons: Patterning and longevity of benefits. *Journal of Mental Deficiency Research, 32,* 1–17.

Gibson, E. J. (1969). *Principles of perceptual learning and development.* New York: Appleton.

Gibson, E. J. (1987). Introductory essay: What does infant perception tell us about theories of perception? *Journal of Experimental Psychology: Human Perception and Performance, 13,* 515–523.

Gibson, E. J. (1992). How to think about perceptual learning: Twenty-five years later. In H. L. Pick, Jr., P. W. van den Broek, & D. C. Knill (Eds.), *Cognition: Conceptual and methodological issues* (pp. 215–237). Washington, DC: American Psychological Association.

Gibson, E. J., & Radner, N. (1979). Attention: The perceiver as performer. In G. A. Hale & M. Lewis (Eds.), *Attention and cognitive development.* New York: Plenum.

Gibson, E. J., & Spelke, E. S. (1983). The development of perception. In J. H. Flavell & E. M. Markman (Eds.), *Handbook of child psychology: Cognitive development* (Vol. 3, pp. 1–76). New York: Wiley.

Gibson, E. J., & Walk, R. D. (1960). The "visual cliff." *Scientific American, 202,* 64–71.

Gibson, E. J., & Walker, A. S. (1984). Development of knowledge of visual-tactual affordances of substance. *Child Development, 55,* 453–460.

Gilligan, C. (1982). *In a different voice.* Cambridge, MA: Harvard University Press.

Gilligan, C., & Attanucci, J. (1988). Two moral orientations: Gender differences and similarities. *Merrill-Palmer Quarterly, 34,* 223–237.

Ginsburg, H. P., & Opper, S. (1969). *Piaget's theory of intellectual development.* Englewood Cliffs, NJ: Prentice-Hall.

Ginsburg, H. P., & Opper, S. (1988). *Piaget's theory of intellectual development* (3rd ed.). Englewood Cliffs, NJ: Prentice-Hall.

Giorgi, P. L., Suskind, R. M., & Catassi, C. (Eds.). (1992). *The obese child.* New York: Karger.

Glaser, R., & Chi, M. T. H. (1988). Overview. In M. T. H. Chi, R. Glaser, & M. J. Farr (Eds.), *The nature of expertise* (pp. xv–xxviii). Hillsdale, NJ: Erlbaum.

Glass, G. V. (1976). Primary, secondary, and meta-analysis. *Educational Researcher, 5,* 3–8.

Glassman, M. (1994). All things being equal: The two roads of Piaget and Vygotsky. *Developmental Review, 14,* 186–214.

Glick, J. (1975). Cognitive development in cross-cultural perspective. In F. D. Horowitz (Ed.), *Review of child development research, Vol. 4* (pp. 595–654). Chicago: University of Chicago Press.

Glick, P. C. (1988). The role of divorce in the changing family structure: Trends and variations. In S. A. Wolchik & P. Karoly (Eds.), *Children of divorce* (pp. 3–34). New York: Gardner Press.

Gnepp, J. (1983). Children's social sensitivity: Inferring emotions from conflicting cues. *Developmental Psychology, 19,* 805–814.

Gnepp, J. (1989). Children's use of personal information to understand other people's feelings. In C. Saarni & P. L. Harris (Eds.), *Children's understanding of emotion* (pp. 151–180). New York: Cambridge University Press.

Gnepp, J., & Chilamkurti, C. (1988). Children's use of personality attributions to predict other people's emotional and behavioral reactions. *Child Development, 59,* 743–754.

Gold, M., & Petronio, R. J. (1980). Delinquent behavior in adolescence. In

J. Adelson (Ed.), *Handbook of adolescent psychology* (pp. 495–535). New York: Wiley.

Gold, M., & Yanof, D. S. (1985). Mothers, daughters, and girlfriends. *Journal of Personality and Social Psychology, 49,* 654–659.

Goldenberg, R. L., & Klerman, L. V. (1995). Adolescent pregnancy— another look. *New England Journal of Medicine, 352,* 1161–1162.

Goldfarb, W. (1943). Effects of early institutional care on adolescent personality. *Journal of Experimental Education, 12,* 106–129.

Goldfield, B. A. (1993). Noun bias in maternal speech to one-year-olds. *Journal of Child Language, 20,* 85–99.

Goldsmith, D. F., & Rogoff, B. (1995). Sensitivity and teaching by dysphoric and nondysphoric women in structured versus unstructured situations. *Developmental Psychology, 31,* 388–394.

Goldsmith, H. H., Buss, A. H., Plomin, R., Rothbart, M. K., Thomas, A., Chess, S., Hinde, R. W., & McCall, R. B. (1987). Roundtable: What is temperament? Four approaches. *Child Development, 58,* 505–529.

Goldsmith, H. H., & Gottesman, I. I. (1981). Origins of variation in behavioral style: A longitudinal study of temperament in young twins. *Child Development, 52,* 91–103.

Goldsmith, H. H., & Harman, C. (1994). Temperament and attachment: Individuals and relationships. *Current Directions in Psychological Science, 3,* 53–57.

Goldstein, J., Freud, A., & Solnit, A. (1973). *Before the best interests of the child* (2nd ed.). New York: Free Press.

Goldstein, J., Freud, A., & Solnit, A. (1979). *Beyond the best interests of the child* (2nd ed.). New York: Free Press.

Goleman, D. (1980, February). 1,528 little geniuses and how they grew. *Psychology Today,* pp. 28–53.

Goleman, D. (1995, March 7). 75 years later, study still tracking geniuses. *The New York Times,* pp. C1, 9.

Golinkoff, R. M. (1983). The preverbal negotiation of failed messages. In R. M. Golinkoff (Ed.), *The transition from prelinguistic to linguistic communication* (pp. 57–78). Hillsdale, NJ: Erlbaum.

Golinkoff, R. M., Shuff-Bailey, M., Olguin, R., & Ruan, W. (1995). Young children extend novel words at the basic level: Evidence for the principle of categorical scope. *Developmental Psychology, 31,* 494–507.

Golombok, S., & Fivush, R. (1994). *Gender development.* Cambridge, England: Cambridge University Press.

Goodlad, J. I. (1984). *A place called school: Prospects for the future.* New York: McGraw-Hill.

Goodnow, J. J. (1988). Children's household work: Its nature and functions. *Psychological Bulletin, 103,* 5–26.

Goodwyn, S. W., & Acredolo, L. P. (1993). Symbolic gesture versus work: Is there a modality advantage for onset of symbol use? *Child Development, 64,* 688–701.

Goossens, F. A., & van IJzendoorn, M. H. (1990). Quality of infants' attachments to professional caregivers: Relation to infant-parent attachment and day-care characteristics. *Child Development, 61,* 832–837.

Gopnik, A., & Meltzoff, A. (1987). The development of categorization in the second year and its relation to other cognitive and linguistic developments. *Child Development, 58,* 1523–1531.

Gopnik, A., & Meltzoff, A. N. (1986). Words, plans, things, and locations: Interactions between semantic and cognitive development in the one-word stage. In S. A. Kuczaj, II, & M. D. Barrett (Eds.), *The development of word meaning* (pp. 199–224). New York: Springer-Verlag.

Gottesman, I. I. (1963). Genetic aspects of intelligent behavior. In N. Ellis (Ed.), *Handbook of mental deficiency* (pp. 253–296). New York: McGraw-Hill.

Gottesman, I. I. (1993). Origins of schizophrenia: Past as prologue. In R. Plomin & G. E. McClearn (Eds.), *Nature, nurture, and psychology* (pp. 231–243). Washington, DC: American Psychological Association.

Gottfried, A. E., Fleming, J. S., & Gottfried, A. W. (1994). Role of parental motivational practices in children's academic intrinsic motivation and achievement. *Journal of Educational Psychology, 86,* 104–113.

Gottfried, A. E., & Gottfried, A. W. (1988). *Maternal employment and children's development.* New York: Plenum Press.

Gottman, J. M. (1983). How children become friends. *Monographs of the Society for Research in Child Development, 48* (3, Serial No. 201).

Gottman, J. M. (1986). The world of coordinated play: Same- and cross-sex friendship in young children. In J. M. Gottman & J. G. Parker (Eds.), *Conversations of friends: Speculations on affective development* (pp. 139–191). Cambridge, England: Cambridge University Press.

Gottman, J. M., & Mettetal, G. (1986). Speculations about social and affective development: Friendship and acquaintanceship through adolescence. In J. M. Gottman & J. G. Parker (Eds.), *Conversations of friends: Speculations on affective development* (pp. 192–237). Cambridge, England: Cambridge University Press.

Gottman, J. M., & Roy, A. K. (1990). *Sequential analysis: A guide for behavioral researchers.* Cambridge, England: Cambridge University Press.

Gould, S. J. (1981). *The mismeasure of man.* New York: Norton.

Gould, S. J. (1995). Curveball. In S. Fraser (Ed.), *The bell curve wars: Race, intelligence, and the future of America* (pp. 11–22). New York: Basic.

Gouze, K. R. (1987). Attention and social problem solving as correlates of aggression in preschool males. *Journal of Abnormal Child Psychology, 15,* 181–197.

Graber, J. A., Brooks-Gunn, J., & Warren, W. P. (1995). The antecedents of menarcheal age: Heredity, family environment, and stressful life events. *Child Development, 66,* 346–359.

Gralinski, J. H., & Kopp, C. B. (1993). Everyday rules for behavior: Mothers' requests to young children. *Developmental Psychology, 29,* 573–584.

Granrud, C. E., Yonas, A., & Opland, E. A. (1985). Infants' sensitivity to the depth cue of shading. *Perception and Psychophysics, 37,* 415–419.

Grantham-McGregor, S., Powell, C., Walker, S., Chang, S., & Fletcher, P. (1994). The long-term follow-up of severely malnourished children who participated in an intervention program. *Child Development, 65,* 428–439.

Graves, T., Meyers, A. W., & Clark, L. (1988). An evaluation of parental problem-solving training in the behavioral treatment of childhood obesity. *Journal of Consulting and Clinical Psychology, 56,* 246–250.

Green, J. A., Jones, L. E., & Gustafson, G. E. (1987). Perception of cries by parents and nonparents: Relation to cry acoustics. *Developmental Psychology, 23,* 370–382.

Green, M. (1989). *Theories of development.* Englewood Cliffs, NJ: Prentice-Hall.

Greenberg, M., & Morris, N. (1974). Engrossment: The newborn's impact upon the father. *American Journal of Orthopsychiatry, 44,* 520–531.

Greenberg, M. T., & Crnic, K. A. (1988). Longitudinal predictors of developmental status and social interaction in premature and full-term infants at age two. *Child Development, 59,* 554–570.

Greenberger, E., & Goldberg, W. A. (1989). Work, parenting, and the socialization of children. *Developmental Psychology, 25,* 22–35.

Greenberger, E., & O'Neil, R. (1992). Maternal employment and perceptions of young children: Bronfenbrenner et al. revisited. *Child Development, 63,* 431–448.

Greenfield, P. M. (1993). International roots of minority child development: Introduction to the special issue. *International Journal of Behavioral Development, 16,* 385–394.

Greenough, W. T., Black, J. E., & Wallace, C. S. (1987). Experience and brain development. *Child Development, 58,* 539–559.

Greenstein, T. N. (1990). Marital disruption and the employment of married women. *Journal of Marriage and the Family, 52,* 657–676.

Greenstein, T. N. (1995). Are the "most advantaged" children truly disadvantaged by early maternal employment? *Journal of Family Issues, 16,* 149–169.

Griffin, S. A., Case, R., & Siegler, R. S. (1994). Right start: Providing the central conceptual prerequisites for first formal learning of arithmetic to students at risk for school failure. In K. McGilly (Ed.), *Classroom lessons: Integrating cognitive theory and classroom practice* (pp. 25–49). Cambridge, MA: Bradford.

Gringlas, M., & Weinraub, M. (1995). The more things change . . . single parenting revisited. *Journal of Family Issues, 16,* 29–52.

Grossmann, K. E., & Grossmann, K. (1990). The wider concept of attachment in cross-cultural research. *Human Development, 33,* 31–47.

Grotevant, H. D. (1992). Assigned and chosen identity components: A process perspective on their integration. In G. R. Adams, T. P. Gullotta, & R. Montemayor (Eds.), *Adolescent identity formation* (pp. 73–90). Newbury Park, CA: Sage.

Grotevant, H. D., & Cooper, C. R. (1985). Patterns of interaction in family relationships and the development of identity exploration in adolescence. *Child Development, 53,* 29–43.

Grueneich, R. (1982). Issues in the developmental study of how children use intention and consequence information to make moral evaluations. *Child Development, 53,* 29–43.

Grunwell, P. (1986). Aspects of phonological development in later childhood. In K. Durkin (Ed.), *Language development in the school years* (pp. 34–56). Cambridge, MA: Brookline Books.

Grusec, J. E. (1992). Social learning theory and developmental psychology: The legacies of Robert Sears and Albert Bandura. *Developmental Psychology, 28,* 776–786.

Grusec, J. E., & Goodnow, J. J. (1994). Impact of parental discipline methods on the child's internalization of values: A reconceptualization of current points of view. *Developmental Psychology, 30,* 4–19.

Grych, J. H., & Fincham, F. D. (1992). Interventions for children of divorce: Toward a greater integration of research and action. *Psychological Bulletin, 111,* 434–454.

Guerra, N. G., & Slaby, R. G. (1990). 1. Cognitive mediators of aggression in adolescent offenders. 2. Intervention. *Developmental Psychology, 26,* 269–277.

Gunnar, M. R., & Nelson, C. A. (1994). Event-related potentials in year-old infants: Relations with emotionality and cortisol. *Child Development, 65,* 80–94.

Gustafson, G. E., Green, J. A., & Cleland, J. W. (1994). Robustness of individual identity in the cries of human infants. *Developmental Psychobiology, 27,* 1–9.

Gustafson, G. E., & Harris, K. L. (1990). Women's responses to young infants' cries. *Developmental Psychology, 26,* 144–152.

Guttentag, R. E. (1984). The mental effort requirement of cumulative rehearsal: A developmental study. *Journal of Experimental Child Psychology, 37,* 92–106.

Guttmacher, A. F., & Kaiser, I. H. (1986). *Pregnancy, birth, and family planning.* New York: New American Library.

Hack, M., & Fanaroff, A. A. (1988). How small is too small? Considerations in evaluating the outcome of the tiny infant. *Clinics in Perinatology, 15,* 773–788.

Hagen, J. W., & Hale, J. A. (1973). The development of attention in children. In A. Pick (Ed.), *Minnesota Symposia on Child Psychology* (Vol. 7, pp. 117–140). Minneapolis, MN: University of Minnesota Press.

Haidt, J., Koller, S. H., & Dias, M. G. (1993). Affect, culture, and morality, or is it wrong to eat your dog? *Journal of Personality and Social Psychology, 65,* 613–628.

Hainline, L., & Abramov, I. (1992). Assessing visual development: Is infant vision good enough? *Advances in Infancy Research, 7,* 39–102.

Haith, M. M. (1980). *Rules that babies look by.* Hillsdale, NJ: Erlbaum.

Hakuta, K. (1986). *Mirror of language.* New York: Basic Books.

Hakuta, K. (1987). Degree of bilingualism and cognitive ability in mainland Puerto Rican children. *Child Development, 58,* 1372–1388.

Hale, S. (1990). A global developmental trend in cognitive processing speed in children. *Child Development, 61,* 653–663.

Halford, G. S., & Boyle, F. M. (1985). Do young children understand conservation of number? *Child Development, 56,* 165–176.

Hall, D. G., & Waxman, S. R. (1993). Assumptions about word meaning: Individuation and basic-level kinds. *Child Development, 64,* 1550–1570.

Hall, J. A., & Halberstadt, A. G. (1980). Masculinity and femininity in children: Development of the Children's Personal Attributes Questionnaire. *Developmental Psychology, 16,* 270–280.

Hallinan, M. T. (1994). School differences in tracking effects on achievement. *Social Forces, 72,* 799–820.

Halpern, D. F. (1992). *Sex differences in cognitive abilities* (2nd ed.). Hillsdale, NJ: Erlbaum.

Hamond, N. R., & Fivush, R. (1991). Memories of Mickey Mouse: Young children recount their trip to Disneyworld. *Cognitive Development, 6,* 433–448.

Hampson, J., & Nelson, K. (1993). The relation of maternal language to variation in rate and style of language acquisition. *Journal of Child Language, 20,* 313–342.

Hanson, D. R., Gottesman, I. I., & Heston, L. L. (1990). Long-range schizophrenia forecasting: Many a slip twixt cup and lip. In J. Rolf, A. S. Masten, D. Cicchetti, K. H. Neuchterlein, & S. Weinraub (Eds.), *Risk and protective factors in the development of psychopathology* (pp. 424–444). New York: Cambridge University Press.

Harkness, S. (1992). Cross-cultural research in child development: A sample of the state of the art. *Developmental Psychology, 28,* 622–625.

Harkness, S., Edwards, C. P., & Super, C. M. (1981). Social rule and moral reasoning: A case study in a rural African community. *Developmental Psychology, 17,* 595–603.

Harkness, S., & Super, C. M. (1985). The cultural context of gender segregation in children's peer groups. *Child Development, 56,* 219–224.

Harlow, H. F., & Mears, C. (1979). *The human model: Primate perspectives.* New York: Wiley.

Harlow, H. F., & Zimmerman, R. (1959). Affectional responses in the infant monkey. *Science, 130,* 421–432.

Harris, P. L. (1983). Infant cognition. In P. H. Mussen (Series Ed.), M. M. Haith & J. J. Campos (Vol. Eds.), *Handbook of child psychology: Vol. 2. Infancy and developmental psychobiology* (4th ed.). New York: Wiley.

Harris, P. L. (1986). The development of search. In P. Salapatek & L. B. Cohen (Eds.), *Handbook of infant perception* (Vol. 2, pp. 155–207). New York: Academic.

Harrison, A. O., Wilson, M. N., Pine, C. J., Chan, S. Q., & Buriel, R. (1990). Family ecologies of ethnic minority children. *Child Development, 61,* 347–362.

Hart, D. (1988). A longitudinal study of adolescents' socialization and identification as predictors of adult moral judgment development. *Merrill-Palmer Quarterly, 34,* 245–260.

Harter, S. (1982). The Perceived Competence Scale for Children. *Child Development, 53,* 87–97.

Harter, S. (1983). Developmental perspectives on the self-system. In

P. H. Mussen (Series Ed.) & E. M. Hetherington (Vol. Ed.), *Handbook of child psychology: Vol. 4. Socialization, personality, and social development* (pp. 275–385). New York: Wiley.

Harter, S. (1985). *Manual for the self-perception profile for children.* Denver, CO: University of Denver.

Harter, S. (1990). Self and identity development. In S. S. Feldman & G. R. Elliott (Eds.), *At the threshold: The developing adolescent* (pp. 352–387). Cambridge, MA: Harvard University Press.

Harter, S., & Monsour, A. (1992). Developmental analysis of conflict caused by opposing attributes in the adolescent self-portrait. *Developmental Psychology, 28,* 251–260.

Harter, S., & Pike, R. (1984). The pictorial scale of perceived competence and social acceptance for young children. *Child Development, 55,* 1969–1982.

Harter, S., Whitesell, N. R., & Kowalski, P. S. (1992). Individual differences in the effects of educational transitions on young adolescents' perceptions of competence and motivational orientation. *American Educational Research Journal, 29,* 777–807.

Hartshorne, H., & May, M. A. (1928–1930). *Studies in deceit* (Vol. 1). *Studies in service and self-control* (Vol. 2). *Studies in the nature of character* (Vol. 3). New York: Macmillan.

Hartup, W. W. (1970). Peer interaction and social organization. In P. H. Mussen (Ed.), *Carmichael's manual of child psychology* (3rd ed., pp. 361–456). New York: Wiley.

Hartup, W. W. (1974). Aggression in childhood: Developmental perspectives. *American Psychologist, 29,* 336–341.

Hartup, W. W. (1983). Peer relations. In P. H. Mussen (Series Ed.) & E. M. Hetherington (Vol. Ed.), *Handbook of child psychology: Vol. 4. Socialization, personality, and social development* (pp. 103–196). New York: Wiley.

Hartup, W. W. (1984). The peer context in middle childhood. In W. A. Collins (Ed.), *Development during middle childhood* (pp. 240–282). Washington, DC: National Academy Press.

Hartup, W. W. (1992). Friendships and their developmental significance. In H. McGurk (Ed.), *Contemporary issues in childhood social development.* Hove, England: Erlbaum.

Hartup, W. W. (1993). Conflict and friendship relations. In C. U. Shantz & W. W. Hartup (Eds.), *Conflict in child and adolescent development* (pp. 186–215). Cambridge, England: Cambridge University Press.

Hartup, W. W., French, D. C., Laursen, B., Johnston, M. K., & Ogawa, J. R.

(1993). Conflict and friendship relations in middle childhood: Behavior in a closed-field situation. *Child Development, 64,* 445–454.

Hartup, W. W., Laursen, B., Stewart, M. I., & Eastenson, A. (1988). Conflict and the friendship relations of young children. *Child Development, 59,* 1590–1600.

Haskins, R. (1985). Public school aggression among children with varying day-care experience. *Child Development, 56,* 689–703.

Hatano, G., & Inagaki, K. (1994). Young children's naive theory of biology. *Cognition, 50,* 171–188.

Hatano, G., Siegler, R. S., Richards, D. D., Inagaki, K., Stavy, R., & Wax, N. (1993). The development of biological knowledge: A multi-national study. *Cognitive Development, 8,* 47–62.

Hauser, R. M. (1995). [Review of the book *The bell curve*]. *Contemporary Sociology, 24,* 149–153.

Hauser, S. T., Powers, S. I., Noam, G. G., Jacobson, A. M., Weiss, B., & Follansbee, D. J. (1984). Familial contexts of adolescent ego development. *Child Development, 55,* 195–213.

Hauth, J. C., Goldenberg, R. L., Parker, C. R., Jr., Phillips, J. B., Copper, R. L., DuBard, M. B., & Cutter, G. R. (1993). Low-dose aspirin therapy to prevent preeclampsia. *American Journal of Obstetrics and Gynecology, 168,* 1083–1091.

Haviland, J. M., & Lelwica, M. (1987). The induced affect response: 10-week-old infants' responses to three emotion expressions. *Developmental Psychology, 23,* 97–104.

Hawkins, J. D., Catalano, R. F., Morrison, D. M., O'Donnell, J., Abbott, R. D., & Day, L. E. (1992). The Seattle Social Development Project: Effects of the first four years on protective factors and problem behaviors. In J. McCord & R. Tremblay (Eds.), *The prevention of antisocial behavior in children* (pp. 140–161). New York: Guilford.

Hay, D. F. (1979). Cooperative interactions and sharing between very young children and their parents. *Developmental Psychology, 15,* 647–653.

Hay, D. F., & Ross, H. S. (1982). The social nature of early conflict. *Child Development, 53,* 105–113.

Hayes, D. P., & Ahrens, M. G. (1988). Vocabulary simplification for children: A special case of 'motherese'? *Journal of Child Language, 15,* 395–410.

Hebb, D. O. (1949). *The organization of behavior.* New York: Wiley.

Hecox, K. (1975). Electrophysiological correlates of human auditory development. In L. B. Cohen & P. Salapatek (Eds.), *Infant perception: From sensation to cognition. Vol. 2. Perception of*

space, speech and sound (pp. 151–191). Orlando, FL: Academic.

Heibeck, T. H., & Markman, E. M. (1987). Word learning in children: An examination of fast mapping. *Child Development, 58,* 1021–1034.

Heller, K. A., & Berndt, T. J. (1981). Developmental changes in the formation and organization of personality attributions. *Child Development, 52,* 683–691.

Henry, L. A., & Millar, S. (1991). Memory span increase with age: A test of two hypotheses. *Journal of Experimental Child Psychology, 51,* 459–484.

Herrnstein, R. J., & Murray, C. A. (1994). *The bell curve: Intelligence and class structure in American life.* New York: Free Press.

Hess, R. D., & Holloway, S. D. (1984). Family and school as educational institutions. *Review of Child Development Research, 7,* 179–222.

Hestenes, S. L., Berndt, T. J., & Gruen, G. E. (1995). *The development of trust in adolescent friendships.* Unpublished manuscript, Purdue University.

Hetherington, E. M. (1972). Effects of father absence on personality development in adolescent daughters. *Developmental Psychology, 7,* 313–326.

Hetherington, E. M. (1988). Family relations six years after divorce. In K. Pasley & M. Ihinger-Tallman (Eds.), *Remarriage and stepparenting: Current research and theory* (pp. 185–205). New York: Guilford.

Hetherington, E. M. (1989). Coping with family transitions: Winners, losers, and survivors. *Child Development, 60,* 1–14.

Hetherington, E. M. (1991). Presidential address: Families, lies, and videotapes. *Journal of Research on Adolescence, 1,* 323–348.

Hetherington, E. M., & Arasteh, J. D. (Eds.). (1988). *Impact of divorce, single parenting, and stepparenting on children.* Hillsdale, NJ: Erlbaum.

Hetherington, E. M., & Clingempeel, W. G. (1992). Coping with marital transitions: A family-systems perspective. *Monographs of the Society for Research in Child Development, 57* (2–3, Serial No. 227).

Hetherington. E. M., Cox, M., & Cox, R. (1982). Effects of divorce on parents and children. In M. E. Lamb (Ed.), *Nontraditional families* (pp. 233–288). Hillsdale, NJ: Erlbaum.

Heyman, G. D., Dweck, C. S., & Cain, K. M. (1992). Young children's vulnerability to self-blame and helplessness: Relationship to beliefs about goodness. *Child Development, 63,* 401–415.

Higgins, A. (1991). The Just Community approach to moral education: Evolution of the idea and recent findings. In W. M. Kurtines & J. L. Gewirtz (Eds.),

*Handbook of moral behavior and development,*
*Vol. 3: Application* (pp. 111–141).
Hillsdale, NJ: Erlbaum.

Higley, J. D., Hopkins, W. D., Thompson,
W. W., Byrne, E. A., Hirsch, R. M., &
Suomi, S. J. (1992). Peers as primary
attachment sources in yearling rhesus
monkeys (Macaca mulatta). *Developmental
Psychology, 28,* 1163–1171.

Hill, J. P., & Lynch, M. E. (1983). The
intensification of gender-related role
expectations during early adolescence.
In J. Brooks-Gunn & A. C. Petersen,
*Girls at puberty* (pp. 201–228). New York:
Plenum.

Hinde, R. A. (1987). *Individuals, relationships,
and culture.* Cambridge, England:
Cambridge University Press.

Hines, M. (1982). Prenatal gonadal
hormones and sex differences in human
behavior. *Psychological Bulletin, 92,* 56–80.

Hines, M., & Kaufman, F. R. (1994).
Androgen and the development of
human sex-typical behavior: Rough-and-
tumble play and sex of preferred
playmates in children with congenital
adrenal hyperplasia (CAH). *Child
Development, 65,* 1042–1053.

Hirsch, B. J., & Rapkin, B. D. (1987). The
transition to junior high school: A
longitudinal study of self-esteem,
psychological symptomatology, school
life, and social support. *Child Development,
58,* 1235–1243.

Hirsch, H. V. B., & Tieman, S. B. (1987).
Perceptual development and
experience-dependent changes in cat
visual cortex. In M. H. Bornstein (Ed.),
*Sensitive periods in development:
Interdisciplinary perspectives* (pp. 39–80).
Hillsdale, NJ: Erlbaum.

Hiscock, M., & Kinsbourne, M. (1995).
Phylogeny and ontogeny of cerebral
lateralization. In R. J. Davidson &
K. Hugdahl (Eds.), *Brain asymmetry*
(pp. 535–578). Cambridge, MA: MIT
Press.

Hoff-Ginsberg, E. (1986). Function and
structure in maternal speech: Their
relation to the child's development of
syntax. *Developmental Psychology, 22,*
155–163.

Hoffer, T. B., Rasinski, K. A., & Moore, W.
(1995). *Social background differences in high
school mathematics and science coursetaking
and achievement.* National Center for
Educational Statistics (NCES 95-206).
Washington, DC: U.S. Department of
Education.

Hoffman, L. W. (1974). Effects of maternal
employment on the child — A review of
the research. *Developmental Psychology, 10,*
204–228.

Hoffman, L. W. (1977). Changes in family
roles, socialization, and sex differences.
*American Psychologist, 32,* 644–657.

Hoffman, L. W. (1979). Maternal
employment: 1979. *American Psychologist,
54,* 859–865.

Hoffman, L. W. (1989). Effects of maternal
employment in the two-parent family.
*American Psychologist, 44,* 283–292.

Hoffman, L. W. (1991). The influence of the
family environment on personality:
Accounting for sibling differences.
*Psychological Bulletin, 110,* 187–203.

Hoffman, M. L. (1970). Moral development.
In P. H. Mussen (Ed.), *Carmichael's
manual of child psychology* (3rd ed., Vol. 2,
pp. 261–359). New York: Wiley.

Hoffman, M. L. (1983). Affective and
cognitive processes in moral
internalization. In E. T. Higgins,
D. N. Ruble, & W. W. Hartup (Eds.),
*Social cognition and social development*
(pp. 236–274). Cambridge, England:
Cambridge University Press.

Hoffman, M. L. (1988). Moral development.
In M. H. Bornstein & M. E. Lamb
(Eds.), *Developmental psychology: An
advanced textbook* (2nd ed., pp. 497–548).
Hillsdale, NJ: Erlbaum.

Hoffman, M. L., & Saltzstein, H. D. (1967).
Parent discipline and the child's moral
development. *Journal of Personality and
Social Psychology, 5,* 45–47.

Hofsten, C. von. (1984). Eye-hand
coordination in the newborn.
*Developmental Psychology, 18,* 450–461.

Hofsten, C. von. (1989). Motor
development as the development of
systems: Comments on the special
section. *Developmental Psychology, 25,*
950–953.

Hoge, D. D., Smit, E. K., & Hanson, S. L.
(1990). School experiences predicting
changes in self-esteem of sixth- and
seventh-grade students. *Journal of
Educational Psychology, 82,* 117–127.

Hoge, R. D., & Renzulli, J. S. (1993).
Exploring the link between giftedness
and self-concept. *Review of Educational
Research, 63,* 449–465.

Hogrefe, G. J., Wimmer, H., & Perner, J.
(1986). Ignorance versus false belief: A
developmental lag in attribution of
epistemic states. *Child Development, 57,*
567–582.

Holden, G. W. (1983). Avoiding conflict:
Mothers as tacticians in the supermarket.
*Child Development, 54,* 233–240.

Holmbeck, G. N., & Hill, J. P. (1991). Con-
flictive engagement, positive affect, and
menarche in families with seventh-grade
girls. *Child Development, 62,* 1030–1048.

Holmes, L. B. (1994). Scope of the problem.
In C. A. Kimmel & J. Buelke-Sam
(Eds.), *Developmental toxicology*
(pp. 3–12). New York: Raven.

Holt, L. H. (1988). Medical perspectives on
pregnancy and birth: Biological risks and
technological advances. In G. Y.

Michaels & W. A. Goldberg (Eds.), *The
transition to parenthood: Current theory and
research* (pp. 157–175). New York:
Cambridge University Press.

Hood, K. E., Draper, P., Crockett, L. J., &
Petersen, A. C. (1987). The ontogeny
and phylogeny of sex differences in
development: A biopsychosocial
synthesis. In D. B. Carter (Ed.), *Current
conceptions of sex roles and sex typing*
(pp. 49–78). New York: Praeger.

Hopkins, B., Beek, P. J., & Kalverboer,
A. F. (1993). Theoretical issues in the
longitudinal study of motor development.
In A. F. Kalverboer, B. Hopkins, &
R. H. Geuze (Eds.), *Motor development in
early and later childhood: Longitudinal
approaches* (pp. 343–371). New York:
Cambridge University Press.

Hopkins, B., & Westra, T. (1990). Motor
development, maternal expectations, and
the role of handling. *Infant Behavior and
Development, 13,* 117–122.

Horgan, J. (1993, June). Eugenics
revisited. *Scientific American, 268,* 122–131.

Horn, J. L. (1985). Remodeling old models
of intelligence. In B. B. Wolman (Ed.),
*Handbook of intelligence* (pp. 267–300).
New York: Wiley.

Horn, J. L., & Cattell, R. B. (1982).
Whimsy and misunderstandings of Gf-
Gc theory: A comment on Guilford.
*Psychological Bulletin, 91,* 623–633.

Horn, J. L., & Hofer, S. M. (1992). Major
abilities and development in the adult
period. In R. J. Sternberg & C. A. Berg
(Eds.), *Intellectual development*
(pp. 44–99). Cambridge, England:
Cambridge University Press.

Horn, J. M. (1983). The Texas adoption
project: Adopted children and their
intellectual resemblance to biological and
adoptive parents. *Child Development, 54,*
268–275.

Horowitz, R., & Schwartz, G. (1974).
Honor, normative ambiguity, and gang
violence. *American Sociological Review, 39,*
238–251.

Hossain, Z., & Roopnarine, J. L. (1994).
African American fathers' involvement
with infants: Relationship to their functioning style, support, education, and
income. *Infant Behavior and Development,
17,* 175–184.

Howe, M. L., & Courage, M. L. (1993). On
resolving the enigma of infantile amnesia.
*Psychological Bulletin, 113,* 305–326.

Howes, C. (1980). Peer play scale as an
index of complexity of peer interaction.
*Developmental Psychology, 16,* 371–372.

Howes, C. (1983). Patterns of friendship.
*Child Development, 54,* 1041–1053.

Howes, C. (1987). Social competence with
peers in young children: Developmental
sequences. *Developmental Review, 7,*
252–272.

Howes, C. (1988). Peer interaction of young children. *Monographs of the Society for Research in Child Development, 53* (1, Serial No. 217).

Howes, C. (1990). Social status and friendship from kindergarten to third grade. *Journal of Applied Developmental Psychology, 11,* 321–330.

Howes, C., & Hamilton, C. E. (1992a). Children's relationships with caregivers: Mothers and child-care teachers. *Child Development, 63,* 867–878.

Howes, C., & Hamilton, C. E. (1992b). Children's relationships with child-care teachers: Stability and concordance with parental attachments. *Child Development, 63,* 867–878.

Howes, C., & Matheson, C. C. (1992). Sequences in the development of competent play with peers: Social and social pretend play. *Developmental Psychology, 28,* 961–974.

Howes, C., Matheson, C. C., & Hamilton, C. E. (1994). Maternal, teacher, and child-care history correlates of children's relationships with peers. *Child Development, 65,* 264–273.

Howes, C., & Olenick, M. (1986). Family and child-care influences on toddlers' compliance. *Child Development, 57,* 202–206.

Howes, C., & Stewart, P. (1987). Child's play with adults, toys, and peers: An examination of family and child-care influences. *Developmental Psychology, 23,* 423–430.

Howes, C., Unger, O., & Seidner, L. B. (1989). Social pretend play in toddlers: Parallels with social play and with solitary pretend. *Child Development, 60,* 77–84.

Howlin, P., & Yule, W. (1990). Taxonomy of major disorders in childhood. In M. Lewis & S. M. Miller (Eds.), *Handbook of developmental psychopathology* (pp. 371–384). New York: Plenum.

Hoy, E. A., Bill, J. M., & Sykes, D. H. (1988). Very low birthweight: A long-term developmental impairment? *International Journal of Behavioral Development, 11,* 37–67.

Hronsky, S. L., & Emory, E. K. (1987). Neurobehavioral effects of caffeine on the neonate. *Infant Behavior and Development, 10,* 61–80.

Hudley, C., & Graham, S. (1993). An attributional intervention to reduce peer-directed aggression among African-American boys. *Child Development, 64,* 124–138.

Hudson, L. M., Forman, E. A., & Brion-Meisels, S. (1982). Role taking as a predictor of prosocial behavior in cross-age tutors. *Child Development, 53,* 1320–1329.

Huebner, A. M., & Garrod, A. C. (1993). Moral reasoning among Tibetan monks: A study of Buddhist adolescents and young adults in Nepal. *Journal of Cross Cultural Psychology, 24,* 167–185.

Huesmann, L. R., Eron, L. D., Lefkowitz, M. M., & Walder, L. O. (1984). Stability of aggression over time and generations. *Developmental Psychology, 20,* 1120–1134.

Hughes, L. A. (1988). "But that's not *really* mean": Competing in a cooperative mode. *Sex Roles, 19,* 669–688.

Hunt, C. E., & Brouliette, R. T. (1987). Sudden infant death syndrome: 1987 perspective. *Journal of Pediatrics, 110,* 669–678.

Huston, A. C. (1983). Sex-typing. In P. H. Mussen (Series Ed.) & E. M. Hetherington (Vol. Ed.), *Handbook of child psychology: Vol. 4. Socialization, personality, and social development* (4th ed., pp. 387–468). New York: Wiley.

Huston, A. C., Donnerstein, E., Fairchild, H., Feshbach, N. D., Katz, P. A., Murray, J. P., Rubinstein, E. A., Wilcox, B. L., & Zuckerman, D. (1992). *Big world, small screen: The role of television in American society.* Lincoln, NE: University of Nebraska Press.

Hyde, J. S. (1984). How large are gender differences in aggression? A developmental meta-analysis. *Developmental Psychology, 20,* 722–736.

Hyde, J. S., Fennema, E., & Lamon, S. J. (1990). Gender differences in mathematics performance: A meta-analysis. *Psychological Bulletin, 107,* 139–155.

Hyde, J. S., & Linn, M. C. (1988). Gender differences in verbal ability: A meta-analysis. *Psychological Bulletin, 104* (1), 53–69.

Hyde, J. S., & Plant, E. A. (1995). Magnitude of psychological gender differences: Another side to the story. *American Psychologist, 50,* 145–158.

Hymel, S., Bowker, A., & Woody, E. (1993). Aggressive versus withdrawn unpopular children: Variations in peer and self-perceptions in multiple domains. *Child Development, 64,* 879–896.

Hymel, S., Wagner, E., & Butler, L. J. (1990). Reputational bias: View from the peer group. In S. R. Asher & J. D. Coie (Eds.), *Peer rejection in childhood* (pp. 156–188). Cambridge, England: Cambridge University Press.

Iannotti, R. J. (1985). Naturalistic assessment of prosocial behavior in preschool children: The influence of empathy and perspective taking. *Developmental Psychology, 21,* 46–55.

Inagaki, K. (1992). Piagetian and post-Piagetian conceptions of development and their implications for science education in early childhood. *Early Childhood Research Quarterly, 7,* 115–133.

Inhelder, B., & Piaget, J. (1958). *The growth of logical thinking from childhood to adolescence.* New York: Basic.

Inhelder, B., & Piaget, J. (1964). *The early growth of logic in the child.* New York: W. W. Norton.

Institute of Medicine. (1990). *Nutrition during pregnancy.* Washington, DC: National Academy Press.

Intons-Peterson, M. J. (1988). *Gender concepts of Swedish and American youth.* Hillsdale, NJ: Erlbaum.

Isabella, R. A. (1993). Origins of attachment: Maternal interactive behavior across the first year. *Child Development, 64,* 605–621.

Isada, N. B., & Grossman, J. H., III. (1991). Perinatal infections. In S. G. Gabbe, J. R. Niebyl, & J. L. Simpson (Eds.), *Obstetrics: Normal and problem pregnancies* (2nd ed., pp. 1223–1299). New York: Churchill Livingstone.

Iyasu, S., Hanzlick, R., Rowley, D., & Willinger, M. (1994). Proceedings of "workshop on guidelines for scene investigation of sudden unexplained infant deaths" *Journal of Forensic Science, 39,* 1126–1136.

Izard, C. E. (1991). *The psychology of emotions.* New York: Plenum.

Izard, C. E. (1994). Innate and universal facial expressions: Evidence from developmental and cross-cultural research. *Psychological Bulletin, 115,* 288–299.

Izard, C. E., Hembree, E. A., & Huebner, R. R. (1987). Infants' emotion expressions to acute pain: Developmental change and stability of individual differences. *Developmental Psychology, 23,* 105–113.

Izard, C. E., & Malatesta, C. Z. (1987). Perspectives on emotional development I: Differential emotions theory of early emotional development. In J. D. Osofsky (Ed.), *Handbook of infant development* (pp. 494–554). New York: Wiley.

Jacklin, C. N. (1989). Female and male: Issues of gender. *American Psychologist, 44,* 127–133.

Jackson, J. F. (1993). Human behavioral genetics, Scarr's theory, and her views on interventions: A critical review and commentary on their implications for African American children. *Child Development, 64,* 1318–1332.

Jacobson, J. L., & Jacobson, S. W. (1994). The effects of perinatal exposure to polychlorinated biphenyls and related contaminants. In H. L. Needleman & D. Bellinger (Eds.), *Prenatal exposure to toxicants: Developmental consequences* (pp. 130–147). Baltimore, MD: Johns Hopkins University Press.

Jacobson, J. L., Jacobson, S. W., Fein, G. G., Schwartz, P. M., & Fowler, J. K.

(1984). Prenatal exposure to an environmental toxin: A test of the multiple effects model. *Developmental Psychology, 20,* 523–532.

Jacobson, S. W., Fein, G. G., Jacobson, J. L., Schwartz, P. M., & Fowler, J. K. (1985). The effect of intrauterine PCB exposure on visual recognition memory. *Child Development, 56,* 853–860.

Jacoby, R., & Glauberman, N. (Eds.). (1995). *The bell curve debate: History, documents, opinions.* New York: Times Book.

Jadack, R. A., Hyde, J. S., Moore, C. F., & Keller, M. L. (1995). Moral reasoning about sexually transmitted diseases. *Child Development, 66,* 167–177.

James, W. (1890). *The principles of psychology.* New York: Dover Publications.

Jaroff, L. (1989, March 20). The gene hunt. *Time,* 62–67.

Jennings, K. D. (1993). Mastery motivation and the formation of self-concept from infancy through early childhood. In D. Messer (Ed.), *Mastery motivation in early childhood: Development, measurement and social processes* (pp. 36–54). New York: Routledge.

Jensen, A. R. (1969). How much can we boost IQ and scholastic achievement? *Harvard Educational Review, 39,* 1–123.

Jiao, S., Ji, G., & Jing, Q. (1986). Comparative study of behavioral qualities of only children and sibling children. *Child Development, 57,* 357–361.

Johnson, B. M., Shulman, S., & Collins, W. A. (1991). Systemic patterns of parenting as reported by adolescents: Developmental differences and implications for psychosocial outcomes. *Journal of Adolescent Research, 6,* 235–252.

Johnson, C. N., & Wellman, H. M. (1982). Children's developing conceptions of the mind and brain. *Child Development, 53,* 222–234.

Johnston, F. E. (1986). Somatic growth of the infant and preschool child. In F. Falkner & J. M. Tanner (Eds.), *Human growth: A comprehensive treatise* (pp. 3–24). New York: Plenum Press.

Jones, L. V. (1984). White-black achievement differences: The narrowing gap. *American Psychologist, 39,* 1207–1213.

Jones, S. S., & Smith, L. B. (1993). The place of perception in children's concepts. *Cognitive Development, 8,* 113–139.

Jonsson, U. (1994). Millions lost to wrong strategies. In United Nations Children's Fund, *The progress of nations 1994* (pp. 7–21). New York: UNICEF.

Joos, S. K., Pollitt, E., Mueller, W. H., & Albright, D. L. (1983). The Bacon Chow study: Maternal nutritional supplementation and infant behavioral development. *Child Development, 54,* 669–676.

Jordan, B. (1978). *Birth in four cultures: A cross-cultural investigation of childbirth in Yucatan, Holland, Sweden, and the United States.* Montreal, Canada: Eden Press.

Jusczyk, P. W. (1993). From general to language-specific capacities: The WRAPSA model of how speech perception develops. *Journal of Phonetics, 21,* 3–28.

Jusczyk, P. W., Friederici, A. D., Wessels, J. M., Svenkerud, V. Y., & Jusczyk, A. M. (1993). Infants' sensitivity to the sound patterns of native language words. *Journal of Memory and Language, 32,* 402–420.

Jusczyk, P. W., Luce, P. A., & Charles-Luce, J. (1994). Infants' sensitivity to phonotactic patterns in the native language. *Journal of Memory and Language, 33,* 630–645.

Justice, E. M. (1985). Categorization as preferred memory strategy: Developmental changes during elementary school. *Developmental Psychology, 21,* 1105–1110.

Kagan, J. (1984). *The nature of the child.* New York: Basic.

Kagan, J. (1989). Temperamental contributions to social behavior. *American Psychologist, 44,* 668–674.

Kagan, J., Arcus, D., & Snidman, N. (1993). The idea of temperament: Where do we go from here? In R. Plomin & G. E. McClearn (Eds.), *Nature, nurture, and psychology* (pp. 197–210). Washington, DC: American Psychological Association.

Kagan, J., Kearsley, R. B., & Zelazo, P. R. (1978). *Infancy: Its place in human development.* Cambridge, MA: Harvard University Press.

Kagan, J., & Klein, R. E. (1973). Cross-cultural perspectives on early development. *American Psychologist, 28,* 947–961.

Kagan, J., Klein, R. E., Finley, G. E., Rogoff, B., & Nolan, E. (1979). A cross-cultural study of cognitive development. *Monographs of the Society for Research in Child Development, 44* (5, Serial No. 180).

Kagan, J., & Moss, H. A. (1962). *Birth to maturity: A study in psychological development.* New York: Wiley.

Kagan, J., Reznick, J. S., Clarke, C., Snidman, N., & Garcia-Coll, C. (1984). Behavioral inhibition to the unfamiliar. *Child Development, 55,* 2212–2225.

Kagan, J., Reznick, J. S., Snidman, N., Gibbons, J., & Johnson, M. O. (1988). Childhood derivatives of inhibition and lack of inhibition to the unfamiliar. *Child Development, 59,* 1580–1589.

Kagan, J., Rosman, B. L., Day, D., Albert, J., & Phillips, W. (1964). Information processing in the child: Significance of analytic and reflective attitudes.

*Psychological Monographs* (Whole No. 578).

Kagan, S., & Madsen, M. C. (1971). Cooperation and competition of Mexican, Mexican-American and Anglo-American children of two ages under four instructional sets. *Developmental Psychology, 5,* 32–39.

Kagan, S., & Madsen, M. C. (1972). Rivalry in Anglo-American and Mexican-American children of two ages. *Journal of Personality and Social Psychology, 24,* 214–220.

Kahn, P. H. (1992). Children's obligatory and discretionary moral judgments. *Child Development, 63,* 416–430.

Kail, R. (1986). Sources of age differences in speed of processing. *Child Development, 57,* 969–987.

Kail, R. (1988). Developmental functions for speeds of cognitive processes. *Journal of Experimental Child Psychology, 42,* 378–391.

Kail, R. (1990). *The development of memory in children* (3rd ed.). New York: Freeman.

Kail, R. (1991). Developmental change in speed of processing during childhood and adolescence. *Psychological Bulletin, 109,* 490–501.

Kail, R. (1993). The role of a global mechanism in developmental change in speed of processing. In M. L. Howe & R. Pasnak (Ed.), *Emerging themes in cognitive development* (Vol. II, pp. 97–119). New York: Springer-Verlag.

Kail, R., & Hall, L. K. (1994). Processing speed, naming speed, and reading. *Developmental Psychology, 30,* 949–954.

Kail, R., & Park, Y. (1994). Processing time, articulation time, and memory span. *Journal of Experimental Child Psychology, 57,* 281–291.

Kamii, C., & Clark, F. B. (1993). Autonomy: The importance of a scientific theory in education reform. *Learning and Individual Differences, 5,* 327–340.

Kamii, C., & DeVries, R. (1978). *Physical knowledge in preschool education: Implications of Piaget's theory.* Englewood Cliffs, NJ: Prentice-Hall.

Kamii, C., & Joseph, L. L. (1989). *Young children continue to reinvent arithmetic—2nd grade: Implications of Piaget's theory.* New York: Teachers College Press.

Kamin, L. (1995, February). Behind the curve [Review of the book *The bell curve*]. *Scientific American, 272,* 99–103.

Kamphaus, R. W., Benson, J., Hutchinson, S., & Platt, L. O. (1994). Identification of factor models for the WISC-III. *Educational and Psychological Measurement, 54,* 174–186.

Kandel, D. B., & Lesser, G. S. (1972). *Youth in two worlds.* San Francisco: Jossey-Bass.

Kaplan, H., & Dove, H. (1987). Infant development among the Ache of eastern

Paraguay. *Developmental Psychology, 23,* 190–198.

Kaplan, R. M. (1985). The controversy related to the use of psychological tests. In B. B. Wolman (Ed.), *Handbook of intelligence* (pp. 465–504). New York: Wiley.

Karniol, R. (1978). Children's use of intention cues in evaluating behavior. *Psychological Bulletin, 85,* 76–85.

Karraker, K. H., & Stern, M. (1990). Infant physical attractiveness and facial expression: Effects on adult perceptions. *Basic and Applied Social Psychology, 11,* 371–385.

Kattwinkel, J., Brooks, J., Keenan, M. E., & Malloy, M. (1994). Infant sleep position and sudden infant death syndrome (SIDS) in the United States: Joint commentary from the American Academy of Pediatrics and selected agencies of the federal government. *Pediatrics, 93,* 820.

Katz, K. S. (1978). Inherited disorders: Down syndrome and phenylketonuria. In P. R. Magrab (Ed.), *Psychological management of pediatric problems. Vol. 1. Early life conditions and chronic diseases* (pp. 89–128). Baltimore, MD: University Park Press.

Katz, P. A., & Ksansnak, K. R. (1994). Developmental aspects of gender role flexibility and traditionality in middle childhood and adolescence. *Developmental Psychology, 30,* 272–282.

Katz, P. A., & Walsh, P. V. (1991). Modification of children's gender-stereotyped behavior. *Child Development, 62,* 338–351.

Katzman, M. A., & Karoly, P. (1988). Strengthening marital relationships via communication training: A critical review of competency-based, preventive interventions. In S. A. Wolchik & P. Karoly (Eds.), *Children of divorce* (pp. 323–367). New York: Gardner Press.

Kaufman, A. S., & Kaufman, N. L. (1983). *Kaufman assessment battery for children: Administration and scoring manual.* Circle Pines, MN: American Guidance Service.

Kaufman, J., & Zigler, E. (1989). The intergenerational transmission of child abuse. In D. Cicchetti and V. Carlson (Eds.), *Child maltreatment: Theory and research on the causes and consequences of child abuse and neglect* (pp. 129–151). New York: Cambridge University Press.

Kazdin, A. E. (1987). Treatment of antisocial behavior in children: Current status and future directions. *Psychological Bulletin, 102,* 187–203.

Kearins, J. M. (1981). Visual spatial memory of Australian aboriginal children of desert regions. *Cognitive Psychology, 13,* 434–460.

Keasey, C. B. (1971). Social participation as a factor in the moral development of preadolescents. *Developmental Psychology, 5,* 216–220.

Keasey, C. B. (1978). Children's developing awareness and usage of intentionality and motives. In H. E. Howe, Jr. (Series Ed.) & C. B. Keasey (Vol. Ed.), *1977 Nebraska symposium on motivation* (pp. 219–260). Lincoln, NE: University of Nebraska Press.

Keating, D. (1990). Adolescent thinking. In S. S. Feldman & G. Elliott (Eds.), *At the threshold: The developing adolescent* (pp. 54–89). Cambridge, MA: Harvard University Press.

Keefe, K. (1994). Perceptions of normative social pressure and attitudes toward alcohol use: Changes during adolescence. *Journal of Studies on Alcohol, 55,* 46–54.

Keefe, K., & Berndt, T. J. (1996). Relations of friendship quality to self-esteem in early adolescence. *Journal of Early Adolescence, 16,* 110–129.

Keenan, T., Ruffman, T., & Olson, D. R. (1994). When do children begin to understand logical inference as a source of knowledge? *Cognitive Development, 9,* 331–353.

Keeney, T. J., Cannizzo, S. R., & Flavell, J. H. (1967). Spontaneous and induced verbal rehearsal in a recall task. *Child Development, 38,* 953–966.

Keil, F. C. (1989). *Concepts, kinds, and cognitive development.* Cambridge, MA: MIT Press.

Keller, A., Ford, L. H., & Meacham, J. A. (1978). Dimensions of self-concept in preschool children. *Developmental Psychology, 14,* 483–489.

Keller, H. (1965). *Helen Keller: The story of my life.* New York: Airmont Publishing.

Keller, H., & Scholmerich, A. (1987). Infant vocalizations and parental reactions during the first 4 months of life. *Developmental Psychology, 23,* 62–67.

Kellman, P. J., Spelke, E. S., & Short, K. R. (1986). Infant perception of object unity from translatory motion in depth and vertical translation. *Child Development, 57,* 72–86.

Kemler Nelson, D. G., Hirsh-Pasek, K., Jusczyk, P. W., & Cassidy, K. W. (1989). How the prosodic cues in motherese might assist language learning. *Journal of Child Language, 16,* 55–68.

Kempe, C. H., Silverman, B. F., Steele, P. W., Droegemueller, P. W., & Silver, H. K. (1962). The battered-child syndrome. *Journal of the American Medical Association, 181,* 17–24.

Kennell, J. H., & Klaus, M. H. (1988). The perinatal paradigm: Is it time for a change? *Clinics in Perinatology, 15,* 01–813.

Kerlinger, F. N. (1986). *Foundations of behavioral research* (3rd ed.). New York: Holt, Rinehart & Winston.

Kern M., Lambert, W. W., & Stattin, H. (1994). Stability of inhibition in a Swedish longitudinal sample. *Child Development, 65,* 128–146.

Kerr, M., Lambert, W. W., Stattin, H., & Klackenberg-Larsson, I. (1994). Stability of inhibition in a Swedish longitudinal sample. *Child Development, 65,* 138–146.

Kessler, J. W. (1988). *Psychopathology of childhood* (2nd ed.). Englewood Cliffs, NJ: Prentice-Hall.

Kiely, J. L., Kleinman, J. C., & Kiely, M. (1992). Triplets and higher-order multiple births: Time trends and infant mortality. *American Journal of Diseases of Children, 146,* 862–868.

Kimmel, D. C., & Weiner, I. B. (1995). *Adolescence: A developmental transition* (2nd ed.). New York: Wiley.

Kinsbourne, M., & Hiscock, M. (1983). The normal and deviant development of functional lateralization of the brain. In M. M. Haith & J. J. Campos (Eds.), *Handbook of child psychology: Vol II. Infancy and developmental psychobiology* (pp. 157–280). New York: Wiley.

Kirkland, R. T. (1994). Failure to thrive. In F. A. Oski, C. D. DeAngelis, R. D. Feigin, J. A. McMillan, & J. B. Warshaw (Eds.), *Principles and practices of pediatrics* (2nd ed., pp. 1048–1051). Philadelphia: Lippincott.

Klahr, D. (1989). Information-processing approaches to cognitive development. In R. Vasta (Ed.), *Annals of child development* (Vol. 6, pp. 133–185). Greenwich, CT: JAI Press.

Klahr, D. (1992). Information-processing approaches to cognitive development. In M. H. Bornstein & M. E. Lamb (Eds.), *Developmental psychology: An advanced textbook* (pp. 273–335). Hillsdale, NJ: Erlbaum.

Klaus, M. H., & Klaus, P. H. (1985). *The amazing newborn.* Reading, MA: Addison-Wesley.

Kline, M., Tschann, J. M., Johnston, J. R., & Wallerstein, J. S. (1989). Children's adjustment in joint and sole physical custody families. *Developmental Psychology, 25,* 430–438.

Klinnert, M. D., Emde, R. N., Butterfield, P., & Campos, J. J. (1986). Social referencing: The infant's use of emotional signals from a friendly adult with mother present. *Developmental Psychology, 22,* 427–432.

Klonoff-Cohen, H. S., Edelstein, S. L., Lefkowitz, E. S., Srinivasan, I. P., Kaegi, D., Chang, J. C., & Wiley, K. J. (1995). The effect of passive smoking and tobacco exposure through breast milk on sudden infant death syndrome. *Journal of the American Medical Association, 273,* 795–798.

Knight, G. P., & Kagan, S. (1977). Development of prosocial and competitive behaviors in Anglo-American and Mexican-American children. *Child Development, 48,* 1385–1394.

Knight, G. P., Tein, J. Y., Shell, R., & Roosa, M. (1992). The cross-ethnic equivalence of parenting and family interactions measures among Hispanic and Anglo-American families. *Child Development, 63,* 1392–1403.

Knight, G. P., Virdin, L. M., & Roosa, M. (1994). Socialization and family correlates of mental health outcomes among Hispanic and Anglo American children: Consideration of cross-ethnic scalar equivalence. *Child Development, 65,* 212–224.

Kochanska, G. (1991). Socialization and temperament in the development of guilt and conscience. *Child Development, 62,* 1379–1392.

Kochanska, G. (1993). Toward a synthesis of parental socialization and child temperament in early development of conscience. *Child Development, 64,* 325–347.

Kochanska, G. (1995). Children's temperament, mothers' discipline, and security of attachment: Multiple pathways to emerging internalization. *Child Development, 66,* 597–615.

Kochanska, G., Casey, R., & Fukumoto, A. (1995). Toddlers' sensitivity to standard violations. *Child Development, 66,* 643–656.

Kochanska, G., DeVet, K., Goldman, M., Murray, K., & Putnam, S. P. (1994). Maternal reports of conscience development and temperament in young children. *Child Development, 65,* 852–868.

Kohlberg, L. (1966). A cognitive-developmental analysis of children's sex-role concepts and attitudes. In E. E. Maccoby (Ed.), *The development of sex differences* (pp. 82–172). Stanford, CA: Stanford University Press.

Kohlberg, L. (1976). Moral stages and moralization: The cognitive-developmental approach. In T. Lickona (Ed.), *Moral development and behavior: Theory, research, and social issues* (pp. 31–53). New York: Holt, Rinehart & Winston.

Kohlberg, L., Boyd, D. R., & Levine, C. (1990). The return of Stage 6: Its principle and moral point of view. In T. E. Wren (Ed.), *The moral domain: Essays in the ongoing discussion between philosophy and the social sciences* (pp. 151–181). Cambridge, MA: MIT Press.

Kohlberg, L., & Candee, D. (1984). The relationship of moral atmosphere to judgments of responsibility. In W. M. Kurtines & J. L. Gewirtz (Eds.), *Morality, moral behavior, and moral development* (pp. 41–51). New York: Wiley.

Kolata, G. (1989, April 9). The medical record on DES emerges after years of research and anxiety. *The New York Times,* p. 26.

Kolata, G. (1995, May 23). Molecular tools may offer clues to reducing risks of birth defects. *The New York Times,* p. C3.

Konner, M. (1975). Relations among infants and juveniles in comparative perspective. In M. Lewis & L. A. Rosenblum (Eds.), *Friendship and peer relations: The origins of behavior series* (pp. 99–130). New York: Wiley.

Konner, M. (1976). Maternal care, infant behavior and development among the !Kung. In R. B. Lee & I. DeVore (Eds.), *Kalahari hunter-gatherers* (pp. 218–245). Cambridge, MA: Harvard University Press.

Kopp, C. B. (1982). Antecedents of self-regulation: A developmental perspective. *Developmental Psychology, 18,* 199–214.

Kopp, C. B. (1983). Risk factors in development. In P. H. Mussen (Series Ed.), M. M. Haith & J. J. Campos (Vol. Eds.), *Handbook of child psychology: Vol. 2. Infancy and developmental psychobiology* (pp. 1081–1188). New York: Wiley.

Kopp, C. B. (1994). Trends and directions in studies of developmental risk. In C. A. Nelson (Ed.), *Threats to optimal development: Integrating biological, psychological, and social risk factors: The Minnesota Symposia on Child Psychology, Vol. 27* (pp. 1–33). Hillsdale, NJ: Erlbaum.

Kopp, C. B., & Kaler, S. R. (1989). Risk in infancy: Origins and implications. *American Psychologist, 44,* 224–230.

Korbin, J. E. (1987). Child abuse and neglect: The cultural context. In R. E. Helfer & R. S. Kempe (Eds.), *The battered child* (4th ed., pp. 23–41). Chicago: University of Chicago Press.

Korner, A. F. (1987). Preventative intervention with high-risk newborns: Theoretical, conceptual, and methodological perspectives. In J. D. Osofsky (Ed.), *Handbook of infant development* (2nd ed., pp. 1006–1036). New York: Wiley.

Korner, A. F., & Thoman, E. B. (1972). The relative efficacy of contact and vestibular proprioceptive stimulation in soothing neonates. *Child Development, 43,* 443–453.

Kramer, L. R. (1991). The social construction of ability perceptions: An ethnographic study of gifted adolescent girls. *Journal of Early Adolescence, 11,* 340–362.

Krebs, D. L., & Van Hesteren, F. (1994). The development of altruism: Toward an integrative model. *Developmental Review, 14,* 103–158.

Kreutzer, M. A. Leonard, C., & Flavell, J. H. (1975). An interview study of children's knowledge about memory. *Monographs of the Society for Research in Child Development, 40* (1, Serial No. 159), 1–58.

Kruger, A. C. (1992). The effect of peer and adult-child transductive discussions on moral reasoning. *Merrill-Palmer Quarterly, 38,* 191–211.

Kuczaj, S. A. (1977). The acquisition of regular and irregular past-tense forms. *Journal of Verbal Learning and Verbal Behavior, 16,* 589–600.

Kuczaj, S. A. (1986). Thoughts on the intentional basis of early object word extension: Evidence from comprehension and production. In S. A. Kuczaj, II, & M. D. Barrett (Eds.), *The development of word meaning.* New York: Springer-Verlag.

Kuczynski, L., Kochanska, G., Radke-Yarrow, M., & Girnius-Brown, O. (1987). A developmental interpretation of young children's noncompliance. *Developmental Psychology, 23,* 799–806.

Kuhl, P. K. (1987). Perception of speech and sound in early infancy. In P. Salapatek & L. Cohen (Eds.), *Handbook of infant perception. Vol. 2. From perception to cognition* (pp. 275–382). Orlando, FL: Academic.

Kuhl, P. K. (1993). Early linguistic experience and phonetic perception: Implications for theories of developmental speech perception. *Journal of Phonetics, 21,* 125–139.

Kuhl, P. K., & Miller, J. D. (1978). Speech perception by the chinchilla: Identification functions for synthetic VOT stimuli. *Journal of the Acoustical Society of America, 63,* 905–917.

Kuhl, P. K., Williams, K. A., Lacerda, F., Stevens, K. N., & Lindblom, B. (1992). Linguistic experience alters phonetic perception in infants by 6 months of age. *Science, 255,* 606–608.

Kuhn, D. (1989). Children and adults as intuitive scientists. *Psychological Review, 96,* 674–689.

Kuhn, D., Nash, S. C., & Brucken, L. (1978). Sex role concepts of two- and three-year-olds. *Child Development, 49,* 445–451.

Kulik, C., & Kulik, J. (1982). Effects of ability grouping on secondary students: A meta-analysis of evaluation findings. *American Educational Research Journal, 19,* 415–428.

Kupersmidt, J. B., & Coie, J. D. (1990). Preadolescent peer status, aggression, and social adjustment as predictors of externalizing problems in adolescence. *Child Development, 61,* 1350–1362.

Kupersmidt, J. B., Coie, J. D., & Dodge, K. A. (1990). The role of poor peer

relationships in the development of disorder. In S. R. Asher & J. D. Coie (Eds.), *Peer rejection in childhood* (pp. 274–305). Cambridge, England: Cambridge University Press.

Kupersmidt, J. B., Griesler, P. C., DeRosier, M. E., Patterson, C. J., & Davis, P. W. (1995). Childhood aggression and peer relations in the context of family and neighborhood factors. *Child Development, 66,* 360–375.

Kurtines W. M., Alvarez, M., & Azmitia, M. (1990). Science and morality: The role of values in science and the scientific study of moral phenomena. *Psychological Bulletin, 107,* 283–295.

Kurtines, W., & Gewirtz, J. L. (Eds.). (1991). Handbook of moral behavior and development. Hillsdale, NJ: Erlbaum.

Laboratory of Comparative Human Cognition. (1983). Culture and cognitive development. In W. Kessen (Ed.), *Handbook of child psychology: Vol. 1. History, theory, and methods* (4th ed., pp. 295–356). New York: Wiley.

Lachiewicz, A. M., Spiridigliozzi, G. A., Gullion, C. M., Ransford, S. N., & Rao, K. (1994). Aberrant behaviors of young boys with fragile X syndrome. *American Journal on Mental Retardation, 98,* 567–579.

Ladd, G. W. (1981). Effectiveness of a social learning method for enhancing children's social interaction and peer acceptance. *Child Development, 52,* 171–178.

Ladd, G. W., & Golter, B. S. (1988). Parents' management of preschoolers' peer relations: Is it related to children's social competence? *Developmental Psychology, 24,* 109–117.

Ladd, G. W., & Hart, C. H. (1992). Creating informal play opportunities: Are parents' and preschoolers' initiations related to children's competence with peers? *Developmental Psychology, 28,* 1179–1187.

Ladd, G. W., & Le Sieur, K. D. (1995). Parents and children's peer relationships. In M. H. Bornstein (Ed.), *Handbook of parenting. Vol. 4. Applied and practical parenting* (pp. 377–410). Mahwah, NJ: Erlbaum.

Ladd, G. W., & Price, J. M. (1987). Predicting children's social and school adjustment following the transition from preschool to kindergarten. *Child Development, 58,* 1168–1189.

La Follette, H. (1991). Personal relationships. In P. Singer (Ed.), *A companion to ethics* (pp. 327–332). Oxford, England: Basil Blackwell.

Lafreniere, P. J., & Sroufe, L. A. (1985). Profiles of peer competence in the preschool: Interrelations between measures, influence of social ecology, and relation to attachment history. *Developmental Psychology, 21,* 56–69.

Lafreniere, P. J., Strayer, F. F., & Gauthier, R. (1984). The emergence of same-sex affiliative preferences among preschool peers: A developmental/ethological perspective. *Child Development, 55,* 1958–1965.

La Greca, A. M. (1993). Social skills training with children: Where do we go from here? *Journal of Clinical Child Psychology, 22,* 288–298.

Lamaze, F. (1970). *Painless childbirth: Psychoprophylactic method.* Chicago: Regnery.

Lamb, M. E., Easterbrooks, M. A., & Holden, G. W. (1980). Reinforcement and punishment among preschoolers: Characteristics, effects, and correlates. *Child Development, 51,* 1230–1236.

Lamb, M. E., & Nash, A. (1989). Infant-mother attachment, sociability, and peer competence. In T. J. Berndt & G. W. Ladd (Eds.), *Peer relationships in child development* (pp. 219–245). New York: Wiley.

Lamb, M. E., Sternberg, K. J., & Prodomidis, M. (1992). Nonmaternal care and the security of infant-mother attachment: A reanalysis of the data. *Infant Behavior and Development, 15,* 71–83.

Lamborn, S. D., Mounts, N. S., Steinberg, L., & Dornbusch, S. M. (1991). Patterns of competence and adjustment among adolescents from authoritative, authoritarian, indulgent, and neglectful families. *Child Development, 62,* 1049–1065.

Lane, D. M. (1980). Incidental learning and the development of selective attention. *Psychological Review, 87,* 316–319.

Lange, G., & Pierce, S. H. (1992). Memory-strategy learning and maintenance in preschool children. *Developmental Psychology, 28,* 453–462.

Langlois, J. H., & Downs, A. C. (1979). Peer relations as a function of physical attractiveness: The eye of the beholder or behavioral reality? *Child Development, 50,* 409–418.

Langlois, J. H., & Downs, A. C. (1980). Mothers, fathers, and peers as socialization agents of sex-typed play behaviors in young children. *Child Development, 51,* 1237–1247.

Larkin, J. H. (1979). Processing information for effective problem solving. *Engineering Education, 70,* 285–288.

Lau, C. S., & Kavlock, R. J. (1994). Functional toxicity in the developing heart, lung, and kidney. In C. A. Kimmel & J. Buelke-Sam (Eds.), *Developmental toxicology* (pp. 119–188). New York: Raven Press.

Lau, S. (1989). Sex role orientation and domains of self-esteem. *Sex Roles, 21,* 415–422.

Laursen, B. (1995). Variations in adolescent conflict and social interaction associated with maternal employment and family structure. *International Journal of Behavioral Development, 18,* 151–164.

Lavatelli, C. S. (1970). *Piaget's theory applied to early childhood curriculum.* Boston: American Science and Engineering.

Lawson, A., & Rhode, D. (Eds.). (1993). *The politics of pregnancy: Adolescent sexuality and public policy.* New Haven: Yale University Press.

Lazar, I., & Darlington, R. (1982). Lasting effects of early education: A report from the consortium for longitudinal studies. *Monographs of the Society for Research in Child Development, 47* (2–3, Serial No. 195).

Lederberg, A. R., Chapin, S. L., Rosenblatt, V., & Vandell, D. L. (1986). Ethnic, gender, and age preferences among deaf and hearing preschool peers. *Child Development, 57,* 375–386.

Lee, K., & Corpuz, M. (1988). Teenage pregnancy: Trend and impact on rates of low birth weight and fetal, maternal, and neonatal mortality in the United States. *Clinics in Perinatology, 15,* 929–942.

Lee, T. F. (1991). *The human genome project: Cracking the genetic code of life.* New York: Plenum.

Lee, V. E., Brooks-Gunn, J., Schnur, E., & Liaw, F. R. (1990). Are Head Start effects sustained? A longitudinal follow-up comparison of disadvantaged children attending Head Start, no preschool, and other preschool programs. *Child Development, 61,* 495–507.

Lee, V. E., Burkam, D. T., Zimiles, H., & Ladewski, B. (1994). Family structure and its effect on behavioral and emotional problems in young adolescents. *Journal of Research on Adolescence, 4,* 405–437.

Lefkowitz, M. M. (1981). Smoking during pregnancy: Long-term effects on offspring. *Developmental Psychology, 17,* 192–194.

Leichtman, M. D., & Ceci, S. J. (1993). The problem of infantile amnesia: Lessons from fuzzy-trace theory. In M. L. Howe & R. Pasnak (Eds.), *Emerging themes in cognitive development* (Vol. I, pp. 195–213). New York: Springer-Verlag.

LeMare, L. J., & Rubin, K. H. (1987). Perspective taking and peer interaction: Structural and developmental analyses. *Child Development, 58,* 306–315.

Lempers, J. D., Flavell, E. R., & Flavell, J. H. (1977). The development in very young children of tacit knowledge concerning visual perception. *Genetic Psychology Monographs, 95,* 3–53.

Lenneberg, E. H. (1967). *Biological foundations of language.* New York: Wiley.

Lennon, R., & Eisenberg, N. (1987). Emotional displays associated with preschooler's prosocial behavior. *Child Development, 58,* 992–1000.

Leon, M. (1984). Rules mothers and sons use to integrate intent and damage information in their moral judgments. *Child Development, 55,* 2106–2113.

Lepper, M. R. (1983). Social control processes, attributions of motivation, and the internalization of social values. In E. T. Higgins, D. N. Ruble, & W. W. Hartup (Eds.), *Developmental social cognition: A socio-cultural perspective* (pp. 294–232). Cambridge, England: Cambridge University Press.

Lerner, R. (1986). *Concepts and theories of human development* (2nd ed.). New York: Random House.

Leventhal, E. A., Leventhal, H., Shacham, S., & Easterling, D. V. (1989). Active coping reduces reports of pain from childbirth. *Journal of Consulting and Clinical Psychology, 57,* 365–371.

Lever, J. (1978). Sex differences in the complexity of children's play and games. *American Sociological Review, 43,* 471–483.

Levin, I. (Ed.). (1986). *Stage and structure: Reopening the debate.* Norwood, NJ: Ablex.

Levine, L. E. (1983). *Mine:* Self-definition in 2-year-old boys. *Developmental Psychology, 19,* 544–549.

Levine, L. J. (1995). Young children's understanding of the causes of anger and sadness. *Child Development, 66,* 697–709.

LeVine, R. A. (1994). *Child care and culture: Lessons from Africa.* New York: Cambridge University Press.

LeVine, R. A., & LeVine, B. B. (1963). Nyansongo: A Gusii community in Kenya. In B. B. Whiting (Ed.), *Six cultures: Studies of child rearing* (pp. 15–202). New York: Wiley.

LeVine, R. A., & Miller, P. M. (1990). Commentary. *Human Development, 33,* 73–80.

Lewis, C., & Osborne, A. (1990). Three-year-olds' problems with false belief: Conceptual deficit or linguistic artifact? *Child Development, 61,* 1514–1519.

Lewis, C. C. (1981). The effects of parental firm control: A reinterpretation of findings. *Psychological Bulletin, 90,* 547–563.

Lewis, M. (1987). Social development in infancy and early childhood. In J. D. Osofsky (Ed.), *Handbook of infant development* (pp. 419–493). New York: Wiley.

Lewis, M., & Brooks-Gunn, J. (1979). *Social cognition and the acquisition of self.* New York: Plenum.

Lewis, M., Feiring, C., McGuffog, C., & Jaskir, J. (1984). Predicting psychopathology in six-year-olds from early social relations. *Child Development, 55,* 123–136.

Lewis, M., Sullivan, M. W., Stanger, C., & Weiss, M. (1989). Self development and self-conscious emotions. *Child Development, 60,* 146–156.

Lewkowicz, D. J. (1994). Development of intersensory perception in human infants. In D. J. Lewkowicz & R. Lickliter (Eds.), *The development of intersensory perception: Comparative perspectives* (pp. 165–203). Hillsdale, NJ: Erlbaum.

Liaw, R. R., & Brooks-Gunn, J. (1994). Cumulative familial risks and low-birthweight children's cognitive and behavioral development. *Journal of Clinical Child Psychology, 23,* 360– 372.

Licht, B. G., & Dweck, C. S. (1984). Determinants of academic achievement: The interaction of children's achievement orientations with skill area. *Developmental Psychology, 20,* 628–636.

Lickona, T. (1976). Research on Piaget's theory of moral development. In T. Lickona (Ed.), *Moral development and behavior: Theory, research, and social issues* (pp. 219–240). New York: Holt, Rinehart & Winston.

Lieven, E. V., Pine, J. M., & Barnes, H. D. (1992). Individual differences in early vocabulary development: Redefining the referential-expressive distinction. *Journal of Child Language, 19,* 287–310.

Liittschwager, J. C., & Markman, E. M. (1994). Sixteen- and 24-month-old's use of mutual exclusivity as a default assumption in second-label learning. *Developmental Psychology, 30,* 955–968.

Linn, M. C., & Hyde, J. S. (1989). Gender, mathematics, and science. *Educational Researcher, 18,* 17–27.

Little, A. H., Lipsitt, L. P., & Rovee-Collier, C. (1984). Classical conditioning and retention of the infant's eyelid response: Effects of age and interstimulus interval. *Journal of Experimental Child Psychology, 37,* 512–524.

Livesley, W. J., & Bromley, D. B. (1973). *Person perception in childhood and adolescence.* New York: Wiley.

Lobel, M., Dunkel-Schetter, C., & Scrimshaw, S. C. (1992). Prenatal maternal stress and prematurity: A prospective study of socioeconomically disadvantaged women. *Health Psychology, 11,* 32–40.

Lobel, T. E., Bempechat, J., Gewirtz, J. C., Shoken-Topaz, T., & Bashe, E. (1993). The role of gender-related information and self-endorsement of traits in preadolescents' inferences and judgments. *Child Development, 64,* 1285–1294.

Locke, J. (1693/1947). Some thoughts concerning education. In *John Locke on politics and education* (pp. 205–388). New York: Walter J. Black.

Lockman, J. J., & Pick, H. L., Jr. (1984). Problems of scale in spatial development. In C. Sophian (Ed.), *Origins of cognitive skills* (pp. 3–26). Hillsdale, NJ: Erlbaum.

Loehlin, J. C., Horn, J. M., & Willerman, L. (1989). Modeling IQ change: Evidence from the Texas Adoption Project. *Child Development, 60,* 993–1004.

Loevinger, J. (1976). *Ego development: Conceptions and theories.* San Francisco: Jossey-Bass.

Lohman, D. F. (1989). Human intelligence: An introduction to advances in theory and research. *Review of Educational Research, 59,* 333–374.

Lorenz, K. (1963). *On aggression.* New York: Harcourt Brace Jovanovich.

Lorenz, K. Z. (1935/1957). 'Der Kumpan in der Umvelt des Vogels.' Eng. Trans. in C. H. Schiller (Ed.), *Instinctive behavior.* New York: International Universities Press.

Lott, B., & Maluso, D. (1993). The social learning of gender. In A. E. Beall & R. J. Sternberg (Eds.), *The psychology of gender* (pp. 99–126). New York: Guilford.

Loveland, K. A., Stehbens, J., Contant, C., Bordeaux, J. D., Sirois, P., Bell, T. S., Hill, S., Scott, A., Bowman, M., Schiller, M., Watkins, J., Olson, R., Moylan, P., Cod, V., & Belden, B. (1994). Hemophilia growth and development study: Baseline neurodevelopmental findings. *Journal of Pediatric Psychology, 19,* 223–239.

Lozoff, B. (1989). Nutrition and behavior. *American Psychologist, 44,* 231–236.

Lozoff, B., Wolf, A., & Davis, N. (1984). Cosleeping in urban families with young children in the United States. *Pediatrics, 74,* 171–182.

Lucariello, J., Kyratzis, A., & Nelson, K. (1992). Taxonomic knowledge: What kind and when. *Child Development, 63,* 978–998.

Lucariello, J., & Nelson, K. (1985). Slot-filler categories as memory organizers for young children. *Developmental Psychology, 21,* 272–282.

Ludemann, P. M., & Nelson, C. A. (1988). Categorical representation of facial expressions by 7-month-old infants. *Developmental Psychology, 24,* 492–501.

Luke, B. (1994). The changing pattern of multiple births in the United States: Maternal and infant characteristics, 1973 and 1990. *Obstetrics and Gynecology, 84,* 101–106.

Lummis, M., & Stevenson, H. W. (1990). Gender differences in beliefs and achievement: A cross-cultural study. *Developmental Psychology, 26,* 254–263.

Luo, D., Petrill, S. A., & Thompson, L. A. (1994). An exploration of genetic *g:* Hierarchical factor analysis of cognitive data from the Western Reserve twin project. *Intelligence, 18,* 335–347.

Luster, T., & McAdoo, H. P. (1994). Factors related to the achievement and adjustment of young African American children. *Child Development, 65,* 1080–1094.

Lutiger, B., Einarson, T. R., Koren, G., & Graham, K. (1994). Relationship between gestational cocaine use and pregnancy outcome. In G. Koren (Ed.), *Maternal fetal toxicology: A clinician's guide* (pp. 353–369). New York: Marcel Dekker.

Lykken, D. T., McGue, M., Tellegen, A., & Bouchard, T. J. (1992). Emergenesis: Genetic traits that may not run in families. *American Psychologist, 47,* 1565–1577.

Lynn, R., & Pagliari, C. (1994). The intelligence of American children is still rising. *Journal of Biosocial Science, 26,* 65–67.

Lyon, T. D., & Flavell, J. H. (1993). Young children's understanding of forgetting over time. *Child Development, 64,* 789–800.

Lyon, T. D., & Flavell, J. H. (1994). Young children's understanding of "remember" and "forget." *Child Development, 65,* 1357–1371.

Lyons-Ruth, K., Alpern, L., & Repacholi, B. (1993). Disorganized infant attachment classification and maternal psychosocial problems as predictors of hostile-aggressive behavior in the preschool classroom. *Child Development, 64,* 572–585.

Lytton, H. (1980). *Parent-child interaction: The socialization process observed in twin and singleton families.* New York: Plenum.

Lytton, H. (1990). Child and parent effects in boys' conduct disorder: A reinterpretation. *Developmental Psychology, 26,* 683–697.

Lytton, H., & Romney, D. M. (1991). Parents' differential socialization of boys and girls: A meta-analysis. *Psychological Bulletin, 109,* 267–296.

Lytton, H., & Zwirner, W. (1975). Compliance and its controlling stimuli observed in a natural setting. *Developmental Psychology, 11,* 769–779.

Maccoby, E. E. (1980). *Social development: Psychological growth and the parent-child relationship.* San Diego, CA: Harcourt Brace Jovanovich.

Maccoby, E. E. (1984). Socialization and developmental change. *Child Development, 55,* 317–328.

Maccoby, E. E. (1988). Gender as a social category. *Developmental Psychology, 24,* 755–765.

Maccoby, E. E. (1990). Gender and relationships. *American Psychologist, 45,* 513–520.

Maccoby, E. E. (1992). Family structure and children's adjustment: Is quality of parenting the major mediator? Commentary on E. M. Hetherington and

W. G. Clingempeel, *Coping with marital transition: A family-systems perspective. Monographs of the Society for Research in Child Development, 57* (2-3, Serial No. 227).

Maccoby, E. E., & Jacklin, C. N. (1974). *The psychology of sex differences.* Stanford, CA: Stanford University Press.

Maccoby, E. E., & Jacklin, C. N. (1980). Sex differences in aggression: A rejoinder and reprise. *Child Development, 51,* 964–980.

Maccoby, E. E., & Martin, J. A. (1983). Socialization in the context of the family: Parent-child interaction. In E. M. Hetherington (Vol. Ed.) & P. H. Mussen (Series Ed.), *Handbook of child psychology: Vol. 4. Socialization, personality, and social development* (pp. 1–101). New York: Wiley.

Maccoby, E. E., & Mnookin, R. H. (1992). *Dividing the child: Social and legal dilemmas of custody.* Cambridge, MA: Harvard University Press.

MacDonald, K. (1992). Warmth as a developmental construct: An evolutionary analysis. *Child Development, 63,* 753–773.

MacDonald, K., & Parke, R. D. (1984). Bridging the gap: Parent-child play interaction and peer interactive competence. *Child Development, 55,* 1265–1277.

MacFarlane, A. (1975). Olfaction in the development of social preferences in the human neonate. *Ciba Foundation Symposium, 33,* 103–117.

Macken, M. A. (1987). Representation, rules, and over-generalization in phonology. In B. MacWhinney (Ed.), *Mechanisms of language acquisition* (pp. 367–398). Hillsdale, NJ: Erlbaum.

Mackenzie, B. (1984). Explaining race differences in IQ: The logic, the methodology, and the evidence. *American Psychologist, 39,* 1214–1233.

MacWhinney, B. (Ed.). (1987). *Mechanisms of language acquisition.* Hillsdale, NJ: Erlbaum.

Madison, L. S., Madison, J. K., & Adubato, S. A. (1986). Infant behavior and development in relation to fetal movement and habituation. *Child Development, 57,* 1475–1482.

Main, D. M., & Main, E. K. (1991). Preterm birth. In S. G. Gabbe, J. R. Niebyl, & J. L. Simpson (Eds.), *Obstetrics: Normal & problem pregnancies* (2nd ed., pp. 829–880). New York: Churchill Livingstone.

Main, M., & Hesse, E. (1990). Parents' unresolved traumatic experiences are related to infant disorganized attachment status: Is frightened and/or frightening parental behavior the linking mechanism? In M. T. Greenberg, D. Cicchetti, & E. M. Cummings (Eds.),

*Attachment in the preschool years: Theory, research, and intervention* (pp. 161–182). Chicago: University of Chicago Press.

Main, M., Kaplan, N., & Cassidy, J. (1985). Security in infancy, childhood, and adulthood: A move to the level of representation. *Monographs of the Society for Research in Child Development, 50* (1-2, Serial No. 209).

Main, M., & Weston, D. R. (1981). The quality of the toddler's relationship to mother and to father: Related to conflict behavior and the readiness to establish new relationships. *Child Development, 2,* 932–940.

Mainstream science on intelligence (1994, December 13) [Letter to the editor, signed by 50 experts in intelligence and allied fields]. *The Wall Street Journal,* p. A19.

Malhotra, K. C. (1990). Changing patterns of disease in India with special reference to childhood mortality. In A. C. Swedlund & G. J. Armelagos (Eds.), *Disease in populations in transition: Anthropological and epidemiological perspectives* (pp. 313–331). New York: Bergin and Garvey.

Malina, R. M. (1979). Secular changes in size and maturity: Causes and effects. In A. F. Roche (Ed.), *Secular trends in human growth, maturation, and development* (pp. 59–102). *Monographs of the Society for Research in Child Development, 44* (3-4, Serial No. 179).

Malina, R. M. (1990). Physical growth and development during the transitional years (9–16). In R. Montemayor, G. R. Adams, & T. P. Gullotta (Eds.), *From childhood to adolescence: A transitional period* (pp. 41–62). Newbury Park, CA: Sage.

Malinosky-Rummell, F., & Hansen, D. J. (1993). Long-term consequences of childhood physical abuse. *Psychological Bulletin, 114,* 68–79.

Mandel, D. R., Jusczyk, P. W., & Kemler-Nelson, D. G. (1994). Does sentential prosody help infants organize and remember speech information? *Cognition, 53,* 155–180.

Mandler, J. M. (1992). The importance of motor activity in sensorimotor development: A perspective from children with physical handicaps. *Human Development, 35,* 246–253.

Mandler, J. M. (1993). On concepts. *Cognitive Development, 8,* 141–148.

Mandler, J. M., Bauer, P. J., & McDonough, L. (1991). Separating the sheep from the goats: Differentiating global categories. *Cognitive Psychology, 23,* 263–298.

Mandler, J. M., & McDonough, L. (1993). Concept formation in infancy. *Cognitive Development, 8,* 291–318.

Mandoki, M. W., Sumner, G. S., Hoffman, R. P., & Riconda, D. L. (1991). A review

of Klinefelter's syndrome in children and adolescents. *Journal of the American Academy of Child and Adolescent Psychiatry, 30,* 167–172.

Mange, A. P., & Mange, E. J. (1990). *Genetics: Human aspects* (2nd ed.). Sunderland, MA: Sinhauer Associates.

Mangelsdorf, S., Gunnar, M., Kestenbaum, R., Lang, S., & Andreas, D. (1990). Infant proneness-to-distress temperament, maternal personality, and mother-infant attachment: Associations and goodness-of-fit. *Child Development, 61,* 820–831.

Maratsos, M. (1983). Some current issues in the study of the acquisition of grammar. In J. H. Flavell & E. M. Markman (Eds.), *Handbook of child psychology: Vol. 3. Cognitive development* (pp. 707–786). New York: Wiley.

Maratsos, M. (1988). Crosslinguistic analysis, universals, and language acquisition. In F. S. Kessel (Ed.), *The development of language and language researchers* (pp. 121–152). Hillsdale, NJ: Erlbaum.

Maratsos, M., Fox, D. E., Becker, J. A., & Chalkley, M. A. (1985). Semantic restrictions on children's passives. *Cognition, 19,* 167–191.

Maratsos, M., & Matheny, L. (1994). Language specificity and elasticity: Brain and clinical syndrome studies. *Annual Review of Psychology, 45,* 487–516.

Marcia, J. E. (1966). Development and validation of ego identity status. *Journal of Personality and Social Psychology, 3,* 551–558.

Marcia, J. E. (1980). Identity in adolescence. In J. Adelson (Ed.), *Handbook of adolescent psychology* (pp. 159–187). New York: Wiley.

Marcia, J. E. (1993). The ego identity status approach to ego identity. In J. E. Marcia, A. S. Waterman, D. R. Matteson, S. L. Archer, & J. L. Orlofsky (Eds.), *Ego identity: A handbook for psychosocial research* (pp. 3–21). New York: Springer-Verlag.

Marcia, J. E., Waterman, A. S., Matteson, D. R., Archer, S. L., & Orlofsky, J. L. (Eds.). (1993). *Ego identity: A handbook for psychosocial research.* New York: Springer-Verlag.

Marcus, D. E., & Overton, W. F. (1978). The development of cognitive gender constancy and sex role preferences. *Child Development, 49,* 434–444.

Marcus, G. F. (1993). Negative evidence in language acquisition. *Cognition, 46,* 53–85.

Marcus, G. F., Pinker, S., Ullman, M., Hollander, M., Rosen, T. J., & Xu, F. (1992). Overregularization in language acquisition. *Monographs of the Society for Research in Child Development, 57* (Serial No. 228).

Marecek, J. (1995). Gender, politics, and psychological gender differences: Another side to the story. *American Psychologist, 50,* 159–161.

Maretzki, T. W., & Maretzki, H. (1963). Taira: An Okinawan village. In B. B. Whiting (Ed.), *Children of six cultures* (pp. 363–539). New York: Wiley.

Marini, Z., & Case, R. (1994). The development of abstract reasoning about the physical and social world. *Child Development, 65,* 147–159.

Markman, E. (1989). *Categorization and naming in children.* Cambridge, MA: MIT Press.

Markman, E. M. (1987). How children constrain the possible meanings of words. In U. Neisser (Ed.), *Concepts and conceptual development: Ecological and intellectual factors in categorization* (pp. 255–287). Cambridge, England: Cambridge University Press.

Markstrom-Adams, A. (1989). Androgyny and its relation to adolescent well-being: A review of the literature. *Sex Roles, 21,* 325–340.

Markus, H. R., & Kitayama, S. (1994). A collective fear of the collective: Implications for selves and theories of selves. *Personality and Social Psychology Bulletin, 20,* 568–579.

Marsh, H. W. (1987). The big-fish-little-pond effect on academic self-concept. *Journal of Educational Psychology, 79,* 280–295.

Marsh, H. W. (1989). Age and sex effects in multiple dimensions of self-concept: Preadolescence to early adulthood. *Journal of Educational Psychology, 81,* 417–430.

Marsh, H. W. (1990). Causal ordering of academic self-concept and academic achievement: A multiwave, longitudinal panel analysis. *Journal of Educational Psychology, 82,* 646–656.

Marsh, H. W. (1993). Relations between global and specific domains of self: The importance of individual importance, certainty, and ideals. *Journal of Personality and Social Psychology, 65,* 975–992.

Marsh, H. W., Chessor, D., Craven, R., & Roche, L. (1995). The effects of gifted and talented programs on academic self-concept: The big fish strikes again. *American Educational Research Journal, 32,* 285–319.

Marsh, H. W., & Craven, R. G. (1991). Self-concepts of young children 5 to 8 years of age: Measurement and multidimensional structure. *Journal of Educational Psychology, 83,* 377–392.

Marsh, H. W., & Holmes, I. W. M. (1990). Multidimensional self-concepts: Construct validation of responses by children. *American Educational Research Journal, 27,* 89–118.

Marsh, H. W., & Shavelson, R. J. (1985). Self-concept: Its multifaceted, hierarchical structure. *Educational Psychologist, 20,* 107–125.

Marshall, W. A., & Tanner, J. M. (1986). Puberty. In F. Falkner & J. M. Tanner (Eds.), *Human growth: A comprehensive treatise* (pp. 171–209). New York: Plenum.

Martin, C. L. (1989). Children's use of gender-related information in making social judgments. *Developmental Psychology, 25,* 80–88.

Martin, C. L. (1993). New directions for investigating children's gender knowledge. *Developmental Review, 13,* 184–204.

Martin, C. L., & Halverson, C. F., Jr. (1981). A schematic processing model of sex typing and stereotyping in children. *Child Development, 52,* 1119–1134.

Martin, C. L., & Halverson, C. F., Jr. (1983). The effects of sex-typing schemas on young children's memory. *Child Development, 54,* 563–574.

Martin, C. L., & Halverson, C. F., Jr. (1987). The roles of cognition in sex role acquisition. In D. B. Carter (Ed.), *Current conceptions of sex roles and sex typing* (pp. 123–138). New York: Praeger.

Martin, C. L., & Little, J. K. (1990). The relation of gender understanding to children's sex-typed preferences and gender stereotypes. *Child Development, 61,* 1427–1439.

Martorell, R., Mendoza, F., Castillo, R. (1988). Poverty and stature in children. In J. C. Waterlow (Ed.), *Linear growth retardation in less developed countries* (pp. 57–74). New York: Raven.

Maruyama, G., Rubin, R. A., & Kingsbury, G. G. (1981). Self-esteem and educational achievement: Independent constructs with a common cause? *Journal of Personality and Social Psychology, 40,* 962–975.

Masten, A. S., Morison, P., & Pellegrini, D. S. (1985). A revised class play method of peer assessment. *Developmental Psychology, 21,* 523–533.

Masters, J. C., Ford, M. E., Arend, R., Grotevant, H. D., & Clark, L. V. (1979). Modeling and labeling as integrated determinants of children's sex-typed imitative behavior. *Child Development, 50,* 364–371.

Masters, J. C., & Furman, W. (1981). Popularity, individual friendship selection, and specific peer interaction among children. *Developmental Psychology, 17,* 344–350.

Masur, E. F. (1993). Transitions in representational ability: Infants' verbal, vocal, and action imitation during the second year. *Merrill-Palmer Quarterly, 39,* 437–456.

Matas, L., Arend, R. A., & Sroufe, L. A. (1978). Continuity of adaption in the second year: The relationship between quality of attachment and later competence. *Child Development, 49,* 47–556.

Matias, R., & Cohn, J. F. (1993). Are max-specified infant facial expressions during face-to-face interaction consistent with differential emotions theory? *Developmental Psychology, 29,* 524–531.

Maurer, D., & Adams, R. J. (1987). Emergence of the ability to discriminate a blue from a gray at one month of age. *Journal of Experimental Child Psychology, 44,* 147–156.

Maurer, D., & Barrera, M. (1981). Infants' perception of natural and distorted arrangements of a schematic face. *Child Development, 52,* 196–202.

Maurer, D., & Maurer, C. (1988). *The world of the newborn.* New York: Basic.

Maurer, D., & Salapatek, P. (1976). Developmental changes in the scanning of faces by young infants. *Child Development, 47,* 523–527.

Mayberry, R., Wodlinger-Cohen, R., & Goldin-Meadow, S. (1987). Symbolic development in deaf children. In D. Cicchetti & M. Beeghly (Eds.), *New directions for child development: Symbolic development in atypical children* (pp. 109–126). San Francisco: Jossey-Bass.

McBride-Chang, C. (1995). What is phonological awareness? *Journal of Educational Psychology, 87,* 179–192.

McCall, R. B. (1977). Challenges to a science of developmental psychology. *Child Development, 48,* 333–344.

McCall, R. B. (1979). The development of intellectual functioning and the prediction of later IQ. In J. D. Osofsky (Ed.), *Handbook of infant development* (pp. 707–741). New York: Wiley.

McCall, R. B. (1983). Environmental effect on intelligence: The forgotten realm of discontinuous nonshared within-family factors. *Child Development, 54,* 408–415.

McCall, R. B. (1994). What process mediates predictions of childhood IQ from infant habituation and recognition memory? Speculations on the roles of inhibition and rate of information processing. *Intelligence, 18,* 107–125.

McCall, R. B., & Carriger, M. S. (1993). A meta-analysis of infant habituation and recognition memory performance as predictors of later IQ. *Child Development, 64,* 57–79.

McCall, R. B., Eichorn, D. H., & Hogarty, P. S. (1977). Transitions in early mental development. *Monographs of the Society for Research in Child Development, 42* (3, Serial No. 171).

McCarthy, J. D., & Hoge, D. R. (1982). Analysis of age effects in longitudinal studies of adolescent self-esteem. *Developmental Psychology, 18,* 372–379.

McCartney, K. (1984). Effect of quality of day care environment on children's language development. *Developmental Psychology, 20,* 244–260.

McCartney, K., & Phillips, D. (1988). Motherhood and child care. In B. Birns & D. Hayes (Eds.), *Different faces of motherhood.* New York: Plenum.

McCauley, E., Kay, T., Ito, J., & Treder, R. (1987). The Turner syndrome: Cognitive deficits, affective discrimination, and behavior problems. *Child Development, 58,* 464–473.

McDevitt, S. C. (1986). Continuity and discontinuity of temperament in infancy and early childhood: A psychometric perspective. In R. Plomin & J. Dunn (Eds.), *The study of temperament: Changes, continuities and challenges* (pp. 27–38). Hillsdale, NJ: Erlbaum.

McDonald, M. A., Sigman, M., Espinosa, M. P., & Neumann, C. G. (1994). Impact of a temporary food shortage on children and their mothers. *Child Development, 65,* 404–415.

McGilly, K. (Ed.). (1994). *Classroom lessons: Integrating cognitive theory and classroom practice.* Cambridge, MA: MIT Press.

McGue, M., Bouchard, T. J., Iacono, W. G., & Lykken, D. T. (1993). Behavioral genetics of cognitive ability: A life-span perspective. In R. Plomin & G. E. McClearn (Eds.), *Nature, nurture, and psychology* (pp. 59–75). Washington, DC: American Psychological Association.

McGuire, K. D., & Weisz, J. R. (1982). Social cognition and behavior correlates of preadolescent chumship. *Child Development, 53,* 1483–1484.

McHale, S. M., Crouter, A. C., McGuire, S. A., & Updegraff, K. A. (1995). Congruence between mothers' and fathers' differential treatment of siblings: Links with family relations and children's well-being. *Child Development, 66,* 116–128.

McKusick, V. A. (1994). *Mendelian inheritance in man: A catalog of human genes and genetic disorders.* Baltimore: Johns Hopkins University Press.

McLoyd, V. C. (1990a). Minority children: Introduction to the special issue. *Child Development, 61,* 263–266.

McLoyd, V. C. (1990b). The impact of economic hardship on Black families and children: Psychological distress, parenting, and socioemotional development. *Child Development, 61,* 311–346.

McNeill, D. (1970). The development of language. In P. H. Mussen (Ed.), *Carmichael's manual of child psychology* (3rd ed., Vol. 1, pp. 1061–1161). New York: Wiley.

Mead, G. H. (1934). *Mind, self, and society.* Chicago: University of Chicago Press.

Mead, M., & Newton, N. (1967). Cultural patterning of perinatal behavior. In S. A. Richardson & A. F. Guttmacher (Eds.), *Childbearing: Its social and psychological aspects* (pp. 142–244). Baltimore, MD: Williams & Wilkins.

Medrich, E. A., Rosen, J., Rubin, V., & Buckley, S. (1982). *The serious business of growing up.* Berkeley: University of California Press.

Meece, J. L., Blumenfeld, P. C., & Hoyle, R. H. (1988). Students' goal orientations and cognitive engagement in classroom activities. *Journal of Educational Psychology, 80,* 514–523.

Meece, J. L., & Holt, K. (1993). A pattern analysis of students' achievement goals. *Journal of Educational Psychology, 85,* 582–590.

Meece, J. L., Wigfield, A., & Eccles, J. S. (1990). Predictors of math anxiety and its influence on young adolescents' course enrollment intentions and performance in mathematics. *Journal of Educational Psychology, 82,* 60–70.

Melton, G. B., & Barry, F. D. (1994). Neighbors helping neighbors: The vision of the U.S. Advisory Board on Child Abuse and Neglect. In G. B. Melton & F. D. Barry (Eds.), *Protecting children from abuse and neglect: Foundations for a new national strategy.* New York: Guilford.

Meltzoff, A. N., & Moore, M. K. (1977). Imitation of facial and manual gestures by human neonates. *Science, 198,* 75–78.

Meltzoff, A. N., & Moore, M. K. (1989). Imitation in newborn infants: Exploring the range of gestures imitated and the underlying mechanisms. *Developmental Psychology, 25,* 954–962.

Meltzoff, A. N., & Moore, M. K. (1994). Imitation, memory, and the representation of persons. *Infant Behavior and Development, 17,* 83–99.

Menn, L., & Stoel-Gammon, C. (1993). Phonological development: Learning sounds and sound patterns. In J. Berko Gleason (Ed.), *The development of language* (3rd ed., pp. 65–114). New York: Macmillan.

Menn, L., & Stoel-Gammon, C. (1995). Phonological development. In P. Fletcher & B. MacWhinney (Eds.), *The handbook of child language* (pp. 335–359). Oxford, England: Blackwell.

Merriman, W. E., & Bowman, L. L. (1989). The mutual exclusivity bias in children's word learning. *Monographs of the Society for Research in Child Development, 54* (3-4, Serial No. 220).

Merz, B. (1987). Matchmaking scheme solves Tay-Sachs problem. *Journal of the American Medical Association, 258,* 2636, 2639.

Meyer-Bahlburg, H. F. L., Ehrhardt, A. A., Rosen, L. R., Gruen, S. G., Veridiano, N. P., Van, F. H., & Neuwalder, H. F. (1995). Prenatal estrogens and the development of homosexual orientation. *Developmental Psychology, 31,* 12–21.

Miele, F. (1995). Interview with Robert Sternberg on *The bell curve. Skeptic, 3,* 72–80.

Miller, A. (1985). A developmental study of the cognitive basis of performance impairment after failure. *Journal of Personality and Social Psychology, 49,* 529–538.

Miller, J. G., & Bersoff, D. M. (1992). Culture and moral judgment: How are conflicts between justice and interpersonal responsibilities resolved? *Journal of Personality and Social Psychology, 62,* 541–554.

Miller, P. H. (1990). The development of strategies of selective attention. In D. F. Bjorklund (Ed.), *Children's strategies: Contemporary views of cognitive development* (pp. 157–184). Hillsdale, NJ: Erlbaum.

Miller, P. H. (1993). *Theories of developmental psychology* (2nd ed.). New York: Freeman.

Miller, P. H., & Aloise, P. A. (1989). Young children's understanding of the psychological causes of behavior: A review. *Child Development, 60,* 257–285.

Miller, P. H., Haynes, V. F., DeMarie-Dreblow, D., & Woody-Ramsey, J. (1986). Children's strategies for gathering information in three tasks. *Child Development, 52,* 1429–1439.

Miller, P. H., & Weiss, M. G. (1981). Children's attention allocation, understanding of attention, and performance on the incidental learning task. *Child Development, 57,* 1183–1190.

Miller, S. A. (1987). *Developmental research methods.* Englewood Cliffs, NJ: Prentice-Hall.

Mills, A. E. (1985). The acquisition of German. In D. I. Slobin (Ed.), *The crosslinguistic study of language acquisition. Vol. 1. The data* (pp. 141–254). Hillsdale, NJ: Erlbaum.

Mills, J. L., McPartlin, J. M., Kirke, P. N., Lee, Y. J., Conley, M. R., Weir, D. G., & Scott, J. M. (1995). Homocysteine metabolism in pregnancies complicated by neural-tube defects. *Lancet, 345,* 149–151.

Millstein, S. G., Petersen, A. C., & Nightingale, E. O. (Eds.). (1993). *Promoting the health of adolescents: New directions for the twenty-first century.* Oxford, England: Oxford University Press.

Minturn, L., & Hitchcock, J. T. (1963). The Rajputs of Khalapur, India. In B. Whiting (Ed.), *Children of six cultures* (pp. 203–361). New York: Wiley.

Minuchin, P. (1985). Families and individual development: Provocations from the field of family therapy. *Child Development, 56,* 289–302.

Mischel, W. (1973). Toward a cognitive social learning reconceptualization of personality. *Psychological Review, 80,* 252–283.

Mischel, W., Shoda, Y., & Rodriguez, M. L. (1989). Delay of gratification in children. *Science, 244,* 933–938.

Mitchell, J. E., Baker, L. A., & Jacklin, C. N. (1989). Masculinity and femininity in twin children: Genetic and environmental factors. *Child Development, 60,* 1475–1485.

Miyake, K., Chen, S., & Campos, J. J. (1985). Infant temperament, mother's mode of interaction, and attachment in Japan: An interim report. In I. Bretherton & E. Waters (Eds.), Growing points of attachment theory and research. *Monographs of the Society for Research in Child Development, 50* (1-2, Serial No. 209).

Mize, J., & Ladd, G. W. (1990). A cognitive-social learning approach to social skill training with low-status preschool children. *Developmental Psychology, 26,* 388–398.

Mize, J., Pettit, G. S., & Brown, E. G. (1995). Mothers' supervision of their children's peer play: Relations with beliefs, perceptions, and knowledge. *Developmental Psychology, 31,* 311–321.

Moely, B. E., Hart, S. S., Leal, L., Santulli, K. A., Rao, N., Johnson, T., & Hamilton, L. B. (1992). The teacher's role in facilitating memory and study strategy development in the elementary school classroom. *Child Development, 63,* 653–672.

Moffitt, T. E., Caspi, A., Belsky, J., & Silva, P. A. (1992). Childhood experience and the onset of menarche: A test of a sociobiological model. *Child Development, 63,* 47–58.

Moffitt, T. E., Caspi, A., Harkness, A. R., & Silva, P. A. (1993). The natural history of change in intellectual performance: Who changes? How much? Is it meaningful? *Journal of Child Psychology and Psychiatry, 34,* 455–506.

Money, J. (1987). Sin, sickness, or status? Homosexual gender identity and psychoneuroendocrinology. *American Psychologist, 42,* 384–399.

Money, J. (1993). Specific neurocognitional impairments associated with Turner (45, X) and Klinefelter (47, XXY) syndromes: A review. *Social Biology, 40,* 147–151.

Money, J., & Ehrhardt, A. A. (1972). *Man & woman, boy & girl.* Baltimore: Johns Hopkins University Press.

Montemayor, R., & Eisen, M. (1977). The development of self-esteem conceptions from childhood to adolescence. *Developmental Psychology, 15,* 314–319.

Moore, K. L. (1988). *The developing human: Clinically oriented embryology* (4th ed.). Philadelphia: W. B. Saunders.

Moore, K. L., & Persaud, T. V. N. (1993). *The developing human: Clinically oriented embryology* (5th ed.). Philadelphia: W. B. Saunders.

Morelli, G. A., Rogoff, B., Oppenheim, D., & Goldsmith, D. (1992). Cultural variation in infants' sleeping arrangements: Questions of independence. *Developmental Psychology, 28,* 604–613.

Morford, M., & Goldin-Meadow, S. (1992). Comprehension and production of gesture in combination with speech in one-word speakers. *Journal of Child Language, 19,* 559–580.

Morgan, M. (1982). Television and adolescents' sex-role stereotypes: A longitudinal study. *Journal of Personality and Social Psychology, 43,* 947–955.

Morgan, M. (1987). Television, sex-role attitudes, and sex-role behavior. *Journal of Early Adolescence, 7,* 269–282.

Morgane, P. J., Austin-LaFrance, R., Brozino, J., Tonkiss, J., Diaz-Cintra, S., Cintra, L., Kemper, T., & Galler, J. R. (1993). Prenatal malnutrition and development of the brain. *Neuroscience and Biobehavioral Reviews, 17,* 91–128.

Morris, W. (1981). *The American heritage dictionary of the English language.* Boston: Houghton Mifflin.

Morrongiello, B. A., & Clifton, R. K. (1984). Effects of sound frequency on behavioral and cardiac orienting in newborn and five-month-old infants. *Journal of Experimental Child Psychology, 38,* 429–446.

Morrongiello, B. A., Fenwick, K. D., & Chance, G. (1990). Sound localization acuity in very young infants: An observer-based testing procedure. *Developmental Psychology, 26,* 75–84.

Mortensen, M. L., Sever, L. E., & Oakley, G. P., Jr. (1991). Teratology and the epidemiology of birth defects. In S. G. Gabbe, J. R. Niebyl, & J. L. Simpson (Eds.), *Obstetrics: Normal and problem pregnancies* (2nd ed., pp. 233–268). New York: Churchill Livingstone.

Moses, L. J. (1993). Young children's understanding of belief constraints on intention. *Cognitive Development, 8,* 1–25.

Moses, L. J., & Flavell, J. H. (1990). Inferring false beliefs from actions and reactions. *Child Development, 61,* 929–945.

Muir, D., & Clifton, R. (1985). Infants' orientation to the location of sound sources. In G. Gottlieb & N. Krasnegor (Eds.), *Measurement of audition and vision in the first year of postnatal life: A methodological overview* (pp. 171–194). Norwood, NJ: Ablex.

Muir, D., & Field, J. (1979). Newborn infants orient to sounds. *Child Development, 50*, 431–436.

Muller, C. (1995). Maternal employment, parent involvement, and mathematics achievement among adolescents. *Journal of Marriage and the Family, 57*, 85–100.

Munroe, R. H., Munroe, R. L., & Whiting, B. B. (Eds.). (1981). *Handbook of cross-cultural human development.* New York: Garland.

Mussen, P. H., Conger, J. J., Kagan, J., & Huston, A. C. (1990). *Child development and personality* (7th ed.). New York: Harper & Row.

Nabarro, D., Howard, P., Cassels, C., Pant, M., Wijga, A., & Padfield, N. (1988). The importance of infections and environmental factors as possible determinants of growth retardation in children. In J. C. Waterlow (Ed.), *Linear growth retardation in less developed countries* (pp. 165–183). New York: Raven.

Nakagawa, M., Lamb, M. E., & Miyaki, K. (1992). Antecedents and correlates of the Strange Situation behavior of Japanese infants. *Journal of Cross Cultural Psychology, 23*, 300–310.

National Commission on America's Urban Families. (1993). *Families first: Report of the National Commission on America's Urban Families.* Washington, DC: U.S. Government Printing Office.

National Research Council. (1993). *Understanding child abuse and neglect.* Washington, DC: National Academy Press.

Neisser, U., Boodoo, G., Bouchard, T. J., Jr., Boykin, A. W., Brody, N., Ceci, S. J., Halpern, D. F., Loehlin, J. C., Perloff, R., Sternberg, R. J., & Urbina, S. (1996). Intelligence: Knowns and unknowns. *American Psychologist, 51*, 77–101.

Nelson, C. A. (1987). The recognition of facial expressions in the first two years of life: Mechanisms of development. *Child Development, 58*, 889–909.

Nelson, K. (1973). Structure and strategy in learning to talk. *Monographs of the Society for Research in Child Development, 38* (1-2, Serial No. 149).

Nelson, K. (1981). Individual differences in language development: Implications for development and language. *Developmental Psychology, 17*, 170–187.

Nelson, K. (1986). *Event knowledge: Structure and function in development.* Hillsdale, NJ: Erlbaum.

Nelson, K. (1993a). Events, narratives, memory: What develops? In C. A. Nelson (Ed.), *Memory and affect in development: The Minnesota Symposia on Child Psychology, Vol. 26* (1–37).

Nelson, K. (1993b). The psychological and social origins of autobiographical memory. *Psychological Science, 4*, 7–14.

Nelson, K., & Gruendel, J. (1981). Generalized event representations: Basic building blocks of cognitive development. In M. Lamb & A. Brown (Eds.), *Advances in developmental psychology* (Vol. 1). Hillsdale, NJ: Erlbaum.

Nelson, K., Hampson, J., & Shaw, L. K. (1993). Nouns in early lexicons: Evidence, explanations and implications. *Journal of Child Language, 20*, 61–84.

Nelson, K., & Hudson, J. (1988). Scripts and memory: Functional relationships in development. In F. E. Weinert & M. Perlmutter (Eds.), *Memory development: Universal changes and individual changes* (pp. 147–168). Hillsdale, NJ: Erlbaum.

Nelson, K. E. (1977). Facilitating children's syntax acquisition. *Developmental Psychology, 13*, 101–107.

Nelson-Le Gall, S. A. (1985). Motive-outcome matching and outcome foreseeability: Effects on attribution of intentionality and moral judgments. *Developmental Psychology, 21*, 332–337.

Neuman, C. G., & Jenks, B. H. (1992). Obesity. In M. D. Levine, W. B. Carey, & A. C. Crocker (Eds.), *Developmental-behavioral pediatrics* (pp. 354–363). Philadelphia: W. B. Saunders.

Newcomb, A. F., & Bagwell, C. L. (1995). Children's friendship relations: A meta-analytic review. *Psychological Bulletin, 117*, 306–347.

Newcomb, A. F., & Bukowski, W. M. (1983). Social impact and social preference as determinants of children's peer group status. *Developmental Psychology, 19*, 856–867.

Newcomb, A. F., & Bukowski, W. M. (1984). A longitudinal study of the utility of social preference and social impact sociometric classification schemes. *Child Development, 55*, 1434–1447.

Newcomb, A. F., Bukowski, W. M., & Pattee, L. (1993). Children's peer relations: A meta-analytic review of popular, rejected, neglected, controversial, and average sociometric status. *Psychological Bulletin, 113*, 99–128.

Nicholls, J. G. (1978). The development of the concepts of effort and ability, perception of own attainment, and the understanding that difficult tasks require more ability. *Child Development, 49*, 800–814.

Nicholls, J. G. (1989). *The competitive ethos and democratic education.* Cambridge, MA: Harvard University Press.

Nicholls, J. G., Patashnick, M., & Mettetal, G. (1986). Conceptions of ability and intelligence. *Child Development, 57*, 636–645.

Nicol, R. (1988). The treatment of child abuse in the home environment. In K. Browne, C. Davies, & P. Stratton (Eds.), *Early prediction and prevention of child abuse* (pp. 213–228). New York: Wiley.

Nicolaides, K., Brizot, M. L., Patel, F., & Snijders, R. (1994). Comparison of chorionic villus sampling and amniocentesis for fetal karyotyping at 10–13 weeks' gestation. *Lancet, 13*, 435–439.

Niebyl, J. R. (1991). Drugs in pregnancy and lactation. In S. G. Gabbe, J. R. Niebyl, & J. L. Simpson (Eds.), *Obstetrics: Normal and problem pregnancies* (2nd ed., pp. 299–327). New York: Churchill Livingstone.

Nilsson, L. (1990). *A child is born.* London: Doubleday.

Ninio, A., & Bruner, J. (1978). The achievement and antecedents of labeling. *Journal of Child Language, 5*, 1–14.

Nisan, M. (1987). Moral norms and social conventions: A cross-cultural comparison. *Developmental Psychology, 23*, 719–725.

Nisan, M. (1988). A story of a pot, or a cross-cultural comparison of basic moral evaluations: A response to the critique by Turiel, Nucci, and Smetana (1988). *Developmental Psychology, 24*, 144–146.

Nisbett, R. (1995). Race, IQ, and scientism. In S. Fraser (Ed.), *The bell curve wars : Race, intelligence, and the future of America.* New York: Basic.

Nolen-Hoeksema, S., Wolfson, A., Mumme, D., & Guskin, K. (1995). Helplessness in children of depressed and nondepressed mothers. *Developmental Psychology, 31*, 377–387.

Norbeck, J. S., & Tilden, V. P. (1983). Life stress, social support, and emotional disequilibrium in complications of pregnancy: A prospective, multivariate study. *Journal of Health and Social Behavior, 24*, 30–46.

Nottelmann, E. D. (1987). Competence and self-esteem during transition from childhood to adolescence. *Developmental Psychology, 23*, 441–450.

Novak, M. A., & Harlow, H. F. (1975). Social recovery of monkeys isolated for the first year of life. I. Rehabilitation and therapy. *Developmental Psychology, 11*, 453–465.

Nowakowski, R. S. (1987). Basic concepts of CNS development. *Child Development, 58*, 568–595.

Nucci, L. (1985). Social conflict and the development of children's moral and conventional concepts. In M. W. Berkowitz (Ed.), *Peer conflict and psychological growth* (pp. 55–70). San Francisco: Jossey-Bass.

Nucci, L., & Turiel, E. (1993). God's word, religious rules, and their relation to Christian and Jewish children's concepts of morality. *Child Development, 64*, 1475–1491.

Nucci, L. P. (1981). Conceptions of personal issues: A domain distinct from moral or societal concepts. *Child Development, 52,* 114–121.

Nunnally, J. C. (1978). *Psychometric theory* (2nd ed.). New York: McGraw-Hill.

Nyiti, R. M. (1976). The development of conservation in the Meru children of Tanzania. *Child Development, 47,* 1122–1129.

Oakes, J. (1985). *Keeping track.* New Haven, CT: Yale University Press.

O'Brien, M., & Huston, A. C. (1985). Development of sex-typed play behavior in toddlers. *Developmental Psychology, 21,* 866–871.

O'Brien, S. F., & Bierman, K. L. (1988). Conceptions and perceived influence of peer groups: Interviews with preadolescents and adolescents. *Child Development, 59,* 1360–1365.

O'Brien, W. F., & Cefalo, R. C. (1991). Labor and delivery. In S. G. Gabbe, J. R. Niebyl, & J. L. Simpson (Eds.), *Obstetrics: Normal & problem pregnancies* (2nd ed., pp. 427–455). New York: Churchill Livingstone.

Oden, S., & Asher, S. R. (1977). Coaching children in social skills for friendship making. *Child Development, 79,* 327–334.

Offer, D., & Offer, J. B. (1975). *From teenage to young manhood: A psychological study.* New York: Basic.

Okagaki, L., & Sternberg, R. J. (1993). Parental beliefs and children's school performance. *Child Development, 64,* 36–56.

Olds, D. L., & Henderson, C. R., Jr. (1989). The prevention of maltreatment. In D. Cicchetti & V. Carlson (Eds.), *Child maltreatment: Theory and research on the causes and consequences of child abuse and neglect* (pp. 722–763). New York: Cambridge University Press.

O'Leary, K. D., & Wilson, G. T. (1987). *Behavior therapy* (2nd ed.). Englewood Cliffs, NJ: Prentice-Hall.

Oller, D. K., & Eilers, R. E. (1988). The role of audition in infant babbling. *Child Development, 59,* 441–449.

O'Loughlin, M. (1992). Rethinking science education: Beyond Piagetian constructivism toward a sociocultural model of teaching and learning. *Journal of Research in Science Teaching, 29,* 791–820.

Olson, G. M., & Sherman, T. (1983). Attention, learning, and memory in infants. In P. H. Mussen (Series Ed.), M. M. Haith & J. J. Campos (Vol. Eds.), *Handbook of child psychology: Vol. II. Infancy and developmental psychobiology* (4th ed., pp. 1001–1080). New York: Wiley.

Olson, S. L., & Hoza, B. (1993). Preschool developmental antecedents of conduct problems in children beginning school. *Journal of Clinical Child Psychology, 22,* 60–67.

Olweus, D., Mattsson, A., Schalling, D., & Low, H. (1980). Testosterone, aggression, physical, and personality dimensions in normal adolescent males. *Psychosomatic Medicine, 33,* 265–277.

Olweus, D., Mattsson, A., Schalling, D., & Low, H. (1988). Circulating testosterone levels and aggression in adolescent males: A causal analysis. *Psychosomatic Medicine, 50,* 261–272.

O'Malley, P. M., & Bachman, J. G. (1983). Self-esteem: Change and stability between ages 13 and 23. *Developmental Psychology, 19,* 257–268.

Opie, I., & Opie, P. (1959). *The lore and language of schoolchildren.* New York: Oxford University Press.

Oppenheim, D., Sagi, A., & Lamb, M. E. (1988). Infant-adult attachments on the kibbutz and their relation to socioemotional development 4 years later. *Developmental Psychology, 24,* 427–433.

Ornstein, P. A., Baker-Ward, L., & Naus, M. J. (1988). The development of memory skill. In F. E. Weinert & M. Perlmutter (Eds.), *Memory development: Universal changes and individual differences* (pp. 31–41). Hillsdale, NJ: Erlbaum.

Osofsky, J. D., Osofsky, H. J., & Diamond, M. O. (1988). The transition to parenthood: Special tasks and risk factors for adolescent parents. In G. Y. Michaels & W. A. Goldberg (Eds.), *The transition to parenthood: Current theory and research* (pp. 209–234). Cambridge, England: Cambridge University Press.

Oster, H., Hegley, D., & Nagel, L. (1992). Adult judgments and fine-grained analysis of infant facial expressions: Testing the validity of a priori coding formulas. *Developmental Psychology, 28,* 1115–1131.

Overton, W. F., Ward, S. L., Noveck, I. A., Black, J., & O'Brien, D. P. (1987). Form and content in the development of deductive reasoning. *Developmental Psychology, 23,* 22–30.

Padden, C., & Humphries, T. (1988). *Deaf in America: Voices from a culture.* Cambridge, MA: Harvard University Press.

Palmer, F. B., & Capute, A. J. (1994) Streams of development. In F. A. Oski, C. D. DeAngelis, R. D. Feigin, J. A. McMillan, & J. B. Warshaw (Eds.), *Principles and practices of pediatrics* (2nd ed., pp. 667–673). Philadelphia: Lippincott.

Parikh, B. (1980). Development of moral judgment and its relation to family environmental factors in Indian and American families. *Child Development, 51,* 1030–1039.

Paris, S. G., & Jacobs, J. E. (1984). The benefits of informed instruction for children's reading awareness and comprehension skills. *Child Development, 55,* 2083–2093.

Paris, S. G., Lindauer, B. K., & Cox, G. L. (1977). The development of inferential comprehension. *Child Development, 48,* 1728–1733.

Park, K. A., Lay, K.-L., & Ramsay, L. (1993). Individual differences and developmental changes in preschoolers' friendships. *Developmental Psychology, 29,* 264–270.

Park, K. A., & Waters, E. (1989). Security of attachment and preschool friendships. *Child Development, 60,* 1076–1081.

Parke, R. D. (1977). Punishment in children: Effects, side effects and alternative strategies. In H. L. Hom, Jr., & A. Robinson (Eds.), *Psychological processes in early education* (pp. 71–97). New York: Academic.

Parke, R. D. (1981). *Fathers.* Cambridge, MA: Harvard University Press.

Parke, R. D., & Bhavnagri, N. P. (1989). Parents as managers of children's peer relationships. In D. Belle (Ed.), *Children's social networks and social supports* (pp. 241–259). New York: Wiley.

Parke, R. D., & Ladd, G. W. (Eds.). (1992). *Family-peer relationships: Modes of linkage.* Hillsdale, NJ: Erlbaum.

Parke, R. D., & Slaby, R. G. (1983). The development of aggression. In E. M. Hetherington (Ed.), *Handbook of child psychology: Vol. 4. Socialization, personality, and social development* (4th ed., pp. 547–641). New York: Wiley.

Parke, R. D., & Tinsley, B. J. (1987). Family interaction in infancy. In J. D. Osofsky (Ed.), *Handbook of infant development* (pp. 579–641). New York: Wiley.

Parke, R. D., & Tinsley, B. R. (1981). The father's role in infancy: Determinants of involvement in caregiving and play. In M. E. Lamb (Ed.), *The role of the father in child development* (pp. 429–458). New York: Wiley.

Parker, J. G., & Asher, S. R. (1987). Peer relations and later personal adjustment: Are low-accepted children "at risk"? *Psychological Bulletin, 102,* 357–389.

Parker, J. G., & Asher, S. R. (1993). Friendship and friendship quality in middle childhood: Links with peer group acceptance and feelings of loneliness and social dissatisfaction. *Developmental Psychology, 29,* 611–621.

Parkhurst, J. T., & Asher, S. R. (1992). Peer rejection in middle school: Subgroup differences in behavior, loneliness, and interpersonal concerns. *Developmental Psychology, 28,* 231–241.

Parsons, J. E., Adler, T. F., & Kaczala, C. M. (1982). Socialization of achievement attitudes and beliefs:

Parental influences. *Child Development, 53,* 310–321.

Parsons, J. E., Kaczala, C., & Meece, J. L. (1982). Socialization of achievement attitudes and beliefs: Classroom influences. *Child Development, 53,* 322–339.

Parten, M. (1932). Social participation among preschool children. *Journal of Abnormal and Social Psychology, 27,* 243–269.

Pascual-Leone, J. (1970). A mathematical model for the transition rule in Piaget's developmental stages. *Acta Psychologica, 32,* 301–345.

Patterson, G. R. (1980). Mothers: The unacknowledged victims. *Monographs of the Society for Research in Child Development, 45* (5, Serial No. 186).

Patterson, G. R. (1982). *Coercive family processes.* Eugene, OR: Castilia Press.

Patterson, G. R., Littman, R. A., & Bricker, W. (1967). Assertive behavior in children: A step toward a theory of aggression. *Monographs of the Society for Research in Child Development, 32* (5, Serial No. 113).

Patterson, G. R., & Stouthamer-Loeber, M. (1984). The correlation of family management practices and delinquency. *Child Development, 55,* 1299–1307.

Paul, P. V., & Jackson, D. W. (1993). *Toward a psychology of deafness: Theoretical and empirical perspectives.* Needham Heights, MA: Allyn and Bacon.

Pearson, J. L., Hunter, A. G., Ensminger, M. E., & Kellam, S. G. (1990). Black grandmothers in multigenerational households: Diversity in family structure and parenting involvement in the Woodlawn community. *Child Development, 61,* 434–442.

Pease, D. M., Gleason, M. B., & Pan, B. A. (1993). Learning the meaning of words: Semantic development and beyond. In J. Berko Gleason (Ed.), *The development of language* (3rd ed., pp. 110–152). New York: Macmillan.

Pedlow, R., Sanson, A., Prior, M., & Oberklaid, F. (1993). Stability of maternally reported temperament from infancy to 8 years. *Developmental Psychology, 29,* 998–1007.

Pellegrini, D. S. (1985). Social cognition and competence in middle childhood. *Child Development, 56,* 253–264.

Pellegrini, D. S., & Urbain, E. S. (1985). An evaluation of interpersonal cognitive problem solving training with children. *Journal of Child Psychology and Psychiatry and Allied Disciplines, 26,* 17–41.

Penner, S. G. (1987). Parental responses to grammatical and ungrammatical child utterances. *Child Development, 58,* 376–384.

Pennington, B. F., Bender, B., Puck, M., Salbenblatt, J., & Robinson, A. (1982). Learning disabilities in children with sex

chromosome anomalies. *Child Development, 53,* 1182–1192.

Perner, J., Ruffman, T., & Leekam, S. R. (1994). Theory of mind is contagious: You catch it from your sibs. *Child Development, 5,* 1228–1238.

Perris, E. E., Myers, N. A., & Clifton, R. K. (1990). Long-term memory for a single infancy experience. *Child Development, 61,* 1796–1807.

Perry, D. G., & Bussey, K. (1979). The social learning theory of sex differences: Imitation is alive and well. *Journal of Personality and Social Psychology, 37,* 1699–1712.

Perry, D. G., Perry, L. C., & Rasmussen, P. (1986). Cognitive social learning mediators of aggression. *Child Development, 57,* 700–711.

Petersen, A. C., & Taylor, B. (1980). The biological approach to adolescence: Biological change and psychological adaptation. In J. Adelson (Ed.), *Handbook of adolescent psychology* (pp. 117–155). New York: Wiley.

Petitto, L. A. (1988). "Language" in the prelinguistic child. In F. S. Kessel (Ed.), *The development of language and language researchers: Essays in honor of Roger Brown* (pp. 187–222). Hillsdale, NJ: Erlbaum.

Petrie, R. H. (1991). Intrapartum fetal evaluation. In S. G. Gabbe, J. R. Niebyl, & J. L. Simpson (Eds.), *Obstetrics: Normal & problem pregnancies* (2nd ed., pp. 457–491). New York: Churchill Livingstone.

Phillips, D. A. (1984). The illusion of incompetence among academically competent children. *Child Development, 55,* 2000–2016.

Phillips, D. A. (1987). Socialization of perceived academic competence among highly competent children. *Child Development, 58,* 1308–1320.

Phillips, D. A., McCartney, K., & Scarr, S. (1987). Child-care quality and children's social development. *Developmental Psychology, 23,* 537–543.

Phillips, D. A., Voran, M., Kisker, E., Howes, C., & Whitebrook, M. (1994). Child care for children in poverty: Opportunity or inequity? *Child Development, 65,* 472–492.

Piaget, J. (1929). *The child's conception of the world.* London: Routledge & Kegan Paul.

Piaget, J. (1936/1952). *The origins of intelligence in children.* New York: International University Press.

Piaget, J. (1937/1954). *The construction of reality in the child.* New York: Basic.

Piaget, J. (1945/1962). *Play, dreams and imitation in childhood.* New York: W. W. Norton.

Piaget, J. (1932/1965). *The moral judgment of the child.* New York: Free Press.

Piaget, J. (1970). Piaget's theory. In P. H. Mussen (Ed.), *Handbook of child psychology* (4th ed., Vol. I, pp. 703–732). New York: Wiley.

Piaget, J. (1926/1971). *The language and thought of the child.* New York: World Publishing.

Piaget, J. (1972). Intellectual evolution from adolescence to adulthood. *Human Development, 15,* 1–12.

Piaget, J. (1983). Piaget's theory. In P. H. Mussen (Series Ed.) & W. Kessen (Vol. Ed.), *Handbook of child psychology. Vol. 1. History, theory, and methods* (pp. 103–128). New York: Wiley.

Piaget, J., & Inhelder, B. (1956). *The child's conception of space.* London: Routledge & Kegan Paul.

Pianta, R. C., & Egeland, B. (1994). Predictors of instability in children's mental test performance at 24, 48, and 96 months. *Intelligence, 18,* 145–163.

Pianta, R. C., Egeland, B., & Erickson, M. F. (1989). The antecedents of maltreatment: Results of the mother-child interaction research project. In D. Cicchetti & V. Carlson (Eds.), *Child maltreatment: Theory and research on the causes and consequences of child abuse and neglect* (pp. 203–253). New York: Cambridge University Press.

Piatelli-Palmerini, M. (Ed.). (1980). *Language and learning: The debate between Jean Piaget and Noam Chomsky.* Cambridge, MA: Harvard University Press.

Pick, H. L. (1992). Eleanor J. Gibson: Learning to perceive and perceiving to learn. *Developmental Psychology, 28,* 787–794.

Pickens, J., & Fields, T. (1993). Facial expressivity in infants of depressed mothers. *Developmental Psychology, 29,* 986–988.

Pinker, S. (1988). Learnability theory and the acquisition of a first language. In F. S. Kessel (Ed.), *The development of language and language researchers* (pp. 97–120). Hillsdale, NJ: Erlbaum.

Pinker, S. (1991). Rules of language. *Science, 253,* 530–535.

Place, K. S., & Becker, J. A. (1991). The influence of pragmatic competence on the likeability of grade-school children. *Discourse Processes, 14,* 227–241.

Plato (1942). *Republic* (B. Jowett, Trans.). New York: Walter J. Black.

Plomin, R. (1987) Developmental behavioral genetics and infancy. In J. D. Osofsky (Ed.), *Handbook of infant development* (2nd ed., pp. 363–414). New York: Wiley.

Plomin, R. (1989). Environment and genes: Determinants of behavior. *American Psychologist, 44,* 105–111.

Plomin, R. (1990). The role of inheritance in behavior. *Science, 248,* 183–188.

Plomin, R. (1993). Nature and nurture: Perspective and prospective. In R. Plomin & G. E. McClearn (Eds.), *Nature, nurture, and psychology* (pp. 459–485). Washington, DC: American Psychological Association.

Plomin, R., DeFries, J. C., & Loehlin, J. C. (1977). Genotype-environment interaction and correlation in the analysis of human behavior. *Psychological Bulletin, 84,* 309–322.

Plomin, R., DeFries, J. C., & McClearn, G. E. (1990). *Behavioral genetics: A primer* (2nd ed.). San Francisco: Freeman.

Plomin, R., Emde, R. N., Braungart, J. M., Campos, J., Corley, R., Fulker, D. W., Kagan, J., Reznick, J. S., Robinson, J., Zahn-Waxler, C., & DeFries, J. C. (1993). Genetic change and continuity from fourteen to twenty months: The MacArthur Longitudinal Twin Study. *Child Development, 64,* 1354–1376.

Plomin, R., Loehlin, J. C., & DeFries, J. C. (1985). Genetic and environmental components of "environmental" influences. *Developmental Psychology, 21,* 391–402.

Plomin, R., & McClearn, G. E. (Eds.). (1993). *Nature, nurture, and psychology.* Washington, DC: American Psychological Association.

Plomin R., Owen M. J., & McGuffin, P. (1994). The genetic basis of complex human behaviors. *Science, 264,* 1733–1739.

Plouffe, L., & Donahue, J. (1994). Techniques for early diagnosis of the abnormal fetus. *Clinics in Perinatology, 21,* 723–741.

Pollitt, E. (1994). Poverty and child development: Relevance of research in developing countries to the United States. *Child Development, 65,* 283–295.

Pollitt, E. P., Gorman, K. S., Engle, P. L., Martorell, R., & Rivera, J. (1993). Early supplemental feeding and cognition. *Monographs of the Society for Research in Child Development, 58* (7, Serial No. 235).

Pollock, L. (1987). *A lasting relationship: Parents and children over three centuries.* Hanover, NH: University Press of New England.

Pool, R. (1994). *Eve's rib.* New York: Crown.

Porter, R. H., Makin, J. W., Davis, L. B., & Christensen, K. M. (1991). An assessment of the salient olfactory environment of formula-fed infants. *Physiology and Behavior, 50,* 907–911.

Porter, R. H., Makin, J. W., Davis, L. B., & Christensen, K. M. (1992). Breast-fed infants respond to olfactory cues from their own mother and unfamiliar lactating females. *Infant Behavior and Development, 15,* 85–93.

Powell, G. F., Low, J. F., & Speers, M. A. (1987). Behavior as a diagnostic aid in failure-to-thrive. *Journal of Developmental and Behavioral Pediatrics, 8,* 18–24.

Power, F. C., Higgins, A., & Kohlberg, L. (1989). *Lawrence Kohlberg's approach to moral education.* New York: Columbia University Press.

Powlishta, K. K. (1995). Gender bias in children's perceptions of personality traits. *Sex Roles, 52,* 17–28.

Powlishta, K. K., Serbin, L. A., & Moller, L. C. (1993). The stability of individual differences in gender typing: Implications for understanding gender segregation. *Sex Roles, 29,* 723–737.

Pressley, M. (1982). Elaboration and memory development. *Child Development, 53,* 296–309.

Pressley, M., & Van Meter, P. (1993). Memory strategies: Natural development and use following instruction. In R. Pasnak & M. L. Howe (Eds.), *Emerging themes in cognitive development* (Vol. 2, pp. 128–165). New York: Springer-Verlag.

Previc, F. H. (1991). A general theory concerning the prenatal origins of cerebral lateralization in humans. *Psychological Review, 98,* 299–334.

Proffitt, D. R., & Bertenthal, B. I. (1990). Converging operations revisited: Assessing what infants perceive using discrimination measures. *Perception and Psychophysics, 47,* 1–11.

Putallaz, M. (1987). Maternal behavior and children's sociometric status. *Child Development, 58,* 324–340.

Putallaz, M., & Heflin, A. (1990). Parent-child interaction. In S. R. Asher & J. D. Coie (Eds.), *Peer rejection in childhood* (pp. 189–216). New York: Cambridge University Press.

Putallaz, M., & Wasserman, A. (1990). Children's entry behavior. In S. R. Asher & J. D. Coie (Eds.), *Peer rejection in childhood* (pp. 60–89). New York: Cambridge University Press.

Pye, C. (1986). Quiche' Mayan speech to children. *Journal of Child Language, 13,* 85–100.

Quenby, S. M., & Farquharson, R. G. (1993). Predicting recurring miscarriage: What is important? *Obstetrics and Gynecology, 82,* 132–138.

Quiggle, N. L., Garber, J., Panak, W. F., & Dodge, K. A. (1992). Social information processing in aggressive and depressed children. *Child Development, 63,* 1305–1320.

Rabiner, D. L., & Gordon, L. V. (1992). The coordination of conflicting social goals: Differences between rejected and nonrejected boys. *Child Development, 63,* 1344–1350.

Rabinowicz, T. (1986). The differentiated maturation of the cerebral cortex. In F. Falkner & J. M. Tanner (Eds.), *Human growth: A comprehensive treatise* (pp. 385–410). New York: Plenum.

Radke-Yarrow, M., Zahn-Waxler, C., & Chapman, M. (1983). Children's prosocial dispositions and behavior. In P. H. Mussen (Series Ed.) & E. M. Hetherington (Vol. Ed), *Handbook of child psychology: Vol. 4. Socialization, personality, and social development* (4th ed., pp. 469–545). New York: Wiley.

Radziszewska, B., & Rogoff, B. (1988). Influence of adult and peer collaborators on children's planning skills. *Developmental Psychology, 24,* 840–848.

Radziszewska, B., & Rogoff, B. (1991). Children's guided participation in planning imaginary errands with skilled adult or peer partners. *Developmental Psychology, 27,* 381–389.

Raffaelli, M., & Duckett, E. (1989). "We were just talking . . ."; Conversations in early adolescence. *Journal of Youth and Adolescence, 18,* 567–582.

Rajecki, D. W., Dame, J. A., Creek, K. J., Barrickman, P. J., Reid, C. A., & Appleby, D. C. (1993). Gender casting in television toy advertisements: Distributions, message content analysis, and evaluations. *Journal of Consumer Psychology, 2,* 307–327.

Ramey, C. (1982). Commentary on "Lasting effects of early education: A report from the Consortium for Longitudinal Studies." *Monographs of the Society for Research in Child Development, 47* (2-3, Serial No. 195).

Ramey, C. (1994). Abecedarian project. In R. J. Sternberg (Ed.), *Encyclopedia of human intelligence* (pp. 1–2). New York: Macmillan.

Ratner, N. B. (1993). Atypical language development. In J. Berko Gleason (Ed.), *The development of language* (3rd ed., pp. 325–368). New York: Macmillan.

Rauh, V. A., Achenbach, T. M., Nucombe, B., Howell, C. T., & Teti, D. M. (1988). Minimizing adverse effects of low birthweight: Four-year results on an early intervention program. *Child Development, 59,* 544–553.

Raven, J. C., Court, J. H., & Raven, J. (1986). *Manual for Raven's progressive matrices and vocabulary scales.* London: Lewis.

Rawlins, W. K. (1992). *Friendship matters: Communication, dialectics, and the life course.* Hawthorne, NY: Aldine de Gruyter.

Rayman, P. (1995). [Review of the book *Failing at fairness: How America's schools cheat girls*]. *Contemporary Sociology, 24,* 87.

Raz, S., Foster, M. S., Briggs, S. D., Shah, F., Baertschi, J. C., Lauterbach, M. D.,

Riggs, W. W., Magill, L. H., & Sander, C. J. (1994). Lateralization of perinatal cerebral insult and cognitive asymmetry: Evidence from neuroimaging. *Neuropsychology, 8,* 160–170.

Reber, M., Kazak, A. E., & Himmelberg, P. (1987). Phenylalanine control and family functioning in early-treated phenylketonuria. *Journal of Development and Behavioral Pediatrics, 8,* 311–317.

Reich, P. A. (1986). *Language development.* Englewood Cliffs, NJ: Prentice-Hall.

Reichenbach, L., & Masters, J. C. (1983). Children's use of expressive and contextual cues in judgments of emotions. *Child Development, 54,* 993–1004.

Reisman, J. E. (1987). Touch, motion, and proprioception. In P. Salapatek & L. Cohen (Eds.), *Handbook of infant perception. Vol. 1. From sensation to perception* (pp. 265–304). Orlando, FL: Academic.

Reissland, N. (1988). Neonatal imitation in the first hour of life: Observations in rural Nepal. *Developmental Psychology, 24,* 464–469.

Renshaw, P. D. (1981). The roots of peer interaction research: A historical analysis of the 1930s. In S. R. Asher & J. M. Gottman (Eds.), *The development of children's friendships* (pp. 1–28). Cambridge, England: Cambridge University Press.

Renshaw, P. D., & Brown, P. J. (1993). Loneliness in middle childhood: Concurrent and longitudinal predictors. *Child Development, 64,* 1271–1284.

Rescorla, R. A. (1988). Pavlovian conditioning: It's not what you think it is. *American Psychologist, 43,* 151–160.

Rest, J. R. (1983). Morality. In P. H. Mussen (Series Ed.) & J. H. Flavell & E. M. Markman (Vol. Eds.), *Handbook of child psychology. Vol. 3. Cognitive development* (pp. 556–629). New York: Wiley.

Rest, J. R. (1986). *Moral development.* New York: Praeger.

Retherford, R. D., & Sewell, W. H. (1991). Birth order and intelligence: Further tests of the confluence model. *American Sociological Review, 56,* 141–158.

Reynolds, A. J. (1994). Effects of a preschool plus follow-on intervention for children at risk. *Developmental Psychology, 30,* 787–804.

Reznick, J. S., & Goldfield, B. A. (1992). Rapid change in lexical development in comprehension and production. *Developmental Psychology, 28,* 406–413.

Rheingold, H. L. (1982). Little children's participation in the work of adults, a nascent prosocial behavior. *Child Development, 53,* 114–125.

Rholes, W. S., & Ruble, D. N. (1984). Children's understanding of dispositional characteristics of others. *Child Development, 55,* 550–560.

Rice, M. L. (1989). Children's language acquisition. *American Psychologist, 44,* 149–156.

Rice, M. L., Huston, A. C., Truglio, R., & Wright, J. (1990). Words from "Sesame Street:" Learning vocabulary while viewing. *Developmental Psychology, 26,* 421–428.

Rice, M. L., & Woodsmall, L. (1988). Lessons from television: Children's word learning when viewing. *Child Development, 59,* 420–429.

Richards, D. D., & Siegler, R. S. (1984). The effects of task requirements on children's life judgments. *Child Development, 55,* 1687–1696.

Richards, M. H., Abell, S., & Petersen, A. C. (1993). Biological development. In P. H. Tolan & B. J. Cohler (Eds.), *Handbook of clinical research and practice with adolescents* (pp. 21–44). New York: Wiley.

Rider, E. A., & Rieser, J. J. (1988). Pointing at objects in other rooms: Young children's sensitivity to perspective after walking with and without vision. *Child Development, 59,* 480–494.

Rieser, J., Yonas, A., & Wilkner, K. (1976). Radial localization of odors by human newborns. *Child Development, 47,* 856–859.

Robinson, J. L., Kagan, J., Reznick, J. S., & Corley, R. (1992). The heritability of inhibited and uninhibited behavior: A twin study. *Developmental Psychology, 28,* 1030–1037.

Robinson, J. P. (1989). Caring for kids. *American Demographics, 11,* 52.

Roche, A. F. (1979). Secular trends in stature, weight, and maturation. In A. F. Roche (Ed.), *Secular trends in human growth, maturation, and development* (pp. 3–27). *Monographs of the Society for Research in Child Development, 44* (3-4, Serial No. 179).

Roche, A. F. (1981). The adipocyte-number hypothesis. *Child Development, 52,* 31–43.

Rodgers, J. L. (1984). Confluence effects: Not here, not now! *Developmental Psychology, 20,* 321–331.

Rodgers, J. L., & Rowe, D. C. (1994). Birth order, spacing, and family size; family environments. In R. J. Sternberg (Ed.), *Encyclopedia of human intelligence* (pp. 204–209). New York: Macmillan.

Rodgers, J. L., Rowe, D. C., & May, K. (1994). DF analysis of NLSY IQ/achievement data: Nonshared environmental influences. *Intelligence, 19,* 157–177.

Rogers, K. B. (1993). Grouping the gifted and talented: Questions and answers. *Roeper Review, 16,* 8–12.

Roggman, L. A., Langlois, J. H., Hubbs-Tait, L., & Rieser-Danner, L. A. (1994). Infant day-care, attachment, and the "file drawer problem." *Child Development, 65,* 1429–1443.

Rogoff, B., & Chavajay, P. (1995). What's become of research on the cultural basis of cognitive development? *American Psychologist, 50,* 859–877.

Rogoff, B., Ellis, S., & Gardner, W. (1984). Adjustment of adult-child instruction according to child's age and task. *Developmental Psychology, 20,* 193–199.

Rogoff, B., Mistry, J., Goncu, A., & Mosier, C. (1993). Guided participation in cultural activity by toddlers and caregivers. *Monographs of the Society for Research in Child Development, 58* (8, Serial No. 179).

Rogoff, B., & Morelli, G. (1989). Perspectives on children's development from cultural psychology. *American Psychologist, 44,* 343–348.

Rogoff, B., & Waddell, J. J. (1982). Memory for information organized in a scene by children from two cultures. *Child Development, 53,* 1224–1228.

Roopnarine, J. L., & Johnson, J. E. (1984). Socialization in a mixed-age experimental program. *Developmental Psychology, 20,* 828–832.

Roper, R., & Hinde, R. A. (1978). Social behavior in a play group: Consistency and complexity. *Child Development, 49,* 570–579.

Rose, A. J., & Montemayor, R. (1994). The relationship between gender role orientation and perceived self-competency in male and female adolescents. *Sex Roles, 31,* 579–595.

Rose, R. M., Bernstein, I. S., & Gordon, T. P. (1975). Consequences of social conflict on plasma testosterone levels in rhesus monkeys. *Psychosomatic Medicine, 37,* 50–61.

Rose, S. A., & Blank, M. (1974). The potency of context in children's cognition: An illustration through conservation. *Child Development, 45,* 499–501.

Rose, S. A., & Ruff, H. A. (1987). Cross-modal abilities in human infants. In J. D. Osofsky (Ed.), *Handbook of infant development* (pp. 318–362). New York: Wiley.

Rose, S. A., Feldman, J. F., Wallace, I. F., & McCarton, C. (1989). Infant visual attention: Relation to birth status and developmental outcome during the first 5 years. *Developmental Psychology, 25,* 560–576.

Rose, S. M., & Feldman, J. F. (1995). Prediction of IQ and specific cognitive abilities at 11 years from infancy measures. *Developmental Psychology, 31,* 685–696.

Rosehan, D. (1970). The natural socialization of altruistic autonomy. In J. Macaulay & L. Berkowitz (Eds.),

*Altruism and helping behavior* (pp. 251–268). New York: Academic.

Rosen, W. D., Adamson, L. B., & Bakeman, R. (1992). An experimental investigation of infant social referencing: Mothers' messages and gender differences. *Developmental Psychology, 28,* 1172–1178.

Rosenberg, A. A. (1991). The neonate. In S. G. Gabbe, J. R. Niebyl, & J. L. Simpson (Eds.), *Obstetrics: Normal & problem pregnancies* (2nd ed., pp. 697–752). New York: Churchill Livingstone.

Rosenberg, M. (1979). *Conceiving the self.* New York: Basic.

Rosenshine, B., & Meister, C. (1994). Reciprocal teaching: A review of the research. *Review of Educational Research, 64,* 479–530.

Rosenzweig, M. R. (1984). Experience, memory, and the brain. *American Psychologist, 39,* 365–376.

Rossi, E. (1992). The future of the obese child. In P. L. Giorgi, R. M. Suskind, & C. Catassi (Eds.), *The obese child* (pp. 240–247). New York: Karger.

Rosso, P. (1990). *Nutrition and metabolism in pregnancy: Mother and fetus.* New York: Oxford University Press.

Rothbart, M. K. (1986). Longitudinal observation of infant temperament. *Developmental Psychology, 22,* 356–365.

Rothbart, M. K., & Ahadi, S. A. (1994). Temperament and the development of personality. *Journal of Abnormal Psychology, 103,* 55–66.

Rothbaum, F., & Weisz, J. R. (1994). Parental caregiving and child externalizing behavior in nonclinical samples: A meta-analysis. *Psychological Bulletin, 116,* 55–74.

Roug, L., Landberg, I., & Lundberg, L. J. (1989). Phonetic development in early infancy: A study of four Swedish children during the first eighteen months of life. *Journal of Child Language, 16,* 19–40.

Rousseau, J. J. (1762/1979). *Emile, or education* (A. Bloom, Trans.). New York: Basic.

Rovee-Collier, C. (1987). Learning and memory in infancy. In J. D. Osofsky (Ed.), *Handbook of infant development* (pp. 98–148). New York: Wiley.

Rovee-Collier, C. (1989). The joy of kicking: Memories, motives, and mobiles. In P. R. Solomon, G. R. Goethals, C. M. Kelley, & B. R. Stephens (Eds.), *Memory: Interdisciplinary approaches* (pp. 151–180). New York: Springer-Verlag.

Rovee-Collier, C. (1995). Time windows in cognitive development. *Developmental Psychology, 31,* 147–169.

Rowe, D. C. (1989). Families and peers: Another look at the nature-nurture question. In T. J. Berndt & G. W. Ladd (Eds.), *Peer relationships in child development* (pp. 274–299). New York: Wiley.

Rowe, D. C. (1994). *The limits of family influence: Genes, experience, and behavior.* New York: Guilford Press.

Rowe, D. C., & Plomin, R. (1981). The importance of nonshared ($E_1$) environmental influences in behavioral development. *Developmental Psychology, 17,* 517–531.

Rowe, D. C., Vazsonyi, A. T., & Flannery, D. J. (1994). No more than skin deep: Ethnic and racial similarity in developmental process. *Psychological Review, 10,* 396–413.

Rowe, D. C., & Waldman, I. E. (1993). The question 'How?' reconsidered. In R. Plomin & G. E. McClearn (Eds.), *Nature, nurture, and psychology* (pp. 355–373). Washington, DC: American Psychological Association.

Rubin, A. R. The baby or the drug? (1995). *U.S. News & World Report, 118,* 59–61.

Rubin, K. H. (1982). Nonsocial play in preschoolers: Necessarily evil? *Child Development, 53,* 651–657.

Rubin, K. H., Fein, G. G., & Vandenberg, B. (1983). Play. In E. M. Hetherington (Ed.), *Handbook of child psychology* (pp. 693–774). New York: Wiley.

Rubin, K. H., & Krasnor, L. R. (1986). Social-cognitive and social behavioral perspective on problem solving. In M. Perlmutter (Ed.), *Cognitive perspectives on children's social and behavioral development: The Minnesota Symposia on Child Psychology* (Vol. 18, pp. 1–68). Hillsdale, NJ: Erlbaum.

Rubin, K. H., LeMare, L. J., & Lollis, S. (1990). Social withdrawal in childhood: Developmental pathways to peer rejection. In S. R. Asher & J. D. Coie (Eds.), *Peer rejection in childhood* (pp. 217–249). New York: Cambridge Press.

Ruble, D. N. (1988). Sex-role development. In M. H. Bornstein & M. E. Lamb (Eds.), *Developmental psychology: An advanced textbook* (2nd ed., pp. 411–460). Hillsdale, NJ: Erlbaum.

Ruble, D. N., Balaban, T., & Cooper, J. (1981). Gender constancy and the effects of sex-typed television toy commercials. *Child Development, 52,* 667–673.

Ruble, D. N., Boggiano, A. K., Feldman, N. S., & Loebl, J. H. (1980). Developmental analysis of the role of social comparison in self-evaluation. *Developmental Psychology, 16,* 105–115.

Russell, G., & Russell, A. (1987). Mother-child and father-child relationships in middle childhood. *Child Development, 58,* 1573–1585.

Russell, J. (1994). Is there universal recognition of emotion from facial expressions? A review of the cross-cultural studies. *Psychological Bulletin, 115,* 102–141.

Russell, J. A., & Bullock, M. (1986). On the dimensions preschoolers use to interpret facial expressions of emotion. *Developmental Psychology, 22,* 97–102.

Rutledge, J. C. (1994). Genetic factors in clinical developmental toxicology. In C. A. Kimmel & J. Buelke-Sam (Eds.), *Developmental toxicology* (2nd ed., pp. 333–348). New York: Raven.

Rutter, D. R., & Durkin, K. (1987). Turn-taking in mother-infant interaction: An examination of vocalizations and gaze. *Developmental Psychology, 23,* 54–61.

Rutter, M. (1972). *Maternal deprivation reassessed.* Harmondsworth, Middlesex: Penguin.

Rutter, M. (1979). Maternal deprivation, 1972–1978: New findings, new concepts, new approaches. *Child Development, 50,* 283–305.

Rutter, M. (1980). *Changing youth in a changing society.* Cambridge, MA: Harvard University Press.

Rutter, M. (1983). School effects on pupil progress: Research findings and policy implications. *Child Development, 54,* 1–29.

Rutter, M., Bailey, A., Bolton, P., & Le Couteur, A. (1993). Autism: Syndrome definition and possible genetic mechanisms. In R. Plomin & G. E. McClearn (Eds.), *Nature, nurture, and psychology* (pp. 269–284). Washington, DC: American Psychological Association.

Rutter, M., Silberg, J., & Simonoff, E. (1993). Whither behavioral genetics? —A developmental psychopathological perspective. In R. Plomin & G. E. McClearn (Eds.), *Nature, nurture, and psychology* (pp. 433–456). Washington, DC: American Psychological Association.

Saarni, C. (1979). Children's understanding of display rules for expressive behavior. *Developmental Psychology, 15,* 424–429.

Saarni, C. (1989). Children's understanding of strategic control of emotional expression in social transactions. In C. Saarni & P. L. Harris (Eds.), *Children's understanding of emotion* (pp. 181–208). New York: Cambridge University Press.

Sachs, J. (1989). Communication development in infancy. In J. Berko Gleason (Ed.), *The development of language* (2nd ed., pp. 35–58). Columbus, OH: Merrill.

Sachs, J. (1993). The emergence of intentional communication. In J. Berko Gleason (Ed.), *The development of language* (3rd ed., pp. 39–64). New York: Macmillan.

Sackett, G. P. (1978). Measurement in observational research. In G. P. Sackett

(Ed.), *Observing behavior: Vol. 2. Data collection and analysis methods* (pp. 25–43). Baltimore, MD: University Park Press.

Sadker, M., & Sadker, D. (1994). *Failing at fairness: How America's schools cheat girls.* New York: Macmillan.

Sadler, T. W., & Hunter, E. S., III. (1994). Principles of abnormal development: Past, present, and future. In C. A. Kimmel & J. Buelke-Sam (Eds.), *Developmental toxicology* (2nd ed., pp. 53–64). New York: Raven.

Sagi, A., Lamb, M. E., Lewkowicz, K. S., Shoham, R., Dvir, R., & Estes, D. (1985). Security of infant-mother, -father, and -metapelet attachments among Kibbutz-reared Israeli children. *Monographs of the Society for Research in Child Development, 50* (1-2, Serial No. 209).

Sagi, A., van IJzendoorn, M. H., Aviezer, O., Donnell, F., & Mayseless, O. (1994). Sleeping out of home in a kibbutz communal arrangement: It makes a difference for infant-mother attachment. *Child Development, 65,* 992–1004.

Sagi, A., van IJzendoorn, M. H., & Koren-Karie, N. (1991). Primary appraisal of the strange situation: A cross-cultural analysis of preseparation episodes. *Developmental Psychology, 27,* 587–596.

Salvioli, G. P., & Faldella, G. (1992). Prevention of childhood obesity. In P. L. Giorgi, R. M. Suskind, & C. Catassi (Eds.), *The obese child* (pp. 235–239). New York: Karger.

Sameroff, A. J., & Chandler, M. J. (1975). Reproductive risk and the continuum of caretaking casualty. In F. D. Horowitz (Ed.), *Review of child development research* (Vol. 4, pp. 187–244). Chicago: University of Chicago Press.

Sanson, A., Oberklaid, F., Pedlow, R., & Prior, M. (1991). Risk indicators: Assessment of infancy predictors of pre-school behavioral maladjustment. *Journal of Child Psychology and Psychiatry and Allied Disciplines, 32,* 609–626.

Sattler, J. M. (1988). *Assessment of children's intelligence and special abilities* (3rd ed.). San Diego: Jerome M. Sattler.

Sattler, J. M. (1994). Individual tests; Stanford-Binet Intelligence Scale, 4th ed. In R. J. Sternberg (Ed.), *Encyclopedia of human intelligence* (pp. 563–570). New York: Macmillan.

Savage-Rumbaugh, E. S., Murphy, J., Sevcik, R. A., Brakke, K. E., Williams, S. L., & Rumbaugh, D. M. (1993). Language comprehension in ape and child. *Monographs of the Society for Research in Child Development, 58* (3-4, Serial No. 233).

Savage-Rumbaugh, S., Sevcik, R. A., & Hopkins, W. D. (1988). Symbolic cross-modal transfer in two species of chimpanzees. *Child Development, 59,* 617–625.

Savin-Williams, R. C., & Berndt, T. J. (1990). Friendships and peer relations during adolescence. In S. S. Feldman & G. Elliott (Eds.), *At the threshold: The developing adolescent* (pp. 277–307). Cambridge, MA: Harvard University Press.

Savin-Williams, R. C., & Demo, D. H. (1984). Developmental change and stability in adolescent self-concept. *Developmental Psychology, 20,* 1100–1110.

Saxe, G. B. (1988a). Candy selling and math learning. *Educational Research, 17,* 14–21.

Saxe, G. B. (1988b). The mathematics of child street vendors. *Child Development, 59,* 1415–1425.

Scarr, S. (1992). Developmental theories for the 1990s: Development and individual differences. *Child Development, 63,* 1–19.

Scarr, S. (1993). Biological and cultural diversity: The legacy of Darwin for development. *Child Development, 64,* 1333–1353.

Scarr, S. (1995). [Review of the book *The bell curve: Intelligence and class structure in American life*]. *Issues in Science and Technology, 11,* 82.

Scarr, S., & Carter-Saltzman, L. (1979). Twin method: Defense of a critical assumption. *Behavior Genetics, 9,* 527–542.

Scarr, S., & Kidd, K. K. (1983). Developmental behavior genetics. In P. H. Mussen (Series Ed.), M. M. Haith & J. J. Campos (Vol. Eds.), *Handbook of child psychology. Vol. 2. Infancy and developmental psychobiology* (pp. 345–433). New York: Wiley.

Scarr, S., & McCartney, K. (1983). How people make their own environments: A theory of genotype-environment effects. *Child Development, 54,* 424–435.

Scarr, S., Pakstis, A. J., Katz, S. H., & Barker, W. B. (1977). Absence of a relationship between degree of white ancestry and intellectual skills within a black population. *Human Genetics, 59,* 69–86.

Scarr, S., Phillips, D., & McCartney, K. (1989). Working mothers and their families. *American Psychologist, 44,* 1402–1409.

Scarr, S., Phillips, D., & McCartney, K. (1990). Facts, fantasies and the future of child care in the United States. *Psychological Science, 1,* 26–35.

Scarr, S., Webber, P. L., Weinberg, R. A., & Wittig, M. A. (1981). Personality resemblance among adolescents and their parents in biologically-related and adoptive families. *Journal of Personality and Social Psychology, 40,* 885–898.

Scarr, S., & Weinberg, R. A. (1976). IQ test performance of black children adopted by white families. *American Psychologist, 31,* 726–739.

Scarr, S., & Weinberg, R. A. (1978). The influence of "family background" on intellectual attainment. *American Sociological Review, 43,* 674–792.

Scarr, S., & Weinberg, R. A. (1983). The Minnesota Adoption Studies: Genetic differences and malleability. *Child Development, 54,* 260–267.

Scarr, S., Weinberg, R. A., & Waldman, I. D. (1993). IQ correlations in transracial adoptive families. *Intelligence, 17,* 541–555.

Schaffer, H. R., & Emerson, P. E. (1964). The development of social attachments in infants. *Monographs of the Society for Research in Child Development, 29* (3, Serial No. 94).

Schiavi, R. C., Theilgaard, A., Owen, D. R., & White, D. (1988). Sex chromosome anomalies, hormones, and sexuality. *Archives of General Psychiatry, 45,* 19–24.

Schneider, B. H. (1987). *The gifted child in peer group perspective.* New York: Springer-Verlag.

Schneider, M. B., Davis, J. G., Boxer, R. A., Fisher, M., & Friedman, S. B. (1990). Marfan syndrome in adolescents and young adults: Psychosocial functioning and knowledge. *Journal of Developmental and Behavioral Pediatrics, 11,* 122–127.

Schneider, W., & Bjorklund, D. F. (1992). Expertise, aptitude, and strategic remembering. *Child Development, 63,* 461–473.

Schneider, W., Korkel, J., & Weinert, F. E. (1989). Domain-specific knowledge and memory performance: A comparison of high- and low-aptitude children. *Journal of Educational Psychology, 81,* 306–312.

Schneider-Rosen, K., & Cicchetti, D. (1991). Early self-knowledge and emotional development: Visual self-recognition and affective reactions to mirror self-images in maltreated and non-maltreated toddlers. *Developmental Psychology, 27,* 471–478.

Schreibman, L., & Charlop, M. H. (1989). Infantile autism. In T. H. Ollendick & M. Hersen (Eds.), *Handbook of child psychopathology* (2nd ed., pp. 105–129). New York: Plenum.

Schuerger, J. M., & Witt, A. C. (1989). The temporal stability of individually tested intelligence. *Journal of Clinical Psychology, 45,* 294–302.

Scialli, A. R. (1994). Clinical care: Preconception and postconception. In C. A. Kimmel & J. Buelke-Sam (Eds.), *Developmental toxicology* (2nd ed., pp. 307–331). New York: Raven.

Scrimshaw, N. S. (1991, October). Iron deficiency. *Scientific American, 266,* 46–52.

Scrimshaw, N. S. (1993). Early supplementary feeding and cognition: A retrospective comment. *Monographs of the Society for Research in Child Development, 58* (7, Serial No. 235).

Sears, R. R. (1977). Sources of life satisfaction of the Terman gifted men. *American Psychologist, 32,* 119–128.

Sears, R. R., Maccoby, E. E., & Levin, H. (1957). *Patterns of child rearing.* Evanston, IL: Row, Peterson.

Sebald, H. (1986). Adolescents' shifting orientations toward parents and peers: A curvilinear trend over recent decades. *Journal of Marriage and the Family, 48,* 5–13.

Seidman, E., Allen, L., Aber, J. L., Mitchell, C., & Feinman, J. (1994). The impact of school transitions in early adolescence on the self-system and perceived social context of poor urban youth. *Child Development, 65,* 507–522.

Seidman, S. A. (1992). An investigation of sex-role stereotyping in music videos. *Journal of Broadcasting and Electric Media, 36,* 209–216.

Selman, R. L. (1980). *The growth of interpersonal understanding: Developmental and clinical analyses.* New York: Academic.

Selman, R. L. (1981). The child as a friendship philosopher. In S. R. Asher & J. M. Gottman (Eds.), *The development of children's friendships* (pp. 242–272). New York: Cambridge University Press.

Selman, R. L., & Byrne, D. F. (1974). A structural-developmental analysis of levels of role-taking in middle childhood. *Child Development, 45,* 803–806.

Selman, R. L., Schorin, M. Z., Stone, C., & Phelps, E. (1983). A naturalistic study of children's social understanding. *Developmental Psychology, 19,* 82–102.

Selman, R. L., & Schultz, L. H. (1989). Children's strategies for interpersonal negotiation with peers: An interpretive/empirical approach to the study of social development. In T. J. Berndt & G. W. Ladd (Eds.), *Peer relationships in child development* (pp. 371–406). New York: Wiley.

Seltzer, J. A. (1994). Consequences of marital dissolution for children. *Annual Review of Sociology, 20,* 235–266.

Sénéchal, M., Thomas, E., & Monker, J. (1995). Individual differences in 4-year-old children's acquisition of vocabulary during storybook reading. *Journal of Educational Psychology, 87,* 218–229.

Sepkoski, C. M., Lester, B. M., Ostheimer, G. W., & Brazelton, T. B. (1992). The effects of maternal epidural anesthesia on neonatal behavior during the first month. *Developmental Medicine and Child Neurology, 34,* 1072–1080.

Serbin, L. A., Connor, J. M., & Citron, C. C. (1981). Sex-differentiated free play behavior: Effects of teacher modeling, location, and gender. *Developmental Psychology, 17,* 640–646.

Serbin, L. A., Powlishta, K. K., & Gulko, J. (1993). The development of sex typing in middle childhood. *Monographs of the Society for Research in Child Development, 58* (2, Serial No. 232).

Serbin, L. A., Tonick, I. J., & Sternglanz, S. H. (1977). Shaping cooperative cross-sex play. *Child Development, 48,* 924–929.

Shantz, C. U. (1983). Social cognition. In J. H. Flavell, E. M. Markman (Eds.), & P. H. Mussen (Series Ed.), *Handbook of child psychology: Vol. 3. Cognitive development* (pp. 495–555). New York: Wiley.

Shapiro, B. L. (1994). The environmental basis of the Down syndrome phenotype. *Developmental Medicine and Child Neurology, 36,* 84–90.

Sharabany, R., Gershoni, R., & Hofman, J. E. (1981). Girlfriend, boyfriend: Age and sex differences in intimate friendship. *Developmental Psychology, 17,* 800–808.

Shatz, C. J. (1992, September). The developing brain. *Scientific American, 267,* 61–67.

Shatz, M. (1983). Communication. In P. H. Mussen (Ed.), *Handbook of child psychology: Vol. 3. Cognitive development* (pp. 841–890). New York: Wiley.

Shatz, M., & Gelman, R. (1973). The development of communication skills: Modifications in the speech of young children as a function of listener. *Monographs of the Society for Research in Child Development, 38* (5, Serial No. 152).

Shayer, M., & Adey, P. S. (1993). Accelerating the development of formal thinking in middle and high school students: IV. Three years after a two-year intervention. *Journal of Research in Science Teaching, 30,* 351–366.

Sherif, M., Harvey, O. J., White, B. J., Hood, W. R., & Sherif, C. W. (1961). *Intergroup conflict and cooperation: The robbers cave experiment.* Norman, OK: Institute of Group Relations.

Shirley, M. M. (1933). *The first two years* (Vol. 2, Institute of Child Welfare Monograph No. 7). Minneapolis: University of Minnesota Press.

Shoda, Y., Mischel, W., & Peake, P. K. (1990). Predicting adolescent cognitive and self-regulatory competencies from preschool delay of gratification: Identifying diagnostic conditions. *Developmental Psychology, 26,* 978–986.

Shonkoff, J. P. (1992). Preschool. In M. D. Levine, W. B. Carey, & A. C. Crocker (Eds.), *Developmental-behavioral pediatrics* (pp. 39–47). Philadelphia: W. B. Saunders.

Shultz, T. R., & Wells, D. (1985). Judging the intentionality of action-outcomes. *Developmental Psychology, 21,* 83–89.

Shultz, T. R., Wright, K., & Schleifer, M. (1986). Assignment of moral responsibility and punishment. *Child Development, 57,* 177–184.

Shure, M. B. (1992). *I Can Problem Solve (ICPS): An interpersonal cognitive problem solving program for children.* Champaign, IL: Research Press.

Shure, M. B. (1993). I can problem solve (ICPS): Interpersonal cognitive problem solving for young children. *Early Child Development and Care, 96,* 49–64.

Shure, M. B., & Spivack, G. (1978). *Problem-solving techniques in child rearing.* San Francisco: Jossey-Bass.

Shweder, R. A. (1990). In defense of moral realism: Reply to Gabennesch. *Child Development, 61,* 2060–2067.

Shweder, R. A., Jensen, L. A., & Goldstein, W. M. (1995). Who sleeps by whom revisited: A method for extracting the moral goods implicit in practice. In J. J. Goodnow, P. J. Miller, & F. Kessel (Eds.), *Cultural practices as contexts for development* (pp. 21–48). San Francisco: Jossey-Bass.

Shweder, R. A., Mahapatra, M., & Miller, J. G. (1987). Culture and moral development. In J. Kagan & S. Lamb (Eds.), *The emergence of morality in young children* (pp. 1–83). Chicago: University of Chicago Press.

Shweder, R. A., & Much, N. C. (1987). Determinations of meaning: Discourse and moral socialization. In W. M. Kurtines & J. L. Gewirtz (Eds.), *Moral development through social interaction* (pp. 197–244). New York: Wiley.

Sibai, B. M., Caritis, S. N., Thom, E., Klebanoff, M., McNellis, D., Rocco, L., Paul, R. H., Romero, R., Witter, F., Rosen, M., Depp, R. National Institute of Child Health & Human Development Network of Maternal-Fetal Medicine Units. (1993). Prevention of preeclampsia with low-dose aspirin in healthy, nulliparous pregnant women. *New England Journal of Medicine, 329,* 1213–1218.

Siegel, L. S. (1989). A reconceptualization of prediction from infant test scores. In M. H. Bornstein & N. A. Krasnegor (Eds.), *Stability and continuity in mental development: Behavioral and biological perspectives.* Hillsdale, NJ: Erlbaum.

Siegler, R. S. (1976). Three aspects of cognitive development. *Cognitive Psychology, 8,* 481–520.

Siegler, R. S. (1978). The origins of scientific reasoning. In R. S. Siegler (Ed.), *Children's thinking: What develops.* Hillsdale, NJ: Erlbaum.

Siegler, R. S. (1983). Information processing approaches to development. In P. H. Mussen (Series Ed.) & W. Kessen (Vol. Ed.), *Handbook of child psychology. Vol. 1: History, theory, and methods* (pp. 129–211). New York: Wiley.

Siegler, R. S. (1987). The perils of averaging data over strategies: An example from children's addition. *Journal of Experimental Psychology: General, 116,* 250–264.

Siegler, R. S. (1988a). Individual differences in strategy choices: Good students, not-so-good students, and perfectionists. *Child Development, 59,* 833–851.

Siegler, R. S. (1988b). Strategy choice procedures and the development of multiplication skill. *Journal of Experimental Psychology: General, 117,* 258–275.

Siegler, R. S. (1991). *Children's thinking* (2nd ed.). Englewood Cliffs, NJ: Prentice-Hall.

Siegler, R. S. (1994). Cognitive variability: A key to understanding cognitive development. *Current Directions in Psychological Science, 3,* 1–5.

Siegler, R. S., & Crowley, K. (1991). The microgenetic method: A direct means for studying cognitive development. *American Psychologist, 46,* 606–620.

Siegler, R. S., & Jenkins, E. (1989). *How children discover new strategies.* Hillsdale, NJ: Erlbaum.

Signorella, M. L., Bigler, R. S., & Liben, L. S. (1993). Developmental differences in children's gender schemata about others: A meta-analytic review. *Early gender-role development. Developmental Review, 13,* 147–183.

Signorella, M. L., & Liben, L. S. (1984). Recall and reconstruction of gender-related pictures: Effects of attitude, task difficulty, and age. *Child Development, 55,* 393–405.

Signorielli, N., & Lears, M. (1992). Children, television, and conceptions about chores: Attitudes and behaviors. *Sex Roles, 27,* 157–170.

Signorielli, N., McLeod, D., & Healy, E. (1994). Gender stereotypes in MTV commercials: The beat goes on. *Journal of Broadcasting and Electronic Media, 58,* 91–101.

Simmons, R. G., & Blyth, D. A. (1987). *Moving into adolescence: The impact of pubertal change and social context.* Hawthorne, NY: Aldine de Gruyter.

Simpson, J. L. (1991). Fetal wastage. In S. G. Gabbe, J. R. Niebyl, & J. L. Simpson (Eds.), *Obstetrics: Normal and problem pregnancies* (2nd ed., pp. 783–807). New York: Churchill Livingstone.

Singer, L. (1987). Long-term hospitalization of nonorganic failure-to-thrive infants: Patient characteristics and hospital course. *Journal of Developmental and Behavioral Pediatrics, 8,* 25–31.

Skaalvik, E. M., & Hagtvet, K. A. (1990). Academic achievement and self-concept: An analysis of causal predominance in a developmental perspective. *Journal of Personality and Social Psychology, 58,* 292–307.

Skinner, B. F. (1957). *Verbal behavior.* New York: Appleton-Century-Crofts.

Skinner, B. F. (1974). *About behaviorism.* New York: Vintage.

Slaby, R. G., & Frey, K. S. (1975). Development of gender constancy and selective attention to same-sex models. *Child Development, 46,* 849–856.

Slaby, R. G., & Guerra, N. G. (1988). Cognitive mediators of aggression in adolescent offenders: 1. Assessment. *Developmental Psychology, 24,* 580–588.

Slater, A. (1995). Individual differences in infancy and later IQ. *Journal of Child Psychology and Psychiatry and Allied Disciplines, 36,* 69–112.

Slater, M. A., Naqvi, M., Andrew, L., & Haynes, K. (1987). Neurodevelopment of monitored versus non-monitored very low birth weight infants: The importance of family influences. *Journal of Developmental and Behavioral Pediatrics, 8,* 278–285.

Slavin, R. E. (1993). Ability grouping in the middle grades: Achievement effects and alternatives. *Elementary School Journal, 93,* 535–552.

Slavin, R. W. (1983). When does cooperative learning increase student achievement? *Psychological Bulletin, 94,* 429–445.

Slobin, D. I. (1985). Crosslinguistic evidence for the language-making capacity. In D. I. Slobin (Ed.), *The crosslinguistic study of language acquisition: Vol. 2: Theoretical issues.* Hillsdale, NJ: Erlbaum.

Smetana, J. G. (1981). Preschool children's conceptions of moral and social rules. *Child Development, 52,* 1333–1336.

Smetana, J. G. (1984). Toddlers' social interactions regarding moral and conventional transgressions. *Child Development, 55,* 1767–1776.

Smetana, J. G. (1989). Toddlers' social interactions in the context of moral and conventional transgressions in the home. *Developmental Psychology, 25,* 499–508.

Smetana, J. G., & Asquith, P. (1994). Adolescents' and parents' conceptions of parental authority and personal autonomy. *Child Development, 65,* 1147–1162.

Smetana, J. G., Killen, M., & Turiel, E. (1991). Children's reasoning about interpersonal and moral conflicts. *Child Development, 62,* 629–644.

Smilansky, S. (1968). *The effects of sociodramatic play on disadvantaged preschool children.* New York: Wiley.

Smiley, P. A., & Dweck, C. S. (1994). Individual differences in achievement goals among young children. *Child Development, 65,* 1723–1743.

Smiley, S. S., & Brown, A. L. (1979). Conceptual preference for thematic or taxonomic relations: A nonmonotonic age trend from preschool to old age. *Journal of Experimental Child Psychology, 28,* 249–257.

Smith, L. B. (1989). A model of perceptual classification in children and adults. *Psychological Review, 96,* 125–144.

Smith, L. B. (1994). Foreword. In D. J. Lewkowicz & R. Lickliter (Eds.), *The development of intersensory perception: Comparative perspectives* (pp. ix–xix). Hillsdale, NJ: Erlbaum.

Smith, L. B., & Thelen, E. (Eds.). (1993). *A dynamic systems approach to development: Applications.* Cambridge, MA: MIT Press.

Smith, M. C. (1978). Cognizing the behavior stream: The recognition of intentional action. *Child Development, 49,* 736–743.

Snarey, J. R. (1985). Cross-cultural universality of social-moral development: A critical review of Kohlbergian research. *Psychological Bulletin, 97,* 202–232.

Snow, C. (1987). Relevance of the notion of a critical period to language acquisition. In M. H. Bornstein (Ed.), *Sensitive periods in development: Interdisciplinary perspectives* (pp. 183–210). Hillsdale, NJ: Erlbaum.

Snow, C. E. (1988). The last word: Questions about the emerging lexicon. In M. D. Smith & J. L. Locke (Eds.), *The emergent lexicon: The child's development of a linguistic vocabulary* (pp. 341–354). New York: Academic.

Snow, C. E., & Hoefnagel-Hohle, M. (1978). The critical period for language acquisition: Evidence from second language learning. *Child Development, 49,* 1114–1128.

Snow, C. W. (1989). *Infant development.* Englewood Cliffs, NJ: Prentice-Hall.

Snow, M. E., Jacklin, C. N., & Maccoby, E. E. (1983). Sex-of-child differences in father-child interaction at one year of age. *Child Development, 54,* 227–232.

Society for Research in Child Development. (1993). *Directory of members and ethical standards.* Chicago: Author.

Soken, N. H., & Pick, A. D. (1992). Intermodal perception of happy and angry expressive behaviors by seven-month-old infants. *Child Development, 63,* 787–795.

Sommers-Flanagan, R., Sommers-Flanagan, J., & Davis, B. (1993). What's happening on music television? A gender

role content analysis. *Sex Roles, 28,* 745–753.

Song, M., Smetana, J. G., & Kim, S. (1987). Korean children's conceptions of moral and conventional transgressions. *Developmental Psychology, 23,* 577–582.

Sonnenschein, S. (1986). Development of referential communication: Deciding that a message is uninformative. *Developmental Psychology, 22,* 164–168.

Sonnenschein, S., & Whitehurst, G. J. (1984). Developing referential communication: A hierarchy of skills. *Child Development, 55,* 1936–1945.

Sophian, C. (1988). Limitations on preschool children's knowledge about counting: Using counting to compare two sets. *Developmental Psychology, 24,* 634–640.

Sorce, J. F., Emde, R. N., Campos, J., & Klinnert, M. D. (1985). Maternal emotional signaling: Its effect on the visual cliff behavior of 1-year-olds. *Developmental Psychology, 21,* 195–200.

Spaccarelli, S. (1994). Stress, appraisal, and coping in child sexual abuse: A theoretical and empirical review. *Psychological Bulletin, 116,* 340–362.

Spangler, G., & Grossmann, K. E. (1993). Biobehavioral organization in securely and insecurely attached infants. *Child Development, 64,* 1439–1450.

Sparrow, S. S., Balla, D. A., & Cicchetti, D. V. (1984). *Vineland Adaptive Behavior scales: Interview edition, survey form manual.* Circle Pines, MN: American Guidance Service.

Spearman, C. (1927). *The abilities of man: Their nature and measurement.* New York: Macmillan.

Speicher, B. (1992). Adolescent moral judgment and perceptions of family interaction. *Journal of Family Psychology, 6,* 128–138.

Speicher, B. (1994). Family patterns of moral judgment during adolescence and early adulthood. *Developmental Psychology, 30,* 624–632.

Spelke, E. S. (1987). The development of intermodal perception. In P. Salapatek & L. Cohen (Eds.), *Handbook of infant perception. Vol. II. From sensation to perception* (pp. 233–274). Orlando, FL: Academic.

Spelke, E. S. (1994). Initial knowledge: Six suggestions. *Cognition, 50,* 431–445.

Spelke, E. S., Born, W. S., & Chu, F. (1983). Perception of moving, sounding objects by four-month-old infants. *Perception, 12,* 719–732.

Spelke, E. S., Breinlinger, K., Macomber, J., & Jacobson, K. (1992). Origins of knowledge. *Psychological Review, 99,* 605–632.

Spence, J. T., & Helmreich, R. L. (1978). *Masculinity and femininity: Their psychological dimensions, correlates, and antecedents.* Austin, TX: University of Texas Press.

Spencer, M. B. (1990). Development of minority children: An introduction. *Child Development, 61,* 267–269.

Spitz, R. A. (1946). Anaclitic depression. *Psychoanalytic Study of the Child, 2,* 313–342.

Spivack, G., & Shure, M. B. (1974). *Social adjustment of young children: A cognitive approach to solving real life problems.* San Francisco: Jossey-Bass.

Sroufe, L. A. (1977). Wariness of strangers and the study of infant development. *Child Development, 48,* 731–746.

Sroufe, L. A. (1979). The coherence of individual development. *American Psychologist, 34,* 834–841.

Sroufe, L. A. (1983). Infant-caregiver attachment and patterns of adaptation in preschool: The roots of maladaptation. In M. Perlmutter (Ed.), *Minnesota Symposia on Child Psychology* (Vol. 16, pp. 41–83). Hillsdale, NJ: Erlbaum.

Sroufe, L. A. (1985). Attachment classification from the perspective of infant-caregiver relationships and infant temperament. *Child Development, 56,* 1–14.

Sroufe, L. A., Bennett, C., Englund, M., Urban, J., & Shulman, S. (1993). The significance of gender boundaries in preadolescence: Contemporary correlates and antecedents of boundary violation and maintenance. *Child Development, 64,* 445–466.

Sroufe, L. A., & Waters, E. (1976). The ontogenesis of smiling and laughter: A perspective on the organization of development in infancy. *Psychological Review, 83,* 173–189.

Sroufe, L. A., & Waters, E. (1977). Attachment as an organizational construct. *Child Development, 48,* 1184–1199.

Sroufe, L. A., & Wunsch, J. P. (1972). The development of laughter in the first year of life. *Child Development, 43,* 1324–1344.

Stahl, S. A., & Murray, B. A. (1994). Defining phonological awareness and its relationship to early reading. *Journal of Educational Psychology, 86,* 221–234.

Stanger, C., Achenbach, T. M., & Verhulst, F. C. (1994). Accelerating longitudinal research on child psychopathology: A practical example. *Psychological Assessment, 6,* 102–107.

Stanway, P., & Taubman, B. (1994). *New guide to pregnancy and child care.* New York: Simon & Schuster.

Starkey, P., Spelke, E. S., & Gelman, R. (1983). Detection of intermodal numerical correspondences by human infants. *Science, 222,* 179–181.

Stattin, H., & Klackenberg-Larsson, I. (1993). Early language and intelligence development and their relationship to future criminal behavior. *Journal of Abnormal Psychology, 102,* 369–378.

Stattin, H., & Magnusson, D. (1989). The role of early aggressive behavior in the frequency, seriousness, and types of later crime. *Journal of Consulting and Clinical Psychology, 57,* 710–718.

Steinberg, L. (1981). Transformations in family relations at puberty. *Developmental Psychology, 17,* 833–840.

Steinberg, L. (1986). Latchkey children and susceptibility to peer pressure: An ecological analysis. *Developmental Psychology, 22,* 433–439.

Steinberg, L. (1987). Single parents, stepparents, and the susceptibility of adolescents to antisocial peer pressure. *Child Development, 58,* 269–275.

Steinberg, L. (1988). Reciprocal relation between parent-child distance and pubertal maturation. *Developmental Psychology, 24,* 122–128.

Steinberg, L., Lamborn, S. D., Darling, N., Mounts, N. S., & Dornbusch, S. M. (1994). Over-time changes in adjustment and competence among adolescents from authoritative, authoritarian, indulgent, and neglectful families. *Child Development, 65,* 754–770.

Steinberg, L., & Silverberg, S. B. (1986). The vicissitudes of autonomy in early adolescence. *Child Development, 57,* 841–851.

Steiner, J. E. (1979). Human facial expressions in response to taste and smell stimulation. In H. Reese & L. P. Lipsitt (Eds.), *Advances in child development and behavior* (Vol. 13, pp. 257–293). New York: Academic.

Stenberg, C., Campos, J., & Emde, R. (1983). The facial expression of anger in seven-month-old infants. *Child Development, 54,* 178–184.

Stern, A. H. (1993). Re-evaluation of the reference dose for methylmercury and assessment of current exposure levels. *Risk Analysis, 13,* 355–364.

Stern, M., & Karraker, K. H. (1989). Sex stereotyping of infants: A review of gender labeling studies. *Sex Roles, 20,* 501–522.

Sternberg, R. J. (1985). *Beyond IQ: A triarchic theory of human intelligence.* New York: Cambridge University Press.

Sternberg, R. J. (1987). A day at developmental Downs: Sportscast for race #2—Neo-Piagetian theories of cognitive development. *International Journal of Psychology, 22,* 507–529.

Sternberg, R. J. (1988). *The triarchic mind: A new theory of human intelligence.* New York: Viking.

Sternberg, R. J. (1994). *Encyclopedia of human intelligence.* New York: Macmillan.

Sternberg, R. J., Conway, B. E., Ketron, J. L., & Bernstein, M. (1981). People's

conceptions of intelligence. *Journal of Personality and Social Psychology, 41,* 37–55.

Sternberg, R. J., & Powell, J. S. (1983). The development of intelligence. In J. H. Flavell & E. M. Markman (Eds.), *Handbook of child psychology: Vol. 3. Cognitive development* (pp. 341–419). New York: Wiley.

Sternberg, R. J., & Wagner, R. K. (Eds.). (1986). *Practical intelligence: Nature and origins of competence in the everyday world.* New York: Cambridge University Press.

Stevens, R. J., & Slavin, R. E. (1995). The cooperative elementary school: Effects on students' achievement, attitudes, and social relations. *American Educational Research Journal, 32,* 321–351.

Stevenson, H. W. (1983). How children learn—The quest for a theory. In W. Kessen (Ed.), *Handbook of child psychology: Vol. 1. History, theory, and methods* (4th ed., pp. 213–236). New York: Wiley.

Stevenson, H. W. (1992, December). Learning from Asian schools. *Scientific American, 267,* 70–76.

Stevenson, H. W., Chen, C., & Lee, S. (1993). Mathematics achievement of Chinese, Japanese, and American children: Ten years later. *Science, 259,* 53–58.

Stevenson, H. W., & Lee, S-Y. (1990). In collaboration with Chuansheng, C., Stigler, J. W., Hsu, C. C., & Kitamura, S. Contexts of achievement: A study of American, Chinese, and Japanese children. With commentary by Giyoo Hatano; and a reply by Harold W. Stevenson and Shin-Ying Lee. *Monographs of the Society for Research in Child Development, 55* (1-2, Serial No. 221).

Stevenson, H. W., Lee, S. Y., & Stigler, J. W. (1986). Mathematics achievement of Chinese, Japanese, and American children. *Science, 231,* 693–699.

Stevenson, M. R., & Black, K. N. (1988). Paternal absence and sex-role development: A meta-analysis. *Child Development, 59,* 793–814.

Stevenson, M. R., & Black, K. N. (1995). *How divorce affects offspring: A research approach.* Madison, WI: Brown & Benchmark.

Stewart, R. B. (1983). Sibling attachment relationships: Child-infant interactions in the strange situation. *Developmental Psychology, 19,* 192–199.

Stewart, R. B., Mobley, L. A., Van Tuyl, S. S., & Salvador, M. A. (1987). The firstborn's adjustment to the birth of a sibling: A longitudinal assessment. *Child Development, 58,* 341–355.

Stigler, J. W., Lee, S. Y., & Stevenson, H. W. (1987). Mathematics classrooms in Japan, Taiwan, and the United States. *Child Development, 58,* 1272–1285.

Stipek, D., Recchia, S., & McClintic, S. (1992). Self-evaluation in young children. *Monographs of the Society for Research in Child Development, 57* (1, Serial No. 226).

Stipek, D. J., & Tannatt, L. M. (1984). Children's judgments of their own and their peers' academic competence. *Journal of Educational Psychology, 76,* 75–84.

Stocker, C., Dunn, J., & Plomin, R. (1989). Sibling relationships: Links with child temperament, maternal behavior, and family structure. *Child Development, 60,* 715–727.

Stolberg, A. L., & Walsh, P. (1988). A review of treatment methods for children of divorce. In S. A. Wolchik & P. Karoly (Eds.), *Children of divorce* (pp. 299–321). New York: Gardner Press.

Straus, M. A., & Kantor, G. K. (1987). Stress and child abuse. In R. E. Helfer & R. S. Kempe (Eds.), *The battered child* (4th ed., pp. 42–59). Chicago: University of Chicago Press.

Streissguth, A. P., Barr, H. M., Sampson, P. D., Darby, B. L., & Martin, D. C. (1989). IQ at age 4 in relation to maternal alcohol use and smoking during pregnancy. *Developmental Psychology, 25,* 3–11.

Streissguth, A. P., Sampson, P. B., Barr, H. M., Bookstein, F. L., & Olson, H. C. (1994). The effects of prenatal exposure to alcohol and tobacco: Contributions from the Seattle Longitudinal Prospective Study and implications for public policy. In H. L. Needleman & D. Bellinger (Eds.), *Prenatal exposure to toxicants: Developmental consequences* (pp. 148–183). Baltimore, MD: Johns Hopkins University Press.

Studdert-Kennedy, M. (1993). Discovering phonetic function. *Journal of Phonetics, 21,* 147–156.

Stunkard, A. J., Sorensen, T. I. A., Hanis, C., Teasdale, T. W., Chakraborty, R., Schull, W. J., & Schulsinger, F. (1986). An adoption study of human obesity. *New England Journal of Medicine, 314,* 193–198.

Suess, G. J., Grossmann, K. E., & Sroufe, L. A. (1992). Effects of infant attachment to mother and father on quality of adaptation in preschool: From dyadic to individual organization of self. *International Journal of Behavioral Development, 15,* 43–65.

Sullivan, H. S. (1953). *The interpersonal theory of psychiatry.* New York: Norton.

Sullivan, K., & Winner, E. (1993). Three-year-olds' understanding of mental states: The influence of trickery. *Journal of Experimental Child Psychology, 56,* 135–148.

Suomi, S. J. (1979). Peers, play, and primary prevention in primates. In G. W. Albee & J. M. Joffe (Eds.), *Primary prevention of psychopathology, Volume III. Social competence in children* (pp. 127–149). Hanover, NH: University Press of New England.

Suomi, S. J., & Harlow, H. F. (1975). The role and reason of peer relationships in Rhesus monkeys. In M. Lewis & L. A. Rosenblum (Eds.), *Friendship and peer relations: The origins of behavior series* (pp. 153–186). New York: Wiley.

Super, C. M. (1981). Behavioral development in infancy. In R. H. Munroe, R. L. Munroe, & B. B. Whiting (Eds.), *Handbook of cross-cultural human development* (pp. 181–270). New York: Garland.

Super, C. M., & Harkness, S. (1986). The developmental niche: A conceptualization at the interface of child and culture. *International Journal of Behavioral Development, 9,* 545–569.

Super, C. M., Herrera, M. G., & Mora, J. O. (1990). Long-term effects of food supplementation and psychosocial intervention on the physical growth of Colombian infants at risk of malnutrition. *Child Development, 61,* 29–49.

Susman, E. J., Inoff-Germain, G., Nottelmann, E. D., Loriaux, D. L., Cutler, G. B., Jr., & Chrousos, G. O. (1987). Hormones, emotional dispositions, and aggressive attributes in young adolescents. *Child Development, 58,* 1114–1134.

Susman, E. J., Trickett, P. K., Iannotti, R. J., Hollenbeck, B. E., & Zahn-Waxler, C. (1985). Child-rearing patterns in depressed, abusive, and normal mothers. *American Journal of Orthopsychiatry, 55,* 237–251.

Swain, I. U., Zelazo, P. R., & Clifton, R. K. (1993). Newborn infants' memory for speech sounds retained over 24 hours. *Developmental Psychology, 29,* 312–323.

Szybist, C. M. (1988). Sudden infant death syndrome revisited. *Journal of Developmental and Behavioral Pediatrics, 9,* 33–37.

Tager-Flusberg, H. (1993). Putting words together: Morphology and syntax in the preschool years. In J. Berko Gleason (Ed.), *The development of language* (3rd ed., pp. 153–196). New York: Macmillan.

Takahashi, K. (1990). Are the key assumptions of the 'Strange Situation' procedure universal? A view from Japanese research. *Human Development, 33,* 23–30.

Tanenbaum, L. (1994). [Review of the book *Failing at fairness: How America's schools cheat girls*]. *The Nation, 258,* 280.

Tanner, J. M. (1978). *Fetus into man.* Cambridge, MA: Harvard University Press.

Tashakkori, A. (1993). Race, gender, and pre-adolescent self-structure: A test of construct-specificity hypothesis. *Personality and Individual Differences, 14,* 591–598.

Tashakkori, A., & Thompson, V. D. (1991). Race differences in self-perception and locus of control during adolescence and early adulthood: Methodological implications. *Genetic, Social, and General Psychology Monographs, 117,* 133–152.

Taylor, M. C., & Hall, J. A. (1982). Psychological androgyny: Theories, methods, and conclusions. *Psychological Bulletin, 92,* 347–366.

Teller, D. Y., & Bornstein, M. H. (1987). Infant color vision and color perception. In P. Salapatek & L. Cohen (Eds.), *Handbook of infant perception. Vol. 1. From sensation to perception* (pp. 185–236). Orlando, FL: Academic.

Terman, L. (1925). *Genetic studies of genius: Vol. 1. Mental and physical traits of a thousand gifted children.* Stanford, CA: Stanford University Press.

Terman, L., & Oden, M. H. (1959). *Genetic studies of genius: Vol. 4. The gifted group at midlife.* Stanford, CA: Stanford University Press.

Termine, N. T., & Izard, C. E. (1988). Infants' responses to their mothers' expressions of joy and sadness. *Developmental Psychology, 24,* 223–229.

Terrace, H. S. (1985). In the beginning was the "name." *American Psychologist, 40,* 1011–1028.

Tesser, A. (1984). Self-evaluation maintenance processes: Implications for relationships and for development. In J. C. Masters & K. Yarkin-Levin (Eds.), *Boundary areas in social and developmental psychology* (pp. 271–299). New York: Academic.

Theilgaard, A. (1984). A psychological study of the personalities of XYY—and XXY—men. *Acta Psychiatrica Scandinavica, 69,* 1–133.

Thelen, E. (1995). Motor development: A new synthesis. *American Psychologist, 50,* 79–95.

Thelen, E., & Cooke, D. W. (1987). Relationship between newborn stepping and later walking: A new interpretation. *Developmental Medicine and Child Neurology, 29,* 380–393.

Thelen, E., Corbetta, D., Kamm, K., Spencer, J. P., Schneider, K., & Zernicke, R. F. (1993). The transition to reaching: Mapping intention and intrinsic dynamics. *Child Development, 64,* 1058–1098.

Thelen, E., & Fisher, D. M. (1982). Newborn stepping: An explanation for a "disappearing" reflex. *Developmental Psychology, 18,* 760–775.

Thelen, E., Fisher, D. M., & Ridley-Johnson, R. (1984). The relationship between physical growth and a newborn reflex. *Infant Behavior and Development, 7,* 479–493.

Thelen, E., Kelso, J. A. S., & Fogel, A. (1987). Self-organizing systems and motor development. *Developmental Review, 7,* 39–65.

Thelen, E., & Ulrich, B. D. (1991). A dynamic systems analysis of treadmill stepping during the first year. With commentary by Peter H. Wolff. *Monographs of the Society for Research in Child Development, 56* (1, Serial No. 223).

Thoman, E. B. (1993). Obligation and option in the premature nursery. *Developmental Review, 13,* 1–30.

Thomas, A., & Chess, S. (1986). The New York longitudinal study: From infancy to early adult life. In R. Plomin & J. Dunn (Eds.), *The study of temperament: Changes, continuities and challenges* (pp. 39–52). Hillsdale, NJ: Erlbaum.

Thomas, A., Chess, S., & Birch, H. G. (1968). *Temperament and behavior disorders in children.* New York: New York University Press.

Thomas, D. R. (1975). Cooperation and competition among Polynesian and European children. *Child Development, 46,* 948–953.

Thomas, J. R., & French, K. E. (1985). Gender differences across age in motor performance: A meta-analysis. *Psychological Bulletin, 98,* 260–282.

Thompson, R. A. (1987). Development of children's inferences of the emotions of others. *Developmental Psychology, 23,* 124–131.

Thompson, R. A. (1990). Vulnerability in research: A developmental perspective on research risk. *Child Development, 61,* 1–16.

Thompson, R. A., & Lamb, M. E. (1983). Security of attachment and stranger sociability in infancy. *Developmental Psychology, 19,* 184–191.

Thorndike, R. L. (1994). *g. Intelligence, 19,* 145–155.

Thorndike, R. L., Hagen, E. P., & Sattler, J. M. (1986). *The Stanford-Binet Intelligence Scale: Guide for administering and scoring* (4th ed.). Chicago: Riverside.

Thrasher, F. M. (1927). *The gang.* Chicago: University of Chicago Press.

Thurstone, L. L. (1938). *Primary mental abilities.* Chicago: University of Chicago Press.

Tienari, P., Kaleva, M., Lahti, I., Laksy, K., Moring, J., Naarala, M., Sorri, A., Wahlberg, K. E., & Wynne, L. (1991). Adoption studies of schizophrenia. In C. Eggers (Ed.), *Schizophrenia and youth: Etiology and therapeutic consequences* (pp. 40–51). Berlin: Springer-Verlag.

Tietjen, A. M., & Walker, L. J. (1985). Moral reasoning and leadership among men in a Papua New Guinea society. *Developmental Psychology, 21,* 982–992.

Tisak, M. S. (1986). Children's conceptions of parental authority. *Child Development, 57,* 166–176.

Tisak, M. S., & Tisak, J. (1990). Children's conceptions of parental authority, friendship, and sibling relations. *Merrill-Palmer Quarterly, 36,* 347–367.

Tizard, B., & Hodges, J. (1978). The effect of early institutional rearing on the development of eight-year-old children. *Journal of Child Psychology and Psychiatry, 19,* 99–118.

Tizard, B., & Rees, J. (1975). The effect of early institutional rearing on the behavior problems and affectional relationships of four-year-old children. *Journal of Child Psychology and Psychiatry, 16,* 61–73.

Toda, M., Shinotsuka, H., McClintock, C. G., & Stech, F. J. (1978). Development of competitive behavior as a function of culture, age, and social comparison. *Journal of Personality and Social Psychology, 36,* 825–839.

Tolson, T. F., & Wilson, M. N. (1990). The impact of two- and three-generational black family structure on perceived family climate. *Child Development, 61,* 416–428.

Tomasello, M., & Barton, M. (1994). Learning words in nonostensive contexts. *Developmental Psychology, 30,* 639–650.

Tomasello, M., & Farrar, M. J. (1986). Joint attention and early language. *Child Development, 57,* 1454–1463.

Tomasello, M., Mannle, S., & Kruger, A. C. (1986). Linguistic environment of 1- to 2-year-old twins. *Developmental Psychology, 22,* 169–176.

Tomlinson-Keasey, C., & Little, T. D. (1990). Predicting educational attainment, occupational achievement, intellectual skill, and personal adjustment among gifted men and women. *Journal of Educational Psychology, 82,* 442–455.

Trehub, S. E. (1976). The discrimination of foreign speech contrasts by infants and adults. *Child Development, 47,* 466–472.

Tronick, E. Z., Morelli, G. A., & Ivey, P. K. (1992). The Efe forager infant and toddler's pattern of social relationships: Multiple and simultaneous. *Developmental Psychology, 28,* 568–577.

Tronick, W. Z. (1989). Emotions and emotional communication in infants. *American Psychologist, 44,* 112–119.

Tudge, J. R., & Winterhoff, P. A. (1993). Vygotsky, Piaget, and Bandura: Perspectives on the relations between the social world and cognitive development. *Human Development, 36,* 61–82.

Turiel, E. (1983). *The development of social knowledge.* Cambridge, England: Cambridge University Press.

Turiel, E. (1989). Domain-specific social judgments and domain ambiguities. *Merrill-Palmer Quarterly, 35,* 89–114.

Turiel, E., Hildebrandt, C., & Wainryb, C. (1991). Judging social issues: Difficulties, inconsistencies, and consistencies. *Monographs of the Society for Research in Child Development, 56* (2, Serial No. 244).

Turiel, E., Nucci, L. P., & Smetana, J. G. (1988). A cross-cultural comparison about what? A critique of Nisan's (1987) study of morality and convention. *Developmental Psychology, 24,* 140–143.

Turner, G. H. (1994). How is deaf culture? Another perspective on a fundamental concept. *Sign Language Studies, 83,* 103–125.

U.S. Bureau of the Census. (1992). *Marriage, divorce, and remarriage in the 1990s.* Current Population Reports, Series P23-180. Washington, DC: U.S. Government Printing Office.

U.S. Bureau of the Census. (1993a). *Marital status and living arrangements: March 1992.* Current Population Reports, Series P20-468. Washington, DC: U.S. Government Printing Office.

U.S. Bureau of the Census. (1993b). *Population profile of the United States: 1993.* Current Population Reports, Series P23-185. Washington, DC: U.S. Government Printing Office.

U.S. Bureau of the Census. (1994a). *How we're changing: Demographic state of the nation: 1995.* Current Population Reports, Series P23-188. Washington, DC: U.S. Government Printing Office.

U.S. Bureau of the Census. (1994b). *Marital status and living arrangements: March 1993.* Current Population Reports, Series P20-478. Washington, DC: U.S. Government Printing Office.

U.S. Bureau of the Census. (1994c). *Statistical abstract of the United States, 14th edition.* Washington, DC: U.S. Government Printing Office.

U.S. Bureau of the Census. (1995a). *United States population estimates, by age, sex, race, and Hispanic origin.* Washington, DC: Author.

U.S. Bureau of the Census. (1995b). *What does it cost to mind our preschoolers?* Current Population Reports, Series P70-52. Washington, DC: U.S. Government Printing Office.

U.S. Bureau of the Census. (1995c). *Population profile of the United States: 1995.* Current Population Reports, Series P23-189. Washington, DC: U.S. Government Printing Office.

U.S. Bureau of the Census. (1995d). *Women in the United States: A profile.* Bureau of the Census Statistical Brief, SB/95-19RV. Washington, DC: Author.

U.S. Department of Education, National Center for Education Statistics. (1994). *The condition of education, 1994.* Washington, DC: U.S. Government Printing Office.

U.S. Department of Education, National Center for Education Statistics. (1995). *The condition of education, 1995.* Washington, DC: U.S. Government Printing Office.

Udry, J. R. (1988). Biological predispositions and social control in adolescent sexual behavior. *American Sociological Review, 53,* 709–722.

UNICEF. (1995). *The state of the world's children 1995.* New York: UNICEF.

Urberg, K. A., Degirmencioglu, S. M., Tolson, J. M., & Halliday-Scher, K. (1995). The structure of adolescent peer networks. *Developmental Psychology, 31,* 540–547.

Usher, J. A., & Neisser, U. (1993). Childhood amnesia and the beginnings of memory for four early life events. *Journal of Experimental Psychology: General, 122,* 155–165.

Valian, V. (1986). Syntactic categories in the speech of young children. *Developmental Psychology, 22,* 562–579.

van den Boom, D. C. (1994). The influence of temperament and mothering on attachment and exploration: An experimental manipulation of sensitive responsiveness among lower-class mothers with irritable infants. *Child Development, 65,* 1457–1477.

van IJzendoorn, M. H. (1995). Adult attachment representations, parental responsiveness, and infant attachment: A meta-analysis on the predictive validity of the Adult Attachment Interview. *Psychological Bulletin, 117,* 387–403.

van IJzendoorn, M. H., Goldberg, S., Kroonenberg, P. M., & Frenkel, O. J. (1992). The relative effects of maternal and child problems on the quality of attachment: A meta-analysis of attachment in clinical samples. *Child Development, 63,* 840–858.

van IJzendoorn, M. H., Juffer, F., & Duyvesteyn, M. G. C. (1995). Breaking the intergenerational cycle of insecure attachment: A review of the effects of attachment-based interventions on maternal sensitivity and infant security. *Journal of Child Psychology and Psychiatry and Allied Disciplines, 36,* 225–248.

van IJzendoorn, M. H., & Kroonenberg, P. M. (1988). Cross-cultural patterns of attachment: A meta-analysis of the Strange Situation. *Child Development, 59,* 147–156.

Vande-Berg, L. R., & Streckfuss, D. (1992). Prime-time television's portrayal of women and the world of work: A demographic profile. *Journal of Broadcasting and Electronic Media, 36,* 195–208.

Vandell, D. L. (1979). Effects of a playgroup experience on mother-son and father-son interaction. *Developmental Psychology, 15,* 379–385.

Vandell, D. L., & Ramanan, J. (1992). Effects of early and recent maternal employment on children from low-income families. *Child Development, 63,* 938–949.

Vandell, D. L., & Wilson, K. S. (1982). Social interaction in the first year: Infants' social skills with peers versus mother. In K. H. Rubin & H. S. Ross (Ed.), *Peer relationships and social skills in childhood* (pp. 187–208). New York: Springer-Verlag.

Vandell, D. L., Wilson, K. S., & Buchanan, N. R. (1980). Peer interaction in the first year of life: An examination of its structure, content, and sensitivity to toys. *Child Development, 51,* 481–488.

Vandenberg, S. G., Singer, S. M., & Pauls, D. L. (1986). *The heritability of behavior disorders in adults and children.* New York: Plenum.

Vandenberg, S. G., & Vogler, G. P. (1985). Genetic determinants of intelligence. In B. B. Wolman (Ed.), *Handbook of intelligence* (pp. 3–58). New York: Wiley.

Vaughn, B. E., Gove, F. L., & Egeland, B. (1980). The relationship between out-of-home care and the quality of infant-mother attachment in an economically disadvantaged population. *Child Development, 51,* 1203–1214.

Vaughn, B. E., Kopp, C. B., & Krakow, J. B. (1984). The emergence and consolidation of self-control from eighteen to thirty months of age: Normative trends and individual differences. *Child Development, 51,* 990–1004.

Vaughn, B. E., & Langlois, J. H. (1983). Physical attractiveness as a correlate of peer status and social competence in preschool children. *Developmental Psychology, 19,* 550–560.

Vaughn, B. E., Lefever, G. B., Seifer, R., & Barglow, P. (1989). Attachment behavior, attachment security, and temperament during infancy. *Child Development, 60,* 728–737.

Vaughn, B. E., Stevenson, H. J., Waters, E., Kotsaftis, A., Lefever, G. B., Shouldice, A., Trundel, M., & Belsky, J. (1992). Attachment security and temperament in infancy and early childhood: Some conceptual clarifications. *Developmental Psychology, 28,* 463–473.

Ventura, S. J., Martin, J. A., Hartin, A., Taffell, S. M., Mathews, T. J., & Clarke, S. C. (1994). Advance report of final

natality statistics, 1992. *National Center for Health Statistics, Monthly Vital Statistics Report, 43.*

Vihman, M. M., & Miller, R. (1988). Words and babble at the threshold of language acquisition. In M. D. Smith & J. L. Locke (Eds.), *The emergent lexicon: The child's development of a linguistic vocabulary* (pp. 151–183). New York: Academic.

Vincent, K. R. (1991). Black/white IQ differences: Does age make the difference? *Journal of Clinical Psychology, 47,* 266–270.

Vlietstra, A. G. (1982). Children's responses to task instructions: Age changes and training effects. *Child Development, 58,* 534–542.

Vogel, D. A., Lake, M. A., Evans, S., & Karraker, K. H. (1991). Children's and adults' sex-stereotyped perceptions of infants. *Sex Roles, 24,* 605–616.

Volling, B. L., & Belsky, J. (1992). The contribution of mother-child and father-child relationships to the quality of sibling interaction: A longitudinal study. *Child Development, 63,* 1209–1222.

von Almen, T. K., Figueroa-Colon, R., & Suskind, R. M. (1992). Psychosocial considerations in the treatment of childhood obesity. In P. L. Giorgi, R. M. Suskind, & C. Catassi (Eds.), *The obese child* (pp. 162–171). New York: Karger.

Vorhees, C. V., & Mollnow, E. (1987). Behavioral teratogenesis: Long-term influences on behavior from early exposure to environmental agents. In J. D. Osofsky (Ed.), *Handbook of infant development* (2nd ed., pp. 913–971). New York: Wiley.

Voyer, D., Voyer, S., & Bryden, M. P. (1995). Magnitude of sex differences in spatial abilities: A meta-analysis and consideration of critical variables. *Psychological Bulletin, 117,* 250–270.

Vuchinich, S., Bank, L., & Patterson, G. R. (1992). Parenting, peers, and the stability of antisocial behavior in preadolescent boys. *Developmental Psychology, 28,* 510–521.

Vurpillot, E. (1968). The development of scanning strategies and their relation to visual differentiation. *Journal of Experimental Child Psychology, 6,* 632–650.

Vurpillot, E. (1976). *The visual world of the child* (W. E. C. Gillham, Trans.). London: Allen & Unwin.

Vygotsky, L. S. (1934/1962). *Thought and language.* Cambridge, MA: MIT Press.

Vygotsky, L. S. (1930/1933/1935/1978). *Mind in society: The development of higher mental processes.* Cambridge, MA: Harvard University Press.

Vygotsky, L. S. (1981). The instrumental method in psychology. In J. V. Wertsch (Ed.), *The concept of activity in Soviet psychology* (pp. 134–143). Armonk, NY: Sharpe.

Wachs, T. D. (1983). The use and abuse of environment in behavior-genetic research. *Child Development, 54,* 396–407.

Wachs, T. D. (1993). The nature-nurture gap: What we have here is a failure to collaborate. In R. Plomin & G. E. McClearn (Eds.), *Nature, nurture, and psychology* (pp. 375–391). Washington, DC: American Psychological Association.

Wachs, T. D., Bishry, Z., Sobhy, A., McCabe, G., Galal, O., & Shaheen, F. (1993). Relation of rearing environment to adaptive behavior of Egyptian toddlers. *Child Development, 64,* 586–604.

Wachs, T. D., & King, B. (1994). Behavioral research in the brave new world of neuroscience and temperament: A guide to the biologically perplexed. In J. E. Bates & T. D. Wachs (Eds.), *Temperament: Individual differences at the interface of biology and behavior* (pp. 307–336). Washington, DC: American Psychological Association.

Waddington, C. H. (1957). *The strategy of the genes.* London: Allen and Unwin.

Wagner, M. E., Schubert, H. J. P., & Schubert, D. S. P. (1979). Sibship-constellation effects on psychosocial development, creativity, and health. *Advances in Child Development and Behavior, 14,* 57–148.

Wahler, R. G. (1990). Who is driving the interactions? A commentary on "Child and parent effects in boys' conduct disorder." *Developmental Psychology, 26,* 702–704.

Wainryb, C. (1993). The application of moral judgments to other cultures: Relativism and universality. *Child Development, 64,* 924–933.

Walker, E., & Emory, W. (1983). Infants at risk for psychopathology: Offspring of schizophrenic parents. *Child Development, 54,* 1269–1285.

Walker, L. J. (1980). Cognitive and perspective-taking prerequisites for moral development. *Child Development, 51,* 131–139.

Walker, L. J. (1984). Sex differences in the development of moral reasoning: A critical review. *Child Development, 55,* 677–691.

Walker, L. J. (1986). Sex differences in the development of moral reasoning: A rejoinder to Baumrind. *Child Development, 57,* 522–526.

Walker, L. J. (1989). A longitudinal study of moral reasoning. *Child Development, 60,* 157–166.

Walker, L. J., De Vries, B., & Trevethan, S. D. (1987). Moral stages and moral orientations in real-life and hypothetical dilemmas. *Child Development, 58,* 842–858.

Walker, L. J., & Taylor, J. H. (1991). Family interactions and the development of moral reasoning. *Child Development, 62,* 264–283.

Walker-Andrews, A. (1994). Taxonomy for intermodal relations. In D. J. Lewkowicz & R. Lickliter (Eds.), *The development of intersensory perception: Comparative perspectives* (pp. 39–56). Hillsdale, NJ: Erlbaum.

Wallerstein, J. S., Corbin, S. B., & Lewis, J. M. (1988). Children of divorce: A 10-year study. In E. M. Hetherington & J. D. Arasteh (Eds.), *Impact of divorce, single parenting, and stepparenting on children* (pp. 215–244). Hillsdale, NJ: Erlbaum.

Wallerstein, J. S., & Kelly, J. B. (1980). *Surviving the breakup: How children and parents cope with divorce.* New York: Basic.

Ward, S. L., & Overton, W. F. (1990). Semantic familiarity, relevance, and the development of deductive reasoning. *Developmental Psychology, 26,* 488–493.

Warren, A. R., & McCloskey, L. A. (1993). Pragmatics: Language in social contexts. In J. Berko Gleason (Ed.), *The development of language* (3rd ed., pp. 195–238). New York: Macmillan.

Warren-Leubecker, A., & Bohannon, III, J. N. (1989). Pragmatics: Language in social contexts. In J. Berko Gleason (Ed.), *The development of language* (2nd ed., pp. 327–368). Columbus, OH: Merrill.

Waterlow, J. C. (Ed.). (1988). *Linear growth retardation in less developed countries.* New York: Raven.

Waterman, A. S. (1982). Identity development from adolescence to adulthood: An extension of theory and a review of research. *Developmental Psychology, 18,* 341–358.

Waterman, A. S. (1992). Identity as an aspect of optimal psychological functioning. In G. R. Adams, T. P. Gullotta, & R. Montemayor (Eds.), *Adolescent identity formation* (pp. 50–72). Newbury Park, CA: Sage.

Waterman, A. S. (1993). Developmental perspectives on identity formation: From adolescence to adulthood. In J. E. Marcia, A. S. Waterman, D. R. Matteson, S. L. Archer, & J. L. Orlofsky (Eds.), *Ego identity: A handbook for psychosocial research* (pp. 42–68). New York: Springer-Verlag.

Waters, E., & Deane, K. E. (1985). Defining and assessing individual differences in attachment relationships: Q-methodology and the organization of behavior in infancy and early childhood. *Monographs of the Society for Research in Child Development, 50* (Serial No. 1-2), 41–65.

Waters, E., Kondo-Ikemura, K., Posada, G., & Richters, J. E. (1991). Learning to love: Mechanisms and milestones. In

M. R. Gunnar & L. A. Sroufe (Eds.), *Self processes and development. The Minnesota Symposia on Child Development. Vol. 23* (pp. 217–255). Hillsdale, NJ: Erlbaum.

Waters, E., Wippman, J., & Sroufe, L. A. (1979). Attachment, positive affect, and competence in the peer group: Two studies in construct validation. *Child Development, 50,* 821–829,

Waters, H. S., & Tinsley, V. S. (1985). Evaluating the discriminant and convergent validity of developmental constructs: Another look at the concept of egocentrism. *Psychological Bulletin, 97,* 483–496.

Watson, J. B. (1928). *Psychological care of infant and child.* New York: W. W. Norton.

Watson, J. B. (1930). *Behaviorism.* New York: W. W. Norton.

Watson, J. D. (1968). *The double helix.* New York: Atheneum.

Watson, J. D., & Crick, F. H. C. (1953). Molecular structure of nucleic acids. *Nature, 171,* 737–738.

Watson-Gegeo, K. A., & Gegeo, D. W. (1989). The role of sibling interaction in child socialization. In P. G. Zukow (Ed.), *Sibling interaction across cultures: Theoretical and methodological issues* (pp. 54–76). New York: Springer-Verlag.

Waxman, S. R., & Hall, D. G. (1993). The development of a linkage between count nouns and object categories: Evidence from fifteen- to twenty-one-month-old infants. *Child Development, 64,* 1224–1241.

Wechsler, D. (1989). *Wechsler Preschool and Primary Scale of Intelligence, Revised.* San Antonio, TX: The Psychological Corporation.

Wechsler, D. (1991). *Manual for the Wechsler Intelligence Scale for Children-III.* San Antonio, TX: The Psychological Corporation.

Wehren, A., & De Lisi, R. (1983). The development of gender understanding: Judgments and explanations. *Child Development, 54,* 1568–1578.

Weinberg, R. A. (1989). Intelligence and IQ: Landmark issues and great debates. *American Psychologist, 44,* 98–104.

Weinberg, R. A., Scarr, S., & Waldman, I. D. (1992). The Minnesota Transracial Adoption Study: A follow-up of IQ test performance at adolescence. *Intelligence, 16,* 117–135.

Weiner, B. (1985). An attributional theory of achievement motivation and emotion. *Psychological Review, 92,* 548–573.

Weinraub, M., Clemens, L. P., Sockloff, A., Ethridge, T., Gracely, E., & Myers, B. (1984). The development of sex role stereotypes in the third year: Relationships to gender labeling, gender identity, sex-typed toy preference, and family characteristics. *Child Development, 55,* 1493–1503.

Weisner, T. S., & Wilson-Mitchell, J. E. (1990). Nonconventional family lifestyles and sex typing in six-year-olds. *Child Development, 61,* 1915–1933.

Weiss, B. (1994). The developmental neurotoxicity of methyl mercury. In H. L. Needleman & D. Bellinger (Eds.), *Prenatal exposure to toxicants: Developmental consequences* (pp. 112–129). Baltimore: Johns Hopkins University Press.

Weiss, B., Dodge, K. A., Bates, J. E., & Pettit, G. S. (1992). Some consequences of early harsh discipline: Child aggression and a maladaptive social information processing style. *Child Development, 63,* 1321–1335.

Weissberg, R. P., & Allen, J. P. (1986). Promoting children's social skills and adaptive interpersonal behavior. In B. A. Edelstein & L. Michelson (Eds.), *Handbook of prevention.* New York: Plenum.

Weisz, J. R., & Zigler, E. (1979). Cognitive development in retarded and non-retarded persons: Piagetian tests of the similar sequence hypothesis. *Psychological Bulletin, 86,* 831–851.

Wellman, H. M. (1988). First steps in the child's theorizing about the mind. In J. W. Astington, P. L. Harris, & D. R. Olson, (Eds.), *Developing theories of mind* (pp. 64–92). Cambridge, England: Cambridge University Press.

Wellman, H. M., Cross, D., & Bartsch, K. (1986). Infant search and object permanence: A meta-analyis of the A-not-B error. *Monographs of the Society for Research in Child Development, 51* (3, Serial No. 214).

Wellman, H. M., & Estes, D. (1986). Early understanding of mental entities: A reexamination of childhood realism. *Child Development, 57,* 910–923.

Wellman, H. M., & Gelman, S. A. (1992). Cognitive development: Foundational theories of core domains. *Annual Review of Psychology, 43,* 337–375.

Wellman, H. M., & Hickling, A. K. (1994). The mind's "I": Children's conception of the mind as an active agent. *Child Development, 65,* 1564–1580.

Wendel, G. D. (1988). Gestational and congenital syphilis. *Clinics in Perinatology, 15,* 287–303.

Wentzel, K. R., & Asher, S. R. (1995). The academic lives of neglected, rejected, popular, and controversial children. *Child Development, 66,* 754–763.

Werker, J. F. (1993). The contribution of the relation between vocal production and perception to a developing phonological system. *Journal of Phonetics, 21,* 177–180.

Werker, J. F., & Lalonde, C. E. (1988). Cross-language speech perception: Initial

capabilities and developmental change. *Developmental Psychology, 24,* 672–683.

Werker, J. F., Pegg, J. E., & McLeod, P. (1994). A cross-language investigation of infant preference for infant-directed communication. *Infant Behavior and Development, 17,* 323–333.

Werker, J. F., & Polka, L. (1993). Developmental changes in speech perception: New challenges and new directions. *Journal of Phonetics, 21,* 83–101.

Werker, J. F., & Tees, R. C. (1984). Cross-language speech perception: Evidence for perceptual reorganization during the first year of life. *Infant Behavior and Development, 7,* 49–63.

Werner, E. E. (1989, April). Children of the Garden Island. *Scientific American,* 106–111.

Werner, H. (1957). The concept of development from a comparative and organismic point of view. In D. B. Harris (Ed.), *The concept of development* (pp. 125–148). Minneapolis: University of Minnesota Press.

Wertsch, J. (1979). From social interaction to higher psychological processes: A clarification and application of Vygotsky's theory. *Human Development, 22,* 1–22.

Wertsch, J. V., & Hickmann, M. (1987). Problem solving in social interaction: A microgenetic analysis. In M. Hickmann (Ed.), *Social and functional approaches to language and thought* (pp. 251–266). New York: Academic.

Wertsch, J. V., & Tulviste, P. (1992). L. S. Vygotsky and contemporary developmental psychology. *Developmental Psychology, 28,* 548–557.

Weston, J. A., Colloton, M., Halsey, S., Covington, S., Gilbert, J., Sorrentino-Kelly, L., & Renoud, S. S. (1993). A legacy of violence in nonorganic failure to thrive. *Child Abuse and Neglect, 17,* 709–714.

White, J. L., Moffitt, T. E., Caspi, A., Bartusch, D. J., Needles, D. H., & Stouthamer-Weber, M. (1994). Measuring impulsivity and examining its relationship to delinquency. *Journal of Abnormal Psychology, 103,* 192–205.

White, L. (1994). Growing up with single parents and stepparents: Long-term effects on family solidarity. *Journal of Marriage and the Family, 56,* 935–948.

White, R. W. (1959). Motivation reconsidered: The concept of competence. *Psychological Review, 66,* 297–333.

Whitebrook, M., Howes, C., & Phillips, D. A. (1990). *Who cares? Child care teachers and the quality of care in America. Final report of the National Child Care Staffing Study.* Oakland, CA: Child Care Employee Project.

Whitehurst, G. J., Falco, F. L., Lonigan, C. J., Fischel, J. E., DeBaryshe, B. D., Valdez-Menchaca, M. C., & Caulfield, M. (1988). Accelerating language development through picture book reading. *Developmental Psychology, 24*, 552–559.

Whitehurst, G. J., & Valdez-Menchaca, M. C. (1988). What is the role of reinforcement in early language acquisition? *Child Development, 59*, 430–440.

Whiteman, M. (1967). Children's conceptions of psychological causality. *Child Development, 38*, 143–155.

Whiting, B. B. (Ed.). (1963). *Six cultures: Studies of childrearing.* New York: Wiley.

Whiting, B. B., & Edwards, C. (1988). *Children of different worlds: The formation of social behavior.* Cambridge, MA: Harvard University Press.

Whiting, B. B., & Whiting, J. W. M. (1975). *Children of six cultures: A psycho-cultural analysis.* Cambridge, MA: Harvard University Press.

Whitley, B. E., Jr. (1983). Sex role orientation and self-esteem: A critical meta-analytic review. *Journal of Personality and Social Psychology, 44*, 765–778.

Wideman, M. V., & Singer, J. E. (1984). The role of psychological mechanisms in preparation for childbirth. *American Psychologist, 39*, 1357–1371.

Widom, C. S. (1989). Does violence beget violence? A critical examination of the literature. *Psychological Bulletin, 106*, 3–28.

Wigfield, A. (1994). Expectancy-value theory of achievement motivation: A developmental perspective. *Educational Psychology Review, 6*, 49–78.

Wigfield, A., & Eccles, J. S. (1992). The development of achievement task values: A theoretical analysis. *Developmental Review, 12*, 265–310.

Wigfield, A., Eccles, J. S., MacIver, D. Reuman, D. A., & Midgley, C. (1991). Transitions during early adolescence: Changes in children's domain-specific self-perceptions and general self-esteem across the transition to junior high school. *Developmental Psychology, 27*, 552–564.

Wilcox, A. J., Weinberg, C. R., & Baird, D. D. (1995). Timing of sexual intercourse in relation to ovulation: Effects on the probability of conception, survival of the pregnancy, and sex of the baby. *New England Journal of Medicine, 333*, 1517–1521.

Wilkinson, L. C., Wilkinson, A. C., Spinelli, F., & Chiang, C. P. (1984). Metalinguistic knowledge of pragmatic rules in school-age children. *Child Development, 55*, 2130–2140.

Williams, C., & Bybee, J. (1994). What do children feel guilty about? Developmental and gender differences. *Developmental Psychology, 50*, 617–623.

Willinger, M., Hoffman, H. J., & Hartford, R. B. (1994). Infant sleep position and risk for sudden infant death syndrome: Report of meeting held January 13 and 14, 1994, National Institutes of Health, Bethesda, MD. *Pediatrics, 93*, 814–819.

Wilson, M. (1986). The black extended family: An analytical consideration. *Developmental Psychology, 22*, 246–258.

Wilson, M. (1989). Child development in the context of the black extended family. *American Psychologist, 44*, 380–383.

Wilson, R. S. (1976). Concordance in physical growth for monozygotic and dizygotic twins. *Annals of Human Biology, 3*, 1–10.

Wilson, R. S. (1983). The Louisville twin study: Developmental synchronies in behavior: *Child Development, 54*, 298–316.

Wimmer, H., Hogrefe, J., & Sodian, B. (1988). A second stage in children's conception of mental life: Understanding informational accesses as origins of knowledge and belief. In J. W. Astington, P. L. Harris, & D. R. Olson (Eds.), *Developing theories of mind* (pp. 173–192). New York: Cambridge University Press.

Wimmer, H., Landerl, K., & Schneider, W. (1994). The role of rhyme awareness in learning to read a regular orthography. *British Journal of Developmental Psychology, 12*, 469–484.

Wimmer, H., & Perner, J. (1983). Beliefs about beliefs: Representation and constraining function of wrong beliefs in young children's understanding of deception. *Cognition, 13*, 103–128.

Windle, M. (1992). A longitudinal study of stress buffering for adolescent problem behaviors. *Developmental Psychology, 28*, 522–530.

Windle, M. (1995). A study of friendship characteristics and problem behavior among middle adolescents. *Child Development, 65*, 1764–1777.

Windle, M., & Lerner, R. M. (1986). The "goodness of fit" model of temperament-context relations: Interaction or correlation? In J. V. Lerner & R. M. Lerner (Eds.), *Temperament and social interaction in infants and children* (pp. 109–120). San Francisco: Jossey-Bass.

Winer, G. A (1980). Class-inclusion reasoning in children: A review of the empirical literature. *Child Development, 51*, 309–328.

Winick, M., Meyer, K. K., & Harris, R. C. (1975). Malnutrition and environmental enrichment by early adoption. *Science, 190*, 1173–1175.

Wittrock, M. C. (Ed.). (1985). *Handbook of research on teaching.* New York: Macmillan.

Wolff, P. H. (1987). *The development of behavioral states and the expression of emotions in early infancy.* Chicago: University of Chicago Press.

Wong, C-M. T., Day, J. D., Maxwell, S. E., & Meara, N. M. (1995). A multitrait-multimethod study of academic and social intelligence in college students. *Journal of Educational Psychology, 87*, 117–133.

Wong, Y. I., Garfinkel, I., & McLanahan, S. (1993). Single-mother families in eight countries: Economic status and social policy. *Social Service Review, 67*, 178–197.

Wood, D. (1988). *How children think and learn.* Oxford, England: Basil Blackwell.

Wood, D., Bruner, J. S., & Ross, G. (1976). The role of tutoring in problem solving. *Journal of Child Psychology and Psychiatry, 17*, 89–100.

Woody-Ramsey, J., & Miller, P. H. (1988). The facilitation of selective attention in preschoolers. *Child Development, 59*, 1497–1503.

Woolston, J. L. (1987). Obesity in infancy and early childhood. *Journal of the American Academy of Child and Adolescent Psychiatry, 26*, 123–126.

Yarrow, L. J., McQuiston, S., MacTurk, R. H., McCarthy, M. E., Klein, R. P., & Vietze, P. M. (1983). Assessment of mastery motivation during the first year of life: Contemporaneous and cross-age relationships. *Developmental Psychology, 19*, 64–100.

Yelland, G. W., Pollard, J., & Mercuri, A. (1993). The metalinguistic benefits of limited contact with second language. *Applied Psycholinguistics, 14*, 423–444.

Yonas, A., & Owsley, C. (1987). Development of visual space perception. In P. Salapatek & L. Cohen (Eds.), *Handbook of infant perception. Vol. II. From sensation to perception* (pp. 80–122). Orlando, FL: Academic.

Younger, B., & Gotlieb, S. (1988). Development of categorization skills: Changes in the nature or structure of infant form categories? *Developmental Psychology, 24*, 611–619.

Younger, B. A. (1993). Understanding category members as "the same sort of thing": Explicit categorization in ten-month infants. *Child Development, 64*, 309–320.

Youniss, J. (1980). *Parents and peers in social development.* Chicago: University of Chicago Press.

Youniss, J. (1992). Antiparticularism in developmental and moral theory. In W. M. Kurtines, M. Azmitia, & J. L. Gewirtz (Eds.), *The role of values in*

psychology and human development (pp. 173–199). New York: Wiley.

Youniss, J., & Smollar, J. (1985). Adolescent relations with mothers, fathers, and friends. Chicago: University of Chicago Press.

Yussen, S. R., & Levy, V. M. (1975). Developmental changes in predicting one's own span of short-term memory. Journal of Experimental Child Psychology, 19, 502–508.

Zahn-Waxler, C., Kochanska, G., Krupnick, J., & McKnew, D. (1990). Patterns of guilt in children of depressed and well mothers. Developmental Psychology, 26, 51–59.

Zahn-Waxler, C., Radke-Yarrow, M., & King, R. A. (1979). Child-rearing and children's prosocial initiations toward victims of distress. Child Development, 50, 319–330.

Zahn-Waxler, C., Radke-Yarrow, M., Wagner, E., & Chapman, M. L. (1992). Development of concern for others. Developmental Psychology, 28, 126–136.

Zajonc, R. B. (1976). Family configuration and intelligence. Science, 192, 227–236.

Zajonc, R. B. (1983). Validating the confluence model. Psychological Bulletin, 93, 457–480.

Zajonc, R. B. (1993). The confluence model: Differential or difference equation. European Journal of Social Psychology, 23, 211–215.

Zajonc, R. B., & Markus, G. B. (1975). Birth order and intellectual development. Psychological Review, 82, 74–88.

Zarbatany, L., Hartmann, D. P., & Gelfand, D. M. (1985). Why does children's generosity increase with age: Susceptibility to experimenter influence or altruism? Child Development, 56, 746–756.

Zeichner, S. L., & Plotkin, S. A. (1988). Mechanisms and pathways of congenital infections. Clinics in Perinatology, 15, 163–188.

Zelniker, T., & Jeffrey, W. E. (1976). Reflective and impulsive children: Strategies of information processing underlying differences in problem solving. Monographs of the Society for Research in Child Development, 41 (5, Serial No. 168).

Zeskind, P. S., & Lester, B. M. (1978). Acoustic features and auditory perceptions of the cries of newborns with prenatal and perinatal complications. Child Development, 49, 580–589.

Zeskind, P. S., Sale, J., Maio, M. L., Huntington, L., & Weiseman, J. R. (1985). Adult perceptions of pain and hunger cries: A synchrony of arousal. Child Development, 56, 549–554.

Zigler, E., Abelson, W. D., Trickett, P. K., & Seitz, V. (1982). Is an intervention program necessary in order to improve economically disadvantaged children's IQ scores? Child Development, 53, 340–348.

Zigler, E., & Hall, N. W. (1989). Physical child abuse in America: Past, present, and future. In D. Cicchetti & V. Carlson (Eds.), Child maltreatment: Theory and research on the causes and consequences of child abuse and neglect (pp. 38–75). New York: Cambridge University Press.

Zigler, E., & Muenchow, S. (1992). Head Start: The inside story of America's most successful educational experiment. New York: Basic.

Zigler, E., & Styfco, S. J. (Eds.). (1993). Head Start and beyond: A national plan for extended childhood intervention. New Haven, CT: Yale University Press.

Zill, N. (1985). Happy, healthy, and insecure. New York: Doubleday.

Zill, N. (1988). Behavior, achievement, and health problems among children in stepfamilies: Findings from a national survey of child health. In E. M. Hetherington & J. D. Arasteh (Eds.), Impact of divorce, single parenting, and stepparenting on children (pp. 325–368). Hillsdale, NJ: Erlbaum.

Zimiles, H., & Lee, V. E. (1991). Adolescent family structure and educational progress. Developmental Psychology, 27, 314–320.

Zuckerman, B. S., & Frank, D. A. (1992). Infancy and toddler years. In M. D. Levine, W. B. Carey, & A. C. Crocker (Eds.), Developmental-behavioral pediatrics (pp. 27–38). Philadelphia: W. B. Saunders.

# CREDITS

## Photographs

### Chapter 1

**Opener:** © Michael Newman/PhotoEdit; **1.4:** © Gesell Institute; **1.5:** Bettmann Archive; **p. 15 top:** © Elizabeth Crews/The Image Works; **p. 15 right:** © Florent Flipper/Unicorn Stock Photos; **p. 17:** © David Frazier Photo Library; **1.7:** Stock Montage; **p. 26:** © Yves DeBraine/Black Star; **p. 27:** © Tony Freeman/PhotoEdit; **p. 32:** © Michael Newman/PhotoEdit

### Chapter 2

**Opener:** © Erika Stone 1996; **2.1 & 2.2:** © Kim Hill/Native Peoples Tropical Conservation Fund; **2.3:** © Ray Stott/The Image Works; **2.4:** © Charles Nelson; **2.7:** Permission of Robert Kail; **p. 55:** © Bob Daemmrich/The Image Works; **p. 71:** © Will & Deni McIntyre/Photo Researchers, Inc.

### Chapter 3

**Opener:** © Renate Hiller/Monkmeyer Press; **p. 80:** © 1993/SPL/Photo Researchers; **3.3:** © Scott Camazine/Photo Researchers; **3.4A&B:** Custom Medical Stock Photos; **3.6A:** © Linda Moore/Rainbow; **3.6B:** Courtesy of Dr. Gail Stetten, Johns Hopkins University Prenatal Diagonistic Center; **3.6C:** © Richard Hutchings/PhotoEdit; **3.7A:** Moore, K.L.: *The Sex Chromatin*, Philadelphia, W.B. Saunders Co., 1966; **3.7B:** © W.B. Saunders Company Courtesy of Dr. M. Ray, Department of Human Genetics, University of Manitoba, Winnipeg, Canada; **p. 91:** © 1995 Joseph R. Siebert, Ph.D/Custom Medical Stock Photo; **3.9:** © Will & Deni McIntyre/Photo Researchers, Inc.; **3.11A:** © Bill Longcore/Photo Researchers, Inc.; **3.11B:** © Bill Longcore/Photo Researchers, Inc.; **p. 103:** © Alan Carey/Image Works

### Chapter 4

**Opener:** © Mark Richards/PhotoEdit; **p. 115:** © Junebug Clark/Photo Researchers, Inc.; **4.3:** © Lennart Nilsson/Bonnier Alba AB; **4.4:** © Lennart Nilsson/Bonnier Alba AB; **4.5:** © Lennart Nilsson/Bonnier Alba AB; **4.6:** © Lennart Nilsson/Bonnier Alba AB; **p. 128:** © Black Star; **p. 133:** AP/Wide World Photos; **4.8:** Streissguth, A.P., Clarren, S.K., & Jones, K.L. (1985, July) Natural History of the Fetal Alcohol Syndrome: A 10-year follow-up of 11 patients. LANCET, 2, 85–92; **p. 135:** © Dan McCoy/Rainbow; **p. 137:** © Ogust/ The Image Works; **p. 140:** © Children's Defense Fund; **p. 143:** © Charles Gupton/ Stock Boston; **4.12:** © Lennart Nilsson/ Bonnier Alba AB; **p. 151:** © Charles Gupton/ Stock Boston

### Chapter 5

**Opener:** © Elizabeth Crews/The Image Works; **p. 157 left:** © Michael Newman/PhotoEdit; **p. 157 middle:** © Myrleen Ferguson Cate/PhotoEdit; **p. 157 right:** © Amy C. Etra/PhotoEdit; **p. 171 left:** © Mary Kate Denny/PhotoEdit; **p. 171 right:** © Mark Richards/PhotoEdit; **p. 179:** © Elizabeth Crews/The Image Works; **p. 183:** © Elizabeth Harris/Tony Stone Images; **p. 187:** © 1996 Laura Dwight; **5.18A&B:** © Enrico Ferorelli

### Chapter 6

**Opener:** © Kramer/The Image Works; **p. 204:** © Photo Media/H. Armstrong Roberts; **6.1A,B&C:** University of Delaware; **p. 214:** © Tony Freeman/PhotoEdit; **6.3:** Harlow Primate Laboratory, University of Wisconsin; **p. 217:** © Sybille Kalas; **6.4:** © Martin Rogers/Stock, Boston; **p. 220:** © Jonathan Nourok/PhotoEdit; **p. 223:** © Mary Ainsworth; **p. 230:** © Michael Newman/PhotoEdit

### Chapter 7

**Opener:** © Elizabeth Glasgow/Monkmeyer; **7.1A:** Central Institute for the Deaf; **p. 250:** Archive Photos; **p. 253:** © Myrleen Ferguson/PhotoEdit; **p. 254:** © Robert Brenner/PhotoEdit; **p. 259:** © Margaret W. Peterson/The Image Bank-Chicago; **p. 260:** © Bob Daemmrich/The Image Works; **p. 265:** © Steve Weber/Tony Stone Images; **p. 269 left:** © Michelle Bridwell/PhotoEdit; **p. 269 right:** © Paul S. Conklin/Uniphoto Picture Agency; **p. 270:** © Laura Dwight/PhotoEdit; **p. 276 left:** © Myrleen Ferguson/PhotoEdit; **p. 276:** © Michael Newman/PhotoEdit; **p. 281:** Savage/Rumbaugh; **p. 282 top:** © Bob Daemmrich/The Image Works; **p. 282 bottom:** © Superstock

### Chapter 8

**Opener:** © Ulrike Welsch; **p. 291 left:** Superstock; **p. 291 right:** © W. Eastep/The Stock Market; **p. 314:** © Robert Daemmrich/Tony Stone Images

### Chapter 9

**Opener:** © Shackman/Monkmeyer; **p. 332:** © Sean Sprague/Impact Visuals; **p. 334:** © Frank Siteman/Picturesque; **9.5:** Courtesy of Jean M. Mandler and Laraine McDonough. Reprinted with permission of Ablex Publishing Corporation; **9.8:** Courtesy of Carolyn Rovee-Collier; **p. 362:** © Amy Etra/PhotoEdit; **9.15:** Courtesy of Tiffany Field

### Chapter 10

**Opener:** © Ulrike Welsch; **p. 378 left:** © Dr. Rose Gantner/Comstock; **p. 378 right:** © 1996 Laura Dwight; **p. 381:** Bettmann Archive; **p. 387 left:** © Alan Carey/The Image Works; **p. 387 right:** © Southern Illinois University/Photo Researchers; **p. 397:** © Myrleen Ferguson/PhotoEdit; **p. 400:** © AP/Wide World Photos; **p. 403:** © David Young-Wolff/PhotoEdit; **p. 407:** © Anna E. Zuckerman/PhotoEdit; **p. 413 bottom right:** © Kay L. Hendrich; **p. 413 top right:** © Robert Brenner/PhotoEdit; **p. 413 left:** © D & I MacDonald/Unicorn Stock Photos; **p. 417:** © H. Yamaguchi/Gamma Liason; **p. 419 left:** © Bob Daemmrich/Image Works; **p. 419 right:** © Laura Dwight

### Chapter 11

**Opener:** © Laura Dwight/Peter Arnold, Inc.; **p. 432:** © Joel Gordon Photography; **p. 438:** © Tony Clark/The Image Works; **p. 442:** © Tony Freeman/PhotoEdit; **p. 444:** © Tony Freeman/PhotoEdit; **p. 465 left:**

© Tony Freeman/PhotoEdit; **p. 465 right:**
© Brian Seed/Tony Stone Images

## Chapter 12

**Opener:** © Sidney/The Image Works; **p. 477 top left:** © David Young-Wolff/PhotoEdit; **p. 477 top right:** © Mary Kate Denny/ PhotoEdit; **p. 477 bottom left:** © Michael Newman/PhotoEdit; **p. 478:** © Suzanne Szasz/Photo Researchers, Inc.; **p. 481:** © David M. Grossman/Photo Researchers, Inc.; **p. 483:** © University of Wisconsin Primate Laboratory; **p. 484:** © University of Wisconsin Primate Laboratory; **p. 487:** © Blair Seitz/Picturesque; **p. 492:** © 1989 Laura Dwight/Peter Arnold, Inc.; **p. 494:** © Myrleen Ferguson Cate/Photo Edit; **p. 501:** © Tony Freeman/PhotoEdit; **p. 512:** © Michael Newman/PhotoEdit; **p. 513:** © Tony Freeman/PhotoEdit; **p. 514 & p. 515:** © University of Oklahoma Institute of Group Relations

## Chapter 13

**Opener:** © Superstock; **p. 524:** © Dan McCoy/Rainbow; **p. 536:** Self Help Book; **p. 539:** © Myrleen Ferguson Cate/ PhotoEdit; **p. 553:** © Suzanne Szasz/Photo Researchers, Inc.

## Chapter 14

**Opener:** © Robert J. Capece/Monkmeyer; **p. 569:** Digital Stock; **p. 571:** © Myrleen Ferguson Cate/PhotoEdit; **p. 584:** © Wisconsin Regional Primate Research Center; **p. 589:** © David Strickler/The Picture Cube; **p. 599:** © Jeff Isaac Greenberg/Photo Researchers, Inc.

## Chapter 15

**Opener:** © Mary Kate Denny/PhotoEdit; **p. 608 top left:** © Doug Vargas/Image Works; **p. 608 top right:** © Robert Bremer/PhotoEdit; **p. 608 bottom right:** © Myrleen Ferguson Cate/PhotoEdit; **p. 611:** © 1996 Laura Dwight; **p. 625:** © Mark Antman/The Image Works; **p. 635:** © George Goodwin/Monkmeyer; **p. 637:** © Martin R. Jones/Unicorn Stock Photos; **p. 646:** © Steve Skjold/PhotoEdit; **p. 647:** Colby & Damonn/Free Press 1992

## Line Art

### Chapter 1

**Figure 1.9:** From R.S. Siegler, "Three aspects of cognitive development," in *Cognitive Psychology*, 8:481–520. Copyright ©

1976 by Academic Press, Orlando, FL. Reprinted with permission of the publisher.

### Chapter 4

**Figure 4.7:** Adapted from K.L. Moore, *The Developing Human: Clinically Oriented Embryology*, 3d ed. Copyright © 1993 W.B. Saunders. Reprinted by permission.

### Chapter 5

**Figure 5.1:** From W.A. Marshall, et al., "Puberty" in F. Falkner and J.M. Tanner, *Human Growth: A Comprehensive Treatise*. Copyright © 1986 Plenum Publishing Corp. Reprinted by permission.
**Figures 5.8 & 5.16:** ©*The Society for Research in Child Development, Inc.*
**Figure 5.17:** From B.I. Bertenthal, et al., "Infants' encoding of kinetic displays varying in relative coherence" in *Developmental Psychology*, 23:171–178. Copyright © 1987 by The American Psychological Association. Reprinted with permission.

### Chapter 6

**Figure 6.8:** ©*The Society for Research in Child Development, Inc.*

### Chapter 7

**Figure 7.4:** ©*The Society for Research in Child Development, Inc.*

### Chapter 8

**Figure 8.1:** Adapted from R. Baillargeon "Object permanence in 3½ and 4½-month-old infants" in *Developmental Psychology*, 23:655–664. Copyright © 1987 by The American Psychological Association. Adapted with permission.
**Figure 8.12:** Adapted from S.L. Ward and W.F. Overton, "Semantic familiarity, relevance, and the development of deductive reasoning" in *Developmental Psychology*, 26:488–493. Copyright © 1990 by The American Psychological Association. Adapted with permission.
**Figure 8.15:** From J. V. Wertsch and M. Hickmann, "Problem solving in social interaction: A microgenetic analysis" in *Social and Functional Approaches to Language and Thought*. Copyright © 1987 by Academic Press, Orlando, FL. Reprinted with permission of the publisher.

### Chapter 9

**Figure 9.1:** From E. Vurpillot, "The development of scanning strategies and their relation of visual differentiation" in *Journal of Experimental Child Psychology*, 6:632–650.

Copyright © 1968 by Academic Press, Orlando, FL. Reprinted with permission of the publisher.
**Figure 9.5:** From M.J. Mandler and L. McDonough, "Concept formation in infancy" in *Cognitive Development* 8:291–318. Copyright © 1993 Ablex Publishing Corp., Norwood, NJ. Reprinted by permission.
**Figure 9.17:** ©*The Society for Research in Child Development, Inc.*

### Chapter 10

**Figures 10.6 & 10.8:** ©*The Society for Research in Child Development, Inc.*

### Chapter 11

**Figure 11.5:** ©*The Society for Research in Child Development, Inc.*

### Chapter 13

**Figure 13.5:** From J. Gnepp "Children's use of personal information to understand other people's feelings" in C. Saarni and P. L. Harris (Eds.), *Children's Understanding of Emotions*. Copyright © 1989 Cambridge University Press. Reprinted with the permission of Cambridge University Press.

### Chapter 14

**Figure 14.6:** From C. P. Benbow, "Sex differences in mathematical reasoning ability in intellectually talented preadolescents: Their nature, effects, and possible causes" in *Behavioral and Brain Sciences*, 11:169–232. Copyright © 1988 Cambridge University Press. Reprinted with the permission of Cambridge University Press.

### Chapter 15

**Figure 15.2:** ©*The Society for Research in Child Development, Inc.*
**Figures 15.3 & 15.4:** From Anne Colby and Lawrence Kohlberg *The Measurement of Moral Judgment, Vol. 1 and 2*. Copyright © 1987 Cambridge University Press. Reprinted with the permission of Cambridge University Press.

# NAME INDEX

## A

Abbott, R. D., 554
Abell, S., 161
Abelson, W. D., 390
Aber, J. L., 529, 530
Abramov, I., 188
Abramovitch, R., 448, 449
Achenbach, T. M., 50, 67, 151
Ackerman, B. P., 278
Acredolo, L. P., 273
Adams, R. J., 188
Adamson, L. B., 210
Adan, A. M., 497
Adey, P. S., 320
Adler, R., 412
Adler, T. F., 413
Adubato, S. A., 347
Ahadi, S. A., 226
Ahrens, M. G., 261
Ainsworth, M. D. S., 177, 178, 217, 220, 221, 222,
    224, 225, 229, 230, 445
Albert, J., 338, 339
Alberts, D. M., 344
Albright, D. L., 138
Allen, J. P., 554
Allen, L., 529, 530
Allison, P. D., 461
Almeida, M. C., 553, 554
Almli, C. R., 174
Aloise, P. A., 547
Alpern, L., 227
Alpert-Gillis, L. J., 598
Alsaker, F. D., 530, 531
Alvarez, M., 645
Alvarez, W. F., 453
Amato, P. R., 456, 457, 461, 462
American Psychological Association, 70
Ames, C., 415
Ames, G. J., 318, 319
Amiel-Tison, C., 149
Ammala, P., 99
Anderson, K. E., 446
Andersson, B. E., 232, 486
Andreas, D., 226
Andrew, L., 149
Andrews, D. W., 496, 497
Anglin, J. M., 252, 257, 261
Anson, A. R., 512
Antell, S. E., 309
Apgar, V., 146
Appleby, D. C., 593
Aquilino, W. S., 457
Arasteh, J. D., 461
Archer, S. L., 534, 535, 536


Arcus, D., 78, 107
Arend, R., 227, 591
Aries, P., 3
Arsenio, W. R., 413
Arvidsson, J., 174
Asendorpf, J. B., 523, 524, 636
Asher, S. R., 51, 502, 503, 507
Asher, S. T., 503
Ashley, C. T., 91
Ashmead, D. H., 182
Aslin, R. N., 185, 187, 194, 246, 333, 339
Asquith, P., 625
Astington, J. W., 548
Astone, N. M., 459
Astor, R. A., 642
Atkinson, J. W., 411
Attanucci, J., 621
Au, T. K., 256
Aumiller, K., 503
Austin-LaFrance, R., 138
Aviezer, O., 230, 231, 232, 238
Azmitia, M., 325, 451, 645
Azuma, H., 259

## B

Bachman, J. G., 530, 531
Bagwell, C. L., 496, 497, 501
Bailey, A., 91, 108
Bailey, C. A., 600
Bailey, J. M., 581
Baillargeon, R., 295, 296, 298, 312, 319
Baird, D. D., 117
Bakeman, R., 210
Baker, J. A., 516
Baker, L. A., 576, 585, 586
Baker-Ward, L., 356
Balaban, T., 595
Baldwin, D. A., 259
Ball, S., 261
Ball, S. J., 415
Balla, D. A., 180
Balsley, J., 132
Baltes, P. B., 67
Bandura, A., 17, 24, 25, 65, 72, 424, 436, 437, 438,
    595, 607, 642, 643
Bank, L., 437, 438, 441
Banks, M. S., 46, 186, 187, 188, 189, 192
Barclay, A., 95
Barenboim, C., 552
Barglow, P., 226, 232
Barker, W. B., 397
Barnard, K. E., 401, 402, 414
Barnas, M. V., 236
Barnes, H. D., 256


Barness, L. A., 160
Barr, H. M., 130, 134, 135, 136
Barrera, M., 189, 209
Barrett, D., 223, 225, 466
Barrett, K., 149, 151
Barrett, K. C., 145, 206, 208, 211, 226, 227, 233,
    235, 417
Barrett, M., 253
Barrett, M. D., 253
Barrickman, P. J., 593
Barry, F. D., 468
Barry, H., III, 54
Barton, M., 256
Bartsch, K., 297, 548, 549
Basham, R. B., 465
Bashe, E., 573
Basinger, K. S., 614
Bass, M., 176
Bates, E., 243, 248, 251, 252, 253, 256, 264, 272,
    273, 274
Bates, J. E., 213, 214, 433, 459, 486
Baudonniere, P. M., 523, 524
Bauer, P. J., 342, 363
Baumann, D. J., 632
Baumeister, R. F., 631, 632
Baumrind, D., 10, 103, 109, 110, 429, 431, 432,
    434, 435, 436, 446, 465, 490
Baydar, N., 453
Bayley, N., 180, 181, 386, 387, 390, 391, 392
Bazin, B., 132
Beach, D. H., 355
Beal, C. R., 361
Bean, R., 531
Beardsall, L., 449
Beartschi, J. C., 174
Becker, J. A., 275, 285
Becker, R. A., 268
Becker, W. C., 428
Beek, P. J., 185
Belden, B., 96
Bell, J. J., 582
Bell, R. Q., 446
Bell, S. M., 177, 178
Bell, T. S., 96
Beller, R., 638
Bellinger, D., 129
Bellugi, U., 266, 267
Belmont, J. M., 367
Belsky, J., 161, 213, 224, 225, 226, 227, 230, 232,
    235, 324, 448, 450, 463, 464, 465, 466
Bem, S. L., 595, 598
Bempechat, J., 573
Benbow, C. P., 580, 585, 586
Bender, B., 90
Benn, R. K., 232

713

Catalano, R. F., 554
Catassi, C., 166, 167
Cattell, R. B., 386
Cauce, A. M., 531
Caulfield, M., 260
Causey, D., 497
Cavalier, L., 362
Cavior, N., 500
Ceci, S. J., 363, 364, 383, 389, 390, 394, 397, 404, 408, 418
Cefalo, R. C., 144
Cernoch, J. M., 196, 347
Chalkley, M. A., 268
Chalmers, J. B., 543, 559
Chan, S. Q., 14
Chance, G., 190
Chandler, M., 550
Chandler, M. J., 127, 140, 227, 537, 542, 543, 559
Chang, J. C., 176
Chang, S., 165
Chao, R. K., 436
Chapin, S. L., 516
Chapman, M., 298, 312, 315, 446, 541, 575, 631, 637, 644, 645
Chapman, M. L., 524
Charkraborty, R., 166
Charles-Luce, J., 247
Charlesworth, W. R., 581
Charlop, M. H., 91
Chase-Lansdale, P. L., 457, 460
Chasnoff, I. J., 147
Chassin, L., 67
Chavajay, P., 309, 322, 326, 327
Chen, C., 418
Chen, I. S., 132
Chen, S., 229
Chen, X., 505
Cherlin, A. J., 457
Chess, S., 211, 213
Chessor, D., 532
Chestnut, D. H., 148, 149
Chi, M. T. H., 343, 357
Chiang, C. P., 275
Chilamkurti, C., 546, 552
Child Care Around the World, 452
Children's Defense Fund, 166
Chinsky, J. M., 355
Chomsky, N., 279, 280, 282, 283, 284
Christensen, K. M., 196
Chrousos, G. O., 584
Chu, F., 197
Cialdini, R. B., 632
Ciaramitaro, V., 195
Cicchetti, D., 223, 225, 466, 524
Cicchetti, D. V., 180
Cillessen, A. H. N., 506
Cintra, L., 138
Citron, C. C., 592
Clark, E. V., 255
Clark, L., 166, 167
Clark, L. V., 591
Clarke, A. M., 8
Clarke, A. O. B., 8
Clarke, C., 212
Clarke, S. C., 134, 135, 139, 140, 147, 148, 149, 151, 458
Clarke-Stewart, K. A., 230, 232, 486
Clasen, D. R., 509, 511
Clausen, J. A., 160
Cleland, J. W., 178
Clemens, L. P., 569, 597
Clifton, R., 194
Clifton, R. K., 182, 194, 195, 348, 363

Clingempeel, W. G., 456, 457, 461, 468, 469
Cloud, J. M., 567, 568
Cluss, P. A., 166
Cochran, W. D., 178, 179
Cod, V., 96
Cohen, J., 476
Cohen, L. J., 221, 577
Cohen, N., 404
Cohn, J. F., 205
Coie, J. D., 51, 499, 502, 503, 504, 506, 507
Colby, A., 606, 614, 615, 617, 618, 619, 620, 624
Cole, M., 340
Coley, J. D., 340
Colgrove, R. W., 96
Collaer, M. L., 583, 584
Collins, N. L., 152
Collins, W. A., 443, 444, 533
Collman, P., 597
Colloton, M., 199
Condry, J., 511
Conel, J. L., 170
Conger, J. J., 565
Conger, K. J., 429, 435, 511
Conger, R. D., 429, 435, 511
Conley, M. R., 125
Connell, J. P., 234, 598
Connolly, J. A., 485, 486
Connor, E. M., 132
Connor, J. M., 592
Contant, C., 96
Conway, B. E., 379, 380, 383, 421
Cook, T. D., 512
Cooke, D. W., 183
Cooley, C. H., 531
Coombs, R., 132
Cooney, G. H., 578
Cooper, C. R., 444, 536
Cooper, H. M., 70
Cooper, J., 595
Cooper, R. L., 131
Coopersmith, S., 429, 431, 432, 527, 530, 533
Corbetta, D., 182
Corbin, S. B., 457
Corley, R., 211, 212
Cornell, E. H., 344, 345
Corpuz, M., 139
Corter, C., 448, 449
Costanzo, P. R., 166
Courage, M. L., 363
Court, J. H., 387
Covington, M. V., 420
Covington, S., 199
Cox, G. L., 358, 359
Cox, M., 455
Cox, M. J., 233
Cox, R., 455
Craig, R. S., 593
Crane, J., 397
Crankshaw, E., 285
Craven, R., 528, 529, 532
Creek, K. J., 593
Crick, F. H. C., 79
Crick, N. R., 554, 556, 558, 560, 640, 641
Crnic, K. A., 149, 465
Crockenberg, S., 213, 226, 433, 434
Crockett, L., 510
Crockett, L. J., 582, 583
Cromer, C. C., 516
Cromer, R. F., 281
Crook, C., 195, 196
Crosby, L., 496, 497
Cross, D., 297
Crossland, J., 250, 251

Crouter, A. C., 105, 450, 454
Crowson, M., 91
Cruikshank, D. P., 121
Cruttenden, L., 298
Culnan, M., 132
Cultice, J. C., 361
Cummings, E. M., 2, 209, 210, 236, 429, 430, 640, 642
Cunningham, F. G., 139, 140, 152
Curwin, A., 259
Cutler, G. B., Jr., 584
Cutter, G. R., 131

# D

Dale, P. S., 243, 248, 251, 252, 253, 256, 264, 273
Dame, J. A., 593
Damon, W., 523, 525, 541, 613
Daniels, D., 214, 450
Dann, S., 492
Dannemiller, J. L., 187, 188, 190
Darby, B. L., 130, 134, 136
Darling, N., 436, 437
Darlington, R., 403, 415
Darwin, C., 29, 206
Dasen, P. R., 54
Davies, C., 463, 464
Davies, P. T., 210, 430
Davis, B., 593
Davis, C. C., 479, 480
Davis, L. B., 196
Davis, N., 4
Davis, P. W., 504
Davis, S. W., 567, 568
Davydov, V. V., 325
Day, D., 338, 339
Day, J. D., 359, 362, 367, 421
Day, L. E., 554
Day, N. L., 129, 133, 134
de Halle, P., 248
De Lisi, R., 594, 595
de Marchena, M. R., 258
De Vries, B., 620, 621
Deane, K. E., 223
Deaux, K., 571
DeBaryshe, B. D., 260
DeCasper, A. J., 194, 198, 365
DeFries, J., 211
DeFries, J. C., 104, 212, 402
Degirmencioglu, S. M., 476
Dehner, L. P., 131
Dekovic, M., 508
Delfraissy, J-F., 132
DeLoache, J. S., 344, 356
DeMarie-Dreblow, D., 336
Demo, D. H., 530
Dempster, F. N., 351, 352
Denham, S. A., 553, 554
Dennis, W., 182, 183, 185
Depp, R., 131, 148
DeRosier, M. E., 504, 507
Detterman, D. K., 392
Deutsch, F. M., 236
DeVet, K., 629, 633
deVries, L. B. A., 90, 91
DeVries, R., 320
Diagne, A., 132
Diamond, A., 297, 298
Diamond, J., 100
Diamond, M. O., 139
Dias, M. G., 626
Diaz, R. M., 129

Diaz-Cintra, S., 138
Dickover, R., 132
Dick-Read, G., 143
Didow, S. M., 479, 480
Dillon, R. F., 134
Dinges, M. M., 509
Diqueland, E. R., 245
Dishion, T. J., 496, 497, 508
Dodge, K. A., 433, 446, 459, 486, 499, 500, 502, 503, 504, 506, 554, 555, 556, 558, 560
Dokecki, P. R., 500
Donahue, J., 99
Donaldson, M., 303, 309
Donaldson, S. I., 512
Donenberg, G. R., 621
Donnell, F., 230, 231, 232, 238
Donnerstein, E., 48, 593, 594, 643
Donovan, W. L., 178
Dorfman, D. D., 396
Dornbusch, S., 436, 460
Dornbusch, S. M., 436, 437
Dorsch, A., 556
Dove, H., 40, 41, 42, 54, 56, 61, 62, 182, 185
Dowd, J. M., 194, 195
Downey, D. B., 458, 459
Downey, J., 582
Downs, A. C., 500
Doyle, A. B., 485, 486
Draper, P., 582, 583
Dronkers, J., 459
Drotar, D., 198, 199
DuBard, M. B., 131
DuBois, D. L., 497
Dubow, E. F., 497
Duckett, E., 510
Dukes, R. L., 530
Dulberg, C. S., 134
Dumas, J. E., 441, 446
Dunham, F., 259
Dunham, P. J., 259
Dunkel-Schetter, C., 141, 152
Dunn, J., 106, 446, 447, 448, 449, 450, 469, 544, 631
Dunn, L. M., 387
Dunphy, D. C., 510
Durand, C., 248
Durkin, K., 272
Duyvesteyn, M. G. C., 225, 228
Dvir, R., 233
Dweck, C. S., 408, 409, 410, 411, 412, 417, 421
Dzur, C., 581

# E

Eagly, A. H., 566, 568, 573, 574, 575, 593, 598
East, P. L., 497
Eastenson, A., 491, 496
Easterbrooks, M. A., 591
Easterling, D. V., 144
Eaton, W. O., 573, 587
Eccles, J., 411, 412, 529, 530
Eccles, J. P., 412
Eccles, J. S., 411, 412, 529, 530
Eckerman, C. O., 478, 479, 480
Eckert, P., 504, 509, 511, 512, 513, 514
Edelstein, S. L., 176
Eder, R. A., 526, 552
Edge, V., 140
Edwards, C., 14, 564, 584
Edwards, C. P., 622
Edwards, J. R., 567, 568

Egeland, B., 224, 225, 226, 227, 229, 230, 236, 401, 463, 464, 465
Ehrhardt, A. A., 582, 583
Eicher, S. A., 509, 511
Eichorn, D. H., 292
Eiferman, R. R., 483
Eilers, R. E., 248
Eimas, P. D., 245, 247
Eisen, M., 525, 526
Eisenberg, N., 501, 547, 575, 587, 607, 631, 632, 637, 638, 639, 640, 644, 645
Ekman, P., 206
Elardo, R., 401
Elder, G. H., Jr., 429, 435, 511
Elicker, J., 490
Elkind, D., 320
Elkins, M., 132
Elliott, E. S., 410, 411, 417, 421
Ellis, S., 322, 516
Ellsworth, C. P., 206
Ellsworth, P., 206
Emde, R., 207
Emde, R. N., 19, 20, 21, 23, 210, 211, 212, 213
Emerson, P. E., 219, 234, 237, 238
Emery, R. E., 458
Emory, E. K., 136
Emory, W., 109
Endsley, R. C., 597
Engle, P. L., 165
Englund, M., 490, 599
Enns, L. R., 573, 587
Ensminger, M. E., 460
Entwistle, D. R., 529
Epstein, L. H., 166, 167
Erel, O., 429
Erickson, M. F., 221, 227, 229, 463, 534, 535
Eron, L. D., 642, 643
Espinosa, M. P., 165
Estes, D., 233, 301
Estrada, P., 413
Etaugh, C., 587
Ethridge, T., 569, 597
Evans, E. G., 497
Evans, S., 586
Eveleth, P. B., 158, 159, 168
Ewart, D. P., 132

# F

Fabes, R. A., 501, 547, 632
Fabricius, W. V., 362
Fagan, J. F., 348, 392
Fagot, B. I., 587, 588, 590, 592, 597, 599
Fairchild, H., 543, 593, 594
Falbo, T., 451
Falco, F. L., 260
Faldella, G., 167
Fandal, W. A., 180, 181
Fantz, R. L., 188, 189
Faranoff, A. A., 149
Farber, E. A., 224, 225
Farmer, M. C., 621
Farquharson, R. G., 140
Farrar, M. J., 259, 342, 346, 358
Feather, N. T., 411
Fein, G. G., 136, 481, 485, 486
Feingold, A., 576, 577, 578, 579
Feinkind, L., 132
Feinman, J., 529, 530
Feinman, S., 237

Feiring, C., 228
Feldman, J. F., 392, 393
Feldman, N. S., 529, 552
Feldman, S. S., 445
Felner, R. D., 497
Fennema, E., 574, 575
Fenson, L., 243, 248, 251, 252, 253, 256, 264, 273
Fenwick, K. D., 190
Fenzel, L. M., 530
Ferguson, L. L., 641
Fernald, A., 259, 270
Ferrara, R. A., 32, 319, 325, 366
Ferree, M. M., 236
Feshbach, S., 642
Fidler, D. S., 594
Field, J., 194
Field, T., 487, 491
Fifer, W. P., 198
Figueroa-Colon, R., 166
Fincham, F. D., 458
Finger, F., 174
Finley, G. E., 156, 163
Fischel, J. E., 260
Fischer, K. W., 292
Fischer, P., 643
Fish, M., 213
Fisher, D. M., 183, 185
Fivush, R., 347, 568, 573, 621
Flannery, D. J., 437
Flavell, E. R., 304, 550
Flavell, J. H., 29, 277, 278, 298, 301, 303, 304, 308, 312, 314, 316, 317, 319, 320, 328, 339, 343, 352, 353, 354, 355, 356, 358, 359, 360, 361, 367, 405, 522, 537, 550
Fleming, J. S., 415, 421, 453
Flerx, V. C., 594
Fletcher, P., 165
Flynn, J. R., 405, 406
Fogel, A., 183
Follansbee, D. J., 537
Ford, L. H., 526
Ford, M. E., 539, 591
Forman, E. A., 326, 542
Forman, G. E., 320
Forsterling, F., 420
Foster, M. S., 174
Fowler, J. K., 136
Fowles, J., 567, 568
Fox, D. E., 268
Fox, N. A., 211, 226, 233
Fraleigh, M. J., 436
Frame, C. L., 554, 556
Frank, D. A., 175
Frankenburg, W. K., 180, 181
Franz, C. E., 429, 435
Fraser, A. M., 139
Fraser, S., 379, 386, 396
Frederick, P. D., 132
Freeman, R. K., 130, 131
Freij, B. J., 129, 131, 132
French, D. C., 47, 48, 58, 71, 496, 516
French, K. E., 574
French, L. A., 346
French, V., 7
Frenkel, O. J., 227
Freud, A., 467, 492
Freud, S., 23, 607, 629
Frey, K. S., 594, 595
Fried, P. A., 134
Friederici, A. D., 247
Friedman, L., 579
Friedrichs, A. G., 360

Friesen, W. V., 206
Fritz, A. S., 550
Fritz, J., 546
Frodi, A. M., 178
Fry, C. L., Jr., 537
Fry, D. P., 56
Frye, D., 311
Fryer, G. E., Jr., 462, 468
Fu, Y-H., 90
Fukumoto, A., 629
Fulker, D. W., 211, 212
Fuller, D., 614
Furman, W., 448, 449, 450, 491, 494, 507
Furstenberg, F. F., Jr., 450, 461
Furstenberg, F. T., 457
Fuson, K., 311

# G

Gabbe, S. G., 152
Gagnon, C., 529
Galal, O., 43, 44, 45, 54, 72, 103
Galbraith, R. C., 400
Gall, C., 170
Gallagher, A. M., 595
Galler, J. R., 138
Gallistel, C., 309
Galotti, K. M., 621
Galperin, C. Z., 259
Gamble, T., 232
Gamoran, A., 415
Gant, N. F., 139, 140, 152
Garber, J., 558
Garcia-Coll, C., 212
Gardner, H., 407, 408
Gardner, W., 322
Garfinkel, I., 459
Gariepy, J.-L., 641
Garrod, A. C., 620
Garvin, R. A., 324
Gauthier, R., 581
Gauze, C., 501
Gay, J., 340
Gegeo, D. W., 451
Geis, F. L., 564
Gelber, R., 132, 309
Gelfand, D. M., 638
Gelman, R., 274, 277, 309, 310, 311, 312, 319
Gelman, S. A., 301, 340, 548, 597
Gentner, D., 258
Gersell, D. J., 131
Gershoni, R., 494
Gesell, A., 182
Gewirtz, J. C., 573
Gewirtz, J. L., 621
Gibbons, J., 212
Gibbs, C. P., 148, 149
Gibbs, J. C., 614, 620, 622
Gibson, D., 88
Gibson, E. J., 192, 193, 197, 334, 336
Gilbert, J., 199
Giles, H., 567, 568
Gilligan, C., 620, 621, 648
Gilstrap, B., 224, 235
Gilstrap, L. C., III, 139, 140, 152
Ginsburg, A. P., 189
Ginsburg, H. P., 308, 311, 320
Giorgi, P. L., 166, 167
Gjerde, P. F., 457
Glaser, R., 343
Glass, G. V., 68

Glass, L., 176
Glassman, M., 328
Glauberman, N., 396
Gleason, M. B., 254, 258
Glick, J., 430
Glick, J. A., 340
Glick, P. C., 461
Glusman, M., 256
Gnepp, J., 545, 546, 552
Gold, M., 498, 510
Goldberg, S., 227
Goldberg, W. A., 454
Goldenberg, R. L., 131, 139
Goldfarb, W., 215
Goldfield, B. A., 252, 256
Goldin-Meadows, S., 266, 273
Goldman, M., 629, 633
Goldsmith, D., 4, 15, 54, 648
Goldsmith, D. F., 323
Goldsmith, H. H., 145, 208, 211, 226, 227, 233, 235
Goldstein, J., 467
Goldstein, W. M., 648
Goleman, D., 421
Golinkoff, R. M., 255, 272
Golombok, S., 568, 573, 621
Golter, B. S., 50, 488, 489
Goncu, A., 326, 327
Goode, S., 92
Goodlad, J. I., 34
Goodman, G. S., 346, 358
Goodman, V., 575, 576
Goodnow, J. J., 434, 435, 578, 588
Goodwin, S. W., 273
Goossens, F. A., 236
Gopnik, A., 252
Gordon, L. V., 556
Gordon, T. P., 584
Gorman, K. S., 165
Gotlieb, S., 348
Gottesman, I. I., 101, 108, 211
Gottfried, A. E., 415, 421, 453
Gottfried, A. W., 401, 402, 414, 415, 421, 453
Gottman, J. M., 44, 491, 494
Gould, S. J., 378, 389, 396
Gouze, K. R., 555
Gove, F. L., 230
Graber, J. A., 161
Graber, M., 295, 298
Gracely, E., 569, 597
Graham, J. W., 512
Graham, K., 134
Graham, S., 556, 557
Gralinski, J. H., 442
Granrud, C. E., 194
Grantham-McGregor, S., 165
Graves, T., 166, 167
Gray, C., 401, 402, 414
Green, F. L., 304, 550
Green, J. A., 177, 178
Green, M., 5
Greenberg, M., 234
Greenberg, M. T., 149, 465
Greenberger, E., 453, 454
Greenfield, P. M., 14
Greenhalgh, J., 214
Greenough, W. T., 169, 170, 171
Greenstein, T. N., 453, 454
Griesler, P. C., 504
Griffin, S. A., 371, 372
Griggs, G. G., 130, 131
Gringlas, M., 459

Gross, R., 460
Grossman, J. H., III, 129, 131, 132
Grossman, K. E., 223, 227, 234
Grossmann, K., 229
Grossmann, K. E., 229
Grotevant, H. D., 444, 536, 591
Grotpeter, J. K., 640, 641
Gruen, G. E., 496
Gruen, R., 582
Gruen, S. G., 583
Gruendel, J., 346
Grueneich, R., 609
Grunwell, P., 249
Grusec, J. E., 24, 434, 435
Grych, J. H., 458
Guerra, N. G., 555, 556, 558, 559, 643
Gulko, J., 453, 568, 569, 581
Gullion, C. M., 90, 91
Gunnar, M., 226
Gunnar, M. R., 211
Guskin, K., 414
Gustafson, G. E., 177, 178
Guttentag, R. E., 368
Guttmacher, A. F., 85, 116, 118, 121, 123, 127, 130, 134, 136, 138, 139, 140, 144, 148, 149, 158

# H

Hack, M., 149
Hagan, R., 590, 597, 599
Hagen, E. P., 386
Hagen, H. W., 337
Hagtvet, K. A., 531
Haidt, J., 626
Hainline, L., 188
Hains, S. M., 206
Haith, M. M., 189
Hakuta, K., 247, 269, 282, 285
Hala, S., 550
Halberstadt, A. G., 576, 577, 598
Hale, C., 362
Hale, S., 354
Halford, G. S., 311
Hall, D. G., 255
Hall, J., 311
Hall, J. A., 337, 576, 577, 598
Hall, L. K., 354
Hall, N. W., 464, 465, 466, 467
Halley, D. J. J., 90, 91
Halliday-Scher, K., 476
Hallinan, M. T., 415
Halpern, D. F., 383, 389, 390, 394, 397, 408, 418, 566, 579
Halsey, S., 199
Halverson, C. F., 597
Halverson, C. F., Jr., 566, 596
Hamilton, C. E., 228, 236, 482
Hamilton, L. B., 368, 371
Hammond, M. A., 401, 402, 414
Hamond, N. R., 347
Hampson, J., 256
Hanis, C., 166
Hanish, L., 501
Hanlon, C., 271, 275
Hansen, D. J., 466
Hansen, W. B., 512
Hanson, D. R., 108
Hanson, S. L., 531
Hanzlick, R., 176
Harkness, A. R., 394

Harkness, S., 13, 14, 54, 599, 622
Harlow, H. F., 215, 218, 483, 484
Harman, C., 226
Harold, R. D., 529, 530
Harris, A., 88
Harris, K. L., 178
Harris, P. L., 290, 297, 298, 548
Harrison, A. O., 14
Hart, C. H., 488, 489
Hart, D., 523, 525, 541, 613, 623
Hart, S. S., 368, 371
Harter, S., 48, 49, 55, 57, 525, 526, 527, 528, 529,
    530, 531, 533, 560
Hartford, R. B., 176
Hartin, A., 134, 135, 139, 140, 147, 148, 149, 151
Hartmann, D. P., 638
Hartshorne, H., 635, 645
Hartup, W. W., 47, 48, 58, 71, 475, 478, 481, 482,
    483, 486, 491, 492, 493, 496, 500, 501, 504,
    506, 511, 516
Harvey, O. J., 515
Haskins, R., 486
Hastorf, A., 560
Hatano, G., 290, 299, 300
Hatcher, R., 147
Hauser, R. M., 396, 398, 400
Hauth, J. C., 131
Haviland, J. M., 209
Hawkins, J. A., 495, 496
Hawkins, J. D., 554
Hay, D. R., 637, 640
Hayes, D. P., 261
Haynes, K., 149
Haynes, V. F., 336
Hays, P. M., 121
Healy, E., 593
Heatherton, T. F., 631, 632
Hebb, D. O., 171
Hecox, K., 194
Hedges, L. V., 70
Heflin, A., 508
Hegley, D., 205, 206
Heibeck, T. H., 256
Heller, K. A., 552, 570, 572, 573, 597
Helmreich, R. L., 576
Hembree, E. A., 207
Henderson, V. K., 233
Henry, B., 212, 213
Henry, L. A., 358
Herrera, M. G., 165
Herrnstein, R. J., 10, 379, 384, 387, 389, 395,
    398, 400
Hess, R. D., 413, 414
Hesse, E., 228
Hesser, J., 451
Hestenes, S. L., 496
Heston, L. L., 108
Heth, C. D., 344, 345
Hetherington, E. M., 455, 456, 457, 461, 462, 468,
    469, 590
Heyman, G. D., 409
Hickling, A. K., 550
Hickmann, M., 321, 323
Hiester, M., 236
Higgins, A., 623
Higley, J. D., 484
Hiilsmaa, V. K., 99
Hildebrandt, C., 626
Hill, J. P., 444, 445, 576
Hill, S., 96
Himmelberg, P., 96
Hinde, R. A., 36, 475, 482
Hinde, R. W., 211

Hines, M., 582, 583, 584
Hirsch, B. J., 530
Hirsch, H. V. B., 170
Hirsch, R. M., 484
Hirsch-Pasek, K., 271
Hiscock, M., 173, 174
Hitchcock, J. T., 114, 115
Hoden, G. W., 432
Hodges, J., 215, 219
Hoefnagel-Hohle, M., 283
Hofer, S. M., 386, 406
Hoffer, T. B., 412
Hoff-Ginsberg, E., 271
Hoffman, H. J., 176
Hoffman, L. W., 433, 434, 435, 446, 453, 454,
    575, 585, 589, 621, 623, 629, 631, 632, 637
Hoffman, M. L., 429, 433
Hoffman, R. P., 90
Hofman, J. E., 494
Hogarty, P. S., 292
Hoge, D. D., 531
Hoge, D. R., 530
Hoge, R. D., 532
Hogrefe, G. J., 549
Hogrefe, J., 549
Holden, G. W., 591
Hollander, M., 265
Hollenbeck, B. E., 630
Holloway, S. D., 413, 414
Holmbeck, G. N., 444, 445
Holmes, I. W. M., 531
Holmes, L. B., 128
Holt, K., 410
Holt, L. H., 121, 123
Hood, K. E., 582, 583
Hood, W. R., 515
Hopkins, B., 184, 185
Hopkins, W. D., 484
Horgan, J., 10
Horn, J. L., 386, 406
Horn, J. M., 394, 395, 398
Horowitz, R., 510
Hossain, Z., 234, 235, 236
Howard, P., 164
Howe, M. L., 363
Howell, C. T., 151
Howes, C., 228, 236, 481, 482, 487, 490, 491, 502
Howlin, P., 91
Hoy, E. A., 151
Hoyle, R. H., 410
Hoyle, S. G., 495, 496
Hoyt, J. D., 360
Hoza, B., 501, 634
Hronsky, S. L., 136
Hryshko, A., 497
Hubbs-Tait, L., 232
Hudley, C., 556, 557
Hudson, J., 346
Hudson, L. M., 542
Huebner, A. M., 620
Huebner, R. R., 207
Huesmann, L. R., 642, 643
Hugdahl, K., 174
Hughes, L. A., 592
Humphries, T., 266, 267
Hunt, C. E., 176
Hunter, A. G., 460
Hunter, E. S., III, 124
Huntington, L., 177
Huntzinger, R. M., 96
Huston, A. C., 261, 565, 566, 567, 568, 569, 573,
    577, 578, 583, 588, 589, 592, 593, 594, 643
Hutchinson, S., 385

Hyde, J. S., 57, 573, 574, 575, 580, 621
Hymel, S., 501, 504

# I

Iacono, W. G., 104
Iannotti, R. J., 2, 209, 210, 429, 541, 640, 642
Ianotti, R. J., 630
Inagaki, K., 290, 299, 300, 320
Inhelder, B., 302, 313, 317, 318
Inoff-Germain, G., 584
Institute of Medicine, 136, 137, 138
Intons-Peterson, M. J., 568, 600, 601
Isabella, R. A., 213, 224, 225
Isada, N. B., 129, 131, 132
Ito, J., 90
Ivey, P. K., 232
Ivy, G., 170
Iyasu, S., 176
Izard, C. E., 205, 206, 207, 209

# J

Jacklin, C. N., 573, 574, 576, 578, 584, 585, 586,
    587, 588, 589, 590, 598
Jackson, D. W., 267
Jackson, J. R., 10, 103, 109, 446
Jacobs, J. E., 369, 370
Jacobson, A. M., 537
Jacobson, J. L., 136, 137
Jacobson, R. L., 132
Jacobson, S. W., 136, 137
Jacobvitz, D., 464, 465
Jacoby, R., 396
Jadack, R. A., 621
James, W., 527
Janssens, J. M. A. M., 508
Jaroff, L., 81
Jarvis, P. E., 537
Jaskir, J., 228
Jeffrey, W. E., 339
Jenkins, E., 371
Jenks, B. H., 166, 167
Jennings, K. D., 417
Jensen, A. R., 403, 405
Jensen, L. A., 649
Ji, G., 451
Jiao, S., 451
Jimenez, E., 132
Jing, Q., 451
Johnson, B. M., 533
Johnson, C. N., 302
Johnson, D. L., 401, 402, 414
Johnson, J. E., 516
Johnson, M. O., 212
Johnson, T., 368, 371
Johnsson, U., 166
Johnston, F. E., 161
Johnston, J. R., 458
Johnston, M. K., 47, 48, 58, 71, 496
Jones, L. E., 177
Jones, L. V., 398
Jones, R. S., 362, 367
Jones, S. S., 342
Joos, S. K., 138
Jordan, B., 114, 151
Joseph, L. L., 320
Juffer, F., 225, 228
Jusczyk, A. M., 247
Jusczyk, P. W., 245, 246, 247, 271
Justice, E. M., 361

# K

Kaczala, C. M., 413, 593
Kaegi, D., 176
Kagan, J., 8, 78, 107, 156, 163, 206, 211, 212, 219, 226, 237, 338, 339, 565, 606, 607, 638
Kagan, S., 638
Kahn, P. H., 621
Kail, R., 28, 52, 353, 354, 360, 361, 368
Kaiser, I. H., 85, 116, 118, 121, 123, 130, 134, 136, 138, 139, 140, 144, 148, 149, 158
Kaler, S. R., 139
Kaleva, M., 109
Kalverboer, A. F., 185
Kamii, C., 320
Kamin, L., 396
Kamm, K., 182
Kamphaus, R., 385
Kandel, D. B., 511
Kane, M. J., 367
Kantor, G. K., 465
Kaplan, H., 40, 41, 42, 54, 56, 61, 62, 182, 185
Kaplan, N., 223, 225
Kaplan, R. M., 389, 390
Karbon, M., 501, 632
Karniol, R., 609, 610
Karoly, P., 458
Karraker, K. H., 586, 587
Kattwinkel, J., 176
Katz, K. S., 95
Katz, P. A., 543, 570, 592, 593, 594
Katz, S. H., 397
Katzman, M. A., 458
Kaufman, A. S., 386
Kaufman, F. R., 583
Kaufman, J., 463, 464, 465
Kaufman, N. L., 386
Kavlock, R. J., 125
Kay, T., 90
Kazak, A. K., 95
Kazdin, A. E., 559
Keane, S. P., 556
Kearins, J. M., 357
Kearsley, R. B., 206, 219
Keasey, C. B., 610, 622
Keating, D., 314
Keating, D. P., 309
Keefe, K., 62, 497, 498, 509, 510
Keefe, L., 511
Keenan, M. E., 176
Keenan, T., 549
Keeney, T. J., 355, 367
Keil, F. C., 342
Kellam, S. G., 460
Keller, A., 526
Keller, H., 252, 272
Keller, M. L., 621
Kellman, P. J., 194
Kelly, J. B., 457
Kelly, T., 486
Kelso, J. A. S., 183
Kemler-Nelson, D. G., 247, 271
Kemper, T., 138
Kennell, J. H., 145
Kenrick, D. T., 632
Kerlinger, F. N., 58
Kerr, M., 212
Kessler, J. W., 86, 88
Kestenbaum, R., 226
Ketron, J. L., 379, 380, 383, 421
Kidd, K. K., 81, 92, 97
Kiely, J. L., 84
Kiely, M., 84

Kiernan, K. E., 457
Killen, M., 646
Kim, S., 625
Kimmel, D. C., 161
Kimmerly, N. L., 233
King, B., 212
King, R. A., 429, 644
Kingsbury, G. G., 531
Kinsbourne, M., 173, 174
Kirke, P. N., 125
Kirklan, R. T., 198
Kiselev, P., 132
Kitayama, S., 646, 648
Klackenbert-Larrson, I., 212, 389
Klahr, D., 28, 29, 317, 319, 332
Klaus, M. H., 145, 175
Klaus, P. H., 145, 175
Klebanoff, M., 131
Klein, R. E., 136, 156, 163, 183, 185
Klein, R. P., 417
Kleinman, J. C., 84
Klerman, L. V., 139
Kline, M., 458
Klinnert, M. D., 210
Klonoff-Cohen, H. S., 176
Knight, G. P., 54, 55, 72, 638
Kochanska, G., 443, 629, 630, 633
Koehler, C., 143, 144
Koeppl, G. K., 507
Kohlberg, L., 298, 566, 594, 597, 599, 606, 607, 614, 615, 616, 617, 618, 619, 620, 621, 622, 623, 624, 636, 640, 645, 647
Kolata, G., 125, 130
Koller, S. H., 626
Kondo-Ikemura, K., 219
Konner, M., 184, 516
Kopp, C. B., 88, 124, 127, 151, 442, 633, 634
Koren, G., 134
Koren-Karie, N., 229
Korkel, J., 342, 343, 357
Korner, A. F., 151, 177
Kotsaftis, A., 224, 226
Kowalski, P. S., 530
Kozberg, S. F., 621
Krakow, J. B., 634
Kramer, L. R., 56
Kramer, S. J., 191
Krantz, D. H., 613
Krasnor, L. R., 502, 554
Kravath, R. E., 176
Krebs, D. L., 640
Kreutzer, M. A., 359, 360, 361
Kreye, M., 237
Kroonenberg, P. M., 227, 229
Krowitz, A., 192
Kruger, A. C., 258, 622
Krupnick, J., 629, 630
Ksansnak, K. R., 570
Kuczaj, S. A., 254, 265
Kuczynski, L., 443
Kuhl, P. K., 246
Kuhn, D., 316, 415, 569
Kulig, J. W., 194, 195
Kulik, C., 415
Kulik, J., 415
Kupersmidt, G. K., 503
Kupersmidt, J. B., 504, 506, 507
Kurland, D. M., 353
Kurtines, W. M., 621, 645
Kurtz, B. E., 356, 368, 369
Kuschner, D. S., 320
Kyratzis, A., 347

# L

La Follette, H., 648
La Greca, A. M., 507
Laboratory of Comparative Human Cognition, 322, 323
Lacerda, F., 247
Lachiewicz, A. M., 90, 91
Ladd, G. W., 50, 488, 489, 490, 507, 508
Ladewski, B., 458
Lafreniere, P., 581
Lafreniere, P. J., 227, 441, 446, 490
Lahti, I., 109
Lake, M. A., 586
Laksy, K., 109
Lalonde, C. E., 243
Lamaze, F., 143
Lamb, M. E., 145, 178, 208, 211, 226, 227, 228, 229, 232, 233, 235, 236, 237, 490, 591
Lambert, W. W., 212
Lamborn, S. D., 436, 437, 514
Lamon, S. J., 574, 575
Lamour, M., 259
Landau, S., 325
Landberg, I., 248
Landerl, K., 250
Lane, D. M., 337
Lang, S., 226
Lange, G., 368
Langer, A., 192
Langlois, J. H., 232, 342, 500
Laros, R. K., Jr., 140
Lau, C. S., 125
Lau, S., 598
Laursen, B., 47, 48, 58, 71, 459, 491, 496, 594
Lauterbach, M. D., 174
Lavatelli, C. S., 320
Lawson, A., 140
Lawton, S. C., 359
Lay, K-L., 491
Lazar, I., 403, 415
Le Crouteur, A., 108
Le Sieur, K. D., 488, 498, 508
Le Vine, B. B., 426
Le Vine, R. A., 54, 426
Leal, L., 368, 371
Lears, M., 593
Leavitt, L. A., 178
Lederberg, A. R., 516
Lee, K., 139
Lee, S., 418
Lee, S. Y., 378, 416, 418
Lee, T. F., 81, 96
Lee, V. E., 403, 405, 458
Lee, Y. J., 125
Leekam, S. R., 549
Lefever, G. B., 226
Lefkowitz, E. S., 176
Lefkowitz, M. M., 135, 642
Leggett, E. L., 410
Leichtman, M. D., 363
Leiderman, H., 460
Leiderman, P. H., 460
Leinbach, M. D., 587, 590, 597, 599
Lelwica, M., 209
LeMare, L. J., 506, 541
Lempers, J. D., 304
Lenneberg, E. H., 173, 174, 282
Lennon, R., 575, 632, 638
Leon, M., 611
Leonard, C., 359, 360, 361
Lepper, M. R., 433
Lerner, R., 56

Meacham, J. A., 526
Mead, G. H., 531
Mead, M., 114, 115, 151
Meara, N. M., 421
Mears, C., 215
Meck, E., 309
Medrich, E. A., 488
Meece, J. L., 410, 412, 413, 593
Meister, C., 326
Melby, J. N., 511
Melton, G. B., 468
Meltzoff, A., 252
Meltzoff, A. N., 365, 366
Mendoza, F., 164, 166, 168
Menn, L., 248, 249
Mercuri, A., 269
Mermelstein, R., 643
Merriman, W. E., 255
Merz, B., 98
Mettetal, G., 379, 420, 494
Meyer-Bahlburg, H. F. L., 583
Meyers, A. W., 166, 167
Michel, G., 205
Midgley, C., 529, 530
Miele, F., 407
Millar, S., 358
Miller, A., 420
Miller, C. L., 507
Miller, J. D., 246
Miller, J. G., 612, 620, 625, 648
Miller, J. L., 247
Miller, K. E., 411, 412
Miller, P. H., 5, 19, 29, 31, 33, 298, 308, 312, 314,
    317, 334, 336, 337, 339, 343, 352, 353, 356,
    358, 368, 522, 547
Miller, P. M., 54
Miller, R., 248
Miller, S. A., 29, 45, 48, 298, 308, 312, 314, 317,
    339, 343, 352, 353, 356, 358, 522
Miller, P. A., 631, 632, 638, 639, 640
Mills, J. L., 125
Millstein, S. G., 511
Milstead, M., 362
Minick, N., 326
Minkoff, H. L., 132
Minturn, L., 114, 115
Minuchin, P., 469
Mischel, W., 24, 607, 635
Mistry, J., 326, 327
Mitchell, C., 529, 530
Mitchell, J. E., 576, 585, 586
Mitchell, S., 401, 402, 414
Miyake, K., 229
Mize, J., 489, 507
Mladinic, A., 568
Mobley, L. A., 447, 448
Moely, B. E., 368, 371
Moffitt, T. E., 161, 212, 213, 394
Molitor, N., 232
Moller, L., 581
Mollnow, E., 124, 130, 133, 134, 135
Money, J., 90, 566, 583
Monker, J., 260
Monsour, A., 560
Montemayor, R., 525, 526, 598
Moore, C. F., 621
Moore, K. L., 86, 116, 117, 118, 121, 126, 129,
    130, 133, 134, 136, 144, 152
Moore, M. K., 365, 366
Moore, W., 412
Mora, J. O., 165
Morelli, G. A., 4, 15, 54, 232, 648
Morford, M., 273

Morgan, G. A., 417
Morgan, M., 593, 594
Morgane, P. J., 138
Morikawa, H., 259
Moring, J., 109
Morishima, A., 582
Morison, P., 50
Morris, N., 234
Morris, W., 16
Morrison, D. M., 554
Morrongiello, B. A., 190, 194, 195
Mortensen, M. L., 125, 128, 130, 136
Moses, L. J., 547, 550
Mosier, C., 326, 327
Moss, H. A., 8
Mounts, N., 514
Mounts, N. S., 436, 437
Moye, J., 132
Moylan, P., 96
Much, N. C., 620
Mueller, W. H., 138
Muenchow, S., 405
Muir, D., 194
Muir, D. W., 182, 206
Muller, C., 454
Mumme, D., 414
Mundfrom, D. J., 149, 151
Munn, P., 544
Munroe, R. H., 14
Munroe, R. L., 14
Murphy, J., 280, 281
Murphy, R. R., 556
Murray, B. A., 250
Murray, C. A., 10, 379, 384, 387, 389, 395, 398,
    400
Murray, F. B., 318, 319
Murray, J. P., 543, 593, 594
Murray, K., 629, 633
Mussen, P. H., 565
Myers, B., 569, 597
Myers, N. A., 363

# N

Naarala, M., 109
Nabarro, D., 164
Nagel, L., 205, 206
Nakagawa, M., 229
Naqvi, M., 149
Nash, A., 228, 490
Nash, S. C., 569
National Commission on America's Urban
    Families, 459, 460
National Research Council, 462, 464, 465, 466,
    467, 468
Naus, M. J., 356
Neckerman, H. J., 641
Needleman, H. L., 129
Neff, C., 178
Neiderman, D., 298
Neisser, U., 363, 383, 389, 390, 394, 397, 408, 418
Nelson, C. A., 208, 209, 210, 211
Nelson, K., 251, 256, 283, 346, 347, 363
Nelson, K. E., 271
Nelson-Le Gall, S. A., 609
Nesselroade, J. R., 67
Neuman, C. G., 166, 167
Neumann, C. G., 165
Neuwalder, H. F., 583
Newberger, A. H., 199
Newcomb, A. F., 64, 496, 497, 498, 499, 500, 501,
    502, 506

Newton, N., 114, 115, 151
Nicholl, J., 311
Nicholls, J. G., 379, 415, 419, 420, 421
Nicol, R., 467
Nicolaides, K., 99
Niebyl, J. R., 125, 132, 134, 136, 152
Niermeijer, M. F., 90, 91
Nightingale, E. O., 511
Ninio, A., 625
Nisan, M., 625
Nisbett, R., 397, 400
Noam, G. G., 537
Nolan, E., 156, 163
Nolen-Hoeksema, S., 414
Norbeck, J. S., 140
Notarius, C. I., 429
Nottelmann, E. D., 530, 584
Novak, M. A., 484
Noveck, I. A., 315, 316
Nowakowski, R. S., 169
Nucci, L., 625, 627
Nucci, L. P., 625, 626
Nucombe, B., 151
Nugent, J. K., 146, 149
Nunnally, J. C., 41, 42
Nunner-Winkler, G., 636
Nyiti, R. M., 309

# O

Oakes, J., 415
Oakley, G. P., Jr., 125, 128, 130, 136
Oberklaid, F., 212, 214
O'Boyle, C., 590
O'Brien, D. P., 315, 316
O'Brien, M., 577, 578
O'Brien, S. F., 513
O'Brien, W. F., 144
O'Connell, B., 272, 273
Oden, M. H., 421
Oden, S., 507
O'Donnell, J., 554
Oetting, E. R., 509
Offer, D., 520
Offer, J. B., 530
Ogawa, J. R., 47, 48, 58, 71, 496
Ogino, M., 259
Okagaki, L., 380, 421
Olds, D. L., 467, 468
O'Leary, K. D., 437
Olenick, M., 490
Olguin, R., 255
Oller, D. K., 248
O'Loughlin, M., 320
Olson, D. R., 548, 549
Olson, G. M., 189
Olson, H. C., 134, 135
Olson, R., 96
Olson, S. L., 634
Olweus, D., 530, 531, 584
O'Malley, P. M., 530, 531
Omelich, C. L., 420
O'Neil, R., 453, 454
O'Neill, E., 132
Oostra, B. A., 90, 91
Opie, I., 278
Opie, P., 278
Opland, E. A., 194
Oppenheim, D., 4, 15, 54, 236, 648
Opper, S., 308, 311, 320
Orlofsky, J. L., 534, 535
Ornstein, P. A., 356

# U

Udry, J. R., 584
Ullman, M., 265
Ulrich, B. D., 183, 185
Unger, O., 482
UNICEF, 164, 166
Updegraff, K. A., 450
Urbain, E. S., 291, 293, 392, 554
Urban, J., 599
Urberg, K. A., 476
Urbina, S., 383, 389, 390, 394, 397, 408, 418
U.S. Bureau of the Census, 16, 452, 455, 459, 460,
    461, 462, 463, 486, 487, 574
U.S. Department of Education, 398, 418
Usher, J. A., 363
Uvebrant, P., 174

# V

Valdez-Menchaca, M. C., 260
Valian, V., 263
Van, F. H., 583
van den Boom, D. C., 225
Van Hesteren, F., 640
van IJzendoorn, M. H., 225, 227, 228, 229, 230,
    231, 232, 236, 238
van IJzendoorn, M. J., 230, 231, 506
van Lieshout, C. F. M., 506
Van Meter, P., 355, 356, 359, 367, 368, 374
Van Tuyl, S. S., 447, 448
Vande-Berg, L. R., 485
Vandell, D. L., 453, 478, 485, 516
Vandenberg, B., 481, 485
Vandenberg, S. G., 391
VanDyke, R., 132
Vaughn, B. E., 224, 226, 230, 232, 500, 634
Vazsonyi, A. T., 437
Ventura, S. J., 134, 135, 139, 140, 147, 148, 149,
    151
Verhulst, F. C., 67
Veridiano, N. P., 583
Vietze, P. M., 417
Vigorito, J., 245
Vihman, M. M., 248
Vincent, K. R., 398
Virdin, L. M., 55, 72
Vitaro, F., 529
Vliestra, A. G., 335, 338
Vogel, D. A., 586
Vogler, G. P., 391
Volling, B. L., 448, 450
von Almen, T. K., 166
Von Hofsten, C., 182
von Koskull, H., 99
von Wendt, L., 174
Voran, M., 487
Vorhees, C. V., 124, 130, 133, 134, 135
Voyer, D., 70, 579
Voyer, S., 70, 579
Vurpillot, E., 334, 335, 336
Vygotsky, L. S., 31, 32, 42, 284, 320, 321, 322,
    323, 324, 332, 373

# W

Waas, G. A., 516
Wachs, T. D., 43, 44, 45, 54, 72, 103, 212, 213,
    399
Waddell, J. J., 357
Waddington, C. H., 163

Wagner, E., 504, 524
Wagner, M. E., 451
Wagner, R. K., 379
Wahlberg, K. E., 109
Wahler, R. G., 446
Wainryb, C., 625, 626
Walchli, S. B., 512
Walder, L. O., 642
Waldman, I. D., 105, 394, 395, 397
Walk, R. D., 192
Walker, A. S., 197
Walker, E., 109
Walker, L. J., 620, 621, 622
Walker, S., 165
Walker-Andrews, A., 198
Wall, S., 217, 221, 222, 224, 225, 229
Wallace, C. S., 169, 170, 171
Wallace, I. F., 392
Wallerstein, J. S., 457, 458
*Wall Street Journal, The,* 384, 396
Walsh, P., 458
Walsh, P. V., 592
Walters, R. H., 437
Walton, O., 95
Ward, R. H., 139
Ward, S. L., 315, 316
Warren, A. R., 274, 275, 276, 277
Warren, S. T., 91
Warren, W. P., 161
Warren-Leubecker, A., 274
Washington, M. L., 459
Wasserman, A., 482, 502
Waterlow, J. C., 164, 168
Waterman, A. S., 534, 535, 536
Waters, E., 4, 98, 207, 217, 219, 221, 222, 223,
    224, 225, 226, 227, 229
Waters, H. S., 539
Watkins, J., 96
Watkinson, B., 134
Watson, J. B., 11, 12
Watson, J. D., 79
Watson-Grego, K. A., 451
Wax, N., 290, 299
Waxman, S. R., 255
Webber, P. L., 105, 106
Wechsler, D., 51, 384
Wehren, A., 594
Wei, L. S., 132
Weinberg, C. R., 117
Weinberg, R. A., 105, 106, 394, 395, 396, 397, 405
Weinberger, J., 429, 435
Weiner, B., 409, 418
Weiner, I. B., 161
Weinert, F. E., 342, 343, 357
Weinraub, M., 459, 569, 597
Weir, D. G., 125
Weiseman, J. R., 177
Weisner, T. S., 591
Weiss, B., 136, 433, 537
Weiss, M., 524
Weiss, M. G., 337
Weissberg, R. P., 554
Weisz, J. R., 292, 446, 497
Wellman, H., 548, 549
Wellman, H. M., 297, 301, 302, 361, 548, 550
Wells, D., 547
Wendel, G. D., 129, 131
Wentzel, K. R., 502, 503
Werker, J. R., 243, 246, 247, 270
Werner, E. E., 150
Werner, H., 5, 6
Wertsch, J., 321, 324

Wertsch, J. V., 31, 33, 320, 321, 323, 327
Wessels, J. M., 247
Weston, D. R., 233, 234
Weston, J. A., 199
Westra, T., 184
Whitbeck, L. B., 429, 435
White, B. J., 515
White, D., 582
White, L., 389, 457
White, R. W., 417
Whitebrook, M., 236
Whitehurst, G. J., 260, 277, 278
Whitesell, N. R., 530
Whiteside, L., 149, 151
Whiting, B. B., 14, 426, 427, 430, 433, 564, 584
Whiting, J. W. M., 426, 427, 430, 433
Whitley, B. E., Jr., 598
Wideman, M. V., 144
Widfield, A., 412, 529, 530
Widom, C. S., 466
Wigfield, A., 411, 529, 530
Wijga, A., 164
Wiklund, L. M., 174
Wilcox, A. J., 117
Wilcox, B. L., 543, 593, 594
Wiley, K. J., 176
Wilfson, A., 414
Wilkinson, A. C., 275
Wilkinson, K. D., 91
Wilkinson, L. C., 275
Wilkner, K., 196
Willerman, L., 394, 395, 398
Williams, C., 631
Williams, J. E., 567, 568
Williams, K. A., 247
Willinger, M., 176
Wilson, G. T., 437
Wilson, K. S., 478, 485
Wilson, M., 460
Wilson, M. N., 14, 460
Wilson, M. S., 547
Wilson, R. S., 162, 393, 398, 399
Wilson-Mitchell, J. E., 591
Wimmer, H., 250, 549
Winer, G. A., 312
Wing, R. R., 166, 167
Winick, M., 138, 139, 165
Winner, E., 548, 550
Winterhoff, P. A., 327
Wippman, J., 227
Witt, A. C., 391
Witter, R., 131
Wittrock, M. C., 416
Wodlinger-Cohen, R., 266
Wolchik, S. A., 587
Wolf, A., 4
Wolff, P. H., 175, 177, 178
Wong, C-M. T., 421
Wong, Y. I., 459
Wood, D., 322, 325
Wood, D. N., 445
Woodsmall, L., 260
Woody, E., 501
Woody-Ramsey, J., 336, 368
Woolston, J. L., 167
Wortham, B., 199
Wright, J., 261
Wright, J. W., 537
Wright, K., 609, 610
Wunsch, J. P., 207
Wynne, L., 109

# X

Xu, F., 265

# Y

Yaffe, S. J., 130, 131
Yanof, D. S., 498
Yarrow, L. J., 417
Yelland, G. W., 269
Yonas, A., 193, 194, 196
Younger, B., 348

Youniss, J., 444, 445, 475, 494, 613, 648
Yu, A. P., 573
Yule, W., 91
Yussen, S. R., 360

# Z

Zahn-Waxler, C., 2, 209, 210, 211, 212, 429, 524, 541, 546, 575, 629, 630, 631, 637, 640, 642, 644, 645
Zajonc, R. B., 400
Zarbatany, L., 638

Zeichner, S. L., 132
Zelazo, P. R., 206, 219, 348
Zelniker, T., 339
Zeskind, P. S., 177, 178
Zigler, E., 232, 292, 390, 405, 463, 464, 465, 466, 467
Zill, N., 461, 577
Zimiles, H., 458
Zimmerman, R., 218
Zuckerman, B. S., 175
Zuckerman, D., 543, 593, 594
Zwirner, W., 433

# SUBJECT INDEX

gene dominance, 92–93
gene-environment interaction, 101–109
genes, **81**
genetic disorders, 93–100
genetic inheritance, process of, 81–85
genotype and phenotype, **85**
Heritability, **104**
Heroin, use in pregnancy, 133
Herpes simplex, effects on fetus, 131–132
Heteronomy, **612**, 615
Heterozygous, **92**
Heuristic value, of theory, **18**
High-amplitude sucking, **245**
HOME (Home Observation for Measurement of the Environment), 401–402
subscales, 401
Homeostasis, in family system, **469**
Homologous, **81**, 83
Homosexuals
childhood activities, 581
and prenatal androgens, 583
Homozygous, **92**
Honesty
development of, 633–635
and moral judgments, 636–637
Hormones
in puberty, 584
and sex differentiation, 582
and sex typing, 583–584
Hostile aggression, **640**
Howes Peer Play Scale, 482
Human Genome Project, 81, 85
Huntington's disease, 94, **95**–96
progression of, 95
Hypotheses, **6**
Hypothetico-deductive reasoning, **314**

# I

Id, **21**
Identification, Freud's theory, **20**
Identity, **534**
Identity achievement, **534**–535
Identity development
Erikson's theory, 534
family influences, 536
stages of, 534–536
Identity diffusion, **534**
Idioms, understanding of, 257–258
Imitation. *See* Observational learning
Implantation, of ovum, **117**–118
Imprinting, **216**–217, 219
Incremental theory of intelligence, **411**
Independent variable, **65**
Inductive discipline, **434**
Infancy
attachment, 214–237
behavioral states, 175–178
cultural factors, 156
emotional development, 205–211
learning in, 365–366
memory, 347–351
motor development, 180–185
parent/child interaction, 442
peer interactions, 478–480
perceptual development, 186–198
reflexes, **178**–180
self-recognition in, 523–524
sensorimotor intelligence, **291**–298
sex differences and behavior, 585
speech perception, 245–247
speech production, 248–250

temperament, 211–214
time span of, 7
Infantile amnesia, **363**
Infant intelligence tests
Bayley Scales of Infant Development, 386–387
and later IQ scores, 391–393
Infant mortality, in India, 142
Information-processing theory, 28–29
approaches in, 28–29
attention, **333**
and developmental issues, 29
human/computer analogy in, 28
learning, 365–374
memory, **347**–364
mental representations, 339–347
perceptual learning, **333**–339
social interaction and learning, 372–374
task performance assessments, 52–53
Informed consent, **70**–71
in developmental research, 70–71
Insecure attachment, 223, 224, 227
Instrumental aggression, **640**
Instrumental traits, **576**
Intelligence
child's theories of, 411
crystallized intelligence, **386**
definitions of, **379**–380
entity theory, **411**
fluid intelligence, 386, **387**
gene-environment interaction, 104–105
incremental theory, **411**
and language development, 281–282
seven intelligences theory, 407–408
social intelligence, **421**
Terman longitudinal study, 421
triarchic theory, 406–407
Intelligence measures
Bayley Scales of Infant Development, 386–387
Binet and Simon scale, 381–382
cultural bias of, 389–390
intelligence quotient (IQ), 382–384
mental age, **382**
Peabody Picture Vocabulary Test-Revised, 387
psychometric approach, **378**
Raven's Progressive Matrices, 387
reliability of, 388–389
Stanford-Binet Intelligence Scale: Fourth Edition, 386
task performance assessments, 51–52
validity of, 389–390
Wechsler Intelligence Scale for Children-III (WISC-III), 384–386
Intelligence quotient (IQ), 382–384
changes in childhood, 393–394
confluence model, **400**
elements of concept, 382–383
environmental influences, 398–405
family influences, 400–402
general intelligence (g), **383**, 384
genetic influences, 394–395, 398–399
program for improvement of, 69
and race, 395–398
raising scores, 405
ratio in, 382
relationship to intelligence, 406
and schooling, 403–405
stability of scores, 390–393
Intentions, inferring in others, 547–548
Intermodal perception, **197**–198
Internal consistency, **57**, 389

Interobserver agreement, **56**
Intervention
example of, 69
research design, **68**
Involvement, parental, **435**
IQ, and maternal cigarette smoking, 135

# J

Jensen, Arthur, 400
Just Communities, 624–625

# K

Kagan, Jerome, 156
Karotypes, **81**, 82
Keller, Helen, 152, 252
Kibbutz, and attachment, 231
Klein, Robert, 156
Klinefelter syndrome, **90**–91
developmental factors, 90
physical characteristics, 90
Knowledge base, and memory, **357**–359
Kohlberg's gender constancy theory, 594–595
Kohlberg's moral development theory, 614–623
assumptions in, 618–619
conventional level, 616
Just Communities, 624–625
moral-judgment interview, 614
postconventional level, 616–617
preconventional level, 615–616
Kwashiorkor, **163**–164

# L

Labor, 144–145
afterbirth, 144
stages of, 144
Laboratory observation
correspondence to real time behavior, 47–48
evaluation of measures, 47–48
and reactivity, 47–48
steps in, 46–47
Lamaze, Ferdinand, 143
Lamaze program, prepared childbirth, 143
Language
grammar, 242
morpheme, **251**
phonemes, **244**
phonology, 242
pragmatics, 242
semantics, 242
Vygotsky's view, 32
Language Acquisition Device (LAD), 279, 282–283
Language Acquisition Support System (LASS), 284
Language development
and bilingualism, 269
and child-directed speech, 468, 470–471
deaf children, 265–267
expressive children, **256**
grammar, **262**–271
idioms, understanding of, 257–258
influencing factors, 258–261, 268, 270–271
and intelligence, 281–282
phonology, 249–250
pragmatics, **271**–278
preschool grammar, 262–265, 268
referential children, **256**
school age children, 256–258, 268

Piaget's theory (continued)
  animism, **299**–300
  assimilation in, **26**
  cognitive organization in, 26
  concrete-operational thought, **307**–309
  conservation, **52,** 305–306
  as constructivist theory, 27, 290
  and developmental issues, 27
  educational implications, 318–320
  egocentrism, 302–303, 539–540
  equilibration in, **27**
  evaluation of, 312
  formal-operational thought, **313**–320
  genetic epistemology, **25**–26
  imitation in, 365
  language development, 279, 280
  logical operations, **306**–308
  moral development, 608–614
  preoperational thought, 299–**307**
  realism, **301**–302
  schemes in, **92**
  sensorimotor intelligence, **291**–298
  task performance assessment methods, 52
Pictorial cues, **193**–194
Placenta, **118,** 121
  afterbirth, 144
  transfer of teratogens, 124
Plasticity, of brain, **174**
Plato, 23, 214
  on nature/nurture issue, 9–10
Play, 480–483
  assessment of, 482
  associative play, **480**
  constructive play, **481**
  cooperative play, **480**
  dramatic play, **481**
  effects of, 485–487
  functional play, **481**
  games with rules, **481**
  onlooker play, **481**
  parallel play, **480,** 482
  rough-and-tumble play, **581**
  same-sex play, 599
  social pretend play, 485–486
  solitary play, **481**
  unoccupied play, **481**
Politeness, in conversations, 274–275
Polychlorinated biphenyls (PCBs), prenatal
  exposure, 136–137
Polygenic inheritance, **97**
Popular children, **499,** 500–504
  and fit with group, 504
  and physical attractiveness, 500–501
  and social behavior, 501–504
Popularity
  cross-cultural view, 505
  parental influences, 508
Positive reinforcement, by parents, 437
Postconventional level, moral development,
  616–617
Power assertion
  negative effects, 433–434
  parental, **433**–434
Pragmatics, meaning of, 242, **271**
Pragmatics development, **271**–278
  age changes, 278
  code switching, **276**
  comprehension monitoring, 277–278
  contingent response, 273–274
  difference rule, **277**
  and egocentrism, **274**
  gestures, use of, 275
  noncontingent response, **273**–274

politeness, 274–275
preverbal communication, 272–273
procedural rules, 277–278
referential communication, **277**
Praise, parental, 428
Precedence effect, **194**–195
Preconventional level, moral development,
  615–616
Preeclampsia, **130**–131
  and aspirin, 130–131
Preferential looking technique, **188**
Prenatal diagnosis, 98–99
  amniocentesis, 98–**99**
  chorionic villus sampling (CVS), **99**
  fetoscopy, **99**
Prenatal period
  adolescent pregnancy, risks in, 139–140
  embryo, **119**–121
  and emotions of mother, 140–141
  fertilization/implantation process,
    117–118
  fetus, **121**–124
  germinal period, **116**–118
  and maternal age, 140
  and maternal nutrition, 137–138
  maternal weight gain, 138
  miscarriage, 118, 121, 122
  placenta, **118,** 121
  teratogens, **124**–137
Preoperational thought, 299–**307**
  animism, **299**–300
  conservation, 305–306
  egocentrism, 302–304
  realism, **301**–302
Prepared childbirth, childbirth education,
  141–144
Preterm birth, **149**–151
  birth weight categories, 149
  intervention programs, 151
  prematurity and child abuse, 464
  special care of, 150–151
  survival outcome, 149
Primary circular reactions, **293**
Primates
  language learning, 280–281
  maternal deprivation, 215, 218–219
  peer deprivation, 483–485
  sex differences, 584
Private speech, 324–325
Problem solving
  and domain-specific knowledge, 343
  interpersonal problem solving, 553–554
Production deficiency, and memory strategies,
  **355**
Prosocial behavior, **426,** 637–640
  and age changes, 637–638
  cross-cultural view, 430–431
  and empathy, 631, 632
  levels of prosocial reasoning, 639
  and moral reasoning, 638–640
Protein-energy malnutrition (PEM), 164
Protein synthesis, and DNA, 81
Protowords, 248
Proximodistal principle, **120,** 160
PSAT (Preliminary Scholastic Aptitude Test),
  578, 579
Psychoanalysis, 19
Psychoanalytic theory
  and developmental issues, 23
  Erikson's theory, 21–23
  Freud's theory, 19–21
Psychometric approach, **378**
Psychosexual stages, Freud's theory, 20–21

Psychosocial stages
  Erikson's theory, **21**–23
  and parent/child relationship, 442–445
Puberty, **159**
  early/late maturation, 160–161
  hormones in, 584
  physical growth, 159, 160
  psychological correlates of, 161
Punishment, effects of, 437–438

# Q

Q-sort, Attachment Q-sort, 224
Qualitative versus quantitative change
  and development, 6–7
  Vygotsky on, 33

# R

Race, and intelligence quotient (IQ), 395–398
Radiation, prenatal exposure, 136
Random assignment, **66**
Random error, **56**
Raven's Progressive Matrices, 387
  example item, 388
Reaction range, **101**–102
Reactivity
  and laboratory observation, 47–48
  and naturalistic observation, 45
Reading
  learning to read, 369–371
  and phonological awareness, 250
  reading strategies instruction, 370–371
  reading to children, positive effects, 260
  and vocabulary development, 261
Realism, **301**–302
  perspective-taking, 302–304
  and theory of mind, **304**
Reasoning, parental control through, 434–435
Recessive gene, **92**
Reciprocal determinism, **25**
Reciprocal teaching, and Vygotsky's theory,
  **32**–33, 325–326
Referential children, language development, **256**
Referential communication, **277**
Reflexes, **178**–180
  Babinski reflex, **179**
  disappearance of, 179–180
  eyeblink reflex, **179**
  Moro reflex, **179**
  palmar grasp reflex, **179**
  rooting reflex, **179**
  sensorimotor intelligence, 292–293
  stepping reflex, **179**
  sucking reflex, 292–293
  withdrawal reflex, **179**
Rehearsal, **354**–355
Reinforcement, and language development, 260
Rejected children, **499,** 500, 502, 503
Rejecting-neglecting parents, **436**
Relational aggression, **641**
Relationships, **36,** 475
  multiple-selves and others, 560
Reliability, **56**–57
  intelligence measures, 388–389
  and internal consistency, **57,** 389
  and interobserver agreement, 56
  and random error, 56
  test-retest reliability, 56
Religious beliefs, and moral development,
  627–628
Replication, in research, **41**

Representational insight, 345–346
Representative samples
    and naturalistic observation, 45
    and research design, 59
*Republic* (Plato), 9–10
Research
    participant/researcher relationship, 72–73
    replication in, 41
Research design, **58**
    cohort-sequential design, **67**–68
    components of, 59
    correlational design, **63**–65
    cross-sectional design, **59**–61
    experimental design, **65**–67
    intervention, **68**
    longitudinal design, **61**–63
    meta-analysis, **68**, 70
    and representative samples, **59**
Research ethics
    guidelines for, 71–72
    informed consent, **70**–71
Research measures
    and cross-cultural research, 54, 56
    laboratory observation, 46–48
    measurement, meaning of, **41**
    naturalistic observation, **42**–45
    reliability of, **56**–57
    steps in use of, **41**–42
    task performance assessments, 51–53
    validity of, **57**–58
    verbal reports, 48–51
Retinal disparity, **193**
Reversal, in experimental design, **66**
Reverse causation, **65**
Robbers Cave experiment, 515–516
Role taking, **537**–543
    and age changes, 540–541
    versus egocentrism, 539–541
    and social behavior, 541–543
    training in, 542–543
    *See also* Perspective taking
Rooting reflex, **179**
Rough-and-tumble play, **581**
Rousseau, Jean Jacques, 7
Rubella, effects on fetus, 132

# S

SAT (Scholastic Aptitude Test)
    math scores, gender differences, 580, 586
    scores and self-control, 635
Scaffolding, **322**
Schemas
    gender schemas, 596–597
    in Piaget's theory, **92**
    social schemas, **555**
Schizophrenia, **108**
    heritability of, **108**–109
Schooling
    and achievement, 415–420
    cooperative learning, 416
    and intelligence quotient (IQ), 403–405
    school climate, influences of, 415–416
    social interaction and learning, 372–374
Scripts, 346–347
    as mental representations, 346
Secondary circular reactions, **293**
Secular trends, and human growth, **167**–168
Secure attachment, 221, 222–223, 224, 227–229
Self-control
    delay of gratification, **634**–635
    and moral behavior, 633–635

Self-efficacy, **24**–25
Self-esteem, **522**, 527
    and achievement motivation, 531–533
    and age changes, 528–530
    cross-cultural view, 530
    family influences, 533
    looking-glass self concept, 531, 533
    measurement of, 527–528
    and significant others, **533**
Self-evaluation
    in adolescence, 526–527
    in early and middle childhood, 525–526, 529
    in infancy, 523–524
Self-Perception Profile for Children (SPPC),
    527–528
Self-reports, 48–49
Semantic development, 251–261
    basic-level categories, **255**
    categorical scope, **255**
    contrast, **255**
    fast mapping, **255**
    influencing factors, 258–261
    mutual exclusivity, **255**
    school age children, 256–258
    underextensions/overextensions, **252**–253
    vocabulary burst, 252
    whole-object rule, **255**
    word inventions, 253
Semantics, meaning of, 242, **251**
Sensitive periods, **125**
    time frame for embryo/fetus, 126
Sensorimotor intelligence, **291**–298
    object permanence, **295**–298
    primary/secondary circular reactions, **293**
    reflexes, 292–293
    structured whole concept, **298**
    tertiary circular reactions, **294**
Sensory primitives, **333**
Separation protest, **219**
Sequential analysis, **45**
Sex chromosomes, **82**–83
    disorders related to, 88–91, 582
Sex differences
    aggression, 574–575
    biological differences, 574
    cross-cultural view, 584
    empathy, 575–576
    interests and activities, 577–578
    longevity, 574
    mathematics ability, 578–580
    moral development, 620–621
    in newborns, 585
    peer relationships, 581
    personality traits, 576–577
    in primates, 584
    research issues, 573–574
    social behavior, 574–575
    and socialization, 585–586
    social relationships, 581
    verbal ability, 578–579
Sex differentiation
    embryo, 120–121
    hormonal factors, 582
    and sex chromosomes, 120–121, 582
Sex-role development, **564**
    *See also* Sex-typing
Sex roles, **564**
    Swedish social policy, 600–601
Sex stereotypes, **565**
    and media, 593–594
    persistence and age, 570–573
    reality based stereotypes, 565
    reinforcement by parents, 587–589

stereotype flexibility, **569**–570, 573
    stereotype knowledge, **567**–569
    and unconventional families, 591
Sex-typing, **564**–567
    androgyny, **598**–599
    biological factors, 566, 582–586
    and cognitive development, 566–567
    components of, 565–567
    family influences, 586–591
    father absence, effects of, 589–590
    gender constancy, 594–595
    gender schemas, 596–597
    hormonal influences, 583–584
    and observational learning, 588–590
    peer influences, 591–592
    and sex chromosome abnormalities, 582
    and socialization, 566
    teacher influences, 592–593
    twin studies, 585
Sexual reproduction, genetic process, 83–84
Shame, toddlers, 208
Shaping, **24**
Shyness, and peer acceptance, 505
Siblings, 446–451
    adjustment to newborn sibling, 447–448
    in adolescence, 448–449
    attachment measurement, 447
    in childhood, 448
    only children, 451
    and parental interactions, 450
    same-sex siblings, 449
    sibling/sibling influences, 450–451
Sickle-cell anemia, **100**
    and malaria, 100
    populations affected by, 100
Significant others, and self-esteem, **533**
Simon, Theodore, 381–382
Single-parent families, 458–460
    and child abuse, 465
    never-married parents, 459
    compared to two-parent families, 459–460
Sister chromatids, **80**
Situational management, **432**
Skinner, B. F., 24, 279
Sleep, infants, 175, 176, 177
Smell, infancy, 196
Smiling, infancy, 206–207, 209
Sociability, meaning of, 211
Social behavior, 552–559
    interpersonal problem solving, 553–554
    and role taking, 541–543
    sex differences, 574–575
    social information processing, 554–559
Social cognition, **522**
    identity development, 534–536
    psychological world, knowledge about,
    543–552
    role taking, **537**–543
    self-evaluation/self-esteem, 523–533
    and social behavior, 552–559
Social conventions
    and moral development, **623**–627
    personal domain of, 624
    as rule, 624, 625
Social-desirability bias, and children's self-reports,
    49
Social development, attachment, 214–237, **217**
Social impact, peer group, **499**
Social information processing, 554–559
    and aggression, 555–558
    and social schemas, **555**
    steps in, 555–556, 558
Social intelligence, **421**